THE CAMBRIDGE HISTORY
OF JAPAN

General editors
JOHN W. HALL, MARIUS B. JANSEN, MADOKA KANAI,
AND DENIS TWITCHETT

Volume 3
Medieval Japan

THE CAMBRIDGE HISTORY OF JAPAN

Volume 3
Medieval Japan

Edited by
KOZO YAMAMURA

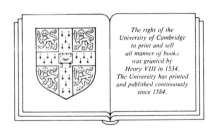

The right of the
University of Cambridge
to print and sell
all manner of books
was granted by
Henry VIII in 1534.
The University has printed
and published continuously
since 1584.

CAMBRIDGE UNIVERSITY PRESS
CAMBRIDGE
NEW YORK   PORT CHESTER   MELBOURNE   SYDNEY

Published by the Press Syndicate of the University of Cambridge
The Pitt Building, Trumpington Street, Cambridge CB2 IRP
40 West 20th Street, New York, NY 10011, USA
10 Stamford Road, Oakleigh, Melbourne 3166, Australia

© Cambridge University Press 1990

First published 1990

Printed in the United States of America

Library of Congress Cataloging-in-Publication Data
(Revised for volume 3)
The Cambridge history of Japan.
Includes bibliographies and index.
Contents: v. 3. Medieval Japan / edited by Kozo
Yamamura   – v. 6. The twentieth century / edited
by Peter Duus.
1. Japan – History.   I. Hall, John Whitney, 1916–
DS835.C36   1990   952   88-2877

British Library Cataloguing in Publication Data
The Cambridge history of Japan.
Vol.3. Medieval Japan
1. Japan, history
I. Yamamura, Kozo
952

ISBN 0-521-22354-7 (V. 3)
0-521-22356-3 (V. 5)
0-521-22357-1 (V. 6)

GENERAL EDITORS' PREFACE

Since the beginning of this century the Cambridge histories have set a pattern in the English-reading world for multivolume series containing chapters written by specialists under the guidance of volume editors. Plans for a Cambridge history of Japan were begun in the 1970s and completed in 1978. The task was not to be easy. The details of Japanese history are not matters of common knowledge among Western historians. The cultural mode of Japan differs greatly from that of the West, and above all there are the daunting problems of terminology and language. In compensation, however, foreign scholars have been assisted by the remarkable achievements of the Japanese scholars during the last century in recasting their history in modern conceptual and methodological terms.

History has played a major role in Japanese culture and thought, and the Japanese record is long and full. Japan's rulers from ancient times have found legitimacy in tradition, both mythic and historic, and Japan's thinkers have probed for a national morality and system of values in their country's past. The importance of history was also emphasized in the continental cultural influences that entered Japan from early times. Its expression changed as the Japanese consciousness turned to questions of dynastic origin, as it came to reflect Buddhist views of time and reality, and as it sought justification for rule by the samurai estate. By the eighteenth century the successive need to explain the divinity of government, justify the ruler's place through his virtue and compassion, and interpret the flux of political change had resulted in the fashioning of a highly subjective fusion of Shinto, Buddhist, and Confucian norms.

In the nineteenth century the Japanese became familiar with Western forms of historical expression and felt the need to fit their national history into patterns of a larger world history. As the modern Japanese state took its place among other nations, Japanese history faced the task of reconciling a parochial past with a more catholic present. Historians familiarized themselves with European accounts of the course of civilization and described Japan's nineteenth-century turn from military to civilian bureaucratic rule under monarchical guidance as part of a larger, worldwide pattern. Buckle, Guizot, Spencer, and then Marx successively provided interpretative schema.

The twentieth-century ideology of the imperial nation state, however, operated to inhibit full play of universalism in historical interpretation. The growth and ideology of the imperial realm required caution on the part of historians, particularly with reference to Japanese origins.

Japan's defeat in World War II brought release from these inhibitions and for a time replaced them with compulsive denunciation of the pretensions of the imperial state. Soon the expansion of higher education brought changes in the size and variety of the Japanese scholarly world. Historical inquiry was now free to range widely. A new opening to the West brought lively interest in historical expressions in the West, and a historical profession that had become cautiously and expertly positivist began to rethink its material in terms of larger patterns.

At just this juncture the serious study of Japanese history began in the West. Before World War II the only distinguished general survey of Japanese history in English was G. B. Sansom's *Japan: A Short Cultural History*, first published in 1931 and still in print. English and American students of Japan, many trained in wartime language programs, were soon able to travel to Japan for study and participation with Japanese scholars in cooperative projects. International conferences and symposia produced volumes of essays that served as benchmarks of intellectual focus and technical advance. Within Japan itself an outpouring of historical scholarship, popular publishing, and historical romance heightened the historical consciousness of a nation aware of the dramatic changes to which it was witness.

In 1978 plans were adopted to produce this series on Japanese history as a way of taking stock of what has been learned. The present generation of Western historians can draw upon the solid foundations of the modern Japanese historical profession. The decision to limit the enterprise to six volumes meant that topics such as the history of art and literature, aspects of economics and technology and science, and the riches of local history would have to be left out. They too have been the beneficiaries of vigorous study and publication in Japan and in the Western world.

Multivolume series have appeared many times in Japanese since the beginning of the century, but until the 1960s the number of professionally trained historians of Japan in the Western world was too small to sustain such an enterprise. Although that number has grown, the general editors have thought it best to draw on Japanese specialists for contributions in areas where they retain a clear authority. In such cases the act of translation itself involves a form of editorial cooperation that requires the skills of a trained historian whose name deserves acknowledgment.

The primary objective of the present series is to put before the English-reading audience as complete a record of Japanese history as possible. But the Japanese case attracts our attention for other reasons as well. To some it has seemed that the more we have come to know about Japan the more we are drawn to the apparent similarities with Western history. The long continuous course of Japan's historical record has tempted historians to look for resemblances between its patterns of political and social organization and those of the West. The rapid emergence of Japan's modern nation state has occupied the attention of comparative historians, both Japanese and Western. On the other hand, specialists are inclined to point out the dangers of being misled by seeming parallels.

The striking advances in our knowledge of Japan's past will continue and accelerate. Western historians of this great and complex subject will continue to grapple with it, and they must as Japan's world role becomes more prominent. The need for greater and deeper understanding of Japan will continue to be evident. Japanese history belongs to the world, not only as a right and necessity but also as a subject of compelling interest.

JOHN W. HALL
MARIUS B. JANSEN
MADOKA KANAI
DENIS TWITCHETT

CONTENTS

General editors' preface   *page* v

List of maps, figures, and tables   xiv

Preface to Volume 3   xvii

Introduction   1
    by KOZO YAMAMURA, *Henry M. Jackson School of*
    International Studies, University of Washington

      Japanese and English works on medieval history   6
      Discussion of the chapters in this volume   12
      Concluding notes   27
      Appendix: Chronology of medieval period   31
      Selected bibliography   39

1 The Kamakura bakufu   46
    by JEFFREY P. MASS, *Department of History, Stanford*
    University, and Oxford University

      The background to the Gempei War   47
      The Gempei War   52
      The Gempei aftermath: *jitō* and *shugo*   59
      The road to Jōkyū   66
      The Jōkyū disturbance and its aftermath   70
      Bakufu governance   74
      Shugo and *jitō*   80
      The bakufu at mid-century   87

2 Medieval *shōen*   89
    by ŌYAMA KYŌHEI, *Faculty of Literature, Kyoto*
    University
    Translated by MARTIN COLLCUTT

The internal structure of medieval provinces   89
The domestic economy of *shōen* proprietors   96
The internal structure of *shōen*   101
The power of the *jitō*   110
Social strata in *shōen*   120
Courtiers and warriors   123

3 The decline of the Kamakura bakufu   128
   by ISHII SUSUMU, *Faculty of Literature, Tokyo
   University*
   Translated by JEFFREY P. MASS and HITOMI
   TONOMURA

   Introduction   128
   The Mongol invasions and the Kamakura bakufu   131
   Japan after the Mongol wars   148
   The fall of the Kamakura bakufu   160

4 The Muromachi bakufu   175
   by JOHN WHITNEY HALL, *Department of History,
   Yale University*

   Introduction   175
   The rise of the Ashikaga house   177
   The founding of the Muromachi bakufu   183
   The path to Ashikaga legitimacy   189
   Shogun, *shugo*, and provincial administration   193
   The Muromachi distribution of power   201
   The Muromachi bakufu: instruments of
   administration and enforcement   211
   Bakufu fiscal and manpower supports   219
   The last hundred years   225

5 Muromachi local government: *shugo* and *kokujin*   231
   by IMATANI AKIRA, *Faculty of Liberal Arts and
   Sciences, Yokohama City University*
   Translated by SUZANNE GAY

   Introduction   231
   Regional administrative officials: *kubō* and *tandai* 232
   Shugo daimyo   235
   The relationship between *shugo* and *kokujin*   253

6   The decline of the *shōen* system   260
    by NAGAHARA KEIJI, *Faculty of Economics,*
    Hitotsubashi University
    Translated by MICHAEL P. BIRT

        Turning points in the decline of the *shōen*   261
        The growth of the *jitō* and *shōkan* as *ryōshu*   265
        The development of the *shugo* domainal system   272
        Peasants' protest and growth   280
        The collapse of the *shōen* proprietors' authority   289
        Conclusion: the disappearance of the *shōen*   298

7   The medieval peasant   301
    by NAGAHARA KEIJI, *Faculty of Economics,*
    Hitotsubashi University
    Translated by SUZANNE GAY

        Status differences among peasants in the *shōen*
        system   303
        Land development and agricultural operations   310
        The peasants, overlord rule, and taxation   315
        The economic life of the peasants   324
        The regional consolidation of peasant society   330
        The *sengoku* daimyo and the peasants   341

8   The growth of commerce in medieval Japan   344
    by KOZO YAMAMURA, *Henry M. Jackson School of*
    International Studies, University of Washington

        The initial conditions   344
        Acceleration of commerce and monetization   360
        Commerce and cities in the Nambokuchō and
        Muromachi periods   376
        Conclusion   394

9   Japan and East Asia   396
    by KAWAZOE SHŌJI, *Faculty of Literature, Kyushu*
    University
    Translated by G. CAMERON HURST III

        Japan's international relations in East Asia   396
        Foreign relations at the founding of the Kamakura
        bakufu   398

Foreign relations during the Hōjō regency   404
The Mongol invasions   411
Foreign relations in the early Muromachi period   423
The tribute system and Japan   432
Changes in the international relations of East Asia   440

10 Cultural life in medieval Japan   447
    by H. PAUL VARLEY, *Department of East Asian
    Languages and Cultures, Columbia University*

    The Kamakura period and the end of Buddhist
    law   447
    The Tale of the Heike and other war tales   449
    The age of *Shinkokinshū* poetry   452
    The revival of Shinto and the late Kamakura period   455
    The early Muromachi period   458
    The noh theater   462
    The evolution of new interior settings for the arts 468
    Social ideals and aesthetic values of the
    Higashiyama epoch   470
    Linked-verse poetry   473
    The Higashiyama epoch and the scholarship of
    nostalgia   481
    Landscape paintings and gardens   485
    The culture of tea   488
    The Azuchi–Momoyama epoch   491
    Decorative screen and door-panel painting   492
    Genre painting and Azuchi–Momoyama humanism   495
    The world of tea   497

11 The other side of culture in medieval Japan   500
    by BARBARA RUCH, *Department of East Asian
    Languages and Cultures, Columbia University*

    Historiographical issues   500
    The case of Mugai Nyodai   502
    Working for a living   511
    Election of the gods   518
    Unheeded voices, winked-at lives   521
    Akashi no Kakuichi   531
    Conclusion   541

12 Buddhism in the Kamakura period   544
    by ŌSUMI KAZUO, *Faculty of Literature, Tokyo*
    Women's College
    Translated, adapted, and expanded by
    JAMES C. DOBBINS

        Introduction   544
        The originators of Kamakura Buddhism   546
        The response of the Buddhist establishment   560
        The formation of religious organizations   571
        Conclusion   580

13 Zen and the *gozan*   583
    by MARTIN COLLCUTT, *Departments of History and*
    East Asian Studies, Princeton University

        The transmission of Ch'an Buddhism to Japan   584
        The development of the Zen monastic institution in
        medieval Japan   596
        Economy and administration of the medieval Zen
        monastery   637
        Changes in Zen practice, culture, and the monastic
        life   643

Works cited   653
Glossary   687
Index   702

MAPS, FIGURES, AND TABLES

MAPS

	Medieval Japan: regions and provinces	*page* xix
	Medieval Japan: major towns, trading centers, and routes	xx–xxi
4.1	The Ashikaga house, ca. 1330	181
4.2	Provinces in central bloc held by Ashikaga collateral *shugo*, ca. 1400	195
4.3	Provinces held by noncollateral houses, ca. 1400	195
4.4	Location of *hōkōnin*, 1444–9	218
4.5	Location of *hōkōnin*, 1565	218

FIGURES

3.1	System of alternate succession between Gofukakusa and Kameyama lines	166
4.1	Ashikaga lineage genealogy	178
4.2	Organization of the bakufu, 1350	212
4.3	Changes in bakufu structure after Tadayoshi's expulsion, 1352	213
5.1	Organization of *shugo* authority in Yamashiro and Kawachi provinces, ca. 1379	249
7.1	Conceptualization of a typical *shōen*	305
11.1	Wooden sculpture of medieval abbess Mugai Nyodai	503
13.1	The growth of Zen schools, thirteenth to sixteenth century	597

TABLES

2.1	*Shōen* in Noto Province	91
2.2	*Gō* and *betchmiyō* in the Wakasa *kokuga* domain	97

2.3 Kumagai family holdings in Miri-no-shō   106
2.4 Management of *jitō–kadota* paddy and dry fields in
     Miri-no-shō   107
4.1 Ashikaga shoguns   177
4.2 Control of provinces by Ashikaga collaterals and
     other families, ca. 1400   194
4.3 Guardsmen holdings by province   221

PREFACE TO VOLUME 3

Nearly eight years elapsed between the initial selection of authors and the submission of the edited manuscript to Cambridge University Press. During those eight rewarding and taxing years I learned a great deal more about the medieval history of Japan and wrote over four hundred letters. As in making good wine, the process of writing, translating, and editing can proceed only slowly. And because of the period covered, coordinating the use and translation of Japanese terms and concepts further lengthened the process.

I feel confident that the volume that emerged is worthy of the years of aging. I believe that the principal goal of producing a volume useful to a wide readership has been attained and that all the chapters in this volume can benefit both beginning and advanced students wishing to deepen and broaden their knowledge of Japan's medieval period. Above all, I believe that these chapters collectively bring Japan's medieval age as a whole into sharper focus.

Conventional romanization is used throughout this volume for Japanese and Korean terms, and the Wade–Giles system is followed for Chinese terms. Japanese and Chinese personal names follow their native form, with surname preceding given name, except in citations of Japanese authors writing English.

I express my sincere gratitude to all who played a vital part in making this volume possible. First to be thanked are the authors who patiently responded to my queries and suggestions and the translators who struggled with many thorny problems. I especially owe a great deal to two of the authors, Jeffrey Mass and Keiji Nagahara, who provided me with valuable advice on many substantive and editorial matters. My deep appreciation is due also to the General Editors, who guided me generously in every step of the long process, and to two of my graduate students, Martha Lane and Karla Pearson, who assisted me tirelessly and ably in all that had to be done to convert fourteen essays written on both sides of the Pacific into a volume that meets the rigorous standards of the General Editors and Cambridge University Press. Finally, I wish to thank the Japan Foundation for grants that covered manuscript fees, costs of translating chapters by Japanese contributors, and editorial expenses and meetings.

The only reward that the authors and editors of this volume seek is that its readers will find studying Japan's medieval period interesting and rewarding, as well as essential to understanding the history of Japan.

KOZO YAMAMURA

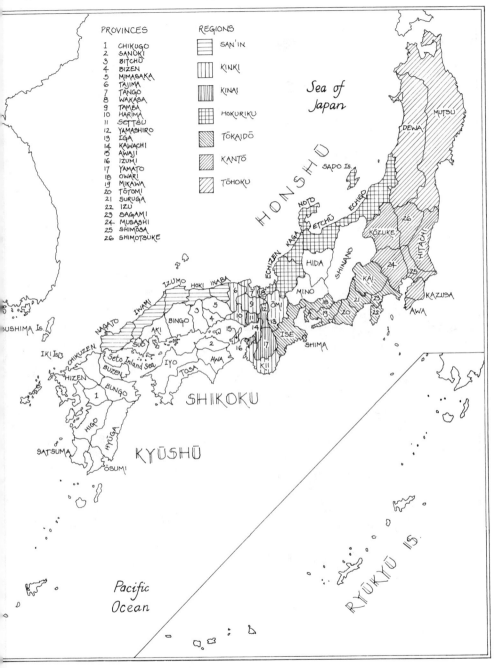

PROVINCES

1 CHIKUGO
2 SANUKI
3 BITCHŪ
4 BIZEN
5 MIMASAKA
6 TAJIMA
7 TANGO
8 WAKASA
9 TAMBA
10 HARIMA
11 SETTSU
12 YAMASHIRO
13 IGA
14 KAWACHI
15 AWAJI
16 IZUMI
17 YAMATO
18 OWARI
19 MIKAWA
20 TŌTOMI
21 SURUGA
22 IZU
23 SAGAMI
24 MUSASHI
25 SHIMŌSA
26 SHIMOTSUKE

REGIONS

SAN'IN

KINKI

KINAI

HOKURIKU

TŌKAIDŌ

KANTŌ

TŌHOKU

Sea of Japan

HONSHŪ

Pacific Ocean

KYŪSHŪ

SHIKOKU

RYŪKYŪ IS.

Seto Inland Sea

Medieval Japan: regions and provinces. (For clarity, numbers are used to indicate names of some provinces.)

Medieval Japan: major towns, trading centers, and routes

TŌKAIDŌ HIGHWAY
SANYŌDŌ HIGHWAY

HONSHŪ

NOETSU

OBAMA   TSURUGA
IMAZU
SAKIMOTO
YAMAGA KYOTO LAKE BIWA
HYOGO   ŌTSU
        UJI
SAKAI   NARA   SHINAGAWA   EDO (TOKYO)
                     KAMAKURA
ŌMINATO

Pacific
Ocean

INTRODUCTION

The subject of this volume is medieval Japan, spanning the three and a half centuries between the final decades of the twelfth century when the Kamakura bakufu was founded and the mid-sixteenth century during which civil wars raged following the effective demise of the Muromachi bakufu.[1] The historical events and developments of these colorful centuries depict medieval Japan's polity, economy, society, and culture, as well as its relations with its Asian neighbors. The major events and the most significant developments are not difficult to summarize.

This was the period of warriors. Throughout these centuries, the power of the warrior class continued to rise, and one political result of this development was the formation of two warrior governments, or bakufu. The first, the Kamakura bakufu, founded in the 1180s, was not able to govern the nation single-handedly. In several important respects, it had to share power with the civil authority of the *tennō* – usually translated as the emperor[2] – and the court. But under the second warrior government – the Ashikaga bakufu that came into being in 1336 and was firmly established by the end of the fourteenth century – the warrior class was able to erode the power of the civil authority. During the first half of the fifteenth century, when the bakufu's power was at its zenith, the warrior class governed the nation in substantive ways. Although the civil authority did not lose all its power and continued to help legitimize the bakufu, it was manipulated and used to serve the bakufu's own political needs almost at will.

The demise of the Kamakura bakufu in 1333 and the beginning of the effective end of the Ashikaga bakufu in the late fifteenth century came about because of political and military challenges to the bakufu's

---

1 Although this volume on medieval Japan deals primarily with the Kamakura and Muromachi periods as dated by most Western scholars, when the period began and ended continues to be debated among Japanese specialists. For a succinct discussion of the debate among Japanese scholars, see Hall (1983), pp. 5–8.
2 An accurate translation of *tennō* is neither "king" nor "emperor," especially as applied to the *tennō* of the medieval period. However, because "emperor" has become an accepted translation, the term is used interchangeably with *tennō* in this volume.

power from within the warrior class. The third and last bakufu in Japanese history, the Tokugawa bakufu, took power in 1600 by unifying the regional warrior powers that had rendered the Ashikaga bakufu powerless and engaged in a century of internal warfare. The establishment of the Tokugawa bakufu, with a 267-year history that could be written with little reference to the civil authority, was the culmination of the warrior power that had first built the Kamakura bakufu nearly 500 years earlier.

Paralleling the continuing rise of the warriors' power was the gradual transformation of the *shōen* – Japan's counterpart to the medieval manors of Europe – and public land into fiefs. *Shōen* were first created in the eighth century from privatized public land, and they had become, by the twelfth century, the principal source of private wealth and income for the emperor himself, nobles, and temples. Along with local and regional officers of the civil government and others, many warriors too played a role in the process of privatization. They either opened new paddies, mostly by reclaiming unused land, or managed to exert their power over nearby public paddies. They then commended these paddies to nobles and temples, which were able to obtain legal grants of immunity from the dues imposed on the paddies. This process gradually reduced the income of the civil government, although it benefited the nobles and temples that shared the income from the paddies with the warriors who commended them. The warriors also increased their income by usurping, in various ways, rights to income from the *shōen* as well as from the public land that continued to provide political and economic bases for the civil authority.

The establishment of the Kamakura bakufu signaled the beginning of more systematic incursion by warriors into *shōen*, as well as into the public land. The process of incursion was at first slow but gathered momentum during the thirteenth century. As a result, more and more of the income from the *shōen* and public land was captured by the warriors at the expense of the emperor, nobles, and temples, as well as the civil government. During the Muromachi period, there was a more systematic and thorough transformation of *shōen* and public land, shifting from these forms of landholding – the basis of the political and economic power of those supporting and benefiting from the civil authority – to fiefs. In contrast with the Kamakura bakufu, the Muromachi bakufu adopted more measures to impose dues on a regional basis and more forcefully promoted the interests of the warrior class as a whole at the cost of the political and economic interests of the nonwarrior elites. In the second half of the fifteenth century and into the sixteenth, as the bakufu's power declined, the warriors in their capacity as regional and local powers were increasingly aggressive in depriving the civil elites of their remaining public land, *shōen,* and other sources of income. By the mid-sixteenth century, few *shōen* and little public land remained.

The growth of institutional capabilities to administer justice and the development of the bureaucracy occurred along with the rise in power of the warrior class and the steady transformation of *shōen* and public land into fiefs. In the Kamakura period especially, but also in the Muromachi period, laws and legal institutions to adjudicate disputes over rights to income from land and over other types of conflicts involving such matters as inheritance, became increasingly important to the polity and society. The bureaucracy and expertise necessary for effective governance also grew over time. Although their effectiveness was reduced as both bakufu lost power, the institutional capabilities to adjudicate and to administer that developed in the Kamakura period and continued to increase in the Muromachi period profoundly affected the course and character of Japan's medieval history.

Aided by the steady growth of productivity and output in agriculture, the medieval period was one of growing commerce and continuing monetization of the economy. Market activities that first increased in the capital in the late twelfth century accelerated from the mid-thirteenth century. By the middle of the Muromachi period, markets became accessible to all villagers across the nation, and the specialization of occupations, which still was limited in the early Kamakura years, progressed substantially, thereby increasing the skill and efficiency of merchants and artisans. As commerce grew, so did cities, nodes of transportation, and economic institutions.

With the growth of commerce and monetization resulting from the rapid increase in the use of coins imported from China, the political and economic conflicts expected in an increasingly market-oriented society became more frequent by the fourteenth century. These included disputes between moneylenders and borrowers (many of whom were warriors), between recipients and payers of dues over the mix of in-kind and cash dues, and between guilds and their would-be competitors. These and many other conflicts often involved, directly or indirectly, the political and economic interests of the bakufu, the civil elite, and the warriors.

The lives of the cultivators, by far the majority of the population, also underwent several significant transformations. Their collective lot improved principally because of the greater agricultural productivity, which resulted from the rising use of double cropping and fertilizer and, most importantly, the more intensive cultivation of paddies over which cultivators enjoyed a slowly increasing degree of managerial freedom and ownership rights. Political developments and wars inevitably affected the cultivators' lives through *ad hoc* imposts, temporary dislocation, newly instituted levies, and other exactions. But by the Muromachi period, their ability to produce more and to benefit from market activities gradually helped them win political and social freedom at the village level, which in turn enabled them to govern their daily lives in matters such as the maintenance of law and order and irrigation. Through mutual aid and more effective collective actions demanding the reduction of dues and mitigation of other political and economic threats to their well-being, cultivators became better able to cope with hardships imposed by nature and by the ruling elites.

A very important part of this medieval history is the new Buddhist sects and Zen Buddhism that became an integral part of Japanese society and culture during the Kamakura and Muromachi periods, as well as the noh plays, tea ceremonies, linked verses, *sansui* paintings, *shoin*-style architecture, and many other cultural pursuits and manifestations that flourished especially in the Muromachi period. Surprising as it may seem, many elements of what we today view as Japanese culture were firmly established in medieval Japan, despite the rise and fall of the two bakufu and all the political turmoil and warfare that the political developments of this period entailed.

The renewed inflow of Buddhist teachings from China and, more importantly, the adaptation of these teachings and the adoption of innovative methods of proselytizing by the leaders of the new sects and Zen Buddhism altered the place of Buddhism in society and in the daily lives of both the elites and the commoners. Kamakura warriors' lives became imbued with Zen Buddhism, and the social and political histories of the fifteenth and sixteenth centuries were changed by the influence of Buddhism on warriors and commoners alike. The best-known results of these developments were the growth of religious institutions led by politically powerful temples, the increase in the number of temples across the nation, and the persistent and often successful rebellions by the followers of a few sects in the waning years of the Muromachi bakufu and into the Sengoku period. The motivations for these rebellions against warrior overlords were not all religious, but it is impossible to explain their character and scope without considering the religious motivations involved in these political uprisings by peasants and some warriors.

The cultural developments in the Muromachi period took various forms and were deeply affected by Buddhism. Under the active patronage of the Ashikaga shoguns – Yoshimitsu and Yoshimasa in particular – the cultural life of the elites reached its height, and the legacies of the elite culture from this period in literature, the performing arts, painting, and architecture continue to form an important core of Japanese culture. Commoners also contributed to the flowering of culture in these centuries. Their dance, music, and songs – often rustic but also affected by the world view of Buddhism – added color and energy to their lives and, as typified in the noh performed for the enjoyment of the elite, villagers' dances and songs often provided the basis from which the highly refined elite culture evolved.

Finally, in outlining the history of medieval Japan, one can hardly fail to note the influence of Japan's East Asian neighbors on Japan's medieval history and that of Japan on China and Korea. Japanese pirates (*wakō*) persistently pillaged the coasts of China and Korea throughout this period. Although partly motivated by trade, the most notable effect of these *wakō* was continual diplomatic friction. China was the source of Buddhist teachings and virtually all the coins used in medieval Japan, and it was Japan's most important trade partner, as evidenced in Japan's efforts to maintain the tally trade (the officially sanctioned and restricted trade) with Ming China. The continent, however, was also the source of medieval Japan's most trying diplomatic and political-military experiences. The Mongol invasions of the last decades of the thirteenth century imposed heavy political and economic burdens on Kamakura Japan, contributing to the fall of the bakufu. The frequent and, at times, threatening demands made by Ming China on the Ashikaga bakufu to accept the status of tributary state forced the shogun and his bakufu to acknowledge that medieval Japan was part of East Asia in which China considered itself the unchallenged hegemonic power.

The collective goal of the authors of this volume is to describe more fully and to analyze more closely the various parts of this history. In this Introduction I shall summarize the methodological orientation of both Japanese and Western specialists in the medieval period. This overview will help acquaint readers with the essential characteristics of Japanese historiography which, for Western specialists, serves as an indispensable source of learning and research. This summary of Japanese historiography may also be useful to nonspecialists who want to read the translated works of Japanese authors cited in the selected bibliography following the Introduction. This bibliography of works in English is presented only to aid nonspecialist readers of this volume and is not intended to be comprehensive. In addition, for discussions of historiographies in Japanese and English, interested readers are invited to examine those works on historiography also cited in the bibliography following the Introduction.[3]

Following these short historiographical notes, I shall discuss, for each chapter of this volume, its historiographical significance and its contents and, in the footnote ending this short discussion, cite the more recent works in English that refer to the topic of the chapter. I shall conclude with some of my reflections on the present state of Western historiography regarding medieval Japan.

A chronology of the main historical events and developments appears as an appendix to this Introduction, and a glossary of Japanese terms is appended at the end of this volume.

JAPANESE AND ENGLISH WORKS ON MEDIEVAL HISTORY

To understand Japanese historiography for the medieval period, one first must be acquainted with two *forces majeures* that shaped the character of the historiography and that had and continue to have profound effects on its essential character.[4] One is Japan's national experience in the past hundred years of having been a latecomer to modernization and industrialization, and the other is the Marxist framework of analysis that was widely adopted by Japanese historians in the early decades of this century. Although the effects of both have been diminishing since the 1960s, even today they continue to mold and affect the works of Japanese historians.

It is not surprising that Japan's national experience of having been a follower of the early industrializers, of having eagerly pursued industrialization and modernization-cum-Westernization, influenced several prewar generations of Japanese historians. The most important question asked by historians around the turn of the century was, How and why did Japanese history differ from those of the industrialized Western nations? This meant that these historians had little choice but to be comparativists, often explicitly and always implicitly.

3 In discussing the historiography, thus the works included in the bibliography following the Introduction, as well as in referring to "Western" scholarship, I refer only to those works published in English. This reflects only the limitations of my linguistic competence and does not suggest that significant works in other Western languages do not exist. Readers should be aware, for example, that many important and useful works on the period have been published in German.
4 Readers who do not read Japanese but wish to gain a further understanding of Japanese historiography can examine Hall (1966, 1968, 1983), Mass (1980), Takeuchi (1982), and Yamamura (1975).

The main topics of study pursued by medievalists, therefore, were the similarities and differences in medieval institutions in Japan and Europe, the reasons for the differences between Japan and Europe in the pace of change in the medieval political economy, and the reasons for the assumed similarities in the patterns of evolution through history, from ancient to medieval and then to modern. In essence, the topics that attracted the most attention from Japanese historians of this period were, they believed, those that helped them see Japanese history as reflected in the historiographical mirror of the West. These and many other comparative questions continued to be asked into the first decades of this century, by pioneering medieval historians who focused on the search for similarities between the institutions and laws of medieval Europe and those of medieval Japan. The scholars who followed the pioneers gradually broadened the scope of their studies to compare and contrast medieval Japan's political and social organizations and patterns of landownership with those of medieval Europe.

Superimposed on this comparativist mold of historiography was the Marxist framework of historical analysis adopted by many Japanese historians and social scientists beginning around the time of World War I. The use of this framework quickly spread, and by the early 1930s it had become firmly established as the dominant method of historical analysis. There were two mutually reinforcing reasons for this development. One was the increasing intellectual and political commitment to leftist ideologies by Japanese historians and social scientists in these decades characterized by political suppression, the prolonged agricultural depression of the 1920s, and the Great Depression and rise of nationalistic militarism of the 1930s. The second reason was to build a broad analytic framework in which to place a methodological foundation for the comparative character of Japanese historiography.

The result was that many of the two generations of historians – those publishing in the interwar years and those in the immediate postwar decades – focused on examining and debating historical questions and issues that are significant within the scope of Marxist analysis. For medievalists, the most important of these questions was when Japan experienced feudalism, a crucial, preindustrial stage in the Marxist analysis. Debates among specialists concerning the periodization and character of Japanese feudalism were intense and often were both academic and political. In these decades, numerous monographs and articles were produced concerning many questions and aspects of medieval history significant within the Marxist framework.

No attempt will be made here to delineate these multifaceted and often heated debates. But it is useful to note that much of the debate within the Marxist framework of analysis focused less on an explicit comparison of Western and Japanese feudalism and their institutional characteristics. Instead, the debate concentrated more on when Japan experienced "pure" feudalism according to each scholar's interpretation of Marx's definition of the term; on the validity of each scholar's characterization of the patterns of landownership, methods and forms of payments of peasant dues, and motivations for interclass struggles; and on how these patterns, forms, and motivations changed over time.

Before the early 1960s, many scholars' works were implicitly motivated by their political ideology, and the Marxist interpretation of medieval history enjoyed its heyday in the late 1940s and 1950s. However, the ideological motivation grew less and less evident in the 1960s, and by the 1970s many scholars used the Marxist framework of analysis and vocabulary merely as familiar and useful tools of historical study that had been generally accepted by their profession.

The preoccupation of two generations of historians with questions and issues within the Marxist framework of analysis had a few other important effects on the historiography of the period. One was that the profession was not hospitable to those who wished to study such aspects of the period as cities, social life, religion, and culture that were not central to the Marxist analysis. An important result was that scholars studying these topics tended to adopt the Marxist framework of analysis and to use as much as possible the Marxist vocabulary.

The other consequence of the profession's preoccupation with Marxist analysis was that economic history became a political-institutional economic history concentrating on interclass politicoeconomic conflicts and the characteristics of production methods in each stage of history that gave rise to and defined the nature of these conflicts. To this day, there is no monograph on Japan's medieval economy that uses the analytic insights of modern (neoclassical) economic theory, as is found in large numbers in the study of the European medieval economy.

But this began to change in the 1960s, becoming more perceptible in the 1970s. The numerous reasons for this change are related, the principal one being that many Japanese began to perceive that Japan had completed its "catch-up" period of industrialization/modernization. Marxist analysis, while still exerting a strong influence on the profession, slowly but steadily lost its former grip, as demonstrated by the increased number of works whose methods of analysis and central questions deviated from those that had preoccupied earlier scholars. This trend has been strengthened, moreover, because the immediate postwar generation of scholars is being replaced by a new generation that generally is not as interested as their predecessors had been in the questions that arose directly from the Marxist framework of analysis. The sudden rise in the number of active professional historians since the 1950s (owing to the larger number of academic posts that became available in universities created after 1945) also has contributed to this trend.

The change, however, is occurring slowly, and so it may be more accurate to characterize the historiography of the medieval period as being in transition. Signs of transition are today found in, for example, the fact that more and more case studies of historical figures, regional political institutions, and forms of economic change are being undertaken, not to provide evidence for the validity of the Marxist analysis, but to offer descriptions and analyses with less and less direct relevance (if any at all) to the Marxist framework of analysis. As yet, extrapolating from such a recent trend is premature. The studies that have appeared in the past fifteen years have not yet challenged in any fundamental ways the Marxist core of the institutional and political-economic history of medieval Japan. Whether or not the process of transition that has begun will gain sufficient momentum to challenge the Marxist framework and rewrite the history of the medieval centuries remains to be demonstrated.

Except for the few instances noted, serious professional study of medieval Japanese history by scholars writing in English did not begin until after World War II. What works were available in the prewar years were limited to naive accounts based on translations of the great Japanese historical narratives such as the *Heike monogatari* or *Azuma kagami*. The history of premodern Japan consisted of the "interweaving of great and petty men and events" and an analysis of what human emotions lay behind the narratives contained in "diaries, war tales, morality pieces, and the more fanciful chronicles." History was to be understood "through dialogue and overt (covert) passion." And in the prewar decades, "the rendering of a famous text was evidently considered task enough." Thus, "there were no monographs, and – lacking these – little experience in learning to use sources critically."[5]

A significant exception to this was the work of Asakawa Kan'ichi,

5 Mass (1980), p. 63.

the Japanese-born Yale scholar, which was published in the 1930s and 1940s. Many of his works were on the medieval land system, and they were the first – and for years the only – studies of the *shōen* system available to Westerners that made extensive use of documentary evidence. Asakawa's studies, however, were comparative; he was searching for similarities between the medieval land systems of Japan and Europe. The other exceptional scholar of the prewar period was George B. Sansom. His major prewar publication, *Japan: A Short Cultural History*, may have relied too heavily on the "history-through-narrative" approach and may not have been comprehensive in coverage, but it provided a vivid picture of Japanese history and numerous interpretive insights.[6]

Although ironically the study of Japan began in earnest as a result of World War II, its medieval history was neglected during the immediate postwar years. The reasons for this include the strong interest in the post-1868 period of a large majority of Western historians of Japan and the linguistic barrier to using original medieval documents. And as is still true today, anyone attempting to begin a serious study of the period must learn the Marxist analysis and vocabulary that the Japanese continue to use.

This neglect of the medieval period ceased rather abruptly in the mid-1970s when, relative to the still very small number of specialists, there was a sudden profusion of works on many aspects of the medieval period. But before describing the works that have appeared during the past fifteen years, we must first discuss John W. Hall's *Government and Local Power in Japan, 500–1700*, published in 1966; this work in a real sense began a new chapter of study of medieval Japan in the United States.

The historiographical significance of Hall's book is that he demonstrated that Japanese history can be written using what he called the concept of familial organization as the fundamental authority-conveying force within the Japanese sociopolitical structure, which he defined as

not a narrowly defined kinship organization, but rather the extended *uji* system in which family and "family-like" bonds extended over branch (*ichimon*), allied (*fudai*) and even subordinate (*kenin*) families surrounding the

6 Some scholars might also include James Murdoch, *A History of Japan*, as an exception. However, Volume I of his work, beginning with the "origins" and ending with the "arrival of the Portuguese in 1542," is of extremely limited interest to the students of the period it covers, despite occasional insights and lively narratives. This is an idiosyncratic work of an able and tireless amateur in the original positive sense of the term, but it is unable to withstand scholarly scrutiny, as Sansom's work still can.

main line of an aristocratic lineage. This *uji*-type structure lay at the heart of any power-holding arrangement, providing the basic framework through which authority was exercised.[7]

Or, as paraphrased by Mary Elizabeth Berry, Hall's concept of familial organization is a major contribution because it helped show "the essential rationality of historical development, the continuity underlying and the integrity discernible in change, the ascendancy of structure over person."[8]

This was Hall's effort to rewrite Japan's premodern history without using feudalism – as used by either the earlier comparativist writers or the Marxists – as the key concept in the study of Japanese history. As Hall himself wrote in 1962, feudalism as a historical concept applied to the analysis of Japan's past caused historians to make facile comparisons of European and Japanese history and to confine their studies to a narrow range of historical aspects readily accommodated by the concept, such as the lord–vassal relationship in its many manifestations and military culture and ethics, and also caused historians "to accept military power as the ultimate determining force in history." His specific objection to the Marxist use of feudalism was that the concept is used "in almost anthropomorphic fashion as a living social organism which can be described as 'taking over' a society, as 'bringing' certain institutions into being, as 'resisting' change or 'leading' to other stages of society."[9] Hall's work showed that non-Japanese scholars using original documents could reinterpret Japanese history and challenge the dominant Marxist view offered by Japanese scholars.

As noted, the study of medieval Japan began to increase in the mid-1970s. The main reason for this growth is the greater number of specialists, many of whom are better trained than were most of the earlier generations of scholars, both in historiography and in their ability to use primary and secondary sources. The better linguistic capabilities of recent entrants to the field is partly a result of the postwar public and private funding that became available for graduate study and extended stays in Japan.

As is evident in the appended bibliography, the recent upsurge of scholarly activities in the field of medieval history took two forms: the publication of several multiauthor volumes, most of which included articles on the medieval period as well as on the Heian, Sengoku, and Tokugawa periods, and the larger number of research

7 Mass (1982a), p. 262.　8 Berry (1987), p. 187.　9 Hall (1968).

monographs and articles on the Kamakura and Muromachi periods by individual scholars.[10]

This section summarizes each chapter in this volume in order of appearance and briefly discusses both the works of the author to date and significant recent works by others that are relevant to the subject of the chapter.

In his numerous works, Jeffrey P. Mass has begun to revise Kamakura history and to present a new vision of the Kamakura bakufu that challenges many of the existing Western interpretations of Japan's medieval history. His chapter in this volume, "The Kamakura Bakufu," summarizes many of his new insights and interpretations and reveals his ability to make extensive and imaginative use of original sources. Mass is careful to identify throughout the chapter the differences in interpretation between his and the more widely held views of both Japanese and Western scholars. For example, he has shown that the once-cherished notion of tyrannic rule by Taira Kiyomori is an exaggeration because Taira was hampered by Emperor Goshirakawa for most of his supposed hegemony; the traditional view of the Jōkyū disturbance of 1221 as a clash between court and bakufu cannot be sustained and must be seen as a war in which disenchanted vassals joined Emperor Gotoba's rebellion; the military estate stewards (jitō) were not a new phenomenon invented by Yoritomo but were appropriated and recast by him to meet his own needs; the office of provincial constables (shugo) were not established in 1185, as the Azuma kagami states, but later and as a means of controlling the jitō; there is a need to distinguish and evaluate more carefully the differing historical significance of jitō appointed before and after the Jōkyū disturbance of 1221 (hompo and shimpo jitō) and the development of the jitō's proprietary control over shōen; and the role of judicial arbitrator is one of the most significant facets of the Kamakura bakufu.

Those who have read Mass's earlier works will note that his chapter shows that his analysis of the Kamakura period is changing. Mass previously viewed the period as one principally of disengagement and innovation instead of continuity with the past or integration with its traditions, but he has now shifted closer to the evolutionary view

---

10 See Hall and Mass, eds. (1974); Hall, Nagahara, and Yamamura, eds. (1981); Hall and Toyoda, eds. (1977); Mass, ed. (1982); Mass and Hauser, eds. (1985); and Yamamura (1975). Some readers may also want to consult Elison and Smith (1981).

espoused by Hall. Mass now views the Heian system of imperial aristocratic rule as still vigorous during the twelfth century but also as remaining the essential framework within which the bakufu was obliged to operate. In this sense, he concludes that the Heian pattern of government survived into the fourteenth century and was destroyed with the Kamakura bakufu rather than by it. However, Mass does point out and discuss those aspects of the period and the bakufu that he believes were revolutionary in nature. One example is Yoritomo's vision, which enabled this Minamoto leader to take advantage of the chaos of the Gempei War to fulfill the most deep-seated desire of the warriors class: to possess guaranteed landholdings outside Kyoto's purview. A second example is Yoritomo's accommodation with the court in 1183 through which, for the first time in Japanese history, a noncentral source of authority provided patronage for central recipients and exerted its power as well in central and western Japan.

Mass stresses that accommodation with the court changed the bakufu's scope of authority from one previously limited to military and police functions to one that became increasingly judicial in tone; that is, the bakufu's major function evolved from simply fulfilling the warriors' desires to restoring political stability, a stability that could be maintained only by protecting equally the rights of warriors and of courtiers. Mass emphasizes that the one-time rebel established a bakufu that became a genuine force for law and order. Indeed, Mass sees a crucial raison d'être for the bakufu's existence in the settlement of land disputes. The bakufu developed a sophisticated legal system that attempted to arbitrate between the local interests of Kamakura vassals, or the *jitō*, and the central elites, the proprietors of *shōen*. As in his earlier writings, Mass discusses the evolution of a legal system that was created to undertake this task. This system of adjudication was based on precedents and in turn developed basic ideas of impartiality, modes of proof, due process, and the right of appeal. Mass's goal here is to show that the Kamakura bakufu maintained peace and stability through the legal system that the bakufu developed with considerable skill and foresight.[11]

Ōyama Kyōhei, who wrote the chapter "The Medieval *Shōen*," is Japan's leading scholar on this subject and has written numerous articles on the *shōen*. Ōyama's interest is broad, and he has studied propri-

---

11 See all of the entries in the selected bibliography for Jeffrey P. Mass; Goble (1982, 1985); Hurst (1982); Kiley (1982); Steenstrup (1979, 1980a, 1980b); Takeuchi (1982); and Varley (1979a).

etorship, management of *shōen*, the *jitō*'s roles in the *shōen*, and the lives of the *shōen* cultivators as payers of dues, defenders of the paddies against nature, and participants in the growing market economy.

Ōyama begins his chapter with an attempt to determine the extent of *shoēn* formation in three provinces, by using the provincial land registers (*ōtabumi*). What he finds from the registers of Noto, Awaji, and Wakasa provinces is that the percentage of the land that contained *shōen* varied from approximately 50 percent in Wakasa to more than 70 percent in Noto and Awaji. Although his observation that the *shōen* system was becoming a fixture in medieval Japanese society is not surprising to students of the period, his finding is significant in that few scholars writing in English have attempted to demonstrate how rapidly and extensively the *shōen* system was spreading during this period.

Ōyama then examines the economic institutions and practices of several *shōen*. On the basis of findings such as that dues were paid in kind to Kyoto-based proprietors, that the mix of dues differed by season and region, and that corvée, too was demanded and received by the *shōen* proprietors, Ōyama concludes that the household economy of *shōen* proprietors in the Kamakura period was basically self-sufficient. The degree of self-sufficiency and how long it lasted have been long, intensively debated subjects, as both pertain to the political and economic reasons for the control over, and growth of, commerce.

The latter half of Ōyama's chapter deals with the internal organization of the *shōen*. He describes in detail a few *shōen* and their landholding patterns–the number of paddies managed and worked by the cultivators themselves (*myō*), office land (*shokan-myō*), and other units of paddies. The position of the *jitō* within the *shōen* is also explained in order to provide a detailed picture of the rights and landholdings of the *jitō*. Ōyama looks at a number of court cases to illustrate the common areas of dispute – excessive corvée imposts, unauthorized taxation, and improper confiscation of fields – between the *jitō* and cultivator and between the *jitō* and proprietor.

Ōyama concludes with a thoughtful discussion of the current scholarly debate among specialists of medieval Japan who emphasize one or the other of the two overlapping land systems of the medieval period: the local overlord–proprietor system (*zaichi–ryōshu*) that provided the warriors' economic base and the *shōen* system as primarily an institution that provided the same for the court nobility in both the Kamakura and Muromachi periods. He argues that those who focus on the former are attempting to draw parallels with the feudalism of medieval Europe, whereas those who concentrate on the latter are favoring an Asian comparison. Ōyama then discusses the recent interest in the Japanese medieval period in its own right, as having non-European structural characteristics. He speculates that the *shōen* system survived in some places well into the sixteenth century because the Kamakura bakufu – and to an extent the Muromachi – supported a policy that created coexistence between the *shōen* and the *zaichi-ryōshu* system.[12]

Ishii Susumu, the author of "The Decline of the Kamakura Bakufu," is an undisputed authority on many aspects of the Kamakura bakufu and an active participant in the debates on the historiographical issues of the medieval period. His contribution to the study of the *shugo* system of the Kamakura period is widely regarded as one of the most important in advancing our understanding of the system and of the character of the Kamakura bakufu.

Ishii first examines the effects of the two Mongol invasions of 1274 and 1281, because the invasions themselves, along with the continued fear of future invasions, put an enormous economic burden on the bakufu which could neither meet the expenses of fortification nor offer rewards to the warriors or religious institutions credited with the *kamikaze* (divine winds) that ultimately drove back the Mongols. Ishii then stresses that the invasions were only one factor in the decline of the bakufu. Other factors included internal dissension within the Hōjō hierarchy, economic difficulties of the warrior class caused by the growing commercialization and exacerbated by the economic burdens imposed on it by the invasions, discontent among rival warrior houses to the Hōjō autocracy and monopolization of bakufu posts, and the rise of domestic unrest evidenced by groups of marauders called *akutō* and by peasants. The dispute over the imperial succession, which divided the court into two factions competing for both the imperial title and rights to *shōen*, also took away support for the bakufu. The bakufu, in the role of arbiter, settled the dispute by introducing a system of alternate succession, but the bakufu's intervention in court affairs was met with enmity and resentment, causing Emperor Godaigo in particular to encourage anti-Hōjō and antibakufu sentiment in his attempt to restore direct imperial rule. Ishii sees the use of *tokuseirei* (debt-abrogation decrees) as an attempt by the bakufu to

12 See Hall (1966); Kiley (1974); Mass (1974b); Nagahara (1975); Sato (1974); Piggott (1982); and Yamamura (1981b).

overcome some of these problems. But such decrees eased the economic difficulties of some warriors and peasants for only a brief period at the cost of further destabilizing the bakufu.[13]

John W. Hall's "The Muromachi Bakufu" is a thorough and critical study of the institutional history of the Muromachi period. Hall begins with a rebuttal of the traditional view that the Muromachi bakufu was weak when judged in terms of effective centralized rule. He points out that recent assessments suggest that even in terms of government efficiency, the Ashikaga should not be dismissed too lightly. Under the auspices of the third and sixth Ashikaga shoguns (Yoshimitsu and Yoshinori), a military government for the first time gained possession of all aspects of secular authority.

The next section of Hall's chapter deals with the *shugo* system, focusing on the steps that led to its increased authority during the period. The most important point of his analysis is that Hall, unlike many other scholars both in Japan and the West, does not view the *shugo*'s increased authority as threatening the survival of the bakufu. Instead, he argues that as long as the *shugo* and the bakufu "worked together in a context that admitted the shogun's primacy, the growth of *shugo* power in the provinces was to the advantage of the bakufu's rule."

Hall next examines the delicate balance of power within the bakufu between the *shugo* and the shogun. Noting that shogunal control increased under Yoshimitsu, Hall offers a number of reasons for this: the end of the fighting over the Southern Court, the development of the *kanrei* (deputy shogun) system, the practice of *shugo* residence in Kyoto, and military action eliminating recalcitrant *shugo*. Shogunal power, Hall emphasizes, was enhanced by the post of *kanrei* which rotated among three primary *shugo* allies, because this practice gave the bakufu the combined military support of the primary allies needed to dominate any would-be challenger of shogunal power.

Hall also explores the economic underpinnings of the bakufu, a subject dealt with only in passing in most histories of the period. He illustrates the diverse income sources used by the bakufu, which included – besides landholdings, taxes on merchants, patronage of *za* (guilds), tolls on roads and borders, and the tribute trade with Ming China – all evidence of the burgeoning medieval economy. After the Ōnin War (1467–77), the bakufu sphere of authority was reduced

13 See Arnesen (1982); Harrington (1982); Hori (1974); and Varley (1971, 1982).

almost solely to the city of Kyoto and its close environs, even though the Muromachi bakufu in form lasted well into the sixteenth century. An important reason for this decline in authority was, according to Hall, the trend toward local autonomy which he describes at various levels. This indeed is a masterful chapter, containing significant insights and reflections by this postwar pioneer and undisputed leader of Japan's premodern history.

Another contribution to the institutional history of the Muromachi period is "Muromachi Local Government: *Shugo* and *Kokujin*," by Imatani Akira, who has in the past dozen years published major works on the subject of this chapter and on other topics in the institutional history of the Muromachi period. In this chapter, Imatani focuses on the decentralization of local authority, an aspect of the institutional history of the period that until very recently was little studied by Western scholars. Imatani's central concern is to analyze the constant battles that Muromachi bakufu had to fight for control of the periphery. He first examines the failure of the regional administrative officials in the Kantō region (*kubō*) and in Kyushu (*tandai*). The post of *kubō* was established by the bakufu in an attempt to maintain control in the region and was considered of such importance that an Ashikaga branch family member was appointed to the position. But instead of strengthening the bakufu's control, the *kubō* became a constant source of trouble and rebellion for the bakufu. After analyzing the development, Imatani concludes that the failure of the *kubō* and *tandai* systems needs to be seen as an important reason for the decentralization in peripheral areas and subsequently for the general state of war that characterized the period.

However, the central intent of Imatani's chapter is to examine the decentralization of power that resulted from the increasing power of the *shugo* despite the bakufu's attempts to control them. He observes that the transformation of the *shugo* into a regional hegemon was due to their increased power to enforce decisions regarding land disputes, to levy *hanzei* and other taxes, as well as to secure other powers. The power to impose a levy taking half of the proprietary dues (*hanzei*) from *shōen* eventually enabled the *shugo* to absorb parts of the *shōen*, thus providing an economic base capable of supporting vassals. The ability to impose a provincewide tax (*tansen*) expanded the *shugo*'s authority throughout the province. Imatani also notes that the post's increasingly hereditary nature further aided in the transformation of *shugo* into hegemon. The analyses offered in this part of the chapter

differ in perspective from that adopted by Hall in the preceding chapter, but they do not counter the substance of Hall's on the changing
relationship between the bakufu and *shugo* and its effects on the stability of the Muromachi polity.

In the final section, which is of great interest to specialists, Imatani
analyzes the relationship between the *shugo* and the *kokujin* (local
overlords). He discusses the scholarly debate between the proponents
of Nagahara Keiji's view of the *shugo* as the axis of political order that
established the *shugo* domain system and the proponents of Kurokawa Naonori's view of the *kokujin* instead of the *shugo* as the central
figure of the time. Imatani concludes that the *shugo* who exerted
power over their respective regions were the principal force behind
the changes that unfolded from the late fifteenth through the early
sixteenth centuries.[14]

Following these two chapters on the institutional developments in the
Muromachi period are two chapters, "The Decline of the Shōen" and
"The Medieval Peasant," by Nagahara Keiji who has written many
scholarly monographs, articles, textbooks, and popular "educational"
books on both the medieval and later periods of Japanese history.
Several of his monographs on the premodern period and on historiography have offered new interpretations, analyses, and insights; some
have been accepted by the profession, and others continue to be
widely debated. Nagahara's scholarly works concentrate on the Muromachi and Sengoku periods, and his articles in English (see the
bibliography to the Introduction) reveal his contributions to the
study of the medieval period.

The first of Nagahara's chapters describes and analyzes the meta-
morphosis of *shōen* into fief. He begins with an outline of the *shōen*
system and concludes that its long success lies in the fact that the *shōen*
answered the economic as well as the social needs of both the ruling
class and the ruled. And turning to the main topic of his essay, he
notes that this successful balance began to be upset because of the
introduction of two new elements, the *jitō* and *shugo*, in which he sees
the manifestation of a process begun in the Kamakura period during
which the power of the central proprietor over the lands, its revenue,
and its inhabitants declined as that of the warrior class increased.

14 See Arnesen (1985); Collcutt (1982a); Davis (1974); Gay (1985); Grossberg (1981a, 1981b);
   Hall (1968, 1981, 1985); Harrington (1985); Hayashi (1977); Kawai (1977); Kuwayama
   (1977); Miyagawa (1977); Murakami (1984); Sato (1977); Varley (1967, 1980); and Wintersteen (1974a, 1974b).

Nagahara concentrates on three pivotal causes of the process that brought about the eventual demise of the *shōen:* the incursion by the *jitō,* that by the *shugo,* and changes at the village level. The *jitō* were able, if only gradually over time, to usurp more proprietary rights over the *shōen* through means of compromises (*wayo*) and contracts (*ukesho*) with the central proprietors which often led to a physical division of the *shōen* (*shitaji chūbun*). Nagahara notes that by the fifteenth century these *jitō* had been transformed into *kokujin-ryōshu* (local overlords) who possessed a contiguous local power base. The *shugo*'s rights over land increased with the establishment of the Muromachi bakufu. New rights concerning the resolution of land disputes were granted to *shugo,* thus widening the scope of their political and economic authority. The *shugo* also received rights to impose taxes (*tansen* and *hanzei*) which gave them the additional lever needed to create a vassal organization of their own. The eventual outcome of these developments was a system of *shugo* domains.

Nagahara then turns to the villages and sees that changes there were also weakening the *shōen* system at the same time. The autonomy of local agricultural communities grew, and there began to appear *sō-mura,* self-governing bodies that evolved into the villages of the Tokugawa period. In the process, many rights of *shōen* proprietors were lost, including those over crimes committed in villages. Large-scale peasant protests (*ikki*), such as the one in 1428 that interfered in the collection of *shōen* taxes and another in 1441 that succeeded in forcing the bakufu to issue a *tokusei* edict abrogating debt obligations, also helped weaken the *shōen* system.

Nagahara also discusses the various means used by the central proprietors to stave off the inevitable. These included appeals to the bakufu and resorts to out-of-court settlements (*wayo*), such as authorizing *jitō* to collect and deliver the annual tax (*ukesho*) and hiring tax collectors (*ukeoi daikan*). Nagahara examines the precarious role played by the bakufu of both the Kamakura and Muromachi periods to placate military supporters and *shōen* proprietors. His conclusion is that the *shōen* system crumbled under the combined pressures from above – the *jitō* and *shugo* – and below – the changes in villages.[15]

Nagahara's second chapter, "The Medieval Peasant," describes peasant life and participation in the political changes of the late medieval period. Convinced that the *shōen* system was pivotal in the creation of

15 See Nagahara (1960, 1979); and Nagahara and Yamamura (1981).

a medieval peasantry, Nagahara believes that the introduction and development of the *shōen* system had a greater impact on the living conditions of peasants in Japan than did the founding of the Kamakura bakufu. The *shōen* system, therefore, is of great significance in peasant history and is the central defining characteristic of the medieval period.

In this chapter Nagahara also expands on a subject introduced in his preceding chapter, that of the growing autonomy of rural communities. The independence of these communities from control by the central proprietor and later by the local overlord was realized gradually as these communities acquired rights of self-governance, welfare, and taxation. Nagahara's unique contribution is his description of everyday peasant life – food, clothing, and shelter – on a *shōen*.

In his chapter, "The Growth of Medieval Commerce," Kozo Yamamura examines the growth of commerce in medieval Japan and the many significant changes that this growth brought to Japanese society. The chapter is organized chronologically and begins with an overview of the initial conditions – the economic and institutional development achieved by the mid-thirteenth century – that the author believes are important to explaining the subsequent rapid growth of commerce. The following sections describe and analyze the reasons for, and the effect of, this growth of commerce, which continued steadily in the Kamakura and accelerated in the Nambokuchō and Muromachi periods.

The principal developments that Yamamura discusses are the growth of agricultural productivity, which provided a basis for the growth of commerce; the increase in the size and number of urban centers; significant institutional developments such as the rise and growth of guilds (*za*) and the increasing use of bills of exchange; the increasing use of Chinese coins even by cultivators in the countryside; the growing practice of commutation; increasing specialization among artisans, merchants, and specialists in transportation, all of whom offered an ever-larger variety of products and services; and the development of a land and water transportation network.

Interwoven in the descriptions of these and other developments are discussions of economic and political conflicts that arose as the direct and indirect results of the growth of commerce and that reflect the changing balance of political and economic powers among the elite recipients of *shōen* dues (the nobles, temples, and shrines); the warrior class (the bakufu and its retainers and regional and local powers); and the commoners (merchants, artisans, and others). The major topics of this chapter are the political and economic conflicts over the *za*, between the *za* and their competitors, and between their old and new patrons (nobles, temples against the bakufu and daimyo); over the *tokuseirei* (debt-abrogation decrees), pitting lenders (rich merchants and other moneylenders) against borrowers (warriors and commoners); and over changing levels and mixes (in-kind versus cash payment) of dues payment by peasants among the recipients of *shōen* dues and between the recipients and the peasants.

In describing these and other closely related developments that occurred as a result of the growth of commerce, Yamamura attempts to show that by enlisting the analytic insights of modern economic theory a few of the questions most frequently debated can be reexamined, resulting in a better understanding of the political and economic motivations of those involved. The two principal subjects reexamined are the reasons that the Ashikaga bakufu or regional powers (*shugo daimyō*) did not mint coins of their own but continued to use Chinese coins, despite a few distinct disadvantages in doing so; and the reasons that commutation was adopted, not always because of demands by the principal recipients of the dues but at times at the request of the cultivators, the payers of the dues themselves.[16]

The chapter by Kawazoe Shōji, "Japan and East Asia," traces Japan's relations with its East Asian neighbors during the Kamakura and Muromachi bakufu. The author is a recognized authority on the subject and a leading student of the domestic and international causes and effects of the Mongol invasions and many other historiographical issues of the Kamakura period. Kawazoe's principal goal is to show the close relationship between international relations and domestic politics. Although Kawazoe's account of Kamakura foreign relations does include some discussion of the role of the headquarters of Kyushu's governor general (*dazaifu*) in the trade with Sung China, his emphasis is on the Mongol invasions and their effects on Japan's polity and society of the time. He explains that the Mongols initially sought to open relations with Japan in order to strengthen their ties with the Koryŏ kingdom of Korea and to prevent the Japanese from aiding the Southern Sung. However, in noting that the Mongol emissaries were constantly rebuffed, Kawazoe speculates that the Japanese did not

16 See Brown (1951); Hall (1974); Hayashi (1977); Hori (1974); Morris (1977); Nagahara and Yamamura (1988); Piggott (1982); Sasaki (1981); Toyoda and Sugiyama (1977); Wakita (1975, 1981); and Yamamura (1973, 1975, 1981a, 1981b).

accede to the Mongol overtures for three reasons: The Japanese considered the Mongol request to be a declaration of war; Japan's information concerning Mongol intentions was biased because it originated
with the Southern Sung, who were at the time at war with the Mongols; and Japan was a society governed by warriors whose innate function predisposed them to war.

Kawazoe stresses that foreign relations in the early years of the
Muromachi bakufu were hindered by the continued existence of the
Southern Court. That is, the traditional trading and diplomatic center,
the Kyushu dazaifu, remained in the hands of the renegade Southern
Court which was brought to an end in 1392. As a result, the bakufu
was unable to gain control of foreign relations until the last two decades of Yoshimitsu's rule (1368–1408).

Turning to the tribute system with Ming China that began under
Yoshimitsu, Kawazoe posits four reasons for Yoshimitsu's desire to
enter the Ming imperial sphere. First, Yoshimitsu needed the income
generated by the tribute trade to defray the enormous expenditures on
art that were made under his auspices. Second, control over foreign
relations gave legitimacy to Yoshimitsu's rule, as evidenced by his
references to himself as "king" in the dispatches he sent to Ming
China. Third, Ming China could prove to be a formidable enemy, and
thus a tribute relationship would eliminate this insecurity and fear.
And fourth, the tribute trade allowed Yoshimitsu to control the
Kyushu tandai which dealt with all legal trade with China. In addition
to his discussion of the Mongol invasion and Japan's relations with
Ming China, Kawazoe examines the Japanese relationship with Korea
and the Ryūkyū Islands, as well as the effect of the omnipresent wakō
(pirates) on international relations in East Asia throughout the medieval period.[17]

H. Paul Varley's "Cultural Life in Medieval Japan" is a rich and
reflective discussion of the elite cultural achievements of the period as
provided by a leading American scholar of the subject who is also an
authority on the institutional history of medieval Japan. He brings to
his chapter the understanding and breadth of knowledge he has acquired over the past two decades in numerous valuable studies ranging
from the Ōnin War, Kamakura intellectual history and folk beliefs,
and selected institutions of the Kamakura and Muromachi periods, to
the many aspects of cultural life in the Muromachi period.

17 See Tanaka (1977); and Yamamura and Kamiki (1983).

Varley's principal intent is to analyze the aesthetic foundations of medieval elite culture which he views as the combined product of the pessimism of the Buddhist concept of *mappō* (literally, "the latter days of Buddhist law," thus a period of historical decline) with a nostalgia for the Heian past. Central to Varley's analysis is the idea that the pessimism evoked by the concept of *mappō* set the dominant tone for the period. This fact, he argues, is evident in one of the great literary works of the Kamakura period, Kamo no Chōmei's *Hōjōki*, and also in the famous war tale, the *Heike monogatari*, a chronicle of the fated destruction of the Taira family during the Gempei War. Varley also credits *mappō* with creating the major aesthetic precepts of the age: *yūgen* (mystery and depth), *sabi* (loneliness), and *wabi* (the plain and humble). The appeal of the "weathered and withered, the desolate and lonely," he shows, is clearly demonstrated in the last major imperial poetry anthology compiled in 1205, the *Shinkokinshū*.

Varley notes that whereas the cultural achievements of the Kamakura age were the product of courtiers, the Muromachi period saw a tremendous outpouring of military patronage. In particular, he credits Yoshimitsu, the third Ashikaga shogun, with the cultural flowering of the Kitayama epoch (1368–1408). The effect of his patronage, Varley argues, was most evident in the development of noh drama which under Yoshimitsu's protégé, Zeami, became the refined and courtly art we know today. Varley speculates that the principal reason for Yoshimitsu's patronage of the arts lay in political ambition; that is, Yoshimitsu wished to combine both the military and civil elements of rule within himself, thus establishing a kind of "feudal kingship." Varley supports this view by noting that Yoshimitsu institutionalized a calendar of formal events mimicking that of the imperial court.

In his conclusion, Varley challenges the traditional view that Zen played a dominant role in molding medieval tastes and sentiments. Instead, he contends that the products of medieval culture – the *Heike monogatari*, *renga* poetry, noh, *sumi-e*, landscape painting, and *shoin*-style architecture – all reflect indigenous Japanese feelings and tastes, with which those of Zen simply coincided. Medieval culture, according to Varley, is a product of an aesthetic longing for, or a nostalgic vision of, the courtier past and aesthetic precepts – *yūgen*, *sabi*, and *wabi* – which too had their roots in the Heian period or earlier.[18]

---

18 See Brazell (1973); Butler (1969); Ito (1977); Keene (1977); McCullough (1966, 1979); Rosenfield (1977); Ruck (1971); Sansom (1943); Smith (1981); Ury (1979); Varley (1972, 1977, 1978, 1979a, 1979b, 1980, 1984); and Varley and Elison (1981).

What Barbara Ruch offers in her chapter, "The Common Culture of Medieval Japan," is the perceptive result of her efforts to revise the cultural history of medieval Japan: an endeavor to broaden our collective image and knowledge of the cultural life of medieval Japan, by focusing on the "common culture" of the nonelite majority which has long remained neglected by Western specialists of the period. Thus this chapter can be seen as an exploration of a *terra incognita* in Western scholarship.

Defining "common culture" as "those attitudes and activities known to all and esteemed by that same majority, high and low. . . . one that has outgrown the exclusive ownership of any gender, group, or coterie in society, high or low, and has become the property of all," Ruch illustrates its development by examining its various aspects – women, itinerant storytellers, and shamans as cultural actors and sources, as well as scrolls, popular songs, and stories. One must be reminded here that written historical sources for her study are extremely scarce and thus she must use what sources exist with insight and imagination.

What Ruch discovered from her examination are the common threads of medieval society. One is the pervasiveness of tonsure. By using the life of one medieval abbess, Mugai Nyodai, Ruch represents the whole complex system of nunhood. Tonsure is viewed not only as a "disposal system for used women" but also as an option for women wishing to express individual talent, a socially acceptable form of deviance from traditional life. Another thread is the creation during the medieval period of common gods shared by a multitude across regional and social lines, the most popular of which were the *kannon*, *jizō*, and gods of fortune. The creation of these common gods, Ruch believes, was "a powerfully unifying social force" during the middle ages.

Ruch also explores everyday life as depicted in various types of scrolls; the role of women as shamans, prostitutes, and entertainers; and the creation of a national myth through the popularization of the *Heike monogatari*. She closes her chapter by noting the limitations inherent in the traditional view of Muromachi culture, the equation of culture with elitism. In short, she argues that concepts such as *yūgen* and *sabi,* said to characterize the arts and literature of the Muromachi period, play no role at all in the common arts of painting, sculpture, song, dance, and musical epic that the specialists have long been studying. She makes the case that those concepts belong to an extremely limited world, to rarefied pockets of medieval society.[19]

Ōsumi Kazuo's chapter, "Buddhism in the Kamakura Period," is a detailed but clearly presented overview and discussion. An undisputed leading Japanese scholar on Buddhism in the medieval period, Ōsumi is working at the forefront of scholarship that is now reacting to and reevaluating the works of the immediate postwar decades, whose principal foci were the linkage between religious teachings and social classes and the teachings and activities of the Kamakura founders of the new sects as reflections of class or regional values.

Ōsumi begins by examining the new schools of Buddhism that developed during this period: Pure Land (Jōdō), True Pure Land (Jōdo Shin), Zen (Sōtō and Rinzai), and Nichiren (Hokke). He provides an extensive outline of the founders, tenets, and the institutional evolution of the new schools. Ōsumi's emphasis, however, is on the nature of Kamakura Buddhism. The new schools were "revolutionary," he feels, because for the first time, Buddhism was fully adapted to Japanese concerns and put down roots among the common people. His view is buttressed by such examples as the Pure Land teachings of Hōnen and Shinran which did not restrict salvation to those with specialized religious training. Ōsumi observes that for the first time, ordinary people could attain enlightenment in the next world through simple chants (*nembutsu*) or through faith. He notes that Nichiren's teachings also appealed to ordinary people, because by propounding a "this-world" form of salvation, Nichiren was able to offer guidance and hope for everyday life. Other religious teachings, too, according to Ōsumi, synthesized Buddhism with various popular beliefs and practices. For example, Ippen absorbed many Shintō practices into his religious teachings, making them more compatible with the spiritual inclinations of ordinary people.

Ōsumi also discusses the impact of the new religions on the Buddhist establishment. The early response of the established schools of Buddhism was persecution, which caused most of the founders of the Kamakura schools to spend years in exile. Later, however, the existence of the new schools acted as a catalyst to a revival of the Buddhist establishment. Thus, in Ōsumi's judgment, Kamakura Buddhism acted as a stimulus forcing the established schools to reassess them-

19 See also Ruch (1977).

selves and to shift their scholastic trends. In short, Ōsumi feels justified in concluding that the religious revolution that occurred in the
Kamakura period not only created new schools of Buddhism but also
transformed the old ones.[20]

The chapter on "Zen and the Gozan" is by Martin Collcutt, author of
both an important book on the subject and significant studies of the
institutional and religious histories of the medieval period. His chapter
provides a perceptive history of Zen in Japan, from its introduction in
the Asuka period (538–710) through the Muromachi period. The first
part of this chapter deals with the transmission of Zen (Ch'an) from
China, a process that, before the Kamakura period, was sporadic.
However, the Kamakura period saw an upsurge in interest in Zen
which Collcutt credits to the perceived decline of the Buddhist estab-
lishment, a belief in *mappō*, and the popularity of Ch'an in Sung
China, where many Japanese monks, including the founders of the
Rinzai and Sōtō Zen (Eisai and Dōgen), traveled for their training.
Collcutt estimates that by the early fourteenth century the practice of
Zen in Japanese monasteries was probably quite similar to that in
Chinese monasteries.

Collcutt then discusses the institutional development of Zen. The
reasons behind the Hōjō and *shugo* patronage of Zen during the
Kamakura period include, according to Collcutt, a variety of cultural,
political, and social factors, as well as spiritual interests. Noting that
these reasons for patronage remained unchanged into the Muromachi
period, Collcutt offers, as an example, the motivations for the development of *ankokuji* (temples for national peace) established by Ashikaga
Takauji in the mid-fourteenth century and built at the urging of an
influential monk of the Rinzai sect, Musō Soseki, who was eager to
close the breach between the supporters of the rival courts and to calm
the restless spirit of Godaigo.

Collcutt also describes the *gozan* network of Rinzai Zen, a three-
tiered hierarchy of temples nationwide and other institutional networks, including the Daiō and Genjū schools of Rinzai and the Sōtō
organization. The fortunes of the networks fluctuated with that of
their patrons, as typified in the *gozan*'s fortunes which rose and fell
with the political power of the Muromachi bakufu. Thus, Collcutt
notes that not surprisingly, when financial support dried up, monaster-

---

20 See Bloom (1965); Kitagawa (1966); Kuroda (1981); Matsunaga (1969); Rodd (1980); and
Weinstein (1977).

ies were gutted in the Ōnin War; their monks were dispersed; and their lands were taken from them.

In the final sections of his chapter, Collcutt discusses the varied sources of income of the Zen establishment (*shōen* proprietorship, donations, prayer fees, *za* sponsorship, medicancy, and moneylending) and the place of Zen in medieval society and culture. He believes that Zen played many roles in the medieval world; for example, apart from giving spiritual and cultural guidance, the Zen monks served as diplomats and political advisers, offered prayers for relief from famines, and conducted funeral services. Their monasteries trained children of warrior families and also made financial loans and organized welfare projects. Collcutt concludes that the *gozan* system, in particular, was seen by the Ashikaga as conducive to national centralization and local surveillance.[21]

CONCLUDING NOTES

Characterizing "an important new feature of Japanese medieval studies in the West," Mass wrote that there is today "a beginning tendency to reassess, even challenge at times, the conclusions of the Japanese historians." He further noted:

This does not mean merely looking at events and institutions through "foreign eyes," but rather reviewing them via the same source materials that led to those conclusions in the first place. Naturally, Western abilities in this area have not progressed very far, but there are the first signs of a genuine dissatisfaction with the citing of a secondary source and then interpreting simply from that. If Western scholarship is to win the respect of historians in Japan, it will be necessary to master the same sources that they use, and also to show greater confidence in our own capacities for originality.[22]

Hideharu Nitta, however, in reviewing *Court and Bakufu in Japan*, which Mass edited and in which Mass made the preceding observations, wrote:

In his editor's introduction, Mass identifies the importance of the practical application of primary documents together with the maintenance of originality, as well as the ability to generalize, as guidelines for American research on Japanese medieval history. However, what one is conscious of as generality in the articles in this volume is that descriptions tend toward general statements, rather than true generalizing. Naturally, some of the articles are heavily under

---

21 See Akamatsu (1977); Collcutt (1981, 1982b); Dumoulin (1969); Kitagawa (1966); Suzuki (1973); and Varley (1981).   22 Mass (1982a), p. xvi.

the influence of Japanese researchers. Thus, anyone expecting novel or different points of view not found in studies made by Japanese will be unsatisfied.
This is probably because American researchers of Japanese medieval history
have not yet developed their own map of the "forest" of the Kamakura
period, a forest which is full of trees, that is, historical facts drawn from
primary documents. Having scrutinized the map made by Japanese researchers, Americans are increasingly forcing their way into the forest, but they are
not yet able to draw their own map.[23]

The juxtaposition of Mass's and Nitta's assessments of American
scholarship on the medieval period offers an important clue to apprais-
ing the current state of Western historiography of the medieval period.
Namely, even though Mass believes that he can now discern Western
scholars' abilities to challenge the conclusions of Japanese historians,
Nitta's words on Mass's qualified assessment are quite harsh and declare that Americans, not having their own map of the forest, see only
trees, as evidenced in the fact that their statements tend toward "general statements" rather than toward "true generalization."

Although these assessments are not contradictory in a strict sense,
their tones differ sharply. I believe that in no small part, what is
suggested by this difference in the perception of the current state of
Western historiography is due to the difference in what Japanese specialists consider "a map" and "true generalizing," in contrast with
what most Western historians believe them to be. As noted earlier in
describing Japanese historiography, despite the wide range of historiographical issues debated among Japanese scholars, their works –
especially in but not limited to institutional history – follow a map
with dimensions and contours by now well delineated because of the
accumulation of Japanese scholarship to date. That map's latitudes
and longitudes are defined basically by the Marxist framework of
analysis, and it is followed by Japanese historians who may no longer
be aware that the issues they debate and the questions they raise have
origins in the Marxist framework of analysis. That is to say, "true
generalizing," in Nitta's usage, means generalized observations that
are meaningful within this broad framework of Marxist analysis.

What Western scholars consider as a map is different. As demonstrated in the recent works of most Western scholars, the contours
and dimensions of the map used by each medieval specialist rarely
overlap with those of the maps used by fellow practitioners. Even the

23 Hideharu Nitta's review appears in the *Journal of Japanese Studies* 10 (1984): 515. [I do not
   wish to suggest that the views expressed in this review accurately reflect Professor Nitta's
   general historiographical approach. In using this review, I also assume that the views expressed in it have been accurately translated from the Japanese.]

rise and decline of feudalism, especially from a comparative perspective, which was used as an underpinning of analysis by the specialists of the prewar years and the immediate postwar decades, today attracts few scholars.

Hall analyzed Japanese history by seeing it as a continuing unfolding of the familial system, whereas Mass offers his vision of the Kamakura bakufu as a living dyarchy, whose true character can be discerned by comparing the relative strength of what was new and revolutionary with the legacies of the past. When reading the best works of other specialists on varied aspects of the institutional and other histories of the period, it becomes clear that each scholar has a map, be it an internally consistent paradigm or an interpretive view of history crafted to meet a particular analytic need.

The general statements offered thus are meaningful within the perspective of the map that each scholar has chosen. Stated differently, Western scholars enjoy the freedom to choose their own analytic frameworks, that is, the freedom to raise fresh questions and answer them in innovative ways. Their Japanese counterparts share a map that yields "true generalizations," but only within the framework of a shared map. The freedom of each Western historian to raise questions of his or her own choosing is a source of creative scholarly energy in the hands of those having visions capable of creating a consistent explanatory analytic paradigm for Japanese history.

However, such freedom can be and has been in some instances misused or abused, because having such freedom can be mistaken for license to expand one's research efforts on ill-conceived analytic bases lacking a substantively formulated vision of history. The results can be studies of limited import and interest. Thus, perhaps it is more accurate to reword the preceding, stating that in rejecting the Marxist analysis and the analytic basis that a comparative analysis of feudalism provided, Western scholars of the period have imposed on themselves the burden of evolving their own analytic approaches of the medieval history of Japan. Although containing a high risk of yielding narrowly conceived works of little interest, this challenge explains the new energy released into the field, which has produced in the West many scholarly works.

Mass's observation that Western students have begun to reassess and even challenge Japanese works and Nitta's remark that some works by Western scholars are still heavily influenced by Japanese scholars are basically the same discovery. That is, both are still correct in referring to or explicitly stating that a large majority of Western works today still rely, and undoubtedly will continue to depend into the foreseeable future, on the works of Japanese scholars. This is inevitable, given the accumulated volume of literature in Japanese, the much larger number of medievalists in Japan, and Japanese scholars' comparative advantage in linguistic facility.

But this should not prevent us from noting, as Mass did, that today's Western scholarship has sufficiently matured to begin to question, reassess, and confront the interpretations and analyses offered by Japanese scholars. Reassessment and reinterpretation can take myriad forms. Restating an event or development without using a Marxist vocabulary and conceptualization, if presented in a form internally consistent and readily comprehensible to Western readers, can constitute a meaningful reassessment of Japanese scholarship. If a specific historical event is reinterpreted on the basis of an *ad hoc* paradigm so that the interpretation advances our understanding of the event, however modestly, and can serve as a valuable input for others who might incorporate the result into a study based on a more comprehensive framework of analysis of medieval history, such a reinterpretation can be seen as a useful historiographical contribution.

To Nitta and to many other Japanese scholars, what reassessments and reinterpretations the Western students produce may appear to be influenced by Japanese works and may be seen as lacking in originality. But to the extent that such restatements enhance the knowledge of Japan's medieval history, they must be considered valuable contributions to the progress of Western scholarship. Similarly, if an event is seen to have had causes different from those commonly accepted by Japanese scholars, however subtle these differences may be, this must be seen as an original contribution, however modest its significance to the sweep of historical change. What I am arguing here is that more Western scholars today have become capable of making such reassessments and original contributions, and a few are challenging parts of Japanese historiography in significant ways.

An important ingredient that has enabled this progress in Western scholarship is the growing ability of Western students to use primary sources. As the works of Collcutt, Hall, Mass, Ruch, Varley, and many others have demonstrated, there is no substitute for using primary sources to make original contributions to historiography. However, at the same time it is no less true that in a young field only slowly developing by most standards of academic endeavors, diverse forms of scholarly contributions are necessary for its growth. This means that we must also welcome "synthetic" works that rely on secondary sources, as they too are often valuable in reinterpreting and, indeed, synthesizing known events, developments, and interpretations. The field must recognize the utility of such efforts by specialists and non-specialists alike, who offer descriptive and interpretive works useful to all interested in the medieval history of Japan.

In the study of medieval history of Japan, the needs of the specialists and the nonspecialists must be balanced. Otherwise, specialists can become self-satisfied students of original sources that yield findings of little broad significance. On the other hand, nonspecialists will be misled if they believe that genuine progress in a field can be made without the demanding tasks of specialists who labor to fill the gaps in our knowledge only a very small part at a time.

I shall conclude this introduction by adding that in the West the field of medieval history of Japan, still young and having few specialists, does not lack in topics and questions for continuing research. Readers of this volume will have little difficulty in suggesting future research topics that they would like to see the specialists pursue. Thus, the task has just begun for institutional historians and especially for others interested in the social, cultural, and economic histories of the period, which are being studied by no more than a handful of specialists.

APPENDIX: CHRONOLOGY OF MEDIEVAL PERIOD

Major political events and developments[a, b, d]	Major sociocultural and economic developments[a, b, d]	Major international events and developments[a-d]
	Pre-Kamakura (before 1185)	
10C Warrior class rises		
	11C Artisans are protected in capital; *za* appear (8)	
	11C Markets appear in Kyoto (8)	[1066 Norman conquest of England]
1087–1192 Insei (cloistered government)		
	12C Artisans begin to trade with cultivators (8)	
Late 11C–Early 12C *Shōen* system now extends throughout Japan (8)		
	1127 *Renga* first appear in imperial anthology	1127–1279 Southern Sung dynasty in China
1150–1200 Taira and Minamoto families become prominent	1151 and 1163 Major fires in Kyoto	
1156 Hōgen conflict: Minamoto challenges Taira position at court and loses		

Major political events and developments[a, b, d]	Major sociocultural and economic developments[a, b, d]	Major international events and developments[a-d]
1159 Heiji War: Minamoto are defeated again by Taira (1)	1163 Kiyomori builds Rengeōin (Sanjūsangendō)	
1167 Kiyomori attains highest court rank		
	1168 Eisai visits China	12C–early 13C Large numbers of Sung and Southern Sung coins are imported (8) E
	Late 1170s–early 1180s Fire, famine, and earthquakes in Kyoto (10)	
1180 Minamoto Yoritomo establishes base in Kamakura	1175 Hōnen founds Jōdo sect (12)	
1180–5 Gempei War: Minamoto achieve victory over Taira (1)		
1181 Kiyomori dies	1181 Famine in Kyoto	
1184–6 Appointment of *hompo jitō* (1)	*Kamakura period (1185–1333)* Around 1185 *Hōgen* and *Heiji monogatari* appear (10)	
	1187 Fujiwara Yoshinori compiles *Senzai wakashū*	
1192 Yoritomo given title of shogun	Late 12C Court decrees prohibit use of coins (8)	1189 Southern Sung attempts to prohibit outflow of Sung copper to Japan (9)
		[1190s Start of first Crusade]
1192 Yoritomo appoints *shugo* (1)	1191 Eisai introduces Rinzai teachings	
1192 *Gokenin* first appears (1)	Late 12C Zen thought, meditation, monastic forms are introduced (10, 12, 13)	
1199 Yorimoto dies		
	1200–7 Bakufu expel fanatic Jōdo sect groups from Kamakura	
	1201–8 Eighth imperial anthology, *Shinkokinshū*, is compiled	
1203 Establishment of *shikken* and rise of Hōjō (1)	Early 13C Marketplaces in Kamakura are authorized by bakufu (8)	
Early 13C Gotoba creates private army later to challenge Kamakura (1)	Early 13C Legal system develops further; more suits are brought against *jitō* (1, 6) P	
	Early 13C *Heike monogatari* appears (10)	
	1207 Hōnen, Shinran, and are others are banished from Kyoto (12)	

Major political events and developments[a, b, d]	Major sociocultural and economic developments[a, b, d]	Major international events and developments[a-d]
1219 Shogun Santeomo is assassinated (1)	1212 Kamo no Chōmei completes *Hōjōki*	[1215 Magna Carta is signed in England]
1221 Jōkyū disturbance: an unsuccessful challenge to the bakufu by Gotoba and dissatisfied warriors (1)	1220 Jien's *Gukanshō* appears Early 13C Use of coins as medium of exchange increases (7)	
1221 Establishment of deputy bakufu headquarters in Kyoto (Rokuhara *tandai*)		1223 First textual reference to Japanese pirates (*wakō*) (9)
1221 Yoritomo appoints *shimpo jitō* to lands confiscated following Jōkyū disturbance (1)	1224 Shinran founds Jōdo Shin sect	
1226 Establishment of *hyōjōshū* and *rensho* (1)	1227 Dōgen brings the Sōtō sect from China	
1227 Bakufu orders *shugo* to suppress *akutō* activities in west		
1230 Establishment of new *shōen* is prohibited	1231 Major famine	
1232 Jōei code and Goseibai *shikimoku* are promulgated (1)	1232 Fujiwara Teika submits *Shin chokusen wakashū* to emperor	
1239 Bakufu prohibits monks, merchants, and moneylenders from becoming deputy *jitō* (8) E	1232 Wake-no-shima is built in Kamakura to facilitate ship docking; becomes base for domestic and foreign trade (9) I	
	1239 Bakufu prohibits use of coins in easternmost provinces	
1249 Establishment of *hikitsuke* (1)	1241 En'ni returns from China with important contributions to Japanese religion and art (9)	
	Mid 13C More Chinese Ch'an masters come to teach Zen; Buddhist doctrines spread to samurai and common people (13)	Mid 13C China attempts to prohibit export of its coins and to restrict Japanese ships in its ports (8) E Mid 13C Genghis Khan builds Eurasian empire (9)
	Mid 13C *Gempei seisuiki* is written	
	Mid 13C *Za* are organized in Kamakura by Hōjō	
	1253 Nichiren founds Nichiren sect (12)	

Major political events and developments[a, b, d]	Major sociocultural and economic developments[a, b, d]	Major international events and developments[a-d]
1264 Bakufu curtails official ships to China (9)	1259 Famine in many provinces	
1266 Kublai Khan seeks relations with Japan (3, 9)	Mid to late 13C Coins become principal medium of trade in large cities; merchants and lenders become common in Kyoto (8)	
1268 Mongol envoys arrive in Japan (3)	Late 13C Bills of exchange begin to be used (8)	[1271–95 Marco Polo visits China]
After 1272 Bakufu orders updating of *ōtabumi* to reassess paddy holdings E	Late 13C *Gozan* institution takes shape (13)	
1274 Mongols attempt first invasion of Japan (Bun'ei) (3)	1280 Abutsu Ni's *Izayoi nikki* appears	
1281 Mongols make second invasion attempt		
1284 *Tokusei* order is issued by shogunate for shogun's retainers (3, 8) E		Post-Mongols: Japanese merchant marine is expanded E
1285 Shimotsuki incident begins period of autocratic rule by *tokusō* (3)		
Late 13C Spread of *do-ikki*, unified cultivator actions (6, 8)		
1293 Heizen-gate disturbance: Taira Yoshitsuna and sympathizers are killed by regent (3)		
1293 Bakufu establishes Chinzei *tandai*		1294 Kublai Khan dies (9)
1297 Bakufu issues Einin *tokuseirei*		
1301 Bakufu implements practice of alternate succession (3)	1306 Japanese pirate ships begin to trade with Chan China	
Late Kamakura *Akutō* become increasingly significant problem	Late Kamakura: Network of markets and ports are developed to accommodate commerce (8)	
14C *Shugo* control of public lands becomes pervasive (6) E	Early 14C Spread of toll barriers (8)	
	1312 *Gyokuyō wakashū* is completed	

Major political events and developments[a, b, d]	Major sociocultural and economic developments[a, b, d]	Major international events and developments[a-d]
1321 Godaigo discontinues *insei*, becomes involved in affairs of state (**6**)		
1331 Genkō disturbance: plotters are arrested	1330s Yoshida Kenkō's *Tsurezuregusa* appears (**13**)	
1332 Emperor Godaigo is exiled to Oki	1333–84 Kan'ami (develops noh under patronage of Yoshimitsu)	
1333 Godaigo escapes from Oki	Early 14C *Jitō uke/ukesho* spread; *jitō* become more autonomous (**6**)	
1333 Kamakura bakufu is overthrown (**3, 4**)		
1333–6 Kemmu restoration: Godaigo attempts to restore direct imperial rule	14C *Shiki* structure is weakened; contiguous local power bases are formed (**6**) P	Late Kamakura/ Nambokuchō: Trading vessels are sent to Yüan China with bakufu's approval for temple and shrine construction (**9**)
	Muromachi period (1336–1467)	
1336 Ashikaga Takauji defeats Godaigo's forces	1336–95 *Shugo* daimyo rise as *shugo's* authority expands (**4, 6**)	
1336 Kemmu *shikimoku*, legal code of Muromachi bakufu, is promulgated	1338 Kyoto replaces Kamakura as focal point of Zen under Ashikaga (**10**)	
1338 Ashikaga Takauji assumes title of shogun, settles bakufu in Kyoto		
1336–92 Nambokuchō era: Northern and Southern Courts both claim imperial legitimacy	Nambokuchō: *Za* appear in rural areas (**8**)	
Muromachi: *Jitō* move to single-heir inheritance, make vassals of peasant leaders (**6**)	Early Muromachi: *Hanzei* laws establish warrior's vested interest in land (**4-6**) P	
	1339–43 Kitabatake Chikafusa's *Jinnō shōtō ki* and other works of similar intent appear (**4, 10**)	
	Muromachi: *Shinden-zukuri* residential style gives way to *shoin-zukuri*	
1348 Kusunoki Masatsura dies in battle of Shijō Nawate	1342 Bakufu institutes *gozan jussetsu* system	[1347 Black Death devastates Europe]

Major political events and developments[a, b, d]	Major sociocultural and economic developments[a, b, d]	Major international events and developments[a-d]
Late Nambokucho: *Kokujin* band together to fight off bakufu-appointed *shugo* (5)	1356 Nijō Yoshimoto and Gusai complete *Tsukubashō*, first imperially sponsored *renga* anthology (10)	1350 Attacks by *wakō* begin in earnest (9)
1352 Bakufu imposes *hanzei* in Ōmi, Minō, and Owari	1367 Bakufu imposes *munabechisen* to build hospital in Kyoto	1366 Koryŏ envoys request bakufu's suppression of *wakō*
1358 Ashikaga Takauji dies		
1368 Yoshimitsu becomes *seii-taishogun*	Mid 14C Commutation is practiced in virtually all regions of Japan (8)	1368–1644 Chinese Ming dynasty (9)
Muromachi: Practice of dividing office of *shugo* begins (5) E	1371 Bakufu levies tax in *sakaya* and *dosō* in Kyoto and *tansen* in many provinces to pay for imperial ascension ceremony	1369, 1370 Ming China sends envoy to establish relations with Japan
	1371(?) *Taiheiki* is completed	
	1376 *Masukagami* is completed, probably by Nijō Yoshimoto	1378, 1380 Yoshimitsu's envoys to Ming China are refused
	1381 Hana no Gosho, headquarters of military aristocracy, is completed	1383 Japan abandons attempt to establish relations with Ming China
	1386 Bakufu settles ranking of *gozan* and selects Nanzenji as the highest-ranked temple	
	1387 *Baishōron* appears	
1391–2 Meitoku rebellion: attempt to overthrow shogunate is put down by bakufu; shogunal dominance of nation is reconsolidated	Late 14C *Gozan* sinification peaks (13)	
1392 Northern and Southern Courts are reconciled by bakufu	1392–1467 Kitayama epoch: a period of stable balance among court, shogun, and *shugo*; Yoshimitsu builds Kinkakuji in Kyoto (1937); noh, *kyōgen*, and *sumi-e* evolve (4)	1392 Koryŏ dynasty collapses in Korea
1394 Yoshimitsu resigns the post of shogun and becomes *dajōdaijin*	1393 Bakufu declares *sakaya* and *dosō* are to pay expenses of *mandokoro* and no longer need to pay dues to their civil protectors	1394 Kyushu *tandai* returns 600 captured Koreans
1390s *Shugo* become local administrators (5)		1397 Bakufu establishes formal ties with Korea
1399 Ōei disturbance: Ouchi Yoshiro is killed in battle in Sakai	Late 14C–early 15C Zeami (1363–1443) elevates noh to a refined art under Yoshimitsu's patronage	

Major political events and developments[a, b, d]	Major sociocultural and economic developments[a, b, d]	Major international events and developments[a-d]
1401 *Machi-gumi* rise in Kyoto (communal organizations of townsmen for internal security) E	Late 14C Sesshū (1420–1506) master of *suiboku* ink landscape painting; develops Japanese style	1404 Official tally trade begins with Ming China (**9**)
1408 Yoshimitsu dies	15C Tea ceremony develops into serious pursuit (**10**)	1404 Envoy is sent to Korea
	15C Popularity of *renga* rises among all classes	1408 Shogun Yoshimochi discontinues relations with Ming China
		1418 First record of tally trade between Japan and Korea
		1419 Ōei invasion: Korean attack on Tsushima is repulsed
1428 Shōchō *dokki: tokusei* are demanded in Kinai		1423 Unification of Ryūkyūs; trade with Japan begins
1432 Yoshinori destroys Kamakura branch of Ashikaga house (**4**)	1431 A major famine results in many deaths in Kyoto; forced sale of rice is ordered	1433 Tally trade with Ming China resumes
1439 Eikyō disturbance: Kanto *kubō* Ashikaga Mochiuji is killed by bakufu troops	1439 Last imperial anthology, *Shinzoku kokinshū*, is compiled (**10**)	
1441 Kakitsu disturbance: Shogun Yoshinori is assassinated, ending strong shogunal rule (**4**)	15C More religious institutions turn to moneylenders (**6**) P	
1447 *Do-ikki* destroys parts of Kyoto	1440s Disease spreads (**8**)	
	1445 Bakufu warriors are prohibited from pawning or selling land	
1449, 1457 Ashikaga attempt to establish branch shogunate in Kantō fails (**4**)	Mid 15C *Shugo* daimyo are able to increase tax revenue by levying *tansen*	
Mid 15C Custom of *gōjichi*, village autonomy, prevails (**4, 6**) E	1450s Deaths from famine are widespread (**4**)	1451 Ming China restricts Japanese tribute missions to one in ten years
	Mid 15C Ichijō Kanera (Kaneyoshi) (1402–81), a prolific scholar of the highest court positions, contributes widely in belles-lettres and studies of Chinese classics and history; also writes (1476) *Renju gappeki shū* on *renga*	[1452–1519 Leonardo da Vinci]
1454 Kyoto is in the grip of unprecedented disorder; thievery is rampant		[1453 Gutenberg Bibles are printed in Mainz]
	1459 Nationwide famine	

Major political events and developments[a, b, d]	Major sociocultural and economic developments[a, b, d]	Major international events and developments[a-d]
1462 Major *tokusei ikki* in Kyoto are suppressed by several *shugo*	1461 Nationwide spread of famine-related diseases	
1467 Ōnin War begins; Kyoto is destroyed	15C/16C Sōtō Zen diffuses nationwide (13)	
	1463 Shinkei's *Sasamegoto* appears (10)	
	Sengoku period (1467–1568) 1467–1568 Higashiyama epoch: artistic culture flourishes at Yoshimasa's Ginkakuji	
1475 Ikkō *ikki* occur in Kaga	1471 Rennyo builds a *dōjō* in Echizen	
1477 Ōnin War ends	Late 15C Shūko develops *wabicha* tea ceremony; further perfected by Takenō Jōō (1502–55) and Sen no Rikyū (1522–91)	
1480s *Shugo* daimyo divorce themselves from bakufu structure, emerge as *sengoku* daimyo		
1485 Yamashiro *kuni ikki* occur; subdued in 1493		
1487 Kaga Ikkō *ikki* stubbornly resists *shugo* forces	1490 *Tokusei ikki* occur in Kyoto and Yamato	
	1491 Sōgi and Kenzai compile *Shinsen tsukubashū (renga)*	
	1491–1500 Famine and diseases occur nationwide; Kyoto fire razes 25,000 houses	[1492 Columbus reaches America]
	Late 15C–16C Financial support for Zen is wanted as result of Ōnin War (13)	
1506 Ikkō *ikki* battle *shugo* forces in Kaga, Noto, and Etchū	1500 Bakufu prohibits *erizeni* by merchants	
1509 *Do-ikki* occur in Yamato and Yamashiro	16C Zen becomes major influence on the arts (10)	1510 Trade with Korea is disrupted
	16C Cotton is imported from India via China and Korea	1512 Trade with Korea is resumed
		[1517 Reformation in Germany begins]

Major political events and developments[a, b, d]	Major sociocultural and economic developments[a, b, d]	Major international events and developments[a-d]
1531 Ikko *ikki* flare up in Kaga	1540 Major nationwide famine	[1522 Magellan's crew completes circumnavigation of world]
1543 Portuguese arrive near Kyushu; guns are introduced P		1547 Last tally ship is dispatched to China
1549 Francis Xavier lands in Kagoshima and begins to proselytize	1550 *Ukiyoe* appears	Mid 16C Trade with Ryūkyūs collapses
1562 Nobunaga concludes alliance with Ieyasu	1568 Nobunaga issues *rakuichi-rakuza* decree in Kanō and orders all toll gates in provinces abolished	1565 Sweet potatoes are introduced to England; to Japan in 1605
1568 Oda Nobunaga captures Kyoto		[1571 Spain occupies Philippines]
	1569 Nobunaga issues *erizeni* decrees	
1573 Nobunaga expels Shogun Yoshiakira from Kyoto		
1588 Exiled shogun resigns		

[a] Centuries are abbreviated, as e.g., 16C, for the sixteenth century.
[b] Boldface numerals in parentheses refer readers to chapters in this volume for further information, e.g. (4) refers to the fourth chapter, by John W. Hall.
[c] Developments in brackets [ ] occurred in the West and are given for reference.
[d] The letters P, E, C, and I following an entry denote that it was also of political, economic, cultural, or international significance, in addition to the category in which it is listed.

SELECTED BIBLIOGRAPHY

Akamatsu Toshihide, with Phillip Yampolsky. 1977. "Muromachi Zen and the Gozan System." In John W. Hall and Takeshi Toyoda, eds., *Japan in the Muromachi Age*. Berkeley and Los Angeles: University of California Press, pp. 313–31.

Arnesen, Peter J. 1985. "The Provincial Vassals of Muromachi Shoguns." In Jeffrey P. Mass and William B. Hauser, eds., *The Bakufu in Japanese History*. Stanford, Calif.: Stanford University Press, pp. 99–129.

1984. "The Struggle for Lordship in Late Heian Japan: The Case of Aki." *Journal of Japanese Studies* 10: 101–41.

1982. "Suo Province in the Age of Kamakura." In Jeffrey P. Mass, ed., *Court and Bakufu in Japan: Essays in Kamakura History*. New Haven, Conn.: Yale University Press, pp. 92–120.

1979. *The Medieval Japanese Daimyo: The Ouchi Family's Rule of Suo and Nagato*. New Haven, Conn.: Yale University Press.

Berry, Mary Elizabeth. 1987. "Review of *The Bakufu in Japanese History*, edited by Jeffrey P. Mass and William B. Hauser." *Journal of Japanese Studies* 13: 186–94.

Bloom, Alfred. 1965. *Shinran's Gospel of Pure Grace*. Tucson: University of Arizona Press.

Boxer, Charles R. 1974. *The Christian Century in Japan, 1549–1650*. Berkeley and Los Angeles: University of California Press.

Brazell, Karen, trans. 1973. *The Confessions of Lady Nijō*. Garden City, N.Y.: Anchor Books.

——— 1971. "Towazugatari, Autobiography of a Kamakura Court Lady." *Harvard Journal of Asiatic Studies* 31: 220–33.

Brown, Delmer M. 1951. *Money Economy in Medieval Japan: A Case Study in the Use of Coins*. New Haven, Conn.: Yale University Press.

Brown, Delmer, and Ichiro Ishida, eds. 1979. *The Future and the Past: A Translation of Gukansho: An Interpretive History of Japan Written in 1219*. Berkeley and Los Angeles: University of California Press.

Butler, Kenneth. 1969. "Heike Monogatari and the Japanese Warrior Ethic." *Harvard Journal of Asiatic Studies* 29: 93–108.

Collcutt, Martin. 1982a. "Kings of Japan? The Political Authority of the Ashikaga Shoguns." *Monumenta Nipponica* 37: 523–30.

——— 1982b. "The Zen Monastery in Kamakura Society." In Jeffrey P. Mass, ed., *Court and Bakufu in Japan: Essays in Kamakura History*, New Haven, Conn.: Yale University Press, pp. 191–221.

——— 1981. *Five Mountains: The Rinzai Zen Monastic Institution in Medieval Japan*. Cambridge, Mass.: Harvard University Press.

Davis, David L. 1974. "Ikki in Late Medieval Japan." In John W. Hall and Jeffrey P. Mass, eds., *Medieval Japan: Essays in Institutional History*. New Haven, Conn.: Yale University Press, pp. 221–47.

Dumoulin, Heinrich. 1969. *A History of Zen Buddhism*. Boston: Beacon Press.

Elison, George, and Bardwell L. Smith. 1981. *Warlords, Artists, and Commoners: Japan in the 16th Century*. Honolulu: University of Hawaii Press.

Gay, Suzanne. 1985. "Muromachi Rule in Kyoto: Administrative and Judicial Aspects." In Jeffrey P. Mass and William B. Hauser, eds., *The Bakufu in Japanese History*. Stanford, Calif.: Stanford University Press, pp. 49–66.

Goble, Andrew. 1985. "The Kamakura Bakufu and Its Officials." In Jeffrey P. Mass and William B. Hauser, eds., *The Bakufu in Japanese History*. Stanford, Calif.: Stanford University Press, pp. 31–49.

——— 1982. "Hojo and Consultative Government." In Jeffrey P. Mass, ed., *Court and Bakufu in Japan: Essays in Kamakura History*. New Haven, Conn.: Yale University Press, pp. 168–90.

Grossberg, Kenneth A. 1981a. *Japan's Renaissance: Politics of the Muromachi Bakufu*. Cambridge, Mass.: Harvard University Press.

——— 1981b. *The Laws of the Muromachi Bakufu*. Tokyo: Sophia University Press.

Hall, John W. 1985. "Reflections on Murakami Yasusuke's 'Ie Society As a Pattern of Civilization.'" *Journal of Japanese Studies* 11: 47–56.

——— 1983. "Terms and Concepts in Japanese Medieval History: An Inquiry into the Problems of Translation." *Journal of Japanese Studies* 9: 1–32.

——— 1981. "Japan's 16th Century Revolution." In George Elison and Bardwell L. Smith, eds., *Warlords, Artists, and Commoners*. Honolulu: University of Hawaii Press, pp. 7–21.

——— 1977. "Muromachi Power Structure." In John W. Hall and Takeshi Toyoda, eds., *Japan in the Muromachi Age*. Berkeley and Los Angeles: University of California Press, pp. 39–44.

——— 1974. "Kyoto As Historical Background." In John W. Hall and Jeffrey P. Mass, eds., *Medieval Japan: Essays in Institutional History*. New Haven, Conn.: Yale University Press, pp. 3–38.

——— 1968. "Feudalism in Japan: A Reassessment." In John W. Hall and Marius B.

Jansen, eds., *Studies in the Institutional History of Early Modern Japan*. Princeton, N.J.: Princeton University Press, pp. 15–55.

1966. *Government and Local Power in Japan 500–1700: A Study Based on Bizen Province*. Princeton, N.J.: Princeton University Press.

Hall, John W., and Jeffrey P. Mass, eds. 1974. *Medieval Japan: Essays in Institutional History*. New Haven, Conn.: Yale University Press.

Hall, John W., Keiji Nagahara, and Kozo Yamamura, eds. 1981. *Japan Before Tokugawa: Political Consolidation and Economic Growth. 1500–1650*. Princeton, N.J.: Princeton University Press.

Hall, John W., and Takeshi Toyoda, eds. 1977. *Japan in the Muromachi Age*. Berkeley and Los Angeles: University of California Press.

Harrington, Lorraine F. 1985. "Regional Outposts of Muromachi Bakufu Rule: The Kanto and Kyushu." In Jeffrey P. Mass and William B. Hauser, eds., *The Bakufu in Japanese History*. Stanford, Calif.: Stanford University Press, pp. 66–99.

1982. "Social Control and the Significance of the Akuto." In Jeffrey P. Mass, ed., *Court and Bakufu in Japan: Essays in Kamakura History*. New Haven, Conn.: Yale University Press, pp. 221–50.

Hayashi Tatsusaburo, with George Elison. 1977. "Kyoto in the Muromachi Age." In John W. Hall and Takeshi Toyoda, eds., *Japan in the Muromachi Age*. Berkeley and Los Angeles: University of California Press, pp. 15–37.

Hori Kyotsu. 1974. "Economic and Political Effects of the Mongol Wars." In John W. Hall and Jeffrey P. Mass, eds., *Medieval Japan: Essays in Institutional History*. New Haven, Conn.: Yale University Press, pp. 184–200.

Hurst, G. Cameron III. 1982. "The Kōbu Polity: Court–Bakufu Relations in Kamakura Japan." In Jeffrey P. Mass, ed., *Court and Bakufu in Japan: Essays in Kamakura History*. New Haven, Conn.: Yale University Press, pp. 3–28.

1974. "Development of Insei: A Problem in Japanese History and Historiography." In John W. Hall and Jeffrey P. Mass, eds., *Medieval Japan: Essays in Institutional History*. New Haven, Conn.: Yale University Press, pp. 60–90.

Ito Teiji, with Paul Norograd. 1977. "Development of the Shoin Style of Architecture." In John W. Hall and Takeshi Toyoda, eds., *Japan in the Muromachi Age*. Berkeley and Los Angeles: University of California Press, pp. 227–40.

Katsumata Shizuo, with Martin Collcutt. 1981. "Development of Sengoku Law." In John W. Hall, Keiji Nagahara, and Kozo Yamamura, eds., *Japan Before Tokugawa*. Princeton, N.J.: Princeton University Press, pp. 101–25.

Kawai Kazuo, with Kenneth A. Grossberg. 1977. "Shogun and Shugo: The Provincial Aspects of Muromachi Politics." In John W. Hall and Takeshi Toyoda, eds., *Japan in the Muromachi Age*. Berkeley and Los Angeles: University of California Press, pp. 65–87.

Keene, Donald. 1977. "Comic Tradition in Renga." In John W. Hall and Takeshi Toyoda, eds., *Japan in the Muromachi Age*. Berkeley and Los Angeles: University of California Press, pp. 241–78.

Kiley, Cornelius. 1982. "The Imperial Court As a Legal Authority in the Kamakura Age." In Jeffrey P. Mass, ed., *Court and Bakufu in Japan: Essays in Kamakura History*. New Haven, Conn.: Yale University Press, pp. 29–44.

1974. "Estate and Property in the Late Heian Period." In John W. Hall and Jeffrey P. Mass, eds., *Medieval Japan: Essays in Institutional History*. New Haven, Conn.: Yale University Press, pp. 109–24.

Kitagawa, Joseph M. 1966. *Religion in Japanese History*. New York: Columbia University Press.

Kuroda Toshio. 1981. "Shinto in the History of Japanese Religion." *Journal of Japanese Studies* 7: 1–21.

Kuwayama Konen, with John W. Hall. 1977. "Bugyōnin System: A Closer Look." In John W. Hall and Takeshi Toyoda, eds., *Japan in the Muromachi Age*. Berkeley and Los Angeles: University of California Press, pp. 65–86.

Mass, Jeffrey P. 1985. "What Can We Not Know About the Kamakura Bakufu?" In Jeffrey P. Mass and William B. Hauser, eds., *The Bakufu in Japanese History*. Stanford, Calif.: Stanford University Press, pp. 13–31.

——— 1983. "Patterns of Provincial Inheritance in Late Heian Japan." *Journal of Japanese Studies* 9: 67–96.

——— ed. 1982a. *Court and Bakufu in Japan: Essays in Kamakura History*. New Haven, Conn.: Yale University Press.

——— 1982b. "Early Bakufu and Feudalism." In Jeffrey P. Mass, ed., *Court and Bakufu in Japan: Essays in Kamakura History*. New Haven, Conn.: Yale University Press, pp. 123–42.

——— 1980. "Translation and Pre-1600 History." *Journal of Japanese Studies* 6: 61–88.

——— 1979. *Development of Kamakura Rule, 1180–1250: A History with Documents*. Stanford, Calif.: Stanford University Press.

——— 1977. "Origins of Kamakura Justice." *Journal of Japanese Studies* 3: 299–322.

——— 1976. *Kamakura Bakufu: A Study in Documents*. Stanford, Calif.: Stanford University Press.

——— 1974a. "Emergence of the Kamakura Bakufu." In John W. Hall and Jeffrey P. Mass, eds., *Medieval Japan: Essays in Institutional History*. New Haven, Conn.: Yale University Press, pp. 127–56.

——— 1974b. "Jito Land Possession in the 13th Century: The Case of Shitaji Chūbun." In John W. Hall and Jeffrey P. Mass, eds., *Medieval Japan: Essays in Institutional History*. New Haven, Conn.: Yale University Press, pp. 157–83.

——— 1974c. *Warrior Government in Early Medieval Japan: A Study of the Kamakura Bakufu, Shugo and Jitō*. New Haven, Conn.: Yale University Press.

Mass, Jeffrey P., and William B. Hauser, eds. 1985. *The Bakufu in Japanese History*. Stanford, Calif.: Stanford University Press.

Matsunaga, Alicia. 1969. *The Buddhist Philosophy of Assimilation*. Tokyo and Rutland, Vt.: Sophia University Press and Tuttle.

McCullough, Helen C., trans. 1979. *The Taiheiki: A Chronicle of Medieval Japan*. Rutland, Vt.: Tuttle.

——— 1966. "Yoshitsune: The Historical Figure, the Legend, Yoshitsune Himself." In Helen C. McCullough, ed., *Yoshitsune: A 15th Century Japanese Chronicle*. Tokyo: University of Tokyo Press, pp. 3–68.

Miyagawa Mitsuru, with C. J. Kiley. 1977. "Shoen to Chigyo: Proprietory Lordship and the Structure of Local Power." In John W. Hall and Takeshi Toyoda, eds., *Japan in the Muromachi Age*. Berkeley and Los Angeles: University of California Press, pp. 89–107.

Morris, V. Dixon. 1977. "Sakai: From Shoen to Port City." In John W. Hall and Takeshi Toyoda, eds., *Japan in the Muromachi Age*. Berkeley and Los Angeles: University of California Press, pp. 145–58.

Murakami Yasusuke. 1984. "Ie Society As a Pattern of Civilization" *Journal of Japanese Studies* 10: 281–363.

Murdock, James. 1910. *A History of Japan*. Vol. 1. Kobe: Asiatic Society.

Nagahara, Keiji. 1979. "The Medieval Origins of the Eta-Hinin." *Journal of Japanese Studies* 5: 385–405.

——— 1975. "Land Ownership Under the *Shōen-Kokugaryō* System." *Journal of Japanese Studies* 1: 269–96.

——— 1960. "The Social Structure of Early Medieval Japan." *Hitotsubashi Journal of Economics* 1: 90–97.

Nagahara, Keiji, and Kozo Yamamura. 1988. "Shaping the Process of Unification:

Technological Progress in Sixteenth- and Seventeenth-Century Japan." *Journal of Japanese Studies* 14: 77–109.

1981. "Sengoku Daimyo and the Kandaka System." In John W. Hall, Keiji Nagahara, and Kozo Yamamura, eds., *Japan Before Tokugawa*. Princeton, N.J.: Princeton University Press, pp. 27–63.

1977. "Village Communities and Daimyo Power." In John W. Hall and Takeshi Toyoda, eds., *Japan in the Muromachi Age*. Berkeley and Los Angeles: University of California Press, pp. 107–23.

Piggott, Joan R. 1982. "Hierarchy and Economics in Early Medieval Todaiji." In Jeffrey P. Mass, ed., *Court and Bakufu in Japan: Essays in Kamakura History*. New Haven, Conn.: Yale University Press, pp. 45–91.

Reischauer, Edwin O. 1956. "Japanese Feudalism." In R. Coulborn, ed., *Feudalism in History*. Princeton, N.J.: Princeton University Press, pp. 26–48.

Rodd, Laurel Rasplica. 1980. *Nichiren: Selected Writings*. Honolulu: University of Hawaii Press.

Rosenfield, John M. 1977. "The Unity of 3 Creeds: A Theme in Japanese Ink Paintings of the 15th Century." In John W. Hall and Takeshi Toyoda, eds., *Japan in the Muromachi Age*. Berkeley and Los Angeles: University of California Press, pp. 205–27.

Ruch, Barbara. 1977. "Medieval Jongleurs and the Making of a National Literature." In John W. Hall and Takeshi Toyoda, eds., *The Muromachi Age in Japanese History*. Berkeley and Los Angeles: University of California Press, pp. 279–309.

1971. "Origins of *The Companion Library*: An Anthology of Medieval Japanese Short Stories." *Journal of Asian Studies* 30: 593–610.

Sansom, George B. 1943. *Japan: A Short Cultural History*. Stanford, Calif.: Stanford University Press.

Sasaki Ginya, with William B. Hauser. 1981. "Sengoku Daimyo Rule and Commerce." In John W. Hall, Keiji Nagahara, and Kozo Yamamura, eds., *Japan Before Tokugawa*. Princeton, N.J.: Princeton University Press, pp. 125–48.

Sato, Elizabeth. 1974. "Early Development of the Shoen." In John W. Hall and Jeffrey P. Mass, eds., *Medieval Japan: Essays in Institutional History*. New Haven, Conn.: Yale University Press, pp. 91–108.

Sato Shin'ichi, and John W. Hall, 1977. "Ashikaga Shogun and the Muromachi Bakufu Administration." In John W. Hall and Takeshi Toyoda, eds., *Japan in the Muromachi Age*. Berkeley and Los Angeles: University of California Press, pp. 45–52.

Shinoda Minoru. 1960. *Founding of the Kamakura Shogunate 1180–1185*. New York: Columbia University Press.

Smith, Bardwell L. 1981. "Japanese Society and Culture in the Momoyama Era: A Bibliographic Essay." In George Elison and Bardell L. Smith, eds., *Warlords, Artists, and Commoners*. Honolulu: University of Hawaii Press, pp. 245–79.

Steenstrup, Carl. 1980a. "Pushing the Papers of Kamakura: The Nitty-Grittiest vs. the Grand Sweepers." *Monumenta Nipponica* 35: 337–74.

1980b. "Sata Mirensho: A 14th Century Law Primer." *Monumenta Nipponica* 35: 405–36.

1979. *Hojo Shigetoki (1198–1261) and His Role in the History of Political and Ethical Ideas in Japan*. London: Curzon Press.

Sugimoto Masayoshi, and David L. Swain. 1978. *Science and Culture in Traditional Japan*, A.D. 600–1854. Cambridge, Mass.: MIT Press.

Suzuki, D. T. 1973. "Zen and the Samurai." In *Zen and Japanese Culture*. Princeton, N.J.: Princeton University Press.

Takeuchi Rizo. 1982. "Old and New Approaches to Kamakura History." In Jeffrey P.

Mass, ed., *Court and Bakufu in Japan: Essays in Kamakura History*. New Haven Conn.: Yale University Press, pp. 269–84.

Tanaka Takeo, with Robert Sakai. 1977. "Japan's Relations with Overseas Countries." In John W. Hall and Takeshi Toyoda, eds., *Japan in the Muromachi Age*. Berkeley and Los Angeles: University of California Press, pp. 159–78.

Toyoda Takeshi and Sugiyama Hiroshi, with V. Dixon Morris. 1977. "Growth of Commerce and Trade." In John W. Hall and Takeshi Toyoda, eds., *Japan in the Muromachi Age*. Berkeley and Los Angeles: University of California, pp. 129–44.

Ury, Marian, trans. 1979. *Tales of Times Now Past: 62 Stories from a Medieval Japanese Collection*. Berkeley and Los Angeles: University of California Press.

Varley, H. Paul, 1984. *Japanese Culture*. 3rd ed. Honolulu: University of Hawaii Press.

——— 1982. "The Hōjō Family and Succession to Power." In Jeffrey P. Mass, ed., *Court and Bakufu in Japan: Essays in Kamakura History*. New Haven, Conn.: Yale University Press, pp. 143–68.

——— 1981. "Zen in Medieval Japan." *Monumenta Nipponica* 36: 463–9.

——— 1980. *A Chronicle of Gods and Sovereigns: Jinnō Shōtōki of Kitabatake Chikafusa*. New York: Columbia University Press.

——— 1979a. "The Place of *Gunkanshō* in Japanese Intellectual History." *Monumenta Nipponica* 34: 479–88.

——— 1979b. "Tea in Japan: From Its Origins to the Late Sixteenth Century." In Seizō Hayashiya, ed., *Chanoyu: Japanese Tea Ceremony*. New York: Japan Society.

——— 1978. "Preeminent Patron of Higashiyama Culture: Ashikaga Yoshimasa." In Hyoe Murakami and Thomas J. Harper, eds., *Great Historical Figures of Japan*. Tokyo: Japan Culture Institute.

——— 1977. "Ashikaga Yoshimitsu and the World of Kitayama: Social Change and Shogunal Patronage in Early Muromachi Japan." In John W. Hall and Takeshi Toyoda, eds. *Japan in the Muromachi Age*. Berkeley and Los Angeles: University of California Press, pp. 183–204.

——— 1972. *A Syllabus of Japanese Civilization*. 2nd ed. New York: Columbia University Press.

——— 1971. *Imperial Restoration in Medieval Japan*. New York: Columbia University Press.

——— 1970. *The Samurai*. London: Weidenfeld.

——— 1967. *The Ōnin War*. New York: Columbia University Press.

Varley, H. Paul, and George Elison. 1981. "The Culture of Tea: From Its Origins to Sen no Rikyū." In George Elison and Bardwell L. Smith, eds., *Warlords, Artists, and Commoners*. Honolulu: University of Hawaii Press.

Wakita Haruko. 1975. "Towards a Wider Perspective on Medieval Commerce." *Journal of Japanese Studies* 1: 321–45.

Wakita Haruko, with Susan B. Hanley. 1981. "Dimensions of Development: Cities in Fifteenth and Sixteenth Century Japan." In John W. Hall, Keiji Nagahara, and Kozo Yamamura, eds., *Japan Before Tokugawa*. Princeton, N.J.: Princeton University Press, pp. 295–326.

Weinstein, Stanley. 1977. "Rennyo and the Shinsu Revival." In John W. Hall and Takeshi Toyoda, eds., *Japan in the Muromachi Age*. Berkeley and Los Angeles: University of California Press, pp. 331–59.

Wintersteen, Prescott B., Jr. 1974a. "Early Muromachi Bakufu in Kyoto." In John W. Hall and Jeffrey P. Mass, eds., *Medieval Japan: Essays in Institutional History*. New Haven, Conn.: Yale University Press, pp. 201–9.

——— 1974b. "Muromachi Shugo and Hanzei." In John W. Hall and Jefrrey P. Mass, eds., *Medieval Japan: Essays in Institutional History*. New Haven, Conn.: Yale University Press, pp. 210–20.

Yamamura, Kozo. 1981a. "Returns on Unification: Economic Growth in Japan 1550–1650." In John W. Hall, Keiji Nagahara, and Kozo Yamamura, eds., *Japan Before Tokugawa*. Princeton, N.J.: Princeton University Press, pp. 327–72.

1981b. "Tara in Transition: A Study of Kamakura Shoen." *Journal of Japanese Studies* 7: 349–91.

1975. "Introduction to the Workshop Papers on the Economic and Institutional History of Medieval Japan." *Journal of Japanese Studies* 1: 255–67.

1973. "The Development of *Za* in Medieval Japan." *Business History Review* 47: 438–65.

Yamamura, Kozo, and Tetsuo Kamiki. 1983. "Silver Mines and Sung Coins – A Monetary History of Medieval and Modern Japan in International Perspective." In J. F. Richards, ed., *Precious Metals in the Later Medieval and Early Modern Worlds*. Durham, N.C.: Carolina Academic Press, pp. 329–62.

CHAPTER 1

THE KAMAKURA BAKUFU

The establishment of Japan's first warrior government, the Kamakura bakufu, represented both a culmination and a beginning. Since the tenth century, an increasingly professionalized class of mounted fighting men had served in local areas as estate administrators and policemen and as officials attached to the organs of provincial governance. By the twelfth century, warriors had come to exercise a dominant share of the total volume of local government, but even after two hundred years they remained politically immature. The most exalted warriors were still only middle-level figures in hierarchies dominated by courtiers and religious institutions in and near the capital. The bakufu's founding in the 1180s thus represented an initial breakthrough to power on the part of elite fighting men, but the fledgling regime was scarcely in a position to assume unitary control over the entire country. What evolved was a system of government approximating a dyarchy. During the Kamakura period, Japan had two capitals and two interconnected loci of authority. The potential of warrior power was clear enough to those who cared to envision it, but the legacy of the past prevented more than a slow progress into the future.

Until quite recently, studies of Kamakura Japan have tended to overstate the warriors' achievement, by equating the creation of a new form of government with the simultaneous destruction of the old. As is now clear, not only was the Heian system of imperial-aristocratic rule still vigorous during the twelfth century, but also it remained the essential framework within which the bakufu, during its lifetime, was obliged to operate. In this sense, the Heian pattern of government survived into the fourteenth century – to be destroyed with the Kamakura bakufu rather than by it. The events of the 1180s were revolutionary insofar as they witnessed the emergence of Japan's first noncentral locus of authority and Japan's first government composed of men not of the most exalted social ranks. But the bakufu, as we shall see, was a military regime dedicated to keeping warriors away from the battle-

46

field and also to finding judicial answers to the feuds and disputes that were plaguing society .

THE BACKGROUND TO THE GEMPEI WAR

Despite its aversion to fighting, the bakufu was created by war, the Gempei (Genji versus Heishi, or Minamoto versus Taira) conflict of 1180–5. This was a much more complex upheaveal than its name implies. Far from being a dispute between two great warrior clans, as it is so often depicted, the Gempei conflict was a national civil war involving substantial intraclan fighting and also pitting local against central interests.[1] Indeed, the character of the violence was responsible for the type of regime that was created. Likewise, the backdrop to the conflict was a product of society's tensions and is therefore integral to the history of the Kamakura bakufu.

To understand the limitations of both the warrior victory and the resulting government, we need to trace the rise of the warrior class in the Heian period as well as the ascendancy of the Taira in the years just before the Gempei War. The original blueprint for imperial government in Japan did not envision a military aristocracy as the mainstay of administration over the countryside. Yet as the courtiers in the capital became more confident of their superiority, they began to loosen their grip over the provinces, exchanging governance over a public realm for proprietorship over its component pieces. The country was divided into public and private estates (the provincial lands known as *kokugaryō*, and the estates known as *shōen*), under the authority of governors and estate holders, respectively, who themselves made up the courtier and religious elite. The owners of land at the topmost proprietary level were thus exclusively nobles and clerics. The purpose of this privatization of land was to secure a flow of revenue that exceeded what was provided by the holding of bureaucratic office. In turn, this permitted an increasingly extravagant life-style in the capital. The division of the country was predicated in this way on the desire of *shōen* owners to be absentee landlords. Yet it was equally dependent on those owners' ability to draft into service a class of willing and obedient administrators.

---

1 See Jeffrey P. Mass, "The Emergence of the Kamakura Bakufu," in John Whitney Hall and Jeffrey P. Mass, eds., *Medieval Japan: Essays in Institutional History* (New Haven, Conn.: Yale University Press, 1974) (hereafter cited as Mass, "The Emergence"). The older view, which underemphasizes the social implications of the war, is ably treated by Minoru Shinoda, *The Founding of the Kamakura Shogunate* (New York: Columbia University Press, 1960).

This loosening of control from above also loosened the cement that bound the provinces to the capital. A degree of local instability ensued, which caused the lower ranks to look to one another for mutual support and protection. Leadership fell to persons of distinction whose principal source of prestige was an ancestry traceable to the capital. Thus, unlike the invaders who promoted the feudalization of Europe, local leaders in Japan were men with long pedigrees. They also retained their central connections, which meant that the developing class of provincial administrators were less members of local war bands than members of groups that were forming to secure the peace. This did not preclude outbreaks of lawlessness. But courtiers could always brand such outbursts as rebellion and enroll others as their provincial agents. In this way, at any rate, local and central remained essentially joined for the duration of the Heian period.

The warriors who were becoming the true captains of local society were called *zaichōkanjin,* or resident officials attached to provincial government headquarters (*kokuga*). Although the governorships themselves continued to rotate among courtiers in Kyoto, positions within the *kokuga* became hereditary. Later, during the early stages of the Gempei War, the developing cleavage of interests here was exploited by the founder of the Kamakura bakufu, Minamoto Yoritomo. However, during the two centuries preceding 1180, patrons in the capital were able to channel the energies of provincial subordinates towards mutually beneficial ends. On the one hand, the locals were given extensive powers in the areas of tax collecting and policing. But on the other hand, these same locals were obliged to work through their superiors to secure new appointments or confirmations of old ones[2] or to secure justice in the frequent legal battles between kin and nonkin rivals. Neither the local chieftain nor the clan head (if this was a different person) was empowered to provide these services on his own authority; he too was dependent on the support of a central patron. The result was that ownership and administration, authority and power, became separable, with little risk to the capital-resident proprietor. So ingrained was the psychology of a hierarchy in which the center dominated the periphery that in the absence of some regionally based patronage source such as the bakufu, courtiers in the capital, no

2 Titles became hereditary and subject to disposition by testament. But wills, in order to be recognized, required probate by the governor. For details, see Jeffrey P. Mass, "Patterns of Provincial Inheritance in Late Heian Japan," *Journal of Japanese Studies* 9 (Winter 1983): 67–95.

matter how effete, could remain the superiors of warriors, no matter how powerful the latter were.[3]

But Kyoto protected its interests in other ways, too. One of the most ingenious was to promote a handful of men as career governors. These persons might then be moved from province to province, much as modern ambassadors are moved today. The origins of this practice have not been adequately studied, but by late in the eleventh century the use of such representatives, now called *zuryō*, had become interwoven with the competition between the Fujiwara and retired emperor patronage blocs in the capital. By this time, governorships had become, in a sense, commodities circulating among the elite. The proprietary province (*chigyōkoku*) system, as it was called, was designed to allow patronage groups to function on both sides of the local land ledger (*shōen* and *kokugaryō*), with the governor as the principal instrument of manipulation. What is important to us is the identity and character of the journeyman governors who now came to be employed by the ex-emperors and Fujiwara. They were from the Taira and Minamoto, particular scions of which were recognized as career troubleshooters for provinces possessed by their patrons. Thus, to cite one example, Taira Masamori received successive appointments to at least nine provinces, as did his son Tadamori after him. And the latter's son, the illustrious Kiyomori, was governor of three provinces before beginning his historic ascent in the capital.[4]

The leaders of the Taira and Minamoto need to be appreciated in this light. They were not, as they are usually depicted, regional chieftains chafing under courtier dominance. Rather, they were bridging figures – military nobles in the truest sense – between the great central aristocrats, who were their patrons, and the great provincial warriors, who were their followers. The leaders' dual character, born out of service to two constituencies, is essential to an understanding of the slow progress of warrior development in its initial phase. It is also basic to the incompleteness of the warrior revolution that was later spearheaded by the bakufu.

The prestige of the Taira and Minamoto names, and the restraining influence they came to exercise, are reflected in still another way. The warrior houses that dominated the provincial headquarters commonly

---

3 In Weberian terms, the system was maintained by a subjective feeling by subordinates that courtier dominance was natural and legitimate. See Max Weber, *The Theory of Social and Economic Organization* (New York: Free Press, 1964), pp. 124ff.
4 Iida Hisao, "Heishi to Kyūshū," in Takeuchi Rizō hakase kanreki kinenkai, ed., *Shōensei to buke shakai* (Tokyo: Yoshikawa kōbunkan, 1969), p. 50.

bore these two surnames, along with one other, Fujiwara. These were seen at the time as connoting an aristocratic ancestry and served to bind provincials to the capital while they also awed truly native families. Not until Kamakura times did houses such as the Chiba, Oyama, and Miura, among others, come to be known by the names with which they are remembered historically.[5]

Unfortunately, this profusion of Taira and Minamoto surnames has led to the view that the chieftains of these two clans were able to fashion ongoing combinations of vassals. The notion of evolving warrior leagues supported the further notion that the histories of the Taira and Minamoto were in fact the proper framework for tracing the rise of the warrior.[6] However, the records of the era tell a much more modest story, forcing us to conclude that what has passed for coherent history is little more than disparate images pulled taut. The chieftains of the two clans did, at times, add a layer of authority that might be effective. But their assignment to a succession of provinces (not to mention long stays in Kyoto) all but ensured that whatever ties they had formed would inevitably weaken. Thus, the unique but ephemeral success of the most famous warrior of the era, Minamoto Yoshiie, needs to be juxtaposed against the peripatetic movements of the succession of Taira chieftains and the mixed success of Yoshiie's own great-grandson, Minamoto Yoshitomo. Yoshitomo was rebuffed as often as he was accepted in the Minamoto's historic heartland region, the Kantō, and he was ultimately defeated in 1160 by an army consisting of only three hundred men.[7]

Even though the saga of the Taira and Minamoto may thus be a weak framework for charting the road to 1180, the histories of the great provincial houses place us on much firmer ground. Here the emphasis is on an expansion of power within the traditional system of rule, along with the lack of any means for circumventing that system. In other words, what was acceptable in the earlier stages of growth did not necessarily remain so, especially as warrior houses came to feel vulnerable to pressures from above. The Chiba, for instance, discovered that the patronage of the Ise Shrine could neither prevent a major

---

5 To cite but one example, the body of documents bearing on the late Heian Chiba house refers only to the Taira. See "Ichiki monjo," in *Ichikawa shishi, kodai-chūsei shiryō* (Ichikawa: Ichikawa shi, 1973), pp. 363–74.

6 For an illustration, see George B. Sansom, *A History of Japan to 1334* (Stanford, Calif.: Stanford University Press, 1958), chap. 12.

7 Yasuda Motohisa, *Nihon zenshi (chūsei 1)* (Tokyo: Tōkyō daigaku shuppankai, 1958), p. 14; and Jeffrey P. Mass, *Warrior Government in Early Medieval Japan* (New Haven, Conn.: Yale University Press, 1974), pp. 35–44 (hereafter cited as *WG*).

confiscation of their holdings by a new governor in the 1130s nor protect them from further seizures by the shrine itself a generation later.[8] To the extent that experiences of this kind led to feelings of resentment, the environment in the provinces was being readied for change.

As we know, it was not the Minamoto who came to experience national power first but, rather, the Taira under the leadership of Kiyomori. Recent historians have amended the traditional view of his ascendancy by emphasizing both its limited nature and duration. Kiyomori is now seen less as a warrior riding the crest of a wave of support from the provinces than as a military noble who attempted, unsuccessfully, to use the scaffolding of imperial offices to achieve his hegemony. Lacking large numbers of warrior followers and also the administrative organization of a central proprietor, Kiyomori failed, until very late, to establish an identifiable "regime." His legacy, as we shall see, was to demonstrate the vulnerability of Kyoto to coercion and to destabilize the countryside. For these reasons, the brief period of his ascendancy must be counted as a direct contributor to the outbreak of war in 1180.

The Taira episode is divisible into two subperiods. From 1160 to 1179, Kiyomori operated in the shadow of his patron, the retired emperor Goshirakawa. Though he himself climbed to the top of the imperial office hierarchy, becoming chancellor in 1167, he remined dependent on the spoils system of the ex-sovereign. Wearying, finally, of established Kyoto's unwavering opposition to his membership in the capital elite, Kiyomori staged a coup d'état in late 1179, which removed the ex-emperor from effective power. Yet this action succeeded also in destroying the basic collegiality of the courtier class, which had always competed according to accepted rules. The damage in Kyoto was further compounded by Kiyomori's seizure of numerous estate and provincial proprietorships. This not only reduced the portfolios of his noble and religious rivals; it also upset the status quo in the countryside. Early in 1180, Kiyomori's own infant grandson became emperor, an event that accelerated a growing sense of malaise everywhere.[9]

While all of this was taking place, the Minamoto leadership was languishing in exile. Twenty years earlier, at the time of the Heiji incident, the sons of Yoshitomo, who was himself killed, were scattered throughout Japan. The eldest, the thirteen-year-old Yoritomo,

8 WG, pp. 48–54.　9 For the Taira ascendancy, see WG, pp. 15–30, 54–56.

was placed in the custody of the eastern-based Hōjō, a minor branch of
the Taira. We have little information on Yoritomo between 1160 and
1180, save for the fact of his marriage to Masako, the daughter of Hōjō
Tokimasa, his guardian. From the perspective of subsequent events,
Kiyomori's leniency in dealing with the offspring of his 1160 enemy
seems impolitic. Yet there was no way the future could have been
foreseen: The heir to the Minamoto name was powerless and had been
absorbed into the Taira by way of marriage to a Taira collateral.

It is in part owing to this absence of any political activity by
Yoritomo that historians have found it difficult to interpret the tumultuous events that lay just ahead. The impediment to understanding
can be removed only by minimizing the importance of the Taira-
Minamoto rivalry, a sentiment evidently shared by Kiyomori as well.
Thus, when Yoritomo raised his banner of rebellion in the eighth
month of 1180, the support he attracted was determined by issues
other than memories of some idealized past. The background of the
Gempei War can be traced to two sources – the perception of vulnerability at court and the condition of warrior houses locally.

THE GEMPEI WAR

Belying true motivations, wars in Japan are waged under strict categories of symbols, none more important than devotion to a higher cause.
In 1180, rebellion was justified on the basis of a call to arms against the
Taira by a prince left out of the imperial succession. Though the
prince himself was dead within several weeks (5/26), his overture
retained great significance. The forces of Yoritomo later cited it as a
pretext for their uprising (8/19), and so did the bakufu's later history
of itself (the *Azuma kagami*) in its opening paragraph.[10] The broader
context encouraging widespread violence yielded in this way to an
official explanation.

Yet just as rectification of the succession had little to do with the
outbreak of war, the outburst also cannot be explained as a spontane-
ous rallying to the Minamoto. As Yoritomo himself discovered, loyalty
proved a singularly noncombustible element. Before a challenge might
be mounted, the warriors of the east required time to gauge their
current situations. The Chiba, with their recent history of setbacks,

---

10 *Azuma kagami (AK)*, 1180/4/9. The most accessible edition of the *Azuma kagami* is that edited
by Nagahara Keiji and Kishi Shōzō (Tokyo: Jimbutsu ōraisha, 1976–7), 6 vols. The *Azuma
kagami* covers the period 1180 to 1266 and was prepared in the early fourteenth century. The
later sections are considered to be more reliable.

joined early (6/17), even though they bore a Taira surname. But for many other houses the issues were more complex, normally centering on inter- and intrafamily relations within their own home provinces. As part of the process, houses segmented into new alignments and subunits, and the provinces themselves became the staging grounds for a series of incipient civil wars.[11] To prevent the east from disintegrating into internecine conflict, Yoritomo was obliged to seek some new common denominator that would bind rather than divide the families under his leadership. The program he evolved was made part of his war declaration on 8/19. Rather than organize a war party to defend the court by dislodging the Taira, Yoritomo designed policies to satisfy the most deep-seated desires of the warrior class in general. The Minamoto chieftain promised what had never before been contemplated: a regional security system that bypassed Kyoto and guaranteed the landed holdings of followers. The vision was revolutionary – and led ultimately to the creation of the Kamakura bakufu.

Though Yoritomo couched his program in procourt and anti-Taira language, the effect of his plan was to disengage the east from central control, by converting its public and private officers into his own vassals. Specifically, he authorized the men of the region to assume possession over the holdings long associated with them and to petition Yoritomo for confirmations. The temper of the program was set when the governor's agent (*mokudai*) of Izu Province, the site of Yoritomo's long exile, was attacked on 8/17 by forces of the Minamoto. Similar campaigns followed (for instance, that of the Chiba against the Shimōsa *mokudai* on 9/13), and this rapidly became a movement to eliminate all representatives of the central government. At the same time, the tide of support, which had been sporadic to this point, now became a ground swell. Resident officials from various provinces pledged themselves to Yoritomo, as did a number of estate-based personnel. The effect of this was to deliver into his hands the potential for rulership over vast areas. This in turn was bolstered by the chieftain's assumption of a protector's role over the region's leading temples and shrines. Yoritomo achieved this latter goal by issuing public directives to the provincial headquarters, in effect, an assumption of the authority – without the title – of the governor. The issuance of such documents began on the same day that he declared war.[12]

---

11 For details, see Mass, "The Emergence," pp. 134–43.

12 "Mishima jinja monjo," 1180/8/19 Minamoto Yoritomo kudashibumi, in Takeuchi Rizō, comp., *Heian ibun* (Tokyo: Tōkyōdō, 1947–80), 15 vols., 9:3782–83, doc. 4883. This is the earliest document bearing Yoritomo's name.

Yoritomo still had many problems to overcome. On 8/23, an army under his command was soundly defeated at the battle of Ishibashi in Sagami Province. His opponents were not forces recruited and sent out by the central Taira but typically were local houses that were opposing other local houses. They called themselves Taira for the same reason that Yoritomo's men from Sagami called themselves Minamoto. Rather quickly, however, the Taira label became obsolete. Owing to Yoritomo's presence in the region, the appeal of his program, and a general rallying to his side, families that had remained neutral or had taken initial positions against him now sought to reverse themselves. Although this necessitated a submergence of hostile sentiments on the part of traditional rivals, the alternative was probably extinction. For his part, Yoritomo showed great leniency in welcoming earlier enemies and showed great understanding by dividing and recognizing new families. By the end of 1180, only the tiniest residue of a "Gempei" War remained in the east, with the task now one of purging and purifying rather than facing an enemy. Kamakura, with historic ties to Yoritomo's forebears, was selected as the seat for his government.

A Taira policy approximating quarantine actually encouraged Yoritomo's preoccupation with the east. A by-product was to make the Chūbu and Hokuriku regions, which were closer to the capital, the next arenas for conflict. Already by 1181, provincial warriors in these areas were seeking to expel Kyoto's representatives by using the same pretext as their eastern counterparts did. They postured themselves as Minamoto engaged in a crusade against the Taira. That Yoritomo was probably ignorant of most of the activities of those invoking his name suggests that the battleground, now of its own momentum, was rapidly expanding in size. At this stage – and until 1183 – Yoritomo was content to limit his personal involvement strictly to the east. For regions beyond the east he delegated a loose authority to two relatives, his cousin Yoshinaka and his uncle Yukiie.

In the meantime, the chieftain in Kamakura was identifying a new enemy. These were the collateral lines of his own house who were refusing to recognize his authority. Even before the end of 1180, Yoritomo demonstrated his unconcern with the Taira by marching east against the Satake, relatives who a generation earlier had refused to submit to his father. The differences between father and son (in effect, between the 1150s and 1180s) are instructive. Whereas Yoshitomo the father had been unable to subordinate recalcitrant Minamoto branches, Yoritomo the son used superior military strength to force the issue. The Satake were destroyed in battle on 1180/11/5. Other lineages were more prudent. The Nitta, for instance, reversed their earlier intransigence (9/30) and submitted to Yoritomo without a fight (12/22). Yet the chieftain in Kamakura remained vigilant. When another collateral, the Shida, showed signs of vacillation, Yoritomo rejected their submission and moved to destroy them (1181/int. 2/20). As we shall see, enmity toward kinsmen continued to be a much stronger inducement to action than did the nonthreatening Taira.

Between 1180 and 1183, Yoritomo worked assiduously to mold the eastern region into a personal sphere of influence. He did this by converting the existing officialdom into a private vassalage, by attempting to make himself the source of all patronage in the area, and by transforming a simple village, Kamakura, into a great center of government. Now when he prohibited local outrages, authorized fiscal exemptions, assigned new lands, or issued orders to provincial officials, he was doing so from a stationary base that he could realistically call his capital. Yet the Minamoto movement could not continue indefinitely to develop in isolation, because the contagion of violence under the Minamoto banner was rapidly spreading. Yoritomo eventually saw this development as an opportunity to inflate his own chieftainship. But he also recognized the danger to his fledgling authority of inaction in the face of warrior outlawry. Though the Taira in Kyoto and the Minamoto in Kamakura were reluctant to confront each other, developments in the provinces eventually forced the issue. They also forced the country's two governmental centers to seek an accommodation.

The years 1183 to 1185 witnessed a convergence of events on several levels. The Gempei War, desultory from the beginning, heated up and reached a sudden climax. The Kamakura bakufu assumed its basic form. The imperial court, with Kamakura's help, began to revive itself. And the warrior class, by means of sustained violence, achieved unprecedented new goals.

The inertia of the war's second and third years was broken in mid-1183 when Yoritomo's Chūbu deputies, Yoshinaka and Yukiie, broke through the Taira defenses and occupied the capital. For their part, the Taira leaders, carrying the child emperor with them, fled westward in an attempt to regroup. Though after the outbreak of war the Taira had made certain modest efforts to establish closer ties with the provinces,[13] they now had to base themselves there for the first time in a generation. At least superficially, the Taira and the Minamoto became comparable, with each side seeking the support of local warriors. In the capital there was general rejoicing over the departure of the Taira and genuine optimism over the prospects of converting the Minamoto into time-honored guardians of the imperial state.

But two major obstacles blocked such hopes – and worked to prevent Japanese history from reassuming its traditional pre-Taira course. The first concerned the nature and level of the upheaval in the countryside, which will be dealt with shortly. The second centered on the condition of the Minamoto leadership. Soon after his arrival in Kyoto, Yoshinaka began to posture himself as the true leader of the Minamoto and to impose his own form of dictatorship on the capital city. Yoritomo, beside himself with rage, did not, however, do the "logical" thing. He refused to abandon his own capital to contest his cousin in the country's capital. Rather, he began negotiating an accord with agents of the retired emperor that would give permanent status to his own government. And he began planning a punitive expedition against Yoshinaka that would be led by his own brother, Yoshitsune.

The accord was eventually hammered out in the intercalated tenth month of 1183 and has been hailed by some scholars as marking the official birth of the Kamakura bakufu. The argument here is that a rebel movement was now being given imperial sanction; a portion of what Yoritomo had earlier seized was now lawfully released to him.[14] The trouble with this view is that it makes Kyoto ultimately responsible for the creation of the bakufu and argues as well for a circumscribed authority. In fact, Yoritomo was already the governing power in the east, and the accord acknowledged that fact even as it called for a restoration of traditional proprietorships in the region. More to the point, as a result of the agreement, the bakufu's range of operations now became countrywide. From this juncture, Kamakura established itself as Japan's preeminent peacemaker, a responsibility that began as a military policing authority but soon became overwhelmingly judicial in nature. As we shall see, the dispensing of justice emerged as the essence of Kamakura's governance and as society's greatest need during the thirteenth century.

13 These efforts centered on the new local titles of *sōkan* and *sōgesu*; see Ishimoda Shō, "Heishi seiken no sōkan shiki setchi," *Rekishi hyōron* 107 (1959): 7–14; Ishimoda Shō, "Kamakura bakufu ikkoku jitō shiki no seiritsu," in Satō Shin'ichi and Ishimoda Shō, eds., *Chūsei no hō to kokka* (Tokyo: Tōkyō daigaku shuppankai, 1960), pp. 36–45.
14 For a discussion, see *WG*, pp. 72–77; and Uwayokote Masataka, "Kamakura seiken seiritsu ki o meguru kingyō," *Hōseishi kenkyū* 11 (1960): 175–81.

The proof for Kamakura's new role lies in the sudden appearance of a type of document hitherto unseen. These were cease-and-desist orders issued by Yoritomo in response to appeals for assistance from traditional estate holders.[15] The development was revolutionary for two reasons. First, for the first time in Japanese history a noncentral source of authority was providing patronage for central recipients; this was a reversal of age-old practice and anticipated a new era of warrior dominance. Second, the decrees themselves provided visual testimony that the bakufu was now active in central and western Japan. This countrywide scope became a permanent feature of Kamakura's authority. At the same time, the language of the edicts made clear that Yoritomo recognized the legitimacy of the traditional proprietors' retaining their positions atop the land system. In a real sense, the one-time rebel was going on record as a force now for law and order. Henceforth, the rights of warriors *and* courtiers would be equally protected, a position adopted as the only realistic way to return the country to stability.

The postures of both Kyoto and Kamakura were in fact a response, not to the exigencies of war, but rather to the unprecedented outpouring of local lawlessness that swept Japan in 1184. Surviving documents reveal Kyoto's attempts to quell these outbursts by threatening traditional sanctions, and the dawning awareness that only Kamakura had any chance to restore true peace.[16] One result is that after disposing of Yoshinaka, Yoshitsune was ordered by his brother to remain in the capital and to establish a Kamakura office there. He was to issue desist orders in response to petitions from proprietors.[17] The effect of this was to reinforce both Kamakura's independence and the interdependence of government in practice.

Now that he was involved in central and western Japan, Yoritomo recognized the need to make contact with as many people and places as possible. He dispatched several of his most trusted followers westward and ordered them to enroll as vassals any who would pledge loyalty. First priority was to be given to the same zaichōkanjin and other local officials who dominated the east's provincial headquarters. These men were to be promised the same confirmations and preferments as their

15 For translated examples of such documents, see Jeffrey P. Mass, *The Kamakura Bakufu: A Study in Documents* (Stanford, Calif.: Stanford University Press, 1976), docs. 1–6 (hereafter cited as *KB*).
16 This is most poignantly depicted in a retired emperor's edict of 1184, in *KB*, doc. 7.
17 For a list of the edicts issued by Yoshitsune, see Mass, "The Emergence," p. 148, n. 71. A general discussion appears in Tanaka Minoru, "Kamakura dono otsukai kō," *Shirin* 45 (1962): 1–23.

eastern counterparts, because they held the potential of delivering to the Minamoto large numbers of subordinates. In this way, sections of territory in hitherto unfamiliar areas could be made the basis of some permanent Kamakura interest in the west.[18] Yoritomo's policy of vassal recruitment could then be joined by his other method of gaining a foothold in public and private estates, providing redress for proprietors' complaints of lawlessness.

Each province and district was different. Some had great families dominating them, others did not. Still others became centers of Taira partisanship. The result was that Kamakura's approach to individual areas required a capacity for flexibility. Likewise, because success, by definition, was bound to be uneven, the potential for influence would forever be mixed. Eventually, Kamakura would need to find a mechanism by which to introduce symmetry into its patchwork presence in the west.

Though the war was an obvious rationale for Minamoto penetration of that region, it is significant that the main-force fighting that now began was largely incidental to Kamakura's efforts at aggrandizement. For example, the battle of Ichinotani in Settsu Province in 1184/2 constituted only the second encounter between what might be called the main Taira and Minamoto armies.[19] Yet the latter's victory did not lead to Settsu Province's becoming a major Minamoto stronghold. Evidently, the pursuit of the war and the contest for control of men and land were separate processes. This is one reason that defeating the Taira, though recognized as necessary, engendered so little enthusiasm. Eventually, however, command of the principal Minamoto armies was placed in the hands of Yoshitsune, and in a series of brilliant maneuvers he pursued the Taira leaders and destroyed them at Dannoura in 1185/3.[20] The Gempei War, from beginning to end more framework than reality, was now over. But the forces that it had unleashed – the real war – were still in development. For Kamakura to carve a permanent place in the authority structure of Japan, it would have to devise strategies both to restore real peace and to satisfy its men. This meant finding ways to restrain and license, confiscate and confer, punish and reward. The institution of *jitō* met each of these several requirements.

18 For this effort in the different provinces of the west, see *WG*, pp. 79–89.
19 The battle of Fujigawa, occurring early in the war (1180/10), was the first such encounter. Taking place in Suruga Province immediately to the west of the Kantō, it led to the "phony war" that ended only at Ichinotani.
20 For an account of the battles and strategy of the war, Shinoda, *The Founding of the Kamakura Shogunate*, is excellent.

THE GEMPEI AFTERMATH: *JITŌ* AND *SHUGO*

The year 1185 is one of the most famous in Japanese history. Its reputation derives from the Minamoto victory over the Taira and from the supposed inauguration of the bakufu's twin officer networks in the field, those of military estate steward (*jitō*) and military governor (*shugo*). As we have just noted, the Gempei denouement was largely an anticlimax, though it did have an unexpected impact on conditions in the countryside. With the war officially over, warriors could no longer use the Gempei labels to justify their private lawlessness. Their aggression was thus more directly an attack on the courtier-dominated estate system. During the middle months of 1185, pressure mounted on Kamakura to quell this rising siege of outlawry.

The bakufu was at a loss as to what to do. Conditions were made even more complicated by a deterioration in the relationship between Yoritomo and Yoshitsune and by the retired emperor's decision to exploit this situation. Thus, not only was there a continuing crisis in the provinces (much of it spearheaded by victorious Minamoto), but there also was a developing rift within Kamakura and between it and Kyoto. The difficulties between the brothers were what eventually brought things to a head. As we have seen, Yoritomo reserved his greatest sensitivity throughout the war for threats that issued from within his own clan. Quite predictably, therefore, when Yoshitsune began to steer a course during the ninth month that was openly rebellious, the Minamoto chieftain determined to seek his destruction.[21] Yoshitsune, however, eluded capture and succeeded in persuading the ex-emperor, Goshirakawa, to brand Yoritomo a rebel and to appoint the hero of the war as *jitō* of Kyushu. The stage was now set for one of Japanese history's most momentous developments.

Yoritomo responded to the crisis by dispatching an armed force to Kyoto that laid before the court a series of demands. Unfortunately, neither the precise content of those demands nor the court's reply can be ascertained, and so we must rely on an account that is now considered suspect. According to the *Azuma kagami*, Yoritomo forced the ex-emperor to authorize Kamakura's appointment of countrywide networks of *jitō* and *shugo*.[22] The importance of this development for

---

21 More has been written on the Yoritomo–Yoshitsune relationship than on any other familial rivalry in Japanese history. See Shinoda, *The Founding of the Kamakura Shogunate*, pp. 121ff; The chapter on Yoshitsune in Ivan Morris, *The Nobility of Failure* (New York: Holt, Rinehart and Winston, 1975); and the relevant sections of Helen Craig McCullough, *Yoshitsune: A Fifteenth Century Japanese Chronicle* (Tokyo: University of Tokyo Press, 1966).
22 *AK*, 1185/11/29. This is the most famous entry in that chronicle.

premodern observers is that Yoritomo's authority to make such assignments was seen as the basis for his government's ongoing presence.
Modern historians go even further than that. The power to appoint *jitō*
and *shugo* represented no less than a merging of the systems of vassalage and benefice. By virtue of his new authority, Yoritomo became a
feudal chieftain, and Japan was thereby launched on its medieval
phase. Japanese history was part of world history, with east and west
exhibiting similar patterns.[23]
     There are many problems (and not a few virtues) in this latter form
of reasoning. One difficulty has been a tendency to conclude too much
from the *Azuma kagami's* description. Not only were there no *shugo* at
all until the early 1190s, but *jitō* countrywide was not the same as *jitō*
everywhere. Moreover, on a different level of argument, a basis for
Kamakura's existence was hardly tantamount to Kamakura's displacement of Kyoto. The bulk of governance in Japan remained in the
hands of traditional proprietors and governors for the duration of the
Kamakura period. On the other hand, the authorization in question
was momentous, first, because it was never rescinded and, second,
because it did mark something strikingly new. Yet even having said
that, feudalism at the end of the twelfth century registered only modest beginnings: Yoritomo's reach remained strictly limited, and more
importantly, the bequests he made were over lands neither owned nor
controlled by him. At all events, the chieftain in Kamakura did come
to exercise a type of authority that was new to Japan. Its precise
limits and nature are bound up with the office of *jitō*, to which we
now turn.
     The term *jitō* originated in the ninth century but did not become a
land officership until the middle of the twelfth. Though its genealogy
and history during the Heian period are the subjects of heated controversy,[24] our concerns are restricted to what happened to the title during the Gempei War. In part owing to its relative newness, local persons found it an attractive cover by which to justify unlawful seizures
of rights and profits from centrally owned estates.[25] That is, they
claimed to be both Minamoto and privately appointed *jitō*, a combina-

23 Perhaps the classic expression of this older view is by Edwin O. Reischauer, "Japanese
   Feudalism," in Rushton Coulborn, ed., *Feudalism in History* (Princeton, N.J.: Princeton
   University Press, 1956), pp. 31–2. For a more recent discussion of the feudal aspects of
   Kamakura's early rule, see Jeffrey P. Mass, "The Early Bakufu and Feudalism," in Jeffrey P.
   Mass, ed., *Court and Bakufu in Japan: Essays in Kamakura History* (New Haven, Conn.: Yale
   University Press, 1982), pp. 123–42 (hereafter cited as Mass, "Feudalism").
24 A useful survey of the several arguments is by Ōae Ryō, "Jitō shiki o meguru shomondai,"
   Hōkei gakkai zasshi 13 (1964): 26–32; also *WG*, pp. 102–11.
25 *WG*, pp. 111–19; *KB*, docs. 6–7.

tion that was designed to immunize them from central control but that actually helped solidify a growing identification of *jitō* with Kamakura. Most of this development occurred during 1184 and 1185, at precisely the same time that the bakufu was assuming its overt stance against warrior lawlessness. It was also the period when Yoritomo was seriously seeking a common denominator on which to erect a full-scale reward–control system. The office of *jitō* was eventually used for this dual purpose. As Yoritomo undoubtedly rationalized it, the most effective means of ridding the countryside of self-styled *jitō* was for Kyoto to authorize a Kamakura monopoly of that post. The bakufu chieftain would then move concertedly against bogus *jitō* while appointing deserving vassals to lawful *jitō* titles whose rights packages had been confiscated from losers in the recent war. In this way, the continuity of services to estates and their proprietors would be ensured, as would managerial tenures for loyal, law-abiding Minamoto. The bakufu would make the actual *jitō* appointments and also guarantee their lawfulness and reliability. Stable conditions would be restored; Kamakura's presence through its *jitō* would be permanently established; and the men of the bakufu would enjoy both security and elite status.

How much of this conception can be credited to Yoritomo in advance of its implementation is difficult to determine. What is clear is that the year 1186 witnessed many appointments to *jitō* posts. At the same time, unauthorized *jitō* continued to be disciplined, as did lawfully appointed persons who exceeded their rights. In many cases, *jitō* were dismissed, whether for unusually serious crimes or owing to unjustified appointments in the first place.[26] One result of this attention to lawfulness and reliability was a network of provincial officers in perpetual motion. Kamakura did not establish its *jitō* corps to have it become static in size or fixed in place. A second result of Yoritomo's willingness to punish even his closest vassals was credibility – with those who served him and with the estate owners who depended on him. A major consequence was the quick appearance of Kamakura's period-long contribution to governance in Japan, its capacity to arbitrate between the local and central elites.

The *shugo* institution, despite being accorded a simultaneous birth with the *jitō* by the *Azuma kagami*, belongs in fact to a slightly later period. Though the bakufu did appoint provincial-level officers from

26 For example, the 1186 cancellation of a *jitō* post in the central region's Tamba Province; *KB*, doc. 30. The loser of the title was none other than Yoritomo's own brother-in-law, Hōjō Yoshitoki.

early in the war, they were evidently not called *shugo* but, rather, *sōtsuibushi*, an older title.[27] This distinction is actually extremely important. Kamakura's wartime *sōtsuibushi* were all-purpose provincial commanders bearing little resemblance to the legally constricted *shugo* of the 1190s and beyond. Indeed, the contexts in which these two officer types flourished is entirely different. Whereas the *sōtsuibushi* belonged to a period of helter-skelter growth on the part of the emerging Kamakura bakufu, the *shugo* were products of a damping-down process by a government seeking greater control of itself. The connection between the two titles, then, is largely superficial. Though both exercised provincewide authority, they had utterly divergent functions. The *Azuma kagami's* assertion of an 1185 authorization to appoint *shugo* is a confusion with *jitō* and a later rationalization by chroniclers intent on creating matching antiquities.

During the later 1180s, the urge to establish a workable division of responsibility with Kyoto gained impetus. The *jitō* institution constituted an important beginning here. Yet the country's proprietors were continuing to deluge Kamakura with undifferentiated appeals for redress, whereas the bakufu, for its part, had little idea as to whom it ought to recognize as permanent vassals. Yoritomo, indeed, became increasingly aware that his government had overextended itself. He therefore began to turn away petitions for assistance of the type he had earlier accepted. He also exhorted Kyoto to assume responsibility for matters now deemed outside his purview.[28] One result was the beginning of a jurisdictional separation between *jitō* and an equivalent managerial title, that of *gesu*. The former were declared men of Kamakura, with bakufu authority over appointments, dismissals, and punishments. The latter, though their perquisites and duties were indistinguishable from those of *jitō*, were now announced to be the responsibility of estate owners. This cutting edge between *jitō* and *gesu* became a prominent feature of the Kyoto–Kamakura dual polity.[29]

The matter of Kamakura's vassalage was an equally thorny problem, though one that did not receive Yoritomo's full attention until after 1190. Until recently, scholars assumed that Yoritomo devised the term *gokenin* at the same time that he launched his drive to power in 1180. The *Azuma kagami* uses the word in its earliest entries, and the currency of the term also made sense historically. Yoritomo was a

27 The finest treatment of the *sōtsuibushi–shugo* problem is by Yasuda Motohisa, *Shugo to jitō* (Tokyo: Shibundō, 1964), pp. 22–42.   28 *WG*, pp. 125–7.
29 The implications of the *jitō–gesu* division are treated in *WG*, pp. 136–42.

feudal chieftain, *gokenin* being the insignia of vassalage appropriate to his warrior movement. But as we now know, the term was not contemporaneous with the Gempei War and was not even used in the later 1180s.[30] Our conclusion is that vassalage remained a highly amorphous concept during the bakufu's first decade. Loyalty itself was often a matter of the moment, and "joining the Minamoto" could literally be done in isolation. Thus, when the war ended, a determination was still in the future as to the composition of a permanent band. The first group to be acknowledged received the initial round of *jitō* appointments, and these mostly were easterners. But each province of the country had warriors claiming to be legitimate loyalists. It was left to Yoritomo to devise a means to test this avowal and to move in the direction of a less disparate following.

It is not surprising, therefore, that the later 1180s witnessed a consolidation drive that was scarcely completed by the end of the century. Apart from the Kantō, the area of first concern was the Chūbu, the bloc of provinces between the country's two capitals. But no region of the country was fully secure, for Kamakura's command structure had never been unified. Numerous warriors remained under traditional chiefs. Yoritomo's solution to these problems was to engage the country's fighting men in yet another military campaign, this time against the north. The north was the site of a major enclave of private governance that had remained aloof from the Gempei War and later had given refuge to Yoritomo's fugitive brother, Yoshitsune. The Kamakura chieftain thus had several reasons to attack the family that dominated the region, the Ōshū Fujiwara.

In preparation for his campaign, Yoritomo authorized selected easterners to initiate a massive recruitment drive in all parts of the country. Though we lack detailed information on most areas, it is clear that warriors answered the call from as far away as Kyushu but that the greatest response came from the Chūbu.[31] Because the campaign itself resulted in a victory for Kamakura in 1189, Yoritomo found himself able to destroy the Fujiwara bloc on his eastern flank and to destroy or subordinate the Chūbu group on his western side. Elsewhere, he rewarded warriors who fought loyally and punished or purged those who did not.[32] A major step was thus taken in the direction of a kind of balance sheet on the country's fighting men. This was not yet a policy

30 Yasuda Motohisa, "Gokenin-sei seiritsu ni kansuru ichi shiron," *Gakushūin daigaku bungaku bu kenkyū nempō* 16 (1969): 81–110. For a discussion, see Mass, "Feudalism," pp. 131–7.
31 Kasai Sachiko, "Ōshū heiran to tōgoku bushidan," *Rekishi kyōiku* 16 (1968): 27–40.
32 This is vividly depicted in a Kyushu investiture of 1192; see *KB*, doc. 37.

of identifying permanent vassals, calling them *gokenin*, and including
their names on vassal registers. But these steps were not very far away.

What was needed to implement such a policy was a corps of deputies
with regular authority and uniform local jurisdiction. Here, then, is
the basis for the *shugo* institution, provincial commanders who might
also function as constabulary officers. The actual process by which the
shugo were first set into place has unfortunately been lost to us, though
a common surmise is that Yoritomo, on the occasion of his first trip to
Kyoto since childhood (1190), forced the court to appoint him *shugo*-
in-chief for the entire country.[33] Although there is no record of such an
arrangement, personnel identifiable as *shugo* do begin to appear
around 1192. This was just at the point that the *gokenin* label also
appears along with indications of the first vassals registers.[34] The connections here can hardly be overlooked: The primary responsibility
for installing and overseeing the *gokenin* system was granted to the
shugo, who were themselves created as extensions of Yoritomo's declared lordship over his new vassalage. Moreover, with the institutionalization of *gokenin* there also appeared a second legal category, *higokenin*
(nonvassals), both of whom may earlier have been "Minamoto." At any
rate, by the early 1190s the three basic local innovations of the
Kamakura bakufu, *jitō*, *shugo*, and *gokenin*, had been established. At
variance with traditional accounts, it is not the *jitō* and *shugo* whose
origins should be closely linked but, rather, the *shugo* and *gokenin*.
Neither of the latter had anything directly to do with the Gempei War.

It has long been assumed that the final pillar in Kamakura's system,
the office of shogun, was likewise set into place in 1192. Because of
that event, this year is almost as well known as 1185. In a sense,
however, the fame here is misplaced. Although Yoritomo was appointed shogun in 1192, he did not understand its significance, which
was established only after his death. Thus, the Kamakura chieftain
resigned the office in 1195, never supposing that posterity would
credit him with starting a tradition of shoguns. For Yoritomo, the title
was important only insofar as it might impress Kyoto; he returned to a
more prestigious office (that of *utaishō*, or commander of the inner
palace guards) in 1195 for precisely that reason.[35] Conversely, in no
ways was the post of shogun a capstone to his system of vassalage. As

33 For a discussion, see Yasuda, *Shugo to jitō*, pp. 45ff.
34 See the list of registers in Tanaka Minoru, "Kamakura shoki no seiji katei–kenkyū nenkan o
  chūshin ni shite," *Rekishi kyōiku* 11 (1963): 23.
35 For Yoritomo and the title of shogun, see Ishii Ryōsuke, "Sei-i tai shōgun to Minamoto
  Yoritomo," reprinted in Ishii Ryosuke, *Taika no kaishin to Kamakura bakufu no seiritsu*
  (Tokyo: Sōbunsha, 1958), pp. 87–94; and Mass, "Feudalism," pp. 126–8.

we shall see, it was left to the Hōjō, in need of an object for a regency, to invest the title of shogun with both a future and a past. Yoritomo thus became the first of a line of shoguns only in the memories of those who followed him.

In the wake of the northern campaign, Yoritomo, as mentioned, traveled to Kyoto for his first visit since childhood. By all accounts it was a triumphant venture. The chieftain of Kamakura was feted everywhere, and he was granted the *utaishō* title to which he later returned after three years as shogun (1192–5). A further preferment allowed him to open a *mandokoro*, a chancellery on the model of those of the great central aristocrats. Hereafter, decrees by his government issued from that organ rather than from Yoritomo personally.[36] This was, in a sense, a concession to bureaucratization, arguably the only one of import that he ever made. More typically, Yoritomo stood firm against the formation of enclaves of private power and shifted men about from one governmental task to another. He also continued his policy of purging warriors whose loyalty he considered suspect. During the 1190s, Yoritomo rid himself of certain province-level vassals in the west and evolved a complementary policy of elevating undistinguished easterners to positions of authority in the same region. As his thinking must have run, men of this type would owe their prestige to the largesse of the chieftain. In ways such as this, Yoritomo's temperament inclined him toward patrimonialism, though the realities of warrior power obliged him to adopt feudal techniques of organization as well.

To conclude this section on the era of Yoritomo, we should note the fluctuations in his relationship with Kyoto. The period covering 1185 to 1200 can be divided into three subperiods. The years between 1185 and 1192 witnessed a contest of sorts between the ex-emperor, Goshirakawa, and Yoritomo. This hardly constituted open warfare. Committed as he was to resuscitating traditional authority, Yoritomo dealt respectfully with the retired emperor throughout. For his part, however, Goshirakawa had little to lose by exploiting this advantage and by attempting to embarrass the rival regime in Kamakura. At any rate, when Goshirakawa died in 1192, there was little sorrow felt in the eastern capital. To prevent further opposition from Kyoto, Yoritomo decided to assume a higher profile in the politics of the court.

In the early stage of this effort, the Kamakura chief worked closely with a ranking ally in Kyoto, Kujō Kanezane. A problem developed,

---

36 For early examples of such edicts, see *KB*, docs. 12, 16–17.

however, when Yoritomo determined that his daughter should occupy the same imperial consort's position held by Kanezane's daughter. Yoritomo's goal was no less than to become grandfather to an emperor, and to promote that cause he undertook a second trip to Kyoto. This occurred in 1195 and was the occasion of his abandonment of the title of shogun in deference to a higher-ranking post, the office of *utaishō*. By this time, however, there were forces in the capital who saw in Yoritomo's gambit an opportunity to rid themselves of both Kanezane's and Kamakura's meddling. The result was exactly as the opposition interests in Kyoto had hoped. With Yoritomo's assistance, Kanezane was removed from power, but the eastern chieftain's plans for his daughter, owing to her untimely death, failed to materialize. Yoritomo, disappointed and chastened, turned his attention back to Kamakura. The period between 1196 and 1199 thus became a time of minimal interaction between the two capitals. The bakufu continued to accept courtiers' complaints alleging lawlessness by *jitō*. But a new power bloc had emerged in Kyoto over which Yoritomo exercised little leverage. When the eastern chieftain died in 1199, he could count as his most conspicuous failure the lack of closer relations with Kyoto.

THE ROAD TO JŌKYŪ

The period 1200 to 1221 has always had a quality of inevitability about it. This is because the Jōkyū disturbance, pitting the two capitals against each other, seemed a logical denouement to the establishment of a warrior regime in a country with only one prior governmental center. In fact, the war was considerably more complex than merely a fated showdown between older and newer authority systems. The lineup of forces in 1221 revealed societies in conflict as much within themselves as against one another; and the outpouring of violence that accompanied and followed the war suggests that the Gempei settlement, embracing various compromises by Yoritomo, had only superficially satisfied many of the country's warriors. A major result of the multisided Jōkyū struggle was thus a shift, if not a restructuring, in the power alignments between and within the two capitals as well as within the warrior class as a whole. For these reasons, the Jōkyū disturbance, belying its brief duration, was the most momentous event of the thirteenth century, rivaled only by the Mongol invasions.[37]

---

37 This multidimensional view of the Jōkyū disturbance is presented in Jeffrey P. Mass, *The Development of Kamakura Rule, 1180–1250: A History with Documents* (Stanford, Calif.: Stanford University Press, 1979), chap. 1 (hereafter cited as *DKR*).

The dominant theme of progress in Kamakura in the generation before Jōkyū was the rise of the Hōjō as hegemons. This was not the relatively easy progress it is often made out to be. The period was punctuated by power struggles and rebellions, and the Hōjō's emergence out of this milieu was anything but certain.[38] The background of the competition was the gap at the political center occasioned by Yoritomo's death. His successors, his sons Yoriie (r. 1199–1203) and Sanetomo (r. 1203–19), were not of the same mettle as their father, which meant that actual leadership fell to a coalition of vassals, itself an unstable arrangement. During the years 1200 to 1203, two families, the Hiki and the Hōjō, presided over this group. The head of the former was the father-in-law of Yoriie, who was himself hostile to his mother's family, the Hōjō. A bloodletting eventually ensued, which resulted in the replacement of Yoriie by the more pliable Sanetomo, as well as the destruction of the Hiki by their rivals, the Hōjō. The way was thus open for the Hōjō scion, Tokimasa, to assume brief but direct command of the Kamakura bakufu.

It has long been assumed that Tokimasa capped this dramatic rise in 1203 by becoming *shikken*, or regent, to the new shogun Sanetomo. According to this tradition, a sequence of *shikken* henceforth paralleled a sequence of shoguns. In fact, there is reason to doubt this version of events, as the title of *shikken*, meaning director of a *mandokoro*, could hardly have been initiated when there was no *mandokoro*. During this period the shogun was of insufficiently high court rank to open a formal chancellery.[39] Nevertheless, Tokimasa did dominate the bakufu until 1205, a fact we know from the regime's edicts, all of which bear his signature alone.[40] In that year he was displaced by his son and daughter, who, because their father's rule had not been institutionalized, failed to inherit all his power. Tokimasa's successors were thus forced to share authority with others, and for a decade after 1209 the *mandokoro*, now open, became the chief decision-making body in Kamakura and the principal issuer of its edicts.[41]

In 1213, another bloodletting occurred in which an old-line *gokenin* family, the Wada, found itself maneuvered into a treasonous position, giving the Hōjō ample reason to lead a bakufu campaign against it.

---

38 The clearest account in English of the rise of the Hōjō is by H. Paul Varley, "The Hōjō Family and Succession to Power," in Mass, ed., *Court and Bakufu in Japan*, chap. 6.
39 The *shikken* post of Tokimasa is noted in *AK*, 1203/10/9; for a critique, see *DKR*, pp. 77–79.
40 For example, *DKR*, docs. 55–59; *KB*, docs. 20, 33–34, 48, 100, 113, 161, 163.
41 For the role of the *mandokoro* during this period, see *DKR*, pp. 75–80.

Yet even now the Hōjō's hold over the governmental apparatus did not become entirely secure; there were fluctuations in the membership of the *mandokoro*, and the Hōjō were not always its directors. All this changed, however, in 1219 when the shogun was assassinated. This development gave the Hōjō a pretext on which to declare an emergency situation, which was close to the truth, as no successor was immediately available. In the absence of a nominal lord, the *mandokoro* ceased its formal activities, and Hōjō Yoshitoki, like his father before him, began issuing Kamakura's edicts under his own name. This time the Hōjō's accession to power within the bakufu proved to be permanent.

While the Hōjō were succeeding, finally, in securing their hegemony, a parallel situation was developing in Kyoto under a new retired emperor. Gotoba was the ultimate beneficiary of Yoritomo's clumsy meddling in court politics during the middle 1190s. When he "retired" in 1198 at the age of eighteen, his immediate task was to neutralize the bloc of supporters that made up his own entourage; it was this group that had engineered the removal of the Kanezane faction and blocked Yoritomo's designs at court. By 1202, Gotoba had succeeded in becoming his own master – and was also well on his way to becoming master of the capital. He established that his chancellery – the *in-no-chō* – was the central decision-making body in Kyoto, and he actively pursued greater wealth, often at the expense of rival proprietors. The result was a growing feeling of restiveness in Kyoto that paralleled a like sentiment in Kamakura.

Gotoba, indeed, attempted to capitalize on the growing warrior unrest, by providing an alternative source of patronage for the country's fighting men. He did this by recruiting both *gokenin* and non-*gokenin* for his private guard units and by distributing to these retainers various rank and office preferments. Although Gotoba might not have been aware of it at first, he was creating, with this activity, the core of an army that would later challenge Kamakura. The members of his guards units were drawn from east and west, a development that the bakufu took little notice of, as relations between the capitals were peaceful, if not unusually warm. In an earlier era, Yoritomo had fought court rewards for Minamoto who failed to be nominated by the chieftain. But now the shogun himself was a conspicuous recipient of court honors, whereas Kamakura remained parsimonious in granting *jitō* awards to most western vassals. In time, relatively large numbers of fighting men came to realize that the bakufu's existence was doing little to benefit them personally. Integrated, as in times past, with the

Kyoto-controlled estate system, warriors of this kind were receptive to Gotoba's call to arms against Kamakura in 1221.

The events that took place in 1219 are generally considered to have contributed to the decision to wage war. During the previous year, Hōjō Masako had traveled to Kyoto to negotiate with Gotoba over the naming of a shogun-designate. Had Sanetomo had an heir, the trip would not have been necessary. But the Hōjō, for whom the post of shogun was the basis for their regency, had already decided to seek a successor from within the imperial family. Such a choice would provide the bakufu (and themselves) with an unimpeachable legitimacy, whereas for Gotoba (whose infant son was the designee) there was the prospect of a bakufu "absorbed" into the imperial state. Early in 1219, however, Sanetomo's assassination prompted a change of heart on the part of the ex-emperor, and he contributed to the crisis in Kamakura by reneging on his earlier agreement. After a show of force in the capital, the bakufu secured a compromise choice – an infant Fujiwara – to be the next shogun. But when the child was brought to Kamakura, the ex-emperor resolved to withhold his formal appointment.

These developments poisoned relations between the two capitals, though, remarkably, the sources fall suddenly silent regarding actual movement toward war. There is no indication of overt steps taken on either side to prepare for any kind of showdown. This silence continued into the spring of 1221, when the ex-emperor had already decided on his course. The magnitude of his error only makes more regrettable our inability to trace events from mid-1219. At any rate, we can imagine a fevered effort, which contributed to the court's debacle, to assemble a fighting force that might acquit itself. In the end, Gotoba's army was a potpourri of warrior society. Drawn mostly from the central and western provinces, but with a number of eastern defectors, the forces of the court had little internal coherence.[42] Whereas fighting for the bakufu meant the prospect of new *jitō* titles, fighting for the court promised nothing in particular. Negative (or passive) feelings toward Kamakura could hardly make up for the absence of a rewards program.

Nor had Gotoba taken account of the fact that like the Hōjō, he had alienated much of his own natural constituency. Presumably, he believed that the central *shōen* proprietors shared his distaste for Kamakura to the point that they would rally to his cause. He must also

---

42 The nature of Gotoba's army is discussed in detail in *DKR*, pp. 16–29.

have expected delivery of the warrior-managers and the mercenaries who served them. In any event, the aristocracy's response was almost as mixed as that of the country's fighting men. Neutrality was the stance adopted by many, whereas others were simply not in a position to guarantee compliance by those living on their estates. A united Kyoto thus proved to be as elusive for Gotoba as it had been for Kiyomori two generations earlier.

Before moving to the Jōkyū encounter itself, it remains to be pondered what the ex-emperor hoped to achieve by his challenge to Kamakura. In his war declaration, he singled out Hōjō Yoshitoki, who was the nearest thing he could find to a common enemy for potential warrior recruits. The Minamoto, whose rule had already ended, could be praised for their service to the court, whereas the Hōjō, with some accuracy, could be condemned as usurpers. Beyond that, Gotoba entreated the men of Kamakura to rely henceforth on the judicial authority of Kyoto, a subtle plea, as it aimed at compromising Kamakura's jurisdiction without threatening to dismantle the bakufu itself. To have sought the support of warriors in overthrowing the warrior government could only have weakened Gotoba's chances for success. Conversely, the *gokenin* who joined the court did not do so out of a desire to destroy the bakufu idea or to end their own elite status. What they must have looked forward to was a reorganized regime with a new warrior leadership and a new form of cooperation with Kyoto. But Gotoba, whatever his rhetoric, could hardly have shared such views; his ultimate aim must have been to end Japan's dual polity, perhaps by placing *shugo* and *jitō* under his own authority. As we know, this potential divergence of goals had no time to surface. The Jōkyū disturbance, if not the violence that it unleashed, was over in less than a month.

THE JŌKYŪ DISTURBANCE AND ITS AFTERMATH

If the *Azuma kagami* is to be believed, Kamakura had no advance warning that Gotoba was preparing for war. Not surprisingly, the bakufu leadership was uncertain at first as to how to respond. The propriety of engaging an imperial army was debated; yet scruples gave way, under urging by the Hōjō, to the threat that was unmistakably at hand. Gotoba's war declaration reached Kamakura on the nineteenth day of the fifth month of 1221. Within a week's time, according to the *Azuma kagami,* a bakufu counterforce of 190,000 men had been assembled.[43]

The recruitment policies devised by the Hōjō had a direct bearing on the outcome of the war and the settlement that followed. Only easterners were called to service, although as Kamakura's armies advanced westward, local vassals were actively recruited. The Kantō-led military campaign thus formed a wedge for greater penetration of the west and also offered a chance for further consolidation of the Chūbu. Unlike the beginning stages of the Gempei War, then, the leadership in Kamakura determined to take the fighting directly to the enemy. The strategy worked splendidly, and on the fifteenth day of the sixth month the victorious bakufu army entered the capital. Brushing aside Gotoba's pleas for mercy, Kamakura scattered into exile the ex-emperor and other members of his war party.

So rapidly had events taken place that at first the bakufu could hardly have appreciated the extent of its victory. The full composition of the ex-emperor's army was a matter to be determined, and probes had to be undertaken to judge degrees of war guilt. Similarly, the bakufu had to examine its own army – who had fought and with what degree of valor. What complicated all of this was a reign of terror that now gripped the countryside. Both vassals and nonvassals interpreted the court's defeat as a license to engage in lawlessness.[44] So savage was this outburst that whatever Kamakura's instinct for revenge against Kyoto, its leadership realized that the traditional authority system could not, without risk to the bakufu, be dismantled. In fact, it would have to be restored, and Kamakura therefore took steps in that direction. It retained most of the governmental apparatus of the court, and it set into place a new retired emperor. At the same time, it undertook to return the countryside to peace by responding to the complaints of violence lodged by the traditional proprietors.

But Kamakura was hardly prepared to oversee a total return to the status quo ante. It replaced its ineffective Kyoto *shugo*'s office with a bakufu branch in the capital, the so-called Rokuhara *tandai.* It also reserved for itself the right to interfere in high-level personnel decisions at court, including the naming of emperors. It further made clear

43 Two translations by William McCullough present a narrative account of the war: "The *Azuma kagami* Account of the Shōkyū War," *Monumenta Nipponica* 23 (1968): 102–55; "Shōkyūki: An account of the Shōkyū War," *Monumenta Nipponica* 19 (1964): 163–215, and 21 (1966): 420–53.
44 For a sampling of the violence in 1221 and 1222, see *DKR*, docs. 21, 24–26; *KB*, docs. 95, 112, 116.

that Kamakura and Kyoto would henceforth work in tandem; the dual polity was a permanent reality that might never be challenged again. To underscore this, the bakufu began issuing legislative pronouncements, demonstrating parity with Kyoto as a lawgiving authority. Finally, Kamakura responded to the desires of its men by flooding the central and western provinces with massive numbers of new *jitō* assignments. This latter development constituted no less than a colonization drive, for the recipients were almost exclusively easterners and the appointment areas were the confiscated holdings of dispossessed westerners. As a result, the demographics of warrior strength in Japan shifted dramatically in favor of elite fighting men from the Kantō.

The restoration of stability, so high on Kamakura's list of priorities, was actually undermined by the introduction of large numbers of new *jitō* into unfamiliar areas. But this was the price that had to be paid to institutionalize a presence countrywide and to satisfy the expectations of a core constituency. A major result was a substantial bolstering of what had long since become Kamakura's principal governmental role, the dispensing of justice. With bakufu men in possession of rights in all parts of the country, it was more important than ever that the policing of *jitō*, immune from the discipline of *shōen* proprietors, be handled with dispatch. At first, Kamakura was hard-pressed to keep up with the demand for judgments, and in fact, its commitment to fairness may have suffered a bit. But these lapses proved momentary, as the bakufu was willing to reverse any mistaken decisions.[45] At any rate, the era was one of adjustment and change in Japan after roughly two decades of equilibrium.

The changes referred to here have less to do with substance and structure than they do with scope and numbers. That is, the Jōkyū disturbance yielded no institutionally new figures comparable to those evolving out of the Gempei War and its aftermath. What occurred after 1221 was an expansion of existing officer networks and authority, not some radical departure into new conceptual space. True, Kamakura now began posing as a lawgiving authority alongside Kyoto, and this was certainly unprecedented. But the enactments themselves did not infringe on the imperial sanction, and in fact, they acknowledged and fortified it. Moreover, Kamakura's efforts as a lawgiver were decidedly modest at first, and the bakufu carved out for itself no new spheres of local or central jurisdiction. What was new after 1221 was

---

45 A classic example, which involved attempts to rectify errors on four separate occasions, was finally put right in 1232; see *DKR*, doc. 33.

the growth of Kamakura's involvement in dispute resolution and its accelerated placement of *jitō*. The number of such *jitō* is perhaps the critical question, and herein lies an interesting tale.

According to a famous datum of history cited in the *Azuma kagami*, Kamakura profited from the confiscation of fully three thousand *shōen* as part of the Jōkyū settlement. If taken literally, a shift of such magnitude would have significantly tilted the court–bakufu balance. Kyoto would have suffered a cataclysmic setback and faced severe revenue shortages followed by immediate decline. In fact, however, the three thousand figure implied far less than it seemed to. In the first place, nowhere near that number of transfers can be corroborated; the total (as with the size of Kamakura's army) is likely exaggerated. Second, even if the number were accurate, it probably implied the total of transfers at all levels of authority. That is, Kamakura and Kyoto shared in this new largesse. The bakufu declared its right to fashion *jitō* assignments from the managerial packages belonging to those warriors caught on the losing side. Likewise, the court, with Kamakura's blessing, shifted an unknown number of proprietary titles from one segment of the traditional aristocracy – Gotoba's war party – to another, those who had remained neutral or shown sympathy for Kamakura. It is in this sense, that the Jōkyū disturbance engendered shifts both within and between Japan's two great power blocs. Research on the "Kyoto settlement" has only just begun, with indications that the major religious institutions came out strongest.[46] By contrast, scholarship on Kamakura is well advanced and shows a small number of proprietorships, against numerous new *jitō* titles.[47] As reflected in the overall settlement, then, the bakufu could be assured that the basic ordering of society was not being impaired. Warriors, difficult to control in the best of circumstances, would remain middle-level land managers.

A final point on this subject is that the postwar era was not limited to a year or two; Jōkyū land transfers are known from as late as the 1240s, though most of the shifts in holdings obviously occurred earlier. By 1225 or 1226, Kamakura was prepared to make structural changes in its organization that pointed the way to a new, mature phase in bakufu operations.

---

46 Kōyasan, in particular, profited from the court's defeat, but so did the Tōdaiji and the shrines of Kamo, Ise, and Iwashimizu; see *DKR*, pp. 38–40.

47 Details on some 129 post-Jōkyū *jitō* appointments appear in Tanaka Minoru, "Jōkyū kyōgata bushi no ichi kōsatsu – rango no shin jitō buninchi o chūshin to shite," *Shigaku zasshi* 65 (1956): 21–48; Tanaka Minoru, "Jōkyū no rango no shin jitō buninchi," *Shigaku zasshi* 79 (1970): 38–53.

BAKUFU GOVERNANCE

In 1224, Hōjō Yoshitoki died and was followed in death by Masako a year later. The new leader of the bakufu was Yoshitoki's son, Yasutoki, by consensus the greatest of the Hōjō regents. Born after the founding of the bakufu and educated in classical Confucianism, Yasutoki left a stamp on the regime's operations that survived until the end of the period. It was under Yasutoki that the bakufu's capacity for mediating disputes achieved new heights and under him also that Kamakura's reputation for good government became a fixture of the historical memory.[48] Kamakura's golden age, which began now, owed much of its luster to the efforts of this extraordinary man.

Yasutoki was an innovator right from the start. Desirous of ending the postwar emergency, he took three steps to place the bakufu on a more regular footing. First, he established the cosigner (rensho) institution wherein a coregent, drawn from his own family, would become part of Kamakura's formal apparatus.[49] Second, he promoted the idea of collegiality by creating a board of councilors (hyōjōshū) to function as the bakufu's ranking governmental organ. Finally, he moved to formalize the elevation of the shogun-designate, a step that his predecessors, even after the Jōkyū victory, had not taken. In the first month of 1226, the eight-year-old Yoritsune became the fourth lord of Kamakura.

These were Yasutoki's public moves. He also moved behind the scenes to ensure that the hyōjōshū would be responsive to his own wishes and become the new high court of Kamakura. Although the council, like the mandokoro before it, was a mixture of old-line gokenin and ex-noble legal specialists, it differed from its predecessor in being the instrument of its founder's will. The mandokoro, which had been founded by the Minamoto and which played such an important role during the period to 1219, was inactive throughout the 1220s and was subsequently divested of its entire judicial authority. In 1232, the shogun was promoted to a court rank high enough to make him eligible to open a mandokoro. But by that time Yasutoki was its director and therefore oversaw the chancellery's principal task of investing and confirming jitō posts. In sum, whereas the mandokoro dated back to

48 Note, for example, the high opinion of Yasutoki's tenure held by Kitabatake Chikafusa, author of the fourteenth-century Jinnō Shōtōki: A Chronicle of Gods and Sovereigns, trans. H. Paul Varley (New York: Columbia University Press, 1980), pp. 228–30.
49 Credit for this innovation used to be given to Hōjō Masako, based on an erroneous entry in the Azuma kagami. The correct attribution was made by Uwayokote Masataka, "Renshosei no seiritsu," in Kokushi ronshū, vol. 2 (Kyoto: Dokushikai, 1959), pp. 625–40.

Heian times and had an existence tied to the court-sponsored rank of the shogun, the *hyōjōshū* was a bakufu invention and a vehicle of the regent. To argue, as many historians have done, that the *hyōjōshū* constituted the beginning of a new conciliar phase in Kamakura history is to overlook the organ's origins and to ignore its subsequent dominance by the Hōjō.[50]

Although the sources do not refer directly to this process, from its beginning the council became the arena for a rapidly modernizing system of justice. As mentioned earlier, the bakufu had been placed in the position of judicial arbiter, literally from the first days of the Minamoto movement. The earliest settlements were edicts issued by Yoritomo himself, but after formation of the *mandokoro*, he centered much of this authority there. With the chieftain's death, however, the Hōjō, under Tokimasa, came to dominate the process (1203–5), though in the decade before Jōkyū the *mandokoro*, as noted, experienced its resurgence. From 1219 to 1226 it was the Hōjō once again who controlled the regime's judgments.[51]

Belying these power shifts at the top level of the bakufu, the techniques of justice were rapidly becoming more sophisticated. Technique, indeed, was emphasized from the start. Because Kamakura had no written laws at first or any philosophical traditions and because the country's estates were accustomed to having individualized precedents (*senrei*) made the basis of judgments, it was natural for the bakufu to stress procedure over principle. On a period-long basis, identifying and confirming local precedents served as the foundation of Kamakura justice. Flowing from this came basic attitudes toward impartiality, modes of proof, due process, and the right of appeal. In its maturity, the system was thus closely calibrated to the needs of a society that was lawless yet litigious, restive yet still respectful of higher authority.

A case in 1187 demonstrates the enormous potential of a system of justice whose principal objective was equity for the litigants rather than aggrandizement by their judges. At stake was the possession of an area in distant Kyushu to which the disputants had conflicting claims. In the words of Yoritomo's settlement edict, "The relative merits of the two parties have been investigated and judged, and [the *jitō*'s] case

---

50 See Andrew Goble, "The Hōjō and Consultative Government," in Mass, ed., *Court and Bakufu in Japan*, Chap. 7, for a rejection of the conciliar view made famous by Satō Shin'ichi.
51 Hōjō control was direct from 1219 to 1226; thereafter it was through the *hyōjōshū*. Either way, judgments between 1219 and 1333 bore Hōjō names exclusively. These have been collected by Seno Seiichirō, *Kamakura bakufu saikyojō shū* (Tokyo: Yoshikawa kōbunkan, 1970–1), 2 vols.

has been found justified." To establish this, proof records (*shōmon*) had been placed in evidence, and the "false claim" (*hiron*) of the challenger was dismissed. Finally, a copy of the edict was sent to the government headquarters (*dazaifu*) in Kyushu, where an additional order executing the decision was handed down.[52]

During the era of Yoritomo, justice, it may be said, remained the prerogative of the chieftain. Though he assigned trusted followers to cases and allowed them some leeway, he did not have professional investigators, much less a class of judges. A "judiciary" in the sense of a separate organ did not appear until later.[53]

The two decades before Jōkyū saw a number of advances in the way that Kamakura handled suits. And these were indeed suits: The system was accusatorial, with litigation initiated by a plaintiff. Moreover, on a period-long basis, the bakufu itself was never a party to such actions and thereby strengthened its reputation as an arbiter and not an inquisitor. It is logical that an investigative agency, the *monchūjo*, should have become active after Yoritimo's death. After conducting inquiries, which now involved a more clearly defined exchange of accusation and rebuttal statements (*sojō* and *chinjō*), along with gathering and analyzing evidence, the *monchūjo* issued a report, which was normally the basis of the judgment. From the beginning, written proof was considered more reliable than witnesses' or litigants' claims, and before long, distinctions among types of documents were introduced. In turn, as verdicts came to rest on documents, the crimes of forging, pilfering, and extorting records correspondingly became a problem. As Kamakura quickly discovered, advances in judicial technique were often followed by attempts to abuse or thwart them.

Integral to the progress in Kamakura was the promotion of a local support system. Because some types of allegations could most effectively be verified locally, *shugo* became the principal agents of investigation in the provinces. As the traffic of directives and responses increased, this served to tighten the bakufu's overall control of its vassalage even as it was expediting the handling of suits. The same end was served by Kamakura's issuance of formal questionnaires (*toijō*) and summonses (*meshibumi*) either directly or indirectly to defendants. As for the suits themselves, these tended to fall into three categories. The most prominent during the early period were actions lodged by

52 *KB*, doc. 14.
53 The standard view, based on the *Azuma kagami*, posits a "board of inquiry" (*monchūjo*) from 1184. I take issue with this version of events; see Jeffrey P. Mass, "The Origins of Kamakura Justice," *Journal of Japanese Studies* 3 (1977): 307–10.

traditional proprietors against *jitō*. Some of these were already quite complex, involving multiple issues, the product of diversified programs of lawlessness by increasingly ambitious *jitō*.[54] The second type of suit, which became far more important later, dealt with intrafamily vassal disputes, generally over inheritances.[55] Finally, there were complaints by or against *gokenin* alleging interfamily infringement.[56] Kamakura's official position against accepting courtier or warrior suits that did not involve vassals was occasionally transgressed by the bakufu itself. Yet the policy of separate jurisdictions with Kyoto remained in force and served as the principal basis for the era's dual polity.

There were, however, certain defects in the system that became more pronounced in the years immediately following Jōkyū. As mentioned earlier, due process was compromised somewhat under the weight of litigation caused by the emergency. This led to a rise in the number of false or frivolous suits and an increasing awareness that Kamakura's judgments did not contain enough information either to prevent repetitions of the same problem or to provide the bakufu with an easy basis for resolving future difficulties. Specifically, the edicts tended not to contain full-enough histories of either troubled areas or families and did not present summaries of the oral and written testimony constituting the basis for the judgment. In addition, by the late 1220s there existed a number of problem estates for which the bakufu had adopted conflicting positions in the past. In order to set the records straight and to line up, as it were, the precedents, Yasutoki was disposed to having Kamakura's highest court, the *hyōjōshū*, rehear such cases. From a handful of settlement edicts surviving from 1227–8, we see that Kamakura justice had taken a major step forward.[57]

Central to the advances made at this time was a new commitment to impartiality, in the form of the *taiketsu*, or face-to-face trial confrontation, and to recording the facts and the reasoning behind a judgment as based on the oral and written testimony. In the past, plaintiff and defendant had been regularly summoned, but it is not certain whether they faced each other and their interrogators simultaneously. Even now, only a minority of cases reached this ultimate test; but the principle of access, so crucial, had been established. The bakufu also made

54 A case in 1216, for example, embraced some sixteen disputed issues; see *KB*, doc. 93.
55 For example, the long-running case involving Ojika Island in Kyushu's Hizen Province. Kamakura first heard the suit in 1196, again in 1204, and thereafter repeatedly until it was settled with some finality in 1228; see *KB*, docs. 19–20; *DKR*, pp. 95–101.
56 For example, cases in Kyushu from 1205 and 1212; see *DKR*, docs. 57, 65.
57 See, in particular, the Ojika Island settlement of 1228, referred to in n. 55. A judgment in 1227/3 is the earliest of the "new" type; see *KB*, doc. 46.

clear that the most extraordinary measures would be used to ferret out the truth. Witnesses, if needed, would be sought from the most remote corners of the land,[58] and summonses would be issued ad nauseum if it was thought they might help.[59] Conversely, Kamakura inculcated the notion that each stage in the judicial process was capable of serving as the final stage; we see no slavish devotion to the full reach of Kamakura's own system. The rationale here was to avoid squandering valuable resources, whether the litigants' or the bakufu's, and to give the system maximum flexibility. Thus, there would be cases when merely the lodging of a suit would induce the defendant to settle "out of court." Or perhaps the same result might occur at the point of acceptance of a suit or the delivery of the charges or of a summons. Under the Kamakura system, justice might be rapid or drawn out; in many instances it was unending, as formal appeals became possible and new suits on old subjects were commonplace. Indeed, it was Kamakura's objective to bottle up potentially explosive situations in litigation; that elite warriors subjected themselves to long-running encounters on the legal field of battle rather than on military battlefields proved to be one of the bakufu's most enduring accomplishments.

Nor did Kamakura justice become static or excessively bureaucratized. Soon after introducing the procedures that would serve as the core of the system, Yasutoki became active as a legislator. Drawing on his Confucian training and his evaluation of current realities, he became the guiding force behind the *goseibai shikimoku*, a behavioral code for *gokenin* that was promulgated in 1232. This formulary was important for several reasons. As the first document of its kind by and for warriors, it gave further evidence of Kamakura's parity with Kyoto and indeed served as the inspiration and precedent for all future warrior codes. Nevertheless, in the context of its own times, the formulary was intended to do less than it has often been given credit for.[60] It represented not so much the creation of binding rules as the establishment of standards; its underlying principle, *dōri*, conveyed reasonableness, not literalness. Thus, a judgment based on the particulars of a

58 For example, a suit in 1244 involving a corner of Kyushu's Hizen Province led to the interrogation of at least twenty local persons; see *DKR*, doc. 144.
59 For example, the reference to seven summonses in a Bizen Province suit in 1255; see *KB*, doc. 50.
60 The existence of an early English translation of the formulary (1904) caused several generations of historians to rely unduly on this document. The potential influence of such translations is discussed by Jeffrey P. Mass, "Translation and Pre-1600 History," *Journal of Japanese Studies* 6 (Winter 1980): 61–88.

case was the closest approximation of *dōri;* Kamakura laws, as summation of current practice, were the next closest.

The *goseibai shikimoku,* then, was a sketch rather than a finished blueprint; its general concerns were more important than its specific content. Had the formulary, by contrast, sought to impose a uniform set of regulations, it would have conflicted with the limitless variety of estate-based customs. This would have rendered justice inoperable, as governance in the thirteenth century (Kamakura's or Kyoto's) could hardly have been reduced to formula. The *shikimoku's* objectives were thus to define the parameters of the *gokenin's* world and to enunciate standards that would both exalt and restrain him. Because the society of the vassal was itself ever-changing, it was readily anticipated that the code, like a constitution, would be supplemented by legislation.

And so it was. Hardly was the ink dry on the 1232 document when new enactments began to pour from Kamakura's lawmakers. Some of these dealt with topics not covered in the *shikimoku,* but others were clearly corrective in nature. The latter condition was promoted by a development that Yasutoki had not foreseen. In its efforts to reconcile two competing social and political orders, Kamakura had forsworn interference in the affairs of *shōen* proprietors, specifically in *shōen* in which *jitō* did not hold land rights. This left non-*jitō gokenin,* who constituted the majority of the native western province vassals, legally unprotected, and estate owners were quick to take advantage of this situation.[61] Moreover, the *shikimoku,* though including *jitō* under its umbrella of protection, also restricted them in a number of explicit ways. Proprietors had merely to study the formulary and then bring suit against a *jitō* for alleged codal violations. Because the *shōen* proprietors themselves were immune from discipline by Kamakura, there was nothing, moreover, to prevent them from bringing trumped-up charges.[62] At any rate, the 1230s and 1240s witnessed a number of adjustments in the bakufu's laws as inequities in the original legislation were deemed needy of correction.

Notwithstanding such difficulties, the post-*shikimoku* era carried Kamakura justice to a new plateau of excellence. From about 1230 the Rokuhara deputyship in Kyoto became an adjunct to the system, fully empowered to judge suits independently of Kamakura. Although in practice Rokuhara functioned mostly as a lower court with appeal eastward regularly used, the bakufu had diversified its judicial machin-

---

61 *DKR,* pp. 108–12, docs. 76–77.
62 For example, a case in which a proprietor ignored an earlier judgment against itself and attempted to reopen the suit; see *DKR,* doc. 78.

ery and strengthened its reputation as Japan's most prestigious court. At the same time, Kamakura was also taking steps to improve its efficiency and overall performance. In 1249, it added another investigative office, the *hikitsuke-shū*, which gradually took its place as the principal organ of inquiry below the *hyōjōshū*.

As indicated earlier, dispute resolution was, from beginning to end, Kamakura's chief contribution to the age. More than policing, the collection of taxes, or any other of a myriad of responsibilities associated with governments, the settlement of land suits, broadly conceived, stood as the raison d'être for the bakufu's existence. On the other hand, this did not mean that Kamakura's authority was simply one-dimensional. It did exercise, for example, certain administrative responsibilities in its base area of the east. Yet this authority was far from fully articulated, and few data survive on Kamakura as a territorial power.

The explanation for this anomaly takes us back to the dual polity. During Kamakura times, the country was not divided into discrete territorial spheres. Authorities were overlapping within the context of the all-encompassing estate system. This meant that *shōen* holders and provincial proprietors maintained contacts with the east, whereas Kamakura, through its *shugo* and *jitō*, exercised influence in the west. Thus, the dual polity was a thoroughly integrated polity which, however, might be unequal. Although the bakufu had arguably the more important contribution to make, Kyoto, it seems clear, had the more varied. Preoccupied with its judicial burden, Kamakura eschewed many of the complementary duties of government, which remained the purview of traditional, court-centered authority.[63]

SHUGO AND JITŌ

The *shugo* and *jitō* were the period-defining figures of the Kamakura age, a condition that was recognized even at the time. The less significant of the two, the *shugo*, was created, as we have seen, as part of the bakufu's effort in the 1190s to inject coherence into its vassal network and to clarify the boundaries of the emerging dual polity. The plan was to assign a trusted easterner to each province of the country and to have this officer represent the bakufu as its ranking agent in that province. The *shugo*'s authority was to be threefold. He was to act as

63 These views are developed by Jeffrey P. Mass, "What Can We Not Know About the Kamakura Bakufu?" in Jeffrey P. Mass and William B. Hauser, eds., *The Bakufu in Japanese History* (Stanford, Calif.: Stanford University Press, 1985), pp. 24–30.

coordinator of his area's *gokenin*, in particular, commanding them in war and leading them in their peacetime guard duty in Kyoto. Second, he was to assume responsibility for controlling local rebellion and crimes of a capital nature, both duties hitherto discharged by the older civil governors. Finally, he was to serve as an adjunct to Kamakura's judicial system, performing in the joint roles of investigator, enforcer, and liaison.[64]

Only the first two duties breached the natural division between Kamakura's and Kyoto's authority, and as such they required official sanction from the court. We do not know the circumstances surrounding this arrangement or when it was secured, but by early in the thirteenth century *shugo* were active in these capacities. The Kyoto guard service, known as *ōbanyaku*, was a legacy from the Heian period that Kamakura inherited and made incumbent on its collective vassalage on a provincial basis. Service periods were normally three or six months, and the duty fell on individual provinces at irregular intervals, sometimes twenty years or more. The *ōbanyaku*, curious as it now seems, was the centerpiece of Kamakura's system of vassal services, which also included tribute obligations (labor, horses, etc.) but not regular taxes or rents. Part of the rationale for doing things in this way derived from the bakufu's ambivalent attitude toward noneastern vassals, relatively few of whom it honored. Although it wished to call these westerners to service from time to time, it did not desire their presence in Kamakura, which had its own *ōbanyaku* limited to easterners. At all events, *shugo* were placed in command of the imperial guard duty.

The *shugo*'s constabulary authority involved them (or their deputies) in fairly frequent conflict with estate owners, who sought immunity from *shugo* entrance. Historians have not been able to agree on the extent of the *shugo*'s jurisdiction here, that is, the stage in the criminal prosecution continuum to which his authority reached, or the precise social classes covered.[65] But it is noteworthy that Kamakura's ranking peace officers in the field, like policemen in other times and places, were the objects of censure rather than praise by the interests ostensibly being served. In this regard, *shugo* were no different from civil governors or their agents from whom estate holders also sought immunity. We may say, at any rate, that *shugo* were

---

64 The Kamakura *shugo* is treated in *WG*, chap. 8.
65 The debate has mostly been between Satō Shin'ichi and Ishii Ryōsuke; for a summary, see *WG*, pp. 213–20.

least successful in this aspect of their duties and were fairly frequently lawbreakers themselves.

These formal responsibilities of the *shugo* (the Kyoto *ōbanyaku*,
rebellion, and murder) were incorporated into Kamakura law under
the curious misnomer of *taibon sankajō*, the three regulations for great
crimes. This was in 1231, long after the three duties, minus the name,
had become an operational definition of the *shugo*'s authority. The
notion of uniformity expressed by such a legalism goes to the very
heart of the *shugo* conception. The holders of this title were viewed as
public officers with responsibilities replicated in all provinces of the
country. In that regard they were like their counterparts, the civil
governors, and unlike the *jitō*, who, following *shōen* custom, all were
perceived to be different. The *taibon sankajō*, with its slender authority, expressed the narrow limits of the *shugo*'s public presence.

As noted, there was a third aspect to the *shugo*'s authority, and this
was centered on duties performed on behalf of the bakufu. In particular, the *shugo* assisted Kamakura in the latter's judicial endeavors. The
range here was impressive – from interrogating local witnesses, sum-
moning defendants, and subpoenaing relevant documents, to forward-
ing investigative reports, issuing enforcement orders, and announcing
judgments. A question arises as to whether such activity (along with
the *ōbanyaku*) allowed *shugo* to develop leverage over *gokenin* as a step
toward fashioning private vassalages. On balance, this probably did
not occur, as *shugo* were commonly obliged to take actions unfriendly
to *jitō*, who were usually the defendants in legal actions, and as
Kamakura was careful to hedge the autonomy of its provincial appointees. *Shugo*, for instance, held tenures that were revocable at will; they
received assignments only in provinces of which they were not natives
(save for the east); their posts were not normally identified with landholding; and they were restricted in the number and functioning of
their deputies.[66] It is hardly surprising, given these conditions, that
few *shugo* bothered to take up residence in their assigned provinces.
With tenures that were considered nonheritable, most appointees remained in their eastern bases or else elected to live in Kamakura itself.

Although a handful of *shugo* did succeed in entrenching themselves
in their provinces, this did not mean that their relations with Kamakura were in any way discordant. They continued to require the
bakufu's active support and patronage, in return for which they pro-

---

66 Among these four, the only point that has been disputed is the landholding issue. Satō
   Shin'ichi argues in the negative, and Ishii Susumu takes the opposing view. I favor Satō here;
   see *WG*, pp. 225–7.

vided valuable and ongoing service. No *shugo* could survive, much less prosper, in isolation. In addition, as the years passed, the bakufu's leading house, the Hōjō, came to gather up an increasingly large portfolio of *shugo* titles, some thirty or more, almost half the national total, by the end of the period. We do not know enough about this development to judge whether it constituted a setback for the *shugo* system or rendered it more efficient. Certainly it limited the potential for the autonomy of other *shugo*, as "Hōjō neighbors" were now a reality for everyone. Our best guess is that the Hōjō aggrandizement of *shugo* posts did not appreciably distort the aims or operations of Kamakura's governance. Localism, society's larger trend, was not occurring at the level of the *shugo* or province anyway and was partly obstructed by them. Thus, far from hastening the decline of higher authority's sanction, the institution of *shugo* functioned as a major support for it. As we shall now see, the same can hardly be said for the Kamakura *jitō*.

If one has to search for multiformity among *shugo*, that condition was built in to the office of *jitō*. *Jitō* appointments could be made to land units of any size or description – or indeed not to land at all. Perquisites and authority were similarly diverse[67] and were expected to conform to the rights packages of the *jitō*'s predecessor, whether another *jitō* or a land manager bearing a different title, usually *gesu*. Once a *jitō* was appointed, he could look on his office as heritable property subject only to Kamakura's probate of his will. He could also expect immunity, as mentioned earlier, from the disciplinary authority of his absentee landlord. If the *jitō* committed any kind of offense against man or property, the estate owner had no recourse but to appeal to Kamakura for redress. This obliging of the *jitō* to manage lands on behalf of a proprietor exercising no direct control over him was what made the office revolutionary. It also ensured an unending need for a bakufu judicial authority.

In the hands of warriors, the post of *jitō* was trouble prone from the start. Kamakura made its appointments without knowledge of, and therefore without specifying, the limits of the managerial authority in question. It admonished its new *jitō* to obey local precedents – and left it to the *jitō* to discover what these were. Not surprisingly, *shōen* proprietors and *jitō* read these practices differently, which became the basis of litigation. Early on, Kamakura thus found itself making historical probes into the customs of remote areas. Where it erred was in not

67 For examples of the limitless variety in both physical shape and range of authority, see *WG*, pp. 171–2.

recording all its findings, not, that is, until Yasutoki's reforms. But even then, resourceful *jitō* were still free to choose new areas of activity to contest or to return to older subjects that retained ambiguities. The problem for the bakufu was that it could hardly afford to move too harshly against too many of its own men. Its judgments against *jitō* were never wavering, but most of its decisions were admonitory rather than overtly punitive. In Kamakura's view, dismissals were possible in extreme cases, but establishing the limits of a *jitō*'s authority would often be punishment enough. Henceforth, the *jitō* would be bound by a legal document that included the particulars of his earlier offenses.

What were some of the specific areas of dispute? *Jitō* received designated land units as compensation for their services. It was a common practice to claim adjacent units as falling within protected regions, to assert lower tax ratios or totals, and to invoke custom as the justification for imposing labor duties on cultivators. Points of quarrel in the sphere of *shōen* management centered on the extent of the *jitō*'s policing authority, the extent of his jurisdiction over local officials, the range of his competence to organize and oversee agriculture, and the nature of his involvement with the collection and delivery of *shōen* dues. Each of these topics was the source of endemic disagreement, as to control all of them was to dominate a *shōen*. Typically, however, the *jitō* enjoyed only a share of that authority, commonly expressed by some kind of formula. Thus, in the area of policing competence, a *jitō* might hold a one-third or one-half share,[68] which meant that confiscated property or fines in those amounts would redound to him. Or again, in regard to a *shōen*'s managerial corps, the *jitō* might control certain titled officials, which gave him the powers of appointment and dismissal over them.[69]

The normal antagonist of the *jitō* in all these areas was a special appointee of the proprietor who exercised the remaining jurisdiction. Thus, many *shōen* had dual tracks of authority, one under the *jitō* and immune from the proprietor, the other controlled by him through his agent. These agents were of two basic origins, either long-time residents of the area in question and possibly the original commenders of some or all of the land composing the *shōen*, or centrally dispatched professional managers. In any event, this bifurcation of authority and responsibility between *jitō* and custodians, as they were called,[70] pro-

68 See *KB*, docs. 90, 89, respectively. Or the share could be total; see *KB*, doc. 88.
69 See, for example, the several titles under a *jitō*'s authority in estates in Satsuma and Aki provinces; *KB*, doc. 78; *DKR*, doc. 41.
70 The term here is *azukari-dokoro*. By mid-Kamakura times, a second term–*zasshō*–was coming

vided the backdrop for some of the era's truly classic, long-running battles. We know a great deal about many of these from the bakufu's judicial edicts, which were the instruments of hoped-for settlement. In fact, we know a vast amount about the *jitō* in general, as they were the primary objects of complaint and control and thus the subjects of thousands of documents.

In their growing desperation, *shōen* proprietors evolved a series of direct approaches aimed at pacifying or constraining the *jitō*. The initiative here was taken by the *shōen* proprietors, who typically offered a compromise. Under the generic name *wayo*, compromises of two types predominated. The first, called *ukesho*, seems unusually remote from reality. Under it the *jitō* were given total administrative control of the *shōen*, even to the point of barring entrance by agents of the proprietor. In return, the *jitō* contracted to deliver a fixed annual tax, regardless of agricultural conditions. By agreeing to underwrite such arrangements, Kamakura was in effect promising that violations could and would be litigated. Yet because delivery of the tax was the *jitō*'s only obligation to the proprietor, amounts in arrears became the sole object of suits. The worst that might happen was that the *jitō*, deeply in debt but with his *ukesho* intact, would simply be ordered to pay, often on lenient terms.[71]

The second device aimed at mollifying the *jitō* was called *shitaji chūbun*, a physical splitting up of *shōen*. As with other divisions of authority, percentage arrangements were the norm here, and maps with red lines through them were drawn to demarcate shares.[72] The bakufu's formal approval, symbolic of its guarantorship, was standard here too.[73] It was long assumed that *shitaji chūbun* represented a more advanced form of settlement than did *ukesho* because ownership, rather than managerial authority, was involved. According to this view, the *jitō* now became Japan's first locally based holders of estate-sized properties, a revolutionary stage in the return of authority to the land. Although the general conclusion here seems accurate in hindsight, perceptions at the time were somewhat different. In particular, *shōen* proprietors, not *jitō*, provided the main impetus toward *shitaji chūbun*. Their objective was to secure an unencumbered share of a

into vogue. Sometimes they implied the same person and were used interchangeably (*DKR*, doc. 103), other times not (*DKR*, doc. 41).

71 The institutions of *wayo* and *ukesho* are treated by Jeffrey P. Mass, "Jitō Land Possession in the Thirteenth Century," in Hall and Mass, eds., *Medieval Japan*, chap. 7. For actual examples, see *KB*, docs. 117–25.

72 For an example, see the photograph on the jacket of Hall and Mass, eds., *Medieval Japan*.

73 For example, see *KB*, docs. 126–8.

property legally theirs but pressured incessantly by a *jitō*. As for the *jitō*, they too were thinking mostly in the present. Thus, they commonly resisted *shitaji chūbun* arrangements, as the loss of an authority embracing entire *shōen* would result. Or the case might be cited of a *jitō* seeking an *ukesho* over a whole *shōen* in place of the *shitaji chūbun* agreed to by his forebears.[74] History – in the concrete – did not always move forward.

Jitō titles, like other forms of property, were heritable within the holder's family. The bakufu permitted its *jitō* to bequeath their titles, in unitary or partible fashion, to legitimate relatives of their own choosing. They were not allowed to bequeath their offices to external parties. In the early part of this period, partible practices were the norm, with women included in the regular inheritance pool. Because distinguished families might hold multiple *jitō* offices, children sometimes received individual titles and established separate lines that gained recognition from Kamakura. Short of that, they received *jitō* portions entitling them to confirmation and protection by the bakufu as well as the right to bequeath shares to their own heirs. During Kamakura times, the tendency was strong to eschew lateral for vertical inheritance, which meant that clannishness in property matters remained relatively undeveloped. Even within the nuclear group there existed the potential for tension, because fathers (and mothers) could write and rewrite wills and progeny might be disinherited. Finally, it was left to the house head to select a principal heir, who might be a younger son. The possibilities were thus rife for family conflict and for recourse to bakufu courtrooms.[75]

Because new *jitō* posts could hardly be expected to keep pace with the number of junior generation candidates for them, practices developed that began to move warrior society toward a more unitary property system. In place of unencumbered, alienable rights to daughters, for example, life bequests and annuities were set up, with reversion to the principal heir or his heir as part of an emerging system of entail. Fathers, moreover, began enjoining inheriting sons to maintain the integrity of family holdings and to reduce or eliminate secondary recipients. Scholars, quite properly, have emphasized such developments. Yet at no time during the Kamakura age did these practices become universal; inheriting daughters and fragmented holdings can

---

74 The division had occurred in 1237; the attempt to replace it with an *ukesho* came sixty years later; see *KB*, doc. 129.

75 Jeffrey P. Mass, *Lordship and Inheritance in Early Medieval Japan: A Study of the Kamakura Sōryō System* (Stanford, Calif.: Stanford University Press, 1989).

always be found.[76] Nor is it clear what Kamakura's attitude was toward the new tendencies. As Seno Seiichirō has shown, the chieftain's authority over his siblings remained undeveloped, and bakufu judgments did not tilt toward him and thus away from his brothers.[77] In any event, the competition for control of *jitō* posts and between these posts and proprietorships constituted the very lifeblood of Kamakura justice. The ambitions of *jitō* were the bane of most everyone, but the office itself marked the clear cutting edge of progress.

THE BAKUFU AT MID-CENTURY

Yasutoki died in 1242 at the age of fifty-nine. His death removed the greatest of the Hōjō from the helm at Kamakura and immediately plunged the bakufu into a period of uncertainty. His successor was his eighteen-year-old grandson Tsunetoki, who soon ran afoul of the shogun Yoritsune, now in his twenties and desirous of ruling in his own name. In 1244, Yoritsune was replaced by his own seven-year-old son, Yoritsugu, but the troubles did not end here. The ex-shogun was still present in Kamakura and began to line up support against the Hōjō. Two years later he was banished to Kyoto, though the faction that had formed around him remained active.

In the meantime, conditions in the capital were also in flux. During the same year that Yasutoki died the emperor also died, and the bakufu promoted a successor, Gosaga, who was not the preferred choice of Kyoto. Four years later Kamakura again forced an issue by elevating Gosaga to the ex-emperorship. In the same year (1246) Tsunetoki himself died and was followed as regent by his more vigorous younger brother, Tokiyori. Yet even with new leadership in the two capitals, harmony did not ensue. A rumor of rebellion by Nagoe Mitsutoki, a branch head of the Hōjō, reached Kamakura in the fifth month of 1246, which led to the dismissal of four anti-Tokiyori members of the *hyōjōshū*. Events came to a head in 1247 when the Adachi, a family allied with the main line of the Hōjō, maneuvered the distinguished house of Miura into challenging for control. The Miura were defeated, thus eliminating the bakufu's second most prestigious house after the Hōjō, and a further housecleaning of recalcitrants followed. As a result of the Miura disturbance, the line of Tokiyori, hereafter known as *tokusō*, was more firmly entrenched than ever, though never

76 For example, an unencumbered bequest to a daughter in 1323; see Mass, *Lordship and Inheritance*, doc. 147.

77 Seno Seiichirō, *Chinzei gokenin no kenkyū* (Tokyo: Yoshikawa kōbunkan, 1975), pp. 375–88.

wholly immune: The deaths of great leaders remained a problem in the absence of a fixed mechanism for succession. Nevertheless, the events of 1247 ushered in a generation of stability, which was not upset until the Mongol threat of the late 1260s.

It is noteworthy that even during the political infighting of the 1240s, Kamakura continued to discharge its judicial responsibilities. After 1247, certain reforms were introduced, whose culmination was the establishment of a new investigative organ, the *hikitsuke-shū*, in 1249. At the same time, with Gosaga as its accomplice, Kamakura encouraged the court to update its own machinery, now on the model of the bakufu. There can scarcely be a more revealing development than the formation in 1246 of a Kyoto *hyōjōshū*, designed as a clearing-house for disputes not affecting Kamakura's interests. In a sense, by this action, the era's dual polity was given its ultimate expression. The court now emulated the bakufu in a major structural advance, but the lines of jurisdiction separating them remained wholly intact. Cooperation between the country's two governments, Yoritomo's goal of an earlier day, had entered a new stage.

In 1252, Gosaga's son Munetaka was installed as Kamakura's first princely shogun. More than thirty years earlier, Hōjō Masako had sought a similar arrangement from a resistant Gotoba, but now at mid-century the Hōjō achieved this objective: The bakufu's leading house secured a puppet in each capital, who were conveniently father and son. Munetaka, indeed, is the final shogun whose name historians remember; his successors appear in lists of bakufu chieftains but are not considered players. The remainder of the era witnessed a number of important developments, among them the rise of lower-class social movements and the impoverishment or enrichment of different groups of warriors. The effects of the the Mongol invasions would be felt at many levels of society. But the bakufu by mid-century had reached its full maturity. Hereafter, the age belonged to the Hōjō, the future to the warrior class as a whole.

CHAPTER 2

MEDIEVAL *SHŌEN*

THE INTERNAL STRUCTURE OF MEDIEVAL PROVINCES

In the opening chapter Jeffrey P. Mass discusses the establishment of warrior government in medieval Japan under the Kamakura bakufu. In an agrarian society the shoguns, regents, and warriors throughout the country – like the emperor and nobles in Kyoto – depended primarily on land and its produce for their support. Thus, to understand early medieval society it is essential to understand the nature of the land system and the subtle but far-reaching changes that were taking place on the land.

The medieval land system is sometimes categorized as a system of private estates, *shōen*, and public domain, *kokugaryō*. The public domain had existed since the Nara period (710–94) when all lands throughout the provinces were subject to the fiscal and administrative authority of the imperial court. During the Heian period (794–1185) absentee proprietors, including nobles, temples, and shrines, and members of the imperial family acquired collections of private rights, *shiki*, in reclaimed or commended holdings scattered throughout the provinces. These holdings, known as *shōen*, were gradually sealed off from the taxing power and administrative supervision of state officials. Thus by the twelfth century most provinces in Japan had complex patterns of landholding in which public and private holdings were intermingled. This chapter will examine the shifting interaction of *shōen* and *kokugaryō* in the Kamakura period, the structure and management of *shōen*, the relations between *shōen* proprietors and their holdings, and the impact of the political emergence of warriors on the control of *shōen*.

In order to understand the role of the private estates (*shōen*) which characterized the landholding system of medieval Japan, it is important to grasp the structure of landholding within each province, the basic administrative unit in medieval Japan. All *shōen*, with the exception of Shimazu-no-shō, were created within a single province as an individual holding (*shoryō*) of a central noble or religious institution.[1]

---

1 Shimazu-no-shō, domain of the Konoe family, included most of the three provinces of Hyūga, Ōsumi, and Satsuma in the southernmost region of Kyushu.

The holdings of these *shōen* proprietors (*shōen ryōshu*), who lived in or near the capital, were often located in distant provinces.

Several land registers listing all the *shōen* of the various provinces they cover have survived from the medieval period. These are commonly known as provincial land registers, or *ōtabumi*, and help explain the medieval landholding system, especially the structure of landholding within an individual province and the relationship between private holdings (*shōen*) and public domain (*kokugaryō*).

Noto Province: the process of shōen formation

Each *ōtabumi* has unique structural characteristics and types of entry. The field register for Noto Province compiled in 1221 is particularly useful in that it lists the *shōen*, *gō* and *ho* (administrative units of public land), and *in* (holdings of the cloistered emperors) in the four districts of the province. The holdings also are classified by the year that they were established with the permission of the central government, the year that immunity was granted by the provincial governor (*kokushi*), or the date that it was first inspected. In the case of holdings for which only the date of inspection is listed, it is believed that at the time the *ōtabumi* was compiled, these lacked documents of foundation or immunity and therefore remained public domain (*kōryō*).[2] Ishii Susumu, who first noticed this while researching the *ōtabumi* for Noto Province, found that of a total of 2,051 *chō* of paddy field, more than 1,437 *chō* made up a total of twenty-eight *shōen* (see Table 2.1). That is, more than 70 percent of the total paddy field area of the province had been organized into *shōen*.[3]

According to Ishii's study, *shōen* began to develop in Noto Province during the period of abdicated rule by Emperor Toba (1129–59). Three early *shōen* of Noto were developed in the Hakui District: The oldest was the Kamo-no-shō, with thirty *chō* of land; in 1051, Keta-no-shō was founded with eighty-five *chō;* and nearly a century later in 1136, Ōizumi-no-shō was created with a total of two hundred *chō*. These were followed by a burst of *shōen* formation. In the Suzu District in 1143, Wakayama-no-shō, the province's largest *shōen* with five hundred *chō*, was established. In 1145, two *shōen* were established in the Fugeshi District, Machino-no-shō with two hundred *chō* and Shimo Machino-no-shō with five *chō*, six *tan*. Several more new *shōen*

---

2 *Kamakura ibun*, no. 2828.
3 Ishii Susumu, *Insei jidai*, vol. 2 of *Kōza Nihon shi* (Tokyo: Tōkyō daigaku shuppankai, 1970), pp. 207–13.

TABLE 2.1
Shōen *in Noto Province*

Period of creation	Number of shōen	Area		
		chō	tan	bu
Ancient shōen	1	30	0	0
1051	1	85	6	7
1136–50	8	1,067	9	5
1184–97	9	197	9	9
1201–75	9	56	0	2
Total	28	1,437 chō	6 tan	3 bu

were created in the following year. The three *shōen* established between 1136 and 1145 – Ōizumi, Wakayama, and Machino – encompassed an area of nine hundred *chō*, 44 percent of Noto's total paddy field area. Thus, the third and fourth decades of the twelfth century marked the height of *shōen* formation in Noto Province.

The situation is not as clear for the other provinces. However, Takeuchi Rizō and Amino Yoshihiko have indicated that the *shōen* of Wakasa and other provinces also began to expand rapidly between 1130 and 1155 or around the time of Toba's rule as a cloistered emperor.[4]

Kokuga *and* shōen *in Awaji Province*

The Awaji *ōtabumi* of 1223 lists the total field area of the province as 1,412 *chō* divided between two districts.[5] Tsuna District contained 777 *chō* and Mihara, 635 *chō*. Both districts were further subdivided into provincial land and private holdings. The *ōtabumi* lists the type of field area for thirty-seven individual holdings within the province. According to the *ōtabumi*, the provincial land in both districts was made up of holdings designated as *gō* and *ho*. The only exception was the village of Nagatamura in the Mihara District which comprised a single independent unit. In contrast, the private holdings were, without exception, *shōen* holdings. Within the two districts, *shōen* made up 72 percent of the total land, with 1,011 *chō*. The remaining 28 percent was *kokugaryō*.

4 Takeuchi Rizō, "In-no-chō seiken to shōen," pt. 2 of *Ritsuryōsei to kizoku seiken* (Tokyo: Ochanomizu shobō, 1958), pp. 392–419; and Amido Yoshihiko, "Wakasa no kuni ni okeru shōensei no keisei," in Takeuchi Rizō hakase kareki kinenkai hen, *Shōensei to buke shakai* (Tokyo: Yoshikawa kōbunkan, 1969), pp. 127–70. 5 *Kamakura ibun*, no. 3088.

The military governor (*shugo*) of Awaji Province, Sasaki Tsunetaka,
led local warriors in support of the cloistered emperor Gotoba against
the Kamakura bakufu in the Jōkyū disturbance of 1221. Most of these
warriors eventually were defeated, and the victorious bakufu appointed new military land stewards (*jitō*). Compiled immediately following the war, the *ōtabumi* records the transfer of warriors and lists
the names of the proprietors of the various private holdings in its
entries for each domain. These entries are representative of the proprietorial relationships of the entire province.

It is clear from the register that many *shōen* in Awaji had close ties
with central temples and shrines or noble families, especially the imperial court. The Kyoto temples and shrines acquired numerous *shōen*
holdings, such as the Ninnaji's Mononobe-no-shō; the three *shōen* of
Takikuchi, Hiraishi, and Torikai belonging to the Iwashimizu
Hachiman Shrine; and Namariho-no-shō and Ayuhara-no-shō of the
Upper Kamo and Katano shrines, respectively.

Many other *shōen* in Awaji Province had ties with the four successive
generations of cloistered emperors (*in*): Shirakawa, Toba, Goshirakawa, and Gotoba. Kokubunji-no-shō, for instance, was part of the
domain of Shōkongō-in built by Shirakawa near Kyoto in 1101. Holdings in Awaji connected with Toba, the next cloistered emperor, included Ama-no-shō in the domain of the Tokuchōju-in; Yura-no-shō
and Tsukusa-no-shō in the Zenrinji Imakumano domain; and Naizen-
no-shō in the domain of the Kangikō-in and Kanimori-no-shō in the
domain of the Gusei-in, both established by Toba's consort Mifu-
kumon'in.[6] Among the holdings connected with Goshirakawa were
Shizuki-no-shō, belonging to the domain of the Imakumano Shrine,
and Kashio-no-shō and Fukura-no-shō, belonging to the domain of
the Kōyasan Hōdō-in. Among the holdings of the Saishōshitennō-in
domain of the cloistered emperor Gotoba were Hikiura and Tsuiigari-
no-shō. Gotoba's personal landholdings also included the Aeka-no-shō
(Sugawara-no-shō).[7] Among the domain holdings of Shūmeimon'in,
Gotoba's wife, was Yoshino-no-shō.

It is easy to see the extent to which *shōen* clustered about the court
during the age of successive cloistered emperors. In addition to these
shōen in Awaji Province, there were also *shōen* belonging to the Fuji-

---

6 Naizen-no-shō, Kanimori-no-shō, Yura-no-shō, and Tsukusa-no-shō later made up the great
   collection of imperial *shōen* known as the Hachijōin domain, as it most likely passed from
   Toba-in to his daughter Hachijōin.
7 Among these, the Kashio-no-shō, Fukura-no-shō, and Igari-no-shō comprised part of the
   great collection of imperial *shōen*, the Chōkōdō domain's *shōen*, linked to Goshirakawa-in.

wara regent family: Kuruma-no-shō in the domain of Matsudono Sōjō
Jisson, the son of Matsudono Motofusa; Shiota-no-shō in the domain
of the Kanshūji in Yamashina; and Uriho-no-shō of the Rokujō Midō
domain and Hirota-no-shō of the Nishinomiya Shrine domain in
Settsu Province.

These twenty-three *shōen* include all *shōen* listed in the *ōtabumi* of
Awaji Province, and all were held by absentee proprietors. Moreover,
although a few of these proprietors (such as Kōyasan in Kii Province
and Nishinomiya in Settsu Province) were some distance from Kyoto,
most were based in Kyoto or its environs. It has often been observed
that centrifugal tendencies were strongly evident in every social phenomenon of medieval Japan, such as in the exercise of political power
and in the economic structure, and *shōen* possession in Awaji Province
supports this observation.

A common characteristic of *shōen* and *kokugaryō* in the Kamakura
period is that in addition to the *shōen* proprietors, *jitō* and various *shōen*
officials were appointed from the ranks of the warrior class to exert
local control over the *shōen*. In Awaji the provincial headquarters
(*kokuga*) were located in the Mihara District. The core of the
kokugaryō in this district was made up of Nohara-ho, Nishijindai-gō,
Higashijindai-ho, and Ueda-ho. During the wars of the Jōkyū era, the
jitō appointments to all of these *gō* and *ho* were usurped by the *shugo*
and became part of his domain. The *shugo*, appointed by Yoritomo,
founder of the Kamakura bakufu, thus came to control the axis of
kokugaryō in Awaji Province. The local officials (*zaichō kanjin*) of the
kokugaryō, however, remained active. Nohara-ho, Nishijindai-gō, and
Ueda-hō, included 55 *chō*, 4 *tan*, 220 *bu* of *zaichō betchimyō*. *Betchimyō*
were various types of private holdings created from *kokugaryō* by obtaining the civil government's official sanction to create an independent administrative unit paralleling the *gō*. The *ōtabumi* records a 14-
chō zaichō betchimyō, known as Shichi-no-shō, in Nishijindai-gō that
made up the residence site of an individual who had previously been
the most powerful local official in the province. Although not the
general case, such unusual *shōen* existed in the medieval period, and in
terms of the land system, *kokugaryō* and their surroundings were at the
core of local politics.

Shōen *and* kokugaryō *in Wakasa Province*

The *ōtabumi* compiled for Wakasa Province in 1265 includes detailed
entries that outline the process by which *shōen* were carved out of

former *kokugaryō* and how the *kokugaryō* themselves were restructured in the Kamakura period.[8]

Wakasa Province was divided into the three districts of Oniu, Ōi, and Mikata. The province's total field area of 2,217 *chō*, 6 *tan* was divided between 1,036 *chō* of *shōen* and 1,181 *chō* of *kokugaryō*, making Wakasa one of the few provinces in which the amount of *kokugaryō* exceeded that of *shōen*. Most *shōen* holdings were divided, depending on when they were established, into two groups: original *shōen* (*honshō*) and new *shōen* (*shinshō*). Kamo-no-shō, four other *shōen*, and two *gō* covering an area of 129 *chō* were included among the *honshō*. Tateishi-no-shō and ten other *shōen* were entered as *shinshō*, for a total area of 474 *chō*.

In Wakasa there were also holdings known as *bimpo-no-ho*, or *ho*, for supplementing officials' income.[9] These holdings were mostly controlled by offices of the central government, such as the Oiryō, Kuraryō, or Tomo-no-ryō. Six *ho*, including Kunitomo-no-ho, accounted for 153 *chō*. These holdings, in cases in which the land in a province was divided into *shōen* and *kokugaryō*, can be treated as *shōen*. Originally, these holdings were written off the registers as not paying the rice tax (*nengu*) to the various offices of the central government, and the proprietory use of these lands was ceded to the relevant offices. From the late Heian period the heads of the government offices controlling such holdings ceded hereditary control over these lands to noble families with whom they had close connections, and so the holdings became, in practice, difficult to distinguish from *shōen*. In addition to the presence of officials from noble lineages, Wakasa Province also felt the powerful influence of the two great Buddhist monastic centers, the Enryakuji and the Onjōji, located in the neighboring province of Ōmi. The Enryakuji had nine holdings, including Tokuyoshi-ho, totaling 132 *chō;* and the Onjōji had three holdings, including Tamaki-gō, totaling 83 *chō*.[10]

Perhaps the most interesting entries in this *ōtabumi* are those related to the remaining *kokugaryō* which reveal the changing structure of *kokugaryō* in the Kamakura period. The three districts of Wakasa – Oniu, Ōi, and Mikata – each had originally comprised several *gō*. The Oniu District had included the four *gō* of Tomita, Shima, Sai, and

---

8 Ōyama Kyōhei, *Nihon chūsei nōson shi no kenkyū* (Tokyo: Iwanami shoten, 1978), pp. 75–101.

9 On *bimpo-no-ho*, see Hashimoto Yoshihiko, "Ōiryō ryō ni tsuite," in *Heian kizoku shakai no kenkyū* (Tokyo: Yoshikawa kōbunkan, 1976).

10 The area of these monastic holdings did not include the 129 *chō* of *honshō*, 474 *chō* of *shinshō*, or 153 *chō* of *bimpo-no-ho*.

Higashi; the Ōi District, the three *gō* of Ao, Saburi, and Hon; and the Mikata District, the two *gō* of Mikata and Miminishi. These *gō* had been thoroughly restructured by the Kamakura period, and a wide variety of different titles for domains, including *gō, ho, ura, shussaku, kanō, tera, sha,* and *miya,* came into use. Some sixty-seven of such holdings can be identified.[11] Moreover, it can be shown that when each of them became independent, it fell under the purview of the tax office of the provincial headquarters (*kokuga*).

The restructuring of the *kokugaryō* of Wakasa Province centered on the *kokuga,* as shown by the proximity of *zaichō betchimyō.* Powerful local men, who became resident officials (*zaichō kanjin*) of *kokugaryō,* participated in the administration of the *kokuga* and thus extended their range of influence, greatly increasing in number throughout Japan during the late Heian period. The strong provincial warrior bands of the medieval period emerged from these local power holders. *Zaichō betchimyō* were the holdings of the *zaichō kanjin* within the *kokugaryō.* In Wakasa Province in the late Heian period, a powerful *zaichō kanjin,* Inaba Gon-no-kami Tokisada, controlled the provincial tax office. He was also the proprietor of a large *betchimyō* of more than fifty-five *chō,* known as Imatomimyō. In addition, it is clear from the *ōtabumi* that there were at least eleven *zaichō* holdings, including Okayasu-myō, Chiyotsugu-myō, and Takeyasu-myō, located near the *kokuga* office.

Within the *kokuga* there were a number of central offices, including a *zeisho* to handle taxation, a *tadokoro* to manage matters relating to paddy fields, and a *fudokoro* to handle official documents. In Wakasa, in addition to the *zeisho* of Imatomi-myō, Yoshimatsu-myō was the *tadokoro-myō* and Chiyotsugo-myō and Tokieda-myō were known as *fudokoro-myō.* (It is also of interest to note that the officials who supervised the *fudokoro* in Wakasa had the name of Hata, the name of a Chinese clan that had earlier immigrated via the Korean peninsula.) In any case, the duties of these *kokuga* offices became hereditary among certain designated families. *Kokugaryō* were divided into various categories on the basis of these duties, and it became difficult to distinguish these once-public holdings from the private holdings controlled by these families. Mid- and low-level officials of the *kokuga* and those who worked in the *kokuga* workshops, such as attendants, stablemen, servants, weavers, carpenters, and woodworkers, were also accorded

11 The *gō* of Wakasa province seem to have originally been about 120 *chō* each in area. Of the nine *gō* mentioned, five come close to this figure. When Ao-gō in the public domain and Ao-ho, a *shōen*-like domain that seems to have been carved out of the former, are added together, they too encompass a total of 120 *chō*.

holdings (*myō*) within the *kokugaryō* and carried out their activities on the basis of income derived from them.

These ancient *gō* that had previously made up the structure of *kokugaryō* in Wakasa Province continued primarily in name only. For example, Shima-gō in the Oniu District originally included 139 *chō* of *kokugaryō*. As restructuring and division proceeded, the paddy field in the *gō* paying taxes to the *kokuga* fell to only 9 *tan* (see Table 2.2). To the extent that public holdings in the Kamakura period still paid taxes to the *kokuga*, they remained public domain. At the same time, the growing reality was that public land was becoming the domain of various levels of functionaries. Moreover, these holdings were becoming the hereditary property of powerful families. In this sense, the *kokugaryō* assumed many features of private *shōen* holdings.

We have now looked at the *ōtabumi* of the three provinces of Noto, Awaji, and Wakasa. Although each reveals different circumstances, they ail indicate that the *shōen* system was spreading and becoming an increasingly important characteristic of medieval Japan. It is probably safe to assume that the other provinces followed a similar course.

THE DOMESTIC ECONOMY OF *SHŌEN* PROPRIETORS

As noted, most proprietors lived in or near the capital, far from their scattered *shōen* holdings. The transportation system linking the provinces with the capital and its environs was of prime importance. The annual tax paid in rice and other commodities and the labor services and dues (*kuji*) received from *shōen* scattered throughout Japan had to be transported to the proprietors in Kyoto. Through the collection of taxes and *kuji*, *shōen* proprietors were basically self-sufficient. The highest civil elites of noble lineage and religious institutions had to observe a constant round of annual ceremonies and festivals. This meant that *shōen* scattered across Japan under the control of absentee *shōen* proprietors of the capital area had to be organized into a single self-sufficient system in order to meet the needs of these ceremonies that occurred throughout the year.

A study of the *shōen* of the Saishōkō-in domain provides a glimpse into the operation of this self-sufficient economic system. The Saishōkō-in temple was built in 1173 by the abdicated emperor Goshirakawa in response to the prayers of his consort Kenshunmon'in Taira-no-Shigeko. After being transmitted as imperial house domain in 1326, it was conferred by Emperor Godaigo on the Kyoto monastery of Tōji. Prior to this bequest in 1325, a register of holdings was

TABLE 2.2

Gō *and* betchimyō *in the* Wakasa *kokuga domain*

	Original paddy (chō)	Number of betchimyō[a]	Remaining paddies (chō)[b]
Oi District			
Ao-gō	60.8	5	24.7
Saburi-gō	120.3	1	64.2
Hon-gō	116.8	0	81.0
Oniu District			
Tomita-gō	128.7	24	6.3
Shima-gō	139.5	28	0.9
Sai-gō	177.5	27	13.5
Tō-gō	88.7	10	5.4
Mikata District			
Mikata-gō	50.9	7	7.1
Miminishi-gō	72.6	0	51.2

[a] *Betchimyō* is a general term for a variety of holdings established through separation from the *gō*.
[b] Remaining paddies indicates the amount of paddy remaining in the public domain and still yielding tax revenues to the central government.

drawn up, listing twenty *shōen* in sixteen provinces and indicating the *nengu* that each *shōen* was to provide. Kuwahara-no-shō in Harima Province, for example, was required to provide rice and figured silk; Yamanobe-no-shō in Settsu provided pine brands and assorted cypress boxes;[12] and Sakai-no-shō in Settsu provided oil.

In addition to detailing the kind and amount of dues – whether rice, silk, silk floss, figured silk, pine brands, cypress boxes, hemp cloth for summer kimonos, *tatami*, white cloth, or rice cakes – the register also lists the burden and duration of military service imposed on each *shōen*. The Saishōkō-in, with the exception of the third, fifth, and ninth months when slightly fewer warriors were needed, required the service of ten warriors supplied in rotation by its *shōen* spread from Shinano and Hitachi provinces in the east to Chikuzen Province in the west.[13]

The same economic considerations can be seen on a much larger scale in the *shōen* of the Chōkōdō acquired by the abdicated emperor Goshirakawa. The Chōkōdō was a Buddha hall established in 1185 by Goshirakawa in his Rokujō Palace in Kyoto. Goshirakawa commended

12 Dried pine branches used for hand-held torches and wooden boxes and containers made from thin boards of cypress or cedar.
13 Uejima Tamotsu, "Tōji jiin keizai ni kansuru ichi kōsatsu," in *Kyōto daigaku bungakubu dokushikai*, ed., *Kokushi ronshū* (Kyoto: Dokushikai, 1959).

numerous *shōen* to the Chōkōdō, principally his own holdings as head of the imperial house. According to the register of *in* holdings, the *in goryō chūshinjo* for 1191, the holdings of the Chōkōdō included seventy *shōen*, four temples, two shrines, and thirteen non-tax-yielding holdings.[14] One of the largest collections of imperial holdings in the medieval period, it subsequently passed through the hands of Goshirakawa's daughter Senyōmon'in and thence from the cloistered emperor Gofukakusa to emperors Fushimi and Gofushimi. During the period of rivalry between the Northern and Southern Courts in the mid- to late fourteenth century, these holdings provided the economic basis for the Northern Court, the Jimyō-in line.

The Chōkōdō, located in the Rokujō section of Kyoto, was a large compound surrounded by streets on all four sides. Each gate to the compound was guarded by warriors drawn from *shōen* who served in rotation. A treasure house inside the compound was also guarded by warriors supplied by the Chōkōdō *shōen*. Various services within the temple were also performed on a monthly basis by attendants from the various *shōen*. The *shōen* were also responsible for providing the vegetables for the meals at the Chōkōdō on certain days each month. For example, Rokka-no-shō in Higo Province was responsible for vegetables on the first and second day of each month; Noguchi-no-shō in Tamba Province supplied them for the third day of each month.[15]

The first three days of each new year were known as *gansan*. Throughout Japan, special ceremonies were carried out, offering prayers for peace in the coming year. The supplies and expenses for these ceremonies were known as *gansan zōji*. The items and quantities of goods to be provided by each *shōen* to support these ceremonies were precisely apportioned among the *shōen*. Yamaka-no-shō in Tōtomi Province, for example, provided seven bamboo blinds, five *tatami*, and ten *ryō* of sand. The Rokka-on-shō of Higo provided four bamboo blinds, twenty-one *tatami*, twenty *ryō* of sand, and three *tan* of cloth hangings for the *samurai-dokoro* (Board of Retainers). In addition to the New Year, many other ceremonies were observed throughout the year. The *shōen* were expected to contribute goods and services for such ceremonies as the Eight Stage Lectures on the Lotus Sutra in the third month, the Buddhist festival of Higan in the eighth month, the

14 Many of these *shōen* were located in the eastern provinces. With Yoritomo's victory in the wars against the Taira, many eastern *shōen* fell under the control of Kantō *bushi*.
15 These vegetables were known as *megurisai*.

ceremonies for the ninth day of the ninth month, the seasonal change of clothing rituals in the tenth month, and the offerings to the gods in the eleventh month.

Additional examples of various items levied on Yamaka-no-shō of Tōtomi Province and Rokka-no shō of Higo for various ceremonies include the following: For the New Year, Yamaka-no-shō was to provide seven *ken* of bamboo blinds, five *tatami* and ten *ryō* of sand; and Rokka-no-shō was to provide four *ken* of bamboo blinds, twenty-one *tatami*, twenty *ryō* of sand, and three rolls of cloth hangings. Both were to provide sand in the third month for the Eight Stage Lectures on the Lotus Sutra in the amount of five *ryō* and twenty *ryō*, respectively. For the Buddhist festival of Higan held in the eighth month, Rokka-no-shō was to donate twenty *tan* of cloth. In the ceremonies for the ninth day of the ninth month, Yamaka-no-shō provided one *hanmono-shōzoku*. In the tenth month during the seasonal change of clothing rituals, Yamaka-no-shō was to provide three *tatami*. For the offerings to the gods in the eleventh month, Yamaka-no-shō was required to provide one-half set of *himorogi*. Rokka-no-shō was responsible for providing vegetables for the first and second days of the month, and Yamaka-no-shō was responsible for the sixth and seventh. The former was to provide three attendants each in the first, eleventh, and twelfth months, and the latter was to provide only three in the sixth month and another as a storehouse guard. Rokka-no-shō was required to send twelve people to serve as gate guards during the sixth month, and Yamaka-no-shō was to send a single guard in the eleventh month. In addition, Yamaka-no-shō was to provide twenty cakes of dye.

The Chōkōdō also gathered various *shōen* dues. Of course, many *shōen* supplied rice, but at the same time, six *shōen* in three provinces offered silk cloth and thread, and two others gave white cloth. Three *shōen* of different provinces provided paper, and others provided gold, horses, copper verdigris, iron, sea bream, and incense. This tax system reflected the special goods produced in the various regions of Japan: silk and thread from Owari, Mino, and Tango; white cloth from Izu and Kai; paper from Tōtomi, Tamba, and Tajima; gold and horses from Dewa; copper verdigris from Yamato; iron from Hōki; sea bream from Settsu; and perfumes from Noto and Yamashiro.

Among the commodities drawn from the Chōkōdō domain were 5,384 *koku* of rice, 1,216 *hiki* of silk, 4,274 *ryō* of silk thread, and 10,000 *tei* of iron. Although much was awarded as a stipend to the attendants of the emperors, a considerable amount must have been exchanged in the markets of Kyoto and elsewhere for other necessary commodities.[16]

It was customary for members of the imperial family or noble houses, as the most powerful lineages, to hold the principal proprietorships (*honke-shiki*) of *shōen*. Beneath the *honke-shiki* were the *ryōke-shiki*, usually held by the middle- and lower-rank nobles who served the powerful lineages. Even in cases in which the *honke* held the actual rights to *shōen* management – as seen in the register of the *shōen* holdings of the Konoe family dated 1253 – there were many cases in which the nobles serving them held these *shōen* as the central proprietor (*ryōke*) or custodian (*azukari-dokoro*).[17] This multilayered system of proprietorships was one characteristic of the medieval Japanese *shōen* system.

The basically self-sufficient character of the *shōen* proprietor system began to change considerably during the late Kamakura period. This phenomenon can be seen in many *shōen*, but it is illustrated clearly in an analysis of the annual tax payments made to the Zen monastery of the Engakuji in Kamakura, established by Hōjō Tokimune in 1283. The Engakuji's holdings at that time consisted of Tomita-no-shō in Owari Province and Kameyama-gō in Ahiru-minami-no-shō of Kazusa Province. From these holdings the Engakuji derived 1,569 *koku*, 8 *to* in rice and 1,575 *kan*, 451 *mon* in cash, mostly from Tomita-no-shō. The necessary cash was raised through the exchange of silk or thread for coins in local markets which were then transported to the monastery. The Engakuji covered its annual outlay by redistributing the rice and cash received from its *shōen* holdings.

On the other hand, the Engakuji had 3,960 packhorse loads of firewood and 500 loads of charcoal directly delivered from Kameyama-gō. The Engakuji disbursed twenty-five *koku* of the tax rice received from Kameyama-gō to cover the costs of transporting this firewood and charcoal to the monastery. An additional four *koku* were used to provide "meals" for the charcoal makers. From distant Tomita-no-shō, the Engakuji also received tax income in the form of silk and thread which was converted into coins before being transported to the monastery. In the relatively closer Kameyama-gō, charcoal makers were hired, and the large amounts of firewood and charcoal used annually were produced locally. In Tomita-no-shō and

16 Nagahara Keiji, *Nihon chūsei shakai kōzō no kenkyū* (Tokyo: Iwanami shoten, 1973), p. 61. Takeuchi, *Shōensei to buke shakai*, p. 417.
17 For instance, of the Konoe family holdings, the Miyata-no-shō in Tamba Province and the Ayukawa-no-shō in Echizen were entrusted to Chōhan as *azukari-dokoro;* and the Tomita-no-shō in Owari, the Enami-Kami-Higashikata in Settsu, and the Shintachi-no-shō in Izumi were likewise entrusted to Gyōyū.

nearby *shōen* along Japan's Pacific coast, the conversion of in-kind dues into cash advanced rapidly starting in the late thirteenth century. This was a major watershed in the economy of *shōen* proprietors.

As described, the household economy of *shōen* proprietors, at least in its ideal form, assumed a self-sufficient structure. At the same time, although there was an effort to spread the tax burden fairly over *shōen* distant from Kyoto and Kamakura, in regard to the actual ability of people on the *shōen* to bear the tax burden or in regard to economic efficiency, stresses and strains appeared with the passage of time. Moreover, market activities steadily increased. Thus, with the development of commerce, medieval *shōen* proprietors came to rely more and more on Kyoto and other markets to supply many of the commodities they needed.

THE INTERNAL STRUCTURE OF SHŌEN

The most useful documents for discerning the pattern of landholdings within *shōen* are the *shōen* land registers. These registers were compiled when *shōen* control was first established, when there was a generational change, or when *shōen* were divided or subject to transfer of proprietorship, and they were frequently accompanied by a survey. In this section I shall use such land records to examine more closely the internal structure of three *shōen* in the provinces of Bingo, Aki, and Higo. Before looking at these individual *shōen*, however, I shall first outline the considerable variation in *shōen* holdings.

The *shōen*'s inner structure was complex. In the simplest terms, *shōen*, especially those of the Kamakura period, were made up of a number of smaller holdings, known as *myō*. *Myō* included paddy fields (or dry fields), known as *myōden*. Each *myō* had a named holder, usually a well-to-do peasant (*myōshu*). The various *myōshu* within a *shōen* were responsible for collecting and delivering to the *shōen* proprietor the annual tax rice and other dues in kind, together with the corvée or services (*kuji*) assessed on each *myō*. *Shōen* proprietors levied dues on the various *myō* within their *shōen* and saw the *myōshu* as the persons responsible for the annual dues and corvée.

In practice, however, the structure of most *shōen* was more complex. There were, for instance, many *shōen* in which a *myō* structure hardly existed, and so the tax burden was borne by local farming households (*zaike*). In *shōen* near the capital, where technological advances in agricultural production were marked and paddy field agriculture was dominant, *myō* were common. However, in *shōen* in Kyushu or the

Kantō, or in mountainous areas such as Kii on the outskirts of the capital region, where dry fields predominated, *shōen* were characterized by the presence of numerous *zaike* holdings.

Ōta-no-shō[18] was located in Bingo Province on the upper reaches of the Ashida River which runs into the Inland Sea. In the Kamakura period it was one of many holdings of the Buddhist monastic complex on Mount Kōya in Kii Province. The structure of this *shōen* is particularly clear because in 1190 the priest Ban'a Shōnin of Mount Kōya wrote a detailed account of Ōta-no-shō and its land system.[19] According to Ban'a, this *shōen* was large, its total area being about 613 *chō*. Because of its size, the *shōen* was divided into two *gō*, Ōta-kata and Kuwabara-kata. In addition, there were pockets of reclaimed farmland, known as detached village fields (*bessakuden*), here and there among the hills.[20]

Shōen *officials'* myō

Among the *myō* of *shōen*, there were two main types: *myō* held by the agents and officials of the central proprietor (*shōkan-myō*) and *myō* held by ordinary peasants (*hyakushō-myō*). In any *shōen* there was a hierarchy of officials with such titles as *geshi*, *kumon*, *tsuibushi*, *tadokoro*, or *kunin*. *Geshi* and *kumon* were generally found in most *shōen*, whereas the *tsuibushi*, *tadokoro*, and *kunin* found in Ōta-no-shō were not characteristic of all *shōen*.

When the cloistered emperor Goshirakawa conferred Ōta-no-shō on Mount Kōya, two local warriors, Ōta Mitsuie and Tachibana Kanetaka, former followers of the Heike clan, controlled Ōta-kata and Kuwabara-kata as *geshi*. According to Ban'a's description, there were four *geshi-myō*, including their two *myō*: Fukutomi-myō (twenty *chō*), Miyayoshi-myō (twenty *chō*), Uga Shigemitsu-myō (three *chō*), and Tobari Miyayoshi-myō (three *chō*). It is apparent that from as early as the Heian period, four individual *geshi* had exercised tight control over this area.

18 The pattern of *shōen* landholding was like a lattice of rights (*shiki*), including the rights of absentee *shōen* proprietors (*honke-shiki* and *ryoke-shiki*), those of *shōen* officials (*geshi-shiki* and *kumon-shiki*), and those of peasants (*myōshu-shiki*). Holders of *shiki* had divided possession at each level of landholding. Ōta-no-shō, which is discussed here, was a *ryoke-shiki* type of *shōen* holding. For an overview of Ōta-no-shō, see Kawane Yoshihira, *Chūsei hōkensei seiritsu shiron* (Tokyo: Tōkyō daigaku shuppankai, 1971), pp. 121–52.

19 Tōkyō daigaku shiryō hensanjo, ed., *Dai Nihon komonjo, Kōyasan monjo*, vol. 1, no. 101.

20 Ōta-kata and Kuwabara-kata were called *gō*, but as I shall explain later, within these two *gō* were several other *gō*.

In addition to these *geshi-myō* there were five *kumon-myō* in Ōta-no-shō, in the *gō* of Uehara, Io, Kosera, Akao, and Uga in Kuwabara-kata of the *shōen*. And because of such expressions as "the *kumon* of the various *gō*,"[21] we can assume that these *kumon* were located within each *gō*. The five *myō* were Shigemasa, Miyamaru, Tsunenaga, Mitsuhira, and Matsuoka. Except for Matsuoka which was two *chō*, all the others were three *chō* in area. Because the area of the *myō* fields roughly reflected the political and economic power of the person holding the *myō*, it reveals the actual balance of power between the *geshi* and the *kumon* within the *shōen*. In both Ōta-kata and Kuwabara-kata there was one *tsuibushi-myō* and one *tadokoro-myō*, each with an area of one *chō*. There were also eleven *kunin-myō*, including Iyaoka-myō, at one *chō;* and each of the remaining ten *myō* was five *tan* in area. It is clear from Ban'a's report that seventy *chō* of land were designated as official *myō* fields in Ōta-no-shō.

Peasants' myō

Apart from the *myō* held by *shōen* officials there was a total of 332 *chō* of *myō* held by peasants, comprising the largest group of fields in the *shōen*. Ban'a also described this peasants' *myō* as land bearing corvée obligations, or *kuji-myōden*. These *myō* were paddy fields allocated among the ordinary peasants (*hyakushō*) of Ōta-no-shō. In addition to providing the daily needs of the *shōen*'s peasants, these fields bore the burden of the annual dues and corvée and were the largest source of income for the *shōen* proprietors. Thus, it is clear why the main aim of the proprietors' *shōen* management was to maintain the stability and cultivation of these peasants' *myō*.

Three types of paddies

Ban'a Shonin pointed to the relationship between the burden of annual tax and corvée as the basis of the rice fields of Ōta-no-shō. He expressed this by using the three terms "tax-bearing fields" (*kanmotsu-den*), "corvée-bearing fields" (*kuji-myōden*), and "exempt fields" (*zōjimen*) to distinguish among the various fields. *Kanmotsu* was another term for dues. Thus *kanmotsu-den* were fields requiring the annual payment of dues. If the payment of dues is taken as the standard, then all fields can be divided into those that were tax bearing

21 *Dai Nihon komonjo, Kōyasan monjo*, vol. 1, nos. 100, 114.

(*kanmotsu*) and those that were not. Not only in Ōta-no-shō, but also in all *shōen*, whether officials' *myō* or ordinary peasants' *myō*, all fields designated as *myōden* were *kanmotsu* fields bearing the burden of dues. As I shall suggest when discussing Sasakibe-no-shō in Tamba Province, this was why those Kamakura-period warriors who had acquired land and the official status of *jitō* by inheriting the *geshi-shiki* in *shōen* originally paid *nengu* to the *shōen* proprietor in the case of their *jitō-shiki*.

Although all *myōden* were tax-bearing fields, in terms of corvée there was a big difference between the *shōen* officials' *myō* and the peasants' *myō*, in that the *shōen* officials were usually exempted from paying corvée dues on their own *myōden*. In Torikai-no-shō in Awaji Province, during a dispute between the *jitō* and an agent of the *shōen* proprietor (*zasshō*), the *jitō*'s proprietorial control over Yasumasa-myō and Tsuneyoshi-myō came to be recognized. But at this time, a special condition was added, that although the *jitō* gained control of these *myō*, the dues paid in rice, *shotōmai*, and the ordinary and extraordinary corvée borne by ordinary peasants should still be paid. This condition was added because these two *myō* had originally been peasants' *myō*.[22] Therefore, fields regarded as officials' *myō* were generally not subject to corvée. Those fields that were exempt from the *shōen* proprietors' corvée (also known as *zōji* or *manzōkuji*) were known as *zōjimen* (*zōmen*). In contrast, ordinary peasants' *myōden* that bore these corvée dues were generally known as *kuji myōden*.

Detached village fields

In Ōta-no-shō, in addition to the aforementioned kinds of official *myō* (*zōjimen*) and peasants' *myō* (*kuji myōden*), there were also approximately 116 *chō* of fields known as detached village fields, or *mura-mura bessakuden*. It appears that in the early Kamakura period, land reclamation was still advancing in the valleys of the mountainous areas of the Chūgoku region, and the detached village fields in Ōta-no-shō were probably of this kind. These lands had not yet been brought into the *myō* system, nor had the *shōen* corvée dues been levied. For this reason, Ban'a equated this land with officials' *myō* and classified it as *zōjimen*. It was most likely recognized that the cultivators had fulfilled their corvée obligation by bringing the detached fields into cultivation under difficult circumstances.

22 *Kamakura ibun*, no. 3088.

In addition, there were twelve *chō* of land known as *tsukuda* in Ōta-no-shō. The common characteristic of these fields, also commonly called *shōsakuden* and *uchitsukuri* in other *shōen*, was that generally they received different treatment than did ordinary *myōden*. As in the case of Sasakibe-no-shō in Tamba, seeds and foodstuffs were allocated to cultivators.[23] Again, in contrast with ordinary *myōden*, on which the rate of annual *nengu* rarely exceeded three or four *to* per *tan*, *tsukuda* were commonly taxed at the very high rate of one or more *koku*. In this sense, *tsukuda* retained the character of fields directly managed by the proprietor.

In addition to this brief overview of the internal land structure of Ōta-no-shō, it is necessary to explain exempted fields (*joden*). In all *shōen*, not simply Ōta-no-shō, a wide variety of people lived according to a wide variety of life-styles. Medium and small village temples and shrines were centers for the *shōen* inhabitants. Moreover, there were many artisans and workers, such as smiths and boatmen, with specialized skills. The maintenance and management of reservoirs and irrigation channels were also essential, and it was common to designate special lands to support these activities. The *shōen* proprietors, calling these lands Buddha and shrine fields, salary fields, or *iryoden*, exempted them from taxation. In addition to artisans and craftsmen, such *shōen* officials as *geshi* and *kumon* were also recognized as the holders of stipendiary fields that were not taxed by the *shōen* proprietor. Among these excluded fields were those from which the proprietor could not collect dues. These lands, known as *kawanari*, had been destroyed by floods or abandoned for various reasons. Because of the period's primitive agricultural technology, such examples could be found in nearly all *shōen*.

Miri-no-shō[24] in Aki Province was a *jitō* holding of the Kamakura *gokenin* Kumagai family. In 1235, the elder and younger brothers of the Kumagai family fought and divided this *shōen* in a ratio of 2 to 1. Judging from the documentary record of division, the Kumagai family's resources included fifty-five *chō*, seventy *bu* of paddy field; nineteen *chō*, seven *tan*, three hundred *bu* of dry field; six *chō*, three hundred *bu* of chestnut woods; various *shōen* shrines; and a hunting range (*karikurayama*). Among the paddy fields, dry fields, and woods in Miri-no-shō held by the Kummagai family were "home fields"

23 *Kamakura ibun*, no. 5315.
24 In contrast with Ōta-no-shō, which was a *ryoke shōen*, Miri-no-shō displays the pattern of a *jitō-shiki shōen*. On Miri-no-shō, see Kuroda Toshio, *Nihon chūsei hōkensei ron* (Tokyo: Tōkyō daigaku shuppankai, 1974), pp. 109–34.

TABLE 2.3

Kumagai family holdings in Miri-no-shō

	Paddy field			Dry field			Woodland		
	chō	*tan*	*bu*	*chō*	*tan*	*bu*	*chō*	*tan*	*bu*
Jitō "home fields" (*kadota-kadobata*)	3	8	0	1	5	0	0	8	180
Jitō-myō	11	4	240	7	2	300	1	2	240
Kumon-shiki									
Residence paddy field	1	3	240	3	9	180		7	0
Kumon-myō	5	3	240						
Cultivators' lots	27	5	6	6	9	180	3	2	0

(*kadota*), *jitō-myo*, official lands known as *kumon-shiki*, and even cultivators' lots (see Table 2.3).

Although not unusual, it is noteworthy that the *jitō* Kumagai family
also held the *kumon-shiki* of Miri-no-shō as part of its holdings.[25] The
jitō's *kadota-kadobata* was outside the purview of the *shōen* proprietor
and in Miri-no-shō included rice paddies and dry fields, together with
the woods attached to the *jitō*'s main residence. The *jitō-myō* fields,
already explained in the case of Ōta-no-shō, technically bore the burden of dues owed the *shōen* proprietor but were exempt from corvée.
The official holding known as *kumon-shiki* in Miri-no-shō included the
kadota attached to the residence of the *kumon* and the *kumon-myō* made
up of the corvée exempt *ryōshu-myō* (*zōjimen*).

The paddy fields, dry fields, and woodlands of the peasants' *myō*
made up the core of Miri-no-shō. Fifty percent of the *shōen*'s paddy
fields were peasants' *myō;* dry fields constituted 35 percent; and woodlands accounted for 53 percent. This comprised the lands of twenty-
seven peasants' *myō*, bearing such names as Tamenao, Takeyuki, and
Tamekage and ranging in size from several *tan* to two or three *chō*.[26] It
was equivalent to the *kuji-myōden* described in the case of Ōta-no-shō;
paddy fields, dryfields, and woodlands all were subject to the *nengu*
and corvée levied by the proprietor. Peasants' *myō* were an important
element in *jitō* holdings. The *jitō* not only had the right to levy small
amounts of supplementary rice tax (*kachōmai*) at the rate of three or
five *shō* per *tan*, but through this right to levy *kachōmai*, the *jitō* also

25 Judging from similar cases in other *shōen*, it is likely that the Kumagai acquired the proprietorship of the *kumon-shiki* through a successful struggle with the *ryōke*.
26 See Kuroda, *Nihon chūsei hōkensei ron*, p. 120.

TABLE 2.4

Management of jitō–kadota *paddy and dry fields in Miri-no-shō*

	Paddy		Dry field		Chestnut woods	
	tan	bu*ᵃ*	tan	bu	tan	bu
Self-cultivated	17	300	3	60	0	186
Karabō	3	180	5	0	2	180
Kurajirō	6	300	4	120	2	180
Kurasaburō	6	0	2	180		
Saburō	3	0				
Mikawadono	1	180				
Nakanyūdō					1	0
Kajitori					1	0
Mikawadono-shitsu					1	0
Total	38	240	15	0	8	6

ᵃ 360 *bu* = *tan.*

was able to demonstrate that he was the legitimate controlling authority over all the *shōen*'s paddy and dry fields.

Of the five *chō*, three *tan* of *kadota-kadobata* belonging to the *jitō* Kumagai family, they directly cultivated only slightly more than two *chō* of paddy and dry fields. The remainder was farmed by the cultivators Karabō, Kurasaburō, and others. This rare piece of data illustrates the *jitō*'s place in a rural warrior band. With regard to the *jitō-myō*, more than eleven *chō* of the *jitō*'s *myōden*, except for 120 *bu* of self-farmed land, was divided among peasants with such names as Saneyori, Ōyamada, Norimasa, and Kunimori. Some of these peasants, such as Kunishige or Myōzen, are mentioned elsewhere as holding Kunishige-myō and Myōzen-myō. It appears that the twenty-seven *jitō-myō* peasants were independent *myōshu* within the *shōen*.[27] As already stated, *jitō-myō* were exempted from the *zokuji* levied by the *shōen* proprietor. The *jitō*, however, held the right to extract *zokuji* from *jitō-myō* peasants in place of the *shōen* proprietor and to retain it as his own income. The *jitō-myō* peasants thus paid dues to the *shōen* proprietor and corvée to the *jitō* (see Table 2.4).

In addition, the *jitō* of Miri-no-shō controlled mountain forests as

27 An interpretation of this phenomenon in Miri-no-shō is difficult. The *shōen* proprietor held the *jitō* responsible for *nengu* owed on *jitō-myō* fields. The *jitō* held the right to allocate the paddy fields within the *jitō-myō*, usually on the basis of a reciprocal relationship between the *jitō* and the cultivators. There may have been special circumstances, but it is not certain that peasants held peasants' *myō* that bore the obligation of *nengu* owed to the *shōen* proprietor.

hunting ranges and, using the river running through the middle of the *shōen* valley as a boundary, divided between elder and younger brothers the lands on both sides of the river up to the mountains. The significance of such hunting ranges within the *shōen* economy will be discussed later in greater detail.

Hitoyoshi-no-shō in Higo Province was part of the domain of the Rengeō-in temple in Kyoto. The holding stretched along the upper reaches of the rapidly flowing Kuma River in Higo Province (now Kumamoto Prefecture). The Sagara family who were *jitō* of the *shōen* came originally from Tōtōmi and were among those *jitō* who moved west and eventually became *sengoku* daimyo.

The *jitō-shiki* of this *shōen* had been divided into north and south in 1244, and the northern half was confiscated from the Sagara by the Hōjō family. According to the division memorandum made at that time,[28] after the division was made, the Sagara family had more than 122 *chō* of paddy legally recognized as belonging in the *shōen* (*kishōden*), more than 41 *chō* of paddy cultivated by *shōen* peasants, which came to be regarded as part of the *shōen* (*shutsuden*), and more than 10 *chō* of new paddy (*shinden*). They also had seventy house lots (*genzaike*), twenty-nine hunting ranges (*karikura*), and river rights (*kawabun*). Their control spread over paddy fields and dry fields, house lots, mountains and hills, rivers, and hunting grounds. Before the division when the eastern *gō* was still attached, Hitoyoshi-no-shō had more than 352 *chō* of *kishōden* paddy fields and 111 *chō* of *shutsuden* fields and, like other *shōen*, established *myō* within its borders. The scale of these *myō* was very large, and they are different from the peasants' *myō* that can be seen in Kinai, the surrounding provinces, or intermediate area. It is thought that they made up the economic base of a small stratum of *jitō* characteristic of Kyushu. Consequently, the income base of this *shōen* was the resident cultivators (*zaike no nōmin*).

These *kishōden* fields were those reported in the 1197 survey; the *shutsuden* fields were noted in the 1212 survey; and the remaining *shinden* were new fields as of 1244. After the division, the lands of Hitoyoshi-no-shō were separated into *kishōden* fields and *shutsuden* fields, with an additional nineteen *myō* or more of shrine fields. Of this, eleven *myō* were from one to five *chō* in scale. These were the most numerous. However, there were a number of *myō* of over twenty *chō*, such as the Keitoku-myō of more than thirty-five *chō*, the

---

28 Tōkyō daigaku shiryō hensanjo, ed., *Dai Nihon komonjo, Sagara-ke monjo*, vol. 1, no. 6.

Matsunobu-myō of more than twenty-nine *chō*, and the Jōraku-*myō* of more than twenty-five *chō*, suggesting that such *myō* had been the established holdings of local proprietors in this area since the Heian period.[29] The scale can be compared with those of the *zaichō betchimyō* as described in reference to the public domain of Awaji and Wakasa provinces. Given the history of this *shōen*'s establishment, it is believed that the structure of *myō* changed little following the establishment of the *shōen* out of public land.

Consequently, compared with the other *shōen* already discussed, the *shōen* proprietor and *jitō* of Hitoyoshi-no-shō held greater control over local cultivator households (*zaike*). The *shōen* proprietor made these *zaike* the target of various levies. In a Sagara family document it is written: "One household. Sō-kumon title holder. Hemp: 7 *ryō*: Mulberries: 48 trees. . . . One household. Kajitori Seitoji. Mulberries: 33 trees."[30] The wide variety of levies imposed on *zaike* were at that time generally called *zaike-yaku* and were usually collected in corvée, that is, labor that the proprietor required on mountains, open land, and dry fields. In some cases when no similar appropriate work could be found for corvée, the proprietor levied silk and silk floss (based on the number of mulberry trees) or hemp in lieu of *zaike-yaku*. At that time, silkworms were bred in many parts of Hitoyoshi-no-shō, and according to the document of division there was a total of 3,775.5 mulberry trees in Hitoyoshi-no-shō.[31] As in the case of exempted paddy fields (*joden*), there seem to have been mulberry trees that were also excluded from the purview of the *shōen* proprietor, and these trees became a source of income for shrines and lower-level *shōen* officials.

Within Hitoyoshi-no-shō there were twenty-nine hunting ranges belonging to the *jitō*. In outlying areas far beyond the *kishōden* and *shutsuden* fields that made up the *myōden*, these were primarily on mountain ridges or in forests. Most ranges were located on the mountain uplands in winter when movement was easiest, but in summer when the trees were dense and entry was difficult, ranges were opened up on the plains at the foot of the mountains. In addition to the upland hunting ranges, fish traps, also tended by corvée, were installed at two fast-flowing parts of the Kuma River. At the Munekawa fish trap three bamboo mats were installed, and at the Oiwase trap as many as thirty

29 Under the policies of Minamoto Yoritomo, the local proprietor stratum in Kyushu was categorized as "small *jitō*" (*shōjitō*), whereas *jitō* from the Kantō such as the Sagara ranked above them, as *sōjitō*.   30 *Dai Nihon komonjo, Sagara-ke monjo*, no. 7.
31 The reason for the indicated fraction for mulberry trees is not clear. It could mean half of the leaves harvested from a tree.

mats were in use. These fish traps were stretched across the entire width of the river, with thirty mats in line, one after the other. When the *shōen* was divided, an imaginary boundary was drawn down the middle of the river, and fifteen mats each were set to north and south.[32]

<h2 style="text-align:center">THE POWER OF THE JITŌ</h2>

There were numerous political struggles within the *shōen* in the Kamakura period, primarily between the *jitō* and the peasants. These disputes, including those over competing interests in paddy fields, dry fields, uplands, commons, rivers, and the sea, were struggles for livelihood, even for existence itself. A close study of such disputes is useful in learning about life in the medieval *shōen*.

In 1207, a judgment by the bakufu (*saikyo*) was issued in regard to Kunitomi-no-shō in Wakasa Province.[33] In this eleven-article judgment the bakufu listed the illegal acts committed by the *jitō* and ordered that in dealing with the *shōen*, he should respect the practices of his predecessor, Tokisada Hōshi, and cease his illegal acts. Tokisada Hōshi was the Inaba-Gon-no-Kami Tokisada mentioned earlier, as well as the largest local official (*zaichō kanjin*) in this province in the late Heian and early Kamakura periods. Among the actions for which precedent was to be followed was cultivating the *jitō*'s private holdings (*tsukuda*) and levying corvée for fishing and raising silkworms. Among the practices the bakufu ordered the *jitō* to cease were collecting monthly expenses for the *jitō*'s official agent, levying labor service for fishing during harvest time, imposing a levy on indigo, requiring the provisioning of horses to be used by his and the *daikan*'s offspring, cutting the peasants' hemp, and imposing corvée for travel by the wives of the *jitō* and *daikan* to and from the *shōen*.

The judgment further ordered the following in regard to the horse-freight levy: The freight of rice from the *jitō*'s fields was a task that could be assigned to the peasants; an annual freight corvée could be levied on peasants, but corvée to transport goods outside Kunitomi-no-shō would be permitted only if there were a precedent; and half the burden of the levy collected in rice in order to transport goods to the Kantō should be borne by the *jitō*. Finally, the judgment decreed that

<hr/>

32 On Hitoyoshi-no-shō, see Nagahara Keiji, "Zaike no rekishi-teki seikaku to sono henka ni tsuite," and Ōyama Kyōhei, "Jitō ryōshusei to zaike shihai," in Nagahara Keiji, ed., *Nihon hōkensei seiritsu katei no kenkyū* (Tokyo: Iwanami shoten, 1961).
33 *Mibu monjo, Kamakura ibun*, no. 1709.

the land and houses of absconded peasants would be divided equally between the *ryōke* and *jitō*. The illegal practices that the *jitō* engaged in within this *shōen* were the source of many similar disputes in other *shōen* in the Kamakura period.

Rounding up *shōen* peasants to work on the *jitō*'s private holdings (*tsukuda*) was also a major cause of conflict between the *jitō* and *shōen* residents in this period. The *jitō* of this *shōen* was attempting to extend his *tsukuda*. The peasants, however, resisted, and so he was ordered to observe the customs of his predecessor. Not only in the cultivation of *tsukuda* but also in many other ways, the *jitō* tried to levy corvée on the peasants. For example, the *jitō* of Kunitomi-no-shō fished on rivers flowing through the *shōen*.[34] Although from ancient times various fishing methods such as weirs, fish traps, and cormorants were used, it is not clear what kind of fishing methods were used in Kunitomi-no-shō. However, it is clear that the *jitō* had direct control over them and that he exacted corvée from the *shōen* peasants for fishing. Accordingly, the bakufu ordered the cessation of this practice during the main agricultural season, as the peasants' resistance to corvée that disregarded their seasonal needs was very strong.

A similar problem arose over silkworm cultivation. The *jitō* did not raise silkworms himself, but rather, they were attended to by women in the houses of the *shōen* peasants where silk thread, floss, and yarn were made. Because the young silkworms consumed enormous quantities of mulberry leaves at the height of the growing season, the peasants appealed to the bakufu to order the *jitō* to stop conscripting their labor during this period.[35] In response to this appeal, the bakufu ordered that the precedent of Tokisada's day be observed.[36]

Corvée employed on the *jitō*'s *tsukuda* or in fishing contributed to the *jitō*'s income, and household or stable services for the *jitō* and his followers helped meet the *jitō*'s domestic needs. Because the *jitō*, his family, and agents always visited the *shōen* on horseback, fodder for their horses was required, as well as firewood and food for the *jitō* and others while they were in the *shōen*. Thus, in Kunitomi-no-shō, household services in the form of provisions for the *jitō*'s wife, *daikan*,

34 The fishing described in this section refers to *ayu* fishing. *Ayu* is a fish similar to trout and is found in the fast-flowing rivers of Japan.
35 The entire peasant family worked during the silkworm season. Some ten years after the *jitō* entered this *shōen*, he "insisted on service" from the peasants, "depending on need." In other words, he demanded service at will.
36 As explained, Tokisada was a local proprietor who had been in this area for a long time, and such a long-time local proprietor usually preserved a balance between the needs of the peasants themselves and his own. Kunitomi-no-shō provides an early example of a new *jitō* disregarding the time-honored balance.

servants, offspring, and horses were also a source of friction. Therefore, the care of only one or two horses limited to the *jitō* himself was
allowed by the bakufu, and the burden was also ordered to be shared
by all the residents of the *shōen*. There is no specific written reference
to these household services, but the same principle most likely prevailed. In the case of offspring of the *jitō* or *daikan*, the *jitō-myō* rather
than the *shōen* had to bear the burden. The corvée levied for the *jitō*'s
wife's travel between the *shōen* and Kyoto was also stopped at this
time. For the purposes of *shōen* management, the *jitō* dispatched an
agent every month, and his monthly expenses were imposed on the
peasants. This too aroused opposition and was eventually stopped.

A third form of corvée was a "horse levy" (*fumayaku*) levied for
transport and freight, on coolies or horses for the transport of humans
and goods between the *shōen* and Kyoto or the Kantō. *Fumayaku* was
limited to hauling rice (*shotōmai*) from the *jitō*'s *tsukuda*. The transport
of other goods, such as produce from the *jitō*'s *myō*, was known as
junyaku and fixed at one levy per year. Most *shōen* of the Kamakura
period to which *jitō* had been appointed levied freight dues to the
Kantō.[37] In Kunitomi-no-shō, the rate for one coolie's *fumayaku* was
set at six *koku* of rice. But because the annual burden was too heavy,
half of it was to be paid from the *jitō*'s income, and the remainder was
to be paid by the peasants.[38]

Before cotton was introduced into Japan, the peasants' clothing was
made mainly with hemp cloth. In Kunitomi-no-shō there was a distinction between cultivated and wild hemp, although both were used in
the production of cloth. Some hemp was cultivated in specific fields by
peasant families and was known as peasants' hemp, whereas wild
hemp was most likely that growing on the mountains. A dispute involving hemp arose between the *jitō* and the peasants in which the peasants
complained to the bakufu that the *jitō* was cutting down the peasants'
hemp. The *jitō* argued that he had never touched the cultivated hemp,
although he had once cut mountain hemp, but now the peasants had
come to cut it. Perhaps because the *jitō* was most likely from the Kantō
and because this was a distant *shōen*, his demands for annual rights to
mountain hemp were not granted, and the peasants of Kunitomi-no-

37 In western *shōen* it was customary to commute the levy into kind. Later, in the Sasakibe-no-
shō in Tamba Province, peasants of the *shōen* paid four *koku*, two *to* in rice and 120 *jō* in
paper, in place of a levy of two men to serve as coolies to travel to the eastern provinces.
Higashi monjo, Kamakura ibun, no. 5315.
38 In 1299, the peasants of Tara-no-shō in Wakasa Province secured an agreement stating that
the Kantō levy would be imposed only when the *jitō* himself went to the Kantō. *Kamakura
ibun*, no. 20139.

shō were able to retain their rights to the hemp growing on the mountain sides.

Indigo was used to dye hemp for clothing, and the plant called *tade* that produced the indigo was cultivated in many provinces of Japan. The Wakasa provincial headquarters had long imposed an indigo levy, but in Kunitomi-no-shō the peasants had appealed for, and been granted, an exemption from it. Later, the *jitō* attempted to reimpose the levy, but because the *ryōke* had previously exempted it, the precedent was recognized in the court decision, and so the *jitō*'s indigo levy was banned.

In the Kamakura period, peasants frequently absconded from *shōen*. In such cases, the disposition of the residence lots (*zaike*) and the cultivated fields was a major source of contention.[39] In Kunitomi-no-shō the *jitō* not only confiscated the *zaike* of absconded peasants but also incorporated their fields into his own *jitō-myōden*. If this occurred each time a peasant absconded, then the amount of *hyakushō-myō* would continually decline, and the amount of *jitō-myō* would increase proportionately. This situation led to disputes in *shōen* all over Japan, but eventually the Kamakura bakufu established the principle that the *ryōke* and *jitō* should divide vacated holdings equally and bring cultivators in from elsewhere to work them. On such occasions the *jitō* was specifically forbidden to install his own servants. The reason was probably that if the newcomers were not independent of the *jitō* and *ryōke*, the continuity of peasants' *myō* would be in jeopardy. The record from Kunitomi-no-shō is one of the earliest examples of the application of this principle, which varied slightly among *shōen*. In the case of Ishiguro-no-shō in Etchū the same principle applied, with *ryōke* and *jitō* sharing the responsibility for bringing in new cultivators, although such fields were administered in a special way.[40] In Miri-no-shō in Aki Province a document mentions that 3 *chō*, 9 *tan*, 240 *bu* of *mandokoro-myō* had been "absconded peasant sites," suggesting that sites vacated by absconding peasants in this *shōen* were taken over by the administrative office of the *ryōke* (*mandokoro*).[41]

The many transgressions by the *jitō* of Kunitomi-no-shō indicate the actual conditions of life in *shōen* during the Kamakura period. Although local conditions changed the character of these transgressions, similar events were occurring in *shōen* throughout Japan. For instance, Sasakibe-no-shō in Tamba was a *shōen* of more than one hundred *chō*

---

39 In the medieval period in Japan, the houses of felons were destroyed and the timbers carried off so that they could not be used again.
40 *Tōyama ken shi, shiryō hen, chūsei.*
41 Tōkyō daigaku shiryō hensanjo, ed., *Dai Nihon komonjo, Kumagai-ke monjo*, no. 16.

of paddy fields under the proprietorship of the Matsuo Shrine in Kyoto. Located in the mid-reaches of the Yura River which flowed into the Japan Sea, cormorant fishing was a common activity in this *shōen*. The *shōen* peasants, who called themselves "divinely protected people" (*jinnin*), made daily offerings of fish (*ayu* and salmon) to the gods of the Matsuo Shrine. The rights of the cormorant fishers of Sasakibe-no-shō as *jinnin* were considerable. Sasakibe-no-shō was located where the Yura River entered Amata District in Tamba Province, but these cormorant fishers crossed the boundaries of the *shōen* and asserted their monopoly of fishing rights on the Yura River as far as the border with Tango Province. With the establishment of the Kamakura bakufu, the powerful Kantō warrior Kajiwara no Kagetoki was awarded this *shōen* as a *geshi* and deputy *jitō*. He did not actually enter the *shōen* but, rather, sent a deputy in his place. When Kagetoki was executed for plotting against the bakufu, a regular *jitō* was appointed. Eventually, in 1237, a *jitō* from the Kantō, accompanying the shogun on a trip to Kyoto, entered the *shōen* and tried for the first time to establish full control.

Immediately after setting foot in Sasakibe-no-shō, the *jitō* attempted to use the labor of the peasants in the *shōen* to build a large new residence. He, however, encountered stiff resistance. Of course, it is possible that the *shōen* proprietor, the Matsuo Shrine, incited the peasants to resist. This was the first in a series of incidents in which the *jitō* attempted to enforce his will in the *shōen* but succeeded only in arousing the peasants' resistance.

The bakufu court at Rokuhara in Kyoto would not support any of the *jitō*'s attempts to strengthen his control.[42] The following *jitō* actions were directly contested: various forms of labor conscription, including labor for the construction of a new *jitō* residence in the *shōen*, nine "permanent coolies" to provide miscellaneous labor service at the *jitō*'s residence in Kyoto,[43] and conscription for service in Kyoto that ignored the precedent of one levy per year per household; several additional levies, including demands for ten cords of firewood, eighty bales of grass for fodder, and a household service levy,[44] enforcement of an extraordinary levy of three hundred *mon* per *tan* for the expenses of residence in Kyoto, and a horse-freight corvée against the headmen

---

42 The Rokuhara *tandai* was established by the Kamakura bakufu in Kyoto to control the western provinces and to handle administrative matters affecting the bakufu.
43 "Permanent coolies" (*nagafu*) were long-term servants.
44 In this matter the Matsuo Shrine was prepared to allow two cords of firewood and two bales of grass, but it rejected outright any household service.

of the twelve groups from Sasakibe-no-shō at the rate of one horse per person;[45] the extension of *jitō* fields (*shōsakuden*) under cultivation to one *chō*, two *tan;* assertion of the claim to half the fishing rights in the Yura River; and the extension of authority over the *kumon* of Sasakibe-no-shō.

Thus the basic points in dispute were the same as those in the case of Kunitomi-no-shō. One new important point in this *shōen* was the extended cultivation of *shōsakuden*. Labor service on the *jitō*'s own fields was known as "hired labor" (*koshi*) and was required three times a year from each individual. It included clearing the fields in early spring, planting rice in early summer, and weeding in midsummer. These three days of labor service were required at the busiest times in the annual cycle of rice production. In this sense, the management method of the *jitō*'s fields (*shōsakuden*) in the Kamakura period was "hired labor" management. The *jitō*, in addition to distributing seed, provided three meals on each labor day in return for the labor. It is most likely in this sense that the character *kō*, meaning "to employ," is used here. This kind of employment in return for foodstuffs or other allowances was characteristic of the labor service in the medieval period.[46]

The *jitō* of Sasakibe-no-shō left his home province of Sagami and went to Kyoto to assert full control over Sasakibe-no-shō. In the *shōen*, however, the *jitō* met an unanticipated degree of opposition from the peasants. It is quite possible that the steps he wanted to take to gain control over Sasakibe-no-shō were common in *shōen* in Sagami and other eastern provinces. In medieval Japan the authority of *jitō* and the actual power of the peasantry differed greatly between the eastern provinces, where the reach of bakufu power was great, and the western provinces.[47] This is clearly revealed by the reactions of both parties when the *jitō* confined the peasants he had brought to Kyoto for labor service in a hut at night to prevent them from fleeing. The Matsuo Shrine appealed to the *jitō* and asserted that "it is unlawful to bind and imprison virtuous people who are protected by the gods." The *jitō* responded that "confining them at night in a hut is not impris-

45 This *shōen* had a system of twelve peasants' responsibility groups. Instead of performing corvée by carrying freight, the twelve headmen (*bantō*) shared the burden of a rice levy (*fukōmai*) and a paper levy at the set rates of three *to*, five *shō* of rice and ten *jō* of paper for each group.
46 Ōyama, *Nihon chūsei nōson shi no kenkyū*, pp. 194–230.
47 There were a number of reasons for the disparity between the power of the *jitō* in the eastern and western provinces. Not least among them were the policies of Minamoto Yoritomo who established the bakufu and set the *jitō* system on its course.

oning them. They are worthless peasants and menials (*genin*). They
are not 'people of the gods.' " The *jitō* from the eastern provinces
probably did not recognize that his actions were unreasonable; the two
parties had completely contradictory opinions of the *shōen* peasants.
The Rokuhara court rejected the excuse offered by the *jitō* of Sasakibe-
no-shō. But many obstacles still remained to prevent the principles of
jitō control, which were beginning to be partially realized in the eastern provinces, from extending more widely throughout Japan.

Torikai-no-shō in Awaji province was a small *shōen* on the Inland
Sea composed of thirty *chō* of paddy and dry fields and a village on a
small bay. It was held by the Iwashimizu Hachiman Shrine located at
the confluence of the Uji, Katsura, and Yodo rivers just south of
Kyoto, enabling close communication with the Inland Sea region.
There was a branch shrine of the Iwashimizu Hachiman within the
shōen. In 1278, following a dispute between the *jitō*, Sano Tomitsuna,
and the chief priest of the branch shrine, a conciliation agreement
was reached, expressed in a twenty-seven-article document.[48] This
agreement illustrates both the growth in the *jitō*'s powers by the
closing decades of the thirteenth century and the limitations still
placed on the *jitō*'s authority.

Many of the western warriors who had supported the cause of the
Kyoto court were destroyed in the Jōkyū disturbance of 1221 and
warriors from the east were installed in their domains as *jitō*. The *jitō*
positions created after the Jōkyū disturbance are known as "new *jitō*"
(*shimpo jitō*) and are usually distinguished from the "original *jitō*"
(*hompo jitō*) who had been installed before the war, although their
status as *jitō* was equal. In principle, *jitō* inherited the powers of their
failed predecessors, such *shōen* officials as *geshi*. In some *shōen*, however, the allotments of income (*tokubun*) and the powers they inherited
were extremely limited. In such cases a set allotment was guaranteed.
In Torikai-no-shō the dispute arose because the *jitō* claimed that he
was entitled to receive the income of both a *hompo jitō* and a *shimpo
jitō*. In the end his claim was rejected, and he was recognized as being
entitled only to the income of a *shimpo jitō*.

The following five principles were recognized with regard to the
jitō's authority as a result of the agreement that generally followed the
prescriptions for awarding *jitō* income (*tokubun*) instituted after the
Jōkyū disturbance: (1) The area of rice paddy and dry fields allotted to

48 Tōkyō daigaku shiryō hensanjo, ed., *Dai Nihon komonjo, Iwashimizu monjo*, vol. 1, nos. 217,
   218. *Kamakura ibun*, no. 3088. On this *shōen*, see Inagaki Yasuhiko, *Nihon chūsei shakai shi
   ron* (Tokyo: Tōkyō daigaku shuppankai, 1981), p. 367.

the *jitō* should be at the ratio of one *chō* in eleven on the basis of the calculations of the official survey conducted in the *shōen* in 1233–4; (2) except for special fields, the rice levy (*kachōmai*) levied by the *jitō* on peasants' *myō* and ordinary fields should be in the ratio of five *sho* per *tan*;[49] (3) the special allotment for apprehending criminals within the *shōen* should be divided: two-thirds for the *ryōke* and one-third for the *jitō*; (4) the *ryōke* and the *jitō* should divide equally the allotment from mountains, rivers, and the sea, apart from the annual tax (*hon nengu*);[50] and (5) *tokubun* from levies on house lots (*zaike yaku*) and mulberry trees and hemp should also be divided equally between the *ryōke* and the *jitō*.

To secure the recognition of these five principles, the *jitō* had to make some significant concessions. The public land that the *jitō* had occupied under a variety of pretexts was returned. Long-term household labor service,[51] five festival offerings, and levies of rice from the public fields were stopped. In particular, the right that the *jitō* had asserted to manage the proprietor's storehouse was rejected. Likewise, the right asserted by the *jitō* to appoint priests and officials to the detached Iwashimizu Shrine was denied.

The proprietor's tax rice was stored in the *shōen* storehouse. Before the 1278 agreement the *jitō* was accused of constantly interfering in the operation of the storehouse, indicating that in this *shōen* the *jitō* was actually involved in collecting the annual tax and that he used his authority to oversee the proprietor's storehouse. For his services the *jitō* retained a set ratio of rice, known as *kyōbunmai*, but this, too, was ended at this time.

The *jitō* was clearly trying to bring the Torikai detached shrine, which comprised the core of the *shōen*, under his own control. To this end the *jitō* attempted to exert the power of appointment over the head priest (*kannushi*) and other shrine priests and to gain control over all the tax income and land of the detached shrine. The *jitō* asserted his right to the annual tax from specially designated fields dedicated to the Sutra of Great Wisdom belonging to the detached shrine and to the management of the land itself. He sought hereditary appointment of

49 With regard to the income fields of the *jitō* of Torikai-no-shō, it says: "It is laid down that with the exception of Buddha and *kami* fields, and *Imizoryo* and ancient tax-exempt rice fields and wells and waterways, it should be collected from the rice fields and dry fields of the *myōden*." With regard to *jitō kachōmai* there is a proviso saying, "On *jōden*." *Dai Nihon komonjo, Iwashimizu monjo*, vol. 1, no. 217.
50 This refers to *kuji*, and likewise for the following.
51 Because in Torikai-no-shō there was a levy of household service (*bōjiyaku*) while the *jitō* was in the shōen, the long-term service referred to here seems to have been equivalent to permanent service (*nagafu*) in Sasakibe-no-shō.

the chief priest of the Yakushi hall and tried to control its fields. He asserted his rights to cut timber in the woods immediately around the shrine. He himself issued orders to the *kannushi* and other shrine officials and tried to regulate shrine functions performed before the gods. All these actions were directed toward monopolizing control over the shrine and its lands.

By the 1270s, in the second half of the Kamakura period, *jitō* power tended to spread in all directions. In Torikai-no-shō, too, the *jitō* – even though he had been subjected to the regulations for new *jitō* and denied intervention in personnel matters – actually interfered, along with the proprietor, in matters affecting the shrine. He issued orders to shrine officials and priests and had some say, albeit limited, in managing the harbor which was a source of contention at this time. He also seemed to have gained considerably more authority than had the *jitō* of Sasakibe-no-shō. However, the *jitō*'s fundamental aim of gaining complete control over the detached shrine had been thwarted. Apart from his legally authorized right to levy *kachōmai*, the *jitō*'s claims to rights of appointing shrine priests, collecting taxes, and taking lumber from the shrine precincts – the basic elements for control of the detached shrine – all were rejected.

In other ways, too, the *jitō*'s powers remained circumscribed. For instance, although when he traveled to the capital, he was permitted to impose levies on the peasants for horse transportation and coolies (*temba-yaku* and *jinpuyaku*), these levies had to be "limited *temba*." Again, the *jitō* was forbidden to be lax in feeding permanent servants and boatmen on journeys to the capital. The *jitō* was permitted to enforce miscellaneous household services in a "limited" way and in accord with precedent, but miscellaneous household service for his *daikan* was not recognized. The case was similar for fodder for his horses. Arrangements in this *shōen* were similar to those in Kunitomi-no-shō and Sasakibe-no-shō. That the *jitō* was enjoined not to monopolize control over irrigation water in the *shōen* and direct it only to his own *myōden* suggests that this was a common situation.

In the medieval period, belief in divination and yin–yang thought flourished, and people were governed by many taboos. Depending on the daily inclination of the stars, there were certain fixed directions from which danger could arise. In order to avoid these inauspicious directions, people frequently traveled via the house of a third party, in what was known as "changing direction" (*katatagae*). The *jitō* of Torikai-no-shō also followed this practice and often seems to have forced his way into the homes of peasants, who bitterly objected to this kind of intrusion. Thus, one of the conditions of the 1278 agreement was that he cease this practice.

In 1237, the *jitō* of Sasakibe-no-shō was ordered to pay within three years over 300 *koku* of unpaid annual tax on the *jitō-myō* that had accumulated unknown to him, though its administration had been left to the *daikan*. In contrast, in the case of the *jitō* of Torikai-no-shō in 1278, although there were many illegalities – such as the *jitō*'s seizing shrine rice at the *shōen* harbor[52] or detaining 310 *koku* of *shotōmai* from various *myō* – all were canceled under the terms of the conciliation agreement. Although there is no doubt that *shōen* were subjected to all kinds of changes, with the advance of the medieval period, conditions tended to favor the *jitō*. At the same time, in the Kamakura period, severe limits were still in effect against the *jitō*'s full control of *shōen*.

Within individual *shōen* there were constant struggles between the *jitō* and the proprietor. Eventually, the *jitō* contracted to collect the proprietor's annual tax (*jitō uke*) and, in practice, came to monopolize actual authority over *shōen* land. The system of tax contracting was adopted commonly from a fairly early period in many eastern *shōen* where the *jitō* tended to have an extremely powerful position vis-á-vis the *shōen* proprietor. For instance in Tomita-no-shō in Owari Province, where the *jitō-shiki* was conferred by the Hōjō family on the Zen monastery of the Engakuji, a *jitō-uke* contract was renewed in 1327. According to this contract, the Engakuji, as the *jitō*, was required to pay 110 *kan* of cash to the proprietor in Kyoto in the eleventh month of each year. The *jitō*'s income from this *shōen* in 1282, however, amounted to 1,248 *koku*, 8 *to* of rice and 1,596 *kan*, 868 *mon* in cash. This disparity shows that under *jitō-uke* contracts, the authority of the *shōen* proprietors could not help but be diluted. Although the amount of the annual tax contract is unknown, in Tomita-no-shō the *jitō-uke* contract itself had been established as early as 1211. In the eastern provinces the dilution of the *shōen* proprietors' authority advanced rapidly from an early period.[53]

Tomita-no-shō was an eastern *shōen* having close ties with the Hōjō and thus was a special case. A similar situation, however, developed in other *shōen*, such as Ōyama-no-shō in western Japan, a holding of the Tōji domain in Tamba Province. In 1266, a *jitō* from eastern Japan, Nakazawa Motosada, exchanged an agreement with the Tōji that he

---

52 The annual tax was loaded for transport to the Iwashimizu Shrine in the harbor.
53 See Ōyama, *Nihon chūsei nōson shi no kenkyū*, p. 324. Martin Collcutt, *Five Mountains: The Rinzai Zen Monastic Institution in Medieval Japan* (Cambridge, Mass.: Harvard University Press, 1981), pp. 255–63.

would submit annually, without fail, two hundred *koku* of tax rice and four hundred *gō* of fruit and other commodities as a supplementary tax. However, in 1295, because the *jitō* continually failed to pay the annual tax, the two parties agreed to divide the *shōen*'s land (*shitaji chūbun*) and not to interfere in the other party's holdings. At this time, fourteen *chō*, four *tan*, ten *shiro* of paddy fields and three *chō* of dry fields in Ichiidani, one *chō*, eight *tan*, thirty-five *shiro* of paddy fields in Kamokukidani, and eight *chō*, seven *tan*, five *shiro* of paddy fields and two *chō* of dry fields in Nishitaimura were left to the Tōji. The Tōji, therefore, was able to maintain its reduced proprietorial rights until the early sixteenth century. The *jitō*, through *shitaji chūbun*, was able to exceed substantially the hitherto narrow framework of the land specifically allotted to him and to gain much more extensive control over a wider area of *shōen* in which the *shōen* proprietor had no authority. This kind of holding was known as "a complete *jitō* holding" (*jitō ichien-chi*) and shows a new development in feudal landholding. However, in the Kamakura period the appearance of *jitō ichien-chi* was still only sporadic.[54]

In 1318, the proprietor of Ōyama-no-shō exchanged a tax contract (*hyakushō-uke*) for an annual tax payment with the peasants of Ichiidani in order to end their continual appeals for its reduction. The amount of tax for which the peasants contracted was slightly less than 62 percent of what they were nominally paying before the agreement. This shows that by the early fourteenth century the peasants' political power had greatly expanded, a development that presaged the beginning of a new age.[55]

SOCIAL STRATA IN *SHŌEN*

Because the surviving documents do not reveal everything, it is not always easy to understand the actual living conditions of the *shōen* residents in the Kamakura period. However, from observations of the various representative *shōen*, it is clear that the *shōen* peasants could act fairly freely and that on occasion they both allied with and resisted the *jitō* and *shōen* proprietors.

With these *shōen* residents in mind, the bakufu promulgated the *goseibai shikimoku*, which stated that "peasants who have paid their annual tax can decide for themselves whether they will stay in the

54 Tōkyō daigaku shiryō hensanjo, ed., *Dai Nihon komonjo, Tōji monjo*, sec. *ni*, nos. 2, 41.
55 *Tōji hyakugō monjo*, sec. *ya*, nos. 3–5. Ōyama, *Nihon chūsei nōson shi no kenkyū*, pp. 256–64.

shōen or leave."[56] To the extent possible, the bakufu clearly wanted to stop *jitō* and local proprietors from binding peasants to the land or from asserting complete proprietorial control over them. If local proprietors became too powerful and independent, they would threaten to undermine the very existence of the bakufu. Thus, the medieval peasant was basically a "freeman" (*jiyūmin*). Under bakufu law, this kind of freeman was defined as a *hyakushō*,[57] as distinguished from those who were not free, such as servants (*genin*) and retainers (*shojū*).

However, there were many kinds of *hyakushō*. Because they lived in *shōen* and *kokugaryō*, the pattern of their existence was determined by their relationship with the particular holding, and especially their relationship with the prevailing system of landholding. Some enjoyed greater independence than others did.

One distinguishing factor in defining social stratification within *shōen* was whether in *shōen* domains in which *hyakushō-myō* existed, peasants had achieved the status of *myōshu*. This is shown most clearly in the case of Tara-no-shō in Wakasa Province. According to the land register, the holdings in this *shōen* included fields known as *isshikiden* (discussed later) and others known as *hyakushō-myō* or *myōbun*, that is, *myōden*. There were five *myōshu* who held *myōden* and part of the *isshikiden*. The majority, however, was allocated to twenty-seven other cultivators with names such as Shigenaga, Sōtsui, and Shinjirō.

Clearly there were two distinct classes in Tara-no-shō: *myōshu* and cultivators. Each member of the *myōshu* group was allotted two *chō*, one *tan* of *myōden* and one *tan* of land controlled directly by the proprietor. In addition, each had a portion of *isshikiden*, for a total holding of a little less than three *chō*.[58] The allocation of *myō* in Tara-no-shō at this time was controlled by a Tōji monk named Jōen who was responsible for managing the *shōen*. As explained earlier, a *myō* was not only the unit of taxation in a *shōen* but was also the unit for such *shōen* officials' proprietory *myō* as *jitō-myō* and *geshi-myō*. Whereas *shōen* were originally established through set legal procedures on the basis of an official connection with the state, there was no such state connection in the establishment of *myō*.

56 This was the basic legal code of the Kamakura bakufu.
57 *Hyakushō* can be translated as "peasant" or "farmer." In this book, "peasants" is used. *Hyaku* literally means "various," whereas *shō* or *sei* means "family name."
58 To be exact, Tokiyasu and Muneyasu had half of other *myō*. They were originally allocated what should have been single *myō*. Within Tara-no-shō, apart from this, there was Suetake-myō, about which there was a dispute as to whether it was *azukari-dokoro-myō* or peasants' *myō*. Also, there was Antsui-myō which enjoyed special circumstances and did not accord with the preceding pattern.

Myō were established on the basis of a more private relationship between the *shōen* proprietor and the small-scale local proprietors and, beneath them, the farming managers and upper-level peasants. As mentioned in regard to the *ōtabumi* for Wakasa Province, *myō* had begun to develop through various private connections within the provincial headquarters (*kokuga*), as tax units of the public domain. During the Kamakura period this kind of private relationship between *myō* and the public domain was generally carried over into *shōen*, although it changed in form and diffused more widely as it matured. In this way it was possible for several types of *shōen* to exist. Most of them were established when the *shōen* was formed, on the basis of the relationship between the *shōen* residents and the proprietor. The *myō* created by Jōen and listed in the Tara-no-shō agricultural register were almost certainly this kind of *myō*. Even so, the peasants' rights to cultivate *myō* were protected, and the fields could be passed on to their descendants as heritable *myōden*.

In the case of *isshikiden*, or partially exempt fields, the cultivator's rights were extremely unstable. This land was also called "floating exemption" (*ukimen*). Unlike peasants working *myō*, the cultivators of such land did not enjoy secure tenure but, rather, could be displaced at any time, depending on the proprietor's interests. In practice there were certainly some cultivators who had settled tenure, but from the proprietor's point of view it was easier to control the land by renewing annual contracts. In this period, when a proprietor permitted a cultivator to work a piece of land for a specified period, it was called a "scattering of fields" (*sanden*). Thus, the *isshikiden* formally was cultivated on an annual basis by the proprietor's "scattering of fields." In Tara-no-shō there were as many as twenty-seven peasants cultivating only *isshikiden*, a far greater number than the number of *myōshu*. However, all the fields they cultivated were, with the exception of a scattered plot held by Shigenaga, limited to two, three, or at the most four *tan* in size. Jōen clearly treated the two types differently, and the peasants of Tara-no-shō were thus divided into the two classes of *myōshu* and *sanden* cultivators.

For other *shōen* in the Kamakura period, the limitations of the documentary record prevent us from getting such a clear picture of the division of peasants. However, it is certain that in each *shōen*, in addition to the *myō* held by *myōshu*, there were a variety of cultivators of the different scattered fields. In some places these cultivators were called *mōto*, and their status in the *shōen* was marginal. Indeed, in times of hardship or distress they tended to move from *shōen* to *shōen*.

In the *shōen* of the Kamakura period there were many holdings that did not take the form of peasants' *myō*. The cultivators of such holdings were, as in the case of Hitoyoshi-no-shō, controlled as individual *zaike*. In Kyushu, *zaike* were also known as *sono*. In a deed referring to the Sagara *jitō* family and the Naritsune *myō* in Buzen Province, there are several references to *sono*. For example, one entry reads, "One holding: Imayoshi-sono."[59] In early research on this period, *zaike* were regarded as dependent peasants originally without land who were units in the proprietor's register of family resources and who could be bought and sold or conveyed by deed. With the passage of time, however, in such documentary references as "*zaike* attached to fields," *zaike* were mentioned in connection with paddy fields.

This fact has been interpreted by some historians to indicate that *zaike* peasants had strengthened their hold on their fields and means of production and that they had become more independent. That the *zaike* were treated separately from the land at the time of transfer of domain holdings was probably because historically their role had been that of direct producers rather than landholders of the *hyakushō-myō* type. However, there is still some question as to whether any direct conclusions can be reached regarding the subordination of peasants in Kyushu or eastern Japan. In the deed of transfer for the Naritsune *myō* in Buzen Province, fourteen *zaike* houses were attached to twenty-two *chō*, nine *tan* of paddy fields. As internal units of Naritsune *myō*, six *myō* are mentioned: Imayoshi-myō, Shōya-imayoshi-myō, Inoue-myō, Taromaru-myō, Iwamaru-myō, and Yoshihiro-myō. Among the fourteen *zaike* residences, seven principal *zaike* (*honzaike*) are listed, including Imayoshi-sono and seven branch *zaike* (*waki zaike*), such as that of the bowmaker Jōbu Saburō-sono, showing the existence of the two strata of *hon* and *waki zaike* in this area. At the same time, of the six *myō*, including Imayoshi-myō but not Tera-sono, they are exactly the same as the names of the six *honzaike* lot titles, suggesting a connection between the *myō* and the *zaike*. In any case, although the pattern of existence of *myō* and *zaike* is the most important problem of the land system underlying the *shōen* system, many elements still remain unclear, and no certain conclusions can be offered.

COURTIERS AND WARRIORS

Two land systems overlapped in the Japanese medieval period: the *shōen* system (or the *shōen–kokugaryō* system) and the local proprietor

59 *Dai Nihon komonjo, Sagara-ke monjo*, vol. 1, no. 26.

system (*zaichi ryōshusei*). Whereas the *shōen* system supported the nobility, the system of local proprietorships supported the warriors.

The earlier studies of the characteristics of medieval Japanese society reveal a shifting interest between European and Asian comparisons. The local proprietor system has been compared with medieval European feudalism, and many specialists have attempted to find a similar feudal structure in Japan's medieval period. In contrast, the *shōen* system has been linked with the long and brilliant cultural tradition of the medieval court nobility and with the politics of civilian bureaucratic primacy. The early research on the *shōen* system tended to focus on the failure of medieval institutions to break out of an "ancient" state structure. More recently, there has been considerable interest in the Japanese medieval period in its own right. This period is increasingly being viewed as embodying non-European structural characteristics, with the medieval emperor system (*tennōsei*) at its apex. Thus the theme of the *shōen* system in Japanese medieval history is enmeshed with the persistence of *tennōsei* in Japanese history. At the same time, students of the Japanese medieval period continue to debate the maturity of the feudal structure in Japan or the "Asian structural characteristics" of medieval society. Although it may seem to have grown weaker with Japan's recent high level of economic growth, the problem of whether medieval Japan resembled in any significant way feudal Europe has been of great interest to the Japanese, who constantly try to catch up with European civilization.[60]

It may seem that everything in medieval society can be expressed as a struggle between warriors (local proprietors) and courtiers (*shōen* proprietors). This effort to portray medieval Japanese society as a struggle between *kuge* and *buke* is a common approach. However, it should be remembered that the central proprietors (*ryōshu*) and the local proprietors (*jitō*) shared proprietory interests in the *shōen*. And at the same time, both had to deal with the peasants living in the *shōen* from and with whom they continued to collect and divide the annual taxes and levies. One interpretation that has recently attracted attention in the Japanese scholarship on medieval Japan has been to see *kuge* and *bushi*, together with the power of the Buddhist religious institutions, as a

60 Having said this, for Japanese historians to deal freely and directly with the historical character of the *tennō* remained taboo even in the period of openness that followed World War II. In this sense, Amino Yoshihiko's recent work, Chūsei tennō-sei to hi-nōgyōmin (Tokyo: Iwanami shoten, 1984) is a major contribution to medieval historical studies even though it deals only indirectly with *shōen*.

single complementary power structure controlling the peasant class. This view, though stressing the non-European development of medieval Japanese society, is seen as offering a new agenda.[61] In practice, cooperation between the central and local proprietors in controlling a single *shōen* was not uncommon.

This tendency was particularly strong in the Kamakura period. In Kunitomi-no-shō in Wakasa Province and Sasakibe-no-shō in Tamba Province, the bakufu often took steps to stop illegal *jitō* acts in cases of conflict between central and local proprietors. I believe that Minamoto Yoritomo's bakufu was instrumental in establishing the pattern of historical coexistence between medieval local proprietorship and the *shōen* system.

The Gempei War was a great crisis for the *kuge* class, although some researchers see it as a temporary phenomenon brought about by civil disturbance that eventually, when peace returned, disappeared. However, the connection between crisis and stability in history is important here. The deeper the roots of civil conflict are, the more deeply the stability that is restored must be defined by the process of that conflict. The effects that the Gempei War, which involved most of the country from Kyushu in the west to the tip of Oshu in the north, had on contemporary Japanese society cannot be measured.

In 1185, the cloistered emperor Goshirakawa, who did not favor the aggrandizement that Yoritomo had achieved through his victory over the Taira, granted to Minamoto Yoshitsune an edict ordering the overthrow of Yoritomo. Goshirakawa hoped to create internal discord within the Minamoto by setting brother against brother. When this attempt ended in failure with the destruction of Yoshitsune, the political position of the cloistered emperor became very tenuous. Yoritomo, who had once dispatched troops to dislodge Yoshinaka from Kyoto, again sent warriors to occupy the city where Yoshitsune was believed to be in hiding and brought pressure to bear on Goshirakawa. Yoritomo forced him to grant the provinces of the Kinai and western Japan to Hōjō Tokimasa and other vassals and to recognize Yoritomo's right to collect a levy of rice to support his troops in the war (*hyōrōmai*), at the rate of five *shō* per *tan* from both *shōen* and *kokugaryō*, and to treat such lands as fief (*chigyō*).

This is known as the appointment of provincial *jitō* to each province (*kuni-jitō*) of the Bunji era. Unlike the civilian provincial governors

---

61 Kuroda Toshio's theory of *Hi-ryōshuteki tenkai* advances this thesis. See his *Nihon chūsei no kokka to tennō* (Tokyo: Iwanami shoten, 1975).

(*kokushi*), the warriors who were appointed as *kuni-jitō* actually governed the assigned province. However, the situation in 1185 did not last for long. In 1186, on the judgment of Yoritomo himself, two of the aforementioned three powers, namely, the collection of *hyōrōmai* and the right to treat lands as fief, on which the *kuni-jitō* depended, were retracted. As a result, the *shōen* system and the local proprietor (*zaichi–ryōshu*) system coexisted in the Kamakura period, although it is important to note that briefly between 1185 and 1186, *shōen* throughout Japan faced a crisis in the startling recognition of the local proprietors' destructive power.

I have already alluded to this case in another essay.[62] In 1185, Doi Sanehira, the *kuni-jitō* of Bingo Province, sent his son Tōhira to govern the province. At this time, Tōhira, as the governor of the province, recognized the claims of the *geshi* of Ōta-no-shō, Tachibana Kanetaka and Ota Mitsuie, to control more than one hundred *chō* of land in Ōta-no-shō. Kanetaka and Mitsuie had been powerful local proprietors in Bingo Province since the Heian period. During the conflict, they forced their way into several hundred *chō* of partially tax-exempted paddies (*zōmen*). They also asserted control over several hundred *zaike* and night and day used a hundred or so ordinary families as servants. Furthermore, they collected *kachōmai* rice at the rate of two *shō*, five *gō* per *tan*. And in mountain plains where the killing of game was prohibited, they hunted wild boar, deer, fish, and birds.

As we learn from an appeal from Kōyasan in 1190, the *shōen* control policy of these two *geshi* toward the *shōen* residents during the period of civil unrest was a determined policy to try to make them into servants. It was also a policy that attempted to convert the *shōen*'s paddy fields and dry fields into land of their own, or *zōmen*. Under the *kuni-jitō* system of 1185–6, Doi Sanehira and Tōhira pressed for *zaichi–ryōshu* control. In response to these actions, Kōyasan stated: "It is customary in the various *shōen* that stipendiary paddies (*kyūden*) and *zōmen* are everywhere from two to three *chō*. Moreover, as customs of the five home provinces and seven circuits [i.e., throughout the entire country] that the exempted houses of *shōen* officials number from four or five to ten houses." It further stated: "Everywhere, *shōen* officials, having servants with exempt houses, oblige them to offer corvée. Kanetaka's and Mitsuie's use of ordinary peasants night and day, ordering them around, should not be allowed." These kinds of preda-

62 Ōyama Kyōhei, "Bunji kuni-jitō no sonzai keitai," in Shibata Minoru sensei koki kinenkai, ed., *Nihon bunka shi ronsō* (Osaka: Shibata Minoru sensei koki kinenkai, 1976).

tory activities by Kanetaka and Mitsuie in Ōta-no-shō continued for six or seven years after 1184 when the civil conflict was at its worst.

This shows clearly that the development of the local proprietor system undermined the *shōen* proprietor system. The fact that from the time of Yoritomo there was a *jitō* policy in effect constantly acted as a brake on illegal acts committed by *jitō* in *shōen*. After Kanetaka and Mitsuie were executed for siding with the Heike, Miyoshi Yoshinobu, who became the *jitō* of Ōta-no-shō, laid down in 1217 the following principles for managing the *shōen:*

1. A rice levy of *kachōmai* on fields graded at a yield of two *to* and three *to* per *tan* should be three *shō* per *tan* and on fields of lesser quality, one *shō* per *tan*.
2. Kantō coolie corvée should be four persons per year.
3. Long-term vegetable offerings should be borne by peasants where the *jitō*'s exemption from corvée is recognized by the proprietor; they should not levied on holders of *hyakushō-myō*.
4. The *myōden* fields of peasants who have absconded should not be absorbed into the *jitō*'s *myō*. If they are included, they should pay annual taxes and other dues (*kuji*) to the proprietor.
5. Intrusions into peasants' homes to avoid inauspicious directions in travel (*katatagae*) should be stopped.
6. With regard to mulberries, the precedent of Kanetaka's and Mitsuie's time should be followed.[63]
7. The *jitō*'s paddies (*tsukuda*) should be allocated to corvée-exempt peasants. The *myōden* of peasants (*hyakushō-myō*) should not be taken.
8. Farming should be encouraged by the deputy *jitō* (*jitō-dai*), who must discuss all matters with the representatives and *azukari-dokoro* of Kōyasan.
9. The *jitō-dai* should not impose fines.
10. Prohibitions against the taking of life should be observed.

This is much the same procedure as seen in *shōen* in other provinces, such as Kunitomi-no-shō in Wakasa. Here, because of the consolidation of the Kamakura bakufu's *jitō* policy (which was at the same time a *shōen* policy), there is none of the rough quality of local proprietorship as in the period of civil conflict. It was thus confirmed that the *shōen* landholding system began to break down during the civil wars of the Nambokuchō period and concluded under the cadastral surveys of Hideyoshi in the sixteenth century.

63 This meant to comply with precedents set before the civil disorder.

CHAPTER 3

THE DECLINE OF THE KAMAKURA
BAKUFU

INTRODUCTION

The 1260s marked the beginning of a decisively new period for the
Kamakura bakufu as it faced a set of increasingly complex problems
caused by changing conditions both at home and abroad.[1] The political structure of the bakufu was about to undergo a major change after

1 I have used the following sources in writing this article: (1) the *Azuma kagami*, a history-
chronicle in diary format written from the viewpoint of the bakufu and covering the years 1180
to 1266. Nothing replaces it after that date. (2) The "Kamakura nendai ki" and "Buke nendai
ki" are helpful, albeit partial, substitutes. I also used other diaries such as (3) "Kenji sannen
ki" and "Einin sannen ki." These and other diaries can be found in Takeuchi Rizō, comp.,
Zoku shiryō taisei, 22 vols. (Kyoto: Rinsen shoten, 1967). For political conditions within the
bakufu, documents in (4) "Kanezawa bunko komonjo," which include letters exchanged
among members of the Kanezawa (Hōjō) family, are important. The most inclusive document
collection for the Kamakura period is (5) *Kamakura ibun, komonjo hen* (thirty-six volumes to
date), compiled by Takeuchi Rizō. Other sources such as (6) *Kanagawa ken shi, shiryō hen*,
vols. 1 and 2; and (7) Seno Seiichirō, comp., *Kamakura bakufu saikyojō shū, jō, and ge* (Tokyo:
Yoshikawa kōbunkan, 1970) are useful. A comprehensive description and index to these and
other published documentary sources can be found in (8) pt. 2 of Jeffrey P. Mass, *The
Kamakura Bakufu: A Study in Documents* (Stanford, Calif.: Stanford University Press, 1976).
There is no index of this magnitude anywhere else. For the Kyoto side of Kamakura history,
diaries by nobles are important historical sources. The following are well known for this
period: (9) "Kitsuzokki" by Yoshida Tsunenaga and "Kanchū ki" by Fujiwara Kanenaka –
both in Sasagawa Taneo, ed., *Shiryō taisei* (Tokyo: Naigai shoten, 1937) – "Sanemikyō ki" by
Sanjō Sanemi (unpublished); and "Hanazono Tennō shinki" by Emperor Hanazono, in
Sasagawa, ed., *Shiryō taisei*. Historical chronicles such as the "Masukagami," "Godai teiō
monogatari," and "Hōryakukan ki" are also helpful. Many of the documents mentioned here
are included in the fifth edition of (10) the *Dai Nihon shiryō*, though the volumes covering the
Kamakura era have reached only 1248. In the meantime, readers are referred to (11) Tōkyō
daigaku shiryō hensanjo, ed., *Shiryō soran*, vol. 5 (Tokyo: Tōkyō daigaku shuppankai, 1965).
    Although there are many secondary works, the following are especially noteworthy: Miura
Hiroyuki, *Kamakura jidaishi*, vol. 5 of *Nihon jidashi* (Tokyo: Waseda daigaku shuppanbu,
1907, 1916), reprinted as *Nihonshi no kenkyū*, vol. 1 (Tokyo: Iwanami shoten, 1982) Ryō
Susumu, *Kamakura jidai, jō, ge* (Tokyo: Shunshūsha, 1957); Satō Shin'ichi, "Bakufu ron," in
Shin Nihon shi kōza, 7th series (Tokyo: Chūō kōronsha, 1949); Satō Shin'ichi, "Kamakura
bakufu seiji no senseika ni tsuite," in Takeuchi Rizō, comp., *Nihon hōkensei seiritsu no kenkyū*
(Tokyo: Yoshikawa kōbunkan, 1955), pp. 95–136; Kuroda Toshio, "Mōko shūrai," *Nihon no
rekishi*, vol. 8 (Tokyo: Chūō kōronsha, 1965); Amino Yoshihiko, *Mōko shūrai*, vol. 10 of *Nihon
no rekishi* (Tokyo: Shōgakkan, 1974); Amino Yoshihiko, "Kamakura makki no shomujun," in
Rekishigaku kenkyūkai and Nihonshi kenkyūkai, comps., *Kōza Nihonshi*, vol. 3 (Tokyo:
Tōkyō daigaku shuppankai, 1970), pp. 21–56; and Nitta Hideharu, "Kamakura kōki no seiji
katei," in *Iwanami kōza Nihon rekishi*, vol. 6 (Tokyo: Iwanami shoten, 1975), pp. 1–40.
Though Miura Hiroyuki's *Kamakura jidaishi* has not lost its value. During the postwar
period, Satō Shin'ichi's work led the field, and most recently, Amino Yoshihiko's "Mōko
shūrai" merits special attention as an innovative history.

the death of Hōjō Tokiyori in 1263, which in effect ended the "Golden Period" characterized by the regency (*shikken*) system. At the same time, changes in the social, economic, and technological spheres were beginning to shake the *shōen* system, which had been flourishing since the eleventh century. As examples of these changes, improved agricultural technology increased arable acreage, and the technique of double cropping – planting wheat after harvesting the rice – also enhanced productivity. The greater surplus in turn led to the diversification of agriculture, and as witnessed by the opening of periodic markets, commerce and trade likewise became more important. Simultaneously, peasants with free time or surplus means produced various handicrafts to be sold at market. A cash economy made advances as a large quantity of coins was imported from China, giving rise to financial middlemen and the practice of paying *shōen* taxes in cash.

These changes could not have taken place without influencing the overall social fabric. In various regions, cultivators rose up against the local *jitō* or *shōen* proprietors. In the meantime, the *jitō* and proprietors themselves began to compete, the worst of such confrontations occurring in the home provinces and the west, often involving military forces. Various groups of marauders, called *akutō*, whether of peasant or warrior origins, upset the peace and undermined the bakufu's original stabilizing aim.[2]

These domestic troubles were compounded by the precarious political conditions prevailing in the neighboring countries of East Asia, which eventually led to an extensive takeover by the Mongols and then to a series of attempted invasions of Japan, the greatest external attack on Japan in premodern times. The bakufu responded to this threat by consolidating its own power, by extending its hitherto weak political influence in western Japan, and by tightening its hold on the affairs of the court in Kyoto. This expansion of power presented an ideal opportunity for factions within the bakufu to strengthen their influence. The Hōjō clan, especially its main (*tokusō*) line, confirmed its already dominant position, whereas the *miuchibito* (private vassals of the *tokusō*) also enhanced their power. The period of so-called autocratic rule by the *tokusō* began after the Shimotsuki incident of 1285, in which a group of powerful *gokenin* represented by Adachi Yasumori was eliminated.

At first, the rise of the *tokusō* and the *miuchibito* factions, accompany-

---

2 The most recent work on the topic of *akutō* is by Koizumi Yoshiaki, *Akutō* (Tokyo: Kyōikusha, 1981).

ing the strengthened national position of the bakufu seemed to mark
the peak of Kamakura political power. However, this proved to be
illusory, as the general trend was toward greater internal strife and
dissatisfaction which soon mushroomed into a serious antibakufu
movement. There were, in fact, many causes for the warriors' dissatisfaction, one being the lack of reward land in the aftermath of the
Mongol invasions. Already by the time of the invasions many *gokenin*
were impoverished, owing to the continued parcelization of landholding under the divided inheritance system, as well as to their involvement in the growing cash economy, which undermined their traditional economic base. Because the warriors were expected to bear the
expenses of their military service, the invasions compounded their
financial difficulties, and many ended up losing their lands, by either
selling or pawning them. The presence of a large number of landless
gokenin thus posed a major problem to the bakufu.

To rescue the small and medium-sized *gokenin* houses in the last
stages of collapse, the bakufu used a radical measure, ordering the
cancellation of the *gokenin*'s debts and the return of their pawned land
at no cost. But this emergency relief measure saved the financially
strained *gokenin* only temporarily, and many houses were subsumed by
others – the *shugo, miuchibito*, or even *akuto* warriors who acquired
wealth through commerce, trade, or financial activities.

Each warrior house was being reorganized as well, adding to the
dissatisfaction of the displaced family members. This transformation
was characterized by two concurrent patterns. First, the divided inheritance gradually gave way to unitary inheritance, which granted the
entire family holding to the head, to whom his siblings were then
required to subordinate themselves. Second, the link between the
family's main line (*honke*) and its branch lines (*bunke*) gradually weakened, as the latter formed strong ties with other warrior houses in their
geographical areas, becoming in the process more independent of their
former blood relations.

Set against this turbulent background, the Hōjō's autocratic rule
further intensified the warriors' dissatisfaction. But the greatest crisis
for the bakufu occurred when a worsening intracourt rivalry propelled
the emperor, Godaigo, to take the lead in an antibakufu movement.
The imperial line had split into two branches which competed for both
the imperial title and rights to *shōen*. Placed in the role of arbitrator,
the bakufu resolved to have the two branches reign in alternate succession. The bakufu's involvement in these matters allowed it tighter
control over the inner workings of the court but at the same time

caused bakufu enmity and resentment from the losers in this competition. Emperor Godaigo, in particular, resented the bakufu's intervention in court affairs, which heightened his desire to return the country to a *tennō*-centered national governance. Godaigo thus took every opportunity to fan the anti-Hōjō and antibakufu sentiments manifested in the *gokenin*'s unrest and the *akuto*'s spreading activities. Godaigo's plan to topple the bakufu was not immediately successful, however, and its failure in 1331 led to his exile to Oki Island. But once this movement was under way, the rebellion spread quickly from the home provinces to the rest of the country. In 1333, the Kamakura bakufu was overthrown.

THE MONGOL INVASIONS AND THE KAMAKURA BAKUFU

The arrival of diplomatic messages from the Yüan

By the early 1260s, Kublai Khan, grandson of the great Genghis Khan, headed the Mongol tribes which had by then built an extensive empire encompassing a large portion of Eurasia.[3] To the Mongols, Japan was desirable owing to its proximity to Korea and its relations with the Southern Sung. In 1266, Kublai made his first overture to Japan by sending a letter through the king of Koryŏ, who was ordered to dispatch an intermediary to accompany the Yüan messenger. This first messenger, however, was prevented from crossing to Japan and

3 Much has been published on topics related to the Mongol invasions. A recent publication, *Mōko shūrai kenkyū shi ron*, by Kawazoe Shōji (Tokyo: Yūzankaku, 1977) contains a nearly complete bibliography that is concisely annotated. Here, I shall list only works of particular importance or those used in this essay. For nonspecialists, the following works are useful: Kawazoe Shōji, *Gen no shūrai* (Tokyo: Popurasha, 1975); Yamaguchi Osamu, *Mōko shūrai* (Tokyo: Jōsha, 1964, 1979); Hatada Takashi, *Genkō–Mōko teikoku no naibu jijō* (Tokyo: Chūō kōronsha, 1965); Abe Yukihiro, *Mōko shūrai* (Tokyo: Kyōikusha, 1980). The works of Yamaguchi and Hatada are important for their view from a wider East Asian perspective. Abe's work is the most recent, but because it is not entirely reliable, I would recommend Kawazoe's work more highly. As for document collections, Yamada An'ei's *Fukuteki hen*, 2 vols. (Tokyo: Yoshikawa kōbunkan, 1981) is still an extremely useful classic, unsurpassed by any later publications. The best compilation of materials related to the defense effort per se appears in Kawazoe Shōji, *Chūkai, Genkō bōrui hennen shiryō–Ikoku keigo banyaku shiryō no kenkyū* (Fukuoka: Fukuokashi kyōiku iinkai, 1971). This is an important work that includes many useful notes.

   Several monographs should be mentioned. A treatment of the Mongols from an East Asian perspective was attempted by Ikeuchi Hiroshi in his *Genko no shin kenkyū*, 2 vols. (Tokyo: Tōyō bunko, 1931). A quarter of a century later Aida Nirō wrote *Mōko shūrai no kenkyū*, which analyzed the invasions from the angle of Japan's internal political conditions (Tokyo: Yoshikawa kōbunkan, 1971) This book had an immense impact on later research. In English, there is an article by Hori Kyotsu, "The Economic and Political Effects of the Mongol Wars," in John W. Hall and Jeffrey P. Mass, eds., *Medieval Japan: Essays in Institutional History* (New Haven, Conn., Yale University Press, 1974).

thus returned to China without accomplishing his diplomatic task. In the following year an angry Kublai issued a strict order to the king of Koryŏ to take responsibility for getting the Yüan letter to Japan. Given no choice, the Korean king attached a letter of explanation to the letter from the Yüan and provided, as before, a guide for the Yüan messenger. The group arrived in Dazaifu, Kyushu, in the first month of 1268.

The letter carried by the Yüan envoy contained roughly the following message:

From time immemorial, rulers of small states have sought to maintain friendly relations with one another. We, the Great Mongolian Empire, have received the Mandate of Heaven and have become the master of the universe. Therefore, innumerable states in far-off lands have longed to form ties with us. As soon as I ascended the throne, I ceased fighting with Koryŏ and restored their land and people. In gratitude, both the ruler and the people of Koryŏ came to us to become our subjects; their joy resembles that of children with their father. Japan is located near Koryŏ and since its founding has on several occasions sent envoys to the Middle Kingdom. However, this has not happened since the beginning of my reign. This must be because you are not fully informed. Therefore, I hereby send you a special envoy to inform you of our desire. From now on, let us enter into friendly relations with each other. Nobody would wish to resort to arms.[4]

At this time, the man governing Dazaifu was Mutō (Shōni) Sukeyoshi, the *shugo* of three northern Kyushu provinces. Upon receiving this message, Sukeyoshi forwarded it to Kamakura.

Changes in the bakufu

The letter from Dazaifu reached Kamakura in 1268. But before examining the bakufu's response, I shall first discuss certain internal changes in Kamakura in the years following Hōjō Tokiyori's death in 1263. In the judicial sector, a new post, the *osso bugyō*, was created to examine judgments that might be appealed. The first appointees were Hōjō (Kanezawa) Sanetoki[5] and Adachi Yasumori, both former heads of courts in the bakufu's main investigatory agency, the *hikitsuke*.

4 Readers are referred to the writings left by the contemporary monk Soshō of Tōdaiji (called 'Mōko koku chō jō'), as well as the following published works: Yamada, An'ei, ed., *Fukuteki hen*, and Takeuchi Rizō, comp., *Kamakura ibun*, vol. 13 (Tokyo: Tōkyōdō, 1977) doc, 9564.
5 The son of Saneyasu, who was in turn the youngest son of Hōjō Yoshitoki. He was called Kanazawa because he had had a villa built in Kanezawa District (Musashi Province) just to the east of Kamakura. Sanetoki is particularly well known for the Kanezawa *bunko* (Kanazawa archive), a library housing a large number of Japanese and Chinese publications that he established at his villa.

Sanetoki was a brother of the new regent, Tokimune's mother, and he had been highly regarded by the late regent Tokiyori. Yasumori was the head of the Adachi family which for many generations had maintained close ties with the Hōjō. He was also the father of Tokisume's young wife. Thus the two men who represented the lines of Tokimune's mother and wife became leading figures in the reorganized bakufu. Inasmuch as they had played dominant roles in the bakufu under Tokiyori, their continuing positions of importance reflected the bakufu's desire to maintain Tokiyori's basic policies, which were strengthening the Hōjō grip over the bakufu's consultative structure and securing the *gokenin*'s trust by improving the operations of the judicial system. The appointments of Tokimune, Sanetoki, and Yasumori fulfilled the first goal, and the establishment of the *osso bugyō* sought to satisfy the *gokenin* who demanded fair judgments.

In general, these efforts were designed to counter certain internal conflicts that began to surface after Tokiyori's death. The Nagoe line of the Hōjō, descended from Yoshitoki's second son, was now in a position to challenge the main Hōjō line, the *tokusō*. The pattern of appointments to major bakufu positions illustrates this internal friction. For instance, in 1264, Tokiaki, the head of the Nagoe, secured the position of chief of the *hikitsuke*, the third most important job in the bakufu following those of regent and cosigner (*shikken* and *rensho*). Nevertheless, Tokiaki was not granted a post in the newly formed *osso bugyō*. Moreover, the *hikitsuke* itself was abolished suddenly in 1266/3, and its responsibilities were diverted to the regent and cosigner, assisted by the Board of Inquiry (*monchūjo*). This action effectively removed Nagoe Tokiaki from his primary base of power in the bakufu.

Several months later a private conference held at Tokimune's residence revealed the composition of a new power bloc. Itself an extension of the *yoriai*, a secret meeting initiated by Tokiyori years earlier to discuss critical matters, the conference was attended by Tokimune, Masamura, Sanetoki, and Yasumori. At the meeting the four men decided to replace the shogun, Prince Munetaka, with his three-year-old son Koreyasu. Although we do not know the motive behind this decision (an alleged affair between the shogun's wife and a certain monk was reported), the explanation given to Kyoto was simply a "rebellion by the shogun." More plausibly, the bakufu's leadership may have sensed a potentially threatening tie between the shogun and the opposition group and so took the offensive to foreclose any trouble.

It was just at the point when Kamakura was astir with rumors regarding the shogun's forced return to Kyoto that the messenger from Koryŏ arrived bearing the letter from the Mongols.

The bakufu's response to the Yüan letter

The Mongols' demand for a peaceful relationship with Japan posed a serious problem to the bakufu. The text of their letter did not seem threatening: It called for peace, not subjugation. In addition, the appended letter from the king of Koryŏ stressed that Kublai's goal was prestige for his dynasty rather than conquest. Yet at the same time, the wording of the Mongol letter could be interpreted more ominously, and thus the bakufu had to contemplate its response carefully.

Kamakura's first consideration may indeed have been Japan's ability to handle diplomatic negotiations. Even though Japan and the Southern Sung maintained commercial ties, formal diplomacy between the two countries had been in abeyance since the late ninth century, which meant that Japan lacked the necessary skill and confidence to assess international conditions. Second, it is likely that Japan's perception of the Mongols was extremely biased, inasmuch as the information it received about China came from either its Sung trading partners or from Buddhist monks, both of whom regarded the Mongols as unwelcome invaders. In particular, the Zen monks, many of whom were patronized by the Hōjō,[6] had come from Southern China and must have been vocal in their opposition to the Yüan request.

Moreover, the bakufu was not the ultimate diplomatic authority in Japan. The Yüan letter had been addressed to the "King of Japan," not to the bakufu, and thus in the second month of 1268 the letter was sent to Kyoto, where it was ignored. This decision, ostensibly made by the ex-emperor Gosaga, probably complied with the bakufu's own view of the matter.

In the meantime, the implementation of actual defense measures rested with Kamakura. Even before the court had reached its formal decision, the bakufu issued a directive to the *shugo* of Sanuki Province in Shikoku, stating: "Recently, we learned that the Mongols have become inclined toward evil and are now trying to subdue Japan.

---

6 Hōjō Tokiyori was a devout follower of Rankei Dōryū, a Chinese Zen monk who migrated to Japan in 1246 and built the Kenchōji in Kamakura. Tokiyori also patronized Gottan Funei, who arrived in Japan in 1260. In subsequent years, both Tokiyori and Tokimune invited Zen monks from the Southern Sung. Among the monks who came to Japan, Mugaku Sogen came to be highly respected among the Ji sect believers. Interestingly, he had been a victim of Yüan suppression in Sung China.

Quickly inform the *gokenin* in your province, and secure the nation's defense." Even though this is the only such directive that survives, we may assume that all *shugo* in the western region received a similar order. The Mongols, of course, were active during this period. In the fifth month of 1268, Kublai ordered Koryŏ to construct one thousand battleships and to conscript ten thousand men, explaining that such preparations were necessary because of the possibility of rebellion by either the Southern Sung or Japan. Despite their public, diplomatic posture, the Mongols were in fact proceeding with their preparations for armed conflict. Nevertheless, Kublai continued to dispatch envoys and letters to Japan via Koryŏ. After the first envoy was forced to return to Koryŏ empty-handed, Kublai sent a second in the eleventh month of 1268. Together with a Korean guide, the Yüan envoy arrived in the second month of 1269 at the island of Tsushima. Instead of completing his mission, however, he had a confrontation with the local Japanese and so returned to Korea, taking with him two Japanese as captives.

The Japanese were taken to the Mongol capital to meet with the khan who stressed once again that his only desires were to have official representatives visit the Japanese court and to have his name remembered for generations thereafter. Kublai then ordered the return of the two Japanese, to be accompanied by another envoy carrying an imperial letter. Koryŏ was again made responsible for delivering the letter, and in the ninth month of 1269, this group arrived in Tsushima. The overture was no more successful than its predecessors – yet the Mongols persisted on the diplomatic front. For example, drafts of letters dated the first and second months of 1270 stated: "The use of military force without reason runs counter to Confucian and Buddhist teachings. Because Japan is a divine country [*shinkoku*], we do not intend to fight with force." Nonetheless, the bakufu advised the court not to respond, and as before, the envoy returned empty-handed.

The invasion's imminence

The timing and actual execution of a plan to invade Japan were closely tied to changing conditions in Koryŏ, which, from the sixth month of 1269, was in disorder, owing to the king's dethronement and reinstallment, and a civil war. By taking advantage of this situation, the Mongols were able to strengthen their hold on Koryŏ and thus facilitate their advance into Japan. In the twelfth month of 1270, Kublai appointed Chao Liang-pi as a special envoy to Japan and simultaneously stationed an army in Koryŏ. This led to Kublai's final campaign to induce a peaceful settlement. In the meantime, he launched a major offensive against rebel elements in Koryŏ itself, using a combined force of Mongols and Koreans. In the fifth month of 1271, these rebel elements were defeated, though some of them relocated to the south and continued their resistance.[7]

In 1271, Japan received a message from Koryŏ that warned of the Mongol advance and requested reinforcements of food and men. Recently discovered evidence suggests that the messenger carrying this letter to Japan was a member of the rebel force. It is evident that the rebels tried to retaliate against the Mongol expansion by warning Japan, even as their own country was serving as Kublai's agent. Although this overture did not yield concrete results, it does reveal the complex international relations of that time.

For their part, the Japanese were now induced to step up their defense by mobilizing even more warriors to protect Kyushu. Accordingly, the bakufu issued an order in the ninth month of 1271 that stated: "We have received news that an invasion is imminent. All *gokenin* who hold land in Kyushu must return to Kyushu immediately, in order to fortify the land and pacify local outlaws [*akutō*]."[8] Before this order was issued, only the *gokenin* living in Kyushu had been held responsible for preparing that island's defense.

Shortly thereafter, the Mongol envoy, Chao Liang-pi, arrived in Dazaifu with a letter. Although its message repeated much of what the previous letters had stated, Chao added the warning that unless Japan replied by the eleventh month, the Mongols were prepared to dispatch their battleships. The court's inclination was to issue an official response, but by the new year Chao was forced to return to Koryŏ without having obtained a reply. It seems that the bakufu had once again vetoed that court's decision to respond – even in the negative. After two more attempts to elicit a response (in 1272/5 and

---

7 Ishii Masatoshi, "Bun'ei hachinen rainichi no Kōraishi ni tsuite – Sanbetsushō no Nihon tsūkō shiryō no shōkai," *Tōkyō daigaku shiryō hensanjo hō* 12 (March 1978): 1–7.
8 It is important to note that the bakufu's order emphasized both the national defense and the suppression of *akutō*. Eastern warriors who were ordered to their holdings in Kyushu did not, however, leave immediately. For example, Shodai, a *gokenin* from Musashi Province, moved to his Higo Province holding only in the fifth month of 1275, and comparatively speaking, this was probably one of the earlier cases. At the end of 1286, the bakufu complained that there were still those who had not made the move. See Gomi Katsuo, "Nitta-gū shitsuin Michinori gushoan sonota," *Nihon rekishi*, no. 310 (March 1974): 13–26. Those warriors who held powerful positions within the bakufu were not obligated to move to Kyushu but were instead to send men of ability in their place.

1273/3), Chao finally notified Kublai of his failure. The Mongols subsequently gave Japan seven more opportunities to change its mind, but Japan's hard-line policy was already fixed. The Mongols eventually realized that force was the only means left for fulfilling their diplomatic goal.[9]

The Kamakura bakufu's response

As invasion seemed more and more inevitable the bakufu decided to consolidate its internal structure. First, it attempted to ease the split in the Hōjō family by reinstituting the *hikitsuke* system in the fourth month of 1269, three years after its abolition. The five units of the *hikitsuke* system now were made to include both main-line and anti-main-line Hōjō members: Nagoe Tokiaki (head of the first unit), Kanazawa Sanetoki (head of the second unit), Adachi Yasumori (head of the fifth unit), and two other Hōjō members. Each unit head represented a branch of the Hōjō, and together they formed a system similar to a coalition government. Nevertheless, the intrabakufu antagonisms intensified and exploded in 1272 in the form of the Nigatsu disturbance, in which many warriors and courtiers who opposed the *tokusō* were murdered. In Kamakura, the victims included Nagoe Tokiaki, his brother Noritoki, and a number of courtiers who had come from Kyoto to serve the shogun. In Kyoto itself, the most prominent person executed was Hōjō Tokisuke, who was the the Rokuhara *tandai* (a shogunal deputy stationed at Rokuhara in southeastern Kyoto to supervise the political, military, and judicial affairs of southwestern Japan) and an aggrieved elder brother of the regent Tokimune.

Soon after Tokiaki's death, the incident took on a new twist: Tokiaki was declared innocent, and instead, the five Hōjō *miuchibito* actually responsible for the murder were eliminated. The murderer of Noritoki received neither praise nor punishment, only ridicule. In sum, the incident was a concrete manisfestation of the serious instability within the bakufu. As far as we can determine, in the wake of the purge of the anti-main-line Hōjō by the *miuchibito*, the *miuchibito* themselves became the targets of condemnation and were accordingly eliminated. This bizarre episode was described as follows by an observer,

9 Some historians interpret the bakufu's rigid attitude toward this matter as a conscious policy to intensify the external crisis in order to deflect the impact of internal problems, such as the rise of *akutō*. This theory implies that the bakufu consciously invited the Mongols to attack Japan. For an example of this view, see Abe Yukihiro, *Mōko shūrai*. I would argue that this interpretation reflects too much the view of the world today.

Kanazawa Akitoki: "After 1269, life became disorderly for one reason or another. Mine or yours, one's life was never safe."

Once the Nigatsu disturbance had been settled, the bakufu issued an order to the provincial authorities to submit land surveys (ōtabumi) detailing the names of owners and the dimensions of local lands used as the basis for taxation and the conscription of gokenin. The timing of this order suggests that the bakufu was finally beginning to investigate the human and economic resources that could contribute to Japan's military potential. As early as 1267, the bakufu had issued an order prohibiting the sale, pawning, or transfer of gokenin land to nonrelatives and had authorized the return of holdings already sold or pawned in exchange for repayment of the original price. This order was rescinded in 1270, but a year after the submission of the ōtabumi, a new regulation was put into effect guaranteeing the return without cost of any pawned gokenin land. The bakufu further attempted to improve its vassals' situations by ordering the submission of lists containing the names of lands that had been lost as well as those of the new owners.

The invasion of 1274

In the second month of 1273, the Southern Sung defense line fell to the Mongols, and a collapse seemed close at hand. In the fourth month, the rebel elements of Koryŏ were finally put down. It had been two years since Kublai had changed the name of his dynasty to Ta Yüan in the Chinese style, and he was now ready to expand his empire even further. There remained no geographical obstacle to his moving forcefully against Japan.

Accordingly, the khan appointed joint commanders of an expeditionary force that was to sail in the seventh month of 1274. Koryŏ was likewise given an order to build and dispatch a fleet of nine hundred battleships and an army of five thousand men. Even though many of the ships of extremely poor quality – the product of hasty workmanship in response to the conqueror's order – the required number was prepared in time.

On the third day of the tenth month, three months later than the original plan, the expeditionary force consisting of 15,000 Yüan soldiers, 8,000 Koryŏ soldiers, and 67,000 ship workers sailed toward Japan. Departing from Koryŏ, they attacked Tsushima two days later and defeated Sō Munesuke, the deputy shugo, and about 80 other mounted soldiers. On the fourteenth day, they attacked Iki Island where the deputy shugo, Taira Kagetaka, fought valiantly with a force of 100 mounted soldiers but was eventually defeated. Two weeks later, the Yüan–Koryŏ allied force settled in Hakata Bay and began landing in the western area of the bay around Imazu, Sawaraura, and Momojibara. From these points, they planned to move east, eventually to attack Hakata.

On the Japanese side, two powerful *shugo*, Ōtomo Yoriyasu and Mutō (Shōni) Sukeyoshi, the bakufu's twin Kyushu deputies (Chinzei *bugyō*), commanded a *gokenin* defense force. The sources do not tell us the size of the Japanese army, but we can assume it was much smaller than the Yüan–Koryŏ expeditionary force. The figure of 100,000 that appears in a Chinese account is obviously exaggerated.[10]

Fatigue from the long voyage seems not to have reduced the skill of the Yüan–Koryŏ soldiers in the art of collective fighting. Moreover, they used poisoned arrows and exploding devices, which the Japanese had never seen before. The Japanese warriors' one-to-one fighting method had little effect here. Despite some minor successes, the defenders were therefore forced to retreat, although in the end they escaped defeat because of a great storm that struck the harbor and destroyed a large part of the Yüan–Koryŏ fleet.

A vivid depiction of this war comes from a picture scroll commissioned by a small-scale *gokenin*, Takezaki Suenaga of Higo Province, to illustrate his meritorious acts. The scroll, called *Mōko shūrai ekotoba*,[11] notes that on the twentieth day of the tenth month, Suenaga mobilized his followers to join the battle of Hakozaki Bay, but because he heard that Hakata was being attacked, he and his men quickly headed there. When they arrived at Okinohama in Hakata, they found that many other warriors were already there. At this point, the commander,

---

10 We know of roughly 120 warriors who received rewards in 1275. Large bands such as those of the Kikuchi and Shiraishi supplied over 100 soldiers and horses, but smaller-scale warriors (like Takezaki Suenaga) could contribute only a handful. If we take the number 50 as a hypothetical average of mounted fighting men per house, the total would have been something over 6,000 defenders. But if we take 30 as the average, then the total would be only 3,600.

11 This is the standard name for the scroll, though *Takezaki Suenaga ekotoba* would be more appropriate, as it reflects Suenaga's point of view exclusively. He commissioned the scroll quite late, around 1293. Over the centuries it has received some damage, and accordingly I have used only those sections whose interpretations are not open to dispute. Several reproductions of the scroll are available: *Gyobutsubon, Mōko shūrai ekotoba (fukusei)* (Fukuoka: Fukuokashi kyōiku iinkai, 1975), which is a reproduction at three-fourths the original size; *Mōko shūrai ekotoba*, in *Nihon emaki taisei*, vol. 14 (Tokyo: Chūō kōronsha, 1978); *Heiji monogatari emaki, Mōko shūrai ekotoba*, vol. 9 of *Nihon emaki zenshū* (Tokyo: Kadokawa shoten, 1964). The first two are in color, and the last two contain descriptions and research notes that are extremely useful. As for the pronunciation and interpretation of the main text of the *ekotoba*, see Ishii Susumu et al., eds., *Chūsei seiji shakai shisō, jō* vol. 21 of *Nihon shisō taikei* (Tokyo: Iwanami shoten, 1972), pp. 415–28.

Mutō Kagesuke (Sukeyoshi's second son), ordered a joint operation to push back the enemy force. Inasmuch as Suenaga had only five mounted soldiers under him, he determined that the situation at Okinohama provided little opportunity for glory, and thus he took his small force to another battle area called Akasaka. There the powerful warrior of Higo Province, Kikuchi Takefusa, was pushing the enemy into retreat, and Suenaga saw his chance. He joined the attack, but soon one of his men was shot, and Suenaga himself and the three others received heavy injuries and lost their horses. He was saved by Shiraishi Michiyasu of Hizen Province, who galloped in at this point at the head of a force of more than one hundred men.

Suenaga's performance exemplified the Japanese manner of fighting, which contrasted markedly with that of the enemy. The soldiers of Yüan–Koryŏ moved collectively in an orderly fashion with spears lined up, following the beat of drums and signals. But this is not to say that all Japanese fighting men were as eager as Suenaga to place personal distinction first. After the invasion, the bakufu complained that some warriors, though present, refused to fight or, in other cases, refused to change locations.

The war reached a climax at dusk on the twentieth day. The Japanese army abandoned the Hakata and Hakozaki areas and retreated to the remains of an ancient fortress at Mizuki in order to defend Dazaifu, located some sixteen kilometers from the shore. The Yüan–Koryŏ force, however, had also suffered losses. In particular, the deputy commander of the Yüan army, Liu Fu-heng, had been wounded by an arrow shot by Mutō Kagesuke. The Mongol leaders made a fateful decision to withdraw, because of manpower and supply problems. By the next morning a major portion of their fleet had simply vanished. It is not clear whether the storm struck while the ships were still in Hakata Bay or when they were passing the Islands of Iki and Tsushima on their way back to Koryŏ. In any case, the force's return trip took more than a month. On the twenty-seventh day of the eleventh month, after spending more than twice the time normally required to cross the channel, the fleet arrived back in Korea. A surviving record shows that more than 13,500 persons, roughly one-third of the entire expeditionary force, did not return. Contemporary Japanese sources called the great storm that saved Japan *kamikaze*, the "divine wind."[12]

12 The accepted theory of Japanese historians in the post-Meiji era is that the Yüan–Koryŏ fleet encountered the storm on the night of the twentieth day of the tenth month. But in 1958, a meteorologist, Arakawa Hidetoshi, published a controversial article entitled, "Bun'ei no eki

Japan after the Bun'ei invasion

The aftermath of any major premodern war in Japan was the occasion for granting rewards for meritorious service. Although this had been an external invasion that did not produce enemy lands to be distributed, the warriors who participated in the defense submitted their demands anyway. In 1275, the bakufu rewarded some 120 deserving warriors for their services in the recent fighting, though for many other there were disappointments. The case of Takezaki Suenaga is illustrative.

In the sixth month of 1275, Suenaga left his home in Higo Province for Kamakura. Despite his brave participation in the defense effort, his deeds had not even been reported to the bakufu. His trip was thus to make a direct appeal. It is interesting that his relatives opposed the plan and refused to give him the needed material support to make the trip. Because he had earlier lost land in litigation and had become otherwise impoverished, he had to sell his horses and saddles in order to earn sufficient traveling money.

In the middle of the eighth month, Suenaga finally reached Kamakura and immediately attempted to contact various officials of the bakufu. But perhaps because of his unimpressive attire he was not even granted an audience. Luck did turn his way, however. In the tenth month, Suenaga succeeded in making his appeal to Adachi Yasumori, chief of the bakufu's rewards office (*go'on bugyō*). Yasumori pressed hard with various questions to which Suenaga replied as follows: "I am not appealing merely because I want a reward. If my claim to having fought in the vanguard be proved false, please cut off my head immediately. I have only one wish: for my merit to be known to the shogun. That would serve as a great encouragement in the event of another war." In the face of such unwavering insistence, Yasumori acknowledged Suenaga to be a loyal servant of the bakufu and promised to inform the shogun and to assist in the matter of rewards.

Suenaga's scroll vividly portrays this meeting, noting that Yasumori apparently kept his word: Among the 120 warriors rewarded, Suenaga was the only one who received the personal investiture (*kudashibumi*)

no owari o tsugeta no wa taifū dewa nai" (It was not a typhoon that ended the Bun'ei war), *Nihon rekishi*, no. 120 (June 1958): 41–45. This article caused a reevaluation of the traditionally accepted theory, and as a result, many new views were introduced. For an introductory summary and critique of these views, see Tsukushi Yutaka, *Genkō kigen* (Fukuoka: Fukuoka kyōdo bunkakai, 1972); and Kawazoe, *Mōko shūrai kenkyū shiron*.

of the shogun. In addition, Yasumori presented Suenaga with a prize horse, an act of benevolence that the recipient did not forget. In the testament that Suenaga left to his heir, he admonished his descendants to continue to honor their noble benefactor.[13]

Anticipating a second invasion, the bakufu quickly moved to strengthen its defense program. In 1275, vassals of the Kyushu region were ordered to organize into combined units of two to three provinces, each of which would serve a defense tour of three months per year. This service, called *ikoku keigo banyaku*,[14] constituted a heavy burden for the warriors of Kyushu, even more so as they had to mobilize instantly – in the event of a crisis – during their off-duty periods.

Aside from the shoreline defense duties, the bakufu enforced a series of measures designed to fortify the nation. Many of these programs, however, were intended at the same time to boost the power of the bakufu vis-à-vis the court, as well as the power of the *tokusō* vis-à-vis other warrior families. An earlier illustration of this double program dates from 1274, just before the withdrawal of the Mongol fleet in the Bun'ei invasion. Taking advantage of the emergency situation, the bakufu ordered the *shugo* of the western provinces to mobilize both *gokenin* and non-*gokenin* alike. This represented a clear expansion of the limits of bakufu jurisdiction nationally and *shugo* jurisdiction locally. Thus, to cite one example, the *shugo* of Aki Province requisitioned more than one hundred ships and confiscated a shipment of rice that had been prepared as a tax (*nengu*) payment to a Kyoto *shōen* owner. Moreover, the bakufu ordered the eastern *gokenin* who held lands in the western part of the Sanyō and San'in areas to proceed to their holdings. This was a further attempt by Kamakura to concentrate more men in the strategic war zones. However, the Mongols retreated before any of these vassals might have been sent to the battle front.

After the Bun'ei invasion, politically influential warriors replaced the *shugo* of certain strategically located provinces. In eight of the eleven cases confirmed by historians, Hōjō family members were appointed as *shugo*. In the other three provinces, Adachi Yasumori and his allies were appointed as *shugo*. This allowed the Hōjō to increase the number of *shugo* posts under their control and meant that the nation's

---

13 The relevant section was appended to the *Mōko shūrai ekotoba* under the title "Yasumori no onkoto" (Honorable matters pertaining to Yasumori).
14 On this topic, see Kawazoe, *Chūkai, Genkō bōrui hennen shiryō*.

defense fell more and more under the direct supervision of the key figures occupying the center of the bakufu.[15]

Kamakura also made new arrangements for protecting the capital. It dispatched to Kyoto the elderly and respected Hōjō Tokimori and other warriors of renown. At the same time, all fighting men – *gokenin* and non-*gokenin* – of Yamashiro Province were made responsible for Kyoto guard duty (*ōbanyaku*), whereas warriors from Kyushu were now exempted. Moreover, so as not to burden the populace unnecessarily, the bakufu encouraged both warriors and courtiers to live frugally. Kamakura also ordered the country's *shugo* to urge provincial temples and shrines to dedicate special prayers for the defeat of the enemy and for protection of the divine land.

Finally, the plans for defense included a retaliatory strategy to attack Koryŏ, the Yüan base for invading Japan. Extant documents from Kyushu and Aki Province show that orders were issued from the last part of 1275 through the following spring to mobilize warriors and prepare battleships, as well as to recruit ships' crews for an expedition. Those recruited included not only *jitō* and *gokenin* but also warriors that were not vassals of the bakufu. From available sources we cannot determine the extent to which these plans were put into effect, although of course there was no actual attack on Koryŏ.

The monument that testifies to the bakufu's effort to secure the country is a series of stone walls along the coastline around Hakata Bay. Although only a portion of the original structure remains today, the walls stretched 20 kilometers east and west of Hakata and generally stood 50 meters inland from the shoreline and were approximately 1.5 to 2.8 meters high and 1.5 to 3.4 meters wide at the bottom. The official schedule for the wall's construction stipulated the third month of 1276 as the beginning date and the eighth month of the same year as the completion date. However, it seems that the construction did not proceed as quickly as planned. For instance, Satsuma Province did not complete its contribution to the project until early in 1277. The responsibility for constructing the wall fell not only on Kyushu *gokenin* but also on various *shōen* officials, the extent of the duty corresponding to the size of individual landhold-

---

15 See Satō Shin'ichi's classic study, "Kamakura bakufu seiji no senseika ni tsuite," in Takeuchi Rizō. ed., *Nihon hōkensei seiritsu no kenkyū* (Tokyo: Yoshikawa kōbunkan, 1955). Subsequently, it was Murai Shōsuke who confirmed that the transfer of these *shugo* occurred in the latter part of 1275. See Murai Shōsuke, "Mōko shūrai to Chinzei tandai no seiritsu," *Shigaku zasshi* 87 (April 1978): 1–43. I have followed Murai's theory.

ings. One document from Ōsumi Province records a ratio of one *shaku* of wall for each *chō* of land held.[16]

In this way, the national mobilization effort permitted the bakufu an unprecedented right of command over officials hitherto outside its jurisdiction. The following example shows Kamakura's changing position in the nation's power balance: In order to provide strong leadership for the Inland Sea defense zone, Hōjō Muneyori, the younger brother of the *tokusō*, was appointed *shugo* of Nagato Province. In 1276, he recruited for service all warriors in the Sanyō and Nankai circuits, irrespective of their vassal status.

At the center of the bakufu during this period were Hōjō Tokimune and Adachi Yasumori. Hōjō Masamura and Kanazawa Sanetoki, the two other prominent figures in the post-Tokiyori era, had already died. Yasumori was Tokimune's father-in-law and had a major impact on policymaking in Kamakura. Miyoshi Yasuari recorded in his diary, *Kenji sannen ki*,[17] that twice during 1277 (in the tenth and twelfth months), Tokimune held private conferences (*yoriai*) at his residence. Tokiyori had started the practice of *yoriai*, which continued during Tokimune's rule, replacing the *hyōjōshū* (deliberative council) as the key arena for decision making. According to the *Kenji sannen ki*, the most important political and personnel decisions were made at the *yoriai*, which were attended by the most influential men of the era. In the same year, the right to recommend *gokenin* for traditional court offices was withdrawn from the *hyōjōshū* and became instead the shogun's sole prerogative. Thus, Tokimune and Miyoshi Yasuari (head of the *monchūjo*) are listed in the *Kenji sannen ki* as having attended four times; Adachi Yasumori, twice; Taira Yoritsuna (who headed a group of *miuchibito*), three times; and two other powerful *gokenin*, twice. The strength of a certain group of *miuchibito* at this time can be attributed to the influence of Adachi Yasumori who, at the conclusion of the Nigatsu disturbance, succeeded in promoting the status of such men despite his initial opposition to them. However, this harmonious balance of interests did not last long, as antagonisms were already beginning to surface between Yasumori and Taira Yoritsuna.

16 Kawazoe Shōji summarizes concisely the present state of research on the wall construction; see his "Kaisetsu," in *Chūkai, Genkō bōrui hennen shiryō*.
17 The main text of "Kenji sannen ki" appears on *Gunsho ruijū, bukebu*, vol. 421, though with a few errata. A better text is Takeuchi Rizō, comp., *Zoku shiryō taisei*, vol. 10 (Kyoto: Rinsen shoten, 1967). Ryō Susumu gives a detailed analysis of this diary in "Kenji sannen ki kō," in *Kamakura jidai, jō*, pp. 217–31.

The second Mongol invasion, 1281

Overtures from the Yüan did not cease after the Bun'ei invasion. In the fourth month of 1275, an envoy arrived in Muronotsu in Nagato, instead of at Dazaifu. The bakufu's response to this mission was harsher than before. The bakufu summoned the entire Yüan entourage in the eighth month and in the following month summarily executed them in the suburbs of Kamakura. In the meantime, the Yüan destroyed the capital of the Southern Sung in 1276 and captured the reigning Chinese emperor. By early 1279, the Southern Sung empire was completely destroyed. At this time, the invasion of Japan was once again put at the top of the Yüan agenda. Destruction of the Sung provided the Yüan with a new approach route to Japan. Instead of going through Korea, the Mongols could use the surrendered Sung navy dispatched from China itself. Another favorable condition for the Yüan was that Koryŏ was growing more complacent as the Yüan expanded their borders ever closer to Korea itself. This new set of circumstances formed the background for the Yüan's plan to attack Japan a second time.

The old Sung territory provided many of the resources for the invasion. In 1279, Kublai ordered the people of the lower Yangtze area to construct six hundred warships and consulted a commander of the Sung army regarding specific plans of action. On the advice he received, the khan sent another envoy to Japan, carrying a message warning that if Japan failed to submit, it would suffer the same fate that had struck the Sung. This envoy arrived in Japan in the sixth month, but as before, the court and bakufu refused to receive him. All the members of his mission were executed in Hakata.

During this period, Koryŏ continued to bear the burden of preparing battleships and their crews. This time, Kublai ordered 900 ships. In China proper, Kublai reinforced his plan administratively by establishing a new governmental organ, the Ministry for Conquering Japan. The official order to attack came in the first month of 1281. The entire army was divided into two divisions – the Eastern Route Division dispatched from Koryŏ and the Chiang-nan Division dispatched from southeast China. The Eastern Route Division had a combined force of 10,000 Koryŏ soldiers and 30,000 Mongols. Some 900 battleships carried 17,000 crew members in addition to the soldiers. The Chiang-nan Division was composed of 100,000 previously defeated Sung soldiers sailing on as many as 3,500 battleships. The two divisions were to merge in Iki and then proceed together to attack Japan proper. Before their departure, Kublai, who was aware of the potential disunity of this invasion plan, strongly emphasized the necessity for cooperation.

Preparations were also under way in Japan. Evidence indicates that Japan knew of the impeding invasion. According to a letter the bakufu sent to the *shugo* Ōtomo Yoriyasu in Kyushu, Kamakura was anticipating the attack before the fourth month of the following year and warned the *shugo* to consolidate their defense strategies. In the same letter, the bakufu noted that there had been a recent tendency for *shugo* and *gokenin* not to cooperate effectively.

The pattern of mobilization in Japan was the same as for the Bun'ei invasion. Kyushu warriors assembled around Hakata Bay. Using the newly constructed stone walls as barriers, they were to fight under the command of the Ōtomo and Mutō. Although the exact size of the Japanese force is unknown, we can assume that this one was larger than the previous one.[18] Adachi Morimune (Yasumori's second son) and the Shimazu of Southern Kyushu also served as generals, and the powerful *miuchibito* Andō and Goda came down from Kamakura to serve as military officials. It is clear that the Hōjō main line was attempting, as before, to consolidate its control. Overall, we can surmise that the proportionate growth in size was much greater for the combined Yüan armies than for the Japanese force.

On the third day of the fifth month of 1281, the Eastern Route Division left Koryŏ and by the end of the month attacked Tsushima and Iki. The original plan had called for the Eastern Route Division to meet the Chiang-nan Division there on the fifteenth day of the sixth month. But in violation of this agreement, the Eastern Route Division moved on toward Hakata Bay early in the sixth month, though owing to the stone walls, it was unable to land and thus occupied Shiga Island instead.

The Japanese army did not hesitate to pursue this fleet that was stationed just off the coastline. By using small boats or running up the causeway connecting the island to the mainland, the Japanese mounted an offensive. Takezaki Suenaga was again present and fought at the forefront of the Higo Province army, and his meritori-

---

18 No extant record reveals the size of the Japanese army in 1281. However, we can identify the names of most warriors who received awards from some seven surviving award listings. During the third granting session alone, Kanazaki estate in Hizen was the site of awards to more than four hundred warriors, a figure that already exceeds by a factor of three the number of known rewards in the Bun'ei war.

ous deeds were recognized by his commander, Adachi Morimune. Before the middle of the sixth month, the Yüan force abandoned Shiga Island and retreated to Iki. The Japanese army chased them, and thus the fighting continued.

In the meantime, because of the death of the Chiang-nan Division's commanding general, it was not able to leave Ningpo until the middle of the sixth month. The plan to merge with the Eastern Route Division was redirected from Iki to Hirado. In the seventh month the two divisions met, and from Hirado they headed toward their original destination, Hakata Bay. By the end of the seventh month, they had arrived at Takashima Island near Hizen Province where they confronted the Japanese army.

But just before the Yüan–Koryŏ force was about to launch its final offensive, a devastating storm hit the bay on the night of the thirtieth day of the seventh month. The generals of the Yüan army commandeered the remaining ships in order to return to Koryŏ, leaving large numbers of stranded soldiers to the mercy of the Japanese. Takezaki Suenaga took part in this phase of the fighting, and the record he commissioned testifies to his gallantry.

In the second Yüan expedition against Japan, the Mongol army lost 69 to 90 percent of its men, a total of more than 100,000 dead. Japan's success was attributed once again to the intercession of the gods. During the crisis, the bakufu continued to strengthen its authority. It received permission from the court to collect a commissariat tax from the public and private estates of Kyushu and the San'in provinces of western Honshū. Moreover, on the ninth day of the intercalary seventh month, the bakufu requested imperial approval to the conscript warriors from nonbakufu lands. Because the news concerning the Mongol retreat reached Kyoto at precisely the same time, this latter request was not immediately granted. However, the bakufu continued to press the emperor on the point, and on the twentieth day, an imperial edict was issued granting the bakufu this new authority. Interestingly, however, the edict was dated the ninth day, instead of the twentieth day, in order to legitimize the bakufu's purported need to expand its control in the name of national security.

Immediately following the defeat of the Yüan–Koryŏ army, Kamakura revived its earlier plan to attack Koryŏ. The plan stipulated that either the Mutō or the Ōtomo would lead a fighting force of *gokenin* from three northern Kyushu provinces as well as *akutō* from the Yamato and Yamashiro provinces. Extant records do not disclose how far this interesting strategy was pursued, but there is no evidence of a counterinvasion. In fact, Japan itself remained under the threat of attack,[19] and as a result, additional Hōjō were dispatched as *shugo* to Kyushu and the Sanyō areas. The *gokenin* of Kyushu, however, were prohibited to travel to Kyoto and Kamakura without the bakufu's authorization. Moreover, the vassals of Kyushu were expected to continue to serve regular defense duty, which now included three to four months of guard service in Kyushu or Nagato, the construction and repair of stone walls, and the contribution of military supplies such as arrows, spears, and flags. These responsibilities now fell on all warriors from Kyushu and not merely the *gokenin*. Some *shōen* proprietors apparently resisted this change, for in 1286 the bakufu decreed that in the event of noncompliance, Kamakura would appoint a *jitō* to the offending estate.

JAPAN AFTER THE MONGOL WARS

The bakufu in the postcrisis period

The years immediately following the second Mongol attack were characterized by innovative regulations, judicial reform, and increasingly intense factional conflicts. In 1284, the regent Hōjō Tokimune died suddenly at age thirty-four and was succeeded by his fourteen-year-old heir, Hōjō Sakatoki. The new regent's advisers immediately enacted changes by issuing new codes and restructuring the judicial organ. In the fifth month of 1284, the bakufu issued a thirty-eight-article "new formulary" (*shin shikimoku*) and then followed this collection of behavioral standards with eighty specific regulations based on these codes.

The new legislation dealt with a wide range of concerns. For example, the shogun was to observe propriety and frugality in all aspects of his life and to devote himself to proper learning. The shogun's lands (the *kantō goryō*) were to be supervised more tightly, and the country's official provincial shrines and temples (*ichinomiya* and *kokubunji*) were to be protected, promoted, and repaired. In Kyushu, not only *ichinomiya* but all shrines received special attention; for instance, shrine land that has been pawned was to be returned to the shrine at

19 In 1283, Kublai established the Office for Advancing East and, at the same time, sent another envoy to Japan who unfortunately encountered a storm and was forced to return to China. After suppressing a rebellion in the Chiang-nan area, Kublai dispatched another envoy in 1284 who got only as far as Tsushima before he was killed. Further plans for an advance against Japan were complicated as the Mongol Empire became increasingly embroiled in domestic rebellions. Kublai's death in 1294 ended further expeditionary attempts. Nevertheless, Japan did not abandon its defense measures until the end of the Kamakura era.

no cost, as an expression of gratitude for the prayers that had been said at the time of the Mongol invasions.

Land rewards were to be granted to those Kyushu *shōen* officers and smaller holders (*myōshu*) who, despite their service during the wars, had not yet received compensation. The regulation further stipulated that land that had been sold or pawned be returned to them without penalty. To implement this provision, the bakufu dispatched a special envoy of three *hikitsuke* magistrates to Kyushu. These officials were called *tokusei no ontsukai* (agents of virtuous rule) and were viewed as the administrators of a rescue mission. There is evidence that around the same time, *gokenin* outside Kyushu were given similar protection.[20] These *tokusei* measures of 1284 were considerably more inclusive than the one issued in 1273, which guaranteed only pawned property.

With respect to the *akutō*, the bakufu dispatched special agents to suppress their activities in the Kinai and neighboring provinces. These agents were to cooperate with local *shugo* in maintaining peace and order in especially troubled areas.

Nevertheless, in 1284 the bakufu focused primarily on consolidating its rule in Kyushu. Until the 1260s, the powerful *shugo* families of Mutō and Ōtomo had jointly held the title of Chinzei *bugyō*. But under the changed circumstance of the invasion era, it was now deemed necessary to establish an autonomous judicial authority in Kyushu to prevent local *gokenin* from traveling to Kyoto or Kamakura to file lawsuits. Thus, the three *tokusei* agents, together with the Mutō and Ōtomo families and Adachi Morimune, came to form a three-unit judicial structure in which each unit was responsible for judging cases from three provinces each. This court was housed in a building in Hakata,[21] and this office served as the governmental organ responsible for enforcing *tokusei* measures as well as delivering judicial decisions.

The judicial system of Kamakura was also reformed in this year. In the eighth month, the bakufu issued an eleven-article code that enjoined the *hikitsu-keshū* and its magistrates to carry out their jobs faithfully and attempted to remove the influence of powerful persons in judicial decision making. Interestingly, much consideration was given to poor *gokenin* who needed to be rescued by the courts. There were some procedural changes as well. Previously, the *hikitsuke* official who

20 Kasamatsu Hiroshi, *Nihon chūsei-hō shiron* (Tokyo: Tōkyō daigaku shuppankai, 1979, p. 104.
21 Satō Shin'ichi, *Kamakura bakufu soshō seido no kenkyū* (Tokyo: Meguro shoten, 1946), pp. 287–91.

was assigned a suit drafted two or three alternative verdicts that were then presented to the *hyōjōshū* for the final decision. But under the new procedure, only a single verdict was forwarded to the *hyōjōshū*, and the authority of the *hikitsuke* was dramatically increased.[22]

Adachi Yasumori, the maternal grandfather of the young regent Sadatoki was influential in promoting these reforms. Since his initial appointment to the post of appeals magistrate (*osso bugyō*) after Tokiyori's death, he had consistently sought to maintain the support of the *gokenin* through efficient administration of the judicial system.[23] Moreover, although the Adachi family had built a strong power base by acting in concert with the Hōjō, they had always stressed as well their continuing close ties with the shogun.[24] In opposition to Yasumori and his followers was a group represented by Taira Yoritsuna, who was a partisan of both the *tokusō* and the *miuchibito*. Before his death, it had been the regent Tokimune who acted as the arbiter between these two contending groups, but after the accession of the youthful Sadatoki in 1284, conditions deteriorated rapidly.

The Shimotsuki incident: the fall of Adachi Yasumori

In the eleventh month of 1285, Taira Yoritsuna suddenly attacked Adachi Yasumori and his followers, claiming to have been ordered to do so by the regent. For half a day a fierce battle was fought in Kamakura, but Yasumori and his followers were surprised in the attack and were soon killed. Because this disturbance occurred in the month of the "frosty moon," a contemporary record referred to it as the "Shimotsuki" incident. The events leading up to the incident are not clear, but according to one theory, Adachi Munekage, Yasumori's heir, was accused of plotting to usurp the shogun's seat on the pretext that his ancestor Kagemori was actually a son of Yoritomo. In view of the traditionally close ties between the Adachi and the Minamoto families, Munekage's decision to change his surname to Minamoto cannot by itself be interpreted as masking some ulterior motive. It is

22 Satō Shin'ichi stresses this point in ibid., pp. 69–76.
23 Yasumori was not only the most remarkable political figure of his era; he was also a learned scholar of the Confucian classics and of Buddhism. For a biographical sketch, see Taga Munehaya, "Akita Jō-no-suke Adachi Yasomuri," in Taga Munehaya, *Kamakura jidai no shisō to bunka* (Tokyo: Meguro shoten, 1946), pp. 247–79.
24 The sister of Yasumori's grandfather Kagemori was the wife of Yoritomo's younger brother Noriyori. Kagemori took Buddhist vows after the death of Sanetomo, the third shogun, and Yasumori himself was highly regarded by Sanetomo's widow. On one occasion, Yasumori found a sword named Higekirimaru that had been left by Yoritomo in Kyoto, and he respectfully returned it to Kamakura.

safer to assume that the confrontation between Yasumori and Yoritsuna had simply attained a level at which an armed struggle could no
longer be avoided.

The impact of this incident was deep and long lasting. According to
extant documents, more than fifty men committed suicide after the
incident. Among these were various members of the Adachi family
and a branch line, the Ōsone, as well as warriors from other influential
houses.[25] The sources also tell of many *gokenin* from the Musashi and
Kōzuke provinces committing suicide and one entry in the record
mentions as many as five hundred victims. But the latter were probably attacked on suspicion of partisanship with Yasumori.

It is understandable that many Kōzuke *gokenin* should have died
along with Yasumori, who held the fourth generation *shugo* post there.
However, the large number of deaths in Musashi, with which the
Adachi had no prior association, deserves special attention. Musashi
Province had long contained several small-scale warrior bands, which
leads us to conclude that Yasumori enjoyed a strong following among
houses of this size. Moreover, Yasumori's ties with those close to the
shogun can be surmised from the suicide of Fujiwara Sukenori, a
courtier in service to the shogun. Thus, by identifying the dead we can
help clarify the overall network of support. Yasumori's partisans consisted mostly of small-scale *gokenin* and those close to the shogun.

Some men who had been on Yasumori's side escaped death but lost
political power. A well-known example here is Yasumori's daughter's
husband, Kanazawa Akitoki, a member of a branch of the Hōjō. He
had been serving as head of the fourth *hikitsuke* unit and held the
third-ranking position in the *hyōjōshū*. Accused of complicity, Akitoki
was removed from his positions and exiled to Shimōsa. The day before
his exile, he sent a letter to a monk of the Shōmyōji, a temple that
might be called the Kanazawa clan temple. He stated, "For the last
decade or so, since 1269, I have lived as though stepping on thin
ice."[26] This statement vividly conveys the degree of insecurity at the
center of the bakufu's political structure. Others who fell from power
included Utsunomiya Kagetsuna and Ōe Tokihide, both members of
the *hyōjōshū* and the husbands of Yasumori sisters. Indeed, we can

25 *Kanagawa ken shi, shiryō hen* vol. 2, nos. 1016–20. For example, the Ogasawara, the maternal
line of Yasumori, lost its chieftain (*sōryō*) and several others. Other suicides and persons
disgraced included the powerful Sagami family of Miura; the Itō of Izu; the Kira, a branch
family of the Ashikaga; Nikaidō Yukikage, a *hikitsuke* member and the hereditary holder of
the *mandokoro shitsuji* post; Mutō Kageyasu, another *hikitsuke;* the Hatta, *shugo* of Hitachi;
and the Ōe, Kobayakawa, Amano, Iga and others. Many of these were famous *gokenin*.
26 *Kanagawa ken shi, shiryō hen* vol. 2, no. 1023.

gauge the extent of Yasumori's influence by noting that five out of sixteen *hyōjōshū* members and seven out of thirteen *hikitsuke* elected to join with the Adachi.[27]

The repercussions from this incident were felt throughout Japan. In Hakata, the second son of Yasumori, Adachi Morimune, who had replaced his father as the deputy *shugo* of Higo, was murdered. Also, in the scattered provinces of Hitachi, Tōtomi, Shinano, and Harima, Yasumori's sympathizers were killed. Not long after, Mutō Kagesuke, the commander who had led Takezaki Suenaga, rebelled at Iwato Castle in Chikunzen, which had been built as a fortress against the Mongols. The Mutō, along with many warriors from northern Kyushu, were defeated in the battle of Iwato.[28]

Autocratic rule by Taira Yoritsuna, a miuchibito *representative*

The immediate outcome of the Shimotsuki incident was the concentration of political power in the hands of Taira Yoritsuna, the leader of the *miuchibito*. A courtier's diary described the situation: "Yoritsuna alone holds power and all live in fear."[29] Yoritsuna himself was said to be a great-grandson of Taira Morikuni who had served Kiyomori during the latter's period of ascendancy. At the time of the Taira defeat, Morikuni was taken to Kamakura as a hostage and placed in the custody of the Miura. Subsequently, Yoritsuna's father, Moritsuna, served Hōjō Yasutoki and wielded significant power as manager of the Hōjō household. Yoritsuna rose by serving Hōjō Tokimune, and his wife was the wet nurse to Tokimune's son Sadatoki. Yoritsuna thus held all the requisite qualifications to be the head *miuchibito*.

Who were these *miuchibito*?[30] From the time of Hōjō Yasutoki, the notable *miuchibito* houses were the Bitō, Andō, Suwa, Nanjō, and Seki. Their residences were located inside Yasutoki's mansion. The families themselves came mostly from outside the east and were originally incorporated into the Hōjō household during the early thirteenth

27 Taga Munehaya was the first to focus on the Shimotsuki incident and analyze it in detail. See "Hōjō shikken seiji no igi," in his *Kamakura jidai no shisō to bunka*, pp. 288–320. Satō Shin'ichi clarified the incident's historical significance in his *Kamakura bakufu soshō seido no kenkyū*, pp. 76–78, 96–97. Also see Ishii Susumu, "Shimotsuki sōdō oboegaki," in *Kanagawa ken shi dayori, shiryō hen* vol. 2 (Yokohama: Kanagawa ken, 1973), pp, 1–4.
28 For a detailed study of this battle, see Kawazoe Shōji, "Iwato gassen saihen – Chinzei ni okeru tokusō shihai no kyōka to Mutō shi," in Mori Katsumi hakase koki kinen kai, ed., *Taigai kankei to seiji bunka*, vol. 2 of *Shigaku rōnshū* (Tokyo: Yoshikawa kōbunkan, 1974), pp. 217–49.   29 "Sanemi kyōki," 1293/4/26.
30 The classic study of *miuchibito* appears in Satō, *Kamakura bakufu soshō seido no kenkyū*, pp. 104–21.

century.[31] Later, a new group of eastern *miuchibito* appeared with base lands in areas once held by shogunal *gokenin*.

This new group of eastern *miuchibito* included the Kudō, Onozawa, Soga, Shibuya, Uji, Shiaku, Aihara, and Homma, among others. The function of these private vassals centered on the management of lands held by the *tokusō* or lands controlled by other Hōjō who were *shugo*. In addition, the *miuchibito* exercised certain administrative duties in Kamakura, for instance, overseeing the paperwork for the Hōjō's growing portfolio of holdings.

As a category, *miuchibito* differed from *gokenin* in several significant ways, as the case of Andō Renshō shows.[32] Renshō was born at the end of Yasutoki's tenure as regent, and he died in 1329, shortly before the fall of the bakufu. He was a near contemporary of Taira Yoritsuna. One of Renshō's special achievements was his patronage of the Kumedadera, a temple in Izumi Province, where his portrait still hangs. Renshō is credited with reviving the temple in 1277, by commending to it three plots of land in Izumi and another in Tajima. With other temples, however, Renshō's activities led to trouble. His inability to collect a loan he had made to a priest of the Ninnaji caused him to seek the assistance of a usurer-monk of the Enryakuji, who in turn attempted to seize certain rents in default of the loan. The affected chapel in Ninnaji brought a suit against Renshō with the bakufu.

In his service to the Hōjō, Renshō held administrative posts in the Tada-in estate of Settsu Province and in three other *shōen*, all belonging to the *tokusō*. He also held the deputy *shugo* post for Settsu. As it happened, two of the three *shōen* under his administrative control bordered Osaka Bay and probably functioned as ports. The port of Fukudomari in Harima Province was constructed in large part by expenditures borne by Renshō alone. The project required more than fifteen years of labor and cash running into the several hundreds of *kan*. Ultimately, Fukudomari developed into a port that was as significant as the older harbor town of Hyōgo in Settsu was. For his part, Renshō collected high rents and dallied in commerce.

Andō Renshō, therefore, was not simply a man of arms but was also a crafty entrepreneur deeply involved in transportation and usury.

31 Like Taira Moritsuna, the Seki were descended from Taira Morikuni. The Bitō came from a family that had lost its holdings at the time of the Gempei War and sought refuge with Yoritomo in Kamakura. The Suwa were Shinto priests from a shrine of the same name in Shinano Province. The only prominent *miuchibito* house originally from the east appears to have been the Nanjō.
32 A number of articles describe Andō Renshō and his activities. For a concise description, see Amino, *Mōko shūrai*, pp. 115–16, 296–300.

Other members of the Andō clan managed additional *tokusō* holdings along the Inland Sea, in Kyushu, and in northern Tōhoku (the Tsugaru peninsula). Members of the Andō family in Tsugaru served as deputies for Ezo (Ezo *daikan*) from the time of Hōjō Yoshitoki and also controlled the premier northern seaport, Tosa, in the same area. Other port towns from Tosa south through Wakasa to Kyoto were likewise controlled by the Hōjō.[33]

The leader of the *miuchibito*, Taira Yoritsuna, occupied the dominant position in the bakufu in the post-Shimotsuki era. He encountered many problems, however, the greatest of which was winning the trust and support of the disaffected *gokenin* class. Instrumental to this effort was the distribution of the post-Mongol reward lands. The reward program began in 1286 when some twenty-five Kyushu warriors (including *shugo* and members of the Hōjō house) were chosen as the first recipients, with the shogun personally administering the operation. Lists of names and rewards were sent down to the Ōtomo and Mutō, but processing them proved complicated, and there was a delay of two years. The rewards themselves were of three sizes – paddy grants of ten, five, and three *chō*, along with proportional awards of residence areas and dry fields.

To solve the problem of land shortages, the bakufu adopted several measures: It utilized a share of the shogun's personal holdings (called *kantō goryō*); it confiscated the landed interests of some *shōen* proprietors; and it exchanged lands outside Kyushu for those located within. Another source of rewards was land confiscated from warriors implicated in the Shimotsuki incident. Because it was the bakufu's policy to confine the grant program to Kyushu, a major shift resulted in the pattern of landholding there. Unfortunately, small-scale warriors were helped little. The greatest tracts of land went either to the Hōjō or to warriors who supported them. It is even possible that for most reward lands, the Hōjō came to hold a superior authority for holdings distributed at a lower level to *gokenin*.

Under Yoritsuna, offices in the bakufu tended to go to persons friendly to the Hōjō, and policymaking was similarly compromised. Thus the *tokusei* measures of 1284, which were aimed at rescuing shrines, *shōen* officials, and *myōshu* (*shōen* cultivators) in Kyushu, were, in effect, nullified when another order was issued to return

---

33 A flag with the Hōjō family emblem that survives from 1272 authorized free passage for ships passing through Tagarasu Bay in Wakasa. Another record from 1306 shows that twenty large ships from the Tsugaru area carried the bakufu's authorization to enter the port of Mikuni in Echizen Province, loaded with salmon and kimono.

conditions to their pre-1284 status. The bakufu also replaced the system of justice by the three *tokusei* agents in Hakata with a new office, the Chinzei *dangijo*, in 1285. This office, staffed by the Mutō and Ōtomo families, Utsunomiya Songaku, and Shibuya Shigesato, was to function as the new central judicial and administrative organ for the entire Kyushu region. Even though the latter two were *gokenin*, their interests were evidently closely tied with those of the *tokusō*.[34] At any rate, the Chinzei *dangijo* was established as a judicial center in Hakata that could handle land-related disputes and criminal cases.

These structural reforms were accompanied by the appointment of *miuchibito* to an ever-increasing number of key positions within the bakufu. For instance, in 1291, two *miuchibito* received supervisory posts in the Chinzei *dangijo;* whereas several other *miuchibito*, from the *hikitsuke*, were given responsibility for justice pertaining to temples, shrines, and courtier landowners. Five powerful Hōjō vassals, including two of Yoritsuna's own sons, came to function in the *hikitsuke*.

Tokusō *autocracy*

Yoritsuna's leadership, however, proved in the end to be ephemeral. In the fourth month of 1293, less than ten years after his rise, he was accused of attempting to advance his son Sukemune to the position of shogun, and so he was killed along with more than ninety of his sympathizers by forces of the regent Sadatoki. This incident, called the Heizen-Gate disturbance after the gate at which the armed conflict took place, ended Yoritsuna's era and ushered in a period of *tokusō* rule by the then-twenty-four-year-old Sadatoki.

Within a month's time, Sadatoki had collected oaths from the membership of the *hyōjōshū*, *hikitsukeshū*, and *bugyōnin* corps. In particular, the last were required to swear that they would not take bribes. Overall, Sadatoki's aim was to assist struggling *gokenin* and to extend favor to honest persons. He thus reconfirmed as vassals those warriors whose great-grandfathers had been recognized as such, irrespective of the present condition of their holdings. In other words, *gokenin* were theoretically secured in that status even if they had pawned or sold lands granted to them by the bakufu.

Contemporary records also called these new measures *tokusei* measures, suggesting an awareness of their similarities to the 1284 policy

---

34 Utsunomiya Songaku came to serve as the deputy *shugo* of Higo Province under a *tokusō*-held *shugo* post. Also, various members of the Shibuya came to be recognized as *miuchibito*.

changes of Adachi Yasumori. There was even a restoration to favor of some of Yasumori's sympathizers. For example, the previously disgraced Nagai Munehide was appointed as an appeals magistrate (*osso bugyō*) along with Hōjō Munenobu. Moreover, in the tenth month, Sadatoki abolished the *hikitsuke* organ and created a system of six "reporters" (*shissō*) in its place, assigning three Hōjō who were previously *hikitsuke* unit leaders, Utsunomiya Kagetsuna, Kanazawa Akitoki, and Hōjō Munenobu, who doubled as *osso bugyō*.[35] In addition Settsu Chikamune, who had been head (*shitsuji*) of the *monchūjo* since the end of 1285, was replaced by Miyoshi Tokitsura, another of Yasumori's sympathizers. Finally, the *mandokoro* leadership was shifted from Nikaidō Yukisada to Nikaidō Yukifuji, who had similarly been close to Yasumori.[36]

This revival of Yasumori's sympathizers, however, proved to be superficial. The new post of *shissō*, for example, was wholly subservient to Sadatoki, with responsibilities limited to the submission of details or reference materials with bearing on cases being litigated. By contrast, the former *hikitsuke* unit heads had had much greater freedom of action under Yasumori's reform measures.

In 1294, Sadatoki decreed that no further awards or punishments would be imposed for participation in the Shimotsuki incident. To Sadatoki, then, the prior affiliation of warriors was less important than their current absolute submission to him. In this year also, he extended the face-to-face confrontation procedure to cover a larger number of suits. Moreover, in the tenth month of 1294 he revived the *hikitsuke* but retained the power to issue independent judgments.[37] He did make one important concession, however, by recognizing second hearings for cases that he himself had judged, a reversal of his prior position on the subject.

Despite Sadatoki's efforts to eliminate factional strife within the bakufu, pressures continued to mount from the *miuchibito* collectively and from the more disadvantaged members of the *gokenin* class. A diary written by Miyoshi Tokitsura in 1295, the *Einin sannen ki*,[38]

---

35 Both Kagetsuna and Akitoki were at one time supporters of Yasumori.
36 For further details, see Ishii Susumu, "Takezaki Suenaga ekotoba no seiritsu," *Nihon rekishi*, no. 273 (1971): 12–32. The year 1293 was also when Takezaki Suenaga, another supporter of Yasumori, began to promote his plan of producing a scroll that depicted his own military valor. The timing of this effort following the Heisen-gate disturbance could hardly have been mere coincidence.
37 The *Kamakura nendai ki* dates the revival of the *hikitsuke* as 1295, and many historians have adopted this. However, the correct date is 1294/10, as first pointed out by Satō Shin'ichi, in "Kamakura bakufu seiji no senseika ni tsuite," pp. 121–22.
38 As noted, Miyoshi Tokitsura was *monchūjo shitsuji*. The text was published and introduced for the first time in 1953 by Kawazoe Hiroshi, "Einin san'nen ki kōshō," *Shichō* 50 (January 1953): 33–51. It also appears in Takeuchi, ed., *Zoku shiryō taisei*, vol. 10.

describes this strife through the following incident: a report by a *miuchibito* of blunders committed by the *hyōjōshū* led to Sadatoki's punishment of his own vassals rather than the perpetrators of the error. Although it can be argued that the *tokusō*'s ultimate aim was to alleviate the suffering of the *gokenin* class, his policies also characteristically promoted his own autocratic rule. This ambiguity is best illustrated by the famous *tokusei* edict of 1297, which stipulated (1) abolition of the appeal suit system (*osso*), (2) prohibition of further pawning or sale of *gokenin* property and a guaranteed return of previously sold property to the original owner at no cost,[39] and (3) refusal by the bakufu to accept any litigation involving the collection of loans, in order to curtail excessive usury practices.

The second and third items represented a bold remedial measure for financial depressed *gokenin*, going one step beyond Yasumori's *tokusei* edict. Responding to these regulations, *gokenin* from many regions demanded the reform of their surrendered lands, and the bakufu regularly supported their claims.[40] The first item, however, was more clearly a device to enhance Sadatoki's rule, for it overturned his authorization of three years earlier confirming the right to appeal. The 1297 *tokusei* edict, at any rate, is symbolic of the ambiguity that characterized this period.[41]

These policies, in fact, remained highly fluid. In the following year, the system of appeal was once again revived, and litigation bearing on the collection of loans was recognized as a legitimate cause for complaint. Only the measure guaranteeing the return of previously pawned or sold *gokenin* land was maintained.

The appeal system underwent further changes. In 1300, two years after its revival, the appeal magistrate's office (*osso bugyō*) was abolished, and instead five *miuchibito* took over that responsibility. Here was an attempt to maintain the appeal system itself while concentrating authority in the hands of the *tokusō*.[42] One year later, however, the *osso bugyō* was reinstituted, a testimony to the difficulties that Sadatoki encountered in seeking to consolidate his rule.

However imperfect this "autocracy," the bakufu under Sadatoki

---

39 Except for land already possessed for twenty years or more.
40 For a more detailed study of this *tokusei* edict, see Miura Hiroyuki, "Tokusei no kenkyū," in Miura Hiroyuki, *Hōseishi no kenkyū* (Tokyo: Iwanami shoten, 1919), pp. 767–835.
41 See Kasamatsu Hiroshi, "Einin tokusei to osso," in Kasamatsu, *Nihon chūsei-hō shiron*, pp. 103–21.
42 According to Kasamatsu, the *miuchibito* decided whether a case warranted reexamination, but the actual review was carried out by the *hikitsuke*. In other words, the *miuchibito* did not handle the entire *osso* process themselves.

was experiencing its most complete domination to date. In 1285, immediately after the Shimotsuki incident, Hōjō house members controlled twenty-nine of the country's sixty-eight *shugo* posts, whereas other families held twenty-two. Five provinces had no *shugo*, and the identity of *shugo* in the twelve remaining provinces is unknown. At any rate, more than half of the known *shugo* posts were held by the Hōjō. By 1333, that family held thirty-six *shugo* titles; other families held twenty-one; five provinces had no *shugo;* and the figures for six provinces are unknown.[43] The provinces in which the Hōjō held their titles were widely distributed.

Not all the *jitō* posts held by the Hōjō have been identified by historians,[44] but most seem to have been concentrated in the Tōhoku region, the eastern part of the Tōkaido (especially Izu and Suruga), and Kyushu. In Kyushu at least sixty *jitō* posts constituting 22,000 *chō* of paddy land, or about 20 percent of the entire paddy total for Kyushu, were under Hōjō control.[45] The overall strength of the Hōjō house derived largely from this ever-expanding portfolio of land.

The akutō

One of the serious problems confronting the bakufu in the late thirteenth century was the rise of the *akutō*. *Shōen* were increasingly requesting Kamakura to suppress this banditry, and in 1296, proprietors, the bakufu ordered the *shugo* to construct policing stations on all major roads and to employ *gokenin* in the growing suppression effort. In 1300, the bakufu dispatched a powerful warrior to each of the provinces of Kyushu, to help the *shugo* maintain the peace. In 1301, to control the pirates, all ships in Kyushu were required to display the name of the shipowner and the port of registry. In 1303, night attacks and piracy, which had previously been punishable by exile, were redefined as crimes punishable by death. Thieves, gamblers, and arsonists were also to receive stricter punishments.

The bakufu's *akutō* control measures did not yield quick results. In 1308, for example, Kōno Michiari, a magnate from Iyo Province posted

---

43 These statistics are based largely on Satō Shin'ichi, *Zōho Kamakura bakufu shugo seido no kenkyū* (Tokyo: Tōkyō daigaku shuppankai, 1971). I have made some minor adjustments.
44 There is currently much local study being done on the landholding patterns of the Hōjō. The most comprehensive study is by Okutomi Takayuki, *Kamakura Hōjōshi no kisoteki kenkyū* (Tokyo: Yoshikawa kōbunkan, 1980), especially the section entitled "Hōjōshi shoryō gairyaku ichiran," pp. 258–78.
45 These figures represent an update of my "Kyūshū shokoku ni okeru Hōjōshi shoryō no kenkyū," in Takeuchi Rizō hakase kanreki kinenkai, ed., *Shōensei to buke shakai* (Tokyo: Yoshikawa kōbunkan, 1969), pp. 331–93.

to Kyushu, was ordered home to assist in the effort to control pirates in the bays of western Japan and especially in Kumano. A year later, warriors from as many as fifteen provinces were mobilized to fight against these same Kumano pirates.[46] On another occasion, in 1301, five *akutō* from Yamato Province refused to submit to the bakufu's conscription order, thereby forcing the bakufu to call out *gokenin* from Kyoto and seven other provinces to attack their fortifications.[47]

Kamakura's increasing reliance on the use of military force came to be reflected in its criminal codes. For example, in 1310, *karita rōzeki* (the pilfering of harvests from property in dispute at court), which had frequently been treated as a land-related issue, was placed under the jurisdiction of the criminal courts. Similarly, in 1315, *roji rōzeki* (the theft of movables as payment for uncollected debts) was also placed under criminal jurisdiction, also a departure from past practice.

Sadatoki continued to attend *hyōjōshū* meetings and maintained his role as the central figure of the bakufu, even after taking Buddhist vows in 1301. His tenure as *tokusō*, however, was beset with internal rivalries. For example, Hōjō Munekata, a member of the *tokusō* line and a cousin of Sadatoki, placed himself in the same functional category as the *miuchibito*, in disregard of his family background, and attempted to steal political power by assuming the position of *uchi kanrei*, an officer of the *samurai-dokoro*. In 1305, Munekata murdered his rival, Hōjō Tokimura, who was cosigner (*rensho*) at the time. Soon thereafter, Munekata himself was killed by a conspirator. This "Fifth-Month disturbance," named after the month of Munekata's death, reveals that even Sadatoki was not able to eliminate the factional disputes among members of the Hōjō. When Sadatoki died, at the age of forty-one in 1311, a contemporary remembered him in his later years as a tired politician but also as a man who had decreed innumerable death sentences.

During Sadatoki's leadership, the bakufu continued to prepare for a Mongol invasion by consolidating its Kyushu region's administrative and judicial organs. In 1292, at the end of the Taira Yoritsuna period, two sets of communications arrived from China: a document from a Yüan official entrusted to a Japanese merchant ship and a messenger from Koryŏ carrying an order from Kublai Khan. Interpreting these messages as premonitory signs of another invasion, the bakufu urgently dispatched Hōjō Kanetoki, a cousin of Sadatoki and a

---

46 Amino Yoshihiko, "Kamakura bakufu no kaizoku kin'atsu ni tsuite – Kamakura makki no kaijō keigo o chūshin ni," *Nihon rekishi*, no. 299 (April 1973): 1–20.
47 "Kōfukuji ryaku nendaiki," in *Zoku gunsho ruijū*, no. 29, *ge*, p. 172.

Rokuhara *tandai*, and Nagoe Tokiie, another Hōjō member, to Hakata. These two men were granted the authority to judge court cases as well as to command military forces. To facilitate the exercise of their authority, the bakufu established the Chinzei *sōbugyō sho* in 1293. Scholars differ as to whether this agency should be regarded as the de facto beginnings of the Kyushu deputyship (Chinzei *tandai*).[48]

Kanetoki and Tokiie returned to Kamakura in 1294. Then Kanazawa Sanemasa, who had been *shugo* of both Nagato and Suō provinces, was delegated to Hakata to judge *gokenin* suits in Kyushu. This transition marked the final step toward full establishment of the Chinzei *tandai*, a powerful political organ in Hakata that administered defense measures against external attack and executed judicial decisions for the entire Kyushu region. Although the scale of the office was smaller than those of the main headquarters in Kamakura or of the Rokuhara *tandai*, the judicial structure of the Chinzei *tandai* came to be equipped with the same lower-level accoutrements, such as a *hyōjōshū*, *hikitsukeshū*, and *bugyōnin*.

Parallel to this development was the strengthening of *shugo* authority in Suō and Nagato provinces on the western extremity of Honshū. The *shugo* in those provinces, who were Hōjō, were granted more extensive authority than that enjoyed by other *shugo* and were sometimes referred to as the Nagato and Suō *tandai*.

The Chinzei *tandai* administered the defense service rotation (*ikoku keigo banyaku*). From 1304, the provinces of Kyushu were divided into a total of five units, with service for each based on one-year tours. This change from the previous mode of duty was implemented in hopes of lightening the service burden, and this system continued until the end of the Kamakura period.

THE FALL OF THE KAMAKURA BAKUFU

Conflicts in the court

Although Tokusō Sadatoki's high-handedness contributed to the general malaise of the late Kamakura era, the more immediate cause for

---

48 Two contrasting theories regarding the establishment of the Chinzei *tandai* are represented by Seno Seiichirō in *Chinzei gokenin no kenkyū* (Tokyo: Yoshikawa kōbunkan, 1975), pp. 391–2; and Satō, *Kamakura bakufu soshō seido no kenkyū*, pp. 304–11. Seno argues that because the power of Kanetoki and Tokiie did not include a definitive authority to issue decisions, the Chinzei *tandai* as such did not yet exist. Satō, on the other hand, advances the notion that even without this definitive authority, the possession of adjudicative powers themselves was tantamount to the beginnings of the Chinzei *tandai*.

the bakufu's demise was the instability at court.[49] In the second month of 1272, immediately after the elimination of the anti-*tokusō* elements in Kamakura, the retired emperor Gosaga died. He (r. 1242–6) had been enthroned at the pleasure of the bakufu and, after a brief reign, had ruled as ex-sovereign for almost thirty years. During this period, the bakufu was dominated by the regents Tokiyori and Tokimune, and court–bakufu relations remained relatively peaceful. The appointment of Gosaga's own son, Prince Munetaka, as shogun in 1252 reflected this absence of tension.

In policymaking as well, there was substantial cooperation between the two capitals. As early as 1246, Gosaga had complied with the bakufu's demand for a general administrative restructuring that included the expulsion of the influential Kujō Michiie. The reforms adopted followed the Kamakura model. Thus, five nobles came to staff a *hyōjōshū*, which served as the highest-ranking organ at court. Two nobles of ability were appointed as "liaison officials" (*densō*), each of whom attended to court business on alternative days. They had the power to decide on daily political matters but were to defer important decisions to the discretion of the Kyoto *hyōjōshū*. Matters concerning court–bakufu relations fell under the authority of the *kantō mōshitsugi*, to which Saionji Saneuji was appointed, replacing the discredited Kujō Michiie. From this time on, the office became a hereditary position within the Saionji family. Reforms initiated by Gosaga set a standard for future retired emperors, and his tenure was known later as the "revered period of Gosaga-in."[50] His death thus caused considerable consternation in both Kyoto and Kamakura.

The first of many problems to develop was the matter of the imperial succession. In many ways this dispute was of Gosaga's own making. Before his death he had shown great affection for his second son, the future emperor Kameyama (r. 1259–74), and had arranged for him to succeed his eldest son, the emperor Gofukakusa (r. 1246–59). Gosaga, moreover, indicated his desire to perpetuate the line of

49 Some of the more prominent works describing conditions at court are the following: Miura Hiroyuki, "Kamakura jikai no chōbaku kankei," in *Nihonshi no kenkyū*, vol. 1 (Tokyo: Iwanami shoten, 1906, 1981), pp. 14–115; Miura Hiroyuki, "Ryōtō mondai no ichi haran," in *Nihonshi no kenkyū*, vol. 2 (Tokyo: Iwanami Shoten, 1930, 1981), pp. 17–36; Yashiro Kuniharu, "Chōkōdō-ryō no kenkyū," in Yashiro Kuniharu, ed., *Kokushi sōsetsu* (Tokyo: Yoshikawa kōbunkan, 1925), pp. 1–115; Nakamura Naokatsu, *Nihon shin bunka shi, Yoshino jidai* (Tokyo: Nihon dentsū shuppanbu, 1942), pp. 41–144; and Ryō Susumu, *Kamakura jidai, ge: Kyoto – kizoku seiji no dōkō to kōbu no kōshō* (Tokyo: Shunshūsha, 1957).
50 For this description of Gosaga's government, I have relied greatly on Hashimoto Yoshihiko, "In no hyōjōsei ni tsuite," in Hashimoto Hoshihiko, *Heian kizoku shakai no kenkyū* (Tokyo: Yoshikawa kōbunkan, 1976), pp. 59–84.

Kameyama by naming the latter's son crown prince (the later emperor Gouda.) Gosaga, however, had failed to designate which of his two sons (Gofukakusa or Kameyama) should control the succession and instead deferred this decision to the bakufu. Inasmuch as Gosaga owed his own enthronement to Kamakura's recommendation, he may have believed that the bakufu should once again intervene.[51] Instead, however, Kamakura asked Gosaga's empress about her late husband's true wish, and in the end Kameyama was chosen. Throughout, the bakufu had attempted to act prudently rather than to risk conflict by making an independent selection.

In this way, the young twenty-four-year-old emperor became the "senior figure" in Kyoto. Although the political center at court was transferred from a retired emperor to a reigning emperor, the administrative structure remained virtually unchanged. The *hyōjōshū*, under Gosaga was renamed the *gijōshū*, but its function remained the same. Likewise, both the *kantō moshitsugi* and the *densō* continued to operate as before. At the apex of this system stood the *chiten no kimi* (supreme ruler), who could now be either a reigning or a retired emperor. Thus for the first time since the eleventh century, a sitting emperor (Kameyama) came to be recognized as dominant over a retired sovereign (Gofukakusa),[52] marking the first in a series of adjustments that eventually led to Godaigo's Kemmu restoration.

In 1274, the year of the first Mongol attack, Kameyama yielded his emperorship to his son Gouda.[53] Gofukakusa registered clear dissatisfaction with this and in 1275 announced his intention to take Buddhist vows. At this point the bakufu suddenly abandoned its earlier indifference and proposed that Kameyama adopt Gofukakusa's son and name him as crown prince. We do not know the exact motive behind this proposition; perhaps Kamakura intended to perpetuate the friction between the two brothers and thereby attenuate the court's potential power. Or perhaps it was the doing of Saionji Sanekane (the *kantō moshitsugi*) who had close ties with the bakufu. He may have wished to exploit this friction in order to undermine the Tōin, a branch of the Saionji recently set up by Sanekane's uncle Saneo, who was wielding much influence through his ties to Kameyama. But the most plausible

51 This sentiment is recorded in "Godai teiō monogatari," a historical writing of Emperor Fushimi. See Yashiro, "Chōkōdō ryō no kenkyū," pp. 50–52.
52 In 1273, Kameyama issued a twenty-five article edict (the "Shinsei" edict) pronouncing this change. See Miura Hiroyuki, "Shinsei no kenkyū," *Nihonshi no kenyū*, vol. 1, pp. 614–18.; and Mitobe Masao, *Kuge shinsei no kenkyū* (Tokyo: Sōbunsha, 1961), pp. 232–41.
53 At this point, the new *gijōshū* organ reverted to a *hyōjōshū*, marking the shift back to a retired emperor.

reason for this sudden intervention was the increasing need of the bakufu, confronted by the Mongol threat, to bring Japan as much as possible under its control. Juggling the imperial succession was just another weapon aimed at national control.[54]

Kameyama complied, but in so doing, he was in fact sowing the seeds of even greater problems. After securing the position of the prince, the supporters of Gofukakusa then demanded that Kamakura enthrone this prince as emperor after Gouda's retirement. In the meantime, perhaps knowing that his own line would not always occupy the imperial seat, the retired emperor Kameyama energetically implemented new policies. In the eleventh month of 1285, Kameyama issued a twenty-article regulation that, for example, prohibited the transfer of temple and shrine land to other temples and shrines or to lay people.[55] This and other articles marked an important advance in the development of legal procedures bearing on land transfers and also marked a radical progress in the formulation of courtier law (*kuge hō*).

In the following month, the *hyōjōshū* of the retired emperor made public a code of behavior prescribing the proper etiquette for inside and outside the palace. It was called the *kōan reisetsu* and included the appropriate format for writing documents. The purpose of these various regulations seems to have been to freeze the hierarchical status system of the day by legalizing the decorum required of each social and official level.[56]

A further reform of Kameyama was to bring courtier justice even more in line with the Kamakura system.[57] Thus in 1286, the *hyōjōshū* classified its responsibilities as follows: (1) *tokusei sata*, for which it met three times a month, to deal with problems relating to religious matters and official appointments, and (2) *zasso sata*, for which it met six times a month, to investigate litigation. Regarding the latter, the *hyōjōshū* set up a system of face-to-face meetings between litigants in an office called *fudono*, at which a judgment might be issued immedi-

---

54 Murai, "Mōko shūrai to Chinzei tandai no seiritsu," p. 11.
55 This edict appears in printed form in *Iwashimizu monjo*, no. 1, doc. 319. Recently it was included in Kasamatsu Hiroshi, Satō Shin'ichi, and Momose Kesao, eds., *Chūsei seiji shakai shisō, ge* vol. 22 of *Nihon shisō taikei* (Tokyo: Iwanami shoten, 1981), along with notes and its Japanese reading, see pp. 57–62. As for analysis of the content of this edict, see Kasamatsu Hiroshi, "Chūsei no seiji shakai shisō," in Kasamatsu Hiroshi, *Nihon chūsei-hō shiron* (Tokyo: Tōkyō daigaku shuppankai, 1977), pp. 178–9.
56 The Kōan *reisetsu* appears in *Gunsho ruijū, zatsu bu*, no. 27. For its historical significance, see Kasamatsu, *Nihon chūsei-hō shiron*, pp. 191–2.
57 See Kasamatsu, *Nihon chūsei-hō shiron*, pp. 157–202; also Kasamatsu Hiroshi, "Kamakura kōki no kuge hō ni tsuite," in Kasamatsu et al., eds., *Chūsei seiji shakai shisō, ge*, pp. 401–16.

164 THE DECLINE OF THE KAMAKURA BAKUFU

ately. Before this, the *fudono* had served as a management bureau for retired emperors' documents, though now it was transformed into a full-scale judicial organ.[58]

The Daikakuji and Jimyō-in lines: a split in the court

Just as the retired emperor Kameyama was reorganizing his government, a rumor spread that he was plotting against the bakufu. The rumor may have originated with the supporters of Gofukakusa at court or with the bakufu itself which may have feared the ex-emperor's potential power. At this time, the bakufu was in the hands of the *miuchibito* under Taira Yoritsuna. At any rate, in 1287 Kamakura demanded the enthronement of Gofukakusa's son as the emperor Fushimi. Although Kameyama pleaded against this, Emperor Gouda was forced to resign and was replaced by Fushimi (r. 1288–98). Gofukakusa then took the position of "supreme ruler" in place of Kameyama. Two years later, at the bakufu's insistence, the son of Fushimi was named crown prince. It was in the same year, 1289, that the shogun, Prince Koreyasu (the son of the former shogun Munetaka, himself the son of Gosaga), was accused of plotting against the bakufu and was sent back to Kyoto. "The prince was exiled to Kyoto," people in Kamakura gossiped. At this point, the thirteen-year-old son of Gofukakusa, Prince Hisaakira, was made the new shogun.

In both Kyoto and Kamakura, then, the Taira Yoritsuna clique succeeded in filling the top hierarchy with members of Gofukakusa's line. The Yoritsuna–Gofukakusa connection was underscored by Yoritsuna's dispatching of his second son, Iinuma Sukemune, to Kyoto to receive the new shogun.

Resentment was felt in many corners. Having been stripped of any real power, Kameyama took Buddhist vows in 1289. For a different reason, Gofukakusa also took Buddhist vows in the following year and yielded his political power to emperor Fushimi. At around this time, a member of a warrior house purged in the Shimotsuki incident attacked the imperial residence and attempted to murder the emperor. Kameyama ultimately was blamed for this intrigue, and he was very nearly confined at Rokuhara, following the example of the Jōkyū disturbance. Only a special plea allowed him to escape this fate.

Unlike his father Gofukakusa, who was a compromiser and follower of precedents, Fushimi, the new supreme ruler, proved to be an ener-

58 Hashimoto, *Heian kizoku shakai no kenkyū*, p. 77.

getic reformer.[59] In 1292 he issued a thirteen-article code regulating judicial procedures.[60] In 1293 a new appeal system called *teichū* was adopted by one of the court's traditional tribunals, the *kirokujo*. *Teichū* proceedings were heard by six courtier judges (*shōkei*), six legal experts (*ben*), and sixteen assistants (*yoriudo*). *Shōkei* and *ben* were each organized into six rotating units, and *yoriudo* into eight rotating units. Each of these units heard appeal cases in rotation for twenty-eight days each month. At the same time, regularized court sessions were held six times a month to hear new cases. These were attended by three rotating units of the *gijōshū* and three other rotating units of *ben* and *yoriudo* who belonged to the *kirokujo*.[61] Fushimi's reforms reflected once again Kamakura's own judicial system and marked a significant advance in court judicial practices.

Fushimi's personal position at court did not remain secure, however, mainly because of a split among those close to him. One of the courtiers closest to Fushimi was Kyōgoku Tamekane. Grandson of the famous poet Fujiwara Teika, Tamekane was a gifted and innovative *waka* poet himself. But this poet had another side. He was notorious as a narrow-minded, unscrupulous politician with extraordinarily high self-esteem.[62] He was resented for having managed to become the husband of the wet nurse to the emperors Fushimi and Hanazono, a position of great influence at court. Among Tamekane's enemies, the most significant was Saionji Sanekane, the *kantō mōshitsugi*. To undermine Tamekane, Sanekane withdrew from Emperor Fushimi and joined Kameyama's supporters. This change in Fushimi's support network in turn endangered his position. Soon enough, Fushimi, too, became the object of the same kind of rumor that caused Kameyama's fall. To counter his precarious position, Fushimi wrote a religious supplication that read, "There are a few who are spreading an unfounded rumor in order to usurp the imperial seat."[63]

By this time, the composition of the bakufu had changed; Taira

59 At this time, the emperor's court set up a *gijōshū*, following the precedent of Emperor's Kameyama in the years 1272–4. A *gijōshū* was equivalent to a retired emperor's *hyōjōshū*. Subsequent governments under incumbent emperors followed this basic pattern.
60 Miura Hiroyuki discusses this edict in "Shinsei no kenkyū," pp. 619–22; also see Mitobe, *Kuge shinsei no kenkyū*, pp. 241–4. Gotō Norihiko gives a full translation in "Tanaka bon Seifu – bunrui o kokoromita kuge shinsei no koshahon," *Nempō, chūseishi kenkyū*, no. 5 (May 1980): 73–86. 61 Hashimoto, *Heian kizoku shakai no kenkyū*, p. 78.
62 Kyōgoku Tamekane has tended to receive fuller treatment as a poet than as a politician. A representative work is by Toki Zenmaro, *Shinshū Kyōgoku Tamekane* (Tokyo: Kadokawa shoten, 1968), which contains a bibliography of related works on Tamekane.
63 Quoted in Miura, *Kamakura jidaishi*, p. 567.

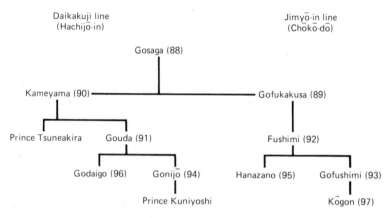

Figure 3.1 System of alternate succession between Gofukakusa and Kameyama lines. (Order of succession is given in parentheses.)

Yoritsuna had fallen, and the autocratic rule of Hōjō Sadatoki was well under way. In 1297, the bakufu arrested Tamekane and exiled him to Sado. Having eliminated this troublemaker, the bakufu then arranged for the resignation of Fushimi and the enthronement of Fushimi's son Gofushimi (r. 1298–1301). The grandson of Kameyama and son of Gouda (the future emperor Gonijō) was designated as the new crown prince. Subsequently, the bakufu began to consider seriously a system of alternate succession between the lines of Gofukakusa and Kameyama.[64] Figure 3.1 shows their lineage and order of succession.

In order to implement the practice of alternate succession, the bakufu demanded Gofushimi's resignation in 1301, only four years after his enthronement. Gonijō, the grandson of Kameyama, then succeeded him. The selection of the crown prince became a major issue, but the bakufu adhered to the practice of alternate succession by designating the younger brother of Gofushimi (later Emperor Hanazono) as the heir apparent.

By this time, the antagonism between the Kameyama and Gofukakusa lines had lasted for thirty years, and it had become a significant part of the imperial institutional tradition. Not only immediate family members but also nobles at court became embroiled in this conflict. The antagonism, moreover, applied to more than just the question of imperial succession. The economic interests of each line, which affected holders of land rights at all levels of the *shōen* hierarchy, deepened the rapidly growing tension at court.

64 Miura, *Nihonshi no kenkyū*, pp. 98–100.

The two lines were identified by the location of their private residences. The line of Kameyama was called the Daikakuji line, taking the name of Gouda's residence, whereas Gofukakusa's line was known by the residence of Fushimi, the Jimyō-in. As many as one hundred to two hundred *shōen* supported each line. *Shōen* units held by each line were collectively named the Hachijō-in-ryō for the Daikakuji line and the Chōkōdō-ryō for the Jimyō-in line.[65]

If the two lines were to share the imperial seat alternately, their economic resources would need to be balanced as well. But sometimes the death of a large property holder could easily upset the balance. In 1300, for example, the ownership of nearly one hundred *shōen* became subject to dispute after Muromachi-in, the previous holder of these lands, died. Muromachi-in's mother had been a member of the Jimyō-in, and after her son's death, her daughter inherited the whole share. But the land slipped out of the Jimyō-in line's possession when this daughter became a wife of Gouda, a member of the Daikakuji line. Fearing further problems of this kind, the bakufu arranged to have the entire portfolio divided in half and assigned to each line.[66]

The deepening hostility between the two lines, which had first begun as a succession dispute, now affected the entire court structure. Even in the cultural and religious spheres, the split was apparent. Whereas the Daikakuji line patronized the new Chinese culture—Sung-style Confucianism, Zen Buddhism, and the Chinese style of calligraphy – the Jimyō-in line preferred the traditional Japanese (Heian) culture in literature, calligraphy, and Buddhism.[67]

The situation at court worsened as the waves of antagonism among courtiers went beyond the original gulf that separated the two camps and caused further splits in each line. In the Jimyō-in line, the retired emperor Gofushimi and his younger brother (the future emperor Hanazono) were showing signs of hostility. The situation was far more grave for the Daikakuji line, however. Initially, the retired emperor Kameyama favored Emperor Gonijō's younger brother, Prince Takaharu (the future emperor Godaigo), as the next emperor. But in 1303, when the daughter of Saionji Sanekane bore Kameyama a son

---

65 The patterns of transfer and division of imperial family holdings, such as the Chōkōdō-ryō and the Hachijō-in-ryō, have been much studied. Among the more important works are the following: Yashiro, "Chōkōdō-ryō no kenkyū"; Nakamura, *Nihon shin bunka shi, Yoshino jidai;* Ashida Koreto, *Goryōchi-shikō* (Tokyo: Teishitsu Rinya kyoku, 1937); Nakamura Naokatsu, *Shōen no kenkyū* (Kyoto: Hoshino shoten, 1931, 1978); and Okuno Takahiro, *Kōshitsu gokeizai shi no kenkyū* (Tokyo: Unebi shobo, 1942).
66 Nakamura, *Shōen no kenkyū,* pp. 382–85.
67 A detailed discussion of this point appears in Miura, *Nihonshi no kenkyū,* pp. 106–7.

(Prince Tsuneakira), Kameyama changed his mind and began to promote this young son for the throne. This change of heart caused those affiliated with the Daikakuji line to split into three smaller factions, supporting Gonijō, Prince Takaharu, and Prince Tsuneakira.

The internal strife at court worsened after the successive deaths of Gofukakusa and Kameyama in 1304 and 1305, followed by the death of Gonijō in 1308. Before these three died, the Saionji family had hoped to enthrone Prince Tsuneakira by forcing Gonijō's abdication. But this proved unnecessary; with Gonijō dead, the principle of alternate succession allowed Emperor Hanazono of the Jimyō-in line to occupy the throne. In the meantime, the retired emperor Fushimi, also of the Jimyō-in line, actually dominated the court and ruled from the office of *in*. The Daikakuji line retained the position of crown prince. With the understanding that the imperial rank and lands would be transferred to the son of Gonijō, Gouda designated Prince Takaharu (Gonijō's brother and the future emperor Godaigo) as the heir apparent.

Godaigo's reign

Fushimi's rule an ex-sovereign was just as energetic as that as emperor. He delegated much responsibility to Kyōgoku Tamekane, who by this time had returned to Kyoto from exile. The organs of justice were further reorganized, and an appeals court (*teichū*) was incorporated into the *fudono*.[68] However, the earlier friction between Tamekane and Saionji Sanekane resurfaced and reduced the effectiveness of Fushimi's rule. Once again, in 1315, Tamekane was accused of plotting against the bakufu and was arrested by the Rokuhara *tandai*. As before, he was exiled to Tosa.

The fall of Tamekane naturally affected the well-being of Fushimi. A rumor spread that Fushimi, too, was involved in an antibakufu plot, and the ex-emperor was forced to prove his innocence by writing a letter of denial in his own hand. It seemed that both the bakufu and Saionji Sanekane were giving greater support to the Daikakuji line than to Fushimi's Jimyō-in line.

In 1317, the bakufu sent a message to the court that recommended Hanazono's resignation and the selection of a new crown prince by way of agreement between the two lines. But the rival lines could not so easily reach an accord. Before a decision could be made on the new crown prince, the retired emperor Fushimi died, leaving the Jimyō-in

---

68 Hashimoto, *Heian kizoku shakai no kenkyū*, pp. 82–83.

line powerless without a central figure. In the following year, 1318, the bakufu proposed to designate the son of Gonijō as the heir apparent and to place Godaigo on the throne. Gouda, the father of Godaigo and Gonijō, thus began his rule as retired emperor. The Daikakuji line thus came to dominate the highest levels of the imperial hierarchy.

But it was not the bakufu's intention to tip the balance permanently. At the same time as the Daikakuji surge, Kamakura set down specific conditions for that line to follow. Later documents reveal the terms of this "*bumpō* mediation": (1)The next succession was to be secured for the Jimyō-in line by designating the son of Gofushimi, Prince Kazuhito (later Emperor Kōgon), as crown prince as soon as the incumbent Prince Kuniyoshi became emperor; (2) the reign of each emperor was not to exceed ten years; and (3) the offspring of Godaigo were not to seek the throne.[69] At his enthronement, therefore, Godaigo faced several limitations. It was particularly unsatisfactory that Godaigo, then in his prime at age thirty-one, should have to surrender all hope of having an imperial heir. And he feared that without an heir, his grandiose plans for reviving "the golden age" of Daigo, an early Heian emperor, would not bear fruit. His strong personality only reinforced the dissatisfaction caused by the circumstances surrounding him. As a first step out of this quandary he sought to become the supreme ruler himself. The resignation of Gouda-in from active politics in 1321 gave Godaigo the opportunity to both reign and rule.

Godaigo began his rule by staffing his court with men of ability. His interest in Sung Confucianism led him to select such famed scholar-politicians as Yoshida Sadafusa and Kitabatake Chikafusa, both of the Daikakuji line, and Hino Suketomo and Hino Toshimoto, men of less prestigious family backgrounds but of equal ability. Moreover, reflecting the changed conditions after Gouda's withdrawal from public life, Godaigo shifted the *teichū* appeals court from the *fudono* of the retired emperor's government back to the *kirokujo* of his own imperial government. Here, Godaigo himself sometimes participated in judging cases.[70]

A noteworthy aspect of the Godaigo's rule was his attempt to consoli-

69 For an extensive description of the "Bumpo no wadan," see Yashiro, "Chōkōdō-ryō no kenkyū," pp. 72–81.
70 A number of works treat topics such as these as the essential historical ingredients presaging the Kemmu restoration. See, for example, Miura, *Kamakura jidaishi;* Tanaka Yoshinari, *Nambokuchō jidaishi* (Tokyo: Meiji shoin, 1922), pp. 23–82; Hiraizumi Kiyoshi, "Nihon chūkō," in Kemmu chūkō roppyakunen kinenkai, comp., *Kemmu chūkō* (Tokyo: Kemmu chūkō roppayakunen kinenkai, 1934), pp. 1–177; and Nakamura Naokatsu, "Godaigo tennō no shinsei," in *Nakamura Naokatsu chosaku shū*, vol. 3: *Nanchō no kenkyū* (Kyoto: Tankōsha, 1978), pp. 55–67.

date imperial power by tapping the growing commercial sector as a source of revenue. In 1322, for example, he ordered imperial officials to collect taxes from saké brewers in Kyoto on a regular basis, the first time that this was ever attempted.[71] The emperor's court, moreover, demonstrated concern over fluctuating prices. During a famine in 1330, he accordingly issued an edict stabilizing prices and also decreed that merchants who were hoarding rice would be required to sell it at a special market. All tariffs were suspended for three months.[72]

Approaching crisis in the bakufu

Meanwhile, Sadatoki's autocratic rule in Kamakura was giving way to renewed *miuchibito* dominance. In 1311, Sadatoki died, and his nine-year-old son Takatoki became *tokusō*. The young *tokusō* had two advisers: Nagasaki Enki (the son of Taira Yoritsuna's brother), who had long been serving as *uchi kanrei*, and Adachi Tokiaki (the grandson of Adachi Yasumori's brother and Takatoki's father-in-law). In 1316, when he was fourteen, Takatoki assumed the post of regent (*shikken*), but he proved to be an effete politician. A contemporary chronicle, the "Hōryaku kanki," noted that Takatoki was "weak-minded and unenergetic . . . it was difficult to call him *shikken*."[73] As a result, the real political power fell to the new *uchi kanrei*, Nagasaki Takasuke, Enki's son. In alliance with other *miuchibito*, Takasuke began to dominate the bakufu.

Takatoki's resignation from the post of regent in 1326 encouraged internal disunity. Nagasaki Takasuke immediately forced Kanazawa Sadaaki (Akitoki's son), who had been serving as cosigner (*rensho*), to become the next *shikken*. This greatly angered Hōjō Sadatoki's widow, who had planned to elevate Yasuie, the younger brother of Takatoki, to the regency. After only a month of service as *shikken*, Sadaaki was forced to resign his post when Sadatoki's widow attempted to have him murdered. In the meantime, Takatoki preoccupied himself with cultural pursuits and completely ignored politics. However, in 1330 Takatoki ordered Nagasaki Takayori and another *miuchibito* to murder Nagasaki Takasuke. Perhaps Takatoki was angered by Takasuke's domination of the bakufu. The plot, nonetheless, was discovered, and Takatoki was forced to pretend complete innocence.

---

71 Amino Yoshihiko provides a detailed treatment of this subject in "Zōshushi kōjiyaku no seiritsu ni tsuite – Muromachi bakufu sakayayaku no zentei," in Takeuchi Rizō hakase koki kinenkai, comp., *Zoku shōensei to buke shakai* (Tokyo: Yoshikawa kōbunkan, 1978), pp. 359–97.
72 Hiraizumi, "Nihon chūkō," pp. 93–100; and Nakamura, "Godaigo tennō no ichi rinji," pp. 76–79.   73 The "Hōryaku kan ki" appears in *Gunsho ruijū, zatsu bu*.

At the same time that conspiracies were rife in the bakufu's capital, the most conspicuous problem in the provinces continued to be the *akutō*. According to records from Harima Province and to the chronicle "Mineaiki," the *akutō* at the turn of the century – whether pirates, mountain bandits, or robbers – were spreading rapidly. They wore outrageous clothing and were equipped with pitiful-looking swords or long bamboo poles, and they also congregated into small groups, gambled regularly, and were talented petty thieves.[74]

The bakufu officially set out in 1318 to bring these people under control in twelve provinces of western Japan (the Sanyō and Nankai regions). Three *miuchibito* of renown were dispatched to each province where they demanded oaths from the *shugo*, deputy *shugo*, and *jitō-gokenin* to destroy existing *akutō* bases. According to the "Mineaiki," in Harima alone, over twenty stone forts were destroyed, and a number of *akutō* members killed. In addition, although arrest warrants for fifty-one famous outlaws were issued, the "Mineaiki" tells us that none was actually captured. At the same time, the bakufu mobilized those warriors holding land along the Inland Sea coastline to defend against pirates and to protect important ports.[75] These efforts produced some positive, but not lasting, results. In Harima, for instance, the *akutō* activities diminished for two or three years but then started up again with even greater vigor.

The style and behavior of the Harima *akutō* changed over the years. In the latter part of the 1330s, previously small and unimpressive *akutō* elements began to appear in large groups of fifty to one hundred, magnificently outfitted men all riding splendid horses. Many of these men came from neighboring provinces to form a band (*tō*) through mutual pledges of loyalty. They were highly imaginative in the violent methods they employed to effect their ends, and most *shōen* in Harima fell prey to their depredations. The "Mineaiki" reports, indeed, that more than half of all warriors in that province sympathized with the *akutō*.

It is now apparent that many of these *akutō* were none other than the local warriors themselves, not "bandits" in the original sense of the word. It is thus understandable that the bakufu's effort to control them by issuing pacification orders would have had little effect. For example, the bakufu's threat in 1324 that it would confiscate *shōen* that failed to hand over captured *akutō* to the *shugo* failed to have much impact.

---

74 The "Mineaiki" appears in *Zoku Gunsho ruijū, Shakuka bu.*
75 Amino, "Kamakura bakufu no kaizoku kin'atsu ni tsuite."

In the northeast the problem was not one of *akutō* but of antibakufu rebellions in a region of the country largely dominated by the Hōjō. In Ezo, for instance, a rebellion that started in 1318 became aggravated two years later when the hereditary officials of the area, the Andō, suffered a severe internal split. Although Kamakura attempted to quell the disturbance by dispatching a large army, the fighting continued unabated.[76]

The demise of the Kamakura bakufu

Because the bakufu was faced with a variety of problems, Emperor Godaigo began to contemplate bringing it down by force. His initial task was thus to tap various sources for potential allies. The monks of the large temples in the Kyoto region were the first to be approached. In particular, Godaigo recognized the potential military power of the Enryakuji monks and accordingly placed his sons, the Princes Morinaga and Munenaga, at the top of the clerical hierarchy, as Tendai *zasu*. Outside the religious orders, Godaigo's close collaborators Hino Suketomo and Toshimoto made contacts with dissatisfied warriors and with *akutō* in the Kinai and neighboring provinces. Gradually, an antibakufu movement began to develop. Sympathizers often assembled in the most casual attire without regard to rank or status and held banquets to discuss strategy and logistics. These meetings were called *bureikō*, that is, discussions without propriety.

There were setbacks at times. In the ninth month of 1324, for example, a plan to mobilize Kyoto warriors under the leadership of the Toki and Tajimi warrior houses of Mino Province was exposed, and a bakufu army dispatched by the Rokuhara *tandai* captured the ringleaders. Significantly, Hino Suketomo and Toshimoto were also implicated and arrested in what became known as the Shōchū disturbance. Godaigo himself fell under suspicion and had to defend his innocence in the matter. The bakufu, at any rate, failed to heed the warning signals in this incident and satisfied itself with blaming Hino Suketomo for the trouble and exiling him to Sado.

Meanwhile at court, a further development in the ongoing imperial succession dispute provided Godaigo with another reason to challenge the bakufu. Crown Prince Kuniyoshi died suddenly in 1326, and there were disagreements as to who should succeed him. There were three

---

76 Kobayashi Seiji and Ōishi Naomasa, comps., *Chūsei ōshū no sekai* (Tokyo: Tōkyō daigaku shuppankai, 1978), pp. 80–82.

candidates: the son of Kuniyoshi, the son of Godaigo, and Prince Kazuhito of the Jimyō-in line. Much to the frustration of the emperor, the bakufu chose Kazuhito, who later became Emperor Kōgon.

In the fourth month of 1331, a second antibakufu conspiracy was exposed, and this time Hino Toshimoto and his followers were arrested. Having lost his commanders, the emperor himself now took the lead in the antibakufu movement, and at the end of the eighth month, he left Kyoto for Nara, where he fortified himself on Mount Kasagi. Godaigo's personal involvement sparked additional support, such as that of Kusunoki Masashige from neighboring Kawachi Province and that of other warriors from the more distant Bingo Province.

Responding to this emergency, Kamakura took the offensive and by the end of the ninth month had captured the emperor. This Genkō incident, as it was called, seemed to mark the end of Godaigo's hopes to destroy the bakufu. In the meantime, Prince Kazuhito had already been enthroned as the new emperor Kōgon, and the retired emperor Gofushimi now became active, restoring power to the Jimyō-in line. Because Godaigo was no longer emperor or an active retired emperor, the bakufu exiled him to Oki, the same punishment meted out to Gotoba for his antibakufu Jōkyū disturbance in 1221. Also following the precedent set by the Jōkyū disturbance, the bakufu punished many of Godaigo's followers with death or banishment. Yet unlike that earlier episode, such forcefulness by Kamakura did not succeed in eradicating all of the antibakufu elements. In the absence of his father, Prince Morinaga, the former Tendai *zasu*, now assumed leadership of the movement.

For some time actually, Morinaga had been secretly encouraging *akutō* in the southern sector of the home provinces. But beginning in 1332, his activities suddenly became overt, and by the eleventh month, he was openly mobilizing warriors in the Yoshino area of Yamato Province. Hearing this news, Kusunoki Masashige came out of hiding and reorganized his army in Kawachi. At the same time, the *akutō* followers of Prince Morinaga became active in the vicinity of Kyoto. By the first month of 1333, Kusunoki advanced from Kawachi into Settsu and there, around Shitennōji, defeated an army of the bakufu's Rokuhara *tandai*.

The bakufu had hardly been routed as yet, and in the second month it took a strategically located castle (Akasaka in Kawachi), seized earlier by Masashige, and then moved its army into Yoshino. In the meantime, Morinaga eluded capture and continued to organize antibakufu forces on his way to Kōyasan in Kii, whereas Masashige fortified his troops at Chihaya Castle on Mount Kongō and – using techniques typical of the *akutō* – fired rocks and branches from the mountaintop on the bakufu army below.

The forces of rebellion now snowballed everywhere. For example, a wealthy local warrior of Harima, Akamatsu Norimura, took up arms late in the first month, whereas the Doi and Kutsuna of Iyo Province rebelled in the second month. The Sanyōdō and Inland Sea areas thus became major battlefields. Continuing their offensive, the Akamatsu moved in the direction of Kyoto and soon pushed into Settsu.

Having been informed of the improving situation, Godaigo escaped from Oki in the second month, arriving on the shores of Hōki Province where he was welcomed by the influential warrior Nawa Nagatoshi. By the third month, the Akamatsu, leading the warriors and *akutō* from Harima and other home provinces, entered Kyoto but were unable to occupy it. A month later reinforcements were provided by Chigusa Sadaaki, a close collaborator of Godaigo, but even then the bakufu succeeded in preventing the imperial loyalists from taking the capital.

At this time the leadership in Kamakura dispatched a new army to Kyoto, led by Ashikaga Takauji. Chief of a distinguished eastern warrior house, Takauji had long held an antipathy toward the Hōjō *tokusō* and his *miuchibito*, and even before entering Kyoto, he was in touch with Godaigo. At first he attacked Kamakura's enemies but soon switched sides, returning to Kyoto to attack the Rokuhara deputyship, which fell early in the fifth month. In disarray, the warriors of Rokuhara fled to Kamakura, carrying Emperor Kōgon with them, but they ran into blockades set up by various *akutō*. On the ninth day of the fifth month, the imperial entourage was captured by these *akutō*, and numerous bakufu fighting men committed suicide.

Exactly one day before this incident, Nitta Yoshisada of Kōzuke Province mounted a challenge against the bakufu in the east, and by the twenty-first day of that month the city of Kamakura fell. There were numerous suicides by the Hōjō and their *miuchibito*, and for all practical purposes the Kamakura bakufu had been destroyed. Four days later the Mutō and Ōtomo families in Kyushu led a successful campaign against the Chinzei *tandai*, and on the same day, Godaigo, who was now heading toward Kyoto, issued an order rejecting Kōgon as emperor. Atop the debris of Japan's first shogunate, the restoration was about to begin.

CHAPTER 4

THE MUROMACHI BAKUFU

INTRODUCTION

The Muromachi bakufu, the second of the three military governments that held power in Japan from 1185 to 1867, was founded between 1336 and 1338 by Ashikaga Takauji (1305–58). The name Muromachi was taken from the district in Kyoto where the Ashikaga residence and administrative headquarters were located after 1378. The end of the regime is dated either 1573, when the last Ashikaga shogun was ousted from Kyoto, or 1597, when the ex-shogun died in exile.

The period in Japanese history defined by the existence of the Muromachi bakufu has been judged in two quite contradictory ways. Measured on the basis of effective centralized rule, it has been seen as a time of political weakness and social unrest. Yet in cultural terms it has been recognized as one of Japan's most creative periods of artistic achievement. There is, of course, no necessary contradiction between political instability and cultural brilliance. And modern historians have tended to play down the apparent paradox. They stress instead the significant social and institutional changes of the time: when military government (the bakufu system) came into its own, when the military aristocracy (the *buke* or samurai estate) became the real rulers of the country, and when profound changes were wrought in the distribution of rights over land and in the organization of the cultivating class. Recent assessments have suggested that even with respect to government effectiveness, the Ashikaga should not be dismissed too lightly. After all, the Muromachi bakufu lasted for more than two hundred years. At the height of its power, under the third and sixth shoguns, a military government for the first time gained possession of all aspects of secular authority. It was only in the exercise of that authority that the Ashikaga shoguns had difficulty.[1]

1 Beginning in the late 1940s, Japanese scholars literally transformed the field of Muromachi studies, along four main lines. (1) Studies by Matsumoto Shimpachiro, Satō Shin'ichi, Ishimoda Shō, Nagahara Keiji, and Kuroda Toshio explored the political institutions of the period to comprehend the balance of power between civil and military, central and local

175

In extending its influence beyond its Kamakura headquarters, the first shogunate had relied on a network of military land stewards (jitō) and provincial constables (shugo), whose reliability was presumably guaranteed by their enlistment, when possible, into the shogun's band of vassals. The Kamakura bakufu's authority, though limited to certain aspects of military recruitment, judicial and police action, and the expediting of estate payments, was exercised effectively within what remained of the legal institutions of imperial provincial administration. The Ashikaga shoguns, however, had less support from this inheritance and were required to depend more upon institutions of their own making; hence their reliance on the provincial constables to whom they delegated much local authority. Under the Muromachi bakufu, the shugo acquired political influence by combining the authority the post had commanded under the Kamakura bakufu with that customarily available to the civil provincial governors under the imperial system. The chain of command among shogun, shugo, and provincial retainers now carried almost the entire burden of government, both nationally and locally.

But the Ashikaga contribution to the evolution of Japanese government has not been easy to define. Although the Muromachi bakufu handled a greater volume of administrative, judicial, and military transactions than the Kamakura system had done, neither shogun nor shugo acquired the capacity for enforcement needed to fully exercise their legal authority. The command imperative and the balance of power on which the Ashikaga house rested its rule was weakened by the fact that the Ashikaga shoguns were not able to perfect either a fully bureaucratic administrative or a fully "patrimonial" delegation of lord to vassal. As chiefs of the military estate, the Ashikaga shoguns did maintain a private bureaucracy and a guard force drawn from their extensive but individually weak jitō-grade vassals. But these direct retainers were limited in number, and in regard to serious military action, or to the staffing of important bakufu offices, the Ashikaga were heavily dependent on the shugo support. And because the ability

interests; (2) studies such as those by Satō Shin'ichi who, in yet another dimension of his work, began analyzing the inner workings of the Muromachi bakufu as a central government – a lead that has been followed most notably by Kuwayama Kōnen; (3) studies by Nagahara Keiji and Sugiyama Hiroshi began the serious exploration of shugo local administration and its articulation with bakufu interests above and with lesser military houses at the provincial level below; and (4) those studies, beginning with Sugiyama Hiroshi's pioneer analysis of the Muromachi bakufu's economic structure, and more recently those by Kuwayama Kōnen, give a more accurate picture of the fiscal practices and policies of the Muromachi regime. Close on the heels of such Japanese historians have come a number of Western specialists in Muromachi history. References to their writings will appear in the later pages of this chapter.

TABLE 4.1
Ashikaga shoguns

Name	Reign as shogun
1. Takauji (1305–58)	1338–58
2. Yoshiakira (1330–67)	1359–67
3. Yoshimitsu (1358–1408)	1368–94
4. Yoshimochi (1386–1428)	1394–1423, 1425–8
5. Yoshikazu (1407–25)	1423–5
6. Yoshinori (1394–1441)	1429–41
7. Yoshikatsu (1434–43)	1441–3
8. Yoshimasa (1436–90)	1443–73
9. Yoshihisa (1465–89)	1473–89
10. Yoshitane (1466–1523)	1490–3, 1508–21
11. Yoshizumi (1480–1511)	1493–1508
12. Yoshiharu (1511–50)	1521–46
13. Yoshiteru (1536–65)	1546–65
14. Yoshihide (1540–68)	1568
15. Yoshiaki (1537–97)	1568–73 (abdicated 1588)

to hold the loyalty of such support shifted over time and circumstance and from shogun to shogun, it is necessary to start any inquiry into the Muromachi bakufu by first looking at the Ashikaga house, its rise as a prominent *shugo* family under the Kamakura bakufu and its role in destroying the Hōjō and in establishing a new bakufu.

THE RISE OF THE ASHIKAGA HOUSE

The Ashikaga house, as seen in Figure 4.1 and Table 4.1, was descended from the same Seiwa branch of the Minamoto lineage as was Yoritomo (1147–99), the founder of the Kamakura shogunate.[2] The name Ashikaga was derived from the family's original landholding, Ashikaga-no-shō in Shimotsuke Province. The Minamoto house began its association with estates, or *shōen*, in Shimotsuke under Yoshiie (1039–1106). His grandson Yoshiyasu (?–1157), after receiving the estate manager's rights (*gesu shiki*) of Ashikaga-no-shō, took the estate's name to identify his newly established branch line. Proprietary rights to the estate were held by the retired emperor Toba (1103–56). Throughout the Kamakura period Ashikaga-no-shō remained an important holding of the estates controlled by the "junior," or Daikakuji,

2 The following description of the Ashikaga house and its early rise relies on Toyoda Takeshi, "Genko tōbatsu no shoseiryoku ni tsuite," in Ogawa Makoto, ed, *Muromachi seiken*, vol. 5 of *Ronshū Nihon rekishi* (Tokyo: Yūshōdō, 1975).

I. The early years

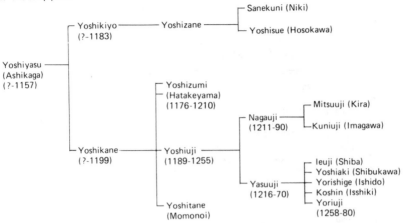

Yoshiyasu (Ashikaga) (?-1157)
— Yoshikiyo (?-1183) — Yoshizane — Sanekuni (Niki); Yoshisue (Hosokawa)
— Yoshikane (?-1199) — Yoshiuji (1189-1255) [with Yoshizumi (Hatakeyama) (1176-1210) and Yoshitane (Momonoi)]
  — Nagauji (1211-90) — Mitsuuji (Kira); Kuniuji (Imagawa)
  — Yasuuji (1216-70) — Ieuji (Shiba); Yoshiaki (Shibukawa); Yorishige (Ishido); Koshin (Isshiki); Yoriuji (1258-80)

II. The Muromachi shogunate years

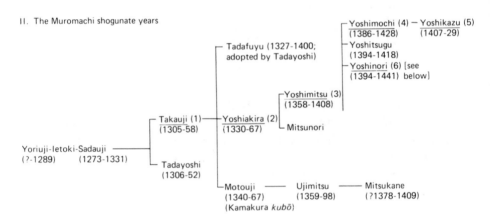

Yoriuji-Ietoki-Sadauji (?-1289) (1273-1331)
— Takauji (1) (1305-58) — Yoshiakira (2) (1330-67)
  — Tadafuyu (1327-1400; adopted by Tadayoshi)
  — Yoshimitsu (3) (1358-1408) — Yoshimochi (4) (1386-1428) — Yoshikazu (5) (1407-29); Yoshitsugu (1394-1418); Yoshinori (6) [see (1394-1441) below]
  — Mitsunori
— Tadayoshi (1306-52)
— Motouji (1340-67) (Kamakura kubō) — Ujimitsu (1359-98) — Mitsukane (?1378-1409)

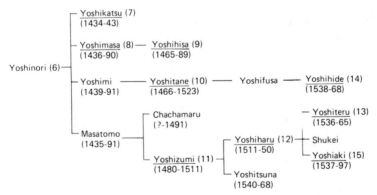

Yoshinori (6)
— Yoshikatsu (7) (1434-43)
— Yoshimasa (8) (1436-90) — Yoshihisa (9) (1465-89)
— Yoshimi (1439-91) — Yoshitane (10) (1466-1523) — Yoshifusa — Yoshihide (14) (1538-68)
— Masatomo (1435-91)
  — Chachamaru (?-1491)
  — Yoshizumi (11) (1480-1511)
    — Yoshiharu (12) (1511-50) — Yoshiteru (13) (1536-65); Shukei; Yoshiaki (15) (1537-97)
    — Yoshitsuna (1540-68)

III. The Kantō branch

Mochiuji (1398-1439) — Shigeuji (1438-97) (Koga kubō) — Masauji (1466-1531) — Takamoto (1485-1535) — Haruuji (?-1560) — Yoshiuji (?-1583)

branch of the imperial house. As a consequence, the Ashikaga family observed two loyalties: one to the shogun and the Hōjō regency and the other to the imperial house. Ashikaga Takauji, whose defection led to the demise of the Kamakura shogunate, made his move in part in the name of Godaigo (1288–1339), head of the Daikakuji line.

It was Yoshiyasu's son, Yoshikane (?–1199), who joined Minamoto Yoritomo's cause in 1180 and thereby brought the Ashikaga family into the service of the Kamakura military government. Before 1180, Yoshikane had married one of Hōjō Tokimasa's daughters. Another daughter, Masako (1157–1225), had married Minamoto Yoritomo. Thus Yoshikane found himself married to the sister of the wife of Yoritomo, the first shogun. The Hōjō connection was actively maintained thereafter, so that during the Kamakura period, of seven generations of Ashikaga chiefs, five took Hōjō wives. Takauji, at the time of his defection, was married to the sister of the last regent. It is significant, however, that Takauji did not have a Hōjō mother; his father had married into the Uesugi, an important military house based in Tamba Province, west of the capital.

In the third generation after Yoshiyasu, the Ashikaga lineage began to segment and spread out beyond the home province. Two of Yoshikane's sons were the first to move out of Shimotsuke. One went to Kōzuke and took the name Momonoi and the other went to Musashi and took the name Hatakeyama. Three members of the next generation moved into Mikawa Province, where they took the place names Niki, Hosokawa, and Togasaki as their own. Then, other members of the lineage established three more branch families, the Kira, Imagawa, and Isshiki in Mikawa. This concentration of holdings in Mikawa probably explains why the head of the house was appointed *shugo* of Mikawa in 1238. The Ashikaga were awarded Kazusa as well, in 1259, but Shimotsuke, the locus of their ancestral holding, remained in the hands of the long-entrenched Koyama family.

Although there is some information about the number of branch families and the location of their holdings, there are almost no data on the size and value of these possessions. Collateral families constituted a first line of support for the chief of the Ashikaga line. By Takauji's generation, these included the Momonoi, Hatakeyama, Niki, Hosokawa, Kira, Imagawa, Isshiki, Ishido, Shibukawa, and Shiba

Figure 4.1 Ashikaga lineage genealogy. (Shoguns are underlined and numbered; names in parentheses are branch family names adopted from location of primary landholding.)

families. Another family that played an important role in the Ashikaga fortunes was the Uesugi, the only family other than the Hōjō that had provided wives for the Ashikaga chiefs. The collaterals provided much of the manpower of the Ashikaga armies. The area of their greatest concentration, Mikawa and adjoining provinces, was clearly a pivotal base, close, but not too close, to Kyoto. Added to this was the fortuitious circumstance that the Uesugi's ancestral holding was in Tamba, just to the west of the capital. It is no accident that Takauji should have started his attack on the Hōjō from Tamba.

Another group that contributed importantly to the Ashikaga power base was the household retainers. Referred to generically as *hikan*, they occupied subordinate positions on the Ashikaga lineage chief's landholdings, serving as estate managers and providing military service. There is little information about this group of families, but a significant piece of documentation in the Kuramochi archives lists what is believed to be the landholdings (*goryō*) of the main Ashikaga house and the stewards serving on them.[3] The document is undated, but internal evidence shows it was drafted between 1293 and 1301.

The Kuramochi document lists thirty-five landholdings located in ten provinces. There is no indication of the size of any of these properties or the income they produced. The locations of those that can be identified are indicated on Map 4.1.[4]

As the map shows, the holdings of the Ashikaga main line were more widely scattered than were the base holdings of its collateral branch families. A correlation between these two sets of holdings makes it clear that the lineage chief could not have depended on his collateral branches to oversee his lands but, rather, had to have them managed by intendants drawn from his own hereditary retainers. The Kuramochi document lists twenty-one such intendants, bearing nineteen surnames.

In 1333, Ashikaga Takauji was called to arms against the threat posed by Emperor Godaigo's machinations. Takauji had already contemplated Godaigo's defection, but Takauji's motives were mixed. First, being of the Minamoto lineage, he felt abused by the Taira Hōjō, who relied on his military support but nonetheless treated him as a vassal, ordering him to commit his troops in defense of Kama-

---

3 The initial analysis of these documents, now held by Tohoku University, is by Kuwayama Kōnen, "Muromachi bakufu no sōsōki ni okeru shoryō ni tsuite," *Chūsei no mado* 12 (April 1963): 4–27.
4 Of the thirty-five pieces referred to in the documents, only some twenty-five can be identified by location.

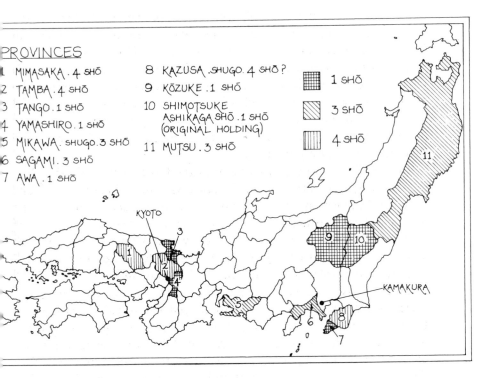

PROVINCES

1 MIMASAKA . 4 SHŌ
2 TAMBA . 4 SHŌ
3 TANGO . 1 SHŌ
4 YAMASHIRO . 1 SHŌ
5 MIKAWA . SHUGO . 3 SHŌ
6 SAGAMI . 3 SHŌ
7 AWA . 1 SHŌ

8 KAZUSA .SHUGO. 4 SHŌ ?
9 KŌZUKE .1 SHŌ
10 SHIMOTSUKE
ASHIKAGA SHŌ .1 SHŌ
(ORIGINAL HOLDING)
11 MUTSU . 3 SHŌ

1 SHŌ

3 SHŌ

4 SHŌ

KYOTO

KAMAKURA

Map 4.1 The Ashikaga house, ca. 1330

kura and requiring him to take a special oath of loyalty. Takauji's
complaint against Hōjō Takatoki, as reported in the *Taiheiki*, was at
first personal:[5]

> Takatoki is but a descendant of Hōjō Tokimasa, whose clan long ago came
> down among the commoners, while I am of the generation of the house of
> Genji, which left the imperial family not long since. Surely it is meant that
> Takatoki should be my vassal instead of contemptuously handing down orders
> such as these![6]

Once Takauji made public his resolve to defect, however, more
justification was needed. He, of course, had every right to consider
Godaigo's call a superior one, particularly as the emperor still held the
proprietary rights to Ashikaga-no-shō. But Takauji could claim a still

5 The *Taiheiki*, written presumably by a priest attached to Godaigo's exiled court in 1345 and
added to as late as 1370, covers events from about 1318 to 1368. Its historical reliability is
moot, but its content is not by any means fictional. Passages quoted in translation are taken
from Helen C. McCullough, trans., *The Taiheiki: A Chronicle of Medieval Japan* (New York:
Columbia University Press, 1959). Hereafter cited as *Taiheiki*.
6 *Taiheiki*, pp. 237–38.

higher cause which was publicized in his prayer to Hachiman, the patron diety of the Minamoto lineage. Passing through the village of Shinomura in Tamba on his way to attack the Hōjō at Rokuhara in 1333, Takauji stopped at a shrine to Hachiman and stated his case. His purpose, he protested, was to destroy the "Eastern descendants of the house of Taira . . . [who] wickedly for nine generations have walked in the ways of violence."[7] But such propagandistic expressions were merely rationalizations. Japan in the 1330s was disturbed by more than private or family rivalries.

Toyoda Takeshi, in his treatment of the forces that undid the Hōjō regency, began with the so-called *akutō* (evil band) phenomenon.[8] The term *evil band* was applied to various types of illegal activities, but the most significant, from the point of view of this analysis, was the work of purposefully organized groups of local warriors who resorted to violence in disputes, usually over land rights. A classic example of such a dispute is that over the Tōdaiji estate of Kuroda in Iga Province. The trouble on this estate was caused by the temple's estate manager (*gesu*). During the 1260s the *gesu* joined with the *jitō* that the bakufu assigned to Kuroda in opposing the temple, withholding dues payments, and the like. The temple appealed for redress to Rokuhara, the bakufu headquarters in Kyoto. To settle the case, Rokuhara called on the deputy *shugo* of adjoining Omi Province and a Kamakura *gokenin* in Iga. But the order had no effect, and Rokuhara was eventually obliged to mobilize a punitive force on its own. Kuroda-no-shō continued to experience trouble periodically until the end of the Hōjō regency.

In the Kuroda case, there is a pattern of growing conflict between central authority and local autonomy. The fact that Rokuhara was unable to suppress the Kuroda *akutō* by calling on the bakufu's regional agents bespoke a growing antagonism between the *jitō*-type of vassals of Kamakura and the Hōjō family that monopolized more and more of these high appointments. In central Japan in particular, local *bushi* houses like these found connections in the imperial court to be a useful device for legitimizing their defection from the Hōjō. Thus, when Godaigo began the plot to rescue the imperial government from domination by the Kamakura bakufu, he received strong support from dissident military houses in all quarters of the country.

Akutō behavior was symptomatic of the two great themes of disaffec-

---

7 Ibid., p. 250.
8 Toyoda, "Genkō," pp. 1–5. For a recent study in English, see Lorraine Harrington, "Social Control and the Significance of Akutō," in Jeffrey P. Mass, ed., *Court and Bakufu in Japan: Essays in Kamakura History* (New Haven, Conn.: Yale University Press, 1982).

tion that led to nearly eighty years of civil war, beginning with the destruction of the Hōjō-dominated Kamakura bakufu in 1333. On the one hand, Godaigo awakened among the court nobility and the major religious establishments the hope that the mounting encroachment of military houses on local administration and land-derived wealth could be stemmed. On the other hand, in the provinces the pressure was toward the reverse – the continuing effort by local houses as estate managers to avoid having to serve the Kyoto nobility and to be able to retain the estates' income for themselves. These two movements were not compatible, and in the final analysis, the second was destined to win out as the powers of lordship passed into the hands of those who could defend them at the village level. During the first half of the Muromachi era, however, the Ashikaga shoguns, by occupying the middle ground between these two positions, managed to stave off the demise of the *shoen*-based nobility for yet another two centuries.

THE FOUNDING OF THE MUROMACHI BAKUFU

Emperor Godaigo, who began his reign in 1318, gave early evidence of his determination to recapture the powers lost by the throne to both the high court nobility (*kugyō*) and the Kamakura bakufu. In 1321, Godaigo discontinued the system of government in which political control was exercised by the retired emperor (*insei*) and by the Fujiwara regency (*sekkan*). Instead, he proposed to engage directly in the affairs of state. As a first step in this direction, he revived the office of land records (*kirokusho*), first established in 1069 to oversee the documentation of *shōen* and to regulate the illegal acquisition of land by noble houses and religious institutions in an effort to prevent the flight of taxable land from the purview of court-designated local officials. Godaigo's plots against the Hōjō came to the attention of the bakufu, and in 1331, he was exiled to the remote island of Oki. But Godaigo had set in motion more than a privately motivated attack on the Hōjō-dominated bakufu. When in 1333 he managed to escape from Oki, he found himself at the center of a broadly based movement of resistance against the Hōjō. Among the many provincial military leaders who came to his support were Ashikaga Takauji and Nitta Yoshisada.

In the winter of 1333, upon word of Godaigo's return to the mainland, Ashikaga Takauji was dispatched from Kamakura in command of a large army to safeguard the Hōjō headquarters at Rokuhara in Kyoto. Already he intended to change his allegiance if the opportunity presented itself. Upon reaching Ōmi Province, he received a written commission from Godaigo that legitimized his defection. Bypassing Kyoto, Takauji marched directly to Tamba, the home province of the Uesugi house. There, in the fourth month of 1333, Takauji raised the banner of Minamoto resistance to the Hōjō and called for supporters. He was joined immediately by warrior bands from all parts of the country. As the *Taiheiki* narrates, a force of twenty thousand in Tamba had swelled to fifty thousand by the time that Takauji was at the gates of Kyoto.[9] To take a local example, in Harima the head of a leading local warrior house, the Akamatsu, destined to be named *shugo* of Harima, was one of the first to join Takauji. Along with him came a band of local samurai families from the neighboring Bizen and Bitchū provinces, among them the Matsuda, who later became *shugo* of western Bizen. Sporadic but fierce fighting ensued, but Takauji had little difficulty in destroying the Hōjō establishment in Kyoto and in capturing the city for Godaigo. At nearly the same time, Nitta Yoshisada led his forces to the destruction of the Hōjō in Kamakura. Thus, the two men were destined to become rival leaders in Godaigo's service.

Godaigo returned to the capital intent on setting himself up as a true monarch. To that purpose he activated the records office and established an awards commission (*onshō-gata*). Through these and other organs of government, he began to make appointments to central and provincial posts and to distribute titles to landholdings. Almost immediately there was a falling out with Takauji. Although they had fought to destroy the Hōjō and to return Emperor Godaigo to the throne, neither Takauji nor his followers were prepared to go along with the emperor's plan to create a government centered on the throne in which military leaders would be of equal or lower rank than the court nobles, men without experience in warfare or statecraft. Takauji personally was well treated by Godaigo. Designated "first to be rewarded," he received the fourth court rank junior grade, the privilege of using one of the characters from the emperor's private name, the governorships of two provinces and the position of *shugo* of another, and numerous landholdings. Takauji, however, had already petitioned for the posts of *seii tai shōgun* (literally, "barbarian-subduing generalissimo)" and *sō-tsuibushi* (constable general), the positions that would give him the authority to establish a new bakufu. Although Godaigo did name Takauji *chinjufu shōgun* (general of the northern pacification command) and, later, *sei-tō shōgun* (general of the eastern pacification command), he refused during his lifetime to grant Takauji's request. In-

9 *Taiheiki*, p. 151. All such figures are, of course, conjectural.

stead, he successively named his sons, the princes Morinaga and Norinaga, to the post, thus giving form to a polity in which civil authority would outrank or displace the military.

Godaigo's conception was bold, but the execution of his plan was inept and highly prejudiced. As the *Taiheiki* records, although men like Takauji and Yoshisada received special attention, "the offices of *shugo* and governor in more than fifty provinces were received by nobles and court officials; likewise confiscated estates and great estates were given them until they became . . . rich and powerful. . . ."[10] Following the destruction of the Hōjō, a considerable amount of vacated land and a large number of provincial posts were available for award to those who had assisted in Godaigo's return to the throne. But by including court nobles among the recipients, the emperor ran out of resources with which to reward his military supporters. Among those poorly treated were local leaders such as Akamatsu Norimura, who, once having been appointed *shugo* of Harima, later had the appointment withdrawn. Such arbitrary action led to a general disillusionment among military leaders in the provinces. Takauji, aspiring chief of the military estate and potential shogun, became the most prominent alternative to Godaigo. But he was not alone, as his rivalry with Nitta Yoshisada was to prove.

In 1333, after crushing the Hōjō in Kyoto, Takauji set up a secretariat (*bugyō-sho*) to administer the city in the manner of the recently destroyed Rokuhara headquarters. As the winning general, Takauji assumed the right to reward his followers with grants of confiscated landholdings and to make appointments to the posts of *shugo* and *jitō*. Obviously there was a conflict of authority and jurisdiction here that could not long remain unresolved. During most of 1334 Takauji and Godaigo managed a precarious coexistence in Kyoto. The emperor publicly announced his plan, called the Kemmu restoration, and established various organs of central government. Takauji did not take office in any of these, nor did he disband his own secretariat. When Godaigo dispatched his young son Prince Norinaga to Kamakura in an effort to assert the imperial presence in the Kantō, Takauji had his brother Tadayoshi appointed military guardian to the prince. When Takauji complained to Godaigo that the newly appointed shogun, Prince Morinaga, was plotting his death, the emperor had Morinaga sent to Kamakura to be placed in Ashikaga Tadayoshi's custody.

---

10 *Taiheiki*, p. 365. In this case, there is good evidence that the *Taiheiki* gives an accurate report.

In 1335, Hōjō remnants recaptured Kamakura and drove out Tadayoshi and Prince Morinaga. In the confusion, Tadayoshi had Prince Morinaga killed. Takauji now led his own army, without imperial orders, to the Kantō and quickly retook Kamakura. This time Takauji remained in Kamakura for a year and began to put on the mantle of shogun, giving out land patents and confirmations. When it was clear that Nitta Yoshisada was siding with Godaigo, Takauji declared Nitta's lands confiscated and began to distribute them to his followers. Godaigo retaliated by declaring Takauji an "enemy of the throne" (chōteki) and stripping him of his titles and honors. He commissioned generals loyal to his cause, among them Nitta Yoshisada and Kitabatake Akiie, to recapture the Kantō.

Takauji was now in full rebellion against Godaigo, and his break with rival military leaders like Yoshisada was complete. Taking to the field again, he fought his way back to Kyoto in the second month of 1336, against heavy opposition from forces supporting Godaigo's cause. Takauji managed to hold the city for only four days before being driven out toward the western provinces. His retreat was not complete until he had reached the island of Kyushu.

Although Kyushu and the western Honshū provinces were not areas in which the Ashikaga had many direct military connections, Takauji used to his advantage a commission of chastisement against Nitta Yoshisada that he obtained from the retired emperor Kōgon-in, head of the senior branch of the imperial house. Also, by representing the Minamoto cause and professing to champion basic warrior interests in the event of his becoming shogun, Takauji was able to build up a considerable following along the path of his retreat. When possible, he found opportunities along the way to place his collateral followers in favorable positions, promising the most powerful local families and the heads of Ashikaga collateral branches who supported him the military governorships of various provinces and districts, depending on the success of his cause. To the Hosokawa he promised the entire island of Shikoku; to the Imagawa, Bitchū; to the Akamatsu, Harima; and to the Niki, Tamba. By the time he arrived in Kyushu, Takauji had already won over most of the local military lords, such as the Shimazu, and only a brief military campaign was needed to gain the support of the remainder.

By the fifth month of 1336, with some of his house retainers and collateral commanders and contingents led by his newly won allies from western Japan, Takauji began the countermarch toward Kyoto. His forces moved by both land and water. At the critical battle of

Minatogawa in Settsu, the Ashikaga won a decisive victory, forcing Nitta back to Kyoto and Emperor Godaigo to take refuge with the monks of Hieizan. Takauji entered Kyoto in the company of Prince Yutahito, the brother of Kōgon-in who had previously given Takauji his imperial mandate. Takauji generously endowed the Kōgon-in faction with lands and guarantees of protected income. Somehow the imperial regalia was obtained from Godaigo. These emblems, which were given to Prince Yutahito, became the basis for his installation as Emperor Kōmyō. Takauji began the construction of a new imperial palace, the first permanent one in many years, which was completed the following year. Takauji had now played the supreme role of having installed an emperor with his military power. He further legitimized himself by taking high court rank and adopting the role of chief of the warrior estate. The secretariat he had established three years before had remained in operation and was now turned into a bakufu in all but name. Takauji's public posture was further enhanced when he promulgated the Kemmu *shikimoku* (the Kemmu injunctions), making public the policy he proposed to follow when named shogun.[11] But the appointment did not come until 1338.

There was work yet to be done. Kyoto was still not safely in Ashikaga hands, nor would the enemies of the new bakufu leave the field. Godaigo, claiming that he had given up only replicas and that he still possessed the authentic regalia, kept his cause alive from the mountainous region of Yoshino. There he set up a court in exile, which, because it was located south of Kyoto, was called the Southern Court. The court that remained in Kyoto, which served to legitimate the Ashikaga shogun, was, by the same token, called the Northern Court. Fighting in the name of these two courts continued until 1392, when a settlement was arranged. The existence of two imperial courts, each claiming legitimacy, each calling on the warrior houses throughout Japan to fight for its cause, justified the resort to arms, often for purely private objectives. The basic motivations were not always apparent, but in the years to follow intense rivalries for power among the most powerful military houses in the provinces were fought out.

Takauji's two primary military rivals from the beginning were Nitta Yoshisada and Kitabatake Akiie, both of whom had their largest bases

11 For a translation of this document and the 452 supplementary laws (*tsuikahō*) that succeeded it, see Kenneth A. Grossberg, ed., and Kenneth A. Grossberg and Nobuhisa Kanamoto, trans., *The Laws of the Muromachi Bakufu: Kemmu Shikimoku (1336) and the Muromachi Tsuikahō* (Tokyo: *Monumenta Nipponica* and Sophia University, 1981). Herewith cited as *Kemmu Shikimoku and Tsuikahō*.

of support east and north of the capital. Although both men were killed in battle in the summer of 1338, and despite Godaigo's death in the summer of 1339, the fighting did not end. Godaigo's son Prince Norinaga succeeded to the "junior" line under the name Gomurakami. In the central provinces, Kusunoki Masatsura, *shugo* of Kawachi, kept the Ashikaga forces on the defensive. In Kyushu, Godaigo's other son, Prince Kanenaga, succeeded in establishing himself at Dazaifu as the chief agent of the capital. The divided polity and the civil war it engendered continued. But the main issue regarding the establishment of a bakufu in Kyoto had been settled.

For a few years the capital area remained sufficiently quiet, so that the work of organizing the new bakufu could move ahead. The Kemmu *shikimoku* was followed by supplementary orders (*tsuikahō*) that sought to resolve the many problems that had been left unsettled during the years of heavy fighting.[12] But in 1350, events took another sudden turn, this time brought on by conflicts within the Ashikaga leadership. For several years, a rift over basic policy had been growing between Takauji and his brother Tadayoshi. This was the consequence of the division of responsibilities that had been worked out between the two men. The division was a natural one to make: Takauji was responsible for military strategy and personnel, and Tadayoshi concerned himself with the bakufu's administrative and judicial organs. But policy differences soon developed between the brothers. Takauji, more sensitive to the interest of the local military houses on whose support he depended, tended to be soft regarding the military encroachment on civil estates. Tadayoshi was more inclined to permit the bakufu courts, staffed to considerable extent by hereditary legal experts, to support the proprietary interests of the capital elite.[13] Eventually factions among the Ashikaga collaterals formed behind the brothers.

In 1349, Takauji, having been persuaded of Tadayoshi's disloyalty, dismissed his brother from his bakufu assignments, withdrawing the expectation that he would be next to inherit the title of shogun. The next year Takauji was forced to take to the field against Tadafuyu, his own troublemaking natural son who had been adopted by Tadayoshi.

---

12 *Kemmu Shikimoku and Tsuikahō*, pp. 25–41. Fourteen *tsuikahō* were issued between 1336 and 1345. But in the year 1346 alone, forty such orders were issued.

13 This analysis was first made by Satō Shin'ichi, "Muromachi bakufu kaisōki no kansei taikei," in Ishimoda Shō and Satō Shin'ichi, eds., *Chūsei no hō to kokka* (Tokyo: Tōkyō daigaku shuppankai, 1960). For a statement in English, see Shin'ichi Sato, with John Whitney Hall, "The Ashikaga Shogun and the Muromachi Bakufu Administration," in John Whitney Hall and Takeshi, Toyoda, eds., *Japan in the Muromachi Age* (Berkeley and Los Angeles: University of California Press, 1977), pp. 45–52.

In the winter of 1351–2, Tadayoshi was captured and killed, presumably by poisoning on Takauji's orders. But Tadayoshi's death only increased the anti-Takauji sentiment in the Kantō. It was not until the spring of 1355 that Takauji, after perhaps the most destructive battle of the civil war, in which several sections of the city were destroyed, retook Kyoto conclusively.

Takauji died in 1358 and was succeeded as head of the Ashikaga house and shogun by Yoshiakira, then in his twenty-eighth year. As might be expected, the second shogun at first had trouble keeping the Ashikaga forces in line, but the intensity of the civil war had subsided. The most powerful *shugo* houses capable of opposing the Ashikaga – the Shiba, Uesugi, Ōuchi, and Yamana – had settled their differences and had joined forces with the bakufu. Yoshiakira died in 1368, to be succeeded by his ten-year-old son Yoshimitsu, who lived to preside over the most flourishing era of the Muromachi bakufu.

THE PATH TO ASHIKAGA LEGITIMACY

One of the major accomplishments of the Ashikaga house was its success in legitimizing the post of shogun within a polity still legally under the sovereign authority of the emperor. We have already noted that Minamoto Yoritomo, the first shogun, did not depend solely on the title of shogun to establish his legitimacy.[14] Rather, it was the Hōjō regents who built up the importance of the title as a device through which to exercise leadership over the *bushi* class. After Yoritomo's death, the office of shogun became identified with the powers that Yoritomo had acquired both as the foremost military leader and by virtue of the high ranks and titles bestowed on him by the court. Although the office of shogun never received written definition or legal formulation, under the Ashikaga the title was recognized as giving to its recipient and holder the status of chief of the military estate (*buke no tōryō*), the keeper of the warriors' customary law, and the ultimate guarantor of the land rights of the *bushi* class.

The concept of *buke* rule, in the context of the imperial tradition of civil government, was the subject of considerable discussion in fourteenth-century Japan. Political philosophers in both Kyoto and Kamakura were fully aware of the issues raised by the emergence of military rule. Godaigo's Kemmu restoration, and the long drawn-out

14 Jeffrey P. Mass, *Warrior Government in Early Medieval Japan: A Study of the Kamakura Bakufu, Shugo, and Jitō* (New Haven, Conn.: Yale University Press, 1974). Also see his chapter in this volume.

civil war that followed, naturally stimulated attempts at special pleading on both sides. One of the foremost efforts to address the issue of
imperial rule was the *Jinnō shōtōki*, written between 1339 and 1343 by
Kitabatake Chikafusa, a supporter of Godaigo in exile.

Chikafusa began with the premise that the *tennō* line, by means of
correct succession from the Sun Goddess, was "a transcendent source
of virtue in government, which was above criticism."[15] On the other
hand, individual emperors were accountable for their private acts and
could be criticized if their intrusion into political and military affairs
should have unfortunate results. According to Chikafusa, not even
Godaigo was above criticism. Having failed to recognize the changed
nature of the time, his appointments to office and his rewards to
courtiers and military leaders had been capricious, and the results
proved harmful to the state.

Statements justifying military rule, written from the point of view of
the *buke* class, were even more direct. The court aristocracy, they
claimed, had had their day and had failed. It was the destiny of the
samurai estate, through its ability (*kiryō*), to bring the state back to a
peaceful and well-administered condition. This essentially was what
Ashikaga Takauji asserted when he prayed publicly before the
Shinomura Hachiman Shrine of Tamba. The same premise underlines
the preamble to the Kemmu *shikimoku* of 1336.[16] Neither statement
was critical of the emperor or his court but, rather, of the maladminis-
tration of the Hōjō regents. As to what constituted good government,
the obvious answer was the maintenance of peace, law, and order, a
condition in which all the people could prosper. The basic intent of the
Kemmu *shikimoku* was to offer guidelines on how to achieve good
government.[17]

Even more philosophically explicit on what constitutes good government is a document known as *Tōji-in goisho* (Takauji's testament) and
written in 1357, though most likely not by Takauji.[18] This document
sets forth in a Confucian manner the proposition that the state (*tenka*)
is not the possession of any person, neither emperor nor shogun, but
of itself and that rulers must conform to the "essence of the polity"
(*tenka no kokoro*). Within the *tenka*, the task of the shogun and his
followers is to ensure peace.

15 H. Paul Varley, *Imperial Restoration in Medieval Japan* (New York: Columbia University
   Press, 1971). 16 *Shigaku kenkyū* 110 (April 1971): 72–97.
17 Henrik Carl Trolle Steenstrup, "Hōjō Shigetoki (1198–1261) and His Role in the History of
   Political and Ethical Ideas in Japan" (Ph.D. diss., Harvard University, 1977), p. 236.
18 Ibid., p. 234.

One is struck by the pragmatic spirit of these general statements on government and statecraft. They clearly stand on a middle ground in placing military rule into the context of a polity that included both an emperor and a large court (*kuge*) community. No model excluded the emperor. Nor was there any thought to bring *kuge* and *buke* together into a single ruling class. *Buke* remained a separate branch of the aristocracy. The shogun, though recognized as chief of the warrior estate, was never conceived of as a self-proclaimed or self-appointed official. The office of shogun was an imperial appointment. Even though the emperor personally might be a creature of the military hegemon, having been assisted to the throne by a victorious military leader, investiture as shogun was an act that only the emperor and his courtiers could perform.

Political ideas of this sort were reflected in the real world. The struggle that preceded the final Ashikaga military victory shaped the complex interdependence between *buke* and *kuge* interests. Takauji had depended on the imperial patent to legitimate his chastisement of Nitta Yoshisada, his own brother, and his natural son Tadafuyu. He had installed Emperor Kōmyō, who in turn had named him *seii tai shōgun*. In the years that followed, the court community became almost totally reliant on military government to preserve its livelihood; yet military leaders avidly competed for apparently hollow court ranks and functionally meaningless court titles. No matter how powerful a military hegemon, if he aspired to recognition as ruler of the entire country, he needed more than a conquering army. He needed also a sufficiently high court status to demonstrate publicly his right to rule.

Having settled in Kyoto, the Ashikaga house was quickly assimilated into the high aristocracy, that is, into the select group of families of third court rank and above who were known as *kugyō*. The third shogun, Yoshimitsu, best illustrates the capacity of the Ashikaga leaders to penetrate court society. Having attained the first court rank in 1380 at age twenty-two, he received successively higher appointments until attaining in 1394 the highest court title available, that of prime minister (*daijō daijin*). Yoshimitsu's successive steps up the ladder of court rank were accompanied by his adoption of a commensurate lifestyle.

In 1378, the Ashikaga house had built a residential palace in the grand manner at Muromachi, soon referred to as the Palace of Flowers (Hana no gosho). This complex of buildings occupied twice the space of the imperial palace that had been built for the emperor by Takauji as a grand gesture of patronage. When in 1381 Yoshimitsu managed to entertain Emperor Goenyu in his own residence, the occasion confirmed his status as *kugyō*. That Yoshimitsu fully understood this is revealed in his conscious adoption of two separate ciphers, one for use as a member of the military aristocracy and the other as a courtier. Increasingly from this time on, he used the latter almost exclusively.

After his successful reconciliation of the rival branches of the imperial house in 1392, Yoshimitsu was in the most exalted position in both the *kuge* and the *buke* worlds. A supreme patron of the arts, he is best remembered for his Kitayama villa and its centerpiece, the Golden Pavilion, built between 1397 and 1407. In 1408 he made known his hopes of having his son Yoshitsugu receive a ceremonial standing comparable to that of an imperial prince, thus setting in motion the rumor that he intended to gain for the Ashikaga house access to the imperial throne itself. But Yoshimitsu died shortly thereafter.

Historians continue to debate whether Yoshimitsu did in fact intend to usurp the throne and whether he could have succeeded. There is not enough documentation to settle the issue on the basis of written evidence. The fact that he did not do so and that his son and successor Yoshimochi dissuaded the court from bestowing on his father the posthumous title of *daijō-hōō* (priestly retired monarch) indicates that an overt act of usurpation would have been difficult, if not impossible, to carry out.

But whether or not Yoshimitsu intended to displace the emperor, he and his successors as shogun did preside over the demise of the tradition of imperial rule as it had been up to that point. As Nagahara Keiji pointed out so clearly, by this time, the warrior aristocracy had absorbed the functions of the imperial government over which the *tennō* and the *kuge* had presided. Yoshimitsu possessed all the formal rights of rulership: to grant or withdraw holdings in land, to staff posts in central and provincial administrations, to establish central and provincial courts, and to maintain the flow of taxes. Yoshimitsu as chief of the *buke* had achieved a general takeover of the functional organs of government.[19]

Can it then be said that Yoshimitsu had attained the status of monarch? As shogun, and hence chief of the *buke* estate, and as prime minister, and thus the highest-ranking official of the noble estate, he held the credentials of ultimate authority in both. Under the Ashikaga,

19 Nagahara Keiji, "Zen-kindai no tennō," in *Rekishigaku kenkyū* 467 (April 1979): 37–45. In English, see Peter Arnesen, "The Provincial Vassals of the Muromachi Bakufu,"in Jeffrey P. Mass and William B. Hauser, eds., *The Bakufu in Japanese History* (Stanford, Calif.: Stanford University Press, 1985), pp. 125–6.

the shogun had become more powerful than any previous secular official. But he was not sovereign, nor were his peers likely to have permitted him to become such.

The monarchical issue is raised in yet another context. Yoshimitsu's acceptance in 1402 of a mission from China that brought to the shogun documents investing him as "King of Japan" and calling on him to adopt the Ming imperial calendar. How did Yoshimitsu justify his break with the Japanese tradition of refusing to acknowledge the sovereignty of a foreign country? Certainly trade was a major consideration. But a final assessment of the encounter may not rest in the field of trade. Tanaka Takeo, for instance, suggests that involvement in trade with the continent was a conscious effort by Yoshimitsu to project Japan into the mainstream of East Asian affairs, an effort to gain recognition as a member of the wider East Asian community. Within Japan, the shogun's successful negotiations with China became a means to confirm the principle that as chief of the military estate, he had full control of Japan's foreign affairs. Yoshimitsu had in fact shielded the emperor from facing the actuality of a letter of investiture from the Ming emperor. But he also made clear that the emperor need not be troubled by diplomatic affairs in the future.[20]

SHOGUN, *SHUGO*, AND PROVINCIAL ADMINISTRATION

It is sometimes claimed that Takauji, in his effort to attract and hold *shugo*-grade warriors in his command, gave away resources vital to the sustenance of his own position as shogun. But the reverse is more likely true. By adding to the stature of *shugo* as provincial administrators, he added equally to the reach of the bakufu's authority. And as long as they worked together in a context that admitted the shogun's primacy, the growth of *shugo* power in the provinces was to the advantage of the bakufu's rule.

At the outset of his attack on the Hōjō, Takauji depended primarily on members of the Ashikaga house, cadet branches, and direct retainers for support in the field. His first appointments to *shugo* were picked from among house retainers like the Kō brothers and were placed over provinces in the Kantō where the Ashikaga already had some reliable bases. As the war spread and Takauji was widely opposed by rival military houses, he was obliged to name trustworthy

20 Takeo Tanaka, with Robert Sakai, "Japan's Relations with Overseas Countries," in Hall and Toyoda, eds., *Japan in The Muromachi Age*, p. 178.

TABLE 4.2

Control of provinces by Ashikaga collaterals and other families, ca. 1400

Province	Family	Province	Family
Yamashiro	Bakufu	Tango	Isshiki
Yamato	Kōfukuji	Tajima	Yamana
Kawachi	Hatakeyama	Inaba	Yamana
Izumi	Niki	Hōki	Yamana
Settsu	Hosokawa	Izumo	Kyōgoku
Iga	Yamana	Iwami	Yamana
Ise	Toki	Iki	Kyōgoku
Shima	Toki	Harima	Akamatsu
Owari	Shiba	Mimasaka	Akamatsu
Mikawa	Isshiki	Bizen	Akamatsu
Totomi	Imagawa	Bitchū	Hosokawa
Suruga	Imagawa	Bingo	Hosokawa
Ōmi	Kyōgoku	Aki	Shibukawa
Mino	Toki	Suo	Ōuchi
Hida	Kyōgoku	Nagato	Ōuchi
Shinano	Shiba	Kii	Hatakeyama
Wakasa	Isshiki	Awaji	Hosokawa
Echizen	Shiba	Awa	Hosokawa
Kaga	Togashi	Sanuki	Hosokawa
Noto	Hatakeyama	Iyo	Kawano
Etchū	Hatakeyama	Tosa	Hosokawa
Echigo	Uesugi		
Tamba	Hosokawa		

collaterals and friendly allies to all the provinces.[21] Between 1336 and 1368 the composition of the Ashikaga house band changed dramatically as a number of the cadet houses who joined the Tadayoshi faction were destroyed and as new allies were put in places of trust. Naturally Takauji sought to bring as many provinces as possible under *shugo* appointed from among Ashikaga kinsmen. By the end of the fourteenth century, of the provinces of central Japan, twenty-three were held by Ashikaga collaterals, twenty by noncollaterals, and two by institutions, as can be seen from Table 4.2[22] (see also Maps 4.2 and 4.3).

It is natural to assume that the collateral houses were the most important in the eyes of the shogun. But as events proved, the

---

21 Imatani Akira, "Kōki Muromachi bakufu no kenryoku kōzō – tokuni sono senseika ni tsuite," in Nihonshi kenkyūkai shiryō kenkyū bukai ed., *Chūsei Nihon no rekishizō* (Osaka: Sōgensha, 1978), pp. 154–183 reveals how in certain strategic but precariously held provinces in central Japan, like Settsu, Yamato, and Izumi, *shugo* were appointed by *kōri* (districts) for strategic reasons.

22 These figures were developed from the listings of *shugo* appointments by Sugiyama Hiroshi in *Dokushi sōran* (Tokyo: Jimbutsu ōraisha, 1966), pp. 115–18.

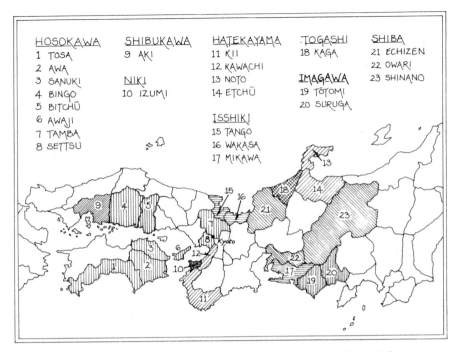

Map 4.2 Provinces in central bloc held by Ashikaga collateral *shugo*, ca. 1400.

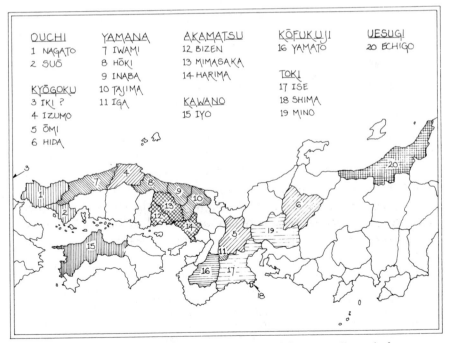

Map 4.3 Provinces in the central area held by noncollateral *shugo* houses, ca. 1400.

noncollateral *shugo*, all being to some extent "creations" of the Ashikaga and having been confirmed or put in place by Takauji or one of his successors, often were even more reliable. The Ashikaga naturally had greater difficulty with entrenched military houses from the Kamakura period that could not be dislodged from their provinces.

Among the noncollateral creations, the Akamatsu house of Harima is typical of the first type.[23] The Akamatsu had served as Kamakura-appointed stewards of the Sayo estate in Harima Province. In 1333, Akamatsu Norimura joined Godaigo and assisted in his escape from exile. In reward Akamatsu was named *shugo* of Harima, but at a later date the reward was withdrawn. Norimura subsequently changed his loyalty to Ashikaga Takauji, and his support in the battles that led to the recapture of the capital placed him high on Takauji's reward list. In 1336 he was appointed *shugo* of Harima, and shortly thereafter his sons were appointed to Settsu and Mimasaka. As the bakufu organization was formalized in the years of the third shogun, Yoshimitsu, the Akamatsu house held the posts of *shugo* in Harima, Bizen, and Mimasaka and was recognized as one of the four families from which the heads of the bakufu's Board of Retainers (*samurai-dokoro*) were chosen.

The Ōuchi of Suō are a good example of the second type of *shugo* house.[24] As the *shugo* of Suō under the Kamakura regime, Ouchi Nagahiro joined the Ashikaga cause in 1336 and assisted in the recapture of Kyoto that year. As reward, Takauji confirmed his possession of Suō. Thereafter the Ouchi were to serve the Ashikaga house, and at the time of its greatest expansion it held six *shugo* posts.

The post of *shugo* had not been fully developed under the Kamakura bakufu. In the provinces the civil governor's office (*kokuga*) and the attached resident officials still provided the machinery of administration and judicial process, and except for the Kantō, these facilities remained accountable to civil officials based in Kyoto. As the power of these civil authorities declined, the need for a greater bakufu presence in the provinces became apparent. The agency through which this was accomplished was the office of *shugo*. When in the later years of their regency, the Hōjō openly attempted to monopolize the *shugo* appointments (they succeeded in filling twenty-eight of the fifty-seven appoint-

23 See John Whitney Hall, *Government and Local Power in Japan, 500–1700: A Study Based on Bizen Province* (Princeton, N.J.: Princeton University Press, 1966), pp. 137–206 for a description of the Akamatsu as *shugo* of Bizen. Kishida Hiroshi offers a detailed study of the Akamatsu rule in Harima. See his "Shugo Akamatsushi no Harima no kuni shihai no hatten to kokuga," in Ogawa, ed., *Muromachi seiken*, pp. 139–76.

24 See Peter Arnesen, *The Medieval Japanese Daimyo: The Ōuchi Family's Rule in Suō and Nagato* (New Haven, Conn.: Yale University Press, 1979), pp. 139–76.

SHOGUN, *SHUGO*, PROVINCIAL ADMINISTRATION   197

ments), it was clear that the importance of the post was being recognized. In the Kantō, where the bakufu possessed broad powers of appointment, the practice of awarding remaining provincial "public lands" to incumbent *shugo* was gaining currency, and Godaigo continued the practice. From the beginning, the Ashikaga shoguns conceived of the provinces as administrative units to be governed by *shugo* who were freely appointed by the shogun.[25]

Article 7 of the Kemmu code of 1336 equated the office of *shugo* with that of provincial governor in the imperial bureaucracy.[26] To that end the Muromachi bakufu sought to make the provincial headquarters and their attached lands (*kokugaryō*) available to the *shugo*. The size of these lands varied widely, but whether or not they were of significant economic value, authority over the seat of provincial government had important political implications. For example, the Akamatsu, as newly appointed *shugo* in Harima, worked steadily to obtain control over the provincial headquarters, by reducing local resident officials to vassalage. By the 1360s they were being referred to as *kunikata*, a recognition that as *shugo* they were the "ruling authority of the province."[27] Contemporary documents record that the Akamatsu chiefs granted land to their subordinates. For a house like the Ōuchi, with a long history of serving as resident officials, the advent of the new bakufu did not demand a radical departure from customary practice.[28]

Most of the newly posted *shugo* in central and western Japan appointed by the first two Ashikaga shoguns were brought in from outside the provinces to which they were assigned. These early appointees did not have ready-made and secure positions in which to settle. The Muromachi bakufu soon realized that it had to give its *shugo* greater administrative, judicial, and fiscal authority. Between 1333 and 1346, important changes were made in the legal nature of the office of *shugo*. Godaigo's policy of naming courtiers as *shugo* or of appointing the same individual (most often a military leader) to both the office of *shugo* and provincial governor had the effect of fusing the two offices into one.

Under the Kamakura bakufu, *shugo* had been given three specific functions: (1) enrolling bakufu retainers for guard duty at Kyoto and Kamakura, (2) suppressing major crimes like murder and piracy, and

25 Kurokawa Naonori, "Shugo ryōgokusei to shōen taisei," in Ogawa, ed., *Muromachi seiken*, pp. 107–22.   26 *Kemmu Shikimoku and Tsuikahō*, pp. 18–19.
27 Kishida, "Shugo Akamatsu," p. 165.
28 Arnesen, *Ōuchi Family's Rule*, pp. 99–115.

(3) punishing treason. In 1346, the Muromachi bakufu added two more important powers. The first conferred the right to deal with the unlawful cutting of crops – a favorite act of *akutō* bands. The second, in practical terms, meant the right to carry out the bakufu's orders to confiscate or redistribute land rights. Together, these legal provisions gave the *shugo* the authority to exercise major judicial and fiscal powers that heretofore had been exercised by organs of the central government.[29] But a number of specific military privileges were still to be defined.

Considering the amount of warfare that accompanied the establishment of the Muromachi bakufu, it is not surprising that the acquisition of supply and support resources would be a primary concern. Those military leaders who, like Takauji or Yoshisada, commanded large house bands, were under constant pressure to underwrite the military expenditures of their followers. Takauji's practice was either to dip into his own family holdings or to promise grants from future acquisitions by conquest. Neither of these sources was fully reliable, nor were land grants in themselves easily or quickly converted into economic products-in-hand. A more immediate source of support thus was needed. The answer was to invoke the precedent of the wartime commissariat surtax.

It had been customary for some time for warriors in the field, or after an extended engagement, to receive from the central authority the right to collect commissariat rice (*hyōrō-mai*) from designated areas. For example, after his victory over the Taira in 1185, Minamoto Yoritomo was empowered to use the newly created military land stewards to collect a nationwide tax of three *shō* per *tan* of cultivated land – about a 3 percent charge on the annual harvest – for commissariat support. When Takauji recaptured Kyoto in 1336, he issued permits to some of his followers to collect extraordinary imposts on certain types of land in areas in which warfare had actually taken place. These permits were issued specifying the lands to which the tax right pertained as military provisions (*hyōrō-ryōsho*). The permits were to be temporary. But privileges of this sort were more easily granted than withdrawn. Before long, the taking of the "military's share" of the country's annual product was institutionalized through the practice of the *shugo*-levied half-tax (*hanzei*).

The adoption of half-tax procedures illustrates the conflicting demands placed on early Muromachi bakufu policy. The first supplemen-

29 Kurokawa, "Shugo ryōgokusei,", pp. 117–19.

tary law, issued in 1337, shows that the bakufu's principal concern was to recall the previously awarded "temporary" tax powers to protect the interests of the most highly placed noble and priestly proprietors. It demanded that lands held by *shugo* and other military officers for commissariat support "be immediately returned to the estate agents of the civil proprietors."[30] A directive issued in 1338 accused the *shugo* of abusing this privilege, by taking permanent possession of lands occupied for military support and even distributing them among their own retainers. The bakufu was clearly in a bind. Its primary interest in the provinces was to build up the strength of its *shugo;* yet it could not deny entirely the interests of the capital nobility and priesthood.

In 1352, in Supplementary Article 56, the bakufu began to protect certain limited and specified proprietary interests.[31] The bakufu order of 1368 singled out for protection "properties of the emperors and empresses, of fully protected shrines and temples, and the hereditary properties of the Fujiwara regents." Moreover, those parts of the estates to which *jitō* rights (*shiki*) had been awarded to the civil proprietor by the bakufu were to remain protected.[32] This policy thus protected the estate incomes of the most prestigious of the court nobility and religious institutions, whose preservation was of vital concern to the Ashikaga. Furthermore, because such a policy of selective application of the half-tax at the provincial level could be carried out only by the *shugo*, the court nobility accordingly became dependent on the shogun as the only authority capable of dealing with the *shugo*.

Already the *shugo* had become involved in another fiscal practice that increased the court's dependence. This was the practice of tax contracting (*shugo-uke*). Under this system, Kyoto-based absentee proprietors entrusted the *shugo* with collecting and delivering the taxes due from their provincial holdings. The amount was generally agreed upon in the abstract as a set figure or quota. Once a proprietor entered into such a relationship, he relinquished all direct contact between him and the estate.

Another fiscal device that derived from the practice of the civil governors was the right to collect provincewide extraordinary taxes (*ikkoku heikin no yaku*). The most common of these, known as *tansen*, were imposts levied to pay for certain special events such as imperial

30 *Kemmu Shikimoku and Tsuikahō*, pp. 25–26; Prescott B. Wintersteen, "The Muromachi Shugo and Hanzei," in John Whitney Hall and Jeffrey P. Mass, eds., *Medieval Japan: Essays in Institutional History* (New Haven, Conn.: Yale University Press, 1974), p. 212; Shimada Jirō, "Hanzei seido no seiritsu," in Ogawa, ed., *Muromachi seiken*, pp. 61–65.
31 *Kemmu Shikimoku and Tsuikahō*, p. 48.   32 *Kemmu Shikomoku and Tsuikahō*, pp. 64–65.

enthronements and abdication ceremonies or for the rebuilding of palaces or important temples. Under the Muromachi bakufu, the *shugo* first served simply as executors of the bakufu's orders to collect such taxes.[33] But gradually the practice was extended so that *shugo* could authorize *tansen* on their own initiative and even convert the tax from an occasional impost to a regular one. The importance of this development cannot be overemphasized. The collection of *tansen* had become a private right. Beyond that it became possible for a *shugo* to grant the use of this right to a subordinate as a "fief," instead of land, to cement a lord–vassal relationship.[34]

The expanded authorities acquired by the *shugo* under the Muromachi bakufu provided them not so much with power in hand as with the tools with which to accumulate such power. A *shugo* could be appointed to a whole province whether or not he possessed a power base in that province. Even if a *shugo* did have such a power base, as in the case of the Ōuchi, many of the proprietary rights in his province of assignment would still be held by court nobles, religious organizations, other *shugo* houses, and other lesser military houses.

The most prevalent practice by which *shugo* sought to gain control of their provinces was not the acquisition of private landholdings but, rather, the enlistment of local warrior families as vassals.[35] In order to accomplish this the *shugo* had to be accepted as the primary lawgivers of the provinces and have the capacity to make, or pass on, grants of office or land to the local warrior families. It is for this reason that the added authority to carry out judicial actions involving land transfers and the awards of *hanzei* or *tansen* privileges were so important to the *shugo*. The ultimate objective of *shugo* policy was to reduce, when possible, all lesser warrior families in the province to a subordinate status.[36] The trend toward the privatization of superior–inferior relations at the provincial level eventually resulted in the appearance of what Japanese of the time called *daimyo* and what modern historians call *shugo* daimyo, a condition in which *shugo* authority had been translated into a considerable amount of actual regional power.

Up to a point, the increase in local influence that the *shugo* acquired was beneficial to the bakufu. But there were limits to the amount of independence that the bakufu could, or should, tolerate from its

---

33 During 1346, a large number of *tsuikahō* dealt with the problems of the violent seizure of crops and property in the provinces. See *Kemmu Shikimoku and Tsuikahō*, pp. 33–47.
34 Arnesen, *Ōuchi Family's Rule*, pp. 165–9.
35 Ibid., p. 23.
36 Sugiyama Hiroshi, "Muromachi bakufu," in *Nihon rekishi kōza*, vol. 3 (1957): 51; Arnesen, *Ōuchi Family's Rule*, pp. 182–4.

shugo. In many instances, the interests of shogun and *shugo* were at odds with each other, and the bakufu would have to assert its primacy. Of course, in principle the shogun himself, or the collective will of his main *shugo* supporters, had the authority to exercise discipline. The Ashikaga shoguns had a number of means for directly intervening into provincial affairs. Unfortunately, we do not yet have sufficient information concerning the shogun's own vassals' serving as *jitō-gokenin* in the provinces, but it does appear that the shogun could go over the heads of his *shugo* by relying on less powerful but more directly controlled provincial houses.[37]

THE MUROMACHI DISTRIBUTION OF POWER

Once the battles of consolidation were over, the major *shugo* houses were put in place, and the division between the Northern and Southern Courts was brought to an end; that is, in the years immediately after 1392 when Shogun Yoshimitsu was in full command of the bakufu, a reasonably stable balance of interests appears to have been achieved among shogun, court, and *shugo*. This condition held for roughly three-quarters of a century. The balance had both territorial and political dimensions.

The usual impression is that the Muromachi bakufu, being located in Kyoto, maintained a more or less uniform hold over the entire country. In actuality, however, the bakufu had to accept a considerable amount of regional variation in its political reach. The debate within the Ashikaga leadership over whether to establish the bakufu in Kyoto or Kamakura had been an issue of real consequence. It was recognized that the Kantō, with its history of separatism from Kyoto and its reputation as the place of origin of the *buke* estate, would be hard to govern from Kyoto. And so it turned out to be. Takauji tried to set up a branch bakufu for the Kantō area at Kamakura but never really succeeded. The bakufu, however, had even greater problems in two other areas: the Ōu district in the far north and Kyushu in the south west. The separatist tendencies of these regions were not caused only by their distance from the capital alone but by political and economic factors as well. The dominant military houses in these regions, left to their own devices, tended to form their own local coalitions through which they tried to ward off outside interference. The difficulty that

---

37 Arnesen, "Provincial Vassals," in Mass and Hauser, eds., *Bakufu in Japanese History*, pp. 99–115.

the Ashikaga shoguns had in maintaining control over the more distant regions of the country was a consequence of their failure both to
develop the necessary machinery of government and to acquire the
power to impose a full military hegemony. Each area had its special
problems.

The Kantō area

It was clearly the intent of the early Ashikaga shoguns to retain direct
control of the Kantō provinces from Kyoto.[38] But this was easier
wished than done. The destruction of the Hōjō regime had been
achieved by men like Takauji, heads of provincial warrior families,
who were seeking to extend their landholdings and their regional influence. Those who survived the lengthy civil war had gained both land
and a sense of local independence. The central authorities were no
longer able to control the provinces by directive or by posting a deputy
there.

As the system of provincial administration by bureaucratic extension from a central authority failed, other forms of command had to be
found. Godaigo had tried to extend his political reach by capitalizing
on the imperial house's charisma. Fortunately for him, eight of his
sons survived into adulthood. In 1334 he sent his son Norinaga to
Kamakura as governor of Kozuke Province. In this instance, Takauji
insisted on supporting with military authority the prestige adhering to
the imperial person, by dispatching his brother Tadayoshi with the
prince to serve as guardian. This practice of combining the prestige of
royalty or of nobility with the enforcement capacity of a powerful
military family was a favorite device. But Tadayoshi lost Kamakura,
making it necessary for Takauji to lead his own forces into the Kantō
to restore the primacy of the Ashikaga house.

When Takauji returned to Kyoto, he left behind his young son,
Yoshiakira, then four years old, as his own representative in the
Kantō. As guardians he appointed three kinsmen related by blood or
marriage: Hosokawa Kiyouji, Uesugi Noriaki, and Shiba Ienaga. It
was expected that this combination of a main-line member of the
Ashikaga house backed by powerful military kinsmen could control
the Kantō. In 1349 Takauji sent his second son, Motouji, to Kama-

---

38 The main source for this section is Itō Kiyoshi, "Muromachi ki no kokka to Tōgoku,"
   Rekishigaku kenkyū (October 1979): 63–72. More recent is Lorraine F. Harrington's study,
   "Regional Outposts of Muromachi Bakufu Rule: The Kantō and Kyūshū," in Mass and
   Hauser, eds., *Bakufu in Japanese History*, pp. 66–88.

kura with the title of Kantō *kanrei* and under the guardianship of Uesugi Noriaki. The jurisdiction of the branch shogunate, now called Kamakura-fu, included the "eight Kantō provinces" plus Izu and Kai. Within these provinces the Kantō *kanrei* was given broad administrative and judicial powers. These included the authority to raise military forces, to make or withdraw grants of land, to make appointments to local offices (including the naming of *shugo*), and to superintend the affairs of temples and shrines. The Muromachi bakufu apparently reserved for itself only the authority to approve succession in the Uesugi house. To carry out its functions, Kamakura-fu created a full assemblage of administrative offices based on the model of the Muromachi headquarters.

Despite these efforts to keep the Kantō subservient to Kyoto, the arrangement never worked well and ultimately failed. The sense of separation remained strong in Kamakura, and this was kept alive by the fact that among the leading Ashikaga collaterals on whom the bakufu had to rely, many had been supporters of Tadayoshi and remained resentful of the manner in which Takauji had brought about his death. Furthermore, after Motouji's death in 1367, members of the Kamakura branch of the Ashikaga house proved ill inclined to take directives from Kyoto. Before long, the head of the Kantō Ashikaga house had adopted the style of *kubō* (an honorific title reserved for the shogun) and had passed the office of *kanrei* to the head of the Uesugi house who had served up to that point only as guardian and chief officer. The Kamakura *kubō* Ujimitsu and his successors, far from keeping the Kantō tranquil, aggressively tried to expand their influence, thereby provoking a series of disturbances. The wide gap between the two branches of the Ashikaga house is symbolized by the Kantō *kubō*'s eventual confiscation of Ashikaga-no-shō. Differences between Muromachi and Kamakura came to a head between the sixth shogun, Yoshinori, and the fourth Kamakura *kubō*, Mochiuji (1398–1439). Mochiuji, who spent much of his time in Kyoto, had hopes of being named shogun himself, to succeed Yoshimochi. He resented the selection of Yoshinori and created trouble by refusing to use the era name (*gengo*) that was identified with Yoshinori's shogunate. Finally, in 1432 Yoshinori felt obliged to send a punitive force into the Kantō to punish Mochiuji for insubordination. Mochiuji was killed and Kamakura-fu destroyed.

The Muromachi bakufu, however, was not prepared to lose the Kantō. In 1449 and again in 1457, members of the Ashikaga shogunal line were sent to the Kantō to reestablish a branch shogunate. But

Kamakura-fu could not be revived. The Uesugi house, having taken the title of Kantō *kanrei*, exerted as much of a centralizing force as was possible under the circumstances. But this was exerted less and less on behalf of Kyoto.

Ironically, despite the Kantō origin of the Ashikaga house, once Takauji had pulled out of the area, he left behind remarkably few supporters. Around 1400, *shugo* appointments in the Kantō provinces were held by eight houses, not one of which was a cadet branch. Clearly, the Kantō was too distant a region to be controlled by proxy from Kyoto, given the means of communication and the military technology of the day. Failure to control the Kantō, however, did not greatly affect the staying power of the Kyoto-based Muromachi bakufu.

The Ōu area

The two large undeveloped provinces of Mutsu and Dewa, known together as the Ōu region, north of the Kantō, suffered even more from its remoteness from Japan's political center.[39] Under the Muromachi bakufu, neither province was brought under the *shugo* system. Yet because the region lay "behind" the Kantō, no government based at Kamakura could ignore its existence and its potential as a place of military buildup or of refuge for enemies of Kamakura. Minamoto Yoritomo had struggled with this problem in the aftermath of the Gempei War and had posted agents there to keep the peace. The provinces played a considerable role in the military action of the Kemmu era, which began when Godaigo sent Kitabatake Chikafusa, one of his important courtier generals, to the region as governor of Mutsu. Takauji countered by naming Shiba Ienaga as the supreme commander of Ōu (Ōu *sotaisho*.) In 1335 Takauji dispatched another of his collateral generals, Ishidō Yoshifusa, to the Mutsu provincial office as protector (Mutsu *chinjō*). In the next few years, Yoshifusa distinguished himself in battles with Southern Court adherents of the region. In 1345, Takauji established the office of governor general for the two provinces, to which he named two house generals, Hatakeyama Kuniuji and Kira Sadaie. But the two generals proved to have irreconcilable differences, having been on opposite sides of the Tadayoshi quarrel. Muromachi next sent Shiba Iekane and Uesugi

39 Endo Iwao, "Nambokuchō nairan no naka de," in Kobayashi Seiji and Ōishi Naomasa, eds., *Chūsei Ōu no sekai* (Tokyo: Tōkyō daigaku shuppankai, 1978), pp. 84–124.

Noriharu to serve jointly as *kanrei*. At one time there were four *tandai* designates in Mutsu contesting for the office. In 1392, the Kantō *kubō*, Ashikaga Ujimitsu, brought Mutsu and Dewa into the jurisdiction of Kamakura-fu and named his son as *kanrei*. But with the end of Kamakura-fu, the office of *kanrei* lost its political meaning and its strategic importance to the Muromachi bakufu.

The Kyushu area

Kyushu presented the Ashikaga with quite different problems of control.[40] Western Japan as a whole had never been securely dominated by military regimes based in central or eastern Japan. Historically, the provinces of Kyushu and of the western end of Honshū had been the domains of strongly entrenched military houses like the Shimazu of Satsuma and Ōsumi; the Shōni of Higo, Buzen, and Chikuzen; the Ōtomo of Bungo; and the Ōuchi of Suō. Takauji and his successors had little choice but to leave these powerful houses in place as *shugo*.

Yet even though the western provinces had their own history of independence from control from either Kyoto or Kamakura, it had been customary to place a representative of the central government in northern Kyushu as an outpost for the conduct of foreign affairs. Since Nara times the Hakata region had been the location of Dazaifu, an office of the central government with authority over foreign relations and trade. The Kamakura bakufu established the post of Kyushu commissioner (Chinzei *bugyō*) to deal with local affairs and to keep peace among the Minamoto vassals. In 1293, in the wake of the Mongol invasions, the office of military governor of Kyushu (Chinzei *tandai*) was created and given powers similar to those of the Rokuhara *tandai*. The office was abolished at the end of Hōjō rule. But during the period of rivalry between the North and South Courts, both sides used these Kyushu regional offices to establish their presence in the western provinces.

As a result of Takauji's retreat to Kyushu in 1336, we find him establishing a regional office, the Kyushu intendant (Kyūshū *tandai*).[41] To this office he appointed a succession of collateral family heads, starting with Isshiki Noriuji. But there was strong support for the Southern Court cause in Kyushu, and this was not easily overcome. Emperor Godaigo had managed to send one of his many sons,

---

40 See Kawazoe Shōji, "Chinzei kanrei kō," in Ogawa, ed., *Muromachi seiken*, pp. 77–106.
41 This office was given a number of names such as Chinzei *kanrei*, Chinzei *tandai*, and Chinzei *taishōgun*. See ibid., pp. 78–79.

Prince Kanenaga, to Kyushu with the title of general of the western pacification command (*sei-sei shogun*). During the next thirty years the Northern Court faction was kept on the defensive against forces mobilized by Prince Kanenaga from local *shugo* families like the Kikuchi and Aso. When envoys sent from China by the Ming emperor reached northern Kyushu in 1369, it was with this office that they negotiated. In 1371 the Muromachi, recognizing its weakness in the west, sent one of its ablest generals, Imagawa Ryōshun, to Kyushu as intendant. After strenuous fighting, in 1381 the Imagawa chief finally managed to defeat the local partisans of the Southern Court. In 1395 he was replaced by Shibukawa Mitsuyori who had less success in maintaining military command. But the office itself remained in the hands of this family for the rest of the Muromachi period. Kyoto was never fully able to rule the western end of the Inland Sea, so critical to the foreign trade that flourished from the fourteenth century on. On the other hand, the *shugo* of Kyushu were more apt voluntarily to support the shogun, taking up residence in Kyoto in order to take part in the cultural life of the capital.

The central provinces

Between the Kantō and northern Kyushu lay the forty-four provinces of central Japan over which the Muromachi bakufu exerted its most direct and effective control. When historians write about the "Muromachi state" or the "Muromachi government" they are usually referring to this more limited portion of the country. *Shugo* appointments to these provinces were drawn from some twenty-two houses. Of these, the majority were collateral branches of the Ashikaga house; the rest were allies by marriage or pledge of loyalty, and as such were considered "outside lords" (*tozama*).[42]

A stable balance among *shugo* appointments was not easily achieved. The war between the Northern and Southern Court factions, which continued for more than fifty years after the founding of the Muromachi bakufu, encouraged flux. The *shugo* were intensely competitive and frequently switched allegiances to pursue their private interests.[43] Even Yoshimitsu was forced to put down rebellions of trusted *shugo*, among them the Akamatsu in 1383, the Yamana in 1394, and the Ōuchi in 1399. Yoshimitsu's successful termination of

---

42 Sugiyama, "Muromachi bakufu," pp. 58–59.
43 Ogawa Makoto, *Ashikaga ichimon shugo hatten shi no kenkyū* (Tokyo: Yoshikawa kōbunkan, 1980), presents the most insightful account of the early competition among the *shugo*.

the rift between the court factions in 1392 removed a major obstacle to the achievement of a general cooperation between the shogunate and the *shugo* of central Japan. The bakufu by that time was functioning effectively as a central government, and the *shugo* found it to be in their best interests to join with, rather than compete against, the bakufu.

Besides the shogun's capacity as chief of the warrior estate to generate superior military force, two administrative practices proved crucial to maintaining this climate of cooperation: One was the requirement that the *shugo* of the central provinces take up residence in Kyoto, and the other was the *kanrei* system of decision making. Given the difficulty of communication in fourteenth-century Japan and the lack of enforcement power in what remained of the court-based institutions of provincial administration, any would-be hegemon was dependent on direct, ideally face-to-face, contact with his subordinates to ensure that his commands were carried out.

Yoshimitsu used various combinations of military force, political manipulation, and intimidation in his efforts to keep the *shugo* in line. His military actions against the Akamatsu, Yamana, and Ōuchi have been noted. His less militant displays of power took the form of grand provincial progresses in the guise of religious pilgrimages, such as his journey in 1389 into the western provinces to visit the Itsukushima Shrine in Aki and, incidentally, to put pressure on the Ōuchi house. The private forces readily available to the shogun, though insufficient to defend unassisted against a determined attack by a major *shugo*, were large enough to turn the balance in the capital area and to impress local military houses. Of course, in the case of punishing a recalcitrant *shugo* or quelling provincial unrest, the shogun had to call on contingents from his *shugo*. The ability of a shogun to assemble mixed armies of this sort depended on his continued success in motivating a sufficient number of *shugo* to obey his commands. And to this end the *kanrei* system proved to be of great value.[44]

During the first few years of the Muromachi bakufu, Takauji and Tadayoshi had used the post of general manager (*shitsuji*) as chief administrative officer, to which a succession of hereditary retainers like Kō Moronao were assigned. In 1362 this office was upgraded and renamed *kanrei* (deputy shogun). The new post was assigned to the heads of some of the most powerful of the shogun's cadet houses in

---

44 Sato, with Hall, "The Ashikaga Shogun," in Hall and Toyoda, eds., *Japan in the Muromachi Age*, pp. 48–49.

hopes of pulling the *shugo* of the central bloc more closely together behind the shogun. In 1367 Hosokawa Yoriyuki was named deputy just as Yoshimitsu became shogun. Because Yoshimitsu was only thirteen years old, Yoriyuki's first years as *kanrei* resembled a regency. But unlike what happened in Kamakura after Minamoto Yoritomo's line ran out, the *kanrei* was not permitted to dominate the Ashikaga shoguns. Nor was the post of *kanrei* allowed to become monopolized by a single family until the end of the fifteenth century. Rather, it became the practice to pass the appointment among the three foremost *shugo* houses of Shiba, Hosokawa, and Hatakeyama. These houses, known as the Sankan (the three *kanrei*), among them held seventeen provinces in Yoshimitsu's day. Together they formed an inner bloc of *shugo* committed to support the Ashikaga house. The *kanrei* functioned in two directions. As head of the assembly of senior *shugo* (*yoriai*), he gave to the *shugo* a sense of involvement in bakufu affairs. To the shogun, the *kanrei* was able to present the *shugo*'s points of view and advise against extreme action that they would resent.

In the early years the *shugo* were naturally preoccupied with establishing their presence in the provinces to which they had been assigned. But by the start of Yoshimitsu's rule, most of the *shugo* of the central bloc had taken up more-or-less permanent residence in Kyoto.[45] Although unlike the *sankin-kotai* requirement of the Tokugawa shogunate, *shugo* residence in Kyoto was not mandated by written precept, by the end of Yoshimitsu's rule such residence had become compulsory in practice. If a *shugo* left his Kyoto residence for his home province without the shogun's permission, it was considered tantamount to an act of rebellion. This obligation of residence in Kyoto appears to have fallen only on the *shugo* of the central provinces; the *shugo* of the Kantō bloc were expected to live in Kamakura. In western Japan, the Kyushu *tandai*, being simply another form of *shugo*, made no residence demands on the other *shugo*. But although not compelled to do so, most of the *shugo* of the Kyushu provinces built residences in Kyoto, both to keep in touch with affairs at the center and to participate in the cultural life of the capital.

Enforced residence away from their assigned provinces meant that the *shugo* themselves had to administer their provinces indirectly through subordinates. The most common practice was to establish one or more deputy *shugo* (*shugo-dai*) from among the *shugo*'s closest retain-

---

45 Masaharu Kawai, with Kenneth A. Grossberg, "Shogun and Shugo: The Provincial Aspects of Muromachi Politics," in Hall and Toyoda, eds., *Japan in the Muromachi Age*, pp. 68–69.

ers to manage local affairs in his absence. Frequently, even the deputy *shugo* was called to Kyoto, thus necessitating the appointment of a subdeputy (*shugo-matadai*). As can be imagined, *shugo* residing in Kyoto found it difficulty to develop a reliable chain of command between capital and province. Vassal *shugo-dai* could play a critical role in either expanding and safeguarding the *shugo*'s local authority or undermining it. The problem was especially acute in situations in which the *shugo* were exercising jurisdiction over an unfamiliar province. In such cases, the *shugo* were often forced to depend on the head of a prominent local family, a *kokujin*, to serve as deputy. In many cases, these families eventually turned against their Kyoto-based superiors so as to grasp local military hegemony.[46]

Contact between *shugo* and shogun was at first personal and direct. But with the adoption of the *kanrei* system, the shogun's relations with the *shugo* were mediated through the *kanrei*, and certain decisions were made subject to the assembly of senior *shugo*. There was, of course, an inherent contradiction in a procedure that put the deputy and the assembly between the shogun and his vassal *shugo*. A strong-minded shogun, like the mature Yoshimitsu or Yoshinori, resented the restrictions this imposed on his freedom of command. The *kanrei–yoriai* system as a check on shogunal absolutism worked well up through the time of Yoshikazu, the fifth shogun. And even the sixth shogun, the strong-willed Yoshinori, was forced to accept from time to time the collective will of the *kanrei* and *yoriai*.

The third shogun, Yoshimitsu, had brought the status and power of the office to its highest level. Yet his grandiose behavior and autocratic rule were tolerated, even admired, by the *shugo*, who were themselves caught up in the heady experiences of aristocratic life in Kyoto. Yoshimitsu's two successors retreated from this autocratic posture and acknowledged a greater acceptance of the *kanrei–yoriai* system. Yoshikazu, living with the knowledge that his father, Yoshimitsu, had intended to pass over him as his heir, was not inclined to offer personal leadership to the bakufu, and so died without naming his own successor. As a result, his successor was determined by lot by the Ashikaga family council, and Yoshinori, Yoshimitsu's sixth son, was chosen. Yoshinori was at the time a mature man of thirty-four. Early in his life, with no apparent hope of becoming shogun, he had entered the priesthood, and at the time he was named shogun he was serving as chief abbot (*zasu*) of the Enryakuji and head of the Tendai sect on Mount

46 Hall, *Government and Local Power*, pp. 227–33.

Hiei. He immediately showed himself to be a leader who intended to become personally involved in bakufu affairs. He was a good politician and was determined to increase the power of the Ashikaga house.

Yoshinori's first move was to change bakufu administrative procedures by reorganizing the Corps of Administrators (*bugyōnin-shū*) and instituting what was called the shogunal hearing (*gozen-sata*).[47] Under this procedure, briefs on policy matters were prepared by the administrators and brought directly to the shogun for decision. This meant that in most instances the *kanrei* was not consulted, as evidenced by the appearance of *bugyōnin* directives that expressed the shogun's will without the customary countersignature of the *kanrei*. This change was correctly perceived as a move toward greater shogunal personal rule.[48]

Another line of action that Yoshinori pursued proved even more disquieting, for it involved the shogun's effort at directly interfering in *shugo* domestic affairs. Using his authority to approve *shugo* appointments and inheritances, Yoshinori began to manipulate the lines of succession among *shugo* houses so as to bring to Kyoto *shugo* more amenable to his direction.[49] One device in particular available to Yoshinori was his authority to enlist the lesser members of *shugo* houses into his private military force as guardsmen. Such appointments were usually of second or third sons in *shugo* families, men not normally in line for the family headship. But as a result of the personal relationship between shogun and guardsmen, the shogun was able to intervene on behalf of those he favored to ensure their succession.

This was the motivation for a series of seemingly arbitrary actions taken by Yoshinori that came to a head in 1441. In that year, the shogun appeared to be taking steps to block the appointment of Akamatsu Mitsusuke's chosen heir to the post of *shugo* in Harima and Bizen. It was to forestall this move that Mitsusuke killed Yoshinori while the shogun was being entertained in the Akamatsu residence in Kyoto. This incident, known as the Kakitsu affair, marks a turning point in Muromachi bakufu history. That a prominent *shugo* could murder the shogun who was a guest in his own house was disquieting enough but that the murderer could survive the incident and return to his provincial base without suffering an immediate punitive attack

---

47 Kuwayama, with Hall, "Bugyōnin," in Hall and Toyoda, eds., *Japan in the Muromachi Age*, pp. 58–61. *Tsuikahō* numbered 183, 184, 189, and 190 to 197 issued in 1428 dealt with this issue.
48 Imatani Akira, *Sengokuki no Muromachi bakufu no seikaku*, vol. 12 (Tokyo: Kadokawa shoten, 1975), pp. 154–6.   49 Arnesen, *Ouchi Family's Rule*, p. 187.

implies that there were strong feelings of sympathy for the Akamatsu leader's actions.[50] Mitsusuke, however, was finally chastized. Having fortified himself in his provincial headquarters, he fought to the finish against a shogunal army led by the Yamana, the *shugo* of several nearby provinces. The Yamana invasion was not in reluctant compliance with bakufu orders, for the Yamana had long coveted the Akamatsu provinces of Mimasaka, Bizen, and Harima. As expected, the Yamana received these provinces as a reward for Mitsusuke's destruction.

The Kakitsu incident brought an end to a brief period of what some have called "shogunal despotism." But the weakening of shogunal power did not lead to a return to *kanrei–shugo* council ascendancy either. As a result of Yoshinori's meddling, one of the three *kanrei* houses, the Shiba, was greatly weakened, and the house served as *kanrei* only once in the ensuing years. In the aftermath of the Kakitsu incident, competition over the post of *kanrei* was largely confined to the Hosokawa and Hatakeyama houses. Moreover, the nature of the post itself changed. After 1441, the post of *kanrei* carried little of its former responsibility of supporting the shogun and mediating with the *shugo*. Rather, the post was regarded as a means to exercise private influence over the bakufu. Because such influence could result in tangible benefits to both the *kanrei* and his favored *shugo*, there was a tendency for the *shugo* houses to divide into factions behind the two remaining *kanrei* houses. How this situation led to the weakening of the bakufu power base became clear during the time of Yoshimasa, the eighth shogun. But before I turn to the events of this period, I shall discuss in more detail the bakufu rule.

THE MUROMACHI BAKUFU: INSTRUMENTS OF ADMINISTRATION AND ENFORCEMENT

The Kemmu *shikimoku*, by announcing the Ashikaga's intent to follow in the footsteps of the previous regime, implicitly laid claim to whatever powers that had accrued to the post of shogun under the Hōjō regents. By 1350, the Ashikaga government had assumed a reasonably stable form in which many of the organs of administration bore the same names as used by the Kamakura shogunate. But identity in name did not necessarily mean identity in function. The Ashikaga leaders approached quite pragmatically the task of building a bakufu.

50 Sugiyama Hiroshi, "Shugo ryōgokusei no tenkai," in *Iwanami koza Nihon rekishi (chūsei 3)* (Tokyo: Iwanami shoten, 1963), pp. 109–69.

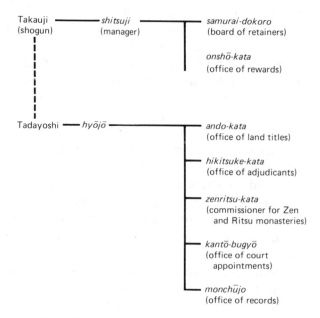

Figure 4.2 Organization of the bakufu, 1350. (Solid horizontal line indicates formal authority relationship; solid vertical line, a more or less equal formal status; and dashed line, an informal equality or division of authority.)

As of 1350, when Tadayoshi was still working closely with his brother, the organization of the bakufu followed the form outlined in Figure 4.2.[51] Satō Shin'ichi has emphasized the importance of the division of responsibility that had been worked out by the Ashikaga brothers.[52] Takauji, the elder brother, as shogun and head of the *buke* estate, assumed the direction of the bakufu organs dealing with such functions as the appointments to military posts, the distribution of rewards for military service, the enlistment of vassal followers, and the management of Ashikaga lands. Satō described these powers as basically feudal. By contrast, Tadayoshi was in charge of what Satō called the more "bureaucratic," or administrative and judicial, functions of government. Under Tadayoshi was organized the deliberative council, consisting of selected professional bureaucrats, and a number of offices that kept land records, adjudicated lawsuits, and handled relations between the bakufu and the imperial court and the religious orders.

51 Imatani, *Sengokuki*, pp. 151–81.   52 Satō, "Kaisoki," pp. 472–86.

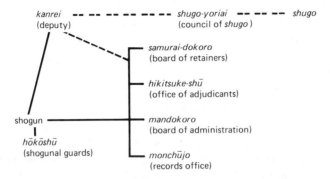

Figure 4.3 Changes in bakufu structure after Tadayoshi's expulsion, 1352. (Lines same as in Figure 4.2; double dashed line indicates an informal authority relationship.)

With Tadayoshi's expulsion from Kyoto in 1352, the bakufu structure underwent a significant change, and many of the offices inherited from Kamakura were either abolished or drastically modified in function. The most important such change, as seen in Figure 4.3, was the conversion of the office of *shitsuji* (the bakufu's chief of operations) into that of *kanrei* (deputy shogun) and the creation of the *shugo* council (*shugo yoriai*).[53]

The top of the Muromachi shogunal government was characterized by both a greater direct involvement in the affairs of state by the shogun and a more influential participation by the *shugo* houses in the decision-making process and in the bakufu administration.

The main bakufu offices with specialized functions were the Board of Retainers (*samurai-dokoro*), the Office of Adjudicants (*hikitsuke-shu*), the Board of Administration (*mandokoro*), and the Office of Records (*monchūjo*). Of these, at the outset the Board of Retainers was the most important. It alone was headed by a major *shugo* house. Charged with controlling the shogun's direct retainers, the Board of Retainers was made responsible for securing the capital area from lawlessness and administering the home province of Yamashiro. With the establishment of the office of *kanrei*, the *samurai-dokoro* lost much of its powers of control over the shogun's household retainers and over the *shugo* houses. But its administrative and judicial functions in the capital area continued to expand. The board, for instance, took over the powers of the Imperial Capital Police (*kebiishi*) and became the main police and

53 Satō, with Hall, "Muromachi Bakufu Administration," in Hall and Toyoda, eds., *Japan in the Muromachi Age*, pp. 47–49.

judicial authority in Kyoto.[54] In 1385, moreover, the chief (*shoshi*) of the Board of Retainers was given the added duty of serving as *shugo* of Yamashiro Province. It became customary to rotate this assignment among four major *shugo* houses: the Yamana, Isshiki, Akamatsu, and Kyōgoku.

The actual day-to-day running of the Board of Retainers was delegated to a deputy chief (*shoshidai*), appointed by the chief from among his own private retainers. Hence the identity of the deputy changed according to who served as chief. As a bureaucratic entity, the board was given a certain stability and continuity of operation by its permanent administrative staff, a group of individuals composed independently of the chief and his deputy, drawn from a class of hereditary administrators or professional bureaucrats, which will be described later.

Despite the many important functions of the Board of Retainers, after the Ōnin War (1467–77), it lost its central importance to the Administrative Council.[55] At first the council was almost exclusively concerned with the shogun's household and its fiscal management.[56] Its first chief officer was a hereditary administrator carried over from the Kamakura bakufu, a member of the Nikaidō house. In 1379, the Nikaidō were replaced by the Ise family, a line of hereditary retainers who, among other duties, had traditionally served as guardians of the Ashikaga shogun's heirs. The council came into its own as the bakufu's main administrative office when the shogun Yoshinori began to use it as the organ through which to bypass the *kanrei*. As the sphere of shogunal government narrowed, however, this single agency was able to handle nearly all of the shogunate's administrative functions. Moreover, as the shogun found fewer and fewer opportunities to assert political initiative, procedures in the bakufu became increasingly routinized under what Kuwayama Kōnen has called the "*bugyōnin* system."[57]

Throughout the Muromachi period there were more than fifty families of professional administrators available for service, many of whom had served the imperial court and the Kamakura bakufu. Such families were now brought into Ashikaga service because of their special

---

54 Haga Norihiko, "Muromachi bakufu samurai dokoro kō," in Ogawa, ed., *Muromachi seiken*, pp. 25–55.
55 Imatani, *Sengokuki*, p. 165.   56 Haga, "Samurai dokoro," p. 50.
57 Kuwayama, with Hall, "Bugyōnin," in Hall and Toyoda, eds., *Japan in the Muromachi Age*, pp. 53–54.

administrative skills. In time they formed the Corps of Administrators, the *bugyōnin-shu*. At any one time, between fifteen and sixty members might be assigned to the finance, justice, and administrative organs of the bakufu.[58] A study of the fluctuating numbers of administrators retained by the Muromachi bakufu shows that in the period before the Ōnin War, the numbers reflected the shifting balance of power between the *kanrei–yoriai* system and the shoguns' effort to exert their own influence on the bakufu. Thus the fewest numbers were in evidence under Yoshimitsu, Yoshikatsu, and Yoshimochi, all of whom followed the *kanrei* principle.[59] Yoshinori's efforts to exert his direct shogunal prerogative was reflected by an immediate increase in the size of the corps. This upward trend continued until Yoshimasa's death. Thereafter, the number of members declined, to remain at around fifteen until the end of the Muromachi bakufu. Members of the corps were drawn from the following eleven families: Iio, Suga, Saitō, Jibu, Eno, Sei, Nakazawa, Fuse, Matsuda, Yano, and Ida.

The drop in staff numbers reflected, first of all, a loss of power by the Ashikaga house and also a change in function. Perhaps because of the shogun's weakening power, the administrators increasingly became an entrenched and self-perpetuating group of families that, more than any other single factor, accounted for the continued existence of the bakufu during its last hundred years. These families became the agents through which members of the capital elite establishment dealt with one another. For instance, administrators serving as members of the Office of Adjudicants were assigned specifically to handle the affairs of important shrines like the Iwashimizu Hachiman Gū or Tsurugaoka Hachiman Gū, and great temples like the Enryakuji, Tōdaiji, Kōfukuji, Tōji, and Tenryuji. In other words, these hereditary administrators had begun to serve as agents of these institutions in case of litigation before the council, receiving retainer fees for serving as their spokesmen.[60] This was obviously a profitable arrangement. To keep it alive, it was to the advantage of all concerned to maintain the prestige of the shogun and the efficacy of the bakufu's remaining organs of adjudication. That this happened is revealed by the fact that the Ashikaga's supplementary laws continued to be issued into the

58 Haga, "Samurai dokoro," p. 27; Kuwayama, with Hall, "Bugyōnin," in Hall and Toyoda, eds., *Japan in the Muromachi Age*, pp. 56–60.
59 Kenneth A. Grossberg, "Bakufu and Bugyonin: The Size of the House Bureaucracy in Muromachi Japan," *Journal of Asian Studies* 35 (August 1976): 651–4.
60 Kuwayama, with Hall, "Bugyōnin," in Hall and Toyoda, eds., *Japan in the Muronmachi Age*, p. 62.

1570s and that there are many records of action taken by the Office of Adjudicants in the last decades of the Ashikaga regime.[61]

But to say that the Muromachi bakufu continued to function until the mid-sixteenth century is also to say that the scope of its competence narrowed. By the time of the last shogun, the scope of the bakufu's control had been reduced almost solely to the city of Kyoto and its close environs. Control of Kyoto, in and of itself, was an important achievement, and the fact that Kyoto became subject to bakufu administration was of major significance for the Ashikaga house's staying ability.

At the time the Ashikaga established their bakufu in Kyoto, the city was still under the control of the civil and religious nobility. Takauji's claim of chieftainship of the military estate gave him the authority to exercise military, judicial, fiscal, and appointment powers over *bushi* but not over the civil elite. The organs of imperial administration that had been revived by Godaigo were soon in disarray. Yet the establishment of the Muromachi bakufu did not automatically rectify the situation.

In Kyoto the imperial house, the high court nobility, and the great religious institutions remained free to govern, through their own house staffs, their estates and other dependent groups like the merchant and craft guilds. In fact, these groups and organizations can be conceived of as a distinct power structure with remarkable staying power, to which modern historians have applied the term *kenmon seika*.[62] Essential to this condition was the maintenance of a secure capital area, a functioning judicial process, and a reasonably effective machinery for the delivery of tax payments. The chief instruments available for this were the Imperial Capital Police (*kebiishi*) and the various management systems maintained by the Kyoto-based headquarters (*honjō*) of the major civil and religious proprietary interests. In its early policy, the bakufu sought only to assist in maintaining law and order in the capital, in order to protect the provincial interests of the most important civil and religious proprietors. Kyoto was administered under what was essentially a dual polity.[63]

61 Kuwayama Kōnen, *Muromachi bakufu hikitsuke shiryō shūsei*, vol. 1 (Tokyo: Kondo shuppansha, 1980).
62 This concept, most closely associated with Kuroda Toshio, is best described in English by Suzanne Gay in "Muromachi Bakufu Rule in Kyoto: Administration and Judicial Aspects" in Mass and Hauser, eds., *Bakufu in Japanese History*, pp. 60–65.
63 Prescott B. Wintersteen, "The Early Muromachi Bakufu in Kyoto," in Hall and Mass, eds., *Medieval Japan*, p. 202.

Tension between the bakufu's Board of Retainers and the capital police was quick to develop, especially in matters of conflicting jurisdiction. The failure of the court-maintained police to carry out their duties effectively induced the bakufu to claim the need to increase its police role in the capital. And the court was inclined to agree. A court decree of 1370, noting the capital police's ineffectiveness in curbing violence against the nobility by religious bill collectors, invited the bakufu to provide assistance. Once the bakufu began enforcing the court decrees, it began also to move into the court's economic affairs. By decree in 1393 the bakufu took over the collection of dues from brewers and moneylenders.

The bakufu relied on several types of personnel to enforce its will. One already noted was the body of professional bureaucrats who served as administrators. The shogun also had at his disposal armed forces with which to ensure compliance with his decisions. Both the *kanrei* and the chief of the Board of Retainers relied on their own armed retainers to provide a military presence in the capital. Resident *shugo* also kept on hand contingents of a few hundred mounted men. In addition, the shogun and the bakufu offices not headed by *shugo* military houses could call on the services of a category of personal retainers of the shogun known as *hōkōnin* (see Maps 4.4 and 4.5).[64]

Those men for whom we might use the term *guardsmen* were direct Ashikaga retainers settled on shogunal lands (*goryōsho*) and accountable to the shogun alone. Their use was political and economic as well as military. The largest number were from lesser branches of Ashikaga cadet and nonkin *shugo* houses. Such were the Hosokawa, Hatakeyama, Isshiki, or Shiba among the cadet houses, and the Sasaki, Toki, Ogasawara, Ōuchi, and Kyōgoku, but not the Akamatsu, among the nonkin *shugo* houses. From these houses the shogun selected individuals who may have borne the same surname as the main house but who were not in line to succeed to the family headship. Another group was recruited from houses that had long served the Ashikaga as hereditary retainers. An outstanding family of this type was the Ise. Finally, some members of provincial houses rose to local prominence, the kind of military proprietor referred to as *kokujin*. The best known of such appointments was the Kobayakawa of Aki Province.[65]

64 Fukuda Toyohiko, "Muromachi bakufu no hōkōshū," *Nihon rekishi* 274 (March 1971). 46–65.
65 See the analysis of the Kobayakawa by Arnesen, "Provincial Vassals," in Mass and Hauser, eds., *Bakufu in Japanese History*, pp. 106–112.

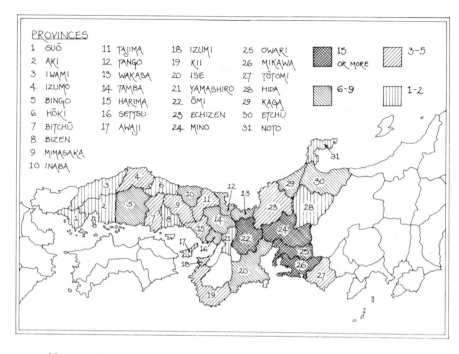

Map 4.4 Location of *hōkōnin*, 1444–9. (Shaded areas indicate number of families per province.)

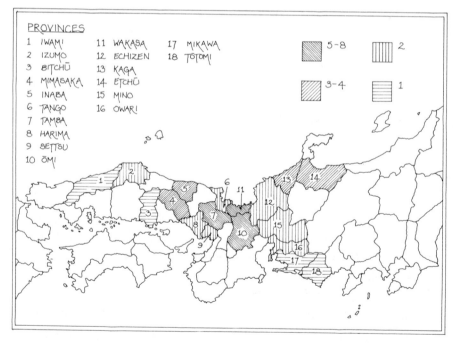

Map 4.5 Location of *hōkōnin*, 1565. (Shaded areas indicate number of families per province.)

Once they reached the capital the guardsmen were mustered into five groups (*ban*) headed by officers drawn from the Hosokawa, Hatakeyama, Momonoi, and Ōdate houses. In the 1450s, guardsmen administered holdings located in thirty-two of the forty-four provinces of central Japan. These were concentrated in the central region, stretching from Mikawa westward to Tango.[66] Interestingly, there were virtually no placements in the closest of the home provinces, such as Yamashiro, Iga, Yamato, very few in Harima, Settsu, Izumi, Kawachi, or Kii, and none at all in Shikoku. The numbers of guardsmen varied over time and circumstances. Takauji is said to have employed 30; Yoshimitsu, 290; and Yoshinori, 180. Satō Shin'ichi estimated that these numbers enabled the shogun to muster at a given time between 2,000 and 3,000 mounted fighters.[67]

All guardsmen were totally dependent on the shogun's favor for the status they held in his service. Thus the guardsmen, like the administrators, comprised an element in the bakufu that was identified with the well-being and continued existence of the Ashikaga house. Although the guardsmen did not constitute a force capable of imposing the shogun's will on even a single hostile *shugo*, in situations in which there was a balance of power, they could swing that balance in the shogun's favor or, as in the years of the Ōnin War, help maintain the shogun's neutrality.

BAKUFU FISCAL AND MANPOWER SUPPORTS

Historians have sought to explain the economic foundations of the Muromachi bakufu in terms of land and landed income. It is troublesome, therefore, not to be able to draw a clear picture of the bakufu's landholdings that might account for the shogunate's fiscal operation. It is on the basis of only a single document in the Kuramochi archives that it is known that as of around 1300 the Ashikaga possessed some thirty holdings (*goryōsho*) located in twelve widely scattered provinces. Beyond this, there is almost no information on what happened to this portfolio in subsequent years. No effort to document a continuous analysis of Ashikaga landholdings has yet succeeded. This failure is partially a result of insufficient diligence on the part of historians and not on the absolute lack of documentation. In the last few years, for

66 Fukuda Toyohiko, "Muromachi bakufu hōkōshū no kenkyū: sono jin'in to chiikiteki bumpu," in Ogawa, ed., *Muromachi seiken*, p. 231.
67 Satō Shin'ichi, "Muromachi bakufu ron," in *Iwanami kōza Nihon rekishi (chūsei 2)* (Tokyo: Iwanami shoten, 1963), p. 22.

instance, the number of identifiable Ashikaga holdings at the end of the fourteenth century has risen from sixty to some two hundred, as reported by Kuwayama Kōnen.[68] And the count is still rising. But how these items came into existence, how they related to earlier holdings, and what their fiscal value was is not at all clear. All the evidence so far has had to be extrapolated from documents that were not drafted to answer such questions directly.

First, as a result of its defeat of the Hōjō, the Ashikaga house's estates were presumably augmented by a package of forty-five pieces in twenty provinces given to Takauji and Tadayoshi by Godaigo. Recent studies have confirmed the retention of a number of these holdings into the 1390s, but not much beyond.[69] A list of sixty holdings dating from shortly before the end of the fifteenth century does not coincide with earlier lists. Clearly, there was a great deal of movement in the bakufu's land base.

The latest scholarship suggests that the search for a "land base" to explain the finances of the Ashikaga house has put its emphasis in the wrong place.[70] The Ashikaga did not create, as did the Tokugawa house, a large bloc of centrally administered lands from which revenues were collected to benefit central bakufu storehouses. Rather, it was the practice to assign landholdings to others to be administered on behalf of the bakufu and also as a means of private support. By far the greatest portion of the goryōsho appears to have been allotted in this way to members of the guards. Such grants tended to become hereditary possessions. But up to the end of the regime, the close relationship between the shogun and his provincial housemen guaranteed at least some return to the shogun from this practice.

Fortunately, there are three sets of documents covering the activities of the shogunal guards for the years 1444 to 1449, 1450 to 1455, and 1487 to 1489. Fukuda Toyohiko, in his careful study of these documents, concludes with the following table (Table 4.3), in which he lists the number of guardsmen holdings, by province.[71] In this table he offers two sets of figures based on the three sets of documents, Column I being a more conservative count than Column II. Column III is based on a roster of guards under Shogun Yoshiteru before his death in 1565 (see Maps 4.4 and 4.5).

The lists of guardsmen's holdings demonstrate graphically the shift-

68 Kuwayama Kōnen, "Muromachi bakufu keizai no kōzō," in *Nihon keizaishi taikei (chūsei 2)* (Tokyo: Tōkyō daigaku shuppankai, 1965), pp. 193–9.   69 Kuwayama, "Sōsōki," p. 18.
70 Imatani, "Sengokuki," pp. 18–22; Kuwayama, "Keizai no kōzō," pp. 219–20.
71 Fukuda, "Hōkōshū," p. 231.

TABLE 4.3

Guardsmen holdings by province

Province	I	II	III
Ōmi	21	25	8
Mikawa	17	44	1
Owari	16	19	2
Mino	15	30	2
Tango	9	18	2
Etchū	9	10	3
Kaga	9	10	4
Wakasa	8	9	7
Tamba	7	11	5
Ise	7	9	–
Inaba	7	9	3
Bingo	7	7	–
Settsu	6	7	2
Mimasaka	5	9	3
Harima	5	6	2
Izumo	5	5	2
Echizen	5	5	2
Tōtōmi	4	6	1
Bitchū	3	4	1
Tajima	3	3	–
Izumi	3	3	–
Kii	3	3	–
Aki	2	4	–
Noto	2	3	–
Yamashiro	2	2	–
Iwami	1	2	–
Suō	1	2	–
Hida	1	1	–
Awaji	1	1	–
Hōki	1	1	–
Bizen	1	1	–
Kawachi	–	1	–
	186	270	50

ing distribution of the bakufu's provincial connections. It is surprising to find such a large number of holdings up to and after the Ōnin War and even more surprising to note how many remained as late as 1565. Of course, distribution alone tells us little about the nature and size of revenues that the bakufu derived from these lands. A number of scattered case studies, however, indicate the pattern of estate management of the *goryōsho* by the guardsmen.

The guards normally resided in Kyoto, and so like the *shugo*, they were obliged to entrust local administration to deputies (*daikan*). A document of about 1450, referring to a *shōen* in Etchū Province, is typical.[72] Out of a total annual tax assessment of 780 *kan*, 340 *kan* were lost through poor harvest and the illegal encroachment of neighbors, leaving 430 *kan* as the reduced tax base. Of this, one-fifth (86 *kan*) was absorbed for managerial services by the guard and his agents, and another one-fifth was spent in transportation fees, leaving three-fifths (250 *kan*) for delivery to the bakufu. No claim can be made that a hard-and-fast rule of one-fifth for the guardsmen and three-fifths for the shogun was enforced. But clearly, besides guard duty the guards were expected to facilitate the delivery of a tangible amount of income to the bakufu. Because these holdings, as seen in Column III, tended increasingly to cluster near the capital, the capacity of the Kyoto-based guards to hold on to them and to derive income from them for their own support and for that of the shogun was relatively high.

Yet another category of land that could benefit the shogun were those that had been donated to patronized temples, like the Gozan. Many properties that the shogun gave to temples as pious gestures were in later years called on to help support the bakufu. In certain locations it appears that members of the Zen monasteries' fiscal administrations, the *tōhanshū*, served as managers of lands that were held in a manner not unlike the regular *goryōsho*.[73]

The fiscal base of the Muromachi bakufu was not limited to income from the *goryōsho*. A growing portion was derived as a consequence of the shogun's authority to levy taxes on special groups and activities in the city of Kyoto and the commercial community at large.

One feature of the Muromachi bakufu's fiscal structure was that several bakufu agencies were supported by direct endowments in land or in rights to income for specific services rendered. For example, as the Administrative Council took over more of the burden of administration in Kyoto, sources of support were sought within the city. In turning to this "inner" source of income, the bakufu took advantage of the urban commercial tax base that had been the historical preserve of the civil and religious aristocracy. One of the main sources of such income came from the categories of merchants known as *sakaya* (saké brewers) and *dosō* (storehouse keepers). The right of the capital police to tax these organizations had been recognized for years on the basis that those responsible for maintaining law and order in the city should be supported by the recipients of this protection. The practice began with the collection of special contributions for special events, such as

---

72 Morisue Yumiko, "Muromachi bakufu goryōsho ni kansuru ichi kōsatsu," in Ogawa, ed., *Muromachi seiken*, pp. 254–5.   73 Imatani, *Sengokuki*, pp. 11–60.

imperial enthronement ceremonies or the rebuilding of temples and palaces. A levy in 1371, to cover the enthronement expenses of Emperor Goenyu, imposed a payment of thirty *kan* per warehouse and two hundred *mon* in cash per vat on the breweries. In 1393, having taken over control of the city's administration, the bakufu made imposts of this kind a regular practice. The 1393 order issued from the council refers to a figure of six thousand *kan* as the amount customarily paid to the monks of the Enryakuji and states that this now should come to the bakufu.[74]

Kuwayama suggests an even closer relationship between the *mandokoro* and the *dōsō*. The latter were at first not so much moneylenders as storehouse keepers, whose fireproof storage houses were used for safekeeping by the aristocracy. Later, as an extension of such a service, *dōsō* began to serve as fiscal managers, extending credit on the basis of stored goods. *Dōsō* also appear to have been appointed as officials of the shogun's treasury (*kubō mikura*). Hence they became both the objects of taxation and the means of tax collection.[75] The bakufu in time developed a number of other commercial and transport taxes derived from the patronage of merchant guilds, the establishment of toll barriers on highways, and the sponsorship of foreign trade. The importance of trade with Ming China to the political, cultural, and economic life of Muromachi Japan has been dealt with extensively elsewhere. It has been suggested that in addition to the "enormous profits" derived from it, the trade gave to the bakufu monopoly control over the Chinese coins imported into Japan and thereby a status equivalent to that of a central mint.[76] But the various benefits that accrued to the bakufu from this trade are still not wholly understood.

Another complex area of bakufu and shogunal house income pertains to revenues derived from the shogun's aristocratic and military status. For instance, the shogun could count on the support of his *shugo* vassals for both military and nonmilitary assistance. For a given military action, it was generally the responsibility of one or more *shugo* to mobilize private forces on the shogun's behalf. Of course, this meant the prospect of tangible reward if the action proved successful. The 1441 Yamana attack on the Akamatsu referred to earlier is a case

74 Prescott B. Wintersteen, "The Early Muromachi Bakufu in Kyoto," in Hall and Mass, eds., *Medieval Japan*, pp. 208–9.
75 Kuwayama Kōnen, "Muromachi bakufu keizai kikō no ichi kōsatsu, nōsen-kata kubō okura no kinō to seiritsu," *Shigaku zasshi* 73 (September 1964). 9–17.
76 Takeo Tanaka, with Robert Sakai, "Japan's Relations with Overseas Countries," in Hall and Toyoda, eds., *Japan in the Muromachi Age*, p. 170.

in point. As a result of the successful campaign, Yamana was made *shugo* of two provinces vacated by the Akamatsu.

In the area of nonmilitary expeditions, the shogun had the right to requisition from his *shugo* contributions for public works, such as the building of shogunal residences. The 1437 requisition of ten thousand *kan* for the shogun's residence was imposed differentially on *shugo* according to the number and size of the provinces that each held. The impost was distributed among twenty-two *shugo* on the basis of two hundred *kan* for those who held only one province and one thousand *kan* for houses holding three or more. Other forms of contribution from *shugo* were the standard practice that *shugo* build their residences in Kyoto, that they maintain their own armed forces of from three hundred to five hundred horsemen, and that when appointed to a bakufu office, such as the Board of Retainers, they staff their offices with their own men. One notable example is the case of Ashikaga Yoshimasa's project to build the Higashiyama villa, the central structure of which was the Silver Pavilion (Ginkaku). The actual fund raising began in 1481, only four years after the termination of the Ōnin War. Yet *shugo* were dunned for contributions as part of their duty toward the shogun. Despite the war-torn condition of the country, the money was collected. As Kawai Masaharu writes, the shogun himself was a person of charismatic prestige who could still expect support of this kind even in the aftermath of a ten-year war that he himself had brought on. It remained a matter of political value for an aspiring provincial daimyo to contribute toward, or build himself, palaces for the *tennō* or shogun in the capital.[77]

Another source of income for the shogun resulted from his powers of appointment. Among aristocratic circles it was standard practice for those appointed to a high court or temple rank by the shogun to pay him a gratuity. Imatani Akira estimates that the flow of treasure into the bakufu coffers from this practice was a major source of support for the bakufu, especially in its declining years. The income from appointments alone has been estimated at 3,600 *kanmon* annually.[78] Of course, this flow of wealth within elite circles was not all in one direction. The shogun himself was obligated to give gifts and to contribute funds for the building of palaces and temples and for the performance of various rituals such as imperial enthronements and funerals. In such situations the shogun was more apt to use his powers to require national compli-

77 Kawai Masaharu, *Ashikaga Yoshimasa* (Tokyo: Shimizu shoin, 1972), pp. 147–50.
78 Martin Collcutt, *Five Mountains: The Rinzai Zen Monastic Institution in Medieval Japan* (Cambridge, Mass.: Harvard University Press, 1981), pp. 235.

ance with bakufu requisitions rather than to draw funds himself from the bakufu's stores.[79] Such requisitions generally took the form of a provincewide *tansen* tax.

For much of the Muromachi period, *tansen* represented a major source of income for the bakufu, to the point that the Administrative Council (*mandokoro*) maintained an officer in charge of *tansen* revenues. The *hōkōshū* were used as collecting agents in the provinces. The picture that emerges, therefore, is one in which land, by being dispersed as private enfeoffments, served mainly to support the many families and institutions that constituted the "governing establishment." The resources that powered the actual functions of government appear to have come from general taxes, like *tansen*, whose collection depended on the continuing prestige of the Ashikaga house as a charismatic entity within what essentially was a structure inherited from the imperial bureaucracy.

THE LAST HUNDRED YEARS

The final century of Muromachi bakufu rule has given historians a number of difficult interpretive problems. During these years the bakufu was obviously in decline, and the shogun was increasingly inconsequential as a political force. In fact, Japanese historians commonly divide the time from the outbreak of the Ōnin War in 1467 until Oda Nobunaga's entrance into Kyoto in 1568, as the Sengoku period, the era of warring provinces, thus shifting the main focus of their attention from the capital and the shogun to the provinces where the daimyo successors to the *shugo* fought among themselves for territorial hegemony. But it is increasingly apparent that the ground swell of change in Japanese government and society that took place in the years following the Ōnin War should not be described simply in terms of denouement or breakdown. The bakufu, as separate from the shogun as person, did retain a function throughout the last hundred years. And although these were times of instability, they gave rise to the structures and institutions that were to support a new, and in many ways revolutionary, centralized order.[80]

Although the political and social order of the mid-Muromachi period may have appeared to differ fundamentally from what it had been

79 Nagahara, "Zen-kindai," pp. 39–40.
80 Mitsuru Miyagawa, with Cornelius J. Kiley, "From Shōen to Chigyō: Proprietory Lordship and the Structure of Local Power," in Hall and Toyoda, eds., *Japan in the Muromachi Age*, pp. 89–105.

at the end of the Kamakura era, the main premises on which Japanese government rested remained basically unchanged. Despite the "encroachment of military government" on civil authority, the polity at large, the *tenka*, was still conceived as before. The same touchstones of legitimation were recognized, and authority was still regarded as a legal right granted or justified from above.

But by the end of the fifteenth century, this order was being challenged by the appearance of groups or communities that sought, from the higher central authority, autonomy in their local affairs. At the upper level, this took the form of "*kokujin* lordships" (*zaichi ryōshu*) whereby local *buke* families became the sole proprietors of their own lands, managing to protect themselves from higher authority by their own strength of arms or by the formation of leagues or compacts (*ikki*) with neighboring *kokujin*. At first, these compacts were small in scale, but as in the case of Aki Province, some were able to counter the interference of both the bakufu and neighboring *shugo*. The revolutionary aspect of such compacts was that they were organized on the basis of territory and were held together by mutual agreement for the purpose of self-defense. By the end of the fifteenth century, local military lords emerged out of the ranks of *kokujin*, many of them heads of *ikki* leagues, whose territory was made large enough to give them the status of daimyo. This, as Kawai has shown, was a major impetus for the formation of the so-called *sengoku* daimyo.[81]

Unlike the *shugo* daimyo whose legitimacy was derived from the bakufu, the *sengoku* daimyo drew their primary authority from their ability to exercise power and to maintain local control over the other *kokujin* and peasant communities within their sphere of command. They might on occasion, however, declare themselves successors to *shugo* or other provincial officials. But their main reliance, besides their own military strength, was on their capacity to secure the loyalty of their military followers and to convince the other inhabitants of their territories of their ability, or at least intent, to work for the good of the territorial community. This situation was reflected in the large body of legal codes issued by *sengoku* daimyo, in which the daimyo territory was conceived of as an organic entity, a *kokka*, over which the daimyo exercised public authority (*kōgi*).[82]

81 Kawai, with Grossberg, "Shogun and Shugo," pp. 80–83.
82 Shizuo Katsumata, with Martin Collcutt, "The Development of Sengoku Law," in John Whitney Hall, Keiji Nagahara, and Kozo Yamamura, eds., *Japan Before Tokugawa: Political Consolidation and Economic Growth, 1500–1650* (Princeton, N.J.: Princeton University Press, 1981), pp. 114–17.

The trend toward local autonomy was evident at the lower levels of Japanese society as well, as the cultivator class underwent a major transformation during the late Muromachi period.[83] One aspect of this was the increased freedom won by agricultural villages to organize their lives according to the community's desire. This was reflected in the appearance of village assemblies (*yoriai*) and village-established codes for internal regulation. It was reflected further in the success of some communities in winning from higher authority the rights to water use, autonomy of internal administration, and adjudication of disputes. Some even earned the right of immunity from entrance by officials of higher authority, as long as an agreed-upon annual tax was delivered. Many of these concessions were won by the use of the only weapons the villages possessed: the organization of village compacts and mass demonstrations, both called *ikki*. It was in this context of local unrest that the incipient daimyo of the Sengoku age recognized the need to accommodate the demands of the peasantry and thus declared themselves the protectors of all classes within their realms (*kokka*). By professing their regard for the common good, they claimed the right to govern their territory on the strength of the support they received from those they governed. Thus they invoked a new legitimacy, not derived from *tennō* or shogun, but established by the implied consent of the public will. This was the making of a new rationale for government, a radically new *tenka*.[84]

Although these changes were taking place in the provinces, their full impact did not reach the capital region until after the mid-sixteenth century. The capital and the surrounding agricultural lands in the provinces of Yamashiro, Ōmi, Kawachi, Settsu, and Yamato and a few other locations made up a central region that retained its own configuration throughout the last century of Ashikaga rule. And in this region in which the economy and society were still dominated by the interests of the court nobility and the central religious orders, the bakufu still had a role to play. During the last century, though the bakufu may have lost its ability to affect national affairs, it still was an important mechanism through which the noble houses, the great temples, and the wealthy merchant houses integrated their interests. Thus the bakufu continued to adjudicate disputes and to issue decrees until 1579.[85]

83 Keiji Nagahara, with Kozo Yamamura, "Village Communities and Daimyo Power," in Hall and Toyoda, eds., *Japan in the Muromachi Age*, pp. 107–23.
84 Ibid., pp. 121–3.
85 Ashikaga legislation, as revealed in the supplementary orders (*tsuikahō*), increasingly narrowed its scope to the capital city and its environs. See items 400–530 (1520–1570) in *Kemmu Shikimoku and Tsuikahō*, pp. 145–64.

The event that so dramatically started the downward slide of the Muromachi bakufu was the "War of Ōnin and Bummei," (1467–77), usually referred to simply as "Ōnin." A war that involved nearly all of the shugo houses of central Japan, it was doubly destructive because it was fought out in the streets of Kyoto. The issue that brought on the war was a conflict between the Hosokawa and Yamana families over the choice of heir to the shogun Yoshimasa. In the fighting, much of central Kyoto and the northern fringe of the city was destroyed, and many courtiers and priests fled the capital for the provinces. The shogun Yoshimasa remained aloof, maintaining his usual standard of aristocratic life.

If Yoshimitsu emerges in Muromachi history as the heroic model of the noble military ruler, Yoshimasa is generally pictured as the tragic ruler whose effete behavior brought on the declining fortunes of the ruling house.[86] Yoshimasa, the second son of the murdered Yoshinori, was named shogun in 1443 at the age of eight. Being a minor at the time, he was placed under the guardianship of the kanrei, Hosokawa Katsumoto. He was declared of age in 1449 and served as shogun until 1473, when he retired in favor of his son Yoshihisa. He lived on until 1489. In Yoshimasa's early years the bakufu had still not recovered from the shock inflicted by the murder of the shogun in 1441. At the same time, the country as a whole was suffering from acute economic problems. Rural mobs frequently broke into the capital, demanding relief from debts and taxation and forcing the bakufu to issue debt cancellation edicts (tokusei-rei). Widespread famine conditions during the 1450s led to death by famine in parts of Japan. Yet Yoshimasa and his kuge and buke colleagues engaged in politics as usual, building costly residences and bickering over court preferment and family inheritance. In 1458, Yoshimasa rebuilt the shogunal palace at great expense.

Meanwhile, political tension among the shugo was building up to the point of general warfare.[87] Yet during the fighting that started in 1467, Yoshimasa built a special residential palace for his mother. He had started in 1465 a retirement residence in the eastern foothills but had dropped the project when war broke out in Kyoto. In 1482, however, he began in earnest to build the Higashiyama villa that was to contain his monument, the Silver Pavilion (Ginkaku). In 1483, Yoshimasa moved to Higashiyama where he lived out his life as a patron of the arts, setting a style that was to leave an enduring mark on Japanese cultural history.

86 Kawai, Ashikaga Yoshimasa, offers the most complete modern biography.
87 Iikura Kiyotake, "Ōnin no ran ikō ni okeru Muromachi bakufu no seisaku," Nihonshi kenkyū (1974). 139–51.

By the end of the Ōnin War, most *shugo* had abandoned Kyoto and returned to their provinces to consolidate their forces. Kyoto itself was no longer a source of power for them. That was to be found in the provinces. As the *shugo* belatedly returned their attention to their provincial bases, most found that the times had already passed them by. Their vassals, being close to the real sources of military support and having for many years served as deputies for their Kyoto-based and increasingly remote *shugo* overlords, were showing signs of insubordination. Under these conditions, only the provincial daimyo domainal lord could survive. *Shugo* houses either were forced to adapt to these conditions or were quickly displaced by stronger provincial leaders. From this point on, affairs in the capital were conditioned on the struggle for power in the provinces.

But the capital and its government, the bakufu, retained some of its importance.[88] Although the last four or five shoguns had no personal power, the Hosokawa family that monopolized the office of *kanrei* managed to give a certain stability to the capital area, at least until the 1530s. During the Ōnin War, the *bugyōnin* had sided with the Hosokawa cause, and after the end of the fighting they remained cooperative with the Hosokawa. The pattern displayed in these years, in which a figurehead aristocratic house was kept alive by provincial military leaders as a means of acquiring national influence, was not new to Japanese history. The story of the last shogun, Yoshiaki, the emperor Ōgimachi, and the rising military hegemon, Oda Nobunaga, reveals how a "puppet shogun" could prove useful and yet cause trouble for his puppeteer.[89]

By the 1560s, the aristocratic houses of Kyoto were faced with more than the usual crises. The last *kanrei*, Hosokawa Ujitsuna, had been ousted by former vassals, the Miyoshi and the Matsunaga. In 1565, this group had assassinated the shogun, Ashikaga Yoshiteru, and had substituted Ashikaga Yoshihide as their puppet shogun. Another potential heir to the Ashikaga shogunate, Yoshiaki, at the time abbot of a subtemple of the Kōfukuji, escaped to the east to find support for his own cause. Oda Nobunaga seemed a likely candidate on whom to rely. Although still unproven as a national leader, he had had a string of notable military successes, especially the defeat in 1560 of a great army led by Imagawa Yoshimoto of Suruga. By 1565, Nobunaga was being

88 Ibid., pp. 142–3.
89 The remainder of what follows relies on Hisashi Fujiki, with George Elison, "The Political Posture of Oda Nobunaga," in Hall, Nagahara, and Yamamura, eds., *Japan Before Tokugawa*, pp. 49–93.

courted by both *tennō* and shogunal claimants to offer his military support on their behalf. Nobunaga responded to these offers in 1568, entering the capital in force "in the interest of" the emperor and "as champion for" Ashikaga Yoshiaki.

Once Nobunaga was in control of the city, the emperor, Ōgimachi, named Yoshiaki as the shogun and gave orders that both Yoshiaki and Nobunaga aid in the restoration of the estates lost by the imperial family. Nobunaga's status was left uncertain, but it appears that Yoshiaki wished to name him as *kanrei*. Had Nobunaga accepted this appointment, he would have become a party to a return to the triangular balance of power that had existed among *tennō*, shogun, and *kanrei* a century or so earlier. But Nobunaga refused to subordinate himself to the shogun. He rejected the offer and instead attempted to dominate the shogun through sheer force. From what transpired during the next few years, it is clear that the shogun was not powerless in such a situation. He could still count on the services of the Ashikaga house retainers, the civil administrators, and the guardsmen. The bakufu continued functioning as a legal office, affirming land grants and inheritances. Moreover, through his staff, the shogun still exercised considerable behind-the-scenes influence by playing factional politics among the provincial daimyo.

In early 1573, Yoshiaki sent out letters to nearby daimyo and religious institutions hostile to Nobunaga, calling for military action against him. He took refuge in a fortification south of Kyoto and waited for developments. Nobunaga made short work of the shogun's move. Yoshiaki was defeated, but not killed, and was allowed to live out his life in exile. But for all intents and purposes, the Ashikaga shogun and the Muromachi bakufu had ceased to exist.

Within a week after disposing of Yoshiaki, Nobunaga managed to have the emperor change the era name to Tensho as a sign of legitimation for a new political order. Nobunaga's *tenka* differed fundamentally from that of the Ashikaga shoguns. Yoshimitsu's or Yoshimasa's *tenka* had envisioned a fusion of *kuge* and *buke* rule conducted through the provincial administration of the shogun's *shugo* vassals. But by the time of Yoshiaki, the Ashikaga mandate to rule had been reduced to the narrowest of private interests, the shogun's simple desire to stay alive. Against this, Nobunaga was able to pose a broader conception of *tenka*, one that included a place for not only the *kuge* and *buke* but also the common people. It was this larger *tenka* that Yoshiaki proved unfit to govern.

CHAPTER 5

MUROMACHI LOCAL GOVERNMENT: *SHUGO* AND *KOKUJIN*

INTRODUCTION

In contrast with that of the Kamakura bakufu, the authority of the Muromachi bakufu expanded rapidly following its establishment in 1336, and the Ashikaga shogun became almost an absolute monarch.[1] In the provinces, *shugo* (military governors) were installed in sixty-six administrative units, or provinces. In Kyushu and in the area from the Kantō eastward, shogunal authority was delegated to regional bakufu headquarters with administrative control over large areas, called the Kantō *kubō* and the Kyushu *tandai*. An intermediate area encompassing the Kinai, or central provinces, was under direct shogunal rule. The authority of the *shugo*, in addition to their three major duties inherited from the Kamakura period – punishing murderers, putting down rebellions, and providing men for guard duty – was enhanced by the addition of jurisdiction over land-related matters. Besides holding nearly all military and administrative authority over the provinces, the *shugo* organized local overlords, called *kokujin*, into retainer bands. This process, called vassalization, progressed as the *shugo* gradually suppressed *kokujin* resistance. In an attempt to contain the increasing power of the *shugo*, the bakufu used control measures such as appointing members of the *shugo*'s collateral family to the shogun's army to serve as captains of the shogun's bodyguard, but from the time of the Ōnin War (1467–77), the *shugo*'s increasing separation and independence from the bakufu became undeniable, and the decentralization of local authority proceeded apace. Most of the *sengoku* daimyo, great sixteenth-century local warriors who controlled their own territories, could trace their lineages back to the Muromachi *shugo* or to their retainers, the deputy *shugo* (*shugodai*).

---

1 Satō Shin'ichi, "Shugo ryōgokusei no tenkai," in *Shin Nihonshi taikei* (Tokyo: Asakura shoten, 1954), p. 107.

REGIONAL ADMINISTRATIVE OFFICIALS: *KUBŌ* AND
TANDAI

During the Nambokuchō disturbance (1336–92), the bakufu's regional administrative headquarters – the Kantō *kubō* and the Kyushu
tandai–were established and had jurisdiction over the *shugo*, chiefly
out of military necessity. The Kantō *kubō* most likely originated during the Kannō disturbance (1350–2), when Shogun Ashikaga Takauji
left Kyoto to go to the Kantō, leaving his son Yoshiakira in his place.
In so doing, Takauji divided the country territorially between east and
west, thus creating a kind of dual government. Later, Takauji returned to Kyoto, but he stationed his fourth son, Ashikaga Motouji,
the younger brother of Yoshiakira, in his place in Kamakura as the
first Kantō *kubō*.

Paralleling the bakufu in Kyoto, a *shitsuji* or chief steward (called
the Kamakura *shitsuji* and, later, the Kamakura *kanrei*) was installed as
an adviser to the *kubō*, to whom the latter delegated all governing
duties. When a serious rift developed between the two, the Kantō
region was gradually brought to a state of disruption and war. The
main line of the Uesugi clan, Yamauchi no Uesugi, came to inherit the
office of Kantō *shitsuji*, which included a concurrent appointment as
the *shugo* of Echigo, Kōzuke, and Sagami provinces. Another official
under the *shitsuji* was in charge of litigation and day-to-day governing.
The office of the *kubō* was thus a smaller replica of the bakufu in
Kyoto. The eight provinces under the jurisdiction of the Kantō *kubō*
included Sagami, Musashi, Shimōsa, Kazusa, Awa, Hitachi,
Shimotsuke, and Kōzuke, but at times the provinces of Shinano, Kai,
Mutsu, and Dewa were also within the purview of the Kantō *kubō*.[2]

Among Japanese specialists, the Kantō governing authority of the
Muromachi period is called the Kamakura-*fu* because its administrative offices were established at Kamakura in Sagami Province.[3] The
branch of the Ashikaga family that served as the Kantō *kubō* maintained an independent stance toward Kyoto, and beginning with the
reign of the third shogun, Yoshimitsu, the Kantō's military activities
were regarded with a wary eye by the authorities in Kyoto,

At the end of 1399, when the powerful western *shugo* Ōuchi
Yoshihiro attacked the bakufu and started the Ōei disturbance,

2 On the Kantō *kubō* system, see Watanabe Yosuke, *Kantō chūshin Ashikaga jidai no kenkyū*
(Tokyo: Yūzankaku, 1926); Itō Kiyoshi, "Muromachi no kokka to Tōgoku," *Rekishigaku
kenkyū*, special issue (October 1979): 63–72.
3 Itō Kiyoshi, "Kamakura bakufu oboegaki," *Rekishi*, no. 42 (April 1972): 17–34.

Ashikaga Yoshimitsu resolved to subjugate the Kantō. The next shogun, Ashikaga Yoshimochi, attempted to check the rebellious Kantō
kubō both openly and by coercive methods. On the one hand he paci-
fied the appeased *shitsuji*, Uesugi Norizane, and at the same time
threw his support to powerful *shugo* and some of the *kokujin* who
dominated areas of the Kantō, calling them the "stipended band of
Kyoto." Accordingly, the *kokujin* and *shugo* of the various areas of the
Kantō split into two factions: those who allied with the bakufu in
Kyoto and thus attempted to widen their own sphere of control, and
those who pledged loyalty to the Kantō *kubō* and broke with Kyoto.

   Antagonism between the shogun Ashikaga Yoshinori and the Kantō
kubō Ashikaga Mochiuji reached a peak in 1428. Finally, in the Eikyō
disturbance of 1438, Mochiuji was defeated and killed by bakufu
troops. Two years later, nearly all of Mochiuji's descendants were
killed in the Yūki disturbance, and the Kantō was left without a *kubō*.
In this conflict, the Kantō *shitsuji* Uesugi Norizane, taking a position
similar to that of the bakufu, tried to dissuade Mochiuji from rebelling, but he was unsuccessful, and finally he left his master and went
into seclusion.

   After the Kakitsu disturbance of 1441, Shogun Yoshimasa appointed the last remaining descendant of Mochiuji, Ashikaga Shigeuji,
to the position of Kantō *kubō* and dispatched him to Kamakura. Since
the Eikyō disturbance, Shigeuji had harbored a deep resentment
against Norizane and his son Uesugi Noritada, who subsequently became the *shitsuji*. In 1454, Shigeuji attacked and killed Noritada in
Kamakura, and the Kantō was plunged into chaos. The next year,
Shigeuji was removed from his post as *kubō* and was driven out of
Kamakura by bakufu troops.

   By now a rebel, Shigeuji set up his resistance headquarters at Koga
in Shimōsa Province. Known as the Koga *kubō*, he attracted many
local military leaders as his retainers.[4] In the conflict that soon broke
out, the town of Kamakura was destroyed, and the Kantō entered the
period of civil wars, the Sengoku period, one step ahead of the rest of
the country. In this way, exactly the opposite of the bakufu's intent in
delegating the Kantō's governing authority to the Kantō *kubō* was
accomplished: It succeeded only in hastening that area's estrangement
from the bakufu.

   The bakufu did not appoint *shugo* to the northern provinces of

4 Satō Hironobu, "Sengokuki ni okeru Tōgoku kokkaron no ichi shiten – Koga kubō
   Ashikagashi to Go-Hōjōshi o chūshin to shite," *Rekishigaku kenkyū*, special issue (October
   1979): 72–75.

Mutsu and Dewa, where in the Nambokuchō period Kitabatake Akiie had gathered a military following and the forces of the Southern Court held sway. First, Ishidō Yoshifusa was appointed *tandai*, and then Shiba Iekane was appointed shogunal deputy (*kanrei*) of the northern region.[5] From then on, Shiba's descendants, the Ōzaki family, were the de facto *shugo* there. At one point in the early fifteenth century, the region came under the jurisdiction of the Kantō *kubō*, and later the *kubō*'s family set up a residence in the southern part of Mutsu, which became known as the Sasagawa Palace. In the early sixteenth century, the *sengoku* daimyo Date was appointed by the bakufu to the office of *tandai* of the northern region, but in fact he held no power, and his office was important in name only.[6]

Kyushu in the Nambokuchō period was an even greater stronghold of the southern forces than was the northern region. Here, in the Kamakura period, the Chinzei *tandai*, the bakufu's Kyushu headquarters, had been located. Isshiki Tōyū, a member of the Ashikaga clan, was appointed to the Muromachi successor of the Kyushu post, now called the Chinzei *kanrei*.[7] Unable to attain control of it as an outpost of the bakufu and the forces of the Northern Court, Isshiki was forced to move his administrative offices north to Dazaifu and Hakata; by the middle of the fourteenth century, the Isshiki family's control of Kyushu had collapsed. There, the bakufu, in the person of the *kanrei* Hosokawa Yoriyuki, appointed Imagawa Sadayo (also known as Imagawa Ryōshun) as the *shugo* of Tōtomi, that is, the Kyushu *tandai*, and he was dispatched to Hakata in 1369.

By 1371, Sadayo had obtained the support of daimyo friendly to the bakufu, like the Matsuura band, the Shimazu and the Ōuchi. Eventually he was able to crush the military leaders of the southern forces, like the Kikuchi, and succeeded in unifying Kyushu under the bakufu's control. Continuing the practice of the Kamakura bakufu, Sadayo established the office of the *tandai* in the Hakata, for Chikuzen Province, and was concurrently appointed *shugo* of the three provinces of Aki, Bingo, and Hyūga. But when Hosokawa Yoriyuki was killed in the Kūryaku disturbance of 1379, Imagawa's position also became precarious. Before long the post of *tandai* passed to Ōuchi Yoshihiro. And after Ōuchi's downfall in the Ōei disturbance of 1399, the

5 Endō Iwao, "Ōshū kanrei oboegaki," *Rekishi*, no. 38 (March 1969): 24–66; Ogawa Makoto, *Ashikaga ichimon shugo hatten shi no kenkyū*, (Tokyo: Yoshikawa kōbunkan, 1980), pp. 525–618.
6 Fujiki Hisashi, *Sengoku shakai shiron* (Tokyo: Tōkyō daigaku shuppankai, 1974), pp. 342–59.
7 Kawazoe Shōji, "Chinzei kanrei kō," *Nihon rekishi*, nos. 205 and 206 (June–July 1965): 2–14 and 29–53, respectively.

Shibukawa, a collateral line of the Ashikaga, inherited the office of *tandai*. Beginning in the early fifteenth century, the powerful *shugo* of northern Kyushu – the Ōuchi, Shōni, and Ōtomo – struggled for hegemony over northern Kyushu. The *tandai* office held by the Shibukawa family ceased to function and became only a nominal position. At the same time, Kyushu entered the Ōnin War and was engulfed in strife for the next thirty years. Like the Kantō, Kyushu entered the Sengoku era early.[8]

The Muromachi bakufu's regional governing mechanisms, called the *kubō* and the *tandai* – which were established in the Kantō, the northern provinces, and Kyushu – entered the Ōnin War early and were stripped of their power before they could reach their full development. This was an important turning point toward decentralization in the peripheral areas and toward a general state of war.

SHUGO DAIMYO

Placement of shugo

The Muromachi *shugo* were the institutional heirs of the Kamakura *shugo* system.[9] Even the short-lived Kemmu government of Emperor Godaigo, an attempt at resurrecting the ancient *ritsuryō* state, pursued a policy of jointly appointing to each province a *shugo* and a governor, the ancient *ritsuryō* post of *kokushi*. The Mongol invasions of the late Kamakura period were an important turning point in the expansion of the *shugo*'s powers. Even Emperor Godaigo's political power cannot be ignored as a factor in the system's entrenchment. In some regions, the Muromachi bakufu, founded in 1336, continued its fight against the forces of the Southern Court, just as before. But in areas where the fighting had ended, the bakufu was able to install powerful military leaders of the Ashikaga clan as *shugo*. To areas where the southern forces remained relatively strong, however, especially in the provinces around Kyoto, the bakufu dispatched "provincial generals" (*kuni daishō*), military commanders quite unlike the *shugo*, who were basically administrative officials. Some provinces had no *shugo* at all; only *kuni daishō*.[10]

8 Kawazoe Shōji, "Kyūshū tandai no suimetsu katei," *Kyūshū bunkashi kenkyūjo kiyō*, no. 23 (March 1978): 81–130.
9 Satō Shin'ichi, *Zōho Kamakura bakufu shugo seido no kenkyū* (Tokyo: Tōkyō daigaku shuppankai, 1971), pp. 243–53.
10 Satō Shin'ichi, *Muromachi bakufu shugo seido no kenkyū – Nambokuchōki shokoku shugo enkaku kōshō hen*, rev. ed., vol. 1 (Tokyo: Tōkyō daigaku shuppankai, 1967), pp. 31–32.

As in the past, in the crucial five provinces of the Kyoto area and particularly in the militarily most strategic province of Yamato, no *shugo* was appointed. Instead, those powers were held by one of the powerful head temples of the Hossō sect of Buddhism, the Kōfukuji.[11] With the historically strong support of the powerful Fujiwara family, the Kōfukuji became the dominant force in Yamato Province and owned extensive estates from which it derived great revenue. To protect its interests, the temple maintained an army of warrior-monks (*sōhei*). Until the *sengoku* daimyo Matsunaga Hisahide conquered it in 1560, Yamato Province generally was able to resist military control. This is not to say that the bakufu's authority did not extend to the province at all: In military crises, *shugo* of the neighboring provinces of Iga, Kōchi, and later Yamashiro temporarily executed the duties of *shugo* there.

Yamato was not the only province lacking *shugo*: In the province of Hida, the bakufu acknowledged the presence of the aristocratic Anekōji family in the capacity of provincial governor, and the Kyōgoku family as *shugo*. Likewise, the Kitabatake family, descendants of the aristocrat Kitabatake Chikafusa, controlled the southern half of Ise Province through the office of provincial governor.[12] After the Ōnin War, only they exercised *shugo* authority there and were even formally appointed *shugo* by the bakufu.

In the Muromachi period, the governors of Ise, Hida, and Tosa (who after the Ōnin War was Ichijō Norifusa, a member of one of the aristocratic regent houses), were known as the "three provincial governors" (*sankokushi*). The lack of a *shugo* in Yamato and the existence of the three aristocratic provincial governors were unusual and not typical of the Muromachi *shugo* system.

As the province where the bakufu itself was located, Yamashiro was of primary importance. In the Kamakura period, no *shugo* had been appointed to this province which was directly administered through the bakufu's Kyoto branch, the Rokuhara *tandai*.[13] This situation continued under the Muromachi bakufu until the end of the Nambokuchō period. From the establishment of the bakufu until the end of the Kannō disturbance in 1352, the *shugo*'s administrative functions were carried out by bakufu vassals in Yamashiro Province, acting

11 Nagashima Fukutarō, "Yamato shugoshiki kō," *Rekishi chiri* 68 (October 1936): 61–66; Nagashima Fukutarō, *Nara bunka no denryū* (Tokyo: Meguro shoten, 1951), pp. 33, 85.
12 Okamura Morihiko, *Hida shikō*, medieval vol. (Tokyo: Okamura Morihiko, 1979), pp. 56–74; Ōnishi Genichi, *Kitabatakeshi no kenkyū* (Mie: Mieken kyōdo shiryō kankokai, 1962), pp. 1–100; Nishiyama Masaru, "Sengoku daimyō Kitabatakeshi no kenryoku kōzō," *Shirin* 62 (March 1979): 51–86.   13 Satō, *Zōho Kamakura bakufu*, p. 1.

as inspection and enforcement officials. In the late fourteenth century, the Board of Retainers the (*samurai-dokoro*) exercised the *shugo*'s authority there.[14] The bakufu, however, was keenly aware of the military importance of Yamashiro and so in 1385 divided it into two administrative sections: Rakuchū, which included the city of Kyoto, and the district (*gunbu*), which was agricultural. Rakuchū was administered by the *samurai-dokoro*, and an office of Yamashiro *shugo* was created for the district as part of a general assignment of *shugo*. Yamana Ujikiyo, the *shugo* of Izumi and Tamba, was appointed to the new office.[15] From then on, the board carried out police functions in most of the capital. After Ujikiyo was defeated in the Meitoku disturbance of 1391, it became customary for the closest vassals of Shogun Yoshimitsu, including Yūki Mitsufuji and Kō no Moronao, to fill the office of Yamashiro *shugo*. But after Yoshimitsu's death, the *samurai-dokoro* again took over the administration of Yamashiro.[16] In the movement of personnel that accompanied the suppression of the provincial governor Kitabatake Mitsumasa's rebellion in 1412, the *kanrei* Hatakeyama Mitsuie was appointed *shugo* of Yamashiro. From then on, Yamashiro for the most part could be considered the domain of the Hatakeyama family, who made the local *kokujin* and wealthy peasants their vassals.

In Ōmi Province as well, where, after Yamato and Yamashiro, the power of the *shōen* proprietors was greatest, a special system was put into effect whereby the *shugo*'s authority was limited and did not extend to the lands of the Enryakuji, the great Buddhist monastery on Mount Hiei. In those areas the *shugo*'s duties were carried out by the Enryakuji's own military organization, the "emissaries of Mount Hiei" (*sanmon shisetsu*), who were even so designated by the bakufu.[17]

Dividing the office of shugo

The *shugo* of the Muromachi bakufu differed from those of the Kamakura period in that their scope of authority was greatly increased. Another change in the office of *shugo* that began in this period was the practice of dividing it between two people. As the Kemmu *shikimoku*, the legal code of the Muromachi bakufu, explained, "The

14 Haga Norihiko, "Muromachi bakufu samurai dokoro tōnin, tsuketafi: Yamashiro shugo bunin enkaku kōshō kō," *Tōyō Daigaku Kiyō*, Faculty of Letters vol., no. 16 (July 1962): 77–98.
15 Gomi Fumihiko, "Shichō no kōsei to bakufu: jūni–jūyon seiki no rakuchū shihai," *Rekishigaku kenkyū*, no. 392 (January 1973): 1–19.
16 Haga, "Muromachi bakufu samurai dokoro," pp. 91–92.
17 Shimosaka Mamoru, "Sanmon shisetsu seido no seiritsu to tenkai: Muromachi bakufu no sanmon seisaku o megutte," *Shirin* 58 (January 1975): 67–114.

post of *shugo* is an office from ancient times," indicating that the bakufu regarded the *shugo* as successors of the provincial governors of the *ritsuryō* system.[18] The Muromachi *shugo* came to be regarded as the administrators of each province's political affairs. The office of *shugo* was first divided into district-level units so that several *shugo* could be concurrently installed in a single province.[19] They were known as "half-province *shugo*" (*hankoku shugo*) or "divided-district *shugo*" (*bungun shugo*) and are thought to be the forerunners of the similar divisions of domains instituted by the Tokugawa bakufu. The initial reason for this division of office was apparently military, and during the Nambokuchō disturbance, military administrative officials like *shugo* were installed as needed. It is not clear exactly when the office of *shugo* for the district level was first divided, but because the two districts of Amata and Ikaruga were taken from the *shugo* of Tamba, Niki Yoriaki, in 1342 and given to the *shugo* of Tango, Uesugi Tomisada,[20] this system may have been instituted immediately after the Muromachi bakufu was established.

In the latter part of the Nambokuchō period, with the rise of powerful *shugo*, the bakufu used this system to check the increasing power of specific *shugo*. In 1383, the bakufu restored Hosokawa Yorimoto (son of Yoriyuki), who was defeated in the Kōryaku disturbance of 1379, as the *shugo* of Settsu Province.[21] But the *kanrei* Shiba Yoshimasa, fearing the rising power of the Hosokawa, then subdivided and allotted nearly half of the province to neighboring *shugo*.[22] Specifically, of Settsu Province's thirteen districts, the districts of Nose, Kawabe, and Arima near Harima Province, as well as Nishinari District, were assigned to the Akamatsu family; Sumiyoshi District near Izumi Province was assigned to the Yamana family; and Higashinari District near Kōchi Province was assigned to the Hatakeyama family. As a result, the Hosokawa family was unable to govern all of Settsu as their own domain or to use the office of *shugo* to cultivate their own military following in order to recover their lost districts. Through political negotiations following the Ōnin War, the Hosokawa regained these districts, except for Arima District. Instead, the Arima family, a collateral branch of the Akamatsu, maintained exclusive control of that

18 Satō, *Muromachi bakufu shugo seido*, p. 46.
19 Imatani Akira, *Muromachi bakufu kaitai katei no kenkyū* (Tokyo: Iwanami shoten, 1985), pp. 225–59.
20 Imatani Akira, *Shugo ryōgoku shihai kikō no kenkyū* (Tokyo: Hōsei daigaku shuppankyoku, 1986), pp. 307–45.
21 Satō, *Muromachi bakufu shugo seido*, vol. 1, pp. 30–52; Ogawa, *Ashikaga ichimon*, pp. 285–9.
22 Satō, *Muromachi bakufu shugo seido*, vol. 1, pp. 30–52; Imatani, *Shugo ryōgoku*, pp. 246–94.

district and indeed, were called "masters of the district" (*gunshu*) until the end of the Sengoku period.[23]

Like Settsu, Aki was a province with several divided districts. The bakufu attached great importance to Aki as a buffer zone between the renowned warrior family of western Japan, the Ōuchi, and the forces of the Yamana family. During the Nambokuchō period the *shugo* of Aki Province was a member of the Takeda family, the great warrior clan based east of Kamakura. But at the end of the Nambokuchō period, as the forces of the Ōuchi and Yamana expanded, the province was internally divided in the following way.

First, the three central districts located near the head of Hiroshima Bay – Satō, Anan, and Yamagata – were assigned as divided districts to the Takeda family. Kamo District and the four islands of Nōmi, Kurahashi, Hidaka, and Gamagari, which made up an archipelago near Anan District, went to the Ōuchi; the remaining five districts of Sasei, Takamiya, Takada, Toyota, and Ahoku were given to the Yamana, who were designated as the official *shugo*; and the Takeda family were named "masters of the district" (*gunshu*).[24] In provinces where the normal *shugo* system was in effect, such a division was rare. Instead, there was a "half-province" *shugo* system in which one province was divided nearly in half and two *shugo* were installed. This half-province *shugo* system was put into effect in the provinces of Bingo, Tosa, Izumi, Ōmi, Kaga, Tōtomi, Suruga, and Hitachi. Except for Tosa and Izumi, the provinces were divided in half, either north to south or east to west, with the border running approximately through the center.

In other words, insofar as the division of the office of *shugo* was territorial, it was only a variation of the divided-district *shugo* system.[25] In the cases of Tosa (from 1400 to 1408 only) and Izumi, however, a peculiar system was instituted whereby the province's military administration was overseen simultaneously by two *shugo*.[26] It is unclear why such a system was devised, but in the case of Izumi, the following explanation seems plausible: The northernmost area of the province was the great trade city of Sakai; a strict territorial division would have resulted in two unbalanced districts, one urban and one agricultural. Moreover, twice during the Meitoku (1391) and Ōei

23 Imatani, *Muromachi bakufu kaitai*, pp. 225–59.
24 Kishida Hiroshi and Akiyama Nobutaka, eds., *Hiroshima ken shi*, medieval vol. (Hiroshima: Hiroshima kenchō, 1984), pp. 301–49; Kawamura Shōichi, "Aki Takedashi kankei monjo mokuroku," pt. 1, *Geibi chihōshi kenkyū*, no. 108 (1975): 26–31.
25 Imatani, *Muromachi bakufu kaitai*, pp. 225–59. 26 Imatani, *Shugo ryōgoku*, pp. 216–45.

(1399) disturbances, powerful *shugo*, using the city of Sakai as their base, rebelled against the bakufu, and so most likely the bakufu took this into consideration when constructing the system.

The shugo'*s duties and scope of authority*

The Kamakura *shugo*'s scope of authority in normal times consisted mainly of recruiting men for guard service and handling criminal matters. The latter included police powers in cases of rebellion, murder, night raiding, robbery, banditry, and piracy. But with the great expansion of the *shugo*'s power brought on by the Mongol invasions and the proliferation of "evil bands" (*akutō*) in the late Kamakura period, the office of *shugo* also took on many administrative duties. For example, the *shugo* had to attend to such things as establishing and maintaining an administrative office for the temples and shrines, as well as for the post stops (lodgings).[27] The *shugo* of the Muromachi period continued this trend, but they were also officially given various powers that the Kamakura *shugo* had not had, such as sending an envoy to the scene of a land dispute (*shisetsu jungyōken*), enforcing the law, allocating *hanzei*, and levying taxes.[28]

The right of enforcement, also called the enforcement of land-related verdicts, included carrying out the litigation procedures pertaining to existing rights over real property (*shomu sōron*, property deliberations), forbidding the trespass on or seizure of the disputed land, and then installing on the land the winner of the lawsuit, that is, the person recognized by the bakufu as the land's rightful owner. This last step was called *satashi tsuku*. The Kamakura bakufu at first would appoint two warriors as emissaries to perform this function, but by the end of the Kamakura period, or before 1330, the *shugo* with jurisdiction over the land in question usually had the duty of enforcement.[29] The Muromachi bakufu also followed these procedures and generally had the *shugo* implement the bakufu decisions regarding land lawsuits. In a Muromachi bakufu decree in 1346, the right of enforcement was added to the *shugo*'s three basic duties.[30]

The legal process itself was as follows: When a verdict was handed down, the bakufu would usually issue it in the form of a shogunal directive stating the verdict, that is, an edict of a judicial settlement.

27 Satō, *Zōho Kamakura bakufu*, pp. 250–2.   28 Ibid., p. 251.
29 Satō, *Muromachi bakufu shugo seido*, vol. 1, pp. 7–9.
30 Satō Shin'ichi and Ikeuchi Yoshisuke, *Chūsei hōsei shiryōshū*, vol. 2: *Muromachi bakufu hō* (Tokyo: Iwanami shoten, 1957), pp. 23–24.

Next, the *kanrei* would receive it and issue an enforcement decree ordering the *shugo* of the province where the land was located to take care of the matter, that is, to enforce the verdict. The winner of the lawsuit would then receive both the shogunal directive and the enforcement decree at the bakufu's office of litigation, take them to the *shugo*'s Kyoto residence, and request that the land be returned to him. If the *shugo* consented, he would issue an enforcement order to the deputy *shugo* residing in the province, charging him with restoring the land to the rightful party. The victorious litigant would then take this document to his province, present it to the deputy *shugo*, and await instructions. The deputy *shugo* would issue an order to turn over the land to an aide or to a district-level official to enforce the verdict on the land itself. When the land had been restored, a guarantee of receipt of the land, that is, a document of reply, would be issued by the deputy *shugo*'s aide and would take exactly the same route in reverse, up to the highest official involved. Finally, all the documents would be handed over to the successful litigant.[31]

This process contained yet another layer of bureaucracy. Many deputy *shugo*, as well as *shugo*, lived in Kyoto, and so in such cases another enforcement edict would be issued from the deputy *shugo* to the junior deputy *shugo* (*koshugodai*) residing in the province. It was also common for the *shugo*'s scribe, who lived in Kyoto in the *shugo*'s absence, to issue an enforcement edict to the deputy *shugo*.[32] Such cases show that the *shugo*'s duty of enforcement, though originally only one part of the bakufu's administration of justice, in fact gave the *shugo* a great deal of room in which to maneuver. Many *shugo* refused to enforce cases that they considered disadvantageous, and many *shugo* collected large fees, known as "offerings," from successful litigants as compensation for this enforcement service.

Another new duty for the *shugo* was to allocate *hanzei*, literally "a half-tax." This means giving to the warriors – the local supporters in the Nambokuchō disturbance – half of the *nengu* (rice tax) of the *shōen* and *kokugaryō*, for their military expenses. This policy was first put into effect in 1352 when Takauji enforced it on the *shōen* of Ōmi, Mino, and Owari provinces. In the beginning it was to be limited to one year, and only *nengu* income would be forfeited by the absentee proprietor. What actually happened, however, was that once the warriors were granted *hanzei*, they developed a vested interest in the land

31 Satō, *Muromachi bakufu shugo seido*, vol. 1, pp. 8–9.
32 Satō, Shin'ichi, *Komonjogaku nyūmon* (Tokyo: Hōsei daigaku shuppankyoku, 1971), pp. 169–70.

and soon began to entertain designs on nearby lands of temples and shrines as well. Thereafter, the *hanzei* decrees that the bakufu intended to use to eradicate the warriors' incursions onto *shōen* met with great resistance by the local warriors.[33]

In 1368, the *kanrei* Hosokawa Yoriyuki issued the famous Ōan *hanzei* decree which recognized *hanzei* on regular *shōen* and exempted only imperial lands, lands of the imperial regent houses, and consolidated holdings of great temples and shrines. This decree was intended to halt permanently the warriors' incursions into *shōen* by dividing not the *nengu* but the land itself into the *shōen* proprietor's sector and the local warrior's sector. This law was important in determining the basic framework of landholding relationships in the Muromachi period. Part of the *shōen* holdings of the aristocratic class were thereby protected and supported by the bakufu, but the rights and interests of the *shugo* and their vassals were also considerable. This decree thus began the consolidation of territorial control by the *shugo* daimyo.[34]

Through this *hanzei* decree the *shugo* were able to acquire enormous amounts of *hanzei* lands, and in accordance with their right to allocate them, they awarded them to favored local warriors and vassals.[35] In 1363, Shogun Yoshiakira issued a directive stating that the custody, that is, disposal, of *hanzei* lands was the right of the *shugo*.[36] This enabled the *shugo* to organize large numbers of prominent peasants into vassal bands.

The third duty assigned to the Muromachi *shugo* was taxation. The tax on the harvest was paid by the peasants to the *shōen* proprietor. Consequently, the *shugo* could not lay claim to the harvest tax or the miscellaneous services tax outside those of their own directly controlled lands. But there was the precedent of the Kamakura *shugo*'s collecting provincewide uniform taxes for the bakufu, with the authorization of the imperial court.[37] This was a tax on temple and shrine buildings, which was called a rice tax, replacing the corvée, as well as a rice tax for an imperial ceremony, the *daijōe*. Both seem to have been instituted in the Insei period (late eleventh through late twelfth centuries). The proceeds from the first rice tax went ot the periodic rebuilding of the Ise Shrine, and the second rice tax was used for the emperor's installation ceremony.

33 Satō Shin'ichi, *Nambokuchō no dōran*, in vol. 9 of *Nihon no rekishi* (Tokyo: Chūō kōronsha, 1965), pp. 328–9.   34 Ibid., pp. 396–7.
35 Satō, *Zōho Kamakura bakufu*, p. 251.   36 Satō, *Muromachi bakufu shugo seido*, vol. 1, p. 38.
37 Ishii Susumu, "Kamakura bakufu to ritsuryō kokka – kokuga to no kankei o chūshin to shite," in Ishimoda Shō and Satō Shin'ichi, eds., *Chūsei no hō to kokka* (Tokyo: Tōkyō daigaku shuppankai, 1960), pp. 135–221.

The Muromachi bakufu continued this taxation procedure, securing imperial edicts and directives from the retired emperor and then ordering the *shugo* to collect the various taxes.[38] Such taxes were levied on assets; one, called *tansen*, was based on land accumulation, and another, called *munabechisen*, was assessed in proportion to the number of posts in one's house. The cadastral register used as the basis for the *tansen* levy was called the *ōtabumi* or *sudenchō*, a comprehensive register of paddy fields compiled in the early Kamakura period.[39] But this registry had not been kept up to date and therefore did not include lands later brought under cultivation. The *shugo* were required to submit only the income from the lands, listed in the *ōtabumi*, but they still taxed all cultivated land and pocketed the excess. In addition, the district or *tansen* officials of the *shugo* routinely entered *shōen* lands for on-site inspections. The *shōen* proprietors resented this and would often pay a large fee to the official in return for exemption from the inspection. In these ways the income of the *shugo* and his officials grew very large.[40]

Thus the *shugo* manipulated the bakufu's *tansen* collection orders and at the same time imposed on the peasants a new tax to cover provincial administrative costs.[41] Japanese scholars refer to this additional tax as *shugo tansen*. This was the tax that the *shugō*, without clearly stating its purpose, converted into a permanent, yearly collection of one hundred *mon* per *tan* of land. This took place roughly around the mid-fifteenth century. The establishment of the *shugo tansen* was in fact a system of tax collection that varied depending on locale and individual *shugo*. This tax was similar to rent for land and marked a new phase in the expansion of *shugo* authority, which now pervaded the entire province, including *shōen* lands, *kokujin* lands, and lands of the provincial governor's office.

In addition to the *tansen* and *munabechisen*, another important *shugo* tax took the form of labor. To cover the costs of the *shugo's* duties in his capacity as the provincial military and police authority, the *shugo* could generally impose the necessary taxes on the villages in his province. These taxes are referred to collectively as *shugoyaku*.[42] Of these, the heaviest was the corvée, which may have originated in the warrior's practice of commandeering peasants to transport provisions and build defenses during the Nambokuchō disturbance. But from the late

---

38 Satō, *Muromachi bakufu shugo seido*, pp. 9–10.
39 Ishii Susumu, *Nihon chūsei kokkashi no kenkyū* (Tokyo: Iwanami shoten, 1970), pp. 118–200.
40 Momose Kesao, "Tansen kō," in Hōgetsu Keigo sensei kanreki kinenkai, ed., *Nihon shakai keizaishi kenkyū*, medieval vol. (Tokyo: Yoshikawa kōbunkan, 1967), pp. 1–34.
41 Tanuma Mutsumi, "Kuden tansen to shugo ryōgoku," *Shoryōbu kiyō*, no. 17 (1965): 16–33.
42 Fukuda Ikuo, "Shugoyaku kō," in *Nihon shakai keizaishi kenkyū*, medieval vol., pp. 147–78.

fourteenth century into the fifteenth, the corvée that the *shugo* demanded of the villages took a variety of forms, depending on the services provided, number of days served, number of people, and so on. In about 1360, the Akamatsu *shugo* pressed the following corvée demands on the peasants of the Tōji's *shōen*, Yano-no-shō, in Harima Province: transport of plaster, lumber, and salt; long-term provision of labor services as standard bearers, armor bearers (especially for transporting baggage for travel), and porters between Kyoto and the provinces; and construction of defenses.

In 1388, peasants on the Tōji's Tamba *shōen*, Ōyama-no-shō, were required to provide a very large amount of corvée to the *shugo*, amounting to 263 people. When such corvée was imposed, the *shugo* would also require the *shōen* proprietor to pay incidental expenses for necessary food and the like. The *shōen* proprietor then passed half of this burden on to the peasants, whose burden became even heavier.[43]

The *shugoyaku* burden was not limited to human labor but extended even to livestock such as oxen and horses and to movable property like boats. Because it was necessary for the *shugo* to maintain constant contact between their provincial office and Kyoto, they would often commandeer horses belonging to the peasants, a practice called *temmayaku*. The horses were usually expropriated for only a few days and then returned to the peasants, but in wartime when such measures were imposed for military reasons, they inflicted serious harm on the peasant families' productivity.[44] In provinces bordering the Inland Sea, fishing villages' boats were apparently commandeered a number of times for military reasons. There are even examples of peasants' everyday items, like pots and pans, being appropriated by *shugo*. In villages like these, peasants unable to endure such impositions often went through the *shōen* proprietor to complain to the bakufu of the *shugo*'s lawlessness.

All of these developments reflected the fact that the authority of the *shugo* was increasing; their oppression of the *kokujin* and peasants was intensifying; and the decentralization of authority in the provinces was advancing.

Making the office of shugo hereditary

In the first half of the Nambokuchō period, in the areas where the fighting was the most severe, *shugo* were frequently shifted about.[45]

---

43 Satō, *Nambokuchō no dōran*, pp. 370–1.   44 Imatani, *Shugo ryōgoku*, pp. 454–71.
45 Satō, *Muromachi shugo seido*, vol. 1, pp. 53, 220; Ogawa, *Ashikaga ichimon*, pp. 1–25; and Satō, *Nambokuchō no dōran*, pp. 378–80.

From the time of the establishment of the bakufu until after the Ōei disturbance during Yoshimitsu's shogunate (from 1336 to 1400), there were only thirteen provinces in which the office of *shugo* remained in the same family: in Satsuma, the Shimazu family; Bungo, the Ōtomo; Tosa, the Hosokawa; Awa and Sanuki, the Hosokawa; Suō, the Ōuchi; Mino, the Toki; Hida, the Kyōgoku; Kai, the Takeda; Suruga, the Imagawa; Shimōsa, the Chiba; Hitachi, the Satake; and Kōzuke, the Uesugi.

Two reasons that the *shugo* were so often moved about are probably that in the Nambokuchō disturbance, they were required to assume military responsibilities where needed and also that the bakufu was plagued by factionalism. In the Nambokuchō period the bakufu leadership divided into two large factions: one led by Kō no Moronao, Ashikaga Tadayoshi, and Niki Yoshinaga and the other by Hatakeyama Kunikiyo, Hosokawa Yoriyuki, and Shiba Yoshimochi. Consequently, dissension and political disturbances became chronic.[46] The first faction derived strength from the fact that they were concentrated in the central Kinai region around Kyoto, an area in which *shugo* were reappointed particularly often. The fate of the second faction, Tadayoshi's "bureaucratic" faction, can be ascertained from the fact that in the Kannō disturbance from 1350 to 1352 they were entirely excluded from appointments, whereas the *shugo* of Hosokawa Yoriyuki's faction were moved about in great numbers. Apart from such major uprisings, there were smaller uprisings of powerful *shugo*, like the Meitoku (1391) and Ōei (1399) disturbances. These were suppressed, and the *shugo* were reassigned. After the Ōei disturbance, the *shugo* of twelve provinces were rotated as follows: from the Shiba family to the Ogasawara family in Shinano Province; from the Hatakeyama to the Shiba in Owari; from the Niki to the Toki in Ise; from Imagawa Sadayo to Imagawa Yasunori in the divided *shugo* office of Tōtomi and Suruga; from the Ōuchi to the Niki in Izumi; from the Kyōgoku to the Yamana in Iwami; from Ōuchi Yoshihiro to Ōuchi Hiroshige in Suō and Nagato; from the Ōuchi to the Hatakeyama in Kii; from a collateral branch of the Hosokawa to the Yamana in Bingo; and from the *sōryō* house of the Hosokawa to a collateral branch of the same family in Tosa.[47]

The Ōei disturbance was the last large-scale movement of *shugo* by the Muromachi bakufu. Subsequently, there were almost no extensive

46 Satō, *Muromachi bakufu shugo seido*, vol. 1, pp. 60–61.
47 Imatani, *Shugo ryōgoku*, pp. 216–45.

reappointments of *shugo*. If the head of a *shugo* family died, a direct heir or some close blood relative would nearly always inherit the office. In this way, from the early fifteenth century on, the office of *shugo* became heritable, which enabled *shugo* to become well established in an area.[48] In the past when the *shugo* were transferred every few years, even when they made vassals of low-ranking warriors and prominent peasants in their provinces, the lord–vassal relationship was necessarily a weak one. But when the office of *shugo* was held continuously by the same family, the most powerful warriors in a province became the *shugo*'s permanent vassals, which allowed the *shugo* to dominate their provinces in fact as well as in name. At about the same time, the *shugo*'s vassals often assumed the duties of a *shōen* manager, a process called *shugo-uke*.[49] Local affairs were such that without the cooperation, direct or indirect of the *shugo*'s vassals, even the proprietor's control of the *shōen* could become precarious.

Thus in the fifteenth century, the term *kunikata*, which in the past had referred to the provincial governor or the provincial office, came to refer solely to the power of the *shugo*. In the late 1420s, when Yoshimochi was shogun and the Muromachi bakufu was at the height of its power, the *shugo* were positioned as follows (including the *shugo* of three or more divided provinces): the Hosokawa *shugo* controlled the provinces of Izumi, Settsu, Tamba, Bitchū, Awaji, Sanuki, Awa, and Tosa; the Yamana *shugo*, Tajima, Inaba, Hōki, Iwami, Bingo, and Aki; the Hatakeyama *shugo*, Kōchi, Ise, Noto, Etchū, and Kii; the Kyōgoku *shugo*, Yamashiro, half of Omi, Hida, Izumo, and Oki; the Ouchi *shugo*, Suō, Nagato, Chikuzen, and Buzen; the Shiba *shugo*, Owari, Tōtomi, and Echizen; the Akamatsu *shugo*, Harima, Mimasaka, and Bizen; and the Isshiki *shugo*, Mikawa, Wakasa, and Tango.

The bakufu would alternate among three of the *shugo* houses, the Hosokawa, Hatakeyama, and Shiba, for individuals to fill its office of *kanrei*.[50] From the four houses of Kyōgoku, Akamatsu, Yamana, and Isshiki, along with the Toki, the *shugo* of Mino, would be chosen the head of the *samurai-dokoro*.[51] When Yoshimochi was shogun, the three *kanrei* houses plus the Yamana, Akamatsu, and Isshiki houses constituted the bakufu's ruling council. They were senior statesmen who made pronouncements on important government matters in response to the shogun's questions. Among the six daimyo were par-

48 Satō, *Nambokuchō no dōran*, pp. 378–80.   49 Ibid., pp. 367–70.
50 Ogawa, *Ashikaga ichimon*, pp. 753–65.
51 Haga, *Muromachi bakufu samurai dokoro*, pp. 77–98.

ticularly experienced *shugo* called *shukurō* (elders); they were deeply trusted by the shogun, and their power exceeded that of the *kanrei*.[52] The Muromachi bakufu's so-called coalition government *(rengō seiken)* of *shugo* daimyo is a reference to these powerful members of the bakufu's ruling council who ran the government through this balance of power.

The governing structure of the ryōgoku

After the Nambokuchō disturbance, the *shugo* changed from military commander to provincial administrator. The bakufu required the official *shugo* – the current heads of the *shugo* houses – to take up residence in Kyoto, the shogun's home base. In particular, the powerful *shugo* who made up the governing council of elders were required to live in Kyoto, barring some great crisis in their own domains.[53] Thus, the person actually managing affairs in the domain itself was the *shugo*'s deputy, or *shugodai*. In the case of powerful *shugo* houses that controlled two or more provinces, even the deputy *shugo* was required to reside in Kyoto. In such cases a proxy of the deputy *shugo*, called the junior deputy *shugo (koshugodai)*, was installed in the province. (The deputy *shugo* might be seen as corresponding to the early modern Edo-period *karō* of the various *han*, whereas the junior deputy *shugo* was like the early modern *kokarō*.)[54] Many of the *shugo* living in Kyoto lacked knowledge and ability, and so they often employed officials as scribes and bureaucrats who actually handled the administrative matters. In regard to the *shugo*'s duty of enforcing the bakufu's land decisions, the enforcement decree was actually issued by the *shugo*'s scribe, with the *shugo* himself simply adding his signature. Even an individual like Hatakeyama Mitsuie, who served as *kanrei* under Shogun Yoshinori and was the greatest of the elders *(shukurō)*, admitted in his diary that he did not completely understand administrative documents.[55]

In nearly all cases in which the office of *shugo* was territorially divided, it was done on a district basis. Therefore, within the divided province, the *shugo* daimyo's administration was probably also divided by district. The *shugo* was the successor of the provincial governor of the

52 Imatani, *Muromachi bakufu kaitai*, pp. 70–91.
53 Tanuma Mutsumi, "Muromachi bakufu, shugo, kokujin," in *Iwanami kōza Nihon rekishi*, vol. 7 (Tokyo: Iwanami shoten, 1976), pp. 1–50.
54 Imatani, *Shugo ryōgoku*, pp. 121–39, 307–45.
55 Tōkyō daigaku shiryō hensanjo, ed., *Dai Nihon kokiroku kennaiki*, vol. 1 (Tokyo: Iwanami shoten, 1963), p. 91.

ancient *ritsuryō* system, and just as the provincial governor had governed through the district official (*gunji*), so too the *shugo*'s domainal organization was the successor to the provincial office (*kokuga*).[56]

Research on provincial offices in the Heian period, however, reveals that starting in about the tenth or eleventh century, the position of district official, which had had great power in the *ritsuryō* provincial administration, lost power because the provincial office took direct control of the district, and gradually the district official became only an agent for the provincial office. Thus by the Kamakura period in most provinces the district officials of the *ritsuryō* system had become mere shadows of their former selves, and in some provinces this office had disappeared completely. In southern Kyushu, however, where the office continued to exist both in name and in reality, the district officials became vassals of the Kamakura bakufu and were organized into the *shugo*'s administrative office, ultimately being transferred into the governing organization of the divided province.[57] But in other parts of Japan the *shugo* had sole authority, and they set up their own military and administrative organizations in the provinces.

Ōmi is believed to be the first place where the *shugo* set up a governing organization based on the district. In an enforcement decree of the Rokuhara *tandai* dated 1284, the official title "deputy *shugo* of Asai District" appears; again, a *shugo* land receipt dated 1285 contains the expression "*shugo* envoy of Asai District." Thus it would appear that envoys of the *shugo* were installed in each district in Ōmi from that time on.[58] In the Nambokuchō period, in several other provinces the *shugo*'s enforcement envoy carried the title "district envoy" and exercised local governing authority resembling that of the district official under the former *ritsuryō* system. In 1400 a district magistrate appeared in Yamashiro Province. In the mid-fifteenth century the same office was called district deputy, and in nearly all provinces those *shugo* vassals who held this official title were given important responsibilities.[59] Usually it was the district deputy who delivered to the local officials the document of enforcement issued under the bakufu's judicial authority. The district official's authority was most apparent in the central Kinai provinces, such as Settsu, Kawachi, Yamashiro, Tamba, Ōmi, and Harima.

56 Yoshie Akio, "Kokuga shihai no tenkai," in *Iwanami kōza Nihon rekishi*, vol. 4 (Tokyo: Iwanami shoten, 1976), pp. 43–80.
57 Tanaka Kenji, "Kamakura bakufu no Ōsumi-no-kuni shihai ni tsuite no ichi kōsatsu," *Kyūshū shigaku*, nos. 65 and 67 (1977, 1979): 1–22 and 1–18, respectively.
58 Imatani, *Muromachi bakufu kaitai*, pp. 225–59.
59 Imatani, *Shugo ryōgoku*, pp. 18–71.

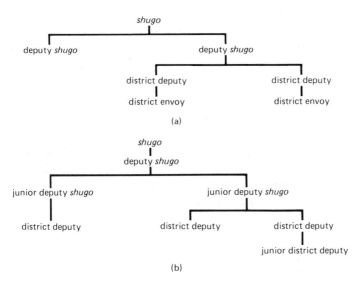

Figure 5.1 Organization of *shugo* authority in (a) Yamashiro and (b) Kawachi provinces, ca. 1379

There were several reasons for the sudden prominence of the district officials: It was at this point that the *shugo* truly took control of the provinces; now that the Nambokuchō disturbance had been resolved, the *shugo* could install permanent administrative officials; and the authority to tax, including provincewide taxes and *tansen*, had shifted from the court to the bakufu and the *shugo*. (This last is said to have occurred at the time of the Kōryaku disturbance of 1379.)[60] The system and organization of the *shugo*'s authority down to the smallest local unit in the divided province are shown in Figure 5.1.[61]

As time passed, the authority of the district deputies increased. They built strongholds on sites that gave them the best view of the district and established substantial fortifications in areas strategic to communication. In addition to taking over the local enforcement of the bakufu's decisions pertaining to land, the district deputies collected *tansen* and *shugoyaku*, and military corvée (*gunyaku*) as well.[62] And the district deputies' role was the most crucial in the suppression of local uprisings in the *shugo*'s jurisdictions. In other words, the district deputy was the official who directly enforced the *shugo*'s military and administrative authority. Although the district deputy domi-

60 Imatani, *Muromachi bakufu kaitai*, pp. 225–59.
61 For Yamashiro Province, see Imatani, *Shugo ryōgoku*, pp. 18–71; and for Kawachi Province, see ibid., pp. 121–39.   62 Imatani, *Muromachi bakufu kaitai*, pp. 225–59.

nated the peasants and had military power far superior to that of prominent local persons, he usually was at odds with these local luminaries.

The *shugo* held the right to appoint the members of his provincial
administration, such as deputy *shugo*, junior deputy *shugo*, and the
district deputies, and except in extraordinary cases, the bakufu did
not intervene. Indeed, in personnel matters, for the bakufu to place
restrictions on the provincial administrative structure was out of the
question.[63]

The district officials of the ancient *ritsuryō* system had been appointed from families whose local prominence predated the Taika reforms of the seventh century. But this was not the case with the district
deputies of the Muromachi period. Deputy *shugo* and district deputies, as members of the *shugo*'s *ryōgoku* organization, lived permanently in the *shugo*'s official compound, serving the *shugo*. Even
among the *shugo*'s subordinates, they constituted a special group of
insiders (*uchishū*).

The ordinary local wealthy peasants were called *kokujin* or *tozama*,
thus distinguishing between the two groups.[64] There were cases in
which powerful *kokujin* who were native to a province acquired hereditary control of the office of deputy *shugo*, as did the Iba family of
Ōmi.[65] But this was an exception; more often *kokujin* were appointed
from outside the province. Examples include the Yusa family of
Kawachi, originally from Dewa; the Ogasawara and Kōzai families of
Tamba, from Awa and Sanuki, respectively; and the Yakushiji family
of Settsu, from Musashi. The Hosokawa family, a branch of the
Ashikaga clan that took its name while still living in Mikawa, moved
to central Japan with the Ashikaga and began establishing a base
there in the Nambokuchō period, centered at first in Awa and Sanuki
in Shikoku. At this point, the Hosokawa incorporated into the upper
echelons of its retainer band powerful *kokujin* from Shikoku, so that
at the end of the Nambokuchō period when the Hosokawa set up the
administrative structure of their Kinai provinces – Settsu, Tamba,
and Izumi – *kokujin* from Shikoku dominated the ranks of the insiders.[66] This was a conscious attempt to exclude local interests from the
administration of the *ryōgoku*, but as a result, it aggravated the divi-
siveness between the *uchishū* (insiders) and the *kokujin* among the
shugo's vassals.

63 Ibid.   64 Ogawa, *Ashikaga ichimon*, pp. 332–58.
65 Imatani, *Shugo ryōgoku*, pp. 372–404.   66 Ogawa, *Ashikaga ichimon*, pp. 332–58.

The governing office of the shugo

At the height of the Muromachi period, the *shugo* were usually required to reside in Kyoto, and the deputy *shugo* or junior deputy *shugo* normally administered local matters. The locus of provincial administration was called the *shugosho*.[67] In the Kamakura period, because the *shugo's* authority had been primarily military, the provincial office (*kokuga*) governed the province. But as the *shugo's* power increased, this responsibility gradually shifted to the *shugosho*. In some provinces, *shugosho* were set up on the very site of the former provincial office or nearby. In such cases, the former provincial office, now transformed into the *shugosho*, was called the *fuchū*.[68] In many areas, like Bungo, Musashi, and Hitachi, the names of the *fuchū* remain even today. But often the *shugosho* were built at military strategic points entirely separate from the old provincial office. For example, in Izumi Province the old provincial office had been located directly in the center of the province, but the *shugosho* was situated in the northernmost part of the province[69] so as to be near the main roads leading to Kawachi and Yamato. As time passed and the *shugo's* administrative functions expanded, the economic center of the entire province grew in importance, and then the *shugosho* were frequently located in post towns and port cities, areas of strategic importance in communications.[70]

Shugosho were not necessarily limited to one per province. As explained earlier, in provinces that contained divided districts, there was a *shugosho* for each head of each divided district. There were two *shugosho* in provinces with two deputy *shugo*, such as Yamashiro and Kawachi (the latter in the Sengoku period), and in provinces under the half-province *shugo* system, such as Ōmi and Kaga.

The *ritsuryō* system also provided for provincial branch offices. Likewise, from the latter half of the Nambokuchō period, local enforcement offices were established as subordinate organs of the deputy *shugo*. They were staffed by junior deputy *shugo* and district officials. In this way, the *shugosho* was divided, and new branch offices were established.[71] In the provinces of Yamashiro and Tamba, there was a *shugosho* branch office in nearly every district. It is not

---

67 Matsuyama Hiroshi, *Nihon chūsei toshi no kenkyū* (Kyoto: Daigakudō shoten, 1973), pp. 65–93.
68 Ibid.   69 Satō, *Muromachi bakufu shugo seido*, vol, I, pp. 14–29.
70 Satō, *Zōho Kamakura bakufu*, pp. 252–3; Matsuyama Hiroshi, *Shugo jōkamachi no kenkyū* (Kyoto: Daigakudō shoten, 1982), pp. 56–76.   71 Imatani, *Shugo ryōgoku*, pp. 405–53.

clear if they were referred to at the time as the offices of the district deputies, but in Izumi the branch offices of both Izumi Otsu and Izumi Sano were called *shugosho* in reference to the *shugo*'s main castle at Sakai. Thus the *shugosho* seemed to be where the *shugo*'s important staff was stationed.

The names of the various *shugosho* of the central Kinai provinces that we know today are listed as follows, according to province:

Yamashiro: Nishishichijō, Shōryūji, Yodo, Makishima, Saga
Kawachi: Tannami, Furuichi, Wakae, Takaya, Iimori
Izumi: Fuchū, Sakai, Otsu, Sano
Settsu: Hyōgo, Ibaragi, Imazato, Hori, Sanda, Koshimizu,
            Akutagawa
Tamba: Hidokoro, Yagi, Yakami, Haji
Harima: Kakogawa, Shirahata, Kinoyama, Sakamoto, Hirose,
            Iwami (Muro)

This list shows that in this period, the *shugosho* were located in the powerful provincial cities; indeed, the main port cities of the Muromachi period such as Sakai, Hyōgo, Yodo, and Muro were built around *shugosho*.[72] Also included among the *shugosho* were cities that emerged as castle towns in the Sengoku period, like Yagi and Yakami, as well as many that became early modern seats of *han* government, such as Yodo, Haji (Fukuchiyama), Tannami, Sanda, Kinoyama (Tatsuno), and Hirose (Yamazaki).

Therefore, the *shugosho* had an urban function as the nucleus of provincial administration, but their economic functions were important as well. One was the function of the district deputy's administrative office as a centralized base for mobilizing labor for military corvée (*gunyaku*) and ordinary corvée (*buyaku*). Post horses, too, were initially requisitioned at the district deputy's office and then sent to the *shugosho*'s main castle or to neighboring provinces, as needed. Thus the number of people and horses that might gather at the district deputy's office must have been considerable. The *shugosho* also functioned as the central location for grain reserves from various taxes such as *tansen*, *tanmai*, and the commissariat tax. Just as under the *ritsuryō* system there had been official storehouses at the provincial and district offices, so too storehouses containing enormous amounts of goods

72 Ibid.

requisitioned from the peasants were located at the *shugosho*. Workshops were also established at the *shugosho*, in which craftsmen, merchants, and those involved in small industries lived and worked.

In 1388 and again in 1410, the *shugo* of Harima Province, the Akamatsu family, commandeered blacksmith's charcoal from Yano *shōen* and ordered that it be sent to the main *shugosho* castle at Sakamoto and to the branch castle at Murozu. Thus in this province there was a foundry or blacksmith's workshop at the *shugosho*, which enabled the monopoly of military technology by the *shugo*.[73] In addition, the famous Shiraga family, artisans of the Shoshanan Engyōji near Sakamoto Castle, belonged to a group of craftsmen serving the *shugo*. Likewise, the Nara *banshō*, the carpenters of the Kōfukuji, also helped the *shugo* of Kawachi, Hatakeyama Yoshinari, construct his main *shugosho* headquarters, Takaya Castle. These craftsmen and technicians were not organized at the beginning of the early modern period by *kokujin* but, rather, by *shugo*, according to their province and district,[74] a practice carried over from the Muromachi period.

THE RELATIONSHIP BETWEEN *SHUGO* AND *KOKUJIN*

The concept of kokujin

The terms *zoku* and *fūzoku* appear frequently in provincial gazetteers of the Nara period. At that time, both words were pronounced *kunihito* and referred to the people indigenous to an area.[75] This is the origin of the word *kokujin*, which in the medieval period generally referred to local overlords native to an area, or native-born *jitō gokenin*. Today, specialists of the period divide *kokujin* into two types, depending on the nature of their activities: "prominent locals" (*dogō*) and *kokujin* in general. The *dogō* were the powerful local overlords with the largest administrative control over an area; some scholars separate them entirely from *kokujin*.

In the Kamakura period, these local overlords, or *jitō gokenin*, enjoyed a feudal bond of vassalage with the shogun. As samurai directly affiliated with the bakufu they held a much higher status than did

73 Ibid.
74 Takagi Shōsaku, "Bakuhan shoki no kuni bugyō ni tsuite," *Rekishigaku kenkyū*, no. 431 (May 1975): 15–62.
75 Murai Yasuhiko, "Kokufū bunka no sōzō to fukyū," in *Iwanami kōza Nihon rekishi*, vol. 4 (Tokyo: Iwanami shoten, 1976), pp. 313–48.

commoners. In a legal sense as well, the *jitō gokenin* received protection from the bakufu. With the rise of a cash economy, the decline of the *sōryō* system, and the tendency for land to be divided up into ever-smaller pieces, many of these local overlords disappeared in the later Kamakura period,[76] and the boundaries between the classes became even more hazy. In such an atmosphere, with the division of offices, anyone who could reach the office of *jitō*, be he commoner or even priest, could enjoy the special rights and privileges of the local overlord.

Starting in the Nambokuchō period, vassals (*gokenin*) in the direct service of the bakufu were incorporated into the shogunal army,[77] and the term *jitō gokenin* gradually became obsolete. Instead, powerful local figures came to be called *kokujin* or *kunishū* (in Yamato Province, *kokumin*), and they differed greatly from the *jitō* of the Kamakura period. There also was a great qualitative difference between these local changes in the central and the peripheral areas. In eastern Japan and in Kyushu, the *shōen* system was eventually dissolved, and the *kokujin* who emerged as local overlords were in a relatively favorable position. Some *kokujin* families later even became *sengoku* daimyo, including the Date of Mutsu and the Mōri of Aki. In central Japan, however, the *shōen* system was reorganized and strengthened, and because the bakufu tried to protect the *shōen* after reorganizing them through the Ōan *hanzei* decree, becoming a powerful *kokujin* overlord was difficult. *Kokujin* were forced to coexist and to some extent compromise with the *shōen* overlord, by means of such measures as exchanging contracts in which the *kokujin* became the *shōen* manager or stipendiary.

The formation of kokujin leagues

From the end of the fourteenth century to the beginning of the fifteenth, the office of *shugo* gradually became hereditary, and the *shugo* domainal system began to develop in earnest. The main problem facing the *shugo* or their subordinate officials who turned their attention to managing the domain was how to handle the *kokujin* who dominated the local area. Among the *kokujin* were powerful local figures whose ancestors had set down roots during the Kamakura period after being

---

76 Satō Shin'ichi, "Kamakura bakufu seiji no senseika ni tsuite," in Takeuchi Rizō, ed., *Nihon hōkensei seiritsu no kenkyū* (Tokyo: Yoshikawa kōbunkan, 1955). pp. 125–34.
77 Fukuda Toyohiko, "Muromachi bakufu hōkōshū no kenkyū – sono jin'in kōsei to chiikiteki bumpu," *Hokkaidō musashi joshi tanki daigaku kiyō*, no. 3 (March 1971): 1–52.

granted land confirmations as vassals of Minamoto Yoritomo. And like the Heian-period provincial governors, the *shugo*, by growing dependent on the *kokujin* to manage the domain, suffered the repercussions of this policy in the coming decades.

In the latter half of the Nambokuchō period, the *kokujin* of various areas banded together in alliances (*kokujin ikki*) in order to resist the *shugo* appointed by the bakufu.[78] Characterized by lateral ties, these *kokujin* alliances even attempted to block physically the entry of *shugo* into the province. The usual image of *ikki* is that of peasant leagues (*do-ikki*) allied for some local cause. But here *ikki* refers to warrior leagues that frequently battled *shugo* in military confrontations. The *ikki* were so effective that it was not unusual for *shugo* appointed by the bakufu to be forced to abandon control of their domain. A typical example of this is the case of Shinano Province.

In this province in 1387, the forces of the Ninomiya family, resident manager for the *shugo* Shiba Yoshimasa, were defeated by the local *kokujin* families Ogasawara and Murakami. From that point on, this area was dominated by an independent *kokujin* class. At the end of 1399, Ogasawara Nagahide (another Ogasawara family which had been *shugo* of Awa in the Kamakura period) was appointed *shugo* in place of the Shiba family. He raised a vassal band and in the following year entered the province. The *kokujin* league led by the Murakami family was bound by a covenant, and so they decided to fight the *shugo*. They achieved a great victory against the *shugo*'s forces in a decisive engagement known as the battle of Ōtō, which resulted in the *shugo* Nagahide's being forced to retreat to Kyoto.[79]

In 1402 the bakufu adopted a conciliatory policy toward the *kokujin* by not posting any *shugo* to Shinano and instead designating it as a direct bakufu province (*goryōgoku*), thereby confirming the *kokujin*'s holdings. Thus the *kokujin* in effect were given preferential treatment, and the matter was resolved without further incident. *Kokujin* leagues that militarily opposed the *shugo* were not always opposed to the bakufu. Rather, they usually formed in order to oust the *shugo* and then sought direct ties with the bakufu. Indeed, this is what was behind the bakufu's making Shinano its own domain and entrusting it to the *kokujin* as a bakufu land.

The peasant class in the central Kinai provinces were particularly

78 Fukuda Toyohiko, "Kokujin ikki no ichi sokumen," *Shigaku zasshi* 76 (January 1967): 62–80.
79 Inagaki Yasuhiko, "Do-ikki o megutte," *Rekishigaku kenkyū*, no. 305 (October 1965): 25–33; Fukuda, "Kokujin ikki," pp. 62–80.

successful in gaining independence. *Shōen* proprietors also held considerable power there. Consequently, it was not easy for the *kokujin*, caught in the middle, to become independent. For these reasons, *kokujin* leagues had difficulty forming in the Kinai, and instead the *shugo*'s management of divided provinces developed on the basis of compromise and balance with the *shōen* proprietors. However, during and after the Ōnin War, particularly in the Kinai provinces of the Hosokawa, *kokujin* uprisings occurred one after another, and the authority of the *shugo* was gravely threatened.

In 1473 a *kokujin* league was organized in Izumi Province. It proved so powerful locally that it was able to impose a commissariat tax even on consolidated *shōen*. Unfortunately, the *shugo*'s reaction to this league is not known. But in 1479, powerful *kokujin* of Suita, Ibaragi, Ikeda, and Itami in Settsu Province allied in a large league in opposition to the *shugo*, the Hosokawa, who had demanded the return of *shōen* taken over by *kokujin* in the Ōnin War. The *kokujin*, however, refused, and they resented being excluded from the local administration of the deputy *shugo* and the district deputies.

Put simply, this was a conflict between the deputy *shugo* class and the *kokujin*. Because the *kokujin* requested help from Hatakeyama Yoshinari, who had rebelled and led an army against the bakufu, the *shugo* Hosokawa reacted by raising a huge army that crushed the uprising. In 1482 he destroyed the home base of the Suita and Ibaragi families, almost entirely annihilating both.[80] Thus in contrast with the Daimonji league of Shinano, in the Settsu uprising, the Hosokawa's military strength was tremendous, and they suppressed the uprising with extreme cruelty.

In 1485 the famous uprising took place in southern Yamashiro Province, seeking to drive the *shugo* Hatakeyama from the province. News of the success of this provincial league spread to Nishigaoka in Yamashiro, a district of the Hosokawa that included the two districts of Otokuni and Kadono. In this area, prominent local families joined to reject the shogun's authority and establish an independent government. Because their league had not attacked his family, Hosokawa Masamoto, the most powerful person in the bakufu, gave it his tacit approval in the beginning. But a large provincial uprising of 1489 in his own province of Tamba changed his response. This time, those in revolt were *tozama kokujin* who had been excluded from the Hosokawa's local administrative system and were considered outsiders

80 Imatani, *Muromachi bakufu kaitai*, pp. 302–13.

lacking important connections. Because this was clearly an anti-*shugo* offensive, Masamoto suppressed it.

A storm of provincial uprisings then spread through the Hosokawa's Kinai provinces of Izumi, Settsu, Yamashiro, and Tamba. *Kokujin* and *shugo* took part in accordance with their own interests, and it became a desperate struggle, a matter of devouring or being devoured. During the fighting the deputy *shugo*, Uehara Motohide, issued a document to the locals stating that "each district deputy shall be consulted and shall be included in the forces suppressing the uprising." The district deputies thus made up the core of the suppressing force. Large numbers of troops from Kyoto also joined the fray. But the rebels resisted, and their strongholds were not easily toppled. For three years this standoff continued, until in 1493 all the powerful *kokujin* of Shūchi and Ogino provinces were defeated, and the great uprising finally ended.[81] Hosokawa Masamoto, shocked and terrified by the force of the *kokujin* uprising, turned his energies to punishing the participants in the Yamashiro uprising. In the ninth month of 1493, he succeeded in eliminating the *kokujin* still resisting in Inayazuma Castle in Yamashiro Province, thereby at last achieving despotic control over all his Kinai provinces.[82]

In short, all the anti-*shugo* provincial uprisings of the Kinai area during and after the Ōnin War were crushed, and subsequently, unaided *kokujin* had great difficulty resisting the *shugo*. They then looked for a new means of opposition, the Ikkō league.

The shugo *domainal system and the* kokujin *overlord system*

The major contribution of the *shugo* domainal system was to define a political order in which the *shugo* daimyo, mainly in the Nambokuchō and Muromachi periods, were the driving force in the feudal overlord system.[83] By making vassals of the *kokujin*, the *shugo* daimyo led the *shōen* system to its demise, and helped establish regional feudal authority. These conclusions, as laid out by Nagahara Keiji, have greatly influenced later scholars. Although some may disagree with them, they did form a conceptual framework for the *shugo* domainal system.

Opposing Nagahara, Kurokawa Naonori in 1961 offered the con-

---

81 Ibid.   82 Ibid.
83 See especially Nagahara Keiji and Sugiyama Hiroshi, "Shugo ryōgokusei no tenkai," *Shakai keizaishigaku* 17 (March 1951): 103–34.

cept of "*kokujin* overlord."[84] Kurokawa first points out that the *shugo* used two methods to encroach on the *shōen:* The first was to obtain funds from outside the *shōen* system, through such taxes as the *tansen* and corvée. The other method was to interfere in the *shōen* system itself and to gain control of the mechanism for collecting the yearly dues. Next, Kurokawa analyzes the activities of the *kokujin* class and postulates that authority over the provincial office's lands played a major role in the *shugo*'s vassalization of the *kokujin*. He asserts that the *shugo* daimyo who could only externally control *shōen* or provincial lands were defeated by the *kokujin*, who were essential to those systems of land control. Thus Kurokawa concludes that it was the *kokujin* overlord system, not the *shugo* domainal system, that formed the power structure of the late medieval period.

Kurokawa's seminal essay, which takes issue with the Nagahara thesis, was for a time, the most widely accepted theory among scholars. But with more research and analysis of the *shugo*'s control of many different regions, it became apparent that some points of Kurokawa's thesis were not valid. For example, his contention that the *shugo* daimyo were subjugated by the *kokujin* does not apply to most of the Kinai provinces, the most advanced region of the country. Rather, the opposite tendency was common.

Another problem in Kurokawa's thesis is that he neglects the military relationship of control between the *shugo* and the *kokujin*. This relationship was characterized by a lack of cohesiveness or a looseness in the feudal relationship in the domain, and it had been pointed out by many scholars even before Kurokawa.[85] When newly appointed *shugo* received from the shogun the decree of appointment, they would make a ritual tour of their new province. In this tour of each *shōen*, they would be given a list of names of the local warriors on each *shōen* and in each subdistrict. In this way, the *shugo* could choose their vassals, and because no documents of appointment were issued – as had been the case in the Kamakura period – it was a very expeditious process. Thus it is possible to agree that the vassal relationship was loose and the feudal system was weak. But on the other hand, collectively a much larger number of warriors could be brought instantly under the *shugo*'s control, as compared with the process of vassalage in the Kamakura period.

An example of this loose feudal relationship can be found in the case

84 Kurokawa Naonori, "Shugo ryōgokusei to shōen taisei – kokujin ryōshusei no kakuritsu katei," *Nihonshi kenkyū*, no. 57 (November 1961): 1–19.
85 Satō, *Nambokuchō no dōran*. pp. 364–8.

of Akamatsu Mitsusuke, the *shugo* of Harima, Mimasaka, and Bizen provinces, who had rebelled against the bakufu in the sixth month of 1441. In only two and a half months he was destroyed, owing to the desertion of his *kokujin*. Another example is Yamana Mitsuyuki, the *shugo* of Tango, who was defeated in the Meitoku disturbance of 1391, again owing to the desertion of his *kokujin*.[86] But there are also examples of exactly the opposite situation. In the ninth month of 1460, Hatakeyama Yoshinari, the *shugo* of Kawachi Province who had been driven out of the bakufu, was able to hold out in his stronghold of Hatakeyama Castle until the fourth month of 1463 – for two years and eight months – owing to the solidarity of his *kokujin* vassals. Therefore, the lord–vassal relationship was not always weak.

In recent years, Japanese scholars have begun to reevaluate the *shugo*'s authority within the entire power structure of the late medieval period. In particular, as the research on the *sengoku* daimyo of nearly all regions has become more complete,[87] the difficult problem of where to draw the line between the *shugo* daimyo and the *sengoku* daimyo once again comes to the fore. The fact that many of the *sengoku* daimyo could trace their lineage to *shugo* or deputy *shugo* has become even more undeniable. The continuity between the Muromachi-period *shugo* and the *sengoku* daimyo has thus been thrown into the spotlight. For scholars, the axis of territorial power from the late fifteenth through the early sixteenth centuries is none other than the *shugo*. Thus the power of the *shugo* reached its peak in the early sixteenth century, and some even apply the term "Sengoku-period *shugo*" to the daimyo authority of this period.[88] At any rate, today we are continuing to make efforts to understand better the relationship between the *shugo* and the *kokujin* and cannot yet claim that the historical evidence refutes the earlier analyses based on the *shugo* domainal system.

86 Nagahara and Sugiyama, "Shugo ryōgokusei no tenkai," p. 19.
87 See Nagahara Keiji, ed., *Sengoku daimyō ronshū* (Tokyo: Yoshikawa kōbunkan, 1986), an eighteen-volume study by region or *sengoku* daimyo.
88 Imaoka Norikazu, Kawaoka Tsutomu, and Yada Toshifumi, "Sengokuki kenkyū no kadai to tembō," *Nihonshi kenkyū*, no. 278 (October 1985). 42–62; Arimitsu Yūgaku, ed., *Sengokuki kenryoku to chiiki shakai* (Tokyo: Yoshikawa kōbunkan, 1986), pp. 207–32, 521–78.

CHAPTER 6

THE DECLINE OF THE *SHŌEN* SYSTEM

The *shōen* system of landholding, one of the most important institutions for organizing the economic life of medieval Japan, was transformed at the end of the eleventh and the beginning of the twelfth centuries. The transformation occurred when Minamoto Yoritomo, who established the Kamakura bakufu, created the offices of *shugo* (military governor) and *jitō* (military estate steward), introducing a new layer of tenurial rights into the *shōen* hierarchy in 1185. Following the Jōkyū disturbance of 1221, the shogunate confiscated the lands of the nobles and warriors who had taken part in the incident and appointed its loyal retainers (*gokenin*) as *jitō* to these lands.[1] Both of these events served to establish firmly a lord–vassal relationship within the proprietary rights structure of the *shōen* system and marked the beginning of a long process that saw the emerging dominance of warrior authority and the declining power of the central proprietor over the land, its revenues, and inhabitants.

The appointment of *jitō* by the Kamakura bakufu was intended to supplement rather than supplant the land rights and political authority of the *shōen* proprietors who traditionally possessed full fiscal and administrative power over these "private lands." This policy did not completely deny the *shōen* as a form of land proprietorship, nor did it mean that the *jitō* acquired exclusive proprietary rights on the *shōen* to which they were appointed. In fact, the Kamakura bakufu struggled to preserve the *shōen* system and to prevent the *jitō* from extending their authority beyond the scope intended by the bakufu.[2] The *jitō*'s main duties, as envisioned by the Kamakura bakufu, were to maintain the flow of income and services to the central proprietor and to keep

---

1 Following the defeat of the Taira in 1185, Minamoto Yoritomo requested and received permission from the emperor to appoint *jitō* to *shōen* and *kokugaryō*. *Jitō* were appointed throughout Japan after the Jōkyū disturbance of 1221.
2 Throughout the Kamakura period, matters involving the control of *shōen* by *jitō* and *shōen* proprietors were adjudicated by the bakufu courts. The fact that the bakufu sought to extend forcibly that authority is borne out by the judicial decisions known as *saikyōjō*. See Seno Seiichiro, *Kamakura bakufu saikyojō-shū*, vols. 1 and 2 (Tokyo: Yoshikawa kōbunkan, 1970).

peace. Once the *jitō* established themselves on the land, however, they sought to extend their authority and control, usually at the expense of the *shōen* officials appointed by the central proprietor to manage *shōen* affairs.

At the end of the thirteenth and the beginning of the fourteenth centuries, important political and military events – the collapse of the Kamakura bakufu in 1333 and the Nambokuchō disturbances between 1335 and 1392 – spurred the decline of the *shōen* system as the *jitō* took advantage of these events to extend their personal control over the *shōen*. By this time neither the civil government of the nobility nor the military government of the bakufu had sufficient power to prevent the *jitō* from extending their control.

I use the fourteenth-century Nambokuchō disturbances, therefore, as a springboard for examining the decline of the *shōen* system. Although greatly weakened and changed in form, the *shōen* system did not collapse entirely during the fourteenth century but continued to function as a basis for land administration and control into the fifteenth and sixteenth centuries. The upheaval of the Ōnin period (1467–9) further eroded the *shōen* system, but the *shōen* were not completely eliminated as a form of landholding until Hideyoshi's cadastral surveys (Taikō *kenchi*) were carried out in the late sixteenth century. Although the focus of this chapter is the events of the fourteenth century that led to the decline of the *shōen* system, my examination will extend also into the fifteenth and sixteenth centuries.

TURNING POINTS IN THE DECLINE OF THE *SHŌEN*

Characteristics of the shōen *landholding system*

The *shōen*, which had developed by the mid-eleventh century, proved to be an extremely successful way of securing a balance between the demands of the ruling class for income and the demands of the populace for a stable means of livelihood. Not only did the *shōen* serve as the primary means through which the ruling class tapped the wealth of the countryside, it also provided the residence, workplace, and source of sustenance for peasants and proprietors alike. The organization of proprietary rights or tenurial hierarchy in the *shōen* system was complex and multilayered. The most widespread means used to expand the *shōen*, and the one that had the greatest impact on the development of tenurial relationships, was commendation.

The *shōen* proprietors or overlords (*ryōshu*) were primarily court nobles who resided in Kyoto (or influential religious establishments of Kyoto and Nara patronized by the court nobility), who attained their right to *shōen* revenue primarily through commendation. The local notables who actually developed the land (*kaihatsu ryōshu*) were mainly small local proprietors who held positions of influence in their area as provincial or district officials of some sort. They used the power and prestige of their offices to extend their landholdings. In doing so, they faced recurrent disagreements with provincial authorities (*kokuga*) over their assertion of fiscal authority over cultivators. Because of the constant threat of provincial interference, these local proprietors sought to protect their interests. The most common way of attaining this protection was through the practice of commendation. The local proprietor commended his rights of ownership to a powerful figure or institution in the capital in return for political influence in securing protection. Therefore, commendation was a means to bypass the power of the provincial offices of the central government.[3]

The *shōen* proprietors were noble-bureaucrats who did not live on the *shōen* under their control; instead, they were absentee landlords residing primarily in Kyoto. From their position as central noble-bureaucrats they were able to supersede the power of the provincial authorities on lands commended to them by a local notable. Consequently, the proprietary rights structure of the *shōen* system was inseparable from the bureaucratic structure of the central government.

The *shōen* held by these court nobles and religious establishments were not necessarily located in a single region but were often scattered throughout the country. The *shōen* held by the Konoe family in 1235, for example, numbered at least 154 and were scattered from Mutsu to Satsuma provinces.[4]

The local notable who developed the land typically initiated the commendation of the *shōen* to the central proprietor. In turning over the title to his lands, he gave up little in terms of income, although he relinquished the title of lord to the central proprietor. It was customary for local proprietors to be appointed as manager of the *shōen* under the

---

3 Land development was carried out by local notables. Even though this land was privately held, the *kokushi* tried to confiscate the land and designate it as *kokugaryō*. The local notable, to avoid this, commended the developed land to a central noble and labored to turn it, along with the nearby *kokugaryō*, into a *shōen*. The local notable often was appointed as a *shōen* official. Collusion between the local and central nobility resulted in the partitioning of the *kokugaryō* and the spread of *shōen* throughout the entire country in the twelfth century.

4 *Konoe-ke ryō shoryō mokuroku*, 1253, in *Konoe Fumimaro shozō monjo*. For an analysis of this form of landholding, see Nagahara Keiji, *Nihon chūsei shakai kōzō no kenkyū* (Tokyo: Iwanami shoten, 1973), p. 57.

terms of the commendation agreement and to continue to oversee local administration as *shōkan* or *jitō*.

The court noble (or religious institution) to whom the land was commended was known as the *ryōke*. The *ryōke* received a specified share of the income from the estate in return for acting as the legal protector of the *shōen*, using his influence to maintain tax immunities and intervening with government authorities when necessary. In order to guarantee possession of the *shōen* and to gain additional weight and prestige from further *shōen* interests, the *ryōke* would often commend a portion of his income share to an even more influential court noble or religious institution, such as the imperial family or the regents' family, who was known as the *honke*, or guarantor. The *honke* acted mainly to lend prestige to an estate's claim and generally took no interest in its administration.

Although the *shoen*'s authority structure varied widely, depending on such factors as its location and the prestige of its proprietors, its general organization can be viewed as a pyramid, with the peasant cultivators at its base. Next came the *shōen* managers who lived on the *shōen*, called *shōkan* or local *ryōshu*, who had developed and commended the land. Above the *shōkan* were the central proprietors, or *ryōke*. At the peak of the hierarchy was the guarantor, or *honke*.

Thus, the *shōen* proprietor's authority – consisting of the right to survey the land and to determine and collect the tax, and authority over judicial affairs – was hierarchically fragmented. The *shōen* system, as a means to derive economic profit from the land, was not based on direct proprietary control of the land but on its revenue. The total income of the *shōen*, which included all the goods and services provided by the cultivators, was divided according to the relationship of each level in the hierarchy. These shares were called *shiki* and represented a specific amount of income due each rank in the *shōen* hierarchy. *Shiki* were classified as *honke shiki*, *ryōke shiki*, *gesu shiki*, and so forth, according to who owned the *shiki* right.

The *shiki* system was based on a relationship in which the holder of a superior *shiki* right granted inferior *shiki* rights, although *shiki* could change hands through sale, inheritance, or donation without disturbing the *shōen*'s economic function. Because *shiki* were alienable and divisible, it was possible for the income from the *shōen* to be widely distributed. Although the *shiki* system was based on a hierarchical structure, it was neither bureaucratic nor feudal but was a comparatively flexible union of superior and inferior rights that did not define a lord–vassal relationship regarding terms of duty and obligation.[5] Therefore, a resident *shōen* manager (*gesu*) appointed to the *gesu shiki* by the *ryōke* could, at the same time, be a *gokenin* of the Kamakura bakufu.

It was difficult for the central proprietor, who usually accumulated numerous *shiki* in many geographically scattered *shōen*, to maintain direct control over each *shōen*. This system of proprietary rights differed dramatically from that of the daimyo of the Edo period, who controlled contiguous domains and whose authority was backed up by independent military forces. The central proprietors, lacking their own military force, were forced to rely on powerful, local officials (*shōkan*). They also relied on the family structure and the state structure formed by the nobility and the bakufu and the legal apparatus of the civil and military governments to maintain the *shiki* system. If a *jitō* committed unlawful acts within the *shōen*, the *shōen* proprietor would usually attempt to resolve the conflict through a legal appeal to the court or bakufu.[6]

Stages in the collapse of the shōen

The collapse of the *shōen* system was closely connected to the tenurial-proprietary structures that characterized the system. As the *shiki* gradually became divorced from the specific tenure function to which they were originally attached and changes occurred at the top of the *shōen* hierarchy, important shifts were taking place at lower levels as well.

Jitō and *shōkan* gradually began to develop their own lordlike authority within the *shōen*, bypassing the *shiki* structure and undermining the *shōen* proprietor's authority. The *shugo* began to usurp the power of the provincial offices and to transform provincial lands (*kokugaryō*) into lands under their personal control (*shugo ryō*). The *shugo* also attempted to extend their authority into the *shōen* of their respective provinces. These two interrelated trends constituted a major shift away from the fragmented *shiki* structure toward regionally contiguous domains.

At a more basic level, the economic relationships that comprised the

5 For a more complete description of the *shiki* structure, see Nagahara Keiji, *Nihon chūsei shakai kōzō no kenkyū*, pp. 28–55.
6 For a general introduction to the *shōen* system, see Nagahara Keiji, *Shōen* (Tokyo: Hyōronsha, 1978). Also, for a general introduction to the social structure of *shōen*, see Kuroda Toshio, *Shōen-sei shakai*, vol. 2 of *Taikei Nihon rekishi* (Tokyo: Nihon hyōronsha, 1967).

foundation of the *shōen* system were changing. This was most visible in the actions of the *shōen* cultivators, the most conspicuous actions being cultivator disputes known as *do-ikki*. In addition, *shugo* and *jitō* recruited upper-level members of the cultivator class as their military vassals (*hikan*). The economic development of the village was at the root of these changes.

As the *shōen* proprietors' control over the *shōen* became more tenuous and the amount of tax rice (*nengu*) they actually collected declined, they began to borrow money from moneylenders (*dosō*) using the next year's taxes as collateral. To collect even these reduced tax receipts, the *shōen* proprietors enlisted local warriors or moneylenders, which led to the development of a system of tax contracting called *ukeoi* and a further decline in the *shōen* proprietors' authority. Their loss of control over the *shōen* proper and the decline in tax receipts were critical factors leading to the collapse of the *shōen* system.

The pattern of the *shōen* system's decline differed among regions. In general, the expanding sphere of authority of the *shugo* and *jitō*, which undermined the position and authority of the *shōen* proprietor, was more constrained in the Kinai region where cultivator rights were most developed and cultivator protests prevalent. In the more remote regions of eastern Japan and Kyushu, the *shōen* proprietor's authority was undercut relatively early, and the *jitō*, *shōkan*, and *shugo* succeeded in taking control of contiguous parcels of land. In the Hokuriku, Tokai, Chugoku, and Shikoku regions, the strength of the *shōen* proprietor was more balanced with that of the *shugo* and *jitō*. In those areas, *shugo* often made the transition to daimyo, but the *shōen* system was maintained for a comparatively long time.[7] Regional differences, therefore, must not be overlooked when examining the decline of the *shōen*.

THE GROWTH OF THE *JITŌ* AND *SHŌKAN* AS *RYŌSHU*

The expansion of the jitō's *shōen* control

Jitō shiki were established on *shōen* and *kokugaryō* in large numbers in two stages. After the Gempei War (1180–5), the emerging Kamakura

---

7 The regional differences in the *shōen* system roughly followed the order of economic development, with the Kinai, western Japan, and Kyoto being the most developed. In addition to economic development, the strength of the central government in a particular region was also a decisive factor. The authority of the *ritsuryō* state penetrated least in eastern Japan.

shogunate secured authorization from the court to appoint *jitō*, called *hompo jitō*, to the lands confiscated from warriors associated with the Taira. After the Jōkyū disturbance of 1221, the shogunate again appointed *jitō* to confiscated lands and termed them *shimpo*, or newly appointed, *jitō*. The authority of the *hompo jitō* was not completely systematized but instead was inherited from the *gesu* who managed the *shōen*. The *shimpo jitō*, on the other hand, were granted benefice land (*kyūden*) amounting to the income produced by one-eleventh of the land under their jurisdiction, in addition to the right to collect a military surcharge (*kachōmai*) of five *shō* per *tan* of paddy.

This authority was not necessarily standardized. Although the *jitō*'s authority was based on a *shiki* right, the *jitō* did not have complete control over the *shōen* or *kokugaryō* to which they were appointed. Moreover, powerful bakufu retainers were often granted geographically scattered *jitō shiki*. In order to maintain these scattered rights, the *gokenin* often dispatched family members to serve as deputies (*daikan*) in overseeing the *shōen*. They might choose a particular *shōen* to be their home base and move their household there. After the Jōkyū disturbance and throughout the Kamakura period, eastern warriors would often acquire *jitō shiki* to *shōen* in western Japan. The Shibuya family, for example, whose ancestral holdings were located in Sagami Province, transferred to Satsuma's Iriki-in. The Mori family of Sagami similarly moved to Yoshida-no-shō in Aki Province.

When *jitō* moved to a new *shōen*, they held the rights indicated by their *shiki* within an existing authority structure. They often came into conflict, however, with the *daikan* dispatched by the *shōen* proprietor, if they tried to increase their share of *shōen* revenue or assume other elements of *shōen* control, such as police and judicial authority.

In one such confrontation between a *jitō* and a *shōen* official, which took place in 1238 on Sasakibe-no-shō in Tamba Province, which was a holding of the Matsuno Shrine, the *shōen* official appealed to the Rokuhara *tandai* – shogunal deputies stationed at Rokuhara in southeastern Kyoto by the Kamakura bakufu who supervised the political, military, and judicial affairs of southwestern Japan – in regard to illegal acts committed by the *jitō*. The appeal charged that in order to construct a new residence, the *jitō* levied unreasonable labor corvée on the *shōen* cultivators; he forced peasants to accompany him to Kyoto under a levy known as the *kyōjōfu;* he forced cultivators to work on his private lands without compensation, not even foodstuffs; and furthermore, the *jitō* was delinquent in his annual payments of twenty-five *koku* of *nengu* from his *jitō myō*, a delinquency that the appeal said amounted to a total of over three hundred *koku* over seventeen years.[8]

A similar confrontation between a *jitō* and a *shōen* official occurred in 1243 on the Daigoji's Ushihara-no-shō in Echizen Province. In this case, the *jitō* disregarded custom by infringing on the traditional authority of the *shōen* proprietor by assuming criminal jurisdiction.[9] Criminal jurisdiction was an important component of the *shōen* proprietor's authority; therefore, the *jitō*'s actions were a direct attack on *ryōshu* control over the *shōen*.

Incidents of this kind occurred repeatedly throughout the country. In many cases, the *shōen* official appealed directly to the bakufu. The bakufu generally sought to suppress these acts by *jitō* that were outside the bounds of *jitō shiki*. Also, because the acts increased the friction with the nobility in Kyoto, who were often the target of these illegal actions, the bakufu's policy was aimed at controlling the *jitō*'s actions. Despite the bakufu's policy, the *jitō* continued to expand their control within the *shōen*. As a result, the *shōen* proprietor, gradually losing control of the *shōen* to the *jitō*, would often turn to settlements known as *wayo* (literally, "peaceful giving"), an out-of-court settlement between *shōen* proprietors and *jitō* regarding the distribution of revenue from the *shōen*.

Two other forms of conciliation, *shitaji chūbun* and *ukesho*, posed an even greater threat to the *shōen* proprietor's authority.[10] *Shitaji chūbun* involved the physical division of *shōen* lands into a part over which the *jitō* would have full authority and derive revenue, and a part under the control of the central proprietor. In 1318, on Koyasan's Kanzaki-no-shō in Bingo Province, in order to resolve an ongoing dispute between the *jitō* and the *shōen* proprietor, the land was divided equally, and each controlled a half of the *shōen*.[11] Although half of the *shōen* was handed over to the *jitō*, the remaining half was left free from *jitō* interference. This system of land division could be carried out in different ways but was generally on a fifty-fifty basis, a major gain for the *jitō* who was originally entitled to only one-eleventh of the revenue.

Ukesho, also called *jitō uke*, often represented an extension of the

8 *Rokuhara saikyojō*, 1238, in *Higashi monjo*.
9 *Rokuhara gechijō*, 1243, in *Hōon-in monjo*.
10 For more information on *shitaji chūbun*, see Shimada Jirō, "Zaichi-ryōshusei no tenkai to Kamakura bakufu hō," in Inagaki Yasuhiko and Nagahara Keiji, eds., *Chūsei no shakai to keizai* (Tokyo: Tōkyō daigaku shuppankai, 1962); and Yasuda Motohisa, *Jitō oyobi jitō ryōshusei no kenkyū* (Tokyo: Yamakawa shuppansha, 1961), pp. 426–60.
11 *Ryōke jitō wayojō*, 1318, in *Kongō sanmai-in monjo*.

jitō's control after *shitaji chūbun*. In this instance the *jitō* contracted with the *shōen* proprietor to send annually a fixed amount of revenue and services to him, regardless of the tax yield actually collected that year. The actual control of the *shōen* was left to the *jitō* and moved him one step closer to being an autonomous local proprietor.[12] On Chibi-no-shō in Bingo Province, the *jitō* Yamanouchi Sudō, who had trans-ferred to the *shōen* from the Kantō, had long been in dispute with the *shōen* proprietor over restoration of the authority to commend land (*shitaji shinshi-ken*). In 1308, Sudō contracted to pay forty-five *kan* annually to the *shōen* proprietor as *jitō uke*.[13] The practice of *jitō uke* began early in the Kamakura period in the eastern provinces where the bakufu's authority was strongest. By the end of the period, however, *ukesho* was increasingly being practiced on *shōen* in the western prov-inces as well.

The *jitō*'s method of expanding their power over the *shōen* relative to that of the *shōen* proprietor, by means of *shitaji chūbun* or *ukesho*, changed over the course of the Kamakura period. During the early to middle Kamakura period, the *jitō* basically operated within the frame-work of the *shiki* structure: They attempted to expand the amount of benefice land granted to them as part of their *shiki;* in order to improve the irrigation on their private lands, they altered the waterways for their personal benefit, or they appropriated labor for the cultivation of their private land. *Shitaji chūbun* and *ukesho*, on the other hand, gave the *jitō* the means to acquire their own proprietorlike authority over the *shōen*'s land and residents.

The shōkan's revolt

The *jitō* were not the only ones to aggrandize the authority of the *shōen* proprietor. The *shōkan*, especially the powerful *gesu*, also attempted to usurp greater control over the *shōen*. On Kuroda-no-shō in Iga Prov-ince, a holding of the Tōdaiji, the *gesu*, a family named Ōe, had held the *gesu shiki* since the twelfth century. At the end of the Kamakura period, Ōe Kiyosada, the current *gesu* of the *shōen*, began to increase his military strength by enlisting local warriors. Kiyosada then seized control of taxation on the *shōen*. The Tōdaiji appealed this act to the Rokuhara *tandai*, and Ōe Kiyosada was arrested and exiled to Izumo province. The Tōdaiji's control over the *shōen*, however, depended on

---

12 Concerning *ukesho*, see Yasuda, *Jitō oyobi jitō ryōshusei*, pp. 339–55.
13 *Rokuhara gechijō* 1308, in *Yamanouchi-Sudo monjo*.

this locally powerful Ōe family. Therefore, the temple subsequently appointed Ōe Kanshun to the post of *gesu* and Ōe Toshisada to the post of *kumon*, a local *shōen* official below the *gesu* in rank.

The new appointees, Kanshun and Toshisada, disregarded the Tōdaiji's orders and continued to commit the illegal acts. In response, the Tōdaiji appointed the son of the former *gesu* Kiyosada, Yasusada, to the *gesu* post. Spared by this appointment, Kiyosada returned from his exile in Izumo, and both father and son undertook seditious actions against the Tōdaiji. Moreover, the residents of the *shōen* community, united with the Ōe family, took action against the Tōdaiji, demanding a reduction in their tax and corvée responsibilities and undermining the Tōdaiji's authority.

In response to this crisis in *shōen* control, the Tōdaiji desperately requested that the *gokenin* warriors of the area and the *shugo* deputy of Iga Province put pressure on the Ōe family. They too, however, only conspired with the Ōe. The Rokuhara *tandai*, finally recognizing the seriousness of the situation, sided with the Tōdaiji. Members of the Ōe family were arrested and its two leaders banished, Kiyosada to Bingo Province and Kakushun to Tango Province. Kiyosada and Kakushun did not remain in exile, however, but returned to plague the Tōdaiji by withholding some three thousand *koku* of *nengu* from the temple.

The Ōe family came to be called *akutō*, a term used by *shōen* proprietors in the Kamakura period to describe lawless groups who banded together for such purposes as forcibly seizing tax rice and other wealth from *shōen* proprietors.[14] *Akutō* were present on many *shōen* and included among their members, *shōkan*, *shōen* cultivators, and *bushi* (warriors). The *akutō* were not successful in attaining complete control over Kuroda-no-shō, however, owing to the vigor of the Tōdaiji's response. Elsewhere, however, the *akutō* pursued a course of aggrandizement similar to the efforts of the *jitō* to increase their personal control over *shōen*.

The growth of the kokujin-ryōshu

The speed with which the *jitō* and *shōkan* usurped the authority of the *shōen* proprietor increased dramatically with the fall of the Kamakura bakufu. Like the Kamakura bakufu, the Muromachi bakufu adopted a

---

14 Concerning the Kuroda *akutō*, see Ishimoda Shō, *Zōho chūseiteki sekai no keisei* (Tokyo: Tōkyō daigaku shuppankai, 1950), pp. 181–302; and Koizumi Yoshiaki, "Iga no kuni Kuroda-no-shō no akutō," in Inagaki and Nagahara, eds., *Chūsei no shakai to keizai*.

policy of suppressing these *jitō* incursions. The Muromachi bakufu lacked the power of its predecessor, however, and was unable to enforce its judicial decisions. The acts by the *jitō* and *shōkan* committed in defiance of the bakufu's judicial decisions were not limited to those against the holdings of the nobles and religious establishments that supported the Southern Court against the bakufu; they extended also to the holdings of the Northern Court which was allied with the bakufu.

Because of the unsettled conditions of the period, those who held rights to widely scattered *shōen* found it difficult to maintain their rights and began to concentrate their power in a single location. In this process, the holder of the *jitō shiki* would choose a particular *shōen* and attempt to make it into a contiguous holding. In addition, he also sought *ukesho* contracts on public lands (*kōryō*) and *shōen* with which he had no prior connection, in order to build a local power base.

The *gokenin* family of Mōri, for example, whose ancestral holding was the Mōri-no-shō in Sagami Province, also held the *jitō shiki* of Sahashi-no-shō in Echigo Province, Kagata-no-shō in Kawachi, and Yoshida-no-shō in Aki. At the beginning of the Nambokuchō period, the main line of the Mōri family entrusted the control of Sahashi-no-shō to a branch family and moved their household to Yoshida-no-shō where they established a new home base. During the Muromachi period, the Mōri created a local power base by means of *ukesho* on *kōryō* and *shōen* in the Takada district of Yoshida-no-shō. They also became *daikan*.[15]

When *jitō* such as the Mōri turned their attention to the formation of a regional power base, they were forced to abandon their rights to their other scattered holdings. In the case of the Mōri, they relinquished their *shiki* held in Kagata-no-shō and Sahashi-no-shō. In another case, a Musashi *gokenin* family by the name of Abo held numerous *jitō shiki* in the provinces of Musashi, Shinano, Dewa, Bitchu, and Harima. During the upheaval of the Nambokuchō period, however, their *jitō shiki* in Bitchu Province was wrestled away from them by locals.[16] The *shiki* structure of the *shōen* began to disintegrate rapidly in the war-torn conditions of the fourteenth century; this involved not only the upper-level *shiki* held by the nobility and the religious establishments but also the scattered *jitō shiki*.

The weakening of the *shiki* structure and the formation of contiguous local power bases during the fourteenth century represented a new

15 *Mōri-ke monjo*, in *Takada-gun shi* (Takada-gun shi hensan iinkai, 1972).
16 *Abo Mitsuyasu okibumi*, 1340, in *Abo monjo*.

trend in landholding – a national reorganization of the landholding system. Changes in landholding patterns were paralleled by changes in inheritance and military organization. In order to construct a system of control over the residents of their newly formed power base, the *jitō* sought to make vassals of the upper-class cultivators. The military force of the Kamakura-period warriors was strongly based on familial relations – unrelated vassals were still quite rare. Under the *sōryō* system, the main family forced branch family members (*ichizoku*) to reside in the villages under their control. In peacetime these branch families managed and developed agricultural production, and in wartime, the head of the main family (*sōryō*) mobilized and led these collateral family members into battle. Unrelated followers called *shojū* and *genin* were often employed but were not part of the military nucleus.[17] After the Nambokuchō period, the *jitō*-level warriors discarded the *sōryō* system and developed a new system of military organization.

Warrior families also discarded the practice of divided inheritance carried out under the *sōryō* system, in order to prevent the opposition from within the family that often accompanied the division of landholdings. An inheritance system under which a sole heir acquired all the land was adopted by many *jitō* families during the Nambokuchō period. Thus the branch family members no longer received a share of the inheritance and were gradually reduced to a position of dependence on the main family. At the same time, the *sōryō* made vassals of the powerful peasant leaders (*dogō*) and upper-class cultivators in their territory, by requiring military service in exchange for a reduction in, or exemption from, *nengu* payments.

The *jitō*'s transition to *kokujin-ryōshu* (local notables who became local or regional overloads) was characterized by three trends: (1) They no longer held scattered *shiki* but controlled contiguous holdings in a single location; (2) they no longer practiced divided inheritance but, rather, switched to the practice of single inheritance in order to avoid diluting their wealth by dividing their landholdings; and (3) they militarized the upper-class cultivators in their area in order to strengthen their military force. The local warriors (*zaichi-ryōshu*) who followed this path were called *kokujin-ryōshu*. The term *kokujin* appears in the documents of the period and refers to those warriors who had deep roots in the provinces.[18]

17 See Haga Norihiko, *Sōryōsei* (Tokyo: Shibundo, 1966).
18 Concerning the *Kokujin-ryōshu*, see Nagahara Keiji, *Nihon hōkensei seiritsu katei no kenkyū* (Tokyo: Iwanami shoten, 1961), pp. 346–56; and Nagahara, *Nihon chūsei shakai kōzō no kenkyū*, pp. 367–93.

In contrast with the *shōen* proprietors, the *kokujin* controlled the *shōen* through their own power. Even so, direct power alone proved insufficient to control the *shōen* residents. The *kokujin* found it essential to persuade the residents that their control was appropriate and that they had a public right to power. Consequently, the *kokujin* did not completely sever their relationship with the *shōen* proprietors, but continued to recognize their position and deliver *nengu* to them, although in reduced amounts. The amount of arable land that had been publicly surveyed and recorded (*kōden*) – on which the *kokujin* based their calculation for *nengu* to be delivered to the central proprietor – however, was far less than the amount of land from which the *kokujin* themselves collected taxes. Moreover, because the *kokujin* assumed the actual control of the *shōen*, the *shōen* proprietor lost all substantive authority over the *shōen* except for the right to collect the tax delivered by the *kokujin*.

The *shōen* proprietor of the Mōri family's Yoshida-no-shō was a Kyoto shrine, Gikansha. The amount of *kōden* on which the *nengu* was computed at the beginning of the fifteenth century was generally no more than forty *chōbu*. The amount of land that the Mōri controlled and on which they levied such imposts as *rinjizei* (a temporary tax), however, exceeded six hundred *chōbu*.[19]

The growth of the *kokujin* took place within the framework of the *shōen* system. The *kokujin* usurped the right to administer the *shōen*, which included the promotion of *shitaji*, the collection of *nengu*, and police authority (*kendan*). The *shōen* proprietor, recognizing his loss of authority, appointed the *kokujin* as an overseer (*daikan*) and took delivery of a fixed amount of *nengu*, as determined by contract. Disputes between *shōen* proprietors and *kokujin* at this time were seldom referred to the legal organs of the Muromachi bakufu. These disputes were not over fragmented rights held by the various *ryōshu*, as we saw in the Kamakura period; instead, *sōryō* was a problem that concerned the proprietor authority itself. In this regard, the growth of the *kokujin-ryōshu* decisively changed control of the *shōen*.

THE DEVELOPMENT OF THE *SHUGO* DOMAINAL SYSTEM

The expansion of shugo *authority*

At the same time that *jitō* and *shōkan* were developing into *kokujin-ryōshu*, the *shugo* was also changing. Under the Kamakura bakufu, the

19 *Mōri-ke monjo*, docs. 28, 29, 47.

shugo's authority was circumscribed by the *daibon sankajō*, empowered only to punish the crimes of murder and rebellion and to muster the imperial guard. In addition, the *shugo* held a power known as *monjo chōshin no yaku*, which gave him the right to request land registers for a province within the jurisdiction of the *kokuga*.[20] The registers proved to be indispensable to the *shugo* in his mobilization of material and manpower, because they listed the amount of public land still held by the *kokuga* within the individual *shōen*, as well as the identities of the *jitō* and *gesu*.

The power of the *shugo* also increased during the Mongol invasions of Japan (1274–81) when the bakufu was forced to mobilize non-*gokenin* warriors and place them under the *shugo*'s command.[21] Normally, the bakufu controlled the *shugo*'s vassalization of the provincial warriors through a policy of making them direct shogunal retainers. But by the end of the Kamakura period, the *shugo*'s own vassalization of the provincial warriors had become common.

The Muromachi bakufu, formed in 1336 after the collapse of the Kemmu restoration, followed its predecessor's policy of limiting the *shugo*'s authority to the *daibon sankajō*.[22] During the fighting in the Nambokuchō period, however, the bakufu had little choice but to grant appropriate powers to the *shugo* so that they could strengthen their military forces by enticing the locally powerful *kokujin* into their vassal organization.

Based on a Muromachi bakufu law issued in 1346, the *shugo* were granted two powers in addition to the *daibon sankajō* – *karita rōzeki* and *shisetsu jungyō*.[23] *Karita rōzeki* gave the *shugo* the authority to suppress provincial warriors who entered *shōen* unlawfully to harvest rice. *Shisetsu jungyō* gave the *shugo* authority to enforce the bakufu judicial decisions in land disputes. Before the 1346 law, the *shugo*'s power was limited mainly to military and police oversight. These new powers, which concerned the resolution of land disputes, increased their political and economic authority.

The bakufu promulgated a *hanzei* law in 1352 that allowed the *shugo* to collect from the *shōen* special tributes for military expenses. The bakufu was divided at this time because of a dispute between the shogun Takauji and his brother Tadayoshi, a division that extended down into the warrior ranks. The bakufu declared that "half of the *honjo-ryō* (lands of the court nobles) in the three provinces of Ōmi,

<hr/>

20 *Azuma kagami* 1187/9/13. See also Ishii Susumu, *Nihon chūsei kokkashi no kenkyū* (Tokyo: Iwanami shoten, 1970), pp. 179–94.   21 *Kamakura bakufu tsuika hō*, no. 463.
22 *Muromachi bakufu tsuika hō*, no. 2.   23 Ibid., no. 31.

Mino, and Owari was designated as commissariat land for the support of the military (*hyōrō ryōsho*) and that one harvest from this year alone may be given to their troops."[24] *Honjo-ryō* referred to land to which a *jitō* had been appointed, to distinguish it from land belonging to temples and shrines (*jisha honjo ichienchi*) and land not under the jurisdiction of a *jitō*. This law allowed the *shugo* to appropriate one-half of the annual tax from the *honjo-ryō*, but for one year only, and to give it to their troops as commissariat rice in order to conduct war. This *hanzei* order was carried out in a total of eight provinces: Ōmi, Mino, Owari, Ise, Shima, Iga, Izumi, and Kawachi.[25]

In 1368, *hanzei* authorization was extended to permit the partitioning of land on a regular basis through the entire country, in contrast with the "from this year alone" status of the earlier *hanzei* order.[26] Because *shugo* and *kokujin* were absorbing *shōen* as their own landholdings at this time, the fact that *hanzei* was limited to *honjo-ryō* and excluded the lands of temples and shrines must be considered part of the policy that the bakufu was then adopting to protect the *shōen*. The national *hanzei* law concerned more than just the collection of rice to meet military needs. Because it loosened restrictions on the partitioning of land from a single harvest a year to allow it on a more frequent basis, the *shōen* proprietors suffered a great setback in their hold over the *shōen*.

Under the *hanzei* law, the *shugo* partitioned the *shōen* and *kōryō* within their province and granted them to their *kokujin* vassals. Although the provincial warriors were the direct beneficiaries of the *hanzei* law, it was the *shugo* who had the power to exercise it. This was one means by which the *shugo* incorporated the *kokujin* into his vassal organization. The *hanzei* law did not mean that the Muromachi bakufu had abandoned its policy of supporting the *shōen* system. Instead, the bakufu pragmatically responded to the *shugo*'s and *kokujin*'s demands for land and, in turn, compelled the *shōen* proprietors to sacrifice their own interests.

Shugo *usurpation of the* kokuga

The *shugo* rapidly expanded their public authority during the Nambokuchō period, a trend underlined by the *shugo*'s usurpation of the *kokuga*'s authority and position. Originally, the *kokuga* held the

24 Ibid., no. 56.   25 Ibid., no. 57.   26 Ibid., no. 97.

most important position of local control in the centralized structure of the *ritsuryō* state. Officials below the fourth rank were appointed as provincial governors for a period of six (and later four) years. In the eleventh and twelfth centuries, however, powerful indigenous families (*zaichi-ryōshu*) made significant inroads into the *kokuga* structure by thrusting themselves upon the *kokuga* as *zaichi kanjin*, local officials of provincial *kokuga*. The provincial governors fought back by appointing their own trusted retainers as higher officials (*mokudai*) and poured their strength into organizing their own military power through the use of warriors that the governors themselves retained (*yakata no tsuwamono*). Thus although the *ritsuryō* state changed greatly in the eleventh and twelfth centuries, the *kokuga* remained the base of local control for the state.

The *kokuga* office was not fundamentally changed even into the Kamakura period. The *shiki* structure, common to both the *shōen* and the *kōryō*, was maintained by the power of the *kokuga*. The *shugo's* power, still based on the *daibon sankajō* in the Kamakura period, limited his ability to interfere directly in *kokuga* affairs. After the mid-Kamakura period, however, the *shugo's* power increased relative to that of the *kokuga*. Although their purpose and function differed, the *kokufu*, which served as the *kokuga's* seat, and the *shugo-sho*, which served as the *shugo's* seat, were often located in close proximity or even adjacent to each other. Both positions were a link in the state's public authority. Backed by his superior military power, the *shugo* gradually began to infringe on the *kokuga's* sphere of control and to insinuate himself with the officials of the *kokuga*.

From a 1257 document issued by the *shugo* of Osumi Province in Kyushu, the *shugo* office was found to include such posts as the *osuke kensaisho* (vice-governor), *oryōshi* (military/police functionaries), and *chōsho* and *shōsho* (administrative and secretarial assistants), in addition to the *shugodai* (*shugo* deputy) post. From as early as the Heian period, these posts had been positions attached to the *kokuga* office, indicating that in this case the *kokuga's* posts and functions had been taken over by the *shugo*.[27] From other such examples, it appears that the *shugo's* usurpation of the *kokuga* office proceeded gradually after the middle of the Kamakura period. Although the *shugo* made inroads into the *kokuga's* authority, they were limited by the Kamakura bakufu's deliberate policy of restraining them. In contrast, the Muromachi

---

27 Tanaka Kenji, "Kamakura bakufu no Ōsumi no kuni shihai ni tsuite no ichi kōsatsu," *Kyūshū shigaku*, nos. 65 and 67 (1977, 1979): 1–22 and 1–18.

bakufu was unable to hold the reins on the stronger *shugo*, and the balance of power shifted even further in the *shugo*'s favor.

The *shugo*'s ascendancy was evidenced by their acquisition of the right to collect a temporary tax levied for such state purposes as the rebuilding of the Ise Shrine's main building every twenty years and the *tansen* (cash tax per *tan* of paddy field) levied to meet the expenses of the emperor's coronation and abdication ceremonies. These *ad hoc* levies had formerly been collected by the *kokuga*, but they later came under the *shugo*'s purview.

The *kokuga* carried out arbitration and enforced the judicial decisions handed down by the court regarding land disputes. The *kokuga* customarily chose a provincial representative (*kunizukai*) who was dispatched to the site of the dispute. When the bakufu assumed those judicial functions previously held by the court, the authority of the *kokuga* in this area was transferred to the *shugo*, and the *shugo*'s representative (*shugozukai*) replaced the *kunizukai* as the local representative of justice.[28]

Under pressure from the *shugo*, the *kokuga* office lost most of its substantive power by the fifteenth century. Although it is impossible to detail the *kokuga*'s fall from power province by province, the loss of power was certain. Even in Harima Province where the *kokuga* maintained power for a relatively long period of time, the shift in the balance of power between *kokuga* and *shugo* was evident by the end of the fourteenth century. The post of *ko-mokudai* (resident deputy of the provincial governor), for example, previously assigned to the *kokuga*, was taken over by the *shugo*, and the holder of the office, Ogawa, became a vassal of the *shugo*.[29] Even in the Kamakura period, this trend was apparent in Harima Province where the power of the central government was relatively secure. It is likely, therefore, that the situation in provinces where the central government's authority was weak was even more advanced.

As the *kokuga* were losing their power in the provinces, the court was losing its control over central Japan. The court's independence had not been severely limited by the establishment of the Kamakura bakufu and military government; it had retained its role as one pillar of the state throughout the Kamakura period. In the Nambokuchō

---

28 Concerning the expansion of the *shugo*'s authority, see Satō Shin'ichi, "Shugo ryōgokusei no tenkai," in Toyoda Takeshi, ed., *Shin Nihonshi taikei dai san kan, chūsei shakai* (Tokyo: Asakura shoten, 1954), pp. 81–127.
29 Kishida Hiroshi, "Shugo Akamatsu-shi no Harima no kuni shihai no hatten to kokuga," *Shigaku kenkyū*, nos. 104 and 105 (1968).

period, however, the court lost its base of control and was rendered powerless in the provinces. This was evidenced by the court's reliance on the *shugo* to collect the *tansen*. By the end of the fourteenth century, the court's authority had been so reduced that even its police authority over the environs of Kyoto was taken over by the bakufu's Board of Retainers (*samurai-dokoro*).

Shogun Ashikaga Yoshimitsu achieved a degree of political consolidation at the end of the fourteenth century when he stepped down in favor of his son Yoshimochi. Yoshimitsu then assumed the post of *daijo daijin*, symbolizing that he stood supreme over both the warriors and the nobility. Furthermore, Yoshimitsu sent an envoy to Ming China, opened formal diplomatic and trade relations, and signed himself "King of Japan" in a letter to the Ming court.

The court lost its independence and authority as a separate state entity. Its powerlessness was indicated by the fact that it was no longer asked to resolve land disputes involving *shōen*. Regardless of the nature of the dispute and the persons involved, the court had no recourse but to rely on the bakufu for its resolution. The bakufu was caught between the desire to preserve the *shōen* system and the need to placate and reward its military supporters. On the one hand, many of its policies encouraged the decline of the *shōen* system such as the issuance of the *hanzei* authorizations that expanded the *shugo*'s authority. On the other hand, the bakufu tried to suppress the *shugo* and adopted a protective policy toward the *shōen* as a means to legitimate its position as the preeminent organ of state. Thus the *shōen* system deteriorated greatly under the Muromachi bakufu, but it was not completely dismantled.

The growth of shugo domains

Yoshimitsu used the *shugo* to achieve his goal of political consolidation. He granted them expanded authority and acknowledged their vassalization of the *kokujin*.

In the fifteenth century, the *shugo* developed into daimyo, powerful regional lords possessing semiautonomous control of a domain (*ryōgoku*). The process of domain building followed many paths. One of the most noteworthy was the *shugo*'s incorporation of "public land" (*kokugaryō*) into his own *shugo* holdings. Although the *shōen* system was the primary form of landholding throughout Japan, it is estimated that *kokugaryō* constituted approximately 40 to 50 percent of the total arable land in some provinces. The entire country was not converted into *shōen* during the twelfth and thirteenth centuries, as might be mistakenly believed. Although the *shōen* had its effects throughout Japan, *kokugaryō* were maintained at the aforementioned ratio and were reorganized into units called *go*, *ho*, or *befu*. Furthermore, *nengu* and *zōkuji* collected from *kokugaryō* provided income for the *chigyō kokushu* – the nobility and powerful religious establishments appointed as the "governor" of a province for the sole purpose of receiving income from it. In other provinces, the *kokugaryō* provided income for the central government. As the *shugo* absorbed the authority of the *kokuga* office, however, the *kokugaryō* increasingly fell under the *shugo*'s control.

The transformation of the *kokugaryō* began in the Kamakura period in the provinces of eastern Japan and Kyushu where the authority of the Kamakura bakufu was strongest. But even in those provinces where the authority of the Kyoto nobility was relatively strong, the process quickly accelerated during the Nambokuchō period. Amidst the desultory fighting of the fourteenth century, the *shugo* took control of the *kokugaryō* through the *kokuga shiki*, and it became part of their own landholdings.[30]

In the fifteenth century, many *shugo* also began to levy *tansen*, once a temporary provincial unit tax, as discussed earlier. The *shugo*, however, did not levy *tansen* as a state tax in their substitute role as a provincial official (*kokushi*); instead, the *shugo* levied *tansen* on the basis of their own political authority. Moreover, although it was originally a temporary levy, it became a permanent tax symbolizing that authority.[31]

In order to strengthen their public authority throughout the entire province, the *shugo* built up their personal military power, primarily by organizing the province's local powers (*kokujin-ryōshu*) as their vassals. The above-mentioned *hanzei* was the most convenient means by which to make vassals of the *kokujin*. The *shugo* also held the right to grant to their *kokujin* vassals the land confiscated from an enemy defeated in battle, as a means to retain or strengthen their loyalty. Thus both *hanzei* and confiscated land provided a source of fief (*chigyō*) by which the *shugo* enticed military service from the *kokujin*.[32]

The relationship between the *shugo* and their *kokujin* vassals was a

30 *Uesugi-ke monjo*, vol. 1, no. 56.
31 Tanuma Mutsumi, "Muromachi bakufu, shugo, kokujin," in Iwanami kōza, ed., *Nihon rekishi (chūsei 3)* Tokyo: Iwanami shoten, 1976), pp. 33–40.
32 Kasamatsu Hiroshi, *Nihon chūsei-hō shiron* (Tokyo: Tōkyō daigaku shuppankai, 1979), pp. 203–38.

tenuous one, as the *hanzei* and confiscated land proved insufficient as a source of *chigyō*. Furthermore, the *kokujin*'s original landholdings had not been granted by the *shugo*. Consequently, the lord–vassal relationship established between the *shugo* and the *kokujin* was not an unbreakable tie, nor did all *kokujin* in a province become *shugo* vassals. Some *kokujin* even tried to avoid becoming *shugo* vassals as in the case of a *kokujin* league (*ikki*) formed in 1404 in Aki Province in order to resist the newly appointed *shugo*, Yamana.[33]

The *shugo* failed to make vassals of all the *kokujin* in their province, but because the *kokujin* were usually much less powerful than the *shugo*, they were unable to prevent the formation of the lord–vassal relationship. This relationship with the *kokujin* was the military foundation of the *shugo*'s provincial control that has been called the *shugo* domainal system (*shugo ryōgokusei*). During the Muromachi period, many of the *shugo* came to be called great lords or daimyo, even by the bakufu.

The *shugo* also extended their control over the *shōen* in their province by means of provincewide levies such as *tansen*. The collection of the *hanzei*, too, as described earlier, was made only in the lands that the *shugo* controlled directly (*honjo-ryō*) and not in the holdings of the religious establishments. In the fifteenth century, however the *shugo* levied *ad hoc* taxes and labor corvée called *shugo yaku*, first on the *honjo-ryō* and then on the holdings of temples and shrines. The *shugo* also made vassals of the *shōen* officials. Once this was accomplished, the *shugo* then proposed *shugo uke* (literally, "*shugo* contract"). Rather than the payment of a small fixed amount of tax to the central proprietor, the *shugo uke* gave the *shugo* complete control over the locale. One case involved Ota-no-shō in Bingo Province, a large *shōen* of at least six hundred *chō* of paddy land under the proprietorship of Kōyasan, a Buddhist monastic complex of the Shingon sect on Mount Kōya. In 1402, the *shugo*, Yamana Tokihiro, contracted to pay 1,000 *koku* in tax to Kōyasan. Tokihiro failed to honor the contract, however, and during the Eikyō period (1429–41), the *shugo* was delinquent on the payment of 20,600 *koku*.[34]

Destruction of the *shōen* system was not the express purpose of the *shugo uke*, but the *shugo*'s acquisition of actual control over the *shōen* greatly aided their rise to the status of daimyo. The *shugo* assigned their vassal *kokujin* to these *shōen* on which the former held *shugo uke*,

33 *Aki no kuni kokujin dōshin jōjō* vol: 1: 1404, no. 24, in *Mōri-ke monjo*. See also Nagahara Keiji, *Chūsei nairanki no shakai to minshū* (Tokyo: Yoshikawa kōbunkan, 1977), pp. 129–57.
34 *Muromachi shōgun-ke migyōsho*, vol: 1: 1402, no. 373, in *Kōyasan monjo*.

giving the latter authority over the *shōen*. Although not a case of *shugo uke*, members of the *shugo* clan were often installed as *daikan* on *shōen*. In a 1393 case involving Miwa-no-shō in Suō Province under the proprietorship of the Tōji, a Suō *shugo* retainer of the Ōuchi, Hirai Nyūdō, acted as an intermediary, and another person, Kutsuya Saemonshigemori, became *daikan* on the *shōen*. Kutsuya, probably a local notable connected to the Ōuchi, was granted the *daikan shiki* for the ten-year period at a fixed salary of forty *kanmon*.[35] This was not, technically speaking, a case of *shugo uke*, but it constituted the same thing.

What kind of attitude did the Muromachi bakufu adopt toward the development of the *shugo* domainal system? From its inception, the bakufu followed the policy inherited from its predecessor and sought both to maintain the *shōen* system and to control the *shugo* and the *jitō*. Both the *shugo* and *jitō* chafed at this policy. Their combined demands for greater power and more land eventually forced the bakufu to retreat from its original stance. It was during the Kannō disturbances in the mid-fourteenth century that the bakufu issued the *hanzei* laws in reaction to the growing dissatisfaction of the *shugo* and *kokujin*. Although the bakufu increased its control during the Nambokuchō period, it was unable to resist by force the *shugo*'s efforts to construct a domainal system, as the *shugo* played a critical role in the bakufu's internal politics.[36]

PEASANTS' PROTEST AND GROWTH

The development of the myōshu kajishi

In addition to the actions of the *shugo* and *kokujin*, the *shōen* system was undermined by the actions of the cultivators and changes in the structure of the village.

An important development in this regard was the establishment of the *myōshu kajishi*. The *myōshu kajishi* was a mid-level right to receive income (*tokubun*), unrelated to the *shōen* proprietor's right to collect *nengu*. In 1385, for example, Fujimatsume of Shimokuze-no-shō in Yamashiro Province sold three *tan* of *myōshu shiki* to a person named Jibukyohōin. According to the contract, the Tōji's *nengu* was set at 742 *shō* of rice and four hundred *mon* in cash, and the buyer received 1.5

---

35 *Saishōkō-in-kata hikitsuke*, 1393/7/10 and 1393/4/7, in *Tōji hyakugō monjo*.
36 Nagahara Keiji, "Muromachi bakufu shugo ryōgokusei ka no tochi seido," in *Nihon chūsei shakai kōzō no kenkyū*, pp. 426–87.

koku of rice as his *myōshu kajishi*.[37] How the *myōshu kajishi* that became prevalent during the Nambokuchō period was originally established is still unclear. As a result of rising agricultural productivity, when the *nengu* obligation and subsistence portion for the cultivators were subtracted from the total yield, the surplus was set aside as the *myōshu kajishi*. This was possible because the *nengu* remained fixed and did not eat away the surplus. A certain amount of surplus remained under the control of the *shōen* proprietor, but as that control weakened, it is thought that the *myōshu kajishi* were bought and sold. The amount of *kajishi* per unit of land was often the same as the *nengu* standard of three to five *to* of rice per *tan* of land.

Under these conditions, well-to-do peasants often bought and accumulated these *myōshu kajishi* rights, and peasants in strained circumstances often became responsible for paying the *myōshu kajishi* in addition to the usual *nengu*. In a 1407 document from the Tōji's Kamikuze-no-shō in Yamashiro Province, we see such notations as the following: I. Heishichi-*myō*, one *tan; myōshu* Hōrindono; and (*sakunin*) Yagorō; and II. Echigo-*myō*, one *tan; myōshu sakunin* Rokurōgorō.[38] In the first entry, Hōrindono, who held the *myōshu kajishi* right, and the *sakunin* Yagorō were two different individuals. In the second entry, the distinction seen in part I between *myōhu* and *sakunin* had not emerged – Rokurōgorō alone was responsible for the *nengu* to be paid by a *sakunin* and *myōshu*.

The *myōshu kajishi* right was not necessarily limited to persons living on the *shōen*. Wealthy peasants on neighboring *shōen*, religious establishments, saké brewers, and moneylenders also bought *kajishi* rights. For example, it is known that a prominent saké brewer by the name of Saikyō Umezakaya acquired in 1434 two *tan* of the *myōshu kajishi* right on Shimokuze-no-shō located southwest of Kyoto.[39] The control of the *shōen* proprietor was inevitably shaken by such transactions. Even though it was called *myōshu kajishi*, if the authority to increase it relative to the *nengu* was acquired by persons outside the *shōen*, then the authority of these outsiders was bound to increase within the *shōen* itself. Consequently, *shōen* proprietors tried to prohibit the sale of *kajishi* rights outside the *shōen*. As early as the mid-fourteenth century, the Tōji proclaimed to the *shōen* manager (*azukari-dokoro*) of Kanno-no-shō in Yamashiro Province that "the sale of lands must be strictly

---

37 *Fujimatsume Shimokuze-no-shō nai myōshu-shiki baiken*, 1385, *me* 11–19, in *Tōji hyakugō monjo*.
38 *Kamikuze-no-shō kumon chūshinjo*, 1407, *wo* 17 and *ge* 18, in *Tōji hyakugō monjo*.
39 *Asahara kannonji jūji keihō mōshijō*, 1435, *wo* 16, in *Tōji hyakugō monjo*.

forbidden without exception" and declared that the *myōden* would be confiscated in cases in which the law was broken.[40]

Shōen proprietors were unable to stop the transfer of *myōshu kajishi* rights by such restrictions alone. The *shōen* proprietors, most of whom resided in Kyoto or Nara, maintained private administrative headquarters (*mandokoro*) in order to control the *shōen* but had no military force of their own. Thus, their power to stop the increasing sales of rights to income from paddies was negligible. As a result, even though agricultural productivity was rising, they were unable to increase the *nengu*, conduct land surveys, or exert control over outsiders who held *kajishi* rights.

The practice of *myōshu kajishi* and its transfer to persons outside the *shōen* were most widely developed on the *shōen* of the Kinai region. The reason for this was that even though these *shōen* were more able to control the growth of the *jitō* and *kokujin*, owing these *shōen*'s proximity to Kyoto and Nara, an independent cultivator class developed in this region and in larger numbers than elsewhere. As I shall describe further later, the *shōen* proprietors, who faced opposition from cultivators in the form of disputes between the proprietors and the cultivators, had to contend with stronger opposition from the cultivators in the *shōen* of this region. And such opposition tended to succeed in gaining more of the agricultural surplus for cultivators in the form of *myōshu kajishi*.

The *myōshu kajishi* developed elsewhere as well, particularly in the provinces near Kyoto. In the mid-fifteenth century the Fun'yōji, a temple located in the Muki District of Mino Province, bought five *tan* of paddy from a person named Nakanishi Hachirō. The temple received four *kanmon* of *nengu* from the *sakunin* and from that amount paid 2.913 *kanmon* for what was known as *kubō nengu* – dues paid to a high-ranking noble (*kubō*) proprietor.[41] In a separate transaction, the temple collected one *koku*, three *to* of rice in *nengu* from two *tan* of paddy, from which it paid six *to* in the form of *kubō nengu*.[42] The *kubō nengu* was paid, but the balance remained in the hands of the Fun'yōji in the form of *myōshu kajishi*. The seller of the *kajishi* right to the Fun'yōji, Nakanishi Hachirō, was probably a *myōshu*, meaning that well-to-do peasants and religious establishments were selling their accumulated *kajishi* rights. In the mid-fifteenth century, a wealthy peasant by the name of Hatamura Gorōzaemon conducted numerous finan-

---

40 *Gakushū bugyō hikitsuke, hōkyō shinyu shojō, mu,* in *Tōji hyakugō monjo.*
41 *Nakanishi Hachirō denchi baiken,* 1460, no. 50 in *Fun'yōji monjo.*   42 Ibid., no. 51.

cial transactions and rapidly accumulated landholdings in the Ōbe-no-shō in Harima Province, a proprietorship of the Tōdaiji. The purchase of *myōshu kajishi* rights was an important source of this new wealth.[43]

Thus over time, the levying and trading of rights to *myōshu kajishi* became increasingly prevalent in the Kinai and neighboring provinces, and this development raised the critical issue of how to guarantee the collection of the *kajishi* and what to do in cases in which the payment of *kajishi* was delinquent. Because the *kajishi* was anathema to the *shōen* proprietors, they could not be expected to lend their authority to ensure payment. Those who held *kajishi* rights were generally well-to-do peasants or religious establishments who, unlike the *kokujin*, did not possess the military power needed to ensure payment. As a result, it proved difficult for the holders of *kajishi* rights to enforce payment. In order to ensure collection of the *myōshu kajishi*, therefore, they developed an organization for this outside the framework of the *shōen* system. Thus, the custom of *gōjichi* ("debt of a village") became prevalent. This custom recognized that the debt of one villager was the responsibility of all villagers and that creditors were allowed to seize the property of villagers other than that of the delinquent debtor himself.[44] These practices and customs were not within the control of the *shōen* proprietors and so served to weaken their control over the *shōen*, whose residents established their own method of administration.

The formation of the sō-mura

The establishment of *myōshu kajishi*, in addition to *nengu*, was prompted by the rise in agricultural productivity brought about by improvements in agricultural techniques, such as the increased use of fertilizer, the development of new strains of rice appropriate to different natural conditions, and the more sophisticated use of land. In the medieval period, significant efforts were made to improve the methods of storing the water necessary to minimize the effect of drought. Agricultural productivity was also spurred by the actions of individual cultivators who sought to manage and protect their land, even though it was also subject to *myōshu kajishi*, which was assessed at a rate roughly equal to the *nengu*.

43 Konishi Mizue, "Harima no kuni Ōbe-no-shō no nomin," *Nihonshi kenkyū*, no. 98 (1968); and Konishi Mizue, "Kyōtoku sannen no Ōbe-no-shō do-ikki ni tsuite," *Hyōgo shigaku*, no. 65 (1976).
44 Concerning *gōjichi*, see Katsumata Shizuo, *Sengoku-hō seiritsu shiron* (Tokyo: Tōkyō daigaku shuppankai, 1979), pp. 37–60.

Until these improvements had begun to be made in the thirteenth century, land was often left uncultivated when damaged by flooding, drought, or breaches in the irrigation system.[45] Under these conditions, the situation of the poorer peasants was extremely tenuous. They borrowed foodstuffs and seed rice from the richer farmers and were able to eke out a living by proffering their labor. If they experienced a disastrous harvest, they were often forced to leave their homes and become indentured agricultural laborers or servants (*genin*) to wealthy peasants.[46]

Agricultural productivity rose, nonetheless, and as conditions improved in the fourteenth century, the number of peasants who accumulated *myōshu kajishi* increased. Even many of the previously insecure peasants gradually improved and strengthened their lot as independent cultivators. That the number of independent cultivators increased was evident in the petitions that the villagers signed. During the stable years of the *shōen* system – the twelfth and thirteenth centuries – appeals to the *shōen* proprietor requesting a reduction in the tax were commonly signed by relatively small number of the *myōshu* who were responsible for collecting the tax and corvée and who acted as the proprietor's representative. It was quite natural then that the *myōshu* were the signatories of these appeals.

But in the fourteenth and fifteenth centuries these petitions came to be signed by all resident cultivators (*sōbyakushō*), not just the *myōshu*. Petitions for a reduction in tax or corvée and complaints against the illegal actions of *shōen* officials often took the form of *sōbyakushō* petitions (*mōshijō*).[47] In order to determine whether the demands were in fact those of all the peasants and to force them to take joint responsibility, the *shōen* proprietor had all concerned make a pledge and swear the veracity of their petition before the divine. Despite the *shōen* proprietor's demands, this new form of petition in the fourteenth and fifteenth centuries indicated the growing self-reliance of the cultivators below the *myōshu* class, that is, the small cultivators (*kobyakushō*) who would not have been signatories in the petitions that had been submitted to the *shōen* proprietor during the thirteenth century.

A petition, dated 1334, from Ōta-no-shō in Wakasa Province, a hold-

---

45 Land was often left fallow (*nen-are*) in twelfth-century Japan. For a discussion of the amount of land cultivated relative to the total amount of existing arable land, see Nagahara Keiji, *Nihon no chūsei shakai* (Tokyo: Iwanami shoten, 1968), p. 160.
46 The cultivators of this period were frequently transients and without a permanent residential structure. See ibid., p. 158.
47 Satō Kazuhiko, *Nambokuchō nairan shiron* (Tokyo: Tōkyō daigaku shuppankai, 1979), pp. 13–43.

ing of the Tōji, charged that the *daikan* illegally assessed an additional labor corvée on the residents for work on his private lands and then seized the *myōden* of the villagers. The beleaguered villagers drew up a detailed list of the *daikan's* transgressions and then gathered at the *shōen's* shrine where they "drank the divine waters of unity" as an indication of their sincerity. The names of fifty-nine *sōbyakushō* were affixed to the petition and sent to the Tōji.[48] The petition was headed by the names of persons with surnames, such as Ōyama Sadashige; below that were the seals of seven persons without surnames, such as Tojirō; and below there were more than fifty names in abbreviated, simple signatures. The former were *myōshu*, and the latter were of the *kobyakushō* class. The status distinctions between *myōshu* and *kobyakushō* were clearly indicated by the use or absence of a surname or seal.

In 1367 on Yano-no-shō in Harima Province, another holding of the Tōji, the residents demanded a reduction in tax from the *shōen* official and asserted that if their demands were not met, they would let the land revert to an uncultivated condition. The petition was entitled "an appeal submitted regarding a great loss" and was signed by forty-six *myōshu* led by the *myōshu* of Yoshinori-myō.[49] *Kobyakushō* and others participated as well, and this villagewide unrest was called a "rising of all of the *sō* (village)" (*sōshō ikki*). In response to the petition, the *daikan* enlisted the help of the *shugo* and brought additional pressure to bear on the petitioners. The *daikan* threatened to arrest thirty-five *myōshu* and others involved, but despite the threat, the petitioners did not give in and soon succeeded in forcing the *daikan's* dismissal.

This kind of unified cultivator action appeared as early as 1298 when the villagers of Tsuda and Okushima in Omi Province drew up a pact (*kimon*) that pledged their unity.[50] This pact involved an agreement over fishing rights on Lake Biwa. A total of thirty-nine persons from Kita-Tsuda village and fifty-eight from Okushima jointly signed the agreement, pledging that they would treat those who broke it as traitors and that those who conspired with the enemy would be banished from the *shōen*. The diversity of the signatories' class origins is indicated by the presence of *kobyakushō* without surnames, such as Tairagorō. This dispute was not directed against the *shōen* proprietor, but it was an instance of unified action by all levels of cultivators.

From these examples, it is clear that unified cultivator action developed in the central provinces of Wakasa, Harima, and Omi. The

48 *Ōta-no-shō hyakushō mōshijō narabi ni kishōmon, ha* 116, in *Tōji hyakugō monjo*.
49 *Yano-no-shō hyakushō mōshijō*, 1367, *kei* 28–37, in *Tōji hyakugō monjo*.
50 *Okushima okutsushima monjo*, 1298, in *Okushima-no-shō murabito ichimi dōshin okibumi*.

cultivators' increased unity lent strength to their defiance of the *shōen* proprietors. This new development, in turn, reflected changes in the villages' social structure that accompanied the social and economic growth of the *kobyakushō*, mainly the establishment of the *sō-mura* – villages that overcame the political, economic, and even geographical constraints imposed on the cultivators by the eroding *shōen* system. The development of the *sō-mura* indicated that a fundamental change had occurred in the village structure to the extent that even the newly emergent *kobyakushō* acquired membership in the village community.[51] The *sō-mura* customarily held general conferences (*shūchū dangō*) or meetings (*yoriai*) to determine the village consensus for collective actions and to draft regulations (*okite*) to maintain peace in the community. These regulations determined how fields and mountains were to be used, prohibited gambling to preserve the peace of the village, and prohibited the lodging of travelers, among other things. The village meetings to draw up these regulations were often held at the local Shinto shrine under the auspices of the various types of "guilds" (*miyaza*) associated with the shrine or Shinto priests, who were also members of the greater village community. The developing autonomy of the greater village community was inextricably connected to such unified cultivator actions as the submitting of petitions (*hyakushō mōshijō*) to the *shōen* proprietors or the *jitō*. These developments caused a further weakening of the *shōen* proprietors' control over the *shōen* and their residents.

Cultivators' protests

The emergence of the *sō-mura* as a foundation for the cultivators' action strengthened their position against the *shōen* proprietors. In the fifteenth century, a variety of cultivator protests erupted in the central provinces, and the strength of these protests ultimately led to the collapse of the *shōen* system.

The demands for *nengu* reductions by the cultivators of Kamikuze-no-shō, a holding of the Tōji situated four kilometers southwest of the temple, became more strident in the fifteenth century. In 1408, residents of the *shōen* requested a waiver of *nengu* for that year because of drought damage to their fields. The Tōji granted a reduction of 8 *koku*, but the residents were still dissatisfied and presented another

---

51 Ishida Yoshito, "Gōson-sei no keisei," in *Iwanami kōza Nihon rekishi*, vol. 8 (1963); and Nagahara Keiji, "Chūsei kōki no sonraku kyōdōtai," in Nagahara, *Chūsei nairanki no shakai to minshū*.

demand. In 1419, 20 *koku* of tax was excused because of wind damage; in 1420, after they thronged to the Tōji, the cultivators received a tax exemption of 12 *koku* because of drought. Over twenty years, the residents of Kamikuze-no-shō demanded and received tax reductions of various amounts: In 1423, wind and water damage resulted in a 22-*koku* reduction; in 1425, 18 *koku* was excused when the cultivators threatened to abandon their fields if their demands were not met; in 1426, they received another 18-*koku* reduction; in 1427, a 31-*koku* reduction was granted; in 1430, by daily visiting the temple with their demands, the cultivators managed to receive a 70-*koku* reduction because of water damage; in 1435, the cultivators obtained a 62-*koku* reduction; and in 1437, sixty *myōshu* and others from Kamikuze-no-shō negotiated with the Tōji and won a 60-*koku* reduction.[52] The tax previously paid by the *shōen* amounted to nearly 230 *koku*, but as these reductions generally became customary, the proprietor was unable to collect the legally established tax.

The most important characteristic of these tax-reduction protests was that they included both the upper-class cultivators, sometimes called *satanin*, who stood at the front of the group, and the lower-class cultivators, the *kobyakushō*, who strongly demonstrated their new-found power. These tax protests, however, were not incited solely by impoverished cultivators. They were often led by powerful individuals in the *shōen* whom the *shōen* proprietor had no choice but to recognize. This gave a political quality to the process. At the same time, the direct participation of lower-class cultivators in the negotiations with the proprietor indicated that the movement included all strata of the cultivating population. These fifteenth-century protests encompassed the upper-class cultivators' desire to obtain as much wealth as possible and the lower-class cultivators' efforts to protect their newly gained agricultural surplus.

In 1428, there was a widespread peasant uprising (*tsuchi-ikki*) throughout the provinces of Omi, Yamashiro, and Yamato.[53] This *tsuchi-ikki* was not in itself a cultivator protests against the *shōen* proprietor. The leaders of the insurrection were teamsters, called *bashaku*, who transported rice and many other goods between Kyoto and Ōtsu. The cultivators of the Kyoto region joined the teamsters and poured

---

52 For more discussion of the actions of the cultivators of Kamikuze-no-shō, see Nagahara Keiji, *Nihon hōkensei seiritsu katei no kenkyū*, pp. 422–41; and Uejima Tamotsu, *Keikō shōen sonraku no kenkyū* (Tokyo: Hanawa shobō, 1970), pp. 318–34.
53 Concerning the Shōchō *do-ikki*, see Nakamura Kichiji, *Do-ikki kenkyū* (Tokyo: Azekura shobō, 1974), p. 156.

into Kyoto, wrecking storehouses (*dosō*), destroying loan papers, reclaiming pawned articles, and demanding that the bakufu issue a *tokuseire* – an edict abrogating debt obligations.

Because the *ikki* was composed of cultivators, the uprising was called a *tsuchi-ikki* or *do-ikki* (the character meaning "land" or "ground" can be pronounced both *do* and *tsuchi* in Japanese). It has also been called a *tokusei-ikki* because it centered on the demand for an abrogation of debts. Other such *tokusei-ikki* occurred repeatedly throughout the fifteenth century. At first glance, the *tokusei-ikki* and the cultivators' protests against the *shōen* proprietor appear unrelated, but such was not the case.

The *shōen* proprietors, hard-pressed by the sharp decline in tax receipts as a result of the cultivators' demands and the *shugo'* s and *kokujin'* s incursions into the *shōen*, borrowed money from moneylenders, using the following year's tax as collateral. In order to collect the tax, the moneylenders themselves became *daikan* on the mortgaged *shōen*. Such *daikan* vigorously collected the tax and, in some cases, treated the delinquent portion of the tax as if it were a cultivator's personal debt.[54] Consequently, a highly antagonistic relationship developed between the cultivator and the moneylender, differing from the usual creditor–debtor relationship. The *tokusei-ikki*, therefore, interfered in the collection of the *shōen* taxes and took on the characteristics of a cultivator revolt. Thus the frequent outbreak of *tokusei-ikki* threatened the moneylenders as well and, by destroying the creditworthiness of the *shōen* proprietor, threatened his already precarious economic position. In this way, the *tokusei-ikki* represented the cultivators' protests against the *shōen* system itself, even though the uprising were ostensibly directed against the moneylenders.

The incidence of the cultivators' protests and *do-ikki* also served to strengthen the position of the upper-class cultivators in the village. As the *shōen* system weakened, the upper-class cultivators cemented their economic position by accumulating *myōshu kajishi* rights. As a result of the cultivators' protests, the amount of tax paid to the *shōen* proprietors declined, and proportionately more of the wealth remained on the *shōen* in the hands of the well-to-do cultivators. These wealthy cultivators, using their increased wealth, armed themselves and took more vigorous actions against the *shōen* proprietors. They often became low-level retainers of the *shugo* or *kokujin* and lent their assis-

---

54 For a discussion of the *ukeoi daikan* system and the *dosō*, see Suma Chikai, "Dosō ni yoru shōen nengu no ukeoi ni tsuite," *Shigaku zasshi*, nos. 80–86 (1971); and Suma Chikai, "Dosō no tochi shūseki to tokusei," *Shigaku zasshi*, nos. 81–83 (1972)

tance to the warriors incursions into the *shōen*. These upper-level cultivators became known as *jizamurai*, or warriors of the land.

The cultivators' recalcitrance did not go unnoticed by the bakufu. The Muromachi bakufu kept a vigilant eye on Kamikuze-no-shō and Shimokuze-no-shō as likely places for a *do-ikki* to form. In 1459, the bakufu investigated the *shōen* residents so as to suppress such an incident. According to the investigation, eleven residents of the two *shōen* were listed as samurai and eighty-nine persons from Kamikuze-no-shō and fifty-six persons from Shimokuze-no-shō as cultivators.[55] Those listed as samurai in the investigation most likely were retainers of the *shugo* who had been recruited into the *shugo*'s military organization. This trend also meant that the cultivators' protests against the *shōen* proprietors were taken up with an armed vigor. In fact, the agrarian protests of this period were gradually connected with the *shugo*'s actions and had a distinctly political flavor.

In 1441, a *tokusei-ikki* composed of cultivators from the Kyoto region succeeded in forcing the bakufu to issue a *tokusei* edict. The outbreak of this *ikki* followed immediately on the heels of the assassination of Shogun Yoshinori by the Harima *shugo*, Akamatsu Mitsusuke, and was tied to the conflict between two powerful *shugo* daimyo, the Hosokawa and Hatakeyama. Vassal warriors connected with the Hatakeyama lent their support to the *ikki* and used it in their battle with the Hosokawa.[56]

Given these circumstances, it is inappropriate to view *do-ikki* as purely agrarian protests, as they also involved the military and political actions of the *jizamurai*. Instead, it was the very complexity of these events that was the primary characteristic of the *do-ikki* and agrarian protests and that shook the foundations of the *shōen* system.

THE COLLAPSE OF THE *SHŌEN* PROPRIETORS' AUTHORITY

The loss of domain and reduction of tax receipts

We shall next examine development relating to tax collection and control of the *shōen*, in order to show how both were undermined by the agrarian protests that contributed to the increased intrusions of the

---

55 *Kamikuze-no-shō/Shimokuze-no-shō hyakushō kishōmon*, 1459, *wo* 14–*jō*, in *Tōji hyakugō monjo*.
56 Concerning the relationship between the Kakitsu *tokusei-ikki* and the struggle between the *shugo* daimyo Hosokawa and Hatakeyama, see Nagahara Keiji, "Kakitsu tokusei-ikki no seikaku ni tsuite," in Nagahara, *Nihon chūsei shakai kōzō no kenkyū*, pp. 394–425.

kokujin and *shugo* into the *shōen* system. Specifically, we shall look at *shōen* under the proprietorship of the Tōji and their transition during the Nambokuchō period. The Shingon sect's Tōji was a large temple built at the end of the eighth century in Kyoto. It received strong imperial support as well as the protection of the Muromachi bakufu, which recognized the temple's military importance. Located in the southern section of the capital, the temple could control the crucial southern approach to Kyoto. In contrast with the holdings of the nobility, those of religious establishments such as the Tōji were to some extent insulated from the incursions of the *kokujin* and *shugo* because of respect for and fear of their religious role. Consequently, the erosion of the Tōji's control over its *shōen* proceeded at a slower pace than did that of the nobility.

The Tōji had at least seventy-one *shōen* at the beginning of the Nambokuchō period. Among them were *shōen* for which Tōji held only the *honke shiki* and not administrative authority, such as the twenty *shōen* of the Saishōkōin-ryō,[57] and the twelve *shōen* of the Hōshōgon' in-ryō,[58] which originally had been imperial lands. The Tōji also held more comprehensive authority over some of its *shōen*. When the Kamakura bakufu was overthrown, Emperor Godaigo confiscated the *jitō shiki* of such *shōen* as Tara-no-shō in Wakasa Province and granted them to the Tōji. Thus there were no warrior *jitō* on these *shōen*. There were also cases in which the Tōji held only the *ryōke shiki* following a *shitaji chūbun* settlement with a *jitō*, as in the case of Ōyama-no-shō in Tamba Province and Niimi-no-shō in Bitchu where *shitaji chūbun* had been carried out in the Kamakura period. Thus the Tōji held various types of authority over the *shōen* under its proprietorship. With this in mind, the *shōen* of the Tōji can be divided into three categories: those held by the Tōji in name only, those from which the delivery of tax rice continued despite the weakening of proprietor authority, and those from which tax rice was regularly collected and authority was maintained.[59]

Of the Tōji's domain, thirty-two of its seventy-one *shōen* were held in name only. The majority were *shōen* to which the Tōji held only the *honke shiki* donated by the imperial family, as evidenced in a 1371 appeal from the Tōji to the bakufu that stated, "In recent years the

57 Saishōkō-in was built by Emperor Goshirakawa for Empress Kenshunmon-in and was granted numerous *shōen*.
58 Hōshōgon-in was built by Emperor Toba and was granted many *shōen*.
59 For a detailed discussion of the Tōji's *shōen*, see Nagahara Keiji, "Shōensei kaitai katei ni okeru Nambokuchō nairanki no shioki," in Nagahara *Nihon chūsei shakai kōzō no kenkyū*, pp. 284–366.

honke have not been paid by any of our *shōen.*"[60] Apart from the dues to the *honke shiki,* nobles and religious establishments were also *ryōke* with the right to administer the *shōen.* The *honke's* relationship to the *ryōke* was based on the receipt of a limited amount of tax rice from the *ryōke.* When the *ryōke* had difficulty in collecting taxes, the role of the *honke* as guarantor was rendered meaningless, and the *honke shiki* became a right in name only. The *shiki* structure no longer operated under these conditions. As explained at the beginning of this chapter, the *shiki* system developed in response to the geographically scattered and hierarchically ordered structure of *shōen* and *kokugaryō.* Consequently, the emasculation of the *honke shiki,* the pinnacle of the *shiki* structure, symbolized the collapse of the *shōen* system.

Based on a number of documents from the Nambokuchō period, it can be established that the proprietor's authority on some *shōen* was imperiled, but the delivery of tax rice did not completely cease. In the case of Shida-no-shō in Hitachi Province during the Kamakura period, the seizure of tax rice by the *jitō* became a severe problem. Because the Tōji's receipt of tax rice was based on a contract with a *jitō* (*ukesho*) in the case of its Okuni-no-shō in Ise Province, as the power of the *jitō* increased, the temple received less and less tax rice. Warfare decreased the tax collected by the Tōji from its Shihi-no-shō in Echizen Province and Himono-no-shō in Omi. The Tōji's authority on these *shōen* was generally based on the *ryōke shiki.* The temple had the right to administer the *shōen,* but income from it fell because of the actions of the on-site *jitō.* The Tōji sent appeals to the bakufu and dispatched envoys to the *shōen* in an attempt to regain its control, but these attempts proved futile. There was little the temple could do to regain its authority over the income from these *shōen.*

Some of the *shōen* under the Tōji's proprietorship remained comparatively stable, and receipts were fairly well maintained during the Nambokuchō period. Although none of these *shōen* continued to deliver *nengu* in the amount stipulated, the Tōji retained its administrative rights. No warrior *jitō* were installed on four of the fourteen *shōen* in this group (Tarumi in Settsu Province, Hirandono in Yamato, and Hayashi and Kanno in Yamashiro), which were part of the Tōji's core holdings located near the temple. Although *shitaji chūbun* had been carried out in the Kamakura period in several *shōen* – Oyama in Tamba Province, Yugejima in Iyo, Yano in Harima, and Niimi in Bitchu – the remaining portions of each of these *shōen* continued to be important

60 *Tōji mōshijō,* 1371, *e* 17–22, in *Tōji hyakugō monjo.*

holdings of the temple. The Tōji also held both the *jitō shiki* and *ryōke shiki* of Wakasa's Tara-no-shō and Yamashiro's Kamikuze-no-shō and Shimokuze-no-shō. The Tōji managed to protect its interests in these holdings – crucial to maintaining its economic base – even during the Nambokuchō period.

On these *shōen*, warriors had been unable to undermine the Tōji's authority. But the temple could not collect *nengu* from these *shōen* in the amount stipulated. Despite the cessation of hostilities and the establishment of the Muromachi bakufu, the trend of declining *nengu* continued. As we saw earlier in the case of Kamikuze-no-shō, the cultivators' protests resulted in an annual reduction of *nengu*.

After the Nambokuchō period, the Tōji's Oyama-no-shō frequently paid only a part of the *nengu* stipulated and even none at all. This development was not unrelated to the great increase in *shugo* imposts such as the *shugo busen* or *shugo tansen*, paid in cash in lieu of corvée or as an assessment per *tan* of paddy. The amount of *nengu* collected by the *shugo* after the first quarter of the fifteenth century exceeded that of the Tōji.[61] The developments on Kamikuze and Oyama, even though they were *shōen* from which the Tōji still collected some *nengu*, indicate that the Tōji's control was seriously threatened during the fifteenth century.

As demonstrated in the developments on the Tōji's *shōen*, only the *honke shiki* was rendered completely meaningless during the Nambokuchō period. Even so, viable control was maintained only on those *shōen* that were part of the temple's core holdings. There were exceptions, of course, in the rate of decline in *shōen* control. The Zen religious establishments of Kyoto's *gozan* (literally, "five mountains," the temples at the apex of the Zen sect's official hierarchy), two of which were the Nanzenji and Shōkokuji, received special support from the Muromachi bakufu in the form of *shōen* donated as temple domain (*jiryō*). These donations to the Zen sect were part of the bakufu's plan to oppose the strong political influence of Hieizan which was traditionally connected to the courtier government. During time of financial crisis, the bakufu turned to these Zen temples and forced them to make donations from the income derived from the donated *shōen* which, in this manner, also served as bakufu domain (*chokkatsuryō*).[62] As a result, the *shōen* of the Zen temples were protected from outside aggression through their relationship with the

61 *Ōyama son-shi*, hombun hen (Tokyo: Hanawa shobō, 1964), p. 199.
62 Concerning the economic ties between the bakufu and Zen temples, see Imatani Akira, *Sengokuki no Muromachi bakufu*, vol. 12 (Tokyo: Kadokawa shoten, 1975), pp. 11–18.

bakufu. But the Tōji, which did not have such a relationship with the bakufu, was not protected in this way.

Even *shōen* that were part of the shogun's domain, however, suffered intrusion by the local *kokujin* and *shugo* during the fifteenth century. The course of decline differed greatly by region. In eastern Japan, for example, the power of the local notables (*zaichi ryōshu*) made it impossible for the *shōen* proprietors to retain administrative control over the *shōen*, even in the Kamakura period. In the provinces around the capital, however, *shōen* continued to survive even into the fifteenth century. Proximity to the capital alone did not guarantee security. Control depended on whether the *shōen* was under the proprietorship of a religious establishment or a noble family and whether or not the *shōen* was the most important part of the proprietor's, such as the Tōji's, holdings. Generally, those *shōen* holders who made the transition from holding only a part of the multilayered *shiki* rights in geographically scattered *shōen* to those holding most of the *shiki* rights in *shōen* located in geographical proximity succeeded in retaining at least a part of their authority over their holdings and continued to receive some income from them.

The ukeoi daikan *system*

As the power of the *shugo* and *kokujin* increased during the fifteenth century, so did their control over the *shōen*. It became more difficult for the *shōen* proprietors to exert their personal authority over the *shōen*, and the *shiki* structure was rendered meaningless. In response to these worsening conditions, the *shōen* proprietors chose "contract stewards" (*ukeoi daikan*) to represent their interests on the *shōen*. These stewards worked outside the *shiki* structure and were chosen for their special talents such as the ability to negotiate with the *shugo* or *kokujin* or for their contacts with bakufu officials who often received money for their sympathetic attention. Basically, *ukeoi daikan* were collectors of *nengu* who differed from the *shugo* and *kokujin ukesho* discussed earlier.

Frequently, a monk from a Zen temple or Hieizan would be chosen to act as an *ukeoi daikan*. This practice may seem somewhat strange, but many monks of the religious establishments of this period were skilled in the conduct of economic affairs. Those with a Hieizan link often managed storehouses which also acted as pawn shops (*dosō*) in such places as Kyoto or Ōtsu, and among them were moneylenders.

In the Zen temples were men skilled in conducting both the *shōen*'s and the temple's financial affairs.[63] In addition to managing the temple's finances, they built up personal fortunes and often lent money to nobility and became *ukeoi daikan* on *shōen* held by the nobles. On the back of stationery used to record daily financial entries, a courtier named Madenokōji Tokiyoki, who became inner minister (*naidaijin*) in 1145, recorded loans made by a Zen monk, Genyū. According to this record, the monthly interest on the loans was as high as 8 percent.[64]

These financially inclined monks contracted the amount of *nengu* to be collected and, when appointed as *ukeoi daikan*, decided when it was to be delivered to the *shōen* proprietor. They customarily took 20 percent of the contracted *nengu* as their own profit. After the contract was drawn up, the *daikan* went to the *shōen* and negotiated with the *shugo* and *kokujin* to collect the *nengu* which was then sold to local merchants for cash and the *shōen* proprietor was paid his share.[65]

When using this method of tax collection, the *shōen* proprietor depended completely on the *daikan*'s services for the collection of the *nengu* and the receipt of his share in cash. His share depended primarily on whether the *daikan* honored the contract and his effectiveness at collecting the *nengu*. If the contract was broken, the proprietor's only recourse was to replace the *daikan* or, abandoning the *ukeoi* method, to manage the *shōen* directly. The latter option, however, differed little from the *ukeoi daikan* method, as the *shōen* proprietor still had to send an individual to negotiate with the *shugo* or *kokujin*.

As the *shōen* proprietors lost power and *nengu* receipts began to fall, both the nobility and the religious establishments turned to moneylenders. Typically this meant that the proprietor mortgaged the *shōen*, using the following year's *nengu* as collateral. Because the *shugo*'s and the *kokujin*'s intrusion into the *shōen* was not yet complete, both the proprietor and the moneylender expected to be able to collect the *nengu*. Even so, the moneylender did not wait passively, hoping that the *shōen* proprietor would collect the *nengu* and pay back the debt he owed to the moneylender. In cases in which payment was not forthcoming, the moneylenders themselves did their best to the collect the *nengu* from the mortgaged *shōen*. In one case, an influential Kyoto shrine, Kamo, had a long-standing financial relationship with a money-

---

63 Ibid., pp. 47–60.
64 Nitta Hideharu, "Muromachi jidai no kuge-ryō ni okeru daikan ukeoi ni kansuru ichi kōsatsu," in Hōgetsu Keigo sensei kanreki kinenkai, ed., *Nihon shakai keizaishi kenkyū*, medieval vol. (Tokyo: Yoshikawa kōbunkan, 1967).
65 The proprietors typically lived in Kyoto ; thus, this *ukeoi* was often known as *kyōsai*, meaning to be paid at the capital, or Kyoto.

lender named Yasui. Near the end of the fifteenth century, the Kamo Shrine mortgaged its Tsuchida-no-shō in Noto Province. One result was that Yasui became the *daikan* on the *shōen* and collected the *nengu* negotiated with the *shugo*.[66]

Warriors also became *ukeoi daikan*. In 1401, a *kokujin* named Niimi Kiyonao, a retainer of the Hosokawa *shugo*, contracted for 60 *kanmon* of the income that the proprietor was to receive in Kyoto from Niimi-no-shō, a holding of the Tōji.[67] The *ryōke*'s share of the *nengu* had previously been 370 *kanmon*. The *kokujin*, therefore, had reduced the *ryōke*'s share to only 60 *kanmon*, from 185 *kanmon*: 370 *kanmon* minus 185 *kanmon* which had been lost as *hanzei* to the *shugo*. The Tōji repeatedly had problems with warrior *daikan* and frequently dismissed them. For example, over the twenty years from 1441 to 1460, a retainer of the Hosokawa named Yasutomi Tokiyasu, who became *daikan*, failed to deliver most of the 150 *kanmon* contracted per year. The records show that he delivered only 791 *kanmon* over the twenty years out of the 3,000 *kanmon* (150 times 20) that the proprietor was to receive under the contract.[68] The *ukeoi daikan* here was a warrior; neither monks nor moneylenders were involved.

The *ukeoi daikan* system, as a method of *nengu* collection that replaced the eroding *shiki* structure in the fifteenth century, was the last attempt of the *shōen* proprietors to stave off the inevitable. The monks, moneylenders, and warriors, in their role as *ukeoi daikan*, further threatened the *shōen* proprietors' authority and income.

The daimyo domainal system and the *shōen*

The *shōen* system was further undermined by the eleven years of the Ōnin War (1467–77). The power of the bakufu was undercut amidst the fighting which originated over a succession dispute within the Ashikaga family and also one involving such powerful *kanrei* (shogunal deputy) houses as the Shiba and Hatakeyama. Even the powerful *shugo* daimyo proved unable to control the seditious actions of the *shugo-dai* and *kokujin* in their domains. In order to weather the storm, the *shugo* daimyo left Kyoto and returned to their respective provinces, pouring their energies into strengthening their military power.

Several political and social developments marked the period follow-

---

66 See Suma, "Dosō ni yoru shōen nengu no ukeoi ni tsuite"; and Suma, "Dosō no tochi shuseki to tokusei."
67 *Niimi-no-shō ryōke-kata shomu-shiki buninjō*, 1401, *yu* 14–21, in *Tōji hyakugō monjo*.
68 *Niimi-no-shō nengu mishin chūmon*, 1461, *kei* 16–24, in *Tōji hyakugō monjo*.

ing the Ōnin War. The *shugo* daimyo divorced themselves from the bakufu structure and attempted to emerge as powerful, independent *sengoku* daimyo. Some *kokujin ryōshu* emerged from the chaos of the Ōnin period as regional overlords who succeeded in making vassals of many of their *kokujin* peers and rose as *sengoku* daimyo. Regional leagues composed of *kokujin, jizamurai*, and cultivators were formed, as in Kaga Province, which were called *ikko-shu*. These organizations were united by an underlying religious belief that fueled their resistance to the *shugo*. In short, various paths were taken in pursuit of the goal of regional control.

Even though the paths chosen were diverse, they all undermined the *shōen* system of land proprietorship. The *sengoku* daimyo, the center of the new trend toward regional control, attempted to organize as many *kokujin* and *jizamurai* as possible into their feudal retainer organizations. In order to determine the amount of military service (*gunyaku*) owned by each retainer, many *sengoku* daimyo used a method whereby the retainer's fief (*chigyō*) was expressed in *kandaka*.[69] *Kandaka* – an amount of cash expressed in *kanmon* – was a means of designating the *nengu* imposed on agricultural land; the retainer's military obligation was also based on this figure.

The *sengoku* daimyo consequently attempted to assign as high a *kandaka* figure as possible to the retainers' land. The retainers, along with the *shōen* proprietors, resisted this drive by the *sengoku* daimyo toward comprehensive control of the region. The daimyo, in an attempt to establish a hierarchical system of land control in which their superior political authority would be based on the right to grant fief, conducted cadastral surveys of the lands of the *kokujin* and religious establishments. At the village level, the daimyos' surveys established a new *nengu* unifying the old *nengu* and the *kajishi* into a single tax. In those cases in which a wealthy cultivator's right to continue to collect *kajishi* was recognized, it was granted by the daimyo as benefice land (*kyūon*). In return, such cultivators were organized into the bottom segment of the daimyo's retainer band and were known as *gunyakushū*.[70] In addition, uncultivated land came under the aegis of the daimyo. New fields that resulted from land development became the daimyo's personal domain (*chokkatsuryō*), even if the fields were

---

69 Concerning the *kandaka* system, see Nagahara Keiji, "Daimyō ryōgokuseika no kandakasei," in Nagahara Keiji, John Whitney Hall, and Kozo Yamamura, eds., *Sengoku jidai* (Tokyo: Yoshikawa kōbunkan, 1978), pp. 1–21.
70 Katsumata Shizuo, "Sengoku daimyō kenchi no shikō gensoku," in Katsumata, *Sengoku-hō seiritsu shiron*, pp. 199–232.

located in the retainer's fief. These new fields, in turn, served as a new supply of land with which to grant fief.[71]

These surveys were not carried out systematically, as most daimyo did not have sufficient power to intrude their own survey teams onto lands held fief by their vassals or by powerful religious proprietors. There was, however, a significant variation in the success of these surveys. In eastern Japan where the *shōen* system had all but collapsed, *sengoku* daimyo such as the Gohōjō, Takeda, and Imagawa thrived. These daimyo conducted comprehensive cadastral surveys and imposed their control throughout the entire domain. In western Japan, however, daimyo such as the Mōri of Aki Province found it much more difficult to conduct such surveys. *Kokujin* in the Mōri domain managed to maintain a relatively high degree of independence, and furthermore, the *shōen* proprietors' rights had not been totally eradicated.[72]

In the central provinces where the *shōen* system was most strongly rooted, *shōen* continued to survive even into the civil war of the sixteenth century. In many cases, warrior *jitō shiki* had not been established on these *shōen*, and the *shōen* proprietors maintained direct control of the *shōen* throughout the medieval period. Even in those cases in which local notables were present, they often were organized into samurai status in service of a religious establishment or noble who continued to hold *shōen* in these provinces. Thus daimyo such as the Rokkaku of southern Ōmi, Matsunaga of Yamato, and Miyoshi of Settsu tried to established a daimyo domainal system on the order of their stronger eastern counterparts but proved incapable of developing a sufficiently durable foundation.[73] Consequently, the *shōen* in central Japan stubbornly persisted.

The *sengoku* daimyos' acquisition of comprehensive political authority in their domains struck hard at the *shōen* system. This development encountered important regional variations connected with the health of the *shōen* in the area concerned. Despite the rise of the daimyo domainal system in the sixteenth century, *shōen* continued to exist in some form.

The rise of the *sengoku* daimyo not only struck at the proprietary

71 Nagahara Keiji, "Daimyō ryōgokusei no kōzō," in *Iwanami kōza Nihon rekishi*, vol. 8 (Tokyo: Iwanami shoten, 1976), pp. 211–60.
72 Matsuoka Hisato, "Saigoku no sengoku daimyō," in Nagahara, Hall, and Yamamura, eds., *Sengoku jidai*, pp. 22–48.
73 For a discussion of the *sengoku* daimyo Rokkaku of Ōmi Province, see Katsumata Shizuo, "Rokkaku-shi shikimoku no shomu rippō," in Katsumata, *Sengoku-hō seiritsu shiron*, pp. 153–74.

rights of the *shōen* system but also undermined its social and economic foundations, as seen in their organizations of craftsmen and their control of markets.[74] Under the *shōen* system, the markets' administration was under the firm control of the religious establishment or *zaichi ryōshu*. During the fourteenth and fifteenth centuries, there was a strong movement toward the local control of the markets in the hands of the *kokujin* or temples. The *sengoku* daimyo, on the other hand, established markets at locations under their direct control, such as the main and satellite castles. By inviting merchants to the domain and assuring them of market activities free of various restraints, the daimyo undermined the local control of the markets by the *kokujin* and religious establishments. Furthermore, the daimyo granted exemptions from trade imposts in order to attract merchants from other areas of the country. In this way, merchants gradually came under the control of the daimyo.

Similar developments occurred with regard to craftsmen. Under the *shōen* system, craftsmen were granted benefice land by the *shōen* proprietors as a means to both protect and control them. This benefice land system, however, declined along with the *shōen* system in the fourteenth and fifteenth centuries, and craftsmen became more independent. In contrast, the *sengoku* daimyo granted fief to the foremen of the various crafts, making them vassals who then controlled the rest of the domain's craftsmen. Rather than grant them an exemption from the payment of *nengu*, the daimyo required the craftsmen to deliver a fixed amount of their specialty goods. As in their control over the land, the *sengoku* daimyo exceeded the authority achieved by the *shōen* proprietors and *kokujin* over the merchants and craftsmen – the daimyo achieved direct control over their actions throughout the domain. Consequently, the self-sufficient *shōen* or land held by *kokujin* was replaced by the daimyo domain, which became a single, self-contained economic unit. This meant that the *shōen* lost their capacity for survival under the daimyo domain system in all respects: the right to administer, land ownership, and market control.

CONCLUSION: THE DISAPPEARANCE OF THE *SHŌEN*

The waning of the *shōen* system advanced in several stages between the fourteenth and sixteenth centuries. The first stage was the beginning

---

74 Fujiki Hisashi, *Sengoku shakai shiron* (Tokyo: Tōkyō daigaku shuppanki, 1974); and Nagahara, "Daimyō ryōgokusei no kōzō."

of the decline of the *shōen* system during the Nambokuchō period. As a result of the conflict after the fall of the Kamakura bakufu, the civil government lost its political viability. It lost the ability to guarantee the scattered, hierarchical *shiki* rights of the *shōen*, and so the *honke shiki*, the pinnacle of this structure, became untenable. At the same time, local powers focused their authority on a single, contiguous piece of land and, in so doing, were transformed into *kokujin ryōshu* with independent control over the area. The *shugo* increased their judicial authority and land control while incorporating the *kokujin* and *jizamurai* into their vassal organization. The *shugo* developed a provincial system based on a feudal lord–vassal power structure, namely, the *shugo* domainal system (*ryōgokusei*).

The second stage proceeded from the political consolidation under Ashikaga Yoshimitsu at the end of the fourteenth century until the Ōnin War. During this period, the *shōen* system experienced a slight respite from the buffeting forces when the Muromachi bakufu adopted a protective policy toward the *shōen*. Despite this policy, the maintenance of the *shōen* system depended on the *ukeoi daikan* system and on the offices of the *shugo, kokujin,* and *dosō*. In this period the *shōen* proprietors lost their ability to administer the *shōen* independently. Furthermore, this period was notable for the appearance of agrarian protests supported by the development of the *sō-mura* and the social and economic growth of the *kobyakushō* class which further spurred the fall of the *shōen* system.

The third stage in the decline of the *shōen* system was the period of civil war in the sixteenth century. The domainal system of the *sengoku* daimyo – the culmination of the *kokujin ryōshu* and *shugo ryōgoku* system – categorically suppressed the *shōen*. The *kandaka* system established by the *sengoku* daimyo was premised on the superiority of the daimyo's political rights throughout the domain. By means of this system, the daimyo implemented a unified measure for *nengu* and the correlation of *chigyō* to the amount of military service owed by the retainer. As a result, the daimyo succeeded in organizing the *kokujin* and *jizamurai* in their domains into a feudal lord–vassal structure.

The *shōen* system passed through these three stages, but there were, as mentioned, significant regional variations in the rate of decline. *Shōen* continued to exist even into the sixteenth century in the Kinai and neighboring provinces where noble and religious authority was most firmly rooted. Although in decline, the *shōen* of those areas resisted the onset of the daimyo domainal system of the Sengoku period. The death knell for these last surviving *shōen* was sounded by the cadastral surveys conducted by Hideyoshi (Taikō *kenchi*). Hideyoshi's surveys drew a curtain on the turbulence of the Sengoku period. Between 1582 and 1598, Hideyoshi conducted cadastral surveys throughout Japan. These surveys measured *nengu* and *chigyō* by a unified standard called *kokudaka* (an assessed base of *nengu* measured in rice). Along with the complete rejection of the collection of *kajishi* by the cultivating class, the surveys eliminated the *shōen* as a unit of land ownership.[75] Even the surviving *shōen* of the nobles and religious establishments in Yamashiro and Yamato provinces were eliminated. In exchange, their new holdings were assessed at a fixed amount of *kokudaka* somewhat lower than the previous amount.

Under the Taikō *kenchi*, the village became the lowest locus of control throughout the country. The village unit existed widely under the *shōen* system, but it was not the exclusive unit, as other administrative units such as *myō* and *gō* were also used. Hideyoshi's surveys completely rejected these other units and replaced them with the village and its functional social value as a rural community as the building block of control. As a result, the *shōen* was rejected as an element of control. In the case of Tara-no-shō in Wakasa Province, a single village community already existed on the *shōen*, which was more and more often referred to as Tara village. The practice of designating an area by the previous *shōen* name continued in some areas even into the Edo period, but this was strictly a popular, unofficial practice.

Hideyoshi's cadastral surveys were inextricably linked to the separation of warriors and cultivators (*heinō bunri*). *Heinō bunri* made a sharp distinction between warrior and peasant (*hyakushō*) status and required that all those of warrior status assemble at the daimyo's castle town. This policy brought an end to the *zaichi ryōshu* system, the hallmark of medieval society. Persons who served as retainers, even though originally of *hyakushō* status, were forced to choose either to remain in the village as *hyakushō* or to leave the village and move to the daimyo's castle town and become warriors. The separation of warrior and cultivator made it possible to establish a permanently mobilized army stationed at the castle and to assemble a ruling class based on centralized power. The emperor, nobility, and religious establishments were consequently pushed out of power, and at the same time, their economic and social foundation, the *shōen*, was eradicated.

75 For a discussion of the Taikō *kenchi*, see Araki Moriaki, *Taikō kenchi to kokudakasei* (Tokyo: Nihon hōsō shuppan kyokai, 1969); and Miyagawa Mitsuru, *Taikō kenchi ron* (Tokyo: Ochanomizu shobō, vol. 1, 1959; vol. 2, 1957; vol. 3, 1963).

CHAPTER 7

THE MEDIEVAL PEASANT

Historians generally date the medieval period in Japanese history as starting at the end of the twelfth century when the Kamakura bakufu was established, marking the emerging dominance of warrior government over aristocratic rule. In peasant history, however, the latter half of the eleventh or early twelfth century, however, is a more appropriate point of division between the ancient and medieval periods. The *shōen* system of land control had extended throughout Japan around that time, bringing entirely new conditions for the peasants and making them henceforth truly "medieval." The introduction and development of the *shōen* system had a much greater impact on the living conditions of peasants in Japan than did the founding of the Kamakura bakufu nearly a century later. The *shōen* system, therefore, is of great significance in peasant history and is the central defining characteristic of the medieval period.[1]

The momentous changes for the peasants brought about by the *shōen* system must be understood in the context of the earlier conditions pertaining to the land of the *ritsuryō* system in the eighth century. Under the *ritsuryō* system, the central government claimed ownership of all land; cultivators were allotted paddies on an equitable basis; and taxes were collected according to specific categories of goods; for example, grain, labor, and silk. But these conditions began to break down rapidly early in the tenth century and had disintegrated entirely by the time the *shōen* system had spread throughout Japan in the late eleventh and early twelfth centuries. Under the *shōen* system, the peasants exhibited characteristics different from those of the earlier *ritsuryō* system. For this reason, the medieval peasant I describe in this chapter can be regarded as simply the *shōen* peasant.

Similar to the controversy among scholars concerning the beginning

---

1 For a comprehensive discussion of the *shōen* system, see Amino Yoshihiko, "Shōen kōryōsei no keisei to kōzō," in Takeuchi Rizō, ed., *Tochi seidoshi*, vol. 1 (Tokyo: Yoshikawa kōbunkan, 1973), pp. 173–274; Nagahara Keiji, *Shōen* (Tokyo: Kōdansha, 1978); and Kudō Keiichi, "Shōensei no tenkai," in *Iwanami kōza Nihon rekishi*, vol. 5 (Tokyo: Iwanami shoten, 1975), pp. 251–98.

of the medieval period in Japan, the date marking the end of this period is also debated. Political historians designate 1573 as the beginning of the early modern period, the year Oda Nobunaga defeated Shogun Ashikaga Yoshiaki and destroyed the Muromachi bakufu. By this time, the *sengoku* daimyo had divided Japan into individual domains, but with Nobunaga's victory over Ashikaga Yoshiaki, the unification process began. Of more importance to the peasants, however, was Toyotomi Hideyoshi, Nobunaga's successor, who undertook to unify the country. In 1582, Hideyoshi ordered a national cadastral survey, the Taikō *kenchi*.[2] This comprehensive system of land registration completely revolutionized land administration and tenure practices in Japan and swept away all previous systems of landholding. I contend that this event and the changes it brought marked the end of the medieval period and the beginning of the early modern period for the peasants in Japan.

Although most scholars of peasant history agree that the medieval period began with the spread of the *shōen* system throughout Japan and ended with the Taikō *kenchi*, it would be an oversimplification to define the entire medieval period, spanning the early twelfth century to 1582, solely in terms of the *shōen* system and its effect on peasant life. For nearly five centuries, until the fall of the Kamakura bakufu in 1333, the *shōen* system was remarkably stable. During the Nambokuchō period (1336–92), however, the *shōen* order began to break down, and in the subsequent Muromachi and Sengoku periods, territorial rule was established by a class of independent local overlords (*ryōshu*) who began by serving as *jitō* (military estate stewards) and *shōen* officials within the *shōen* system. At the same time, the *shugo* (provincial military governor) in each province consolidated their control as military and civil authorities over these local overlords. These developments in territorial control culminated in the emergence of the *shugo* daimyo in the fifteenth century and the *sengoku* daimyo in the following century. Therefore, the peasants of the latter half of the medieval period – the fourteenth through the sixteenth centuries – are defined less by the *shōen* system than by the territorial authority system built up by these local overlords. Agricultural productivity increased dramatically in the second half of the medieval period, providing the economic foundation on which to base territorial rule. For this reason, the study of the medieval peasant must consider, in addition to the *shōen* system and its effects on the peasant, the later system

2 For a more complete description of the Taikō *kenchi*, see Araki Moriaki, *Taikō kenchi to kokudakasei* (Tokyo: Nihon hōsō shuppankyokai, 1969).

of territorial control, which took its most mature form as the daimyo *ryōgoku* system of the Sengoku period.

Even in the early medieval period there were local overlords. They were closely tied to the *shōen* system, however, as *jitō* or officials. Thus, although there were clear distinctions between the authority systems of the early and late medieval period, there was also continuity in that a local overlord system existed throughout the entire period, if at greatly different levels of development. The life of the peasants was defined by the continuities and changes in the authority systems of the medieval period.

Variations in medieval peasant life can be attributed not only to these changes during the medieval period but to geographical location as well. Agricultural productivity in the central Kinai area was considerably higher than in the peripheral areas in eastern Japan and Kyushu, implying a higher standard of living for the peasants of this region. Proximity to large cities, Kyoto and Nara in particular, also played a role, in that residing near these cities enriched the lives of the peasants both economically and culturally. The life of the peasants in the Kinai region, therefore, differed dramatically from that of those in eastern Japan or Kyushu.

With these variations in mind, I shall portray the medieval peasants mainly as they existed under the *shōen* system in the central Kinai region. The development of the *shōen* system in this region was stable and, therefore, the most appropriate setting for a study of peasant activities. I shall also consider regional differences within the peasant class, as well as changes during the medieval period.

STATUS DIFFERENCES AMONG PEASANTS IN THE *SHŌEN* SYSTEM

The shōen *as a place to live*

The first *shōen* emerged in the mid-eighth century, chiefly in the form of newly opened lands that aristocratic families and the religious establishment developed with the assistance of the state. A grain tax on these lands had to be submitted to the central government, but possession of the land itself was recognized as a private right. By contrast, the *shōen* that spread throughout Japan in the eleventh and twelfth centuries – the so-called commended *shōen* – were lands opened by prominent local families who then commended them to aristocrats or great religious establishments. It was common practice not only to commend such newly opened lands but also to divide up and absorb into the *shōen* the adjacent vast holdings of the provincial office – land still subject to public taxation. Therefore, both cultivated fields and uplands and peasant settlements were part of the commended *shōen*, creating a contained, comprehensive environment for daily life. The well-known Tara-no-shō of Wakasa Province under the Tōji's proprietorship was located in a mountainous area and included thirty-two *chō* of cultivated land, uplands, and a fairly contained community.[3] Ota *shōen*, a Kōyasan holding in Bingo Province, included the eastern half of Sera District and comprised six hundred *chō* of paddy land, over ten communities, and extensive uplands.[4] Although the early *shōen* were simply privately owned cultivated fields, by the eleventh and twelfth centuries, commended *shōen* constituted an all-inclusive setting for medieval peasant life.

In nearly all cases, *shōen* proprietors were high-ranking aristocrats or representatives of powerful temples and shrines in Kyoto or Nara. These proprietors held rights to numerous *shōen* scattered throughout Japan and collected taxes from them with which to support themselves. Taxes took the form of rice (*nengu*) and miscellaneous dues in the form of nonrice products and labor (*zōkuji*). The actual administration of individual *shōen* was left to local *shōen* officials. Most local *shōen* officials were members of prominent local families who owned their own land and often had held the rank of subdistrict head on the lands of the provincial office before the establishment of the *shōen*. Although they often commended their privately held land to aristocrats or religious establishments, these local officials converted into *shōen* the land of the provincial office on which they held official posts, and they themselves became *shōen* managers responsible for administering *shōen* affairs and consolidated their power in the area. *Shōen* were thus established within the local power structure and, through high-level aristocratic or religious patronage, avoided taxation by the provincial office.

The central layout of a typical *shōen* is represented by concentric circles in Figure 7.1. Section A includes the house and the land immediately surrounding (usually two or three *chō*) belonging to the local *shōen* official. These immediate lands included dry and wet fields and

3 For more information on Tara-no-shō, see Amino Yoshihiko, *Chūsei shōen no yōsō* (Tokyo: Tachibana shobō, 1966); and Kozo Yamamura, "Tara in Transition: A Study of a Kamakura *Shōen*," *Journal of Japanese Studies* 7 (Summer 1981): 349–91.
4 For more information on Ōta-no-shō, see Kawane Yoshihira, "Heian makki no zaichi ryōshusei ni tsuite," in *Chūsei hōkensei seiritsu shiron* (Tokyo: Tōkyō daigaku shuppankai, 1971), pp. 121–52.

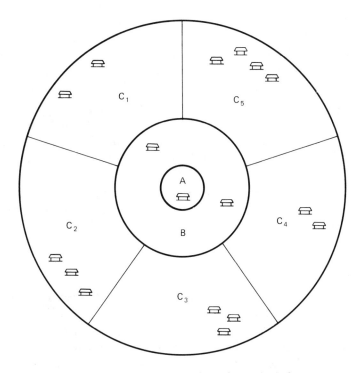

Figure 7.1 Conceptualization of a typical *shōen*

were usually surrounded by a moat or earthen embankment. They were exempt from the taxes exacted by the central proprietor and were cultivated by *genin* (lowly people). The *shōen* official, as well, held allotted fields that were also tax exempt and cultivated by peasants. These privately held lands varied greatly in size, depending on the official's real power, but most were larger than the lands immediately surrounding his house.

Section B includes the *shōen* official's allotted *myō* and miscellaneous exempt lands; both were subject to *nengu* but not *zōkuji*. The size of this section also varied, depending on the official's power; large ones were some tens of *chō* or more. These allotments were not necessarily concentrated in one geographical location. The miscellaneous exempt lands were privately developed holdings and the base of the *shōen*. The peasants who lived in this section were called *zōmenbyakushō* (cultivators of miscellaneous exempt lands) and *menke* (exempt households), to distinguish them from other cultivators. These cultivators were obligated to pay dues in kind (*zōkuji*), including labor, to the *shōen* official.

Section C comprises the core of the *shōen*. Originally part of the public lands of the provincial office before the establishment of the *shōen*, these lands were brought under the direct control of the *shōen* proprietor. This section was usually divided into one to five communities (denoted C_1 through C_5 in Figure 7.1). The peasants living on these lands were required to submit both *nengu* and *zōkuji* to the *shōen* proprietor. Although they were not privately subordinate to the local official but, rather, directly under the control of the *shōen* proprietor, it was within the local official's authority to oversee the land and peasants of Section C.

The *shōen* was home not only to the local official and peasants but also to the artisans, craftsmen, and merchants who submitted their commodities as taxes. Grant lands were set aside for these people, and each plot was designated by function; for example, pottery, leather goods, carpentry, metalwork, and boat transportation. The craftsmen supported by these lands did not necessarily live on the *shōen* but might live elsewhere and produce goods for the *shōen* in return for income from these lands. Markets served as places of exchange on the *shōen* and on large *shōen* were held on prescribed days each month. Through these grant lands and markets, the *shōen* acquired the commodities it did not produce. It is clear that *shōen* were not self-sufficient and that the division of labor was quite advanced.[5]

Status subdivisions of the peasantry

The peasants living on the *shōen* were divided into subgroups based on a complicated status system. These subgroups included *myōshu, kobyakushō, zōmenbyakushō, mōto,* and *genin,* each indicating the group's relative degree of freedom or subordination. These status levels reflected the great economic variation within the peasant class and the various rights of the peasants and the duties they owed to the *shōen* proprietor and local official.

Myōshu were powerful peasants who held much of the cultivated land in Section C of the *shōen*. The proprietor divided this land into *myōden* (the basic unit of land on which the yearly tax was calculated, also called *hyakushōmyō*), consisting of one or two *chō* or sometimes more. The *myōshu* had to submit a tax on each *myōden*. For example, the Tōji's Tara-no-shō in Wakasa Province had six *myōden* on a total of thirty-two

---

5 Concerning the problems surrounding markets and craftsmen on *shōen*, see Sasaki Ginya, *Shōen no shōgyō* (Tokyo: Yoshikawa kōbunkan, 1964).

chō of arable land, and the Tōji's Kamikuze-no-shō in Yamashiro Province had thirteen *myōden* on a total of about sixty *chō* of cultivated land. Most of the *myōden* were lands held by *myōshu*, but some were held by other peasants. For convenience in tax collection, however, the proprietor often consolidated the individual peasant-held lands into a single *myōden* and appointed a prominent peasant as *myōshū*. In this sense, *myōshu* were similar to low-ranking officials in the *shōen* administrative organization. But primarily, *myōshu* were powerful peasants administering their own lands, part of which were cultivated by other peasants.

Kobyakushō were small cultivators living in Section C of the *shōen*. In addition to the *myōden*, the *shōen*'s cultivable land was organized into *isshikiden*, land from which only *nengu* was exacted, but at a relatively high rate. As wet paddy land exempt from *zōkuji*, these lands were under the proprietor's direct administration. The actual labor on *isshikiden* was provided mostly by small cultivators who also worked part of the *myōden*. Compared with the *myōshu*, these cultivators had little economic power, and because their ownership rights to *isshikiden* were not guaranteed, their financial condition was precarious. Small cultivators generally outnumbered *myōshu*, as evidenced by Kamikuze-no-shō southwest of Kyoto. This *shōen* was divided into thirteen *myō* but in the mid-fourteenth century had fifty-two households. In the mid-fourteenth century, Tara-no-shō had six *myōshu* households out of a total of fifty, the remaining belonging to small cultivators. *Kobyakushō* were weak compared with *myōshu*, insofar as rights over land or agricultural administration were concerned, but they shared with the *myōshu* the status of *hyakushō*, peasants directly subordinate to the *shōen* proprietor.[6]

Zōmenbyakushō lived on and cultivated the exempted lands of Section B of the *shōen* allotted to the *shōen* official. These peasants were also called *menke no genin*, or lowly people of exempted households. They were obligated to submit *zōkuji* to the *shōen* official and were directly subordinate to him and not to the proprietor. *Zōmenbyakushō* were not so numerous as *myōshu* or small cultivators, amounting at most to only a few households on each *shōen*. In the late twelfth century, an official on Koyasan's Ota-no-shō in Bingo Province was chastised by the proprietor for using questionable methods to increase the number of *zōmenbyakushō* under his direct jurisdiction. In attempt to justify the increased number of *zōmenbyakushō*, this official stated that these cultivators consisted of "lowly people" and were "exempted

6 On some *shōen*, this *hyakushō* status was referred to as *heiminbyakushō*.

households for free use, morning and night." In other words, the official freely imposed taxes in goods and labor on them and considered them his own personal subordinates. Ordinarily, peasants of exempted households could be used by the *shōen* official as personal subordinates only with the proprietor's permission. Thus, *genin* rather than *hyakushō* best expresses the status of such peasants.

The peasants' subordinate character was especially evident in peripheral areas in eastern Japan and Kyushu. In these remote areas, powerful peasants did not become *myōshu*. Instead, the higher-ranking local *shōen* official designated as one *myō*, the area over which his own control extended, and himself became the *myōshu*. In such cases the *myō* – the land unit under *myōshu* control – was subject to taxation (*nengu*) but was exempt from *zōkuji*. The *zōkuji* collected from peasants living on the *myō* was kept by the *shōen* official himself. In other words, for the *myōshu*, the *myō* was entirely tax exempt. In that respect, the peasants living on the *myō* were strongly and personally subordinate to the *myōshu*. This type of *myō* is distinct from *hyakushōmyō* or proprietor *myō*, from which *zōkuji* was submitted to the proprietor. The peasants' subordination to local officials in peripheral areas was widespread, and proprietors unable to oversee administration directly had no choice but to recognize that fact.[7]

Myōshu, *kobyakushō*, *zōmenbyakushō* and *menke no genin* differed in degree of administrative control and subordination, but all were clearly sedentary peasants. By contrast, the fourth level of peasant, the *mōto*, were transients whose relations with the ruling class were not clearly defined. *Mōto* did not necessarily remain on any one *shōen;* those who did were unusual. In documents concerning Tara-no-shō there is a reference to "a *mōto* who arrived yesterday or today," implying that he had drifted in from another place or had not lived there for long.[8] The *mōto* had probably settled on a *shōen* at one time, living in a hut, developing a bit of wasteland, and making ends meet by working for a well-to-do peasant family. Such *mōto* were most likely disdained by the sedentary peasants. For example, on Tara-no-shō, a *mōto* was arraigned by the *jitō* for taking in a beggar who had wandered into the *shōen* and stolen from the residents.[9] From this it can be surmised that *mōto* were similar to beggars and were similarly despised.

7 For more information on the *myō* of remote areas, see Nagahara Keiji, *Nihon hōkensei seiritsu katei no kenkyū* (Tokyo: Iwanami shoten, 1961), pp. 243–62.
8 Amino, *Chūsei shōen no yōsō*, pp. 76–79.
9 Beggars (*kojiki*) were a despised group in medieval Japan. See Nagahara Keiji, "Fuyū na kōjiki," in *Nihon chūsei shakai kōzō no kenkyū* (Tokyo: Iwanami shoten, 1973), pp. 280–3.

STATUS DIFFERENCES AMONG PEASANTS 309

In the case of famine or natural disaster, when cultivation was
difficult if not impossible, transients were not an unusual phenomenon. Faced with bleak prospects for the future, many were forced
to move on to another place and settle down for a time in a corner
of a community, appealing to various connections and human sympa-
thies. Whether or not the term *mōto* was used uniformly throughout
Japan, it is evident that temporary residents of agricultural communities who were neither vagabonds nor sedentary were probably
quite common.

Genin occupied the bottom level of the peasant class and had no
independent control over land. These peasants served *shōen* officials as
well as *myōshu*. Household bequests of *shōen* officials indicate that
genin were inherited as part of the estate. *Genin* of either sex were often
bought and separated from their parents while still children or were
sometimes left with their mother. Even when a husband and wife of
this status had children, they were not normally allowed to live as a
family unless they had been in service to a master for many years. In
such cases they would often be lent a small amount of land to support
their family, in addition to serving their master.

The life of a *genin* could take a variety of forms, but they were
basically manual laborers of a master household. They were virtual
slaves and could be bought, sold, or inherited at their master's will.
Often they would escape. Although they could be treated as chattel,
they were not accumulated in great numbers of forced to work under
cruel conditions but, rather, were treated as part of the family in the
patriarchal system. It is not clear why most medieval *shōen* officials
and *myōshu* owned *genin*, but they were generally used for large-scale
agricultural work and land development.

These five categories constitute the major status divisions of the
medieval peasant class. In addition, there were *eta, hinin,* and *sanjo*, all
of whom suffered social discrimination.[10] *Eta* were primarily involved
in catching birds, disposing of animal carcasses, and making leather
goods – activities generally considered "unclean." *Hinin* were people
expelled from their communities for committing a crime. Neither
group can be included in the peasant class. *Sanjo* were involved in
transporting water or cleaning temples, shrines, or the residences of
aristocrats. They, too, strictly speaking, were not peasants. However,

10 On social discrimination in the medieval period, see Buraku mondai kenkyūjo, ed.,
Burakushi no kenkyū, premodern vol. (Kyoto: Kenkyūjo, 1978); and Keiji Nagahara, "The
Medieval Origins of the Eta-Hinin," *Journal of Japanese Studies* 5 (Summer 1979): 385–403.

these groups formed communities on the outskirts of villages and were often closely connected with village peasant life.

LAND DEVELOPMENT AND AGRICULTURAL OPERATIONS

Forms of land development

In the medieval period most of Japan, with the exception of the central Kinai region, was still undergoing land development. In the ancient period, the provincial and district offices of the *ritsuryō* estate organized large-scale projects using peasant labor as a form of tax to open paddy land on nearby level ground. The government maintained that this land was state owned because it was public (*kōden*), publicly irrigated (*kōsui*), and developed with state-organized labor (*kōkō*). Peasants were allotted parcels of paddy land but in return could be forced to participate in state land-opening activities. Powerful peasants often abandoned their public paddy land and opened their own lands in the mountainous back country. It was not difficult to maintain private rights to such lands, and in doing so, they easily avoided the labor demanded by the state. Tiny pockets of valley land tucked away among the hills were suitable for such individual development because water was readily available from springs and streams. This paddy land, called *yachida*, is found throughout Japan.

Leading peasant families chose land suitable for development near a water source in the valley, where the wind was light and there was no danger of flooding. Powerful peasants would gain control of the water source and then develop paddy lands, extending from the area nearest the water source deep in the valley to the level land below. They would also maintain dry fields in the hilly areas adjacent to the valley in order to supplement their diet by raising buckwheat and other grains besides rice. Even in the early *shōen* period, these valley paddy lands were not beyond the proprietor's reach but were organized into *myōden*, and leading peasant families were usually given the status of *myōshu*.

Local *shōen* officials undertook activities similar to the *myōshu*'s land opening, although they had access to more labor and capital. These officials developed large areas of land suitable for cultivation with the labor of peasants. These lands were then divided among the relatives in the area, and with the combined strength of the family group, the peasants were pressed into *zōmenbyakushō* status. On Kōyasan's Otano-shō in Bingo Province, the *shōen* official's exempted lands were generally in low, damp areas along a large river, whereas nearly all the *myōden* of ordinary peasants were *yachida* scattered throughout the valleys. *Shōen* officials most likely reclaimed the low, damp lands that had first been opened in the ancient period and had since fallen into neglect. These they designated as privately opened lands with exemption rights.

Both *yachida* – the paddies in the valleys – and the low-lying paddy land had their disadvantages. The *yachida*, dependent on local water sources, frequently suffered drought. The low-lying lands, on the other hand, were often flooded when the river overflowed its banks. Therefore, even though crops had been planted, in some years there was no harvest, and in especially bad years planting itself was impossible. Documents from this period contain expressions like *eifu* (former paddy land unusable for some time) and *nenfu* (land on which planting did not take place in that year).[11] The term *kata arashi* was used frequently to refer to infertile paddy land, part of which was left fallow.[12]

For these reasons, the dependability of developed, arable lands was important to the medieval peasant. On the central Kinai plain in Yamato and Yamashiro provinces, many reservoirs and irrigation and drainage ditches were built under the direction of the *ritsuryō* state or *shōen* proprietors. As a result, agricultural conditions in this area were particularly stable. In other areas, land-developing communities strove to make the water supply more dependable by pooling their resources to build irrigation ponds near springs in high and middle-lying areas to offset the water shortage on the flood plain at the foot of the valley. On the Tōji's Ota-no-shō in Tamba Province, the problem was solved by creating an irrigation pond to store water in the center of the valley. Even today an irrigation pond called Hoshi-maruike can be found there. It was built by peasants in the late thirteenth century to alleviate the water shortage problems of the lower portion of the valley.[13]

Land development began in earnest in the twelfth century in eastern Japan, the part of Japan slowest to develop. Here, the local warrior overlord class, with its strong ties to the provincial office, took a leading role. The Kantō plain was covered by natural forests, and small peasant communities were usually unable to clear it. The local

11 For a more detailed discussion of the low cultivation rate of arable land, see Nagahara Keiji, *Nihon no chūsei shakai* (Tokyo: Iwanami shoten, 1968), pp. 160–1.
12 For more discussion of the term *kata arashi*, see Toda Yoshimi, *Nihon ryōshusei seiritsushi no kenkyū* (Tokyo: Iwanami shoten, 1967), pp. 168–91.
13 Ōyama Kyōhei, *Nihon chūsei nōsonshi no kenkyū* (Tokyo: Iwanami shoten, 1978), pp. 231–87.

overlords adopted two approaches. They would develop paddy lands in the alluvial valleys of the plain and cut down forests to establish agricultural settlements. Most peasants were subordinate to the local overlord and were granted cultivation rights to the newly opened lands as members of the community. These warriors, who later became vassals of the Kamakura bakufu, were almost without exception the center of such land development communities.[14] Those peasants who became subordinate to these local developers could not establish independence as *myōshu*.

Local warrior overlords and powerful peasants were central to medieval land development and reclamation, although the actual labor was generally carried out by small communities of peasants. Medieval land-opening communities were quite different from early peasant society which was characterized by large-scale agricultural communities under one leader. These later medieval "communities" were hardly worthy of the name, generally being small villages of a few scattered cultivator households under the direction of a powerful peasant or local overlord. *Shōen* were an amalgamation of many small communities and were not in themselves organic groups. The *myōshu* at the center of each small community cooperated with the *shōen* official in punishing unlawful behavior on the *shōen*, but daily functions were for the most part carried out within the individual community.[15] Gradually, the peasants of these small communities became more independent and increased in number. As a result, community relations became more tightly knit. In the fourteenth century, village communities called *sōson* were formed, in which even the small cultivators had membership rights.

Agricultural operations and techniques

Because they had access to labor, the local overlords and powerful peasants were able to gain control of fertile, well-irrigated paddy land. As a result, their agricultural operations were generally stable and prosperous, unlike those of the small cultivators. The peasants' first obligation was to furnish labor to the local overlord and *myōshu*, in

---

14 The Miura family, which became a powerful vassal (*gokenin*) of the Kamakura bakufu, divided the entire Miura peninsula in Sagami Province among its members. They controlled the highly developed valley lands throughout the peninsula and continued the process of development. They often took place names as surnames, for example, Ashida, Ōwada, Wada, Nagai, and Nobi.

15 On the situation in small communities, see Nagahara Keiji, "Shōensei shihai to chūsei sonraku," in *Nihon chūsei shakai kōzō no kenkyū*, pp. 169–254.

return for which they could borrow food, seeds, and, in lean years, rice.

Wet paddy lands were very important to the agricultural operations of powerful peasants who were prosperous enough to use oxen for spring plowing. For weak, poor peasants, however, the wet paddy lands were of little consequence, and dry fields or *yakihata* were the most common form of cultivable land.[16] Wet paddy lands were developed using a compost of grass trampled by oxen and horses and cut grass containing saplings and young leaves. During the second half of the medieval period, they also discovered that the crop yield improved when ashes from burnt trees were used. The average yield of one *tan* of paddy land cannot be accurately estimated, but uplands generally yielded about one *koku*, two or three *to* of rice. Dry fields were usually planted with barley, and *yakihata* were usually planted with millet and buckwheat. Paddy land with much richer soil and higher productivity was planted with rice.

Various technological advances improved the agricultural output starting in about the second half of the thirteenth century. New and improved varieties of wetland rice were developed, and depending on the climate, even triple cropping was possible. Run-off ditches were built in both valley lands and moist lowlands. After the wetland rice was harvested, the water was drained off, and barley was planted as a second crop. Needless to say, the productivity of wet paddy lands increased with such concentrated usage.[17]

A variety of crops were planted in dry fields: grains such as barley and soybeans, vegetables, hemp, mulberry for sericulture, and the *perilla* plant. Until the mass production of cotton began in the sixteenth century, hemp was the most widely used fabric for clothing.[18] Sericulture, including removing the silk from cocoons and making silk floss and silk goods, was another endeavor of the peasants, although strictly a luxury line. Silk floss was referred to as *gofukumen* (dry goods cloth) and was taxed as *nengu* in many areas. The raising of cocoons was difficult because in some years disease killed all the silkworms.[19]

16 On *yakihata*, see Kuroda Hideo, "Chūsei no kaihatsu to shizen," in *Seikatsu, bunka, shisō*, vol. 4 of *Ikki* (Tokyo: Tōkyō daigaku shuppankai, 1981), pp. 91–130.
17 Double cropping was already being practiced in some areas by the end of the Heian period, but in the late Kamakura period the problem arose concerning whether *nengu* should be exacted in the form of barley, the second crop on wet paddy lands.
18 Echigo Province was noted for its hemp thread in the Muromachi period, and hemp cloth was one of its major products. The production of hemp, however, was not limited to Echigo but took place throughout Japan.
19 The *ritsuryō* government required that mulberry, along with lacquer trees, be cultivated in orchards and taxed the silk thread taken from the cocoons. In the medieval period, however,

Oil for lamps was increasingly produced as a commodity in the fourteenth century because of its expanding demand in the cities.[20]

In order to prepare dry fields for planting, wood was burned on top of the soil. Later, millet, buckwheat, and soybeans were sown. A single plot was planted for a period of two or three years before rotating to another plot. The first plot was then burned again in preparation for another planting. Because these lands were not under the proprietor's control and were outside the tax structure, such practices, believed to have been common in the medieval period, were rarely mentioned in *shōen* documents. Small and marginal cultivators (*kobyakushō* and *genin*) with families relied on these fields as a crucial source of food.

Medieval agriculture took place on a combination of wet paddy lands, dry fields, and *yakihata*. In addition to drought and flood damage, which was unavoidable given the peculiar characteristics of medieval cultivable land, insects and animals were also a frequent cause of crop damage. The worst, and unpreventable, insect damage was suffered when great swarms of locusts ate the water-planted rice seedlings. Sparrows ate rice seedlings, and wild boars and deer caused much damage as well. Devices such as clappers and deer fences were used to combat the problem, but these methods by no means eliminated the loss of crops caused by these animals.[21]

Such unpredictable catastrophes often destroyed small cultivators and *zōmenbyakushō*. On Kōyasan's Ategawa-no-shō in Kii Province, a 1246 document records that only one-sixth (three or four) of the households on the entire *shōen* were living with plenty, whereas untended, fallow *myō* numbered thirteen in the upper village and eight in the lower village.[22] In addition to being located on inferior mountain land, this *shōen* was cursed with an abusive *jitō* who engaged in illegal activities. At the same time, it provides a good illustration of the volatile agricultural conditions of the time. Peasants whose crops failed were called *mibiki* (literally, "thinning") and were often forced to sell themselves and their families and become *genin* of a local overlord or power-

mulberry was gathered mainly in the wild. It was again cultivated in orchards during the Edo period.
20 Starting in about the fourteenth century, the production and sale of the oil extracted from the *perilla* plant were a specialty in several areas of the central Kinai region, such as Ōyamazaki in Yamashiro Province, Yagi in Yamato, and Abiko in Settsu.
21 Locusts, birds, and leafhoppers (*unka*), a rice insect, caused great crop damage. In mountain fields where damage by boars and deer was great, deer fences made of bamboo and twigs were erected around the fields.
22 *Kōyasan monjo, vol. 6, Yūzoku hōkanshū*, no. 1433 (1276) in Shiryō hensanjo, ed., *Dai Nihon komonjo, iewake*, vol. 1, pt. 6 (Tokyo: Tōkyō teikoku daigaku, 1906), pp. 501–2.

ful *myōshu*. Or they might become transients and drift into lodgings for *hinin*. The unpredictability of agricultural conditions in the medieval village also created the peasant equivalent of *rōnin*, or "masterless samurai."

THE PEASANTS, OVERLORD RULE, AND TAXATION

Nengu, zōkuji, *and labor service*

The medieval peasant was required to submit two types of taxes to the *shōen* proprietor: *zōkuji* and *nengu*. *Zōkuji* is generally understood to include labor service (*buyaku*), in addition to miscellaneous dues on various nonrice products. To avoid confusion, *zōkuji* will be defined more narrowly here as additionally taxed products and separate from labor service. *Nengu*, on the other hand, was the tax paid by the *myōshu* to the proprietor on *myōden*, locally held rice fields constituting the major part of the shōen's cultivable land. The usual rate of taxation per *tan* of wet paddy land was three to five *to* of rice.[23] This form of taxation differed greatly from that of the *ritsuryō* system, in which peasants were taxed by categories of goods, and each *tan* of land was assessed a grain tax amounting to no more than 3 percent of its total yield.

The state depended on a tax on various products levied on individuals for income and on a labor tax called *zōyō*, about sixty days' service per year for adult males. The household registry system, however, declined along with the *ritsuryō* system, and the assessment and collection of taxes on individuals became impossible. Gradually, both labor taxes and taxes on goods came to be calculated according to the area of arable land. In addition, in the tenth century the provincial office renewed efforts to collect taxes in kind, especially in rice. As a result, the basis of taxation was changed from imposts estimated by categories of goods to miscellaneous labor and rice submitted to the officials. The latter, in most cases, amounted to three *to* of rice per *tan* of land. The labor tax came to encompass a wide variety of goods and services. The *shōen* system of taxation, including *nengu*, *zōkuji*, and *buyaku*, descended from this Heian system of taxation by the provincial office. This was a natural development, given that most *shōen* were created

---

23 One medieval *tan* was equivalent to 360 *bu* or about 12 *are*. (An *are*, a French unit of measure, is equal to 100 square meters.) In Hideyoshi's cadastral survey, 1 *tan* was redefined as equal to 300 *bu*; 1 *to* of rice is equal to about 15 kilograms.

when the lands of the provincial office were partitioned, and the overlord's right of control over the *shōen* evolved from the provincial governor's right of control over the province.

The *nengu* tax rate of three to five *to* of rice per *tan* of land probably comprised, on average, one-third to one-half of the assessed total yield, which was a rather high rate considering that yields were often reduced by natural disasters and other conditions. On the other hand, the land from which *nengu* was collected was by no means all the land under cultivation. The *shōen* proprietor formally recorded in his land registries the amount of cultivable land based on surveys. But in *shōen* documents, the phrase "land on which *nengu* is not assessed" appears frequently, suggesting that there were "hidden lands" whose entire yield went directly to the peasants. In addition, dry fields were not taxed comprehensively. The *ritsuryō* government considered dry fields to be an extension of immediate residential lands and, thus, were privately owned and not directly taxed. Given this precedent, the *shōen* proprietor could not be excessively strict about taxation in such areas. Under these circumstances, peasants of the *myōshu* class could make ends meet, even though the *nengu* rate was high. The life of the small cultivators, however, was difficult. For the most part, they worked land on which only *nengu* was collected, but at a relatively higher rate than *myōden* and usually amounted to seven or eight *to* per *tan*. Many small cultivators also worked part of a *myōden* and were therefore unable to avoid the labor tax. In addition, they were often required to perform private labor services for the *myōshu*.

In most cases *nengu* was collected in rice, but it could take the form of other products as well. For example, on *shōen* in eastern Japan, *nengu* was often exacted in silk or cotton. The reasons were both the paucity of paddy lands and the relatively undeveloped state of the eastern transportation routes, particularly the water routes, which made the transportation of heavy items like rice difficult. *Nengu* from *shōen* in the Inland Sea area often took the form of salt, marine products, or lumber. The form of *nengu* was often determined by the products of the particular region and by the condition of the transportation routes.

The *shōen* proprietor also collected income from *zōkuji*. In the Kamakura period, *zōkuji* on the Tōji's Oyama-no-shō in Tamba Province took a surprising number of forms, for example, vegetables, chestnuts, barrels, and oil. It differed from *nengu* in that anything from the village could be taxed, produce as well as finished goods, such as thread, fabric, and confections. Thus *zōkuji* consisted of important items of daily consumption exacted by the proprietor from his various *shōen*. From *shōen* on the Chōkōdō lands belonging to the imperial family, for example, products such as vegetables, fruit, saké, flowers used for dying, pine torches, and bamboo blinds were collected for the annual New Year's ceremonies.[24] The type of product demanded depended on such factors as the specialized product of the region, distance from the *shōen* to the capital, and the state of the transportation system. These products collected from individual *shōen* made the proprietor virtually self-sufficient. There were a variety of ways to apportion this burden on the peasants. A common method, called *myōbetsukuji*, was to collect *zōkuji* from each *myōden*, although this was a cumbersome method.

The typical *shōen* proprietor was an urban aristocrat who lived in the capital. He almost never lived on the *shōen* itself, nor did he demand large amounts of labor for operations on directly managed lands. One exception was land called *tsukuda*, found on *shōen* near the capital. *Tsukuda* were under the proprietor's direct control, although he did not generally manage them personally. Instead, he forced the peasants to cultivate them at a high *nengu* rate of one or two *koku* per *tan* of land. Normally, the proprietor did not require labor service of the peasants, but they were often required to transport *zōkuji* to his residence in the capital or to serve guard duty there on a rotating basis. According to the diary *Yamashina keraiki*, even in the early fifteenth century when the proprietor's authority was at its lowest, peasants from *shōen* in areas relatively near the capital, such as Settsu and Mino, took turns serving the proprietor at his Kyoto residence.[25]

Peasants also provided customary labor service. Peasants often accompanied *shōen* officials on extended stays in the capital and provided three-day service, which involved ministering to the needs of the proprietor's representative when he visited the *shōen*. But compared with the labor service exacted by *shōen* officials and *jitō*, the burden was not heavy.

In addition to the *nengu*, *zōkuji*, and labor demanded by the *shōen* proprietor, there were also exactions by *shōen* officials and *jitō*. As explained earlier, *shōen* officials were allotted paddies that were ex-

---

24 The Chōkōdō was a private chapel erected by the retired emperor Goshirakawa at his residence. Numerous *shōen* lands were subsequently attached to it. Most imperial *shōen* were of this type.
25 *Yamashina keraiki*, edited and annotated by Toyoda Takeshi and Iikura Harutake, 5 vols. (Tokyo: Zokugunsho ruijū kanseikai, 1967–73).

empt from the proprietor's *nengu* and *zōkuji*, as well as *myō* from which only *nengu* was required. *Shōen* officials also had the right to collect a set amount of income from the *shōen* as a whole. This included *kachōmai*, a tax in addition to *nengu*, amounting to about one-tenth of the *nengu*, or about three to five *shō* per *tan*. By comparison, there was a great deal of labor service required. As stated earlier, *shōen* officials were free to exploit *zōmenbyakushō*, and they could also exact a set amount of labor from the *myōshu* and peasants directly subordinate to the proprietor. A local official of the Kangiji's Wasa-no-shō in Kii Province demanded that *shōen* inhabitants provide agricultural labor ranging from spring planting to fall harvest, including plowing, weeding, cutting grass, and pounding the rice.[26] This labor service could be demanded "as needed."

With the establishment of the Kamakura bakufu, limits were set on the rights of *jitō* on a case-by-case basis, but generally they were determined by the limits established by those administering the *shōen* on behalf of the proprietors. In reality, however, because the *jitō* was a warrior, he could make oppressive labor demands. According to documents of 1238, the *jitō* of Sasakibe-no-shō, a holding of the Matsuno Shrine in Tamba Province, made the peasants serve him in a wide variety of ways. He forced the peasants to cultivate the land without giving them food or land in return; he used nine peasants daily as his servants; he made the peasants build his residence; and he requisitioned peasants to accompany him on a journey to the capital.[27] Because relations between *jitō* and peasants were strained by such demands, in 1262 the Kamakura bakufu ruled that although the *jitō*'s use of peasants for cultivation and farmwork could continue within the bounds of custom, during the three summer months (four to six months in the lunar calendar), peasant labor could not be used privately by the *jitō*.[28] In addition, *shōen* officials and *jitō* frequently collected various commodities resembling the *zōkuji* of the *shōen* proprietor. Therefore, small cultivators and *myōshu* under the proprietor's direct control were subject to two tiers of taxation, one by the proprietor and the other by the local *shōen* officials and *jitō*.

26 A 1327 income report by the recordkeeper (*kumon*) of Shimomura on Wasa-on-shō, in *Kangiji monjo*.
27 This 1238 account of a dispute between the *shōen* administrator (*zasshō*) and the *jitō* on Matsuno Shrine's Sasakibe-no-shō is found in *Higashi monjo*, vol. 1.
28 Kamakura bakufu supplementary law no. 424, in Satō Shin'ichi and Ikeuchi Yoshisuke, eds., *Chūsei hōsei shiryōshū*, vol. 1 (hereafter cited as *CHS*) (Tokyo: Iwanami shoten, 1955; reprinted 1978), p. 222.

Governance of shōen

The rule of the *shōen* proprietor over the peasants may be divided into three broad areas: collection of taxes, jurisdiction over land, and jurisdiction over criminal matters. The first category, the collection of taxes, has already been described. Taxes were originally collected by *shōen* officials, but once *jitō* were installed, they usually became the tax collectors.[29] The authority to collect taxes gave the *shōen* officials and *jitō* close personal control over the peasants. When peasants did not pay their taxes, the proprietor would exert various types of pressure – expressed as "delivering a reprimand" (*kenseki o kuwaeru*) – and if that did not produce results, he would physically restrain the defaulting peasant. This was known as "binding one's person" (*migara o karametoru*). In some cases, the *jitō* would make the delinquent cultivator his *genin*. The *jitō*, as tax collectors, applied physical restraint to *myōshu* as well as to small cultivators and restricted their freedom of movement. The peasants had previously had little freedom of movement anyway, but if taxation became too severe and official control too oppressive, they would often abscond. The *jitō* would then forbid such behavior and bind the peasants to the land, collecting taxes and labor by force. Because this was a major cause of conflict between *jitō* and peasant, the legal code of the Kamakura bakufu, the *goseibai shikimoku*, stipulated that once they had paid the *nengu*, peasants were to be allowed freedom of movement.[30]

The second area of proprietor rule, jurisdiction over land, refers to the right to administer the land within the *shōen*. The proprietor had the right to survey the cultivated land in the *shōen* in order to measure the area of land from which *nengu* would be exacted, reorganize locally held peasant lands, and reassign the lands of peasants who had fled.

Because jurisdiction over the land was an important component of the proprietor's control, once *jitō* were installed on *shōen*, severe conflicts arose between proprietor and *jitō* concerning this right. According to a 1247 decree of the Kamakura bakufu:

There are many conflicts in which *jitō* insist that though *nengu* must be submitted to the *shōen* proprietor from local lands of *shōen* officials and peasants, the right of jurisdiction over land is the *jitō*'s. Meanwhile, *shōen*

---

29 On the various limitations on *jitō* controlling *shōen*, see Yasuda Motohisa, *Jitō oyobi jitō ryōshusei no kenkyū* (Tokyo: Yamakawa shuppansha, 1961).
30 *Goseibai shikimoku*, art. 42, in *CHS*, pp. 24–26.

officials hold that the *jitō*'s allotment fields are under his jurisdiction but that lands in local possession (*myōden*) are under the *shōen* proprietor's. However, "originally appointed *jitō*" [those appointed to lands that had had *jitō* before the Jōkyū disturbance] must abide by the limitations set on their rights long ago, and "newly appointed *jitō*" are limited to one *chō* for every eleven *chō* as allotment fields.[31]

In this way the Kamakura bakufu attempted to restrain the *jitō*'s increasing power over land jurisdiction.

Such repeated clashes between *shōen* officials and *jitō* over matters of land jurisdiction, as well as over the right of jurisdiction in criminal matters, had a decisive effect on peasant control. These were, for instance, various ways to dispose of fields abandoned by absconding peasants. Such fields could be allotted to other peasants or absorbed into the *jitō*'s holdings. Or they might be given as *myō* to a so-called *rōnin*, someone who was not a regular resident of the *shōen*. Because the disposal of such land was based on the right of jurisdiction over land, the person who held this right had considerable authority. In 1185 Minamoto Yoritomo incurred the wrath of the aristocracy and the religious establishment when first reporting to the emperor the installation of *jitō*, he negotiated to be allowed to grant *jitō* the right of jurisdiction over land.[32] Throughout the Kamakura period, there was nothing uniformly regarded as embodying *jitō* authority, and so the importance of possessing the right of jurisdiction over land cannot be underestimated.

The right of jurisdiction in criminal matters, the third area of proprietor rule, combined police and judicial powers. This included the authority to take punitive action against *shōen* peasants who violated the law. In addition, it allowed the proprietor to enforce criminal sentences, including acquiring confiscated land and property for himself. According to contemporary law, in some cases the guilty party could be driven off the *shōen*, his land confiscated, and his dwelling destroyed. The right of acquiring confiscated land and property was recognized as belonging to the person who exercised the right of criminal jurisdiction. For this reason, there was intense rivalry among *shōen* officials and *jitō* for the right of criminal jurisdiction.

A Kamakura bakufu law of 1223 designated that items confiscated in a criminal case were to be divided between the *shōen* proprietor

---

31 Kamakura bakufu supplementary law no. 259, in *CHS*, p. 162.
32 The aristocrat Kūjo Kanezane of the regency house expresses his surprise over this matter in his diary, *Gyokuyō:* "Not only will they impose a military rice tax, but they will also gain complete control over the land."

and the *jitō*, with the former receiving two-thirds and the latter one-third.[33] The *jitō*, however, attempted to take over by force the entire right of criminal jurisdiction. When a peasant defaulted on taxes and absconded, the wife and children left behind were made *genin*. Even in the case of a very small theft, a large penalty was often imposed. There were many cases of penalties of unprecedented severity. In Yamada and Befu villages in the Taniyama District of Satsuma Province in 1300, the *jitō* and district head clashed over peasant control. The *jitō* invoked the right of criminal jurisdiction in forty-one separate, minor incidents involving peasants, such as stealing potatoes, committing slander, killing dogs, and stealing horses. He seized the culprits, their wives, and children and exacted overly harsh penalties.[34] Such extreme enforcement of the right of criminal jurisdiction by the *jitō* was denounced by the peasants and *shōen* oficials as "new and illegal practices" or unprecedented, illegal acts. By applying such pressure, the *jitō* was attempting to gain direct and personal control over the peasants.

Jitō and *shōen* officials competed for control of the peasants in all three of the areas discussed: the collection of taxes and jurisdiction over land and criminal matters. The *jitō* attempted to monopolize local control over the *shōen*'s land and peasants; the *shōen* officials tried to prevent the private subordination of the peasants to the *jitō;* and the peasants were caught in the middle of this conflict.

Peasant resistance

Control over peasants in the *shōen* system was divided between the proprietor, in his ability to collect all the taxes, and the local *shōen* officials and *jitō*, in their jurisdiction over land and criminal matters. In the fourteenth century, the peasants began to demand a reduction in, or even an exemption from, *nengu*. On *shōen* near Kyoto, in many cases even the local *shōen* officials united with the peasants to press these demands on the proprietor. However, at this point the *shōen* system itself had begun to decline amidst antiproprietor movements led by *shōen* officials in league with *shugo*. Demands for reductions or exemptions from taxes were due less to the peasants' inability to pay them than to their desire to deny the proprietor's right to collect them.

---

33 Kamakura bakufu supplementary law no. 14, in *CHS*, p. 66.
34 The judicial decree of 1300 of the Kyushu office of the Kamakura bakufu is found in *Yamada monjo*.

In the twelfth and thirteenth centuries, by contrast, there were virtually no peasant movements demanding tax relief from the proprietor. Rather, the peasants' dissatisfaction and resistance were turned against the arbitrary rule of the *shōen* officials and *jitō*. This early medieval peasant resistance to oppressive *jitō* rule most typically took the form seen in a 1275 peasant complaint (*sojō*) on Atekawa-no-shō, directed against the proprietor, the Jakurakuji temple in Kyoto.[35] This *shōen* was located in the mountains on the upper reaches of the Arita River in Kii Province. A powerful provincial family, the Yuasa, had come to dominate the *jitō* office, and its power spread accordingly. The Yuasa's methods of control over the peasants were so crude that the peasants rose up and submitted a thirteen-article protest to the proprietor written in their own faltering handwriting. The following matters were brought to light in this document.

Upon discovering that the peasants had concealed the existence of certain fields from him, the *jitō* levied his own *nengu*, even though this was a privilege of the proprietor alone. In addition, he imposed a fine of two hundred *mon* in copper coins per year per *tan* of land. On one occasion, the *jitō* dispatched over twenty people from his own house to collect hemp and cotton from the peasants. He also mobilized the peasants to cut and transport trees, imposing on them many hours of arduous labor. Most seriously, he hunted down and forcibly returned fleeing peasants, whom he then punished by making them sow barley on their recently abandoned land. He furthermore threatened that if they did not comply, he would take their female children and cut off their ears, slice off their noses, cut their hair like nuns, tie them up, and then parade them around. He forced the peasants to take care of his horses morning and night and required them to submit one *to*, three *shō* of hay as fodder for them. He totally ignored precedent in his dealings with the peasants and displayed no concern for the stability of their lives but thought only of his own gain. He required an inordinate amount of service from the peasants and showered them with abuse. These are few documented cases of peasants directly protesting the *jitō*'s actions, but from those that exist it can be inferred that around the thirteenth century, peasants were no longer content either to accept abusive treatment or to flee but began to resist harsh rule by *jitō* by pressing complaints against them.

---

35 The petition by the peasants of Ategawa-no-shō, dated the tenth month of 1275, can be found in *Kōyasan monjo*, vol.6, *yūzoku hōkanshū*, no. 1423, pp. 486–90.

In a similar example in 1334 on Tara-no-shō, a Tōji holding in Wakasa Province, peasants protested the illegal activities of a *shōen* official, Wakibukuro Hikotaro.[36] The appeal document, signed by all fifty-nine *myōshu* and small cultivators of the *shōen*, requests Wakibukuro's dismissal. According to their complaint, he was guilty of numerous outrages. He mobilized six hundred people yearly for agricultural labor on his directly managed lands (over three *chō*). He dispatched peasants daily to work in a place called Wakibukuro near the *shōen* where his residence was located, required twenty peasants to serve and accompany him when he went to Kyoto, and confiscated peasant holdings and incorporated them into his official lands. In addition, he failed to submit dues on *myō* as required, used peasant labor to build a fortress, destroyed peasant dwellings, and engaged in countless other illegal activities.

The peasants in these two examples were no longer willing to bear the excesses of the *jitō* and *shōen* officials and therefore appealed directly to the proprietor. But this is not typical of the early medieval period. In general, if the *jitō* exceeded the legal bounds of his office, the *shōen* officials would lodge a complaint with the Kamakura bakufu. In such cases, the wrath of the peasants was obscured in the litigation of the *shōen* officials and failed to surface directly.

Another point merits attention here. Although the *jitō* and local officials lived on or near the *shōen*, the proprietor lived far away in the capital and, therefore, did not appear to the peasants to be their tormentor. For this reason, the peasants persisted in seeing the *jitō* as a villain whereas the proprietor was considered a force for good. Even in the fourteenth and fifteenth centuries, when the *shōen* system was declining and peasant struggles were increasing, the peasants usually opposed the local warriors who were gaining dominance over the *shōen* by taking control of taxation. On the other hand, the peasants welcomed direct rule by the shōen proprietor. This does not imply that the proprietor's rule over the *shōen* was particularly enlightened but only that it was weak and much more lenient, and therefore, the peasants preferred it to warrior rule. A major reason that the *shōen* system survived longer than conditions would have predicted was that peasants resisted warrior incursions while they supported the proprietor.

36 The petition and deposition submitted by the peasants of Tara-no-shō in the eighth month of 1334 are found in Shiryō hensanjo, ed., *Tōji hyakugō monjo*, vol.1, *ha*, no. 116, *Dai Nihon komonjo, iewake*, vol. 10, pt. 1 (Tokyo: Tōkyō teikoku daigaku, 1925), pp. 709–13.

THE ECONOMIC LIFE OF THE PEASANTS

Clothing, food, and shelter

There is still a dearth of research regarding specific aspects of medieval peasant life, including their clothing, food, and shelter, but I shall present a summary of what little is known to date.

Clothing. The fabric most widely used for clothing by medieval peasants was hemp or ramie (*karamushi*). Hemp was a perennial plant that could be cultivated anywhere in Japan. The process of producing thread from the plant was not difficult, and so it was widely used as a component in peasant clothing. Several steps, however, were involved in producing the fabric. The hemp stalk had to be finely shredded, tied together, and twisted into thread. Then, it had to be placed on a wooden stand, a pulling block, and beaten with a mallet to soften it. This work was usually done at night during the winter season. In the late medieval period, Echigo Province became a center of hemp production, and a *za* (guild) was established there that monopolized the production of blue hemp (*aoso*). Its guarantor was the aristocratic Sanjōnishi family. This *za* also produced Echigo crepe, a high-quality product made of blue hemp, aimed at the city market.

Other fabric used for clothing included fabrics made from raw silk thread from either cultivated or wild silkworms. Sericulture, however, was technically quite difficult, and compared with that of hemp, the process of making silk thread and weaving fabric was much more time-consuming. Consequently, peasants did not commonly use silk fabric. Silk floss and silk wadding, however, easily produced by boiling the cocoons and then spreading them out to dry, offered good insulation and was most often used as a winter fabric. It is known that in the Muromachi period, silk floss was often among the products carried by merchants selling in peasant markets.[37] In eastern Japan in particular, a method known as *tsumugi* was developed, whereby silk floss was twisted by hand into a thick thread and woven on a primitive loom instead of being spun into raw silk thread. Because it was thick and sturdy, this fabric provided excellent insulation. Of all the silk fabrics, fabric produced in this manner was the most likely to be used by the peasants.

37 For example, it is known that in order to sell it in local markets the merchants of Imahori village in Ōmi Province kept fabric (*gofukusen*) from Ise in stock. See Nakamura Ken, ed., *Imahori Hie jinja monjo* (Tokyo: Yūzankaku, 1981).

Cotton, which offered the best insulation and was the most pleasing to the touch, was produced in Korea in the fifteenth century and subsequently exported to Japan. The cultivation, spinning, and weaving of cotton did not begin in Japan until the sixteenth century. Therefore, cotton fabric was not available to medieval Japanese peasants. Similarly, sheep were not raised in Japan, and so there was no wool.

It is clear that the choice of fabrics available to the medieval Japanese peasant for clothing was limited, although there may have been other self-subsistent fabrics that do not appear in the sources. For example, it is quite likely that deer and antelope hides were used for clothing. And the seeds may have been stripped off cattails and inserted into cotton bedding as wadding. Folk studies of mountain communities have revealed that a fabric made from wisteria vines was widely used in clothing. This natural fiber, gathered in the wild, may have been a common component in medieval clothing as well. In any case, there were few fabrics that were produced in mass quantities in the medieval period.

Food. Since the beginning of sedentary agriculture in Japan, food production has centered on rice cultivation, for several reasons. The nutritional properties of rice are excellent compared with those of other grains; the preparation and maintenance of rice paddies are relatively easy; a large amount of fertilizer is not necessary for cultivation; consecutive planting is usually feasible; and the harvest is quite dependable. Given these attributes, it is understandable that the ancient *ritsuryō* state considered rice paddies central to its policy on the control of cultivable land. Later, *shōen* proprietors too put most of their efforts into maintaining their control over rice paddies, whereas dry fields were of only secondary importance.

But despite the emphasis on rice production, rice was not the primary staple in the peasants' diet. The state's and later the proprietor's control over the paddies meant that the peasants did not have reliable access to rice. In addition, small cultivators could not secure enough paddy land in the first place to ensure a stable rice income. Consequently, only the privileged *myōshu* class had enough rice for a year after paying their taxes. In addition, most of the small cultivators did not have time to maintain their own paddies while providing mandatory labor service to the proprietor, as well as to their direct overseer, the local *myōshu*. Cultivators also incurred debts of food and seed each year at a high interest. As a result, there were precious few days in the year when peasants ate rice. Most of the time they ate inferior grains such as millet and wild grasses. In medieval lists of items submitted as *zōkuji*, the term *tokoro* appears frequently. *Tokoro* was a wild plant similar to a yam; its stalk and root were edible once cooked to remove the bitterness. These plants were evidently part of the proprietors' diet. It is possible that *tokoro* also figured prominently in peasants' diet. According to the *Myōhōji ki*, a late medieval journal kept by the priests of a mountain temple in Kai Province, the peasants raised rice, barley, wheat, and millet, but by spring they had usually consumed these harvested foods. After that, ferns and plant roots kept them alive until the summer barley harvest.[38] They also ate fish, birds, and other animals when available. Food brought in from the outside, however, was limited to salted fish a few times a year.[39]

Shelter. The residential lands of *shōen* officials and *jitō* occupied an area of about one hundred square meters surrounded by an earthen embankment with a moat or ditch along the outer slope. Archaeological digs of medieval structures, as well as scroll depictions of warrior houses (such as the *Hōnen shōnin eden* of the late Kamakura period), suggest that there were outbuildings for servants and animals in addition to the main residence. The house of the average small cultivator, in contrast, consisted of two small rooms without a partition which opened onto a dirt-floored room used for cooking and storing farm implements. Such peasant houses are depicted in the *Kōmyō shingon ekotoba*, dated 1398, and in the thirteenth-century *Ise shinmeisho uta-awase emaki*.[40] Foundation stones were not used; instead, support posts were placed directly into holes dug in the ground. Only the homes of well-to-do peasants had wooden flooring; poor households had only straw mats or straw spread on the bare ground. The roof was built with oblong planks of lumber cut short and split, instead of tile. The outside walls of the house were constructed of mud or stacked logs and mud plaster. Making boards was difficult, and not until the Muromachi period were there craftsmen who specialized in making boards by splitting logs lengthwise with a large saw. Before that, wooden panels were not used in peasant houses, and carpenters were

---

38 *Zatsu no bu* in *zoku gunshō ruijū*.
39 Refers to salt curing, fish markets, and the like, dealing mostly in salmon and yellowtail (*buri*).
40 These picture scrolls are reproduced in *Nihon emakimono zenshū*, 32 vols. (Tokyo: Kadokawa shoten, new ed., 1977–81); and *Nihon emaki taisei*, 29 vols. (Tokyo: Chūō kōronsha, 1977–81).

rarely found on *shōen*. Instead, members of the village communal organization got together to build the necessary dwellings. Sources from this period frequently cite incidences of *shōen* officials and *jitō* dismantling the houses of peasants banished for illegal activities, because lumber was a precious commodity in the medieval village and old boards were reused repeatedly.

The peasants and the market

The preceding account portrays the economic existence of the medieval peasant as nearly self-sufficient; however, trade was also important to obtaining such necessary items as salt, iron implements used in farming, and pottery to store and water. Many of these items had to be purchased from those specializing in producing them. Markets where such items could be bought were held three times a month on prescribed days, such as those with numbers containing a three or six.[41] Markets held six times a month proliferated in the fifteenth century. In some cases, markets were located on *shōen*, but it was not unusual for them to be held in remote areas as well. In general, markets were located near the residence of a *jitō* or *shōen* official, in a conveniently located place, or adjacent to a temple.[42]

Markets were originally the means by which *shōen* officials and *jitō* sold part of all of the *nengu* they received and acquired luxury goods such as fabric and swords from the capital. Until the early fourteenth century, *nengu* was usually sent in kind to the capital, with part of it first exchanged at the market to defray local expenses. In later periods, however, all the *nengu* was sold to merchants in the local market, and the proceeds were sent in currency to the proprietor in the capital.[43] Peasants, too, used these markets to exchange modest amounts of rice, barley hemp, and other fabrics for other necessary items.

In the fourteenth century, beginning in Yamato and Yamashiro provinces, it became common in the villages of central Japan to manufacture products for sale in cities like Nara, Kyoto, Sakai, and Ōtsu. Such

---

41 A market held three times a month is called *sansai ichi*, and that held six times a month, *rokusai ichi*.

42 According to a late-Kamakura-period map of Okuyama-no-shō in Echigo Province, found in the archives of Chūjōchō of Niigata Prefecture, a market was located near the *jitō*'s family residence.

43 Sasaki Ginya, "Shōen ni okeru daisennōsei no seiritsu to tenkai," in *Chūsei shōhin ryūtsūshi no kenkyū* (Tokyo: Hōsei daigaku shuppankyoku, 1972), pp. 250–362.

products included noodles made from wheat flour, rice derivatives such as vinegar and malt, lamp oil produced from the *perilla* plant, and blinds crafted from bamboo.[44] The peasants who made such products often formed *za* and placed themselves under the protection of a powerful religious patron. The *za* submitted a business tax in return for monopoly rights over their product. Eventually some *za* members made their way to cities like Kyoto to sell their goods. In the late medieval period, the production and sale of such commodities were not limited to central Japan but could be found in all areas linked with a port city or a castle town of a daimyo.

As peasants became involved in market activities, their use of coins also increased. The ancient *ritsuryō* state had borrowed the T'ang monetary system, minted coins, and encouraged their circulation. However, the actual area where coins were in circulation was extremely limited and, in time, all but disappeared. Until near the end of the twelfth century, barter was the rule. Even land transactions between aristocrats and priests were conducted in rice.[45]

In the thirteenth century, coins imported from Sung China gradually came into common usage, and by the end of the century, this practice had spread to the village level. Merchants from the capital purchased with coins products from the villages. In the fourteenth century it became common practice to exchange *nengu* for coins and submit it to the proprietor in that form. Individual peasants, however, did not submit *nengu* in coins by selling their rice and products to merchants. Rather, the *shōen* officials or an agent contracted by the proprietor sold the *nengu* rice in the local market at a profit and then submitted it in coins to the proprietor at a lower conversion rate. Local officials benefited from the lucrative conversion arrangement and therefore welcomed merchants to markets in areas under their control. As a result, the peasants were involuntarily exposed to the market and gradually acquired coins with which they could purchase goods. Not only in the economically developed villages of central Japan but even in the poorer villages it became possible for peasants to acquire coins by producing woodwork and charcoal and collecting firewood for sale.[46] Even in the late-developing villages of eastern Japan in the

44 Wakita Haruko, *Nihon chūsei shōgyō hattatsushi no kenkyū* (Tokyo: Ochanomizu shobō, 1969), pp. 419–522.
45 A cursory survey of twelfth-century bills of sale for cultivated land reveals that outside one or two exceptions, transactions were conducted in rice, silk, and hemp. See Nagahara Keiji, "Heian makki kōhi baiken no bunseki," in *Nihon chūsei shakai kōzō no kenkyū*, pp. 159–68.
46 Ōyama Kyōhei, *Nihon chūsei nōsonshi no kenkyū* (Tokyo: Iwanami shoten, 1978), pp. 288–319.

fifteenth century, there were cases of local temples' collecting from the cultivators the land rent in cash.

Land as property

In the early medieval period, peasants did not hold land as private property in the true sense of the word. The *shōen* proprietor formally registered *myōden* and *isshikiden* in the land registry, and because this land was the basis for *nengu* and *zōkuji*, peasants were forbidden to buy and sell it without permission. This was not the only reason that such land was not privately owned, however. From the peasant's point of view, cultivable land was not always a highly valued "possession." The peasants invested a great deal of labor in opening arable land, and even if initially compensated, once the proprietor began to exact taxes and labor service, the property value of such land was indeed low. Cultivation rights were not in high demand for land burdened with excessive imposts, particularly in the case of famine or natural disaster.

In villages near Nara and Kyoto, the sale of the peasants' right to possess arable land began early. This included selling land outright, using it as collateral for a loan, and, in many cases, becoming a tenant on the land as a result of debt default. In most areas, however, even if the peasants left the land because it no longer provided a sufficient income, there were not the changes in ownership commonly seen later. Instead, in the early medieval period, entire families would pack up and start wandering as *mibiki*, or they would become *genin*. For this reason, land abandoned and left vacant was common. It was the task of the *shōen* official to see that vacant land was not left fallow for long. To that end, it was necessary to install on the land, as quickly as possible, another transient cultivator. Under these circumstances, it is unlikely that such land could have maintained much property value.

In the mid to late medieval period in central Japan and other nearby economically advanced areas there was a great change in the perceived value of land. A bill of sale dated 1381, found in the document collection of the Daitokuji, records that a person named Meuko of Settsu Province sold two *tan* of land of the Takehisa *myō* in Gūke District for five *kanmon* to one Anshu of Naruo.[47] Subsequently, Meuko paid one *koku* of rice yearly as a cultivation fee (*kajishi*) to Anshu, and the

---

47 Bill of sale dated 1381, intercalary ninth month, for land referred to as Meuko, in *Daitokuji monjo*, vol. 3, in Tōkyō daigaku shiryōhensanjo, ed., *Dai Nihon komonjo iewake*, vol. 17 (Tokyo: Tōkyō daigaku shuppankai, 1954), pp. 328–9.

contract stated that in addition he was to submit the *nengu* directly to the Daitokuji. In other words, Meuko sold his land to Anshu and each year paid Anshu one *koku* in order to continue to cultivate the land. It is probable that Meuko, the cultivator, even though he was bearing both the *nengu* and the cultivation fee, derived some profit from this arrangement. One *koku* was paid as a cultivation fee for two *tan* of land; the *nengu* probably amounted to about the same. Even given such a heavy tax burden, if the cultivator could be assured of productivity, the land would have real salable property value. For Anshu, too, the situation had definite advantages. Precisely because the land was highly productive, he bought it for the income derived from the *kajishi*. In other words, he bought it as property with value to him as its landlord. Meuko and Anshu, then, each had rights to land with definite property value, in contrast with the early medieval peasant who could be brought to ruin by a combination of unstable agricultural and economic conditions.

Therefore, as land productivity rose, its value to the peasant as property increased commensurately. When land was sold, an economic relationship was established between the lowly peasant cultivator who paid the cultivation fee and the *myōshu* landlord who received the fee. In the early medieval period, *myōshu* expanded their agricultural operations by using collateral family members and *genin*. Then, they gradually reduced the amount of land under their direct management and became primarily landlords who exacted a fee from the peasant cultivators. Many former relatives or *genin* of *myōshu* who had never been independent became peasant cultivators, thereby achieving some economic stability. By the fifteenth century, such changes in the real value of land as property meant that *shōen* officials no longer had to worry about land lying fallow.

THE REGIONAL CONSOLIDATION OF PEASANT SOCIETY

The village and peasant self-rule

Great economic and social changes took place during the medieval period, especially during the crucial fourteenth century. The conditions that encouraged widespread abandonment of land by peasants were alleviated, and it became possible for the village to retain a certain portion of wealth. Along with these developments came the establishment of a surtax relationship between the upper and lower strata of the peasant class. Small, weak peasants subordinated themselves to powerful peasants of the *myōshu* class; indeed, only by placing themselves in this position of dependence were they able to survive. This arrangement was not without benefit to the poor peasant; it gradually stabilized his livelihood and strengthened his ties to the land. This social trend was national in scope, but it was particularly pronounced in central Japan. In the 1334 case cited earlier, both *myōshu* and small cultivators submitted a petition to protest the illegal actions of the *shōen* official, Wakibukuro. This indicates that even small cultivators were major, independent participants in activities against their overlords.

In 1346, on Sugaura-no-shō on the northern shore of Lake Biwa in Omi Province, twelve people issued a joint statement on the disposal of local land: "Concerning the dry fields of Hisashi and Morokawa, for a limited period of one to two years there is no objection to buying and selling, but selling in perpetuity is forbidden. Anyone who goes against this will cease to hold membership in the village communal organization (*sō-mura*)".[48] At this time there was a bitter dispute between Sugaura-no-shō and the neighboring Oura-no-shō over the jurisdiction of Hisashi and Morokawa. The statement was issued by the residents of Sugaura, who were most likely members of the *myōshu* class and its "main residents" (*honzaike*), to prevent the sale of these lands to the other *shōen*. According to other sources, such *honzaike* generally kept two or three families of subordinate cultivators who were "subsidiary residents" (*wakizaike*). The statement, however, applied to all residents of what they referred to as the "place" (*tokoro*) and threatened transgressors with expulsion from the village communal organization (*sō*).

The use of the terms *tokoro* and *sō* should be noted here. *Tokoro* means "place" but also connotes "that land" and corresponds to an old word frequently used in Kansai region even today, *zaisho*. This word is used by people of an area to indicate closeness to their land, regardless of local politics. The use of the word *tokoro* in this sense came into being only in the late medieval period. The term *tokorojichi*, having the same connotation, also came into widespread use in the late medieval period.

Tokorojichi is nearly synonymous with *gōjichi*, which refers to situations in which a creditor, faced with a reneging debtor, could, in retaliation, seize the property of a person living in the same area or

48 The 1346 village *okibumi* (property testament) of Sugaura-no-shō can be found in Shiga daigaku Nihon bunka kenkyūjo shiryōkan, ed., *Sugaura monjo* (Tokyo: Yūhikaku, 1960–7), vol.1, no. 180, p. 67.

district as the debtor.[49] In the medieval period, even if a person were not the cosigned guarantor on the written debt agreement, simply by living in the same area or district, he could be required to repay the debt. This practice clearly presupposes the communal nature of the local unit. It was generally accepted that people in the same communal group must bear mutual responsibility for the debts of their neighbors. A more positive way of characterizing this late medieval communal relationship is an expression of the local communities' close land-based ties. The *sō* was also the communal expression of social solidarity of the people of an area. In the Sugaura statement, the phrase "membership in the *sō*" clearly refers to a social organization. The more specific meaning of the word *sō* here is not clear, but it most likely refers to a regional communal organization in which all the people of an area could take part. (The character with which *sō* is written can also mean "all.")

One of the day-to-day functions of the *sō* was to solve problems of common concern. In 1367, on the Tōji's Yano-no-shō in Harima Province, forty-six peasants jointly issued a pledge swearing by the deities that the harvest that year had failed and therefore were requesting a survey of damage by the proprietor in order that a reduction in, or exemption from, the *nengu* could be granted. Later in 1377, the *myōshu* and small cultivators staged a *shōen*-wide uprising and denounced the *shōen* officials. Concerning the uprising, one *myōshu* complained: "When some tens of *myōshu* of the entire *shōen* press their complaints and sign jointly, 'of one intent' (*ichimi dōshin*), how could I alone raise an objection? If I should resist the uprising, I would without a doubt be attacked."[50] As can be seen from this example, once the *sō* arrived at a decision by group consensus, the members were bound by it. Anyone who went against the decision "of one intent" would not be tolerated and would most likely be killed.

In addition to bringing action against the proprietor, the village communal organization dealt with internal affairs. In the Nambokuchō period, for instance, in Imabori District of Ōmi Province, the peasants established a communal religious organization called a *miyaza* (shrine guild) for holding religious ceremonies at Imabori Hie Shrine, the village shrine. In 1383, the group established rules governing responsibility for a ceremony held on the fourth day of the first month

49 Katsumata Shizuo, "Kunijichi gōjichi ni tsuite no kōsatsu," in *Sengoku-hō seiritsu shiron* (Tokyo: Tōkyō daigaku shuppankai, 1979), pp. 37–60.
50 Satō Kazuhiko, "Sōshō ikki no tenkai," in *Nambokuchō nairan shiron* (Tokyo: Tōkyō daigaku shuppankai, 1979), pp. 73–124.

each year. In 1403, it was decreed that those who did not pay guild dues, which covered the shrine's operating expenses, would be barred from membership. In 1448, again, a six-article regulation was handed down. In addition to matters of a purely religious nature, general matters of village life were also addressed. Examples of the articles include: "Do not give lodging to travelers," and "No villager shall perform the coming-of-age ceremony of a child brought in from the outside with the intent of making the child a village resident." In 1489, a longer, twenty-article regulation was issued that dealt with local matters of daily life: "Outsiders without a guarantor are not allowed in the village"; "Keeping dogs is forbidden"; and "Adopted children over the age of seven will not be accepted into the guild." Many of the articles concerned the use of the *sō*'s communally owned mountain. Taken as a whole, these regulations range broadly over the communal affairs and daily life of the people of Imabori District and provide a comprehensive look at village law.[51]

To the extent that the *sō* created such regulations, as the village communal organization it also assumed judicial powers in the event of a transgression. Sugaura provides a case in point. Lake Biwa lay to the south and the mountains to the north, leaving only the east and west for access to the village. Gates that survive to this day were erected at these points of entry, clearly defining the village's boundaries. Anyone who disobeyed the *sō* communal regulations and committed an illegal act was banished outside these gates and thus effectively isolated from the village. Under the *shōen* system, officials frequently banished residents who had committed illegal acts, but in this case it was the *sō*, not the officials, that imposed the punishment. Sugaura's local law code of 1483 also contains a regulation stating that if a person commits an offense and is put to death or banished, it is acceptable and tolerable if his child is allowed to inherit his property. From this it can be surmised that the *sō* not only banished offenders but could even put them to death.

The *sō*'s ability to impose sanctions on offenders was a clear sign that the proprietor's power of jurisdiction in criminal matters had declined and that the *sō* had, in effect, assumed that right. In 1568, the leaders of the Sugaura *sō* posted a decree impeaching four *sō* members. In it they wrote, "Though the *jitō* may not enter Sugaura and we claim jurisdiction in all criminal matters ourselves, these four have in the

<hr />

51 Nakamura, ed., *Imahori Hie Jinja monjo*.

name of the *jitō* behaved improperly toward the *sō*."[52] By refusing entry to *shugo*, Sugaura-no-shō was exerting its right of self-jurisdiction in criminal matters. The *sō* usurped this important right from the proprietor and severely limited his power. This shift in power constituted a dramatic expansion in *sō* self-government.

The development of sō leagues

Sō self-rule, as a means of protecting community interests, developed from first gaining the right of self-jurisdiction in criminal matters. As time went on, the *sō* increasingly took other matters into its own hands, including such economic concerns as debt amnesties and declarations of local cancellations of debts.[53] On the Okushima and Kitatsuda *shōen* on the eastern shore of Lake Biwa, such an amnesty was granted in the eight month of 1441. A six-article decree was issued, requiring that pawned items be returned to debtors even if only one-tenth of the debt had been repaid. All rice and cash loans were to be written off.[54] In the same month, rebellions demanding the cancellation of debts erupted in many villages in the Kyoto area. The bakufu was thrust into the controversy and, in the following month, issued a debt-abrogation decree for the entire Kyoto area. Shortly thereafter, the bakufu issued a more comprehensive nationwide decree, the historic Kakitsu debt abrogation.[55]

There was most likely a connection between the circumstances of the uprisings of the *shōen* of Okushima and Kitatsuda and those leading to the Kakitsu decree. The connection, however, should not be overemphasized. After all, the Okushima–Kitatsuda regulations were issued a month before the bakufu decided to issue the Kakitsu debt amnesty. Moreover, those who signed the earlier decree were local, powerful peasant leaders of Kitatsuda and Okushima who took the lead in the uprising and then issued the local amnesty. Unlike internal matters decided by the village communal organization, debt amnesties affected entire regions within which creditors operated. There must have been at least some communications among the groups in the area demanding amnesty. This was certainly the case in the documents cosigned by *sō* leaders of both Okushima and Kitatsuda *shōen*. Local

---

52 The 1568 decree posted in the village of Sugaura can be found in *Sugaura monjo*, vol.2, no. 925, p. 126.
53 Seta Katsuya, "Chūsei makki no zaichi tokusei," *Shigaku zasshi* 77 (September 1968): 1–52.
54 This debt cancellation decree is found in the archives of Oshima Okutsushima *jinja*.
55 Nagahara Keiji, "Kakitsu tokusei ikki no seikaku ni tsuite," in *Nihon chūsei shakai kōzō no kenkyū*, pp. 394–425.

representatives of the two *shōen* reached an agreement and put into effect a debt amnesty applying to both. This illustrates the scope of *sō* self-government and how it expanded to the extent of infringing on the proprietor's traditional sphere of authority. As this occurred more often, the need arose for an organization – a *sō* league – that could deal with the peasants' social and political problems, transcending the bounds of a single *shōen* to encompass a larger region.

In 1494, forty-six prominent peasants in Oyamato District of Ise Province signed a pledge, whose gist was that "if there is a dispute among us, we shall together come to a decision after examining all sides of the case." This document was presented to the priest Shinsei of the Jōganji, the major temple and focal point of the district.[56] In the Edo period, Oyamato Province encompassed twelve village administrative units. Therefore, this agreement represents the decision of several *sō* organizations. The forty-six delegates were leaders of several *sō* in Oyamato District who formed a collegial organization that agreed to avoid confrontation by solving problems as a group.

At the same time, another pledge containing five articles related to communal matters of village life was signed by 350 peasants from the entire district. The pledge contained five prohibitionary regulations such as "there shall be no falsifying boundaries for paddies, fields, mountains, or forests," "no taking another's right of cultivation," and "no stealing of crops." It appears that the *sō* leagues of Oyamato District encouraged cooperation in order to resolve matters of common concern. It is likely that the district's leaders who signed the first pledge had issued a ruling to all the peasants of the area and, to make sure they complied, had them sign the latter, five-article pledge. In other words, in establishing self-rule throughout the district, not all district residents participated directly and equally to draw up these articles. Rather, a group of leaders together controlled the peasants as a whole. In Oyamato District, there was a local debt amnesty in the mid-sixteenth century, and a group of local elders arbitrated the matter. It is probable that the forty-six signers of the first pledge were also such elders.

The *sō* leagues went beyond the single village communal organization, and as regional alliances sprang up, the scope of the problems they faced expanded. As a result the leagues needed leaders to take charge of the central operations. As can be seen clearly in the Oyamato

56 Seta, "Chūsei makki no zaichi tokusei."

case, this led to distinction among the leadership group and the rest of the peasants, as illustrated by the *sō* of Kōga District in Ōmi Province. The *sō* was made up of the Yamanaka, Minobe, and Ban. Local warriors and small-scale village overlords, who lived in the vicinity of the *shōen* belonging to the Kashiwagi Shrine. Each family formed its own organization, called a *dōmyō-so,* or a *sō* whose members shared the same surname. They then formed the Kashiwagi *sanbōsō,* a three-member league, and established a districtwide *sō* by allying with similar local *sō* organizations.[57] This Kōga District *sō* took charge of the communal management of waterways for the regional irrigation of wetlands and served a military function in defending the area and preserving peace.

There are other examples of *sō* organizations expanding to encompass entire provinces. An undated petition submitted by peasants of a provincewide *sō* in Yamato Province most likely some time in the late fifteenth or early sixteenth century, contains a request for a debt moratorium owing to extensive drought damage throughout the province.[58] The request was directed to the Kōfukuji, the great Nara temple that held the *shugo* office of Yamato at the time. If their request was not granted, the peasants threatened to stop working. The request is signed, "respectfully submitted by the peasants of the Yamato provincial *sō*," but the handwriting is of a quality far superior than that of ordinary peasants. Most likely a member of the local overlord class organized the movement and wrote the document as representing the entire province. The provincial *sō* was also found in Yamashiro and Iga provinces. The village *sō* expanded into leagues to encompass entire districts and provinces, the local administrative units of ancient times. In this sense, the *sō* came to control public matters in a given region.

From being the village's basic unit, the *sō* expanded into leagues and, from the fifteenth through the sixteenth centuries, grew particularly strong in the central provinces. These organizations were led by small-scale village overlords (*jizamurai*) and contained the seeds of new hierarchical relationships.[59] Nevertheless, they had a strong popular, democratic flavor not found in the rule of the bakufu, *shugo,* or *sengoku* daimyo. Phrases used constantly by the *sō,* like *shūchū dangō*

---

57 Ishida Yoshito, "Sōteki ketsugō no shoruikei," *Rekishi kyōiku* 8 (August 1960); Murata Shūzō, "Chiiki masu to chiiki kenryoku," in *Shirin* 55 (1972); and Murata Shūzō, "Yōsui shihai to shōryōshu rengō," *Nara joshi daigaku bungakubu kenkyū nempō,* no. 16 (1973).
58 *Hōryūji monjo.*
59 These small-scale overlords lived in the village, and although only of peasant (*hyakushō*) status, they privately dominated the village communal organization by means of their economic and social power. Based on my research, I have found that they constituted the upper stratum of the peasant class yet had overlord characteristics.

(mass discussion) and *ichimi shinsui* (group pledge), are symbolic of the organization's communal workings. Figuratively speaking, the *sō* was an original democratic institution distinctive of Japan.[60]

Peasant entertainment

The development of the village communal organization gave life to peasant culture in the form of festivals and public entertainment. Literary sources like *kyōgen* plays provide a glimpse into peasant life in the Muromachi period. Villagers would often meet to compare regional varieties of tea and engage in linked-verse (*renga*) parties. The immense popularity of such village cultural recreation was characteristic of the Muromachi period. It is interesting to note that these all were group activities. Indeed, the collective aspect cannot be ignored.

A leading form of village entertainment was Yamato *sarugaku*, a kind of drama that had already evolved to a high degree of perfection by the Nambokuchō period. Originally a service in the religious festivals of the Kasuga Shrine and the Kōfukuji, *sarugaku* became a form of peasant entertainment performed in Yamato villages. It gradually attained great popularity and received widespread acclaim. In time, four schools of *sarugaku* were established – Kongō, Konparu, Hōshō, and Kanze – and great masters like Kan'ami and Zeami emerged under the patronage of the shogun Yoshimitsu.

The dance (*kagura*) troupes and other accomplished performers in the village formed guilds (*miyaza*) under the protection of a village shrine and performed in shrine festivals. Until the Sengoku period, Hine-no-shō in Izumi Province was a major holding of the Kujō family, one of the five regency houses. A local overlord, Kujō Masamoto, who saw the *kagura* performed at the Hine Shrine festival was so impressed by its quality that he remarked, "This entertainment by country folk is not to be sneered at."[61] Hine-no-shō was located in an agriculturally advanced area, and each village had a *sō* council that enjoyed the right of self-jurisdiction. It is not surprising that an area with well-established *sō* would also be a center of peasant culture.

Village women of this period also took part in group activities. Official documents offer little on the life of peasant women, but contemporary illustrated scrolls suggest that nearly all the spring planting, the fall threshing, and the hulling were done by women. The women

60 Nagahara Keiji, "Gekokujō to shūchū dangō," in *Chūsei nairanki no shakai to minshū* (Tokyo: Yoshikawa kōbunkan, 1977), pp. 158–88.
61 Kunaichō Shoryōbu, ed., *Kujō Masamotoko tabi hikizuke* (Tokyo: Yōtokusha, 1961).

of villages in the Kyoto area also went out to sell vegetables, firewood, and farm products.

Several *kyōgen* plays in which peasant couples appear depict the husbands as good-for-nothings who do nothing but carouse, whereas the wives are dependable and hardworking. Evidence from central Japan shows that lowly peasants, fearful of the ever-present possibility of ruin, began to seek improvements and stability in their lives. As they became more active, women also shared this ambition. The Imabori *sō* of Ōmi Province, for instance, had a wives' guild apart from the all-male shrine guild.[62] Its specific function is not clear from the sources but was most likely in part for recreation, with the members bringing food to religious functions and spending the whole day at the shrine gossiping. Although these groups may seem trivial, they represented a degree of independence for medieval peasant women not found among the women of the strongly patriarchal warrior class.[63]

Ikki *and religion*

Ikkō ikki were the base on which the *sō* leagues were built and were representative of peasant solidarity. Located mainly in central Japan and the Japan Sea coast region from the late fifteenth through sixteenth centuries, *ikkō ikki* were concentrated forces of peasants and local warriors, linked by their belief in the True Pure Land (*Jōdo Shinshū*) sect of Buddhism and united in their struggle against *shugo* and *sengoku* daimyo. This religious and social movement constituted the largest organized peasant struggle in Japanese history.[64] A problem that historians face is determining the nature of the peasants' religious faith in the early medieval period. In regard to the new forms of Buddhism that emerged in the thirteenth century, it is certain that Shinran of the True Pure Land sect and Ippen of the Ji sect, a mendicant order of Pure Land Buddhism, vigorously proselytized among the peasants.

Around the mid-fourteenth century, just before the Ōnin War, these religions were putting down roots among the peasants, and their members were beginning their struggle against the ruling authorities by forming *ikki* leagues. Rennyo, the head priest of the True Pure Land

---

62 *Imahori Hie jinja monjo.*
63 Nagahara Keiji, "Joseishi ni okeru Nambokuchō Muramachi ki," in *Nihon joseishi*, medieval vol. (Tokyo: Tōkyō daigaku shuppankai, 1982), pp. 137–71.
64 Kasahara Kazuo, *Ikkō ikki no kenkyū* (Tokyo: Yamakawa shuppansha, 1962); and Inoue Toshio, *Ikkō ikki no kenkyū* (Tokyo: Yoshikawa kōbunkan, 1968), are representative works.

sect, was persecuted by the Tendai monks on Mount Hiei. As a result, he moved to adjacent Ōmi Province where he began to spread his teachings. In 1471, Rennyo again moved his headquarters, this time from Ōmi to Yoshizaki in Echizen Province on the Japan Sea. There he pursued even more vigorous proselytization. The key to Rennyo's success lay in taking over the *sō* organizations of the peasant villages of Ōmi Province. Believers in the True Pure Land sect were organized into groups or congregations called *kō*, which meshed well with the existing *sō* organizations. A meeting place, called a *dōjō*, was established at the home of a powerful village resident, and every month the believers assembled there to discuss their complaints against the proprietor, in addition to religious matters. Rennyo himself said at the time that the most important thing for the sect's survival was to have the village elders at its center. To this end, the *sō* was absorbed to the extent possible without change into the *kō* organization. Likewise, establishing *dōjō* at the homes of powerful peasants, instead of building conventional temples, was an excellent way to organize a popular religion.

Concentrations of True Pure Land peasant believers proliferated in rapid succession in Echizen and Kaga provinces on the Japan Sea. Many of these religious groups were led by members of the local overlord class, who organized the members militarily into a true peasant movement. Even more threatening to the ruling establishment was the fact that when the peasants joined the religion, they believed that by making contributions to the head temple of the sect, the Honganji, they would be saved. This made them less willing to pay taxes to their own proprietor or warrior overlord. For this reason, the conflict between the *shugo* and the *ikkō ikki* was particularly intense in Kaga Province. In 1488, the *ikkō ikki* went so far as to force the *jitō* to commit suicide. This incident dealt a blow to the ruling establishment, including the Muromachi bakufu and the *shugo* domain system. The *ikkō ikki* peasant organization was held together to a great extent through religious faith, but it also achieved impressive political gains. In Kaga Province the *ikki* toppled the *shugo*'s authority, seized power, and created a provincewide *sō*.

By the sixteenth century, *ikkō ikki* were no longer limited to the Japan Sea area but had spread to Hida, Mikawa, and other areas near Nagoya. The movement also spread rapidly throughout central Japan to Owari, Ise, Ōmi, Settsu, and Kawachi. Later, Mikawa Province produced Tokugawa Ieyasu, who established the Tokugawa bakufu. His father, Matsudaira Hirotada, was dealt a severe blow by the *ikkō ikki* of Mikawa. Even Oda Nobunaga, the first of the national unifiers, was continuously harassed by the *ikkō ikki* of Nagashima on the border of Owari and Ise provinces; his younger brother was killed in one of the confrontations. The aggravation of the ruling class was expressed by Rokkaku, initially the *shugo* of Ōmi and later a *sengoku* daimyo, who lamented, "The *ikkō ikki* do not make the slightest effort to pay taxes, and if pressed to do so, each district and village threatens to abandon cultivation. They are thoroughly uncontrollable!"[65] To the *sengoku* daimyo and leaders like Nobunaga and Ieyasu, the *ikkō ikki* had developed into a most fearsome force.

One reason for the *ikkō ikki*'s prominence was that many mid-level members of the warrior class – *kokujin* and *jizamurai* – became True Pure Land adherents and played a major role in organizing the peasants. However, a more fundamental reason was that in the *ikki*, religious conviction and communal self-government (*sō* leagues) neatly coalesced, bestowing great power on the peasants. The emergence of the *ikki* coincided with expanding village industry and commerce, and thus the *ikki* could bring this economic power to bear in a sustained, long-term manner against the *shugo* and daimyo authorities.

Proselytization in the True Pure Land sect was aimed not only at the peasants but also at those with social power. In some cases, it was even aimed at the most despised of merchants and craftsmen. One explanation for this is that all the main bastions of *ikkō ikki* strength – Nagashima in Ise, Saikai in Kii, and Ishiyama (Ōsaka) where the Honganji was located – were situated at the mouth of a large river where such merchants and craftsmen tended to congregate. In addition, the areas in front of the gate of great True Pure Land temples in central Japan were gradually built up as temple towns (*jinaimachi*) whose merchants gravitated toward membership in the sect.[66] The temple towns originated from the markets held on specified days of the month. These towns developed close economic ties with the surrounding villages, providing a link between peasant and merchant believers. Thus the religious *ikki*, in combination with the merchant community and the *sō* leagues, cemented the area's economic and social solidarity.

The fifteenth and sixteenth centuries were the most noteworthy in Japanese peasant history. The development of village and regional self-government and *ikkō ikki* allowed the peasants to oppose successfully

---

65 *Rokkakushi shikimoku* is a basic primary source showing the territorial control of the *sengoku* daimyo Rokkaku. See *CHS*, vol. 3, pp. 259–76.
66 Wakita Osamu, "Jinaimachi no kōzō to tenkai," *Shirin* 41 (1958): 1–24.

the ruling authorities, and the *ikkō ikki*'s collective strength played an immense role.

THE *SENGOKU* DAIMYO AND THE PEASANTS

The increasing strength of the *ikkō ikki* posed a great threat to the *sengoku* daimyo. Although *ikki* rebellions appeared to be occurring haphazardly in various parts of Japan, the Honganji in fact acted as a central headquarters, which enabled the local *ikki* to maintain contact with one another and to coordinate their activities. Even Oda Nobunaga was virtually trapped after entering Kyoto, because of the *ikki* of Settsu and Ōmi provinces. Consequently, the *sengoku* daimyo were extremely cautious in their dealings with the *ikkō ikki*. The daimyo of Aki, Mori Motonari, adopted a tolerant policy toward True Pure Land proselytizing. In fact, he extended his protection to the sect in opposing Nobunaga. When he moved into Etchū and Noto provinces, Uesugi Kenshin of the adjacent Echigo Province clashed with the *ikkō ikki* there and continued to be tormented by them. Seeing this, Takeda Shingen of Kai, Uesugi's rival, established contact with the *ikkō ikko* of Etchū and Noto in an attempt to topple Uesugi. In the Kantō, Hōjō Ujiyasu took an extreme step and suppressed True Pure Land proselytization in his domain.

As these examples illustrate, the *sengoku* daimyo adopted various tactics in an attempt to deal with the *ikkō ikki*. They all were aware, however, of the *ikki*'s power. Although the *ikkō ikki* can be seen merely as a religious group, its essence was the peasant league with its well-established roots in the village communal organization. The daimyo were aware that a well-organized peasant class brought with it the threat of rebellion.

In order to stamp out the peasant *ikki*, it became necessary for the daimyo not only to suppress the *ikki* militarily but also to create an alternative institution to rule the peasants. The *sengoku* daimyos' policy toward the peasants had three major components. First, to reestablish control of the land, cadastral surveys were carried out, and a system was set in place for the daimyos' income which included *nengu*, labor service, and *tansen* (a daimyo impost on lands directly controlled by the daimyo and the allotment lands of retainers). Many peasants, disliking the higher taxes levied by the daimyo, fled to the cities or to other domains. The daimyo sought to prevent this, both to avoid the loss of tax revenue from the peasants and to strengthen the status system of which the peasant was a vital part. In doing so, the daimyo bound the peasants to the land and restricted the peasant movement to an extent not seen under the rule of *shōen* proprietors or warrior overlords.

Second, the daimyo sought to destroy the source of leadership in the peasant movement by including in their band of retainers the upper stratum of the peasantry, the *jizamurai*. As we have already seen, these well-to-do peasants had acquired the right to collect *kajishi* and, in addition to becoming landlords or small-scale overlords, were also the leaders of the village communal organization and, frequently, of peasant *ikki* as well. The daimyo, by means of cadastral surveys and reports submitted by the peasants, closely investigated the *kajishi* relationship within the peasant class. Instead of allowing the situation to continue, the daimyo began to look upon the *kajishi* as a grant to rich peasants and required public military service of them in return. In other words, the *sengoku* daimyo usurped control over this *kajishi* relationship, which had hitherto been solely between rich and poor peasants, without interference from the *shōen* proprietor or daimyo. Once the *sengoku* daimyo seized control of the *kajishi* and made it an obligatory payment, their control of land became pervasive. Upper-class peasants became low-level retainers of the daimyo and were often enlisted as military subordinates. Although they normally performed only agricultural labor, in time of war, the daimyo mobilized these peasants as warriors.

The third component of daimyo policy included using peasant labor to build river embankment and irrigation works and to encourage agriculture, including the opening of new paddy lands. The *shōen* proprietor had been an aristocrat living in the capital who had shown no interest in encouraging agriculture. By contrast, the *sengoku* daimyo, in an attempt to promote a stable agricultural sector in his domain, encouraged agriculture and actively mediated disputes over water use. Such actions were tantamount to public rule by the *sengoku* daimyo over the peasants' livelihood. To the peasants, the *sengoku* daimyo were not simply "privileged robbers" but were rulers who offered valuable assistance in agricultural development. The *sengoku* daimyo themselves frequently referred to their rule as *kōgi*, the highest public authority in their territories. Their control of peasant labor and encouragement of agriculture reinforced their authority.

The three main components of *sengoku* daimyo policy toward the peasants strengthened the daimyo's control by organizing them into a hierarchical power structure. At the same time, this policy destroyed the *sō* leagues by transforming upper-class peasants into low-level retainers of the daimyo and by encouraging agriculture, it gave the daimyo's authority over the peasants a public aspect. By means of various strategems, then, the daimyo gradually eliminated the threat of the peasant *ikki*. Peasants became mere agricultural producers under the daimyo's control, a trend dominant under Oda Nobunaga's and Toyotomi Hideyoshi's regimes. With Hideyoshi's national cadastral survey of 1582, the Taikō *kenchi*, the history of the medieval peasant came to an end.

CHAPTER 8

THE GROWTH OF COMMERCE IN
MEDIEVAL JAPAN

Japanese society changed in many significant ways between the mid-twelfth century when the Taira were reveling in the final decades of their power and the close of the fifteenth century when the tenth Ashikaga shogun Yoshiki was ignominiously forced into a long exile. One of the most important changes was the rapid growth of commerce which affected in myriad ways both daily lives and the course of history.

This chapter describes and analyzes how market activities began and grew, leading to specialization among merchants, artisans, those engaged in transportation, and others and, as a result, raising the efficiency of both production and distribution. This chapter will pay special attention to the emergence and growth of several important economic institutions such as markets and guilds; the rise of Kyoto as the center of medieval commerce; the appearance of cities, port towns, and other urban centers and the increase in both their number and size; and other consequences of market activity and monetization that caused political and economic conflict between recipients and payers of dues and between lenders and borrowers.[1]

THE INITIAL CONDITIONS

This section discusses (1) the extent and nature of market activities during the late Heian and early Kamakura periods in agricultural communities; (2) such activities in the "capital trade region" of Kyoto, Nara, and several smaller satellite cities and port towns; (3) the emergence of guildlike institutions called *za* during the eleventh and twelfth centuries; (4) the growth of cities and port towns, in both their

---

1 Because the subject of this chapter is a large one on which numerous works already exist in Japanese, not all of the important topics can be discussed as fully as desirable, and some significant developments will receive only passing attention. Readers wishing to pursue a specific topic or an analysis of a specific development are advised to consult the sources cited in the following footnotes. Note also that this chapter is written assuming that readers are familiar with the history of the period that it discusses.

physical dimensions and the institutional capabilities necessary for the growth of commerce; and (5) the increasing inflow and use of coins from China before the end of the twelfth century, presaging the significant effects monetization had on medieval Japan's economy.

The agricultural communities

Even as late as the early decades of the thirteenth century, most cultivators continued to live on what they planted and could obtain from nearby mountains, forests, and waters. But compared with their ancestors in the preceding century, cultivators were now acquiring more nonagricultural goods, such as pottery, agricultural implements and household items made of iron (hoes, pots and pans, and the like), and some wooden products (such as kegs, bowls, and tubs). These goods required skills to produce, and cultivators bartered for them with rice, cloth, local products, and possibly even their own services. Coins were not unfamiliar, but in agricultural communities they were still scarce and little used in daily life.[2]

Who provided these nonagricultural products to the cultivators? The answer, deduced from documents written for and by government officials or by the elites who were receiving dues from the *shōen*, is that three principal groups of artisans and traders provided nonagricultural goods and services in agricultural communities on "public land" (*kokugaryō*) and in the *shōen*.

Perhaps the most important of these three groups were the artisans who produced specialized products in exchange for stipendiary paddies from the provincial governors of the *kokugaryō*. We know, for example, that as late as 1255 the governor of Iyo Province was

2 No scholarly monograph has been written by a Western scholar on the growth of commerce or the economy of medieval Japan. However, we have in English several textbooks and a dozen research monographs on political and institutional aspects of the period that contain informative descriptions and discussions of various aspects of the growth of commerce. Among the textbooks, those most useful for readers interested in the subject of this chapter are by John Whitney Hall, *Japan from Prehistory to Modern Times* (New York: Dell, 1970); Edwin O. Reischauer and Albert M. Craig, *Japan: Tradition and Transformation* (New York: Houghton Mifflin, 1973); and George Sansom, *A History of Japan, 1334–1615* (Stanford, Calif.: Stanford University Press, 1961). Also containing several essays valuable as background to the topics discussed in this chapter is the book by John Whitney Hall and Takeshi Toyoda, eds., *Japan in the Muromachi Age* (Berkeley and Los Angeles: University of California Press, 1977). For research monographs, readers are referred to the Introduction to this volume.

There are many important or useful books and scholarly articles in Japanese on several aspects of the growth of commerce during the medieval period. The most important among them are referred to in the footnotes of this chapter. Those readers wishing to obtain a more comprehensive bibliography of the Japanese works on the growth of commerce and economy in the medieval period are referred to my articles cited in footnotes 14, 21, 32, and 98 which present full citations of nearly two hundred Japanese works.

providing stipendiary paddies to artisans, including several weavers, a plasterer, a dyer, a singing puppeteer, a few carpenters, and a dozen artisans making leather, paper, saddles, umbrellas, pottery, and copper products. The amounts of the stipendiary paddies given to these artisans were very large by the standard of the period. Whereas many cultivators would have considered themselves fortunate to work half a *chō*, the weavers jointly received as much as 25 *chō;* carpenters and their assistants together were given 5 *chō;* and the stipendiary paddies of the rest of the artisans ranged from 3 *tan* to 4.5 *chō*, with most receiving 1 to 2 *chō*. All told, the governor was providing a total of 52 *chō* to these artisans for their specialized products and services.

On the strength of this evidence and similar documents found for Wakasa and Tango provinces, which show that they respectively gave about forty *chō* and slightly more than thirty-four *chō* to their provincial artisans, Sasakai Ginya speculates that most provincial governors must also have allocated paddies to their artisans in amounts roughly proportional to the size of each province. We have no means to establish exactly when such paddies began to be provided or whether the artisans actively engaged in their cultivation. Because it is known that artisans traveled throughout the province, or even to other provinces, offering their services and products, it is likely that their paddies were worked by local cultivators.[3]

The fact that these artisans traveled suggests that during the twelfth century, if not earlier, they produced more specialized products than the provincial governor required. That is, the artisans were allowed to trade a part of what they produced to cultivators in exchange for agricultural products, shelter, or labor.

Artisans and others given stipendiary paddies by the *shōkan* (the *shōen* administrator) or the *jitō* were a second source of specialized products and services. In this case too, we have only a few documents concerning these artisans, and all are for *shōen* belonging to temples. However, according to documents regarding the Tōdaiji's Niimi-no-shō in Bitchu Province, in 1271 a *jitō* administering half the *shōen* provided stipendiary paddies ranging in amounts from one to eight *tan*, amounts far smaller than those given to artisans by provincial governors. The recipients of these paddies included a smith, a founder, carpenters, persons engaged in shipping, and others who

3 Sasaki Ginya, *Chūsei shōhin ryūtsūshi no kenkyū* (Tokyo: Hōsei daigaku shuppankyoku, 1972), pp. 146–58.

provided "miscellaneous services from morning to night." These documents show that the artisans' paddies constituted only between 3.6
and 26.5 percent of the total amount of paddy that each was then
cultivating. Records relating to other *shōen* provide similar evidence.
The mix of artisans receiving stipendiary paddies differed slightly in
each *shōen* – a few had potters, dyers, and other artisans, but no shippers or founders.[4]

Clearly, only a few paddies were offered, because these artisans were
primarily cultivators who produced their specialized products and provided their skilled services on a part-time basis and only for the benefit
of the *jitō*, the *shōkan*, and the *shōen* proprietor. Here, too, we can
assume that the cultivators, in exchange for their goods and services,
obtained the products and services of these specialists.

The last group of artisan-traders were those known to travel long
distances. Some undoubtedly were still receiving or had received stipendiary paddies from a province, but clearly many were not. All the
artisans receiving paddies and/or under the protection of the court,
nobles, or temples were skilled and gradually became more independent of this protection. This meant that these highly skilled smiths,
founders, sword makers, and many others had both the need and the
freedom to sell their products, which were likely to be superior in
quality to those offered by the local artisans.[5]

Among these traveling merchants, some of those who changed the
cultivators' lives were the peddlers of pots, pans, needles, hoes, plows,
knives, sesame oil, various household items made by the skilled carpenters and potters, and other goods. Many of them were skilled
producer-merchants from the capital region who, during the twelfth
century, traveled to more and more distant provinces.[6] Some of them
undoubtedly had been under the protection of the court, nobles, and
temples. Although no direct evidence exists, it is most likely that
many of these merchants traded their goods for cash in and around the
capital during the twelfth century and the early decades of the thirteenth century.

In regard to the period before the second half of the thirteenth

---

4 Ibid., pp. 155–6. Also see Sasaki Ginya, "Sangyō no bunka to chūsei shōgyō," in Nagahara
   Keiji, ed., *Chūsei: Nihon keizaishi taikei*, vol. 2 (Tokyo: Tōkyō daigaku shuppankai, 1965), pp.
   145–50.
5 Toyoda Takeshi and Kodama Kōta, *Ryūtsūshi* (Tokyo: Yamakawa shuppansha, 1969), pp. 46–
   54.
6 Ibid., pp. 47–54; and Ishii Susumu, *Kamakura bakufu*, vol. 7 of *Nihon no rekishi* (Tokyo: Chūō
   kōronsha, 1971), pp. 459–72.

century – for which there are more historical sources concerning commercial activities in agricultural communities – we have only limited information about the means by which the cultivators obtained specialized products. Cultivators, artisans, and merchants left little record of their daily lives.

The capital trade region

In and around the capital, some goods and services were traded during the Heian period, and trade is known to have increased steadily during the twelfth century. Even for this region, much of our knowledge of commercial activities is restricted to those of court members, high-ranking nobles, and monks of major temples – the authors of most of the medieval documents. Although we can obtain various important facts from these documents concerning some groups of artisans and merchants, they tell us little about the nature and extent of market activities. We know even less about the economic lives of the warriors and the many other residents of the region. What follows therefore is a summary of what the documents and the fragmentary evidence tell us about the late Heian and early Kamakura periods.

The elites living in and around the capital – the members of the court, the nobles, and the monks – obtained their food and other daily necessities from shōen dues paid in kind; from those artisans, fishermen, and others under their protection; and from the markets offering an increasing variety of goods. Though the proportion of daily necessities obtained from the market must have risen slowly over time, there is little doubt that many of the elites' needs were met by the shōen.

For example, we learn from the records of the Tōdaiji, a major temple in Nara, that as late as 1250 it was receiving many goods from Ōyama-no-shō in Tamba, one of the many shōen belonging to the temple. The dues consisted of 142.4 koku of rice; 10 koku of barley; varying quantities of several kinds of paper, cloth, nuts, fruits, and vegetables; carefully specified quantities of roasted barley, rice cakes, dried persimmons, mushrooms, sesame oil, hemp, Japanese lacquer, dried bracken, yams, burdock, horsetails, wooden buckets and ladles, straw mats, firewood, and thread; and half a dozen other items.[7] Although such a detailed record is not available for other shōen of the Tōdaiji, there is no doubt that the temple obtained various combina-

7 Ōyama Kyōhei, *Kamakura bakufu*, vol. 9 of *Nihon no rekishi* (Tokyo: Shōgakkan, 1974), pp. 214–16.

tions of the goods it required from all of its *shōen*, adjusting the dues from each in regard to the climate and other limitations, as well as the distance of each *shōen* from Nara. The existing documents show that *shōen* far from the temple paid a large part of their dues with more readily transportable and nonperishable items such as rice and cloth, and a *shōen* on the Inland Sea even paid all of its dues in salt.[8]

The Daigoji, another large temple in Nara, not only varied the dues according to each *shōen*'s distance from Nara and its climatic limitations but also rotated by month and year which *shōen*, among those located near Nara, was to supply the temple with vegetables, other perishable products, and the labor services required for various ceremonial occasions. The products supplied to the temple from its *shōen*, scattered around the capital and to the north in the Hokuriku region, included saké, seaweed, earthenware, straw mats, charcoal, lumber, straw, hay, and several other items.[9]

Most of the records for *shōen* held by the emperor and nobles are less informative. However, an unusually detailed record concerning some of the seventy-six *shōen* belonging to the Chōkōdō – a temple built by the cloistered emperor Goshirakawa – reveals that the dues included such items as oxen, silk, and cotton batting, in addition to vegetables, rice, and many of the goods listed in the preceding examples. In this case, too, the mix of dues varied according to distance and presumably the ability of each *shōen* to produce various products.[10]

These and other examples show that even in the mid-thirteenth century, the elite were still obtaining most of their daily necessities from their *shōen*. This, however, did not mean that markets were not becoming more important. In fact, the evidence indicates that these markets gradually developed from sometime in the eleventh century to satisfy the needs of lesser nobles, warriors, and various commoners residing in the capital region.

One group of producer-merchants who began to sell goods in the market were *kugonin*, persons supplying the court with such daily necessities as fish, vegetables, fruit, charcoal, straw mats, and the like in exchange for exemption from taxes and corvée. Even after they had begun to sell some of their products in the market sometime in the late Heian period, they continued to provide their products to the court.[11]

8 Nagahara Keiji, "Shōen ryōshu keizai no kōzō," in Nagahara, ed., *Chūsei*, pp. 57–70.
9 Ibid., pp. 75–80. Also see Sasaki, "Sangyō no bunka to chūsei shōgyō" in Nagahara, ed., *Chūsei*, pp. 151–2.
10 Nagahara, "Shōen ryōshu keizai no kōzō," in Nagahara, ed., *Chūsei*, pp. 60–63.
11 Wakita Haruko, *Nihon chūsei shōgyō hattatsushi no kenkyū* (Tokyo: Ochanomizu shobō, 1969), pp. 112–22; and Toyoda and Kodama, *Ryūtsūshi*, pp. 78–79.

Another group of producer-merchants who used the market were those former part-time cultivators who had supplied, in exchange for reduced *shōen* dues and corvée, specific goods to the elite of the capital region. These producer-merchants were allowed to sell their goods in the market as long as they continued to supply goods to the elite. As these part-time suppliers of daily necessities began to sell more of their products in the market, they eventually became full-time producer-merchants permitted to provide the nobles and temples with the products they produced in order to compensate for the dues (often rice) and corvée that they no longer paid.

There was yet another group of persons who sold goods in the capital region. These were the fisherman and cultivators of the region who, while remaining primarily fishermen and cultivators, came to Kyoto, Nara, and other satellite towns to sell their goods. Although we learn more about the activities of these part-time merchants as they begin to play a more important role in the region's commerce after the mid-thirteenth century, all we know of them until then is that they were one of the groups of producer-merchants who came to trade their products in the region.[12]

To summarize, the elites living in the capital region were obtaining, even in the mid-thirteenth century, most of their daily necessities from the *shōen* located in and around the capital region. However, *shōen* dues and what was supplied by the *kugonin* and others as a part of the dues were not the only source of many of the goods that these elites consumed. As the *kugonin* and others, including nearby fishermen and cultivators, began to sell their goods in the markets, the elites could acquire more goods more easily to supplement what they were receiving from the *shōen*, the *kugonin*, and others.

Little is known of how warriors and commoners in the capital region obtained their daily necessities. But we can surmise, from what we have just observed, that they too acquired a significant and increasing portion of these goods from the markets, where more and more goods were being sold in response to the residents' growing demands. However, as with the elites, an increasing number of warriors residing in the capital region also undoubtedly obtained many items from *shōen*, the portion of output they were entitled to as *shugo* or *jitō*. It is also quite likely that some warriors living or staying for a limited time in and around the capital must also have received dues in kind from cultivators working their lands located some distance from the capital.

12 Wakita, *Nihon chūsei shōgyō*, pp. 116–20.

These dues in kind from distant landholdings must have consisted of rice, cloth, and other products that could be readily transported to Kyoto and exchanged in the market for numerous goods that the warriors consumed daily. We can be reasonably certain that by the early decades of the thirteenth century, warriors – and elites – in the capital region used cash more frequently than they had in the late twelfth century.[13]

The artisans under the protection of elites obtained their daily necessities in the form of in-kind payments from elites and by using their products to barter among themselves or with cultivators in the region. Beginning in the early thirteenth century, they may have received some cash from the elites and others through their market transactions, and they may have used money to buy the goods they consumed.

In contrast with the market activities, which were growing only slowly, trading in specialized products grew more visibly throughout the twelfth century. By the early decades of the thirteenth century, elites in the capital region could acquire many specialized products from artisans and merchants. The reason was that market activities expanded steadily in the twelfth century as artisans and others who had been providing their products and services exclusively to the elites began to sell more of their products and services in the capital region and even in the surrounding provinces. And a growing number of commoners were becoming, albeit slowly, consumers of these products and services.

The emergence of the za

The producer-merchants of these specialized products, who first appeared in the capital region far ahead of those who later appeared in the agricultural communities, were also the first to give birth to the za, a counterpart to the European medieval guild, which played an increasingly important role in the growth of commerce in medieval Japan.[14]

The origins of the capital region's producer-merchants can be traced to the groups of artisans and others who, sometime during the

---

13 Takenaka Yasukazu and Kawakami Tadashi, *Nihon shōgyōshi* (Tokyo: Minerva shobō, 1965), pp. 42–43; and Oyama, *Kamakura bakufu*, p. 378.

14 Because the *za* has long been studied by many Japanese specialists, there are numerous works on the subject. See Kozo Yamamura, "The Development of *Za* in Medieval Japan," *Business History Review* 47 (Winter 1973): 438–65, and the works cited in this article.

eleventh century, had begun to be "protected" by the most powerful elites. The protection of artisans began because the weakened central government had become unable to provide the desired goods and services to the elites. This protection may also have been offered because the elites, whose political and economic powers had been increasing at the expense of the government, had the power to protect or exempt artisans and others from government taxes and could supply them with food, shelter, and even cash payments. The elites holding high positions in government were able to "privatize" groups of artisans so that both patrons and artisans could benefit at the expense of the government.

Such actions by the powerful elites are exemplified in the well-known case of the *sekkanke*, the several collateral lines of the highest-ranked nobles. Sometime during the eleventh century they created, for their respective lines, workshops and offices that oversaw the activities of artisans who had previously provided specialized services to the government. The workshops were for smiths, founders, and other artisans who worked with metals; carpenters, several groups of weavers and those who made silk, cloth, thread, and the like; makers of Buddhist statues and other goods used in religious services; scroll makers and painters; papermakers; dye makers and dyers; and several other groups of artisans. Offices were established to oversee porters and litter bearers, cooks, those who tended horses and orchards, those responsible for acquiring fish and other food products (perhaps those not directly obtained from *shōen* dues), cleaners and sweepers, and the like.[15] Though few records remain for other high-ranked and well-off nobles, we know that they too created such workshops and offices – fewer in number and smaller in scale than those of the *sekkanke* – to meet their needs.

By the twelfth century, the elites had much less need to rely on their "protected" artisans. One reason for this was that more of the protected artisans began to produce more goods for sale in the market in addition to those supplied to their protectors. Recent studies by Japanese scholars show that as early as the mid-eleventh century such artisans as papermakers, weavers, scroll painters, smiths, founders, and several other highly skilled specialists who had been protected by the government and the highest-ranked nobles began to produce their products "privately" and to sell them in the market.[16] The other rea-

---

15 Wakita, *Nihon chūsei shōgyō*, pp. 199–234, contains an excellent description of the *za*'s origins.   16 Ibid., pp. 204–5.

son was that an increasing number of other artisans in and around the region began to produce for the markets. Though the origins of these artisans remain obscure, many had probably produced their products in exchange for the stipendiary paddies given to them by temples and *shōen* administrators.

As soon as these artisans began to sell their goods in the markets, *za* began to appear under the protection of the court, high-ranking nobles, and temples, because such protection benefited both the patrons and the producer-merchants. The protection consisted of using the patrons' political and religious power to reduce or eliminate the competition that each *za* might face and to enable the *za* merchants to engage in their market activities in the region, and even in nearby provinces, with a minimum of hindrance (such as the levying of various taxes in kind or in cash by the government, provincial governors or other nobles, and temples). This meant that the *za* enabled merchants to enjoy substantial monopolistic or monopsonistic power that could increase their income and ability to engage more freely in market activities in the capital region and nearby provinces. The benefit to the patrons was that they could share in the *za*'s economic gains, by continuing to receive the goods they required from the *za*. The patrons also could demand more goods as the *za*'s profits rose.[17]

Although the historical evidence does not indicate a precise date when the first *za* emerged, it seems certain that they began to appear during the last decades of the eleventh century and throughout the twelfth, initially in and near the capital and then elsewhere. The oldest-known description of a *za* occurs in a petition requesting a reduction in woodcutting dues, written in 1092.[18] According to this source and others dated later, woodcutters belonging to the Seiren-in temple voluntarily formed a group that was allowed to sell firewood in the capital in exchange for providing litter-bearing services to the temple. This group, the Yatsusesato-*za*, apparently had been formed to increase the income of its members, by selling firewood in Kyoto. Further, the presumably exclusive privilege of doing so was granted by the temple, which then received litter-bearing services in addition to

17 Japanese specialists discussing the *za* do not consider the gains that the consumers of the products sold by the *za* might have realized. However, it is important to note that the *za*, not being literal monopolists who could price their products at will (as if facing a totally inelastic demand), would in most cases have increased output and caused the price to fall. Thus, to the extent that this occurred, the consumer would have gained what economists call "consumers' surplus"; that is, consumers could have obtained a product at prices below those that they would have been willing to pay.
18 For the original document relating to this *za*, see Yamamura, "The Development of *Za*," p. 441.

the woodcutters' usual work (i.e., cutting wood and supplying fire-wood in lieu of *shōen* dues).

There is no doubt that several *za*, similar in origins and functions to the one just described, existed by this period. Two *za*, one for selling charcoal and the other for selling needles, were authorized by the Shirakawa-in before 1095. The first record of a *za* belonging to the Tōdaiji is dated 1097; this was a *za* for the temple's woodcutters. There is mention of a *za* for lamp oil in Kyoto and another in Kyushu, but the records are too sketchy to establish much more than their existence. Documents from the mid-eleventh century also state that some groups of *sanjo* residents "ceased to pay *shōen* dues" and "entered into the protection of the powerful." The *sanjo*, which grew in number throughout the Heian period, reflecting the growth of *shōen*, literally meant "scattered places" in regard to the *honjo*, the "main place" where the *shōen* administrators resided. The *sanjo* referred to the residences of those persons providing the *shōen*, often on a part-time basis, with various nonagricultural products and specialized services. Because of the tasks that these persons at the *sanjo* performed, *sanjo* were usually located at local nodes of transportation, and they grew in number, first in and around the capital and then in Kinai and else-where. We cannot be certain whether de facto *za* were created between the *sanjo* residents and "the powerful" who protected them. However, it appears that the protection was quite similar to that of the producer-merchants of the capital region.[19]

The most important fact for this chapter, however, is that the num-ber of *za* grew during the twelfth century. A document written in 1127 indicates that two lamp-oil *za* – one belonging to the Daigo temple in Kyoto and the other sanctioned by a branch shrine of the Hachimangu in Kyushu – functioned as bona fide *za*. The evidence indicates that *miyaza* (*za* formed by those providing services to shrines) and some groups in the *sanjo* formed *za* during the twelfth century.

The powerful temples and court nobles also sanctioned more *za* as the twelfth century progressed. For example, a large temple, the Gionsha, had cotton batting, cloth, lumber, and tangerine *za* by 1185. The total number of *za* at the end of the century cannot be established precisely, but a reasonable estimate would be a few dozen. In any event, by the end of the twelfth century the *za* had developed to the point that an entry in a court noble's diary referred to a demand made by a rush-mat *za* of Yamato that competitors be restrained. In addi-

---

19 Japanese specialists also often refer to the residents of the *sanjo* as *sanjo*, as well.

tion, in 1195 the members of a *za* of mercury sellers in Ise petitioned that competition by "many" outsiders be restricted.[20]

To understand the historical setting in which the *za* emerged and grew in number during these centuries, we should note that two closely related and historically significant changes – one political and the other economic – were taking place between the mid-eleventh century and the end of the thirteenth century. The political change consisted of the gradual rise of the warrior aristocracy, which gained sufficient strength to form the Kamakura bakufu in 1185. The rise of the warriors was accomplished at the expense of the central government and of those court nobles and temples whose political power was derived from the legitimating authority of the throne.

The economic change resulted mainly from a slow but steady rise in agricultural productivity and was spurred by the growing number of *myōden* (paddies registered in the name of the head of a patriarchally organized group of cultivators, or *myōshu*, within a *shōen*), a significant step toward increasing the rights of cultivators in specific strips of paddies.[21] The *myōshu*, who could share more effectively in any increases in output, had additional incentives to raise productivity. They therefore began to hasten the process of improving seeds, irrigation, and agricultural management. Double cropping began to be practiced during the early Kamakura period. These developments, in turn, helped augment the economic power of the warrior class, as many of them were also *myōshu* or *myōshu*-turned-warriors. Many were also *shōen* administrators and thus were in positions to share in the increasing agricultural output at the expense of the *shōen* owners in Kyoto. Thus, what both enabled and motivated these warriors to join forces to establish the Kamakura bakufu was an increase in their economic power and the desire to legitimate their hold on that power.

During the early stage of these changes, that is, during the latter half of the eleventh and most of the twelfth century, most of the *shōen* belonging to court nobles and temples remained basically secure. The challenge to the *shōen* proprietorship by local military powers had begun, but it did not yet seriously threaten the existence of the *shōen* or the economic well-being of the *shōen* owners. Increases in productiv-

20 The diary referred to is *Sanchōki* by Sanjō Nagakane. See Yamamura, "The Development of *Za*," p. 442.
21 On the rise of agricultural productivity in the twelfth and thirteenth centuries and for further discussion of the *myōden* as an important institutional development contributing to the growth of productivity, see Kozo Yamamura, "Tara in Transition: A Study of a Kamakura Shōen," *Journal of Japanese Studies* 7 (Summer 1981): 349–91.

ity also proceeded slowly, and a marketable surplus was just beginning to appear.

However, these political and economic changes were sufficient to enable the court nobles and the temples to recognize the emerging trend: a decline in their political power and thus a decline in their tax revenues. At the same time, in the economically most advanced capital region, some producers began to see that they could earn larger incomes if they specialized in the production of certain goods and limited their competition. The *za* thus emerged as an institutional means by which to raise the income of the producers and to compensate for the falling income of the patrons.

Cities, ports, and markets

To encourage market activities in the capital trade region, the number of marketplaces in Kyoto rose, and various economic activities in the several satellite towns and ports increased. In Kyoto, the east market of the Heian period, located in the eastern half of the city (the Sakyō), became the principal marketplace. That is, a larger number of artisans and traders came to trade in the Sakyō, especially on Sanjō, Shichijō, and Hachijō, the major east–west avenues enjoying easy access to major thoroughfares to other parts of the region and located close to the warrior residences to the south. The Sakyō was also more conveniently situated for several important and economically active temples on the eastern edge of the city that had long held small markets, the *monzenmachi* (literally, "markets in front of the temple gates").[22]

What we know of the economic activities of Nara, the city of temples, is limited to the fact that it was a city consisting principally of the *monzenmachi* of two powerful temples: the Tōdaiji and the Kōfukuji.[23] Although there are few medieval documents referring to port towns, we know that many of them – such as Katsura and Toba adjacent to the capital; Yodo and Kizu on the Yodo River; Imazu, Ōtsu, and Sakamoto on Lake Biwa; and Hyōgo on the Seto Inland Sea – played important roles in the economic activities of the capital trade region during the eleventh and twelfth centuries. These were centers for transshipping government taxes and *shōen* dues to the capital and for some market activities.

22 A good discussion of medieval cities can be found in Wakita Haruko, *Nihon chūsei toshiron* (Tokyo: Tōkyō daigaku shuppankai, 1981).
23 Takenaka and Kawakami, *Nihon shōgyōshi*, p. 25; and Endō Motō, *Nihon chūsei toshiron* (Tokyo: Hakuyōsha, 1940), pp. 108–9.

Many port towns were also important because it was there that elites had their own *toi* who engaged in shipping and even perhaps in some trading on their behalf in exchange for stipendiary paddies or stipends in kind.[24] These *toi* were the precursors of the *toimaru* (shippers who also engaged in other activities), who will be discussed later in this chapter. Although supporting evidence is even more scarce, there is little doubt that market and other economic activities steadily increased in the cities outside the capital trade region during the late Heian and early Kamakura periods. The most important of such cities was Kamakura, which grew rapidly after it became the seat of the newly established bakufu. Yoritomo and his retainers in Kamakura received most of the dues from the paddies of the nine surrounding provinces, and combined with the fact that Kamakura was blessed with an excellent harbor, commerce in that city could not but expand – as did the population – to serve the warriors' needs. Although we have no details, we do know that seven (or nine, depending on the source) "marketplaces" were authorized by the bakufu by the beginning of the thirteenth century to facilitate the expanding market activities. Several *za* had already appeared, though little is known of their origins and activities.[25] Coins must also have become an increasingly prevalent medium of exchange in commercial transactions among the merchants and warriors in Kamakura.

We should not underestimate the extent of commercial activities in Kamakura by the early decades of the thirteenth century. After all, this was a city in which the bakufu had to destroy as many as 32,274 saké jars when it temporarily prohibited the sale of saké in 1252. We also know that Kamakura's population had grown so rapidly that the city had to be subdivided into *ho*, as was Kyoto, beginning in 1240 and that an earthquake in 1293 was reported to have killed 23,024 of its inhabitants.[26]

Throughout the twelfth century and into the early decades of the thirteenth, virtually all other important cities outside the capital region were also port cities having access to shipping services. Some became points of transshipping for the provincial taxes and *shōen* dues headed to the capital region. Given that the principal means of transportation, especially for agricultural products, was by water, many cities became both important ports and centers of commerce, includ-

---

24 Even today, the best discussion on *toimaru* is still Toyoda Takeshi's *Chūsei Nihon shōgyōshi no kenkyū* (Tokyo: Iwanami shoten, 1952), pp. 194–263.
25 Ishii, *Kamakura bakufu*, pp. 472–86.   26 Ibid., p. 474.

ing Hakata, Hakozaki, Urado, and a few others in Kyushu and Akama-zeki (Shimonoseki), and Yamasaki, Onomichi, Wakasa, Naoetsu, and a dozen others in western to northern Honshū. There must have been, as well, other smaller nodes of transportation, including provincial capitals in which commercial activities were increasing, but no reliable records for them exist.[27]

Finally, it is known that following the establishment of the Kamakura bakufu, nearly thirty *shukuba* – towns that grew up around inns for travelers – developed on the Tōkaidō, the main route for those making the two-week journey between Kyoto and Kamakura. Although the increased traffic on the Tōkaidō diminished travel on the Sanyōdō (the route connecting Kyoto and Hakato), the latter route too is known to have had fifteen to twenty *shukuba*.[28]

Sung coins and trade with China

Throughout the late Heian and early Kamakura periods, trade with the continent – Sung and Southern Sung – continued, and two results of this trade are especially significant in the context of this chapter. One was that trade with China offered elites many products unobtainable in Japan; the other was that the trade brought in a large quantity of Sung coins. The latter was by far more important because it led to the monetization of the Japanese economy, which in turn had profound effects on the political, economic, and social history of Japan during the Kamakura and Muromachi periods.

By the late Heian period, the power of the Dazaifu to control trade with the continent had diminished, reflecting the weakened government in the capital. Thus, the trade, conducted primarily through ports in northern Kyushu, was mostly private trade carried on by elites for their own economic gains. After the Kamakura bakufu was established, private trade continued because Yoritomo chose not to impose restrictions on it. During this period, as well as into the second half of the Kamakura period, Japan exported gold, pearls, mercury, sulfur, scrolls, folding screens, fans, and other craft products and imported several kinds of luxury cloth; numerous varieties of incense and fragrances; writing materials (brushes, ink sticks, and ink stones); various art objects and decorative furnishings made of ivory, gold,

27 Toyoda, *Chūsei Nihon shōgyōshi no kenkyū*, pp. 226–38.
28 Ishii, *Kamakura bakufu*, p. 459.

silver, and precious stones; Buddhist writings of many kinds; and a large number of Sung coins.[29]

Although there are no reliable data on the quantity of coins imported through private trade, there is no doubt that the amount was extremely large – large enough to cause Sung China to issue, in 1199, an unsuccessful decree to prohibit the export of its coins to Japan. It is also known that Saionji Kintsune, a high-ranking noble, imported as many as 100,000 *kan* of Sung coins in 1242, an amount equivalent in that period to the cost of building the complex of a dozen or so buildings needed to establish a major Buddhist temple.[30]

The effects of the continuing inflow of coins in such magnitudes were felt throughout the twelfth century and even more so in the early decades of the thirteenth. This is perhaps best illustrated by the fact that a series of decrees prohibiting the use of coins was issued by the court in 1179, 1187, 1189, and 1192. The futility of these decrees is evident in that although the first two prohibited the use of imported coins, the second two attempted only to limit their use in marketplaces in the capital.[31] The reasons stated for the prohibition included such inconsistent facts as that imported coins were no more legal than the prohibited, privately minted coins and that the use of coins caused undesirable price fluctuations. However, the real reason must have been that the large inflow of coins was causing both inflation, an unwelcome development for the elites who had to buy more and more goods and services in the markets, and a drop in the relative value of the coins that the elites received when selling a part of the *shōen* dues paid in kind, thus reducing the real income of the court and the elites.[32]

However, such official reactions began to change in the beginning of the thirteenth century. As the inflow of Chinese coins continued to increase, the use of money – the "money sickness" as contemporaries called it – spread rapidly. Nobles, and later the bakufu, had no choice but to come to terms with the fact that coins were far more convenient than was bartering or using cloth or rice as a medium of exchange.

---

29 Oyama, *Kamakura bakufu*, pp. 370–81, describes the trade with Sung China and the effects of a large inflow of Sung coins.   30 Ibid., pp. 379–80.   31 Ibid., p. 379.

32 Of course, an empirical verification is required to establish the observation made in the text. However, given the quantity of Sung coins then flowing into Japan, there is little doubt that inflation was occurring during this period. See Kozo Yamamura and Tetsuo Kamiki, "Silver Mines and Sung Coins: A Monetary History of Medieval and Modern Japan in International Perspective," in J. F. Richards, ed., *Precious Metals in the Later Medieval and Early Modern Worlds* (Durham, N.C.: Carolina Academic Press, 1983), pp. 329–62.

Thus, the court declared in 1226 that exchange using coins was to be encouraged in preference to that using cloth. And by 1240, the use of coins was prohibited by the bakufu only in the northernmost Ou region, effectively conceding to the use of coins in all other parts of the nation.[33] Simply put, as trade – commercial activities – grew, this convenient medium became a necessity.

Foreseeing the various difficulties to arise as a result of the economy's continuing monetization, in 1239 the bakufu was forced to issue a decree prohibiting the appointment of monks, merchants, and moneylenders to the position of deputy *jitō* (*jitō-dai*). Some in the warrior class had begun to appoint these men to collect dues directly from the *shōen* so that those who had lent money against the warriors' land could be repaid. To prevent such a development, the bakufu in 1240 admonished its retainers living in Kyoto not to indulge in luxury beyond their means.[34] These developments, however, were only the harbinger of the much more serious consequences of monetization.

ACCELERATION OF COMMERCE AND MONETIZATION

From the mid-thirteenth century, the pace of commercial activities accelerated first in the large cities and then in the provinces. In and around the capital and in a few larger cities, including Kamakura, the number of shops selling specialized products and daily necessities rose; an increasing number of merchants and artisans selling specialized products frequented the cities from nearby towns and villages as well as from distant provinces; and the *za* steadily grew in number. More markets appeared in ports, towns, and at other nodes of transportation in most parts of the nation, and as a result, cultivators too were able to participate in commerce. Although the cultivators' participation was limited during the second half of the Kamakura period, there can be no doubt that their economic lives were changing fundamentally as their visits to local markets grew more frequent and they traded more goods at these markets. And to facilitate the expanding trade between the largest cities and the provinces, transportation capabilities, over both land and water, improved, thereby increasing the number of teamsters, porters, and other specialists engaged in shipping.

A no less visible and significant change that accompanied these

33 Ōyama, *Kamakura bakufu*, p. 379; and Takenaka and Kawakami, *Nihon shōgyōshi*, p. 42.
34 Takenaka and Kawakami, *Nihon shōgyōshi*, pp. 42–43.

commercial activities was the continuing monetization of the economy, which spread from cities to villages with profound effects. The use of coins made trading much more efficient: When coins were used as a medium of exchange, the relative values of goods could be established more readily, and the desired mix of what one consumed could be obtained far more easily than through bartering. In short, what economists call *transaction costs* were significantly reduced. Another effect was the rapid spread of commutation (payment of dues in cash), enabling the cultivators to plant more efficient mixes of grains, vegetables, and other cash crops. No longer forced to plant specific mixes of products in order to pay their dues, cultivators could make better use of their resources. Another effect common to all monetized economies was the emergence of borrowers and lenders of money, forcing the bakufu to adopt policies to aid the borrowers, many of whom were warriors.

Commerce and the za in Kyoto

In the latter half of the Kamakura period, the growth of commerce was nowhere more evident than in Kyoto. Although most shops were located in the city's commercial section, between Sanjō and Hachijō in the Sakyō, small shops selling such daily necessities as rice, fish, and the like could be found throughout the city. Many of these merchants were former *kugonin* and artisans who had once supplied the needs of the court and the nobles but who, throughout the Kamakura period, gradually became more independent. The court and elite had no need to discourage their growing independence. As independent suppliers, the *kugonin* and artisans required no economic assistance, and as they produced more for the market, their productive efficiency and skills also rose. Furthermore, there was an additional economic incentive for the patrons in permitting, if not encouraging, such independence: In many cases, these newly independent producers formed *za* of their own and paid more dues in kind and services in exchange for their patron's protection.[35]

The residents of the capital also enjoyed many goods and services supplied by artisans, fishermen, and cultivators who came to sell their wares from both the surrounding regions and distant provinces. By the mid-Kamakura period, more and more merchants – those special-

---

35 Endō, *Nihon chūsei toshiron*, pp. 99–103; Wakita, *Nihon chūsei toshiron*, pp. 77–84.

izing in trading and not those selling what they produced, as was often the case before the mid-thirteenth century – appeared in Kyoto. The growth of commerce in Kyoto can also be confirmed by the greater number of *za* during the thirteenth century. We can establish from documents written in the 1220s that at least a dozen *za* were organized, including those for selling lamp oil, lumber, straw mats, and several types of cloth. Many were sponsored by the Kōfukuji, Tōdaiji, Hachimangu, other temples and shrines, and some court nobles. During the mid-thirteenth century *za* were organized to sell firewood, fish, dried fish, roof tiles, and various "metal products," as well as *za* for various skilled craftsmen such as carpenters, painters, and smiths. And during the final decades of the century, *za* were established among the sellers of dyes, sickles, silk, "birds" (the Buddhist euphemism for small game), and others. Although we cannot be sure of the exact number of *za* in Kyoto at the end of the Kamakura period, it was easily more than a few score. We also know that by the end of the century, a few *za* began to appear in regional urban centers as well.[36]

The *za* continued to increase in number when, as suggested earlier, they discovered that they could make a higher profit if potential competitors were prevented from infringing on their monopolistic or monopsonistic rights. The case of the Oyamazaki-*za*, organized in Yamashiro to sell lamp oil under the protection of the Hachiman Shrine, is an example of how a *za* emerged under the protection of a patron.

This *za* was initially sanctioned to permit a group of men providing various services to the shrine to sell lamp oil in the capital in exchange for dues paid in kind. But because these men found that they could earn more profits by becoming full-time merchants, they began to expand their markets from Kyoto to the regions on both sides of the Yodo River and into Hyōgo. Such expansion was possible because the shrine's political power extended to many regions through its branch shrines and its *shōen* holdings. The fact that the shrine exempted members of the *za* from tolls (which were beginning to be levied by various court nobles and temples during this period) in exchange for higher dues paid in lamp oil also helped discourage potential competitors.[37]

The *za* of this period emerged and grew in similar ways. However,

36 Toyoda and Kodama, *Ryūtsūshi*, pp. 80–87; and Wakita, *Nihon chūsei shōgyō hattatsushi*, pp. 235–74.   37 Takenaka and Kawakami, *Nihon shōgyōshi*, pp. 39–40.

from the mid-thirteenth century, the circumstances encouraging the *za*'s continued development became more pronounced. Many *shōen* proprietors – temples and nobles – suffered a continued decline in tax revenue owing to the rising power of the warriors, and at the same time, the marketable surplus was steadily rising because of the higher agricultural productivity that occurred primarily as a result of more intensive land cultivation. That is, just when the *shōen* owners felt the need for additional income from the *za*, the producers of marketable goods and the merchants were able to meet that need at a profit. Under such circumstances, the *za*, benefiting all concerned, could not but proliferate.

One might wonder why the warriors allowed the court nobles and temples to capture the lion's share of the income earned by the *za*. The answer to this puzzle can be readily found. As evidenced by Minamoto Yoritomo's desire for a formal appointment to the Kyoto-based government, the bakufu had to remain within the legitimate framework of the imperial government in order to maintain the delicate balance between Kyoto and Kamakura. This meant that the Kamakura bakufu still had to respect the interests of the court nobles and the temples, whose political power reflected the waning but still substantial power of the throne. In other words, the warriors had to allow the court nobles and the temples to profit from the *za* as the price for supporting the imperial authority in this delicate balance. Of course, it is also true that some temples had enough military power to rebuff all but a major attempt by warriors to wrestle away the benefits being realized by the *za*. In short, the power of the ascending warrior class was still insufficient during the thirteenth century to permit it to capture the gains from the *za*'s expanding activities.

Finally, it is important to note that despite their monopolistic or monopsonistic activities, the *za* undoubtedly contributed to the growth of commerce during the Kamakura period. Given the still-limited demand, free entry and the consequent competition would have caused specialization to occur more slowly. Although most of the benefits resulting from specialization – increased efficiency in production and marketing – were undoubtedly shared by the sponsors and the *za* members, some of those benefits must have been shared by the consumers as well.

One reason for making this speculation is that the *za* sponsors, usually collecting only a fixed sum from the *za*, left the benefits of increased specialization to be shared by *za* members and consumers. Another reason is that to the extent the *za* monopoly was not yet securely established and consumers could exercise their prerogative to buy fewer products sold by *za* if prices were raised, consumers enjoyed some of the benefits of the *za*'s increased efficiency. Even the economic gains accruing to the *za*'s members were not totally private because such gains would help improve skills and the efficiency of production and distribution, thus benefiting the society as a whole in the long run.

The growth of markets, towns, and transportation

There is no doubt that the number of markets – most of them having only three market days per month (*sansai-ichi*) – steadily increased across the nation during the second half of the Kamakura period. When we count the number of local markets mentioned in historical records, we find that there were only six between 1200 and 1250, increasing to nineteen between 1250 and 1300, and to twenty-one between 1300 and 1331.[38] Such data, though limited, are a useful indicator of the rise in the number of local markets. These markets frequently sprang up at or near the nodes of transportation – ports and the more important crossroads – and in such places as provincial capitals and the larger local temples.

Reflecting the importance of sea transportation in commerce, port towns continued to proliferate. The most important among them were those located on the Seto Inland Sea and Lake Biwa. These port towns developed as the entrepôts for goods bound for the capital region. For example, Ōtsu and Sakamoto in Ōmi Province grew in importance as the transshipping centers of such products as rice, lumber, salt, paper, and fish brought from the eastern provinces in the Togoku and Tōkaidō regions. Hyōgo, Sakai, and Yodo on the Yodo River were active ports for many goods shipped to the capital region from Kyoto and several ports on the Inland Sea. Most of the products coming from San'in and Hokuriku passed through Wakasa to ports around Lake Biwa and then to the capital region. By the end of the Kamakura period, the capital region, the local markets, and these port towns constituted a commercial network.[39]

The foregoing shows that transportation, especially over water, was

38 Sasaki, *Chūsei shōhin ryūtsūshi*, pp. 74–97; Toyoda, *Chūsei Nihon shōgyōshi no kenkyū*, pp. 112–18; and Takenaka Yasukazu and Sakudō Yōtarō, *Nihon keizaishi* (Tokyo: Gakubunsha, 1972), pp. 29–30.
39 Takenaka and Sakudō, *Nihon keizaishi*, pp. 26–28; and Toyoda, *Chūsei Nihon shōgyōshi no kenkyū*, pp. 254–7.

indispensable, and specialists in both sea and land transportation helped improve this capability. Those specialists meriting our attention were the *toi*, more frequently referred to as *toimaru* during the Kamakura period, who performed managerial functions (including the supervision of ship captains, crew, and stevedores) and also engaged in the warehousing and delivery of cargo (including dues in rice or other products).[40] Many of the *toimaru* were either large enterprising *myōshu*, minor retainers, or relatives of *jitō* and *shōkan* who received, for performing these roles, rights to yields of rice and other crops from designated rice paddies within a *shōen* or a *kokugaryō*.[41] The *toimaru* were also responsible for supervising porters (many of whom were cultivators discharging their corvée obligations) and other specialists of land transportation.

Also contributing to transportation capabilities in the thirteenth century was the gradual increase, beginning in mid-century, of *kaisen*, literally, "ships making rounds." These ships were chartered to carry cargo on consignment or were used by their owners for trading of their own. They were most frequently found in the Seto Inland Sea, but during the second half of the Kamakura period, many traveled from distant northern ports to ports on the Japan Sea near Lake Biwa. Though some of these ships were manned by fishermen, as were those of Sugaura on Lake Biwa, by the end of the Kamakura period, many others were operated by full-time specialists. The growing importance of *kaisen* in the commerce of the thirteenth and fourteenth centuries can be confirmed by frequent references to them in contemporary records.[42]

Perhaps because most bulk goods were transported by water, there are few historical records of the Kamakura period that refer to specialists in land transportation. This does not mean, however, that these specialists did not exist. It is known that by the mid-thirteenth century the *shōen* administrators and proprietors were beginning to engage the services of *shariki* (teamsters using carts) and others because the cultivators were not providing all of the necessary land transportation. The need for these specialists, however, rose only slowly. Even by the end of the Kamakura period, the scale of their business was such that most merchants and artisans were still able to transport their wares without

---

40 Toyoda's *Chūsei Nihon shōgyōshi no kenkyū*, pp. 196–354, still is one of the best sources on *toimaru*. For a good description, also see Kodama and Toyoda, *Ryūtsūshi*, pp. 57–62.
41 Toyoda, *Chūsei Nihon shōgyōshi no kenkyū*, pp. 196–206.
42 Ibid., pp. 221–5; and Kodama and Toyoda, *Ryūtsūshi*, pp. 103–11.

their assistance. It was not until the Muromachi period that the number of specialists in land transportation rapidly increased.

Monetization and commutation

The importation and use of Chinese coins, which had begun to increase in the early decades of the thirteenth century, accelerated from mid-century. Japan's importation of Sung coins indeed became so large that copper coins frequently disappeared from the cities of the T'ai-chou region of China within a day after Japanese traders came in search of them. In an attempt to stem this outflow, Sung China issued decrees that prohibited the export of coins and in 1254 limited the number of Japanese ships allowed to call on its ports to only five per year. But these measures did not succeed, because "forty to fifty Japanese ships, coming every year to exchange lumber, sulphur, and other products for coins, were helped by inspectors who took bribes, hid coins at the bottom of ships . . . or loaded coins after the inspection."[43]

Although trade between Japan and China declined sharply after the collapse of Southern Sung in 1279, and especially because of the Mongol attempts to invade Japan, the importation of Chinese coins continued, albeit at a reduced level. Unauthorized Japanese merchant ships continued to trade with the coastal cities of China and brought back coins well into the fourteenth century.[44] The largest amount of these coins were imported during the century or so preceding the demise of the Southern Sung. According to a study of large (non-overlapping) collections of Chinese coins found in Japan, approximately 85 percent consisted of Sung and Southern Sung coins.[45]

There is no doubt that by the middle of the thirteenth century, coins were being used daily by residents of the capital and other large cities as the principal medium of trade. The use of coins also grew in towns and villages throughout the second half of the Kamakura period. With Kyoto at the center, the use of money expanded from Kinai to the distant provinces and from the nobles and the temples to the cultivators. The record shows that even as early as the 1240s, coins were used in the remote Ou region in the north.[46] The monetization of the econ-

43 Kobata Atsushi, Nihon kahei ryūtsūshi (Tokyo: Tōkō shoin, 1969), p. 48.
44 Takenaka and Kawakami, Nihon shōgyōshi, pp. 48–49.
45 For a discussion and analysis of these studies, see Yamamura and Kamiki, "Silver Mines and Sung Coins," pp. 336–8.   46 Takenaka and Kawakami, Nihon shōgyōshi, p. 42.

omy was proceeding in response to, as well as promoting, the development of markets in provinces throughout the nation.

Attesting to the degree of monetization achieved by mid-century, documents show that nobles and temples paid cash for most wages, stipends, clothing allowances, ceremonial costs, some transportation costs, and the like. For example, Tōdaiji documents dated between 1261 and 1279 confirm that by this time most of the temple's allowances to its monks were paid in cash and only a small part in kind.[47]

As well-known study of land sales records in the Kinai region shows that the use of cash became more important as a medium of exchange throughout the Kamakura period. This study found that between 1186 and 1219, of a sample of 187 land sales, 139 were conducted using rice as the medium of exchange, 7 using cloth, and the remaining 40 using cash. Between 1220 and 1283, of a sample of 331 land sales, cash was used in 143 cases, rice in 181, and cloth in 7. Finally, between 1284 and 1333, of a sample of 189 land sales, 124 used cash, 64 used rice, and only 1 sale used cloth. In short, over these three periods, the proportion of the transactions conducted in cash went from 21 percent to 42 percent and then to 66 percent.[48]

The importance of money for residents of large cities and even for others is also evident in the appearance of bills of exchange and moneylenders. Bills of exchange began to be used sometime during the second half of the thirteenth century to alleviate the costs and risks of transporting cash over long distances for trading, paying dues in cash, and meeting expenditures incurred by litigants forced to remain in Kamakura for the duration of court proceedings.

The oldest surviving evidence of a bill of exchange – called variously *kawashi*, *saifu*, or *warifu* – is dated 1279. This bill enabled the holder, a local power (a person who had reclaimed some amount of land and exercised political and military authority in the region) in Kii Province (modern Wakayama Prefecture) to receive cash in Kamakura. Although most of the remaining documents show that these bills were used by litigants and by *jitō* and *shōen* administrators sending dues to the capital, there are a number of documents, especially during the final decades of the Kamakura period, demonstrating that bills

---

47 Sasaki, *Chūsei shōhin ryūtsūshi*, p. 262.
48 This study was made by Tamaizumi Tairyō and is described and discussed in Kobata, *Nihon kahei ryūtsūshi*, pp. 40–46. Also see Toyoda, *Chūsei Nihon shōgyōshi no kenkyū*, pp. 101–8; and Nagahara Keiji, "Shōen ryōshu keizai no kōzō," in Nagahara, ed., *Nihon keizaishi taikei*, vol. 2, pp. 80–85.

were also used for trading between sellers (producers and merchants) of specialized products and buyers (nobles and temples).[49]

However, an even more important result of the rapid monetization was, as noted in an official bakufu document issued in 1255, a visible increase in the number of moneylenders, beginning in the middle of the thirteenth century. These moneylenders, who were called *kashiage* or *kariage* and who usually took pawns, consisted of *sansō* (literally, "mountain monks," monks of the powerful Enryakuji temple on Mount Hiei in Kyoto), some *toimaru* of larger port towns, some monks from other temples, and a number of richer merchants. The *sansō* became moneylenders because of the availability of a large and steady cash income from *shōen* dues owed to the temple and collected in cash and donations of coins from worshipers and because the *sansō* were in a position to remind borrowers that failure to repay the loans could bring about the wrath of God. The *toimaru* began to engage in moneylending as a natural sideline to their occupation. The larger among them had enough cash income and warehouses in which to store the pawns and were strategically located in port towns where the need for loans was greater.[50] This proliferation of moneylenders reflected the degree to which the economy's monetization had proceeded.

Yet another important development brought about by monetization was *daisennō* (paying dues in cash instead of in kind; commutation) which became prevalent during the latter half of the Kamakura period. The following data are useful as a quantitative indicator of the popularity of commutation.

Sasaki Ginya collected 170 historical records of the 1230–1350 period containing references to at least partial commutation and classified them by date. He found that only 6 of these records belonged to the 1230–50 period, 38 to the 1251–1300 period, and 126 to the 1301–50 period. Although we cannot assume that these records accurately reflect the speed with which commutation increased, this study provides valuable evidence indicating how quickly commutation became popular during the final decades of the Kamakura period.[51] An exami-

49 Toyoda, *Chūsei Nihon shōgyōshi no kenkyū*, pp. 264–300, contains an excellent description of numerous original documents. Takenaka and Sakudō, *Nihon keizaishi*, pp. 30–31, provides a useful example showing how a specific *kawase* was used.
50 See Toyoda, *Chūsei Nihon shōgyōshi no kenkyū*; and Kodama and Toyoda, *Ryūtsūshi*.
51 The data were first presented and analyzed by Sasaki Ginya, "Shōen ni okeru daisennō-sei no seiritsu to tenkai," in Nagahara Keiji and Inagaki Yasuhiko, eds., *Chūsei no shakai to keizai* (Tokyo: Tōkyō daigaku shuppankai, 1962), which was later expanded and published in Sasaki's *Chūsei shōhin ryūtsūshi*.

nation of Sasaki's original sources also reveals that commutation began early and was practiced most frequently in Owari and the surrounding provinces on the Tōkaidō route, in Harima and nearby provinces on the Sanyōdō route, and in the northern provinces of Kyushu. The number of *shōen* practicing commutation also continued to rise most rapidly in those provinces into the fourteenth century.

There is an ongoing debate among Japanese specialists concerning why commutation began to be practiced and why it increased during the thirteenth century. The older generation of specialists generally explain the increase in commutation as the inevitable outcome of the fact that as local markets developed, enabling the dues payers to obtain cash, the dues recipients in the capital demanded commutation. The relatively early and more extensive growth of the local markets in *shōen* located on the major routes and in the northern provinces of Kyushu is offered as evidence supporting this view. Toyoda Takeshi, one of these specialists, also cites the relative difficulties and higher costs of transporting bulky dues in kind as contributing to the increase in commutation.[52]

In more recent studies, however, a few Japanese historians have begun to argue that these explanations are unsatisfactory and leave several questions unanswered. First, if the dues recipients' demand for cash was the reason for commutation, why does a recent examination of nearly a dozen *shōen* reveal that commutation was initiated by the *jitō* or even the cultivators themselves? Second, if the relative difficulties and higher costs of transporting dues in kind was a factor in encouraging commutation, would not the same factor inhibit the ability of local merchants to buy products from dues payers, inasmuch as most of what they bought would have to be transported to the capital and other centers of consumption? That is, the authors of the recent studies assert that the difficulties and costs of transporting bulky goods could also have reduced market activities in the provinces, and this in turn would have made it more difficult for the cultivators to obtain the cash needed to pay dues. Third, although the earlier generation of historians assumed that rice – the most important product that the cultivators sold to obtain cash – was transported to Kyoto for sale, was there sufficient demand for rice in the capital where many recipients of dues were still receiving rice from their *shōen* located in neighboring provinces? Finally, if local markets had been

---

52 On this debate, the best sources are Kodama and Toyoda, *Ryūtsūshi*, pp. 71–74; and Sasaki, *Chūsei shōhin ryūtsūshi*, pp. 250–362.

developing across the nation, why did the *shōen* of more distant regions not pay dues in cash, which would have been easier and less costly than bulky dues in kind to transport over long distances?[53]

Those historians who question the long-accepted views readily concede that their own answers are still far from satisfactory, primarily because of the few case studies that they have been able to make (in part because of the scarcity of pertinent historical records). However, the results of their case studies and subsequent analyses are worthy of attention.

In regard to the first question, Sasaki's study of six *shōen* that adopted partial commutation at the insistence of the *jitō* and his analysis of this development are important. These *shōen* were located in the eastern and central provinces and belonged to such proprietors as the highest-ranked nobles (including the Fujiwara) and the Tōdaiji. Sasaki establishes that commutation was adopted between 1240 and 1331 against the proprietors' wishes when the bakufu ruled in favor of the *jitō*, who demanded that cash payment of dues be allowed. Why did the *jitō* opt for commutation? Sasaki posits that the *jitō* demanded commutation either because the cultivators themselves were demanding cash payment or because the *jitō*, acting as middlemen, could benefit from commutation. The dues payers might demand commutation for two reasons. First, the proprietors were demanding dues in kind in a mix of products not produced by the cultivators themselves (thus forcing them to incur the costs of selling the products they produced and buying the mix of products the proprietor demanded). Second, paying cash was more advantageous, as the *jitō* would have made certain that the conversion rate between the products was paid in kind and that their cash value was set in favor of the cultivators (the prices of rice, cloth, and other in-kind dues in the local markets were higher than those used in the *jitō*'s conversion rate).[54]

One obvious question that Sasaki felt obliged to answer was why the *jitō* (except when they demanded commutation for the obvious reason of increasing their own income as middlemen) battled the proprietors, to the point of necessitating the bakufu's intervention on behalf of the cultivators. His answer is that the *jitō*'s economic welfare depended on having cultivators better able to meet the *jitō*'s demands, even at the

53 See Kodama and Toyoda, *Ryūtsūshi*; Sasaki, *Chūsei shōhin ryūtsūshi*; and Kamiki Tetsuo, "Chūsei shōhin ni okeru kahei," *Kokumin keizai zasshi* 120 (1963): 50–65, for an analytic discussion.
54 See Sasaki, "Shōen," in Nagahara and Inagaki, eds., *Chūsei no shakai to keizai*; Kodama and Toyoda, *Ryūtsūshi*; and Sasaki, *Chūsei shōhin ryūtsūshi*.

proprietors' expense. Even if the *jitō* did not benefit economically by the adoption of commutation, they would have fewer political problems if the cultivators felt indebted to them because of the *jitō*'s actions on their behalf. Sasaki recognizes that he is not, based on only a few case studies, in a position to refute the long-accepted interpretation that commutation was initiated by the *shōen* proprietors. He thus suggests that what is needed is a careful reexamination, and not a refutation, of the old views.[55]

On the second question concerning the relative costs and difficulties of transporting goods versus cash, the existing empirical evidence is far from sufficient to settle the issue. Although there are a few specific historical references to the high cost of transporting goods, which are emphasized by the older historians, a careful examination by Sasaki of a dozen historical documents citing the costs of transporting goods and cash demonstrates that it is not possible to conclude that the cost of transporting cash was lower than that of shipping various products. Thus, Sasaki is prepared to argue on the analytic ground noted earlier that the relative costs of transportation need not and should not be considered a factor in the increase of commutation.[56]

On this point, however, the older view has not gone undefended. More recently, Toyoda responded to Sasaki's criticism by contending that those merchants and specialists of transportation engaging in long-distance trade were more experienced in overcoming the difficulties of transporting goods over both land and sea; they knew how to bribe the pirates and brigands and how to protect their wares. They might also have been better organized in the use of ships and manpower so that their costs and risks would have been lower than those incurred by the nonspecialists retained by the *shōen* owners. Because Toyoda's rebuttal is based on assertions, the controversy on this point must also remain unresolved, awaiting further case studies and analyses of quantitative evidence.[57]

The third question regarding Kyoto's ability to consume the large quantity of rice transported there, owing to the prevalence of commutation, also cannot be answered unequivocally. Even the recent studies recognize that rice as a proportion of the total dues paid to the proprietors residing in Kyoto was falling, whereas the population of Kyoto was rising. Therefore, the answer to this question depends on each historian's educated assessment as to whether the amount of rice

55 Sasaki, *Chūsei shōhin ryūtsūshi*, pp. 350–2.
56 Ibid., pp. 329–30. 57 Kodama and Toyoda, *Ryūtsūshi*, p. 72.

being transported to Kyoto from the local markets exceeded the demand.[58]

The last question pertaining to the regional distribution of *shōen* that practiced commutation must also remain unsettled because this also concerns the relative costs and risks of transporting goods versus cash. Furthermore, there have not been enough case studies to establish the validity of the assertion, made in recent critiques of the old view, that local markets in distant regions were sufficiently developed by this time to enable dues payers to obtain the necessary cash by selling their products.

Abrogation of debts

The continuing growth of commercial activities, accompanied by the accelerating use of cash and adoption of commutation, had familiar and predictable effects on the cultivators. Trading in markets gave them opportunities to increase their income. They could now produce more of those products in which they had a comparative advantage and make more efficient use of labor, land, and other resources in response to changes in the prices of various products. Commutation, to the extent that it was adopted, freed them from the burden of producing predetermined, often disadvantageous, mixes of products.

Involvement in a cash economy, however, subjected the cultivators to price fluctuations. Inevitably there were periods of low prices that forced some to borrow money at a high interest rate, often more than 25 percent per year, in order to pay cash dues. The market-oriented economy, on the other hand, tended to favor the large *myōshu* and others who worked a large amount of land; they could better withstand the risks of price (and yield) fluctuations and even take advantage of them. They were also able to augment their economic resources by becoming village moneylenders. The most successful among them were beginning to accumulate enough cash to acquire more *kajishiki* (the right to receive rents from paddies).

However, even in the second half of the Kamakura period, market activities, monetization, and commutation affected the lives of cultivators only to a limited extent. Market days were still few; commutation was far from universal; many cultivators were still paying all or part of their dues in kind; and the paddies of most cultivators did not yield

58 Sasaki, *Chūsei shōhin ryūtsūshi*, pp. 328–30.

large or reliable surpluses that could be sold. Most of the cultivators' lives were still dictated more by the rhythms of nature than by the widening ripples of the cash nexus.

The situation was quite different for an increasing number of warriors, to whom cash with which to buy goods and services was becoming indispensable by the early decades of the thirteenth century. This was one reason that some warriors in their capacity as *jitō* took the initiative in adopting commutation and that some with more than one landholding (*shoryō*) began to appoint monks (*sansō*), merchants, and other commoners "wise in the ways of cash" as *daikan* (magistrates) to collect the cash dues from their lands.[59]

It did not take long for some warriors to spend more than their income. By the early decades of the thirteenth century they began to borrow, often mortgaging their lands, so that they could buy the goods and services that the markets offered. But this was a development that the bakufu could not allow to continue, especially when it saw that more and more of the *gokenin* – the direct retainers of the shogun – were beginning to incur large debts. In 1239, therefore, the bakufu issued a decree prohibiting *jitō*, many of whom were *gokenin*, from appointing moneylenders to the position of *daikan* or *jitō-dai* for the purpose of collecting dues. The bakufu issued this edict because a part or even all of the dues that the moneylenders collected were being retained by them as payments on loans they had advanced to the *jitō*. In the following year the bakufu, hoping to eliminate the problem at the source, issued another decree forbidding the *gokenin* from mortgaging or selling land to any non-*gokenin* or any commoner, as well as from indulging in such luxuries as riding in ox-drawn carriages.[60]

Obviously, these admonitions and prohibitions had little effect, and many *gokenin* continued to lose their lands. As a result, the bakufu issued yet another decree in 1267 to undo the damage already done. The decree gave the *gokenin* who had lost their mortgaged land the right to regain it by repaying the loans in cash or kind. That is, the decree forced the lenders, who had acquired land from the *gokenin*, to accept overdue repayment on the loans. Furthermore, the decree repeated the prohibition against all sales of land by *gokenin* and added new restrictions disallowing former wives and widows of *gokenin* to

59 Amino Yoshihiko, *Mōko shūrai*, vol. 10 of *Nihon rekishi* (Tokyo: Shōgakkan, 1974), pp. 112–16.
60 Takeuchi Rizō, ed., *Tochi seidoshi*, vol. 1 (Tokyo: Yoshikawa shuppansha, 1973), pp. 286–301.

transfer land received from their husbands to new husbands and void-
ing the ownership of land by any women except the wives and daughters of *gokenin*. Also in 1267, the bakufu abolished its office in charge
of appeals concerning decisions made on cases involving sold or mortgaged land.[61]

Not surprisingly, this decree caused great confusion and created
many problems. Even the few surviving records show that the problems thus created were widespread and serious. For example, the
Tōdaiji vigorously protested a *gokenin*'s demand to regain possession
of his land by making an overdue payment; some *gokenin* took possession of the land they had lost, without repaying their debt; and bitter
disputes arose concerning the ownership of crops growing on land
whose ownership was forcibly changed by the decree.[62] It quickly
became apparent that the bakufu's decree had seriously undermined
the sanctity of the contracts on which these economic transactions
were based. In order for the bakufu to preserve the political structure,
however, the *gokenin*, who occupied a central position, had to be
"saved" from the undesirable effects of accelerating monetization, despite the consequences.

The dilemma grew even worse after the Mongol invasions in 1274
and 1281. The invasions themselves and the threats of future attack
forced the *gokenin* to carry an extremely heavy economic burden, first
in fighting the Mongols and then in waiting, combat-ready, for nearly
two decades in fear that another invasion could come at any time.
What made this economic burden on the *gokenin* such a grave crisis for
the bakufu was that unlike in civil wars, it could not in this case
confiscate land from defeated enemies in order to reward the *gokenin*,
now even more hard-pressed because of the newly incurred debts. The
bakufu thus once again came to the aid of the *gokenin* by issuing a
limited decree in 1284 and another, more sweeping decree in 1297.

The decree of 1284 was issued only for the benefit of the *gokenin* in
northern Kyushu, where the effects of the invasion were especially
noticeable. The decree ordered that the *myōshu-shiki* (rights to dues
from *myōden*) acquired from *gokenin* be returned immediately and
unconditionally. Throughout the remainder of the century, more and
more *gokenin* went into debt and lost their lands owing to the costs of
maintaining a defense against the Mongols and living beyond their
means – borrowing in order to acquire desired goods and services
from the market. Thus, by the end of the century, the bakufu realized

61 Amino, *Mōko shūrai*, pp. 136–60.   62 Ibid., pp. 141–2.

that it had no choice but to issue a decree to prevent further deterioration of the *gokenin*'s economic condition.[63]

The result was the Einin *tokuseirei* of 1297. The three articles of this decree that survive today made the following provisions: Appeals of decisions concerning the ownership of land would no longer be accepted (the same prohibition against appeals issued in 1267 had just been lifted in 1294, causing a flood of appeals). One appeal was permitted to nobles and temples, and the litigation for those cases for which appeals were already in process was allowed to continue. The *gokenin* were prohibited from selling or pawning their land, and all the land that the *gokenin* lost, by sale or by failure to redeem pawned land, was to be returned to the *gokenin*, even of they were unable to repay the money they had received. The only exceptions to this article were cases in which more than twenty years had elapsed since the land in question had been lost and cases in which the land transactions occurred under the bakufu's explicit written permission. Finally, the bakufu court would henceforth no longer accept any legal case concerning the nonpayment of loans. The only exceptions were those cases in which pawns were currently held by the lenders.[64]

Although with apparent political concessions to the interests of the nobles, temples, and moneylenders (in whose economic well-being the nobles and temples were very much interested), the decree was an undisguised application of bakufu power to protect the *gokenin*. Important also is the fact that the decree's third article – the nonacceptance of legal cases concerning loans – applied, unlike all previous decrees, to everyone, including both warriors and commoners. The reason for this was that the bakufu, in its apparent attempt to justify its protection of the *gokenin* and to call this decree *tokusei*, benefiting all, felt it necessary to allow "all those impoverished" to come under this article's protection.

Again, a predictable amount of confusion ensued that forced the bakufu to issue detailed directives concerning the sale of crops, uses of promissory notes, goods borrowed or kept for safekeeping, and numerous other circumstances. Worse still, the decree allowing the *gokenin* to regain ownership of land without repayment caused the nobles, temples, moneylenders, and many commoners to appeal to the court in Kyoto, forcing the bakufu to negotiate specific cases and to make exceptions.

---

63 Ibid., pp. 325–34.
64 Ibid., pp. 329–34. Hall, *Japan;* Reischauer and Craig, *Japan;* and Sansom, *A History of Japan* all contain discussions of these major *tokuseirei*.

The bakufu was forced to rescind the decree in February 1298; it had been in effect for only eleven months. The repossession of land that had occurred during these eleven months, however, remained valid, and so the *gokenin* who were able to take advantage of the decree gained from it.[65] No more *tokuseirei* were issued during the Kamakura period, not because the need declined but because the bakufu was too weak by the end of the thirteenth century to defy the dictates of a monetized economy. For the Kamakura bakufu in the final decades of its power, monetization acted like an illness suffered by an already deteriorating body. The illness made the effects of the Mongol invasion even more grave, and the warriors' greater dependence on the markets too became a truly debilitating affliction. In the final decades, the bakufu, further weakened by this illness, was not even able to use the anodyne called *tokuseirei*.

COMMERCE AND CITIES IN THE NAMBOKUCHŌ AND MUROMACHI PERIODS

Building on the momentum generated in the latter half of the Kamakura period and, more importantly, on the continuing rise in agricultural productivity, the economy in the Nambokuchō and Muromachi periods continued to grow. This momentum continued unabated into the fourteenth and fifteenth centuries, scarcely slowed by the demise of the Kamakura bakufu and the prolonged political and military disturbances that culminated in the rise of the Ashikaga bakufu. The increasing market activities in these periods led to further specialization, which in turn made production and distribution more efficient, and the resultant gains were shared, though not without conflicts, by all classes.

The growth of agricultural productivity was the foundation on which the commerce of these periods flourished. Japan during this time specialized more and more in products in which each cultivator and region had a comparative advantage; it improved its irrigation, used more fertilizer, and adopted new varieties of rice and other crops. A new variety of rice, known as Champa, reached Japan from Indochina by way of China in the Muromachi period and was especially important to raising productivity. This rice, which was more resistant to both drought and insects than were existing varieties,

---

65 Amino, *Mōko shūrai*, pp. 332–3; and also see, for a useful discussion of the political background of these *tokuseirei*, Nitta Hideharu, *Kamakura kōki no seiji katei*, vol. 6 (*chūsei* 2) of *Iwanami kōza Nihon rekishi* (Tokyo: Iwanami shoten, 1975), pp. 1–40.

enabled cultivators in western Japan to double crop and even triple crop their paddies.[66] The market forces exerted an ever-stronger hold on the cultivators, forcing as well as motivating them to become more efficient.

Growth of commerce and za in Kyoto

From the short-lived Kemmu restoration to the fall of the Ashikaga bakufu, Kyoto remained the seat of power. This meant that during the fourteenth and fifteenth centuries Kyoto grew both in population and wealth, and its commerce expanded even more rapidly. But the protracted civil wars of the Nambokuchō period and the Ōnin War in the second half of the fifteenth century made the city a battleground, intermittently slowing or even halting its commerce. Recurring famines and disease, especially during the 1440s, also eroded both population and commerce.

Even with civil war, famine, and disease, the population of Kyoto is estimated to have grown to more that 200,000 by the time of the Ōnin War. If this estimate is correct, it was, in the mid- to late fifteenth century, one of the largest cities in the world. London, for example, had no more than 50,000. The large population and commercial sector gradually transformed the capital. In the Sakyo, from Sanjō in the north to Gojō and Shichijō in the south, more and more merchants and artisans engaged in trade, and an increasing number of za, to which most of them belonged, congregated. Where the major north-south and east-west roads crossed, machi – administrative units enjoying a degree of self-government – appeared in the Nambokuchō period and continued to proliferate throughout the fifteenth century. The best-known and largest machi were Sanjō, Rokkaku, Nishikōji, Shijō, Gojō, Shichijō, and Kujō-Omiya.[67]

Although most of the merchants and artisans were small and their establishments humble, some merchants became quite wealthy during the fourteenth and fifteenth centuries, so much so that the Ashikaga bakufu began to depend on their wealth to meet its fiscal needs.[68] It is

66 Kuroda Hideo, "Chūsei nōgyō gijutsu no yōsō," in Nagahara Keiji and Yamaguchi Keiji, eds., Nōgyō to nōsan kakō, vol. 1 of Nihon gijutsu no shakaishi (Tokyo: Nihon hyōronsha, 1983), pp. 67–76.
67 Wakita, Nihon chūsei toshi ron, pp. 280–317; Endō, Nihon chūsei toshi ron, pp. 99–108; and Akiyama Kunizō and Nakamura Ken, Kyoto "machi" no kenkyū (Tokyo: Hōsei daigaku shuppankai, 1975), which describes the growth of Kyoto from the Heian period to the eighteenth century.
68 This is a well-known fact discussed in all textbooks. See also Wakita Haruko, Muromachi-ki no keizai hatten, vol. 7 (chūsei 3) of Iwanami kōza Nihon rekishi (Tokyo: Iwanami shoten,

known that in 1393, the bakufu began to collect an annual due of six thousand *kanmon* – a huge sum considering that the cash value of the total annual dues of many *shōen* was less than one hundred *kanmon* – from the *dosō* and *sakaya* in and around Kyoto.[69]

The magnificent cultural life during this period would not, of course, have been possible without this wealth. The most prosperous among these merchants were the *dosō* who were pawnbrokers and moneylenders and who also engaged in warehousing and other commercial ventures; the *sakaya*, who sold saké and used their earnings for moneylending; and other merchants who accumulated wealth by importing luxuries from the continent and controlling profitable *za*. These most successful merchants, led by about 370 *sakaya* and 300 to 400 *dosō*, came to be called *utokunin* (literally, "men of virtue"). In this age of commerce in which the *langage des halles* commanded respect, "virtue" was an appropriate and mellifluous synonym for wealth.

The services and products provided by the majority of the humbler merchants, artisans, and other specialists expanded throughout the Nambokuchō and Muromachi periods. By the mid-fifteenth century, a roster of their occupations was long indeed. Toyoda Takeshi, who examined the composition of the population in a part of Kyoto, using various local records, wrote:

One cannot but be surprised by the large number of small merchants and artisans. In 1460 . . . one finds on both sides of the Gion *ōji* [a central north-south main road] a very large number of persons serving the needs of the temples and shrines . . . their occupations included, among the artisans, carpenters, keg makers, smiths, *tatami* makers, makers of Buddhist statues, and others, and among the merchants, those selling rice, brooms, combs, needles, rice cakes, dyes, oils, threads, and saké.[70]

Toyoda's observation can be applied to the entire city because we have learned from the documents how rapidly the number of *za* in Kyoto multiplied in the Nambokuchō and Muromachi periods. The growth of *za*, called "new" *za* as opposed to "old" *za* that had existed since the previous century, was especially noticeable during the Nambokuchō period. Although it is impossible to ascertain the precise increase in the number of these *za* in both periods, there is no doubt that it was large.

1976), pp. 88–93; and Sasaki Ginya, *Muromachi bakufu*, vol. 13 of *Nihon rekishi* (Tokyo: Shōgakkan, 1975), pp. 129–38.
69 Inoue Mitsusada et al., eds., *Nihon rekishi taikei*, vol. 2 (*chūsei*) (Tokyo: Yamakawa shuppansha, 1985), p. 622. See pp. 621–26 for a good general description of the *utokunin* of this period.   70 Toyoda, *Chūsei Nihon shōgyōshi no kenkyū*, pp. 363–4.

One example useful in demonstrating the greater number of *za* is the case of the Shifu litter bearers who had formed a few *za* during the thirteenth century under the protection of the nobles in charge of the imperial guards. The number of *za* that they organized in and around Kyoto rose to no fewer than twenty by the end of the Nambokuchō period. Although not by such a large number, similar increases of *za* continued in the Muromachi period under the protection of a dozen high-ranked nobles and the Hachimangu, Gionsha, Tōdaiji, and other temples, as has been documented by Japanese scholars. The products of these new and old *za* in Kyoto included salt, silk, cotton batting, dyed cloth, fresh fish, dried fish, salted fish, dyes, candies, leather, sickles, lamp oil, lumber, bamboo, noodles, a few types of clothing, various vegetables, and a dozen other products. No better evidence exists than such a "mushrooming" of the *za* to indicate that Kyoto in the Muromachi period dominated commerce more than it had at any time in the past.[71]

Cities, towns, and markets

Throughout the fourteenth and fifteenth centuries, cities and towns increased in both number and size. Many were located in and around the capital region, but the number of towns on the coastlines and in the countryside grew even more, so much so that there is little exaggeration in saying that most of the cultivators in Muromachi Japan could reach and return from a town within a day.[72]

Because the principal impetus for the growth of cities and towns came from the growth of commerce, many of these urban centers were port towns and the *monzenmachi* of temples. Those port towns that grew fastest during these centuries were the best-located and better-established towns of Yodo and Yamasaki to the south of Kyoto on the Yodo River; Sakamoto, Ōtsu, Funagi, Imazu, and a few others on Lake Biwa; Hyōgo, Sakai, and Amagasaki on the Inland Sea; Obama, Tsuruga, Mikuni-Minato, and Noetsu on the Japan Sea coast; Kuwana, Ōiso, Ōminato, Numazu, Shinagawa, and Matsuura on the Pacific coast; and Hakata on the northern coast of Kyushu.[73] There also were some new port towns, although it is difficult to date exactly when some of them emerged. One can, however, assume that at least a

71 Yamamura, "The Development of *Za*," pp. 447–54, and the Japanese sources cited therein.
72 Toyoda, *Chūsei Nihon shōgyōshi*, pp. 364–86; Sasaki, *Muromachi bakufu*, pp. 260–71; and Nakamura Kichiji, ed., *Shakaishi*, vol. 1 (Tokyo: Yamakawa shuppansha, 1974), pp. 328–44.
73 Ibid.

score of them were established sometime in the fourteenth century. Many were satellite towns of the larger urban centers that appeared on or near the principal water-transportation routes.

Most of these old and new towns grew mainly because of the rising volume of interregional trade, owing to the interregional specialization in agriculture and crafts. Some of the port towns' trade was mainly with the continent. In all of these towns were the *toimaru* managing the flow of goods and providing warehousing and other necessary services, as well as the merchants and artisans, captains, crews, and stevedores. The port facilities, such as wharves, also improved over those of the past.[74]

The *mozenmachi* were another group of towns that grew in both number and size. The main reason for this was the higher incomes of the cultivators, merchants, and artisans, giving them the necessary wherewithal and leisure to make pilgrimages to the temples and shrines, a favorite pastime during the medieval period. By the end of the Muromachi period, prospering *monzenmachi* included, in addition to Nara, such towns as Sakamoto and Uji-Yamada in the capital region and Zenkōji and Suwa in Shinano province. The *jinaimachi*, towns that grew up within the temple grounds, should perhaps be regarded as a variant of *monzenmachi*. Most *jinaimachi* were located in and around the capital region, the best known being six in Osaka-Ishiyama and others in Yamashina, Imai, and Tondabayashi.[75]

Za also began to appear outside Kyoto, Nara, and Kamakura. These *za*, first recorded in the Nambokuchō period, were called *sato-za* or *inaka-za*, the *za* of the villages and countryside. Most of them first were started near the capital and, later, during the fifteenth century, in towns around the nation. Records of some *za* dating from the fifteenth century, have been found for towns in Ōmi, Bizen, Chikuzen, and Kaga provinces. By mid-century, several *za* had appeared in the larger towns of a dozen other provinces as well.[76]

The emergence and growth of *za* are evidence that market activities were increasing in most towns as well as at other nodes of transportation, the principal crossroads, and in more established towns at or near the administrative centers of local governments. More villagers were going to markets and more frequently. To respond to this need, by the mid-fifteenth century, market days, which had typically been three

---

74 Toyoda, *Chūsei Nihon shōgyōshi no kenkyū*, pp. 238–42; and Sasaki, *Muromachi bakufu*, pp. 172–3.
75 See Wakita, *Nihon chūsei toshi ron*; Endō, *Nihon chūsei toshi ron*; Akiyama and Nakamura, *Kyoto "machi" no kenkyū*; Toyoda, *Chūsei Nihon shōgyōshi no kenkyū*; Sasaki, *Muromachi bakufu*; and Nakamura, *Shakaishi*, vol. 1.
76 Yamamura, "The Development of *Za*," pp. 447–51.

times a month, had expanded to six in many markets thereby creating the *rokusai-ichi*. Both pieces of unequivocal documentary evidence we have for these markets are dated 1469: one for the Oyada market in Mino Province and the other for Uji-no-go Rokkado-ichi in Yamashina Province. One specialist, however, speculates on the strength of indirect evidence that the earliest six-day market was likely to have been held as early as the mid-fourteenth century in the capital of Hitachi Province.[77] In short, although we cannot be certain either of the date when six-day markets first appeared or when they began to spread throughout Japan, no one doubts that they became prevalent in many parts of the nation by the end of the fifteenth century.

The increase in six-day markets indicates that with the market activities, the local towns were also growing. The number of towns with populations of less than 1,000 was rising steadily, and those with more than 1,000 were also increasing. Although reliable data are not available, we can, using various contemporary descriptions, offer reasonable "guesstimates" of the population of the following cities during the second half of the fifteenth century: Nara, 10,000 to 15,000; Tennōji in Kawachi Province, 35,000; Sakai, at least 20,000; Sakamoto in Ōmi Province, 15,000; Kuwana and Ōminato in Ise Province, 15,000 and 5,000, respectively; Yodo near Kyoto, 5,000; and Hakata in northern Kyushu, 30,000 to 50,000. If we use the contemporary sources of the early sixteenth century, we can easily add a score of cities and port towns with populations in excess of 10,000 and even more urban centers with at least 5,000 residents.[78]

Development of a transportation network

The growing commerce of the fourteenth and fifteenth centuries led to the development of a better organized and more systematic transportation network on both land and sea. This network was served by specialists consisting of *toimaru*, captains, crew, teamsters, carters, and the like.

The heart of the network was the part that linked Kyoto with the rest of Japan. From western Japan, rice, paper, salt, lumber, fish, sesame, sumac, and many other products were shipped to Kyoto via Hyōgoseki, Amagasaki, and Sakai, with the Yodo River the main waterway between these ports and Kyoto. From the east, fish, silk,

---

77 Sasaki, *Chūsei shōhin ryūtsūshi*, pp. 10–26.
78 See Toyoda, *Chūsei Nihon shōgyōshi no kenkyū*, Sasaki, *Muromachi bakufu*; and Nakamura, *Shakaishi*, vol. 1.

seaweed, lumber, cotton cloth, and other products of the Tohoku and San'in regions were brought to the capital through the ports of Obama, Tsuruga, and others. These products then were carried over-land to Imazu and Umizu on Lake Biwa and shipped south across the lake to Sakamoto and Otsu which were only a short distance from Kyoto. Prized products of the neighboring, commercially active prov-inces of Mino and Owari – paper, china, lumber, and a variety of cloth – were brought in on roads.[79]

Most goods that needed to be transported across the nation were carried over water when possible. This is why as many as nine major sea routes were established during these periods. An examination of these routes makes it clear that not only was Kyoto linked with all parts of Japan but even distant Kyushu, Hokuriku, and Ou enjoyed ready sea access to the capital region, the Kantō basin, and other commercially active provinces on the Inland Sea.[80]

Such a network called for more *toimaru*, whose roles in the seaborne transportation became even more important. Thus, these maritime entrepreneurs were found in those port towns mentioned earlier and in Katsura, Toba, Kizu, Uji, and Settsu on the Yodo River; Kiinada and Onomichi on the Inland Sea; Nagahama, Yawata, Funagi, and several others on Lake Biwa; Mikuni, Tsuruga, Izumo, Noetsu, Oya-minato, and a few others facing the Japan Sea; and Mikawa, Ōminato, Kuwana, Shinagawa, and a half-dozen others on the Pacific coast.[81]

Along with the development of ocean-transportation capabilities, Muromachi Japan improved its ability to transport goods over land. The major participants in overland transportation were teamsters us-ing carts *(shariki)* or horses *(bashaku)*. In addition to performing these crucial functions, they constituted a potent economic and political force. Teamsters were capable of inciting mass uprisings, demanding, for example, the abrogation of debts or the abolition of trade restric-tions imposed by *za*, and of manipulating the prices of rice and other important products in Kyoto by disrupting delivery and otherwise affecting the flow of products to and from the capital.

As can be expected, the teamsters were most commonly found in the port and satellite towns in the capital region. Records also establish that each port town around the nation had a number of teamsters

79 Sasaki, *Muromachi bakufu*, pp. 171–7. Also see Tokuda Ken'ichi, *Chūsei ni okeru suiun no hattatsu* (Tokyo: Gannandō shoten, 1966).   80 See ibid.
81 See Wakita, *Nihon chūsei toshi ron;* Endō, *Nihon chūsei toshi ron;* Akiyama and Nakamura, *Kyoto "machi" no kenkyū*, Toyoda, *Chūsei Nihon shōgyōshi*, Sasaki, *Muromachi bakufu;* and Nakamura, *Shakaishi*, vol. 1.

commensurate with the size of the port. Some scholars believe that these teamsters were most likely to have originated from the *sanjo*, destitute *kawaramono* (literally, "those living on river beds"), and other persons displaced from villages for various reasons who had little choice but to become teamsters or carters.[82] Some small cultivators living in agricultural villages along transportation routes also became part-time teamsters who carried freight in the off-season.

Some transportation over land was provided by the merchants themselves. Many merchants traveling long distances organized themselves into caravans (*taishō*), chiefly to increase the security of their travel. The most famous of these caravans were those of the Ōmi merchants who traveled from Ōmi to Kyoto and other more distant regions. These caravans typically consisted of tens and sometimes hundreds of merchants. Itinerant peddlers, traveling shorter distances, carried their wares in backpacks. Such groups of peddlers were called *renjaku* for the packs they carried or *takani* for piling many packs on their backs.[83] Some of them also traveled in large groups for protection from thieves, mutual assistance, and greater leverage in negotiating lower market taxes from local lords.

The swelling tide of commerce was such that even the toll barriers (*sekisho*) failed to discourage it. These barriers, which began to increase in number in the early fourteenth century, were erected mostly by nobles, temples, and shrines whose *shōen* income had dwindled and by the *toimaru* and others who collected tolls on behalf of local powers, including some *shugo* and *jitō*. The number of barriers continued to grow throughout the fifteenth century. In some instances, the tolls imposed by these *sekisho* were so heavy it was impossible for merchants and others to pay them. Thus, for example, the bakufu forced a temple in 1471 to abandon its toll barriers, which were causing a substantial hardship for the *bashaku* of Sakamoto; and Ōmi merchants, angered by the increasing burden of these tolls, set fire in 1512 to new barriers in northern Ōmi.[84]

Monetization and commutation

In the 1430's, a Korean envoy was surprised to discover the prevalent use of money in Muromachi Japan. Even those traveling from one end

---

82 For descriptions of these specialists of land transportation in the Muromachi period, see Sasaki, *Muromachi bakufu*, pp. 164–71; and Kodama and Toyoda, *Ryūtsūshi*, pp. 107–9.
83 Kodama and Toyoda, *Ryūtsūshi*, pp. 107–8.
84 Toyoda, *Chūsei Nihon shōgyōshi no kenkyū*, p. 403.

of the country to the other, he noted, did not carry provisions because coins were accepted everywhere at inns and post stations and even by toll collectors at bridges, who were accepting "five *mon* or ten *mon* depending on the length of the bridge." He was especially amazed to find that people were paying fees in cash for public bathhouses.[85]

With this high degree of monetization, commutation, too, spread even more widely. All Japanese specialists agree that commutation, either for a part or all of the dues, was being practiced in virtually all regions of Japan by the mid-fourteenth century. However, as in the debate concerning the reasons for adopting commutation, important questions above commutation in the Muromachi period remain unanswered. The reasons for this are similar to those accounting for the other ongoing debate. There still are few case studies, and the analytic methods remain restricted to asking who among those in a position to coerce dues payers – *shōen* owners, *shōkan*, local powers, and the bakufu – gained the most by adopting or not adopting commutation.[86] As a result, no consensus has emerged among specialists to answer such questions as why commutation grew more prevalent. And why do there seem to have been so many differences, across regions and over time, in the specific terms of commutation?

What is needed to answer these questions is an economic analytic perspective. That is, if we are to understand why commutation became more prevalent in the ways it did during the Muromachi period, we must ask (1) who converted dues in kind to cash (cultivators, *myōshu*, or *shōkan*); (2) how the amount of commutation was specified (in market prices or in fixed money terms); (3) how prices were determined in local markets (freely or under some degree of manipulation or control by local powers or *shōen* administrators); (4) what differences existed in the prices of commodities between markets in Kyoto or elsewhere (where the recipients of dues resided) and local markets (where the same commodities produced by dues-paying cultivators were sold); (5) how large the costs of transportation of dues in kind (determined by distance and availability of sea transport) were relative to the price differences; and (6) what the price trend was – the rate of exchange between cash and goods – prevailing in this period. A diffi-

85 Kodama and Toyoda, *Ryūtsūshi*, p. 74.
86 In contrast with this established analysis of *daisennō*, emphasizing the coercion or "exploitation" by the dues recipients, Wakita Haruko was the first in 1976 to state that the prevailing view is erroneous in not recognizing that the *daisennō* "began responding to the demand made for it by the local powers and the cultivators." Wakita, "Muromachi-ki no keizai hatten," p. 53. She also makes it clear that she is aware of needing to raise economic analytic questions in discussing the issues involved in *daisennō* (pp. 53–61).

cult task is weighing the relative importance of, and assessing the relationships existing among, each variable in these questions.

The significance of such questions becomes apparent when we learn, for example, that in 1438 the Tōji in Kyoto demanded payment of dues in rice from its *shōen* located in and near the capital, because the rice price in Kyoto was then nearly double that in the markets where the *shōen* were located.[87] With such an incentive, the temple was willing to go against the tide of commutation and shoulder the costs of selling and transporting rice. We must remember, however, that from the early fourteenth century to the end of the fifteenth, the prices of rice and other major products were steadily falling and that in such a period of chronic deflation, anyone with political power would be demanding dues in cash.[88]

Thus, though there were many exceptions caused by economic and political circumstances, commutation became widely practiced by the beginning of the Muromachi period. Even with the deflationary trend, dues payers generally preferred commutation because it enabled them to raise their income by planting those crops that made the most profit. But this motivation on the part of the cultivators would, of course, be lost – as happened in many cases studied by the participants in this debate – if the *shōen* administrators or local powers (who became more powerful politically during the fifteenth century) fixed the dues in money terms thereby ignoring the changes in market prices caused by deflation or price manipulation.[89]

The reason for presenting this short discussion of commutation in the Muromachi period is only to describe the current state of study by Japanese specialists and to indicate how much more study is needed to understand the real economic and political significance of the commutation that so affected the lives of both the collectors and the payers of dues.

Even in this brief summary of monetization and its effects in the fourteenth and fifteenth centuries, there remains one more important question to ask. Why did the bakufu not mint coins, especially when the need for them was obvious and when Japan had both the raw materials and the technological capability to do so? Japanese specialists have offered two answers to date. One is that Japan in the medieval

---

87 Ibid., pp. 53–54.
88 Because of the limits placed on importation of coins from China (i.e., restrictions on the "tally" trade) and an increasing demand for cash (owing to the growth of the economy and monetization), the shortage of coins (deflation) was chronic during the fifteenth century. See Yamamura and Kamiki, "Silver Mines and Sung Coins," pp. 339–42.
89 This refers to the *erizeni* decrees discussed later in the text.

period was not yet a full-fledged nation-state in the international community and was only a member of the East Asian political economic sphere dominated by China; thus it was to be expected that Japan would use Chinese coins as its medium of exchange. The other, a more recent answer, is that no government after the ninth century, even the Muromachi bakufu at its zenith, had the political power, thus "the power that commanded commerce on a nationwide basis," necessary to have coins accepted and used nationally.[90]

The partial validity of both these answers cannot be denied. Muromachi Japan was a part of the East Asian political order maintained by a much more powerful China, and the bakufu perhaps did not have the political power necessary to have its own coins accepted nationally. These answers also appear to be supported by a later historical development: It took the strong unifying power of the Tokugawa bakufu to accomplish what the Ashikaga bakufu was unable to do.

These answers, however, are not completely satisfactory. Explanations that depend on "sufficient" or "necessary" political power cannot escape the charge of being tautological. Furthermore, there are many examples of European cities, small "states," and others that had less political power than did the bakufu, that were located near much stronger neighbors, that issued their own monies, and that used them within their boundaries as well as in surrounding cities and states.

Clearly, further explanations are needed to answer the question adequately. Thus, not to replace but to supplement the explanations offered by Japanese specialists, let me offer the following hypothesis: Because a large number of Chinese coins had already been in circulation and had been accepted for over two centuries, the bakufu and those who supported the Muromachi polity – the *shugo* and other local powers (many of whom also were *shōen* administrators) – found it economically advantageous to have a large variety of coins. It was advantageous because using both varying qualities of Chinese coins and illegal (privately minted) Japanese coins enabled the recipients and collectors of dues to maintain or increase their income by dictating or manipulating the acceptable mix of coins. For the dues recipients, demanding a more lucrative mix of coins (containing a larger proportion of higher-quality coins) on an *ad hoc* and incremental basis was usually easier and required less political power than did imposing higher dues on the cultivators.

90 The former view was first expressed by Satō Shin'ichi in his "Muromachi bakufu ron," vol. 7 (*chūsei* 3) of *Iwanami kōza Nihon rekishi* (Tokyo: Iwanami shoten, 1965); and the latter is found in Wakita, "Muromachi-ki no keizai hatten," p. 91.

More specifically, changing the real burden of dues by changing the acceptable mixes of coins either explicitly (formally) or in an *ad hoc* fashion had the following advantages over raising the dues by changing the rates on rice yields: (1) The political and economic costs would be lower because no cadastral survey was required, as there usually would have been if new dues rates were imposed; (2) changing the mix of coins would offer flexibility in changing the real burden of the dues in small increments, in order to respond to changing economic conditions (to the extent that local economic conditions differed, this advantage was especially significant to the *shugo* and other local powers in the late Muromachi period); (3) changing the mix of coins could act as a quasi income tax in that the mixes of acceptable coins could be changed so as to share in the gains realized by dues payers from their increasing involvement in commercial activities (because the degree of market activities differed by region, this advantage made the second advantage even more significant); and (4) dues payers would have difficulty in accurately assessing how much their real dues burden was rising over time and whether they were paying more dues than were others living on lands taxed by neighboring *shugo* or local powers. This difficulty of obtaining accurate comparative information would make it easier for a *shugo* or a local power to impose a desired level of dues with less risk of upsetting the dues payers.

In short, coins of more uniform quality issued by the bakufu would have robbed the dues recipients of opportunities to increase their income by dictating or manipulating the acceptable mix of coins for dues payment. Furthermore, increasing the supply of coins – adding bakufu-minted coins while Chinese coins were slowly withdrawn from circulation – would have reversed the deflationary trend of these centuries. When dues were paid in coins, it was to the advantage of the dues recipients not to inflate the economy.[91]

As noted, the foregoing is only a hypothesis. It should be examined for both its political and its economic ramifications and it should consider the *erizenirei* – decrees issued, beginning in the late Muromachi period, by the bakufu and regional and local powers,

91 There was a large difference among the values of copper coins in Japan and China, which might have contributed to Japan's continued importation of Chinese coins in large quantities. For more discussion and evidence, see Yamamura and Kamiki, "Silver Mines and Sung Coins," pp. 352–8. For those interested in monetization and its effects during the medieval period, this article contains a bibliography of all relevant English and Japanese sources. Also see Kenneth A. Grossberg, *Japan's Renaissance: The Politics of the Muromachi Bakufu* (Cambridge, Mass.: Harvard University Press, 1981), pp. 82–83. This is the only recent source in English that asks why the Muromachi bakufu did not mint coins and offers speculative answers similar to those I present in this text.

specifying the acceptable mixes of "good" and "inferior" coins of varying values for paying dues – and informal practices adopted by the dues collectors in order to achieve the same goal.[92] However, doing all this will be difficult for the same reason as for the study of commutation. That is, the studies to date by Japanese scholars of the *erizenirei* and other methods of specifying the acceptable mixes of coins also need further empirical and analytic research.[93]

Commerce and political change

From the turbulent Nambokuchō period to the Ōnin War that soon engulfed Japan in civil war, the prolonged political conflicts and the rise and gradual decline of the bakufu could not help but affect the course of history. What follows is a brief discussion of the *tokuseirei* issued by the bakufu and the change in the relationship between a *za* and its patron, in order to illustrate how the political reality of the period interacted with the growth of commerce.[94]

As in the Kamakura period, the *tokuseirei* (debt-abrogation decrees) of the fifteenth century were issued by the bakufu to relieve the debt burden of commoners and warriors. However, reflecting both the degree of monetization achieved and the decline in the bakufu's power, the demand for these decrees, made more and more frequently beginning in the early decades of the fifteenth century, was more intense and came from a much larger number of commoners. It was common for the demand to take the form of *do-ikki* (uprisings of cultivators and other commoners) involving several thousand persons. To illustrate these *do-ikki*, I shall describe one of the biggest which occurred in 1428 to demand a *tokuseirei*.

The uprising was begun by the teamsters of Ōmi Province whose meager livelihood were readily affected by the value of the goods they

92 Takizawa Takeo, "Erizeni," in Nagahara Keiji et al., eds., *Chūseishi Handbook* (Tokyo: Kondō shuppansha, 1973), pp. 67–69, explains what is meant by *erizeni* (also called *erisen* and *sensen*) and summarizes how the issues involved in *erizeni* and *erizenirei* have been analyzed to date by Japanese specialists. Issues relating to *erizeni* of the Muromachi period receive far less attention from the Japanese specialists than do those of the Sengoku period, as indicated by the fact that Sasaki's *Muromachi bakufu* does not even mention this topic at all.

93 Wakita was again the first to suggest the need for an analysis of the *erizenirei* from both a political-institutional perspective and an economic analytic perspective. However, such an analysis has yet to be made. See Wakita, "Muromachi-ki no keizai hatten," p. 91.

94 *Tokuseirei* and *ikki* (uprisings) are described in all English textbooks. For an especially interesting and insightful discussion of them, see Katsumata Shizuo, *Ikki* (Tokyo: Iwanami shoten, 1982).

transported to Kyoto.[95] They were quickly joined by several thousand cultivators from Ōmi and neighboring provinces. Although no historical document tells exactly why this uprising began and spread so quickly, there is no doubt that the main reason was the poor harvest of the previous year that caused disease to spread and the debt burden of the teamsters and cultivators to become even heavier. The cultivators involved in the uprising "took the records of their debt and burned them" and "attacked, in the name of *tokusei* [virtuous rule], *sakaya*, *dosō*, and temples and robbed them of valuables." They had to be subdued by the warriors dispatched by several daimyo in response to the urgent request of the shaken bakufu.[96]

Although only a few *ikki* were as large as this one,[97] there were twenty-six large *ikki* each involving at least a few hundred people, between 1428 and the end of the century. A dozen or so of the later uprisings involved more and more warriors, indicating both the effects that monetization and the growth of commerce had on their economic lot and the further weakening of the bakufu. The *tokuseirei* of the fifteenth century were perhaps the offspring of a marriage between a growing commerce that made money even more essential to the daily lives of all and a central political authority that was gradually becoming less central and less authoritative.

The Kitano saké-malt (*kōji*) *za* demonstrates the effects of the changing political reality of the period on commerce in general and on the *za* in particular.[98]

Sanctioned by the Kitano Shrine, a branch of the powerful Enryakuji, by the mid-fourteenth century, this *za* was actively engaged in selling malt. Documents written during the 1390s, however, show that its exclusive right to supply malt to about 350 saké makers in most parts of Kyoto was no longer "protected" by the shrine alone. In 1388, the bakufu began to levy taxes in exchange for a decree supporting the *za*'s continued monopoly rights. Clearly, even with the backing of the Enryakuji, the shrine by this time had become unable to prevent the bakufu from sharing in the *za*'s profits.

Then, during the early decades of the fifteenth century, the *za*

95 This is the so-called Seichō *do-ikki*. An excellent description of it can be found in Sasaki, *Muromachi bakufu*, pp. 178–81. 96 Ibid., p. 179.
97 Another major *ikki* occurred in 1441 and is called Kakitsu *do-ikki*. A short but good summary of it can be found in ibid., pp. 181–3.
98 For descriptions of this *za*, see Yamamura, "The Development of Za," pp. 454–63, and the works of Japanese scholars that it cites.

found that many saké makers were providing their own malt instead of buying it from the za. This apparently occurred because the demand for saké had risen so that it became more profitable for each saké maker to build a malt chamber rather than to buy malt from the za and because the saké brewers evidently judged the Enryakuji's power to have so declined that they could safely challenge the za's monopoly rights.

The saké makers had, however, underestimated the bakufu's reluctance to become involved at this time in open conflict with the Enryakuji. In 1419, the bakufu affirmed its support of the za and allowed it to destroy nearly fifty malt chambers that had been constructed by the saké makers. But as the bakufu continued to show signs of increasing strength and stability in the early decades of the fifteenth century, the saké makers, motivated by the possibility of larger profits, continued to build malt chambers as if to test the limits of the delicate balance of political power then existing between the bakufu and the large temples. Between 1420 and the mid-1440s, the bakufu continued to allow the za to destroy malt chambers when they were discovered, thus indicating that the bakufu, at least on the surface, was still maintaining its political stance of not challenging the Enryakuji's hold on the za.

The saké makers saw the bakufu's actions as an indication of less than wholehearted support for the za and assumed that sooner or later the bakufu would choose to support them. They knew that they were a more lucrative source of tax income for the bakufu than was the za which owed its primary allegiance to the temple. Meanwhile, malt chambers continued to be built and destroyed.

This, then, was the background of the celebrated malt incident of 1444-5. In the fall of 1444, the saké makers openly disregarded the za's monopoly rights and ceased to buy malt. The za members immediately petitioned the bakufu to enforce their monopoly. They locked themselves in the Kitano temple to await a favorable decision. Despite this drastic measure, the occupation of a sacred temple, the bakufu wavered. To abandon the za was the more profitable alternative, but the bakufu was uncertain whether it wished to risk an uprising of temples, which could prove costly to subdue. After sixty days of indecision, the bakufu resolved to support the za. However, because the bakufu had clearly shown by its delay that it might be persuaded to rule against the za, the saké makers of eastern Kyoto presented a counterpetition asking for permission to make their own malt. Hearing of this, the members of the za again locked themselves in the temple, vowing not to leave until the bakufu reaffirmed its decision favorable to the *za*.

This time it was the *za* that miscalculated the remaining power of the Enryakuji and the extent to which the bakufu could be coerced. Angered by the *za*'s action, the bakufu ordered one of its leading supporters, Hatakeyama, to drive the *za* members out of the temple. Hatakeyama's troops clashed with the *za* members, who failed to win the support of the Enryakuji's well-known soldier-monks. The skirmish left forty dead, and the surviving *za* members fled the temple. Some of the *za* members fleeing the conflict set fire to large structures in western Kyoto, causing a major blaze that reduced much of the western half of the city to ashes. The *za* was abolished, and it was not until after the Ōnin War that some of its members were allowed to return to Kyoto. This episode tells us that a political force powerful enough to secure the profits from the increased sale of a product or from increased commerce in general found it more profitable to forgo a share in the monopolistic profits of a *za* that had clearly become detrimental to the growth of commerce.

To be sure, many *za* in Kyoto continued to operate by paying more to the bakufu, and many survived because they did not have a competing group able to promise more to the bakufu. In many regions, this century of transition was a period of *ad hoc* arrangements that depended on the strength of the regional warrior class, on the degree to which the bakufu's authority was felt, and on the residual strength of court nobles and temples. In many cases, as the price for survival, the *za* paid more dues to the bakufu or to the regional power, and in others, temples and court nobles were forced to forgo dues from some regions while continuing to receive income from others. The trend, however, was unmistakable – the amount of dues that the *za* received from temples and court nobles was fast diminishing. This happened simply because as the fifteenth century progressed and the *za* monopolies were more often challenged, each *za* had to appeal to the bakufu or a regional power for the support that its original sponsors could no longer provide.

Finally, as the growth of commerce continued, integrating more markets within a region and even across regions, the political powers and all who traded in the markets came to realize that the varying measures of weight, length, and volume being used seriously impeded market transactions. The absence of a uniform measure of volume (cubic measure) was especially troublesome.

Even though nearly a dozen measures of weight and length were used (to measure land and such widely traded commodities as silk, cloth, and iron), this problem could be overcome: All these measures could, if necessary, be converted and made comparable. In most cases, these were measures used since the *ritsuryō* period, and the specialized use of some measures, such as those for cloth and iron, were pertinent to only a few specialists.

But the same was not the case for a cubic measure, which was important during this period because it was used by all who measured rice in paying and receiving taxes and rents and also in trading generally. Stated simply, the cubic measure of rice, the *masu* (square wooden container), had grown over time; that is, for measuring the same nominal quantity of rice, the *masu* increased by a factor of approximately 2.5 during the medieval period. For example, in terms of the measure used in the Tokugawa period, one *shō* of rice had changed from approximately 0.4 *shō* in the tenth century to almost 1.0 *shō* by the mid-fifteenth century. And to compound the problem, any precise conversion was virtually impossible because the size of the *masu* grew gradually from the tenth century to the early sixteenth century by region and even by *shōen*. Some large temples also used differing sizes of *masu*, depending on the purposes for which each was used.

It is not difficult to speculate why this occurred. Because rice was principally a means of paying dues, it was to the advantage of each dues recipient to enlarge the *masu* used in measuring those dues. Undoubtedly the rate and rapidity of the increase in size closely reflected the political or military power of each recipient.

Here, it is useful to recall the hypothesis offered earlier to explain the use of *erizeni* by various levels of political powers to increase the real burden of dues with minimal political costs. This situation is analogous in that enlarging the size of *masu* gradually over time was also a means to enlarge the real burden of the dues with minimal political costs. Such a hypothesis also explains why the effort made by Emperor Gosanjō in 1072 to standardize the size of the *masu* – an attempt to require the use of the "decreed *masu*" (*senji-masu*) – had little effect and why no political power, either the bakufu or the *shugo* daimyo who were in positions to standardize the measure, did not make a similar effort.

It is unlikely that the dues payers failed to detect the change in the size of the *masu* by which their dues were measured. Possible explanations for their accepting the larger *masu* from dues payers range from the dues recipients' power over the dues payers, to the latter's willingness to accept this means of increasing dues rather than more explicit and potentially more burdensome means such as increasing the rate of dues or resurveying the arable land. Or it might have been a mixture of these two reasons. The second reason should not be rejected, because agricultural productivity was rising from the mid-thirteenth century on and dues payers were better able to accept the de facto increase in the dues through the larger size of the *masu*. And there is no record of uprising or petition expressing dissatisfaction with the bigger dues resulting from the *masu*'s increased size.

However, by the mid- to late fifteenth century and into the sixteenth century, more and more *shugo* daimyo and then *sengoku* daimyo began to try to standardize such measures. Their motivation was to encourage the growth of commerce, as typified by their adoption of *rakuichi-rakuza* (promotion of less impeded commerce and limitation of the *za*'s power), a policy they adopted beginning in the mid-sixteenth century. And it is known that before an effective nationwide standardization of measures of weight and length was adopted in the Tokugawa period, several *shugo* daimyo and *sengoku* daimyo actively promoted standardized measures their respective domains.

Again, the cubic measure was the most difficult to standardize. Although limited historical evidence makes it difficult to make any definite observations, it appears that from the mid-fifteenth century on, the regional powers and especially Nobunaga, the first of the unifiers, encouraged the use of *kyō-masu* (Kyoto *masu*), the *masu* that by then was widely used in the capital, the center of commerce as well as the seat of the Muromachi bakufu. The *kyō-masu* differed slightly in size (with a maximum margin of nearly 5 percent), but one *shō* of *kyō-masu* was roughly equivalent to one *shō* by the Tokugawa measure (the *kyō-masu* later became the basis on which the Tokugawa cubic measures were established).

In addition, because of the problems with cubic measures in this period, in virtually no cases is it possible to ascertain correctly the exact amount of dues collected in rice. If an estimate is to be made over any length of time, even for a single *shōen*, let alone broader interregional and intertemporal comparisons, one must allow for the growth in the size of the *masu* at differing paces and magnitudes throughout most of the medieval period.[99]

99 The most useful source on the medieval measures is by Hashimoto Mampei, *Keisoku no bunkashi* (Tokyo: Asahi Shimbunsha, 1982), pp. 269–334. The seminal study on the subject is by Hōgetsu Keigo sensei kanreki kinenkai, ed., *Chūsei ryōseishi no kenkyū* (Tokyo: Yoshikawa kōbunkan, 1961). The latter contains analyses of all of the significant historical evidence relating to the medieval measures.

CONCLUSION

This chapter has examined the growth of commerce in medieval Japan and how the many changes that resulted from it transformed the economy from one with only limited market activities in the capital region into an economy with an increasing number of six-day markets throughout the nation.

This transformation was accompanied by such readily visible results as an increase in both the size and number of urban centers; significant institutional developments typified by the rise and growth of *za* and *toimaru;* the spread of monetization from the capital to villages throughout the nation; increased specialization of merchants and artisans who produced more and more products; and the development of a transportation network linking all parts of the nation and including a growing number of persons engaged in transporting goods by both water and land.

Less visible but fundamental to this transformation was a steady and at times rapid increase in agricultural productivity which began in the second half of the thirteenth century. This was enabled principally by the more intensive use of paddies, including double cropping and even triple cropping in some regions, and to a decreasing number of paddies lost to flooding or drought, owing to improvements in irrigation and water control. In addition, the economy as a whole was more productive and efficient. People became much more aware of the effects that changes in prices could have on their lives, of markets where they could buy many more goods that others produced more efficiently than they themselves could; and of the many ways that they could increase their income, by selling products or services or lending money.

To be sure, the benefits of commercialization and monetization also produced conflicts of interest between the *za* and their challengers, between lenders and borrowers, and between dues recipients and payers. Such conflicts took many forms. The *za* sought protection from would-be competitors, and the *za* patrons attempted to gain a greater share of their profits. Through *tokuseirei,* bakufu tried to protect warriors indebted to moneylenders, and dues payers and others who felt victimized by the changes in the economy expressed their dissatisfaction and demands through *ikki.* The prevailing political realities of these three and a half centuries played a crucial role in determining the specific forms these symptoms would take and the degree to which their costs would affect the polity's future course.

Sengoku Japan inherited a highly commercialized and monetized economy, but one that was still coping with rapid political and economic change and the symptoms and costs of such growth. The most interesting aspect of sixteenth-century Japanese history is how the *sengoku* daimyo, who reaped the benefits of the growing commerce, were forced to deal with both.[100]

100 On the *erizeni* issues and other politicoeconomic developments in the Sengoku period, see Kozo Yamamura, "Returns on Unification: Economic Growth in Japan, 1550–1650," in John Whitney Hall, Nagahara Keiji, and Kozo Yamamura, eds., *Japan Before Tokugawa* (Princeton, N.J.: Princeton University Press, 1981), pp. 327–72.

CHAPTER 9

JAPAN AND EAST ASIA

In this chapter I shall describe and analyze Japan's relations during the Kamakura and Muromachi periods with various countries of East Asia and their governments, including the Sung, Yüan, and Ming dynasties of China, the Koryŏ and Yi dynasties of Korea, and the Ryūkyū Islands. My descriptions and analyses focus primarily on Japan's international political relations, particularly Japan's relationship with its Asian neighbors, the effect of this relationship on Japan's internal political developments, and, conversely, the influence of Japan's internal politics on its international relations.[1] Because my research interests lie mainly in the Kamakura period, I shall discuss developments of that period more extensively than those of the later Muromachi period.

JAPAN'S INTERNATIONAL RELATIONS IN EAST ASIA

Around the tenth century the motive force in East Asia shifted from the Han People of China to the northern nomadic tribes, often called the conquest dynasties. In the thirteenth and fourteenth centuries, East Asian history centered on the rise and fall of the Mongol Empire. The Southern Sung (1127–1279) was reestablished after China's territory was reduced by the consecutive invasions of the Liao and Chin, which generated a financial crisis owing to the massive military expenses. The Southern Sung, whose resources and level of productivity were lower than those of northern China, inherited the developments that took place in various industries during and following the domi-

---

1 There are a number or works on the methodology of studying East Asian relations; the following cover the thirteenth through the sixteenth centuries: Nakamura Hidetaka, "Jūsan, yonseki no Tōa jōsei to Mongoru no shūrai," in *Iwanami kōza Nihon no rekishi*, vol. 6 (chūsei 2) (Tokyo: Iwanami shoten, 1963), pp. 4–9; *Nissen kankeishi no kenkyū*, vol. 1 (Tokyo: Yoshikawa kōbunkan, 1965), pp. 2–7 (reprint of the preceding); Tōma Seita, *Higashi Ajia sekai no keisei* (Tokyo: Shunjūsha, 1966); Tanaka Takeo, *Chūsei taigai kankeishi* (Tokyo: Tōkyō daigaku shuppankai, 1975), pp. 10–20; Sasaki Ginya. "Higashi Ajia bōekiken no keisei to kokusai ninshiki," in *Iwanami kōza Nihon rekishi*, vol. 7 (chūsei 3) (Tokyo: Iwanami shoten, 1976), pp. 100–10.

nance of the Northern Sung (960–1127) and vigorously promoted foreign trade in hopes of resolving its financial crisis.

Japan did not have official diplomatic relations with either the Southern Sung or the Koryŏ (918–1391) dynasties. But it did enjoy close cultural and economic ties with both China and Korea, especially the Southern Sung dynasty, through its commercial maritime activity along the China seacoast which formed one link in the East Asian trading sphere. This was the reason that the Mongols – who had dominated Koryŏ in creating a new international order in East Asia after their conquest of Southern Sung – tried first to entice Japan into the new order and then to conquer it. Thus, the Mongol invasions were attempts to force Japan to enter international politics.

The Kamakura bakufu assumed diplomatic powers during the invasions and undertook official trade with the Yüan dynasty of China (1279–1368) in response to the Mongol's official intensification of its trade policy during the late Kamakura period. This presaged the diplomacy of the succeeding Muromachi bakufu which received investiture from China's Ming dynasty (1368–1644) and was included in the Sinocentric international order. The Mongol invasions strengthened the authoritarian tendencies of the Hōjō family, which held the real power in the Kamakura bakufu, and presented the Hōjō with a number of problems beyond their administrative capabilities, finally causing the bakufu to topple in 1333.

The Kemmu regime, which destroyed the Kamakura bakufu and lasted only two years, led Japan into the protracted internal conflict between the Northern and Southern Courts during the Nambokuchō period (1333–92). During this sixty-year period Ashikaga Takauji founded the Muromachi bakufu. The war between the courts during the fourteenth century served to consolidate the power of the Muromachi bakufu. During this struggle in 1350, the attacks of Japanese pirates (wakō) began in earnest, spreading from the Korean peninsula south along the China coast.[2] The wakō's activities spanned four centuries and occurred in two phases.

The early phase of wakō activity began in the thirteenth century and extended to the second half of the fourteenth, corresponding to the Nambokuchō and early Muromachi periods in Japan, the late Koryŏ

---

2 There are many works dealing with the wakō, and a number of works on Koryŏ, Choson, and Ming relations with Japan also touch on the wakō. See especially Tanaka Takeo, Chūsei kaigai kōshōshi no kenkyū (Tokyo: Tōkyō daigaku shuppankai, 1959) and Wakō to kangō bōeki (Tokyo: Shibundō, 1961); Kobata Atsushi, "Kangō bōeki to wakō," in Iwanami kōza Nihon rekishi, vol. 7 (chūsei 3) (Tokyo: Iwanami shoten, 1963); and Ishihara Michihiro, Wakō (Tokyo: Yoshikawa kōbunkan, 1964).

and early Yi (1392–1910) in Korea, and the late Yüan to early Ming in China. Although the Korean peninsula was their main theater of activity, the *wakō* reached the China coast as well. During the first phase of *wakō* activity, the indigenous Chinese Ming dynasty emerged in China after destroying the intruding Mongol Yüan dynasty, and on the Korean peninsula, the Yi dynasty succeeded the Koryŏ dynasty. The *wakō* problem was a force in the founding of both these dynasties in China and Korea, and it is evident that relations among Japan, Korea, and Ming China were established as a result of the *wakō* problem. In Southeast Asia, several new kingdoms were established in the fourteenth and fifteenth centuries, ushering in an era of revolution and disorder previously unknown. The second major phase of *wakō* activity occurred in the early to mid-sixteenth century.

The different stages of political, economic, and cultural development in these Asian countries occurred within a unified international order revolving around Ming China. This order was referred to as the *tribute system* and involved the exchange of tribute and largess between China and other "barbarian" nations. Ming policy forbade Chinese citizens to leave the country as part of this tribute system, but this only stimulated the development of a flourishing trade in the newly risen Ryūkyū kingdom (present-day Okinawa) and the overseas Chinese communities to the south. The Ryūkyūs achieved unmatched prosperity as an intermediary in the trade among Southeast Asia, Japan, and Korea. The Ming policy forbidding overseas travel failed, and in the sixteenth century during the Chia-ching era (1522–66), *wakō* flourished along the southeastern China coast. But with the arrival of European ships, East Asian international relations underwent a dramatic change.

FOREIGN RELATIONS AT THE FOUNDING OF THE
KAMAKURA BAKUFU

Kyushu had been a base of political power for the Taira family. During the Gempei War (1180–5), however, Minamoto Yoritomo's younger brother Noriyori overthrew the Heishi forces in Kyushu. In 10/1185 Noriyori left Kyushu to return to Kamakura and presented the retired emperor Goshirakawa and Yoritomo with many gifts imported from the mainland to Kyushu, reconfirming for both men the importance of Kyushu in foreign trade.[3] Although initially an eastern power, the

3 These gifts included Chinese brocade, damask, silks, Sung silver coins, tea, ink, utensils, and matting. There is also mention of the Southern Court in a deed of sale of some land belonging

Kamakura bakufu sought quite early to establish Kyushu as a base for foreign trade, by gaining control of Dazaifu, which handled both internal politics and foreign relations in Kyushu. This control, however, was not achieved quickly.

Nakahara Hisatsune and Kondō Kunihara were sent earlier in the same year (7/1185) as envoys from Kamakura bearing an order from Goshirakawa to check the malicious actions of the warriors in Kyushu.[4] In addition, Amano Tōkage went to Kyushu as commissioner for the subjugation of Kyushu.[5] Tōkage was appointed to serve with influential officials at Dazaifu, and so his authority did not extend to the entire administration there.

The chronology is not entirely clear, but Tōkage's involvement in foreign affairs began soon after his move to Kyushu, with Dazaifu's unprecedented seizure of the cargo of a Chinese vessel that had landed in Shimazu-no-shō, an estate belonging to the Fujiwara clan's main line, the Konoe house.[6] Shimazu estate officials complained to the Konoe house, which in turn requested that Yoritomo intervene. Yoritomo ordered Tōkage to return the goods to the Konoe house. Shimazu-no-shō was an enormous estate that encompassed land in the three provinces of Hyūga, Ōsumi, and Satsuma. Bōnotsu, located within Shimazu-no-shō on the southwest coast of the Satsuma peninsula, was one of Japan's principal trading ports.

The foreign trade centering on Bōnotsu was of considerable economic importance to the estate.[7] Tōkage attempted to usurp the right to control trade from the central noble proprietor of Shimazu-no-shō, in the name of Dazaifu. But Minamoto Yoritomo overruled Tōkage's action, choosing instead to recognize and protect the right of the central proprietor to control the estate's trade. The Kamakura bakufu had just been established and had not yet officially assumed authority over foreign relations and trade. Thus, it could not deny the trade of

---

to the priest Eishō in Fukuoka's *Aoyagi monjo*, dated 5/3/1226. The *Aoyagi monjo* is included in Fukuokashi kyōiku iinkai, *Iimori jinja kankei shiryōshū* (Fukuoka: Fukuokashi kyōiku iinkai, 1981).

4 *Azuma kagami*, 7/12/1185, 8/13/1185, in *Shintei zōhō kokushi taikei*, vol. 32 (Tokyo: Yoshikawa kōbunkan, 1932), pp. 162, 164. Hereafter cited as *AK*.

5 *AK*, 12/15/1186, 11/5/1187, 1/15/1191. pp. 249, 281, 432.

6 *Shimazu-ke monjo*, vol. 1, no. 298, 5/14. "Minamoto no Yoritomo kahan Taira no Moritoki hōshoan," in *Dai Nihon komonjo, Iewake* 16, vol. 1 (Tokyo: Tōkyō daigaku shiryō hensanjo, 1942), p. 257.

7 For example, according to the 11/10/1147 entry in Fujiwara Yorinaga's diary (*Taiki*), Regent Fujiwara no Tadamichi presented a peacock and a parrot from Shimazu-no-shō to ex-Emperor Toba. See *Zōho shiryō taisei*, vol. 23 (Kyoto: Rinsen shoten, 1975), p. 232.

the court nobility, in this case the trading of the *shōen* officials of Shimazu-no-shō, as it did not yet control Dazaifu.

In 6/1182, Yoritomo canceled the *jitō* appointments in thirty-seven provinces, but he adopted special measures in Kyushu directing the provisional governor general of Dazaifu, Fujiwara (Yoshida) Tsunefusa, to administer the area, quell any rebellions, and rectify misdeeds.[8] Yoritomo's action thus must be seen in the light of his close relationship with Tsunefusa; his decision limited Tōkage's authority and reaffirmed the court's previous control over Dazaifu. Dazaifu, thus, was under the dual control of the nobles of Kyoto and the warriors of Kamakura.[9]

Fujiwara Noriyoshi became senior assistant governor general in the first month of 1190.[10] During his tenure in 1191, the following incident took place:[11] A Dazaifu report to the court stated that two Sung traders, Yang Yung and Chen Ch'i-t'ai, had committed a crime in the Southern Sung and that the Sung court had issued an order stating that henceforth anyone traveling from Japan to Sung China would be arrested. This presented an alarming situation for Japan. Consequently, Dazaifu recommended that Yang and the others be severely punished and that a report of their punishment be sent to the Sung court. The nationality of Yang and the other traders presented a problem, however. Yang had been born in Japan, and it was clear that he could be punished in Japan. But Chen had been born in Sung China, and so the court felt that it might be inappropriate to punish him in Japan. The exact crime committed, the decision reached by the court, and the punishment meted out are not known. It is clear, however, that Sung traders born in Japan, most likely in Hakata, were important to the trade between the two countries. Questions regarding an international legal order, including matters of territorial jurisdiction and trade, had now been raised, and Japan became a much stronger force than before in the development of East Asian history.

The authority to resolve this kind of foreign-policy issue lay not

---

8 In fact, from 1186 to 1190, we can point to at least six Dazaifu actions, that is, acts by Fujiwara no Tsunefusa, in which Amano Tōkage was not involved. See Takeuchi Rizō, "Chinzei bugyō ni tsuite no ichi, ni no kōsatsu," in *Uozumi-sensei koki kinen kokushigaju ronsō* (Osaka: Kansai daigaku, 1959), p. 423.

9 Seno Seiichirō, *Chinzei gokenin no kenkyū* (Tokyo: Yoshikawa kōbunkan, 1975), p. 38. Fujita Toshio, "Kamakura shoki no Dazaifu kikō ni tsuite," *Kumamoto shigaku* 55 (May 1981).

10 The following are useful source material collections on Dazaifu during the establishment of the Kamakura bakufu: Takeuchi Rizō, ed., *Dazaifu, Dazaifu temmangū shiryō*, vol. 7 (Fukuoka-ken: Daizaifu temmangū, 1971).

11 *Gyokuyō*, vol. 3, 2/15/1191, 2/19/1192, 6/12/1192 (Tokyo: Kokusho kankōkai, 1907), pp. 660–61, 710.

with the Kamakura bakufu but with the court. Dazaifu, which handled its own foreign relations directly, was divided between its responsibility to the court and that to the bakufu. It seems, however, that Tōkage did not play a decisive role in managing foreign-policy issues.[12] During an earlier discussion of matters involving commodity prices in 7/1179, the court had prohibited trade in Sung coins, regarding them as equivalent to privately minted coins.[13] In 7/1193, the court further forbade the circulation of Sung coins, in order to stabilize prices.[14] This was an attempt to manage foreign relations in a very broad sense of the term. Both the 2/1227 Koryŏ affair[15] and the 4/1240 communiqué from Koryŏ were discussed in council at the court.[16]

How did the incident involving Yang and the other Sung traders arise? A better understanding of the incident requires a discussion of Sung residents in Japan. A number of persons from Sung China had formed relationships with the great Japanese temples and shrines as yoriudo (outside laborers) and jinin (shrine dependents), carrying out trade and accumulating wealth. The Hakozakigū shrine, located in present-day Fukuoka City, is a good example.[17] According to a 1219 document, Sung people owned twenty-six chō of paddy field, and these fields were exempt from taxes and levies.[18] We know that the Sung provided Chinese goods such as saddles and silk cloth to the Hakozakigū. In addition, these Sung traders were responsible for paying various levies to the shrine. The Hakozakigū formed this relationship with foreign-trading merchants residing in Hakata and received a portion of their profits. This trade was further connected to the main shrine, Iwashimizu Hachimangū.

In 1218 an absentee official of the main shrine, Gyōhen, and his son, Mitsusuke, killed Chang Kuang-an, a yoriudo of Dazaifu and a jinin of the Daisenji, as well as a translator and a boat captain. The motive for the murder is unknown, but we can deduce that it was somehow

12 Kawazoe Shōji, ed., Umi kara yomigaeru wakō (Fukuoka: Asahi shimbum seibu honsha kikakubu, 1981), p. 39.   13 Gyokuyō, vol. 2, 7/25/1179, 7/27/1179, pp. 290–91.

14 "Hōsō shiyōshō," suiko, in Gunsho ruijū, vol. 4, (Tokyo: Keizai zasshisha, 1898), p. 873. Takeuchi Rizō, ed., Kamakura ibun, vol. 2 (Tokyo: Tōkyōdō, 1972), p. 78. Hereafter cited as KI.

15 Kokusho kankōkai, comp., Meigetsuki, vol. 3, 2/18/1227 (Tokyo: Kokusho kankōkai, 1912), p. 14.

16 Hyankurenshō, 1240/4/3, vol. 11 of Shintei zōho kokushi taikei (Tokyo: Yoshikawa kōbunkan, 1939), p. 187. Heidoki, 1240/4/12–14, 17, vol. 32 in Zōho shiryō taisei (Kyoto: Rinsen shoten, 1975)), pp. 48–49, 52–53.

17 Mori Katsumi, Shintei Nissō bōeki no kenkyū (Tokyo: Kokusho kankōkai, 1975), pp. 245–51. Kawazoe Shōji, Chūsei Kyūshū no seiji to bunka (Tokyo: Bunken shuppan, 1981), pp. 62–66.

18 This was written on the reverse side of the 6/1219 entry in the Ruijū kokushi owned by Iwashimizu Hachimangū. See KI, vol. 4, pp. 339–40.

related to a dispute over trade profits. Gyōhen was the deputy of Sosei, the provincial governor of Iwashimizu. The priests of the Enryakuji, the Daisenji's main temple, threatened the court with the sacred palanquins of the Hie, Kitano, and Gion shrines, demanding that Sosei be handed over to the Enryakuji and that the ports of Hakata and Hakozaki be made possessions of the Enryakuji. There was also a conflict within Iwashimizu Hachimangū between Sōsei and Yusei. The affair ended with some underlings being jailed, but nothing more. It was a bold attempt by the Enryakuji to check the power of the Iwashimizu Hachimangū, to place the Hakozakigū under its own control, and to seize the profits from foreign trade.

Also in 1218, Hsiu-an, a translator and ship captain, and an estate official of Kanzaki-no-shō in Hizen attacked the deputy administrator of the Hakozakigū and an envoy of Dazaifu. This incident was related to another in 11/1219, in which estate officials of Kanzaki-no-shō requested that Chang Kuan-an's death place, Hakata, and its holdings be made possessions of Kanzaki-no-shō. It appears that Chang had some sort of profit arrangement in Kanzaki-no-shō. He had holdings in Hakata and clashed with the Hakozakigū over a matter of rights, thus beginning the fight between the Daisenji's main temple, the Enryakuji, and the Hakozakigu's main shrine, Iwashimizu Hachimangū.[19]

Another case illustrating the life of the Sung Chinese in Japan was that of Hsieh Kuo-ming, who built the Jōtenji in Hakata.[20] The temple was founded by Shoichi Kokushi En'ni Ben'en (1202–80) and built in the late thirteenth century adjacent to the Shōfukuji, which Eisai had built in Hakata. En'ni was the first priest in Japan to be given the title of national teacher (kokushi). The temple's chief financial supporters were the trader Hsieh Kuo-ming and a member of the Mutō house, claimed to be Mutō Sukeyori, who served as junior assistant governor (shōni) of Dazaifu. The temple was constructed against a background of connections between these two financial backers in the Japan–Sung trade. En'ni was a native of Suruga Province who had received his ordination at the Tōdaiji. After entering the service of Eichō at the Chōrakuji in Kōzuke, he moved to Hakata in 1233 in preparation for a trip to China. He stayed in Hakata for two years, and it was probably during those years that he came to know Hsieh Kuo-ming and the

---

19 See Takeuchi, ed., Dazaifu, Dazaifu Temmangū shiryō, vol. 7, pp. 344ff.
20 Hirowatari Masatoshi, Hakata jōtenjishi (Tokyo: Bunka shuppan, 1977) and Hakata jōtenjishi (Fukuoka: Fukuoka-ken bunka kaikan, 1981).

Mutō (Shōni) family. In 1235 he went to China and entered the service of Wu-chun Shih-fan at Mount Ching-shan in the northern part of Linan-fu of Kang-chou in Chiekiang Province. He returned to Japan in 1241 with many Chinese volumes and made an important contribution to Japanese religion and arts. En'ni was in Hakata for about three years and became known to Fujiwara no Michiie, under whose protection he opened the Tōfukuji, establishing the foundation for the rise of Zen Buddhism in Kyoto.

En'ni went to the capital after his stay in Hakata, but he soon returned to China where he was in close contact with his teacher, Wu-chun Shih-fan. En'ni played a major role in the cultural interchange between Sung China and Japan. For example, at the urging of people like Hsieh Kuo-ming he contributed to the restoration of Ching-shan, which had suffered a calamity. And when the Jōtenji caught fire in 1248, he quickly returned to Hakata and rebuilt the temple with Hsieh's assistance.

The Mutō family was a Kantō *gokenin* family based in Musashi with special bakufu authority over Kyushu. Because the family served in the Dazaifu post of *shōni*, they came to be called the Shōni family. Family members concurrently held *shugo* posts in Chikuzen, Buzen, Hizen, Tsushima, and Iki. The Mutō family is said to have been the patron family of the Jōtenji, to which they commended certain lands, but there are no extant documents confirming this. However, as the Dazaifu officials directly responsible for foreign relations, the Mutō were most likely involved with En'ni's trips to Sung and the Sung–Japan trade of Hsieh Kuo-ming. Therefore, the claim that the Mutō cooperated with Hsieh to build the Jōtenji is quite likely true.

Hsieh Kuo-ming, known variously as "trade leader," "boat captain," and "Japanese trade envoy" (*Nihon gōshi*), was a Hakata-based merchant active in the Sung–Japan trade. His extraordinary wealth is attested to by his construction of the Jōtenji and the restoration of Ching-shan, although he probably had help from other Sung merchants like himself. We know that Hsieh held the *jitō-shiki* for certain lands in Oro-no-shima belonging to the Munakata Shrine (Munakata District, Fukuoka Prefecture). This reveals part of his economic base as a trader. When the Jōtenji was built, Hsieh bought land owned by the Hakozaki Hachimangū in the Aka District of Chikuzen and donated it to the temple. This indicates both Hsieh's wealth and his dependent relationship with the Hakozakigū. He enjoyed close connections with the Munakata and the Hakozakigū shrines, both occupying important positions in foreign trade. It is said that in 1242 Hsieh restored the Jōtenji after it was destroyed by fire, rebuilding eighteen structures in one day. There is also a letter from Wu-chun Shih-fan addressed to Hsieh, thanking him for contributing lumber to the reconstruction of the Ching-shan. Built by Chinese trade leaders to revive the faith of their homeland, the Jōtenji was an entirely appropriate Zen temple for Hakata, a center of foreign trade.

The construction of the Jōtenji is significant in the context of cultural interchange between Japan and Sung China. The Shōfukuji, supposedly built by Eisai, marks the appearance in Hakata of Sung-style Zen *garan*, the first step in a change in the city's urban landscape. But the subsequent construction of the Jōtenji brought the powerful styles of Sung's Tendai Zen and accelerated urban Hakata's sinofication. Along with the Dazaifu's Sōfukuji and the Hizen's Manjuji, the Jōtenji formed the center of the Rinzai sect's development in northern Kyushu. Temples and shrines represent the culture of medieval Hakata, and the majority of these institutions were centers of foreign trade. Consequently, it was from that quarter that the culture of Hakata took its direction. The remarkable roles played by En'ni and Hsieh Kuo-ming in the history of cultural interchange between Sung China and Japan indicate the tremendous significance of the founding of the Jōtenji in the history of Japan's adoption of a foreign culture.

FOREIGN RELATIONS DURING THE HŌJŌ REGENCY

Mutō (Shōni) Sukeyori came to Kyushu shortly after 3/1196 to govern the island for the bakufu. He inherited Amano Tōkage's position of leadership over the influential local officials at Dazaifu and also established the Dazaifu *shugo-shō*, with jurisdiction over the constabulary provinces of Chikuzen, Buzen, and Hizen. It was only after his appointment[21] as *Dazai no shōni* (junior assistant governor of Dazaifu) in 10/1226 that Mutō Sukeyori became the ranking local official in Dazaifu.

Sukeyori had gradually accumulated power within the Dazaifu structure before this appointment. Furthermore, his appointment as *shōni* (the post with the highest authority over foreign contacts at Dazaifu)

---

21 Takeuchi, ed., *Dazaifu, Dazaifu temmangū shiryō*, vol. 7, p. 390.

was related to the bakufu's consolidation after the Jōkyū disturbance under Hōjō Yasutoki. Succeeding his father Yoshitoki as regent, Yasutoki[22] moved toward a councilor type of rule, first by appointing one of his most trustworthy kinsmen, Hōjō Tokifusa, as cosigner, and then by designating eleven men to serve on a board of councilors in 12/1225. Mutō Sukeyori, a bakufu *gokenin*, became *Dazai no shōni* ten months later. During this interval the bakufu had successfully negotiated Sukeyori's appointment with the court. Although, Sukeyori's appointment was connected with the Kamakura bakufu's political consolidation, foreign policy considerations made the court's approval mandatory.

The 5/1223 entry in the twenty-second *kwon* of the *Koryosa*[23] states that "Japanese (pirates) attacked Kumjo." This is the first textual reference to *wakō*. The 4/1225 entry states further that Koryŏ dispatched troops and captured two *wakō* boats that had attacked the coast of Kyongsangdo. These accounts are quite detailed, indicating Koryŏ's increasing concern about piracy. *Wakō* again attacked the coast of Kyongsangdo in the first month of the next year, 1226, and in the sixth month again invaded Kumjo. These raids were on a smaller scale than those beginning in 1350 and are best thought of as a prelude to those later attacks.[24] Nevertheless, their impact was significant. Especially troublesome was the 6/1226 attack, in which the majority of pirates were Tsushima islanders. Koryŏ complained strongly to Dazaifu in 2/1227,[25] and Fujiwara Sada'ie expressed fear of a Koryŏ attack.[26] It was because of this sense of foreign crisis generated by the *wakō* problem that the court agreed to the appointment of Mutō Sukeyori as *shōni*, because he enjoyed special authority for bakufu control of Kyushu and moreover he was *shugo* of Chikuzen, Chikugo, Buzen, and Hizen.

Sukeyori became *shōni* under confused circumstances, but how he dealt with the foreign problem in Dazaifu is relatively clear from the sources. In his diary, *Meigetsuki*, Fujiwara Sada'ie relates in a 10/17/1226 entry that because the Matsura-tō, a pirate band from Kyushu, had attacked Koryŏ with several dozen warships, Koryŏ had raised a force and taken revenge by burning some Japanese ships used for

22 Uwayokote Masataka, *Hōjō Yasutoki* (Tokyo: Yoshikawa kōbunkan, 1958).
23 For the *Koryosa*, see Tokyo, *Kokusho kankōkai*, 1908 ed.
24 Tanaka, *Wakō to kangō bōeki*, p. 3.   25 *AK*, 1227/5/14, vol. 33, p. 56.
26 *Meigetsuki*, vol. 2, 1226/10/16–17, pp. 544–5.

travel to Sung China. This was the 6/1226 raid attributed to the inhabitants of Tsushima. In 2/1227 Koryŏ vehemently complained of this in a communiqué, to Dazaifu. In response, Mutō Sukeyori opened the Koryŏ communiqué, had ninety pirates beheaded in front of the Koryŏ envoy, and secretly sent back his own reply.[27] In the twenty-second *kwan* of *Koryosa* an entry for 5/17/1227 records that "Japan sent a letter apologizing for the crime of the pirate ship invasions and seeking to improve relations." The entire matter was debated in council at court, where Sukeyori's actions were considered "an embarrassment to our nation," and the Koryŏ communiqué, a breach of etiquette. Mutō Sukeyori tried to restore good relations by controlling the pirate attacks through severe reprisals, but the Kyoto nobles, placing great value on honor, criticized him.

By the middle of the eleventh century, the relationship between Japan and Koryŏ had progressed from merely returning each other's shipwrecked sailors into a full trading relationship. However, in the twelfth century there were no diplomatic relations at all. The goods that Koryŏ exported to Japan consisted of basic raw materials, whereas Japan's exports to Koryŏ were finished goods requiring detailed craftsmanship. The reason that the Japan–Koryŏ trade rose to a peak and then declined rapidly can be attributed to an imbalance in the levels of the countries' productive capacities. Koryŏ's relationship with Japan into the thirteenth century soured and was limited, as we have seen, by the agreement on annual trading missions. The primary reason for this was Koryŏ's low level of productivity and lack of commercial development.[28] In addition, the *wakō* problem limited cultural interchange between Japan and Koryŏ in the thirteenth century. Through foreign-policy negotiations with Dazaifu and Mutō Sukeyori, Koryŏ hoped to control Tsushima and the Matsura-tō, to limit trade as far as the Shōni were concerned, and to stabilize its own economy, whose productive capacity was as yet undeveloped.

Although Japanese pirate attacks against Koryŏ decreased after the 6/1226 raid on Kumjo, they did not cease. Koryŏ's Ungjin District was raided in the fifth month of the following year,[29] the same month in which Mutō Sukeyori beheaded the criminals in front of the Koryŏ

27 Takeuchi, ed., *Dazaifu, Dazaifu temmangū shiryō*, vol. 7, pp. 399–400.
28 Aoyama Kōryō, *Nichirai kōshōshi no kenkyū;* (Tokyo: Meiji daigaku bungakubu bungaku kenkyūsho, 1955), p. 25. Tamura Hiroyuki, *Chūsei Nitchō bōeki no kenkyū* (Kyoto: Sanwa shobō, 1967), p. 13.
29 Source materials on Japanese–Koryŏ relations are collected in Shiryō shūsei hensankai, *Chūgoku–Chōsen no shiseki in okeru Nihon shiryō shūsei, Sankoku, Kōrai no bu* (Tokyo: Kokusho kankōkai, 1978).

envoy. In 1232, residents of Kagamisha in Hizen Province invaded Koryŏ and stole many rare treasures. The *azukari-dokoro* of Kagamisha complained of interference by the *shugo*, but the Kamakura bakufu ordered the *shugo-sho* of Hizen (Mutō Sukeyori's son Sukeyoshi) to investigate the criminals, as well as their vessels and contraband.[30] In 9/1243, Japan offered goods to Koryŏ and also returned some Koryŏ castaways; this was in all likelihood the work of the Mutō. Likewise, the Mutō order to Shigehisa, said to be the founder of the Sō clan, to attack the Ahira family of Tsushima in 1245 or 1246 was probably an attempt to control pirate activity.

In the latter half of the reign of Koryŏ's King Kojong, there were fewer Japanese pirate raids on Koryŏ because of both Koryŏ's increased diplomatic pressures on Japan and its strengthened defense. But it was after 1231, when Koryŏ was invaded by the Mongols, that the pirate attacks declined most significantly. In 11/1251, Koryŏ prepared for pirate raids by constructing a castle at Kumju,[31] and immediately after surrendering to the Mongols in 7/1259, Koryŏ sent an envoy to Japan requesting that the pirates be suppressed.[32] The *Koryosa* entry for 2/1260 records that Sung merchants and "island *wae*" (meaning Japanese from Tsushima) continued to visit Koryŏ, and as a result Koryŏ dispatched a defense commissioner to prepare for emergencies. In 1263 a number of priests and secular people entering Sung China in search of the Buddhist law came to Koryŏ ports, and merchant vessels returning to Japan from Sung also docked in Koryŏ. Koryŏ sent these travelers away and strengthened its defenses.[33]

In 2/1263, Japanese *wakō* again at Ungjin, seizing cloth and rice from tribute vessels from various administrative centers. Koryŏ sent an envoy bearing a communiqué to Japan strongly protesting this action and requesting that the pirates suppressed. Koryŏ maintained that Koryŏ–Japan relations were limited by agreement to two ships per year and that the Japanese pirate activities were in flagrant violation of this.[34] Thus pressured, Japan's negotiators (most likely from the Mutō family) reconfirmed the policies of limiting trade and prohibiting piracy. A Dazaifu investigation of the raid established clearly that the guilty parties were Tsushima people, and so the Koryŏ envoy confiscated rice, horse fodder, and leather before returning to Korea. The *Aokata monjo* contains a fragmentary document pertaining to

30 *AK*, vol. 33, 1232/9/17, p. 121.   31 Shiryō shūsei hensankai, *Nihon shiryō shūsei*, p. 266.
32 Ibid., p. 69.   33 Ibid., p. 70.   34 Ibid., p. 70.

this affair that indicates that the Matsura-tō was at the center of things.[35]

The Mongols, having terrorized Koryŏ for thirty years, enthroned Kublai Khan, who then dealt less harshly with Koryŏ because of its political instability at the time of his accession. But in 7/1265, the year after Koryŏ entered into tribute relations with the Mongols, the Japanese attacked the coasts of Koryŏ southern provinces. Koryŏ defended against these attacks by employing its most powerful military force, the *sampyol'cho* (third special unit).[36] These problems surrounding the *wakō* were related to the Mongol invasions of Japan, which I shall discuss later in this chapter.

From late Heian to early Kamakura times, the court had forbidden metal currency and prohibited the circulation of "new coins,"[37] that is, Southern Sung coins, in order to control prices. In 7/1199, the year of Minamoto Yoritomo's death, the Southern Sung also prohibited the export of Sung copper coins by Japanese and Koryŏ merchants.[38] At that time copper coins were not used as money in trade transactions but were exchanged for goods of equivalent value. Southern Sung intellectuals, lamenting the flow of Sung coins out of the country, made numerous plans and proposals. The severe outflow of copper coins during the Southern Sung resulted in deflationary conditions referred to as "scarcity of money" (*ch'ien-huang*). In Japan, prices had previously been calculated in amounts of cloth, but in 1226 the Kamakura bakufu abolished the cloth equivalence and ordered the use of copper coins.[39] Money had not been minted in Japan since the twelve imperial coins (*kōchō junisen*) of Nara times, and from late Heian, Sung coins circulated unchecked by legislative action. However, with the development of various forces of production and the expansion of commerce, the demand for a circulating currency increased. The court was thus forced to recognize the great importance of the Sung coins, whose circulation had been prohibited until early Kamakura.

It was said that traffic between Sung and Japan was never less than forty to fifty ships annually and that the Japanese especially desired

35 Seno Seiichirō, ed., *Aokata monjo*, vol. 1 (Tokyo: Zoku gunsho ruijū kanseikai, 1975), p. 68.
36 Shiryō shūsei hensankai, *Nihon shiryō shūsei*, p. 71   37 *Gyokuyō*, vol. 3, 1187/6/13, p. 375.
38 The following section on the flow of Sung coins into Japan relies on Mori Katsumi, *Shintei Nissō bōeki no kenkyū* (Tokyo: Kokusho kankōkai, 1975); and Sogabe Shizuo, *Nissō kinkahei kōryūshi* (Tokyo: Hōbunkan, 1949).   39 *AK*, 1226/8/1, vol. 33, p. 45.

copper coins. The money that was imported and circulated was predominantly Northern Sung coins; that from Southern Sung comprised an insignificant amount. In 1242, a merchant vessel belonging to Saionji Kintsune returned from Sung China carrying 100,000 *kan* worth of coins, along with parrots and water buffalo. This 100,000 *kan* of Sung coins was equivalent to the entire amount of coins minted annually in the Southern Sung. Thus, the importation of these coins had a significant impact on the economies of both Sung China and Japan.

The tremendous outflow of Sung coins to Japan as well as to various parts of Asia aggravated the economic crisis throughout the Southern Sung, causing the government to adopt stringent regulations to curtail the flow of copper coins to Japan. The excessive exporting necessary to obtain the Sung coins also disrupted the Japanese economy. For example, according to the *Teiō hennenki*,[40] the export of rice from the western provinces mentioned in the edict probably means most of it was Chinzei *mai* (Kyushu rice), which was favored by the Kyoto nobles. Because of Japan's chronic natural disasters and frequent famines, this measure was most likely adopted out of fear that the export of rice to China would exceed productive capacity and so reduce the income from the *shōen* and *kōryō*.

While the history of foreign relations to the mid-thirteenth century was evolving around these problems, the power structure of the Kamakura bakufu was consolidated; the Hōjō family regency system was secured; and the bakufu's control over the western provinces – the base for foreign relations – was strengthened. The transport route for the continental goods from Hakata along the Seto Inland Sea to Kyoto expanded to reach the warrior stronghold at Kamakura, which became the terminus. Kamakura received a large amount of material goods from the continent by two routes: from Kyoto and from Hakata through the Inland Sea. This movement of goods increased from mid- to late Kamakura times, and economic circulation and regional culture developed throughout the entire century.

The *Kaidōki* of 1223 records that Yuihama in Kamakura was crowded with houses and had several hundred ships anchored there. Ten years later, in 1232, during the regency of Hōjō Yasutoki, a small island – Wake no shima – was constructed with contributions solicited by the priest Oamidabutsu to facilitate ship docking, and it became a base for both domestic and foreign trade. Subsequently, the

---

40 *Shintei zōhō kokushi taikei* (Tokyo: Yoshikawa kōbunkan, 1932), p. 409.

importation of continental goods into Kamakura increased further. And along with the consolidation of water routes – the opening of the Asahina canal between Kamakura and Musashi Matsura in 1241, for example – the warrior government at Kamakura increased in prosperity, supported by wealth acquired through trade. When we consider the growth of the cities during the Kamakura period in the light of Japan's relations with East Asia, we must take special note of the prosperity of the port cities along the Inland Sea, such as Hakata, Kamakura, and Kusado Sengen,[41] which, is contrast with Kyoto, served as entrepôts for foreign trade.

The bakufu issued legislation to limit foreign traffic on the Inland Sea linking Hakata and Kamakura when it became too active. In 4/ 1254 a bakufu document addressed to Nikaidō Yukiyasu and Ota Yasutsura prohibited the possession of more than five Chinese vessels ordered the destruction of ships beyond that number.[42] According to the *Kentō hyōjōshū-den*, Yasutsura was a member of the Council of State (*hyōjōshū*) and head of the Board of Inquiry (*monchūjo*) and Yukiyasu administered the fifth *hikitsuke* and head of the Administrative Board (*mandokoro*). If we accept the interpretation that "suits by commoners and nonhousemen in Kamakura were administered by the *mandokoro* and suits by such individuals from the provinces were handled by the *monchūjo*," then this law must have been intended to limit private trade among trading merchants in both Kamakura and the provinces.[43] Thus, the earlier interpretation that this ordinance was addressed to Dazaifu requires reexamination. If we consider the way the law was transmitted, as well as the state of communications between Japan and the continent, then the law must have extended even to Dazaifu and Hakata.

What exactly was this ordinance? Koryŏ and Sung China were suffering from *wakō* attacks and an excessive outflow of coins. Japan faced several problems: an international legal order[44] necessitated by the residency of foreigners in Japan; an outflow of rice exceeding productive capacity which was destroying the income structure of the *shōen* and *kōryō* and fanning the crisis of famine; and the rapid increase of Chinese imports into Kamakura. Furthermore, Japan's internal

41 Murakami Masana, *Maboroshi no Kusado Sengenchō* (Tokyo: Kokusho kankōkai, 1980).
42 *AK*, 1254/4/29, vol. 33, p. 561.
43 For the various theories about the 1254 regulation, see Osa Setsuko, "Kenchō rokunen 'tōsen' seigenryō ni kansuru shomondai," in *Chūkyō tanki daigaku ronsō 1* (March 1966).
44 Along with this we must also consider that there were then a rather large number of Japanese residents in Ningpo. See Sogabe, *Nissō kinkahei kōryūshi*, pp. 166–67.

politics were shifting toward Hōjō authoritarianism. These problems were probably considered when writing the ordinance.

We must recognize, however, that this law was an attempt by the Kamakura bakufu (the Hōjō) to protect its own official trade vessels and to strengthen its own control over trade while limiting trade with Sung China in general. We should also consider the course leading toward the bakufu's monopolization of public trading vessels in the late (post-Mongol invasion) Kamakura period. Although the limitation ordinance certainly is significant to the history of Kamakura foreign relations, this does not mean that it was immediately and permanently enforced. Judging from later conditions, it did not seem to limit private foreign trade. But in 4/1264 the bakufu did order Dazaifu to stop the official trade vessels.[45] This action was probably taken in light of the Mongols' imminent conquest of the Southern Sung.[46]

THE MONGOL INVASIONS

In 1206 the Mongol unifier, Genghis Khan (1162–1227), unleashed a stormlike campaign of warfare, utilizing incomparably powerful cavalry forces. The campaign lost force by the mid-thirteenth century, but in the process it created a new political situation. A great new empire emerged, encompassing the nomadic pasture lands of the northern plains, the Islamic cultural sphere, large parts of East Asia, and even a portion of Europe. By the era of the fourth khan, Mongke (1208–59), control of the Mongol Empire had shifted from the Ogotei line to the descendants of Tului, exacerbating a tendency toward disintegration. When Kublai (1215–94) succeeded his brother Mongke as Great Khan, the situation became critical. Mongke appointed Kublai as commander in chief with authority to rule northern China; of all the Mongol leaders, Kublai was the most friendly toward China. After Mongke's death, Kublai fought for the position of Great Khan with his younger brother Arighbugha (?–1266) who placed primary importance on the Mongol homeland. Calling together the great council (Khuriltai), Kublai proclaimed his own succession. Thus, at least in name, Kublai became the leader of the Mongols. But in reality he had

---

45 Satō Shin'ichi and Ikeuchi Yoshisuke, eds., *Chūsei hōsei shiryōshū* (Tokyo: Iwanami shoten, 1955), p. 222.
46 Concerning the cultural interchange during the Kamakura period, see Kawazoe Shōji, "Kamakura jidai no taigai kankei to bunbutsu no inyū," in *Iwanami kōza Nihon rekishi*, vol. 6 (*chūsei* 2) (Tokyo: Iwanami shoten, 1975).

to create his own authority, the Yüan dynastic order, whose political base lay in the Chinese agricultural region.[47]

The Yüan dynasty attacked Japan twice – first in 1274 and then again in 1281. The attackers were called Yüan pirates (*genkō*). In this chapter, I shall call these attacks Mongol invasions (*Mōkō shūrai*), as they are referred to in contemporary sources. The two wars themselves are known from the era names as the Bun'ei and Kōan campaigns. One can consider the significance of the Mongol invasions in Japanese history in two ways. The first is to look at them in the context of East Asian history, using a time frame from the Mongol invasions themselves to the end of the Kamakura period, during which the bakufu, fearing yet another attack, kept its defense structure intact. This would be, in other words, a cross-sectional analysis. But such an approach has two problems: how to regard the Mongol invasions from the standpoint of Japan's relations with Yüan, Koryŏ, and Southern Sung and how to analyze Japan's internal situation in terms of politics, economics, society, thought, and culture. The second approach reveals how this unprecedented foreign attack functioned in terms of the Japanese consciousness of foreign peoples, that is, in the formation of a national consciousness. This is a sort of vertical analysis.[48] Because I cannot use both approaches here, I shall first describe the international situation leading to the Mongol invasions, and then explain the reasons behind them.[49]

Because the Japanese–Mongol negotiations were initiated through Koryŏ, the relationship between the Mongols and Koryŏ requires some clarification.[50] This relationship began when the Mongols attacked the Tungusic Jurchin kingdom of Chin (1115–1234). The Chitan people, previously subject to the Chin, had revolted and ravaged the northern area of Korea; consequently, in 1219, Koryŏ joined the Mongols to subdue them. Later, however, Mongol envoys periodically visited Koryŏ, demanding and collecting large amounts of tribute. But in 1225, when Ogotei (1168–1241) succeeded Genghis Khan,

47 Murakami Masatsugu, "Mongoru teikoku no seiritsu to bunretsu," in *Iwanami kōza sekai rekishi*, vol. 9 (*chūsei* 3) (Tokyo: Iwanami shoten, 1970).

48 There are numerous studies dealing with the Mongol invasions, and for a history of these studies, see Kawazoe Shōji, *Mōkō shūrai kenkyū shiron* (Tokyo: Yūzankaku, 1977).

49 The following discussion is based mainly on Kawazoe, *Chūsei Kyūshū no seiji to bunka*, pp. 103–33. Consequently, I have not listed each document. Two representative works on the Mongol invasions are by Ikeuchi Hiroshi, *Genkō no shinkenkyū* (Tokyo: Tōyō bunko, 1931); and Aida Nirō, *Mōkō shūrai no kenkyū* (Tokyo: Yoshikawa kōbunkan, 1971). For more details, see Kawazoe, *Mōkō shūrai kenkyū shiron*.

50 The following discussion of Japanese–Koryŏ relations is based on the first two chapters of Ikeuchi, *Genkō no shin kenkyū*.

Mongol ambassadors returning to China with Koryŏ tribute goods were attacked and murdered. Under the pretext of punishing the murderers, Ogotei appointed Sartag as commander in 1231 and sent him to invade Koryŏ. Thus began the Mongol invasions of Koryŏ which continued for the next three decades. Koryŏ moved its capital to Kanghwa Island and continued a heroic resistance. But the people and land of Koryŏ were trampled under the hooves of the Mongol cavalry; corpses covered the fields; and after the Mongols passed through, nothing was left behind.

At the time of the fourth Mongol ruler, Mongke, the Koryŏ court left Kanghwa and surrendered to the Mongols. Prince Chon departed for an audience with Mongke, but Mongke died suddenly at his battle headquarters in Szechuan Province, and the prince instead met Kublai, who was proceeding north. In order to defeat his younger brother Arighbugha, Kublai found it necessary to win over Koryŏ. So he altered his earlier policy of successive attacks and adopted a moderate policy toward Koryŏ, while continuing to rely on the success of those raids.

Koryŏ's King Kojong died after hearing that the fortress on Kanghwa Island had been destroyed by the Mongols, and Crown Prince Chon succeeded as King Wonjong, securing his position with Mongol backing. Peace seemed to have returned to Koryŏ. However, when Kublai defeated Arighbugha and consolidated his position as the Mongol ruler, he reversed his moderate policy and instead demanded strict compliance with the heavy obligations he imposed on the Koreans. Thus the Mongols assigned to Koryŏ the responsibility of negotiating with Japan. As the base for the invasion of Japan, Koryŏ was forced once again to face difficult times.

While Kublai and Arighbugha were fighting each other, a man known as Li T'an held sway in Shantung Province. In 1262 the Southern Sung persuaded him to raise a rebellion against the Mongols. However, Li's rebellion was put down in only half a year, and the Southern Sung's calculation that they could weaken Mongol power proved inaccurate. Before that, just a month after his accession, Kublai dispatched envoys to the Southern Sung, demanding the formal establishment of peace negotiations, but the Sung imprisoned the envoys. With this they had assisted Li T'an's rebellion, which constituted a challenge to the Mongols.

Kublai began to raise an army to invade the Sung. In 1268 he attacked Hsiang Yang in Hupei and, after a five-year assault, finally forced its surrender. The Mongol army then seized Ngo Chou (Hupei

Province, Wu Chang) and in 1275 occupied the Southern Sung capital of Lin'an (Hangchou). There were attempts to revive the Southern Sung, but in 1279, two years before the Kōan campaign, the young Sung emperor Ping perished at sea in the battle of Yaishan. Kublai had at last defeated the Southern Sung and brought all of China under his control. Thus my conclusion is that the Mongol threat to and invasion of Japan was related to this attack on the Southern Sung.

In Kangan (south Kyongsang Province), a part of Koryŏ close to Japan, lived a man named Ch'oe I who enjoyed Kublai's favor. He reported information he had heard about Japan to Kublai, telling him that the country's laws and government were superior, and advised him to open negotiations with Japan, which had been in communication with China since Han and T'ang times. Ch'oe further recommended that Koryŏ guide the Mongols to Japan. This is the background of Kublai's dispatch of emissaries to Japan requesting diplomatic relations. Thus in 1265 negotiations commenced between Japan and the Mongols.

A document from the Mongols (dated 8/1266 and arriving in Japan on 1/1268) first described the Mongols' might and then recounted how they had brought peace to Koryŏ, explaining that the Mongol–Koryŏ relationship was like lord and vassal or father and son: Koryŏ was the Mongols' "eastern vassal state." Japan is close to Koryŏ, the document continued and, since Japan's founding, had normally had exchanges with China but had not yet concluded peace with it. Saying that perhaps "your honorable country" is unaware of these circumstances, the document expressed the Mongols' wish to establish friendship between the two states. The wording was courteous and did not demand Japan's submission, but it concluded that if there were no other way, the Mongols would resort to force of arms. Reminiscent of the edicts issued by the emperor in the Han Chinese state,[51] this document coupled the Mongol sense of superiority with a Chinese moral view, following traditional Chinese foreign-policy forms. From ancient times China had, in return for the tribute goods that neighboring kingdoms brought and presented at the Chinese court, granted these states "gifts" of a higher value than the tribute, preserving a China-centered foreign-policy structure. Ever mindful of Chinese tradition, Kublai naturally patterned his actions after that policy. The type of

51 Ishihara Michihiro, "Gendai Nihonkan no ichi sokumen," in Wada hakase kanreki kinenkai, ed., *Tōyōshi ronsō* (Tokyo: Wada hakase kanreki kinenkai, 1951).

relationship that Kublai first sought with Japan was probably this sort of tribute–gift exchange,[52] one that combined politics, foreign relations, and economics.

Why did Kublai seek peace with Japan in 1266? The Mongols were preparing to attack the Southern Sung, and Kublai, judging the Sung to be strong, proceeded carefully with his attack plans. Part of these plans required strengthening control over Koryŏ. In his document Kublai referred to Koryŏ as the Mongols' "eastern vassal state." With Kublai's military backing, Koryŏ's King Wonjong had suppressed the military officials who had previously controlled national politics and had increased his own authority as sovereign. Thus, from Kublai's point of view, Koryŏ was indeed a newly attached country. Using the negotiations with Japan as a tool, Kublai was able to intensify his domination over Koryŏ. Also, in preparing to invade Southern Sung, Kublai had come to realize that Japan, even though it was a small eastern island really not worth taking, it could not be left alone. Japan traded with the Southern Sung and therefore continuously added to the Sung's financial strength. Seen in this light, Japan had to be cut off from the Sung and added to Kublai's empire. And this would be possible if Koryŏ were used as a go-between. Even in the event that Japan did not reply positively, Kublai would have a good excuse to punish Koryŏ. There is no way to know whether Kublai did think in these terms, but it is reasonable to suppose that he did.

One view regards Kublai's dispatch of envoys to Japan as stemming from his desire for trade through amicable relations.[53] But even granting that motive, there was still the matter of the attack on the Southern Sung, and so trade alone could not have been the chief reason. The aforementioned Mongol document came about because of the prevailing circumstances, and it expressed a conciliatory foreign policy. In any case, Kublai's attempt to negotiate with Japan was linked to his invasion of Southern Sung, which was itself related to his Koryŏ policy. Therefore, he had not definitely decided from the outset to invade Japan. Rather, that decision emerged during the six Japan–Mongol negotiations covering nearly eight years.

The Koryŏ party, led by P'an Pu, arrived at Dazaifu as envoys of the Mongols in the first month of 1268. The Mongol and Koryŏ documents were given to the provincial governor Mutō Sukeyoshi, went through the Kamakura bakufu, and then to the court at Kyoto. Au-

52 Tanaka, *Chūsei taigai kankeishi*, p. 19.
53 Kayahara Shōzō, "Mōko shūrai no ichi hihan," *Rekishi to chiri* 10 (August–October 1922).

thority for foreign relations lay with the court, but the decision to reply or not was actually controlled by the bakufu. Kamakura decided not to respond, and so the party of envoys returned without receiving an answer. The Mongols sent more envoys, but Japan was unyielding in its refusal, and this eventually resulted in the Mongol invasion. What explains the bakufu's persistent refusal? The answer will also explain the reason for the Mongols' attack on Japan.

From the moment the Kamakura bakufu received the Mongol document, it considered it a declaration of war and therefore strengthened Japan's defenses. Nichiren's famous treatise *Risshō ankoku-ron* (The establishment of the legitimate teaching for the security of the country) expressed the same interpretation of the document,[54] emphasizing that it was not only the bakufu administrators who interpreted the communiqué as a declaration of war. To understand the reasons for such an interpretation and the adoption of a firm attitude, we need to consider how Japan obtained information about the Mongols and what that information was.

Information concerning international relations was learned primarily from the Southern Sung, through Japanese priests who had visited Sung, Sung priests who came to Japan, and merchants. But Sung was constantly pressured by the Mongols, and its hatred for the Mongols was strong. For Sung, the Mongols were nothing but invaders and conquerors. The person responsible for formulating Japan's Mongol policy was Hōjō Tokimune. He was strongly influenced by the patriotic and nationalistic religious thought of the Sung priests and based his foreign policy on information from these priests. The authoritarian control of the Hōjō family's main line had increased from the time of Tokimune's father, Tokiyori, and the rejection of the Mongol communiqué was decided by a very small group led by Tokimune. We must remember that the bakufu, which held the real power over Japan's political and military affairs, represented the warriors. Thus the Mongol invasions were a meeting between a people with strong tendencies toward conquest and a society governed by warriors.

The nobles deliberating how to respond to the Mongols lived in a closed society clinging to ancient practices. Because Japan's relations with the continent had long since ceased, the nobles were not able to make an informed judgment on Japan's international relations. Most of their debate, therefore, was devoted to interpreting the Mongol

54 Kawazoe Shōji, *Nichiren-sono shisō, kōdō to Mōko shūrai* (Tokyo: Shimizu shoin, 1971), p. 55.

document. In addition, the real power at court, the retired emperor Gosaga, was made emperor by the Hōjō family after the Jōkyū disturbance, and thus Kamakura's wishes were directly reflected in the court's deliberations. The Koryŏ document that accompanied the Mongol communiqué appealed to the Japanese to accept the Mongol request, as the Mongols only sought recognition of their moral influence. But this had no decisive influence on Japan's decision. We should not overlook the fact that in its continental relations, Japan had a tradition of familiarity with southern China and an estrangement from the north. Further, Japan's traditional attitude was to confront China as an equal or superior, which was the principal reason for Tokimune's unyielding attitude.

Kamakura adopted its own plan for foreign conquest, appointing the provincial governors Mutō Tsunesuke and Otomo Yoriyasu as commanders in an attack on Koryŏ, the base for the Mongol attack on Japan. In addition, the bakufu constructed a stone wall along the entire Hakata Bay coastline as a defense against the Mongols. The Japanese selected the third month of 1276 as the date for their attack. The plan was to prepare troops and boats primarily in Kyushu but this idea was ultimately abandoned, and Kamakura instead concentrated on strengthening its defenses. Immediately after the second Mongol invasion, the bakufu drew up a second plan to invade Koryŏ, using outlaw bands from Yamato and Yamashiro provinces. But this plan was abandoned too.

Both of these plans attempted to use a foreign-policy issue to help solve internal political problems. In 9/1274, claiming that there was a rumor of an impending invasion by the Mongols, Kamakura ordered the descendants of the Kantō warrior Shodai Shigetoshi to proceed to their holdings in Higo Province and the deputy of Nikaidō Ninsho, the *jitō* of Ata Kitakata in Satsuma Province, likewise to proceed to that holding. The bakufu also ordered them to subdue the local outlaw bands (*akutō*) in those holdings.[55] Just before this order, Nichiren and his followers, whose teaching of the supremacy of the Lotus Sutra continued to spread rapidly throughout society in light of the Mongol problem, intensified their criticism of the bakufu. Nichiren was regarded as perpetrating unlawful acts under the very noses of the Kamakura military leaders and accordingly suffered tremendous persecution. The Kamakura bakufu, that is,

55 For the "foreign defense" (*ikoku keigo*) against the Mongol invasions, see Kawazoe Shōji, *Chūkai, Genkō bōrui hennen shiryō – ikoku keigo banyaku shiryō no kenkyū* (Fukuoka: Fukuokashi kyōiku iinkai, 1971).

the Hōjō main line under Tokimune, saw its political task as resolving the various internal social contradictions that were eroding the existing social structure. These social contradictions, as expressed by the outlaw bands, coincided with the Mongol problem and continued to become more serious. Clearly the Mongol threat was used to try to solve these internal political problems, chief among them that of the *akutō*.[56] The unyielding bakufu attitude – Hōjō Tokimune's "resolute" attitude toward the Mongols – resulted from these circumstances.

All of these conditions on the continent and in Japan ultimately led to the Mongol invasion. The first Mongol invasion, the Bun'ei campaign, came in 10/1274. Combined Mongol-Koryŏ forces of some 28,000 men and 900 ships passed through Tsushima and Iki before landing at Hakata. They immediately withdrew when it appeared useless to continue fighting, and tremendous damage from the so-called divine wind (*kamikaze*) forced them to return home. The second Mongol invasion, the Kōan campaign, came in the fifth month of 1281 and lasted for three months. The Mongols attacked with an eastern-route force composed of 40,000 Mongols, Chinese, and Koreans, and a Kiang-nam force of 100,000 (composed primarily of conquered Southern Sung troops), and 3,500 ships. But this time as well the Mongols suffered a destructive blow from the *kamikaze* in which the greater part of their force sank to the bottom of the sea.

The origins and course of the Kōan campaign differ in many respects from those of the Bun'ei campaign. The Yüan dynasty regarded the first attack as unsuccessful but not as a defeat; the second invasion was intended to rectify the failure of the first. Several important considerations were involved in the second invasion. At the time of the first attack, the Yüan attached considerable importance to its Koryŏ policy, as it was closely linked to the task of subjugating the Southern Sung. But in the second invasion, the Mongols were pressed to resolve a number of problems that followed their defeat of the Sung, such as the treatment of a large number of captured Sung mercenaries. The Mongol's activities also included redirecting already-conquered peoples toward a new area for conquest, and so they used many defeated Sung professional soldiers, the basis of their mercenary system, to invade Japan.[57]

56 Abe Yukihiro, *Mōko shūrai* (Tokyo: Kyōikusha, 1980), pp. 20–21.
57 Atagi Mitsuo, *Ajia no seifuku ōchō*, vol. 11 of *Sekai no rekishi* (Tokyo: Kawade shobō 1969).

The problem of Koryŏ was also important. Koryŏ adopted passive tactics throughout the first Mongol invasion, attempting to evade control by the Mongols, who were primarily intent on conquering Japan.[58] Then, shifting tactics to support the Mongol attack, King Chungyul hoped that the Mongol subjugation of Japan would alleviate the exhaustion of his own country. Some scholars argue that this shift was actually to prepare for the Japanese *wakō*.[59] I disagree, for as I showed earlier, Koryŏ's problem with the *wakō* was rather severe, and I believe that Koryŏ tried to solve it by relying on the Mongols' power.

Many scholars hold that the Mongols invaded Japan to obtain its wealth. They are particularly taken with the idea that the Mongols wished to conquer a Japan that was believed to have been full of gold, as related in *The Travels of Marco Polo*. The fact that Japan exported gold dust to Sung supports this contention. With the defeat of the Southern Sung, the Yüan dynasty no longer needed to concern itself with maritime trade between Japan and Southern Sung; furthermore, it had seized the prosperous port cities of Kiang-nam. These ports traded extensively with Japan, and naturally the rumor that Japan was a country rich in gold circulated widely. Gold was especially coveted by the Mongols, although it was also well known that Japan produced pearls and many other prized goods. The desire for wealth from the conquest of Japan became a much clearer motive in the second Mongol attack.[60]

Kublai's proclamation to his generals leading the invasion clearly indicates the Yüan's intentions in the second invasion. In his proclamation, Kublai indicated that the first reason for the invasion was Japan's internment of his envoys. By executing the Mongol envoys, Japan blocked the Mongols' attack for a long time, but this action had catastrophic effects stemming from the differences in foreign-policy outlook between Japan and the Yüan. In response, therefore, Kublai called for seizure, invasion, and conquest of the Japanese people and lands.

A third invasion of Japan was impossible. The Yüan court was plagued with both a factional struggle characteristic of the Mongol Empire and continual widespread wars of resistance by its conquered peoples. The burden of the people under Mongol control was over-

58 Nakamura Hidetaka, *Nissen kankeishi no kenkyū*, vol. 1, p. 78; Tamura, *Chūsei Nitchō bōeki no kenkyū*, p. 24.
59 Aoyama, *Nichirai kōshōshi no kenkyū*, p. 32; Ikeuchi, *Genkō no shin kenkyū*, p. 200.
60 Atagi, *Ajia no seifuku ōchō*, p. 314.

whelming,[61] as it included those from the invasions of Japan, Champa (South Vietnam), and Chiao Chih (Kingdom of Annam and North Vietnam). Moreover, the economy of the Yüan court was racked by unrelenting inflation.[62]

In the era of King Chungyol, Koryŏ suffered under Mongol demands related to the planned third invasion of Japan, but scattered entries in the *Koryosa* in the reigns of King Chungyol and his successor King Chungson point to a relatively peaceful relationship with Japan. However, while Japan was planning an attack on Koryŏ during the Mongol invasion, a bellicose and deprecatory view of Koryŏ was forming among the Japanese people, which revived and even strengthened the legend of Empress Jingū's "conquest of the three Han countries."

The Mongol invasions strengthened the Hōjō family's control over Kyushu. With the Mutō family's position diminished as the main support of bakufu control in Kyushu, however, they were unable to check the *wakō*'s activities. In the late Kamakura period, the various contradictions of the prevailing social order became severe. The national power of Koryŏ itself also was weakened. Under these circumstances, the *wakō* became very active. In the seventh month of 1323, a large-scale pirate raid took place, and one hundred *wakō* were beheaded in Cholla Province. In the Nambokuchō period, these raids developed into full-scale pirate attacks.[63]

After the Kōan campaign, despite Japan's and the Yüan's adversary relationship, trading vessels traveled back and forth openly, and there was a brisk economic and cultural interchange. In the year following the Kōan campaign, 1282, the Yüan began cutting timber to use for ships to attack Japan and several times issued orders for the construction of vessels. They planned to invade in the eighth month of 1283. But the peoples of Kiangsu and Anhwei had suffered military conscription and the harsh labors of ship construction for many years, and in more than two hundred localities they rose in revolt, forcing abandonment of the plan. Nonetheless, the preparations for the attack continued, albeit on a smaller scale. But rebellions arose in Fukien, Kwantung, and other areas, and in 1284 the office responsible for coordinating the attack was abolished. But the preparations still contin-

61 Hatada Takashi states that the major reason for the frustration and failure of the Mongol attacks on Japan was the resistance of the various Asian peoples under Mongol domination. Hatada Takashi, *Genkō – Mōko teikoku no naibu jijō* (Tokyo: Chūō kōronsha, 1965).
62 Iwamura Shinobu, "Gen jidai ni okeru shihei infurēshon," in *Tōyō gakuhō*, vol. 34 (March 1964).   63 Ikeuchi, *Genkō no shin kenkyū*, chap. 12.

ued, and the office was revived in 1285. The Mongols planned to attack from Happo in the eighth month of 1286. But the Yüan dynasty had been sending troops for several years to Champa and Chiao Chih, and so this plan had to be abandoned because of a severe lack of manpower. It is said that when they heard this, the conscripted soldiers from south China raised shouts of joy that resounded like thunder. Even though the uprisings continued in both the north and east, Kublai Khan would not give up the conquest of Japan but continued with the preparations. With his death in 1/1294, however, the conquest of Japan was no longer possible.

While Kublai continued to prepare for conquest, he also tried to effect Japan's subjugation through diplomatic means, and these attempts continued even after his death. Following the Kōan campaign, the Mongols sent at least four ambassadors to Japan carrying royal edicts: Ju Chih and Wang Chun-chih in 8/1283; Ju Chih and Wang Chi-weng in 5/1284; Chin You-ch'eng and Kuo Lin in 10/1292; and I-shan I-ning in 3/1299. However, the first and second missions failed to reach Japan, and on the third mission Chin You-ch'eng was detained for years in Japan, where he subsequently died. On the fourth mission I-shan I-ning won over Hōjō Sadatoki in Kamakura and ex-Emperor Gouda in Kyoto and contributed to the development of Japanese culture through his broad knowledge. The Mongols' purpose in dispatching the envoys, however, was never achieved.

Even as the Yüan dynasty attempted to invade Japan on two occasions and continued to seek a military solution, they established a monopolistic trade system that permitted trade by Japanese merchant vessels. However, in 10/1292 when a Japanese merchant ship landed at Ch'ing-Yuan (Ningpo) seeking trade, weapons were discovered hidden on board. Accordingly, the Yüan immediately strengthened its coastal defenses and appointed a commander in chief, intensifying their cautionary attitude toward Japan. Soon thereafter, however, Kublai died.

The edict of 1298 failed to sway Japan, and rumors of Japanese revenge against the Mongols circulated. The Mongols' fear of Japan increased, and Mongol court officials began to adopt a firm attitude toward Japanese trading vessels. In response to this, and to illegal persecution by Yüan court officials, the Japanese found it necessary to arm themselves for self-defense, and a kind of forced trade ensued. In addition, Japanese pirate attacks on the Yüan continued. Thus the Yüan forbade private trade and repeatedly sent out commercial officials to regulate it.

While the Yüan dynasty prepared for a third attack on Japan, or attempted to lure the Japanese to its side, Japan did not dismantle the defense structure prepared for the Mongol invasions. The institutional exemplification of this was the establishment of the Chinzei *tandai* (western defense command)[64] in Hakata to rule on lawsuits (mainly civil suits) in Kyushu where warriors were forced to devote their entire attention to foreign defense. Hōjō family members were successively appointed to head the office. Previously, the center of Kyushu government had been at Dazaifu, but now it shifted to Hakata. The Chinzei *tandai* was organized around 7/1300, the year after the Yüan envoy I-shan I-ning came to Japan. Because the Chinzei *tandai* was a Kamakura bakufu organ for controlling Kyushu and hinged on foreign defense, it was granted authority primarily over foreign relations. Because the Chinzei *tandai* also functioned as a link in the Hōjō's control of the entire country, it meant that the control of foreign relations was directly connected from Hakata to Kamakura within the Hōjō family itself. However, as it became obvious that it was merely a local office for Hōjō family authoritarian control, the Chinzei *tandai* gradually lost the support of Kyushu warriors and suffered the same fate as did the bakufu.

In 4/1264 the Kamakura bakufu had curtailed its official ships to China as the conditions leading to the Mongol invasions began to take shape. But in 4/1290 the bakufu allotted "money seized from Chinese ships" to construct the Raizan Sennyoji, a temple in Chikuzen. Therefore, nine years after the Mongol invasions, Japanese trading vessels were entering China with the official approval of the Kamakura bakufu. Documents 70 through 73 in Volume 1 of the *Aokata monjo* pertain to a Chinese vessel wrecked in Hizen in 4/1298; the greater portion of the cargo was consigned to the Hōjō family. This is a partial indication of why Kamakura was excited about the importation of Chinese goods.

Thus, from the end of the Kamakura period into the Nambokuchō era, trading vessels for the purpose of constructing temples and shrines were dispatched to Yüan China with the approval of the Kamakura bakufu. Among these, for example, were a vessel for the construction of the Kenchōji (departed in 1325 and returned the next year) and one for the construction of the Great Buddha at Kamakura in 1329. A ship for the construction of Sumiyoshi Shrine in Settsu was also dispatched under bakufu protection in the final years of this

---

64 For Chinzei *tandai*, see Satō Shin'ichi, *Kamakura jidai soshō seido no kenkyū* (Tokyo: Unebi shobō, 1943), chap. 5; Seno, *Chinzei gokenin no kenkyū*.

period. The ship for the construction of the Tenryūji temple dispatched by the Muromachi bakufu during the Nambokuchō era is well known.[65] Temple and shrine construction projects of this magnitude required enormous wealth, and so Japan relied on foreign trade, from which it was easy to obtain great profits. And we should not forget that it was the Hōjō family's control over Japan's coastlines along the Inland Sea and Kyushu that enabled the dispatch of these trading vessels.

Thus, in regard to Japanese-Mongol relations after the invasions, even while the Mongols prepared for a third invasion (a military solution) and attempted to induce Japan's surrender (a diplomatic solution), there were also cultural exchanges, and trade was brisk.[66] The bakufu publicly authorized the trading vessels so that they would not be mistaken for *wakō*, and these ships became the precedent for the later tally trade with Ming China. On the other hand, the *wakō* trade also increased. So in postinvasion Japanese–Yüan relations we see two trends developing that served as forerunners of the trading structure of the succeeding era: authorized trade and piracy.[67]

FOREIGN RELATIONS IN THE EARLY MUROMACHI PERIOD

The Muromachi bakufu was presented with its first diplomatic problem in 1366 with the arrival of the Koryŏ envoys,[68] requesting in the name of the Yüan dynasty the suppression of *wakō* raids which had become especially fierce after 1350. Koryŏ periodically dispatched envoys to Japan in response. The Muromachi bakufu saw the Koryŏ mission as significant, for two reasons. First, this was the first time that Koryŏ had sent a mission requesting the suppression of piracy since the fall of the Kamakura bakufu. The Muromachi bakufu dispatched its own envoy privately and achieved a peaceful relationship with Koryŏ, thus taking the first steps toward seizing authority for foreign relations. Second, although the Muromachi bakufu acceded to

65 Miura Hiroyuki, "Tenryūji-bune ni kansuru shin kenkyū," in *Shigaku zasshi* 25 (January 1914), reprinted in *Nihonshi no kenkyū*, vol. 1 (Tokyo: Iwanami shoten, 1922).
66 Kimiya Yasuhiko, *Nikka bunka kōryūshi* (Tokyo: Fuzambō, 1955), is the most comprehensive work dealing with the Sino-Japanese cultural interchange this era. Tsuji Zennosuke, *Nisshi bunka no kōryū* (Osaka: Sōgensha, 1938), describes the cultural exchange between the two countries from ancient times to the early modern period.
67 Mori, *Shintei Nissō bōeki no kenkyū*, p. 525.
68 On this subject, see Aoyama, *Nichirai kōshōshi no kenkyū*, pp. 91–97; and Nakamura, *Nissen kankeishi no kenkyū*, vol 1, pp. 203–26.

Koryŏ's desire to establish diplomatic ties, it did not do so as Japan's official representatives. Because Kyushu, the local agency of Japanese foreign policy, was under the sway of the Southern Court, the Kyushu *tandai* – who controlled the bakufu's forces on the island – could not exercise his authority and thus could scarcely suppress the pirates as requested by Koryŏ. And this forced the Muromachi bakufu to consider in earnest the subjugation of Kyushu.

The next diplomatic problem to arise for the Muromachi bakufu was the arrival of Chinese envoys following the founding of the new Ming dynasty. These envoys did not initially approach the bakufu but negotiated with Prince Kaneyoshi, the Southern Court's general for the conquest of the west (*seisei shogun*).

In the first month of 1368, Chu Yuan-chang (1348–98), having toppled the Yüan dynasty, was enthroned as emperor at Yungt'ien-fu (Nanking). He called his new dynasty Ta-ming (Great Ming) and changed the era name to Hung-wu (Vast militance). The Grand Progenitor (T'aitsu) Chu Yuan-chang based his state on Confucianism, which regarded the Ming as the center of the world, and he expected to establish an international order in which the surrounding barbarian states would bring tribute to the Ming as the Middle Kingdom. In the eleventh month of the same year, T'aitsu sent envoys to Annam, Champa, Koryŏ, and Japan announcing the founding of the dynasty.[69] He aimed for the restoration of a Chinese world order based on exchange (gifts or trade, allowed by the Ming in return for tribute from the foreign states).[70] This exchange represented a form of etiquette demonstrating friendly political relations between states and, at the same time, having an economic aspect as it involved an exchange of goods.[71] The Ming accordingly revived the appointment of commis-

69 *Ming shih-lu* records dealing with Japan are collected in Nihon shiryō shusei hensankai, ed., *Chūgoku–Chōsen no shiseki ni okeru Nihon shiryō shūsei, Min jitsuroku no bu* (Tokyo: Kokusho kankōkai, 1975), vols. 1–3 (abbreviated as *Min jitsuroku*). Likewise, *Ming shih* (abbreviated as *Minshi*) is included in the same collection in *Rekishi no bu*, vol. 1. Ishihara Michihiro, *Yakuchū Chūgoku seishi Nihonden* (Tokyo: Kokusho kankōkai, 1975), which includes the Japan-related sections of the *Ming shih*, provides a valuable overview of Sino-Japanese relations from Chinese official histories, from the *Wei chih* to the *Ch'ing shih*.

70 The following are studies on Sino-Japanese relations in the early Ming: Ikeuchi Hiroshi, "Minsho ni okeru Nihon to Shina to no kōshō," *Rekishi to chiri* 6 (May–August 1904); Sakuma Shigeo, "Minsho no Nitchū kankei o meguru ni, san no mondai," in *Hokkaidō daigaku jimbun kagaku ronshū*, no. 4 (February 1966); and Imaeda Aishin and Murai Shōsuke, "Nichimin kōshōshi no jomaku," in *Tōkyō daigaku shiryō hensanjohō*, no 11 (March 1977). Also see the following studies that deal with Japanese–Ming relations: Akiyama Kenzō, "Nichimin kankei," in *Iwanami kōza Nihon rekishi*, vol 1 (1933); Kobata Atsushi, *Chūsei Nisshi tsūkō bōekishi* (Tokyo: Tōkō shoin, 1941); and Tanaka, *Chūsei taigai kankeishi*.

71 Sakuma, "Minsho ni okeru Nihon to Shina to no kōshō," p. 8.

sioners at Ningpo (Ming chou), Ch'uan chou, and Kuang chou, to oversee the exchange.

T'aitsu's first envoy to Japan was killed en route by pirates. He dispatched another in 2/1396 and, in a threatening manner, pressed the Southern Court general Prince Kaneyoshi to send tribute and to suppress the pirates.[72] Prince Kaneyoshi, however, had the Ming envoy killed and refused the demands. One reason that the Ming had chosen to negotiate with the outpost of the Southern Court was its geographical proximity in Kyushu's Chikuzen Province, but they also thought that it was the successor to Dazaifu, Japan's traditional local agency for foreign relations.[73] However, when the Ming sent a third envoy to Japan in 3/1370, Prince Kaneyoshi presented a *hyōsen* (*piaochien*, a foreign-policy document presented to a Chinese emperor) in which he referred to himself as "subject." He sent his vassal Sorai and others with tribute to Ming in 10/1371, at which time he returned more than seventy men and women who had been captured at Mingchou and Tai-chou.[74] Prince Kaneyoshi thereby completely reversed his previous attitude, accepting the Ming international order and entering into a subject relationship.

Representative bakufu warriors from Kyushu traveled to Kyoto pleading with the bakufu to develop a plan to revive its declining power in Kyushu. One reason that the Muromachi bakufu did not earlier subjugate the Southern Court's last fortress of Seiseifu and its ruler was that the bakufu was not recognized by foreign countries as sovereign in Japan, and thus the bakufu leaders prepared with great care their plan for pacifying Kyushu. At the center of this plan was Hosokawa Yoriyuri, aiding the young shogun Ashikaga Yoshimitsu. It also involved the appointment as Kyushu *tandai* of the Ashikaga kinsman Imagawa Ryōshun, who possessed both civil and martial abilities. After thorough preparations, Ryōshun set off for Kyushu in the second month of 1371. Because the Muromachi bakufu concentrated its power on overthrowing the Southern Court in Kyushu, an attack on the Seiseifu fortress at Dazaifu became a necessity. Prince Kaneyoshi's change of attitude toward the Ming was quite natural under the circumstances.

When Prince Kaneyoshi's envoy arrived at the Ming capital, T'aitsu accepted him as Japan's official ambassador and treated the prince as

72 *Min jitsuroku no bu*, vol. 1, pp. 1–2.   73 Tanaka, *Chūsei taigai kankeishi*, p. 55.
74 *Min jitsuroku no bu*, vol. 1, p. 8; *Ming shih*, p. 284.

"Japan's true ruler." During T'aitsu's era, Japan dispatched about ten envoys to China. Among them, the 6/1374 and 9/1380 missions sent by Ashikaga Yoshimitsu were turned back because they did not have proper documents. The 6/1374 Shimazu Ujihisa mission was also turned back because the Ming said he was not a ruler but only a vassal. Two missions are of uncertain nature, and all the other six were from the "Japanese King Ryokai" (Yoshikane) in 10/1371, 4/1378, intercalary 5/1379, 5/1380, 7/1381, and 11/1386.[75] In the first three, Japan forwarded a *hyōsen* under Prince Kaneyoshi's name and offered horses, swords, armor, sulfur, and other items. However, the fourth mission was turned back for insincerity; the fifth's tribute was rejected; and the sixth had both its documents and tribute rejected. Prince Kaneyoshi's name, "King of Japan," was credible with the Ming up until the third mission; thereafter, even though rejected by the Ming, the Japanese attempted diplomatic contacts with the Ming under his name. Those in charge of foreign affairs actually believed that under Prince Kaneyoshi's name, relations would be acceptable to the Ming. Because it appears that Prince Kaneyoshi resigned the post of *seisei* shogun in 4/1374[76] and died in 1384, the only mission that he unquestionably dispatched to China was that of 1371. The other missions were probably dispatched by Kaneyoshi's successor, the *goseisei shogun no miya*, using the prince's name as he had already been recognized by the Ming as "Japan's true ruler," although this is not known for certain. By this time the Southern Court's influence in Kyushu was already on the wane, and these may have been bogus envoys to Ming China sent by pirate forces.

The Ming envoys to Prince Kaneyoshi at Dazaifu arrived in Hakata in the fifth month of 1372. This was during Imagawa Ryōshun's siege of the Seiseifu at Dazaifu, and so the envoys were detained at Hakata and could not present the prince with the Ming calendar and other items symbolic of his status as a subject of the Ming. Responding to the changed political situation, the Ming envoys instead went to Kyoto and entered into negotiations with the Northern Court. In 8/1373 Ashikaga Yoshimitsu sent them home to China and then dispatched his own ambassador with a reply, returning at the same time some 150 Chinese and Korean captives. However Ming T'aitsu refused to accept the tribute relationship on the grounds that it lacked proper documentation. Thus, the Muromachi bakufu's initial negotiations with the

75 Kawazoe Shōji, *Imagawa Ryōshun* (Tokyo: Yoshikawa kōbunkan, 1964).
76 Kawazoe Shōji, "Kaneyoshi Shinnō o meguru Kyūshū no Nambokuchō," in *Rekishi kōron 5* (September 1979): 92–99.

Ming ended in failure.[77] In this incident, the Muromachi bakufu under the Ashikaga shogun was keenly aware that it had not received recognition as Japan's representative in the Sinocentric East Asian international order. To do so, the bakufu would have to defeat Prince Kaneyoshi – whom the Ming recognized as "Japan's true ruler" – and suppress the *wakō*. Thus the pacification of Kyushu became even more urgent. Only after the political opposition between the two courts had been settled in favor of the Northern Court did Ashikaga Yoshimitsu become "King of Japan."

In 2/1375 Koryŏ's King U sent an envoy to Japan requesting that it suppress the *wakō* raids. In response, Japan dispatched an envoy offering Koryŏ dyed cloth, painted folding screens, long swords, wine vessels, and other items. On that occasion the Tenryūji monk Tokusō Shūsa sent the following letter expressing the bakufu's intention: "Kyushu is broken apart by rebelling subjects and does not pay tribute; the stubborn subjects of the Western seacoast have become pirates. But these are not the doing of the bakufu. We are planning to dispatch a general to Kyushu to pacify the area and can promise to suppress the pirates."[78] This indicates that the Muromachi bakufu was counting on Imagawa Ryōshun's operations in Kyushu and hoping to use his success in negotiations with Koryŏ.

In 8/1372, Imagawa Ryōshun forced Dazaifu's surrender and captured Prince Kaneyoshi and his chief military supporters, the Kikuchi family, at Kikuchi in Higo Province, and in 8/1375, he killed Shōni Fuyusuke at Mizushima in Higo. The Shōni family had held *shugo* appointments since Kamakura times and had inherited the office of *Dazai no shōni* the highest post of local responsibility within the Dazaifu structure. Imagawa Ryōshun secured the supremacy of the bakufu force in Kyushu by first proceeding from Dazaifu to Seiseifu and then defeating Shōni Fuyusuke, the warrior of highest local authority in Dazaifu. Shimazu Ujihisa, who brought Shōni Fuyusuke to Imagawa Ryōshun, subsequently found himself having to follow Ryōshun's orders. However, he not only came into control of Chikuzen Province, the Shōni's home territory and the base for administering Kyushu; he also seized the Shōni's authority over foreign affairs. As the real successor to Dazaifu, Imagawa Ryōshun came into control of Japan's foreign policy.

---

77 Imaeda and Murai, "Nichimin kōshōshi no jomaku"; and Murai Shōsuke, "Muromachi bakufu no saisho no kenminshi ni tsuite," in Imaeda Aishin, ed., *Zenshū no shomondai* (Tokyo: Yūzankaku, 1979).   78 *Koryosa, kwan* 133, *Yolchon* 46, *Shin U.*

Ashikaga Yoshimitsu secured shogunal authority only after Kyushu had been subjugated. Except for his reception of the Ming envoy in 1372, Imagawa Ryōshun's dealings with Ming are not mentioned in any sources. It was natural that Ming would not conduct formal negotiations with Ryōshun, as he was only a vassal. But it also goes without saying that there were always hidden problems stemming from the Ming's relations with the Southern Court in Kyushu.

That being the case, Imagawa Ryōshun's public diplomatic dealings were with only the two Korean dynasties, Koryŏ and Choson. The 9/1377 visit of the Koryŏ envoy Ch'oe Mong-ju seeking suppression of the *wakō* was an epoch-making event in Ryōshun Koryŏ negotiations.[79] Ch'oe Mong-ju, a noted scholar and high government official of the pro-Ming faction, was praised as the greatest statesman of his day. Ryōshun received Ch'oe warmly, returned several hundred prisoners captured by the *wakō*, and suppressed the pirates of Tsushima, Iki, and Matsura. From then on, Koryŏ dealt directly with the real power holder in Kyushu, "the Kyushu defense commander Minamoto no Ryōshun," when seeking the suppression of pirate attacks. Ryōshun, taking advantage of this role, dealt directly with Koryŏ without consulting the bakufu. At this point, the Muromachi bakufu recognized that direct control over foreign relations was necessary to crush the Southern Court in Kyushu, and fortunately for the bakufu, Ryōshun's supporter, Hosokawa Yoriyuki, was the real power in bakufu politics. Ryōshun's return of the captives was an "enterprise similar to a commercial act contracted to obtain compensations,"[80] and in this sense his dealings with Koryŏ were a kind of "trade" appropriate to the *wakō* period.

However, Shogun Ashikaga Yoshimitsu, aspiring to become "King of Japan," could not be expected to allow the situation to continue forever. When Ryōshun's protector, Hosokawa Yoriyuki, was toppled from power in the Ōryaku incident of 1379, the repercussions affected Ryōshun's position as Kyushu *tandai*, and Yoshimitsu's designs on control of foreign policy intensified. A shogunal order of 6/8/1381 in the *Nejime monjo*, addressed to Ryōshun as *shugo* of Ōsumi, prohibited the *akutō* (outlaws) of that province from crossing over to Koryŏ and committing outrages; that is, the order prohibited pirate activities.[81]

79 Shiryō shūsei hensankai, *Chūgoku–Chōsen no shiseki ni okeru Nihon shiryō shūsei, Sangoku, Kōrai no bu*, p. 238.   80 Tanaka, *Chūsei taigai kankeishi*, p. 99.
81 Kawazoe Shōji, ed., *Nejime monjo*, vol. 3 (Fukuoka: Kyūshū daigaku bungakubu, Kyūshū shiryo kankōkai, 1955), p. 56.

This is the only Muromachi bakufu order dealing with the suppression of *wakō*. The document clearly expressed Yoshimitsu's intention to arrange the suppression of the *wakō* under the chain of command from shogun (bakufu) to Kyushu *tandai (shugo)*.

The final epoch of Imagawa Ryōshun's foreign policy was marked in Korea by the fall of Koryŏ and the founding of Choson, and in Japan by the unification of the Northern and Southern Courts. On the Korean peninsula, in the seventh month of 1392, Yi Song-gye (1334–1408), who had achieved some success in suppressing the *wakō*, received the abdication of King Kong Yang and was "installed by the ministers" as king (reigned 1392–98?). He was the dynastic founder, Taijo, of the Yi dynasty's Choson. In Japan, in the intercalary tenth month of the same year, the fifty-seven year conflict between the Northern and Southern Courts was brought to an end with the victory of the Northern Court.

From the outset Choson adopted a conciliatory policy toward Japan. Taejo inherited from the former dynasty the task of subjugating the *wakō*, but he aimed for amicable relations with the outside world and also reorganized the country's own military system and strengthened defenses.[82] In the year of Taejo's accession, the new dynasty sent an envoy to Japan requesting that the "government of the *seii taishogun*" (the Muromachi bakufu) suppress the *wakō*.[83] The bakufu responded that it was ordering the Kyushu *tandai* to subjugate these *wakō* in its name. As Kyushu *tandai*, Imagawa Ryōshun's dealings with Choson, as with Koryŏ, involved the return of captives in response to Korean requests for piracy control and his interest in obtaining such items as the Buddhist Tripitaka. The number of captives returned to Choson increased greatly. But when the courts were reunified, the coincidental link between defeating the Southern Court in Kyushu and suppressing piracy disappeared. Shogunal restrictions on the Kyushu *tandai* as a subordinate local officer of the Muromachi bakufu became stronger. The *tandai*'s growing wealth from trade, conducted in the guise of returning Korean captives, was exceeding the limits appropriate to a local bakufu official and was arousing the shogun's jealousy. Thus, Imagawa Ryōshun was removed from his post as Kyushu *tandai* in 1395.

82 Nakamura, *Nissen kankeishi no kenkyū*, vol. 1 p. 149. Nakamura Hidetaka, *Nihon to Chōsen* (Tokyo: Shibundō, 1966), provides a good summary of Japanese-Korean relations from ancient times through the Tokugawa period.
83 Zuikei Shūhō, *Zenrin kokuhōki* (Tokyo: Kokusho kankōkai, 1975), pp. 91–92. This work, written in 1466, is an invaluable source for the study of Muromachi-period foreign relations.

The problem of suppressing piracy and the development of the tribute system that accompanied the founding of the Ming dynasty were the common threads running through Japan's relations with Koryŏ, Choson, and Ming China in the Nambokuchō period. When considering the East Asian international order centered on the Ming, one must examine the Ming policy of prohibiting overseas travel which was inseparable from the tribute system.[84] This policy prohibited all Chinese from going abroad; whereas the tribute system was foreign policy, the overseas prohibition was domestic policy. Together the two had a significant influence in East Asian international relations. The impetus for Emperor T'aitsu Hung-wu's issuance of the overseas prohibition order lay in his fear that internal political divisions might link up with foreign powers, leading to a domestic political crisis. This fear was directly related to the Japanese *wakō* problem. In concrete terms, it was generated by two incidents, which I shall discuss next.

After the defeat of the late Yüan-period rebels, Fang Kuo-chin and Chang Shin-cheng, who had held sway in the Kiangsu and Chekiang areas, some of their surviving followers established bases on the coastal islands. They tried to revive their influence by joining with people on the mainland and, moreover, by linking up with the *wakō*.[85] Thus, for the Ming, the *wakō* were not simply a foreign concern but also a problem linked to internal discontent. This is why the Ming insisted that Japan control the *wakō*.

The second incident, involving Hu Wei-yung and Lin Hsien, brought about a decisive rupture in Japanese-Ming relations.[86] One of the meritorious subjects involved in the founding of the dynasty, Hu Wei-yung, had risen to become left chancellor, or head, of the Secretariat because of his superior political talent. But after becoming left chancellor, Hu exercised authoritarian policies and planned to usurp the throne. Attempting to enlist Japan's aid in this endeavor, Hu linked up with Lin Hsien, the leader of Ningpo-wei (Yin District in the province of Chekiang). Hu falsely accused Lin of a crime and banished him to Japan, where he put him in touch with Japanese leaders. Next, Hu Wei-yung announced the restoration of Lin Hsien to his former post, and he dispatched a messenger to bring Lin back, secretly sending a message to the "King of Japan" seeking military

84 Sakuma Shigeo, "Minchō no kaikin seisaku," in *Tōhōgaku*, no. 6 (1953).
85 This incident is recorded in the *Mingshih, Chuan* 91, treatise 67 (military 3, section on coastal defense).
86 This incident is outlined in *Mingshih, Chuan* 322, in pt. 3, "Foreign Lands." Also see Sakuma, "Minsho no Nitchū kankei o meguru ni, san no mondai."

support. This king of Japan sent four hundred soldiers under the priest Nyoyo, misrepresenting them as an envoys merely bringing a tribute of large candles. Within this tribute, however, he concealed gunpowder and swords. But when Nyoyo landed in China, he found that Hu Wei-yung and his group had been executed in the first month of 1380, based on a tip from an informer. Six years later in 1421, it became clear that Nyoyo and the "King of Japan" were involved in the affair, and Lin was executed along with his whole clan. Emperor T'aitsu was enraged over Japan's actions and severed relations; he reinforced the policy forbidding Chinese to go overseas and strengthened China's coastal defenses.

These is some doubt concerning the details of this affair, but the real problem is identifying the "King of Japan" who colluded with Hu Wei-yung and Lin Hsien. One view is that it was perhaps a leader of the wakō.[87] In Chuan 13 of Ming T'aitsu shihlu (Veritable records of Ming T'aitsu), in an entry for 7/1381, we learn that the King of Japan, Ryōkai (Prince Kaneyoshi), dispatched the priest Nyoyo and others to Ming, bearing goods and ten horses as tribute, but the Ming emperor did not accept their offering. So Nyoyo appeared as Prince Kaneyoshi's messenger, but at that time the prince was no longer leader of the Southern Court in Kyushu. This role had passed to goseisei shogun no miya. As in the case described earlier, it was only a matter of using Prince Kaneyoshi's name. Nyoyo may well have had connections with the Kyushu Southern Court, but he might also have been connected with the wakō. Therefore, the "King of Japan" at the time of the Hu Wei-yung incident could have been the leader of the Kyushu Southern Court (goseisei shogun no miya), Southern Court forces with wakō connections, or wakō simply using the name of the Southern Court in Kyushu.

The Ming regarded the "King of Japan" as a pirate, and his connection with an internal Chinese plot was truly a serious problem. Because this incident followed so closely on the last one, Emperor Hung Wu's distrust of Japan grew stronger, and he also cut off diplomatic relations and intensified the ban on Chinese going abroad. This prohibition had been carried out at one point during the late Yüan, but from the beginning of the Ming it became permanent and was continued for some two hundred years. Furthermore, the plotting of Hu Wei-yung and Liu Hsien was a convenient opportunity for the Ming emperor to complete his authoritarian structure. Here we can see a

87 Tsuji Zennosuke, Nisshi bunka no kōryū, p. 123.

pattern by which *wakō* or *wakō*-like forces helped define Ming internal politics.

The tribute system and the ban on overseas travel represented a unified internal-external relationship, and together they exerted a great influence on East Asian international relations. Tribute brought by various foreign lands to the Ming was rewarded by Ming gifts in return,[88] which is properly termed tribute trade. Virtually all the tribute items were either luxury goods for China's upper class or military necessities. The Ming government monopolized the import and purchase of these resources and allowed only a very small portion to be traded by general merchants under government supervision. Overseas trips by Chinese were forbidden under the formal prohibition in force from the beginning of the Ming dynasty. Through the tribute system and this ban, the Ming government was able to protect itself against piracy and to monopolize trade. Both policies were in accord with its political and economic goals. The travel prohibition struck a blow against the Ming trading merchants, but on the other hand, it expanded the area of activity for overseas Chinese to the south and for merchants from the newly risen Ryūkyū kingdom.

THE TRIBUTE SYSTEM AND JAPAN

Ashikaga Yoshimitsu dispatched envoys to Ming China in 1374 and 1380 in order to establish relations, but his offers were rebuffed. Subsequently, Yoshimitsu reunited the two courts and rose to the highest position in the civilian bureaucracy, that of prime minister. He dismissed Imagawa Ryōshun, who had succeeded in pacifying Kyushu, and now placed that island – the base for foreign relations – under his own control. Yoshimitsu furthermore subdued Ōuchi Yoshihiro, a warrior with considerable power in foreign affairs who held several *shugo* appointments and was becoming a rival force to the shogun. By these actions, Yoshimitsu achieved control over Japan's politics. However, he resigned from his public offices and became a free agent and therefore was not in a position to open formal relations with the Ming as the representative of Japan. In 1401, Yoshimitsu dispatched a mission to the Ming headed by Soa, a member of his coterie of artists and aesthetes (*dōbōshū*), as chief envoy, with a Kyushu merchant as his assistant. This appointment of shogunal

88 Momose Hiromu, *Minshin shakai keizaishi kenkyū* (Tokyo: Kenkyū shuppan, 1980), p. 6; Tanaka, *Chūsei taigai kankeishi*, p. 86.

dōbōshū and merchants as envoys was an exception, however, and never occurred again.

Ashikaga Yoshimitsu sent a document addressed to the emperor of the Great Ming dated 5/13/1401 under the title *Nihon jusangō Dōgi* ("equivalent in rank to imperial family").[89] In it, Yoshimitsu sought to establish relations in accord with the customary practices of the past, and he listed the tribute goods he was sending. He also returned a number of Ming citizens who had been captured by *wakō*. In the eighth month of the next year, 1402, Soa's party returned to Japan, accompanied by a Ming envoy whom Yoshimitsu received warmly. They brought with them an edict from the second Ming emperor, Chien Wen, which began with the words, "you, King of Japan, Minamoto no Dogi," and invested Yoshimitsu as ruler and ordered him to accept the Ming calendar. In other words, the edict proclaimed that Japan should be vassal to the Ming. However, three years earlier a war had broken out between Chien Wen and his uncle (later Emperor Ch'engtsu Yung Lo); and only two months before his envoy reached Japan, the city of Nanking had fallen, and Chien Wen had perished in the flames. Yung Lo, known as the greatest warrior-emperor in Chinese history, had toppled his nephew and seized the throne for himself.

In 3/1403 a party of Japanese envoys headed for China with the returning Ming envoy. Japan's document to the Ming was also in the form of an edict. Opening with the words, "King of Japan, Your Subject, Minamoto," it congratulated Emperor Ch'engtsu on his enthronement and offered gifts. The document mentions many military items: twenty horses, one thousand spears, one hundred large swords, and ten thousand *kin* of sulfur. It seems that some of the three hundred people accompanying the mission were carrying weapons to trade. These were probably sent to gain profits, anticipating an increase in Chinese military requirements for internal purposes.[90] Ch'engtsu received this tribute just when he was on the verge of sending an envoy to announce his accession. He was exceedingly pleased and sent back the envoy with a reply. In contrast with T'aitsu, Ch'engtsu had a positive attitude toward the outside world,

89 The document is found on p. 97 of the *Zenrin kokuhōki*. A draft can be found in the diary of Gon no daigeki Nakahara Yasutomi, "Kōfuki," in *Zōho Shiryō taisei*, vol. 37 (Kyoto: Rinsen shoten, 1965), p. 3. For an overview of Japanese foreign relations documents, see Kawazoe Shōji, "Kodai–Chūsei no gaikō monjo," in Kagamiyama Takeshi sensei koki kinenkai, ed., *Kobunka ronkō* (Fukuoka: Kagiyama Takeshi sensei koki kinen ronbunshū kankōkai, 1980).
90 Sakuma Shigeo,"Eirakutei no taigai seisaku to Nihon," in *Hoppō bunka kenkyū*, no. 2 (1967): 121.

which accounts for the subsequent development of active Ming foreign relations.

Ashikaga Yoshimitsu had referred to himself as "King of Japan, Your Subject, Minamoto" when corresponding with the emperor of China; in return he received from the Ming a gold seal investing him as the king of Japan. This was a shift away from Japan's traditional policy of regarding China as an equal and accepting the Ming tribute system: Japan was incorporated into the East Asian international order centering on the Ming emperor. It was on this occasion that one hundred Yüan Lo tallies were brought, commencing the so-called tally trade (kangō bōeki).

Yoshimitsu's relations with Ming China

During the era of T'aitsu (Japan's Nambokuchō era), Yoshimitsu twice tried to establish relations with the Ming but was rebuffed. The Ming joined instead with Prince Kaneyoshi, head of the Seiseifu, which could also be called the successor to Dazaifu. Ming relations with Japan became active in the reign of the Yung Lo emperor Ch'engtsu who was quite positive regarding foreign affairs. In comparison with T'aitsu, who devoted his energy to internal institutional consolidation, Ch'engtsu planned to maintain internal institutions by working actively in the foreign arena.[91] In the case of Japan, the wakō problem was directly connected with China's internal security, and so the matter of reducing Japan to the position of a vassal state was a task of some urgency. The first half of the Ch'engtsu's twenty-two-year reign corresponded to the era of Ashikaga Yoshimitsu's negotiations with the Ming: The relationship between the two countries was normalized according to the Chinese model, and a friendly relationship was preserved. Ch'engtsu never ceased to praise Yoshimitsu's successful efforts to suppress the wakō.

In opening diplomatic relations with the Ming, Yoshimitsu hoped to develop normal trade. This policy reflected the inclinations of the merchants in northwestern Kyushu, especially Hakata. It was also congenial to the ryōshu class of the west Japan seacoast and the farmers of Tsushima, Iki, and Matsura. Yoshimitsu established an internal control structure, and the political situation generally stabilized. By successively dismissing and overthrowing Imagawa Ryōshun and Ōuchi Yoshihiro, Yoshimitsu absorbed their real authority in foreign

91 Ibid., pp. 118, 136.

affairs and strengthened a base from which he could open normal relations with Ming and Choson. However, the Ming would not permit direct trade by vassals, as was clear from the case of Shimazu Ujihisa: Trade was allowed only to the king. This was why Ashikaga Yoshimitsu sent tribute to Ming China as the "King of Japan."

Yoshimitsu's adoption of the title King of Japan represented a denial of the traditional foreign-policy concepts of Japan's ruling class, which had considered Japan to be China's equal, and it was criticized by contemporaries. In his *Zenrin kokuhōki*, Zukei Shūhō claimed that Yoshimitsu was wrong to call himself the king of Japan, to use the character for *subject,* and to write the Chinese era name. Most contemporary specialists on ceremony shared this criticism. In more recent times there have been several criticisms of Yoshimitsu's action as being disrespectful of the sovereign or as being a "national shame," criticisms based on the ideal of supreme loyalty.[92] In contrast, members of the nobility and those close to Yoshimitsu argued that any change in the form of the documents could destroy Japan's traditional foreign-policy course and the sense of equality between Japan and the Ming. But they did not fault Yoshimitsu out of any concern over loyalty to the emperor. Rather, their concern lay in a fear that Yoshimitsu's policies might lead to subjugation to the Ming. The title King of Japan was problematic because it indicated that Ashikaga Yoshimitsu had transformed his position from warrior hegemon to ruler of a feudal state.

Yoshimitsu's motive in reversing the traditional course of foreign policy and initiating relations with Ming China has also been debated. One thesis argues that his motive was to acquire trading profits. Suganuma Teifu's *Dainihon shōgyōshi* (first published in 1892) explained Yoshimitsu's relations with the Ming exclusively from the standpoint of trade, and many since have contended that it was the income that could be gained from missions to China that motivated Yoshimitsu to open relations with the Ming.[93] Enormous sums were required to build such projects as the Kitayama villa, said to have cost 100,000 *kan,* and for the frequent Buddhist ceremonies. The large gifts of copper coins, silk, brocades, and so forth that the Ming envoys brought to the shogunal court were certainly a major economic attraction. This tribute–gift exchange was in reality simply trade, and

Ashikaga Yoshimitsu's Japan–Ming relations represented his own personal monopoly of it.

That Yoshimitsu was motivated by a desire for trading profits is generally accurate. However, the actual role of Ming trade in shogunal and bakufu finances, which included income from the goryōsho (the bakufu's direct holdings) and levies on pawnbrokers and saké dealers in and around the capital, is unclear. Moreover, even though the Ming "gifts," that is, the importation of Chinese goods, may have satisfied the desires of Yoshimitsu and his followers, it is unclear how they were related to the bakufu's finances. In any event, it is too narrow to attribute Yoshimitsu's motive in opening Japan–Ming relations solely to profits.

Others have sought a political explanation for Yoshimitsu's actions. Satō Shin'ichi argues that by representing himself to the Ming emperor as "King of Japan, Your Subject, Minamoto no Dogi," Yoshimitsu brought the various lords of Kyushu under his control and through them brought stability to the central political arena, thereby forcing the diverse factions participating in Ming trade to recognize his position as king. In other words, Ashikaga Yoshimitsu's position as king was guaranteed by the Ming emperor.[94] This is the Ming tribute-system theory. Satō examined the importation of copper coins in terms of its political function, whereas earlier scholars had focused only on its economic aspects. He also viewed Yoshimitsu's control of trade through the tally system as an attempt to increase his own political power. Satō's study was a breakthrough, explaining Yoshimitsu's Ming relations in terms of political history when previously scholars had emphasized Yoshimitsu's profit motivation. We should also note Miura Keiichi's thesis that the Ming tally system – and the system whereby the king of Choson received books from and granted posts to traders – functioned as a kind of overseas shiki (rights) system that augmented Japan's internal shiki system. It was used, Miura feels, to maintain Japan's internal ruling structure.[95]

Yet questions remain: Why did Ashikaga Yoshimitsu, who had come to wield absolute power, feel the need to seek an even higher – and foreign – guarantee?[96] The theory of control over private trade was criticized for overemphasizing political factors and ignoring other

94 Satō Shin'ichi, "Muromachi bakufu ron," in Iwanami kōza Nihon rekishi, vol. 7 (chūsei 3) (Tokyo: Iwanami shoten, 1963).
95 Miura Keiichi, "Chūsei kōki no shōhin ryūtsū to ryōshu kaikyū," in Nihonshi kenkyū, no. 65 (March 1963).
96 Haga Norihiko, "Muromachi bakufu ron," in Nihon rekishigaku kenkyūkai, ed., Nihonshi no mondaiten (Tokyo: Yoshikawa kōbunkan, 1965).

forms of economic income to the bakufu.[97] Furthermore, Sasaki Ginya raises a question that is indeed difficult to answer: In the turbulent international situation of the late fourteenth and early fifteenth centuries, did Ashikaga Yoshimitsu and the ruling class really grasp, in any coherent political and international way, the relationship between national trade and their own political power?[98]

Sasaki's view of the motivation behind Japan–Ming relations is that Japan hoped to eliminate the insecurity caused by fear of a Chinese invasion. In order to do so, Japan, already a latecomer, had to become part of the Ming tribute system as soon as possible and thus cease to be the "orphan" of East Asia.[99] For centuries the Japanese had feared attack by the Silla, and the Mongol invasions provided real grounds for fearing a Ming attack. Then too, the Ming had tried to use the Mongol invasions to China's advantage in the negotiations with Japan. Sasaki sees Yoshimitsu's adoption of the title King of Japan not only as stemming from his own personal predilection to "serve the great" but also as an honest expression of the almost traditional uncertainty and fear toward "Great T'ang" or "Great Ming" which derived from his responsibility and position as Japan's feudal monarch and ruler. Sasaki's argument is, in a broad sense, an explanation in terms of political motives, but he sees it as a political response, albeit uncertain, at a stage when Japan could not yet understand Ming Chinese foreign policy.

Most studies of Yoshimitsu's motives start from the end product of the entire history of Japan–Ming relations and argue back toward the origins; they try to surmise actual conditions from the surviving documents. As Sasaki stated, it is difficult to prove that Yoshimitsu dealt with the situation from a clear political and international perspective. That he had a fuzzy perception of Chinese foreign policy can be seen from the fact that he dispatched an envoy during the Chingnan incident (1399–1402). When considering Yoshimitsu's motivation, we must recognize the importance of that first 1401 mission. I have already explained that there was a strong demand for normal trade from the trading merchants of western Japan, and that in responding to this demand, Ashikaga Yoshimitsu was himself eager for profits. In his document to the Ming emperor, Yoshimitsu emphasized his establishment of control over the entire country and proclaimed his qualifications to open relations with China. Furthermore, besides the required

97 Tanaka, *Chūsei taigai kankeishi*, pp. 78–79.
98 Sasaki "Higashi Ajia," p. 113.   99 Ibid., p. 114.

tribute, Yoshimitsu also returned the Ming prisoners captured by the *wakō*, an act that Sasama Shigeo has called a kind of primitive slave trade.[100]

These, then, are the various theories concerning Yoshimitsu's motives in establishing relations with Ming China amidst the political and economic conditions of Japan at the turn of the fifteenth century. We cannot simply select only one of these theories as correctly identifying the motive; rather, we must adopt a syncretic and comprehensive view. It is true that trading profits were in large measure misdirected toward the extravagant life-style of Yoshimitsu and his coterie, but it is also true that they stabilized the bakufu's finances. Thus we can see that such profits from trade did work to the advantage of what the *Zenrin kokuhōki* and Miura Hiroyuki call "the country,"[101] that is, the Muromachi bakufu structure. Furthermore, Japanese–Ming relations conducted in the name of Ashikaga Yoshimitsu and the Muromachi bakufu were of obvious help in controlling Kyushu. Even though the title King of Japan is ambiguous when considered in regard to the court, it did clearly indicate the primary agent of Ming relations, Japan's feudal ruler. Through Yoshimitsu's action, Japan joined the East Asian Sinocentric tribute system and achieved a guarantee of international security. The *wakō* problem was the real intermediary in this relationship as far as Ming China was concerned.

The tally trade system

Tally refers to a certificate of proof that authenticated an envoy or mission.[102] Already in Yüan times there was a system of tallies for · foreign-trade purposes, called *panyin kongho wenpu* (half-seal tally register), which was also used for domestic trade. The Ming practice of issuing tallies to foreign trading vessels, a blend of these two systems, began in 1383, and was first applied to Japan in 1404. The Ming tally system was one in which some two hundred tallies and four volumes of records were collected and kept in each country. In Japan's case, the tallies were divided into two sets, labeled *nichi* and *hon*. One hundred of the *nichi* tallies and one volume each of the *nichi* and *hon* tally records were kept in the Board of Rites at the Ming capital in Peking, and one hundred of the *hon* tallies and a volume of the *nichi* tally

---

100 Sakuma, "Eirakutei no taigai seisaku to Nihon," p. 124.
101 Miura Hiroyuki, *Nihonshi no kenkyū*, vol 2 (Tokyo: Iwanami shoten, 1930), p. 973.
102 Among the early inclusive studies of the tally trade was that by Kayahara Shōzō, "Nichimin kangō no soshiki to shikō," in *Shigaku zasshi 31* (April, May August, and September 1920).

records were sent to Japan. A set of the *hon* tally records was also placed in the Chekiang provincial governor's office (which handled popular and financial affairs).

When a ship went from Japan to China, it sailed with the proper *hon* tally, which was then checked against the record book at the Board of Rites in Chekiang and Peking. When the checking was completed, the tally was collected. The converse, Ming ships going to Japan bearing *nichi* tallies, did not in fact occur. None of these tallies exists today, but according to a sketch in the *Boshi nyūmin-ki*, the "*hon* character number 1" was stamped in red ink on the tally sheet. On the reverse side were various pieces of information, such as the number of tribute items presented, the auxiliary gifts for the envoy and members of his party, and the cargo, number of ships, and sailors of the "official merchants" (those merchants recorded on the tally). These writings on the reverse side were called *p'i-wen* or *pieh-fu*.

Over the century and a half from Ashikaga Yoshimitsu to 1547, nineteen missions were sent to the Ming.[103] The fourth Ashikaga shogun, Yoshimochi, severed relations with Ming China, and in the latter half of the Yung Lo emperor's reign, the *wakō* incursions became severe. The sixth shogun, Ashikaga Yoshinori, restored the tribute relationship with the Ming. The Muromachi bakufu monopolized trade until the eighth mission in 1401, but starting with the ninth mission to Ming in 1433, temples, shrines, and daimyo joined in. The sixteenth mission during the tenure of the eighth shogun, Yoshimasa, was the largest in the course of Japan–Ming relations. On this occasion, the Ming concluded the Hsuan Teh treaty, which stipulated that from then on there could be one mission every ten years, each consisting of three ships and three hundred people.

A conflict regarding the Ming trade developed between the Hosokawa and Ouchi houses, based respectively in Sakai and Hakata. This confrontation became severe during the sixteenth and seventeenth missions to the Ming in 1511 and 1523, and on the latter

---

103 Here I follow Tanaka, *Chūsei taigai kankeishi*, pp. 159–60. There are many other studies of Japan–Ming relations after Yoshimitsu's time. See Kayahara Shōzō, "Nichimin kangō bōeki ni okeru Hosokawa Ōuchi nishi no kōsō," *Shigaku zasshi* 25 and 26 (September–October 1914, February–March 1915); Akiyama Kenzō, *Nisshi kōshō shiwa* (Tokyo: Naigai shoseki kabushiki kaisha, 1935); Fujita Motoharu, *Nisshi kōtsū no kenkyū, chū-kinsei hen* (Tokyo: Fuzambō, 1938); Akiyama Kenzō, *Nisshi kōshōshi kenkyū* (Tokyo: Iwanami shoten, 1939); Makita Tairyō, *Sakugen nyūminki no kenkyū* (Kyoto: Hōzōkan, 1959); Sakuma Shigeo, "Mindai chūki no taigai seisaku to Nitchū kankei," *Hokkaidō daigaku jimbun kagaku ronshū*, no. 8 (1971); Kobata Atsushi, *Kingin bōekishi no kenkyū* (Tokyo: Hōsei daigaku shuppankyoku, 1976). See also the short but useful guide by Sakai Tadao, "Mindai bunka no Nihon bunka ni ataeta eikyō," *Rekishi kyōiku 11* (October 1963).

occasion the struggle reached a peak, resulting in the Ningpo disturbance. The eighteenth and nineteenth missions in 1540 and 1549 came
during a period when the Ouchi monopolized the trade, and with their
defeat, trade with the Ming was abolished. Thus, the dispatch of ships
to Ming China is a wonderful barometer of the rise and fall of the
Muromachi bakufu's power.

CHANGES IN THE INTERNATIONAL RELATIONS OF
EAST ASIA

The Kyushu *tandai* after the dismissal of Imakawa Ryōshun was
Shibukawa Mitsuyori (priestly name Dōchi), but the real focus of
relations with Choson was Ōuchi Yoshihiro, known as the "head of the
six countries of Japan." Yoshihiro attempted in the name of the shogun or bakufu to subdue the *wakō* and to acquire such items as the
Buddhist Tripitaka. As "King of Japan," Ashikaga Yoshimitsu carried
on relations separately from the Ōuchi,[104] and we know about the
shogun's relations with Choson until the mission dispatched by
Ashikaga Yoshiaki in the mid-sixteenth century. From the Korean
point of view, Japan participated in the Ming-centered East Asian
relationship as an equal with Choson, but Japan's warrior government
viewed itself as superior to the Korean government. Moreover, dealings between Japan and Korea were not conducted solely between the
two central authorities, as in the Japan–Ming situation. Instead, a
number of local lords in western Japan, as well as the Muromachi
bakufu, had connections with the Yi government, the sole interest on
the Korean side. The bakufu was only one of the traders and did not
direct the entire trade. Japanese–Korean relations were not like the
one-dimensional Japan–Ming relationship predicated on Japan's subordinate position. Furthermore, the Ming dynasty would not recognize any relation with vassals of the king of Japan. On the other hand,
Japan and Choson were on an equal footing within the tribute system.
The Yi dynasty understood Japan's political situation. It did not regard the shogun's power as the only force able to control the *wakō*, and
it knew that the bakufu was limited by the differences in the productive capacity of the different areas (especially the west) and classes.
  The Yi government initiated a variety of policies to bring the *wakō*,
under control and achieved great success during the reigns of T'aejo,

---

104 For accounts of relations with Japan in the *Yijo sillok*, see Nihon shiryō shūsei hensankai,
    ed., *Chūgoku–Chōsen no shiseki ni okeru Nihon shiryō shūsei, Richō Jitsuroku no bu*, vols. 1–5
    (Tokyo: Kokusho kankōkai, 1976–81).

T'aejong, and Sejong. One was a conciliatory policy toward the *wakō* wherein the Yi government granted official posts, rice lands, and other property to those who surrendered. However, as a result, the number of defectors became so large that the Yi had to limited trading areas to the ports of Pusan-p'o and Naei-p'o. In 1426, the system was relaxed to include Yon-p'o as well. The Japanese who lived in these three ports were referred to as "permanently resident Japanese" (*hangko waein*). There were others living in Japan who received appointments from the Yi government and came once a year to trade in Korea; these people were called "appointment-receiving Japanese" (*jusik waein*). In 1407 trading vessels (called *hungnison* or "profit-raising ships") from various Japanese daimyo were made to bear passports (*gyōjō* or *fumihiki*) as proof of their origin. The Yi government also established rules for people on the vessels.[105] The issuance of these documents became the exclusive monopoly of the Sō family of Tsushima. This was the initial step allowing the Sō to occupy a special position in Japan–Korea trade until the middle of the nineteenth century and was one of the primary causes leading to their complete control of Tsushima.

The Yi dynasty also undertook military action, in the form of an attack on Tsushima in 1419, to annihilate the *wakō*. In Japan this attack is known as the Ōei invasion.[106] However, after the primary agent behind the attack, King T'aejong, died, his successor King Sejong moved Japanese-Korean relations toward normalization, and for about a century the two countries remained comparatively peaceful trading partners.[107] However, all the various classes in Japan wished to expand their trading with Korea unilaterally. The Yi dynasty continued to be mindful of checking further occurrences of *wakō* raids and tightened control by consecutively adding restrictive regulations. This trade policy emerged in the first years of Sejong's reign and was virtually complete by Songjong's rule. A senior Yi official in charge of foreign affairs, Shin Suk-ji, wrote the *Haedong Chegukki* (A record of countries to the east), which brought together all the existing rules and

105 For the Yi dynasty's limitation regulations, see Nakamura, *Nissen kankeishi no kenkyū*, vol. 1.
106 See the following works on the Ōei-period pirates: Miura, *Nihonshi no kenkyū*, vol. 2, pp. 1086–1121; Takagi Shintarō, *Ōei gaikō no zengo* (Tokyo: Yagi shoten, 1942); and Nakamura, *Nissen kankeishi no kenkyū*, vol. 1. pp. 227–310.
107 Among the works on Japanese and Korean trade are Nakamura, *Nissen kankeishi no kenkyū;* Tanaka, *Chūsei taigai kankeishi;* and Tamura, *Chūsei Nitchō bōeki no kenkyū.* Tamura Hiroyuki has also compiled three useful works of source materials on Japan's relations with the Koryŏ and Yi dynasties: *Nichirai kankei hennen shiryō* (Kyoto: Mine shobō, 1967); *Taiso-Teisō-Taisō jitsuroku Nitchō kankei hennen shiryō* (Kyoto: Sanwa shobō, n.d.); and *Sesō jitsuroku Nitchō keizai shiryō* (Tokyo: Kōseikaku, n.d.).

agreements concerning association and trade.[108] It includes data on
internal conditions in Japan and the Ryūkyū Islands as well as histories of these nation's relations with Korea.

Choson adopted a policy combining favorable treatment of Japanese
travelers with restrictive legislation. The main restrictions consisted of
control by granting official tally seals, edicts, passports, limitations on
the number of ships per year, and a system of communication seals.[109]
The first bronze seals to be used bore the name of the recipient and
were known in Japan as tally seals (kangōin). This system was initiated
at Japan's request and is first recorded in documents in 1418. The
recipients of these seals were called jutō shomin. Edicts, the second
measure, were confirmations stamped with the seals. This measure
was implemented through the position and influence of the Kyushu
tandai and the Sō family lord of Tsushima. It originated in 1419 as a
request from Choson to the Kyushu tandai Shibukawa Mitsuyori.
After that date, simple trading vessels could no longer travel between
Japan and Korea: Trade was instead carried out as a subsidiary business of the official vessel traveling under the ambassador's name.
Under the system of passports, missions not bearing passports from
the Sō lord of Tsushima were treated as pirates. This system first
appeared in 1426 at the request of Sō Sadamori. It was organized after
1435 and firmly established in 1436.

The fourth item was a system for limiting the number of official
ships that could visit annually, which began in 1424 with a suggestion
by Kyushu tandai Shibukawa Yoshitoshi that there be two ships per
year.[110] In 1443 the famous Kyehae (Kakitsu) treaty established the
right of the Sō to send fifty ships annually and to dispatch special ships
when necessary. This was the culmination of Korea's control policy;
the treaty confirmed the Sō's monopolistic position regarding trade
with Korea and thus represented the very heavy restrictions on trade
for Japan as a whole.

Japanese traders required permission to trade, from someone like the
"King of Japan" (the Ashikaga shogun or the head of the Ōuchi fam-

108 Shin Shuku Shū, Kaitō shokokki (Tokyo: Kokusho kankōkai, 1975).
109 Nakamura, Nissen kankeishi no kenkyū, vol. 1. pp. 112–14.
110 For the Kyushu tandai in Japanese-Korean relations, see Akiyama Kenzō, "Muromachi
    shoki ni okeru wakō no chōryō to Kyūshū tandai," Rekishi chiri 57 (April 1931),
    "Muromachi shoki ni okeru Kyushu tandai no Chosen to no kōtsō," Shigaku zasshi 42 (April
    1931), and "Muromachi shoki ni okeru wakō no chōryō to Ōei gaikō jijō," Shigaku zasshi 42
    (September 1931); Kawazoe Shōji, "Kyūshū tandai to Nitchō kōshō," in Seinan chiikishi
    kenkyū, vol. 1 (Tokyo: Bunken shuppan, 1977), and "Kyūshū tandai no suimetsu katei,"
    Kyūshū bunkashi kenkyūsho kiyō, no. 23 (March 1978): 81–130.

ily). Communication seals, the fifth control, were used to prevent the forgery of such permission. In addition to the aforementioned restrictions, Korea instituted the port restrictions mentioned earlier, designated a special route to the capital, and issued stipulations regarding the reception of envoys.

In the article dealing with envoys in the "Choping ungjopgi" ("Record of reception for court visitors") of the *Haedong chegukki*, four categories of Japanese travelers involved in trade were enumerated: (1) envoys of the king of Japan (Ashikaga shogun); (2) envoys of the various daimyo, called *koch'u* or "great chieftain," (3) envoys from the Kyushu *chuldosa* – *tandai* – or lord of Tsushima; and (4) Tsushima people and *jusikin*. The envoys of the second category – the various daimyo – were actually traders. Japanese–Korean trade took three main forms. The first was trade via the ceremonial exchange of tribute goods and gifts; the second was official trade in which the Yi government traded with government goods; and the third was private trade carried out under the Yi government's supervision. Outside these legally established forms, there was an illicit trade that could not be eliminated despite stringent controls. When private trade was outlawed, it flourished all the more.

According to the *Yijo sillok*, which records Japanese–Korean trade relations in comparative detail, there were, on the average, twenty-two missions per year in the first half of the fifteenth century, but in the second half of the century, the number more than tripled, reaching sixty-seven.[111] The amount of cargo per shipment was small, and the prices were low in comparison with those of the Japan–Ming trade, but the number of ships and missions, that is, the total amount of trade, far outstripped that between Japan and China.

Japanese-Korean trade held a very important place in Japan's overseas relations in the fifteenth century. The main items exported from Japan to Korea included cinnabar and other Southeast Asian dyes, medicines, sulfur, and spices; metals such as brass, gold, tin, and lead; and military and cultural items like swords and folding screens. Southeast Asian items were imported in large quantities to Choson directly from the Ryūkyūs or via Hakata.[112] Merchant ships from the Ryūkyūs and Southeast Asia frequently put in at Hakata; with many traders from Choson and Ming, the port prospered as an international city.

---

111 Tanaka, *Chūsei taigai kankeishi*, p. 167.
112 For the details of this affair, see Arimitsu Yūgaku, "Chūsei kōki ni okeru bōeki shōnin no dōkō," *Shizuoka daigaku jimbun gakubu jimbun ronshū*, no. 21 (January 1971).

Japanese–Korean trade clearly formed an important link in the East Asian trading sphere.

The kinds of goods imported into Japan from Korea included such things as tiger skins, boar skins, floral-patterned woven mats, ginseng, and honey. In the beginning, trade was largely in ramie and hemp cloth, but later cotton cloth became more important. Cotton was not yet being produced in Japan, and so became the central item in Japanese–Korean trade, as Japan's strong demand for cotton coincided with an increase in Korea's cotton production. Besides these items, a considerable number of Buddhist sutras and religious items were imported, primarily by those people referred to as "great chieftains" (the *shugo* daimyo).

If one considered the Japanese–Korean trade relationship by stages in accord with Tanaka Takeo's scheme, it would be as follows:[113] The first period (1392–1419) lasted from T'aejo to the Ōei raid in Sejong's first year. It was the era after the height of the *wakō* attacks, when trade relations with Korea finally got started and traders from different parts of Japan could cross over to Korea freely. Having already opened Japanese–Ming relations, Ashikaga Yoshimitsu was actively pursuing trade.

The second period (1419–50) corresponds to the latter part of Sejong's rule. This was the era in which the Muromachi bakufu deemphasized the importance of Korean trade and the Sō family of Tsushima enhanced its position through the restoration of amity after the Oei raids. Sejong adopted a policy of equality based on peaceful relations, set up a number of trade controls, and put relations between Tsushima and Choson on course.

The third period (1450–1510) runs from Munjong's reign to the first year of Chungjong and the Three Ports disturbance. Continuing in the same vein as the previous stage, the controls on trade were consolidated, but the discrepancy in Japan's and Korea's stages of economic development influenced trade, which subsequently foundered. The outbreak of violence in the Three Ports, involving the permanent Japanese residents, proved to be a turning point in trade relations between the two countries.

The fourth period (1510–92) lasted from the Three Ports disturbance until the outbreak of the Bunroku campaign (Hideyoshi's invasions of Korea). Although Japanese–Korean relations revived early in

113 Tanaka, *Chūsei taigai kankeishi*, p. 166.

this period through the efforts of the Sō family, contacts became less frequent because of declining interest on the part of the Japanese. Relations were totally severed with the invasion. This period in East Asian history witnessed the failure of the Ming policy forbidding overseas travel, the arrival of European vessels, and *wakō* incursions, all of which strongly influenced Japanese–Korean relations.

The Ryūkyū Islands (present-day Okinawa) also was a link in the East Asian trading sphere.[114] After engaging in a three-cornered struggle, the three Ryūkyū kingdoms of Hokuzan, Chūzan, and Nanzan were unified by Shō Hashi in 1429. This unification hinged on the issue of offering tribute to Ming China. The Ryūkyūs had been sending about one tribute mission to the Ming annually since 1372. At the outset they presented such southern products as spices and pepper, and also Japanese swords and fans, but later their tribute was limited to horses and sulfur produced in the Ryūkyūs. From the Ming, Okinawa received pottery, iron, textiles, and coins. Because Okinawa sent students to study in Ming China and received some thirty-six Ming immigrant families from Fukien, the Chinese cultural influence in the islands was significant.

The Ryūkyūs enjoyed trading relations with Southeast Asia from at least the latter half of the fourteenth century, and from then through the sixteenth century they advanced to such places as Siam (present-day Thailand), Palenpan, Java, Malacca, Sumatra, Patani, Vietnam, and Sunda, with the Siam trade being especially brisk. This trade was actively pursued only by the Ryūkyū side, and it was mainly official trade directly controlled and managed by the kingdom. This was some 150 years before Japan's venture into the south. The demand for, and expansion of trade in, products from the south in Ming, Choson, and Japan was supported largely by the Ryūkyūs' relationship with the various countries of Southeast Asia.

The Ryūkyūs' relations with Choson began in 1389 when the Ryūkyū's sent back some Koryŏ people captured by *wakō*, along with offerings of sulfur, pepper, and sapon wood.[115] Even after the establish-

114 See the following studies of the Ryūkyū foreign trade: Akiyama, *Nisshi kōshō shiwa;* Higaonna Kanjun, *Reimeiki no kaigai kōtsūshi* (Tokyo: Teikoku kyōikukai shuppanbu, 1941); Miyata Toshihiko, "Nichimin, Ryūmin kokkō no kaishi,"*Nihon rekishi*, nos. 201–3 (February–April 1965); Kobata Atsushi, *Chūsei nantō tsūkō bōekishi no kenkyū* (Tokyo: Tōkō shoin, 1968); and Miyagi Eishō, *Okinawa no rekishi* (Tokyo: Nihon hōsō shuppan kyōkai, 1968).

115 Kobata Atsushi, *Nihon keizaishi no kenkyū* (Kyoto: Shibunkaku shuppan, 1978), pp. 559–79.

ment of the new Yi dynasty by T'aejo Yi Song-gye, the Ryūkyūs
continued to send envoys to Korea, trading Southeast Asian and Chinese goods. But this was unilateral, active trade by the Ryūkyūs; the
Korean side remained inactive. The Ryūkyūs dispatched envoys to
Choson who traveled on the merchant ships from Hakata, Tsushima,
or other ports in Kyushu. Sometimes the Kyushu merchants themselves became Ryūkyū envoys. But this kind of trade was ended by
Satsuma's invasion of the Ryūkyūs in 1609.

Japan and the Ryūkyūs opened mutual trading relations through the
medium of Ming tribute. For the Ryūkyūs, Japan and Korea were
places to resell items imported from China, and later they became
trading partners to which Okinawa could reexport trade goods from
Southeast Asia. It was a classic case of intermediary trade. Thus,
Ryūkyū boats called at such ports as Bōnutsu, Obi, and Hakata in
Kyushu; Hyōgo and Sakai in the Kinki region; and Matsura in
Musashi Province of eastern Japan. The Muromachi bakufu appointed
a Ryūkyū commissioner to administer and control the trade. The
Ashikaga shogun and the king of the Ryūkyūs exchanged documents
written in Japanese *kana*, and they had a superior–subordinate rela-
tionship based on a common script and common race.[116] Because the
Ōnin–Bunmei War in Japan brought an end to the visit of the Ryūkyū
ships to Hyōgo, Sakai merchants seeking trade began instead to venture to the Ryūkyūs. However, the Hakata merchants, backed by the
Ōuchi, opposed these Sakai merchants, who were supported by the
Muromachi deputy shogun of the Hosokawa house, and restrained
their activities. They were able to confine the Japanese mainland base
for the Ryūkyū trade to Kyushu, where Bōnotsu and Hakata became
the principal centers.

The Ryūkyū Islands were able to carry out such extensive trading
activity because Chinese traders were hampered by the Ming policy of
forbidding overseas travel. But when this policy broke down, illicit
international trade focusing on the southeast China coast commenced.
Oceangoing traders engaged in this illicit trade increased in number,
and the period of the great *wakō* raids of the Chia-ching (1522–67) era
ensued. However, when European vessels began to arrive, the
Ryūkyūs' glory based on its extensive trade came to an end.

116 Tanaka Takeo, "Muromachi bakufu to Ryūkyū to no kankei no ichikōsatsu," *Nantō shigaku*,
no. 16 (November 1980).

CHAPTER 10

CULTURAL LIFE IN MEDIEVAL JAPAN

After senior retired emperor Toba died on the second day of the seventh
month of 1156 (the first year of Hōgen), fighting and strife began in Japan,
and the country entered the age of warriors.[1]

This laconic statement came from the brush of the Buddhist priest
Jien (1155–1225), the author of *Gukanshō*, an early-thirteenth-century
history of Japan. Jien was a member of the ascendent northern branch
of the Fujiwara and wrote *Gukanshō* in part to justify the historical
success of his family as regent-rulers at the Heian court. But Jien is
probably best remembered as the first historian in Japan to view the
past in distinct terms of cause and effect and as a progression from one
stage to another. Although earlier writers had not been totally oblivi-
ous to historical causality, none had sought to analyze Japanese history,
as Jien did, within an overall, interpretive framework.

Jien's emphasis on the progress of history was not an aberrant view
but, rather, emerged from a heightened awareness of the momentous
historical changes that he himself witnessed. As observed in
Gukanshō, Japan in the late 1100s was transformed from a comparatively peaceful and tranquil country under the rule of the imperial
court to a tumultuous, strife-filled "age of warriors." Yet the anguish
that Jien and other members of the courtier elite experienced as a
result of this transition was accepted fatalistically because of a belief in
its inevitability: They were convinced that the period of *mappō*, or
"the end of the Buddhist law," had already begun a century before.
According to this pessimistic notion, which set the dominant tone for
the outlook of the medieval age, Japan had entered into a final, cataclysmic stage of its history, in which people ceased to follow the Buddhist law, turmoil replaced order in society, and life became sub-

---

1 Okami Masao and Akamatsu Toshihide, eds., *Gukanshō*, vol. 85 of *Nihon koten bungaku taikei*
(Tokyo: Iwanami shoten, 1967), p. 206.

merged in darkness and suffering. Under such circumstances, it was hardly surprising that warriors should arise to reimpose, even by brutal force, some semblance of order in the land.

The *mappō* concept of historical decline, strongly held in the early medieval age, was nurtured by the traditionally keen sensitivity of the Japanese to the mutability and evanescence of all things. The central ideal of beauty in Japan had always been a beauty of perishability, found most typically in the changes in nature brought about by the passage of the seasons. Buddhism, with its belief that the world is in constant flux, deepened and rendered more poignant this native feeling for change. Thus, when we read the following passage:

> The flow of the river is ceaseless and its water is never the same. The bubbles that float in the pools, now vanishing, now forming, are not of long duration: so in the world are man and his dwellings. It might be imagined that the houses, great and small, which vie roof against proud roof in the capital remain unchanged from one generation to the next, but when we examine whether this is true, how few are the houses that were there of old. . . . The city is the same, the people are as numerous as ever, but of those I used to know, a bare one or two in twenty remain. They die in the morning, they are born in the evening, like foam on the water.[2]

we are struck by its poetic imagery and the profoundly sad vision it presents of the fleeting nature of humans and their works.

Standing alone, this passage provides no clue to the period of its composition: It expresses feelings that the Japanese have always been wont to articulate. In fact, it is the opening to Kamo no Chōmei's *Hōjōki* (An account of my ten-foot square hut), a brief miscellany written in 1212, and is prelude to a narrative that is characteristically medieval in it description of the sufferings of this life and the pension for salvation in Amida's Pure Land paradise after death.

Chōmei (1153–1216) was a member of the lower-court aristocracy whose family served as Shinto priests at the Kamo Shrine in Kyoto. A gifted poet, he was nevertheless denied – probably because of his inferior social standing – full membership in the literary salon at court; and in middle age he took Buddhist vows and withdrew from life in the capital, eventually moving into reclusive retirement in a meager, "ten-foot square" hut on Mount Hino on the city's outskirts.

The first half of *Hōjōki* describes the grief and hardships of life in this world and relates a series of calamities, including earthquake, fire, and famine, that afflicted Kyoto during the late 1170s and early 1180s.

2 Donald Keene, ed., *Anthology of Japanese Literature* (New York: Grove Press, 1955), p. 197.

These were the epochal years when the Taira and Minamoto contended for military hegemony of the land and a warrior government (bakufu) was established at Kamakura. But Chōmei, the poet, said scarcely a word about these events, even though at least one of his calamities – the famine of 1181 – was in part caused by the disruption of food shipments to the capital, owing to fighting in the nearby province of Ōmi, the "breadbasket" of Kyoto.

Against this backdrop of disaster and suffering, Chōmei turned in the second half of Hōjōki to an account of his personal quest for religious salvation. Increasingly he sought to disentangle himself from worldly ties, both social and material, and in the end sequestered himself in the ten-foot square hut. Yet pathetically, he was forced to confess that even his attachment to the tiny hut might hinder his salvation and rebirth in the Pure Land of Amida.

Perhaps the most striking feature of Hōjōki is the conflict revealed within the author himself who, even as he denounced this existence and yearned for rebirth in Amida's Pure Land, found beauty almost everywhere in life, even in his wretched hut. Although the hut was supposed to represent rejection of material values, it became instead a focal point for Chōmei's aesthetic sensibilities as a poet. Later in the medieval age, the "hut" became an important aesthetic ideal for many poets and artists, but few were ostensibly as torn as Chōmei was in the desire to renounce the beauty of the world in order to achieve religious salvation.

THE TALE OF THE HEIKE AND OTHER WAR TALES

Although Hōjōki is one of the finest literary expressions of the intensified awareness of change that accompanied the advent of medieval times, it is not concerned with the larger course of history and Japan's inexorable descent into the age of mappō. This is the central theme of Gukanshō, but Gukanshō is a rather drily written historical record and does not reflect the popular imagination of its age. Instead, it is the great war tale, Heike monogatari (Tale of the Taira, or Heike), that provides us with the richest legends and the most vivid impressions of the medieval mind at the time when the high civilization of the Heian court waned and the country was plunged into an age of warriors.

There is no simple definition for the literary genre of war tales (gunki monogatari) that became so important to the narrative tradition of the medieval age. In subject matter they deal with warriors and battle, and by that criterion the earliest war tales are Shōmonki (or

Masakado-ki), which recounts the rebellion of Taira no Masakado (d. 940) in the Kantō in 935–40, and *Mutsu waki* (Tale of Mutsu), a record of the Former Nine Years War fought in the northern Mutsu–Dewa region in the mid-eleventh century. Both of these works, however, although abundant in the lore and ethos of the emerging samurai class, are written in Chinese and are therefore quite different linguistically from the war tales of the medieval age. In contrast, the language of the medieval war tales was Japanese (transcribed with Chinese characters and the native *kana* syllabary), enriched by a heavy admixture of Chinese loan words, including many that were used to express Buddhist ideas.

The authorship and dates of most of the war tales are either unknown or disputed. We do not even know, for example, by whom and in what order the three major tales of the Kamakura period (1185–1333) – *Hōgen monogatari*, *Heiji monogatari*, and *Heike monogatari* – were written or compiled. Perhaps there was no "order"; for although the first two tales are relatively short, focused on restricted events (the Hōgen and Heiji disturbances of 1156 and 1159–60), and possibly written by single authors at specific times, *Heike monogatari* is an enormously long and episodic record of the rise and fall of the Taira clan that evolved over a century (from the late 1100s to the late 1200s) from both written and oral sources.

Scholars hypothesize that the original *Heike monogatari* was written in the early thirteenth century by a former courtier named Yukinaga who came under the patronage of the priest-historian Jien, then abbot of the Enryakuji temple on Mount Hiei. This suggests that *Gukanshō* and *Heike monogatari* (in its first form) were compiled at roughly the same time and that Yukinaga was strongly influenced by Jien's fatalistic ideas and philosophy of *mappō*.

If there was an "original" *Heike*, it was most likely a fairly brief, chronological account of the events and developments that have always constituted the book's principal narrative: the rise of the Taira under Kiyomori (1118–81) to dominance of the Heian court in the late 1170s and the family's fall from grace and power and final destruction during the Gempei War (1180–5). But the *Heike* we have today is a vastly expanded work, containing many miscellaneous stories and legends from diverse sources. Most important, the *Heike* was extensively revised and reshaped by the contributions of blind itinerant priests who traveled the countryside chanting their tales to the accompaniment of a *biwa*, or lute.

Whereas the opening lines of *Hōjōki* plaintively observe the sadness of change and the passage of time, the introduction to *Heike monogatari* strikes a much more somber and ominous tone:

In the sound of the bell of the Gion Temple echoes the impermanence of all things. The pale hue of the flowers of the teak tree shows the truth that they who prosper must fall. The proud ones do not last long, but vanish like a spring-night's dream. And the mighty ones too will perish in the end, like dust before the wind.[3]

We are informed that the Taira are fated for a fall, and the text assumes a tone of tragic inevitability that is sustained until the end. The fall of the Taira is one of the great themes in the Japanese cultural tradition, and the reasons for and the manner of their decline, as presented in *Heike monogatari*, tell us much about differing attitudes toward the historical displacement of courtiers by warriors as rulers in this age.

The views of *Heike's* original author (let us assume it was Yukinaga) represent those of the courtier-centered *ancien régime*. Kiyomori, the Taira chieftain, was the vilest of men. Not only was he excessively proud and haughty, but he also repeatedly breached the tenets of the unwritten but sacred "imperial law" (*ōhō*), violating both the persons and offices of the emperor and other members of the imperial family. In a sense, the *Heike* portrait of Kiyomori – which cannot be accepted as historically accurate – represents a *cri de coeur* against the entire warrior class as usurpers of national power from the emperor and his court. But the depiction of the Taira clan as a whole, especially after Kiyomori's death in 1181 (at the end of the first half of *Heike*), can be interpreted quite differently. In the sections in the second half of the book in which the Taira are forced to flee Kyoto and are relentlessly pursued by the Minamoto to final destruction at the battle of Dannoura in 1185, they subtly become surrogates for the courtier class, and their pitiful fate represents the demise of the courtiers as rulers in the medieval age.

This portrayal of the Taira as courtiers may be found in the famous passage in "The Death of Atsumori" in which the Minamoto retainer Kumagai Naozane, having captured the young Taira general Atsumori on the beach at Ichinotani, is forced to behead him in order to save him from crueler treatment at the hands of other Minamoto partisans. When Naozane discovers a flute in Atsumori's sash, he exclaims in anguish that not a single member of the myriad forces of the Minamoto would have thought to carry such a thing into battle. But it is not merely the refined courtly tastes in music, poetry, and the like attrib-

3 Ibid., p. 78.

uted to the Taira that transforms them into surrogates for the courtiers. It is also the tone and literary qualities of certain key sections that
relate the humiliations, agonies, and deaths of leading Taira during the
Gempei War. Whereas most of *Heike monogatari* is written in the
strong, vigorous style of the new genre of war tales, these sections
evoke the mood and feelings of the fictional tales (*tsukuri monogatari*)
of the Heian period.

Although the Taira may be viewed as both warriors and courtiers,
the Minamoto who appear in the pages of *Heike monogatari* are, with
few exceptions, clearly drawn as the dynamic military leaders of the
new age. The book's pervasively tragic tone is sustained even in the
treatment of these victors: for example, in the vivid detailing of the
death in battle of the first great Minamoto field general of the Gempei
War, Yoshinaka (1154–84), and in the foreshadowing of the doom of
the second, Yoshitsune (1159–89). But otherwise the Minamoto represent the future, and indeed some of them and their followers are
portrayed in terms of the exaggeratedly superior prowess and courage
that were to become stereotypical of the war tales of the medieval age.[4]

THE AGE OF *SHINKOKINSHŪ* POETRY

The nostalgia for the courtier past that we find in both *Gukanshō* and
Heike monogatari (and less explicitly, in *Hōjōki*) was not merely a passing, futile yearning for something that could never be recaptured but
was part of a growing sentiment that endured throughout the medieval
age. In part, this sentiment was sustained because the courtier class
itself survived the traumatic transition to warrior times. Although
eventually stripped of all political power and most of their economic
wealth, the courtiers retained their unique social status as aristocrats
and their custodianship of the still greatly admired classical culture
that their forebears had produced.

The heart of the classical culture was *waka* poetry, the art on which
the courtiers lavished their greatest love and in whose cadences they
sought to express their highest sense of beauty. The *waka* tradition's
range of poetic expression, vocabulary, and social sentiment was established in the early to mid-Heian period, about the time of the compilation in 905 of *Kokinshū* (Anthology of ancient and modern poems), the

---

4 See Kenneth Dean Butler, "The *Heike Monogatari* and the Japanese Warrior Ethic," *Harvard
Journal of Asiatic Studies* 29 (1969): 93–108. Butler has analyzed how, contrary to the facts of
history, oral-tale singers created stereotyped, "ideal heroes" of famous warriors who appear in
the *Heike monogatari*.

first imperially authorized *waka* anthology. Later court poets deeply venerated *Kokinshū* and identified it and other works of tenth and early eleventh centuries – especially *Ise monogatari* and *Genji monogatari* – as models of the aesthetic and cultural values of court life. In earlier times the "classical past" had been essentially a Chinese past; now the Japanese looked back increasingly to the mid-Heian period of their own history for artistic guidance and inspiration.

Keen awareness of a classical Japanese past was a major feature of the efflorescence of *waka* that occurred, ironically perhaps, during the twelfth and early thirteenth centuries when the court was a declining governmental institution. This period may be called the age of *Shinkokinshū*, as its finest achievement was the compilation of the eighth imperial anthology, the "new *Kokinshū*," in 1205. The *Shinkokinshū* poets, who included Fujiwara no Shunzei (1114–1204), the priest Saigyō (1118–90), and Shunzei's son Teika (1162–1241), spoke of expressing "new feelings with old words" (*kotoba furuku, kokoro atarashi*) and sought to achieve resonance in their poetry by both alluding to earlier poems (*honkadori*) and using suggestion rather than explicit statement. A poem by Fujiwara no Teika illustrates some of these techniques:

> As I look about,
> I see neither cherry blossoms
> Nor crimson leaves.
> A straw-thatched hut by the bay
> At evening the Autumn.[5]

Teika alludes to two traditional subjects, the cherry blossoms of spring and the changing maple leaves of autumn, but instead of celebrating them directly, he describes a setting in late autumn or early winter in which they are conspicuously absent. The setting itself, a monochromatic scene of a lowly fisherman's hut by the bay, is untraditional and suggests some of the new tastes of the medieval age. It is made familiar through reference to the blossoms and leaves that poets had always praised, and our impression of the bleak landscape is enhanced by the reminder that it has been and will again be suffused with color.

Two aesthetic values that guided the *Shinkokinshū* poets and set much of the artistic tone of the medieval age were *yūgen* (mystery and depth) and *sabi* (loneliness). I leave the discussion of *yūgen* to the section on the noh theater in the Muromachi period. Here let me note some of the tastes connoted by *sabi*.

5 *Shinkokinshū*, vol. 4, no. 363.

Heian-period poets had given their attention chiefly to the new and fashionable (*imamekashi*) and to nature's more conventionally regarded beauties, such as spring's blossoms and autumn's leaves. By the age of *Shinkokinshū*, an aesthetic appeal was growing – perhaps encouraged by the somber sentiments of *mappō* pessimism and the mounting awareness that a great era was coming to an end – for the weathered and withered, the desolate and lonely – *sabi*. Teika's hut by the bay at eveningtime in late autumn is a good example of *sabi*. An even better example is the following well-known poem by Saigyō:

> Even one who has renounced
> His worldly feelings
> Knows of the pathos of life.
> A shrike rises from the marsh;
> Autumn at dusk.[6]

Both the Teika and Saigyō poems have the same last line (*aki no yūgure*, autumn at evening or dusk) and are therefore set at the same time of day in the same season. Teika's verse is almost purely descriptive, whereas Saigyō's speaks also, in intensely personal terms, of the desolation and loneliness of life.

Fujiwara no Teika and his compeers were not only poets but also scholars. The scholarship they pursued, essential to the "allusive depth" of their poetry, was itself one of the most important products of the nostalgia for the past that evolved in the medieval age. Usually called *wagaku*, or Japanese scholarship (to distinguish it from *kangaku*, or Chinese scholarship), it consisted of two general areas of study. One was the corpus of *waka*-centered, classical court literature, especially the mid-Heian-period masterworks *Kokinshū*, *Ise monogatari*, and *Genji monogatari;* the other was "court ceremonial and practice" (*yūsoku kojitsu*), the accumulated rituals, customs, and minutiae of court life. *Wagaku* reached its peak of development in the mid-Muromachi period in the late fourteenth and fifteenth centuries.

The compilation of *Shinkokinshū* in the early thirteenth century was one of the last major achievements in the arts that was primarily the work of the courtier class. It is fitting that its leading compiler was the senior retired emperor Gotoba (1180–1239), who later schemed to overthrow the Kamakura bakufu and precipitated the Jōkyū disturbance of 1221. As a result of this brief war, Kamakura military rule was vastly expanded, and perhaps most important in terms of cultural history, the bakufū's control over Kyoto was firmly established.

6 *Shinkokinshū*, vol. 4, no. 362.

THE REVIVAL OF SHINTO AND THE LATE KAMAKURA PERIOD

After 1221, the court ceased to control even its most important affairs. Major decisions, including the selection of successors to the throne, were made either directly by the bakufu or through its representatives, the Rokuhara *tandai*. Under these circumstances, a stultifying atmosphere settled over Kyoto, and for the remainder of the Kamakura period the arts did not shine as brilliantly as they had during the first three decades or so of the medieval age. Meanwhile, Kamakura came under the firm administration of the Hōjō shogunal regents (*shikken*), who became ever more confident of their newly acquired status as rulers and who wished to enhance their seat of power by elevating its cultural life. This was achieved primarily through the patronage of Zen Buddhism. The Hōjō invited Chinese Zen (Ch'an) priests to Kamakura and helped them establish major Zen centers, such as the Kenchōji and Engakuji temples.

Much of the intellectual vigor of the Kamakura period was devoted to Buddhism, and the finest works in learned writing were those by the founders of the new Buddhist sects, including Hōnen, Shinran, Eisai, Dōgen, and Nichiren. But there was also a revival in Shinto in Kamakura times. Although it did not stimulate much great writing, it greatly influenced the attitudes of at least the higher levels of society during the late thirteenth and early fourteenth centuries, when Japan was attacked by two Mongol invading forces (1274 and 1281), the Kamakura bakufu gradually faltered and was finally overthrown (1333), and Emperor Godaigo (1288–1339) attempted to "restore" imperial rule in the Kemmu restoration (1333–6).

One aspect of the Shinto revival was renewed interest in Japan's origins. Jien began his history in *Gukanshō* with the first earthly emperor, Jimmu, and the so-called age of humans. But others began to study the long-neglected history of the "age of the gods," thus preparing the way for articulating the concept of *kamikaze* during the period of the Mongol invasions – the "winds of the gods" that arose at times of great peril to protect Japan. This concept asserted the primacy of Shinto over Buddhism, which for many centuries had been viewed as the supreme "protector of the state."[7]

Another aspect of the Shinto revival was the commencement of new research into the history of the imperial institution. This research

7 *Chingo kokka.*

coincided with disputes over succession to the throne that erupted among the descendants of the senior retired emperor Gosaga (1220–72) upon his death in 1272. The most important product of this research was *Jinnō shōtōki* (Chronicle of the direct descent of gods and sovereigns), a history of Japan written in 1339 by the courtier-general Kitabatake Chikafusa (1293–1354). To understand the historical setting of *Jinnō shōtōki*, it is necessary first to note the circumstances surrounding the failure of the Kemmu restoration and the subsequent founding of the Ashikaga bakufu (1336–1573).

The Kemmu restoration was essentially a futile, ahistorical effort to reinstitute the conditions of an age some five hundred years earlier when emperors supposedly exercised personal rule over the country. Probably the most grievous failure of the restoration government in Kyoto was its inability to meet the demands for rewards by warriors who had aided in overthrowing the Kamakura bakufu. The restoration government was also divided from its inception by intense rivalries among the chieftains who were its principal military supports. In 1335 one of these chieftains, Ashikaga Takauji (1305–58), the head of a major branch of the Minamoto clan, turned against the government and occupied Kyoto, forcing Emperor Godaigo and his backers to flee to Yoshino in the mountainous region south of the capital. Thus began the period of war between the courts (1336–92), an unprecedented time in Japanese history when there were two rival seats of emperorship: Godaigo's "Southern Court" at Yoshino and the "Northern Court" in Kyoto headed by emperors of another branch of the imperial family. The Northern Court was a mere pawn of the Ashikaga bakufu, which Takauji established in Kyoto in close proximity.

Kitabatake Chikafusa, a follower of Emperor Godaigo, became the de facto leader of the Southern Court after Godaigo's death in 1339. It has long been speculated that he wrote *Jinnō shōtōki* to instruct the emperor's son and youthful successor, Gomurakami (1328–68). Recently, however, it has been suggested that Chikafusa intended his history primarily as a means to recruit support for the Southern Court.[8] Whatever Chikafusa's purpose may have been, *Jinnō shōtōki* is mainly remembered as a history whose author argued the legitimacy of the Southern over the Northern line of emperors during the war be-

8 I have discussed this new interpretation in H. Paul Varley, trans., *Jinnō Shōtōki: A Chronicle of Gods and Sovereigns* (New York: Columbia University Press, 1980), pp. 30–31.

tween the courts. Yet even more fundamentally, Chikafusa emphasized the continuity of imperial succession, which in his mind set Japan apart from other countries and made it superior. Whereas Jien began *Gukanshō* with the reign of the first human sovereign, Jimmu, Chikafusa traced a line of unbroken rulership from the age of the gods.[9]

A principal theme in *Gukanshō* is the interrelationship between *ōhō* (imperial law) and *buppō* (Buddhist law) in Japanese history. Jien believed that imperial law was headed toward extinction and had, in fact, been propped up for centuries by the imported law of Buddhism. By contrast, Chikafusa eschewed the use of the term *ōhō* with its connotations of imperial decline and extinction.[10] Although he said a great deal in *Jinnō shōtōki* about Buddhism, he did not acknowledge that it exerted any influence on the imperial institution. Chikafusa, whose thinking emerged from the Shinto revival of the late Kamakura period, also rejected the concept of *mappō*. Although recognizing the debased state of civil war into which the country had fallen in his own time, he insisted that it could be revived through the restoration of proper (i.e., time-honored and legitimate) principles of rule and that the imperial institution would endure eternally through the mandate of Amaterasu.[11]

Kitabatake Chikafusa's thinking was more significant to the Shinto ideologues and nationalists of later centuries than it was to his contemporaries. With his call for the restoration of "proper principles," Chikafusa was already an anachronism in his own lifetime. We know in retrospect that after the failure of the Kemmu restoration, there was no real chance of reviving imperial rule in the sense of returning political power to the emperor or his ministers.[12] The warriors' long process of displacing the courtiers as the ruling elite, which began in the late twelfth century, was complete by the fourteenth century.

---

9 This emphasis on continuous rule from the age of the gods is announced in the opening lines of the *Jinnō shōtōki:* "Great Japan is the divine land. The heavenly progenitor founded it, and the Sun Goddess bequeathed it to her descendants to rule eternally. Only in our country is this true; there are no similar examples in other countries. That is why our country is called the divine land."

10 Rather than imperial law (*ōhō*), Chikafusa stressed imperial succession.

11 The mandate given to Ninigi by Amaterasu in the *Jinnō shōtōki* when she bestowed the regalia upon him and sent him down from heaven to rule Japan was, "Go there and rule. Go, and may your line prosper eternally, like heaven and earth."

12 The emperor and ministers of the Northern Court were dominated by the Ashikaga bakufu. The emperors and ministers of the Southern Court seemed to have had no real chance of reinstalling themselves as leaders of the entire country.

THE EARLY MUROMACHI PERIOD

A major result of the founding of the Ashikaga bakufu and the commencement of the Muromachi period (1336–1573) was the reestablishment of Kyoto as the country's unchallenged administrative and cultural center. With the bakufu located in Kyoto instead of Kamakura, courtiers and warriors began to intermingle socially to a much greater degree than before and to share patronage of the arts. In addition, Kyoto replaced Kamakura as the focal point of Zen, and the Kyoto Zen temples assumed a new leadership among the religious institutions of the central provinces in encouraging art and learning.

This period also witnessed the emergence of Kyoto as a commercial center and the rise of a newly affluent merchant class that increasingly participated in the city's cultural life. Until the end of the Heian period, culture and the arts had been monopolized by the courtiers. It was a sign of the dynamic social changes that occurred in the early medieval age that by the beginning of the Muromachi period, not only warriors and merchants but also members of the lower orders in the provinces came to play meaningful roles in cultural development. A truly national culture was taking shape for the first time in Japan, a culture that derived from both elite and popular sources and was increasingly shared and enjoyed by all classes.

The war tale *Taiheiki* (Chronicle of great peace) is the single best source describing the political, social, and cultural changes that occurred during the Kemmu restoration and the first three decades or so of the Muromachi period.[13] This lengthy chronicle covers the time from Godaigo's accession to the throne in 1318 until about 1368, when Yoshimitsu became the third Ashikaga shogun, and ranks with *Heike monogatari* as one of the two most important medieval war tales. In literary terms, however, *Taiheiki* is far inferior to *Heike monogatari*. The first third of *Taiheiki* deals with Godaigo's plot against the Kamakura bakufu and is reasonably well structured and presented. But later sections are loosely organized and full of digressions, trivial anecdotes, and repetitious and stereotypical battle scenes. *Taiheiki* lacks a great unifying theme. Whereas *Heike monogatari*, from its opening lines until its somber closing pages, narrates the tragically portended decline and annihilation of the Taira family, *Taiheiki* comes closer to a simple narrative of events.

13 One theory is that "great peace" expressed the wish for termination of the strife that the *Taiheiki*, in fact, records.

Japanese critics over the centuries have categorized *Taiheiki* as a propaganda text of the Southern Court. If anything, the work is distinctive for the cumulative criticism that its author or authors directed against all parties to the dynastic warfare of the fourteenth century.[14] Nevertheless, there is a certain validity to this perception of *Taiheiki* as a Southern Court work; the episodes most frequently extracted from it by later storytellers were those dealing with the heroic exploits and steadfast loyalty of the adherents of Emperor Goidago and the Southern Court. By the modern age such men as Nitta Yoshisada (1301–38), Prince Morinaga (1308–35), and especially Kusunoki Masashige (d. 1336), all of whom died fighting for the unsuccessful Southern side, had been apotheosized in the Japanese folk tradition as the most exemplary of loyalist heroes. The characters most beloved in both *Heike monogatari* and *Taiheiki* were those whom Ivan Morris termed "failed heroes," characters who made their greatest appeal to the Japanese sentiment by destroying themselves or otherwise going resolutely to their ends for noble but losing causes.[15]

The pages of *Taiheiki* introduce a great variety of characters and social types. Most notable, apart from the loyal heroes of the Southern Court, are the military leaders, led by the Ashikaga, who sponsored the Northern Court and emerged as the new ruling elite in Kyoto. These men came to share, along with the courtiers and Buddhist prelates (especially of the Rinzai Zen sect), patronage of the arts and culture in the early Muromachi period. Many of them came from the central and western provinces and were quite a different breed from the chieftains who had supported the Kamakura bakufu. Rising to prominence at a time when regional pulls made centralized control of the country exceedingly difficult, they were far more independent and far more apt to challenge traditional authority than were their Kamakura-period predecessors. In Kyoto, where the new leaders took up residence, they became the most prominent figures in a social life that was severely criticized by some contemporary chroniclers as ostentatious and extravagant. A term that came into currency about the time of the Kemmu restoration and connoted such ostentation and extravagance was *basara*,[16] and the chieftains who subscribed to it were dubbed *basara* daimyo.

The most conspicuous *basara* daimyo portrayed in *Taiheiki* was

14 I have discussed this point in H. Paul Varley, *Imperial Restoration in Medieval Japan* (New York: Columbia University Press, 1971), chap. 5.
15 Ivan Morris, *The Nobility of Failure* (New York: Holt, Rinehart and Winston, 1975).
16 *Basara* also meant disruptive or potentially destructive.

Sasaki Dōyo, a *shugo* from Ōmi Province. At parties held at Dōyo's residence, the seating places were lavishly adorned with leopard and tiger skins, damask, and gold brocade, and works of art were ostentatiously displayed. Guests were regaled with munificeni quantities of food and saké, and there was music, singing, and dancing. The parties (which were said to project a glitter not unlike the "radiance of a thousand Buddhas") also included gambling in the form of *tōcha* or tea-judging contests.[17]

Tea had first been introduced to Japan from China in the early Heian period, but tea drinking was not permanently accepted by the Japanese until after its reintroduction by the Zen priest Eisai in the late twelfth century. By the Muromachi period, all classes in Japan drank tea. The *tōcha* were contests in which the participants, backed by wagers, sought to identify the tea of Togano'o, a place northwest of Kyoto where the most highly regarded tea of that time was grown, by drinking from unmarked cups that contained it as well as the products of other tea-producing regions.[18] As we shall see, *tōcha* was the precursor to the classical tea ceremony (*chanoyu*) of later Muromachi times.

Another connotation of *basara* was exoticism, manifested especially in this age by the desire to acquire works of art and craft (*karamono*) from China. There had been a hiatus in relations with the continent following the Mongol invasions of Japan in the late thirteenth century. But the Ashikaga, beginning with the bakufu's founder, Takauji, gradually renewed trade with China, which was formalized and made official from the time of the third shogun, Yoshimitsu (1358–1408). Much of the story of the importance of this trade in cultural terms belongs to the chapter on the *gozan* (Chapter 13), because until the late fifteenth century, the Zen monks of these temples managed most of the trade under the sponsorship of the bakufu. In addition to trading, the *gozan* Zen monks also inquired eagerly into Chinese art, literature, and scholarship. But for our discussion the most important aspect of the new China trade was the *karamono*, including paintings, calligraphic scrolls, ceramic wares, fine porcelains, and lacquerware brought to Japan in ever-greater quantities beginning in the mid-fourteenth century.

People like Sasaki Dōyo vied aggressively for *karamono* and dis-

---

17 These contests were a form of *monoawase* or "comparison of things" and had been popular from at least the Heian period, when the courtiers engaged in a great variety of *monoawase*, from the comparison or judgment of things such as flowers, incense, roots, and seashells to artistic creations such as poems and paintings.

18 By the end of the fourteenth century, Uji had replaced Togano'o as the leading tea-producing region of Japan.

played them proudly at parties and other social functions. Scenes from late-fourteenth-century scrolls show *karamono* lined up on view at gatherings.[19] But there is little indication, either in the scenes themselves or in the writings of the time, that the owners were qualified to judge the quality of their treasures. The process by which the Japanese gradually developed a connoisseurship for *karamono* and evolved canons of taste for displaying both these and their native works of art and craft (*wamono*) is a major theme of cultural history in the fifteenth century and is closely related to the creation of the earliest settings for the performance of *chanoyu*.

Sasaki Dōyo was a flamboyant man who opportunistically played the shifting politics of his age. He also possessed considerable learning and artistic discrimination. He was, for example, a major contributor to the first imperially authorized linked-verse (*renga*) anthology, *Tsukubashū* (1356), and was an authority on incense and the purported author of a book on flower arrangement.[20] Dōyo may also have been the first person of prominence to discover Kan'ami (1333–84) and Zeami (1363–1443) who, under the patronage of the shogun Yoshimitsu, created the classical noh theater.

The Ashikaga bakufu reached its greatest influence during the time of Ashikaga Yoshimitsu, who acceded to the office of shogun at the age of ten in 1368 and about a decade later became the real as well as the titular head of the bakufu. Yoshimitsu's time (from 1368 until his death in 1408) is known as the Kitayama or "Northern Hills" epoch, named for the location of the residential retreat he built in his later years in the hills north of Kyoto. There were few other epochs in Japanese history when a ruler was so important to shaping cultural developments. The principal reason for this, apart from Yoshimitsu's personal proclivities, was his desire to establish himself as "king" of the bakufu by combining in himself both the supreme military (*bu*) and the civil or cultural (*bun*) aspects of rule. Yoshimitsu's pursuit of the *bun* of rule involved both the extension of patronage to the arts in general and the adoption of a policy of simultaneous assimilation with and domination of the courtiers, the traditional possessors of *bun*. I shall discuss Yoshimitsu's relations with the courtiers first, as they were a major influence on the character of his patronage of the arts.

Yoshimitsu sought to transform himself into a courtier and encour-

---

19 For example, a scene from the fifteenth-century narrative scroll *Sairei zōshi* shows *karamono* vases and an incense burner aligned on shelves extending the lengths of two walls of a room in which people are gathered waiting to be served food.
20 This book was entitled *Rikka kuden daiji*.

aged his leading vassals to adopt courtier tastes and the courtly style of life. Perhaps the most conspicuous aspect of Yoshimitsu's personal transformation was his acquisition of ever-higher court ranks and offices. By 1380, at the age of twenty-two, he had attained the junior first rank (*ju-ichii*), the highest level of the courtier ranking system. A year later he received the position of minister of the center (*naidaijin*), and in 1394 he was made great minister of the Council of State (*daijō-daijin*), an office that, with the exception of Taira no Kiyomori, had not been held previously by a warrior. In addition, Yoshimitsu took a wife from the noble Hino family,[21] obliged prominent courtiers to become members of his entourage, and constructed a splendid palace, the Hana no Gosho (Palace of Flowers), where he held court in a kingly manner.

We are most interested in Yoshimitsu's cultivation of courtier taste, however, and the main influence on him in this area was Nijō Yoshimoto (1320–88), a leading Fujiwara and imperial regent who is probably best known as the compiler of the *renga* anthology *Tsukubashū*. Yoshimoto personally tutored the young shogun in courtier customs, etiquette, and art and was frequently at his side to guide him in the conduct of cultural affairs.

THE NOH THEATER

Seldom in cultural history are single events of great significance, but one exception was the visit by Yoshimitsu to Imakumano Shrine in Kyoto in 1374 to attend his first performance of *sarugaku* (an early form of noh drama). At Imakumano he saw Kan'ami and his young son (the later Zeami), was totally entranced, and promptly provided the patronage that enabled them to become the leading theatrical figures of the Kitayama epoch and the principal creators of noh.[22] We see here one of Yoshimitsu's first and most important acts in his patronage of the arts and, as can be deduced from the subsequent career of Zeami, who eagerly sought to satisfy his grand patron, probably the best example of the influence of Yoshimitsu's courtier tastes on the evolution of a major art.

The two main types of early medieval theater were *sarugaku* and *dengaku* (field music), both of whose performers were organized into troupes or guilds (*za*) that received the patronage of great religious

---

21 The Hino were related to the northern branch of the Fujiwara.
22 It may have been another actor-playwright, Nan'ami, who arranged to have Yoshimitsu go to Imakumano Shrine.

institutions, including the Tōdaiji and Kōfukuji temples and the Kasuga Shrine. Little is known about the shows given by *sarugaku* and *dengaku* players, although it is assumed that they included music, dance, and other types of entertainment such as acrobatics and juggling. Because the troupes traveled throughout the provinces, performing at various temples and shrines and from town to town, they presumably presented material that appealed chiefly to popular tastes. But *dengaku*, at least, was also much appreciated by members of the upper classes, including the military leaders of the Kamakura and Ashikaga bakufu. For example, the last of the Hōjō regents, Takatoki (1303–33), is said in *Taiheiki* to have brought to ruin his house and the military regime at Kamakura because of his passion for dogfighting and *dengaku*.[23]

By Yoshimitsu's time, *sarugaku* and *dengaku* had quite likely become similar to each other. Yoshimitsu was drawn to *sarugaku* mainly because of Kan'ami's fame as both a playwright and an actor, about whom he may have first heard from Sasaki Dōyo. Yoshimitsu's extension of patronage to Kan'ami, the twelve-year-old Zeami, and their Kanze troupe of Yamato Province is the most conspicuous example of a process whereby the patronage of both *sarugaku* and *dengaku* troupes was largely shifted from religious institutions to warrior leaders.

A courtier writing in his diary expressed outrage that Yoshimitsu not only gave material support to *sarugaku* performers, whom he dismissed as lowly fellows "little better than beggars," but also consorted with them. The direct cause of the courtier's outrage was an occasion when Yoshimitsu, attending the Gion festival, shared his mat with Zeami and ate with the boy from the same plate.[24] Yoshimitsu's liking for the young Zeami seems to have been exceeded only by that of Nijō Yoshimoto who, in a remarkable letter recently discovered, spoke of him in terms that could only have sprung from a passionate love. To Yoshimoto, Zeami was a dreamlike vision who had stepped out of *Genji monogatari*, a youth of infinite grace and elegance of manner who was not only wonderfully talented as an actor but was also skilled in *kemari* (football) and the composition of *waka* and *renga*.[25]

There are at least two important points to be noted regarding Zeami's personal relationship with Yoshimitsu and Yoshimoto. First, it was possible during the medieval age for an actor like Zeami, even though of

23 Helen Craig McCullough, trans., *The Taiheiki: A Chronicle of Medieval Japan* (New York: Columbia University Press, 1959), pp. 131–3.
24 From *Gogumaiki*, the journal of Sanjō Kintada.
25 See Toita Michizō, *Kan'ami to Zeami* (Tokyo: Iwanami shoten, 1969), pp. 152–53.

humble birth, to attain access to members of both the warrior and the courtier elites solely on the basis of talent and professional achievement. (Other commoner artists, such as *renga* masters, shared this opportunity to mingle with the elite of the land and also enjoyed much greater freedom of activity and movement than did the lower classes as a whole.) Second, access to courtiers and warrior leaders helps explain how Kan'ami, Zeami, and their fellow playwrights acquired the classical education – indeed, erudition – necessary to compose the masterpieces of the noh theater that have come down to us today. Nijō Yoshimoto spoke in his letter as though Zeami was already learned when he met him, but surely Yoshimoto himself played an instrumental role in educating the precocious youth in the literature and other arts of the court tradition.

The major elements of the noh theater as it evolved from Yamato *sarugaku* during the Kitayama epoch were a type of acting known as *monomane* (the "imitation of things"), a style of dance called *kusemai*, and the aesthetic quality of *yūgen*. From what we can judge of the plays of Kan'ami and his contemporaries (most of Kan'ami's extant plays were reworked by Zeami), they were centered on *monomane* in the form of dramatic narratives based on the lives of such perennially popular figures of history and legend as Ono no Komachi, the Soga brothers, and Minamoto Yoshitsune and his mistress Shizuka.[26] Although gods, demons, and other unearthly characters appeared in them, these plays were essentially "realistic plays" (*genzaimono*), insofar as the main personages were usually portrayed as living humans.

Kan'ami is given chief credit for transforming Yamato *sarugaku* into noh by incorporating into it, first, the *kusemai* dance and, second, the *yūgen* aesthetic, which had theretofore been associated with the *sarugaku* troupes of Ōmi Province rather than those of Kan'ami's Yamato.[27] But Kan'ami remained committed, even after he received the patronage of Yoshimitsu, to *sarugaku* as a theater for all classes, and he continued to travel and perform in the provinces up to his death in distant Suruga in 1384. It was Zeami who accepted immersion in the elite social world of Kyoto and who, under the tutelage and

---

26 Ono no Komachi was a poet and famous beauty of the late ninth century, about whom many legends grew. The Soga brothers were warriors of the late twelfth century who carried out a celebrated vendetta against their father's killer. Their tale is told in *Soga monogatari*. Legends dealing with Yoshitsune and Shizuka can be found in the Muromachi-period work entitled *Gikeiki* (the record of Yoshitsune).
27 There were four *sarugaku* troupes in Yamato: the Hōshō, Komparu, Kongō, and Kanze troupes.

influence of people like Yoshimitsu and Yoshimoto, elevated noh to the supremely refined and courtly art we know today.

Two categories of plays that best illustrate how Zeami changed noh are "warrior plays" (*shuramono*) and "woman plays" (*kazuramono*).[28] Before Zeami, warrior plays, as they were to be later categorized, did not exist; it was no doubt in part to appeal to and flatter Yoshimitsu and other warriors that Zeami created the *shuramono*, which had as their main characters (*shite*) historical personages of the samurai class. Zeami's source for nearly all of his *shuramono* was *Heike monogatari*. But even as he recreated famous samurai heroes from this great war tale, he stressed their courtier rather than their martial qualities and used them as a means to evoke the past world of the courtiers.

A brilliant technique that Zeami employed in his plays to turn back time to the courtier past was *mugen*, the apparitional or ghostly dream, wherein the *shite*, often after first appearing on stage in such humble guise as a boatman, a reaper, or a village girl, reappears in the second act as the ghost of the famous person on whom the play is based. A good example of such a play by Zeami employing *mugen* is *Atsumori*, whose plot was drawn from the pathetic death (as told in *Heike monogatari*) of the young Taira general Atsumori at the hands of Kumagai Naozane at the battle of Ichinotani. The play begins with Kumagai, called by the Buddhist name Rensei which he took after becoming a priest to pray for Atsumori's spirit, announcing that he is going to visit the site of the battle of Ichinotani. The site, quickly reached by means of noh convention,[29] is on the shore of Suma on the Inland Sea, a place rich with associations from *Genji monogatari*, and the time is dusk.[30] Rensei meets a young reaper, whom he hears playing a flute just as Atsumori had the night before the Ichinotani conflict, and, on inquiring, learns that he is related to the Taira.[31] In the second act, as Rensei prepares to spend the night praying for Atsumori, the reaper reappears in a dreamlike sequence as the ghost of the fallen general. Announcing that ties to the world still bind him in death, Atsumori recounts the rise and fall of the Taira and his own destruction at the hands of Rensei (Kumagai). After performing the *kusemai* dance that is the climax to most noh plays, he attains salvation through the prayers of his former foe, Rensei.

---

28 The five categories of plays are god plays, warrior plays, woman plays, miscellaneous plays, and devil plays. 29 A few short steps can indicate the taking of a distant journey.
30 Prince Genji was exiled to Suma but later returned triumphantly to the court.
31 In the *Heike monogatari*, Kumagai says that he heard the sound of the flute at dawn on the day of the battle.

Nonomiya (The shrine in the fields) is a woman play by Zeami similar in structure to *Atsumori*. This play also begins with the ubiquitous traveling priest, although in this case one who remains nameless. He visits the shrine outside Kyoto where, in *Genji monogatari*, Prince Genji had once called on Lady Rokujō, his most jealous lover.[32] There the priest meets a village girl who later shows herself to be Rokujō's ghost, and by earnest prayers he helps the ghost overcome her still burning passion for Genji and gain release from the delusion of earthly existence.

The priest playing the secondary role (*waki*)[33] in each of these plays represents the audience or, indeed, all living people, and it is through this character that we are drawn into a mysterious world of death, dreams, and a remote past. It is above all an aristocratic world, for most of its main characters are taken from Heian history or literature, and its language at the highest moments is the language of *waka* poetry. Moreover, in its resplendent costuming and the elegant movements of the actors, some of them wearing masks, it is a visual recreation of the age of courtier glory.

In Zeami's woman plays, in particular, there is very little action in the conventional theatrical sense and virtually no conflict among the characters. These plays, which are regarded as the principal repositories of Zeami's ideal of *yūgen*, deal primarily with the emotions of the *shite*. Zeami achieved *yūgen* through poetic resonances cultivated from the age of *Shinkokinshū* and evocation of the courtier past by means of the ghostly dream. This is not to suggest that *yūgen* is to be found in Zeami's plays only in poetic resonances that brought depth and ghostly dreams with their intense sense of mystery, but simply that they were particularly important methods by which he created this aesthetic quality.

An aspect of the *yūgen* of Zeami and other noh playwrights that has received less emphasis by critics is its relationship to *sabi*. We noted examples of the *sabi* aesthetic of loneliness in poems from *Shinkokinshū*, one of which was by the priest Saigyō. *Sabi* was particularly associated in the medieval age with traveling priests, like Saigyō, whose journeys took them to desolate, remote areas, and who were thought to be especially sensitive to the insubstantiality and inherent pathos of life. Thus the *waki* in plays like *Atsumori* and *Nonomiya*, as they set out to visit sites near and far, but always lonely, establish from

---

32 The jealous spirit of Lady Rokujō was believed to have caused, for example, the death of Genji's first wife, Aoi.   33 A noh play usually focuses on only one main character, the *shite*.

the outset a strong atmosphere of *sabi*. In *Nonomiya* the sense of desolation and loneliness is also quickly advanced by the first entrance of the village girl, who declaims:

> Autumn has drawn to a close
> And the harsh winds blow;
> Colors so brilliant they pierce the senses
> Have faded and vanished.
> What remains now to recall the memories of the past?

The past that the girl yearns to recall was a time of "color and perfume"; but *Nonomiya*, representing the present, is described again and again in the play as lonely and desolate, a place "of withered stalks and leaves."[34] As one writer has observed, the balance between spring and autumn found in *Kokinshū* shifted in favor of the latter with the coming of the medieval age and *Shinkokinshū*.[35] By the time of Zeami and noh, autumn was by far the preferred season of poets, and a preponderance of plays, of the warrior and woman categories in particular, are set in that time of year.

The *sabi* of noh, whether or not regarded as a component of *yūgen*, is often presented in explicitly religious terms, and it is important to note that aesthetics and religion were virtually inseparable in plays of this kind. Death was always near at hand in the tumultuous medieval centuries, and *mugen* plays display an almost morbid fascination with the realm of the dead and the agonies that people may be forced to endure before achieving salvation.

Although Zeami was one of the brightest stars in the artistic firmament of the Kitayama epoch, his ascendancy rested largely on the personal patronage of Yoshimitsu, and when the latter died suddenly at the age of fifty in 1408, Zeami fell precipitously from favor. One reason was that the next shogun, Yoshimitsu's oldest son, Yoshimochi (1386–1428), bitterly resented his father and all who were associated with him because of the greater love that Yoshimitsu had bestowed upon another son, Yoshitsugu. Yoshimochi seems also to have genuinely preferred *dengaku* to *sarugaku*, and his taste was evidently indicative of a broad and continued liking for the more narrative, *monomane*-centered plays of both *dengaku* and *sarugaku*, in contrast with Zeami's highly aestheticized works with virtually no action.

34 "The Shrine in the Fields," in Donald Keene, ed., *Twenty Plays of the Nō Theatre* (New York: Columbia University Press, 1970).
35 Umehara Takeshi, "Yūgen to shi," in Hayashiya Tatsusaburō and Okada Yuzuru, eds., *Ami to machishū* vol. 8 of *Nihon bunka no rekishi* (Tokyo: Gakkyū, 1969), p. 190.

The misfortune that Zeami encountered after Yoshimitsu's death followed him for the remainder of his life, reaching its nadir with his exile in 1434. For reasons that are not clear, he was exiled to the island of Sado by Yoshimochi's successor as shogun, the cruel and tyrannical Yoshinori (1394–1441). Meanwhile, the famed Kanze troop of *sarugaku* noh also fell on hard times and was left nearly leaderless after the death in 1432 of Zeami's son and chosen successor, Motomasa. Yet Zeami never ceased working, and it was during these years that he wrote most of his critical works on noh that constitute the finest legacy of theoretical writing on art from the medieval age.

A form of theater that emerged simultaneously with noh was *kyōgen* (literally, "wild words"). One kind of *kyōgen* was simply an interval or separate scene (*ai-kyōgen*) in a noh play, generally used as a device by which a "person of the vicinity" appears to provide the *waki* with the background information necessary to understand the story of the main character. Another kind of *kyōgen* also evolved. These were independent skits of a farcical nature that were often presented on the same programs with noh. As suggested by the character for *kyō* in *kyōgen*, which connotes odd or unorthodox behavior, these skits probably first arose from informal mimicry and satirizing by noh players. In any event, broad, slapstick satire became the staple of this kind of *kyōgen* and can best be observed in skits in which servants outwit their daimyo masters. Some people in the mid-medieval age railed against these skits, claiming they encouraged insubordinate behavior. But the warrior authorities, who enthusiastically patronized *kyōgen*, evidently regarded them as harmless.

THE EVOLUTION OF NEW INTERIOR SETTINGS FOR THE ARTS

The practice of adopting professional names that included the syllables *ami* (a shortened form of *amida-butsu*, Amida Buddha), such as Kan'*ami* and Ze*ami*, was very common during the Muromachi period, especially among actors and artists. The first to adopt such names were members of the Ji sect of Pure Land Buddhism, some of whom attached themselves to armies during the war between the courts and, in addition to ministering to the wounded after battles, gathering up bodies, and conducting funeral services, also served as entertainers for the warriors during lulls in the fighting. By the Kitayama epoch the adoption of *ami* names had become conventional practice for artists and the like and did not necessarily imply formal association with the Ji or any other Buddhist sect.[36] Some of those who took *ami* names entered into the direct service of Shogun Yoshimitsu and his successors and formed a group known as the *dōbōshū* (companions). Although there are still many unanswered questions concerning the role of the *dōbōshū* during the Muromachi period, it appears that they began simply as menials who ran errands and performed miscellaneous chores for the shogun. They became important to cultural history when they were given responsibility for arranging and overseeing the social and ceremonial functions of the bakufu.

One manner in which Yoshimitsu attempted to transform the office of shogun into what I call a feudal kingship was the institutionalization of a calendar of formal events for warriors imitating the annual events (*nenjū-gyōji*) of the imperial court. Perhaps the most conspicuous of these events was the procession of the shogun (*onari*) at New Year's and other times to the Kyoto mansions of his leading vassals, who by this time were obliged to maintain nearly full-time residency in the capital. There were also important events held on special occasions, such as the six-day visit of Emperor Goen'yū (1358–93) to the Hana no Gosho in 1381 and the twenty-day visit of Emperor Gokomatsu (1377–1433) to Yoshimitsu's Kitayama estate in 1408.

The parties and celebrations that were arranged during such events were similar to the social affairs held by the earlier *basara* daimyo and included music, dance, *dengaku* and *sarugaku* (noh) performances, *waka* and *renga* compositions, and the drinking of tea. Besides promoting these arts, they helped create a new interior setting, known from contemporary records as the *kaisho* (banquet chamber), for socializing among members of both the warrior and courtier elites. The evolution of this new setting in the late fourteenth and early fifteenth centuries was so significant that historians often discuss the period in terms of *kaisho* culture. This is because several of the most important forms of Muromachi art and culture, such as *renga* and *chanoyu*, were premised on intimate social intercourse for which the *kaisho* and, from the late fifteenth century on, the *shoin* served as settings.[37] Moreover, as the *kaisho* and *shoin* rooms and appropriate decorations evolved, other

36 H. Paul Varley, "Ashikaga Yoshimitsu and the World of Kitayama: Social Change and Shogunal Patronage in Early Muromachi Japan," in John Whitney Hall and Takeshi Toyoda, eds., *Japan in the Muromachi Age* (Berkeley and Los Angeles: University of California Press, 1977), pp. 188–9.   37 The *shoin* room will be described later in this chapter.

arts, including ink painting (*sumi-e*) on vertical hanging scrolls and flower arranging, were also greatly advanced.

The shogun's *dōbōshū* played a central role in the development of both the *kaisho* and *shoin*. Although many *dōbōshū*, such as the famous "three *ami*" (Nōami, 1397–1471; his son Geiami, 1431–85; and his son Sōami, d. 1525), were artists in their own right,[38] their main function as a group was to establish criteria for the evaluation and display of *karamono*. The best source for information about these criteria and the work of the *dōbōshū* in this area is *Kundaikan sōchōki*. Begun by Nōami and completed by Sōami, it contains three sections: a listing and evaluation of some 150 Chinese artists and their works, illustrated descriptions of ways to display paintings and other *karamono*, and a discussion of the kinds of Chinese works of art and craft that should be shown to guests.

In the last years of his life, Yoshimitsu devoted much time to the construction of his Kitayama estate, where he lived after 1397 in the manner of a retired emperor. Of the many buildings that once made up this estate, only the Kinkakuji (Golden Pavilion) has been preserved into modern times, and it remains a striking symbol of the brilliance of the Kitayama epoch of cultural history.[39] Architecturally, the Kinkakuji is an amalgam of the older courtier (*shinden*) style of construction and newer features associated with the buildings of medieval Zen temples. Perhaps the strongest impression one receives when viewing the Kinkakuji, with its low ceilings and gently sloping roof, is of a much greater intimacy that in earlier Japanese buildings. Such intimacy seems quite in keeping with the new habits of social intercourse and standards of artistic tastes than brought about the *kaisho* during this same period.

SOCIAL IDEALS AND AESTHETIC VALUES OF THE HIGASHIYAMA EPOCH

Study of the cultural history of the mid-Muromachi period usually focuses on the two peaks of Yoshimitsu's Kitayama epoch and the late-fifteenth-century Higashiyama, or "Eastern Hills," epoch of the eighth Ashikaga shogun, Yoshimasa (1436–90). The obvious danger in concentrating on these two periods of cultural brilliance is the implication that little of significance occurred during the three intervening

38 For example, both Geiami and Sōami were noted painters.
39 The Kinkakuji was burned down by a deranged monk in 1950 but was rebuilt a few years later.

decades. Because shogunal patronage was so important to both the Kitayama and Higashiyama epochs, we might suppose that the shoguns of the interim period, Yoshimochi and Yoshinori, were less earnest in their support of the arts. This was by no means the case. Both Yoshimochi and Yoshinori were men of great artistic discrimination and taste, and they actively continued the *bun* policies inaugurated by Yoshimitsu.[40] For example, Yoshimochi and Yoshinori markedly expanded the warrior calendar of annual events, instituting, among other things, monthly *waka* and *renga* gatherings. Yoshinori was also responsible for urging the compilation of the twenty-first and last imperially authorized *waka* anthology, *Shinzoku kokinshū*, which was completed in 1439. Also, it was during Yoshinori's bakufu rule that Nōami became a member of the *dōbōshū* and played a leading role, along with the shogun, in the evolution of the first major form of the tea ceremony, *denchū chanoyu* (the aristocratic tea ceremony).

A simple division between the fourteenth and fifteenth centuries provides a periodization more meaningful than that yielded by focusing only on the Kitayama and Higashiyama eras, for the new century brought important developments that led to the Higashiyama flowering. These developments included the establishment of standards for evaluating and appreciating *karamono*, evolution of the *shoin* room setting, formalization of the preparation and serving of tea, a deepening nostalgia for the past, and the rise in popularity of linked verse among all classes to a nearly consuming passion.

We can also observe, by the beginning of the fifteenth century, a new emphasis on certain social ideals and aesthetic values of earlier origin but that collectively gave the Higashiyama epoch its special coloration. The main social ideals were those of the *inja* (or *tonseisha*, a person who has taken Buddhist vows and placed himself outside the official class ordering),[41] the wandering priest, and life in a hut (*sōan*). The aesthetic values included *sabi*, *wabi* (the austere and irregular), and *hiekareru* (cold and withered).

People who took Buddhist vows in early and medieval Japan did so with various intentions, the most important distinction being between those who joined particular sects or temples and devoted themselves to the true life of religion and those who took vows either to break free of the restraints imposed by a class system based almost exclusively on

---

40 Zeami, who had no reason to love Yoshimochi, said that he possessed finer taste than did Yoshimitsu.

41 *Inja* means, literally, a "hidden person," whereas *tonseisha* means a "person who has withdrawn from the world." The closest English equivalent to these terms is *eremite*.

birth or to avoid the normal duties and responsibilities of society. The second group of priests are commonly known as *inja* or *tonseisha* and included (among those who have already appeared in this chapter) Saigyō, Kamo no Chōmei, Kan'ami and Zeami, and the members of the shogunal *dōbōshū*. Some *inja*, such as Saigyō, gained distinction through their frequent travels throughout the country. In the Japanese literary tradition, traveling implied at least two important things. First, it meant the opportunity to visit the famous sites of history and literature, view them firsthand, and express one's feelings about them, usually in verse. Second, it symbolized release from the ordinary social and material attachments of life and acceptance of human existence for what, in Buddhist terms, it really was – fleeting and insubstantial, a state of ceaseless flux.

The *inja* were also associated with the renunciation of material things by retirement to reclusive life in a hut. One of the most famous *sōan* in Japanese literature is Kamo no Chōmei's "ten-foot square" hut. Chōmei's desire, expressed so movingly in *Hōjōki*, to prepare himself for rebirth in the Pure Land by rejecting all worldly possessions and retreating to a bare existence in a tiny hovel, however, was not shared by most other *inja*. Rather, as we shall see in the discussion of *renga* and *chanoyu*, the *sōan* became more of an aesthetic than a religious ideal: It was not conceived by *inja* as a mean hovel but as a microcosmic setting of beauty based on *sabi*, *wabi*, and similar aesthetic tastes.

Sabi and *wabi* are probably the two key aesthetic terms of the fifteenth century. I wish to reserve further analysis of *wabi* until I discuss the *wabi* form of *chanoyu* that was first evolved by Murata Shukō (d. 1502) in the Higashiyama epoch. But it should be noted here that the two terms are commonly used together to connote a wide range of Muromachi-period tastes, including a preference for the austere, the old, the worn, the irregular, the imperfect, and the lonely. In general, we may think of *sabi* and *wabi* as representing the monochromatic aspect of the Muromachi period, as contrasted with the vividly colorful quality of Heian-period court culture.

One of the earliest depictions of the *sabi–wabi* realm of Muromachi culture is to found in *Tsurezuregusa* (Essays in idleness), written in the early 1330s by Yoshida Kenkō (1283–1350), a minor-ranking courtier and poet who became an *inja*. *Tsurezuregusa* is a miscellany (*zuihitsu*, or flowing brush) in the tradition of the mid-Heian-period *Makura no sōshi* (Pillow book) of Sei Shōnagon. It is characteristic of the *zuihitsu* genre that the author writes impressionistically rather than with any clear attempt to be logical. Kenkō certainly did not present a consistent or overall philosophy in *Tsurezu-regusa*, and commentators over the centuries have variously regarded it as a work of didacticism, aesthetics, and even social criticism.[42] Yet we can note some significant consistencies in *Tsurezuregusa*. Kenkō was always nostalgic for times gone by, proclaiming "a longing in all things for the past," and he was driven by an urge to preserve even the smallest of ancient practices and customs (*yūsoku kojitsu*).[43] In addition, Kenkō rigorously criticized ostentation and repeatedly urged simplicity of taste and moderation in behavior.

Perhaps the most important thing to be said about Kenkō is that he possessed an excellent "eye" for things, and in this sense his book is a treasure trove of medieval aesthetics. The following passages exemplify Kenkō's *sabi–wabi* sensibility:

A house, though it may not be in the current fashion or elaborately decorated, will appeal to us by its unassuming beauty – a grove of trees with an indefinably ancient look; a garden where plants, growing of their own accord, have a special charm; a verandah and an open-work wooden fence of interesting construction; and a few personal effects left carelessly lying about, giving the place an air of having been lived in. Somebody once remarked that thin silk was not satisfactory as a scroll wrapping because it was so easily torn. Ton'a replied, "It is only after the silk wrapper has frayed at the top and bottom and the mother-of-pearl has fallen from the roller that a scroll looks beautiful." This opinion demonstrated the excellent taste of the man. People often say that a set of books looks ugly if all volumes are not in the same format, but I was impressed to hear the Abbot Kōyū say, "It is typical of the unintelligent man to insist on assembling complete sets of everything. Imperfect sets are better." In everything, no matter what it may be, uniformity is undesirable. Leaving something incomplete makes it interesting, and gives one the feeling that there is room for growth.[44]

LINKED-VERSE POETRY

One of the most characteristic arts, and indeed fervid preoccupations, of the medieval age was linked-verse (*renga*) poetry. Because the greatest *renga* master, Sōgi (1421–1502), lived his life almost entirely during the fifteenth century, it is fitting to discuss the development of linked verse here.

The technique of dividing the *waka* into two discrete links of three

42 The Japanese of the Tokugawa period generally regarded *Tsurezuregusa* as a didactic work, whereas during the Meiji period its aesthetic content was stressed. More recently, scholars have made much of what they perceive as the social criticism in Kenkō's writing.
43 Donald Keene, trans., *Essays in Idleness* (New York: Columbia University Press, 1967), p. 29.
44 Ibid., pp. 10, 70.

lines of five, seven, and five syllables and two lines of seven syllables each dates back to the *Kojiki*, the oldest extant Japanese book.[45] But there was little experimentation in the use of such links until the Heian period. True *renga*, wherein several poets gathered together and alternately composed links of verse and joined them into chainlike sequences of a hundred or even a thousand or more, did not evolve until the early thirteenth century in the salon of the retired emperor Gotoba, compiler of the *Shinkokinshū*.

Renga remained popular among court poets for the rest of the Kamakura period. Meanwhile, the composition of linked verse also spread among members of the lower classes and was sometimes called *renga* "under the blossoms," because of the practice of holding parties on temple grounds in the spring to compose verses beneath the blossoming trees.

The widespread growth of a commoner tradition in *renga* caused considerable variations in the methods, purpose, and general quality of composition throughout the country. For example, an anonymously written satirical tract posted in Kyoto in 1334, a year after the overthrow of the Kamakura bakufu and during the Kemmu restoration, claimed that in the capital the vulgar Kamakura and elegant Kyoto styles of *renga* were being freely intermixed, distinctions between hereditary and newly formed *renga* schools were being ignored, and everyone deemed himself qualified to serve as a judge at versing competitions.[46] The authors of Kemmu *shikimoku*, a brief formulary of admonitions issued by the Ashikaga bakufu in 1336, asserted that people then were "addicted to the pleasure of loose women, and engage in gambling. . . . Under the pretext of holding tea parties and *renga* competitions, they make great wagers, and their expenses are beyond calculation."[47] We can deduce from this that *renga* versifying, like tea competitions, had become a popular diversion among the *basara* daimyo and others in the early Muromachi period.

Yet developments were also under way that merged *renga*'s aristocratic and commoner strains and established it as a recognized, serious art. The two people chiefly responsible for the *renga*'s success at this time were Nijō Yoshimoto (1320–88), the imperial regent and later confidant-adviser of Yoshimitsu, and the *inja* poet Gusai (or Kyūsai).

45 See Donald L. Philippi, trans., *Kojiki* (Princeton, N.J.: Princeton University Press, 1969), pp. 242–3. This so-called oldest *renga* contains the place name Tsukuba, and linked-verse poetry later became known as the way of Tsukuba.

46 The Nijō–Kawara lampoons in *Kemmu nenkan ki* in Hanawa Hokinoichi, ed., *Gunsho ruijū* (Tokyo: Zoku gunsho ruijū kanseikai, 1933), vol. 25, pp. 503–4.

47 *Gunsho ruijū*, vol. 22, pp. 33–34.

Working together, they compiled *Tsukubashū,* whose appearance in 1356 gave *renga* a status in poetry that had previously been reserved exclusively for *waka.* Although lacking the ancient tradition of *waka, renga* was thereafter regarded as a pursuit of significance and high artistic purpose.

Nijō Yoshimoto who wrote several pieces on the history and art of *renga,* expressed the belief that the work he, Gusai, and their contemporaries were doing was a coming-of-age for *renga,* an achievement of poetic maturity that would serve as a model for all linked verse in the future. Yoshimoto also sought to distinguish between the *renga*'s tradition (or relative lack of it) and that of the *waka:* "Although the way of *waka* is transmitted orally and in secret, *renga* – which has no fixed rules for versification from ancient time – is intended to give pleasure merely by arousing the emotions of those who join together in composition."[48] Yoshimoto further explained the essence of *renga* in these words:

The poet of *renga* does not seek to tie the idea of one moment in with that of the next but, like this fleeting world, shifts through phases of both waxing and waning, of sadness and joy. No sooner does he reflect on yesterday than today has passed; while thinking about spring it becomes autumn; and even as he admires a scene of new blossoms it turns into one of crimson leaves. Is this not proof that everything is impermanent, like scattered flowers and fallen leaves? In ancient times poets of *waka* pursued their way with such zeal that we have examples of one person who offered his life in return for the inspiration to write a superior poem and of another who died from criticism of his poetry. But in *renga* such things do not happen. Because the sole aim is to give pleasure to those who have gathered to compose verse, there is no room for such attachments and zeal. And because the poets exclude all extraneous thoughts from their minds, bad notions are not apt to arise.[49]

Above all, *renga* was conceived as a means for expressing the constant flow and changeability of life. As we have seen, impermanence was a religious and philosophical concept that underlay nearly all the thinking of the medieval age, and it evoked intense feelings about the evanescence of the beauties of nature on the one hand and of the fundamental pathos of human existence on the other. Yet, to the *renga* poet, nature's beauties were not entirely evanescent nor human existence entirely pathetic, and to dwell even on these presumed verities was to distort reality. In *renga,* the highest value was placed on movement and progression, and strict rules were formulated to ensure that

48 *Tsukuba mondō,* in Kidō Saizō, ed., *Renga ronshū* (Tokyo: Iwanami shoten, 1961), p. 80.
49 Ibid., pp. 82–83.

poets steadily advanced from one theme to another. Some scholars have likened *renga* to modern jazz. In much the same way as jazz musicians harmonize extemporaneously, medieval *renga* poets sought to blend their verses with those of others, even to the point of subordinating their own creativity.

Although some famous *renga* are contained within multiverse sequences, many anthologies, such as *Tsukubashū*, have their verses arranged in pairs. As a rule, the first verse of each pair is anonymous, and the second is identified by its composer's name. *Renga* poets were thus given the opportunity to respond to the verses of others. Here, for example, is an anonymous verse and Nijō Yoshimoto's response:

> Flying squirrels
> Screeching in the mountains!
> The moon sinks
> Below the treetops
> Of the forest at dawn.[50]

In this poem Yoshimoto used a device he much favored when composing responses to action or sound-oriented verses. Rather than seek to explain why the squirrels were screeching or what their screeching might mean, he simply provided a visual setting for the verse. The image of the moon sinking as dawn breaks over the forest creates an eerie impression that heightens our awareness of the sound of the squirrels.

As Yoshimoto and others were advancing the literary status of *renga* in the late fourteenth century, an important institutional basis was also established through its association with the Kitano Shrine in Kyoto. This shrine was dedicated to the spirit of the Heian-period scholar and statesman Sugawara no Michizane (845–903), and the Ashikaga had formed close affiliations with it. It became the location of poetry sessions known as Kitano *hōraku renga*, or "linked verse for the entertainment of the gods," that were regarded in Muromachi times as the most important formal occasions for *renga* composition.

Kitano *hōraku renga* began about 1391, when the shogun Yoshimitsu sponsored and attended, along with his usual kingly retinue of courtiers, daimyo, ecclesiastics, and others, a gala affair that not only set the precedent for an annual *renga* event at Kitano but also inspired daimyo to hold similar affairs at the shrine. In this way, the Kitano Shrine became the undisputed center of *renga*, with sessions most commonly held on the twenty-fifth of the month, the day when Michizane, who

50 *Tsukubashū*, no. 384.

became apotheosized as the god of *renga*, died. To handle such bustling *renga* activity, the bakufu founded an office entitled Magistrate of the Kitano *kaisho* (Kitano *kaisho bugyō*) and, by combining appointment to it with the designation of *renga* master (sōshō), made the office tantamount to poet laureate of *renga* in Japan.

It was the *renga*'s good fortune to be championed by so illustrious a courtier as Nijō Yoshimoto, who may have been individually responsible for its acceptance as a major art. Interestingly, the commoner strain represented by Gusai also had its most pronounced influence on *renga* during Yoshimoto's day. Although many linked-verse masters of later times were of low social origin, they often became the leading advocates of a more classically oriented, aristocratic poetry. In other words, they sought to elevate *renga* to elite status in much the same way that Zeami raised *sarugaku*.

Linked-verse poets of the Higashiyama epoch regarded the Eikyō period (1429–40) of the shogun Yoshinori as the starting point of a new flourishing of *renga* that climaxed during their own age. One reason for this flourishing was the active patronage of Yoshinori. More fundamentally, it occurred as part of the antiquarianism in scholarship (*wagaku*) and culture in general that grew in intensity from about this time. In their study of the ancient literary masterpieces of the Heian period, *wagaku* scholars (some of the best known of whom, like Sōgi, were also *renga* masters) strongly influenced the aesthetic tastes of the age by contributing to a reenunciation of the classical courtier vision of beauty. In this regard, we should keep in mind that Zeami did most of his theoretical writing on aesthetics and the art of noh during roughly the same period.

The enduring ties between *waka*, the richest repository of the courtier vision of beauty, and *renga* may be illustrated by reference to Sōzei (d. 1455), one of the leading linked-verse poets of the Eikyō period, and his relationship to the *waka* master Shōtetsu (1380–1458). It was said that "upon meeting the noted master Shōtetsu, he [Sōzei] studied *Genji monogatari* and acquired a deep understanding of the way of poetry. He selected his models for *renga* on the basis of the great knowledge he came to possess and prized especially the *ushin-yūgen* style of ancient times."[51]

Another student of Shōtetsu and one of the finest linked-verse poets in Japanese history was Shinkei (1406–75), who not only stressed the

---

51 These remarks were made by Sōgi. *Azuma mondō* in Kidō, ed., *Renga ronshū*, pp. 208–9. *Ushin* means "elegant."

inseparability of *waka* and *renga* but also asserted that poetic inspiration was equal to Buddhist enlightenment. Such an assertion was in keeping with the syncretic thinking of the Muromachi period, when it was commonplace, for example, to argue the congruence of Buddhism, Shinto, and Confucianism or to seek to enhance one's artistic way – whether it be poetry, flower arrangement, or incense – by enshrouding it with the divine.

As analyses of medieval taste, Shinkei's critical writings on *renga*, including *Sasamegoto* (Whisperings, 1463), are second in quality only to the works of Zeami on noh. Imbued with the aesthetic of *yūgen* through his study of *waka* under Shōtetsu, Shinkei expressed the conviction that the highest level of *yūgen* was in the sphere of the cold, withered, and lonely:

When a master poet of the past was asked how poetry should be composed, he replied: "Grasses on the withered moor/The moon at dawn."
This was his way of saying that one should concentrate on things that cannot be expressed with words and should become aware of the sphere of the cold and lonely (*hie-sabi*). The poems of those who have attained the highest level in the art of poetry are invariably in the cold and lonely style. Thus, in response to a verse like "Grasses on the withered moor," one should always reply with a line of similar feeling such as "The moon at dawn."
In teaching poetry, the ancients urged that the following poem [by Minamoto no Saneakira] be kept in mind as a model for composing in this style:

> Faintly it beams,
> The light of the moon
> At dawn.
> Crimson leaves blow down
> With the piercing mountain wind.[52]

Shinkei entered Buddhist orders in infancy, but unlike the more typical artist-priest kind of *inja*, he remained devoutly committed to his priestly responsibilities throughout his life. This was one reason that he participated in public *renga* gatherings to a much lesser degree than did most other poets. Another reason, it appears, was that Shinkei was less interested in the composition of multiverse *renga* sequences than in the construction of the basic statement-and-response links (known as *tanrenga*, or short *renga*). He approached linked verse with an extraordinary intensity and evidently felt ill at ease in sessions where it was necessary to mute this intensity of feeling to achieve an overall emotional balance among the participants.

---

52 Shinkei, *Sasamegoto*, in Kidō, ed., *Renga ronshū*, p. 175.

Like many others of the world of art and culture in Kyoto, Shinkei left the capital at the outbreak of the Ōnin War (1467–77), a conflict that reduced the city almost totally to ashes. Filled with a longing for Kyoto, Shinkei traveled through the eastern and northern provinces and finally died, a virtual exile, in the province of Sagami in 1475. It was a fitting, if poignant, end for a poet so inspired by the aesthetic values of the cold and lonely.

During his travels in the east and north, Shinkei frequently met and perhaps gave instruction to Sōgi, a person and poet of a considerably different stamp. Almost nothing is known about Sōgi's birth and early life, as he did not mention them in his writings, a fact that suggests he was of low origin. There is, however, evidence that at a young age he took Zen vows at the Shōkokuji, one of the Kyoto *gozan* temples. Unlike Shinkei, Sōgi used his *inja* status primarily to move in social circles from which he would otherwise have been barred. Thus, we find him meeting and studying with such luminaries of Kyoto society, art, and religious life as the *waka* poet Asukai Masachika (1417–90), the *wagaku* scholar Ichijō Kanera (1402–81), and the Shinto theologian Urabe Kanetomo (1435–1511).

Like Saigyō, Sōgi was one of the great traveling poets of Japanese history. In his journeys he visited the domains of such prominent daimyo as Saitō Myōshun of Mino, Ōta Dōkan (1432–86) of Musashi, and Ōuchi Masahiro of Yamaguchi. But probably Sōgi's closest relationship in the provinces was with the Uesugi clan of distant Echigo, which he visited on nine occasions between the late 1470s and 1500. Provincial chieftains cherished the visits of people like Sōgi, who were bearers of Kyoto art and culture, and they undoubtedly recompensed them well. In this sense, Sōgi's traveling was good business. But it also greatly nourished his art in a very special way. Poets like Saigyō, Sōgi, and Bashō (1644–94) did not journey into the provinces simply in quest of random inspiration from the beauties of nature. Rather, they "sought what the ancients sought"; they attempted to experience nature through classical eyes, as the great poets of the past had experienced it.

Sōgi's fame as a *renga* master was equaled by his eminence as a *wagaku* scholar. *Wagaku*, as we shall see in the discussion of Ichijō Kanera, came especially into demand during and after the Ōnin War, when nostalgia for the past became ever greater as a result of the war's appalling destruction. Sōgi lectured on such works as *Genji monogatari* and *Ise monogatari* to both courtiers and warriors and wrote, among other things, a tract on *Genji monogatari* that has been recognized as the first attempt to deal with a *wagaku* masterpiece in terms of its overall structure and content.[53]

Whereas Shinkei was noted for the brilliance of his short *renga*, Sōgi's greatness as a poet lay in the fact that he treated *renga* as truly *linked* verse. Of the major surviving *renga* sequences from the fifteenth century, nearly all were composed either by Sōgi independently (*dokugin*) or by poetic groups in which he participated. Sōgi was invariably the central figure at any *renga* gathering because he devoted himself so fully to the spirit of linking verses together. Rarely intruding his personal sentiments, he sought in his poetry to reveal the classical vision of beauty he cherished most and, at the same time, to maintain the poetic rhythm that was the essential quality of *renga*.

The most famous of all *renga* sequences is known as "The Three Poets at Minase" (Minase *sangin*) and was composed in 1488 by Sōgi and his disciples Shōhaku (1443–1527) and Sōchō (1448–1532) at a palace once used by Emperor Gotoba at Minase Village, Settsu Province. The opening verses of this one-hundred-link poem illustrate the best qualities of medieval renga:

Sōgi:	Snow clinging to slope, On mist-enshrouded mountains At eveningtime.
Shōhaku:	In the distance water flows Through plum-scented villages.
Sōchō:	Willows cluster In the river breeze As spring appears.
Sōgi:	The sound of a boat being poled In the clearness at dawn.
Shōhaku:	Still the moon lingers As fog o'er-spreads The night.
Sōchō:	A frost-covered meadow; Autumn has drawn to a close.
Sōgi:	Against the wishes Of droning insects The grasses wither.[54]

When Sōgi was at home in Kyoto, he lived in a *sōan* called Shugyokuan, which he had built in a bamboo grove in the Muromachi

53 Konishi Jin'ichi, *Sōgi* (Tokyo: Chikuma shobō, 1971), pp. 34–35. Previous *wagaku* studies had been restricted to analyses of word usage and the like.
54 See the next in Ichiji Tetsuo, ed., *Renga shū* (Tokyo: Iwanami shoten, 1960).

section of the capital. His construction of a *sōan* was in keeping with his status both as a Zen priest, however minimal his religious affiliations may have been, and as an *inja* poet. Although we know little about Shugyokuan, we can imagine that it was a hut only in name and was actually a residence, whatever its size, of the best quality. It was also sufficiently well appointed to be suitable, the records indicate, for entertaining guests from the most elite circles of Kyoto society. Shugyokuan was destroyed by fire in 1500, and in that same year Sōgi set out on what was to be his last journey. He died at Hakone in the eastern provinces in 1502, having dreamt the night before, we are told, of Fujiwara no Teika.

I have limited my discussion of *renga* to its development as an elegant (*ushin*) form of art. By Sōgi's time, elegant *renga* was certainly dominant, but we should note that an inelegant (*mushin*), comic type of linked verse evolved alongside the more conspicuous *ushin renga* and led the way to the emergence of both *haikai* and *haiku* in later centuries. A leading figure in the evolution of *mushin renga* was Sōchō, one of Sōgi's companion poets at Minase in 1488.

THE HIGASHIYAMA EPOCH AND THE SCHOLARSHIP OF NOSTALGIA

The shogun Yoshimasa is as closely associated with the Higashiyama epoch in medieval culture as Yoshimitsu is with the Kitayama. The differences in personality between the two men reflect the changes in tone and quality of the bakufu from one epoch to the other. Whereas Yoshimitsu was strong willed and domineering and exercised power more broadly than did any other Ashikaga shogun, Yoshimasa was negligent and careless in his duties and was easily swayed by others. Yet even a more forceful ruler could have done little, for by Yoshimasa's time the Ashikaga hegemony, founded on a balance of power between the shogun and the *shugo* daimyo, was in rapid decline. It was Yoshimasa's fate to preside over the bakufu as it moved toward and met disaster in the Ōnin War.

The Higashiyama epoch may be defined broadly as the second half of the fifteenth century or, more narrowly, as the decade and a half following the Ōnin War, when Yoshimasa, having retired as shogun, pursued a life of elegant leisure and reigned as the foremost patron of the arts and culture from his retreat in the Eastern Hills of Kyoto. Perhaps the narrower definition is preferable, because it emphasizes the horrendous consequences of the Ōnin War, during which Kyoto, the heart of Japanese cultural life, was virtually destroyed. The world must indeed have seemed a "cold and lonely" place as strife and disorder spread and the country fell into the age of war in the provinces (Sengoku *jidai*, 1478–1568). One reaction, at least among the elite circles of Japanese society, was to look to the past with ever-greater nostalgia, especially to the golden age of court life in the mid-Heian period. This nostalgia can be observed in nearly all the arts and drew increasing attention to *wagaku* scholarship, which had been evolving throughout the medieval age. It was such attention that elevated Ichijō Kanera, the greatest of the *wagaku* scholars, to the pinnacle of cultural life in the Higashiyama epoch.

A grandson of Nijō Yoshimoto, Kanera served for three terms as imperial regent. He established his reputation as a scholar during the 1420s and 1430s in the field of courtier customs and ceremonial (*yūsoku kojitsu*), and in 1438 he received the exceptional honor of being selected by Emperor Gohanazono (1419–70), probably at the urging of the shogun Yoshinori, to write both the Chinese and Japanese prefaces to the last imperially authorized anthology of *waka*, *Shinzoku kokinshū*.

One of the most productive periods of Kanera's life as a scholar was the decade of the Ōnin War, which he spent in Nara. Like many other prominent persons of religion, art, and culture, he fled Kyoto at that time, thus contributing to a movement of culture outward from the capital that continued long after the end of hostilities in 1477.[55] Meanwhile the provinces, where a new breed of independent warrior chieftains were establishing territorial controls, beckoned. Because they were conscious of the need to bolster their de facto military positions with an aura of cultural legitimacy and sincerely desired to advance their knowledge and artistic appreciation, these chieftains invited people like Kanera, Sōgi, and the painter Sesshū (1420–1506) to their domains to participate in and lend authority to their cultural activities. Such invitations gave tremendous impetus to the spread of higher learning and art throughout the country and demonstrated that fighting men in the medieval age were sensitive to the need to combine the *bun* and *bu* in rulership.

During his decade in Nara, Kanera completed major studies of *Genji monogatari* and *Nihon shoki*. He also visited the Kitabatake family in Ise Province and Saitō Myōchin, deputy constable to the daimyo

---

55 Others who left Kyoto during the Ōnin War were the *renga* master Shinkei, the Zen priest Ikkyū (1394–1481), the noh master Komparu Zenchiku (1405–68), and the painter Sesshū (1420–1506).

family of Toki, in Mino Province. As the Ōnin War neared its end, Kanera received repeated calls from Kyoto imploring him to return. Yoshimasa and his wife, Hino Tomiko (1140–96), were particularly insistent, and in the twelfth month of 1477 Kanera finally made his way back to the capital. He found himself in constant demand at both the imperial and shogunal palaces, where he regularly lectured on *wagaku* topics, and when he died in 1481 at the age of seventy-nine, he was hailed by one diarist as the finest scholar in Japan in five hundred years.[56]

After Kanera, the leadership of *wagaku* study at court fell to Sanjōnishi Sanetaka (1455–1537). A courtier of upper-middle rank, Sanetaka is remembered less for the quality of his scholarship than for the detailed diary he kept from 1474, during the Ōnin War, until 1536, a year before his death. *Sanetaka Kō ki* (The record of Lord Sanetaka) provides us with a fascinating view not only of Sanetaka's day-to-day activities but also of Kyoto during more than a half-century of the darkest and most tumultuous period in its history. Although there is no reason to suppose that all courtiers reacted to the events of the period precisely as Sanetaka did, his diary, as the record of a man who was at the center of cultural life, can be taken as a fair depiction of how the courtier class looked upon its world during the first half of the age of war in the provinces.

Sanetaka Kō ki provides a grim chronology of the grief inflicted on the residents of Kyoto during this age. In addition to the fighting of armies, there were constant outbreaks of fire (often set by arsonists), attacks by robbers, and pillaging by armed bands (*ikki*). In the seventh month of 1500, for example, fire swept through the city, destroying twenty thousand homes, including Sanetaka's; and in the fifth month of 1531 robbers were even able to make their way into the imperial palace.

Sanetaka and other members of the courtier and warrior elites sought escape from the harsh realities of life through a seemingly constant round of parties, noh performances, poetry gatherings, and other forms of entertainment. For the courtiers, however, even escape into pleasure brought sad reminders of their fallen state: On the occasion of a lavish affair at the shogunal palace in the third month of 1475 held by Yoshimasa's wife, Tomiko, and attended by the emperor, Sanetaka was obliged to remain in a separate room because he did not

56 *Jurin-in naifu ki*, 1481/4/2. Cited in Tōkyō teikoku daigaku, ed., *Dai Nihon shiryō* (Tokyo: Shiryō hensan gakari, 1927), ser. 8, vol. 13, p. 171.

have proper clothing. And when the shogun Yoshitane (1466–1523) departed from Kyoto in the eight month of 1491 on a military campaign to Ōmi, some courtiers could not call on him because their clothing was inadequate. By contrast, according to *Sanetaka Kō ki*, Yoshitane and his commanders attired themselves in dazzling finery.

To Sanetaka and his circle, a particularly fearful danger of the times was the destruction of books and manuscripts. Ichijō Kanera lost his personal library in the early days of the Ōnin War, and Sanetaka recorded similar losses by others during the years covered in his diary. The feeling grew that measures were required to ensure preservation of the cultural legacy of the past. One result was a mounting demand that copies be made of such classics as *Genji monogatari*, *Ise monogatari*, and both *waka* and *renga* anthologies. Sanetaka, who was both a scholar and fine calligrapher, was much sought after as a copyist by emperors, shoguns, and others. Brief works, like *Ise monogatari*, could be readily reproduced, and Sanetaka recorded in his diary having copied *Ise* many times. The reproduction of *Genji monogatari*, on the other hand, was a major undertaking that usually required a team of copyists, and Sanetaka, we learn, frequently took the lead in organizing teams to copy this most revered of all courtly writings.

One of the most interesting stories that Sanetaka tells in his diary is his relationship with the *renga* master Sōgi. Sōgi, thirty-four years Sanetaka's senior, had studied the *wagaku* classics with Ichijō Kanera, and in his later years he lectured on these to Sanetaka. It is a testament to the relative social mobility possible in the field of the arts and learning in the medieval age that we find a person of Sōgi's humble origins giving scholarly instruction to a courtier of Sanetaka's stature.

A major benefit to Sanetaka of his association with Sōgi was the receipt from the older man of the "*Kokinshū* Transmission" (*Kokin denju*). This transmission was a collection of arcane interpretations of obscure words, phrases, and names in the poems of the tenth-century anthology *Kokinshū* that had been passed down from early medieval times by the descendants of Fujiwara no Teika.[57] There were many such collections of arcana during the medieval age, but the *Kokinshū* Transmission was the most famous, and possession of it was thought to endow one with an almost magical insight into poetry. When Sanetaka received the written transmission in 1501, a year before Sōgi's death, he recorded the event in his diary in almost hushed tones of awe:

---

57 The *Kokinshū* transmission was passed down by the Nijō line of poets descended from Teika. It later came into the hands of the Tō, a warrior family from the Kantō that had married into the Nijō. Tō no Tsuneyori (1401–94) gave the transmission to Sōgi.

"Priest Sōgi's materials of the *Kokinshū* Transmission, including his notes . . . were delivered today in their entirety in sealed boxes . . . it was all handled in the greatest secrecy."[58]

Sanetaka obtained much-needed supplements to his income from Sōgi and others, who took copies he had made of the classics and other samples of his writing into the provinces, where they were eagerly awaited by the daimyo, their families, and their leading vassals. It is a plaintive commentary on the times that we find an entry in *Sanetaka Kō ki*, such as the one on 1509/2/4, in which Sanetaka records having sent passages copied from *Genji monogatari* by Emperor Gokashiwabara (1464–1526) to the wives of the Imagawa daimyo of Suruga and the Asakura daimyo of Echizen. "Appreciation money" was soon forthcoming from both Suruga and Echizen and was presumably forwarded by Sanetaka, through discreet channels, to the emperor.[59]

Unlike Ichijō Kanera, Sanetaka himself never ventured into the provinces. Yet his fame spread from one end of the country to the other, owing as much as anything else, it seems, to the yearning of people in these dark times for the classical culture and values of the ancient courtly tradition.

LANDSCAPE PAINTINGS AND GARDENS

A major theme of medieval aesthetics was the trend toward the monochromatic, toward a realm "transcending color," as the *renga* master Shinkei might have put it. Great encouragement was given to this trend by the importation from China of a form of painting in black ink that evolved during the Sung dynasty.

Works of Sung-style ink painting (*sumi-e*) were brought to Japan throughout the medieval age and were among the most prized of *karamono* during the Kitayama epoch. These paintings dealt with a variety of traditional Chinese subjects – people, flowers and birds, and landscapes – but it was the landscapes that most influenced the aesthetics of medieval Japan.

The Japanese, of course, already had a highly developed sense of landscape, articulated especially in their poetry. But nothing in their poetry or the other native arts prepared them to deal with the vast scale of many Sung landscapes, in which mountains tower awesomely

58 *Sanetaka Kō ki*, 1501/9/15.
59 Haga Kōshirō, *Sanjōnishi Sanetaka*, vol. 43 of *Jimbutsu sōsho* (Tokyo: Nihon rekishi gakkai, 1960), p. 159.

and craggy masses recede, one behind the other, into the remote distance. The landscape of Japan is less imposing, and when the Japanese began painting in the manner of the Sung landscape in the early fifteenth century, they succumbed entirely to the subject matter of their foreign models and reproduced monumental scenes based on what they imagined settings in China to look like.

The three most famous landscape painters of the fifteenth century were also monks of the Kyoto Zen temple Shōkokuji. The first, Josetsu, is a shadowy figure remembered primarily because of his "Catching a Catfish with a Gourd," a painting commissioned by the shogun Yoshimitsu. The inspiration for this painting came from a Zen riddle about catching a slippery fish with such an unlikely object as a gourd. The main historical interest of "Catching a Catfish," however, lies not in the foreground depiction of a man in tattered clothes, with gourd in hand, approaching a fish swimming in a stream but, rather, in the setting, which includes a hazy view of mountains in the distance. The picture as a whole conveys a feeling of spatial depth not found in earlier ink works by Japanese artists.

Josetsu's disciple and successor as painter-monk at the Shōkokuji was Shūbun, who flourished in the second quarter of the fifteenth century but is otherwise nearly as dim a person in history as is his teacher. Many extant paintings are attributed to Shūbun, but not one has been authenticated as his. For this reason, it is probably better to speak of paintings "in the Shūbun style" than of the paintings of Shūbun. The Shūbun style is an impressionistic, highly atmospheric way of representing imagined Chinese landscapes. Mountains appear to be suspended; cliffs jut precariously into space; and a pervasive mistiness makes it impossible to judge how the various elements in a painting might actually fit together. Painters in the Shūbun style did not intend to be realistic but aimed at capturing the essences of idealized Chinese settings. It was not until the time of Sesshū (1420–1506), the third great Shōkokuji painter of the fifteenth century, that the art of ink landscape finally became truly Japanese in both subject matter and feeling.

In 1467, the year the Ōnin War began, Sesshū went to Yamaguchi at the western end of Honshū and, under the patronage of the daimyo family of Ōuchi, even journeyed to China, where he was able to observe *sumi-e* at its source. Back in Japan, Sesshū never returned permanently to Kyoto but spent the remainder of his life either in the Yamaguchi region or traveling elsewhere in the provinces. He may be likened to Saigyō, Sōgi, and others of the medieval age, whose artistic awarenesses were enhanced by visiting famous sites and by long exposure to provincial life. Such exposure was evidently especially important to Sesshū, inspiring him to break free of the Shūbun school's imaginary visions of China and to depict landscapes from a distinctly Japanese perspective.

Rather than to the panoramic landscape work of the early Sung masters, Sesshū was attracted to the more narrowly focused, asymmetrically composed paintings of such later Sung artists as Ma Yüan and Hsia Kuei. In addition, Sesshū tended to flatten the surfaces of his landscapes, thus reducing the feeling of depth even in his depictions of distant vistas. The Japanese had always approached nature intimately, and we may speculate that Sesshū's de-emphasis of depth was more comprehensible and inherently congenial to Japanese tastes than were the vast scenes of the Shūbun style.

Ink painting influenced another major art of the Muromachi period, the *kare-sansui* or "withered landscape" garden. A Heian-period text on gardening, *Sakuteiki*, informs us that the chief concern in garden construction during the courtier age was the handling of water, both its flow in the form of streams and its coalescence as ponds. Several of the finest gardens of the Muromachi period, including the Saihōji (moss) garden and the gardens of Yoshimitsu's Golden Pavilion and Yoshimasa's Silver Pavilion, featured streams and ponds. From about mid-Muromachi times, however, primary attention was shifted from the element of water to the use of rocks in gardens. At the same time, partly as a result of the Kyoto region's limited sources from springs and mountain streams, water was represented increasingly by the use of sand. The *kare-sansui*, as they evolved in the later Muromachi period, were constructed mainly, and in some cases exclusively, of sand and rocks.

All the remaining *kare-sansui* of the Muromachi period are situated on the grounds of Zen temples, and the great majority are in Kyoto or its suburbs. The two most famous are the gardens at Daisenin of the Daitokuji temple and at the Ryōanji temple. The Daisenin garden contains unusually shaped and textured rocks that are arranged to depict mountains, islands, and a bridge under which sand (representing water) flows. Although the garden, which is L-shaped, is exceedingly small – no more than a few yards in any direction – it gives the feeling of great height and depth and may be likened to a painting in the Shūbun style. The Ryōanji garden, on the other hand, is severely abstract – only fifteen rocks scattered about on a surface of raked sand. It is comparable, perhaps, to a Sesshū painting in its minimization of depth.

THE CULTURE OF TEA

The medieval age in Japan brought a great diversification in the arts and culture, both in terms of new and more varied pursuits and of participation by new classes, including samurai, merchants, and even peasants. But equally significant was the fact that within this diversity, there was an exceptional degree of aesthetic unity, made possible chiefly through the continued appreciation of, and nostalgic yearning for, the courtier past. The main aesthetic terms of the medieval age – *yūgen, sabi, wabi* – had their roots in the Heian period or earlier. Although these terms led in the fourteenth, fifteenth, and sixteenth centuries to a stress on the monochromatic and the "cold, withered, and lonely" that seems outwardly to reject the Heian passion for color, the richness of these aesthetic concepts derives from the fact that they so strongly resonate the color and warmth of classical courtier tastes.

This aesthetic unity is nowhere better seen than in the culture of tea and the classic tea ceremony *(chanoyu)* around which it developed. As noted, tea was adopted as a beverage by all classes in Japan during the early medieval age. In the late fourteenth century it was used conspicuously in judging competitions *(tōcha)* at the social affairs of the *basara* daimyo. During the fifteenth century, the drinking of tea was removed from the realm of game playing and was gradually transformed into a serious pursuit.

The evolution of the *chanoyu* was inseparably linked to the creation of the *kaisho* and *shoin* rooms, for the *chanoyu* was never conceived as an activity to be pursued outside a carefully arranged and decorated setting. In the *kaisho* form of *chanoyu*, which first appears in the records during the time of the shogun Yoshinori, tea was prepared in another room or outside corridor and brought to the host and his guests in the *kaisho*. The utensils employed in the *chanoyu* and the works of art used to decorate the *kaisho* were "Chinese pieces" *(karamono)*, and their selection and handling reflected the more restrained, discriminating taste for *karamono* established by the *dōbōshū* and others in the fifteenth century.

A paucity of records makes it impossible to determine precisely when and how the *kaisho* tea ceremony was transformed into the *wabicha,*[60] although credit for the transformation is traditionally given to Shukō (or Jukō, d. 1502), a semilegendary person from the merchant class of Nara. The setting for the *wabicha* was the *shoin*. This room, which came into fashion during the Higashiyama epoch, had as its principal features *tatami* floor matting, *shōji* sliding doors, the *tokonoma* alcove, the *shoin* writing desk, and asymmetrical shelves (*chigaidana*). It has remained to the present day the prototype of the main room of a Japanese dwelling.

Shukō's preferred *shoin* was a four-and-a-half-mat (approximately nine-foot-square) room. In its confines he created a microcosmic world within which the host, in a precisely arranged aesthetic setting, prepared and served tea to his guests. As the process of serving tea evolved from Shukō's day, it became an act symbolizing the renunciation of the material and the celebration of the spiritual values of life. These spiritual values had both religious and aesthetic origins and were most commonly articulated by the late medieval Japanese in terms of Zen Buddhism and the aesthetic of *wabi*.

One of the most difficult problems in the study of medieval culture is to assess the influence on it of Zen Buddhism. The problem arises primarily because of the tendency of many commentators in the centuries since the medieval age to give excessive credit to Zen for molding medieval tastes and sentiments. If there is a single point that stands out most clearly in a survey of the culture of medieval Japan, it is that aesthetics of the age evolved directly from earlier times. The criteria of Zen in the arts – simplicity, suggestion, irregularity – coincided with feelings that were also indigenously Japanese and had always governed native tastes. Thus Zen (Ch'an) Buddhism, brought from China in the late twelfth and thirteenth centuries, found a particularly congenial environment in which to flourish culturally. But it was not until the sixteenth century that Zen was truly extolled as a major influence on the arts, especially on the culture of tea. We can see this, for example, in a phrase that gained wide currency at the time, that "tea and Zen have the same flavor" (*cha-Zen ichimi*).

Wabi derives from the verb *wabu*, whose original meaning was "to decline into a sad and helpless state." An early use of *wabu* as a term of aesthetic value appears in the noh play *Matsukaze* by Kan'ami (reworked by Zeami). In the play, an itinerant priest (the *waki*) visits Suma, where he meets two sisters, Matsukaze and Murasame, who

---

60 I know of no single word in English that can serve as a translation for *wabi*, although "austerity" is probably as good as any. *Cha* means tea.

had once received the affections of a courtier exiled to their lonely coast and are now consigned to live as ghosts because of their ceaseless yearning for him. The priest requests that the sisters put him up for the night, but they at first refuse because their hut, "with its rough pine pillars and bamboo fence," is too wretched to accommodate a guest. But the priest persuades the sisters to let him in, by assuring them that he is accustomed to poverty. He further observes that any sensitive person would derive pleasure from living "humbly and in solitude" in such a setting. Although the use of *wabu* in its adverbial form as *wabite* in this passage from *Matsukaze* is vague and could easily be translated with words other than "humbly and in solitude," it conveys much of the tone of the *wabi* aesthetic that later became central to the culture of tea.[61]

In a letter to one of his disciples, Shukō wrote:

In pursuing this way [of tea], greatest attention should be given to harmonizing Japanese and Chinese tastes. How absurd it is these days for those who are inexperienced to covet with self-satisfaction such things as Bizen and Shigaraki wares on the grounds that they possess the quality of being "cold and withered" (*hiekareru*).[62]

From these remarks we can deduce that Shukō opposed outright rejection of the aesthetic values of the *kaisho* tea ceremony, based on the connoisseurship of *karamono*, and disapproved of too impetuous an espousal of the *wabi* range of tastes. Many commentators have interpreted the remarks to mean that Shukō, although he may have originated *wabicha*, still had one foot in the earlier world of *karamono*.

The historical role of perfecting *wabicha* as the classic tea ceremony fell to two men of merchant stock from the city of Sakai, Takeno Jōō (1502–55) and Sen no Rikyū (1522–91). Rikyū, the most celebrated tea master in Japanese history, preferred as a setting for *wabicha* a room of only two mats in size, which could accommodate no more than two or three people. He dispensed with the customary tea stand (*daisu*) and placed his utensils, including dark *raku* bowls and bamboo whisks and ladles, directly on the floor. Rikyū also espoused a philosophy of tea that came to be regarded as the very essence of *wabicha*. His sentiments, as recorded by a disciple, were as follows:

Chanoyu performed in a plain hut is above all an ascetic discipline, based on the Buddhist law, that is aimed at achieving spiritual deliverance. To be

---

61 "Matzukaze," in Keene, ed., *Twenty Plays of the Nō Theatre*, pp. 26–27.
62 "The Furuichi Letter," in Hayashiya Tatsusaburō, ed., *Kodai-chūsei geijutsu ron* (Tokyo: Iwanami shoten, 1973), p. 448.

concerned about the quality of the dwelling in which you serve tea or the flavor of the food served with it is to emphasize the mundane. It is enough if the dwelling one uses does not leak water and the food served suffices to stave off hunger. This is in accordance with the teachings of the Buddha and is the essence of the *chanoyu*. First, we fetch water and gather firewood. Then we boil the water and prepare tea. After offering some to the Buddha, we serve our guests. Finally, we serve ourselves.[63]

The achievements of Jōō and Rikyū in the evolution of *wabicha* signified the prominence of members of the rich merchant class in the cities of Kyoto, Nara, and Sakai in late medieval art and culture. Jōō's wealth enabled him to study literature with Sanjōnishi Sanetaka, the great *wagaku* scholar of the early sixteenth century. Rikyū was one of several tea masters of Sakai employed by Oda Nobunaga and Toyotomi Hideyoshi as they led the way to the unification of Japan in the second half of the sixteenth century.

Rikyū's greatest fame came in the service of Hideyoshi, when he not only assumed the role of grand arbiter of taste in matters concerning the culture of tea but also wielded substantial power as an intimate of the hegemon. Rikyū's power was made possible by practices of the age of unification that can collectively be called the "politics of tea" and that gave rise to the use of a tea master in political negotiations as well as in the ceremonies of rule.

THE AZUCHI−MOMOYAMA EPOCH

If a date must be selected to mark the end of the medieval age, the best choice is probably 1568, for this was the year when Nobunaga entered Kyoto and began the process of unification that was completed by his successor, Hideyoshi, in 1590. The period of unification under Nobunaga and Hideyoshi was a heroic time of growing self-confidence and expansiveness of spirit. Warlords built great castles and decorated them with painted screens and door panels suffused with brilliant colors; new vistas to the outside world were opened by the arrival of European traders and missionaries; and the establishment of order on a national scale promised joys in this life that served to dispel the gloom and other-worldliness of the medieval age.

It is fitting that this new age should be known in cultural history by the name of Azuchi−Momoyama, a name taken from the location of No-bunaga's principal castle at Azuchi on Lake Biwa and of one of Hide-

---

63 *Nambōsōkei*, *Nambōroku*, in Sen Sōshitsu, ed., *Sadō koten zenshū*, vol. 4 (Kyoto: Tankōsha, 1956), p. 3.

yoshi's strongholds at Momoyama to the south of Kyoto.[64] The castle was the preeminent symbol of these exciting times and represented the tangible glories of the chieftains who led the way to unification. Despite their imposing appearances, the castles of the Azuchi–Momyama epoch were not constructed only for defense. Daimyo wished to develop commercially thriving towns around their fortresses and therefore often selected castle sites more on the basis of economic than military considerations. But above all, the typical Azuchi–Momoyama daimyo conceived of the castle as a means to impress the world with his grandeur and power. Thus, although castles of the time were noteworthy because of their broad, deep moats and huge protective walls made of stone, their most distinctive features were multistoried donjons or keeps, which were of little use militarily but were highly decorative and showy. Designed to dazzle the eye and give the appearance of "reaching to heaven," the donjons were often painted a glistening white or, as in the case of Nobunaga's Azuchi castle, were rendered in colors. Luis Frois, a Jesuit missionary who spent many years in Japan, gave the following description of the exterior appearance of the donjon at Azuchi Castle:

> Some of the stories are painted white with their windows varnished black according to Japanese usage and they look extremely beautiful, others are painted red, others blue, while the uppermost one is entirely gilded. This *tenshu* (donjon) and all the other houses are covered with bluish tiles which are stronger and lovelier than any we use in Europe; the corners of the gables are rounded and gilded, while the roofs have fine spouts of a very noble and clever design. In a word the whole edifice is beautiful, excellent and brilliant.[65]

The interiors of the donjons were also decorated for conspicuous display. Indeed, donjon rooms and the rooms in other castle buildings were among the most important settings for the visual arts in the Azuchi–Momoyama epoch and, in them, on the formats of folding screens and sliding doors, could be found the work of the leading artists of the day.

DECORATIVE SCREEN AND DOOR-PANEL PAINTING

The main kind of painting in the late medieval age was, as noticed, landscape work in a monochrome ink style (*sumi-e*) that had developed

---

64 The dates most commonly used for the Azuchi–Momoyama epoch are 1568, when Nobunaga began unification, and 1615, the year when Hideyoshi's heir was destroyed by Tokugawa Ieyasu at the battle of Osaka Castle.
65 Michael Cooper, ed., *They Came to Japan* (Berkeley and Los Angeles: University of California Press, 1965), p. 134.

in China during the Sung and Yüan dynasties. Landscapes by medieval Japanese masters like Shūbun and Sesshū were suffused with a deeply religious feeling that emerged from the pervasive Buddhist sentiment of impermanence and from the desire of painters, poets, and other artists to discover some ultimate truth about life beyond this transitory existence. Although certain paintings revealed the more violent aspects of nature and the weather, for the most part the medieval ink landscapes depicted tranquil, quietistic scenes.

The form of decorative screen and door-panel painting that evolved in the Azuchi–Momoyama epoch differed from the preceding, mainstream work of medieval artists, in several important respects: (1) Its principal subject matter was "flowers and birds," which, along with "landscapes" and "people," was a traditional category of Chinese art; (2) it was rendered chiefly in brilliant colors, including a dazzling gold leaf used for backgrounds; (3) it showed little if any of the religiosity of medieval painting; (4) its artists frequently imbued their works with a great dynamism, through such means as the posturing of animals and the configuration of enormous trees, that was strikingly different from the quietism of most medieval landscapes; (5) it was decorative in the sense that objects were deliberately placed to achieve balance (or a conscious imbalance) of design; and (6) it was a monumental art because the artists often had to paint on huge formats, such as door panels (*fusuma*) that comprised entire walls of castle rooms.

The spectacular return of color to art distinguished, perhaps more dramatically than anything else, the aesthetic difference between the medieval age and the Azuchi–Momoyama epoch. Yet even during the flourishing of the monochrome ink landscape, color had not been entirely absent from Japanese painting. Throughout the medieval age, for example, artists of the ancient Yamato-e school, represented especially by the Tosa line of artists, had continued to paint in colors, producing studies based on themes from classical Heian-court literature, the lives of great religious leaders, and the histories of Buddhist temples and Shinto shrines. In stylistic terms, the decorative screen and door panel art of the Azuchi–Momoyama epoch was a blending of the monochromatic Sung–Yüan Chinese school, which had produced the great medieval landscapes (although artists of this school also painted flowers and birds and people), and the color-oriented Yamato-e tradition.

This blending was achieved chiefly by the Kanō line of painters, of whom Eitoku (1543–90) was the dominant figure in the first half of the Azuchi–Momoyama epoch.[66] The most important event in Eitoku's career was undoubtedly his selection by Nobunaga to decorate the interiors of the rooms in the donjon of Azuchi Castle. Regrettably, Azuchi Castle was destroyed shortly after Nobunaga's assassination in 1582, and none of the screen and door-panel paintings done by Eitoku and his assistants survived. But we do have a rather detailed catalogue of these paintings and can surmise what they looked like from other contemporary works by Eitoku and the Kanō line.[67] By far the most numerous of the Azuchi paintings were those of "flowers and birds," although there were also a number in the "people" category, consisting primarily of pictures of famous hermits, sages, and immortals of Chinese history and legend. Interestingly, there appears to have been only one pure landscape in all of the Azuchi works.

One reason for the preference for flowers and birds in the new decorative art of the Azuchi–Momoyama epoch was that this subject lent itself particularly well to filling up large spaces, as Eitoku effectively demonstrated in such famous paintings as the cypress tree screen. This screen, consisting of eight panels, depicts the bottom portion of a massive tree whose twisted trunk and limbs spread out from the lower right side of the painting and reach nearly to the opposite, left side. In a manner characteristic of Azuchi–Momoyama decorative art, Eitoku's cypress tree is set against a brilliant background of gold-leaf clouds, a stream of dark blue water, and carefully detailed rocks.

Eitoku's greatness lay in the fact that his art forcefully conveyed the spirit of the age of unification. It was he who took the last major step away from the restraint and quietude of medieval painting into the realm of gorgeous colors and dynamic motifs rendered on monumental screen and door-panel formats. Fittingly, Eitoku died in 1590, the very year that Hideyoshi completed Japan's unification. His successors, living in a new state of national peace (which was secured in 1600 by the founding of the Tokugawa bakufu), modified the raw energy of Eitoku's style and produced a type of painting, subdued and refined by the standards of decorative screen and door-panel art, that was perhaps more suitable to the sentiment of their age of political and social stability.

66 The Kanō family line was begun by Masanobu (1434–1530), who in the late fifteenth century was appointed by the Ashikaga bakufu as the official artist in the Chinese manner of painting.
67 The catalogue appears in *Shinchōkō ki* (Public chronicle of Nobunaga). Its contents are summarized by Tsugiyoshi Doi, *Momoyama Decorative Painting* (New York: Weatherhill–Heibonsha, 1977), pp. 69–79.

GENRE PAINTING AND AZUCHI–MOMOYAMA HUMANISM

A second major form of painting that evolved in the Azuchi–Momoyama epoch was genre art, or the depiction of people in their everyday activities of work and play. Genre scenes can be found in earlier Japanese paintings, especially in the narrative scrolls of the Yamato-e tradition. But it was not until the sixteenth century that such scenes became a principal subject of painting.

One of the earliest types of genre painting was the *rakuchū–rakugai zu* or "scenes inside and outside Kyoto."[68] These scenes, originally done as distant panoramas, gradually became intimate views of the city, its buildings, and the bustling activities of its inhabitants. Kanō Eitoku, using essentially the same style and colors as in his decorative work, did an especially fine *rakuchū–rakugai zu* on a pair of six-panel screens that contain some fifteen hundred people in an intricate mosaic of movement and behavior. These screens are a brilliant piece of art and place Eitoku in the forefront of the genre as well as the decorative painting of his day.

There is a theory that the first "scenes inside and outside Kyoto" paintings were commissioned by wealthy merchants to celebrate their role in the rebuilding of Kyoto after the Ōnin War. It is also generally assumed that townsmen patrons and artists were prominent in the production of genre paintings, as great emphasis is given in these works to commercial and craft activities. Yet fully half of the genre paintings extant from the Azuchi–Momoyama epoch are either signed by or attributable to the Kanō line of artists, who had been patronized by the military aristocracy for more than a century. The fact that such "aristocratic" artists and their samurai patrons should be keenly interested in the activities of all classes of society testifies to the new humanism that so distinguished Azuchi–Momoyama times culturally from the preceding medieval age.

The humanism that emerged in the late sixteenth century and continued into the Tokugawa period (1600–1867) was not based on the individualism – the idea of the inherent worth of the individual – that was spawned in Renaissance Europe, and therefore it must not be confused with what is usually regarded as humanism in the Western tradition. Japanese humanism was, first, a secular movement that rejected the other-worldly Buddhism that had dominated the medieval centuries. Second, it was a kind of joyous rekindling of interest in the

68 The oldest extant *rakuchū–rakugai zu* dates from about 1525.

lives and doings of people – all people – in this world. The genre art of the Azuchi–Momoyama epoch thus constituted the first portion of what became a vast and fascinating pictorial record of the lives of the early modern Japanese. This art reached its culmination in the "pictures of the floating world" (*ukiyo-e*) of the middle and late Tokugawa period.

Of all the many categories of genre art, the most interesting from the standpoint of cultural history are those that deal with the activities of people at leisure and play, including the depictions of festivals, picnicking, flower viewing, horseracing, dancing, theatrical performances, bathing, wrestling, and the promenading of women of the pleasure quarters. These pictures attest to a great increase in leisure time, especially in the larger cities, which helped create the conditions that gave rise to the flourishing of a bourgeoise culture in the Tokugawa centuries.

A special kind of genre art, unique in subject matter, is the *namban*, or "southern barbarian," screen paintings that portray the Portuguese traders and Jesuit missionaries who first arrived in Japan during the 1540s. These paintings, which in style are purely Japanese (they are similar to the other genre and the decorative work of the time), are of two varieties: single-scene paintings and split-scene paintings. The single-scene paintings show the Portuguese carrack arriving in Nagasaki harbor and its passengers walking into town to be greeted by the Japanese and the missionaries. The split-scene paintings depict, on one side (e.g., on the left screen of a pair of six-panel screens), the Portuguese in one of their overseas ports, presumably Goa or Macao, either in some kind of genre setting – such as observing the training of horses – or departing for Japan in their great ship and, on the other side (e.g., the right screen), the ship's arrival in Nagasaki.

The detail with which the Europeans and their things are shown in the *namban* screens tells of the lively interest that the Japanese of the Azuchi–Momoyama epoch had in foreign people and exotic ways. Intercourse and trade flourished in this age, not only with Europeans but also with the people of other Asian countries, making Japan more international and cosmopolitan than at any other time in its premodern history. (Such "internationalism," it should be noted, also led to two Japanese invasions of Korea in 1592 and 1597.) The rest of the story of European and other foreigners in Japan, of trade in the late sixteenth and early seventeenth centuries, and of the Korean invasions must be left for the next volume of this *History of Japan*. Let us simply note here that the humanism that evolved in the Azuchi–Momoyama epoch in Japan seems to have made the Japanese more curious and perhaps more receptive than they might earlier have been to the intrusion of outsiders and of new, alien ideas.

THE WORLD OF TEA

A topic in the cultural history of the age of unification that is especially difficult to assess is the *chanoyu*, the tea ceremony. This is because it was far more than just a ceremony. It was also a philosophy, an art, and a unique style of social intercourse, and in the Azuchi–Momoyama epoch it entered its finest phase.

As a philosophy, the *chanoyu* had come to be equated, as we have seen, with Zen Buddhism. This aspect of the *chanoyu* was authentically medieval and underlay the concept and practice of *wabicha*. It is ironic that *wabicha* was perfected in the Azuchi–Momoyama epoch after the medieval age had ended. Yet this is what was achieved through the efforts of the great master Sen no Rikyū, and it served to accentuate the dualism that had long been characteristic of the *chanoyu*. On the one hand, there was in the *chanoyu* an urge to ostentation, as when it was used in the early fifteenth century as a setting for the display of *karamono*. On the other hand, there evolved that sentiment, from at least the late fifteenth century, that drew the *chanoyu* more and more to Zen and the *wabi* realm of aesthetic taste.

Shukō, as noted, appears to have stood at the turning point between the "ostentation" period of the *chanoyu* and its evolution toward *wabicha*. But although the creation and perfection of *wabicha* became the main line of development in the *chanoyu* during the sixteenth century, the "urge to ostentation" was never lost and led in the Azuchi–Momoyama epoch to a new outburst of display, especially by the warlords, which was in keeping with the "display" character of the epoch as a whole.

This tendency in the *chanoyu* was closely related to the treasuring and collecting of tea articles, including paintings and scrolls of calligraphy as well as the actual tea utensils. Thus *karamono*, many of which were colorful and showy and therefore antithetical to *wabicha* taste, remained popular and much sought after throughout the medieval age. Because *wabicha* was based on a philosophy that rejected materialism, we might suppose that its practitioners disdained any attachment to the physical articles of tea. But in fact, they were as covetous of these as was everyone else in the *chanoyu*. The "famous articles" of *wabicha*, along with the best of the *karamono*, came to be regarded as virtual national treasures, and their prices were driven up by demand to astronomical levels.

Nobunaga reflected the national mania for tea articles when, shortly after entering Kyoto with his army in 1568 and taking the first major step toward unification, he launched a "hunt for famous tea articles" (*meibutsu-gari*), acquiring either by payment or, if necessary, by confiscation, many of the finest articles in the country. Nobunaga proudly displayed these tea articles at banquets and other special gatherings, and on occasion he bestowed one or another of them on a subordinate for meritorious service. Thus, in 1577, he gave Hideyoshi a famous kettle as a reward for his attack on and destruction of a castle.[69]

The tea-article mania of the Azuchi–Momoyama epoch is perhaps best illustrated by the story of Matsunaga Hisahide (1510–77), a chieftain of the central region around Kyoto who made peace with Nobunaga in 1568 by rendering to him a prized tea caddy. Eleven years later, when Hisahide had joined a plot against Nobunaga and was about to be killed, he deliberately smashed another coveted tea article, a kettle, to prevent it from falling into Nobunaga's hands.

Hideyoshi, when he became hegemon, also avidly collected tea articles and displayed them with even more enthusiasm than did Nobunaga. Very likely it was because of his desire to show off his tea articles on a grand scale that Hideyoshi conceived the idea of the Great Tea Party held at the Kitano Shrine in Kyoto in 1587, a spectacular affair to which he invited everyone and promised to exhibit his collection of articles "without leaving any out."[70] Hideyoshi was indeed the champion displayer of all, and his exhibitionist instincts reached a pinnacle not only in the Great Kitano Tea Party but also in his construction of a tea room covered entirely with gold, which was portable and could be taken on military campaigns and other sojourns.

As a style of social intercourse, the *chanoyu* gave rise in the Azuchi–Momoyama epoch to the politics of tea. Of course, the *chanoyu* was used for political purposes when its articles were bestowed as rewards on allies (or, conversely, given to seduce or appease an enemy) and when the articles or *chanoyu* itself were conspicuously displayed in the same way that castles, decorative screens, and other things were displayed to enhance the power and prestige of the warlords. But the essence of the politics of tea was the exploitation of the special social

69 Nobunaga also made the holding of formal tea parties by his subordinates an exclusive right that only he could authorize. Hideyoshi gained this right in 1578.
70 The party was scheduled to last for ten days, and guests were required only to bring a few utensils and mats to sit on. In fact, the party was suspended after only one day.

function of the *chanoyu* and the deliberate use by warlords of the tea master as a go-between, a negotiator, and even a diplomat. It was the tea master Imai Sōkyū (1520–93), for example, who finally arranged the peaceful submission of the city of Sakai to Nobunaga during the latter's march to power in 1568. Both Nobunaga and Hideyoshi employed tea masters, including Sen no Rikyū, to perform various political as well as cultural services for them. Rikyū, we are told, became so influential under Hideyoshi that no one could see the hegemon without first securing his approval.

Sen no Rikyū is the most fascinating figure of the Azuchi–Momoyama epoch because he symbolizes more than anyone else the clashes and pulls of the cultural history of the waning medieval age and the beginning of the early modern period. Even as he perfected *wabicha*, he abetted Hideyoshi the parvenu in his penchant for vulgar display. But in the end Rikyū ran afoul of Hideyoshi, who was ever capable of acting on a tyrannical whim, and in 1591 he was condemned to commit suicide.[71] With Rikyū's death the last major force of medieval culture was spent, and there was nothing left to impede further development of the more "modern" aspects of Azuchi–Momoyama culture.

---

71 Historians cannot determine the precise reasons for this severe punishment. Included among the possibilities are that Rikyū personally offended Hideyoshi's vanity or that he was sacrificed to appease a political faction that opposed him.

CHAPTER 11

THE OTHER SIDE OF CULTURE IN MEDIEVAL JAPAN

HISTORIOGRAPHICAL ISSUES

Historians transform lived life into narrated life, and in this sense they are not unlike novelists. Intent notwithstanding, neither history nor novel copies human experience but, rather, selects, focuses, and retells and thereby inevitably reshapes. Even subtraction adds something new. And so though we go to both historians and novelists for "truth," both are inherently disposed to falsification.

By selecting and subtracting, the interpretations of Japanese cultural history to date, particularly those of the Kamakura and Muromachi eras (roughly the twelfth through the sixteenth centuries) have focused on the "high" culture of the period; on the activities of the political, religious, and intellectual leaders of the time; and on the achievements of their close associates, eminent artists, architects, writers, and performers. Even those historians who are interested in the culture of ordinary people tend to view them in comparison with the upper classes, and their accounts are thereby riveted to the same high–low polarity as are those of the historians with whom they are ideologically at odds. Ironically, therefore, an elite veneer stretches over the history of the middle ages, obscuring the texture and contours of the daily life of the great majority of medieval men and women, while leaving in darkness those creators of Japanese culture who have failed to qualify under these preferred definitions of history.

It is not that such lives are beyond historical retrieval. On the contrary, throughout the middle ages the daily life of ordinary citizens was often a subject of note, even in the diaries and historical records of the elite; it is therefore much more easily resurrected than might be imagined. We are fortunate, further, in having a rich tradition of medieval paintings, statues, fiction, and songs, all of which preserve a realistic depiction of the period's life. Through these works we are

This chapter was originally presented and discussed in European and American forums under the title "The Other Side of History: In Search of the Common Culture of Medieval Japan."

able to look in on the common culture of medieval Japan and to perceive it as it was experienced by men and women from all levels of society. This chapter will aim, therefore, at revision. It will examine significant concerns of the Japanese middle ages – indeed, significant creators of Japanese culture – that have gone unnoted, unheeded, or even disdained. I do not refer here to the culture of commoners as opposed to that of courtiers, nor do I contrast "popular" with "elite," as I am not convinced that primary sources permit so convenient a dichotomy. If I use the word *popular,* I shall do so with regard to those aspects of a nation's culture valued by most of its citizens, crossing all lines of class, sex, and generation. The common culture that I seek are those attitudes and activities known to all and esteemed by that same majority, high and low. A common culture is one that has outgrown the exclusive ownership of any gender, group, or coterie in society, high or low, and has become the property of all.

We must recognize that historical constructs have been built around a conceptual vocabulary frozen by class, gender, and status preclusions. This had led to a favoring of certain topics of research and a denigration of other features of Japan's culture that do not fit the dominant paradigm. History, like court poetry, has been written from a canonized list of preselected topics, with most aspects of ordinary life excluded.

To complicate matters, the Japanese middle ages comprised not an elite and a popular culture but a variety of cultures – those of farmers, warriors, fisherfolk, courtiers, urban working people, and religious practitioners, for example – and within each, the cultures of the young, the middle-aged, the old, and so on. But if there is one marked characteristic of the medieval years, it is the clear sense of a coming together for the first time, of a sense of national community. Emanating from the expressive arts of song, dance, mime, and narrative are self-perceptions, community perceptions, revelations regarding social contracts, and struggles with the margins of tolerated behavior that help us see better those perimeters.

The use of such "fictions" as painting, song, and narrative in the writing of history has, for some critics, occasioned inordinate skepticism. Yet historians have embraced historical records far more contaminated; for example, "In the *Gukanshō* it is impossible to separate the history from the dogma."[1] And genealogical forgery, even the buying

---

1 Toshio Kuroda, "Gukanshō and Jinnō Shōtōki: Observations on Medieval Historiography," in John A. Harrison, ed., *New Light on Early and Medieval Japanese Historiography* (Gainesville: University of Florida Monographs, Social Sciences no. 4, Fall 1959), p. 39.

of family trees, was a common way of life for some during various centuries in Japanese history.[2] On the other hand, to be accepted by medieval Japanese citizens, fiction, painting, and song had to ring true. Thus, they are useful to historians precisely because behind their narratives are implicit agreements about the nature of the social experience; they organize what is deemed significant and represents knowledge of the daily universe. Knowledge of this kind is no less true than the symbolic representation in a statistical account. Literature and art are, in effect, the staging of collective experience. And they perhaps have an even greater authenticity than does fact because they represent the "truth" as fidelity to social expectation.

The story of every nation is that of both unique historical events and recurring events, events that are the habits of a people.

For medieval Japan, such recurring patterns include the tonsure (cutting or shaving off the hair and taking religious vows), the selling of children, pilgrimage, the enjoyment of dance, the need to talk to the spirits of the dead, or the talismanic function of the vocalized word. The great power of the medieval song or the bard's narrative, like that of their counterparts today, lies wholly in this generic nature, in the likelihood of the tale it tells. One is moved because one knows that this is the way things really are.

THE CASE OF MUGAI NYODAI

In 1976 Nishikawa Kyōtarō published a book on the subject of *chinsō*,[3] or what I shall term "proxy statues," a genre of sculpture devoted to the realistic, three-dimensional portrayal of the seated figures of historical Zen priests, whose function was to convey the essence of the master of his disciples after his death. The wooden statues depicted were largely similar-looking ecclesiastics in Buddhist robes with shaved heads. But one, despite the uniform presentation, somehow seemed different from the rest. Astonishingly, it was the figure of a thirteenth-century female Zen master. No remnant of feminine culture can be seen in her figure; with shaved head and Buddhist robes, she looks almost identical to her male colleagues. Yet the flesh of the face and shoulders is incontrovertibly matronly; it is indeed the portrait of a woman (see Figure 11.1).

2 Toyoda Takeshi, "Tenkanki no shakai," in *Otogizōshi*, vol. 13 of *Zutsetsu Nihon no koten* (Tokyo: Shūeisha, 1980), p. 196.
3 Nishikawa Kyōtarō, *Chinsō chokoku*, in *Nihon no bijutsu*, no. 123 (Tokyo: Shibundō, 1976).

Figure 11.1 Wooden sculpture of medieval abbess Mugai Nyodai

This medieval abbess's religious name was Mugai Nyodai,[4] and she lived from 1223 to 1298. An unknown artist captured in wood the quiet, life-worn face and dignified meditative posture of a serious woman in her seventies, who looks out through glimmering eyes of inlaid crystal in so uncanny a fashion that she seems alive, about to reply to something of great importance that one has asked. Once seen, Mugai's face is unforgettable. The great master who made this statue must have known Mugai Nyodai very well. Like the best of *chinsō* sculpture, it is not mere likeness; it emanates the powerful life spirit of the Zen master herself and must truly, as intended, have served as her proxy after her death.

During the past decade this statue has become the object of study and analysis. The woman it depicts, however, has not, nor has the important religious association of Zen convents she headed and, in effect, launched.

In Japanese medieval history as it is now written, women appear, when they do at all, because they are the mother, wife, mistress, or daughter of an important man. Almost all the rare exceptions are

4 Also apparently known as Mujaku.

women who have written outstanding literary works that somehow have survived. Mugai Nyodai, however, represents a challenging case. Here is a woman of superb accomplishments in the ecclesiastical world, and yet no one seems certain just which "important man" might have been her father or her husband. What were the facts of this woman's life, and what was the nature of the institution she headed? From this perspective, her life takes on an importance beyond the historical; it has generic ramifications.

The tonsure was as widespread in female culture as it was in male culture, and possibly more so, for even at that time, if they lived through childbearing, women tended to outlive their husbands – sometimes by a great many years when the occupational hazards of the wars thinned out the male population. There were also a variety of nunhoods, ranging from a status that permitted a spiritual life of ascetic devotion, to a welfare system for the abused or impoverished, to a disguise for prostitution. Indeed, just what was nunhood in medieval society? And what was the institution of the convent? No one knows. It is hard to find reliable information on even the lives of eminent nuns.

The standard references on Japanese history and Buddhism reveal the woeful state of current research on ecclesiastic women in Japan. Each authority assigns to Mugai a different Hōjō-connected father and husband. Further inquiry reveals one husband to have been twenty-five years her junior, another thirty-five years younger – unthinkable liaisons for that time. Her alleged fathers, too, are incongruously intriguing, as one was born eight years after she was and another was born when she was twenty-five![5]

Such neglect is not due to Mugai's failure to fulfill the traditional qualifications for history. An extraordinary person from well-connected *bushi* stock, born into the Adachi family, given the name Chiyono when she was young, married into a branch of the Hōjō clan, highly educated in both Japanese and Chinese, Mugai was a woman to be reckoned with. Owing to circumstances as yet unclear, in mid-life she studied Zen under the Chinese priest Mugaku Sogen (also called Bukkō Kokushi, 1226–86), who had come to Japan in 1279 at the invitation of the regent Hōjō Tokimune to head the Kenchōji temple in

5 *Nihon rekishi daijiten* (Tokyo: Kawade shobō shinsha, 1956); *Sanshū meiseki shi* 21 and *Fusō keika shi* 2, in *Shinshū Kyōto sōsho*, vols. 2 and 9 (Kyoto: Kōsaisha, 1967); *Koji ruien*, vol. 44 (Tokyo: Yoshikawa kōbunkan, 1969); and *Dai Nihon jiin sōran* (Tokyo: Meiji shuppansha, 1917). As of this writing no published accounts concerning Mugai's family should be taken as reliable. Even the most recent contain inherent inconsistencies and errors, and many problems remain to be solved.

Kamakura. After Mugaku Sogen founded the Engakuji in 1282 and began laying the groundwork for the establishment of Rinzai Zen in Japan, Mugai continued as his proselyte. Before his death in 1286, he recognized her as the heir to his teachings and gave her the character *mu* from his own name. Mugai thus became the first woman in Japan fully qualified not as a nun but as a Zen priest (Zen *sō*).

After her years under Mugaku Sogen, Mugai Nyodai founded, and served as the abbess of, the Keiaiji temple and its subtemples in northern Kyoto, which throughout the Muromachi period stood at the pinnacle of the developing network of Zen convents known as the Niji (Amadera) Gozan, or the Five-Mountain Convents Association, an institution organized concurrently with the Gozan (five-mountain) Monasteries established for male priests.[6] Mugai's Keiaiji headed the Niji Gozan network, which in her day had more than fifteen subtemples. In the generation after her death, the Five-Mountain Convents expanded to include the Keiaiji, Tsūgenji, Danrinji, Gonenji, Erinji, and their subtemples in Kyoto, as well as five convents in Kamakura: the Taiheiji, Tōkeiji, Kokuonji, Gohōji, and Zemmyōji. Keiaiji, it is said, was burned down in the Ōnin War during the mid-fifteenth century, at which time Mugai's *chinsō* and other relics were removed to one of Keiaiji's subtemples in Kyoto, the Hōji-in (also known as Chiyonodera), where they remain today.[7]

Mugai was born during a short but receptive time in Japanese history for the participation of women in official religious institutions. Buddhism, like Christianity, has had a dismal history of discrimination against women. Theologically women were viewed as inherently flawed, as both defiled and defiling; they were forbidden to enter even the grounds of the major Buddhist centers of learning and worship, such as Mount Hiei and Mount Kōya, and they were also barred by doctrine from attaining Buddhahood. Now suddenly, in Mugai's lifetime, momentous and major changes were afoot. All of the newly founded and growing sects of reform Buddhism (Pure Land, Nichiren, and Zen) were asserting that the old sects had erred and that Buddha's compassion extended to the salvation of all sentient creatures.

The statements of the Zen priest Dōgen (1200–53), in particular, were world-shaking. Indeed, Stanley Weinstein's fine studies of re-

6 See Martin Collcutt, *Five Mountains: The Rinzai Zen Monastic Institution in Medieval Japan* (Cambridge, Mass.: Harvard East Asian Monographs no. 85, 1981). No research has yet been published in any language on the Niji Gozan system of Zen convents.
7 A name taken from what is thought to have been her childhood name, Chiyono.

form Buddhism reveal that Dōgen, of all the new religious leaders, was "by far the most uncompromising on asserting complete equality between the sexes."[8] In his treatise *Shōbōgenzō*, Dōgen describes the new world into which Mugai was fortunate enough to be born:

> When we speak of the wicked there are certainly men among them. When we talk of noble persons, these surely include women. Learning the Law of Buddha and achieving release from illusion have nothing to do with whether one happens to be a man or a woman.[9]
> A nun who has attained the Way is entitled to receive the homage of all the arhats, *pratyeka*-buddhas and bodhisattvas who would seek to learn the Dharma from her. What is so sacred about the status of a man? . . . The four elements that make up the human body are the same for a man as for a woman. . . . You should not waste your time in futile discussions about the superiority of one sex over another.[10]

Zen was then virtually a new sect of Buddhism in Japan. Known early to the Japanese, it made no lasting impression for centuries and no inroads into Japanese religious life until Eisai (1141–1215) introduced Rinzai teachings in 1191 and his student Dōgen introduced Sōtō thought in 1227, just four years after Mugai was born. Her life was fundamentally changed by this new wave of social thought, and the path she chose was one that affected the lives of thousands of other women who joined the Five-Mountain Convents.

Mugai lived during a time when the foundations of modern Japanese society and culture were taking shape. Women and men from every stratum of society were taking part in its design. Studying Mugai's life, then, illuminates this period from a different perspective than has been available to us before.

Dōgen went to China the same year that Mugai was born. While she was still an infant, Shinran (1173–1262) had begun actively to propagate the Jōdo Shin faith. Dōgen returned from China when Mugai was four and wrote his *Shōbōgenzō* when she was ten. The great courtier-poet Fujiwara no Teika (1162–1241) was still alive throughout her teens, and numerous famous *waka*-poetry collections appeared as she grew up. In her adolescence, the *Uji shūi monogatari* and *Azuma kagami* were written, and *biwa*-priests were chanting narratives around the country that recounted episodes from the cataclysmic Gempei War of a half-century earlier. In Mugai's middle years, Ippen

8 Stanley Weinstein, "The Concept of Reformation in Japanese Buddhism," in Saburo Ota, ed., *Studies in Japanese Culture*, vol. 2 (Tokyo: P.E.N. Club, 1973), p. 82.
9 Weinstein, "Concept of Reformation," p. 82, trans. from *Shōbōgenzō*, Iwanami bunko ed. (Tokyo: Iwanami shoten, 1939), vol. 1, p. 128.
10 Weinstein, "Concept," p. 82, trans. from *Shōbōgenzō*, vol. 1, p. 124.

(1239–89) was at work spreading early Jishū teachings, and Nichiren (1222–81) was writing his *Risshō ankokuron*. Mujū was at work on his collection of Buddhist *setsuwa*, the *Shasekishū*. *Ban Dainagon ekotoba* and one of the famous sets of *Kitano Tenjin engi* scrolls were being painted. The Mongols attacked Japan twice. The central structure of the Sanjūsangendō temple and the Great Buddha of Kamakura were built. The restless ghosts of the Soga brothers were being placated by enshrinement in Hakone. And when Mugai died, Yoshida Kenkō (1283–1350) was only a fifteen-year-old boy.

In addition to the particular details of her life, Mugai also offers us a glimpse into that silent other side of elite culture. No understanding of medieval Zen, its values or practices, can be complete without knowing something of her contribution to it. Mugai represents the vast and complex socioreligious institution of the convent and of nunhood itself, a culture rarely represented in history at all, elite or otherwise. She stands for the founder-abbesses of history and also for all those women who took the tonsure and thereafter moved not to the cloister but out into the world of commerce and the arts. They, too, played a fundamental role in creating Japan's emerging national culture.

If there is a single dominant paradigm in medieval life, it is the tonsure as an acceptable option, a pervasive dynamic in the common culture of medieval Japan, in the lives of all, men and women alike. In offering religiosecular severance (and liberation) from the requirements (and impositions) of society, the tonsure proved to be one of the most creative forces in Japanese history. Eventually discredited by Neo-Confucian thought and social changes during the Edo period, the tonsure has today virtually ceased to exist as a socially creative factor in society. It can be hypothesized, however, that during the middle ages, it was one of the most important contexts for Japan's artistic, intellectual, and even entrepreneurial freedom and originality.

No history of medieval Japan has yet been written in which tonsured males (*inja* and *tonseisha*), representing a wide range of religiosity, did not appear prominently in every realm of activity, from the imperial top to the outcast, mendicant bottom of society. Their role – not only in the religious domain but also in politics, art, the performing arts, commerce, literature, and even the military – is so ubiquitous as to constitute a major characteristic of the age. Yet the sociological background of this option of the tonsure has not been explored, for men or for women.

Curiously, those few prominent medieval nuns who have succeeded in attracting historians' attention were alive during Mugai's years. The nun Eshin (1182–1270s), the first official wife of a priest in Japan, actively supported the work of her husband, Shinran, in his Jōdo Shin teachings. Both Lady Nijō (1258–1306?), the author of *Towazugatari*, and Abutsu (1233?–83?), the author of *Utatane no ki* and *Izayoi nikki*, were traveling throughout Japan as nuns during Mugai's lifetime, though they had taken the tonsure with considerably different aims than did either Mugai Nyodai or Eshin. Both women wrote notable autobiographies whose contents are self-absorbed and concerned to varying degrees with literary ambition.[11] Indeed, their work has been of historical interest primarily because of its literary value; the religious consciousness they express is only elementary. Nijō's pilgrimage appears to have been the traditional medieval tourist course; Abutsu's tonsure, which took place in her late teens, was hardly a religious decision, but an act of despair akin to suicide over a dying love affair. During her brief stay in a convent, it was the man who had grown indifferent to her who obsessed her thoughts. Nevertheless, neither woman would probably have achieved what she did in her day had she not taken the liberating step of choosing the tonsure.

It is troubling that although the lives of these two aristocratic women have been studied, no one has yet examined their nunhood or tried to explore its meaning in the context of medieval society. Nunhood, after all, was not an elite pursuit. Nijō encountered several nuns who had previously made their living as prostitutes; one was a former brothel owner. If we are to believe the overwhelming statistical evidence of medieval fiction, diaries, poetry, songs, paintings, and drama, then nunhood must have been common in medieval life from the top to the bottom of society, an acceptable alternative in the popular culture of medieval Japan.

Becoming a nun in childhood was rare, but taking the tonsure in late middle age was common among all classes and geographical areas. Indeed, when one was widowed, society expected it. Some widows clearly "acquiesced" to nunhood, in Emile Durkheim's sense of the word.[12] Widows' becoming nuns also had an important secular socio-

11 For English translations of these works, see Karen Brazell, trans., *The Confessions of Lady Nijō* (New York: Anchor Books, 1973); and Edwin O. Reischauer, trans., "The *Izayoi Nikki*," in Edwin O. Reischauer and Joseph K. Yamagiwa, eds., *Translations from Early Japanese Literature* (Cambridge, Mass.: Harvard University Press, 1951), pp. 3–135. Donald Keene recounts Abutsu's diary, *Utatane no ki*, written when she was about seventeen years old, in "Diaries of the Kamakura Period," *Japanese Quarterly* 32 (July–September 1985): 186–9.
12 Emile Durkheim, *The Rules of Sociological Method* (Glencoe, N.Y.: Free Press, 1950), p. 104.

political, and even economic role in the medieval family: It was, in effect, a disposal system for used women.

There were other types of nunhood, however. Medieval fiction provides a rich array of tonsured women whose motivations varied widely and include defiance, resignation, religious fervor, love of poetry and travel, flight from crime, and passionate attachment to deceased loved ones on whose souls they wished to concentrate their attention through prayer. Paintings show us the commercial side of nunhood as well. Depicted in the city streets, in the countryside, and in marketplaces are nuns with diverse affiliations plying their trades as peddlers, artisans, brokers, singers, and proselytizers.

Like the various monastic options for males (*shukke-tonsei*), nunhood also could simply be an opportunity to escape from the unwelcome pressures of life – to become independent, to get away, and to take up appealing avocations – provided one had the means. Interdependence and dependence are favorite themes in analyses of Japanese society, but a closer look at the tonsure will cast much light on the often disregarded but equally important anatomy of *in*dependence at work in the Japanese social system.

In *Shichinin bikuni*, the activities of one particular nun are illuminating:

[She] . . . cut off her hair, and changed her flower-like appearance to that of a nun. In linen robes, carrying a mendicant's bag, her make-up gone, her natural complexion revealed, she wandered through the provinces as a tattered beggar. . . . She visited learned monks in various temples and listened to sermons. . . . After some years during which she lived amongst other religious itinerants and social outcastes, she decided to go to Zenkōji. There was a sub-temple to one side, the abbot of which was greatly revered as someone who had obtained enlightenment. She felt this was the kind of place she had been looking for and stayed in the area for two years. Sometimes she secluded herself in mountain valleys, sometimes she begged with other mendicants. She did not neglect the practices of either the completely enlightened cleric (Daiin) or the partially enlightened one (Shōin).[13]

This is a woman who demonstrates a familiarity with a wide range of sutras and Buddhist treatises and has a fine grasp of religious doctrine. As she departs from the company of other nuns at the end of the story, the words she tosses back over her shoulder strike a sympathetic chord

13 Margaret Helen Childs, "Religious Awakening Stories in Late Medieval Japan: The Dynamics of Didacticism" (Ph.D. diss., University of Pennsylvania, 1983), p. 283. For the original, see *Shichinin bikuni*, in vol. 1 of *Kindai Nihon bungaku taikei* (Tokyo: Kokumin tosho, 1928), pp. 171–226. At one time believed to be a seventeenth-century work, it is now generally agreed to be from the Muromachi period.

even in the modern reader: "Rather than spending my time with small-minded people and staying in cramped houses, I just take an old straw hat and begging bag and go."[14]

In another medieval story, *Akimichi*, Kitamuki is asked by her husband to seduce and trap the professional thief who has murdered his father so that he can take revenge. Outraged, she protests vigorously her husband's willingness to use her in this way, but in the end she can find no alternative but to succumb to his wishes. The wary thief, though swiftly seduced, does not let down his guard until she has been with him for a year and borne him a son. Ultimately she succeeds in leading her husband to the thief's secret hiding place, and the revenge is accomplished. Her husband is delighted and showers her with words of love. She is revolted. Her husband has asked her to prostitute herself, and in the end her actions have led to the death of the man who, though repulsive to her, is the father of her child. Thus in chagrin and defiance, Kitamuki leaves her husband and becomes a nun.[15]

Medieval Japanese society considered nunhood to be an acceptable form of deviation from the behavior it normally required of its women of childbearing age. It was indulged disengagement, lamented but not punished. Insofar as nunhood was a liberation from the requirements of socially expected life roles, it represented freedom in a society that otherwise presented few social choices. To become a nun was, throughout Japan's middle ages, one of the few decisions a woman could make about her own life. Suicide was another; flight and prostitution a third. For example, in *The Tale of Genji*, the father of Lady Akashi observed: "I have had high hopes for [my daughter] since she was born. I have been determined that she go to some noble gentleman in the city. . . . I have said to her that . . . if I die before my hopes are realized she is to throw herself into the sea."[16]

That his daughter might not wish to die, as she was, after all, healthy and even beautiful and talented, that she might wish instead to devise a life for herself even in the environment of a cloister, never occurred to this father. This was still the eleventh century, but by the time of Nijō and Mugai, medieval fact and fiction show the positive value of both the cloistered and the itinerant religious life for tonsured women. Convents were certainly places of shelter and respectable occu-

14 Childs, "Religious Awakening Stories," p. 277.
15 For an English translation of the full story, see Childs, "Religious Awakening Stories," pp. 191–212. For the original, see *Akimichi* in *Otogizōshi*, vol. 38 of *Nihon koten bungaku taikei* (Tokyo: Iwanami shoten, 1965), pp. 394–410.
16 Edward G. Seidensticker, trans., *The Tale of Genji* (New York: Knopf, 1978), p. 257.

pation for women in a day when wars were numerous and the result was a surplus of widows and orphans left without male support. Convents were also places of learning, especially for women such as Mugai Nyodai. We cannot be certain whether it was widowhood that led her to "acquiesce" to becoming a nun or whether it was spiritual or intellectual drive. Nor do we know what circumstance caused her to become a learned Zen master. In any case, the temples she founded and the institution she led had major political and economic ramifications for her day. In 1973, the Japanese National Research Institute of Cultural Properties designated her statue as an "important cultural property," but today Mugai Nyodai continues to sit before us as an important cultural challenge, reminding us of that other side of gender that has for so long gone unheeded and unstudied.

WORKING FOR A LIVING

I'm Saru Genji
From Akogi Bay.
Buy my sardines, you hear!
Buy my sardines, ei![17]

From *Saru Genji sōshi* sounds the plucky call of an audacious Muromachi-period entrepreneur.

One of the most delightful aspects of mid- and late-medieval literature and painting are the glimpses they give us of the flow of activity in the streets and marketplaces of medieval Japan and the insight they offer into the lives of those ordinary (and some extraordinary) men and women who had to work for a living.

If Kyoto was an aristocratic center of religiopolitical power, it also became a city of commerce. Despite its agricultural base, Japanese society was developing its mercantile side, and a network of trades and services fanned out across the land. The capital and the provincial centers, production sites and marketplaces, were linked by medieval entrepreneurs in all their guises. Pilgrim's routes became peddlers' circuits; itinerant poets' paths became tourists' tracks; and mendicant proselytizers' courses turned into commercial trade routes.

From early times, the Japanese elite have been fascinated by the activities of ordinary working people. Heian-period paintings on fan-shaped paper, the *Ōgimen Hokekyō zōshi* owned by Shitennōji, depict scenes from daily life. Shops can be seen where fish and dumplings are

---

17 *Saru Genji sōshi*, in *Otogizōshi*, vol. 38 of *Nihon koten bungaku taikei* (Tokyo: Iwanami shoten, 1965), p. 180.

sold and people with bundles on their heads are busily transporting items here and there. Among the earliest twelfth-century hand-scroll paintings are narrative scrolls such as the *Shigisan engi* and *Ban Dainagon ekotoba* in which everyday people can be found going about their business either as background to the central action of the story or as part of the main events themselves. Such narrative hand scrolls, or *emaki*, are one of the most conservative of all Japanese art forms, in the sense that they seem to have been designed less to embellish than to preserve the literary, religious, military, and ceremonial heritage.

That desire to preserve has given us a vivid view of the medieval world. Women doing laundry, men hauling wood, children devising games, elegant urban dwellings, simple rural farmhouses – the panorama goes on and on and reveals in detail how Japanese from all walks of life dressed, did their hair, furnished their houses, cooked, ate and drank, and pursued their pleasures. There are people running, falling, dancing, peeing, blowing their noses, playing, sleeping, buying and selling, carting, peddling, begging, and in general engaged in the sorts of activities that absorb men and women everywhere in all ages and cultures. Yet here we see the Japanese variations on these themes. Thirteenth-century scrolls recounting the histories and miracles of religious centers such as the *Taima mandara engi* or the lives of famous priests such as the *Ippen shōnin eden* offer excellent depictions of not only religious activities but also daily secular life in cities, regional markets, and the countryside.[18] Other genres of painting are valuable as well: illuminated works of fiction, records of annual ceremonies, battle tales, and even paintings of sacred sites, such as the Nachi Shrine crowded with pilgrims. Medieval painting, in the form of hand scrolls, hanging scrolls, and screen paintings, was more than an elite avocation or investment, it was a public art, a national art in the deepest sense. In intimate detail the entire known population of the country, from beggars to deities, is depicted, with sacred and profane in wholly comfortable continuity – indeed, even when such categorical dichotomies are out of place.

Late in the thirteenth century, a new genre of hand scroll emerged in which working people became the central focus. Known as *shokunin uta awase e,* or poetry contests among people from various occupations, these scrolls normally pair one representative each of two similar types of profession; a poem or two on a preestablished theme is in-

---

18 These paintings are reproduced in their entirety in *Nihon emakimono zenshū,* 24 vols. (Tokyo: Kodokawa shoten, 1958–69).

scribed beside each; and a judgment is recorded as to which poem is superior. The oldest of the genre is the *Tōhokuin shokunin uta awase*, probably made in the late thirteenth century. This work was followed by similar poetry-contest scrolls illustrating an increasing array of occupations, such as the *Tsurugaoka hōjō e shokunin uta awase* and the Muromachi-period *Sanjūniban shokunin uta awase*. The most detailed of them all is *Nanajūichiban shokunin uta awase*, which depicts 142 professions.[19] The majority show trades and crafts found in Kyoto and its environs, but a few merchants from other locales are included as well.

Without any question, such works were composed, painted, and inscribed by educated members of the higher levels of society for their own pleasure. These works also contain, however, religious and poetic nuances that remain unstudied and unclear to us. I believe that the rules for the pairing as well as the painting of the professions were more complex than has been recognized and that indeed they may be a kind of "linked-painting," related in a fashion similar to linked verse *(renga)*. The artists' delight in depicting the working people of their society, in pairing up "similar" types, in being sure to include in the picture the tools of each trade, and in general making poetic play with the figures' names and functions have resulted in what is for us today an invaluable array of portraits of medieval working people.[20]

Simply to invoke the names of those depicted in these paintings is to bring back to life the lively street action of medieval Kyoto. From early in the day echo the calls of the fishmongers, herb sellers, incense and medicine vendors, and peddlers of firewood, charcoal, brooms, footgear, salt, oil, and fresh greens. In a city constantly being renewed, there was always somewhere the sound of sawing and hammering as the carpenters, roof tilers, stone cutters, and plasterers ply their trades. On street corners passersby delight in the antics of monkey trainers, word tricksters, and puppeteers. Hard at work in their homes and shops are the armor makers, indigo dyers, wig makers, sword sharpeners, hat lacquerers, comb makers, needle sharpeners, fabric weavers, embroiderers, cord weavers, rosary makers, metal workers,

---

19 The most convenient and informative reproductions of the *shokunin uta awase e* mentioned here can be found in Ishida Hisatoyo, "Shokunin zukushi e," *Nihon no bijutsu*, no. 132 (May 1977); and the special issue, "Shokunin uta awase no sekai," *Kobijutsu*, no. 74 (April 1985).
20 For an important and detailed historical study of the meaning of *shokunin* in medieval society, see Amino Yoshihiko, "Nihon chūsei no heimin to shokunin," *Shisō*, pt. 1, no. 680 (April 1980): 1–25; pt. 2, no. 681 (May 1980): 73–92. Until the middle of the fourteenth century, the word *shokunin* referred to a wide variety of nonagricultural workers, including fishermen, hunters, craftsmen, merchants, fortune-tellers, and performing artists. Only later did the word narrow to mean only craftsmen. See Amino, "Nihon chūsei no heimin," pt. 2, p. 73.

blacksmiths, and religious image makers, among many others. Were you to venture to the marketplace you would find vendors of rice and beans, tofu and yeast, saké, wooden pillows, rouge and face powder. The big fish market is along Rokkaku Street; you can watch the carters come into town and unload at Gojō and Muromachi; they stable their animals there and also find lodgings nearby.[21] Should you tire, there are vendors of whisked tea or brewed tea, rice cakes or dumplings along the thoroughfares. The high-class pleasure houses are at Higashi no Tōin, but if you wander over to Hell's Alley (Jigoku ga Tsuji) or Earning-a-living Lane (Kasegi ga Tsuji) any time of the day or night there will be girls waiting on street corners or in back-alley enclaves to satisfy prurient impulses. If in trouble, you will find, here and there in public places, doctors, mediums, soothsayers, and geomancers at your service. Inevitably you will also run into a variety of holy men and women, fund collectors, sutra readers, touring *yama-bushi* and Kōya *hijiri*, and prayer chanters intoning rhythmically while beating time on bowls or gourds or even on their bare chests.

Such nonagricultural working people were a sign of the entrepreneurial flavor of urban medieval life. Unlike rigidly stratified seventeenth-century Japan, there was as yet no particular differentiation among an artisan, manufacturer, peddler, merchant, or a worker engaged in providing services, except perhaps in their economic success or failure.

By the late sixteenth century a new genre of paintings, the *rakuchū rakugai zu byōbu*, or screen paintings of Kyoto and its environs, added another dimension to the depiction of the daily life of ordinary people. From a bird's-eye perspective, the painters of these screens reveal a flourishing Kyoto completely recovered from the wars. We see in exquisite detail its hills and temples, rivers and canals, and streets and alleys and look telescopically into shops at fan sellers and writing-brush dealers and even into public baths to watch people having their backs scrubbed. The streets are animated by people buying snacks – broiled sparrow-on-a-stick – or watching cockfights; street girls paw reluctant customers; a mother holds her tiny child's bare bottom encouragingly over a street-side ditch while friends dawdle tolerantly nearby.[22]

21 Toyoda Takeshi, "Otogi ni arawareta minshū," in *Otogizōshi*, vol. 13 of *Zusetsu Nihon no koten* (Tokyo, Shūseisha, 1980), p. 132.
22 The pair of six-panel screens known as the Uesugi screens were made by Kanō Eitoku (1543–90). In 1574 Oda Nobunaga gave them to Uesugi Kenshin (1530–78), the daimyo of Echigo. The political psychology behind such a gift to one who lived so far from the capital should not be overlooked. The Uesugi screens are reproduced in detail in Okami Masao and Satake Akihiro, eds., *Rakuchū rakugai byōbu: Uesugibon* (Tokyo: Iwanami shoten, 1983).

The picture of working people that emerges also from contemporary fiction and popular songs enriches these painted portraits of the medieval Japanese. Muromachi fiction – usually referred to as *otogizōshi*, or companion stories – describes life-styles and human situations that corroborate the sorts of activities and concerns depicted in paintings and recorded in contemporary diaries and chronicles. Fact and fiction are more than contiguous; they have a redundancy that historians can count on. In painted portrayals of working people and their environments, fantasy had no place. Prosperity might be exaggerated for aesthetic or even political ends, but the aim was to convey the real, not to invent the imaginary. Likewise, in medieval Japan, readers of fiction would not countenance stories that did not somehow ring true. Even flights of fantasy tell us much about the actual contexts from which escape is sought.

As there had been for centuries, we find, of course, stories of ineffectual princesses and their premarital problems. But they are joined in the medieval repertory by sexually tormented priests and their anguished love affairs with one another, by warriors who are easily offended and do not hesitate to use young girls badly. The picture is consistent with the essayists' laments of a less-than-ideal world. By and large, however, the world of ordinary people in *otogizōshi* is felicitous: smile inducing, hope inspiring, and reassuring. Despite literary shortcomings, which will not be our concern here, these stories, like the contemporary comic plays (*kyōgen*) and popular songs (*kouta*), reveal a people down to earth, unwilling to pine away in the face of hardship, entrepreneurial, imaginative, hardworking, combative, ambitious, self-reliant, persistent, and even brazen.

The sardine peddler Saru Genji, whose bold street call sounded at the start of this section, was not about to let his lowly occupation stand in the way of his getting the one woman in the world he wanted after a love-at-first-sight look at her on the street one day. Never mind that she was Keika, one of the highest ranking courtesans in Kyoto, who catered only to the elite of that city's society. Never mind that he would have to impersonate a daimyo, spread rumors of his own arrival in town, find himself an entourage, carry the whole thing off with improvisation and aplomb once inside the door of her elegant establishment. And never mind that he is ingenious and clever at poetic double entendres; he almost ruins the whole thing by doing exactly what one imagines peddlers or salesmen would be likely to do: when he talks in his sleep it is to recite his daily call: "Buy my sardines, Ei!" But the story ends felicitously. Keika is a woman of wisdom. We are not informed about how she got where she is, but she is smart enough to recognize a hardworking, intelligent, entrepreneurial winner; leaving Kyoto's high life, she goes off to set up a home with Saru Genji in his fishing village. They prosper as fish merchants, and their descendants enjoy their wealth.

Clearly not all made millions. The old nun who makes a living as a broker of secondhand goods and odd-job services in *Oyo no ama* seems just above indigence. Nonetheless, her work and style clearly show the same qualities of ingenuity and boldness so highly valued in the sardine merchant story. On her rounds one day she convinces an old priest that he needs a girl to look after his needs; she knows just the one. Tottering with anticipation, excited and befuddled all the more by a touch of saké, the old man that night gives an overwhelming welcome to his new companion, who has arrived modestly swathed in robes. Dawn reveals her to be the old peddler-nun herself. Why not, she says. We are perfectly matched; here is a good way to look after each other in our declining years. Two can live as cheaply as one. And with other such assurances, the story ends on a felicitous note for each of them.

In the *kyōgen* play *Imajimmei*, however, a husband and wife have had no luck in any of the small businesses they try to start. Hearing that a new deity has appeared in Uji, they decide to set up a tea shop near the sacred site and start out afresh. But their burner is too small, and they cannot seem to keep the tea hot; they can afford only one tea cup, and so they have a dishwashing problem; then, too, the wife is not pretty enough to attract customers. In the end, the small business fails.

The nouveau riche appear in many forms in medieval fiction, and in some instances the entrepreneur emerges as a cultural hero. Perhaps the most famous such manufacturer-merchant is Bunshō, the salt maker, from the story *Bunshōsōshi*. Beginning as a servant to the head priest at the Kashima Shrine in Hitachi, the hero is one day tested by dismissal. Stopping at a salt maker's house, he earns his keep by helping around the salt kilns and proves able to work as hard as six men. Rewarded by his employer with the gift of two kilns, he begins to manufacture and sell salt himself. His product proves extremely tasty and of good medicinal effect; he is also able to increase his production to thirty times that of his rivals! Hardworking, ambitious, with a better product and higher productivity, he soon becomes a millionaire. At this point the story turns to questions of progeny and the marrying of his two daughters to the court. In the end, Bunshō himself becomes the senior councilor of state.[23]

It has been common to interpret such stories as a sign of the commercial class's burgeoning self-consciousness, their drive for upward mobility, for control of commercial activity, and also for the attainment of political powers. Yet we would do well to notice that, here, Bunshō's success is not attributed to his self-awareness or even to his hard work, but to the blessings of the deity of the Kashima Shrine.

As is clear from the few stories described here, upward social mobility is not the aim of characters in medieval fiction; what they want is economic security. No one is looking for power; everyone is looking for wealth. If one's life ends in high rank and aristocratic marriage, these are just the natural results of having money. And having money is good fortune bestowed on one by the gods. Bunshō and his daughters are supremely indifferent to government. They want merely to prosper and be as rich as possible. And indeed they succeed. So well suited was this story to the dreams of the Japanese people that it took on talismanic qualities. In merchant homes during the Edo period, it became standard practice to read this story aloud at New Year's time as the year's "first reading" – an act of invocation, as it were, to induce wealth and good fortune to enter the home.

Felicitous words end many works of medieval fiction, and laughter and/or good-natured reconciliation can be found in many *kyōgen* (comic plays) and noh plays. Indeed, felicitous words remain in the mainstream of Japanese sociolinguistic life and continue as a fundamental dynamic in both the Japanese family and work mentality. Throughout the middle ages there were those who worked for a living as performers of felicitous words. Such itinerant *shōmonji*, or "front-gate performers," as the *senzu manzai*, *shishi mai*, and others whose words, dances, and rituals warded off evil, expressed gratitude, and were of a felicitous nature, reflected the great importance the populace assigned to inviting good forces and good fortune into the home and workplace. Modern Japanese men and women in their homes and workplaces today continue this pattern of felicitous gestures and word formulas designed in the middle ages to elicit and maintain good fortune.

---

23 For a translation of this story, see James T. Araki, "Bunshō sōshi: The Tale of Bunshō, the Saltmaker," *Monumenta Nipponica* 38 (Autumn 1983): 221–49.

ELECTION OF THE GODS

Underlying the struggle to earn a living during the middle ages was a perception that success or failure depended not only on one's own efforts and talents but also on the deities, who either cleared the way for good fortune or interfered by means of their disgruntlement. Shinto deities had always been this-world oriented, and Buddhism, too, was not exclusively concerned with salvation or rebirth into a paradise in the next world. It is customary to comment on Buddhism's "next-world"orientation, its emphasis on the concept of *mūjo*, or transience of this world, and its doctrine of *mappō*, or the degeneracy of the latter days of the Buddhist law. Conversely, however, during the middle ages, Buddhist deities came to play a more overtly philanthropic role in the daily "this-world" activities of ordinary men and women, a role that transcended theology or orthodox doctrine. For example, Jizō muddies his feet helping believers plant rice (*Jizō engi*), and Kannon bleeds from the blow of a sword endured on a devoted believer's behalf (*Munewari Kannon*).

On the other side of the history of religious doctrine, therefore, lies the question of how these daily perceptions and practices were related to the spiritual and sacred forces in which the medieval Japanese believed. How, in daily life, did lay people on all levels of society perceive such supernatural forces? To which deities did they usually turn for help in affairs pertaining to this world? In view of all the buddhas and boddhisattvas and the many Shinto deities, we should ask which ones fell by the wayside and which the Japanese elected to keep at the center of their daily, active faith. Which ones became the national gods of an entire people?

With increased travel, the pilgrim's circuit and the merchant's route, and the influence of the here-and-now needs of mercantilism, we find emerging those deities who, serving this world and not the next, transcended their role as local tutelary gods and became national gods.

Fiction, song, and drama illuminate those deities who came first to everyone's mind and on whom all seemed to rely. Although various Buddhist and Shinto divinities were magnets of devotion in certain locales and were the principal features in fiction as well, no deities had greater general nationwide appeal in the daily life of the Muromachi period than did Kannon, Jizō, and the seven gods of good fortune, especially Daikoku, Ebisu, and Bishamon.[24]

24 Toyoda Takeshi, "Otogi ni arawareta minshū," p. 129.

Kannon appears more often in medieval literature than does any other deity, and the *kannon* of Kiyomizu Temple, granter of good marriages and healthy children, is ubiquitous. The temple had a proxy pilgrimage path on its premises, and so one could worship before all the thirty-three manifestations of Kannon there. But the real attraction was the temple's own *kannon*, before whom, throughout the centuries, there was always a steady stream of petitioners. In literature perhaps only the *kannon* of the Hase Temple begins to approach that of Kiyomizu in serving this-worldly needs for good mates and healthy progeny.

Bishamon, as the protector from all evil, had a natural appeal. Daikoku, on the other hand, looking like a plump and prosperous Chinese tradesman, was a deity who seemed made to order for the medieval businessman. Standing on overstuffed bales of rice, holding out the promise of his coin-producing magic mallet, he exuded prosperity, and the strength of even his name led numerous medieval tradesmen to adopt it for the name of their own establishments. Poetry and dance genres such as Daikoku *renga* and Daikoku *mai* are indicative of this deity's widespread popularity. Money in this world, not promises of comfort in the next, was a major concern of Daikoku's devotees. Another divinity who emerged directly from medieval Japan was Ebisu. Looking unmistakably like a wealthy Japanese entrepreneur – mild mannered, fair dealing, and with his leisure-time fishing pole – Ebisu was a deity who promised wealth, fair business management, and the good life.[25]

Dreams of wealth, so important to those who worked for a living, are reflected in *kyōgen* plays through the frequent appearance of Daikoku, Ebisu and Bishamon. The grounds of Kyoto's temples contained shrines dedicated to one or more of the lucky gods. At Tōji, the shrine to Daikoku had an endless line of daily petitioners. On Bishamon's festival day, tens of thousands visited shrines associated with him. And the 1480s witnessed the notorious case of some burglars who disguised themselves as the seven lucky gods and broke into a house where they were welcomed with open arms and loaded down

25 The appearance and accoutrements of both Daikoku and Ebisu evolved over time, probably to accommodate various occupational groups. From early times, Daikoku was a guardian of harvests and kitchens, and Ebisu was especially revered by those in fishing and industry. For essays in English on these deities, see Ichirō Hori, "Mysterious Visitors from the Harvest to the New Year," pp. 76–103, and Katsunori Sakurada, "The Ebisu-gami in Fishing Villages," pp. 122–132, both in Richard M. Dorson, ed., *Studies in Japanese Folklore* (Bloomington: Indiana University Folklore Series, no. 17, Indiana University Press, 1963).

with treasure by the rejoicing residents, who believed they had been blessed by a holy visitation.[26] These were the divinities with which medieval men and women lived intimately, with whom they shared the troubles of their daily work, and on whom they relied for the blessings of whatever good fortunes their lives might bring. Depictions of these deities today continue to smile out at customers from shop fronts throughout Japan.

Throughout the middle ages the business of selling charms was a source of support for both Shinto and Buddhist institutions. Such talismans included small woodprint images of Buddhist deities (inbutsu), miniature wooden strips shaped like stupas (kogata sotoba), pieces of wood with religious phrases written on them (kokeragyō), and wood or paper strips acknowledging the receipt of a contribution (kanjin fuda). To obtain charms, contributors donated rice and other staples as well as money. The most wealthy even donated land.

A visit to a religious site usually included the invoking of the deities and prayers for some longed-for wish. The prayers were often written out and left at the temple, much as they are today, written on the kinds of wooden plaques (ema) or paper strips that are also depicted in medieval picture scrolls. These strips, of no monetary value to religious institutions, were usually burned when they took up too much space, and so few survive. But those discovered at Gangōji-gokurakubō give a vivid picture of the petitions of ordinary men and women – usually prayers for benefits in both this world and the next.[27]

Medieval literature mentions again and again those few Buddhist sites of the thousands nationwide that drew the greatest numbers of both the devout and the curious. Most famous, if we are to trust their omnipresence in fiction, drama, and jongleurs' tales, were Mount Kōya (present-day Wakayama Prefecture), to which the bones of so many of the nation's dead were carried and interred; the Shitennōji, closely associated with the founding patron of Japanese Buddhism, Prince Shōtoku; the so-called Nara Three: Tōdaiji, Hasedera, and Taimadera; the two most beloved temples in Kyoto: Kiyomizudera and Seiryōji; the great Nagano center, Zenkōji, rich in legends and associated with the activities of tonsured women; and farthest of all from the capital, Risshakuji, in northwestern Japan (present-day

---

26 Toyoda, "Otogi ni arawareta," p. 130.
27 Gorai Shigeru, Gangōji–Gokurakubō chūsei shomin shinkō shiryō no kenkyū – chijō hakkenbutsu hen (Kyoto: Hōzōkan, 1964).

Yamagata Prefecture). The shrines on the sacred mountains of Kumano and the Ise Shrine, destined to attract imperial focus in later years, appear constantly in fiction, song, and drama, attesting to the magnetism they evinced in medieval society. The middle ages also gave birth to Japan's common gods. Across regional and social lines, pilgrimage, work, and the narratives spawned by both drew people everywhere together into a kind of nationwide network of believers. Having gods in common is a powerfully unifying social force, and during the middle ages, the Japanese people began, for the first time, to become shareholders of beloved national gods.

Shamans

Like popular songs in most times and places, the medieval Japanese popular song (imayō, or "modern style," and later kouta, or "short song") was a genre full of clichés. Nevertheless, from among the hundreds of lyrics that survive, some touch on areas of deep human concern, startle and move us with their authenticity, and bear witness to history. The following is Song 364, from Ryōjin hishō (ca. 1170):

> My child by now
> Must be more than ten.
> Soothsayer she's become, I hear,
> Out wandering the land.
> They say she walks the tide's edge
> Out by Tago Bay.
> Will fisherfolk there gather
> To hear her auguries?
> Or will they say "Too young!" and scoff
> With this or that remark?
> Will they close in and taunt her?
> Oh my beloved child![28]

Across the centuries we hear the grief-stricken voice of a still-young mother tormented by anxiety and desolate in the loneliness of eternal separation that fate and the curse of poverty have inflicted on her and her child. It is a stunning piece. Eight hundred years later – maybe a thousand, who can say? – we cannot doubt this was a "true" song.

This song confirms other sources and helps us reconstruct an impor-

---

28 Usuda Jingorō and Shimma Shin'ichi, eds., *Kagura uta, saibara, Ryōjin hishō, Kanginshū*, vol. 25 of *Nihon koten bungaku zenshū* (Tokyo: Shōgakkan, 1985), p. 295.

tant, yet mysterious, ancient profession, the itinerant woman shaman, or *aruki-miko*, "shaman who walks." Unlike the settled, institutional shaman, this was a nomad.

Shamans came in many varieties.[29] Some were clearly attached to shrines, whereas others were independent, self-employed urban dwellers. Still others were migrant, following routes that are as yet unclear. *Miko, agato-miko, azusa miko, ichiko, itako, aruki-miko, kannagi, jisha:* we are not really sure how to distinguish definitively among them. Yet the many names need not necessarily imply fundamentally different species. It is possible to imagine that in a still linguistically splintered country, different locales, though merging dialectically, still had their own favorite names for the same familiar person.

The position of shaman was predominantly held by females, and shamans are widely depicted in medieval literature and painting, where they range from elegant city women in business for themselves to impoverished mendicants on the road who seem just one step ahead of starvation and who, in some instances, have fallen into prostitution. Also shown are *jisha,* who may have been male shamans impersonating females, a phenomenon still alive in Korean shamanism today.[30]

In the Muromachi-period story *Kachō Fūgetsu,* the two sisters named in the title are reputable professional shamans who are called in as consultants when an affluent fan-comparing party comes to a halt because no one can decide whether the figures depicted on the fan are of Ariwara no Narihira – the poet-hero of *The Tales of Ise* – or of Hikaru Genji – the hero of Lady Murasaki's novel *The Tale of Genji.* In the Tenri Library *Nara ehon* hand-illuminated book version, although the paintings are extremely simple and unaffected, the two sisters are clearly depicted as beautiful, fashionably dressed women, wearing on their heads gold crowns from which projections in the shape of half-moons rise in the front, reminiscent of early Korean aristocratic embellishments.[31] They are requested to consult the spirits

29 Carmen Blacker's study of present-day shamanistic practices in Japan, *The Catalpa Bow* (London: Allen's Unwin, 1975), deals with prehistoric shamanism and then jumps to twentieth century practices. She gives a select bibliography of the best works, in both English and Japanese, on the subject. Hori Ichirō's *Nihon no shamanizumu* (Tokyo: Kōdansha, 1971) is a major contribution. Almost all of these works take a religious phenomenological approach. For the premodern period, there are virtually no studies of the social institution or of individual practitioners.

30 Yanagita Kunio's classic study of shamanism, "Miko kō," published under a pseudonym in 1913, discusses many manifestations of shamanism. It has been republished in *Teihon Yanagita Kunio shū* (Tokyo: Chikuma shobō, 1982), vol. 9, pp. 223–301.

31 See Plate 39, p. 38 of Ichiko Teiji, ed., *Otogizōshi,* vol. 13 of *Zusetsu Nihon no koten* (Tokyo: Shūseisha, 1980).

to determine the true identity of the portraits. Kachō calls down the spirit of the long-dead Narihira; he speaks through her and denies involvement. Next, using a mirror on a stand, they call up the spirits of the figures in the picture, and suddenly in the mirror appear Hikaru Genji and Lady Suetsumuhana. They begin to talk. Lady Suetsumuhana, mild-mannered in the novel, turns on Genji the full force of her unexpressed and unrelieved fury at his promiscuous love life. Through this seance, the identity of the painting on the fan is thus confirmed to be Genji.

The shamans in this story are well known, successful professionals on call in the capital. In a matrilinear profession in which the skill is taught from woman to young girl and in which adoption into the female group was the most common method, the identification of Kachō and Fūgetsu as "sisters" is wholly natural and reflects social reality.

The "soothsayer" song quoted earlier, though it gives few details, makes clear a great deal. Behind the remorse and pain and love, we see a parent separated from her child against all will and feeling. Yet the child is neither lost nor abducted, as in the noh play *Sumidagawa*, but was given to others when she was very young. The bereft mother tries to follow the news of her over the years and always keeps her ears open for rumors of the child's whereabouts. She hears that now she has been adopted into a shamans' group that is at work around the Tago Bay area. She wonders whether now that the child is almost ten, she will have already been called to try out her newly learned skills. With such hints of the child's whereabouts, the parent of a kidnapped child would be off at once to retrieve it. But this mother gave up her little girl out of need. All she can do now is hope to keep track somehow, to look out longingly over the hills in the little girl's direction, pray that the gods will somehow protect her and bless her with the skill to talk with the spirits, and hope that people (and especially men) will be kind.

The importance of shamanism in ancient as well as medieval life has been underestimated and essentially ignored in contemporary historical discourse. Female dominated and individual oriented, it was in marked contrast with male-dominated and institution-oriented Buddhism. Yet from early on, shamanism was a part of the daily life of Japanese on all levels. The statesman Fujiwara no Kaneie (929–90), for instance, would not make a move without consulting the *uchifushi no miko* (shaman who falls into a trance) attached to the Kamo shrine in Kyoto.[32] Eleventh-century novels invariably include discussions of shamanistic consultations, and in twelfth- and thirteenth-century songs and paintings, shamans appear frequently.

The influence of shamanism on the fourteenth- and fifteenth-century performing arts was enormous. Talking with the spirits is the basis of the world view of the playwright Zeami Motokiyo (1363–1443), whose *mugen* noh plays depend on the principles of shamanism. Even the structure of Zeami's plays and the manner of their casting (the *mae-jite*, a borrowed local body, and the *nochi-jite*, the spirit of the dead made manifest and speaking in authentic voice) derive almost wholly from shamanistic ritual.

But for the ordinary shaman working for a living, it was not an easy profession. See Song 324, from *Ryōjin hishō* (ca.1170):

> Sorceress Tōta!
> Shaking the bells that way!
> Bells are to be shaken
> High above the eye:
> Jingle, jangle, jingle,
> Shake them way up high.
> If you shake them low like that
> Down below the eye,
> The spirits will scold, "You're dawdling!"
> Oh how frightful
> When they're mad![33]

Shamans were ascetic and virginal, wedded to the spirits. Such shamans continued to work in shrines and to travel the land as spiritual mediums and soothsayers, sacred women with spiritual powers, hired for those services alone. During the middle ages, however, if not before, the shaman path split in several directions, as indeed had the career of mendicant, itinerant nuns. Those who could not survive in their trade shook their bells for show, took to being itinerant entertainers of sorts, or as the last option, became *ukareme* or "drifters," a euphemism for prostitutes.

In the several versions of the early-thirteenth-century *shokunin* poetry – contest scrolls, for instance, a very old woman with an archer's bow – the standard diviner's tool of the *azusa miko* – is identi-

---

32 A seminal and revisionist work on attitudes toward medieval professional women, including entertainers and shamans, is by Wakita Haruko, "Chūsei ni okeru seibetsu yakuwari buntan to joseikan," in vol. 2 of *Nihon josei shi – chūsei* (Tokyo: Tōkyō daigaku shuppankai, 1983), pp. 65–102. Wakita (p. 69) calls attention to *Konjaku monogatari*, book 31, story 26, in which can be found the account of Kaneie. The original can be found in Yamada Yoshio et al., eds., *Konjaku monogatari* 5, vol. 26 of *Nihon koten bungaku taikei* (Tokyo: Iwanami shoten, 1963), p. 293.   33 Usuda and Shimma, eds., *Kagura uta*, vol. 25, p. 283.

fied as a *miko* or shaman, but her poem is erotic and belongs to the world of prostitution. She is both shaman and singing girl, a combination of skills that seems to have become endemic in medieval life.

At the lower edges of the shaman profession, as indeed of all professions in which women were central, hovered the slave trade, a source of young girls for any of the matrilinear professions (shamans, entertainers, prostitutes) that could afford the purchase. See Song 131, from the *Kanginshū* (ca. fourteenth century):

> A slave trader's boat
> Rows in the offing.
> "In any case I will be sold,
> Tossed about from hand to hand,
> So just for now, row gently,
> Mr. Boatman, please."[34]

The voice of a young girl, specific in her predicament, heartrending in her acceptance of the suffering that lies ahead, rises to meet us across the years, and we know her inner heart better than that of her more illustrious countrymen, whose higher status caused the recording of their names and ranks and dates and around whom we weave our histories. This song struck a poignant chord in the hearts of medieval men or women, and the lyrics were later quoted and adopted in a variety of forms by the writers of later poetic and dramatic genres. As late as the Tokugawa period this song was still sung in many forms by the women of the Yoshiwara brothels.[35] Did this young girl end up shaman, entertainer, or prostitute? Who can say?

Female entertainers

As we have seen, the working people that we can resurrect from medieval sources fall into three groups: those known for the products they grow, make, sell, or repair; those known for their spiritual powers or religious activities; and those known for their performing arts. It is from this last group that there emerged some of the most influential artists in all of Japanese history: the Japanese hetaerae or female companions – the singers, dancers, and inamorata of emperors, prime ministers, generals, and priests.

---

34 Ibid., p. 424. A different translation can be found in Frank Hoff, *Song, Dance, Storytelling: Aspects of the Performing Arts in Japan* (Ithaca, N.Y.: Cornell University East Asian Papers, no. 15, Cornell China–Japan Program, 1978), p. 36, in which the *Kanginshū* is translated in full.
35 Kitagawa Tadahiko, ed., *Kanginshū, Sōan kouta shū*, vol. 53 of *Shinchō Nihon koten shūsei* (Tokyo: Shinchōsha, p. 76, n. 131.

Yet because dancers, singers, and shamans shared a matrilinear professional line, mother to daughter or female-adept to adopted daughter-disciple; because the repertories of singers of tales and songs included some sacred subject matter; because shaman ritual usually included dance; because all three types tended to be without husbands, independent, and unregulated and to travel in small groups, observers throughout history have tended to confuse them. The brothel, too, was structured in a similar fashion: The female manager played the role of mother to the adopted girls. In the popular mind, therefore, shaman, entertainer, and prostitute were often not distinguished. Modern historians writing about this period, too, have so far treated them as degrees of one kind.

It should be noted that the professional troupes of musicians and dancers (*gagaku* and *bugaku* artists) maintained by the court, and the musicians or ritual dancers used by temples, were male. Only the Shinto shrines supported female ritual dancers, and they were not in any way considered entertainers. Virtually every female performing artist in premodern Japanese life, therefore, was outside the institutionalized structure – until later in the Muromachi period, when brothels were institutionalized and taxed, and the skilled singers or dancers located there came under their support and regulation.

The great singers and dancers of the early medieval period, who virtually created Japan's great traditions of secular song and dance, have not fared well in historical accounts. Usually swept into the anonymous category of "lowly entertainer" or "prostitute," their names obscured by those of their elite patrons, women such as Otomae, Ishi, and Kamegiku have been lost to the Japanese consciousness.

We are not yet at that stage in scholarship that we can distinguish among the many types of female entertainers who brought pleasure to medieval life and became the stars of medieval public stage and private mansion. Their varieties were enormous, and the quality of their professional achievement ranged from brilliant to mere pretense. The most prominent and artistically influential types, however, appear to have been the *kugutsu (kairaishi)*, women thought traditionally to be associated with puppet troupes but especially identified with composing and singing the popular songs known as *imayō*, or "present style," during the Heian and Kamakura periods; the *shirabyōshi* ("white-beat") dancers thought to have originated from the ranks of *kugutsu*[36]

36 Wakita, "Chūsei in okeru seibetsu yakuwari," p. 94.

after one entertainer made a sensation costumed in white male attire and dancing to a strong beat; and finally the *yūjo* (or *asobime*), which means "female entertainer" but is most commonly translated as "courtesan" or "prostitute." On the higher levels, *yūjo* were elegantly attired singers of the medieval popular "short song" who accompanied themselves on the *tsuzumi* or hand drum.

The early and medieval Japanese *yūjo* suggest parallels with the professional hetaerae of fourth-century B.C. Greece. Women such as the Athenian Muesarette (nicknamed Phyrne), Praxiteles' lover and model for the artist Appelles, might well be compared with Otomae, the *kugutsu* singer under whom Emperor Goshirakawa studied and collected popular songs, or Kamegiku, the *shirabyōshi* dancer and inamorata of Emperor Gotoba, who accompanied him into exile, or the *yujo*, Takahashi-dono of Gojō Avenue and famous consort to the shogun Yoshimitsu. Skilled entertainers living fashionably alone or in small groups, their origins ranging from slave to free professional woman, patronized by wealthy men, hired to perform at public and family affairs, and taxed by the state, the hetaerae of Corinth and Athens have many characteristics in common with their counterparts in Muromachi Japan.

The origins of the *kugutsu* remain clouded.[37] A Heian observer, Ōe no Masafusa (1041–1111), describes *kugutsu* women who play the hand drum, dance, sing, intone prayers that bestow good luck and good fortune, and worship the "hundred gods" – a description that would also fit some types of shamans.[38] Scholarly debate continues among those who perceive *kugutsu* women as foreigners or gypsies who sold combs and engaged in prostitution;[39] those who see them originally as shamans who sang magic invocations, were vehicles for the voices of the dead, and manipulated dolls;[40] and those who view them as highly skilled, admired, itinerant shamanistic singers who from early in history became members of imperial households and gave birth to princess.[41] Clearly they were sufficiently respectable and pow-

---

37 The *kugutsu* are traditionally thought to have been primarily entertainers who manipulated puppets. The activities of the women in the *kugutsu* troupes, however, remain a subject of debate.
38 Wakita analyzes Masafusa's account in terms of later evidence available in the song collections and concludes that *aruki miko*, *yūjo*, and *kugutsu* all were similarly organized social groups and engaged in similar religious practices. See Wakita, "Chūsei ni okeru seibetsu yakuwari," pp. 69–70. 39 Amino, "Nihon chūsei no heimin," pt. 2, pp. 81–84.
40 Gorai Shigeru, "Chūsei josei no shūkyōsei to seikatsu," in *Nihon josei shi – chūsei* (Tokyo: Tōkyō daigaku shuppankai, 1983), vol. 2, pp. 103–8.
41 Wakita, "Chūsei ni okeru seibetsu yakuwari," p. 94.

erful in the thirteenth century for one group of them to have been able to win a lawsuit in Kamakura against a high-ranking warrior.[42]

Otomae

Otomae (1085–1169), a *kugutsu* singer of *imayō* songs, was the voice teacher to Emperor Goshirakawa (1127–92). The great collection of favorite popular songs of the past centuries, the *Ryōjin hishō* (Secret selection of songs that make the rafter dust dance),[43] is considered to be Emperor Goshirakawa's work. It was his love of these songs that led him to study, collect, and commit them to writing. It would be better, however, to refer to these as essentially Otomae's songs. She was a professional singer whose life work was learning, performing, proba-bly composing, and then teaching these songs. Goshirakawa was her student and amanuensis.

Already retired and known as the nun of Gojō Avenue, Otomae was in her early seventies when Emperor Goshirakawa, then just entering his thirties, called her to court in 1157 and apprenticed himself to her so as to learn her repertory. Widely admired in the capital as a master of the *imayō*, Otomae's lineage can be traced through four generations of female masters: Her own teacher, Mei, was the disciple of Shisan, who in turn was taught by the *imayō* master Nabiki, who had been trained by Miyahime.[44]

Goshirakawa had loved music above all else since childhood, was an avid attender of musical affairs, and had studied various types of vocal and instrumental music himself, such as Buddhist *shōmyō* liturgical music and the lute. His passion, however, was the *imayō* popular song, which, by his day, had become almost classical in its form.[45]

When first called to become Goshirakawa's *imayō* teacher, Otomae declined, considering herself too old and his wish to become her disci-ple inappropriate. But he prevailed and proved a serious and deter-

---

42 The group of *kugutsu* involved in this suit dressed as Buddhist nuns and adopted ecclesiasti-cal names. It is quite possible that they were wealthy hetaerae, as their establishment had been in operation for several generations. The suit is discussed both by Wakita in "Chusei ni okeru seibetsu yakuwari," p. 95, and by Amino in "Nihon chūsei no heimin," pt. 2, p. 83.

43 At the end of the first volume of this work the collector explains its curious title. In ancient China, it is said, there were two singers whose performances were so marvelous even the dust on the rafters above them was excited and continued to dance for three days after they had left. Usuda and Shimma, eds., *Kagura uta*, vol. 25, p. 202. The texts of 566 songs from the collection are still extant.

44 Ibid., pp. 172–3. When actual maternal blood lines could not be maintained in these relation-ships, mother–daughter adoption was practiced, much as paternal lines governed *sarugaku* noh.   45 Ibid., pp. 170 ff.

mined student. He became devoted to her. In a moving gesture some ten years later, when she was in her eighties and had fallen ill, Goshirakawa sat at her bedside and performed the *imayō* related to the healing buddha, Yakushi Nyorai (song 32 in the *Ryōjin hishō*),[46] a song believed to help invoke a cure for serious illnesses. Greatly stirred, Otomae wept at her student's (and her emperor's) effort and at his faith.

Many of Otomae's *imayō* had religious themes. As generations passed, however, the secular songs prevailed. The popular songs of the Muromachi age can best be imagined from the 1518 collection, the *Kanginshū*, which contains 311 of the most beloved songs covering the 350-year period following Otomae's death around 1169, when Goshirakawa had completed the *Ryōjin hishō*. The *Kanginshū* draws on the great array of vocal music that circulated during the middle ages: short songs, longer narrative songs, folk songs, songs from stage plays, professional entertainer's songs, and dance songs. We do not know how such songs were sung, as the melodies have been lost, and the meter cannot be reconstructed. But we do know that most were accompanied by a hand drum or the tapping of a closed fan against the palm of the hand.

The shirabyōshi *and* kusemai *dancers*

Better known to history than are the *kugutsu*, the *shirabyōshi* dancers are represented by many famous names: Shizuka Gozen, Giō, Hotoke, Iso no Zenji, Ishi, Kamegiku, and so on; yet we understand and can reconstruct little of their dance art. At the peak of its popularity during the thirteenth century, it proliferated into various forms and came to include not only solo but chorus dancing as well.

The unexpected boldness, the soft touch of the erotic, the poignant – all these qualities in a woman putting on the garb of a man and dancing, especially electrifying when the items of clothing belong to her lover – are the elements, I would suggest, that inspired Zeami, who added death and deranged passion to the formula. The result was a riveting form of choreographed drama. In the noh play that bears her name, Matsukaze, in desolate loneliness at having lost him, puts on the robe and lacquered court hat left behind with her as a keepsake by her lover Yukihira, now dead. Enclosed in his fragrant robes, she loses herself in derangement and in dance. In *Izutsu*, a

---

46 See ibid., p. 206, for the text of the song.

young woman dons the hat and robes of her lost lover Ariwara no Narihira and in lonely grief, dances; the sight of her own reflection glimpsed on the surface of the water in the well gives her the deranged joy of believing it is Narihira himself returned. Indeed, her dance persuades the viewer that she may, in shamanlike fashion, be possessed by his ghost.

Although it has not been customary to view them so, Zeami's woman plays should be regarded as a natural evolution of the *shirabyōshi* art. *Shirabyōshi* dancers themselves appear as heroines in the plays of both Kan'ami (*Yoshino Shizuka*, for instance) and Zeami (*Futari Shizuka, Futari Giō, Hotoke no hara*, and so forth). Indeed, Zeami's father, Kan'ami Kiyotsugu (1333–84), was famed for his performances portraying the dancer Shizuka, and Zeami, in his "Three Elements" treatise of 1423, puts *shirabyōshi* dancers such as Giō, Gijo, and Shizuka on the same level of artistic accomplishment as such Heian-period poetesses as Lady Ise and Ono no Komachi.[47]

Out of the *shirabyōshi* dancer's art evolved the *kusemai* dance, a form that more fully integrated dance and song. When Kan'ami adapted the *kusemai* musical style into his *sarugaku* noh performance, he revolutionized it and laid the foundation for the emergence of noh as Zeami later developed it. Zeami made the famous *kusemai* dancer, Hyakuman, the central figure in his play that bears her name.

The label *prostitute*, however, hangs over the lives of all of these several types of medieval female artists in a way that it does not in the lives of male artists who were sometimes also, like Zeami, involved sexually with their patrons. Shizuka Gozen, for example, the most outstanding *shirabyōshi* dancer of her generation at the time of the Gempei War, is known to us primarily not as an artist but as Yoshitsune's mistress.[48] Yet we would do well to notice that every major vocal and choreographed genre of literature and music from the twelfth century on (*imayō, kouta, shirabyōshimai, kusemai, enkyoku, heikyoku*, noh, *Kōwaka bukyoku, etoki, goze-gatari, sekkyō-bushi*,

---

47 *Nōsakusho*, in Hisamatsu Sen'ichi and Nishio Minoru, eds., *Karonshū, Nōgakuronshū*, vol. 65 of *Nihon koten bungaku taikei* (Tokyo: Iwanami shoten, 1961), pp. 470–1. For an English translation of the whole work, see J. Thomas Rimer and Masakazu Yamazaki, trans., *On the Art of the Nō Drama: The Major Treatises of Zeami* (Princeton, N.J.: Princeton University Press, 1984).

48 Not only entertainers and shamans but also merchants and proselytizers – as long as they were female – were labeled prostitutes at some time in the medieval period. Itinerant merchants called *Katsurame*, women from Katsura who peddled *ayu* fish in Kyoto; *Ōharame*, women from Ōhara who sold charcoal; Kumano *bikuni*, nuns from Kumano who performed painting recitations and raised money for the religious centers on Mount Kumano; *uta bikuni*, mendicant singing-nuns; *goze*, blind hand drum – playing singers of religiosecular narratives – none has escaped the judgment of history that if not overt, then behind the scenes, their real service was sex.

kojōruri, and, later, *senryū*, *ningyō-jōruri*, kabuki, and samisen-*gatari*) bears the distinctive marks of the female entertainer. "Tea, men, and poetry" has a very different ring than does "wine, women, and song." The first three constitute the main ingredients in the history of Muromachi Japan as commonly depicted today. Yet the history of medieval life and literature, and indeed of Japanese culture as we know it today, is inconceivable without the ceremonials and liberations of saké, the fascinations of female artistry, and the social bonding of song.

AKASHI NO KAKUICHI

> The islands of our small country,
> Scattered like grains of millet
> At the ends of the earth,
> Are poisoned by troubles.
> Let me take you away
> To paradise, where all is exultation.[49]

If in our discussions of nuns and shamans, singers and dancers, we have reviewed cases of historical apathy, inattention, and disregard, they pale in comparison with the neglect showered on the creator of Japan's greatest medieval narratives, *The Tale of the Heike*. On the twenty-ninth day of the sixth month of 1371, one of the greatest composer-performers in history died, and yet there are few today who even know his name. Blind and no doubt sensing that he had little time left, Akashi no Kakuichi had, three months earlier, dictated to his chosen disciple, Teiichi, the mammoth libretto of the masterpiece that had been the life work of his mature years and that he had spent his last decades perfecting.[50] It has not been sufficiently appreciated

---

49 Kiyomori's widow to her eight-year-old grandson, Emperor Antoku. For the original, see Takagi Ichinosuke et al., eds., *Heike monogatari*, vol. 33 of *Nihon koten bungaku taikei* (Tokyo: Iwanami shoten, 1960), p. 438. I have modified Hiroshi Kitamura's and Paul T. Tsuchida's translation, as found on p. 777 of their complete translation: *The Tale of the Heike* (Tokyo: University of Tokyo Press, 1975).

50 Takagi Ichinosuke et al., eds., *Heike monogatari*, vols. 32 and 33 of *Nihon koten bungaku* (Tokyo: Iwanami shoten, 1959–60), pp. 51 and 443, respectively. Data are based on the *okugaki* of Kakuichi's text as well as on information recorded in *Jōrakuki*, an anonymous fifteenth-century historical work. Biographical material on Akashi no Kakuichi can be found in Takagi et al., eds., *Heike monogatari*, vol. 32, pp. 5–51; and in Tomikura Tokujirō, "Akashi no Kakuichi o megutte," *Kokugo kokubun* 21 (1952): 37–46. The best works in English on the *Heike* are by Kenneth Dean Butler. See particularly "The Texual Evolution of the *Heike monogatari*," *Harvard Journal of Asiatic Studies* 26 (1966): 5–51; and "The *Heike monogatari* and the Japanese Warrior Ethic," *Harvard Journal of Asiatic Studies* 29 (1969): 93–108. In addition, outstanding scholars of the *Heike* whose works should not be missed are Atsumi Kaoru and Yamashita Hiroaki. (Helen McCullough's translation appeared after this chapter was in page proofs.)

that no single work of Japanese literature or music has had a greater impact on subsequent literary genres, theater, and music – indeed on the Japanese people's very sense of their own past history – than has Akashi no Kakuichi's *Heike monogatari*. In the six hundred years since his death, alterations in his libretto have been small and subtle, not unlike the changes that conductors and soloists today make in a composer's work. In effect, with Kakuichi, the *Heike* was completed. Yet today his great achievement as a national bard is relegated largely to footnotes. I speak here not of cultural disappearance but of historical neglect. The very popularity of Kakuichi's *Heike* as a musical art meant that during the middle ages it lay outside the normal purview of elite scholars, whose interests centered on written canon designed for reading and poetic study. Only after the *Heike* was published during the Edo period as history to be read was it considered an appropriate subject of scholarly examination. And not until the twentieth century was it treated as literature, the only masterwork of classical literature to have been ignored academically so long and to have been accepted as a masterpiece so late.

Kakuichi's *Heike* is an oratoriolike work made up of some 182 cantatas for solo bass voice and *biwa* accompaniment, each lasting for thirty to forty minutes. Its subject is the conditions leading up to and following the cataclysmic Gempei War between the Genji and Heike clans. It recounts the rise to glory and then the decline and fall and eventual annihilation of the Taira, the clan known as Heike. It sings of the political maneuvering and subsequent rise of the Heike leader Kiyomori (1118–81); his arrogance and obliviousness to criticism; his clan's bloody battles with their rough, east-country rivals, the Minamoto clan, called Genji; and the lives of the men and women who witnessed, and were caught up in, the havoc wrought by the pride and vainglorious ambition of the powerful.

No one was unaffected by the battles. The Gempei Wars shocked the nobility, cracked the social structure, disrupted normal agricultural and commercial life, tore apart families on all levels of society, and left whole segments of the country widowed, orphaned, or disabled by the loss of economic support or normal employment. The downfall of the Heike was everyone's history. As the generations passed, however, it could have become mere history had not two things happened. First, the wars of the 1330s divided the imperial reign into two rival courts and brought the downfall of the shogunate that had been established by the victors of the Gempei War. The old story of the fall of the Heike thus gained a freshness and new relevance. Second, Akashi no Kakuichi's great genius transformed the story into art. Kakuichi's *Heike* sang so movingly about the Gempei War that it became the war with which all subsequent wars were compared. It brought both recognition and perspective to the present. Though tradition assigns the *Heike* to the genre of war tales, the work is so far superior in conception, scope, and quality to all others in that category that it is better thought of as a unique work. Nor should it be described, as it so often is, as a work representative of or belonging to the warrior classes. Kakuichi grasped the essential quality of the terrifying historical event about which he sang: its generic nature, its universality, and its metaphorical meaning for all Japanese. Yet he also knew the inherent power the story had to bring healing, even beatification. His *Heike* was not mere narrative; it was liturgy, sung before audiences when such liturgy was deeply needed. The incantations abolished time. Its ritual retelling united hearers, pulling them into participation in the past, causing them to "remember" things they had never experienced at first hand. It is fair to say that the power of Kakuichi's great composition was such that it did not preserve the past but, rather, replaced it with a redesigned collective memory.

Scholars generally agree that the first version of *Heike monogatari* was written between 1219 and 1222 by Nakayama (Hamuro) no Yukitaka's son, Yukinaga (born around 1164), a minor court noble who became a monk in 1218. Unfortunately, this *Heike monogatari* has been lost, though several subsequent texts have survived.

One of Kakuichi's great achievements was to purge earlier, more primitive versions of the narrative of much of their partisan defense of ancestors and their oppressive sermonizing. The Buddhistic themes and motifs that resound in his version give the work a reassuring quality, a serenity and universality. Kakuichi attempts neither to glamorize nor to vilify: The great oratorio is on the side of all those who fell and died.

One thousand or more people make their appearance in Kakuichi's *Heike*. Some pass through quickly, but others have names that to this day, owing to the work's influence on Japan's society and its performing arts, stir the hearts of all Japanese. Giō, Kumagai, Sanemori, Tomoe, Atsumori, Nasu no Yoichi, Yoshitsune, Benkei, Shizuka, Koremori, Kenreimonin: These names are beloved; they are Japan's heroes and heroines of the past, not because they can be read about in history (though of course most can), but because Kakuichi's *Heike* thrust them into the mainstream of myth and somehow sanctified them.

The historical truth of Kakuichi's *Heike* lies also in its inclusiveness.

Labeled as a war tale, described as a story of the rise and fall of men, it is fundamentally a tale about women. Although Kakuichi's version supplements history by giving mythicofictional flesh to the bones of historical men, he has also done something even more extraordinary. Threading their stories throughout the work like beads on a rosary, he has framed the entire *Heike* with the victorious salvation of women. The chord is struck in the opening movement by the work's longest single canto, which recounts the tragedy of Kiyomori's hetaera, the professional *shirabyōshi* dancer Giō. Her downfall is Kakuichi's first restatement of the major theme of impermanence that was announced in the prelude's opening stanzas.

The Giō canto, too, with the tonsures of Giō, her mother, sister, and her rival Hotoke, contains the first sounding of the salvation motif in a work that offers intricate variations on that theme. Kakuichi concludes the *Heike* with the nun Kenreimonin, her tonsure, her retreat to the Jakkōin cloister, the visit there of the ex-emperor, and her story and confession. Kakuichi's finale presents the fall of the Heike – indeed all that has come to pass – through this guiltless yet haunted woman's eyes. It was her voice that spoke for the age. It is as if the whole fall of the Heike, and indeed of humankind is subsumed into her pain:

> Verily, all this
> That came to pass
> Before my very eyes
> Has been none other than
> A complete turning of the eternal wheel –
> The Six Realms of sentient pain.[51]

In the end there is salvation for the "mother of the nation" and her two attendants. The imagery of the three women is reminiscent of Amida and his two attendants, Kannon and Seishi. So powerful are the five concluding movements that make up the finale that it has been customary for a master to burn incense when teaching this canto to a student.[52]

In many ways, despite their different traditions and the fact that Akashi no Kakuichi lived almost four centuries earlier, the role he played in Japanese culture was not unlike that of Johann Sebastian Bach (1685–1750) in the Western tradition. Both men lived in an environment of sacred music. They began by following those tradi-

---

51 Takagi et al., *Heike monogatari*, vol. 33, p. 439.
52 Kindaichi Haruhiko, "Heikyoku – sono rekishi to ongaku," in *Heike monogatari*, vol. 9 of *Zusetsu Nihon no koten* (Tokyo, Shūseisha, 1980), p. 11.

tions but in the end went further, to creative choice. They also were exposed to the several secular and folk-music traditions within traveling distance of their homes. Both were professional music makers, for hire, who arranged and performed for a living. Although the perspective of time permits us now to view each as the founder of the musical tradition that flowed from their genius, in their own periods they were admired primarily as outstanding performers, Kakuichi as a virtuoso bard playing the *biwa*, Bach on the organ. Both men appeared at propitious moments in time when their genius could flower; both were men of great conceptual talent. Able to survey and bring together the principal styles and regional manifestations of music and vocalized texts that had developed before them, they enriched them all in a synthesis that set the future direction of their national traditions.

The biwa-*priests*

Because it was the occupation to which Kakuichi turned to make a living after he lost his sight, the profession of *biwa*-playing narrative singers that nurtured the evolution of the *Heike* texts deserves a brief note here. The *biwa*-priests (*biwa-hōshi*) were engaged in a service profession whose origins lie in the obscurities of early history.[53] They seem to have begun by performing rituals to placate unsettled spirits attached to home or village, during which the plucking and striking of the strident-sounding lutelike instrument, the *biwa*, played an important role. Its sound was believed to reach across to the spirit world and dissipate malignant forces (much as was the sounding of the string of an archer's bow in other shamanistic connections).

Numerous medieval picture scrolls show *biwa*-priests. Their casual appearance as part of the scenery must be taken as representative of their ubiquitous presence in medieval Japanese life. The depictions imply an itinerant existence on the edges of poverty. Invariably, *biwa*-priests are portrayed as blind, a misfortune attributed in those days to karmic hindrances originating in a previous existence. Blindness was certainly lamented, but it was also perceived as a sort of fortunate early warning that in this life one should at once occupy oneself with activities conducive to improved karma and salvation, or rebirth in paradise, depending on doctrinal proclivities. The *biwa*-priests' exorcistic

53 Barbara Ruch, "Medieval Jongleurs and the Making of a National Literature," in John W. Hall and Takeshi Toyoda, eds., *Japan in the Muromachi Age* (Berkeley and Los Angeles: University of California Press, 1977), pp. 279–309.

services, though surely intended to accumulate merit for themselves, also provided spiritual service to a society that universally embraced a belief in *onryō*, malignant spirits of the dead.

We do not know when or how *biwa*-priests changed from being purely exorcistic mediums who chanted incantations and played the *biwa* to being artist-performers of vocal narratives. Their function both as local exorcists and eventually as chanters of sacred liturgies over the dead on battlefields provided a natural background from which might evolve the intoning of accounts of the last moments of the dead and finally longer tales about these battles themselves. At least by the tenth century, *biwa*-priests who chanted narratives were noted as mendicant street entertainers, though what they chanted we do not know.

By the eleventh century there were at least two main strains of *biwa*-priests. One type, active especially in Kyushu and eastern Japan, followed the troops and sang battle tales. The other type was attached to temples, mostly around Kyoto, where they sang Buddhist pieces to small audiences.

After the Gempei War many of the battle singers seem to have gathered at Shoshazan, a Buddhist monastic center in Harima Province, west of the capital. Composed of several temples related to the Tendai sect, Shoshazan was an enclave where interest in the composition of vocal narratives flourished and whose library would have contained materials relevant to historic and religious accounts. A veritable melting pot for different strains of chanting and instrumentalizing and for tales from the widely separated battlefield regions from northeast to southwest, the Shoshazan environment played a vital role in the evolution of early versions of the *Heike*. It was also the monastery where Kakuichi himself studied and where, after he lost his sight, he trained to be a *biwa*-priest.

During the same period in *Heike* history, temple priests in Kyoto had begun to introduce canticles from other circulating *Heike* accounts into their own singing, in which history was made an example and the powers of Buddhism were offered as the answer to history's woes.

It is into this milieu that Kakuichi was born, a man who rose from the ranks of a thousand nameless composer-performers to become bard to a whole nation. But his life remains mostly mystery. Because he died in 1371 and was at that time over seventy, we may assume that he was born shortly after Mugai Nyodai died, sometime around 1300. We do not know his secular name, though records indicate that he was referred to as Akashi-dono.[54] Nor do we know the priestly name he used when, at a fairly youthful age, he became a monk at Shoshazan, which was located in the mountains not far from Akashi. Known as "the western Mount Hiei," Shoshazan attracted traveling monks from throughout Japan. Judging from the later quality of his literary and musical genius, Kakuichi obtained a good liturgical and musical education there. In addition to scriptural study, he probably also learned the Shoshazan-style of Tendai *shōmyō*, or liturgical vocal music for the incantation of scriptural texts, as well as a rather fast-paced rhythmical method of reading sutras, then considered a Shoshazan specialty. He was surely also familiar with certain styles of *enkyoku*, or Buddhist festive melodies, a kind of rhythmic prose song enjoyed by priests in a party environment at the end of important religious services. Somehow he also learned the songs called *imayō*, of the sort Otomae had in her repertory, as he incorporated them into the *Heike*.

We have no way to resurrect the melodies or rhythms or the preferred vocal timbres of these various works, as the system used at the time to record them constituted merely signs to indicate relative durations and the general direction of melodic line; music was learned orally by imitating a teacher. We can only hope that the conservative nature of religious forms of music makes it possible to hear echoes of the past in the present forms of Tendai *shōmyō* and in the vocalization of such performing arts as noh that were influenced by early Buddhist music.

After studying at Shoshazan for some years, Kakuichi lost his eyesight while he was still fairly young – no later than his early thirties – under circumstances that cannot be reconstructed at the present time.[55] For a priest in a scholarly center where sacred texts were central to life's daily activities, the blow must have been great. Nonetheless, Shoshazan was also a gathering place for *biwa*-priests; that Kakuichi had readily available such a creative option to turn to and that there were musician-chanters at Shoshazan under whom to study, was a momentous confluence of circumstances and a turning point in Japanese cultural history.

While still a Shoshazan, Kakuichi learned how to perform an early version of the *Heike*, now called the Kamakura-*bon Heike*, that most likely had been created by *biwa*-playing priests there when he was still a child. In effect, it was a kind of Shoshazan *Heike*. After learning to

54 According to the fourteenth-century *Heike kammon roku*, quoted by Tomikura Tokujirō, *Heike monogatari kenkyū* (Tokyo: Kadokawa shoten, 1967), p. 283.
55 From the *Saikai yōteki shū*, quoted by Tomikura, "Akashi no Kakuichi," p. 39.

perform it, Kakuichi left Shoshazan and moved to Kyoto, probably in the 1330s. Despite the political turbulence, Kyoto was a good place for a *biwa*-priest to make a living. The best talent was there, and audiences were readily available.

Kakuichi may have been urged to come to Kyoto by Joichi, a *biwa*-priest from Kyushu who had spent some time at Shoshazan; they might have become acquainted there. By about this time Joichi had become the most famous reciter in Kyoto of what is now called the Yashiro-*bon Heike*, one of the earliest extant reciter's versions. He must have been a talented innovator as well, as he and his associates were responsible for creating sometime before 1340 what is now called the Chikuhakuen-*bon* version.

Although he planned to make a living in Kyoto performing his Shoshazan *Heike*, Kakuichi nonetheless apprenticed himself to Joichi, which means he soon became familiar with at least the two other *Heike* compositions performed by his teacher. The association must have been a felicitous one for the two talented men, as both were interested in innovative composition and performance techniques. It is around this time that Joichi and Kakuichi, with one or two others, took the character *ichi* (first) as part of their names, a step that indicates an important bond.

Kakuichi's talent flowered. Soon the new "Kakuichi variations" were mentioned in diaries, and his name began to dominate the Kyoto scene. In 1340, Nakahara no Moromori recorded his attendance at a *Heike* recital by Kakuichi and stated that it was a "different form" of the work.[56] Moromori must have enjoyed it, as from then on until 1362 he attended numerous recitals of this new Kakuichi *Heike*. Recitals were held throughout the city, largely at such shrines or temples as the Rokujō Mido, the Yata Jizō Hall, the Yakushi Hall at the corner of Gojō and Takakura, and the Kitano Tenjin shrine.

By this time Kakuichi had attracted students. In the chronicle *Taiheiki*, written when Kakuichi was quite elderly, there is an account of Kakuichi and another *biwa*-priest, Shin'ichi, being called to the bedside of Musashi no kami Kō no Moronao (d. 1351), who was then greatly distracted from his discomfort by their performance of the *Heike* canto concerning, appropriately, a terrible night spirit called *nue*. Several *nue* had made an emperor ill until they were shot out of

---

56 Quoted from Moromori's diary, *Shishuki*, by Takagi et al., eds., *Heike monogatari*, vol. 32, p. 50; and Tomikura, *Heike*, p. 284.

the sky; thereupon the emperor's possession was broken, and he was restored to health.

The *biwa*-priests' performance before Moronao is described as a *tsure-Heike*, which seems to have been an intricate style of duet performance in which the elder Kakuichi vocalized the bass lines and the somewhat younger Shin'ichi the higher tenor lines. It is likely that *tsure* indicates an antiphonic rather than a harmonic arrangement, but because both men were by this time highly ranked *biwa*-priests, this must have been a virtuoso performance.

During Kakuichi's years in Kyoto, or at least by 1340, the *biwa*-priests had formed a guild and had established ranks of *kengyō*, *bettō*, *kōtō*, and *zatō*, the last and lowest coming to refer in later years to any blind person with a shaved head in a low-level entertainment or service job. From 1363 on, Kakuichi was referred to as *kengyō*, and he was probably soon thereafter made *sōkengyō* or "head *kengyō*," master of the entire guild, a rank he kept until his death.[57]

Kakuichi had at least four major disciples and was the main force in the establishment of the Ichikata style, or school of *Heike* performers, all of whom took the character *ichi* in their names and were singers of Kakuichi's *Heike*. For one hundred years after his death, Kakuichi's *Heike* was the principal *Heike* and represented one of the mainstays of the country's common culture. A rival style, the Jōkata (or Yasaka) school, which was using the Yashiro version of the *Heike* that Joichi had once used, was no match. Although it survived for some generations, it had virtually disappeared by the end of the Muromachi period. Written librettos of the Yashiro and the Kamakura variations once used by Kakuichi dropped out of sight at around the same time and were not rediscovered until the twentieth century.

Other battle tales such as the *Hōgen monogatari* and *Heiji monogatari* had been a part of the repertory of some *biwa*-priests up to Kakuichi's time, but by the late fourteenth century, *Hōgen* and *Heiji* had been dropped, and Kakuichi's *Heike* dominated all else.

Before, during, and after the Ōnin War in the fifteenth century, Kakuichi's disciples and their descendants flourished. Public performances of the *Heike* were often held as fund-raising activities for shrines and temples. The most famous *biwa*-priests played at court and before shoguns, and itinerant performers traveled the length of the nation. In 1462, it was estimated that five hundred to six hundred

57 Tomikura, *Heike*, pp. 282–3, 287.

biwa-priests were active in Kyoto alone.[58] It is doubtful that all of them were capable of performing Kakuichi's mammoth, complex masterpiece. Rather, according to contemporary records, the *biwa*-priests' repertories included other types of storytelling as well as the singing of the popular *kouta*, or "small song." Nonetheless, the popularity of Kakuichi's work is reflected in the greatly increased numbers of performer-disciples associated directly with it.

After Kakuichi's death, however, a new genre became popular: choreographed narratives such as noh and Kōwaka *mai*, both of whose subjects drew on Kakuichi's vocal narrative. Indeed, Kakuichi supplied Zeami with a cast of men and women characters of enormous power and aesthetic potential. Zeami himself revealed the awe with which he held Kakuichi's masterpiece: "In warrior plays, when it comes to the depiction of famous Genji and Heike warriors, we must without fail write the script in absolute faithfulness to the *Heike monogatari*."[59] Indeed, without Kakuichi's and his disciples' achievements, the appearance of such narrative works as *Taiheiki*, *Soga monogatari*, and *Gikeiki* is inconceivable.

Kakuichi had created the national myths. Yet in the face of intense competition from narrative forms with visual choreographed effects, the *Heike* priests faltered. Their revival in the Momoyama period had a kind of antiquarian interest (Kakuichi's *Heike* was by then viewed as an old national classic), and they never succeeded in taking center stage again. Although the *Heike* performers tried innovations – in 1598, for example, seven outstanding *biwa*-priests gave a "choral" performance of the *Heike*[60] – these could not compete with the more visually spectacular performing arts then fashionable. With the general burgeoning of the printing industry during the Edo period, Kakuichi's *Heike* circulated, with Momoyama-period revisions, as a reading text. It was at this time that the term *heikyoku* first came into usage, to distinguish the vocal composition from the new book-for-reading.

A definitive blow was struck in 1871, ironically marking the five-hundredth anniversary of Kakuichi's death: The government sponsorship and protection of guilds of blind *biwa*-players as preservers of a national tradition ended in the flush of "modernization" and "Westernization." Kakuichi's *Heike* was mortally wounded. Practitioners

58 Naramoto Tatsuya and Hayashiya Tatsusaburō, eds., *Kyōto no rekishi* (Tokyo: Gakugei shorin, 1968), vol. 3, p. 666.
59 *Nōsakusho*, in Hisamatsu and Nishio, eds., *Karonshū, Nōgakuronshū*, p. 475.
60 Tomikura Tokujirō, *Shintei Heike monogatari*, vol. 1 of *Nihon koten zenshū* (Tokyo: Asahi shimbunsha, 1984), p. 75.

sank into poverty and could not attract enough new disciples to earn a living; most scattered to the few alternative occupations open to the blind.[61]

The Tale of the Heike represents the first and surely the finest articulation of Japan's earliest truly nationwide catastrophe and is a compendium of religious, aesthetic, ethical, and psychological responses to it as intuited by Kakuichi. To accounts of battles he added details of heroic action that are entirely fictitious, thereby synthesizing a national ethic and creating a national myth.[62] No other work before it spoke of or to such a broad spectrum of people. Carried from one end of the country to the other and performed by religiosecular jongleurs, the *Heike* addressed men and women on all levels of society in all localities. Indeed, another of Kakuichi's important additions to the earlier *Heike* versions was his accounts of the great temples of Nara and Kōya and of the sacred sites of Itsukushima, Chikubushima, and Kumano, through which these sacred sites left sectarian history and became national monuments.

Kakuichi succeeded where the writers of such Western medieval epics as *Beowulf*, *The Poem of Cid*, or the *Song of Roland* did not. The events and personalities he crafted inspired hundreds of later literary works in every conceivable genre, from noh drama to *Kōwaka bukyoku; kojōruri; otogizōshi;* Meiji, Taishō, and Showa novels; and modern cinema. They are alive today as the central national myth of Japanese society.

CONCLUSION

Gekokujō ("inferior overthrows superior") is a favorite term of Japanese historians,[63] and among twentieth-century scholars it has become the fashion to call the late middle ages, especially the post–Ōnin War

---

61 There are still surviving two or three conservators – chiefly in Sendai and Nagoya – who are preserving Kakuichi's living *Heike* and are recording parts of it. For example, Nippon Columbia cassette tape CAY-9040 (*Heike biwa*), "Gion shōja" and "Yokobue"; Nippon Columbia record AL-5046 (*Heike biwa*), "Gion shōja" and "Kogō"; and Philips (Nippon Phonogram Co.) PH-7511–2 (*Heike Biwa*), "Chikubushima mōde," "Nasu no Yoichi," and "Susuki."

62 The *Heike* provided a model for personal conduct in war throughout the middle ages and even well into the twentieth century. The process whereby such ethical concepts as loyalty, sacrifice, and honor were incorporated into Kakuichi's *Heike* is discussed in Butler, "The *Heike monogatari* and the Japanese Warrior Ethic."

63 The concept came from China in the *Book of Changes*, which describes each of the five elements (wood, fire, earth, metal, water) as capable of overpowering one of the others. In human relations as well, nature had ordained similar powers of control for lord over vassal, husband over wife, and the like, and any reversal was a dangerous aberration.

years, the age of *gekokujo*. Yet the rise of ordinary persons to economic consequence and political effectiveness in the fourteenth or fifteenth century cannot be explained in such simplistic terms as the rise and fall or overturn of classes. Furthermore, in writing the history of culture, we must keep in mind that culture is not benign. It is passionate and irrational and is based on deeply felt choices. Beyond individual eccentricity and class, common national preferences spring from shared social ritual, and for the medieval Japanese the central rituals were classless: the tonsure, pilgrimage and travel, wine and song, rites to activate good and nullify evil forces, communication with the spirits of the dead, and rituals to ensure an afterlife in paradise or beyond the pain of this life.

Concepts such as *yūgen* and *sabi*, said to characterize Muromachi-period arts and literature, play no role at all in the common arts of painting, sculpture, song, dance, and musical epic that we have been discussing. Those values belong to an extremely limited world, to rarefied pockets of society. But the elements that can be found everywhere, in those same rarefied enclaves as well as in the world outside, include attitudes, values, and conceptions characteristic of the popular songs and narratives discussed earlier. Such basic life attitudes emerged and coalesced during the middle ages; they were transmitted nationwide and have never left Japanese society to this day.

The list is long and could be easily expanded: *gense no go-riyaku* (a focus on the present world with a belief in the personal compassion and efficacy of deities in this life), *akirame* (a sense of security in resignation), the need for *shugyō* (a belief that suffering is normal and necessary, that one must drive oneself to the point of suffering for any good to emerge), the compulsion for *tabi* or *mōde* (an obsession with travel coupled with a sense of its inevitable discomfort that makes it akin to *shūgyō*, yet with a deep appreciation of its liberating qualities), *hōgan biki* (a sympathy for the underdog, altered in the face of twentieth-century pressures and practicality to a distaste for the very powerful or the sure winner), *seijitsu* (an admiration for the impetuously sincere act despite any irrational outcome), *gisei* (a deep sense of self-worth and even pleasure in sometimes devastating self-suppression, a complete confidence that happiness or salvation can lie in a sublimated existence), *shi* (a belief that sometimes death is a ready, necessary, and socially accepted alternative), and *shūgen* (a belief in the talismanic power of felicitous words to move both the gods and one's fellows to good effect). These are but a few of the major values and attitudes of medieval Japan, classless, and rendered national through the social rituals of song, dance, festival, and vocalized myth.

The men and women, the images that here have been drawn from the unheeded other side of history – the other side of gender, work, faith, and national image – all add up to a medieval society that is passionate and practical and brazen, a far cry from the subdued and reticent elegance of the elite ideal. The shared national heritage certainly included a courtier past. In the popular mind, the age of Genji was a vision of the nation's artistic accomplishment; yet it was all the more treasured because it was both greatly idealized and wholly irretrievable.

If we leave these pages having categorized Mugai Nyodai as woman or nun, Saru Genji as fisherman or merchant, or Akashi no Kakuichi as blind priest and national bard, we will have merely substituted classification for meaning. Though orthodox constituents of the social structure, these men and women, like shamans, have traditionally been excised from the pages of official history. Because they were perceived as existing outside the processes of power, the notion was that they therefore could not have been important to the nation's past.

Japan has not one past, however, but many pasts, all of which are indispensable to the public whole and all of which contributed to society and culture. Our emphasis here on recovering lost histories of neglected groups is not advocacy of further segmenting scholarship but, rather, a suggestion that our search for the larger synthetic patterns in cultural history will fail if half the lights are out. When our history matures, it will thus be the interrelationships of all these groups in the formulation of Japanese culture that will be the object of our best analyses.

CHAPTER 12

BUDDHISM IN THE KAMAKURA PERIOD

INTRODUCTION

Buddhism has had a long and illustrious history in Japan, but it was in the Kamakura period that Buddhism in Japan came into full flower. The forms of Buddhism that emerged at that time – Pure Land, Zen, and Nichiren – were largely responsible for the dissemination of Buddhist beliefs and practices throughout Japanese society. The success of this movement lay in tailoring the ideas and goals of Buddhism to the concerns of the populace at large. Hence, Kamakura Buddhism, as the entire religious movement is called, has left an indelible mark on Japanese history and has made Buddhism a lasting and pervasive component of Japanese culture.

Buddhism originated in India and spread to China about four centuries after the time of the historical Buddha Śākyamuni (ca. fifth to fourth century, B.C.). It was transmitted to Japan from China via the Korean peninsula around the middle of the sixth century.[1] The cultural gulf that existed at that time between Japan on the one hand and China and Korea on the other was considerable. Japan's ruling class accepted Buddhism as the embodiment of an advanced and superior civilization, and in order to gain control over the concepts and technology that Buddhism brought to Japan, the elite provided a succession of large temples where Buddhism could put down roots. A community of priests supported by the state and the aristocracy belonged to each of these temples. The priests pursued activities in a variety of fields: They learned how to read the Chinese version of the Buddhist scriptures that had been translated from Sanskrit; they became experts in engineering, architecture, and medicine – fields of knowledge that were concentrated in the temples – and they performed the various ceremonies and prayers requested by the imperial court and the aristocracy for

---

1 *Nihon shoki*, in *Nihon koten bungaku taikei*, vol. 68 (Tokyo: Iwanami shoten, 1957–67), p. 100. Hereafter *Nihon koten bungaku taikei* is cited as *NKBT*.

their spiritual and material well-being. As temples became better organized and acquired control over vast estates (*shōen*), their operation
became more complex and internal power struggles more prevalent.
Japan absorbed Buddhism as a comprehensive and advanced cultural medium from the outside but did not, at first, give substantial
weight to its religious concerns per se. Three centuries after Buddhism's arrival, however, around the middle of the Nara period, there
was an awakening to Buddhism's actual teachings. Priests became
more and more involved in specifically religious activities. Some withdrew from the temples and secluded themselves in mountainous regions, proselytizing among the common people.[2]

At the popular level, various types of beliefs and practices with
indigenous Japanese roots circulated among the people, and among
them, the priests who left the temples gradually found a receptive
audience for their teachings. The Buddhism that they introduced into
these circles contained more sophisticated doctrines and more refined
rituals than the native traditions did. Buddhism was thus used to give
greater form and expression to Japan's simpler folk beliefs and practices. The *kami*, or indigenous deities, were explained using Buddhist
doctrines, and the native practices were further ritualized through
contact with Buddhism.

From late in the tenth century, aristocratic society in Japan started
to become stagnant and closed. Important government positions were
monopolized by a few families, and many aristocrats and members of
the literati could not find positions appropriate to their skills, even
when they possessed superior ability and extensive knowledge. Individuals frustrated by this situation began to show greater interest in
Buddhism. They were attracted to its teaching of the relative and
conditional nature of this world and to its goal of transcending it. They
studied Buddhism's complex doctrines, which up to that time had
been the exclusive pursuit of scholar-priests. Aristocrats and the literati sought out priests to lecture on the scriptures, particularly priests
active outside the temples. These events paved the way for
Kamakura's new movements to appear in Buddhist history.

During this period a number of large temples had close ties with
aristocratic society through the religious ceremonies they performed
on its behalf. Among them were the Enryakuji on Mount Hiei and the
Tōdaiji and the Kōfukuji of Nara, all major centers of Buddhist learn-

---

2 One example of these priests is Gyōki, described in the *Shoku Nihongi*, in *Kokushi taikei*, vol. 2
(Tokyo: Yoshikuwa kōbunkan, 1929–64), pp. 68–69. Hereafter *Kokushi taikei* is cited as *KT*.
Other examples can be found in the *Nihon ryōiki*, *NKBT*, vol. 70.

ing. The temples of Nara preserved the orthodox teachings of the Kegon and the Hossō schools, whereas Mount Hiei preserved the teachings of the Tendai school. Mount Hiei also became a center for the formulation of the new doctrines that popularized Buddhism throughout Japan. The priests who established ties with the aristocracy and literati in Kyoto were also those living at Mount Hiei or in its vicinity. Among them, there arose a tendency to interpret Buddhism not in a scholarly vein but, rather, in subjective religious terms. As beliefs and practices spread among the aristocrats, the stage was set for the emergence of Kamakura's revolutionary Buddhist movements.

From the end of the twelfth century through the middle of the thirteenth – that is, in the first half of the Kamakura period – some of Japan's foremost religious figures appeared, in quick succession. The schools of Buddhism that today claim them as their founders have long had considerable influence in Japan. From their inception in the Kamakura period, these schools stood as a separate religious movement from the eight schools that existed before them. These new schools came to be known collectively as Kamakura Buddhism. The establishment of Kamakura Buddhism was a pivotal event in Japanese history, because through it Buddhism was adapted to Japanese ways and thus made accessible to the common people.

THE ORIGINATORS OF KAMAKURA BUDDHISM

Hōnen and Shinran

Kamakura Buddhism criticized the formalism of the Buddhist establishment of its day and instead emphasized belief and practice.[3] The person at the forefront of this new movement was Hōnen (1133–1212).[4] He was born in the province of Mimasaka (present-day Okayama Prefecture), and while still a child, he lost his father in a local political dispute. As a result of that experience, Hōnen was moved to enter the Buddhist clergy as a novice. Some years later he went to Mount Hiei to receive intensive religious training. During Hōnen's lifetime, one of the few ways for people from the provinces to penetrate Japan's elite intellectual circles was to become a priest. This

3 Scholars since the Meiji period have frequently compared the new Buddhism of Kamakura Japan to the Christian Reformation of Europe. See, for examples, Hara Katsurō, "Tōzai no shūkyō kaikaku," in Nihon chūseishi no kenkyū (Tokyo: Dōbunkan, 1929), pp. 304–21; and Matsumoto Hikojirō, Nihon bunka shiron (Tokyo: Kawade shobō, 1942).
4 Concerning Hōnen's life, see Tamura Enchō, Hōnen (Tokyo: Yoshikawa kōbunkan, 1959); and Bukkyō daigaku, ed., Hōnen Shōnin kenkyū (Kyoto: Heirakuji shoten, 1961).

is precisely the route that Hōnen took. He went to Mount Hiei and received training first in Tendai doctrine. Later he took as his teacher a priest named Eikū (d. 1179), who had distanced himself from the mainstream of Mount Hiei's religious organization. Hōnen followed Eikū's example of withdrawing from Mount Hiei's political entanglements and secluding himself on a remote part of the mountain for study and religious training. Under Eikū, Hōnen studied the Buddhist scriptures and doctrinal treatises. For a time he concentrated on the Vinaya, containing the rules of conduct for Buddhist clergy, and he began to reflect on what it meant to be a priest. He also read the Ōjōyōshū by Genshin (942–1017), which exposed him to the Pure Land teachings that the Tendai school had integrated into its religious system.[5] In addition, Hōnen traveled to Nara and received instruction in the doctrines of Hossō and the other philosophies of Nara Buddhism. In short, Hōnen received a classical education in the teachings of the established Buddhist schools.

In 1175, after thirty years on Mount Hiei, Hōnen happened to read the Kuan ching shu, a commentary by the Chinese master Shan-tao (613–81) on the Pure Land Meditation Sutra (Kanmuryōjukyō).[6] Hōnen also had a revelatory vision of Shan-tao, and as a result of this experience, he began to expound the doctrine of the "exclusive nembutsu" (senju nembutsu). Shan-tao, who formulated his teachings in seventh-century China, advocated the practice of intoning Amida Buddha's name in the form "I take refuge in the Buddha Amida." This practice, known in Japan as the nembutsu, was emphasized even more by Hōnen as the single and exclusive act leading to enlightenment in Amida's resplendent and transcendent realm called the Pure Land.

The basic scripture describing Amida and his Pure Land paradise is the Larger Pure Land Sutra (Muryōjukyō). According to this scripture, Amida framed forty-eight vows in a previous lifetime when he was living as the ascetic monk Hōzō, before becoming a Buddha. He phrased the vows in such a way as to make their fulfillment a condition for his own enlightenment and Buddhahood.[7] In the eighteenth

5 Ōjōyōshū, in Genshin, Nihon shisō taikei, vol. 6 (Tokyo: Iwanami shoten, 1970–82), pp. 9–322, is the most representative work of Pure Land beliefs and practices in the Heian period. It was written in 985 by the Tendai priest Genshin, on Mount Hiei. Hereafter, Nihon shisō taikei is cited as NST.
6 Kuan ching shu, in Taishō shinshū daizaōkyō, vol. 37 (Tokyo: Taishō shinshū daizōkyō kankōkai, 1924–32), pp. 245–78. Hereafter Taishō shinshū daizōkyō is cited as TD. For the Pure Land Meditation Sutra itself, see Kanmuryōjukyō, TD, vol. 12, pp. 340–6. Shan-tao was the foremost Pure Land thinker in China during the T'ang period and was very active in Pure Land proselytization.   7 Muryōjukyō, TD, vol. 12, pp. 267–9.

vow, known as the principal vow (hongan), he stated that everyone who invokes his name will be born in their next lifetime in the Pure Land.[8] The scripture stated that in fact the monk Hōzō had achieved Buddhahood as Amida and that the Pure Land he created now exists. Consequently, Hōnen believed that anyone intoning Amida's name is assured of birth in that paradise after death in this world.[9] Amida Buddha shows no partiality in welcoming human beings into his Pure Land. Thus, what binds them to Amida must be an act that can be performed by any person. Hōnen considered the spoken nembutsu – that is, uttering the name of Amida Buddha – to be that very act.[10]

Hōnen believed that among Buddhism's innumerable religious practices, nembutsu could be singled out as the simplest and most efficacious one.[11] Therefore, it is the most fundamental Buddhist practice of the present age, and it stands in perfect accord with the essence of Buddhism. This was an epoch-making teaching in Japan, because for the first time Buddhism's path of salvation was opened to people without specialized religious training or discipline. When Hōnen left Mount Hiei and began to expound this new teaching in Kyoto, he attracted the interest of many people, but he also elicited doctrinal criticism from Buddhist authorities. In an attempt to defend himself, Hōnen presented a doctrinal systematization of his own, in his magnum opus, the Senjakushū.[12] In this work, written for the benefit of those aristocrats who had accepted his ideas, Hōnen indicated why it was essential to adopt the Pure Land teachings: Through them one is drawn in faith to Amida Buddha's principal vow, which will deliver all people into the Pure Land. One is inspired to intone Amida's name because one is the beneficiary of his compassion. Hōnen maintained that if these points are understood, then none of Buddhism's other doctrines will be necessary.[13]

Hōnen's assertions were based on the pessimistic assumption that the human beings in his time were mired in foolishness and wrongdoings. A time long ago, he believed, humans were capable of attaining Buddhahood through their own efforts, but in the present age that is

8 Ibid., p. 268.
9 Muryōjukyōshaku, in Hōnen Ippen, NST, vol. 10, p. 50.
10 Senjaku hongan nembutsushū, in Hōnen Ippen, NST, vol. 10, pp. 94–100.
11 Ibid., pp. 101–9; and Ichimai kishōmon, in Kana hōgoshū, NKBT, vol. 83, p. 53.
12 The full title of this work is Senjaku hongan nembutsushū. For standard editions of the text, see Hōnen Ippen, NST, vol. 10, pp. 87–162; and TD, vol. 83, pp. 1–20. Hōnen composed the work in 1199.
13 Senjaku hongan nembutsushū, in Hōnen Ippen, NST, vol. 10, pp. 103–5.

no longer possible, as Śākyamuni Buddha's time has long passed.[14] This kind of pessimism emerged in Japan around the mid-Heian period, based on a sober introspective view of the human condition. Aristocrats and the literati tended more and more to perceive human existence in its actual state rather than in the idealized form for which humans were supposed to strive. Various literary works produced in the Heian period echo these sentiments, including Japanese poetry (waka), diaries (nikki), and narratives (monogatari).[15] Hōnen carried this introspective view of the human condition one step further. He moved from human foolishness and wrongdoing to Amida Buddha's perfection and all-pervading compassion. In perceiving the dramatic gulf between the two, Hōnen concluded that total reliance on Amida was the only hope for humans in the present age.

Shinran (1173–1262) inherited Hōnen's teachings and developed them even further.[16] A member of the lower aristocracy, Shinran was probably born in Kyoto. Like Hōnen, he became a monk at a young age. He spent some twenty years of his life on Mount Hiei but found unsatisfying the Buddhism espoused there. In 1201, Shinran secluded himself for religious practices in a temple in Kyoto known as the Rokkakudō. During this seclusion he received a nocturnal revelation that created for him a new religious outlook. This event marked the turning point in Shinran's life, at which time he devoted himself single-mindedly to Hōnen's teachings. The master–disciple association between them, nonetheless, was short-lived. Shinran was separated from Hōnen during a suppression of the new Pure Land movement in 1207, which was sanctioned by the imperial court. Shinran was banished to Echigo Province (present-day Niigata Prefecture).[17] Several years later, when he was pardoned, Shinran moved to Hitachi Province (present-day Ibaragi Prefecture) instead of returning to Kyoto. There he became an active proselytizer of the Pure Land teachings. From the time of his banishment, Shinran described himself as neither priest nor layman.[18]

14 This eschatological way of thinking is usually referred to as mappō shisō, "decline of the Dharma" thought. One Heian-period work that is representative of this way of thinking is the Mappō tōmyōki, in Shinshū zenshū, vol. 58 (Tokyo: Kokusho kankōkai, 1915 and 1975), pp. 495–502.
15 Examples are Kagerō nikki, Murasaki Shikibu nikki, and Sarashina nikki. Genji monogatari is an exception to this pattern.
16 Concerning Shinran's life, see Akamatsu Toshihide, Shinran (Tokyo: Yoshikawa kōbunkan, 1961); and Matsuno Junkō, Shinran: sono shōgai to shisō no tenkai katei (Tokyo: Sanseidō, 1959).
17 Concerning the suppression, see the appendix of the Tannishō, in Shinran-shū Nichiren-shū, NKBT, vol. 82 p. 265, n. 175.
18 Kyōgyōshinshō, in Shinran, NST, vol. 11, p. 258.

He openly took a wife, in clear violation of the vow of celibacy he took when ordinated as a Tendai priest. Shinran perceived in his own life the very image of human existence that Hōnen had preached, one mired in foolishness and wrongdoings. It was in this humble and self-effacing frame of mind that Shinran established himself as a religious seeker and Pure Land teacher in the community of ordinary peasant farmers in the Kantō region.

The introspective views of Hōnen and Shinran were an indirect product of the decline in social mobility in Japan's aristocracy. Consequently, it was not easy to propagate these views among the peasant farmers of the Kantō, who had grown up amid more superstitious and less introspective beliefs. Shinran thus attempted to adapt Pure Land ideas to the concerns of the lower classes by using the dual concepts of "this world" and the "next world" that Hōnen had used. Hōnen originally presented the *nembutsu* as the religious act that one must perform in order to be born into the next world where Buddhahood will be achieved.[19] Shinran stressed the same idea in a slightly different way to show that one is blessed also while living in this world. That blessing comes in the form of an assurance, that one will attain Buddhahood without fail when born into that next world.[20]

Thus, the reward of Buddhahood in one's next life is paralleled in this life by personal assurance and peace of mind. Shinran taught that whoever enters into this belief is assured of salvation from the first *nembutsu* spoken. After that, whenever the *nembutsu* is invoked, it is not a repetition of this assurance but, rather, an act of gratitude for salvation already assured.[21] In Shinran's later years, this idea developed further into the doctrine that a person of correct faith is equal to the buddhas and the bodhisattvas.[22] In other words, faith accords one the most exalted status possible in this world, even though enlightenment itself has not yet been achieved. In this way, Shinran conveyed the idea of immediate benefits that the Pure Land path offered, without endorsing the mechanistic, superstitious, and magical rewards that the peasant population typically sought in religion. The heart of his teaching, however, was that faith leads to enlightenment in the next world.

Shinran arrived at his beliefs through ever-deeper introspection on

19 *Shōsokumon*, in *Hōnen Ippen, NST*, vol. 10, p. 175.
20 *Kyōgyōshinshō*, in *Shinran, NST*, vol. 11, pp. 97–100; and *Mattōshō*, in *Shinran-shū Nichiren-shū, NKBT*, vol. 82, p. 115.
21 *Shinran Shōnin goshōsokushū*, in *Shinran-shū Nichiren-shū, NKBT*, vol. 82, p. 167.
22 *Sanjō wasan* and *Mattōshō*, in *Shinran-shū Nichiren-shū, NKBT*, vol. 82, pp. 62 (*wasan* no. 94), pp. 120–1.

THE ORIGINATORS OF KAMAKURA BUDDHISM   551

the human condition. While living in his fallen state with his wife and children among the peasant farmers of the Kantō, Shinran focused his attention on the nature and capacity of human beings. Hōnen had asserted that all sentient beings are objects of Amida's salvation, but Shinran continued to seek their true inner nature. In the end, he perceived humans as incapable of anything but wrongdoing. He categorically denied that they had the power to save themselves, and he thus added another dimension to the idea of faith. That is, faith is not a path to salvation through one's own efforts. It is defined, instead, by "other power" (*tariki*), a total reliance on the power of Amida Buddha.

Around the age of sixty, Shinran left the Kantō region and returned to Kyoto, where he spent the last thirty years of his life. There he composed a number of religious works, the foremost of which is his *Kyōgyōshinshō*.[23] Shinran continued to maintain contact with his Kantō disciples through letters and to give them guidance in religious matters. It is clear, however, that he shunned the personal aggrandizement and veneration that his followers often accorded him. Shinran believed that all human beings are equal before Amida Buddha, and he thus refused to accept the exalted role of religious master in which others cast him. His self-abnegation suggests that Shinran had no desire to organize a religious sect of his own. Indeed, that enterprise was undertaken only after his death by his spiritual successors and blood descendants.

Eisai and Dōgen

Shinran and Hōnen formulated their new religious ideas by concentrating on the internal nature of human beings. In their proselytization activities, they separated themselves from the major temples and turned their attention more to the common people and those living in the provinces. Zen, however, emerged along very different lines. During the late Heian period, one segment of Japan's aristocracy began to study the orthodox traditions of Chinese thought, as a way of reinvigorating society. Chinese learning had long been considered the foundation of civilization, especially by the aristocracy, but in the middle of the Heian period, interest in things Chinese waned or existed only in the abstract. By the end of the period, however, interest reemerged in some circles, and priests began to travel to China to visit the important

---

23 The formal title of this work is the *Ken jōdo shinjitsu kyōgyōshō monrui*. A first draft of the text was completed by Shinran in 1224. For standard editions of the text, see *Shinran, NST*, vol. 11, pp. 7–260; and *TD*, vol. 83, pp. 589–643.

temples and Buddhist sites there.[24] Eisai (1141–1215), Chōgen (d. 1195), and Shunjō (1166–1227) were among those who went to China at the beginning of the Kamakura period. They differed in their individual religious views, but they all were united in their attraction to the thought and culture of Sung China. By importing Chinese learning and synthesizing it with their own religious traditions, they hoped to revitalize Buddhism in Japan. It was in this context that Zen was imported from China.

The first person to play an important role in the adoption of Zen was Eisai.[25] He was born in 1141 into a prominent family of Shinto priests in Bitchū Province (present-day Okayama Prefecture). Instead of following the family tradition, Eisai entered a Buddhist temple at a young age and was eventually ordained as a Buddhist priest. In his early career he studied Tendai doctrine and *mikkyō* or esoteric Buddhism. Unlike Hōnen, Eisai was not inclined toward withdrawal or religious seclusion on Mount Hiei. Rather, he had strong ambitions to make a name for himself in the Tendai establishment. While studying on Mount Hiei, Eisai began to dream of restoring the Tendai school to the state of religious creativity from which it had declined. That aspiration prompted him to make the arduous journey to China twice and to seek out Buddhism's orthodox teachings there. On his first visit, Eisai discovered that Zen was the dominant form of Buddhism in China. During his second visit, he actually studied Zen. His teacher was Hsüan Huai-ch'ang (Kian Eshō), a master in the Huang-lung (Ōryō) branch of the Lin-chi (Rinzai) school.[26]

Zen had some influence on the Japanese Tendai school at the time of its founding by Saichō (767–822). This school is often described as an amalgamation of four Buddhist traditions: Tendai doctrine, Zen meditation, Vinaya rules, and *mikkyō* ritual. Eisai believed that among the four, Zen and Vinaya had lapsed into disuse, and Mount Hiei had thus fallen into stagnation.[27] Hence, Zen was the first thing he sought to reintroduce from China. The controlling powers at Mount Hiei were not aware of Zen's ascendant position in China and therefore refused to recognize the new teachings that Eisai propounded and even attempted

24 Mori Katsumi, *Mori Katsumi chosaku senshū*, vol. 4: *Nissō bunka kōryū no shomondai* (Tokyo: Kokusho kankōkai, 1975), pp. 167–202.
25 Concerning Eisai's life, see Taga Munehaya, *Eisai* (Tokyo: Yoshikawa kōbunkan, 1965).
26 *Kōzen gokokuron*, in *Chūsei Zenka no shisō*, NST, vol. 16, pp. 53–54; and *Genkō shakusho, KT*, vol. 31, pp. 43–46. The Lin-chi branch was founded by Lin-chi I-hsüan (d. 867) and was the most powerful branch of Zen in China during the Sung period.
27 *Kōzen gokokuron*, in *Chūsei Zenka no shisō*, NST, vol. 16, pp. 16–48.

to suppress them. In response to their opposition, Eisai wrote his primary work, the *Kōzen gokokuron*, in which he defended Zen as a teaching that would preserve and uphold the nation rather than undermine it.[28] Despite his protestations, the established authorities on Mount Hiei were unwilling to permit Zen to be taught there. Fortunately, however, the leaders of the newly established bakufu, or military government, in Kamakura expressed an interest in it and accorded Eisai the institutional support and patronage necessary to establish Zen as a religious tradition in Japan. The bakufu recognized the power and influence of Sung China and hoped to use Eisai's knowledge of Chinese thought and culture to lend prestige and authority to its own rule.

Zen originated in China in the mid-T'ang period. As a school of Buddhism, it bore the strong imprint of Chinese culture. China and Japan had close ties during the Nara period, and Zen was first introduced into Japan at that time. But it was difficult for the Japanese to comprehend Zen because of its mystical qualities and its highly developed mental training. Zen was reintroduced on several other occasions during the Heian period, but it never managed to take root as an independent school. Only in the late Heian period, when the religious authority of Mount Hiei was shaken and Kamakura's religious revolution took shape, was the climate right for Zen to be accepted.

Eisai and other early Zen priests in Japan inherited the fundamental Zen principle that the absolute must be grasped through direct intuitive experience within the mind, not through the aid of the written word. But they tended to couch Zen's mystical aspects in the context of *mikkyō*, or esoteric Buddhism. The two were similar in that both preserved their teachings through private master–disciple transmissions, and they conveyed the absolute through symbolic acts of ritual and discipline. The arrival of Zen from China, therefore, played a role in reshaping and bolstering esoteric Buddhist thought, which had flourished throughout the Heian period. With the appearance of Dōgen, however, Zen assumed a more revolutionary guise and began to emerge as a strain of Kamakura Buddhism itself.

Dōgen (1200–53) was the son of the court noble and politician Tsuchimikado Michichika.[29] As a child, Dōgen was surrounded by

---

28 This was Eisai's most important treatise and the first work on Zen composed in Japan. For standard editions of the text, see *Kōzen gokokuron*, in *Chūsei Zenka no shisō*, *NST,* vol. 16, pp. 7–97; and *TD*, vol. 80, pp. 1–17.
29 Concerning Dōgen's life, see Imaeda Aishin, *Dōgen: sono kōdō to shisō* (Tokyo: Hyōronsha, 1970); and Ōkubo Dōshū, *Dōgen zenji den no kenkyū* (Tokyo: Iwanami shoten, 1953).

high-ranking aristocrats and well-known literary figures, and so he received a superior and extensive education. Both of his parents died while he was still young, and as a result, Dōgen decided to take up the life of a priest on Mount Hiei. In disposition, Dōgen was fervent in his religious pursuits and intent on discovering Buddhism's essence, but the Buddhism he found on Mount Hiei failed to give satisfying answers to the questions he asked.

Dōgen's entire experience on Mount Hiei differed significantly from that of the other originators of Kamakura Buddhism: First, by Dōgen's time Mount Hiei was beginning to lose credibility as the hub of Buddhism in Japan. Second, Dōgen was never dependent on Mount Hiei for social mobility, as were Hōnen, Eisai, and other priests from the provinces. For them, Mount Hiei was an entry into Japan's intellectual and cultural circles. But for Dōgen, who came from the highest aristocracy, studying the doctrines of Buddhism and mastering the scholarship of the Chinese and Japanese classics were never the only alternative. Hōnen and Shinran spent considerable time in doctrinal training on Mount Hiei, and the scriptures and commentaries they encountered there became, through reinterpretation, the springboard for their own religious ideas. Dōgen, by contrast, quickly abandoned Mount Hiei in his search for true Buddhism, and his disillusionment with Buddhism there prompted him to travel to China in 1223.

In China, Dōgen was not attracted to the most popular form of Zen, the Lin-chi (Rinzai) school, which had extensive ties with the highest echelons of secular society. Instead, he gravitated toward the Ts'ao-tung (Sōtō) school, which had maintained a strong monastic and antisecular flavor since its inception in the T'ang period. After training in Zen meditation at the T'ien-t'ung-shan monastery under the Ts'ao-tung master Ch'ang-weng Ju-ching (Chōō Nyojō, 1163–1228) Dōgen underwent a religious experience that his master certified as a state of enlightenment.

Dōgen then returned to Japan to impart the Zen teachings there. Earlier, Eisai had propounded a brand of Zen that was intermixed with other forms of Buddhism. Dōgen, by contrast, rejected other types of Buddhism and maintained that the religious absolute could be realized only through Zen in its purest form.[30] His claim was that a person achieves enlightenment only by sitting in meditation and that meditation itself is indistinguishable from the actual state of enlightenment.[31]

---

30 *Fukan zazengi*, *TD*, vol. 82, pp. 1–2.
31 *Shōbōgenzō*, "Bendōwa" chapter, in *Dōgen*, pt. 1, *NST*, vol. 12, p. 20.

In Japan, Dōgen first made his religious base at a temple in Uji on the outskirts of Kyoto. There he offered instruction in meditation to an ever-increasing number of Zen aspirants. But because of Mount Hiei's opposition to his teachings, Dōgen was eventually forced to retreat to Echizen Province (present-day Fukui Prefecture) to continue his activities.

Dōgen's primary work, the *Shōbōgenzō*, is a collection of essays presented as lectures to his disciples.[32] The essays date from the time he resided at Uji until shortly before his death. The *Shōbōgenzō* reveals the sophisticated level of speculative thought of which Dōgen was capable. In it he addresses some of Buddhism's fundamental questions: What is the essence of Buddhahood? What constitutes true religious practice? What is the nature of time? In addition to the *Shōbōgenzō*, Dōgen composed several works defining the rules and etiquette governing monastic conditions and the daily life of religious practitioners.[33] He formulated these in an attempt to put into practice what his teacher had taught him in China. Dōgen sought to separate Zen from the political intrigues in which the religious authorities on Mount Hiei and the great temples of Nara engaged. Even though they had dominated Japanese Buddhism throughout the Heian period, Dōgen considered Sōtō Zen to be the quintessential form of Buddhism. The basic theme of his teachings was that one should fervently seek the absolute and diligently practice meditation. Based on that principle, Dōgen scrupulously avoided dealing with the secular powers, and he produced one of Japan's most sublime religious philosophies.

Nichiren and Ippen

The last of Kamakura Buddhism's seminal figures, Nichiren and Ippen, appeared well after the religious revolution began. Although their teachings differed profoundly from each other, the way that they adapted them to the Japanese context was similar. This element of adaptation and concern for the immediate world stands out more prominently in their ideas than in those of earlier Kamakura thinkers. The Pure Land teachings of Hōnen and Shinran, for example, present

---

32 The *Shōbōgenzō*, written in classical Japanese, is the most comprehensive account of Dōgen's ideas. Its contents were assembled from his sermons and lectures. For the standard seventy-five and ninety-five fascicle editions of the *Shōbōgenzō*, see *Dōgen*, pts. 1 and 2, *NST*, vols. 12–13; and *TD*, vol. 82, pp. 7–309.   33 *Eihei shingi, TD*, vol. 82, pp. 319–42.

salvation as occurring not in the present world but in the Pure Land after death. Dōgen's teachings are built around the experience of an ineffable absolute and thus display little concern for the existing secular order or for guiding people in how to live in it. Nichiren and Ippen, on the other hand, couched their ideas in down-to-earth terms and formulated a religious path that melded Buddhism with the immediate experiences of the Japanese.

This last stage in the development of Kamakura Buddhism occurred amid conditions different from those of the first stage. Major changes were at work in Japan's social and religious spheres in the middle of the thirteenth century, some fifty years after Hōnen appeared on the scene. The first important change was in the aristocracy. In Hōnen's time, new forms of religious thought came directly out of the aristocracy. They arose from a deep sense of alarm among the aristocrats and literati over the crumbling of the established order. But by the middle of the thirteenth century this situation had changed. It was no longer possible to hide the fact that the aristocracy itself was in a state of precipitous decline. The aristocrats withdrew from the religious forefront to work out their convictions in isolation. They came to view themselves as the bastion of Japanese culture and the preservers of tradition. At this stage, the aristocrats no longer functioned as active agents in creating Japan's new religious ideas.

The second change was the widespread dissemination of Buddhist doctrines among the samurai and common people. This occurred primarily through the efforts of the Kamakura Buddhist proselytizers. The rise of Kamakura Buddhism was paralleled by the emergence of a new social order in which the samurai class asserted considerable influence. But successful samurai were not the only ones attracted to the new Buddhist movement. Even samurai who languished on the fringes of the new social order, as well as ordinary peasants, found comfort and salvation in the new teachings.

The third change was the appearance of new religious organizations. As various branches of Pure Land and Zen Buddhism became more active, they generated rudimentary religious organizations that offered an alternative to the orthodox schools of Mount Hiei and Nara. The more people that affiliated with these groups, the more that the Buddhist establishment lost its monopoly over organized religion.

The fourth and final change was the redefinition of Shinto beliefs in the light of Buddhism. There was widespread social turmoil in the villages from the end of the Heian period through the Kamakura. During the fourteenth century, new villages came into existence, and the villages' social structure as a whole was transformed. Amid this ferment, Shinto, the villages' indigenous religion, also began to change. Shinto shrines were the functional centers of people's faith, and so tales were compiled about the origins of the shrines and the miraculous works of their *kami*. These tales were used to proclaim the power of local *kami* to people living in distant regions. Buddhism provided the conceptual framework for these tales.[34] All of the changes that occurred during the mid-Kamakura period created a climate favorable to religious innovation, quite unlike that encountered by Hōnen and the early Kamakura religious figures.

Nichiren (1222–82) played an important role in this last stage of Kamakura Buddhism's development.[35] He was born into a family of minor samurai in Awa Province (present-day Chiba Prefecture). In order to receive an education, Nichiren entered a temple near his birthplace and studied Tendai doctrine. Eventually, he went to Mount Hiei for training. Nichiren's principal doctrinal interest was not in a "next-world" form of salvation, such as rebirth in the Pure Land, but rather in a "this-world" form of salvation that would perfect and liberate the Japanese, both individually and as a nation. Therefore, the teachings that Nichiren propounded were meant to guide both spiritual and political affairs and also to ensure the country's peace and tranquility.[36] While studying the Tendai doctrine, Nichiren discovered in the Lotus Sutra (Hokekyō) the image of the absolute that would become the basis of his teachings.[37] He came to believe that the truth and power of the Lotus Sutra are concentrated in the title of the sutra itself, and he therefore taught that salvation can be attained by chanting, "I take refuge in the Lotus Sutra." In structure, his teachings bear certain similarities to those of Hōnen and Shinran, in that all claim that a person is confirmed in faith by intoning a sacred name.

Nichiren became convinced that he had been assigned the task of realizing the Lotus Sutra's ideal in this world, and he stood ready to do battle with anyone who obstructed that end. Perceiving himself to be a specially ordained prophet, Nichiren launched vitriolic attacks against

---

34 *Chūsei Shintō ron*, *NST*, vol. 19; and *Jisha engi*, *NST*, vol. 20.
35 Concerning Nichiren's life, see Takagi Yutaka, *Nichiren: sono kōdō to shisō* (Tokyo: Hyōronsha, 1970).
36 *Risshō ankokuron*, in *Shinran-shū Nichiren-shū*, *NKBT*, vol. 82, p. 293.
37 The Lotus Sutra, known in Sanskrit as the Saddharma Puṇḍarīka Sūtra, is one of the most important religious texts in Mahāyāna Buddhism. It was translated from Sanskrit into Chinese by Kumārajiva in 406. The complete title of the scripture in Japanese is *Myōhō rengekyō*, *TD*, vol. 9, pp. 1–62. This sutra has been extremely popular as a religious text throughout Chinese and Japanese history. It is the fundamental scripture of the Tendai school.

the teachings of the Pure Land, Zen, Shingon, and Ritsu schools. The
harshness of his diatribes was unprecedented in Japan's religious history, and eventually Nichiren was arrested by the Kamakura bakufu
and exiled for three years to the island of Sado (in present-day Niigata
Prefecture).[38] Nichiren believed that through chanting the title of the
Lotus Sutra persons in this world would be bound together in a perfect and transformed society. Despite the many teachings of Buddhism, he embraced the Lotus Sutra exclusively, and he asserted that
anyone is capable of the simple practice of chanting its title.[39] This
exclusiveness of outlook and simplicity of practice are what place
Nichiren's teachings within the framework of Kamakura Buddhism.

Among the Kamakura Buddhist thinkers, Nichiren was the first to
integrate secular matters and Shinto *kami* into his Buddhist scheme,
for he believed that Buddhism undergirds reality in all its dimensions.
The writings of Hōnen, Shinran, and Dōgen rarely address the immediate concerns of ordinary people. Instead, they focus on doctrinal
questions such as Amida Buddha's compassion or on transcendent
experiences such as Zen enlightenment. Nichiren, by contrast, actively propounded an ethic for life in this world that was relevant to
both the samurai class and the common people. His teachings, in fact,
incorporated various elements from Confucian morality and Shinto
piety. Before Nichiren's time, Buddhist priests tended to concentrate
on scripture, exegesis, and doctrine. Nichiren departed from this pattern by trying to explain Buddhism in more pedestrian terms and by
amalgamating it with other varieties of thought popular in his day.
Among the schools of Kamakura Buddhism, Nichiren's in particular
helped create a form of Buddhism well adapted to the Japanese context. Through this adaptation, Buddhism became accessible to far
more people than ever before.

Ippen (1239–89), a proponent of Pure Land Buddhism and a contemporary of Nichiren, was another religious figure who synthesized Buddhism with various popular beliefs and practices.[40] Ippen was the son
of a samurai in Iyo Province (present-day Ehime Prefecture). He was
ordained at a young age and at first studied Tendai doctrine. Later he
went to study under someone named Shōtatsu, who had been a follower of Hōnen's disciple Shōkū (1177–1247).

38 *Shuju gofurumai gosho*, in *Shōwa teihon Nichiren Shōnin ibun*, vol. 2 (Minobu-san, Yamanashi-
ken: Kuonji, 1953), p. 963.
39 *Senjishō* and *Hōonshō*, in *Nichiren, NST*, vol. 14, pp. 233, 297.
40 Concerning Ippen's life, see Ōhashi Shunnō, *Ippen* (Tokyo: Yoshikawa kōbunkan, 1983).

Ippen eventually formulated his own version of the Pure Land teachings, and he is commonly recognized as the last of the originators of Kamakura Buddhism. Ippen's initial inspiration was an oracle he received from the Shinto deity at Kumano Shrine in Kii Province (present-day Wakayama Prefecture). This *kami* had long been identified in popular culture as a manifestation of Amida Buddha. Ippen's experience at Kumano reflects the strong affinity between his teachings and the indigenous Japanese beliefs. The oracle stated that rebirth in the Pure Land is assured only if one chants Amida's name fervently. It does not matter whether one has faith or whether one is tainted with wrongdoings.[41] The *nembutsu* that one chants transcends all human intention. It should be intoned single-mindedly and without distraction. Ippen maintained that one should set aside all religious practices except the *nembutsu*, for then one's trust in it will be perfect.[42] He himself discarded all other practices and thus came to be known as the *sutehijiri*, "the discarding holy man." To propagate these beliefs, Ippen traveled the length of Japan, from Kyushu in the south to Tōhoku in the north, and distributed amulets inscribed with the *nembutsu* to every person he met.[43]

Ippen's teachings stress first and foremost a simple religious practice, as do all forms of Kamakura Buddhism. In the case of Hōnen and Shinran, however, the need for introspection and reflection underlies this simple practice. Ippen, by contrast, did not focus on the believer's underlying mental state. Rather, he emphasized the primacy of religious practice and its power to elicit "single-mindedness without distraction" from the believer. This stress on religious practice was well suited to Ippen's style of proselytization.

In the villages that Ippen and his religious cohorts visited, he would gather congregations to intone the *nembutsu* and dance to its rhythm.[44] Ordinary people were thus exposed to the elements of religion as they participated in the dancing and *nembutsu* chanting. These were easier for them to assimilate than were the subtle teachings of Hōnen and Shinran, even though they also presented a message with strong popular appeal. Ippen, more than any of the priests before him, came into direct contact with the masses as he traveled from place to place in an

41 *Ippen Shōnin goroku*, in *Hōnen Ippen*, *NST*, vol. 10, p. 305. Kumano Shrine, located in the southern half of the Kii peninsula in Wakayama Prefecture, has been regarded as a sacred spot since ancient times and has been visited by countless pilgrims over the centuries.
42 *Ippen hijirie*, in *Nihon emakimono zenshū*, vol. 10 (Tokyo: Kadokawa shoten, 1960), "Shisho," p. 66.
43 Ibid. This work gives a pictorial image of Ippen as he traveled to these various regions.
44 Ibid., p. 66.

endless evangelistic sojourn. He managed to communicate Buddhism to the people as a path of salvation, by integrating it with practices they could understand. Even while seeking salvation in Buddhism, the common people retained their native Shinto religious beliefs. Ippen was open and responsive to Shinto, and he incorporated various beliefs and practices associated with the *kami* into his own religious paradigm.[45] In so doing, he made his teachings compatible with the spiritual inclinations on the ordinary people. Throughout Japanese history, it was necessary for Buddhism to come to terms with Japan's indigenous religious traditions in order for it to spread widely. Nichiren's and Ippen's teachings accomplished this synthesis better than those of the earlier Kamakura thinkers, as both molded Buddhism to fit the popular religious consciousness of the Japanese.

THE RESPONSE OF THE BUDDHIST ESTABLISHMENT

An awakening in the traditional schools

The various groups that arose out of Kamakura Buddhism generated formal religious organizations during the Muromachi period. From that time on, they have been the most powerful schools of Buddhism in Japan. In reflecting on their origins, all of these schools hark back to the Kamakura period as their institutional starting point, and they claim a continuous and unbroken existence since that time. There is a tendency among them to overestimate the power and influence of Kamakura Buddhism at this embryonic stage in its history. Their perspective is one of historical hindsight – that is, looking back on the period from the vantage point of later times. If one looks at the Kamakura period without this sectarian predilection, one will find that the various schools of Kamakura Buddhism had no institutional influence at that time, for their religious organizations had not yet taken substantive shape. The earlier schools of Buddhism from Nara and Heian times were, in fact, still paramount in the Kamakura period. These established schools were both challenged and threatened, however, by the rise of Kamakura Buddhism, and they responded vigorously with political and religious initiatives of their own.

The Tendai school exerted the greatest influence in Buddhist circles throughout the Heian period. By Kamakura times the elite within the

45 In every region to which Ippen traveled, he would visit the local Shinto shrine and pray to its *kami*. See Tamura Enchō, *Nihon Bukkyō shisōshi kenkyū: Jōdokyōhen* (Kyoto: Heirakuji shoten, 1959), pp. 403–4.

school, like much of Japan's aristocratic elite, was locked in a conservative mind-set dedicated to preserving the status quo, but up to the
mid-Heian period, when the talented scholar-priest Annen lived, the
school had been a vibrant, creative center of grand doctrinal formula-
tions. The doctrinal system that gained the greatest prominence in the
Tendai school was the philosophy of original enlightenment (*hongaku
shisō*). Original enlightenment, which has always been a central tenet
in Mahāyāna Buddhism, refers to the idea that every living being has
the innate capacity to attain Buddhahood. One is saved at the very
moment that one comprehends this fact. Hence, enlightenment is
immanent and immediate, although people do not ordinarily realize its
presence.[46] The concept of original enlightenment directly contrasts
with the idea of acquired enlightenment (*shigaku shisō*). According to
this doctrine, enlightenment requires one to progress through stages
of religious practice from the time one enters the Buddhist path until
one attains Buddhahood. The religious practices at each stage are
geared to the individual's abilities.

In the Tendai school the doctrine of original enlightenment resulted
in the belief that enlightenment is omnipresent. All things are vessels
of enlightenment, even though they may appear to be discrete and
unrelated objects. Even things that stand in diametric opposition to
one another are not ultimately at odds. At base they are identical, for
they embody the same essence. This philosophy provided a rationale
for affirming all things in their present state, and it fit well with
Tendai's mystical aspect, wherein every form, just as it is, is perceived
as a manifestation of the absolute. Mystical truths of this kind were
not to be revealed capriciously, as religious preparation and training
were necessary to understand them. Consequently, secret oral transmissions developed in the Tendai school as a way of imparting these
truths between master and disciple.

Various fragmentary works that appeared in the early Kamakura
period came out of this tradition, containing teachings that hitherto
had been transmitted either orally or in secret.[47] The Tendai school
suffered a decline in doctrinal creativity during the second half of the
Heian period, at the same time that Mount Hiei increased its involvement in worldly affairs. Kamakura Buddhism arose in part as a critique of these involvements and as a search for a purer form of reli-

46 Tamura Yoshirō, "Tendai hongaku shisō gaisetsu," in *Tendai hongaku ron, NST,* vol. 9, pp.
  477–548.
47 Some examples of these works are the *Tendai Hokkeshū gozu hōmon yōsan* and the *Kankō ruijū,*
  in *Tendai hongaku ron, NST,* vol. 9, pp. 23–40, 187–286.

gion. Nonetheless, the Tendai philosophy of original enlightenment exerted a strong influence on the new and emergent forms of Buddhism. In fact, all the originators of Kamakura Buddhism studied on Mount Hiei at one time or another.

The other powerful schools of Buddhism in the Kamakura period were the Shingon school and the schools affiliated with the major temples in Nara, such as the Kegon, Hossō, Sanron, and Ritsu schools. All of these schools boasted long traditions, and each exercised considerable authority in both doctrinal and political affairs. In the Nara schools a large number of monk scholars continued the venerable enterprise of articulating and elaborating sectarian doctrine.

One representative figure from Nara who was active at the beginning of the Kamakura period was Jōkei (1155–1213).[48] He is best known as a systematizer of Hossō doctrine, but he was interested in Pure Land and Zen teachings as well. He attempted to incorporate the *nembutsu* and Zen meditation into the religious practices of his school in order to adapt it to the changing times. Jōkei's disciple Ryōhen (1194–1252), who was instrumental in formulating a system of Hossō doctrine that was uniquely Japanese, followed a similar pattern. He was a student of Zen and was also attracted to the new trends found in the *nembutsu* teachings and in Tendai.[49]

Another important figure, Myōe (1173–1232) of the Kegon school, was likewise influenced by Zen and the *nembutsu*.[50] Myōe wrote a work entitled *Zaijarin* that criticized Hōnen's major treatise, the *Senchakushū*.[51] He did so not because he rejected the *nembutsu* as a practice but because he disagreed with Hōnen's unorthodox interpretation of it.

The Buddhism centered at the great temples in Nara has come to be known as "old Buddhism" (*kyū Bukkyō*), in contrast with the "new Buddhism" (*shin Bukkyō*) of the Kamakura period. There is a tendency to regard the former as a reactionary form of Buddhism opposed to the revolutionary trends of Kamakura Buddhism. But it is clear that the very people defending the traditional doctrines and criticizing the new schools were also heavily influenced by Zen and the *nembutsu*, and they were likewise working toward a practicable form of religion. In short, the religious revolution that occurred in the Kamakura period

---

48 Concerning Jōkei, see Tanaka Hisao, "Chosakusha ryakuden," in *Kamakura kyū Bukkyō, NST,* vol. 15, pp. 461–9.
49 Concerning Ryōhen, see Tanaka, "Chosakusha ryakuden," pp. 480–8.
50 Concerning Myōe's life, see Tanaka Hisao, *Myōe* (Tokyo: Yoshikawa kōbunkan, 1961).
51 *Zaijarin*, in *Kamakura kyū Bukkyō, NST,* vol. 15, pp. 43–105. This work, containing three fascicles, was composed in 1212, one year after Hōnen's death.

not only created new schools of Buddhism but also transformed the old ones.

One other trend that surfaced in the established Buddhist schools as a result of this revolution was a movement to reassert adherence to religious precepts (*kairitsu*).[52] Prominent figures in this movement included Jōkei, his disciple Kakushin (1168–1243), Myōe, and Shunjō (1166–1227), a priest of the Ritsu school who resided in Kyoto.[53] There were two motives for emphasizing religious precepts. One was to reestablish spiritual purity as the aim of the Buddhist priests. In that state, priests could function as role models for the populace at large and thereby could once more assume their proper place as spiritual leaders in society. This social role was connected to the second reason for administering religious precepts: to lead all people, as the objects of proselytization, to salvation.[54] Implicit in the first reason was an attack on Buddhism's laxity and worldliness. Implicit in the second was the idea that priests are the propagators of Buddhism and should be active among the people. The goal of this movement was to propel the established Buddhist schools out of their moribund state.

A widely acclaimed figure in the precept movement was the Ritsu priest Eizon (1201–90).[55] He revived the Saidaiji temple in Nara and strove to make it a center of the Ritsu school where religious precepts in one form or another were administered. One distinguishing feature of Eizon's proselytization efforts was a ceremony that he instituted in which people would promise to uphold the precepts. Gradually there emerged the popular belief that anyone who underwent this ceremony would be saved. Eizon's disciple Ninshō (1217–1303) was also involved in the movement, but instead of trying to save people individually by administering precepts to them, he emphasized the broader social responsibilities incumbent on the clergy because of their precepts.[56] Ninshō organized a wide variety of social works such as building roads and bridges, digging wells, and looking after the sick. In order to make the most out of these social activities, Ninshō established ties with political authorities and enlisted

52 Concerning this movement, see Ishida Mizumaro, *Nihon Bukkyō ni okeru kairitsu no kenkyū* (Tokyo: Nakayama shobō, 1976).
53 Concerning Shunjō's life, see *Sennyūji Fukaki Hōshi den*, in *Zoku gunsho ruijū*, vol. 9 (Tokyo: Zoku gunsho ruijū kanseikai, 1927), pp. 45–58.
54 Ōsumi Kazuo, "Kamakura Bukkyō to sono kakushin undō," in *Iwanami kōza Nihon rekishi*, vol. 5 (Tokyo: Iwanami Shoten, 1975), p. 232.
55 Concerning Eizon's life, see Wajima Yoshio, *Eizon Ninshō* (Tokyo: Yoshikawa kōbunkan, 1970).   56 Concerning Ninshō's life, see Wajima, *Eizon Ninshō*.

their assistance and protection in implementing his programs. In this way he differed from most of the leaders of Kamakura Buddhism, who wished to have as little contact as possible with the world of politics.

The suppression of Kamakura Buddhism

The established schools of Buddhism were challenged by the innovations of Kamakura's new religious movements, and they responded with such activities as those described, in an attempt to revitalize their own religious traditions. Buddhist authorities were also disturbed by certain beliefs and practices circulating in Kamakura Buddhism, and they reacted aggressively in the name of Buddhist orthodoxy to suppress them. One early example of suppression was their response to Hōnen's followers.

Within the Pure Land movement, some converts to Hōnen's teachings formed fanatic *nembutsu* groups. Their claim was that if one simply practiced the *nembutsu* and had faith in Amida Buddha's compassion, then one would be assured of rebirth in Pure Land, no matter what evil deeds or wrongdoings one might commit.[57] Such views were anathema to both the Buddhist establishment and the civil authorities. Therefore, they frequently joined forces to institute measures that would check the spread of the Pure Land movement. The first measure was instituted in 1200 when the Kamakura bakufu ordered the expulsion of all *nembutsu* priests from Kamakura.[58] The next came in 1204 when Mount Hiei led the other major temples in petitioning the imperial court to ban Hōnen's teaching of the exclusive *nembutsu*. Hōnen defended himself by declaring that what he taught in no way undermined the established order, and he warned his followers not to act in an inflammatory way.[59] On that occasion Hōnen followers managed to escape suppression. In 1206, however, the Kōfukuji temple in Nara submitted to the imperial court a set of nine accusations against Hōnen and his cohorts, entitled the *Kōfukuji sōjō*, drafted by Jōkei.[60] As support for Hōnen eroded among court nobles, suppression became inevitable. It finally occurred in the following year when Junsai and several other disciples of Hōnen were sentenced to death and

---

57 Inoue Mitsusada, *Nihon kodai no kokka to Bukkyō* (Tokyo: Iwanami shoten, 1971), pp. 280–8.
58 *Azuma kagami, KT*, vol. 32, p. 574. See also Inoue, *Nihon kodai no kokka to Bukkyō*, pp. 284–5.
59 *Shichikajō kishōmon*, in *Hōnen Ippen, NST*, vol. 10, pp. 231–5.
60 *Kōfukuji sōjō*, in *Kamakura kyū Bukkyō, NST*, vol. 15, pp. 31–42.

when Hōnen, Shinran, and other *nembutsu* proponents were banished from the capital to different parts of Japan.[61] One of the unexpected consequences of this suppression was that it provided the context for Shinran's own religious maturation. The suppression set in motion a sequence of events that led Shinran to settle in the Kantō region and to work out his religious convictions there.[62] To the extent that these convictions were established in an atmosphere of religious duress, the tenets of Kamakura Buddhism were often framed in opposition to established Buddhist doctrines. These doctrinal divergences only heightened the reputation of the new Buddhist schools as opponents of ecclesiastical authority.

Suppression was by no means limited to the Pure Land movement. Zen was also a periodic target in the early Kamakura period. The first attacks on Zen were directed not at Eisai or Dōgen but at a priest named Nōnin, who studied Zen meditation independently before Eisai became an active proponent. Nōnin formed his own sectarian group known as the Daruma school, named after the semilegendary founder of Zen in China.[63] Soon after its formation, Mount Hiei expressed its opposition to the school and initiated repressive measures against it. The reasons given were similar to the charges leveled against Hōnen: that Nōnin stressed Zen meditation to the exclusion of all other religious practices, that he attached little importance to the religious precepts that priests were obliged to obey, and that he denounced other schools of Buddhism. Mount Hiei was the greatest defender of orthodoxy among the eight schools of Buddhism and enjoyed the official recognition of the imperial court. It thus was determined to defend the religious system of the eight against anyone who threatened their authority or deviated from their norm. Hence, it was only natural that after its attack on Nōnin, Mount Hiei would attack Eisai and Dōgen as well.

Eisai first began propagating Zen after his return from Sung China. In 1194 the imperial court, at the behest of Mount Hiei, issued an order banning Nōnin's Daruma school, and this ban was applied to Eisai activities also.[64] Although Eisai's Zen was originally a target for suppression, he was determined to lift it into the ranks of socially

61 *Dai Nihon shiryō*, pt. 4, vol. 9 (Tokyo: Tōkyō teikoku daigaku, 1909), pp. 504–89 (entry for Jōgen first year, second month, eighteenth day).
62 Kasahara Kazuo, *Shinran to tōgoku nōmin* (Tokyo: Yamakawa shuppansha, 1957), pp. 145–85.
63 Concerning Nōnin, see Tsuji Zennosuke, *Nihon Bukkyōshi*, vol. 3 (Tokyo: Iwanami Shoten, 1960), pp. 61–66.
64 *Hyakurenshō, KT*, vol. 11, p. 125. See also Tsuji, *Nihon Bukkyōshi*, vol. 3, pp. 70.

acceptable religion, by demonstrating that Zen is not detrimental to the nation but, rather, beneficial. Eisai insisted that the efflorescence of Zen would revitalize the Tendai school. As aristocrats came to realize that Zen occupied the mainstream of Buddhism in China, they had a gradual change of heart toward it.[65] Eisai's Zen ceased to be an object of suppression when he received official patronage and protection from the Kamakura Bakufu.

Dōgen, on the other hand, differed from Eisai in that he propounded a pure form of Zen, not mixed with beliefs and practices from the orthodox schools. Because of his unyielding devotion to Zen, Dōgen became subject to various kinds of pressure and coercion, especially from Mount Hiei. Dōgen preferred to avoid open confrontation, and so he withdrew to Uji, on the outskirts of Kyoto, to remove himself from Mount Hiei's watchful gaze. In the ensuing years, however, Mount Hiei continued to put pressure on him, even from that distance, and ultimately forced Dōgen in 1242 to retreat to the remote province of Echizen (present-day Fukui Prefecture) to continue his teaching.[66] Although Dōgen eventually was recognized by the imperial court and the Kamakura bakufu as an eminent Buddhist master, he spent most of his career harassed by Mount Hiei for his uncompromising advocacy of Zen.

These early figures in Kamakura Buddhism all presented teachings that departed in one way or another from orthodox doctrine in Japan. Because of their differences they were suppressed as agitators against the established Buddhist order. Nichiren appeared slightly later than the others, but he suffered a similar fate. In fact, Nichiren received the harshest treatment of all, stemming in part from his abrasive personality. Nichiren was notorious for his fierce and unmitigated attacks, not only on the established Buddhist schools, but also on the *nembutsu* and Zen. These attacks earned Nichiren the wrath of civil and religious authorities, but they also helped him hammer out and define his own convictions and teachings.

The first suppressive measure against Nichiren was his banishment to Izu Province (present-day Shizuoka Prefecture) in 1261.[67] This action was prompted by Nichiren's presentation to the bakufu of his treatise *Risshō ankokuron*, in which he vehemently denounced the gov-

65 Taga, *Eisai*, pp. 224–84.
66 Imaeda, *Dōgen: sono kōdō to shisō*, pp. 88–89, 137–41.
67 Nichiren was exiled to Izu Province from 1261 to 1263 and to Sado Island from 1271 to 1274. See Takagi, *Nichiren: sono kōdō to shisō*, pp. 75–79.

ernment's policies.[68] The religious ideal that Nichiren propounded had a strong social and political dimension. In this way it differed from the salvation found in Pure Land and from the experience of enlightenment achieved through Zen meditation. Hence, his suppression may have been more political than religious.

Notwithstanding Nichiren's social and political pronouncements, his teachings had a religious message at their core – that one is saved by chanting the title of the Lotus Sutra. It was this conviction that led Nichiren to criticize the other schools of Buddhism. Many people who embraced his teachings likewise assailed the existing Buddhist system, and their precipitous actions contributed to its decline. The government's second suppression of Nichiren occurred in 1271, just as the Mongols were launching their attack on Japan. Nichiren was arrested for fomenting social unrest, and it was decided that he would be executed. According to Nichiren's own account, however, he managed to escape death because of a miraculous intervention, and instead he was sent into banishment on Sado Island (in present-day Niigata Prefecture). In Sado's desolation and harsh environment Nichiren developed his religious teachings to their fullest.[69] Thus, as in the case of Shinran, suppression only deepened Nichiren's inner religious experience and propelled him to work out his provocative system of thought.

The harsh reaction of the religious and political establishment to Kamakura Buddhism is demonstrated by the various instances of suppression cited here. The reasons for this response differed according to the particular circumstance of each case and the particular agents instigating each suppression. In some instances, suppression signified an imperially sanctioned assault against those who slighted Buddhism's role as supplicator and ensurer of national tranquillity. In other instances, the attacks arose from doctrinal issues, especially when the teachings of Kamakura Buddhism violated or ignored the formalities of orthodox dogma. In still other instances, suppression was used as a precautionary measure to preclude any acts detrimental to the traditional order that people attracted to Kamakura Buddhism were inclined to commit. The intensity with which some of the suppressions were carried out reflects how determined Mount Hiei and the major temples of Nara were to preserve the traditional Buddhist order they had created.

68 Risshō ankokuron, in Shinran-shū Nichiren-shū, NKBT, vol. 82, pp. 291–318.
69 Inoue, Nihon kodai no kokka to Bukkyō, pp. 339–54.

New scholastic trends

In its capacity as the ecclesiastical authority, the Buddhist establishment reacted adversely to various beliefs and practices of Kamakura Buddhism. But Kamakura's radical innovations also spurred many priests, who held fast to the orthodox teachings, to reflect on their own religious traditions. This was truer of the Nara schools than of Mount Hiei. The Tendai school on Mount Hiei was caught up in diverse secular affairs stemming from its extensive connections with aristocratic society in Kyoto during the latter half of the Heian period. Kamakura Buddhism emerged partially in reaction to Mount Hiei's involvements. The major temples in Nara, by contrast, had kept Buddhist scholarship alive and moved toward comprehensive systematizations of Buddhist doctrine. They produced a succession of eminent scholar-priests such as Jōkei and Ryōhen of the Hossō school, Myōhen of the Sanron school, and Myōe of the Kegon school. Together they began a movement that is often described as "the revival of Nara Buddhism" (*Nantō Bukkyō no fukkō*). Without a doubt the appearance of Kamakura Buddhism stimulated Nara's new systematizations of traditional Buddhist doctrine, which were the response of the Nara priests to the changes occurring around them in society.

The resurgence of Buddhist scholasticism was part of the broader current of scholarly pursuits in elite society. Beginning in the mid-Heian period, aristocrats attempted to organize and classify the various forms of knowledge that had developed so far. Editorial projects aiming at the systematic compilation of information became very common. This trend extended to the field of Buddhist doctrine as well. In the latter half of the Heian period, priests at the Kōfukuji temple in Nara began compiling catalogues of Buddhist works such as the *Tōiki dentō mokuroku*[70] by Eichō (1012–95) and the *Hossō-shū shōso mokuroku*[71] by Zōshun (1104–80). Compiling catalogues relating to Buddhist doctrine helped give order to the vast store of knowledge that Japanese Buddhism had amassed since the Nara period. The catalogues had the effect of making Buddhist doctrinal studies more organized and accessible to outsiders, and they were valuable tools in efforts to systematize Buddhist doctrine. Through the process of doctrinal systematization, the foremost scholar-priests of the early

70 *Tōiki dentō mokuroku, TD*, vol. 55, pp. 1145–65.
71 *Hossō-shū shōso mokuroku, TD*, vol. 55, pp. 1140–4.

Kamakura period produced a uniquely Japanese version of traditional Buddhist philosophy.

By the end of the Kamakura period, many scholars began to construct outlines of various doctrinal and ritual systems. They provided comprehensive and sometimes encyclopedic overviews of the specific elements in Japanese Buddhism. Chōzen (1217–97) of the Sanron school and Gyōnen (1240–1321) of the Kegon school are good examples of such scholars.[72] Gyōnen's Hasshū kōyō, for instance, outlines the fundamental doctrines of the traditional Buddhist schools in Japan.[73] Also, the Kakuzenshō[74] by Kakuzen and the Asabashō[75] by Shō-chō (1205–82), which were compiled about this time, give encyclopedic coverage of the ceremonies and monastic decorum of the Tendai and Shingon schools, respectively. Because of their scope, such works became valuable references for Buddhist beliefs and practices. These attempts to systematize all knowledge relating to Japanese Buddhism eventually aroused an interest in Buddhist history also. Shūshō (1202–92) of the Kegon school, for instance, composed a work entitled Nihon kōsōden yōmonshō, in which he collected the biographies of eminent priests who had played important roles in the history of Buddhism in Japan.[76] His disciple Gyōnen also left behind a number of works on Buddhist history, such as the Sangoku Buppō denzū engi.[77] Hence, the systematization of Buddhist doctrine eventually led scholars to historiographical questions as well.

Buddhist scholastic trends over the Kamakura period reveal a gradual shift from the cataloguing of doctrinal literature, to the systematization of diverse forms of knowledge, and finally to the study of Japanese Buddhist history.[78] When these enterprises are compared with the concerns of the new schools of Kamakura Buddhism, a distinct contrast emerges. The originators of Kamakura Buddhism formed their ideas by making religious experience paramount. They drew their inspiration from their own personal realizations, and they sought a path of salvation that each and every individual could follow. Hence, none of them considered the systematization of traditional Buddhist

---

72 Concerning Gyōnen's life, see Ōya Tokujō, Gyōnen Kokushi nempu (Nara: Tōdaiji kangakuin, 1921).
73 Hasshū kōyō, in Dai Nihon Bukkyō zensho, vol. 3 (Tokyo: Dai Nihon Bukkyō zensho hakkōjo, 1912–22), pp. 7–40. Hereafter Dai Nihon Bukkyō zensho is cited as DNBZ.
74 Kakuzenshō, DNBZ, vols. 45–51.   75 Asabashō, DNBZ, vols. 35–41.
76 Nihon kōsōden yōmonshō, KT, vol. 31, pp. 1–92.
77 Sangoku Buppō denzū engi, DNBZ, vol. 101.
78 Takagi Yutaka, Kamakura Bukkyōshi kenkyū (Tokyo: Iwanami shoten, 1982), pp. 177–241.

doctrine to be a matter of overriding concern.[79] The Buddhist establishment, however, regarded doctrinal questions as fundamental, and
as a result it frequently condemned Kamakura Buddhism for its neglect of Buddhist doctrine.[80]

The founders of Kamakura Buddhism did not derive their tenets
from analytical interpretation or rational treatment of existing doctrine. Nor did they attempt to couch their ideas in perfect harmony
with traditional systems of Buddhist thought.[81] What is more, few of
them had any interest in the relationship of their own ideas to other
philosophies and religions such as Confucianism, Taoism, and Shinto.
Nichiren was the only Kamakura originator to show a strong interest
in such questions.[82]

The original teachings of the founders of Kamakura Buddhism
therefore diverged from the interest in Buddhist history that arose in
the traditional schools during the latter half of the Kamakura period.
In the case of the Kamakura innovators, their starting point was a
profound longing for salvation and the religious experience that undergirds it. When they sought to explain their experiences intellectu-
ally, they were led back to Buddhist doctrine to discover the concepts
and rationale for their beliefs. Traditional priests, on the other hand,
considered the study of Buddhist doctrine to be fundamental and
accepted its doctrinal framework as the parameters of their inquiry.
Only within that framework did they attempt to innovate or to explore
variations on basic themes.[83]

As Kamakura Buddhism emerged with its diverse new movements
and as various types of religious and intellectual activities began to
appear, the priests at the major temples in Nara were prompted to
reflect on the nature of Buddhism in Japan. They sought to comprehend the place of Buddhism and its differing systems of thought.[84]
The interest in Buddhist history that grew out of these circumstances
was eventually inherited by such figures as the Rinzai Zen priest

79 Ōsumi, "Kamakura Bukkyō to sono kakushin undō," in *Iwanami kōza Nihon rekishi*, vol. 5,
   pp. 236–8.
80 See, for example, *Kōfukuji sōjō*, in *Kamakura kyū Bukkyō, NST*, vol. 15, pp. 32–42.
81 The Kamakura founders adopted only those things from traditional doctrine that seemed
   applicable to and effective in clarifying their own ideas. Hōnen's *Senchaku hongan
   nembutsushū*, in *Hōnen Ippen, NST*, vol. 10, pp. 87–162, exemplifies this idiosyncratic and
   selective approach to Buddhist doctrine characteristic of them.
82 Tokoro Shigemoto, *Nichiren no shisō to Kamakura Bukkyō* (Tokyo: Fuzambō, 1965), pp. 233–
   70.
83 Ōsumi Kazuo, "Kamakura Bukkyō to sono kakushin undō," in *Iwanami kōza Nihon rekishi*,
   vol. 5, pp. 236–8.
84 The works of Gyōnen in particular are good examples of this trend. See *Hasshū kōyō, DNBZ*,
   vol. 3, pp. 7–40; and *Sangoku Buppō denzū engi, DNBZ*, vol. 101.

Kokan Shiren (1278–1346), who modified the approach to Buddhist history pioneered by Shūshō and Gyōnen.[85] Kokan's work *Genkō shakusho* is a history of Japanese Buddhism in condensed form.[86] With works of this type, the Japanese first attempted to look at Buddhism in Japan in its entirety and as objectively as possible.[87]

THE FORMATION OF RELIGIOUS ORGANIZATIONS

The attitude of the Kamakura innovators

All of the schools of Kamakura Buddhism passed through various formative stages and eventually succeeded in developing highly structured religious organizations. None of them originated from a schism within the older schools of Buddhism. They had as their starting point the teachings of the Kamakura innovators, who voluntarily severed ties with the established religious institutions of their day. Even during the lifetime of these innovators, rudimentary religious organizations began to coalesce around them. These groups were, by and large, charismatic religious movements based on their teachings. They had specific religious tenets at their core, and they were composed of believers of like conviction. From these loosely structured beginnings, full-fledged religious organizations gradually evolved, known today as the Kamakura schools of Buddhism. This entire process extended many years beyond the lifetime of the innovators, and it resulted not only in the institutionalization of their teachings but also in the idealization of them as founders. Whether or not they ever intended to establish formal sectarian bodies, they ultimately became venerated as the founding fathers of the Kamakura schools.

Kamakura Buddhism presents clear-cut instances in which religious teachings acted as the consolidating agent in the creation of religious organizations. This may seem only natural, but it was not a universal pattern in Japanese history. There are numerous examples before the Kamakura period in which religious organizations developed from communities of priests with special privileges or, in the case of folk religion, from certain well-defined groups in society. Also, in some instances, organized movements arose on the periphery of major religious institutions and incorporated their beliefs and practices.[88] Beginning only in

85 Concerning Kokan, see Fukushima Shun'ō, *Kokan* (Tokyo: Yūzankaku, 1944).
86 *Genkō shakusho, KT*, pt. 2, vol. 31, pp. 1–454.
87 Ōsumi Kazuo, "*Genkō shakusho* no Buppō kan," *Kanezawa bunko kenkyū* 271 (1983).
88 Examples of such groups are the Pure Land societies that arose in the mid-Heian period,

the Kamakura period, believers straddling various social classes, including the commoner class, banded together around set religious tenets.
Social status, institutional ties, and geographical proximity may have
been other factors in their consolidation, but the teachings of the
Kamakura innovators provided the strongest bond uniting believers in
one body. The organizations that they created reached full institutional
development later as the schools of Kamakura Buddhism.

With the exception of Ippen, all of the originators of Kamakura
Buddhism left behind writings revealing a sophisticated knowledge of
Buddhist doctrine. Most of them studied on Mount Hiei while it was
still in the twilight of its doctrinal heyday, a time when priests in
training might devote ten or twenty years to study. Generally, the
Kamakura innovators propounded their new teachings after undergoing some type of revelatory or mystical experience. Hence, they
tended to stress the primacy of religious experience. But to the extent
that they all were versed in Buddhist scriptures and doctrine, they
attempted to undergird these experiential elements with doctrinal explanations. The religious organizations coalesced around their teachings seldom attracted followers with a profound knowledge of Buddhist doctrine. Consequently, believers looked to these originators as
the religious specialists of the group. But the articulation of religious
tenets per se did not make the Kamakura thinkers the actual founders
of a religious body in the sense that later adherents portrayed them.
Rather, their teachings simply functioned as a magnet bringing believers together as a group. The more structured and hierarchical aspects
of the religious organizations emerged sometime later, after the reputed founders had passed from the scene. During their own lifetime,
however, the founders' attitude toward the creation of independent
sectarian organizations was far more mixed and varied.

Hōnen and, especially, Shinran present interesting cases in the problems of institutional development in the Kamakura schools. Both of
them preached a form of salvation requiring total reliance on the
power of Amida Buddha and complete denial of self. Implicit in that
view is the repudiation of any qualitative difference between teacher
and follower and, by logical extension, the rejection of the hierarchy
necessary for setting up a religious organization. This attitude is exhibited in its purest form in Shinran's assertion, preserved in the
Tannishō, that he was on the same plane with other believers and that

primarily around the Tendai monk Genshin, and the bands of pilgrims that frequented
kannon sites from the end of the Heian period on.

he shared with them the same faith.[89] The resistance to formal religious organization intimated in Shinran's statement was one of
Kamakura Buddhism's revolutionary characteristics.

Notwithstanding these antiorganizational inclinations, religious bodies did take shape, with the Kamakura originators at their center. This
process of formation is seen in the examples of Hōnen and Shinran
alike. They themselves functioned as guides and advisers in matters of
religious faith but around them revolved a great number of organizers
and proselytizers. These people were the ones who consolidated the
institutional dimension of Kamakura Buddhism. The originators
themselves had no grand vision of organizational expansion. Based on
their attitudes, the Pure Land schools did not overtly express any
intention of competing with established social organizations, but at the
same time they commanded enough popular appeal to create formidable religious bodies.

Compared with those for the Pure Land schools, the conditions for
the emergence of the Zen schools differed in may ways. Zen is predicated on the experience of enlightenment. Because of the subtle and
elusive nature of enlightenment, various doctrines were devised to
explain it, and monastic practices centering on Zen meditation were
developed to induce it. Because specialized training and understanding are part of Zen, it is impossible for ordinary members of the
organization to stand above the teacher or master. A hierarchy is inherent in the system, and both Eisai and Dōgen received training in these
technical aspects of Zen during their travels to monasteries in China.

Eisai, for his part, sought to combine Zen with other forms of
Buddhism once he returned to Japan. He regarded Zen as a revitaliz-
ing form of religious authority, and he strove to create a place for it
within the existing Buddhist schools. Eisai introduced what he had
learned in China into the administration of monasteries in Japan, and
he attempted to inaugurate a revival of Buddhism by doing so. The
new religious organization that Eisai established therefore had roots
firmly planted in the old. Consequently, Eisai must be characterized as
a reformer at heart who attempted to resuscitate the Tendai school
through the importation of Zen.[90]

Dōgen, on the other hand, was critical of combining Zen with other
religious elements, as Eisai proposed. Dōgen idealized a strict form of
clerical monasticism, and he was not expressly interested in the organi-

89 *Tannishō*, in *Shinran-shū Nichiren-shū*, *NKBT*, vol. 82, p. 196.
90 Yanagida Seizan, "Eisai to *Kōzen gokokuron* no kadai," in *Chūsei Zenka no shisō*, *NST*, vol. 16,
     pp. 450–80.

zation or expansion of a school of Buddhism. Instead, he confined his attention to the practice of meditation and the attainment of enlightenment, and he tailored his teachings to the needs of the individual monks he trained.[91] Hence, Dōgen's monastic organization, though hierarchical like Eisai's, was not integrated into the established social and religious network as Eisai's was. The differing institutional concerns of the two are best reflected in the fact that Eisai actively sought ties with the political authorities, whereas Dōgen turned his back on the world of secular affairs.

Nichiren, who appeared late in Kamakura Buddhism, differed considerably from the other four religious innovators before him. He was a religious genius in his own right who produced Buddhist ideas that were totally new and unique to Japan. But compared with that of the other Kamakura originators, Nichiren's period of formal doctrinal training was somewhat shorter. As a result, his ideas were not as fully systematized into traditional doctrinal form.[92] Nichiren tended to stress religious experience more than doctrinal matters, and hence he was more directly involved in creating a religious sect. In this respect he was closer to being an actual sectarian founder than were the other Kamakura innovators.

The last of the Kamakura figures, Ippen, was an exception to the general pattern established by his predecessors. He differed, first, in that his original inspiration contained a Shinto dimension: a revelation received from the Shinto deity of Kumano Shrine. Ippen's second difference was that he repudiated doctrinal systematization and instead invested his energies in proselytization activities.[93] His third difference was that in his proselytization efforts he did not root himself in a single location but traveled continuously from place to place. Neither Ippen's peripatetic life-style nor his lack of a doctrinal corpus of writings lent itself to the establishment of a religious organization.

The institutional evolution of the Kamakura schools

Religious organizations took embryonic shape around the originators of Kamakura Buddhism, but the Kamakura schools themselves achieved full institutional form only through the efforts of countless religious organizers, long after the founders were gone. What reli-

91 *Shōbōgenzō*, in *Dōgen*, pt. 1, *NST*, vol. 12, pp. 165–231; and in *Dōgen*, pt. 2, *NST*, vol. 13, pp. 298–302.
92 Ienaga Saburō, *Chūsei Bukkyō shisōshi kenkyū* (Kyoto: Hōzōkan, 1957), pp. 66–109.
93 *Ippen Shōnin goroku*, in *Hōnen Ippen*, *NST*, vol. 10, p. 348.

gious organizers had to do in order to give structure to these movement was to universalize the ideas that the Kamakura originators
derived from personal experiences and to refashion them in a logical
way that would appeal to the largest number of people. Part of that
was actually accomplished by the originators themselves in their
doctrinal writings. Among them Ippen was the only one who did not
translate his experience into doctrinal tenets. Immediately before his
death he burned all the writings and religious texts that he possessed.
Nevertheless, Ippen's successor Shinkyō (1237–1319), who had long
traveled with Ippen on his religious sojourns, set about framing his
beliefs in a doctrinal format that would be passed down in subsequent periods.[94]

In instances in which the originator did formulate his doctrine,
there was no assurance that it would preserve organizational cohesion in the movement he left behind. For example, Hōnen, the pioneer of Kamakura Buddhism, produced a distinct doctrinal corpus,
but soon disagreements arose among his followers as to how to interpret his ideas. In the end there emerged sharp doctrinal differences
among his major disciples: Kōsai (1163–1247), Ryūkan (1148–1227),
Shōkū (1171–1247), Benchō (1162–1238), and Shinran. Many of
these priests drew concepts that they had learned before they ever
met Hōnen, in order to recast his beliefs into a systematic body of
doctrine.

As a result, interpretive differences put Hōnen's disciples at odds
with one another after his death. The influential ones ultimately produced religious organizations of their own and were recognized as
sectarian founders in their own right.[95] The unity that Hōnen's religious organization had while he was still living was quickly shattered
once he was gone. The same tendency was quite pronounced in
Nichiren's following, too. There were many elements in Nichiren's
thinking that were not spelled out doctrinally. Furthermore, his career
was filled with upheaval and commotion, and so his own ideas
changed frequently according to the events of his life. The result was
that his disciples differed in how they comprehended his teachings and
what elements they were attracted to, depending on what period of his
life they spent with him. Soon after Nichiren's death, his religious
organization was divided into six branches, each with a major disciple
at its head: Nisshō (1221–1323?), Nichirō (1243–1320), Nikkō (1246–

94 Ōhashi Shunnō, *Jishū no seiritsu to tenkai* (Tokyo: Yoshikawa kōbunkan, 1973), pp. 83–99.
95 Yasui Kōdo, *Hōnen monka no kyōgaku* (Kyoto: Hōzōkan, 1968); and Itō Yuishin, *Jōdoshū no
   seiritsu to tenkai* (Tokyo: Yoshikawa kōbunkan, 1981), pp. 135–97.

1332), Nikkō (different characters, 1253–1314), Nitchō (1252–1314), and Nichiji (b. 1250).[96]

Despite the fragmentation in Hōnen's and Nichiren's movements, the tendency toward sectarian splintering did not emerge prominently in other Kamakura schools. Part of the reason was the nature and content of the founders' teachings. In the case of Shinran, there was little schism in his following, even though he himself was the founder of a separate sect within Hōnen's religious movement. In the case of Zen, its doctrines were not conducive to sectarian division. That is, they stressed the importance of Dharma lineage through which the enlightenment experience is kept alive in a continuous master–disciple transmission. In the case of Ippen, his teachings were not even formulated into doctrine at his death, and so there was no palpable issue from which one could dissent.

As stated previously, the Kamakura schools of Buddhism were distinctive in that they did not revolve so much around doctrinal studies as the earlier schools did but, rather, stressed experience and religious practice. Their religious organizations, therefore, were geared to provide a context for religious practice. What constituted religious practice was gradually broadened to include not only the exclusivistic practices, such as the *nembutsu*, which are the hallmark of Kamakura Buddhism, but also the practice of venerating the founders themselves. Examples of this new trend are found in the memorial services to the founders established in the Kamakura schools. The Chionkō ceremony to Hōnen and the Hōonkō ceremony to Shinran originated only decades after their death, but as time wore on they were elevated to become one of the most important rituals in their respective schools.[97]

It also became popular to venerate iconic images of the founders and to build memorial halls (*mieidō*) in the major temples to enshrine these images.[98] Religious leaders and organizers in the Kamakura schools contributed to the founders' deification by composing idealized biographies of them, which often were read aloud at memorial services for

96 Takagi Yutaka, *Nichiren to sono montei* (Tokyo: Kōbundō, 1965), pp. 291–307.
97 Each year the Chionkō service is held on the anniversary of Hōnen's death day, and the Hōonkō on the anniversary of Shinran's death day. The liturgy for such a service is called a *kōshiki*. *Kōshiki* were composed for a number of the Kamakura innovators. The one for Shinran, known as the *Hōonkōshiki*, in *Shinshū shōgyō zensho*, vol. 3 (Kyoto: Kōkyō shoin, 1941), pp. 655–60, was written by his great-grandson Kakunyo in 1294.
98 The memorial hall to Shinran at the Honganji, the head temple of the Shinshū school, is larger than the hall in which the image of Amida Buddha is enshrined. Concerning the development of *mieidō*, see Akamatsu Toshihide, *Kamakura Bukkyō no kenkyū* (Kyoto: Heirakuji shoten, 1957), pp. 337–55.

them. Some were expanded into illustrated editions (*emakimono*) to be used in teaching believers about the greatness of the founders.[99] For example, Hōnen's religious organization, which divided into branches early on, produced several different biographies of him. Over time, many of these biographies were embellished and enlarged so as to aggrandize the lives of the founders as much as possible.

In looking at these biographies and at the veneration of the founders in general, one can discern both the religious inclinations of ordinary believers and the institutional designs of sectarian organizers. Believers willingly and enthusiastically incorporated reverence for the founders into their religious outlook and practice. Indeed, organizers found this reverence to be a crucial element in establishing sectarian control. The deification of Shinran, for instance, helped strengthen the authority of his school's organizers, who were his blood descendants. They made their base of operations the Honganji temple, founded at Shinran's grave site, and they claimed the position of *hossu*, or chief priest of the temple, as the hereditary office of their family.[100] Many other organizers attached themselves to the memory of the founders through the use of religious writings, images, or other objects that they had received from them. These articles became potent symbols of authority, imparting a special privilege or status to their possessors.

Facilities where religious practices were performed were the institutional backbone of the Kamakura religious organizations. In the case of Shinran's school, these facilities were small religious meeting places called *dōjō*.[101] The religious organization was gradually built in a pyramid fashion, with countless *dōjō* at its base. In other schools, temples were the first institutions around which religious organizations took shape.

Organizers sought to occupy key positions in the school by taking charge of the administration of major temples that had close connections with the founder. Struggles over administration and authority arose in the Nichiren school at the Kuonji temple on Mount Minobu where Nichiren had retired and in the Sōtō Zen school at the Eiheiji monastery that Dōgen had founded.[102] In Shinran's Shinshū school,

99 For examples of illustrated biographies of Kamakura Buddhist figures, see *Nihon emakimono zenshū*, vol. 10: *Ippen Hijiri e;* vol. 13: *Hōnen Shōnin eden;* vol. 20: *Zenshin Shōnin e, Boki e;* and vol. 23: *Yugyō Shōnin engi e* (Tokyo: Kadokawa shoten, 1960–8).
100 Matsuno Junkō, "Honganji no seiritsu," in Akamatsu Toshihide and Kasahara Kazuo, eds., *Shinshūshi gaisetsu* (Kyoto: Heirakuji shoten, 1963), pp. 83–94.
101 Kasahara, *Shinran to tōgoku nōmin*, pp. 271–5.
102 Imaeda Aishin, "Dōgen Sōhō Kanzan no monryū," and Fujii Manabu, "Tōgoku Hokke kyōdan no seiritsu to tenkai," in Akamatsu Toshihide, ed., *Nihon Bukkyōshi*, vol. 2 (Kyoto: Hōzōkan, 1967), pp. 201–3, 245–6.

fierce competition emerged not over temple administration but over
dōjō. Rival factions tried to incorporate as many *dōjō* congregations as
possible into their respective religious organizations. After various ups
and downs, the Honganji temple, established by Shinran's great-
grandson Kakunyo (1270–1351), prevailed over the other factions and
unified the school under its religious authority.[103] In the case of
Ippen's Jishū school, it was difficult for a religious organization to
emerge while he was still living because of the peripatetic life he led.
His successor Shinkyō, while preserving religious itinerancy as a practice of the Jishū clergy, established a domicile base for proselytization,
in the form of *dōjō* and temples. Once these institutions were in place,
the school quickly gained definition.[104] In short, even the most loosely
organized movements of Kamakura Buddhism developed a sectarian
structure through fixed institutions where doctrine could be refined
and symbols of authority housed.

The role of lay believers

Kamakura Buddhism began as a movement by turning away from
traditional Buddhist doctrine and severing ties with established Buddhist temples. It took shape as a formal religious organization by
consolidating believers around institutions of its own. With the exception of Zen in the early period, particularly the Sōtō Zen school of
Dōgen, all the schools of Kamakura Buddhism actively proselytized
among lay people. Hence, as the religious organizations gained greater
structure, groups of believers had considerable say in the school's
operation. The clerical organizers of the schools functioned primarily
as leaders of ritual and religious practice, but the people who oversaw
the organization's economic affairs were often lay adherents. Through
their combined efforts the Kamakura schools gained a high degree of
institutional stability, though the power and vitality of their teachings
were sometimes diluted by institutional concerns.

The Shinshū school in its early decades is a striking example of the
prominent role that the laity could play in sectarian affairs. Shinran
taught that all people are equal in the sight of Amida Buddha. He was
critical of the clerical ideal that existed in the established Buddhist
schools, and he described himself as neither priest nor layman.[105]

103 Concerning Kakunyo's life, see Shigematsu Akihisa, *Kakunyo* (Tokyo: Yoshikawa
   kōbunkan, 1964).   104 Ōhashi, *Jishū no seiritsu to tenkai*, pp. 79–99.
105 *Kyōgyōshinshō*, in *Shinran, NST*, vol. 11, p. 258; and *Tannishō*, in *Shinran-shū Nichiren-shū,
   NKBT*, vol. 82, p. 196.

Because of this outlook, the Shinshū religious organization, during its formative period at least, consisted of nothing more than individual congregations. In congregational *dōjō* there was no great difference between *dōjō* leaders and ordinary believers, in either intellectual capacity or economic means. But this idyllic period of Shinran's school did not last long, for a master–disciple relationship gradually evolved between the *dōjō* head and the average adherent. The *dōjō* leader was at first merely a representative chosen from the ranks of congregational members. But as he became more specialized in his religious functions, the intellectual and economic gap between him and the other members widened.[106] The expansion of the *dōjō* leader's power gradually accorded him a superior status, and ultimately it fit well into the hierarchical sectarian pyramid that developed under the Honganji.[107] Among the various Kamakura schools, congregations of this type were most prominent in the Shinshū. Their egalitarian character derived not simply from Shinran's teachings but also from the fact that there was a greater social homogeneity of believers in Shinshū congregations than in other schools.

In other Kamakura schools, temples commonly functioned as the rallying point for the formation of religious organizations. Therefore, the people who were most involved in the construction of the temple usually emerged as the dominant figures among the laity. In Hōnen's Jōdoshū school and Eisai's Rinzai Zen school, for example, aristocrats and powerful samurai became major donors and supporters, and so they exerted considerable influence on the organization's affairs.[108] The role of the religious organizers was limited more or less to the religious functions of the school. There gradually emerged a gap between the influence of these supporters and that of ordinary believers, who comprised the wider membership of the schools. Ordinary adherents had little say in the organization's administration, and so whatever activities they initiated had minimal impact.

Powerful supporters also began to place members of their own families in positions of influence as religious leaders and organizers in the temples. As a result, the power of other groups of believers within the school was circumscribed even more. The tendency in these religious

106 Ōsumi Kazuo, "Kamakura Bukkyō to sono kakushin undō," in *Iwanami kōza Nihon rekishi*, vol. 5, p. 245.
107 For an overview of the development of the Shinshū school in this context, see Akamatsu, and Kasahara, eds., *Shinshūshi gaisetsu;* and Kasahara, *Shinran to tōgoku nōmin.*
108 The Tōfukuji in Kyoto is an example of a temple in which aristocratic adherents became influential. The Jufukuji and the Engakuji in Kamakura are examples in which samurai became influential.

organizations was to revert to the pattern of the traditional schools of Buddhism wherein a small elite controlled the religious organization. The Nichiren school varied somewhat from this pattern. Its major supporters were mostly samurai, but there was not as pronounced a difference between them and the other believers. Thus, a broad spectrum of adherents was involved in the school's religious activities. Because of the greater number of parties initiating action and exerting influence, the religious organization was pulled in several different directions at the same time. These internal dynamics may have contributed to the sectarian schisms that plagued the Nichiren school more than the other Kamakura schools.[109]

There has been considerable research on the specific classes in society that became the social foundations of the various schools of Kamakura Buddhism. Investigation into the organization of the schools and the circumstances of the believers who were attracted to them has been extensive in the postwar period. Although a number of controversies still remain, the prevailing views concerning the social origins of the Kamakura schools are as follows: Hōnen's teachings made their greatest inroads among aristocrats and commoners living in the increasingly complex urban environment of Kyoto and its vicinity.[110] Shinran's teachings were disseminated primarily among the farming peasants of the Kantō countryside.[111] The Nichiren school received its principal support from the samurai residing along the coastal belt of the eastern provinces.[112] Eisai's Rinzai school of Zen appealed to urban aristocrats and upper-class samurai, whereas Dōgen's Sōtō school spread among the samurai of the outlying regions.[113] These are the dominant theories concerning the social composition of the Kamakura schools, but debate continues over many of their finer points.[114]

CONCLUSION

The period from the middle of the twelfth century through the middle of the thirteenth was a pivotal juncture in the history of Japanese

109 Nakao Takashi, *Nichirenshū no seiritsu to tenkai* (Tokyo: Yoshikawa kōbunkan, 1973), pp. 28–84.
110 Inoue Mitsusada, *Nihon Jōdokyō seiritsushi no kenkyū* (Tokyo: Yamakawa shuppansha, 1956), pp. 283–333; and Tamura, *Nihon Bukkyō shisōshi kenkyū*, pp. 58–123.
111 Kasahara, *Shinran to tōgoku nōmin*, pp. 277–303.
112 Kawazoe Shōji, "Nichiren no shūkyō no seiritsu oyobi seikaku," in *Nihon meisō ronshū*, vol. 9: *Nichiren* (Tokyo: Yoshikawa kōbunkan, 1982), pp. 2–28.
113 Imaeda Aishin, *Zenshū no rekishi* (Tokyo: Shibundō, 1966), pp. 13–213.
114 For alternative views and variations on these points, see Ienaga, *Chūsei Bukkyō shisōshi kenkyū*, pp. 2–109; and Akamatsu, *Kamakura Bukkyō no kenkyū*, pp. 60–72.

Buddhism. A number of priests broke ties with Mount Hiei, the citadel of established Buddhism, and became critical of the Buddhism espoused there. They believed that the religious ideal propounded in the traditional schools made it impossible for people to be saved in the present age, and they spawned a movement that sought to address the human condition in its actual state. This movement concentrated on the weakness of humans in their current situation, and it generated a new religious path containing a heavy component of faith. The leaders of this religious revolution steadfastly maintained that no person is excluded from enlightenment, and so they focused on how the Buddha can save even those overwhelmed by wrongdoings and defilements. In the process they produced forms of religious thought oriented toward the internal experience of human beings.

This new movement of thought, though creative in its own right, was built on ideas inherited from the literati of the Heian period, as well as on doctrinal principles produced at Mount Hiei. The context for its appearance was the profound social, political, and economic changes of the late Heian and Kamakura periods – that is, the decline of the aristocracy, the expansion of samurai control, the emergence of a new urban class of townsmen, and the transition from *shōen* to autonomous villages in the countryside. Kamakura Buddhism turned its back on the authority of earlier Buddhism; it exerted a strong influence on samurai society, which itself strove to create a new culture; and it spread its teachings aggressively among the common people.

Kamakura Buddhism generally refers to those schools with roots in the Kamakura period. They have had a pervasive influence on the religious thought and sentiment of the Japanese people even into modern times. The significance of Kamakura Buddhism in Japanese history is that for the first time Buddhism, which entered Japan as a foreign religion, was fully adapted to Japanese concerns and put down roots among the common people. Buddhist thought, transmitted with great difficulty from India, was boiled down to a few essentials. It was rendered into simple and comprehensible teachings and couched in the context of religious practices that ordinary people could perform. Admittedly, the Japanese adaptation of Buddhism made it diverge in several ways from its original form. From the beginning the Japanese fused Buddhism with Shinto and with their own long-held cosmology of the spirit world. In the Kamakura schools themselves the veneration of religious teachers and sectarian founders also distinguished Japanese Buddhism from its antecedents in other parts of Asia. Nonetheless, the streamlined and simplified tenets produced by the Kamakura originators had a distinctly Buddhist message at their core.

The emphasis on belief and practice found in Kamakura Buddhism displaced a luxurious aesthetic sensibility that had been a part of Buddhism in the Heian period. Buddhism in the Kamakura period did not produce artistic works in the fields of painting, sculpture, architecture, or even literature. The only exceptions to this rule were the artistic images of the schools' founders used in the memorial services and the illustrated biographies of them used in religious teaching. The Rinzai Zen school, which had close ties to the bakufu, was later influential in the creation of Japan's literature, art, and culture of daily life, but such involvements of Rinzai did not exist in the Kamakura period. They emerged only in the Muromachi period that followed.

Notwithstanding Kamakura Buddhism's divergence from the fine arts, its impact on other spheres of society and culture was extensive. Its teachings stimulated Japan's most widespread propagation of Buddhism among the lower classes and fostered for the first time organizations that could rightly be called religious institutions of the people. It also challenged the earlier schools of Buddhism so profoundly that they were inspired to initiate various religious activities of their own. These consequences and others, as they worked their way through all levels of society, carved out an indisputable place for Kamakura Buddhism in Japanese history.

CHAPTER 13

ZEN AND THE *GOZAN*

The medieval centuries can fairly be described as the great age of Japanese Buddhism. Hōnen, Eisai, Shinran, Dōgen, Nichiren, Ippen, Rennyo, and thousands of lesser-known but equally dedicated religious leaders took Buddhism out of its traditional place in monastic cloisters under elite patronage, found new possibilities for personal salvation, and carried their message to common people throughout Japan. During these centuries, the foundations were laid for those new schools of Buddhism – Pure Land, True Pure Land, Nichiren, and Zen – that still claim the spiritual allegiance of the majority of Japanese. In response to these surges of reform, innovation, and popularization, some of the older schools of Buddhism produced reformers who called for a return to stricter monastic discipline and tried to make their teachings more accessible to ordinary men and women.

The social ramifications of this religious upsurge were enormous. Thousands, perhaps tens of thousands, of monasteries, nunneries, hermitages, and "training places" (*dōjō*) for lay devotees were established. Monasteries, monks, and wandering preachers looked for, and found, new patrons; received donations and grants of land; served as bearers of culture and learning as well as advocates of Buddhist spirituality; acted as political advisers; and engaged in commerce and diplomacy. Some of the older monastic centers remained powerful political and military forces in society. And some of the newer groups, especially the Nichiren and True Pure Land followers, displayed a militant edge.

The general development of Buddhism in the medieval period is discussed in Chapter 12 of this volume. This chapter will examine the introduction and spread of Zen Buddhism as one aspect of the larger development of Buddhism and of changes in medieval society. The growth of Zen was rapid and striking. In 1200, there were no more than a handful of small Zen temples in Japan, in most of which Zen meditation was practiced in conjunction with Tendai or Shingon Buddhist ceremonies. By 1600, the Rinzai and Sōtō schools of Zen had developed clear sectarian identities, and there were literally thousands of Zen monasteries in Japan, some having populations of a thousand monks. The impact of this expansion of Zen on the religious, social and cultural life of the age can hardly be overestimated.

The development of medieval Zen in all its religious and social manifestations cannot be dealt with in a single chapter. Here, therefore, I shall concentrate on five topics: the transmission of Zen from China to Japan, the institutional growth and diffusion of the major branches of Zen and the patronage that made this possible, the administration and economy of the medieval Zen monastery, the transformation of Zen thought and practice in the Japanese context, and the contribution of Zen monks to medieval Japanese culture.

THE TRANSMISSION OF CH'AN BUDDHISM TO JAPAN

The Asuka, Nara, and Heian periods

Before the mid-twelfth century, few monks claimed to be bearers of Zen. Meditation in one form or another is part of the spiritual practice of most schools of Buddhism. However, Japanese monks and some of their imperial patrons during the Nara and Heian periods were aware that some Chinese monks emphasized meditation (*dhyana* or *ch'an*) as a path to enlightenment more direct than such traditional Buddhist practices as sutra study, prayer and ritual, and the accumulation of merit through good works. The Japanese monk Ennin (793–864) recorded in his journal several encounters with Ch'an monks during his pilgrimage to Chinese Buddhist monasteries in the mid-ninth century. But he was not impressed by the Ch'an devotees nor inspired to study Ch'an:

> After we had eaten, we drank tea, and then, heading due north, we went twenty-five *li* to Hsing-t'ang hsien in the territory of Chen-chou and went to the Hsi-ch'an-yüan inside the walled town and spent the night. There were over twenty Zen monks who were extremely unruly men at heart.[1]

Ennin journeyed to China to study what he believed to be the mainstream of T'ang-dynasty Buddhism – T'ien-t'ai teachings and tantric practices. Ch'an was clearly peripheral to his interest, and on this occasion at least, he seems to have been repelled by the boisterousness of the Ch'an practitioners he met.

---

1 For Ennin's comments, see Edwin O. Reischauer, trans., *Ennin's Diary: The Record of a Pilgrimage to China in Search of the Law* (New York: Ronald Press, 1955), p. 210.

Other Japanese monks during these early centuries were more favorably disposed that Ennin was toward Ch'an Buddhism. Dōshō (629–700), one of the founders of the Hossō school of Buddhism in Japan, went to China in 653 as part of an official embassy. Together with Hossō teachings, he also studied Ch'an and after his return to Japan established a meditation hall in his monastery, the Gankōji. Saichō (766–822), the founder of the Tendai (T'ien-t'ai) school in Japan, is said to have received a Ch'an transmission from a Ch'an master on Mount T'ien-t'ai. He incorporated meditation into a fourfold Tendai practice that involved sutra study, esoteric rituals, study of the Vinaya precepts, and contemplation (*shikan*). Saicho's receptivity to Ch'an was to have significant consequences for later phases of the Zen transmission. In the late Heian period, many monks who had been trained in the Tendai monastery of the Enryakuji renewed their interest in meditation and sought to use Zen to revive Japanese Tendai Buddhism. But this impulse toward reform was rejected by the Tendai establishment. Had the Tendai leadership been more accommodating to the advocates of Zen, it is possible that Zen would have continued to develop within a Tendai framework rather than emerging as an independent school of Japanese Buddhism.

Several Chinese exponents of Ch'an found their way to Japan during the Nara and Heian periods. Around 736, the monk Tao-hsuan (Dōsen) arrived. He was an adherent of the Vinaya school who had studied Ch'an under masters of the Northern school of Ch'an. Tao-hsuan received imperial patronage and established a meditation hall within the Nara monastery of Daianji. A century later the Ch'an monk I-k'ung (Gikū) was invited to Japan by Empress Tachibana, a consort of Emperor Saga and an enthusiastic patron of Buddhism. She had heard from Kūkai that Ch'an Buddhism was in vogue in T'ang China and had requested that a Ch'an master be sent to Japan. I-k'ung was installed in the newly built monastery of Danrinji. He lectured on Zen before the imperial court and instructed some Japanese monks in Ch'an, but then he eventually returned to China.[2]

Thus, although Zen was known in Japan in the Nara and Heian periods, the transmission was sporadic and did not lead to any sustained development. Ch'an was only one among many expressions of T'ang Buddhism and was certainly not the most clearly defined or

---

2 Biographical information on Dōshō, Saichō, Tao-hsuan (Dōsen), and I-kung (Gikū) is drawn from Komazawa daigaku zengaku daijiten hensanjo, ed., *Zengaku daijiten*, 3 vols. (Tokyo: Taishūkan shoten, 1978).

ZEN AND THE *GOZAN*

socially influential.[3] The Japanese monks accompanying the official
embassies to China during these centuries sought out masters of the
major philosophical schools of Buddhism – T'ien-t'ai, Hua-yen, or
Fa-hsian – or monks who could instruct them in monastic precepts or
esoteric practices. It was these monks, not the Ch'an practitioners,
who dominated the great metropolitan monasteries of the T'ang empire. If they displayed an interest in Ch'an, it was as a complementary
practice. Dōshō combined Ch'an meditation practice with Hossō meta-
physics. Saichō blended it into a syncretism in which devotion to the
Lotus Sutra and the conduct of tantric rituals played major roles.
Many Chinese monks came to Japan during the Nara and early Heian
periods, and some, like the Vinaya master Ganjin, attracted many
followers. Few of these Chinese masters were specialists in Ch'an
meditation or philosophy, however, or advocated Ch'an as an exclusive
practice. Tao-hsuan combined Ch'an with Vinaya discipline. I-k'ung
came as a Ch'an master, but he left Japan before establishing anything
resembling an independent meditation practice.

Opportunities for the transmission of Zen were drastically reduced
with the abandonment of official embassies to China after 894 because
of the expense involved and the political disorder on the continent.
Thereafter, until the twelfth century, the only contacts were sporadic
ones made by traders, pirates and a few pilgrim monks. One Japanese
monk, Jōjin, is known to have journeyed to China and studied Ch'an
during the Northern Sung period. There is no evidence, however, that
he ever returned to Japan.

The Kamakura period

The number of monks transmitting Ch'an teachings to Japan during the
late twelfth and thirteenth centuries increased dramatically. This transmission was hardly interrupted by the Mongols' invasion attempts in
1274 and 1281. During this period, Japanese and Chinese monks introduced to Japan not only Zen thought and meditation techniques but
also monastic forms and cultural idioms. A few of the monks who
journeyed from Japan to China during the Kamakura period studied
Vinaya (Ritsu) or Pure Land teachings, but most were bearers of Zen.

Why, when there had been so little interest in Ch'an during the Nara

---

3 The general character of T'ang-dynasty Buddhism is discussed by Stanley Weinstein, "Imperial Patronage in the Formation of T'ang Buddhism," in Arthur F. Wright and Denis
Twitchett, eds., *Perspectives on the T'ang* (New Haven, Conn.: Yale University Press, 1973),
pp. 265–306.

and Heian periods, should there have been so much enthusiasm demonstrated in the Kamakura period? By the late Heian period, monks and lay people alike were convinced that Tendai and other branches of established Buddhism were in serious decline. Monastic regulations were flouted; monks and nuns lived like aristocrats and indulged in political intrigues; and monastic armies periodically threatened the capital, fought among themselves, or challenged the military power of the new warrior bands. The growing awareness of social dislocation and political disorder in the eleventh and twelfth centuries heightened these feelings of religious decline. So did the belief that beginning in 1052 Japan had entered the Later Age of the Buddha's Law (mappō), a phase of cosmic spiritual degeneration in which the remoteness of the Buddha's teaching made salvation by such traditional methods as the accumulation of merit extremely difficult.

By the late twelfth century, Japanese Buddhist circles were showing signs of revitalization. The lead was taken by Tendai monks seeking to reform traditional Buddhism and extend the promise of salvation to the common people. One powerful current developing in Tendai Buddhism emphasized the compassion of the Amida Buddha as the surest recourse in the age of mappō. Hōnen (1133–1212), for instance, stressed that sincere devotion to Amida, expressed through the invocation of his sacred name (nembutsu), offered the easiest path to rebirth (ōjō) in the Pure Land of Amida's Western Paradise. Other Tendai monks came to believe that they could revitalize Tendai practice by reasserting the centrality of the Lotus Sutra or by reemphasizing the Vinaya discipline. Others believed that revival could best be accomplished by bringing the latest and best in Buddhist teachings from Sung China. Like their predecessors in the Asuka and Nara periods, a few determined monks made the dangerous sea crossing to study in the great Buddhist centers of the Southern Sung empire.

When they reached China, however, they quickly discovered that most of the Chinese monks they encountered no longer advocated T'ien-t'ai or Hua-yen doctrines but were devotees of Ch'an. In the intervening centuries, while the older schools of Chinese Buddhism had languished, Ch'an had flourished and had become the most vital branch of Chinese monastic Buddhism. This vitality was expressed in a sharply focused spiritual practice based on rigorous meditation, a carefully ordered monastic life, an active intellectual and cultural influence throughout Chinese society, and institutional growth based on generous secular patronage. Purges of established metropolitan Buddhism of the kind witnessed by Ennin in the mid-ninth century had left Ch'an and Pure Land communities – with their provincial roots, loose organization, and relative lack of wealth or reputation for wealth – virtually unscathed. In fact, by attacking established Buddhism as alien, opulent, and antisocial, the purges helped clear the way for the spread of Ch'an and Pure Land teachings and practices that could easily be reconciled with Chinese sensibilities. Even if they had not impressed the Japanese monks, T'ang Ch'an masters like Matsu (709–88) and Lin-chi (d. 867) had attracted able monks and intrigued many laypersons through their direct approach, cryptic responses, and vigorous advocacy of the possibility of immediate enlightenment through meditation and self-negation.[4] In the centuries following the collapse of the T'ang dynasty, while Pure Land devotion spread widely at the popular level, Ch'an won the support of large numbers of monks, literati, and provincial military governors:

With the diffusion of political power after the An Lu-shan Rebellion, the military governors came to share with the imperial court the patronage of Buddhism. The governors and the men around them were attracted to the ideas of the school of meditation (Ch'an), and this school flourished in many provincial centers.[5]

Thus, monasteries that had once been filled with T'ien-t'ai, Lü (Ritsu), Fa-hsiang, or Hua-yen monks were now dominated by Ch'an monks and headed by Ch'an masters. During the Sung dynasty, some thirty Ch'an centers thoughout the empire were organized in a hierarchy, culminating in five great monasteries, or mountains (*wu-shan*), in Hangchow. These monasteries had great wealth and prestige. Of course, together with official sponsorship went alignment with the secular bureaucracy. The lives of the monks were carefully regulated, and the appointments of their abbots were subject to official confirmation. It was to these thriving Ch'an monasteries in and around Hangchow and the lower Yangtze River region that Japanese monks came in the late twelfth and thirteenth centuries.[6]

When they enrolled in the monks' halls of these Chinese monasteries and recovered from their surprise at the pervasiveness of Ch'an, the Japanese monks found that they had much to learn. The Ch'an teachings that I-K'ung introduced to Japan during the T'ang dynasty had

4 The growth of Ch'an Buddhism is introduced by Heinrich Dumoulin, *A History of Zen Buddhism* (New York: Pantheon, 1963).
5 Wright and Twitchett, eds., *Perspectives on the T'ang*, p. 21.
6 Brief discussions of the role of Ch'an Buddhism in Sung-dynasty society can be found in Araki Kengo, "Zen," in Kubo Noritada and Nishi Junzō, eds., *Shūkyō*, vol. 6 of *Chūgoku bunka sōsho* (Tokyo: Taishūkan shoten, 1968), pp. 106–114; and Tamamura Takeji, "Zen," in Bitō Masahide, ed., *Chūgoku bunka to Chūgoku* (Tokyo: Taishūkan shoten, 1968), pp. 151–71.

been those of the Northern school of Ch'an. By the Sung dynasty, the rather contemplative Northern teaching had been outstripped by the Southern school deriving from Hui-neng, the sixth Ch'an patriarch, which stressed a dynamic meditation leading to "sudden enlightenment."[7] In the late twelfth and early thirteenth centuries, Southern-school masters tracing their Ch'an lineage from Lin-chi were the most influential. Their Ch'an practice harnessed mind-breaking "cases" (kung-an, kōan), shouts, and even slaps to intensify their students' meditative quest. Japanese monks also found that this meditation practice was conducted in a novel monastic setting in which the monks' hall, where they practiced communal meditation, and the Dharma, or lecture, hall, where the monks debated Ch'an publicly with their masters, were among the most important buildings. They found that Ch'an masters stressed the Vinaya precepts and that a detailed code of monastic regulations for the Ch'an communities, the Ch'an-yuan ch'ing-kuei, had recently been compiled (1103) and was in force in many Ch'an communities.[8] Those monks who stayed longer in China discovered that many Ch'an masters shared the intellectual and cultural interests of the secular literati with whom they consorted. They also learned that monastic life included not only meditation and study of Ch'an Buddhist traditions and texts but also a wide range of cultural avocations such as poetry, painting, and scholarship, many of which blended Ch'an and secular taste.

Young Japanese monks found the Ch'an Buddhism in the monasteries of Hangchow to be vigorous and impressive. It was natural that they should have viewed Ch'an as the highest expression of Sung Buddhism and sought to use it to revitalize Japanese monastic Buddhism. When they discovered that the Tendai establishment in the capital resisted such reform, that Zen as a single practice was denounced as vociferously as Hōnen's exclusive nembutsu practice had been, the Zen pioneers were forced to try to establish Zen as an independent branch of Buddhism in Japan under the patronage of new groups in medieval society.

The first monks to introduce Sung Ch'an teachings to Japan were Myōan Eisai (1141–1215) and Kakua (1143–?). Eisai made two journeys to China, the first in 1168 and the second in 1187. His first stay in

---

7 The place of Hui-neng and the differences between the northern and southern branches of Ch'an Buddhism are discussed by Philip Yampolsky in his introduction to The Platform Sutra of the Sixth Patriarch (New York: Columbia University Press, 1967), pp. 1–57.

8 Kagamishima Genryū, Satō Tatsugen, and Kosaka Kiyū, eds., Yakuchū Zen'on shingi (Tokyo: Sōtōshū shūmuchō, 1972), pp. 1–25.

China lasted for only a few months and was devoted to visiting traditional Buddhist sites and collecting Tendai and Shingon texts. Eisai's
interest in Ch'an had been whetted, but after his return to Japan he
seems to have continued to advocate Tendai Buddhism. His second
pilgrimage to China lasted for three years and brought him into much
deeper contact with Ch'an. Having been refused permission to proceed through China to visit the Buddhist sites in India, Eisai made his
way to Mount T'ien-t'ai where he studied Ch'an under Hsu-an Huai-
chang of the Huang-lung lineage of the Lin-chi school. Hsu-an gave
Eisai a certificate of enlightenment and urged him to spread Zen
throughout Japan. Eisai was able to establish several meditation halls
in Kyushu, but when he tried to promote Zen in the capital, suggesting that it be given pride of place in Tendai practice and arguing that
the secular patronage of Zen would contribute to the country's security, he ran afoul of the monks and supporters of the Enryakuji and
was driven out of Kyoto. Making his way to eastern Japan, Eisai
secured the patronage of Hōjō Masako and the young shogun Minamoto Sanetomo. With their backing Eisai eventually was able to return to Kyoto and establish the Kenninji, where Zen meditation was
taught together with Tendai and Shingon Buddhist practices.[9]

Kakua may have introduced Sung Zen teachings to Japan even
before Eisai. In 1171, he learned that Ch'an was in vogue in China and
made a four-year journey to the continental monasteries. He had returned to Japan before Eisai made his second visit to China. According
to the *Genkō shakusho*, a history of Buddhism compiled in 1322 by the
Zen monk Kokan Shiren, Kakua bemused emperor Takakura by responding to his questions about Zen with a melody on the flute. But
because Kakua did not establish an enduring lineage, the credit for
founding Rinzai Zen in Japan went to Eisai.[10]

By the mid-thirteenth century at least thirty Japanese monks had
journeyed to China in search of Zen. A number of them studied at the
Hangchow monastery of Ching-shan under the guidance of Wu-chun
Shih-fan (1177–1249) of the Yang-ch'i lineage of Rinzai Zen.[11] In the

---

9 Yanagida Seizan, *Rinzai no kafū* (Tokyo: Chikuma shobō, 1967), pp. 28–88, offers a biographical study of Eisai (or, as he is also known, Yōsai).
10 Kokan Shiren, "Genkō shakusho" in Kuroita Katsumi, ed., *Shintei zōho kokushi taikei* (Tokyo: Yoshikawa kōbunkan, 1930), vol. 31, p. 100.
11 The fine portrait of Wu-chun given to Enni and carried back by him to Japan is illustrated in
   the catalogue for the exhibition The Arts of Zen Buddhism held at the Kyoto National
   Museum, October–November 1981. See Kyoto kokuritsu hakubutsukan, ed., *Zen no bijutsu*
   (Kyoto: Kyōto kokuritsu hakubutsukan, 1981), pp. 25, 55. An example of his calligraphy is
   discussed in Jan Fontein and Money L. Hickman, eds., *Zen Painting and Calligraphy* (Boston: Boston Museum of Fine Arts, 1970), pp. 24–26.

transmission of Zen to Japan, the most influential of these monks were Dōgen Kigen, Enni Ben'en, and Muhon (Shinchi) Kakushin. Dōgen (1200–53) entered the Tendai monastery of Enryakuji at the age of thirteen. Not finding answers to his religious questioning in Tendai Buddhism, he moved to the Kenninji to study Zen with Eisai. In 1223, in company with Eisai's most senior disciple Myōzen, Dōgen journeyed to China. After studying under several Ch'an masters, Dōgen met T'ien-t'ung Ju-ching (1163–1228), a Ts'ao-tung (Sōtō) Zen master reputed for his austere personal life and severe Zen practice. The elderly Chinese master and the enthusiastic young Japanese monk established an immediate rapport. Before Dōgen returned to Japan, Ju-ching recognized Dōgen's enlightenment and transmitted to him the teachings of Sōtō Zen. Dōgen found it difficult, however, to gain acceptance for his Zen in the capital. He returned at first to the Kenninji, but Eisai had died, and the Zen training there had deteriorated. Dōgen's advocacy of single-minded meditation (*shikan taza*) as the best form of Buddhist practice aroused the hostility of the Enryakuji monks. Their opposition eventually forced him to leave the capital and establish his community in the mountains of Echizen. With the exception of one brief visit to Kamakura, where he discussed Zen with the regent Hōjō Tokiyori, he spent the remainder of his life there, building the monastic center of Eiheiji, training the few disciples who came to study with him, and writing his treatises on Zen and the monastic life, the *Shōbō genzō*.[12]

Enni Benn'en (1202–80) was more successful than Dōgen had been in gaining acceptance for Zen in Kyoto. As a young monk, Enni studied Zen with Eisai's disciple Eichō after becoming dissatisfied with Tendai Buddhism. In 1235, he set out on a six-year pilgrimage to China. There he became a disciple of Wu-chun Shih-fan at Ching-shan. Wu-chun gave to Enni a robe and bowl symbolizing the legitimate transmission of Zen enlightenment and urged him to spread Zen throughout Japan. On his return to Japan in 1241, Enni brought with him many Zen-related texts, as well as portraits of Wu-chun and examples of his calligraphy.

Eisai, Kakua, and Dōgen had not been readily accepted in Kyoto. Enni, however, secured a stronger beachhead for Zen in the capital largely because he enjoyed the sponsorship of one of the most influential nobles of the day, Kujō Michiie. In 1243, Enni was invited to

---

12 This biographical sketch of Dōgen is based on Imaeda Aishin, *Dōgen: zazen hitosuji no shamon* (Tokyo: NHK Books, 1981); and Hee-jin Kim, *Dōgen Kigen – Mystical Realist* (Tucson: University of Arizona Press, 1975).

Kyoto to serve as the founding abbot of a grandiose new monastery, the Tōfukuji, that Michiie had built. The Tōfukuji was not at first exclusively a Zen monastery. Rather, Enni was forced to compromise with established Buddhism and, like Eisai at the Kenninji, to teach Zen alongside Tendai and esoteric Buddhism. Enni, however, made it clear that he considered Zen the fundamental Buddhist practice and worked to convert the Tōfukuji into a full-fledged Zen monastery. Enni's learning, his firsthand knowledge of Chinese Buddhism, and the patronage of the Kujō family guaranteed his acceptance by the Buddhist circles close to the court. On several occasions, Enni lectured on Zen to Emperor Gosaga and his entourage and taught Zen to the warrior rulers of eastern Japan. In his long lifetime, Enni attracted large numbers of disciples, many of whom in their turn went to study under Wu-chun and his successors.[13]

Muhon (Shinchi) Kakushin (1207–98) was in his thirties before he began to practice Zen with Eisai's disciples Gyōyū and Eichō in eastern Japan. In 1249, he traveled to China where he studied Ch'an under the Lin-chi master Wu-men Hui-k'ai (Mumon Ekai), the compiler of the collection of *kōan*, (literally, "public cases") known in Japanese as the *Mumonkan* (Gateless gate). *Kōan* were conundrums or propositions used as an aid to Buddhist meditation and enlightenment. Kakushin was certainly one of the first monks to use *kōan* from this collection in his training of Zen monks in Japan. Unlike Enni, however, he had little desire to head a great temple in the capital. Although he was invited to Kyoto by the cloistered emperors Kameyama and Gouda, who wished to learn about Zen and offered to build temples for him, Kakushin preferred an eremitic life at a small mountain temple, the Kōkokuji, in Kii Province.[14]

Japanese monks like Mukan Fumon or Tettsū Gikai, who had studied Zen under Enni and Dōgen, respectively, continued to journey to China during the second half of the thirteenth century. But by the time Kakushin returned to Japan in 1254, a new and important stage in the transmission of Sung Zen was under way. Chinese Ch'an masters were beginning to come to Japan to teach Zen and the conduct of Zen monastic life. The young Japanese monks enrolling in Chinese monasteries had conveyed to the Chinese monks both their enthusiasm for

13 For the life of Enni, see the chronology compiled by his follower Enshin, "Shōichi kokushi nempu," in Suzuki gakujutsu zaidan, ed., *Dai-Nihon Bukkyō zensho* (Tokyo: Kōdansha, 1972), vol. 73, pp. 147–56; and the section by Tsuji Zennosuke in *Nihon Bukkyō-shi (chūsei 2)* (Tokyo: Iwanami shoten, 1970), pp. 98–124. A painting of the Tōfukuji in the early sixteenth century is illustrated and described in Fontein and Hickman, eds., *Zen Painting and Calligraphy*, pp. 144–8.   14 Entry on Kakushin in *Zengaku daijiten*.

Zen and the information that Zen was taking root in Japan. As a result, some Chinese Ch'an masters came to view Japan as a possible field for the transplanting of Zen.

The first of these Chinese monks to come to Japan was Lan-ch'i Tao-lung (Rankei Dōryū, 1213–78). Although still only in his early thirties when he landed in Kyushu in 1246, Lan-ch'i was a recognized Ch'an master who had practiced meditation under the guidance of Wu-chun Shih-fan and Wu-ming Hui-hsing, the leading Lin-chi masters of that time. The young Chinese monk made his way to Kamakura where he won the favor of the regent Hōjō Tokiyori. Tokiyori studied Zen with Lan-ch'i and installed him as the founding abbot of a new Zen monastery, the Kenchōji, in Kamakura. The completion of the Kenchōji in 1253 was an important milestone in the transmission of Zen to Japan. Unlike the Kenninji and Tōfukuji in Kyoto, it did not begin by compromising with the older schools of Buddhism. The temple bell and the plaque over the main gate proclaimed that it was a Zen monastery. Unlike Dōgen's community at Eiheiji, which had rejected any accommodation with Tendai or other forms of Buddhism and as a result had discouraged elite patronage, the Kenchōji had the backing of the country's warrior rulers.

The establishment of the Kenchōji signaled that Zen Buddhism was now a major force in Japanese religious life. But Lan-ch'i did not restrict himself to Kamakura. In 1265, in response to an imperial request, he went to Kyoto and lectured at the court. While in the capital he revitalized Zen practice at Eisai's old monastery, the Kenninji, and helped Enni transform the Tōfukuji into a full Zen monastery. During the Mongols' first invasion attempt in 1274, it was rumored that Lan-ch'i was a Mongol spy. Subsequently, when he was exiled to Kai Province, he took the opportunity to spread Rinzai Zen among the local warriors. Lan-ch'i was allowed to return to the Kenchōji shortly before his death. In recognition of his contribution to the transmission of Zen, he was granted the posthumous title of Daikaku Zenji, Zen master Daikaku. His disciples and successors in the Daikaku lineage, with Kenchōji as their base, carried his Zen teachings throughout the Kantō region.[15]

Lan-ch'i had been followed before the close of the Kamakura period by more than a dozen fully trained Chinese Ch'an masters. This was a

15 Lan-ch'i Tao-lung and Kenchōji are discussed in Daihonzan Kenchōji, ed., *Kyofukuzan Kenchōji* (Kamakura: Daihonzan Kenchōji, 1977), pp. 23–82. Portraits of Lan-ch'i and Tokiyori, temple ground plans, and examples of Lan-ch'i's calligraphy and monastic regulations are also included in this source.

rare phenomenon in Sino-Japanese cultural relations, and after the Nara period there was no other comparable influx of fully trained, high-ranking monks. Some came because they felt uprooted by the Mongol conquest of China. Others responded to invitations from the Hōjō regents. Others came simply because, like Lan-ch'i, they had heard that Zen was in the ascendant in Japan. A few of these émigrés, for instance, Wu-an P'u ning (Gottan Funei, 1197–1267), returned to China disappointed with their Japanese students' incomprehension of Zen. Most, however, spent the remainder of their lives in Japan, training monks and lay persons in Kamakura, Kyoto, and the provinces, where they were invited to establish temples by powerful local *shugo* warriors. Through their efforts, the practice of Zen in the Japanese monasteries by the early fourteenth century was probably equivalent to that in the Chinese monasteries.[16]

The Muromachi period

Throughout the fourteenth and fifteenth centuries, Japanese monks – now well trained in Zen before their departure – continued to travel to Chinese Ch'an centers in search of teachings, monastic codes, and cultural expressions of Zen. Some of them spent more than a decade in China and rose to high ranks in Chinese monasteries. Others were sent by their temples or by the Ashikaga shoguns to head embassies, to act as interpreters, and to handle foreign trade and cultural exchanges. These latter may have made very little contribution to the transmission of Zen.

By 1350, the Zen monastic establishment in Japan was so large, well organized, and self-sustaining that there was less incentive for Chinese monks to come to Japan or for Japanese monks to undergo training in Chinese monasteries. Monks who had been to China were highly respected, not least by provincial warrior chieftains eager to sponsor Zen in their domains, but it was no longer essential to have studied Zen in China or to have had one's enlightenment certified (*inka*) by a Chinese master in order to be a leading figure in Japanese Zen circles.

The influential monk Musō Soseki (1275–1351) represented this first generation of self-confident Japanese Rinzai masters. Musō had begun his Zen practice under the guidance of the Chinese émigré monk I-shan I-ning (Issan Ichinei, 1247–1317) but had failed to attain

---

16 Information on some of these Chinese masters and their patrons can be found in Tsuji, *Nihon Bukkyō-shi (chūsei* 2), pp. 125–264; and Martin Collcutt, *Five Mountains: The Rinzai Zen Monastic Institution in Medieval Japan* (Cambridge, Mass.: Harvard University Press, 1981), pp. 57–78.

I-shan's recognition of his enlightenment. I-shan described Musō's approach to Zen as too bookish. After further wandering and intense meditation, Musō attained enlightenment at dawn in a mountain hut, on seeing dying embers burst into renewed fire. This experience was accepted as a true enlightenment by the Japanese Zen master Kohō Kennichi (1241–1316), a son of Emperor Gosaga. Musō subsequently became one of the most influential Zen monks in medieval Japan. He was patronized by emperors and shoguns, headed many of the leading Zen monasteries in Kyoto and Kamakura, and attracted many hundreds of disciples. Some of these disciples went to China. Musō, however, never made the journey. He declared that with Zen so well rooted in Japan, there was no longer any need to look to China as a source of transmission.[17] Musō's contemporaries Daitō and Kanzan, the founders of the Daitokuji and the Myōshinji, likewise never visited China.

War in Japan and piracy in East Asian waters during the late fifteenth and sixteenth centuries virtually ended the direct transmission of Zen from Chinese monasteries. Beginning in the late sixteenth century, however, commercial contacts between Japan and China recovered, and a community of Chinese merchants settled in Nagasaki. In the seventeenth century, in response to their requests for spiritual leadership, Chinese monks from Fukien Province began to come to Nagasaki. Among them was Yin-yüan Lung-chi (Ingen Ryūki, 1592–1673), an eminent Ch'an master of the Huang-po (Ōbaku) school.

Yin-yüan came to Nagasaki in 1654 to serve as the abbot of the Kōfukuji. His reputation soon came to the attention of the fourth Tokugawa shogun, Ietsuna, who first invited him to Edo and then sponsored the building of a new monastery at Uji, near Kyoto, called the Mampukuji, a Japanese reading of the name of the monastery in Fukien from which Yin-yüan had come. Yin-yüan and the Chinese masters of the Huang-po school who followed him to Japan to head the Mampukuji or its branches introduced a new type of Zen common in Ming Chinese monasteries in which Zen meditation and *kōan* study were allied with Pure Land *nembutsu* devotion.[18] Ōbaku Zen did not become a very large school, however. At its peak it probably included no more than several hundred temples. The novel syncretic Ming Zen teachings and monastic practices, nonetheless, presented a challenge to the established Rinzai and Sōtō schools which were sunk in a late medieval lethargy. Many Rinzai and Sōtō monks were strongly attracted by *nembutsu* Zen. Others, like Hakuin Ekaku (1685–1768),

---

17 Tamamura Takeji, *Musō Kokushi* (Kyoto: Heirakuji shoten, 1969).
18 On Yin-yüan, the Ōbaku school, and Mampukuji, see Fuji Masaharu and Abe Zenryō, eds., *Mampukuji* (Kyoto: Tankōsha, 1977).

vigorously rejected such syncretic tendencies, but in doing so they encouraged a revival of serious Zen practice in both the Rinzai and Sōtō monasteries.

THE DEVELOPMENT OF THE ZEN MONASTIC
INSTITUTION IN MEDIEVAL JAPAN

When Eisai returned from his second pilgrimage to China in 1191, no Zen monasteries existed in Japan. But, a century later, Zen had taken root, and by 1491 there were many thousands of Rinzai and Sōtō Zen monasteries, subtemples, branch temples, nunneries, and hermitages scattered throughout the country.

Figure 13.1 presents an overview of the growth and institutional relationships of the major branches of Japanese Zen between the twelfth and sixteenth centuries. One major institutional division was that between the Rinzai monasteries, dominated by monks who traced their Zen lineage from Eisai, Enni, Chinese émigré monks, and their successors, and the Sōtō monasteries, whose monks traced their Zen from Dōgen and his disciples. A third branch of Zen, the Ōbaku school, was not, as I have already mentioned, introduced to Japan until the seventeenth century and thus falls outside the scope of this chapter. The division between Rinzai and Sōtō was significant, and I shall return to it frequently in this chapter, but it must be stressed that divisions within Rinzai and Sōtō were equally significant in the institutional development of medieval Zen. These institutional subdivisions reflected different attitudes toward Zen itself and differences in patterns of patronage, in economic well-being, and in cultural involvement. It is through an understanding of these groupings that we can most easily grasp the institutional development of medieval Zen.

Rinzai Zen: the gozan

Until at least the mid-fifteenth century, the largest, most prosperous, and most influential Rinzai monasteries were those comprising the nationwide network headed by the so-called five mountains (*gozan*), the great metropolitan monasteries of Kyoto and Kamakura.[19] Especially during the fourteenth and early fifteenth centuries, the *gozan* group was both the most vigorous branch of Rinzai Zen and one of the most vital sectors of the entire metropolitan Buddhist establishment.

19 Unless otherwise indicated, the ensuing discussion of the *gozan* branch of medieval Zen follows Collcutt, *Five Mountains*, pp. 76–125.

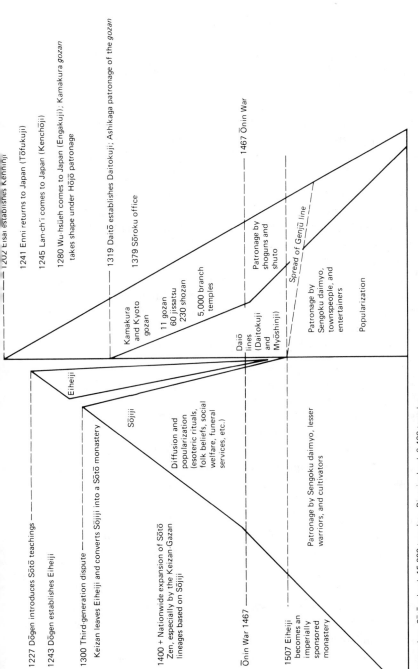

Present-day: Sōtō school, 15,000 temples; Rinzai school, 6,400 temples.

Figure 13.1 The growth of Zen schools, thirteenth to sixteenth century. (From Kawasaki Tsuneyuki and Kasahara Kazuo, eds., *Shūkyō-shi*, vol. 18 of *Taikei Nihon-shi sōsho*, p. 219. Tokyo: Yamakawa shūppansha, 1966.)

The development of the *gozan* institution was of great significance, not merely for the diffusion of Zen, but also for the cultural, political, and economic life of the age. *Gozan* monasteries had as their patrons members of the warrior and courtly elites. They were major landholders and collectively were one of the largest holders of private domain (*shōen*) interests in medieval Japan. Their monks, who must be counted among the intellectuals of the age, were well versed in Chinese culture as well as in Zen and served as cultural and political advisers to shoguns and emperors besides being mentors in Zen to the sons and daughters of warrior families. The *gozan* group comprised a three-tiered hierarchy of monasteries. All adopted the same basic organizational structure, and although they differed greatly in size and importance, they all were regulated by the same monastic codes, and were subject to the same control by warrior laws. A youth entering one of the small provincial monasteries making up the lower tier of the *gozan* system might in time become a Zen master or monastic official in one of the Kamakura or Kyoto *gozan*. Conversely, Zen teachings or Chinese cultural tastes adopted by the metropolitan *gozan* quickly spread to the system's provincial extremities.

The *gozan* institution began to take shape in the late thirteenth century. By 1299, the Kamakura monastery of Jōchiji was being referred to as one of "five mountains." A Kenchōji document of 1308 states that that monastery was then regarded as the "head of the five peaks." At about the same time, the newly established Kyoto monastery of Nanzenji was also being described as one of the five mountains. Details of the early *gozan* network are unclear, but the surviving records indicate that the Hōjō regents in Kamakura took the initiative in honoring and regulating the new Zen monasteries that they were building, by adopting the Southern Sung practice of organizing an official three-tiered hierarchy of Zen monasteries. Together with the appointment of monasteries to *gozan* status, the Hōjō also designated smaller monasteries in Kamakura, Kyoto, and the provinces to the second and third tiers of the hierarchy as *jissatsu* ("ten temples") and *shozan* ("various mountains"). Most of the monasteries included in the *gozan* were Rinzai monasteries dominated by those schools of Zen derived from Eisai, Enni, or Chinese émigré masters that had taken root in Kamakura and Kyoto. Sōtō Zen was represented in the *gozan* system by a very small number of monasteries that had been founded in Kamakura.

Why should the Hōjō have shown such interest in creating a Zen monastic establishment? In part they were probably responding to suggestions by Chinese and Japanese monks who were eager that their monasteries be given official recognition and warrior protection, thus relieving them of some of the hostility of the Enryakuji and other powerful and long-established rivals. The warrior regents would have been receptive to arguments that it would add to their prestige and that of Japan to create a nationwide network of official Zen monasteries similar to the system established in Sung China. But the Hōjō could also have seen other benefits deriving from the elaboration of an official Zen monastic system. They were thus asserting their predominant influence over, and co-opting to their service, a new and increasingly influential branch of Japanese Buddhism.

For centuries, the imperial court had created client relationships with certain Buddhist monasteries, by granting them the status of *jōgakuji* or *monzeki*. Other monasteries in Kyoto and Nara were linked to the imperial family or the Fujiwara and other noble houses through the family connections of their abbots. Such ties of monastic status and personal connection kept the older monasteries firmly within the sphere of court influence and resistant to warrior control.

By creating an official network of Zen monasteries, the Hōjō were, therefore, building their own countersystem of client monasteries, in which warrior interests would be heeded and the sons of warrior families who entered the monastic life could rise to positions of leadership. The Hōjō were also painfully aware that many of the older monasteries maintained powerful armed bands that were sources of political violence and monastic unruliness and corruption. By asserting their control over the metropolitan Zen monasteries, the Hōjō were thus trying to ensure that the new Zen institution would not become yet another militant branch of monastic Buddhism. Warriors from the bakufu with the title of superintendent of Zen monasteries (*jike gyoji*) were given authority over the *gozan* network, and the bakufu began to issue detailed regulations for the various *gozan* monasteries, including strong prohibitions against the acquisition of weapons by Zen monks.

Although the Hōjō took the lead in elevating to official status the new Rinzai monasteries they sponsored, members of the imperial family were quick to follow suit. The Kyoto monastery of Nanzenji was established in 1291 when the cloistered emperor Kameyama converted one of his detached palaces into a Zen monastery. At the urging of the court, it was quickly accorded *gozan* status. Emperor Godaigo (1288–1339) demonstrated that, like the Hōjō, he too could discern political advantage in the patronage and control of the growing *gozan* Zen institution. When he came to power after the destruction of the Kamakura bakufu in 1333, he deliberately shifted the leadership of the *gozan* monasteries from Kamakura to Kyoto, by promoting to the

highest rank within the *gozan* group those monasteries like the
Nanzenji or the newly established Daitokuji that had strong imperial
connections. Godaigo had relied heavily on the support of the older
Buddhist monasteries like the Enryakuji in his efforts to topple the
Hōjō. His promotion of a Kyoto-centered *gozan* was thus an indication
that he fully recognized the social influence of metropolitan Zen and
was eager to use that influence to help restore imperial rule.

Godaigo's imperial restoration was short-lived. Ashikaga Takauji, a
warrior leader who had helped him overthrow the Kamakura bakufu,
ousted him from the capital in 1336, installed a rival emperor on the
throne, and set himself up as shogun. The Ashikaga family came from
the Kantō where they had already been patrons of Rinzai Zen monks.
Takauji, his brother Tadayoshi, and the Ashikaga shoguns carried on
from the Hōjō the practice of promoting metropolitan Zen monasteries to the various ranks of the *gozan* system. With their bakufu based
in Kyoto, it was natural that the Ashikaga should have particularly
favored newly established Kyoto monasteries like the Tenryūji or
Shōkokuji, with which they had close ties and which were dominated
by monks from Zen lineages that they patronized such as that of Musō
Soseki. The Kamakura *gozan* survived, but for the next century or
more it was the Kyoto *gozan* monasteries, their subtemples and provincial satellites patronized by the Ashikaga and their leading vassals and
headed by monks of the Musō and Shōichi lineages that dominated the
gozan network and the whole Zen establishment.

As an institution, the *gozan* network grew rapidly under the patronage of the Ashikaga shoguns and their provincial agents, the *shugo*.
Among the *shugo* families that became generous patrons of *gozan*
monks and monasteries during the fourteenth and fifteenth centuries
were the Akamatsu, Asakura, Hosokawa, Imagawa, Kikuchi, Kira,
Ogasawara, Ōtomo, Ōuchi, Sasaki, Satake, Takeda, Toki, Uesugi,
and Yamana. Both Akamatsu Norimura (1277–1350) and his son
Norisuke (1314–71), for instance, studied Zen under Sesson Yūbai
(1290–1348). For Sesson and his followers, they established several
Rinzai monasteries in Harima, among them the Hōunji and Hōrinji,
both of which were designated *jissatsu* by the Muromachi bakufu.[20]
Hosokawa Yoriyuki (1329–92), who served as a senior bakufu official
(*kanrei*) and as *shugo* in Shikoku and Bingo, was an enthusiastic patron
of monks of the Musō lineage and a vigorous sponsor and reformer of
gozan monasteries.[21] Imagawa Ryōshun, who served the Ashikaga as

20 Kōsaka Konomu, *Akamatsu Enshin, Mitsusuke* (Tokyo: Yoshikawa kōbunkan, 1970). pp.
    60–71.
21 Ogawa Makoto, *Hosokawa Yoriyuki* (Tokyo: Yoshikawa kōbunkan, 1972), pp. 243–73.

governor of Kyushu (Kyushu *tandai*) and as *shugo* of Tōtōmi and Suruga, was a patron of Bukkai and other monks of Enni's lineage from the Tōfukuji.[22] The Ōuchi made their provincial headquarters, Yamaguchi in Suō, into a major cultural center during the Muromachi period and invited to it some of the most famous Zen masters of the age. Of the Rinzai temples that they sponsored, the bakufu ranked the Jōfukuji, Kōshakuji, and Kokuseiji as *jissatsu* and the Eikōji as a *shozan*.[23] The Ōtomo established half a dozen Rinzai temples in Bungo during this period. Most of them were headed by monks of Enni's line, the Shōichi branch of the *gozan*, and had close ties with Tōfukuji. Among these monasteries, one was ranked as a *jissatsu*, the remainder as *shozan*. Of eleven *jissatsu* and *shozan* monasteries in Mino, at least five were established by the Toki family, the *shugo* of the province.

The expansion of the *jissatsu* and *shozan* tiers of the *gozan* network clearly owed a great deal to patronage of the *gozan* lineages of Rinzai Zen by warriors of *shugo* rank. It seems fair to ask, therefore, why the majority of *shugo* should have become such eager sponsors of *gozan* monks and the *gozan* institution.

Certainly they were attracted by the new Chinese Zen teachings and by the novel practice of meditation (*zazen*). The writings of the Zen masters of that time reveal that *shugo* and other provincial warriors not only discussed Zen with them but also sat in meditation and came to them to discuss *kōan* – that is, they sought enlightenment. Many *shugo* placed their younger sons or daughters in Zen monasteries and nunneries and some, like Ōtomo Ujiyasu, rose to high positions in the *gozan*.

In addition, as in the case of the Hōjō regents and Ashikaga shoguns, cultural, political, and social factors, as well as spiritual interests, were involved in *shugo* patronage. Many *shugo* spent at least part of their time at the shogun's court in Kyoto, where they associated both with other warriors and with nobles and Zen prelates from the *gozan* monasteries. The patronage of *gozan* monks and the establishment of Zen monasteries in their domains kept these provincial warriors in direct touch with the cultural style of Kyoto and, beyond that, with the cultural interests of the Chinese literati.

It is clear from the surviving documents that the Zen monks whom warriors were most eager to patronize and invite to their territories were monks who had recently returned from China or who enjoyed a reputation in Kyoto for spiritual insight or cultural accomplishment.

22 Kawazoe Shōji, *Imagawa Ryōshun* (Tokyo: Yoshikawa kōbunkan, 1964), pp. 49–52.
23 Ouchi patronage of Zen and the arts is detailed in Yonehara Masayoshi, *Sengoku bushi to bungei no kenkyū* (Tokyo: Ōfūsha, 1976), pp. 511–814.

Imagawa Ryōshun, the Akamatsu, Ogasawara, Ōtomo, and many other *shugo* studied Neo-Confucianism and Chinese poetic styles under Zen monks. Ogasawara Sadamune (1291–1347) is believed to have developed his code of warrior etiquette (Ogasawara-ryū) partly under the guidance of Ch'ing-cho Cheng-ch'eng (Seisetsu Shōchō, 1274–1339), from whom he learned the rules of Zen monastic etiquette and the cultural ideals of Chinese literati.

The Ōuchi family, learning from the printing activities of the Kyoto *gozan*, sponsored the printing of Buddhist texts, Confucian classics, and treatises on Chinese poetry at Zen temples in Suō. Like other wealthy provincial warrior families, they were collectors of Chinese paintings and other art objects (*karamono*), in regard to whose appreciation they sought the guidance of Zen monks. Indeed, it was with the backing of the Ōuchi, and on an Ōuchi vessel, that the painter Sesshū Tōyō (1420–1506), who had begun his painting career as a monk in the Kyoto *gozan* monastery of Shōkokuji, was able to make his way to China for further study.

By the mid-fourteenth century it was obvious to the *shugo* and other provincial warrior families that Rinzai Zen was politically very much in the ascendant and that the Ashikaga and members of the imperial family were showing particular favor to those lineages of Rinzai Zen that were represented in the newly designated *gozan*, *jissatsu*, and *shozan* monasteries. As vassals of the Ashikaga, the *shugo* were encouraged to establish Zen monasteries in their provinces, and they found it politically expedient to have those monasteries ranked as *jissatsu* or *shozan*.[24] In doing so they were not only winning favor with the bakufu; they were also opening up channels of communication with the capital and doors for the advancement of those of their offspring who chose to enter the Zen monastic life. Socially, by installing prestigious Zen monks from the *gozan* schools as heads of their family temples (*ujidera*), the *shugo* hoped to raise their own local prestige among the warrior families in their province and perhaps contribute to a greater sense of cohesion among their family members and vassals. Certainly, the proliferation of *jissatsu* and *shozan* monasteries was achieved in many cases not by building new foundations but by converting former Tendai, Shingon, and Pure Land family temples into Zen monasteries in response to the rapidly growing religious and social interest in Zen.[25]

24 On the provincial diffusion of the *gozan*, see Imaeda Aishin, *Chūsei Zenshū-shi no kenkyū* (Tokyo: Tōkyō daigaku shuppankai 1970), pp. 137–268.
25 Kawai Masaharu, *Chūsei buke shakai no kenkyū* (Tokyo: Yoshikawa kōbunkan, 1973), p. 120.

The *shugo*'s patronage was also instrumental in carrying Rinzai Zen into the provinces. Their example prompted other local warrior families (*gōzoku* or *kokujin*) to establish Zen monasteries, some of which were ranked among the *jissatsu* and *shozan*.

By the mid-fifteenth century, the *gozan* network included some three hundred monasteries, many of which had their own subtemples (*tatchū*) and branch temples (*matsuji*). Eleven monasteries were ranked as full *gozan*. After the reorganization of the *gozan* ordered by Ashikaga Yoshimitsu in 1386, the five Kamakura *gozan* monasteries, in descending order of seniority, were the Kenchōji, Engakuji, Jufukuji, Jōchiji, and Jōmyōji. The Kyoto *gozan* included the Tenryūji, Shōkokuji, Kenninji, Tōfukuji, and Manjuji. Nanzenji was set in a special position "above" the *gozan*.

In 1386 Yoshimitsu had also named ten monasteries from Kyoto and ten from Kamakura as *jissatsu*. By the mid-fifteenth century, however, the principle that this category should include only ten monasteries or ten ranks was being neglected. The Ashikaga shoguns awarded *jissatsu* ranking to important provincial monasteries until more than forty were included in this tier. There had never been any restriction on the number of *shozan*, or "various mountains," and so the Ashikaga were able to show favor to provincial warrior families and monks of the *gozan* schools by according *shozan* status to their monasteries. By the mid-fifteenth century more than 250 *shozan* had been designated throughout Japan. In most provinces there was at least one monastery of *jissatsu* and five or six *shozan*. These carried *gozan* Zen practices and the cultural values of Kyoto into the most remote parts of the country.

Gozan Zen was also carried into the provinces through the system of *ankokuji*, or "temples for peace in the realm." At the urging of Musō Soseki, Ashikaga Takauji and his brother Tadayoshi, starting in 1345, gave the title of *ankokuji* to one important Zen monastery in each province, provided it with a Buddha relic, and required its monks to offer prayers for the memory of Godaigo and those warriors who had fallen in the fighting between the Northern and Southern Courts. At the same time, for the same purpose, they gave the title *rishōtō*, "pagoda of the Buddha's favor," to a Tendai, Ritsu, or Shingon monastery in each province. In doing this, Musō and the Ashikaga may have taken a hint from the Nara-period *kokubunji* system of provincial monasteries, but they were also motivated by contemporary concerns. Musō was eager to close the breach between the supporters of the rival courts and put at ease the restless spirit of Godaigo. By establishing the *ankokuji*, the Ashikaga were publicly expressing their repentance for their treatment of Godaigo and the Southern Court and were playing for popular sympathy by a nationwide offering of prayers for those who had died in the civil war. They were also honoring Musō, promoting *gozan* Zen, and tightening their links with the provincial warrior families whose family temples were designated as *ankokuji*. Many of the *ankokuji* were later included in the *gozan* network as *jissatsu*-rank monasteries. The appointment of non-Zen monasteries as *rishōtō* gave the bakufu one means of surveillance over these influential provincial monasteries.[26]

Limitations of space preclude a detailed discussion of the *ankokuji* system or of the frequent promotions and demotions of temples within the *gozan* system. It does seem important, however, before considering the institutional development of the other branches of Rinzai and Sōtō Zen, to mention some of the features characterizing the operation of the *gozan* as a bureaucratic institution.

Under the Hōjō and the early Ashikaga, the *gozan* monasteries were supervised by warrior officials of the bakufu who held the title of *jike gyōji* or *Zenritsugata* (commissioners for Zen and Ritsu monasteries). In 1379, Ashikaga Yoshimitsu gave supervisory control over the *gozan* to the Zen monks when he appointed Shun'oku Myōha, a leading disciple of Musō Soseki, to the office of *sōroku* (registrar general of monks). Yoshimitsu may well have borrowed this idea from a similar office supervising the Ch'an monasteries in Ming China. He was also demonstrating that he believed that the *gozan* was a mature institution capable of regulating itself. Beginning in 1383, the *sōroku* office was headed by the chief monk of the Rokuon'in subtemple within the Shōkokuji. The original intention seems to have been that the *sōroku* would be responsible for all Zen monasteries, but in practice, his authority was limited to the *gozan* network, especially the Kyoto *gozan*. The duties of the *sōroku* included the nomination to the bakufu of monks qualified for appointment as abbots and senior monks of *gozan* monasteries, the collection of fees for such appointments, and the enforcement of Zen monastic regulations and bakufu prohibitions. The *sōroku*'s authority was limited because the monastic assemblies in each monastery maintained considerable autonomy and the bakufu continued to deal directly with individual *gozan* monasteries and to interfere in the policymaking of the *gozan*. When Kamakura *gozan* monasteries were unable to settle their disputes, the bakufu urged them to look for redress not to the *sōroku* but to the Kantō *kubō*.

During the fifteenth and sixteenth centuries, the *sōroku* office was

26 Imaeda, *Chūsei Zenshū-shi no kenkyū*, pp. 77–138.

held by a number of influential monks, most of whom belonged to the Musō lineage, including Zekkai Chūshin (1336–1405), one of the most accomplished *gozan* monk poets; Zuikei Shūhō (1391–1473), poet and compiler of the collection of diplomatic documents known as the *Zenrin kokuhōki;* the bakufu representative who settled a dispute between the Kamakura *kubō* Ashikaga Mochiuji and the Kantō *kanrei* Uesugi Norisada; and Keijo Shūrin (1440–1518), a confidant of Ashikaga Yoshimasa, the eighth shogun. During much of the sixteenth century, the office of *sōroku* was eclipsed by that of the Inryōken. The Inryōken was a hermitage built by the sixth shogun, Yoshinori, within the Rokuon'in. As shogunal appointees, the heads of the Inryōken came to exert considerable religious and political influence and to extend their authority over the *gozan*. In 1615, both the *sōroku* and Inryōken office were abolished by the Tokugawa bakufu as part of its policy of regularizing Buddhism. The last holder of the *sōroku* office was the influential monk Ishin Sūden (1569–1633) of the Nanzenji, who had served as an adviser to Tokugawa Ieyasu and played a major role in drafting policy toward Buddhist temples, in handling foreign relations, and in compiling codes regulating the nobility and the samurai.[27]

The *gozan* monasteries comprised an officially sponsored system. Following Sung Chinese practice, the ideal was that these official monasteries be "open monasteries" (*jippōsatsu*), their abbots nominated by the *sōroku*, from among the most qualified monks available, and confirmed by the bakufu, irrespective of their Zen lineage. In practice, in the *gozan* rank, the Nanzenji and Kenninji in Kyoto and the Engakuji and most of the Kamakura *gozan* took their abbots from one of the *gozan* Zen lineages. Some *gozan* and many *jissatsu*, however, were virtually closed temples (*tsuchien*), headed and filled by monks of a particular lineage. In Kyoto, for instance, the Tenryūji and Shōkokuji among the *gozan* and the Rinsenji and Tōjiji of the *jissatsu* category were enclaves of the Musō school. The Tōfukuji and its many provincial offshoots were generally headed by monks of the Shōichi lineage, successors of Enni Ben'en. In Kamakura, the Kenchōji was dominated by monks who traced their Zen lineage through Lan-ch'i Tao-lung.[28]

Subtemples (*tatchū*) proliferated around the great metropolitan Zen monasteries. These began as private retreats for senior monks who had

27 Ibid, pp. 269–366.
28 Toshihide Akamatsu, and Philip Yampolsky, "Muromachi Zen and the Gozan System," in John W. Hall and Takeshi Toyoda, eds., *Japan in the Muromachi Age* (Berkeley and Los Angeles: University of California Press, 1977), pp. 324–5.

completed their term as abbot and, instead of returning to the monks' hall, had retired to build a small hermitage (*in, ken,* or *an*) in or near the main compound, where they lived quietly with a few close disciples. At his death, the Zen master's cremated remains would be kept in the *tatchū* for veneration, and the hermitage would be treated as a memorial temple in which his spirit was kept alive. These subtemples, too, naturally became the enclaves of particular lineages. They were not unique to Japan or to the *gozan*, but the lavish patronage enjoyed by the *gozan* monasteries and the relatively short terms of appointment by their abbots – generally two years – meant the existence of a substantial pool of well-supported venerable monks eager to establish their own subtemples. Monasteries like the Nanzenji and Tenryūji in Kyoto or the Engakuji in Kamakura were, by the sixteenth century, surrounded by twenty or thirty *tatchū*. The Hōjō regents and the Ashikaga shoguns tried, but with little success, to restrict the growth of *tatchū*, as they were a drain on the resources and manpower of the main monastery, not always responsive to bakufu regulation or monastic discipline, and prone to feuding among themselves.

Many of the Zen masters who established subtemples also had cultural interests: They were poets, painters, connoisseurs of Chinese art objects, devotees of tea, designers of gardens, and students of Confucian, Taoist, and Buddhist thought. Their subtemples, therefore, tended to become close-knit salons in which their cultural interests were transmitted to their disciples and given free rein, often at the expense of rigorous Zen practice.[29]

As an officially sponsored monastic system, the *gozan* institution was subjected to close regulation by the warrior rulers. The Hōjō regents Sadatoki and Takatoki issued sets of prohibitions for the Kamakura *gozan* monasteries in 1294, 1303, and 1327. Similar codes were issued periodically by the Ashikaga shoguns for the various tiers of the *gozan* hierarchy and for individual monasteries. It was the *sōroku*'s responsibility to secure compliance with these regulations by the *gozan* monasteries and their subtemples. In these regulations the shogunate sought to maintain monastic discipline and prohibit luxury and immorality, to prevent the excessive growth of Zen monastic populations, and to ensure that the Zen monasteries did not follow the example of some of the older monastic centers and become armed camps.

29 Tamamura Takeji, "Gozan sōrin no tatchū ni tsuite," *Rekishi chiri* 76, nos. 5 and 6 (1940): 44–58, 33–64.

The basic legal codes of the Muromachi bakufu, the Kemmu *shikimoku*, and their supplementary regulations, the *tsuikahō*, give considerable attention to the regulation of the *gozan*. A sampling of these regulations will indicate some of the rulers' concerns in their relations with the Zen monasteries. Article 72 of the *tsuikahō*, issued around 1352, attempted to deal with certain flagrant breaches of monastic discipline:

Up to now monks have wandered about day and night outside the temple at will. They have schemed to make money in the temple precincts and such moneylending activities have multiplied. This has become a subject of rumors, causing a decline from the Buddha's law, and must be admonished. The abbot and temple council acting in concert must make an inspection, and a violator must be expelled from the temple without delay. If he refuses to leave the temple, he will be considered a criminal and the Kantō government must be notified.[30]

By the late fourteenth century, as *gozan* life became formalized, secure, and culturally oriented, some monks were becoming casual in the performance of their religious practice of prayer and meditation. Yoshimitsu and his successors thereupon issued sharp admonitions to delinquent monks, as in the *tsuikahō*, Article 141:

Both elders and ordinary monks must be carefully checked for [attendance at] the three daily services. [If they are absent,] they must be removed from the temple rolls, and elders must not be promoted. In the Zen sect, advancement comes with the practice of Zen discipline (*zazen*), and those who have been repeatedly negligent shall be expelled from the temple.[31]

As a new, growing, and generously patronized institution, the *gozan* monastic population swelled rapidly from the late thirteenth century. The novelty of Zen practice, the fame of Chinese Ch'an masters, the reputations of Japanese monks like Enni, Musō, and Gidō Shūshin (1325–88), the splendor of the new *gozan* monasteries, their close ties with the warrior elite and the imperial court, and their cultural style all helped draw monks away from other branches of Buddhism and convince provincial warriors that their younger sons could find advancement in the *gozan* cloisters. The Hōjō and the Ashikaga had no desire to see the *gozan* Zen monasteries rival in size the older monastic institutions like the Enryakuji, Kōyasan, or Negoro with their thousands of monks, monastery servants, and armed bands. Such huge complexes were unruly, badly disciplined, and hungry for land and donations to

30 Kenneth A. Grossberg and Kanamoto Nobuhisa, trans., *The Laws of the Muromachi Bakufu* (Tokyo: Sophia University Press, 1981), p. 55.   31 Ibid., p. 79.

support their populations. The Kamakura and Muromachi bakufus, therefore, tried to contain the growth of *gozan* monastic populations. They ruled that major *gozan* like the Engakuji in Kamakura or the Nanzenji in Kyoto should have no more than between three hundred and five hundred monks, one hundred or fewer *jissatsu*, and no more than around fifty *shozan*. That their efforts to control the growth of *gozan* monastic population were unavailing is clear from the many references to this problem in the *tsuikahō* and other codes pertaining to Zen monasteries. Article 138 of the *tsuikahō*, for instance, reflects the situation around 1380:

In the Jōji law it was set at 500 men for large monasteries. However, we hear that [monasteries of] from seven and eight hundred to one and two thousand [monks] exist, and all must know that this will cause the destruction of Hyakujō's standards. The abbots must strictly obey the [Jōji] law and reduce the number of monks. There should be thirty novices in regular residence, fifty as visitors from other temples, and all others must be removed from temple rolls.[32]

The large numbers of novices, boys of fifteen or under, in the *gozan* monasteries created several problems. First, although they contributed little to the monastic economy, they had to be fed. Those of them who came from wealthy warrior families vied with one another in flaunting the luxury of their robes and personal effects. And many of them became the objects of sexual attention and rivalry by older monks.

One recurrent problem confronting the bakufu and the *sōroku* in their efforts to regulate the swelling *gozan* monastic institution was that of maintaining capable and dedicated leadership and administration for *gozan* monasteries of all levels. Many of the bakufu's regulations were directed at correcting abuses by abbots and by monks in the eastern and western ranks of the monastic bureaucracies. The authorities were forced repeatedly to warn about powerful families seeking monastic office for their protégés and to criticize monks appointed to office for neglecting their duties in one office while seeking appointment to a higher post in the monastic hierarchy. One bakufu regulation of 1352, for instance, provides early evidence of these problems:

In recent years men of no ability have been indiscriminately appointed to office, either because it was requested by the Bakufu or because of ties to a powerful person. Furthermore, it is widely heard that in the course of a year

32 Ibid., p. 78.

several men have alternately held the same post. This is unpardonable. . . .
They must choose and appoint men who will hold a post for half a year. Those
who hold an office for less than half a year will not have their names entered
on the roster.[33]

The same problem is raised even more acutely in the regulations of
1376:

Concerning the period of service for both ranks in recent years, we hear that
there are those who serve for only three or five days, or even change posts
three and five times in one day. This is not the Zen church that Hyakujō
intended. The previous rank must not be recognized. . . . The Shogun will
also not issue an order of appointment to such priests.[34]

The abbot's choice and behavior was particularly important to effective monastic leadership, administration, and order. Even the bakufu
recognized that "the rise and fall of temples depends on the abbot."
Abbots were expected to serve for at least three years. Many, however,
retired "after only four or five months" (Article 98) or less.[35] The
installation expenses for a new abbot were a heavy drain on a monastery. The bakufu's regulations repeatedly stressed that gift giving and
entertainment at such installation ceremonies should be kept to a
minimum: "Installation ceremonies must not be extravagant. Temples
are ruined primarily by such expenses, and therefore they are to be
specially prohibited. Abbots must also completely cease gift-giving
because of the great expense involved."[36]

High office in one of the gozan monasteries brought distinction to
a monk, his family, and patrons. Clearly, many monks wanted the
title of abbot or senior administrator but not the obligations that
went with the office. Finding and maintaining talented monastic
leadership thus remained a critical problem for the gozan institution
and its secular sponsors. And the problem was compounded by the
fact that the shogunate collected a fee each time it issued a certificate
of appointment to an abbot. The fee varied from five kanmon for
installation as abbot of a shozan-rank monastery to fifty kanmon for
installation at the Nanzenji. This represented a substantial income
from the whole gozan system. During the fifteenth century, the
bakufu undermined its own regulations by indiscriminately issuing
such certificates of appointment (kumon) as a means of maximizing
income from the gozan.

Another area of grave concern to warrior rulers and Zen monastic
administrators in their regulation of the gozan institution was that

33 Ibid., p. 55.   34 Ibid., p. 77.   35 Ibid., p. 65.   36 Ibid., p. 77.

these populous Zen monasteries not become armed camps, as had many of the older Japanese monastic centers. Article 76 (1352) and Article 234 (ca. 1445), respectively, reveal that Zen temples were not always havens of meditative tranquillity:

Recently we have heard repeatedly that groups of monks are shedding blood among themselves within temple precincts. This is unpardonable. The wounded parties must be forthwith expelled from the temple, no matter what their excuse. As for the offenders, the case must be thoroughly investigated, and in addition to being expelled from the temple, they shall not be allowed to live in any other temple. If it becomes clear that the investigation is being delayed, litigation concerning the temple in question and its various retreats shall not be heard.

In recent years monks and novices of the Gozan [monasteries] have frequently brought their demands into the temples, using force and bearing arms. This is unpardonable. Hereafter, even if they have a justifiable grievance, they will be punished by the Shogun if they attempt to petition using force in this manner. If such individuals exist, then the Eastern rank and priests of *tsūbun* and lower ranks shall protect the temple by catching those using force and by searching for their hiding places. They must search *tatchū* temples to find the ringleaders. In addition, whenever monks and novices bear arms at night, the temple's lay employees shall be ordered to capture them.[37]

On the whole, the shogun's efforts to prevent the militarization of the Zen monasteries were successful. Although there was brawling and an occasional resort to arms in the monasteries or between *gozan* monks and those of other monasteries or schools, as in the clash between the Nanzenji monks and those of the Onjōji and Enraykuji during the Nanzenji-gate incident of 1367, neither the *gozan* nor any other branch of medieval Zen was so militarized as to become a decisive armed force in the power struggles of that time.

Rinzai Zen: the Daiō school

Although the *gozan* institution was extensive and influential, it did not include all the Rinzai monasteries in medieval Japan. The monasteries of Daitokuji, Myōshinji, and their affiliates in the Daiō school of Zen were excluded from the *gozan* or chose to remain outside it. But their independence of the *gozan* meant no patronage by the shogun, a very frugal monastic life, and a consequent emphasis on rigorous Zen practice. The monks of the Daitokuji and Myōshinji found their patrons

---

37 Ibid., pp. 56 and 103, respectively. Other examples of bakufu regulation of *gozan* monasteries can be found in Collcutt, *Five Mountains*, pp. 165–70.

among members of the imperial court, lesser provincial warrior families, and the wealthy townspeople of Kyoto and Sakai. Ties of patronage played a significant role in shaping the development of Rinzai Zen schools in medieval society. While the Ashikaga shoguns were in reasonably firm control of the country and able to dominate the bakufu–*shugo* alliance during the fourteenth century and the first half of the fifteenth, the *gozan* schools were in the ascendant. They enjoyed great social prestige, generous economic support, and the protection of their extensive landholding rights. However, in the late fifteenth and sixteenth centuries, when the authority of the Ashikaga shogunate and the *shugo* was undercut by assassination, civil war, and the restlessness and ambition of local warrior families, *gozan* monasteries at all levels suffered. Financial support dried up, monasteries were gutted in the Ōnin War, their monks were dispersed, and their lands were taken from them. The Daitokuji and Myōshinji also suffered destruction in the warfare of the late fifteenth century, but the patrons they were attracting among the local warrior families and townspeople were a waxing rather than a waning force in Japanese society. In the sixteenth century, many of the warriors who toppled *shugo* and emerged as warlords (*sengoku* daimyo) were patrons of the Daitokuji and Myōshinji monks. The Daitokuji, in particular, benefited from its close connections with the daimyo and the merchant community of Sakai. During the sixteenth century, the merchant houses in Sakai grew rich on trade with China and Europe. Some of their wealth was used to buy Chinese art objects or to indulge in the arts related to the tea ceremony, under the guidance of the Daitokuji monks. As links were forged between merchants and Zen masters, some Sakai townsmen studied Zen, sponsored the building of subtemples in the Daitokuji, or sent their sons to study Zen there.

The Daiō school takes its name from the Japanese Zen monk Nampo Jōmyō (Daiō Kokushi, 1235–1308). Nampo began his Zen practice under Lan-ch'i Tao-lung at the Kenchōji. In 1259 he journeyed to Sung China where he studied Ch'an under many masters before attaining enlightenment under the Lan-ch'i master Hsu-t'ang Chih-yü, whose teaching he transmitted to Japan. In 1267 Nampo returned to Kamakura to assist Lan-ch'i. He then spent thirty years heading temples and teaching Zen in northern Kyushu. His reputation as a stern Zen master eventually reached the court, and in 1305, he received an imperial invitation to head the Manjuji in Kyoto. There he tried to establish his own Zen monastery, the Kigenji in Higashiyama, but was frustrated by opposition from the Enryakuji's monks. Accepting an invitation from Hōjō Sadatoki in 1307, he moved to Kamakura where he headed the Kenchōji until his death.[38] Daiō's numerous disciples included Shūhō Myōchō (Daitō Kokushi, 1282–1337) whose vigorous Zen and six years as a beggar under the Gojō Bridge in Kyoto attracted the interest and patronage of Akamatsu Norimura, *shugo* of Harima, the cloistered emperor Hanazono, and Emperor Godaigo. Daitō lectured to his patrons on Zen and the *Blue Cliff Koan Collection*. With their backing he was able to establish the monastery of Daitokuji on the site of his hermitage at Murasakino in the northern part of the capital in 1326.

Although it is unclear whether Daitō welcomed Godaigo's plans to make the Daitokuji, along with the Nanzenji, the head of a Kyoto-centered, pro–Southern Court *gozan* system during the Kemmu restoration, it is very clear that he sought imperial acknowledgment that the Daitokuji should be named "protector of the nation" and "place of imperial worship" and that it should always be headed by monks of his own lineage. Daitō was a contemporary of Musō, who served as adviser and Zen master for the Hōjō, Godaigo, and the Ashikaga. But Daitō was critical of Musō's Zen and probably of Musō's ability to be all things to all men. He thus never established close ties with the Ashikaga, who were admirers of Musō. Daitō's death followed by only a year Godaigo's flight from Kyoto. Throughout its history, the Daitokuji maintained a strong imperial connection.[39]

After Daitō's death, the Daitokuji was headed by his disciple Tettō Gikō (1295–1369), a skilled administrator. In his codes for the Daitokuji and its subtemples, the *Seven Article Code* (1337), *Daitokuji hatto*, *Shōden'an hatto*, and *Tokuzenji hatto* (all compiled in 1368), Tettō laid down the regulations by which abbots should be selected and by which the monastery and its lands should be administered by a monastery council comprising the abbot, the officers of the eastern and western ranks, and older monks.[40] The Daitokuji was not included in the revised list of Kyoto *gozan* monasteries issued by the bakufu in 1341, presumably because the monastery was regarded as a *tsuchien*, or temple exclusive to the members of a single lineage.

38 Biographical details for Nampo Jōmyō are taken from Ogisu Jundō, "Nampo Jōmyō no Nihon zenshū shijō no chii," in *Nihon chūsei zenshū-shi* (Kyoto: Mokujisha, 1965), pp. 202–20.
39 Shūhō Myōchō and the Daitokuji are discussed in Haga Kōshirō et al., eds., *Daitokuji to sadō* (Kyoto: Tankōsha, 1972); and by Ogisu Jundō, "Shūhō Myōchō to sono Zen," *Nihon chūsei zenshū-shi*, pp. 222–36.
40 Tettō's role in providing an administrative framework for the early Daitokuji community is examined by Takenuki Genshō, "Rinka ni okeru kyōdan keiei ni tsuite," *Bukkyō shigaku* 15 (July 1971): 225–63.

Both the Daitokuji and Ryūshōji, a Kyoto monastery established by Daiō Kokushi, were included in a 1385 listing of Kyoto *jissatsu* issued by Ashikaga Yoshimitsu. They were ranked at the lowly ninth place among the *jissatsu* and were undoubtedly ill at ease among the official monasteries. After several appeals to the bakufu, the Daitokuji was permitted to withdraw from the *jissatsu* on the grounds that its charter by the emperors Godaigo and Hanazono had recognized it as a training center exclusively for monks of the Daitō lineage. It is likely that the Ryūshōji withdrew from the *gozan* system at the same time. From this point, Daitokuji abbots were permitted to wear purple robes, as granted by the imperial court.

In 1453, the Daitokuji was almost completely destroyed by fire. Before it could be fully rebuilt, it was again put to the torch during the Ōnin War. But even while the Daitokuji was in ashes, the basis for its recovery and expansion was being laid by the monks Yōsō Sōi (1376–1458) and Ikkyū Sōjun (1394–1481). Both Yōsō and Ikkyū began their Zen training in *gozan* monasteries. But like growing numbers of monks in the late fourteenth and fifteenth centuries, they quickly became dissatisfied with what they perceived as the formalism, and aestheticism of the official monasteries and so turned to masters of the Daiō school like Kasō Sōdon (1352–1428) for training in a more rugged Zen. When in 1410 Ikkyū left the *ankokuji*, he expressed in a poem his disgust at the *gozan* monks who, he felt, were more like merchants than Buddhist priests and who carried their family snobberies into the cloister:

> Amidst Zen sermons and lectures they talk of family.
> Filled with shame I struggle to remain silent.
> But, when Zen talk fails the challenge,
> Demon-victories perpetuate spiritual ignorance.[41]

Ikkyū was an irreverent, unconventional monk who preferred the camaraderie of drinking places and brothels to the constraints of monastic administration. Quite apart from his attacks on the *gozan*, he was ambivalent about Zen at the Daitokuji. In 1440 he was persuaded, perhaps by Yōsō, to become abbot of the Nyoi'an subtemple, but he quit after only a few days, complaining about the frivolousness of the monks and the endless bureaucratic demands of the office.

> "Interesting donations" are dragged into the hermitage;
> they decorate the east wall with wooden ladles and rustic baskets.

41 Translated by James H. Sanford, *Zen-man Ikkyū* (Decatur, Ga.: Scholars Press, 1981), p. 14.

> I have no use for such useless stuff,
> A straw raincoat beside rivers and lakes has long been
> my style.[42]

and

> Only ten fussy days as abbot,
> and already my feet are tangled in red tape.
> If, someday, you want to look me up,
> Try the fish-shop, the tavern, or the brothel.[43]

Ikkyū and Yōsō could hardly have been less alike as Zen monks. Yōsō seems to have been everything that Ikkyū was not: a gentle, sober, monk-administrator who devoted his energies to training Daitokuji monks and restoring the monastery. For some reason Ikkyū developed a violent dislike of Yōsō and took every opportunity to denounce him as a counterfeit Zen master, eager only for imperial recognition, who had betrayed the tradition of Daitō and Kasō. When in 1457 Yōsō was awarded the title of Sōe Daishō Zenji by Emperor Gohanazono in recognition of his labors in rebuilding the Daitokuji, Ikkyū honored him with the following verse:

> A purple robe and high title that impoverish our line.
> An imperial appointment is just so much cash in hand.
> A clear counterfeit, this master from the Daiyō Hermitage
> Come and see him, a real West China highwayman.[44]

But Ikkyū and Yōsō had at least one thing in common. Both, in very different ways, were extremely effective in winning patrons for the Daitokuji among the Sakai merchants. Yōsō popularized Zen and raised donations in the process, by granting certificates of enlightenment to lay people who attended mass meditation sessions at which *kōan* were "solved" by esoteric transmission rather than through rigorous self-directed meditative enquiry. Although Ikkyū denounced these practices as a prostitution of Zen by "selling the Dharma" and ridiculed Yōsō and the townsmen who supported him, Ikkyū's own wild antics, unconventional Zen, and direct, outspoken approach won him a devoted following in Sakai. When in 1474, late in life, Ikkyū accepted the abbacy of the Daitokuji and the burden of restoring it after the ravages of the Ōnin War, his prestige and wide-ranging connec-

42 Ibid., p. 47.   43 Ibid., p. 48.   44 Ibid., p. 50.

tions attracted donations from Sakai merchants, tea masters, *renga* masters, and daimyo.[45]

The links between the Daitokuji and Sakai that had been forged by Yōsō Sōi and Ikkyū in the mid-fifteenth century were strengthened as Sakai prospered in the sixteenth, by the townspeople's passion for Chinese luxury items, Zen, and the tea ceremony. The Daitokuji's branch temples were established in Sakai; Daitokuji prelates were frequent visitors to the city; and in time, some of the younger sons of the merchant families enrolled as monks in the Daitokuji or its subtemples. After the fire of 1453, a Sakai merchant with the Buddhist name of Sōkan, a patron of Yōsō, paid for the rebuilding of the Dharma hall (*hatto*). Some twenty years later, the merchant Owa Shiroraemon Sōrin, a disciple of Ikkyū, bore most of the cost of rebuilding the abbot's building, the Buddha hall, the Dharma hall, and several of the older *tatchū* after their destruction in the Ōnin War. He also persuaded other Sakai merchants to contribute to the establishment of the Shinju'an as a memorial temple for Ikkyū and bequeathed mortuary funds (*shidōsen*) to be used as capital for moneylending ventures by the Daitokuji. The documents recording the many small "incense donations" for the thirteenth and thirty-third-year memorial services for Ikkyū held at the Shinju'an in 1494 and 1514 include the names of many Sakai and Kyoto merchants, as well as warriors and wealthy peasants.[46]

Whereas the backing of Sakai merchants helped the Daitokuji recover from the effects of the Ōnin War in the late fifteenth century, it was the patronage of the daimyo that ensured its prosperity and ushered in its golden age in the sixteenth century. Before 1500, the Daitokuji had seven subtemples. Between 1500 and 1812, another eighteen were established, most of them by *sengoku* daimyo or by Toyotomi Hideyoshi. Many of these daimyo *tatchū* combined the character of the daimyo family temple (*bodaiji*) with that of the memorial temple (*tatchū*) for a revered Zen master and were generously supported, at least while their warrior patrons were successful in the wars and political intrigues. The daimyo patrons shared with the Daitokuji monks and Sakai merchants a common passion for the tea ceremony, as well as an interest in Zen, and many *tatchū* assumed the character of cultural salons.

Here I need mention only a few examples to convey the character of

45 Izumi Chōichi, "Sakai chōnin to Zen," *Rekishi kōron*, no. 10 (1977): 89–91.
46 Hayashiya Tatsusaburō et al., *Kyōto no rekishi* (Kyoto: Gakugei shorin, 1968), vol. 3, pp. 128–9.

daimyo patronage in the growth of the Daitokuji school.[47] The Kōrin'in, for instance, was built and patronized by the Hatakeyama of Noto and later patronized by the Maeda of Kaga. In 1597, Hatakeyama Yoshimoto bestowed on the subtemple holdings in two villages in Noto, producing an annual tax income of 100 *kanmon*. The Kōrin'in also preserved a list of those secular patrons granted Buddhist names (*hōmyō*) between 1525 and 1535. This *hōmyōchō* lists sixty-four males and thirty-six females, mostly from Kyoto, its environs, and Hokuriku. The fact that, apart from the Hatakeyama, most were the deputies (*hikan*) of daimyo, merchants and artisans, or wealthy peasants indicates something about the Daitokuji monks' social influence. Ōbai'in was built by Kobayakawa Takakage (1533–85), one of Hideyoshi's leading generals, and granted an annual income of one hundred *koku*. Subsequently, the Ōbai'in came under the patronage of the Mōri (Chōshū), who were related to the Kobayakawa, and during the Tokugawa period the head monks of the Ōbai'in were treated as if they were members of the Mōri family. Finally, the Kōtō'in in was built in 1602 by Hosokawa Tadaoki (1563–1645) as a memorial to his famous father Hosokawa Yūsai (1534–1610).

Tadaoki's career was one of the success stories of the age. His wife, the Christian convert Gracia, was the daughter of Akechi Mitsuhide (1528–82). Tadaoki refused to help Mitsuhide assassinate Oda Nobunaga and later served Hideyoshi and Ieyasu with distinction. For his services at the battle of Sekigahara and in the Osaka campaigns, Tadaoki was awarded the Kokura *han* (390,000 *koku*) as a fief. Like his father, Yūsai, Tadaoki combined literary with martial skills. He was an accomplished painter and *waka* poet, one of the leading students of the tea master Rikyū, and the compiler of a guide to the conduct of the tea ceremony, the *Hosokawa Sansai chaso*. Gyokuho Jōsō, the monk for whom the Kōtō'in was built, was Yūsai's younger brother. *Sengoku* daimyo did not limit their patronage to Kyoto. Many daimyo, like the Hōjō of Odawara, invited Daitokuji monks to their domains and built provincial branch temples for them. With this kind of backing, the Daitokuji school of Zen spread rapidly throughout Japan in the sixteenth century. By the late sixteenth century, the Daitokuji had more than two hundred branch temples, many of them former members of the *gozan* hierarchy.

A third group of sponsors who contributed in the sixteenth century

---

47 Further information on these and other Daitokuji *tatchū* can be found in Kawakami Mitsugu, *Zen'in no kenchiku* (Kyoto: Kawara shoten, 1968), pp. 127–265.

to the prosperity of the Daitokuji and its subtemples were the men of culture of that period: the linked-verse (*renga*) poets and tea masters. The *renga* poet Saiokuken Sōchō (1448–1532), who had studied Zen with Ikkyū, built a single-story great gate (*sanmon*) at the Daitokuji. To help raise the money, he sold a precious copy of *The Tale of Genji*. According to documents belonging to the Shinju'an, a total of 731 *kan* and 500 *mon* were spent in 1525 and 1526 on the construction of this gate.[48] Sōchō's fellow poet, Yamazaki Sōkan (1465–1553) was among those who contributed "incense money" at the memorial services for Ikkyū. Most of the leading tea masters of the age – men like Murata Jukō (1422–1502), Takeno Jōō (1502–55), Tsuda Sōkyū (?– 1591), Imai Sōkyū (1520–93), and Sen no Rikyū (1522–91) – studied Zen and the tea ceremony with the Daitokuji monks, contributed generously to the monastery and helped make the Daitokuji one of the leading cultural centers in Japan.[49] In 1585, Hideyoshi held an ostentatious tea ceremony at the Daitokuji, in which Sen no Rikyū and Tsuda Sōkyū played leading roles and to which large numbers of daimyo and townsmen were invited. This assertion of cultural hegemony by Hideyoshi established the Daitokuji as the center for the tea ceremony and brought fame and favor to Sen no Rikyū. In 1559, Rikyū rebuilt the great gate at his own expense, adding a second story and installing a statue of himself. This presumption aroused Hideyoshi's anger, led to Rikyū's suicide, and almost resulted in the Daitokuji's destruction.[50]

As this incident suggests, Hideyoshi's relations with the Daitokuji were usually tempestuous, blending ostentatious liberality with sudden bursts of anger and changes of mind. It was undoubtedly under his example that many *sengoku* daimyo developed an interest in the monastery. Hideyoshi continued Nobunaga's policy of tightening control over the Buddhist institutions while using Buddhism as a counter to Christianity and extending patronage to compliant monasteries and Buddhist groups.[51]

Although Hideyoshi was by no means an exclusive, or particularly dedicated, devotee of Zen, he had great respect for the Daitokuji monk Kokei Sōchin. In the tenth month of 1582, Hideyoshi held

---

48 Yamada Sōbin, "Sanmon shūfuku no kiroku," in Haga et al., eds., *Daitokuji to sadō*, pp. 264–73.   49 Hayashiya et al., *Kyōto no rekishi*, vol. 3, p. 130.
50 Yamada, "Sanmon shūfuku no kiroku," pp. 273–9.
51 For a brief general discussion of Hideyoshi's attitude toward Buddhism and his treatment of the various branches of the Buddhist institution, see Kuwata Tadachika, *Toyotomi Hideyoshi kenkyū* (Tokyo: Kadokawa shoten, 1975), pp. 341–58.

lavish funeral obsequies at the Daitokuji for his slain overlord, Nobunaga, at which Kokei officiated. To pay for the ceremonies, Hideyoshi made a gift of ten thousand *kan* in cash to the monastery.[52] In the same year, he ordered the construction of the Sōken'in subtemple as a memorial to Nobunaga and installed Kokei as the founding abbot. In 1588, he had the Tenzuiji built at Daitokuji as a memorial for his mother and, at about the same time, gave Kokei Sōchin four thousand *kanmon* to build a new temple, the Tenshōji. Construction had hardly begun when Hideyoshi, angered by Kokei's use of the funds, banished the monk to Kyushu and abandoned work on the new temple.[53]

Hideyoshi's land surveys and reforms, however, were much more significant to the Daitokuji than were his temple-building activities, as they restructured the Daitokuji's whole economy and largely defined the economic base on which the monastery was to operate during the Edo period. Without detailed overall figures for the period before the land reforms, it is impossible to know exactly how the Daitokuji fared under Hideyoshi. But compared with monasteries like Negoro or Kōyasan, which were stripped of many of their holdings, the Daitokuji seems to have been treated generously and may even have gained a little. In the spring of 1585, when widespread cadastral surveys of Buddhist monastic holdings were being made, the Daitokuji's domains were granted full confirmation (*ando*).[54] Later in the same year, Hideyoshi ordered the consolidation of the Daitokuji's scattered holdings into three major areas with an assessed yield (*kokudaka*) of 1,545 *koku*.[55] This was increased to 2,010 *koku* by Tokugawa Ieyasu in 1615, a level of income that was maintained during the Tokugawa period. Although this was not a particularly large allowance by contemporary standards – it compared with the stipends of high-ranking Tokugawa bannermen – it was greater than the incomes allotted to the principal *gozan* monasteries. The wheel of fortune for the Daitokuji had come full circle.

The other major branch of the Daiō school was the line tracing its descent from the monk Kanzan Egen (1277–1360), disciple of Daitō and founder of the Myōshinji monastery in Kyoto. After a difficult history in the fourteenth and early fifteenth centuries, the Myōshinji line expanded dramatically under the patronage of the *sengoku* daimyo in the late fifteenth and sixteenth centuries. By the close of the sixteenth century, it was outstripping the *gozan* and Daitokuji lineages. At least one key to the rapid growth of the Myōshinji school in the sixteenth century was an effective monastic organization begun under the abbot Sekkō Sōshun.

Kanzan began his Zen studies in the *gozan* monastery of the Kenchōji in Kamakura. There, he found no monk who could steer him toward enlightenment. He did, however, hear of Shūhō Myōchō (Daitō) in Kyoto. Kanzan immediately left the Kenchōji and practiced Zen under Daitō's guidance for several years until he attained enlightenment by resolving a *kōan* by Yun-men Wen-yen (Unmon Bun'en, 864–949) hinging on the single character *kan* (barrier). From this he took his name, "Barrier-mountain." Although Kanzan fell out with Daitō and left the Daitokuji, he had learned from Daitō a severe Zen based on rigorous meditation. In his own Zen practice and teaching, Kanzan earned a reputation for austere meditation and total indifference to personal advancement, monastic prosperity, and cultural accomplishments. Like Daitō, Kanzan was patronized by Godaigo and especially by Hanazono who practiced Zen under Kanzan's guidance and converted a detached palace into the Zen monastery of Myōshinji, naming Kanzan as the founding abbot. According to all the surviving accounts, Kanzan remained indifferent to his environment. During his lifetime, it was said that the Myōshinji's roof leaked, that there was nowhere comfortable to sit, and that when he entertained the eminent prelate Musō he sent out a monk to buy a few cheap rice cakes. These accounts may be apocryphal. What is important, however, is that they had currency in Kanzan's day and shaped his reputation within the Myōshinji lineage as a stern Zen master who set the highest standards of effort in *zazen* and *kōan* study. The term *Ō-Tō-Kan school* applied to his line reflects his prestige as heir to, and equal of, Daiō and Daitō.[56]

The first century or so of the Myōshinji's history was troubled and unpromising. The Myōshinji was a branch temple of the Daitokuji, but the discord between Kanzan and Daitō had created tensions in the relationship between the two communities. The monks who succeeded Kanzan as heads of the Myōshinji, Juō Sōhitsu (1296–1380) and Muin Sōin (1326–1410), maintained his ideal of a reclusive, frugal monastic life and spartan Zen practice. Although Muin had come to

56 For a more detailed biography of Kanzan and the early history of Myōshinji, see Ogisu Jundō, "Kanzan Egen no shomondai," in *Nihon chūsei zenshū-shi*, pp. 332–431; and Kawakami Kozan, *Myōshinji-shi* (Kyoto: Shibunkaku, 1975), pp. 25–60.

the Myōshinji from the *gozan* monastery of the Kenninji and introduced strict monastic regulations of the kind found in the *gozan* codes,
the Myōshinji was never included at any level of the *gozan* hierarchy.
But it was in its relationship with the shogunate that the greatest
difficulty for the community lay.

Never on very close terms with the Ashikaga shoguns, in 1399 the
Myōshinji became the object of the anger of Ashikaga Yoshimitsu,
who accused its abbot Setsudō Sōboku of being in league with the
warrior rebel Ōuchi Yoshihiro (1356–99), *shugo* of six provinces in
western Japan. Setsudō was dismissed; the temple's lands were confiscated and placed under the control of Yoshimitsu's relatives in other
monasteries; the Myōshinji's monks scattered to the provinces where
they looked to local warrior families for patronage; and the monastery's buildings were allowed to fall into ruin. Even the name
Myōshinji was erased when the compound was renamed the Ryūunji
and reclassified as a branch temple of the Tokuun'in *tatchū* in the
Nanzenji. Because Kanzan had been a disciple of Daitō, some
Myōshinji monks naturally tried to find refuge in the Daitokuji. But
with rivalry already evident between the two branches of the Daiō
school, they received a very cool reception.[57]

This hiatus in the Myōshinji's development lasted for more than
thirty years. During the 1430s, part of the Ryūunji's former holdings
were restored; monks began to return from the provinces; and the
community again assumed the name Myōshinji. This recovery began
under the leadership of the monks Kongai Sōri, Myōkō Sōei, and
Nippō Sōshun (1368–1448) and with the backing of the imperial court
and the Hosokawa family. Kongai was successful in appealing to Shogun Yoshimochi to restore some of the Myōshinji's former holdings.
Myōkō, who was a son of the cloistered emperor Sukō and had served
as abbot of temples in Suō Provinces after the breakup of the
Myōshinji, secured the interest of the imperial court and the Ōuchi
family in the Myōshinji's restoration.

Nippō had spent much of his early life running temples in Mino.
There he had earned a popular reputation as a great Zen master and
had come to the attention of Hosokawa Mochiyuki and his son
Katsumoto (1430–73). This connection prove to have inestimable
value in the Myōshinji's recovery. The Hosokawa not only were the
most powerful warrior family in the Kantō; they also frequently held
the office of *kanrei*, the most powerful position in the shogun's bureau-

---

57 Kawakami, *Myōshinji-shi*, p. 81.

cracy. Mochiyuki, for instance, was the *kanrei* from 1432 to 1442, and Katsumoto held the office three times: from 1445 to 1449, 1452 to 1464, and 1468 to 1473. Thus with Mochiyuki's support, Nippō was able to secure the return of much of the Myōshinji's property and to rebuild some of the monestary's deteriorating buildings.[58]

But Nippō's popularity and success in restoring the Myōshinji renewed its tensions with the Daitokuji. In 1444, Nippō received an imperial appointment as the abbot of the Daitokuji. Yōsō Sōi, Ikkyū, and the whole Daitokuji community protested unsuccessfully that this was a breach of the intentions of Daitō and his imperial patrons that the abbacy of their monastery be restricted solely to monks of Daitō's line. The court and the bakufu, however, held that the lineage also included Kanzan's followers. Thus, Nippō was installed as abbot of the Daitokuji, the first of many coming from the revived Myōshinji line.[59]

Nippō attracted as disciples many of the monks who had left the *gozan* monasteries. For instance, both of his successors as heads of the Myōshinji, Giten Genshō (1393–1462) and Sekkō Sōshin (1408–86), had left the Kenninji. These monks continued to enjoy the devoted patronage of Hosokawa Katsumoto, who practiced Zen meditation under their guidance. Indeed, for Giten, Hosokawa built the Ryōanji with its famous stone garden. Like the Daitokuji and many of the Kyoto *gozan* monasteries, both the Myōshinji and the Ryōanji were destroyed during the Ōnin War. It fell to Sekkō to organize their rebuilding. Again, the Hosokawa family offered their aid. Katsumoto persuaded all branches of the Hosokawa family and many of their allies to contribute to the reconstruction effort. Although he died before the reconstruction was complete, his son Masamoto (1466–1507), who gained control of the shogunate after the Ōnin War, oversaw the work to its completion.

Sekkō was not only responsible for restoring the Myōshinji as a monastery; he is also given credit for introducing important administrative reforms that contributed both to better management of the Myōshinji itself and to the rapid provincial expansion of the Myōshinji line.

From about the time of Sekkō's incumbency, the Myōshinji began to use an extremely detailed system for keeping the monastic accounts. The monastery has in its archives some 250 account books known as

58 The Hosokawa patronage of Myōshinji is discussed by Kawakami, *Myōshinji-shi*, pp. 84–112. See also Tsuji, *Nihon bukkyō-shi (chūsei* 4), pp. 87–124.
59 Sanford, trans., *Zen-man Ikkyū*, p. 54.

the *Shōbōzan Myōshin Zenji beisen nōgechō*. Covering the period from the 1480s to the 1830s, the account books contain a detailed monthly record of the Myōshinji's income and expenditures. Like many other Zen masters in China and Japan, Sekkō seems to have recognized that the maintenance of communal Zen practice in the meditation hall depended in large measure on the stability of the monastic economy and the careful husbanding of resources.

Another institutional development for the Myōshinji following Sekkō's administrative reforms was the system of rotating the headship of the main monastery among the senior members of its four principal subtemples. Sekkō had four able disciples: Keisen Sōryū (1426–1500), Gokei Sōton (1416–1500), Tokuhō Zenketsu (1419–1506), and Tōyō Eichō (1428–1504). These monks and, in turn, their disciples established four subtemples within the Myōshinji: the Ryōsen'in, Tōkai'an, Reiun'an, and Shōtaku'an. The subtemple heads jointly supervised the Myōshinji's administration and accounts, and they, or members of their provincial branch temples, alternated in the headship of the Myōshinji itself. Institutionally, therefore, the Myōshinji had an effective oversight committee and a pool of senior monks from which to draw talented leadership. Each subtemple also took its turn supervising the monastic accounts (*nōgechō*), which were checked and countersigned each year by the heads of all four subtemples, as well as by the abbot and monk officers of the Myōshinji itself.[60]

As the four disciples of Sekkō attracted their own followers, their subtemples became bases for the diffusion through the provinces of the Myōshinji school. The Hosokawa remained devoted patrons, but by mid-sixteenth century the Myōshinji monks were attracting the patronage of many other *sengoku* daimyo, especially those in central Japan. Saitō Toshifuji and his wife, who later became the nun Ritei-ni, the Toki family in Mino, Imagawa Yoshimoto in Suruga, Oda Nobunaga from his days in Owari, and Takeda Shingen in Kai were only a few of the daimyo patrons that established temples for the Myōshinji monks within their domains or built subtemples around the Myōshinji in Kyoto.

By the end of the sixteenth century, several hundred provincial monasteries had been established by Kanzan's successors. At least fifty of these were former *gozan* monasteries. With strong leadership and the backing of *sengoku* daimyo, the Myōshinji school was growing as rapidly as that of the Daitokuji. Growth was helped by populariza-

60 Hayashiya et al., *Kyōto no rekishi*, vol. 3, pp. 132–3.

tion. By simplifying the *kōan* and meditation practices, introducing Pure Land devotional practices, and conducting prayer meetings and funeral services, the Myōshinji monks made their teachings more attractive not only to daimyo but also to the lesser warriors, farmers, wandering jongleurs, *renga* poets, and craftsmen with whom they also consorted.[61]

The Myōshinji remained an influential temple under the Tokugawa. In the eighteenth century the monk Hakuin Ekaku (1685–1768) of the Shōtaku branch of the Myōshinji reemphasized Kanzan's *zazen*-centered practice. Indeed, Hakuin's Zen revival was so powerful that it spread to the Daitokuji and the *gozan* monastic circles. Kanzan's teachings thus became the source of modern Japanese Zen.

Rinzai Zen: the Genjū school

Before leaving the Rinzai lineages, we should look briefly at the Genjū (Huan-chu) school.[62] In the late Kamakura period, a number of Japanese monks who visited China studied Zen with the famous Ch'an monk Chung-feng Ming-pen (Chuhō Myōhon, 1263–1323) at his hermitage called the Huan-chu-an (Genjūan). Chung-feng was a scholarly recluse whose Zen was influenced by Pure Land teachings. Chung-feng's teachings were introduced to Japan by Enkei Soyū (1286–1344), Kosen Ingen (1295–1374), Muin Genkai (d. 1358), and other monks, most of whom had been trained in *gozan* monasteries before their travel to China but forsook them after their return to Japan in order to follow Chung-feng's ideal of the hermit. They carried Zen teachings to remote mountain valleys in northern and central Japan. Their very reclusiveness militated against their developing a strong sectarian identity, and during the late Kamakura and Nambukuchō periods they were overshadowed by the highly organized and expansive *gozan* lineages.

During the Muromachi period, however, monks of the Genjū lineage began to return to *gozan* monasteries where their very ecumenical attitudes toward the Zen transmission won them considerable influence. The Kyūshū monk Ichige Sekiyu (1447–1507) was one of the first to set in motion this "return to the *gozan*." Like other medieval Zen monks, Ichige studied Zen under masters of different lineages. Unlike most of his fellows, however, he did not commit himself to a

61 Ibid., p. 134.
62 See Imaeda Aishin, *Zenshū no rekishi* (Tokyo: Shibundō, 1962), pp. 209–12.

single lineage but received certificates of transmission (*inka*) from several different masters, Sōtō as well as Rinzai. Ichige's appointment in 1504 as the abbot of the *jissatsu*-level monastery Shōfukuji in northern Kyūshū was only the first of many appointments of Genjū-lineage monks to the headship of *gozan* affiliates.

The tolerant attitude by monks of the Genjū lineage toward other branches of Zen was seen as a source of strength and possible integration in the faltering early-sixteenth-century *gozan*. Not only were monks of the Genjū line invited to head *gozan* monasteries, but also many *gozan* monks combined the Genjū transmission with their own *gozan* affiliations. This practice spread also into the Daitokuji and Myōshinji branches of Rinzai Zen, and so by the mid-sixteenth century many of the leading Rinzai monasteries in Japan had as their abbot a monk who had at least a partial affiliation with the eclectic tradition of Chung-feng. Ironically, however, the successors of those monks who had left the *gozan* in disgust at its formalism and literary pretensions had rejected their eremitic ideal and assumed the leadership of the Rinzai Zen establishment. On the positive side, their eclecticism encouraged the breaking down of artificial barriers between the many lineages or transmissions of Rinzai Zen. But on the negative side – that is, from the viewpoint of the "purity" of Zen as a self-directed struggle for enlightenment – they injected into Rinzai practice a strong dose of Pure Land devotionalism.

Sōtō Zen

While the Rinzai Zen of the *gozan* and Daiō schools was spreading outward from Kamakura and Kyoto and winning the enthusiastic patronage of shoguns, emperors, *shugo*, *sengoku* daimyo, and merchants, Sōtō Zen was spreading less obtrusively but equally pervasively among the families of local samurai and farmers throughout the provinces. By the sixteenth century, the Sōtō monks, like those of the Daitokuji and Myōshinji schools, were winning adherents among members of the imperial court, *sengoku* daimyo, and townspeople and were making inroads into *gozan* monasteries in the provinces and the capital.

There were two major transmissions of Sōtō (Ts'ao-tung) Zen to Japan. The first was made by Dōgen who returned from China in the autumn of 1227; the second by the Chinese monk Tung-ming Hui-jih (Tōmyō Enichi, 1272–1340) who came to Japan in 1309 at the invitation of Hōjō Sadatoki.

The institutional development of Dōgen's lineage during the medieval period occurred in four fairly clear-cut stages. The first of these covered Dōgen's lifetime and included the establishment of the Kōshōji and Eiheiji communities and the compilation by Dōgen of comprehensive regulations for the monastic institution he had in mind. The second, beginning around 1300, saw a sectarian schism among the third generation of Dōgen's followers and the growth of the Sōjiji as a rival to the Eiheiji. The third stage included the movement for the popularization of Sōtō Zen teachings and their widespread provincial diffusion during the Muromachi period. The fourth stage witnessed the recovery of the Eiheiji as the central temple (*honzan*) of a nationwide Sōtō school.

Dōgen and the early development of Sōtō Zen

Dōgen returned from China in 1227 convinced that the Zen practice of concentrated meditation (*shikan taza*) that he had inherited from the Ts'ao-tung master T'ien-t'ung Ju-ching was the "true Dharma" (*shōbō*). In the first works he wrote after his return to Japan, the *Fukan zazengi* (Principles for the universal promotion of *zazen*) and *Bendōwa* (Distinguishing the Way), he advocated *zazen* (seated meditation) as the supreme Buddhist practice for both monks and laypersons.[63] This assertion of the primacy of Zen aroused the anger of the Enryakuji monks, who succeeded in driving Dōgen from the Kenninji where he had settled after his return to the capital.

In 1231, Dōgen moved to Fukakusa, just south of Kyoto. There he established the Kōshōji. Dōgen's strict training under Ju-ching had made him an admirer of Zen monastic life as he believed it to have been shaped by the regulations enforced by the T'ang-dynasty Ch'an master Pai-chang. For some time after his return to Japan, Dōgen held an ideal of universal monkhood in the broadest terms. Enlightenment through *zazen*, he argued in *Fukan zazengi*, was open to all men and women, lay as well as clerical. And access to this enlightenment was facilitated by the scrupulous, mindful observance of the Zen monastic regulations.

In time, however, when Dōgen was excluded from the capital – confronted with the practical difficulty of spreading his teachings in the face of bitter opposition from the established Buddhist schools, deprived of elite patronage, and becoming more pessimistic about the

63 For translations of these two works, see Masao Abe and Norman Wadell, trans., "Dōgen's *Bendōwa*," *The Eastern Buddhist* 4 (May 1971): 124–57; and Masao Abe and Norman Wadell, trans., "Dōgen's *Fukanzazengi*," *The Eastern Buddhist* (October 1973): 121–6.

responsiveness of ordinary people to his message – Dōgen's thoughts shifted increasingly toward the reassertion of an exclusively monastic tradition: the training of a few select monks who were prepared to devote themselves single-mindedly to attaining enlightenment in a remote, strictly regulated monastic community.

At the Kōshōji, Dōgen worked to create the first pure Zen monastery on Japanese soil. Eisai's monastery of the Kenninji had allowed the practice of a mixed Zen in which Tendai and Shingon prayers and rituals were conducted alongside *zazen*. But Dōgen rejected this accommodation with other streams of Buddhism. The core of the Kōshōji complex contained two characteristic Ch'an monastic buildings: the communal monk's hall (*sōdō*), the room where communal *zazen* was carried on day and night, and the Dharma hall (*hatto*) where the abbot and senior monks debated Zen with the members of the community.

During the thirteen years he remained at the Kōshōji, Dōgen produced more than forty treatises on Zen, which were later included in the *Shōbō genzō* (The eye-treasury of the true Dharma). These included not only instructions for *zazen* and commentaries on the Lotus Sutra and other texts but also detailed regulations for Zen monastic life. Through these regulations Dōgen introduced to the Kōshōji the administrative organization of Sung-dynasty Ch'an monasteries and the ideals of Pai-Chang. His regulations shaped the institutional character of Sōtō Zen.

One of the earliest of Dōgen's treatises was the *Tenzo kyōkun* (Instructions for the monastery cook), in which Dōgen explained the attitude to be maintained by those monks charged with preparing the meals that sustained the community. He stressed that the simple acts of washing rice or cooking vegetables, if performed mindfully, were conducive to the Zen practice of the individual himself and the whole community and that the vegetables used should, therefore, be treated with the greatest reverence: "Simple vegetables feed the seeds of the Buddha and nurture the buds of the Way."[64]

In the *Jūundōshiki* (Regulations for the layered cloud hall), Dōgen provided twenty-one basic regulations for the annex that had been built to take the overflow from the monks' hall at the Kōshōji. To realize the "true Dharma," monks should use the hall solely as a place for meditation, not for reading the sutras or, worse, gossiping or quar-

---

64 *Tenzo Kyōkun*, in Ōkubo Dōshū, ed., *Dōgen Zenji zenshū* (Tokyo: Chikuma shobō, 1970), pp. 295–303.

reling. The monks' robes should be coarse, and the monks should avoid spitting or blowing their noses loudly. Saké and spicy foods were, of course, forbidden. *Semmen* (Washing the face) and *Senjō* (Purification) emphasized the importance of purification rituals in Zen practice and monastic life. For Dōgen, such activities as washing the face, bathing the body, cleansing the mouth and teeth, washing robes and bowls, and using the latrine all could be ritualized expressions of Zen and Buddha-nature if they were performed scrupulously according to the regulations laid down by Ch'an patriarchs and interpreted by Dōgen:

In the Buddha-dharma the principles of cleansing with water are always prescribed. To wash the body, to wash the mind, to wash the feet, to wash the face, to wash the eyes, to wash the mouth, to wash the two acts of urination and excretion, to wash hands, to wash a bowl, to wash a robe, or to wash the head – all these acts comprise the right Dharma of the Buddhas and patriarchs of the three periods.[65]

In these and many other writings on Zen monastic life, Dōgen laid the basis for a rigorous Zen practice in which careful observance of the rules and precepts sustained *zazen* and maintained harmonious community life. It should be stressed that although Dōgen was extremely critical of some Chinese schools of Rinzai Zen and their monastic discipline and reinterpreted traditional regulations in the name of faithfulness to Pai-chang or to suit Japanese conditions, he was drawing on the same corpus of Ch'an monastic codes (*shingi*) as did the Rinzai masters, Chinese and Japanese, who were active in the Kamakura and Kyoto *gozan* monasteries.

The need to build an annex for the monks' hall suggests that under Dōgen's leadership the Kōshōji community grew rapidly. Dōgen attracted to the Kōshōji laymen and monks from other schools of Buddhism. Among those who came were a group of followers of the monk Dainichibō Nōnin who had also been driven from Kyoto for advocating Zen as the supreme Buddhist practice. For its continued survival, this expanded community needed patrons. Here Dōgen's own aristocratic family connections were of help. Shōgaku-ni, a nun from an aristocratic family who may have been a relative of Dōgen's, paid for the construction of the Dharma hall. Kujō Noriie, a cousin, also made generous donations. These and other noble sponsors helped build the Kōshōji and sustain the community's day-to-day life. Their patronage

65 Cited in Kim, *Dōgen Kigen*, p. 234.

allowed Dōgen to remain undisturbed at the Kōshōji for more than a decade and to lay the foundations of traditional Zen community life.[66] As the community at Kōshōji expanded, it again attracted the attention of the Enryakuji's supporters. Dōgen refused to dilute his Zen with Tendai or Shingon elements. In 1242, in an effort to defend his position and assert the importance of Zen for the country, he wrote a short apologia entitled *Gokoku shōbōgi* (Principles of the true Dharma in defense of the country). The text of this work has not survived, but it seems likely that in it Dōgen not only made a case for Zen as the essence of the Buddha's teaching but also argued that its promotion would bring spiritual benefits and protection to its sponsors and the nation at large. If anything, the presentation of this defense only made Dōgen's position more critical. The Enryakuji monks counterattacked by prevailing on the court to outlaw Dōgen's teachings as a dangerous heretical interpretation of Buddhism that could only lead people astray and thus do harm to the Dharma and the country. To make things more difficult for Dōgen, a new monastery, the Tōfukuji, headed by Enni Ben'en and supported by Kujō Michiie, had been established near the Kōshōji. The Tōfukuji had close relations with the Enryakuji, where the very kind of syncretic Tendai–Zen that Dōgen had criticized was being advocated. Dōgen must have felt that his small community at the Kōshōji was being squeezed between the Enryakuji and this powerful new Rinzai Zen monastery.[67]

In 1243, before the Enryakuji monks could carry out their threats to have the Kōshōji destroyed, Dōgen and his followers moved north to the mountains of Echizen. The move was made possible by the enthusiastic patronage of the warrior Hatano Yoshishige, a retainer of the Kamakura bakufu and the military steward (*jitō*) of the Shihi-no-shō in Echizen. Yoshishige gave Dōgen land and resources for a new monastery, the Eiheiji. Here, except for a brief visit to Kamakura in 1247 to lecture on Zen to the regent Hōjō Tokiyori, Dōgen spent all but the last few months of his life. He wrote prolifically on Zen, compiled and enforced monastic regulations, instituted a monastic administration composed of senior eastern and western monks, and oversaw the building of a true Zen monastic complex. Undoubtedly, the remoteness and harsh winters of Echizen intensified the shift in Dōgen's thought from the advocacy of *zazen* as a universal practice easily accessible to all men

66 On Dōgen's patrons, see Ōkubo Dōshu, *Dōgen zenji-den no kenkyū* (Tokyo: Chikuma shobō, 1966).
67 The incidents surrounding the writing of the *Gokoku shōbōgi* are discussed in Imaeda, *Dōgen: zazen hitosuji no shamon*, pp. 138–40.

and women to the reiteration of a traditional Ch'an monastic ideal in which his guidance would be offered to the few dedicated monks who sought him out and could endure the rigorous conditions.

After Dōgen's death, the Eiheiji community developed slowly and peacefully for half a century under the leadership of two of Dōgen's closest disciples, both of whom had been with him from the Kōshōji and had played active roles in organizing the move to Echizen and the building of the Eiheiji.

Koun Ejō (1198–1280), Dōgen's immediate successor, was from the Kujō branch of the Fujiwara family. Before joining Dōgen at the Kōshōji, he had studied Tendai, Pure Land, and esoteric Buddhism and had begun the practice of Zen as a follower of Dainichibō Nōnin. As a secretary for Dōgen, Koun helped copy many of the books included in the *Shōbō genzō*. He accompanied the ailing Dōgen on his last journey to Kyoto and brought back his ashes to the Eiheiji. Koun was thus close to Dōgen in life and familiar with his ideas and teachings on Zen and monastic practice. He strove to continue those teachings in his leadership of the community.[68]

Tettsū Gikai (1219–1309), who succeeded Koun in 1267 for the first of several terms as abbot of the Eiheiji, was a member of a branch of the Fujiwara family from Echizen and had begun his religious career in the Tendai monastery of the Enryakuji. Tettsū's family connections with Echizen may have been crucial in persuading Dōgen to move to that remote province. At the Eiheiji, Tettsū served as cook (*tenzo*) and one of the officers in charge of monastery finances (*kanzu*). In 1259, he journeyed to China where he spent four years studying Zen and recording Ch'an monastic architecture, ceremonies, and religious utensils. The sketches he made of Ch'an monastery buildings were used as models for the Eiheiji, and on the basis of his other observations, he revised many of the rituals and regulations in force at the monastery.[69]

The peaceful development of the Eiheiji community was broken in the year 1300 by a bitter dispute over the succession to the monastery's leadership and over the character of the Zen practiced there. The struggle pitted Tettsū's followers Keizan Jōkin (1268–1325) and Gazan Shōseki (1275–1368) against a group of monks led by Gien. Gien secured the leadership and drove Tettsū's followers from the Eiheiji by presenting himself as the heir to Dōgen's strict Zen tradition

---

68 *Zengaku daijiten*.   69 Ibid.

and attacking his rivals as advocates of the dilution and distortion of that tradition.[70]

There was some justice in Gien's charges: Both Keizan and Gazan wanted to spread Sōtō Zen outside the Eiheiji cloister. They could argue that efforts to proselytize were in keeping with the universalism implicit in the *Fukan zazengi* and *Bendōwa*, but they must also have been aware that popularization could be attained only by relaxing the strict, exclusive monastic practices enforced at the Eiheiji. Keizan was, by disposition, a syncretist. He had studied Tendai Buddhism and had close ties with many of the monks and mountain ascetics (*yamabushi*) in the Tendai center at Hakusan. He had also studied esoteric Buddhism and practiced Zen under Muhon Kakushin and *gozan* masters. After Keizan was excluded from the Eiheiji, he established two new monasteries, the Sōjiji and Yōkōji, in Noto. The former was converted from a Shingon temple, the latter from a Ritsu (Vinaya) school center. Keizan's willingness to make accommodations with other branches of Buddhism, to offer funeral and prayer services for local warriors and farmers, and to hold mass meetings at which lay people could do *zazen* or take the precepts all helped to set in motion a rapid expansion of Sōtō Zen based on the Sōjiji.[71]

Keizan's work of popularization and diffusion was carried further by Gazan, who attracted monks from all over Japan to study Zen under his guidance at the Sōjiji and Yōkōji. Gazan is said to have had twenty-five brilliant disciples. Among them, five monks – Daigen Sōshin (d. 1371), Tsūgen Jakurei (1322–91), Mutan Sokan (d. 1387), Daitetsu Sōrei (1333–1408), and Jippō Ryōshū (d. 1405) – established subtemples within the Sōjiji. As in the case of the Rinzai monastery of the Myōshinji, these subtemples provided abbots and supervision for the Sōjiji and became the nuclei for the diffusion of these branches of Sōtō Zen throughout the provinces.

With the Daigen and Tsūgen branches in the vanguard, Sōtō Zen witnessed a dramatic, nationwide diffusion during the fifteenth and sixteenth centuries. The details of that diffusion go beyond the scope of this chapter. Some indication of its pace and extent, however, is provided in the number of monasteries belonging to the Sōtō school. At Gazan's death there were probably no more than 30 or 40 Sōtō foundations. But a document dated 1745 refers to 16,554 Sōtō tem-

---

70 This "third-generation dispute" is analyzed by Takeuchi Michio, "Nihon ni okeru Sōtō Zen no tenkai," in *Kōza Zen*, vol. 4 (Tokyo: Chikuma shobō, 1967), pp. 152–5.
71 For a more detailed account of this expansion, see Takeuchi, "Nihon ni okeru Sōtō Zen no tenkai."

ples, most of which were almost certainly established in the phase of rapid growth during the Muromachi period.[72]

It is natural to ask what lay behind this rapid growth. Obviously, Sōtō monks like Keizan, Gazan, and their successors gave their Zen teachings a mass appeal. A few Sōtō monks came to the attention of the Ashikaga shoguns. Out of respect for Gazan, Ashikaga Takauji and Tadayoshi designated the Yōkōji as the *ankokuji* for Noto. And Baizan Monbon (d. 1417) of the Daigen branch earned such a reputation as a Zen master that Ashikaga Yoshimitsu invited him to Kyoto. When Baizan pleaded illness, Yoshimitsu is said to have sent a painter to Baizan's monastery to produce a portrait of the monk. The portrait had to be painted secretly, as Baizan would not receive the painter. When it was unveiled before the shogun, the legend goes, the hall was shaken by an earthquake, and so the portrait was returned to the reclusive monk.[73]

For the most part, however, the Sōtō monks and monasteries did not enjoy shogunal or imperial patronage. Rather their patrons were farmers and local warriors, some of whom emerged as *sengoku* daimyo from the wars of the late fifteenth century. In many cases, they were supported by the same daimyo that were patronizing Rinzai monks of the Daitokuji or Myōshinji lineages. Among the early patrons of Sōtō monks were substantial provincial warrior families, some of them of *jitō* rank. Hatano Yoshishige's successors, for instance, remained patrons of the Eiheiji. The monk Daichi (1290–1366) established several monasteries under the patronage of both the Kikuchi in Kyushu and Fujiwara Shigemuni, a *jitō* in Kaga, who conferred domains on the Gidaji.[74]

In the sixteenth century, a roster of Sōtō Zen patrons would have included most of Japan's warlords. Among these *sengoku* daimyo patrons were the Uesugi in northern Japan; the Hōjō, Ōta, and Yūki in the Kantō; the Imagawa and Tokugawa on the Pacific coast; the Uesugi, Takeda, Asakura, Hatakeyama, Oda, Asai, and Maeda in central Japan; the Ōuchi, Mōri, and Yamana in the west; and the Ōtomo and Shimazu in Kyushu. In the late fifteenth and early sixteenth centuries alone, several hundred Sōtō temples were estab-

72 Yokozeki Ryōin, *Edo jidai tōmon seiyō* (Tokyo: Bukkyōsha, 1950), pp. 524–5.
73 Cited in Nakamura Hajime et al., *Muromachi Bukkyō*, vol. 6 of *Ajia Bukkyō-shi* (Tokyo: Kosei shuppansha, 1972), p. 87.
74 On Daichi and his patrons, see Mizuno Yahoko, *Daichi*, vol. 9 of *Nihon no Zen goroku* (Tokyo: Chikuma shobō, 1978), pp. 9–68; and Sugimoto Hisao, *Kikuchi-shi sandai* (Tokyo: Yoshikawa kōbunkan, 1966), pp. 129–51.

lished in territories controlled by the Imagawa family. Both the Takeda family and Tokugawa Ieyasu, learning from the *gozan* organization, appointed Sōtō monks as registrars (*sōroku*) of the temples in their domains.[75]

The patronage by farmers is more difficult to define. The records that survive from Sōtō temples all over Japan and the diaries and letters of Sōtō monks include lists of donations from villagers and references to meetings and ceremonies attended by Sōtō monks and farming families. Some Sōtō temples were established in Kyoto, Kamakura, Sakai, and other urban centers, but overall, the great expansion of Sōtō Zen was made in rural areas.

The key to this expansion was popularization: the development of practices that made Sōtō Zen and Sōtō monks welcome in the domains of *sengoku* daimyō and in farming villages. (The popularization of Zen practice will be discussed later in this chapter.) But there were ways other than the simplification of Zen itself by which Sōtō monks established close ties with warriors and villagers. Some Sōtō monks, like Sensō Esai (d. 1475), revived the Ch'an ideal of labor that had been expressed centuries before by Pai-chang: "A day without work, a day without food." Perhaps partly from necessity but also from conviction, these monks farmed the temple lands as did the villagers around them. Other monks engaged in local welfare work, organizing the building of bridges, the construction of irrigation channels, the digging of wells, or the provision of relief services in time of drought or floods. The surviving diaries and sermons of Sōtō monks reveal that they also provided simplified funeral services, prayer meetings for the exorcism of restless spirits, and ceremonies to pray for rain, relief from sickness, and other immediate benefits. They were, in almost every way, more in touch with the day-to-day life of the ordinary people than were their counterparts in the *gozan*.[76]

For much of the Muromachi period, Sōtō Zen lacked the institutional centralization of the *gozan* schools or the Daitokuji and Myōshinji lineages. The rift between the Eiheiji and the Sōjiji persisted for decades, and the Eiheiji languished as the Sōjiji and other temples in Keizan's lineage flourished. But even among the rapidly spreading branches of the various Sōjiji offshoots, there was little unity or central organization.

75 For a detailed presentation of the provincial diffusion of Sōtō Zen under daimyo patronage, see Suzuki Taizan, "Sōtō Zen no kōfū to sono gegosha," in *Kokumin seikatsu-shi kenkyū* (Tokyo: Yoshikawa kōbunkan, 1959), pp. 223–76.
76 Nakamura et al., *Muromachi Bukkyō*, p. 98.

By the late fifteenth century, however, a process of centralization was taking place as monks from the Keizan lineages began to serve as abbots of the Eiheiji, to rebuild its reputation, and to make it, alongside the Sōjiji, the main temple (*honzan*) of the Sōtō school. The prestige of the Eiheiji and the Sōtō school was further enhanced when, beginning early in the sixteenth century, its leading abbots received the honorary title of "Zen master" (Zenji) from the imperial court. Throughout most of the sixteenth century, the Eiheiji overshadowed the Sōjiji as its abbots received imperial appointments, such as those of the *gozan* monastery of the Nanzenji, and were permitted to wear purple robes. Under the imperially granted title "principal training place for the Sōtō school in this realm" (Honchō Sōtō daiichi dōjō), the Eiheiji recovered the primacy it had enjoyed under Dōgen and his immediate successors.[77]

Although the huge Zen school derived from Dōgen and Keizan was the mainstream of Sōtō Zen in medieval Japan, there was another and very different transmission. The Chinese monk Tung-ming Hui-jih (Tōmyō Enichi, 1272–1340), who came to Japan in 1309 at the invitation of Hōjō Sadatoki, has already been mentioned. Tung-ming was already a renowned monk in Chinese Ch'an monasteries before he departed for Japan. He belonged to the Tsao-tung lineage of Hung-chih Cheng-chueh (Wanshi Shōgaku, 1091–1157) and had held high office in several leading Ch'an monasteries. In Kamakura he received a much warmer reception than Dōgen had received on his return to Kyoto. At the request of the Hōjō, Tung-ming served as the abbot of the Engakuji and most of the Kamakura *gozan* monasteries. Emperor Godaigo invited him to Kyoto, where he headed the Kenninji and Nanzenji. Tung-ming, who shared many of the literary interests of the *gozan* monks, was clearly at home in the Japanese *gozan* environment. At his death his remains were enshrined in the Hakuunan subtemple in the Engakuji, which became the spiritual center for monks of the Wanshi Sōtō lineage.

Tung-ming's followers included cultured monks like the poet-monk Betsugen Enshi (1294–1364), who was patronized by the Shiba and Asakura warrior families and served as the abbot of the *gozan* monastery of the Kenninji in Kyoto. Betsugen and a number of other Wanshi school monks visited Mongol China and were known as experts on the latest cultural developments in Chinese literary circles. After the destruction of the Hōjō, the Wanshi school found patrons among the

77 Ibid., pp. 98–100; and Takeuchi Michio, *Nihon no Zen* (Tokyo: Shunchōsha, 1976), p. 290.

Asakai and Nijō, *kuge* families and the Asakura warrior house in Echizen. The Asakura connection was particularly important. Wanshi school monks remained within the orbit of the *gozan* but were able, with the support of the Asakura who became *sengoku* daimyo, to survive the decline of the *gozan* that resulted from the weakening of the bakufu and *shugo* in the late fifteenth century. However, when the Asakura were crushed by Oda Nobunaga in 1573, the fortunes of the Wanshi school declined rapidly.[78]

Before ending this rather extended discussion of the institutional development and nationwide diffusion of the various branches of medieval Zen, several questions remain to be addressed. We have shown that Rinzai and Sōtō Zen spread rapidly – the words "explosive development" would perhaps not be an exaggeration – and found patrons at all levels and in all sectors of medieval society. But why were shoguns, emperors, *shugo*, *jitō*, *sengoku* daimyo, farmers, townspeople, merchants, tea masters, and wandering entertainers, not to mention the monks and nuns from other schools of Buddhism, drawn to Zen and to the monks who advocated it? And how deep and exclusive was their commitment?

Their motivations, not surprisingly, were complex. People from all these groups took a spiritual interest in Zen, accepting the assertion that *zazen* was indeed the most direct means to realize the enlightenment attained by Śākyamuni. The regent Hōjō Tokiyori, the cloistered emperor Hanazono, and the provincial warrior Akamatsu Norimura were only three of many millions of lay people of all classes who, during the medieval period, engaged in what Zen masters described as a "life-and-death struggle" for enlightenment (*satori*) through *zazen*. As Suzuki Daisetsu and many other scholars have pointed out, Zen had a particularly strong appeal for Japanese warriors: *Zazen* is physically demanding; an encounter with a Zen master involves a frank and penetrating probe of the seeker's sincerity and attainment; Zen practice calls for a direct, intuitive understanding of self rather than book learning or the recitation of sutras; and for the Zen practitioner, enlightenment must be grasped by one's own efforts, not conferred by some compassionate Buddha. All of these qualities appealed to Japanese warriors and help explain why they were the most numerous and enthusiastic patrons of Zen monks. But it would be a mistake to suggest that all warriors practiced Zen – many were devoted followers

---

78 The growth of the Wanshi line is described by Imaeda Aishin, "Sōtō-shū Wanshi-ha to Asakura-ke," in *Chūsei zenshū-shi no kenkyū*, pp. 483–503.

of Nichiren, Shinran, and other Pure Land preachers – or that the patronage of Zen was restricted to warriors.

Cultural factors also contributed to the widespread acceptance of Zen. The Hōjō regents, Ashikaga shoguns, members of the imperial court, provincial warriors, and wealthy merchants of Kyoto, Sakai, and Hakata all were eager to learn from Zen monks the latest in cultural styles from China. Most *gozan* monks were advocates of the "unity of the three creeds." Although Zen remained for them the most direct path to personal salvation, they also recognized the validity of Confucianism and Taoism. Chinese Zen monks who came to Japan, and those Japanese monks who stayed for more than a few years in China, were fully conversant with the intellectual and cultural interests of the Chinese literati. In Japan they were happy to discuss with their patrons the ideas of Confucian or Taoist thinkers, often as a means of introducing Zen Buddhist ideas. Many Zen monks were calligraphers, composers of Chinese verse (*kanshi*), and painters of ink monochromes, reflecting their spiritual insights and intellectual gatherings. At literary gatherings and tea ceremonies, monks were in great demand as mentors and arbiters of cultural styles. Members of the imperial court were interested in the Chinese culture made accessible through Zen monks. But for the Hōjō regents and Ashikaga shoguns, access to Chinese culture was particularly important. Some familiarity with the latest in continental styles gave them a greater sense of confidence in their social dealings with the nobility, who remained the arbiters of taste in the Japanese cultural tradition.

Political factors also played a part in the motivations of Zen's patrons, especially in the patronage of the *gozan* by the Hōjō and Ashikaga families. Close political regulation by the Kamakura and Muromachi bakufus ensured that the Zen monasteries never became an independent political or military force in medieval society. From the beginnings of its development in Japan, the Zen monastic institution, unlike the monasteries of the older schools of Japanese Buddhism, proved amenable to warrior control. At least part of the motivation for patronage lay in the fact that Zen, as a new institution in Japanese society, did not have ingrained social and political ties with the court, the nobility, and the powerful monasteries clustered around the capital. For the early Ashikaga shoguns seeking to establish themselves in Kyoto, their deliberate promotion of the *gozan* was a means of offsetting the influence over the capital exerted by the Enryakuji, Onjōji, and other long-established Tendai and Shingon monasteries.

Imaeda Aishin has shown in his studies of the *ankokuji* and *rishōtō* and the provincial diffusion of the *gozan* that Ashikaga Tadayoshi and Takauji regarded these networks as a means of showing favor to specific local temples and their patrons, of linking them more closely to the capital, and of exercising surveillance over them. When both *shugo* and local warriors saw that Zen was in the ascendant under the shogun's patronage, they must have found it politically expedient to sponsor Zen monks and establish Zen monasteries their domains. During the fourteenth and fifteenth centuries, when the bakufu was in the ascendant, *gozan*, *jissatsu*, and *shozan* monasteries were the beneficiaries of the most generous provincial patronage. In the late fifteenth century, with the bakufu reduced to political impotence, the *gozan* in decline, and the country in turmoil, those branches of Zen – the Myōshinji, Daitokuji, Sōtō – that had strong provincial roots and weaker ties with the shogunate came into greater favor with the upsurge of local warlords, the *sengoku* daimyo. Like the Hōjō and Ashikaga before them, the daimyo quickly appreciated that Zen monasteries were disciplined and orderly, politically and militarily docile, and sources of astute advisers, spartan training, and basic literary education for the warriors' children.

After the fourteenth century, the imperial court lacked the financial means to be a major patron of Zen. Godaigo, however, had seen some political advantage to be gained by trying to bring the *gozan* monasteries under his wing. Later emperors maintained close ties with the Nanzenji and some of the Kyoto *gozan*. The granting of purple robes to abbots of the Daitokuji, Myōshinji, and Eiheiji was, of course, the court's recognition of their spiritual stature, but as the Tokugawa bakufu realized in the seventeenth century, it also had the effect of creating political ties between the court and the major Zen monasteries.

In regard to the exclusiveness of the commitment to Zen, patrons like Hōjō Tokiyori and Ashikaga Tadayoshi practiced Zen assiduously until their deaths and displayed little inclination to promote other branches of Buddhism. Most patrons of Zen, at least among the elite, however, seem to have adopted a more eclectic attitude, combining practice and patronage of Zen with devotion to other Buddhist schools. Ashikaga Takauji and Yoshimitsu are counted among the great patrons of the *gozan*, but in their spiritual lives they were also strongly attracted by the message of salvation carried by Pure Land preachers. Godaigo's patronage was not unusual, blending, as it did, the occasional practice of *zazen*, the Chinese learning and culture available through Zen monks, and the politically motivated sponsorship of certain Zen monasteries with the continued patronage of Shingon and Tendai Buddhism.

ECONOMY AND ADMINISTRATION OF THE MEDIEVAL ZEN MONASTERY

The growth and maintenance of a Zen community of several hundred monks depended on the existence of a stable monastic economy. The economic basis of all Zen monasteries in the medieval period – Rinzai and Sōtō, *gozan* and non-*gozan* – was income from land, either the annual rice taxes (*nengu*) derived from holdings in *shōen* or the rents (*kajishi*) from cultivators of monastic lands. Income from landholdings was supplemented by a variety of other sources. Among these were donations from patrons for the construction and repair of buildings; the conduct of ceremonies; the provision of texts, paintings, and statues; fees for funeral services and prayer ceremonies; the proceeds from foreign trading ventures, from the sale of monastery produce, or from market fees; the fruits of mendicancy; and the profits of moneylending. The amount of income and the various elements in the economic "mix" naturally varied with the size of the monastery, its location, the wealth and enthusiasm of its patrons, and the period. In general, the income from *shōen* holdings provided the mainstay for Zen monastic economies in the Kamakura period, whereas the income from rents, commerce, and small donations came to play a greater role in the Muromachi period as the *shōen* were dismembered and alienated from their proprietors.

Unfortunately, the sporadic quality of the documentary record makes it impossible to provide a detailed picture of the economic life of any single Zen monastery over the whole medieval period. By piecing together information on different monasteries at different times, however, we can form an impression of the main features of the larger monasteries' economic life and of the ways in which these may have changed over time in response to changing political and economic circumstances in the country at large.

The *gozan* monasteries, under the patronage of the Kamakura and Muromachi shogunates, were generously endowed and enjoyed huge incomes from landholdings, mostly *jitō shiki*, in *shōen* scattered throughout the country.[79] The Tenryūji, in 1387, for instance, enjoyed

---

79 The economies of the Engakuji, Nanzenji, and Daitokuji are discussed at somewhat greater length in Collcutt, *Five Mountains*, pp. 255–75.

an income of "8,123 *kanmon* in rice and cash" from more than twelve *shōen* holdings in eight different provinces.[80] The Nanzenji in the same period was receiving an annual income of well over four thousand *koku* in rice from domains in Kaga and half a dozen other provinces.[81] By the standards of the age, these were very substantial incomes, greater perhaps than those enjoyed by some *shugo*. The *jissatsu* and *shozan* monasteries, likewise, were granted extensive *shōen* rights by shoguns, members of the imperial court, and *shugo* and were protected by the bakufu.[82]

Although the provincial monasteries in the *gozan* system remained dependent on income from landholdings, donations, and local mendicancy, the metropolitan *gozan*, especially the Kyoto *gozan*, had other important sources of income. The capital was the hub of a growing commercial economy, and some Zen monasteries were active participants in this growth. The Tenryūji, for instance, derived income from a thriving saké-brewing enterprise, and the Tōfukuji sponsored and taxed a merchant community at its gates. Zen monks from the Kyoto *gozan* led many of the official trading embassies to China on behalf of the bakufu, the Ōuchi, or the Hosokawa. Some *gozan* monasteries, notably the Shōkokuji, sent monks as traders on these missions and may have derived an occasional income of several thousand *kanmon* from the proceeds of such ventures.

A steadier source of income for *gozan* monasteries and some individual Zen monks in Kyoto was provided by moneylending. Many *gozan* monks came from wealthy families or were able to use administrative offices in the *gozan* to amass private fortunes. They were not averse to lending money to needy nobles or warriors at high rates of interest. One Shōkokuji monk in the mid-fifteenth century, known as Sei *tsūbun*, accumulated funds through the management of Shōkokuji *shōen* holdings and made substantial loans to other Kyoto temples and nobles at interest rates of between 3 and 8 percent per month.

In addition to private usury, some Zen monasteries also used "mortuary contributions" (*shidōsen*) that had been donated by patrons to pay for memorial services as capital for more public low-interest loans. Interest rates on *shidōsen* were 2 or 3 percent per month. They were in considerable demand, but because interest rates would mount rapidly if the loan were extended, they were sources of fric-

---

80 *Tenryūji monjo*, cited by Imatani Akira, *Sengoku-ki no Muromachi bakufu* (Tokyo: Kadokawa shoten, 1975), p. 54.
81 Sakurai Keiyū and Fujii Manabu, eds., *Nanzenji monjo* (Kyoto: Nanzenji, 1972), vol. 1, docs. 2, 93, 189.   82 Imatani, *Sengoku-ki no Muromachi bakufu*, pp. 51–54.

tion as well as profit. Among the rioters' demands in the uprisings (*ikki*) of the fifteenth century was relief (*tokusei*) from the payments on overdue *shidōsen* loans. Involvement in usury thus exposed Zen monasteries to the anger of disgruntled citizens, some of whom sought revenge by pillaging monasteries when the chance arose during the Ōnin War.[83]

In addition to direct donations and endowments of land, the *gozan* system benefited indirectly from the bakufu's protection. Under the umbrella of bakufu sponsorship, *gozan* monasteries and their *shōen* holdings enjoyed military protection, exemption from such bakufu and *shugo* levies as *yakubuku-mai* (rice paid in lieu of corvée) and *tansen*, immunity from intrusion by warrior officials and tax collectors, freedom from barrier fees, and favorable treatment in litigation. This protection allowed the *gozan* economies to prosper until well into the fifteenth century and for *gozan* monastic populations to swell far beyond the numbers that the bakufu thought desirable. The Tōfukuji in the early fifteenth century, for instance, had more than 600 monks enrolled, although the bakufu regulations permitted only 350.[84]

But the close association between *gozan* and bakufu did not always work to the advantage of the Zen monasteries. During the fifteenth century, when the Muromachi bakufu was having financial difficulties and beginning to lose its grip over the country, the *gozan* monasteries were being exploited financially and losing important landholdings. By the mid-fifteenth century, the Ashikaga shoguns were forcing the *gozan* monasteries to give them loans and gifts, and these exactions increased as the bakufu's finances weakened.

In 1435, for instance, Ashikaga Yoshinori collected at least twenty *kan* from the Rokuon'in and fifty *kan* from the Tōjiji. According to Imatani Akira, in 1458 there were sixty incidents of forced "gift giving" by *gozan* monks, providing more than fifteen hundred *kanmon* for the shogun. In 1459, the shogunate borrowed two thousand *kanmon* and in 1463 six thousand *kanmon* from monks of the eastern rank of the Kyoto *gozan*.[85] It is unlikely that these loans were ever repaid. Exactions on this scale were a heavy drain on *gozan* coffers, and from

83 On the questions of moneylending by Zen temples and the activities of monks of the eastern rank, see Fujioka Daisetsu, "Gozan kyōdan no hatten ni kansuru ichi kōsatsu," *Bukkyō shigaku* 6 (March 1957): 47–66; and Fujioka Daisetsu, "Zen'in nai ni okeru tōhanshū ni tsuite," *Nihon rekishi*, no. 145 (July 1960): 19–28.
84 Hiraizumi Kiyoshi, *Chūsei ni okeru shaji to shakai to no kankei* (Tokyo: Shibundō, 1934), p. 49, states that the Tōfukuji maintained a population of nearly 700 monks, despite repeated efforts by the bakufu to hold down the number to 350.
85 Imatani, *Sengoku-ki no Muromachi bakufu*, pp. 35–39.

the 1460s, *gozan* monk administrators protested that they could no longer afford to make loans to the shogunate.

Moreover, the wealth that the *gozan* monasteries had derived from their extensive *shōen* holding was drastically reduced when, from around the time of the Ōnin War, the bakufu began to disallow exemptions from *yakubuku-mai* and *tansen* levies and the local warriors began to intrude with impunity into *gozan* landholdings. In the spreading provincial disorder of the late fifteenth and sixteenth centuries, *gozan* monasteries like the Tenryūji, Nanzenji, Engakuji, and Rinsenji lost control over most of their *shōen* holdings. This continued until Oda Nobunaga and Toyotomi Hideyoshi restored order to the provinces and began to rebuild the stricken *gozan* monasteries, restoring, though on a much smaller scale, their economic base. In 1591, for instance, Hideyoshi confirmed the Nanzenji's holdings in and around Kyoto, with an income of 592 *koku*. Tokugawa Ieyasu later raised this to 892 *koku*.[86] This income was probably sufficient to support a community of several hundred, but it was a far cry from the more than 4,000 *koku* that the Nanzenji had received from its landholdings in the late fourteenth century.

Whereas the economies of the *gozan* monasteries generally traced a parabola of growth through the thirteenth, fourteenth, and early fifteenth centuries, followed by disintegration in the late fifteenth and sixteenth centuries, the economies of the Daiō branches of Rinzai Zen and the Sōtō monasteries followed a contrary curve, coming into their own as the *gozan* declined.

In the late fourteenth century, none of the leading non-*gozan* Rinzai or Sōtō monasteries – Daitokuji, Myōshinji, Eiheiji, and Sōjiji – compared in wealth with their *gozan* counterparts. The Daitokuji had fared well under the patronage of Godaigo in the early 1330s. It was granted full control and immunity (*ichien fuyu*) over six *shōen* and from one of them, Tomono-no-shō in Shinano Province, derived (if the documents can be believed) the enormous income of 7,600 *koku*.[87] The Daitokuji did not, however, find favor with the Ashikaga, and without the shogun's support, the monastery found it difficult to hold on to its scattered *shōen* holdings during the civil wars of the fourteenth century. In 1371, the Daitokuji appears to have received an income of only 433 *kanmon* from two *shōen*.[88] This was sufficient to sustain a community of thirty or so monks and attendants, in contrast with the more

---

86 *Nanzenji monjo*, vol. 2, docs. 303, 378, 384.
87 *Daitokuji monjo*, vol. 1, doc. 25 and vol. 2, doc. 643.   88 *Daitokuji monjo*, vol. 1, doc. 124.

than one thousand members of the Nanzenji community. The scale of the Myōshinji's economy in the fourteenth century was even smaller than that of the Daitokuji, and as we have already seen, what landholdings it did possess were confiscated by Yoshimitsu when the community was disbanded in 1339.

When the Daitokuji and Myōshinji began to recover in the mid-fifteenth century, their economies reflected their ties with new patrons and changing economic and commercial possibilities. Most of their subtemples were built by *sengoku* daimyo and endowed not with *shōen* holdings but with income from lands under the daimyo's own control. Cash donations from daimyo, merchants, townspeople, and entertainers helped finance monastic ceremonies, construct buildings, and install abbots. The Daitokuji's connections with tea masters and merchants from Sakai were a valuable source of support. Most of the thirty-odd contributions made at the installation ceremony for Kokei Sōchin as the 117th abbot of the Daitokuji in 1573, for instance, came from Sakai. Among the contributors were Sen no Sōeki (Rikyū), who gave one hundred *kanmon;* Tennojiya Tsuda Sōkyū, fifty *kanmon;* Aburaya Shōsa, thirty *kanmon;* and Takeno Shōga, twenty *kanmon.*[89]

Sasaki Ginya analyzed the economies of four Daitokuji subtemples: the Ryōshōji, Nyoi'an, Yōtoku'in, and Shōgen'in. He concluded that although these subtemples continued to derive some of their income from consolidated *shōen*-type holdings in distant provinces until well into the sixteenth century, they also developed various alternative sources of income to compensate for the relentless erosion of their *shōen* interests by local warriors. Among the most important of these new sources of support were the supplementary rents (*kajishi*) paid by the cultivators of numerous small holdings, rents (*jishi*) from house lots in the city of Kyoto, income from the holdings of a growing number of branch temples, mortuary funds (*shidōsen*), and the sale in the markets of such temple produce as rice, bamboo, or lumber. Some *tatchū* may have managed to subsist on income from landholdings throughout the sixteenth century. Others, like the Shōgen'in, relied heavily on income from the loan of mortuary funds or rental income from smallholdings, or, like the Ryōshōji, on the sale of commercial produce.[90]

All of the temples were obliged to respond, in some measure at least, to the changing economic circumstances, in which *shōen* were an

89 Cited in Haga et al., eds., *Daitokuji to sadō*, p. 151.
90 Sasaki Ginya, *Chūsei shōhin ryūtsū-shi no kenkyū* (Tokyo: Hōsei daigaku shuppan kyoku, 1972), pp. 95–250.

increasingly precarious and inaccessible means of support. But new opportunities were being made available by the growth of commercial activity in and around the Kinai region. Documentary evidence for the economic life of the main monastery, the Daitokuji, in the fifteenth and sixteenth centuries is disappointingly sketchy, but we may assume that it too acquired small-holding rights and lent money to supplement its income from donations and meager *shōen* interests. Income from donations, land, rents, and moneylending all may have helped swell the Daitokuji's coffers. But the monastery was placed on a solid financial footing again only by the patronage of daimyo, and especially by Hideyoshi's grant in 1585 of an income of 1,545 *koku* from three holdings.

The major Sōtō monasteries, like those of the Daiō school, were less populous than their *gozan* counterparts and less generously endowed with *shōen* holdings. Located as they were in the provinces, they had no access to involvement in foreign trade and only limited opportunities for commercial activities or moneylending. These communities remained heavily dependent on the patronage of warrior families and on small donations for funeral and prayer services.

Over centuries of development in China and Japan, the Zen monasteries had refined their effective administrative structure. The characteristic Zen bureaucracy – with five or six senior monks in each of the eastern and western ranks assisting the abbot in running the monastery – was used in the Hangchow monasteries visited by Eisai, Dōgen, and Enni and was described in detail in such Ch'an codes as the *Ch'an-yuan ch'ing-kuei*. It was adopted in Japan without substantial modification by Rinzai and Sōtō monasteries.

Whereas the monks of the western rank, or *chōshu*, supervised the religious, ceremonial, and literary aspects of the monastic life, the *chiji* of the eastern rank managed the day-to-day administration of the monastery and its lands. In medieval society, Zen monk administrators were known for their managerial expertise. Indeed, some of the bursars and estate overseers from Zen monasteries were employed by the bakufu as *daikan* or by non-Zen temples to oversee rebuilding projects. Bursars of *gozan* monasteries, in particular, had opportunities to accumulate capital for their monasteries and for themselves. And it was to these monks that the shoguns turned for advice and loans when the bakufu's finances crumbled in the fifteenth century.[91]

91 For a fuller treatment of eastern-rank activities, see Fujioka, "Gozan kyōdan no hatten ni kansuru ichi kōsatsu"; Fujioka, "Zen'in nai ni okeru tōhanshū ni tsuite"; and Collcutt, *Five Mountains*, pp. 239–43, 275–85.

CHANGES IN ZEN PRACTICE, CULTURE, AND THE
MONASTIC LIFE

Even though the Zen pioneers strove to achieve a full and true transmission of Ch'an practice, monastic discipline, and culture from China, the very success of Zen in Japan brought changes, accommodation, and divergence from the Chinese ideal espoused by Eisai, Dōgen, and the Chinese émigré monks. These concluding pages will point to some of the ways in which Zen practice and Zen-related culture were transformed in the medieval Japanese context.

At the outset it must be stressed that the Japanese and Chinese monks who brought Ch'an teachings to Japan during the Kamakura period wanted to recreate in Japan a complete and faithful replica of the Zen monastic life, or the best traditions of that monastic life, as they had experienced it in Chinese monasteries. During their training in Ch'an monasteries, Eisai, Dōgen, Enni, and their successors did not simply practice *zazen* or engage in *kōan* study. From their writings and the materials they brought back to Japan, it is clear that they took an interest in all aspects of Ch'an monastic life, from Buddhist texts and ceremonies to the details of monastic architecture and the secular cultural interests of the Chinese monks. Eisai's advocacy of the efficacy of tea derived from the Ch'an monastic use of tea ceremonies to promote community harmony, bodily well-being, and wakefulness during long periods of meditation.[92] Enni brought back to Japan a library of Buddhist texts used in Ch'an monasteries, portraits and calligraphy of his master Wu-chun, and Chinese secular writings. His long stay in China allowed him to study Sung Confucianism as well as Zen. In Japan, he lectured on Confucianism before the imperial court, no doubt intending to lead his audiences on to a deeper interest in the superior insights of Zen Buddhism. Dōgen, too, in the *Shōbō genzō*, *Eihei shingi*, and *Tenzo kyōkun*, displays an intense concern for the full transmission of the detailed rules of authentic Ch'an monastic practice. He was convinced that the monastic regulations enforced by Pai-chang and the Chinese patriarchs reflected the Buddha's teaching and were intrinsic to the practice of *zazen*.[93]

The many Chinese monks who came to Japan in the late thirteenth

---

92 On the role of Eisai and other Zen monks in popularizing the Chinese custom of tea drinking in Japan, see Theodore M. Ludwig, "Before Rikyū: Religious and Aesthetic Influences in the Early History of the Tea Ceremony," *Monumenta Nipponica* 36 (Winter, 1981): 367–90; and Nishibe Bunjō, "Zen Monks and the Formation of the Way of Tea," *Chanoyu*, no 28 (1981): 7–46.   93 Kim, *Dōgen Kigen*, pp. 228–308.

century and headed the Rinzai monasteries in Kamakura and Kyoto naturally insisted on what they knew as orthodox Sung Ch'an monastic practice in those Japanese communities. Under the guidance of Lan-ch'i Tao-Lung and Wu-hsueh Tsu-yuan, monasteries like the Kenchōji were built in the traditional Ch'an style on a north-south axis, with the central line of great ceremonial buildings – great gate, Buddha hall, and Dharma hall – flanked east and west by the monks' communal hall (*sōdō*) – where the monks meditated, took their meals, and slept – and the kitchen – office building that housed the monastery's administrative functions. Monastic life was regulated by codes that were also in force in the Chinese monasteries: The monks wore Chinese dress, studied the Chinese language, and moved to the sounds of bells, gongs, and clappers used in Ch'an monasteries. Following Chinese Ch'an practice, meditation sessions (*zazen*) were held four times daily, interspersed with discussion of *kōan* in the Dharma hall or abbot's quarters and the conduct of prayer ceremonies in the Buddha hall.[94]

Both Lan-ch'i and Wu-hsueh stressed unremitting *zazen* and discouraged literary pursuits. But as Chinese monks came to Japan in growing numbers and Chinese art objects (*karamono*) flowed into temples and warrior mansions in Kamakura, Zen monasteries also became centers for the study and promotion of secular Chinese culture. For example, in order to be accepted as a student by Issan Ichinei, the Japanese monk Musō Soseki was tested on his command of Chinese verse.[95] In Issan's day, Chinese émigré monks in the *gozan* monasteries instructed their Japanese disciples in those arts that were esteemed by Ch'an masters and their Chinese literati patrons. This *gozan* cultural movement embraced calligraphy, ink painting, poetry, philosophy, book printing, the enjoyment of tea, and garden design. Among the Japanese monks who studied with Issan and became enthusiastic advocates of Chinese culture were Kokan Shiren (1278–1348) and Sesson Yūbai (1290–1346). Although he never visited China, Kokan was an admirer of Chinese civilization. His *Genkō shakushō*, the first attempt at a comprehensive history of Buddhism in Japan, was based on Chinese collections of the biographies of eminent monks and Confucian historical classics. Kokan was a poet and, in addition to his scholarly writings on Zen and the Lankāvatāra Sutra, produced the first Chinese rhyming dictionary for use by Japanese and a handbook of

94 A more detailed treatment of the introduction of Chinese monastic regulations and the character of the Zen monastic life is provided by Collcutt, *Five Mountains*, pp. 133–51.
95 Tamamura, *Musō kokushi*, p. 18.

phrases from the Confucian classics useful in composing the kind of Chinese parallel prose that was fashionable in Zen monasteries.[96]

After meeting Issan in Kamakura, Sesson traveled to China where he spent more than twenty years wandering from Ch'an monastery to Ch'an monastery. For a time he was imprisoned as a spy. During his long stay in China, Sesson became expert in the composition of Chinese verse in both the *lü-shih* (regulated-verse) and the freer *ku-shih* (ancient-verse) styles. The following "irregular verse" reflects on Sesson's experiences in China and conveys something of his independence and spiritual detachment from Zen:

> The praises of others do not move me,
> Their slanders have no bite,
> With a heart as free as flowing water,
> My ties with the world are slight.
> Surviving the grip of prison fetters,
> I stayed on three years in Ch'ang-an;
> When I feel in the mood to sing,
> I speak out straight: What need of fancy phrases?[97]

Throughout the fourteenth century, the Chinese literary and cultural tone of the *gozan* monasteries thickened, and even while the number of monks actually traveling between Japan and China decreased. *Gozan* monasteries were recognized as centers for the diffusion of Chinese culture and Zen monks, considered by shoguns, emperors, and provincial warriors as experts in the Chinese language, literature, and values. The peak of Sinification in the *gozan* was probably reached in the late fourteenth century with Gidō Shūshin and Zekkai Chūshin, both fine poets whose work was praised in China and who would have been as much at home in Chinese literary circles of the day as they were in the Kyoto *gozan*.

But Japan was very different from China. And even though a concerted effort was being made to recreate Chinese Ch'an monastic practice in Japan and raise the level of Chinese cultural awareness in the *gozan* monasteries, there were also signs of accommodation with the prevailing religious and cultural conditions in Japan. This accommodation with Japanese conditions was most striking in the transformation of Sōtō Zen after Dōgen's death, but it was also evident in Rinzai Zen from an early period.

---

96 *Zengaku daijiten.*
97 Yamagishi Tokuhei, ed., *Gozan bungaku-shū, Edo kanshi-shū Nihon koten bungaku taikei* (Tokyo: Iwanami shoten, 1968), vol. 89, p. 73; and Marian Ury, *Poems of the Five Mountains* (Tokyo: Mushinsha, 1977), p. 36.

Although Dōgen was critical of the lax standards he had observed in contemporary Chinese monasteries – monks who did not practice meditation wholeheartedly, who were dirty and smelled or who failed to cut their hair or trim their nails – he remained throughout his life a vigorous advocate of the monastic ideal of Pai-chang and of the severe meditation practice he had engaged in under the guidance of Ju-ching:

> After hearing this truth [of the sole importance of *zazen*] from my master, I sat in *zazen* day and night. Other monks, afraid that they might fall ill at time of great heat and cold, abandoned their meditation temporarily but I only urged myself harder with the thought: "I should devote myself to *zazen* even at risk of death from serious illness."[98]

Dōgen warned his followers against the temptations of building for themselves a lavish monastic environment that would stifle the energy of their Zen practice: "Don't be foolishly impressed with magnificent monastery buildings. The Buddhas and Patriarchs never sought fine temples. If you put up temples or monasteries without attaining true vision, you are not consecrating havens for the Buddhas but merely providing caves for your own glory and wealth."[99] But from his writings and his building activities at the Kōshoji and Eiheiji, it is clear that Dōgen wanted his communities to prize those buildings – especially the monks' hall, Dharma hall, and library – that had provided the traditional setting for meditation, *kōan* discussion, and study in Chinese Ch'an monasteries.

Although he was sometimes forced to modify regulations that had been written for large Chinese monasteries to suit his small community at Eiheiji, Dōgen took pains to preserve, or recover, what he believed to be authentic Ch'an monastic discipline as it had been instituted by Pai-chang and other T'ang masters. Even a trivial daily routine such as cleansing the teeth could be an expression of Zen performed in the proper manner: "Although in the Ch'an monasteries of great Sung nowadays the use of the wooden toothpick has gone out of fashion, and hence no place is provided for it, there is now a place for the wooden tooth cleaner here at Eiheiji. . . ."[100]

Thus Dōgen conceived of his ideal Zen community as one in which *zazen* would be the paramount activity. The setting might be simple, but it should at least include a meditation hall, library, and lecture

---

98 Nishio Minoru, *Zuimonki*, book 1, vol. 82 of *Shōbōgenzō, Shōbōgenzō zuimonki, Nihon koten bungaku taikei*, (Tokyo: 1965). An English translation of the *Zuimonki* is provided by Thomas Cleary, trans., *Record of Things Heard from the Treasury of the Eye of the True Teachings* (Boulder, Colo.: Shambala, 1982).
99 Dōgen, *Shōbōgenzō, Gyōji.*   100 Dōgen, *Shōbō genzō, Senmen.*

hall. Furthermore, though regulations might be modified to suit Japanese conditions, every effort should be made to preserve the monastic spirit of the Chinese patriarchs. Dōgen rejected accommodation with Confucianism and Taoism, with branches of Buddhism that did not accord primacy to *zazen*, and with popular or folk religious practices common around the Eiheiji.

The rapid expansion of Sōtō Zen was achieved only by a deliberate shift away from the exclusive, *zazen*-centered, Chinese-inspired monastic practice that Dōgen had espoused regarding a popular Zen that took into account the interests of ordinary lay people and was willing to combine with local Japanese religious conditions.

Whereas Dōgen had rejected opportunities to proselytize, declaring that all who sincerely wished to practice Zen would find his community, Keizan and his successors seized every opportunity to take their teachings to the people. Whereas Dōgen had avoided syncretism in the interest of preserving the centrality of *zazen*, his successors accepted into daily Sōtō practice the Tendai and Shingon texts and prayer ceremonies; Pure Land invocations; devotion to the *kannon* and to local mountain cults; and healing, exorcism, and funeral rites.

In Sōtō monasteries the forms of *zazen* were preserved, and Dōgen's writings and Chinese *kōan* collections were studied, but over time the *zazen* practice was diluted. The interviews between master and disciple (*sanzen*), which had been the core of Dōgen's Zen practice, were formalized and esotericized as model answers circulated among monks and secret oral and verbal transmissions were made from master to disciple. As *sanzen* lost its spontaneity, it was increasingly replaced by ceremonial public expressions of Zen, especially mass meetings for *gōkoe* and *jukai* at which hundreds of monks and lay people gathered for formalized meditation ceremonies or publicly to profess the Buddhist precepts. Undoubtedly these changes helped Sōtō Zen win large numbers of adherents and respond to the religious needs of peasants and samurai. At the same time, however, the more energy that the Sōtō monks put into popular ceremonial functions and large-scale public activities, the less that they could devote to private *zazen* and *sanzen*, and the further Sōtō Zen shifted, for good or ill, from the type of community that Dōgen had wished to establish at the Kōshōji and Eiheiji on the basis of his experience in China.[101]

In the development of Rinzai Zen, too, there was a growing tendency toward accommodation with Japanese medieval society and cul-

101 Takeuchi, *Nihon no zen*, p. 273.

ture. This process was less sharply defined than in the case of Sōtō Zen after Dōgen, but it can be detected in the areas of Zen thought and practice, the monastic life, and Zen-related cultural activities. Although Eisai and Enni had carefully observed Ch'an monastic life in China and sought to recreate it in Japan, pressure from supporters of established Buddhism, especially of the Enryakuji, obliged them to incorporate Tendai and Shingon buildings and rituals into their monasteries, the Kenninji and the Tōfukuji. Moreover, Eisai's *Kōzen gokokuron* (The promotion of Zen in defense of the country), for instance, argued that Zen was fully in accord with the ideals of Saichō, the founder of Tendai Buddhism in Japan, and that in return for support by political authorities, Zen monks, through their meditation and prayers, could provide the spiritual protection for the state that Tendai had traditionally claimed to offer.[102]

The influx of Chinese monks into Kamakura's and Kyoto's *gozan* monasteries in the late thirteenth century contributed to an emphasis on pure Sung monastic practice and unadulterated *kōan* Zen. Lan-ch'i set the tone by having the Kenchōji built in the Sung style and stressing, in particular, the importance that the communal life of meditation in the monks' hall (*sōdō*) had played in Ch'an Buddhism. All of the *gozan* monasteries built after the Kenchōji were built on the basic seven-hall layout characteristic of Sung Ch'an centers and regulated by the *Ch'an-yuan* and others codes governing the Chinese monasteries.

But despite this effort to adopt Chinese models, the Japanese features of monastic life could not be entirely eliminated. The ground plans of the early Kenchōji and Engakuji reveal that although all the public buildings of those monasteries – the great gate, Buddha hall, Dharma hall, monks' hall, kitchens, and bathrooms – were built in the Sung Chinese style of Ch'an monastic architecture, on the basis of drawings of actual Chinese monasteries, their abbot's buildings (*hōjō*) were in the Japanese residential style, including elements derived from Heian aristocratic buildings and gardens.[103] It has already been pointed out that from the late Kamakura period there was a proliferation of subtemples (*tatchū*) around the compounds of major Zen monasteries. Like the *hōjō* buildings, these too were built in the Japanese style.

Although Chinese masters stressed the primacy of *zazen* and *kōan* study as the core of Zen monastic life, during the frenzied years of the

---

102 *Kōzen gokokuron*, in Ichikawa Hakugen et al., eds., *Chūsei zenke no shisō* (Tokyo: 1972).
103 See, for instance, the ground plan of the medieval Kenchōji included in Yokoyama Hideya, *Zen no Kenchiku* (Tokyo: Shōkokusha, 1967), p. 282.

threatened Mongol invasions, the Zen monks, too, like the monks of
other schools of Japanese Buddhism, conducted frequent prayer ceremonies for the country's delivery. These introduced esoteric rituals
into the monastic timetable and thus inevitably reduced the time that
could be devoted to *zazen* and *sanzen*.

As the role of Chinese masters declined from the early fourteenth
century, Japanese influences, especially from Shingon Buddhism,
grew stronger in the *gozan*. Shingon practices had been incorporated
into the Rinzai Zen teaching of Muhon Kakushin and his followers,
but it was under the powerful influence of Musō Soseki that they
permeated *gozan* Zen monastic practice.

Musō's earliest religious training had been in Tendai and Shingon
Buddhism. He had begun his Zen practice under the Chinese monk I-
shan I-ning and had received recognition of his enlightenment after
studying with the Japanese monk Kōhō Kennichi. Kōhō, a member of
the imperial family, had a strong interest in esoteric Buddhism; Musō
never visited China, and thus it is not difficult to detect in his writings
an indifference to many of the contemporary trends in Chinese Ch'an
Buddhism and a receptivity to Japanese religious practices. In his
Muchū mondō, Musō argued that "although Zen teachings offered the
most direct way to grasp the root of enlightenment," esoteric prayers
and rituals provided a valuable expedient means (*hōben*) of attaining
the gateway to enlightenment, which could then be deepened by Zen
practice.[104] Musō's tolerance of Shingon practices had far-reaching
ramifications. Although there is no evidence that Musō himself conducted such rituals – in *Muchū mondō* and elsewhere he warned that
their excessive use would dilute Zen practice – he associated with
Shingon monks and had among his "ten thousand disciples" many
monks who combined Zen and esoteric Buddhism. The esoteric Japanese tone in the Zen teachings of Musō and his followers made them
particularly attractive to members of the court nobility as well as to
warriors. The readiness of the Musō school's monks to perform rituals
and prayer ceremonies for the welfare of the country, the recovery of a
shogun from sickness, and for relief from drought or famine made the
gozan monasteries that much more useful as religious agents of the
bakufu.

During the fourteenth and fifteenth centuries, many Zen monks
adopted the Pure Land practice of *nembutsu*. Some of these Pure Land

---

104 Musō Soseki, *Muchū mondō*, vol. 1, stage 15 in Satō Taishun, ed., *Muchū mondō* (Tokyo:
Iwanami shoten, 1934).

influences came from medieval Japanese religion, in which devotion to Amida was a powerful current. Other influences came from China. One branch of Ch'an Buddhism during the Yüan and Ming dynasties combined an eremitic ideal with Pure Land devotion. A few Chinese monks of this school found their way to Japan. But many more Japanese monks who visited China in the fourteenth century adopted Pure Land beliefs. Some *gozan* monks, like Nankō Sogan (1397–1463), remained hostile to any accommodation with Pure Land. In a long poem from which the following lines are taken, Nankō heaped scorn on the practitioners of the dancing *nembutsu* (*odori nembutsu*) that had become popular in Kyoto:

> They suddenly leap up, arms flailing hands never at rest,
> As mile after mile booms with empyrean thunderclaps.
> Men dress in women's clothes, women imitate men,
> In red kerchiefs, white caps, torn and tattered shifts,
> Their mouths swell with cries of "*Namu Amida Butsu!*"
> Till their "butsu-butsu-butsu" sounds like a pot bubbling over.[105]

Although he was less interested in Pure Land than in Shingon Buddhism, Musō was tolerant of the *nembutsu* teaching, regarding it as a means of approaching the deeper truth of Zen for those people who were not yet ready to commit themselves fully to *zazen*. Many of his followers thus recited the *nembutsu* as part of their daily Zen practice.[106]

Just as the "pure Sung Zen monastic practice" of the Kamakura period was colored by Japanese religious elements in the Muromachi period, so too was the Chinese tone of *gozan* culture tinged by the influence of Japanese aesthetics and literary taste. What we think of as the typical Zen garden, using stones and moss instead of trees and water, reflects a blending of the Ch'an monastic garden and Japanese taste and garden design. Zen-inspired ink painting and portraiture, based at first on Sung ideals, acquired a Japanese character at the hands of Shūbun and Sesshū. The tea ceremony, which had been nurtured in Zen monasteries before it became a passion among merchants and daimyo, saw the introduction of Japanese tastes and utensils alongside prized Chinese ware.

In literature, too, Japanese influences were evident in *gozan* circles from the fourteenth century. Musō's mentor Kōhō Kennichi composed *waka* and had verses included in imperial anthologies. Musō

---

105 Translated by David Pollack, *Zen Poems of the Five Mountains* (Decatur, Ga.: Scholars Press, 1985), p. 80.   106 Tamamura, *Musō Soseki*, pp. 137–43.

himself seems to have been more at home with Japanese verse than with Chinese poetry. Even Gidō and Zekkai, who were acknowledged masters of Chinese versification, were active participants in mixed Japanese-Chinese *renga* gatherings with courtiers and high-ranking samurai. They and other *gozan* monks read the Japanese literary classics and composed verses on Japanese themes, such as the following reflection by Zekkai on the destruction of the Taira:

Akamagaseki:
The scene before me brings sorrow night and day,
A cold tide battering the Red Walls;
Among weird crags and fantastic boulders, a temple in the clouds,
Between the new moon and the setting sun, boats on the sea.
A hundred thousand valiant warriors have turned to empty silence,
Three thousand swordsmen are gone forever;
Heroes' bones rot in a soil of shields and lances –
Thinking of them, I lean on the balustrade, watch the white gulls.[107]

Finally, looking back over the role of Zen in medieval society, what have we seen? Most obviously, of course, the history of medieval Zen involved the importation and growth of an institution that, by the fifteenth century, embraced thousands of temples and tens of thousands of monks, nuns, novices, and monastery servants. In the early phase of its development, Zen encountered determined opposition from monks belonging to the established schools of Japanese Buddhism. It prevailed only with the backing of enthusiastic sponsors at all levels of society. The various branches of the Zen schools reached from Kyoto and Kamakura into almost every village in Japan. Zen monastic landholdings were scattered throughout the country, and the Zen monastic economy reflected the economic possibilities and problems of the age. Zen monks consorted with shoguns, emperors, *shugo*, provincial warriors, *sengoku* daimyo, townspeople, artists and entertainers, and peasants. They were among the spiritual pioneers and leading educators of the time, spreading not only the Buddhist meditation practice of *zazen* but also a broader understanding of Buddhism in general and of Chinese and Japanese secular culture.

From the viewpoint of their secular patrons, Zen monks and monasteries played many roles. Apart from providing spiritual and cultural guidance, monks served as diplomats and political advisers, offered prayers for relief from famines, and conducted funeral services. Monasteries trained the children of warrior families, contributed to family

107 Translated by David Pollack, *Zen Poems of the Five Mountains*, p. 105.

and local unity and stability, and in some cases made financial loans or organized welfare projects. The *gozan* system, in particular, was seen by the Ashikaga as conducive to national centralization and local surveillance. But other Rinzai and Sōtō monasteries played similar roles in daimyo domains. Responsive to these many demands, Zen monasteries became deeply enmeshed in the fabric of medieval society.

Medieval Zen was neither monolithic nor static. The *gozan* schools, the Daitokuji and the Myōshinji, and Sōtō Zen all had their own characteristics and followed different patterns of development. In their diverse ways, however, they came to terms with the society in which they had taken root. The expansion of Sōtō Zen and the Daiō branches of Rinzai Zen was based on a deliberate effort to take Zen to local warriors, peasants, and townspeople, even at the cost of diluting the traditional Ch'an monastic ideal and the strict meditation practice advocated by their founders. Under the patronage of the shogunate, the *gozan* was better able to preserve its elite Chinese, meditation-centered monastic ideal. But even the *gozan* monasteries were not totally isolated from the cultural ebb and flow of medieval Japanese society.

WORKS CITED

Abe, Masao, and Waddell, Norman, trans. "Dōgen's *Bendōwa*." *The Eastern Buddhist* 4 (May 1971): 124-57.

Abe, Masao, and Waddell, Norman, trans. "Dōgen's *Fukanzazengi*." *The Eastern Buddhist* 6 (October 1973): 121-6.

Abe Yukihiro 阿部征寛. *Mōko shūrai*. 蒙古襲来. Tokyo: Kyōikusha 教育社, 1980.

Aida Nirō 相田二郎. *Mōko shūrai no kenkyū*. 蒙古襲来の研究. Tokyo: Yoshikawa kōbunkan 吉川弘文館, 1971.

Akamatsu Toshihide 赤松俊秀. *Kamakura Bukkyō no kenkyū* 鎌倉仏教の研究. Kyoto: Heirakuji shoten 平楽寺書店, 1957.

Akamatsu Toshihide 赤松俊秀. *Shinran* 親鸞. Tokyo: Yoshikawa kōbunkan 吉川弘文館, 1961.

Akamatsu Toshihide 赤松俊秀, ed. *Nihon Bukkyōshi* 日本仏教史, vol. 2. Kyoto: Hōzōkan 法蔵館, 1967.

Akamatsu Toshihide 赤松俊秀, and Kasahara Kazuo 笠原一男, eds. *Shinshūshi gaisetsu* 真宗史概説. Kyoto: Heirakuji shoten 平楽寺書店, 1963.

Akamatsu Toshihide, and Yampolsky, Philip. "Muromachi Zen and the Gozan System." In John Whitney Hall and Toyoda Takeshi, eds. *Japan in the Muromachi Age*. Berkeley and Los Angeles: University of California Press, 1977.

Akiyama Kenzō 秋山謙蔵. "Muromachi shoki ni okeru Kyūshū tandai no Chosen to no kotsu" 室町初期における九州探題の朝鮮との交通. *Shigaku zasshi* 史学雑誌 42 (April 1931).

Akiyama Kenzō 秋山謙蔵. "Muromachi shoki ni okeru wakō no chōryō to Kyūshū tandai" 室町初期における倭寇の跳梁と九州探題. *Rekishi Chiri* 歴史地理 57 (April 1931).

Akiyama Kenzō 秋山謙蔵. "Muromachi shoki ni okeru wakō no chōryō to Ōei gaikō jijō" 室町初期における倭寇の跳梁と応永外寇事情. *Shigaku zasshi* 史学雑誌 42 (September 1931).

Akiyama Kenzō 秋山謙蔵. "Nichimin kankei" 日明関係. In *Iwanami kōza Nihon rekishi* 岩波講座日本歴史, vol. 1. Tokyo: Iwanami shoten 岩波書店, 1933.

Akiyama Kenzō 秋山謙蔵. *Nisshi kōshō shiwa* 日支交渉史話. Tokyo: Naigai shoseki kabushiki kaisha 内外書籍株式会社, 1935.

Akiyama Kenzō 秋山謙蔵. *Nisshi kōshōshi kenkyū* 日支交渉史研究. Tokyo: Iwanami shoten 岩波書店, 1939.

Akiyama Kunizō 秋山国三, and Nakamura Ken 仲村研. *Kyōto "machi" no kenkyū* 京都「町」の研究. Tokyo: Hōsei daigaku shuppankyoku 法政大学出版局, 1975.

Amakasu Ken et al. 甘粕健他, eds. *Nihon gijutsu no shakaishi* 日本技術の社会史, vol. 1. Tokyo: Nihon hyōronsha 日本評論社, 1983.

Amino Yoshihiko 網野善彦. *Chūsei shōen no yōsō* 中世荘園の様相. Tokyo: Tachibana shobō 橘書房, 1966.

Amino Yoshihiko 網野善彦. "Wakasa no kuni ni okeru shōensei no keisei" 若狭の国における荘園制の形成. In Takeuchi Rizō hakase kanreki kinenkai 竹内理三博士還暦記念会, comp. *Shōensei to buke shakai* 荘園制と武家社会. Tokyo: Yoshikawa kōbunkan 吉川弘文館, 1969.

Amino Yoshihiko 網野善彦. "Kamakura makki no shomujun" 鎌倉末期の諸矛盾. In Rekishigaku kenkyūkai and Nihonshi kenkyūkai 歴史学研究会・日本史研究会, comp. *Kōza Nihonshi* 講座日本史, vol. 3. Tokyo: Tōkyō daigaku shuppankai 東京大学出版会, 1970.

Amino Yoshihiko 網野善彦. "Kamakura bakufu no kaizoku kin'atsu ni tsuite – Kamakura makki no kaijō keigo o chūshin ni" 鎌倉幕府の海賊禁圧について – 鎌倉末期の海上警護を中心に. *Nihon rekishi* 日本歴史, no. 299 (April 1973): 1-20.

Amino Yoshihiko 網野善彦. "Shōen kōryōsei no keisei to kōzō" 荘園公領制の形成と構造. In Takeuchi Rizō 竹内理三, ed. *Tochi seidoshi* 土地制度史, vol. 1. Tokyo: Yoshikawa kōbunkan 吉川弘文館, 1973.

Amino Yoshihiko 網野善彦. *Mōko shūrai* 蒙古襲来. Vol. 10 of *Nihon no rekishi* 日本の歴史. Tokyo: Shōgakkan 小学館, 1974.

Amino Yoshihiko 網野善彦. "Zōshushi kōjiyaku no seiritsu ni tsuite – Muromachi bakufu sakayayaku no zentei" 造酒司麹役の成立について – 室町幕府酒屋役の前提. In Takeuchi Rizō hakase koki kinenkai 竹内理三博士古希記念会, comp. *Zoku shōensei to buke shakai* 続荘園制と武家社会. Tokyo: Yoshikawa kōbunkan 吉川弘文館, 1978.

Amino Yoshihiko 網野善彦. "Nihon chūsei no heimin to shokunin" 日本中世の平民と職人. *Shisō* 思想, no. 670 (1980): 1-25 and no. 671 (1980): 73-92.

Amino Yoshihiko 網野善彦. *Chūsei tennō-sei to hi-nōgyōmin* 中世天皇制と非農業民. Tokyo: Iwanami shoten 岩波書店, 1984.

Aoki Michio et al. 青木美智男他, eds. *Seikatsu, bunka, shisō* 生活・文化・思想. Vol. 4 of *Ikki* 一揆. Tokyo: Tōkyō daigaku shuppankai 東京大学出版会, 1981.

Aoyama Kōryō 青山公亮. *Nichirai kōshōshi no kenkyū* 日麗交渉史の研究. Tokyo: Meiji daigaku bungakubu bungaku kenkyūsho 明治大学文学部文学研究所, 1955.

Arakawa Hidetoshi 荒川秀俊. "Bun'ei no eki no owari o tsugeta no wa taifū dewa nai" 文永の役の終りを告げたのは台風ではない. *Nihon rekishi* 日本歴史 120 (June 1958): 41-45.

Araki, James T. "*Bunshō sōshi*: The Tale of Bunshō, the Saltmaker." *Monu-

menta Nipponica 38, no. 3 (Autumn 1983): 221-49.

Araki Kengo 荒木健吾. "Zen" 禅. In Kubo Noritada 窪徳忠, and Nishi Junzō 西
順三, eds. *Shūkyō* 宗教. Vol. 6 of *Chūgoku bunka sōsho* 中国文化叢書. Tokyo:
Taishūkan shoten 大修館書店, 1968.

Araki Moriaki 安良城盛昭. *Taikō kenchi to kokudakasei* 太閤検地と石高制.
Tokyo: Nihon hōsō shuppan kyōkai 日本放送出版協会, 1969.

Arimitsu Yūgaku 有光友学. "Chūsei kōki ni okeru bōeki shōnin no dōkō" 中世
後期における貿易商人の動向. *Shizuoka daigaku jimbun gakubu jimbun ronshū*
静岡大学人文学部人文論集, no. 21 (January 1971).

Arimitsu Yūgaku 有光友学, ed. *Sengokuki kenryoku to chiiki shakai* 戦国期権力
と地域社会. Tokyo: Yoshikawa kōbunkan 吉川弘文館, 1986.

Arnesen, Peter. *The Medieval Japanese Daimyo: The Ōuchi Family's Rule in Suō
and Nagato*: New Haven, Conn.: Yale University Press, 1979.

Arnesen, Peter. "The Provincial Vassals of the Muromachi Bakufu." In Jeffrey
P. Mass and William B. Hauser, eds. *The Bakufu in Japanese History*. Stanford, Calif.: Stanford University Press, 1985.

Ashida Koreto 蘆田伊人. *Goryōchi-shikō* 御料地史考. Tokyo: Teishitsu Rinya
kyoku 帝室林野局, 1937.

Atago Matsuo 愛宕松男. *Ajia no seifuku ōchō* アジアの征服王朝. Vol. 11 of *Sekai
no rekishi* 世界の歴史. Tokyo: Kawade shobō 河出書房, 1969.

Bitō Masahide 尾藤正英, ed. *Nihon bunka to Chūgoku* 日本文化と中国. Tokyo:
Daishūkan shoten 大修館書店, 1968.

Blacker, Carmen. *The Catalpa Bow: A Study of Shamanistic Practices in Japan.*
London: Allen & Unwin, 1975.

Brazell, Karen, trans. *The Confessions of Lady Nijō.* New York: Anchor Books,
1973.

Bukkyō daigaku 仏教大学, ed. *Hōnen Shōnin kenkyū* 法然上人研究. Kyoto:
Heirakuji shoten 平楽寺書店, 1961.

Buraku mondai kenkyūjo 部落問題研究所, ed. *Burakushi no kenkyū* 部落史の研
究, premodern vol. Tokyo: Buraku mondai kenkyūjo 部落問題研究所, 1978.

Butler, Kenneth Dean. "The Textual Evolution of the *Heike monogatari.*" *Harvard Journal of Asiatic Studies* 26 (1966): 5-51.

Butler, Kenneth Dean. "The *Heike Monogatari* and the Japanese Warrior
Ethic." *Harvard Journal of Asiatic Studies* 29 (1969): 93-108.

Childs, Margaret Helen. "Religious Awakening Stories in Late Medieval
Japan: The Dynamics of Didacticism." Ph.D. diss., University of Pennsylvania, 1983.

Chūgoku bunka sōsho 中国文化叢書. 10 vols. Tokyo: Daishūkan shoten 大修館書
店, 1967-78.

Cleary, Thomas, trans. *Record of Things Heard from the Treasury of the Eye of
the True Teachings.* Boulder, Colo.: Shambala, 1982.

Collcutt, Martin. *Five Mountains: The Rinzai Zen Monastic Institution in
Medieval Japan.* Cambridge, Mass.: Harvard University Press, 1981.

Cooper, Michael, ed. *They Came to Japan.* Berkeley and Los Angeles: University of California Press, 1965.

Coulborn, Rushton, ed. *Feudalism in History*. Princeton, N. J.: Princeton University Press, 1956.

Daihonzan Kenchōji 大本山建長寺, ed. *Kyofukuzan Kenchōji* 巨福山建長寺. Tokyo: Daihonzan Kenchōji 大本山建長寺, 1977.

Dai Nihon Bukkyō zensho 大日本仏教全書, 160 vols. Tokyo: Dai Nihon Bukkyō zensho hakkōjo 大日本仏教全書発行所, 1912-22.

Dai Nihon jiin sōran 大日本寺院総覧. Tokyo: Meiji shuppansha 明治出版社, 1917.

Dai Nihon komonjo, Ie wake 大日本古文書家わけ 16, vol. 1. Tokyo: Tōkyō daigaku shiryō hensanjō 東京大学史料編纂所, 1942.

Dai Nihon shiryō 大日本史料, vol. 9. Tokyo: Tōkyō teikoku daigaku 東京帝国大学, 1909.

Doi, Tsugiyoshi. *Momoyama Decorative Painting*. New York: Weatherhill-Heibonsha, 1977.

Dorson, Richard M., ed. *Studies in Japanese Folklore*. Bloomington: Indiana University Folklore Series, no. 17, Indiana University Press, 1963.

Dumoulin, Heinrich. *A History of Zen Buddhism*. New York: Pantheon, 1963.

Durkheim, Emile. *The Rules of Sociological Method*. Glencoe, N. Y.: Free Press, 1950.

Endō Iwao 遠藤巌. "Ōshū kanrei oboegaki" 奥州管領おぼえ書. *Rekishi* 歴史, no. 38 (March 1969): 24-66.

Endō Iwao 遠藤巌. "Nambokuchō nairan no naka de 南北朝内乱のなかで. In Kobayashi Seiji 小林清治 and Ōishi Naomasa 大石直正, eds. *Chūsei Ōu no sekai* 中世奥羽の世界. Tokyo: Tōkyō daigaku shuppankai 東京大学出版会, 1978.

Endō Motoo 遠藤元男. *Nihon chūsei toshi ron* 日本中世都市論. Tokyo: Hakuyōsha 白楊社, 1940.

Fontein, Jan, and Hickman, Money L., eds. *Zen Painting and Calligraphy*. Boston: Boston Museum of Fine Arts, 1970.

Fuji Masaharu 富士正晴, ed. *Mampukuji* 万福寺. Tokyo: Tankōsha 淡交社, 1977.

Fujii Manabu 藤井学. "Tōgoku Hokke kyōdan no seiritsu to tenkai" 東国法華教団の成立と展開. In Akamatsu Toshihide 赤松俊秀, ed. *Nihon Bukkyōshi* 日本仏教史, 1967.

Fujiki Hisashi 藤木久志. *Sengoku shakai shiron* 戦国社会史論. Tokyo: Tōkyō daigaku shuppankai 東京大学出版会, 1974.

Fujiki, Toyohiko, with Elison, George. "The Political Posture of Oda Nobunaga." In John Whitney Hall, Keiji Nagahara, and Kozo Yamamura, eds. *Japan Before Tokugawa: Political Consolidation and Economic Growth, 1500-1650*. Princeton, N. J.: Princeton University Press, 1981.

Fujioka Daisetsu 藤岡大拙. "Gozan kyōdan no hatten ni kansuru ichi kōsatsu" 五山教団の発展に関する一考案. *Bukkyō shigaku* 仏教史学 6 (March 1957): 47-66.

Fujioka Daisetsu 藤岡大拙. "Zen'in nai ni okeru tōhanshū ni tsuite" 禅院内にお

ける東班衆について. *Nihon rekishi* 日本歴史, no. 145 (July 1960): 19-28.

Fujita Motoharu 藤田元春. *Nisshi kōtsū no kenkyū chū-kinseihen* 日支交通の研究, 中近世編. Tokyo: Fuzambō 冨山房, 1938.

Fujita Toshio 藤田俊雄. "Kamakura shoki no Dazaifu kikō ni tsuite" 鎌倉初期の太宰府機構について. *Kumamoto shigaku* 熊本史学 55 (May 1981).

Fujiwara Kanenaka 藤原兼仲. "Kanchū ki" 勘仲記. In Sasagawa Taneo 笹川種郎, comp. *Shiryō taisei* 史料大成. Tokyo: Naigai shoseki 内外書籍, 1937.

Fukuda Ikuo 福田以久男. "Shugoyaku kō" 守護役考. In Hōgetsu Keigo sensei kanreki kinenkai 宝月圭吾先生還暦記念会編, ed. *Nihon shakai keizaishi kenkyū* 日本社会経済史研究, medieval vol. Tokyo: Yoshikawa kōbunkan 吉川弘文館, 1967.

Fukuda Toyohiko 福田豊彦. "Kokujin ikki no ichi sokumen" 国人一揆の一側面. *Shigaku zasshi* 史学雑誌 76 (January 1967): 62-80.

Fukuda Toyohiko 福田豊彦. "Muromachi bakufu no hōkōshū" 室町幕府の奉公衆. *Nihon rekishi* 日本歴史, no. 274 (March 1971): 46-65.

Fukuda Toyohiko 福田豊彦. "Muromachi bakufu no hōkōshū no kenkyū - sono jin'in kōsei to chiikiteki bumpu" 室町幕府の奉公衆の研究－その人員構成と地域的分布. *Hokkaidō musashi joshi tanki daigaku kiyō* 北海道武蔵女子短期大学紀要, no. 3 (March 1971): 1-52.

Fukuda Toyohiko 福田豊彦. "Muromachi bakufu hōkōshū no kenkyū - sono jin'in to chiikiteki bumpu" 室町幕府奉公衆の研究－その人員と地域的分布. In Ogawa Makoto 小川信, ed. *Muromachi seiken* 室町政権. Vol. 5 of *Ronshū Nihon rekishi* 論集日本歴史. Tokyo: Yūshōdō 雄松堂, 1975.

Fukuokashi kyōiku iinkai 福岡市教育委員会. *Iimori jinja kankei shiryōshu* 飯盛神社関係史料集. Fukuoka: Fukuokashi kyōiku iinkai 福岡市教育委員会, 1981.

Fukushima Shun'ō 福島俊翁. *Kokan* 虎関. Tokyo: Yūzankaku 雄山閣, 1944.

Gay, Suzanne. "Muromachi Bakufu Rule in Kyoto: Administration and Judicial Aspects." In Jeffrey P. Mass and William B. Hauser, eds. *The Bakufu in Japanese History*. Stanford, Calif.: Stanford University Press, 1985.

Goble, Andrew. "The Hōjō and Consultative Government." In Jeffrey P. Mass, ed. *Court and Bakufu in Japan: Essays in Kamakura History*. New Haven, Conn.: Yale University Press, 1982.

Gomi Fumihiko 五味文彦. "Shichō no kōsei to bakufu: jūni-jūyon seiki no rakuchū shihai" 使庁の構成と幕府: 12〜14世紀の洛中支配. *Rekishigaku kenkyū* 歴史学研究, no. 392 (January 1973): 1-19.

Gomi Katsuo 五味克夫. "Nitta-gū shitsuin Michinori gushoan sonota" 新田宮執印道教具書案その他. *Nihon rekishi* 日本歴史, no. 310 (March 1974): 13-26.

Gorai Shigeru 五来重. *Gangōji-Gokurakubō chūsei shomin shinkō shiryō no kenkyū-chijō hakkenbutsu hen* 元興寺−極楽房中世庶民信仰資料の研究-地上発見物編. Kyoto: Hōzōkan 法蔵館, 1964.

Gorai Shigeru 五来重. "Chūsei josei no shūkyōsei to seikatsu" 中世女性の宗教性と生活. In Joseishi sōgō kenkyūkai 女性史総合研究会, ed. *Nihon joseishi* 日本女性史, vol. 2. Tokyo: Tōkyō daigaku shuppankai 東京大学出版会, 1983.

Gotō Norihiko 後藤紀彦. "Tanaka bon seifu - bunrui o kokoromita kuge shinsei no koshahon" 田中本政府 - 分類を試みた公家新制の古写本. *Nempō, chūseishi kenkyū* 年報, 中世史研究, no. 5 (May 1980): 73-86.

Grossberg, Kenneth A. "Bakufu and Bugyonin: The Size of the House Bureaucracy in Muromachi Japan." *Journal of Asian Studies* 35 (August 1976): 651-4.

Grossberg, Kenneth A. *Japan's Renaissance: The Politics of the Muromachi Bakufu.* Cambridge, Mass.: Harvard University Press, 1981.

Grossberg, Kenneth A. ed., and Kanamoto, Nobuhisa, trans. *The Laws of the Muromachi Bakufu: Kemmu Shikimoku (1336) and the Muromachi Tsuikahō.* Tokyo: *Monumenta Nipponica* and Sophia University, 1981.

Gunsho ruijū 群書類従, vol. 4. Tokyo: Keizai zasshisha 経済雑誌社, 1898.

Gyobutsubon, Mōko shūrai ekotoba (fukusei) 御物本・蒙古襲来絵詞（複製）. Fukuoka: Fukuokashi kyōiku iinkai 福岡市教育委員会, 1975.

Gyokuyō 玉葉, vols. 2 and 3. Tokyo: Kokusho kankōkai 国書刊行会, 1907.

Haga Kōshirō 芳賀幸四郎, ed. *Daitokuji to sadō* 大徳寺と茶道. Kyoto: Tankōsha 淡交社, 1972.

Haga Kōshirō et al. 芳賀幸四郎, eds. *Sanjōnishi Sanetaka* 三条西実隆. Vol. 43 of *Jimbutsu sōsho* 人物叢書. Tokyo: Yoshikawa kōbunkan 吉川弘文館, 1960.

Haga Norihiko 羽下徳彦. "Muromachi bakufu samurai dokoro tōnin, tsuketari: Yamashiro shugo bunin enkaku kōshōkō" 室町幕府侍所頭人付山城守護補任沿革考証稿 *Tōyō daigaku kiyō* 東洋大学紀要, Faculty of Letters vol., no. 16 (July 1962): 77-98.

Haga Norihiko 羽下徳彦. "Muromachi bakufuron" 室町幕府論. In Nihon rekishigaku kenkyūkai 日本歴史学研究会, ed. *Nihonshi no mondaiten* 日本史の問題点. Tokyo: Yoshikawa kōbunkan 吉川弘文館, 1965.

Haga Norihiko 羽下徳彦. *Sōryōsei* 惣領制. Tokyo: Shibundō 至文堂, 1966.

Haga Norihiko 羽下徳彦. "Muromachi bakufu samurai dokoro kō" 室町幕府侍所考. In Ogawa Makoto 小川信, ed. *Muromachi seiken* 室町政権. Vol. 5 of *Ronshū Nihon rekishi* 論集日本歴史. Tokyo: Yūshōdō 雄松堂, 1975.

Hall, John Whitney. *Government and Local Power in Japan, 500-1700: A Study Based on Bizen Province.* Princeton, N. J.: Princeton University Press, 1966.

Hall, John Whitney. *Japan from Prehistory to Modern Times.* New York: Dell, 1970.

Hall, John Whitney, and Craig, Albert M. *Japan: Tradition and Transformation.* New York: Houghton Mifflin, 1973.

Hall, John Whitney, and Mass, Jeffrey P., eds. *Medieval Japan: Essays in Institutional History.* New Haven, Conn.: Yale University Press, 1974.

Hall, John Whitney, Nagahara, Keiji, and Yamamura, Kozo, eds. *Japan Before Tokugawa: Political Consolidation and Economic Growth, 1500-1650.* Princeton, N. J.: Princeton University Press, 1981.

Hall, John Whitney, and Toyoda Takashi, eds. *Japan in the Muromachi Age.* Berkeley and Los Angeles: University of California Press, 1977.

Hanawa Hokinoichi 塙保巳一, comp. *Gunsho ruijū* 群書類従, vols. 22 and 25. Tokyo: Zoku gunsho ruijū kansei kai 続群書類従完成会, 1933.

Hara Katsurō 原勝郎. *Nihon chūseishi no kenkyū* 日本中世史の研究. Tokyo: Dōbunkan 同文館, 1929.

Harrington, Lorraine F. "Social Control and the Significance of Akutō." In Jeffrey P. Mass, ed. *Court and Bakufu in Japan: Essays in Kamakura History.* New Haven, Conn.: Yale University Press, 1982.

Harrington, Lorraine F. "Regional Outposts of Muromachi Bakufu Rule: The Kantō and Kyūshū." In Jeffrey P. Mass and William B. Hauser, eds. *The Bakufu in Japanese History.* Stanford, Calif.: Stanford University Press, 1985.

Harrison, John A., ed. *New Light on Early and Medieval Japanese Historiography.* Gainesville: University of Florida Monographs in Social Sciences, no. 4, University of Florida Press, 1959.

Hashimoto Mampei 橋本万平. *Keisoku no bunkashi* 計測の文化史. Tokyo: Asahi shimbunsha 朝日新聞社, 1982.

Hashimoto Yoshihiko 橋本義彦. *Heian kizoku shakai no kenkyū* 平安貴族社会の研究. Tokyo: Yoshikawa kōbunkan 吉川弘文館, 1976.

Hatada Takashi 旗田巍. *Genkō – Mōko teikoku no naibu jijō* 元寇 – 蒙古帝国の内部事情. Tokyo: Chūō kōronsha 中央公論社, 1965.

Hayashiya Tatsusaburō 林屋辰三郎, ed. *Kodai-chūsei geijutsu ron* 古代中世芸術論. Tokyo: Iwanami shoten 岩波書店, 1973.

Hayashiya Tatsusaburō 林屋辰三郎 et al., *Kyōto no rekishi* 京都の歴史. Kyoto: Gakugei shorin 学芸書林, 1968.

Hayashiya Tatsusaburō 林屋辰三郎, and Okada Yuzuru 岡田譲, eds. *Ami to machishū* 阿弥と町衆. Vol. 8 of *Nihon bunka no rekishi* 日本文化の歴史. Tokyo: Gakushūkenkyūsha 学習研究社, 1969.

Heiji monogatari emaki, Mōko shūrai ekotoba 平氏物語絵巻, 蒙古襲来絵詞. Vol. 9 of *Nihon emakimono zenshū* 日本絵巻物全集. Tokyo: Kadokawa shoten 角川書店, 1964.

Higaonna Kanjun 東恩納寛惇. *Reimeiki no kaigai kōtsūshi* 黎明期の海外交通史. Tokyo: Teikoku kyōikukai shuppanbu 帝国教育出版部, 1941.

Hiraizumi Kiyoshi 平泉澄. *Chūsei ni okeru shaji to shakai to no kankei* 中世における社寺と社会との関係. Tokyo: Shibundō 至文堂, 1934.

Hiraizumi Kiyoshi 平泉澄. "Nihon chūkō" 日本中興. In Kemmu chūkō roppyakunen kinenkai 建武中興六百年記念会, comp. *Kemmu chūkō* 建武中興. Tokyo: Kemmu chūkō roppyakunen kinenkai 建武中興六百年記念会, 1934.

Hirowatari Masatoshi 広渡正利. *Hakata jōtenjishi* 博多承天寺史. Tokyo: Bunka shuppan 文化出版, 1977.

Hirowatari Masatoshi 広渡正利. *Hakata jōtenjishi* 博多承天寺史. Fukuoka: Fukuoka-ken bunka kaikan 福岡県文化会館, 1981.

Hisamatsu Sen'ichi 久松潜一, and Nishio Minoru 西尾実, eds. *Karonshū, Nogakuronshū* 歌論集, 能楽論集. Vol. 65 of *Nihon koten bungaku taikei* 日本文学古典大系. Tokyo: Iwanami shoten 岩波書店, 1965.

Hoff, Frank. *Song, Dance, Storytelling: Aspects of the Performing Arts in Japan.* Ithaca, N. Y.: Cornell University East Asian Papers, no. 15, Cornell University Press, 1978.

Hōgetsu Keigo sensei kanreki kinenkai 宝月圭吾先生還暦記念会, ed. *Chūsei ryōseishi no kenkyū* 中世量制史の研究. Tokyo: Yoshikawa kōbunkan 吉川弘文館, 1961.

Hōgetsu Keigo sensei kanreki kinenkai 宝月圭吾先生還暦記念会, ed. *Nihon shakai keizaishi kenkyū* 日本社会経済史研究, medieval vol. Tokyo: Yoshikawa kōbunkan 吉川弘文館, 1967.

Hori Ichirō. "Mysterious Visitors from the Harvest to the New Year." In Richard M. Dorson, ed. *Studies in Japanese Folklore*. Bloomington: Indiana University Folklore Series, no. 17, Indiana University Press, 1963.

Hori Ichirō 堀一郎. *Nihon no shamanizumu* 日本のシャーマニズム. Tokyo: Kōdansha 講談社, 1971.

Hori, Kyotsu. "The Economic and Political Effects of the Mongol Wars." In John Whitney Hall and Jeffrey P. Mass, eds. *Medieval Japan: Essays in Institutional History*. New Haven, Conn.: Yale University Press, 1974.

Ichiji Tetsuo 伊知地鉄男, ed. *Renga shū* 連歌集. Tokyo: Iwanami shoten 岩波書店, 1960.

Ichikawa Hakugen 市川白弦 et al., comps. *Chūsei zenka no shisō* 中世禅家の思想. Tokyo: Iwanami shoten 岩波書店, 1972.

"Ichiki monjo" 一木文書. In *Ichikawa shishi, kodai-chūsei shiryō* 市川市史, 古代・中世史の研究. Ichikawa: Ichikawa shi 市川市, 1973.

Ichiko Teiji 市子貞次, ed. *Otogizōshi* 御伽草子. Vol. 13 of *Zusetsu Nihon no koten* 図説日本の古典. Tokyo: Shūeisha 集英社, 1980.

Ienaga Saburō 家長三郎. *Chūsei Bukkyō shisōshi kenkyū* 中世仏教思想史研究. Kyoto: Hōzōkan 法蔵館, 1957.

Iida Hisao 飯田久夫. "Heishi to Kyūshū" 平氏と九州. In Takeuchi Rizō hakase kanreki kinenkai 竹内理三博士還暦記念会, comp. *Shōensei to buke shakai* 荘園制と武家社会. Tokyo: Yoshikawa kōbunkan 吉川弘文館, 1969.

Iikura Harutake 飯倉晴武. "Ōnin no ran ikō ni okeru Muromachi bakufu no seisaku" 応仁の乱以降における室町幕府の政策. *Nihonshi kenkyū* 日本史研究, no. 139-40 (March 1974): 140-55.

Ikeuchi Hiroshi 池内宏. "Minsho ni okeru Nihon to Shina to no kōshō" 明初における日本と支那との交渉. *Rekishi to chiri* 歴史と地理 6 (May-August 1904).

Ikeuchi Hiroshi 池内宏. *Genkō no shinkenkyū* 元寇の新研究. 2 vols. Tokyo: Tōyō bunko 東洋文庫, 1931.

Ikki 一揆. 5 vols. Tokyo: Tōkyō daigaku shuppankai 東京大学出版会, 1981.

Imaeda Aishin 今枝愛真. *Zenshū no rekishi* 禅宗の歴史. Tokyo: Shibundō 至文堂, 1962.

Imaeda Aishin 今枝愛真. "Dōgen Sōhō Kanzan no monryū" 道元, 宗彭, 関山の門流. In Akamatsu Toshihide 赤松俊秀, ed. *Nihon Bukkyōshi* 日本仏教史, vol. 2. Kyoto: Hōzōkan 法蔵館, 1967.

Imaeda Aishin 今枝愛真. *Chūsei Zenshū-shi no kenkyū* 中世禅宗史の研究. Tokyo: Tōkyō daigaku shuppankai 東京大学出版会, 1970.

Imaeda Aishin 今枝愛真. *Dōgen: sono kōdō to shisō* 道現, その行動と思想. Tokyo: Hyōronsha 評論社, 1970.

Imaeda Aishin 今枝愛真, ed. *Zenshū no shomondai* 禅宗の諸問題. Tokyo: Yūzankaku 雄山閣, 1979.

Imaeda Aishin 今枝愛真. *Dōgen: zazen hitosuji no shamon* 道元, 坐禅ひとすじの沙門. Tokyo: Nihon hōsō shūppankyōkai 日本放送出版協会, 1981.

Imaeda Aishin 今枝愛真, and Murai Shōsuke 村井章介. "Nichimin kōshōshi no jomaku 日明交渉史の序幕." *Tōkyō daigaku shiryō hensanjo hō* 東京大学史料編纂所報, no. 11 (March 1977).

Imaoka Norikazu et al. 今岡典和他. "Sengokuki kenkyū no kadai to tembō" 戦国記研究の課題と展望. *Nihonshi kenkyū* 日本史研究, no. 278 (October 1985): 42–62.

Imatani Akira 今谷明. *Sengokuki no Muromachi bakufu no seikaku* 戦国期の室町幕府の性格, vol. 12. Tokyo: Kadokawa shoten 角川書店, 1975.

Imatani Akira 今谷明. "Kōki Muromachi bakufu no kenryoku kōzo-tokuni sono senseika ni tsuite" 後期室町幕府の権力構造 - 特にその専制化について. In Nihonshi kenkyūkai shiryō kenkyū bukai 日本史研究会史料研究部会, ed. *Chūsei Nihon no rekishi zō* 中世日本の歴史像. Tokyo: Sōgensha 創元社, 1978.

Imatani Akira 今谷明. *Muromachi bakufu kaitai katei no kenkyū* 室町幕府解体過程の研究. Tokyo: Iwanami shoten 岩波書店, 1985.

Imatani Akira 今谷明. *Shugo ryōgoku shihai kikō no kenkyū* 守護領国支配機構の研究. Tokyo: Hōsei daigaku shuppankyoku 法政大学出版局, 1986.

Inagaki Yasuhiko 稲垣泰彦. "Do-ikki o megutte" 土一揆をめぐって. *Rekishi-gaku kenkyū* 歴史学研究, no. 305 (October 1965): 25–33.

Inagaki Yasuhiko 稲垣泰彦. *Nihon chūsei shakaishi ron* 日本中世社会史論. Tokyo: Tōkyō daigaku shuppankai 東京大学出版会, 1981.

Inagaki Yasuhiko 稲垣泰彦, and Nagahara Keiji 永原慶二, eds. *Chūsei no shakai to keizai* 中世の社会と経済. Tokyo: Tōkyō daigaku shuppankai 東京大学出版会, 1962.

Inoue Mitsusada 井上光貞. *Nihon Jōdokyō seiritsushi no kenkyū* 日本浄土教成立史の研究. Tokyo: Yamakawa shuppansha 山川出版社, 1956.

Inoue Mitsusada 井上光貞. *Nihon kodai no kokka to Bukkyō* 日本古代の国家と仏教. Tokyo: Iwanami shoten 岩波書店, 1971.

Inoue Mitsusada 井上光貞 et al., eds. *Nihon rekishi taikei* 日本歴史大系, vol. 2. Tokyo: Yamakawa shuppansha 山川出版社, 1985.

Inoue Toshio 井上鋭夫. *Ikko ikki no kenkyū* 一向一揆の研究. Tokyo: Yoshikawa kōbunkan 吉川弘文館, 1968.

Ishida Hisatoyo 石田尚豊. "Shokunin zukushi e" 職人尽絵. *Nihon no bijutsu* 日本の美術, no. 132 (May 1977): 94–114.

Ishida Mizumaro 石田瑞麿. *Nihon Bukkyō ni okeru kairitsu no kenkyū* 日本仏教における戒律の研究. Tokyo: Nakayama shobō 中山書房, 1976.

Ishida Yoshito 石田善人. "Gōson-sei no keisei" 郷村制の形成. In *Iwanami kōza Nihon rekishi* 岩波講座日本歴史, vol. 6. Tokyo: Iwanami shoten 岩波書店, 1963.

Ishida Yoshito 石田善人. "Sōteki ketsugō no shoruikei" 惣的結合の諸類型. *Rekishi kyōiku* 歴史教育 8 (August 1969): 24–38.

Ishihara Michihiro 石原道博. "Gendai Nihonkan no ichisokumen" 現代日本観 の一側面. In Wada hakase kanreki kinenkai 和田博士還暦記念会, ed. *Tōyōshi ronsō* 東洋史論叢. Tokyo: Wada hakase kanreki kinenki 和田博士還暦記念会, 1951.

Ishihara Michihiro 石原道博. *Wakō* 倭寇. Tokyo: Yoshikawa kōbunkan 吉川弘 文館, 1964.

Ishihara Michihiro 石原道博. *Yakuchū Chūgoku seishi Nihon den* 訳注中国正史 日本伝. Tokyo: Kokusho kankōkai 図書刊行会, 1975.

Ishii Masatoshi 石井正敏. "Bun'ei hachinen rainichi no Kōraishi ni tsuite-Sanbetsushō no Nihon tsūkō shiryō no shōkai" 文永八年来日の高麗使につい て‐三別抄の日本通交史料の紹介. *Tōkyō daigaku shiryō hensanjo hō* 東京大学 史料編纂所報, no. 12 (March 1978): 1-7.

Ishii Ryosuke 石井良助. *Taika no kaishin to Kamakura bakufu no seiritsu* 大化の 改新と鎌倉幕府の成立. Tokyo: Sōbunsha 創文社, 1958.

Ishii Susumu 石井進. "Kamakura bakufu to ritsuryō kokka‐kokuga to no kankei o chūshin to shite" 鎌倉幕府と律令国家‐国衙との関係を中心として. In Satō Shin'ichi 佐藤進一, and Ishimoda Shō 石母田正, eds. *Chūsei no hō to kokka* 中世の法と国家. Tokyo: Tōkyō daigaku shuppankai 東京大学出版会, 1960.

Ishii Susumu 石井進. *Insei jidai* 院政時代. Vol. 2 of *Kōza Nihon shi* 講座日本史. Tokyo: Tōkyō daigaku shuppankai 東京大学出版会, 1970.

Ishii Susumu 石井進. *Nihon chūsei kokkashi no kenkyū* 日本中世国家史の研究. Tokyo: Iwanami shoten 岩波書店, 1970.

Ishii Susumu 石井進. *Kamakura bakufu* 鎌倉幕府. Vol. 7 of *Nihon no rekishi* 日 本の歴史. Tokyo: Chūō kōronsha 中央公論社, 1971.

Ishii Susumu 石井進. "Takezaki Suenaga ekotoba no seiritsu" 竹崎季長絵詞の 成立. *Nihon rekishi* 日本歴史, no. 273 (1971): 12-32.

Ishii Susumu 石井進. "Shimotsuki sōdō oboegaki" 霜月騒動おぼえ書き. In *Kanagawa-ken shi dayori, shiryō hen* 神奈川縣史だより，資料編, vol. 2. Yokohama: Kanagawa ken 神奈川県, 1973.

Ishii Susumu 石井進 et al., eds. *Chūsei seiji shakai shisō zō* 中世政治社会思想像. Vol. 21 of *Nihon shisō taikei* 日本思想体系. Tokyo: Iwanami shoten 岩波書店, 1972.

Ishimoda Shō 石母田正. *Zōho chūseiteki sekai no keisei* 増補中世的世界の形成. Tokyo: Tōkyō daigaku shuppankai 東京大学出版会, 1950.

Ishimoda Shō 石母田正. "Heishi seiken no sōkan shiki setchi" 平氏政権の総官 職設置. *Rekishi hyōron* 歴史評論, no. 107 (July 1959): 7-14.

Ishimoda Shō 石母田正. "Kamakura bakufu ikkoku jitō shiki no seiritsu" 鎌倉 幕府一国地頭職の成立. In Satō Shin'ichi 佐藤進一, and Ishimoda Shō 石母田 正, eds. *Chūsei no hō to kokka* 中世の法と国家. Tokyo: Tōkyō daigaku shup-pankai 東京大学出版会, 1960.

Itō Kiyoshi 伊藤喜良. "Kamakura bakufu oboegaki" 鎌倉幕府覚書. *Rekishi* 歴史 42 (April 1972): 17-34.

Itō Kiyoshi 伊藤喜良. "Muromachi ki no kokka to Tōgoku" 室町期の国家と東

国. *Rekishigaku kenkyū* 歴史学研究, special issue (October 1979): 63-72.

Itō Yuishin 伊藤唯真. *Jōdoshū no seiritsu to tenkai* 浄土宗の成立と展開. Tokyo: Yoshikawa kōbunkan 吉川弘文館, 1981.

Iwamura Shinobu 岩村忍. "Gen jidai ni okeru shihei infurēshon" 元時代における紙幣インフレーション. *Tōyō gakuhō* 東洋学報 34 (March 1964).

Iwanami kōza Nihon rekishi 岩波講座 日本歴史. 23 vols. Tokyo: Iwanami shoten 岩波書店, 1962-64.

Iwanami kōza Nihon rekishi 岩波講座 日本歴史. 26 vols. Tokyo: Iwanami shoten 岩波書店, 1975-77.

Izumi Chōichi 泉澄一. "Sakai chōnin to Zen" 堺商人と禅. *Rekishi kōron* 歴史公論 10 (1977): 89-91.

Joseishi sōgō kenkyūkai 女性史総合研究会, ed. *Nihon joseishi* 日本女性史. 5 vols. Tokyo: Tōkyō daigaku shuppankai 東京大学出版会, 1982-83.

Kachō Fūgetsu 花鳥風月. Vol. 3 of *Muromachi jidai monogatari taisei* 室町時代物語大成. Tokyo: Kadokawa shoten 角川書店, 1975.

Kagamishima Genryū et al. 鏡島元隆他, eds. *Yakuchū Zennen shingi* 訳注禅苑清規. Tokyo: Sōtōshū shūmuchō 曹洞宗宗務庁, 1972.

Kagamiyama Takeshi sensei koki kinenkai 鏡山猛先生古稀記念会, ed. *Kobunka ronkō* 古文化論考. Fukuoka: Kagamiyama Takeshi sensei koki kinen ronbun-shū kankōkai 鏡山猛先生古稀記念論文集刊行会, 1980.

Kamiki Tetsuo 神木哲男. "Chūsei shōen ni okeru kahei" 中世荘園における貨幣. *Kokumin keizai zasshi* 国民経済雑誌 120 (1963): 50-65.

Kasahara Kazuo 笠原一男. *Shinran to tōgoku nōmin* 親鸞と東国農民. Tokyo: Yamakawa shuppansha 山川出版社, 1957.

Kasahara Kazuo 笠原一男. *Ikkō ikki no kenkyū* 一向一揆の研究. Tokyo: Yamakawa shuppansha 山川出版社, 1962.

Kasai Sachiko 笠井幸子. Ōshū heiran to tōgoku bushidan" 奥州兵乱と東国武士団 *Rekishi kyōiku* 歴史教育 16 (1968): 27-40.

Kasamatsu Hiroshi 笠松宏至. *Nihon chūsei-hō shiron* 日本中世法史論. Tokyo: Tōkyō daigaku shuppankai 東京大学出版会, 1977.

Kasamatsu Hiroshi 笠松宏至, Satō Shin'ichi 佐藤慎一, and Momose Kesao 百瀬今朝男, eds. *Chūsei seiji shakai shisō* 中世政治社会思想. Vol. 22 of *Nihon shisō taikei* 日本思想大系. Tokyo: Iwanami shoten 岩波書店, 1981.

Katsumata Shizuo 勝俣鎮夫. *Sengoku-hō seiritsu shiron* 戦国法成立史論. Tokyo: Tōkyō daigaku shuppankai 東京大学出版会, 1979.

Katsumata Shizuo 勝俣鎮夫. *Ikki* 一揆. Tokyo: Iwanami shoten 岩波書店, 1982.

Katsumata Shizuo, with Collcutt, Martin. "The Development of Sengoku Law." In John Whitney Hall, Keiji Nagahara, and Kozo Yamamura, eds. *Japan Before Tokugawa: Political Consolidation and Economic Growth, 1500-1650*. Princeton, N. J.: Princeton University Press, 1981.

Kawai Masaharu 河合正治. *Ashikaga Yoshimasa* 足利義政. Tokyo: Shimizu shoin 清水書院, 1972.

Kawai Masaharu 河合正治. *Chūsei buke shakai no kenkyū* 中世武家社会の研究. Tokyo: Yoshikawa kobunkan 吉川弘文館, 1973.

Kawai Masaharu, with Grossberg, Kenneth A. "Shogun and Shugo: The Provincial Aspects of Muromachi Politics." In John Whitney Hall and Toyoda Takeshi, eds. *Japan in the Muromachi Age*. Berkeley and Los Angeles: University of California Press, 1977.

Kawakami Kozan 川上孤山. *Myōshinji-shi* 妙心寺史. Kyoto: Shibunkaku 思文閣, 1975.

Kawakami Mitsugu 川上貢. *Zen'in no kenchiku* 禅院の建築. Tokyo: Kawahara shoten 河原書店, 1968.

Kawamura Shōichi 河村昭一. "Aki Takedashi kankei monjo mokuroku" 安芸武田氏関係文書目録, pt. 1. *Geibi chihōshi kenkyū* 芸備地方史研究, no. 108 (1975): 26-31.

Kawane Yoshihira 河音能平. *Chūsei hōkensei seiritsu shiron* 中世封建制成立史論. Tokyo: Tōkyō daigaku shuppankai 東京大学出版会, 1971.

Kawasaki Tsuneyuki 川崎庸之, and Kasahara Kazuo 笠原一男, eds. *Shūkyō shi* 宗教史. Vol. 18 of *Taikei Nihon-shi sōsho* 体系日本史叢書. Tokyo: Yamakawa shūppansha 山川出版社, 1966.

Kawazoe Hiroshi 川副博. "Einin san'nen ki kōshō" 永仁三年記考証. *Shichō* 史潮 50 (January 1953): 33-52.

Kawazoe Shōji 川添昭二, ed. *Nejime monjo* 禰寝文書, vol. 3. Fukuoka: Kyūshū daigaku bungakubu and Kyūshū shiryō kankōkai 九州大学文学部・九州史料刊行会, 1955.

Kawazoe Shōji 川添昭二. *Imagawa Ryōshun* 今川了俊. Tokyo: Yoshikawa kōbunkan 吉川弘文館, 1964.

Kawazoe Shōji 川添昭二. "Chinzei kanrei kō" 鎮西管領考. *Nihon rekishi* 日本歴史, nos. 205 and 206 (June and July 1965): 2-14 and 29-53.

Kawazoe Shōji 川添昭二. *Chūkai, Genkō bōrui hennen shiryō - ikoku keigo banyaku shiryō no kenkyū* 注解元寇防塁編年史料 - 異国警護番役史料の研究. Fukuoka: Fukuokashi kyōiku iinkai 福岡市教育委員会, 1971.

Kawazoe Shōji 川添昭二. *Nichiren-sono shisō, kōdō to Mōko shūrai* 日蓮 - その思想・行動と蒙古襲来. Tokyo: Shimizu shoin 清水書院, 1971.

Kawazoe Shōji 川添昭二. "Iwato gassen saihen - Chinzei ni okeru tokusō shihai no kyōka to Mutō shi" 岩戸合戦再編 - 鎮西における得宗支配の強化と武藤氏. In Mori Katsumi hakase koki kinen kai hen 森克己博士古稀記念会編, ed. *Taigai kankei to seiji bunka* 対外関係と政治文化. Vol. 2 of *Shigaku ronshū* 史学論集. Tokyo: Yoshikawa kōbunkan 吉川弘文館, 1974.

Kawazoe Shōji 川添昭二. "Chinzei kanrei kō 鎮西管領考. In Ogawa Makoto 小川信, ed. *Muromachi seiken* 室町政権. Vol. 5 of *Ronshū Nihon rekishi* 論集日本歴史. Tokyo:Yūshōdō 雄松堂, 1975.

Kawazoe Shōji 川添昭二. *Gen no shūrai* 元の襲来. Tokyo: Popurasha ポプラ社, 1975.

Kawazoe Shōji 川添昭二. "Kamakura jidai no taigai kankei to bunbutsu no inyū" 鎌倉時代の対外関係と文物の移入. In *Iwanami kōza Nihon rekishi* 岩波講座日本歴史, vol. 6. Tokyo: Iwanami shoten 岩波書店, 1975.

Kawazoe Shōji 川添昭二. *Mōko shūrai kenkyū shiron* 蒙古襲来研究史論. Tokyo:

Yūzankaku 雄山閣, 1977.

Kawazoe Shōji 川添昭二. *Seinan chiikishi kenkyū* 西南地域史研究, vol. 1. Tokyo: Bunken shuppan 文献出版, 1977.

Kawazoe Shōji 川添昭二. "Kyūshū tandai no suimetsu katei" 九州探題の衰滅過程. *Kyūshū bunkashi kenkyūjo kiyō* 九州文化誌研究所紀要, no. 23 (March 1978): 81-130.

Kawazoe Shōji 川添昭二. "Kaneyoshi Shinnō o meguru Kyūshū no Nambokuchō" 懐良親王をめぐる九州の南北朝. *Rekishi kōron* 歴史公論 5 (September 1979): 92-99.

Kawazoe Shōji 川添昭二. "Kodai-chūsei no gaikō monjo" 古代中世の外交文書. In Kagamiyama Takeshi sensei koki kinenkai 鏡山猛先生古稀記念会, ed. *Kobunka ronko* 古文化論考. Fukuoka: Kagamiyama Takeshi sensei koki kinen ronbunshu kankōkai 鏡山猛先生古稀記念論文刊行会, 1980.

Kawazoe Shōji 川添昭二. *Chūsei Kyūshū no seiji to bunka* 中世九州の政治と文化. Tokyo: Bunken shuppan 文献出版, 1981.

Kawazoe Shōji 川添昭二, ed. *Umi kara yomigaeru wakō* 海から甦る倭寇. Fukuoka: Asahi shimbun seibu honsha kikakubu 朝日新聞西部本社企画部, 1981.

Kawazoe Shōji 川添昭二. "Nichiren no shūkyō no seiritsu oyobi seikaku" 日蓮の宗教の成立及び性格. In *Nichiren* 日蓮. Vol. 9 of *Nihon meisō ronshū* 日本名僧論集. Tokyo: Yoshikawa kōbunkan 吉川弘文館, 1982.

Kayahara Shōzō 栢原昌三. "Nichimin kangō bōeki ni okeru Hosokawa Ōuchi nishi no kōsō" 日明勘合貿易における細川大内二氏の抗争. *Shigaku zasshi* 史学雑誌 25 and 26 (September-October 1914 and February-March 1915).

Kayahara Shōzō 栢原昌三. "Nichimin kangō bōeki no soshiki to shikō" 日明勘合貿易の組織と使行. *Shigaku zasshi* 史学雑誌 31, nos. 4, 5, 8, and 9 (April, May, August, and September 1920).

Kayahara Shōzō 栢原昌三. "Mōko shūrai no ichihihan" 蒙古襲来の一批判. *Rekishi to chiri* 歴史と地理 10 (August-October 1922).

Keene, Donald, ed. *Anthology of Japanese Literature*. New York: Grove Press, 1955.

Keene, Donald, trans. *Essays in Idleness*. New York: Columbia University Press, 1967.

Keene, Donald, ed. *Twenty Plays of the Nō Theatre*. New York: Columbia University Press, 1970.

Keene, Donald. "Diaries of the Kamakura Period." *Japan Quarterly* 32 (July-September 1985): 281-9.

Kemmu chūkō roppyakunen kinenkai 建武中興六百年記念会, comp. *Kemmu chūkō* 建武中興. Tokyo: Kemmu chūkō roppyakunen kinenkai 建武中興六百年記念会, 1934.

Kidō Saizō 木藤才蔵, ed. *Renga ronshū* 連歌論集. Tokyo: Iwanami shoten 岩波書店, 1961.

Kim, Hee-jin. *Dōgen Kigen - Mystical Realist*. Tucson: University of Arizona Press, 1975.

Kimiya Yasuhiko 木宮泰彦. *Nikka bunka kōryūshi* 日華文化交流史. Tokyo: Fuzambō 冨山房, 1955.

Kindai Nihon bungaku taikei 近代日本文学大系. 25 vols. Tokyo: Kokumin tosho kabushiki kaisha 国民図書株式会社, 1928-31.

Kindaichi Haruhiko 金田一春彦. "Heikyoku-sono rekishi to ongaku" 平曲－その歴史と音楽. In *Heike monogatari* 平家物語. Vol. 9 of *Zusetsu Nihon no koten* 図説日本の古典. Tokyo: Shūeisha 集英社, 1980.

Kishida Hiroshi 岸田裕之. "Shugo Akamatsu-shi no Harima no kuni shihai no hatten to kokuga" 守護赤松氏の播磨国支配の発展と国衙. *Shigaku kenkyū* 史学研究, nos. 104 and 105 (1968).

Kishida Hiroshi 岸田裕之. "Shugo Akamatsu-shi no Harima no kuni shihai no hatten to kokuga" 守護赤松氏の播磨国支配の発展と国衙. In Ogawa Makoto 小川信, ed. *Muromachi seiken* 室町政権. Vol. 5 of *Ronshū Nihon rekishi* 論集日本歴史. Tokyo: Yūshōdō 雄松堂, 1975.

Kishida Hiroshi 岸田裕之, and Akiyama Nobutaka 秋山伸隆, eds. *Hiroshima kenshi* 広島県史, Medieval 中世 vol. Hiroshima: Hiroshima kenchō 広島県庁, 1984.

Kitagawa Tadahiko 北川忠彦, ed. *Kanginshū. Sōan koutashū* 閑吟集・宗安小歌集. Vol. 53 of *Shinchō Nihon koten shūsei* 新潮日本古典集成. Tokyo: Shinchōsha, 1982.

Kitamura, Hiroshi, and Tsuchida, Paul T., trans. *The Tale of the Heike.* Tokyo: University of Tokyo Press, 1975.

Kobata Atsushi 小葉田淳. *Chūsei Nisshi tsūkō bōekishi* 中世日支通交貿易史. Tokyo: Tōkō shoin 刀江書院, 1941.

Kobata Atsushi 小葉田淳. "Kangō bōeki to wakō" 勘合貿易と倭寇. In *Iwanami kōza Nihon rekishi* 岩波講座日本歴史, vol. 7. Tokyo: Iwanami shoten 岩波書店, 1963.

Kobata Atsushi 小葉田淳. *Chūsei nantō tsūkō bōekishi no kenkyū* 中世南島通交貿易の研究. Tokyo: Tōkō shoin 刀江書院, 1968.

Kobata Atsushi 小葉田淳. *Nihon kahei ryūtsūshi* 日本貨幣流通史. Tokyo: Tōkō shoin 刀江書院, 1969.

Kobata Atsushi 小葉田淳. *Kingin bōekishi no kenkyū* 金銀貿易史の研究. Tokyo: Hōsei daigaku shuppankyoku 法政大学出版局, 1976.

Kobata Atsushi 小葉田淳. *Nihon keizaishi no kenkyū* 日本経済史の研究. Kyoto: Shibunkaku shuppan 思文閣出版, 1978.

Kobayashi Seiji 小林清治, and Ōishi Naomasa 大石直正, comps. *Chūsei Ōu no sekai* 中世奥羽の世界. Tokyo: Tōkyō daigaku shuppankai 東京大学出版会, 1978.

Koizumi Yoshiaki 小泉宜右. "Iga no kuni Kuroda-no-shō no akutō" 伊賀の国黒田の庄の悪党. In Inagaki Yoshihiko 稲垣泰彦, and Nagahara Keiji 永原慶二, eds. *Chūsei no shakai to keizai* 中世の社会と経済. Tokyo: Tōkyō daigaku shuppankai 東京大学出版会, 1962.

Koizumi Yoshiaki 小泉宜右. *Akutō* 悪党. Tokyo: Kyōikusha 教育社, 1981.

Koji ruien 古事類苑, vol. 44. Tokyo: Yoshikawa kōbunkan 吉川弘文館, 1969.

Kokan Shiren 虎関師練, "Genkō shakusho" 元亨釈書. In Kuroita Katsumi 黒板

勝美, ed. *Shintei zōho kokushi taikei* 新訂増補国史大系, vol. 31. Tokyo: Yoshikawa kōbunkan 吉川弘文館, 1930.

Kokushi taikei 国史大系. 66 vols. Tokyo: Yosikawa kōbunkan 吉川弘文館, 1929-64.

Kokusho kankōkai 国書刊行会, comp. *Meigetsuki* 明月記, vol. 3. Tokyo: Kokusho kankōkai 国書刊行会, 1939.

Komazawa daigaku zengaku daijiten hensanjo 駒沢大学禅学大辞典編纂所, ed. *Zengaku daijiten* 禅学大辞典. 3 vol. Tokyo: Taishūkan shoten 大修館書店, 1978.

Konishi Jin'ichi 小西甚一. *Sōgi* 宗祇. Tokyo: Chikuma shobō 筑摩書房, 1971.

Konishi Mizue 小西瑞恵. "Harima no kuni Ōbe-no-shō no nōmin" 播磨国大部庄の農民. *Nihonshi kenkyū* 日本史研究, no. 98 (May 1968): 1-28.

Konishi Mizue 小西瑞恵. "Kyōtoku sannen no Ōbe-no-shō do-ikki ni tsuite" 享徳三年の大部庄土一揆について. *Hyōgo shigaku* 兵庫史学, no. 65 (1976).

Kōsaka Konomu 高坂好. *Akamatsu Enshin, Mitsusuke* 赤松遠心・満祐. Tokyo: Yoshikawa kōbunkan 吉川弘文館, 1970.

Kubo Noritada 窪徳忠, and Nishi Junzō 西順蔵, eds. *Shūkyō* 宗教. Vol. 6 of *Chūgoku bunka sōsho* 中国文化叢書. Tokyo: Taishūkan shoten 大修館書店, 1968.

Kudō Keiichi 工藤敬一. "Shōensei no tenkai" 荘園制の展開. In *Iwanami kōza Nihon rekishi* 岩波講座日本歴史, vol. 5 Tokyo: Iwanami shoten 岩波書店, 1975.

Kunaichō Shoryōbu 宮内庁書陵部, ed. *Kujō Masamotokō tabi hikizuke* 九条政元公旅引付. Tokyo: Yōtokusha 養徳社, 1961.

Kuroda Hideo 黒田日出男. "Chūsei no kaihatsu to shizen" 中世の開発と自然. In Aoki Michio et al., eds. *Seikatsu, bunka, shisō* 生活・文化・思想. Vol. 4 of *Ikki* 一揆. Tokyo: Tōkyō daigaku shuppankai 東京大学出版会, 1981.

Kuroda Hideo 黒田日出男. "Chūsei nōgyō gijutsu no yōsō" 中世農業技術の様相. In Nagahara Keiji 永原慶二, and Yamaguchi Keiji 山口啓二, ed. *Nōgyō to nōsan kakō* 農業と農産加工. Vol. 1 of *Nihon gijutsu no shakaishi* 日本技術の社会史. Tokyo: Nihon hyōronsha 日本評論社, 1983.

Kuroda, Toshio. "Gukanshō and Jinnō Shōtoki: Observations on Medieval Historiography." In John A. Harrison, ed. *New Light on Early and Medieval Japanese Historiography*. Gainesville: University of Florida Monographs in Social Sciences, no. 4, University of Florida Press, 1959.

Kuroda Toshio 黒田俊雄. "Mōko shūrai" 蒙古襲来. In *Nihon no rekishi* 日本の歴史, vol. 8. Tokyo: Chūō kōronsha 中央公論社, 1965.

Kuroda Toshio 黒田俊雄. *Shōen-sei shakai* 荘園制社会. Vol. 2 of *Taikei Nihon rekishi* 大系日本歴史. Tokyo: Nihon hyōronsha 日本評論社, 1967.

Kuroda Toshio 黒田俊雄. *Nihon chūsei hōkensei ron* 日本中世封建制論. Tokyo: Tōkyō daigaku shuppankai 東京大学出版会, 1974.

Kuroda Toshio 黒田俊雄. *Nihon chūsei no kokka to tennō* 日本中世の国家と天皇. Tokyo: Iwanami shoten 岩波書店, 1975.

Kuroita Katsumi 黒板勝美, ed. *Shintei zōho kokushi taikei* 新訂増補国史大系, vol. 31. Tokyo: Yoshikawa kōbunkan 吉川弘文館, 1930.

Kurokawa Naonori 黒川直則. "Shugo ryōgokusei to shōen taisei-kokujin ryōshusei no kakuritsu katei" 守護領国制と荘園体制－国人領主制の確立過程. *Nihonshi kenkyū* 日本史研究, no. 57 (November 1961): 1-19.

Kurokawa Naonori 黒川直則. "Shugo ryōgokusei to shōen taisei" 守護領国制と荘園体制. In Ogawa Makoto 小川信, ed. *Muromachi seiken* 室町政権. Vol. 5 of *Ronshū Nihon rekishi* 論集日本歴史. Tokyo: Yūshōdō 雄松堂, 1975.

Kuwata Tadachika 桑田忠親. *Toyotomi Hideyoshi kenkyū* 豊臣秀吉研究. Tokyo: Kadokawa shoten 角川書店, 1975.

Kuwayama Kōnen 桑山浩然. "Muromachi bakufu no sōsōki ni okeru shoryō ni tsuite" 室町幕府の草創期における所領について. *Chusei no mado* 中世の窓 12 (April 1963): 4-27.

Kuwayama Kōnen 桑山浩然. "Muromachi bakufu keizai kikō no ichi kōsatsu, nōsen kata kubō mikura no kinō to seiritsu" 室町幕府経済機構の一考察－納銭方・公方御倉の機能と成立. *Shigaku zasshi* 史学雑誌 73 (September 1964): 9-17.

Kuwayama Kōnen 桑山浩然. "Muromachi bakufu keizai no kōzō" 室町幕府経済の構造. In *Nihon keizaishi taikei* 日本経済大系, vol. 2. Tokyo: Tōkyō daigaku shuppankai 東京大学出版会, 1965.

Kuwayama Kōnen 桑山浩然. *Muromachi bakufu hikitsuke shiryō shūsei* 室町幕府引付史料集成, vol. 1. Tokyo: Kondō shuppansha 近藤出版社, 1980.

Kuwayama Kōnen, with Hall, John Whitney. "The Bugyōnin System: A Closer Look." In John Whitney Hall and Toyoda Takeshi, eds. *Japan in the Muromachi Age*. Berkeley and Los Angeles: University of California Press, 1977.

Kyōto daigaku bungakubu dokushikai 京都大学文学部読史会, ed. *Kokushi ronshū* 国史論集. Kyoto: Kyōto daigaku bungakubu dokushikai 京都大学文学部読史会, 1959.

Kyōto kokuritsu hakubutsukan 京都国立博物館, ed. *Zen no bijutsu* 禅の美術. Kyoto: Kyōto kokuritsu hakubutsukan 京都国立博物館, 1981.

Kyōto no rekishi 京都の歴史. 9 vols. Kyoto: Gakugei shorin 学芸書林, 1968-76.

Ludwig, Theodore M. "Before Rikyū: Religious and Aesthetic Influences in the Early History of the Tea Ceremony." *Monumenta Nipponica* 36 (Winter 1981): 367-90.

McCullough, Helen Craig. trans. *The Taiheiki: A Chronicle of Medieval Japan*. New York: Columbia University Press, 1959.

McCullough, Helen Craig. *Yoshitsune: A Fifteenth Century Japanese Chronicle*. Tokyo: University of Tokyo Press, 1966.

McCullough, William H. "Shōkyūki: An Account of the Shōkyū War of 1221." *Monumenta Nipponica* 19 (1964): 163-215.

McCullough, William H. "The *Azuma kagami* Account of the Shōkyū War." *Monumenta Nipponica* 23 (1968): 102-55.

Makita Tairyō 牧田諦亮. *Sakugen Nyūminki no kenkyū* 策彦入明記の研究. Kyoto: Hōzōkan 法蔵館, 1959.

Mass, Jeffrey P. "The Emergence of the Kamakura Bakufu." In John Whitney

Hall and Jeffrey P. Mass, eds. *Medieval Japan: Essays in Institutional History*. New Haven, Conn.: Yale University Press, 1974.

Mass, Jeffrey P. "Jitō Land Possession in the Thirteenth Century." In John Whitney Hall and Jeffrey P. Mass, eds. *Medieval Japan: Essays in Institutional History*. New Haven, Conn.: Yale University Press, 1974.

Mass, Jeffrey P. *Warrior Government in Early Medieval Japan*. New Haven, Conn.: Yale University Press, 1974.

Mass, Jeffrey P. *The Kamakura Bakufu: A Study in Documents*. Stanford, Calif.: Stanford University Press, 1976.

Mass, Jeffrey P. "The Origins of Kamakura Justice." *Journal of Japanese Studies* 3 (Summer 1977): 299-322.

Mass, Jeffrey P. *The Development of Kamakura Rule, 1180-1250: A History with Documents*. Stanford, Calif.: Stanford University Press, 1979.

Mass, Jeffrey P. "Translation and Pre-1600 History." *Journal of Japanese Studies* 6 (Winter 1980): 61-88.

Mass, Jeffrey P, ed. *Court and Bakufu in Japan: Essays in Kamakura History*. New Haven, Conn.: Yale University Press, 1982.

Mass, Jeffrey P. "The Early Bakufu and Feudalism." In Jeffrey P. Mass, ed. *Court and Bakufu in Japan: Essays in Kamakura History*. New Haven, Conn.: Yale University Press, 1982.

Mass, Jeffrey P. "Patterns of Provincial Inheritance in Late Heian Japan." *Journal of Japanese Studies* 9 (Winter 1983): 67-95.

Mass, Jeffrey P. "What Can We Not Know About the Kamakura Bakufu." In Jeffrey P. Mass and William B. Hauser, eds. *The Bakufu in Japanese History*. Stanford, Calif.: Stanford University Press, 1985.

Mass, Jeffrey P. *Lordship and Inheritance in Early Medieval Japan: A study of the Kamakura Sōryō System*. Forthcoming.

Mass, Jeffrey P, and Hauser, William B., eds. *The Bakufu in Japanese History*. Stanford, Calif.: Stanford University Press, 1985.

Matsumoto Hikojirō 松本彦次郎. *Nihon bunka shiron* 日本文化史論. Tokyo: Kawade shobō 河出書房, 1942.

Matsuno Junkō 松野純考. *Shinran: Sono shōgai to shisō no tenkai katei* 親鸞, その生涯と思想の展開過程. Tokyo: Sanseidō 三省堂, 1959.

Matsuno Junkō 松野純考. "Honganji no seiritsu" 本願寺の成立. In Akamatsu Toshihide 赤松俊秀, and Kasahara Kazuo 笠原一男, eds. *Shinshūshi gaisetsu* 真宗史概説. Kyoto: Heirakuji shoten 平楽寺書店, 1963.

Matsuoka Hisato 松岡久人. "Saigoku no Sengoku daimyō" 西国の戦国大名. In Nagahara Keiji 永原慶二, John Whitney Hall ジョン・ホイットニイ・ホール, and Kozo Yamamura コーゾー・ヤマムラ, eds. *Sengoku jidai* 戦国時代. Tokyo: Yoshikawa kōbunkan 吉川弘文館, 1978.

Matsuyama Hiroshi 松山宏. *Nihon chūsei toshi no kenkyū* 日本中世都市の研究. Kyoto: Daigakudō shoten 大学堂書店, 1973.

Matsuyama Hiroshi 松山宏. *Shugo jōkamachi no kenkyū* 守護城下町の研究. Kyoto: Daigakudō shoten 大学堂書店, 1982.

Mitobe Masao 水戸部正男. *Kuge shinsei no kenkyū* 公家新制の研究. Tokyo: Sōbunsha 創文社, 1961.

Miura Hiroyuki 三浦周行. "Tenryūji-bune ni kansuru shinkenkyū" 天龍寺船に関する新研究. *Shigaku zasshi* 25 (January 1914).

Miura Hiroyuki 三浦周行. *Hōseishi no kenkyū* 法制史の研究. Tokyo: Iwanami shoten 岩波書店, 1919.

Miura Hiroyuki 三浦周行. *Nihonshi no kenkyū* 日本史の研究, vols. 1 and 2. Tokyo: Iwanami shoten 岩波書店, 1930, reprinted in 1981.

Miura Keiichi 三浦圭一. "Chūsei kōki no shōhin ryūtsū to ryōshu kaikyū" 中世後期の商品流通と領主階級. *Nihonshi kenkyū* 日本史研究, no. 65 (March 1963).

Miyagawa Mitsuru 宮川満. *Taikō kenchi ron* 太閤検地論, 3 vols. Tokyo: Ochanomizu shobō お茶の水書房, 1957-63.

Miyagawa Mitsuru 宮川満, with Kiley, Cornelius J. "From Shōen to Chigyō: Proprietary Lordship and the Structure of Local Power." In John Whitney Hall and Toyoda Takeshi, eds. *Japan in the Muromachi Age*. Berkeley and Los Angeles: University of California Press, 1977.

Miyagi Eishō 宮城栄昌. *Okinawa no rekishi* 沖縄の歴史. Tokyo: Nihon hōsō shuppan kyōkai 日本放送協会出版協会, 1968.

Miyata Toshihiko 宮田俊彦. "Nichimin, Ryumin kokkō no kaishi" 日明琉明国交の開始. *Nihon rekishi* 日本歴史, nos. 201-3 (February-April 1965).

Mizuno Yahoko 水野弥穂子. *Daichi* 大智. Vol. 9 of *Nihon no zen goroku* 日本の禅語録. Tokyo: Kōdansha 講談社, 1978.

Mōko shūrai ekotoba 蒙古襲来絵詞. Vol. 14 of *Nihon emaki taisei* 日本絵巻大成. Tokyo: Chūō kōronsha 中央公論社, 1978.

Momose Hiromu 百瀬弘. *Minshin shakai keizaishi kenkyū* 明清社会経済史研究. Tokyo: Kenkyū shuppan 研究出版, 1980.

Momose Kesao 百瀬今朝男. "Tansen kō" 段錢考. In Hōgetsu Keigo sensei kanreki kinenkai 宝月圭吾先生還暦記念会, ed. *Nihon shakai keizaishi kenkyū* 日本社会経済史研究, medieval vol. Tokyo: Yoshikawa kōbunkan 吉川弘文館, 1967.

Mori Katsumi 森克己. *Nissō bunka kōryū no shomondai* 日宋文化交流の諸問題. Vol. 4 of *Mori Katsumi chosaku senshū* 森克己著作選集. Tokyo: Kokusho kankōkai 国書刊行会, 1975.

Mori Katsumi 森克己. *Shintei Nissō bōeki no kenkyū* 新訂日宋貿易の研究. Tokyo: Kokusho kankōkai 国書刊行会, 1975.

Mori Katsumi hakase koki kinen kai 森克己博士古希記念会, ed. *Taigai kankei to seiji bunka* 対外関係と政治文化. Vol. 2 of *Shigaku ronshū* 史学論集. Tokyo: Yoshikawa kōbunkan 吉川弘文館, 1974.

Morisue Yumiko 森末由美子. "Muromachi bakufu goryōsho ni kansuru ichi kōsatsu" 室町幕府御料所に関する一考察. In Ogawa Makoto 小川信, ed. *Muromachi seiken* 室町政権. Vol. 5 of *Ronshū Nihon rekishi* 論集日本歴史. Tokyo: Yūshōdō 雄松堂, 1975.

Morris, Ivan. *The Nobility of Failure*. New York: Holt, Rinehart and Winston, 1975.

Murai Shōsuke 村井章介. "Mōko shūrai to Chinzei tandai no seiritsu" 蒙古襲来と鎮西探題の成立. *Shigaku zasshi* 87 (April 1978): 1-43.

Murai Shōsuke 村井章介. "Muromachi bakufu no saisho no kenminshi ni tsuite" 室町幕府の最初の遣明使について. In Imaeda Aishin 今枝愛真, ed. *Zenshū no shomondai* 禅宗の諸問題. Tokyo: Yūzankaku 雄山閣, 1979.

Murai Yasuhiko 村井康彦. "Kokufū bunka no sōzō to fukyū" 国風文化の創造と普及. In *Iwanami kōza Nihon rekishi* 岩波講座日本歴史, vol. 4. Tokyo: Iwanami shoten 岩波書店, 1976.

Murakami Masana 村上正名. *Maboroshi no Kusado Sengenchō* 幻の草戸千軒町. Tokyo: Kokusho kankōkai 国書刊行会, 1980.

Murakami Masatsugu 村上正二. "Mongoru teikoku no seiritsu to bunretsu" モンゴル帝国の成立と分裂. In *Iwanami kōza sekai rekishi* 岩波講座世界歴史, vol. 9. Tokyo: Iwanami shoten 岩波書店, 1970.

Murata Shūzō 村田修三. "Chiiki masu to chiiki kenryoku" 地域舛と地域権力. *Shirin* 史林 55 (January 1972): 38-76.

Murata Shūzō 村田修三. "Yōsui shihai to shōryōshu rengō" 用水支配と小領主連合. *Nara joshidaigaku bungakubu kenkyū nempō* 奈良女子大学文学部研究年報, no. 16 (1973).

Nagahara Keiji 永原慶二, ed. *Nihon hōkensei seiritsu katei no kenkyū* 日本封建制成立過程の研究. Tokyo: Iwanami shoten 岩波書店, 1961.

Nagahara Keiji 永原慶二. "Zaike no rekishi-teki seikaku to sono henka ni tsuite" 在家の歴史的性格とその変化について. In Nagahara Keiji, ed. *Nihon hōkensei seiritsu katei no kenkyū* 日本封建制成立過程の研究. Tokyo Iwanami shoten 岩波書店, 1961.

Nagahara Keiji 永原慶二, ed. *Chūsei* 中世. Vol. 2 of *Nihon keizaishi taikei* 日本経済史大系. Tokyo: Tōkyō daigaku shuppankai 東京大学出版会, 1965.

Nagahara Keiji 永原慶二. "Shōen ryōshu keizai no kōzō" 荘園領主経済の構造. In Nagahara Keiji 永原慶二, ed. *Chūsei* 中世, Vol. 2 of *Nihon keizaishi taikei* 日本経済史大系. Tokyo: Tōkyō daigaku shuppankai 東京大学出版会, 1965.

Nagahara Keiji 永原慶二. *Nihon no chūsei shakai* 日本の中世社会. Tokyo: Iwanami shoten 岩波書店, 1968.

Nagahara Keiji 永原慶二. *Nihon chūsei shakai kōzō no kenkyū* 日本中世社会構造の研究. Tokyo: Iwanami shoten 岩波書店, 1973.

Nagahara Keiji 永原慶二. "Daimyō ryōgokusei no kōzō" 大名領国制の構造. In *Iwanami kōza Nihon rekishi* 岩波講座日本歴史, vol. 8. Tokyo: Iwanami shoten 岩波書店, 1976.

Nagahara Keiji 永原慶二. *Chūsei nairanki no shakai to minshū* 中世内乱期の社会と民衆. Tokyo: Yoshikawa kōbunkan 吉川弘文館, 1977.

Nagahara Keiji 永原慶二. "Daimyō ryōgokuseika no kandakasei" 大名領国制下の貫高制. In Nagahara Keiji 永原慶二, John Whitney Hall ジョン・ウイットニィ・ホール, and Kozo Yamamura コーゾー・ヤマムラ, eds. *Sengoku jidai* 戦国時代. Tokyo: Yoshikawa kōbunkan 吉川弘文館, 1978.

Nagahara Keiji 永原慶二. *Shōen* 荘園. Tokyo: Hyōronsha 評論社, 1978.

Nagahara Keiji 永原慶二. "The Medieval Origins of the Eta-Hinin." *Journal of*

Japanese Studies 5 (Summer 1979): 385-403.

Nagahara Keiji 永原慶二. "Zen-kindai no tennō" 前近代の天皇 *Rekishigaku kenkyū* 歴史学研究, no. 467 (April 1979): 37-45.

Nagahara Keiji 永原慶二. *Nihon joseishi* 日本女性史, medieval vol. Tokyo: Tōkyō daigaku shuppankai 東京大学出版会, 1982.

Nagahara Keiji 永原慶二, ed. *Sengoku daimyō ronshū* 戦国大名論集. 18 vols. Tokyo: Yoshikawa kōbunkan 吉川弘文館, 1986.

Nagahara Keiji 永原慶二 et al., eds. *Chūseishi handobukku* 中世史ハンドブック. Tokyo: Kondō shuppansha 近藤出版社, 1973.

Nagahara Keiji 永原慶二, Hall, John Whitney ジョン・ウイットニィ・ホール, and Yamamura, Kozo ヤマムラ・コーゾー, eds. *Sengoku jidai* 戦国時代. Tokyo: Yoshikawa kōbunkan 吉川弘文館, 1978.

Nagahara Keiji 永原慶二, and Kishi Shōzō 貴志正造, eds. *Azuma kagami* 吾妻鏡. 6 vols. Tokyo: Jimbutsu ōraisha 人物往来社, 1976-77.

Nagahara Keiji 永原慶二, and Sugiyama Hiroshi 杉山博. "Shugo ryōgokusei no tenkai" 守護領国制の展開. *Shakai keizai shigaku* 社会経済史学 17 (March 1951): 103-34.

Nagahara Keiji 永原慶二, and Yamaguchi Keiji 山口啓二, eds. *Nōgyō to nōsan kakō* 農業と農産加工. Vol. 1 of *Nihon gijutsu no shakaishi* 日本技術の社会史. Tokyo: Nihon hyōronsha 日本評論社, 1983.

Nagahara Keiji, with Yamamura, Kozo. "Village Communities and Daimyo Power." In John Whitney Hall and Toyoda Takeshi, eds. *Japan in the Muromachi Age*. Berkeley and Los Angeles: University of California Press, 1977.

Nagashima Fukutarō 永島福太郎. "Yamato shugoshiki kō" 大和守護職考. *Rekishi chiri* 歴史地理 68 (October 1936): 61-6.

Nagashima Fukutarō 永島福太郎. *Nara bunka no dentō* 奈良文化の伝統. Tokyo: Meguro shoten 目黒書店, 1951.

Nakamura Hajime et al. 中村元他, eds. *Muromachi Bukkyō* 室町仏教. Vol. 4 of *Ajia Bukkyō-shi* アジア仏教史. Tokyo: Kōsei shuppansha 佼成出版社, 1972.

Nakamura Hidetaka 中村栄孝. "Jūsan-yonseki no Tōa jōsei to Mongoru no shūrai" 十三, 四世紀の東亜情勢とモンゴルの襲来. In *Iwanami kōza Nihon rekishi* 岩波講座日本歴史, vol. 6. Tokyo: Iwanami shoten 岩波書店, 1963.

Nakamura Hidetaka 中村栄孝. *Nissen kankeishi no kenkyū* 日鮮関係史の研究, vol. 1. Tokyo: Yoshikawa kōbunkan 吉川弘文館, 1965.

Nakamura Hidetaka 中村栄孝. *Nihon to Chōsen* 日本と朝鮮. Tokyo: Shibundō 至文堂, 1966.

Nakamura Ken 仲村研, ed. *Imahori Hie jinja monjo* 今堀日枝神社文書. Tokyo: Yūzankaku 雄山閣, 1981.

Nakamura Kichiji 中村吉治. *Do-ikki kenkyū* 土一揆研究. Tokyo: Azekura shobō 校倉書房, 1974.

Nakamura Kichiji 中村吉治, ed. *Shakaishi* 社会史, vol. 1. Tokyo: Yamakawa shuppansha 山川出版社, 1974.

Nakamura Naokatsu 中村直勝. *Nihon shin bunka shi, Yoshino jidai* 日本新文化史 吉野時代. Tokyo: Nihon dentsū shuppanbu 日本電通出版部, 1942.

Nakamura Naokatsu 中村直勝. *Nanchō no kenkyū* 南朝の研究. Vol. 3 of *Nakamura Naokatsu chosaku shū* 中村直勝著作集. Kyoto: Tankōsha 淡交社, 1978.

Nakamura Naokatsu 中村直勝. *Shōen no kenkyū* 荘園の研究. Kyoto: Tankōsha 淡交社, 1978.

Nakao Takashi 中尾堯. *Nichirenshū no seiritsu to tenkai* 日蓮宗の成立と展開. Tokyo: Yoshikawa kōbunkan 吉川弘文館, 1973.

Nanjō Bunyū 南條文雄, ed. *Dai-Nihon Bukkyō zenshū* 大日本仏教全集, vol. 95. Tokyo: Kōdansha 講談社, 1972.

Naramoto Tatsuya 奈良本辰也, and Hayashiya Tatsusaburō 林屋辰三郎, eds. *Kinsei no taidō* 近世の胎動. Vol. 3 of *Kyōto no rekishi* 京都の歴史. Tokyo: Gakugei shorin 学芸書林, 1968.

Nihon bunka no rekishi 日本文化の歴史. 16 vols. Tokyo: Gakkyū 学究, 1969-70.

Nihon emaki taisei 日本絵巻大成. 29 vols. Tokyo: Chūō kōronsha 中央公論社, 1977-81.

Nihon emakimono zenshū 日本絵巻物全集. 24 vols. Tokyo: Kadokawa shoten 角川書店, 1958-69.

Nihon emakimono zenshū 日本絵巻物全集. 32 vols. Tokyo: Kadokawa shoten 角川書店, 1977-81.

Nihon keizaishi taikei 日本経済史大系. 6 vols. Tokyo: Tōkyō daigaku shuppankai 東京大学出版会, 1965.

Nihon koten bungaku taikei 日本古典文学大系. 100 vols. Tokyo: Iwanami shoten 岩波書店, 1957-67.

Nihon meisō ronshū 日本名僧論集. 10 vols. Tokyo: Yoshikawa kōbunkan 吉川弘文館, 1982-83.

Nihon rekishi daijiten 日本歴史大辞典. 20 vols. Tokyo: Kawade shobō shinsha 河出書房新社, 1956-60.

Nihon rekishigaku kenkyūkai 日本歴史学研究会, ed. *Nihonshi no mondaiten* 日本史の問題点. Tokyo: Yoshikawa kōbunkan 吉川弘文館, 1965.

Nihon shiryō shūsei hensankai 日本史料集成編纂会, ed. *Chūgoku-Chōsen no shiseki ni okeru Nihon shiryō shūsei* 中国朝鮮の史籍における日本史料集成, vols. 1-5. Tokyo: Kokusho kankōkai 国書刊行会, 1975-81.

Nihon shisō taikei 日本思想大系. 67 vols. Tokyo: Iwanami shoten 岩波書店, 1970-82.

Nihonshi kenkyūkai shiryō kenkyū bukai 日本史研究会史料研究部会, ed. *Chūsei Nihon no rekishi zō* 中世日本の歴史像. Osaka: Sōgensha 創元社, 1978.

Nishibe, Bunjō. "Zen Monks and the Formation of the Way of Tea. *Chanoyu*, no. 28 (1981): 7-46.

Nishikawa Kyōtarō 西川杏太郎. "Chinsō chōkoku" 頂相彫刻. *Nihon no bijutsu* 日本の美術, no. 123 (August 1976): 1-98.

Nishio Minoru 西尾実 et al. *Shōbōgenzō, Shōbō genzō zuimonki* 正法眼蔵・正法眼蔵隋聞記. Vol. 82 of *Nihon koten bungaku taikei* 日本古典文学大系. Tokyo: Iwanami shoten 岩波書店, 1965.

Nishiyama Masaru 西山克. "Sengoku daimyō Kitabatakeshi no kenryoku kōzō"

戦国大名北畠氏の権力構造. *Shirin* 史林 62 (March 1979): 51-86.

Nitta Hideharu 新田英治. "Muromachi jidai no kuge-ryō ni okeru daikan ukeoi ni kansuru ichikōsatsu" 室町時代の公家領における代官請負に関する一考察 In Hōgetsu Keigo sensei kanreki kinenkai 寶月圭吾先生還暦記念会, ed. *Nihon shakai keizaishi kenkyū* 日本社会経済史研究, medieval vol. Tokyo: Yoshikawa kōbunkan 吉川弘文館, 1967.

Nitta Hideharu 新田英治. "Kamakura kōki no seiji katei" 鎌倉後期の政治過程. In *Iwanami kōza Nihon rekishi* 岩波講座日本歴史, vol. 6. Tokyo: Iwanami shoten 岩波書店, 1975.

Ōae Ryō 大饗亮. "Jitō shiki o meguru shomondai" 地頭職をめぐる諸問題. *Hōkei gakkai zasshi* 法経学会雑誌 13 (1964): 26-32.

Ogawa Makoto 小川信. *Hosokawa Yoriyuki* 細川頼之. Tokyo: Yashikawa kōbunkan 吉川弘文館, 1972.

Ogawa Makoto 小川信, ed. *Muromachi seiken* 室町政権. Vol. 5 of *Ronshū Nihon rekishi* 論集日本歴史. Tokyo: Yūshōdō 雄松堂, 1975.

Ogawa Makoto 小川信. *Ashikaga ichimon shugo hatten shi no kenkyū* 足利一門守護発展史の研究. Tokyo: Yoshikawa kōbunkan 吉川弘文館, 1980.

Ogisu Jundō 荻須純堂. *Nihon chūsei zenshū shi* 日本中世禅宗史. Kyoto: Mokuji-sha 木耳社, 1965.

Ōhashi Shunnō 大橋俊雄. *Jishū no seiritsu to tenkai* 時宗の成立と展開. Tokyo: Yoshikawa kōbunkan 吉川弘文館, 1973.

Ōhashi Shunnō 大橋俊雄. *Ippen* 一遍. Tokyo: Yoshikawa kōbunkan 吉川弘文館, 1983.

Okami Masao 岡見正雄, and Akamatsu Toshihide 赤松俊秀, eds. *Gukanshō* 愚管抄. Vol. 85 of *Nihon koten bungaku taikei* 日本古典文学大系. Tokyo: Iwanami shoten 岩波書店, 1967.

Okami Masao 岡見正雄, and Satake Akihiro 佐竹昭広, eds. *Rakuchū rakugai byōbu: Uesugibon* 洛中洛外屏風・上杉本. Tokyo: Iwanami shoten 岩波書店, 1983.

Okamura Morihiko 岡村守彦. *Hida shi kō* 飛騨史考, medieval vol. Tokyo: Okamura Morihiko 岡村守彦, 1979.

Ōkubo Dōshū 大久保道舟. *Dōgen zenji-den no kenkyū* 道元禅師伝の研究. Tokyo: Iwanami shoten 岩波書店, 1953.

Ōkubo Dōshū 大久保道舟. *Dōgen zenji-den no kenkyū* 道元禅師伝の研究. Tokyo: Iwanami shoten 岩波書店, 1966.

Ōkubo Dōshū 大久保道舟, ed. *Dōgen zenji zenshū* 道元禅師全集. Tokyo: Chikuma shobō 筑摩書房, 1970.

Okuno Takahiro 奥野高廣 Kōshitsu gokeizai shi no kenkyū 皇室御経済史の研究. Tokyo: Unebi shobō 畝傍書房, 1942.

Okutomi Takayuki 奥富敬之. *Kamakura Hōjōshi no kisoteki kenkyū* 鎌倉北条氏の基礎的研究. Tokyo: Yoshikawa kōbunkan 吉川弘文館, 1980.

Ōnishi Genichi 大西源一. *Kitabatakeshi no kenkyū* 北畠氏の研究. Mie: Mieken kyōdo shiryō kankōkai 三重県共同資料刊行会, 1962.

Osa Setsuko 長節子. "Kenchō rokunen 'tōsen' seigenryō ni kansuru shomon-dai" 建長六年「唐船」制限令に関する諸問題. *Chūkyō tanki daigaku ronsō* 中京短期大学論叢 1 (March 1966).

Ōsumi Kazuo 大隅和雄. "Kamakura Bukkyō to sono kakushin undō" 鎌倉仏教とその革新運動. In *Iwanami kōza Nihon rekishi* 岩波講座日本歴史, vol. 5. Tokyo: Iwanami shoten 岩波書店, 1975.

Ōsumi Kazuo 大隅和雄. "*Genkō shakusho* no Buppō kan" 元亨釈書の仏法観. *Kanezawa bunko kenkyū* 金沢文庫研究, 271 (1983).

Ota, Saburo, ed., *Studies in Japanese Culture*, vol. 2. Tokyo: P.E.N. Club, 1973.

Ōya Tokujō 大屋徳城. *Gyōnen Kokushi nempu* 凝然国師年譜. Nara: Tōdaiji kangakuin 東大寺勧学院, 1921.

Ōyama Kyōhei 大山喬平. "Jitō ryōshusei to zaike shihai" 地頭領主制と在家支配. In Nagahara Keiji 永原慶二, ed. *Nihon hōkensei seiritsu katei no kenkyū* 日本封建制成立過程の研究. Tokyo: Iwanami shoten 岩波書店, 1961.

Ōyama Kyōhei 大山喬平. *Kamakura bakufu* 鎌倉幕府. Vol. 9 of *Nihon no rekishi* 日本の歴史. Tokyo: Shōgakkan 小学館, 1974.

Ōyama Kyōhei 大山喬平. "Bunji kuni-jitō no sonzai keitai" 文治国地頭の存在形態. In Shibata Minoru sensei koki kinen 柴田実先生古稀記念, ed. *Nihon bunkashi ronsō* 日本文化史論叢. Osaka: Shibata Minoru sensei koki kinenkai 柴田実先生古稀記念会, 1976.

Ōyama Kyōhei 大山喬平. *Nihon chūsei nōsonshi no kenkyū* 日本中世農村史の研究. Tokyo: Iwanami shoten 岩波書店, 1978.

Philippi, Donald L., trans. *Kojiki*. Princeton, N. J.: Princeton University Press, 1969.

Pollack, David, trans. *Zen Poems of the Five Mountains*. Decatur, Ga.: Scholars Press, 1985.

Reischauer, Edwin O., trans. "The *Izayoi Nikki*." In Edwin O. Reischauer and Joseph Yamagiwa, eds. *Translations from Early Japanese Literature*. Cambridge, Mass.: Harvard University Press, 1951.

Reischauer, Edwin O., trans. *Ennin's Diary: The Record of a Pilgrimage to China in Search of the Law*. New York: Ronald Press, 1955.

Reischauer, Edwin O. "Japanese Feudalism." In Rushton Coulborn, ed. *Feudalism in History*. Princton, N. J.: Princeton University Press, 1956.

Reischauer, Edwin O., and Craig. Albert M. *Japan: Tradition and Transformation*. New York: Houghton Mifflin, 1973.

Reischauer, Edwin O., and Yamagiwa, Joseph. *Translations from Early Japanese Literature*. Cambridge, Mass.: Harvard University Press, 1951.

Rekishigaku kenkyūkai 歴史学研究会, and Nihonshi kenkyūkai 日本史研究会, comps. *Kōza Nihonshi* 講座日本史, vol. 3. Tokyo: Tōkyō daigaku shuppankai 東京大学出版会, 1970.

Richards, J. F., ed. *Precious Metals in the Later Medieval and Early Modern Worlds*. Durham, N. C.: Carolina Academic Press, 1983.

Rimer, J. Thomas, and Yamazaki, Masakazu, trans. *On the Art of the Nō Drama: The major Treatises of Zeami.* Princeton, N. J.: Princeton University Press, 1984.

Ronshū Nihon rekishi 論集日本歴史. 12 vols. Tokyo: Yūshōdō 雄松堂, 1973-77.

Ruch, Barbara. "Medieval Jongleurs and the Making of a National Literature." In John Whitney Hall and Toyoda Takeshi, eds. *Japan in the Muromachi Age.* Berkeley and Los Angeles: University of California Press, 1977.

Ryō Susumu 龍肅. *Kamakura jidai, ge: Kyoto-kizoku seiji dōkō to kōbu no kōshō* 鎌倉時代, 下：京都 - 貴族政治の動向と公武の交渉. Tokyo: Shunjūsha 春秋社, 1957.

Sakai Tadao 酒井忠夫. "Mindai bunka no Nihon bunka ni ataeta eikyō" 明代文化の日本文化に与えた影響. *Rekishi kyōiku* 歴史教育 11 (October 1963): 11-23.

Sakuma Shigeo 佐久間重男. "Minchō no kaikin seisaku" 明朝の海禁政策. *Tōhōgaku* 東方学 6 (1953).

Sakuma Shigeo 佐久間重男. "Minsho no Nitchū kankei o meguru ni, san no mondai" 明初の日中関係をめぐる二, 三の問題. *Hokkaidō daigaku jimbun kagaku ronshū* 北海道大学人文科学論集, no. 4 (February 1966).

Sakuma Shigeo 佐久間重男. "Eirakutei no taigai seisaku to Nihon" 永楽帝の対外政策と日本. *Hoppō bunka kenkyū* 北方文化研究 2 (1967).

Sakuma Shigeo 佐久間重男. "Mindai chūki no taigai seisaku to Nitchū kankei" 明代中期の対外政策と日中関係. *Hokkaidō daigaku jimbun kagaku ronshū* 北海道大学人文科学論集, no. 8 (1971).

Sakurada, Katsunori. "The Ebisu-gami in Fishing Villages." In Richard M. Dorson, ed. *Studies in Japanese Folklore.* Bloomington: Indiana University Folklore Series, no. 17, Indiana University Press, 1963.

Sakurai Keiyū 桜井景雄, and Fujii Manabu 藤井学, eds. *Nanzenji monjo* 南禅寺文書, vol. 1, docs. 2, 93, and 189; vol. 2, docs. 303, 378, and 384. Kyoto: Nanzenji shūmu honsho 南禅寺宗務本所, 1972.

Sanford, James H., trans. *Zen-man Ikkyū.* Decatur, Ga.: Scholars Press, 1981.

Sansom, George B. *A History of Japan to 1334.* Stanford, Calif.: Stanford University Press, 1958.

Sansom, George B. *A History of Japan, 1334-1615.* Stanford, Calif.: Stanford University Press, 1961.

Saru Genji sōshi 猿源氏草紙. *Otogizōshi* 御伽草紙. Vol. 38 of *Nihon koten bungaku taikei* 日本古典文学大系. Tokyo: Iwanami shoten 岩波書店, 1965.

Sasagawa Taneo 笹川種男, comp. *Shiryō taisei* 史料大成. Tokyo: Naigai shoseki 内外書籍, 1937.

Sasaki Ginya 佐々木銀弥. "Shōen ni okeru daisennō-sei no seiritsu to tenkai" 荘園における代銭納制の成立と展開. In Inagaki Yasuhiko 稲垣泰彦 and Nagahara Keiji 永原慶二, eds. *Chūsei no shakai to keizai* 中世の社会と経済. Tokyo: Tōkyō daigaku shuppankai 東京大学出版会, 1962.

Sasaki Ginya 佐々木銀弥. *Shōen no shōgyō* 荘園の商業. Tokyo: Yoshikawa kōbunkan 吉川弘文館, 1964.

Sasaki Ginya 佐々木銀弥. "Sangyō no bunka to chūsei shōgyō" 産業の分化と中

世商業. In Nagahara Keiji 永原慶二, ed. *Chūsei* 中世. Vol. 2 of *Nihon keizaishi taikei* 日本経済史大系. Tokyo: Tōkyō daigaku shuppankai 東京大学出版会, 1965.

Sasaki Ginya 佐々木銀弥. *Chūsei shōhin ryūtsūshi no kenkyū* 中世商品流通史の研究. Tokyo: Hōsei daigaku shippankyoku 法政大学出版局, 1972.

Sasaki Ginya 佐々木銀弥. *Muromachi bakufu* 室町幕府. Vol. 3 of *Nihon no rekishi* 日本の歴史. Tokyo: Shōgakkan 小学館, 1975.

Sasaki Ginya 佐々木銀弥. "Higashi Ajia bōekiken no keisei to kokusai ninshiki" 東アジア貿易圏の形成と国際認識. In *Iwanami kōza Nihon rekishi* 岩波講座日本歴史, vol. 7. Tokyo: Iwanami shoten 岩波書店, 1976.

Satō Hironobu 佐藤博信. " Sengokuki ni okeru Tōgoku kokkaron no ichi shiten - Koga kubō Ashikagashi to Go-Hōjō shi o chūshin to shite" 戦国期における東国国家論の一視点 - 古河公方足利氏と御北条氏を中心として. *Rekishigaku kenkyū* 歴史学研究, special issue (October 1979): 72-5.

Satō Kazuhiko 佐藤和彦. *Nambokuchō nairan shiron* 南北朝内乱史論. Tokyo: Tōkyō daigaku shuppankai 東京大学出版会, 1979.

Satō Shin'ichi 佐藤進一. *Kamakura jidai soshō seido no kenkyū* 鎌倉時代訴訟制度の研究. Tokyo: Unebi shobō 畝傍書房, 1943.

Satō Shin'ichi 佐藤進一. *Kamakura bakufu soshō seido no kenkyū* 鎌倉幕府訴訟制度の研究. Tokyo: Meguro shoten 目黒書店, 1946.

Satō Shin'ichi 佐藤進一. "Bakufu ron" 幕府論. In *Shin Nihon shi kōza* 新日本史講座. Tokyo: Chūō kōronsha 中央公論社, 1949.

Satō Shin'ichi 佐藤進一. *Shin Nihonshi taikei* 新日本史大系. Tokyo: Asakura shoten 朝倉書店, 1954.

Satō Shin'ichi 佐藤進一. "Shugo ryōgokusei no tenkai" 守護領国制の展開. In Toyoda Takeshi 豊田武, ed. *Shin Nihonshi taikei dai san kan, chūsei shakai* 新日本史大系第三巻・中世社会. Tokyo: Asakura shoten 朝倉書店, 1954.

Satō Shin'ichi 佐藤進一. "Kamakura bakufu seiji no senseika ni tsuite" 鎌倉幕府政治の専制化について. In Takeuchi Rizō 竹内理三, ed. *Nihon hōkensei seiritsu no kenkyū* 日本封建制成立の研究. Tokyo: Yoshikawa kōbunkan 吉川弘文館, 1955.

Satō Shin'ichi 佐藤進一. "Muromachi bakufu kaisōki no kansei taikei" 室町幕府開創期の官制体系. In Satō Shin'ichi 佐藤進一, and Ishimoda Shō 石母田正, eds. *Chūsei no hō to kokka* 中世の法と国家. Tokyo: Tōkyō daigaku shuppankai 東京大学出版会, 1960.

Satō Shin'ichi 佐藤進一. "Muromachi bakufu ron" 室町幕府論. In *Iwanani kōza Nihon rekishi* 岩波講座日本歴史, vol. 7. Tokyo: Iwanami shoten 岩波書店, 1963.

Satō Shin'ichi 佐藤進一. *Nambokuchō no dōran* 南北朝の動乱. Vol. 9 of *Nihon no rekishi* 日本の歴史. Tokyo: Chūō kōronsha 中央公論社, 1965.

Satō Shin'ichi 佐藤進一. *Muromachi bakufu shugo seido no kenkyū-Nambokuchōki shokoku shugo enkaku kōshō hen* 室町幕府守護制度の研究 - 南北朝期諸国守護沿革考証編, vol. 1. Tokyo: Tōkyō daigaku shuppankai 東京大学出版会, 1967.

Satō Shin'ichi 佐藤進一. *Komonjogaku nyūmon* 古文書学入門. Tokyo: Hōsei daigaku shuppankyoku 法政大学出版局, 1971.

Satō Shin'ichi 佐藤進一. *Zōho Kamakura bakufu shugo seido no kenkyū* 増補鎌倉幕府守護制度の研究. Tokyo: Tōkyō daigaku shuppankai 東京大学出版会, 1971.

Satō, Shin'ichi, and Hall, John Whitney. "The Ashikaga Shogun and the Muromachi Bakufu Administration." In John Whitney Hall and Toyoda Takeshi, eds. *Japan in the Muromachi Age*. Berkeley and Los Angeles: University of California Press, 1977.

Satō Shin'ichi 佐藤進一, and Ikeuchi Yoshisuke 池内義資, eds. *Chūsei hōsei shiryōshū* 中世法制史料集, vols. 1 and 2. Tokyo: Iwanami shoten 岩波書店, 1955-57, reprinted in 1978.

Satō Shin'ichi 佐藤進一, and Ishimoda Shō 石母田正, eds. *Chūsei no hō to kokka* 中世の法と国家. Tokyo: Tōkyō daigaku shuppankai 東京大学出版会, 1960.

Satō Taishun 佐藤泰舜, ed. *Muchū mondō shū* 夢中問答集. Tokyo: Iwanami shoten 岩波書店, 1934.

Seidensticker, Edward G., trans. *The Tale of Genji*. New York: Knopf, 1978.

Sen Sōshitsu 千宗室, ed. *Sadō koten zenshū* 茶道古典全集, vol. 4. Kyoto: Tankōsha 淡交社, 1956.

Seno Seiichirō 瀬野精一郎. *Kamakura bakufu saikyojō shū* 鎌倉幕府裁許状集. 2 vols. Tokyo: Yoshikawa kōbunkan 吉川弘文館, 1970.

Seno Seiichirō 瀬野精一郎, ed. *Aokata monjo* 青方文書, vol. 1. Tokyo: Zoku gunsho ruijū kanseikai 続群書類従完成会, 1975.

Seno Seiichirō 瀬野精一郎. *Chinzei gokenin no kenkyū* 鎮西御家人の研究. Tokyo: Yoshikawa kōbunkan 吉川弘文館, 1975.

Seta Katsuya 瀬田勝哉. "Chūsei makki no zaichi tokusei" 中世末期の在地徳政. *Shigaku zasshi* 史学雑誌 77 (September 1968): 1-52.

Shibata Minoru sensei koki kinenkai 柴田実先生古稀記念会, ed. *Nihon bunka shi ronsō* 日本文化史論叢. Osaka: Shibata Minoru sensei koki kinenkai 柴田実先生古稀記念会, 1976.

Shichinin bikuni 七人比丘尼. Vol. 1 of *Kindai Nihon bungaku taikei* 近代日本文学大系. Tokyo: Kokumin tosho 国民図書, 1928.

Shiga daigaku Nihon keizai bunka kenkyūjo shiryōkan 滋賀大学日本経済文化研究所史料館, ed. *Sugaura monjo* 菅浦文書, vol. 1, no. 180. Tokyo: Yūhikaku 有斐閣, 1960.

Shigematsu Akihisa 重松明久. *Kakunyo* 覚如. Tokyo: Yoshikawa kōbunkan 吉川弘文館, 1964.

Shimada Jirō 島田次郎. "Zaichi-ryōshusei no tenkai to Kamakura bakufu hō" 在地領主制の展開と鎌倉幕府法. In Inagaki Yasuhiko 稲垣泰彦, and Nagahara Keiji 永原慶二, eds. *Chūsei no shakai to keizai* 中世の社会と経済. Tokyo: Tōkyō daigaku shuppankai 東京大学出版会, 1962.

Shimada Jirō 島田次郎. "Hanzei seido no seiritsu" 半済制度の成立. In Ogawa Makoto 小川信, ed. *Muromachi seiken* 室町政権. Vol. 5 of *Ronshū Nihon rekishi* 論集日本歴史. Tokyo: Yūshōdō 雄松堂, 1975.

Shimosaka Mamoru 下坂守. "Sanmon shisetsu seido no seiritsu to tenkai:

Muromachi bakufu no sanmon seisaku o megutte" 山門使節制度の成立と展開・室町幕府の山門政策をめぐって. *Shirin* 史林 58 (January 1975): 67-114.
Shin Shuku Shū 申叔集. *Kaitō shokokki* 海東諸国記. Tokyo: Kokusho kankōkai 国書刊行会, 1975.
Shinoda, Minoru. *The Founding of the Kamakura Shogunate*. New York: Columbia University Press, 1960.
Shinshū Kyōto sōsho 新修京都叢書, vols. 2, 9. Kyoto: Kōsaisha 光彩社, 1967.
Shinshū seikyō zensho 真宗聖教全書. 5 vols. Kyoto: Kōkyō shoin 興教書院, 1941.
Shinshū zenshu 真宗全集, vol. 58. Tokyo: Kokusho kankōkai 国書刊行会, 1915 and 1975.
Shintei zōho Kokushi taikei 新訂増補国史大系, vols. 11, 32. Tokyo: Yoshikawa kōbunkan 吉川弘文館, 1932-39.
Shiryō shūsei hensankai 史料集成編纂会, ed. *Chūgoku-Chōsen no shiseki ni okeru Nihon shiryō shusei, Sankoku, Kōrai no bu* 中国朝鮮の史籍における日本史料集成, 三国, 高麗の部. Tokyo: Kokusho kankōkai 国書刊行会, 1978.
Shōbōgenzō 正法眼蔵, vol. 1. Tokyo: Iwanami bunko 岩波文庫, 1939.
"Shokunin uta awase no sekai" 職人歌合絵の世界. *Kobijutsu* 古美術, no. 74 (April 1985).
Sogabe Shizuo 曽我部静雄. *Nissō kinkahei kōryushi* 日宋金貨幣交流史. Tokyo: Hōbunkan 宝文館, 1949.
Steenstrup, Henrik Carl Trolle. "Hōjō Shigetoki (1198-1261) and His Role in the History of Political and Ethical Ideas in Japan." Ph.D. Diss., Harvard University, 1977.
Sugimoto Hisao 杉本尚雄. *Kikuchi-shi sandai* 菊池氏三代. Tokyo: Yoshikawa kōbunkan 吉川弘文館, 1966.
Sugiyama Hiroshi 杉山博. "Muromachi bakufu" 室町幕府. In *Iwanami kōza Nihon rekishi* 岩波講座日本歴史, vol. 3. Tokyo: Iwanami shoten 岩波書店, 1957.
Sugiyama Hiroshi 杉山博. "Shugo ryōgokusei no tenkai" 守護領国制の展開. In *Iwanami kōza Nihon rekishi* 岩波講座日本歴史, vol. 7. Tokyo: Iwanami shoten 岩波書店, 1963.
Sugiyama Hiroshi 杉山博. *Dokushi sōran* 読史総覧. Tokyo: Jimbutsu ōraisha 人物往来社, 1966.
Suma Chikai 須磨千頴. "Dosō ni yoru shōen nengu no ukeoi ni tsuite" 土倉による荘園年貢の請負について. *Shigaku zasshi* 80 (June 1971): 1-43.
Suma Chikai 須磨千頴. "Dosō no tochi shūseki to tokusei" 土倉の土地集積と徳政. *Shigaku zasshi* 史学雑誌 81 (March 1972): 1-40.
Suzuki Taizan 鈴木泰山. "Sōtō Zen no gubu to sono gegosha" 曹洞禅の弘布とその外護者. In Itō Tasaburō 伊東多三郎, ed. *Kokumin seikatsu-shi kenkyū* 国民生活史研究. Tokyo: Yoshikawa kōbunkan 吉川弘文館, 1959.
Taga Munehaya 多賀宗隼. *Kamakura jidai no shisō to bunka* 鎌倉時代の思想と文化. Tokyo: Meguro shoten 目黒書店, 1946.
Taga Munehaya 多賀宗隼. *Eisai* 栄西. Tokyo: Yoshikawa kōbunkan 吉川弘文館, 1965.

Taishō shinshū daizōkyō 大正新修大蔵経. 85 vols. Tokyo: Taishō shinshū daizōkyō kankōkai 大正新修大蔵経刊行会, 1924-32.

Takagi Ichinosuke et al. 高木市之助他, eds. *Heike monogatari* 平家物語. Vols. 32 and 33 of *Nihon koten bungaku taikei* 日本古典文学大系. Tokyo: Iwanami shoten 岩波書店, 1959-60.

Takagi Shintarō 高木真太郎. *Ōei gaikō no zengo* 応永外寇の前後. Tokyo: Yagi shoten 八木書店, 1942.

Takagi Shōsaku 高木昭作. "Bakuhan shoki no kuni-bugyō ni tsuite" 幕藩初期の国奉行について. *Rekishigaku kenkyū* 歴史学研究, no. 431 (May 1975): 15-62.

Takagi Yutaka 高木豊. *Nichiren to sono montei* 日蓮とその門弟. Tokyo: Kōbundō 公文堂, 1965.

Takagi Yutaka 高木豊. *Nichiren: Sono kōdō to shisō* 日蓮 - その行動と思想. Tokyo: Hyōronsha 評論社, 1970.

Takagi Yutaka 高木豊. *Kamakura Bukkyōshi kenkyū* 鎌倉仏教史研究. Tokyo: Iwanami shoten 岩波書店, 1982.

Takenaka Yasukazu 竹中靖一, and Kawakami Tadashi 川上雅. *Nihon shōgyōshi* 日本商業史. Tokyo: Minerva shobō ミネルヴァ書房, 1965.

Takenaka Yasukazu 竹中靖一, and Sakudō Yōtarō 作道洋太郎. *Nihon keizaishi* 日本経済史. Tokyo: Gakubunsha 学文社, 1972.

Takenuki Genshō 竹貫元勝. "Rinka ni okeru kyōdan keiei ni tsuite" 林下における教団経営について. *Bukkyō shigaku* 仏教史学 15 (July 1971): 225-63.

Takeuchi Michio 竹内道雄. "Nihon ni okeru Sōtō Zen no tenkai" 日本における曹洞禅の展開. In *Kōza Zen* 講座, 禅, vol. 4. Tokyo: Chikuma shobō 筑摩書房, 1967.

Takeuchi Michio 竹内道雄. *Sōtō-shū kyōdan shi* 曹洞宗教団史. Tokyo: Kyōiku shinchōsha 教育新潮社, 1971.

Takeuchi Michio 竹内道雄. *Nihon no Zen* 日本の禅. Tokyo: Shinchōsha 新潮社, 1976.

Takeuchi Rizō 竹内理三, comp. *Heian ibun* 平安遺文. 15 vols. Tokyo: Tōkyōdō 東京堂, 1947-80.

Takeuchi Rizō 竹内理三, ed. *Nihon hōkensei seiritsu no kenkyū* 日本封建制成立の研究. Tokyo: Yoshikawa kōbunkan 吉川弘文館, 1955.

Takeuchi Rizō 竹内理三. *Ritsuryōsei to kizoku seiken* 律令制と貴族政権. 2 vols. Tokyo: Ochanomizu shobō 御茶ノ水書房, 1957-58.

Takeuchi Rizō 竹内理三. "Chinzei bugyō ni tsuite no ichi, ni no kōsatsu" 鎮西奉行についての一, 二の考察. In *Uozumi-sensei koki kinen kokushigaku ronsō* 魚住先生古稀記念国史学論叢. Osaka: Kansai daigaku 関西大学, 1959.

Takeuchi Rizō 竹内理三, comp. *Zoku shiryō taisei* 続史料大成. 22 vols. Kyoto: Rinsen shoten 臨川書店, 1967.

Takeuchi Rizō 竹内理三, ed. *Dazaifu, Dazaifu temmangū shiryō* 太宰府・太宰府天満宮史料, vol. 7 Fukuoka-ken: Dazaifu temmangū 太宰府天満宮, 1971.

Takeuchi Rizō 竹内理三, ed. *Kamakura ibun* 鎌倉遺文. 36 vols. Tokyo: Tōkyōdō 東京堂, 1971-88.

Takeuchi Rizō 竹内理三, ed. *Tochi seidoshi* 土地制度史, vol. 1. Tokyo: Yoshikawa kōbunkan 吉川弘文館, 1973.

Takeuchi Rizō hakase kanreki kinenkai 竹内理三博士還暦記念会, ed. *Shōensei to buke shakai* 荘園制と武家社会. Tokyo: Yoshikawa kōbunkan 吉川弘文館, 1969.

Takeuchi Rizō hakase koki kinenkai 竹内理三博士古稀記念会, comp. *Zoku shōensei to buke shakai* 続荘園制と武家社会. Tokyo: Yoshikawa kōbunkan 吉川弘文館, 1978.

Takizawa Takeo 滝沢武雄. "Erizeni" 撰銭. In Nagahara Keiji 永原慶二 et al., eds. *Chuseishi handobukku* 中世史ハンドブック. Tokyo: Kondō shuppansha 近藤出版社, 1973.

Tamamura Takeji 玉村竹二. "Gozan sōrin no tatchū ni tsuite" 五山叢林の塔頭について. *Rekishi chiri* 歴史地理 76 (1940): 44-58 and 33-64.

Tamamura Takeji 玉村竹二. "Zen" 禅. In Bitō Masahide, ed. *Nihon bunka to Chūgoku* 日本文化と中国. Tokyo: Taishūkan shoten 大修館書店, 1968.

Tamamura Takeji 玉村竹二. *Musō Kokushi* 夢窓国師. Kyoto: Heirakuji shoten 平楽寺書店, 1969.

Tamura Enchō 田村円澄. *Hōnen* 法然. Tokyo: Yoshikawa kōbunkan 吉川弘文館, 1959.

Tamura Enchō 田村円澄. *Nihon Bukkyō shisōshi kenkyū: Jōdokyōhen* 日本仏教思想史研究・浄土教編. Kyoto: Heirakuji shoten 平楽寺書店, 1959.

Tamura Hiroyuki 田村洋幸. *Chūsei Nitchō bōeki no kenkyū* 中世日朝貿易の研究. Kyoto: Sanwa shobō 三和書房, 1967.

Tamura Hiroyuki 田村洋幸, comp. *Nichirai kankei hennen shiryō* 日麗関係編年史料. Kyoto: Mine shobō 峰書房, 1967.

Tamura Hiroyuki 田村洋幸, comp. *Sesō jitsuroku Nitchō keizai shiryō* 世宗実録日朝経済史料. Tokyo: Koseisha Koseikaku 恒星社厚生閣, n. d.

Tamura Hiroyuki 田村洋幸, comp. *Taiso-Teisō-Taisō jitsuroku Nitchō kankei hennen shiryō* 大祖・定宗・太宗実録日朝関係編年史料. Kyoto: Sanwa shobō 三和書房, n. d.

Tamura Yoshirō 田村芳郎' "Tendai hongaku shisō gaisetsu" 天台本覚思想概説. In *Tendai hongaku ron* 天台本覚論. Vol. 9 of *Nihon shisō taikei* 日本思想大系. Tokyo: Iwanami shoten 岩波書店, 1973.

Tanaka Hisao 田中久夫. *Myoe* 明恵. Tokyo: Yoshikawa kōbunkan 吉川弘文館, 1961.

Tanaka Hisao 田中久夫. "Chosakusha ryakuden" 著作者略伝. In *Kamakura kyū Bukkyō* 鎌倉旧仏教. Vol. 15 of *Nihon shisō taikei* 日本思想大系. Tokyo: Iwanami shoten 岩波書店, 1971.

Tanaka Kenji 田中健二. "Kamakura bakufu no Ōsumi no kuni shihai ni tsuite no ichi kōsatsu" 鎌倉幕府の大隅国支配についての一考察. *Kyūshū shigaku* 九州史学, nos. 65 and 67 (1977 and 1979): 1-22 and 1-18.

Tanaka Minoru 田中稔. "Jōkyū kyōgata bushi no ichi kōsatsu-rango no shin jitō buninchi o chūshin to shite" 承久京方武士の一考察－乱後の新地頭補人地を中心として. *Shigaku zasshi* 史学雑誌 65 (1956): 21-48.

Tanaka Minoru 田中稔. "Kamakura-dono otsukai kō" 鎌倉殿御使考. *Shirin* 史

林 45 (November 1962): 1-23.

Tanaka Minoru 田中稔. "Kamakura shoki no seiji katei-kenkyū nenkan o chūshin ni shite" 鎌倉初期の政治過程 - 建久年間を中心にして. *Rekishi kyōiku* 歴史教育 11 (1963): 19-26.

Tanaka Minoru 田中稔. "Jōkyū no rango no shin jitō buninchi" 承久の乱後の新地頭補任地. *Shigaku zasshi* 史学雑誌 79 (1970): 38-53.

Tanaka Takeo 田中健夫. *Chūsei kaigai kōshōshi no kenkyū* 中世海外交渉史の研究. Tokyo: Tōkyō daigaku shuppankai 東京大学出版会, 1959.

Tanaka Takeo 田中健夫. *Wakō to kangō bōeki* 倭寇と勘合貿易. Tokyo: Shibundō 至文堂, 1961.

Tanaka Takeo 田中健夫. *Chūsei taigai kankeishi* 中世対外関係史. Tokyo: Tōkyō daigaku shuppankai 東京大学出版会, 1975.

Tanaka Takeo 田中健夫. "Muromachi bakufu to Ryūkyū to no kankei no ichi kōsatsu" 室町幕府と琉球との関係の一考察. *Nantō shigaku* 南島史学, no. 16 (November 1980).

Tanaka, Takeo, with Sakai, Robert. "Japan's Relations with Overseas Countries." In John Whitney Hall and Toyoda Takeshi, eds. *Japan in the Muromachi Age*. Berkeley and Los Angeles: University of California Press, 1977.

Tanaka Yoshinari 田中義成. *Nambokuchō jidaishi* 南北朝時代史. Tokyo: Meiji shoin 明治書院, 1922.

Tanuma Mutsumi 田沼睦. "Kuden tansen to shugo ryōgoku" 公田段銭と守護領国. *Shoryōbu kiyō* 書陵部紀要, no. 17 (1965): 16-33.

Tanuma Mutsumi 田沼睦. "Muromachi bakufu, shugo, kokujin" 室町幕府, 守護, 国人. In *Iwanami kōza Nihon rekishi* 岩波講座日本歴史, vol. 7. Tokyo: Iwanami shoten 岩波書店, 1976.

Tayama Hōnan 田山方南, ed. *Daitokuji* 大徳寺. Tokyo: Kōdansha 講談社, 1968.

Toda Yoshimi 戸田芳実. *Nihon ryōshusei seiritsushi no kenkyū* 日本領主制成立史の研究. Tokyo: Iwanami shoten 岩波書店, 1967.

Toita Michizō 戸板道蔵. *Kan'ami to Zeami* 観阿弥と世阿弥. Tokyo: Iwanami shoten 岩波書店, 1969.

Toki Zenmaro 土岐善麿. *Shinshū Kyōgoku Tamekane* 新修京極為兼. Tokyo: Kadokawa shoten 角川書店, 1968.

Tokoro Shigemoto 所重基. *Nichiren no shisō to Kamakura Bukkyō* 日蓮の思想と鎌倉仏教. Tokyo: Fuzambō 富山房, 1965.

Tokuda Ken'ichi 徳田釼一. *Chūsei ni okeru suiun no hattatsu* 中世における水運の発達. Tokyo: Gannandō shoten 巌南堂, 1966.

Tōkyō daigaku shiryō hensanjo 東京大学史料編纂所, ed. *Dai Nihon komonjo, iewake* 大日本古文書家わけ, vol. 1, pt. 6. Tokyo: Tōkyō teikoku daigaku 東京帝国大学, 1906.

Tōkyō daigaku shiryō hensanjo 東京大学史料編纂所, ed. *Tōji hyakugō monjo* 東寺百合文書, vol. 1. *Dai Nihon komonjo, iewake* 大日本古文書家わけ, vol. 10, pt. 1. Tokyo: Tōkyō teikoku daigaku 東京帝国大学, 1925.

Tōkyō daigaku shiryō hensanjo 東京大学史料編纂所, ed. *Daitokuji monjo* 大徳寺

文書, vols. 1-3. Vol. 17 of *Dai Nihon komonjo, iewake* 大日本古文書家わけ.
Tokyo: Tōkyō daigaku shuppankai 東京大学出版会, 1954.

Tōkyō daigaku shiryō hensanjo 東京大学史料編纂所, ed. *Dai Nihon kokiroku kennaiki* 大日本古記録建内記, vol. 1. Tokyo: Iwanami shoten 岩波書店, 1963.

Tōkyō daigaku shiryō hensanjo 東京大学史料編纂所, ed. *Shiryō sōran* 史料総覧, vol. 5. Tokyo: Tōkyō daigaku shuppankai 東京大学出版会, 1965.

Tōkyō teikoku daigaku 東京帝国大学, ed. *Dai Nihon shiryō* 大日本史料, series 8, vol. 13. Tokyo: Shiryō hensan gakari 史料編纂掛, 1927.

Tōma Seita 藤間生大. *Higashi Ajia sekai no keisei* 東アジア世界の形成. Tokyo: Shunjūsha 春秋社, 1966.

Tomikura Tokujirō 冨倉徳次郎. "Akashi no Kakuichi o megutte" 明石覚一をめぐって. *Kokugo kokubun* 国語国文 21 (1952): 37-46.

Tomikura Tokujirō 冨倉徳次郎. *Heike monogatari kenkyū* 平家物語研究. Tokyo: Kadokawa shoten 角川書店, 1967.

Tomikura Tokujirō 冨倉徳次郎. *Shintei Heike monogatari* 新訂平家物語. Vol. 1 of *Nihon koten zenshū* 日本古典全集. Tokyo: Asahi shimbunsha 朝日新聞社, 1984.

Toyoda Takeshi 豊田武. *Chūsei Nihon shōgyōshi no kenkyū* 中世日本商業史の研究. Tokyo: Iwanami shoten 岩波書店, 1952.

Toyoda Takeshi 豊田武, ed. *Shin Nihonshi taikei dai san kan, chūsei shakai* 新日本史大系第三巻・中世社会. Tokyo: Asakura shoten 朝倉書店, 1954.

Toyoda Takeshi 豊田武. "Genkō tōbatsu no shoseiryoku ni tsuite" 元寇討伐の諸勢力について. In Ogawa Makoto 小川信, ed. *Muromachi seiken* 室町政権. Vol. 5. of *Ronshū Nihon rekishi* 論集日本歴史. Tokyo: Yūshōdō 雄松堂, 1975.

Toyoda Takeshi 豊田武. "Otogi ni arawareta minshū" お伽に現れた民衆. In Ichiko Teiji 市古貞次, ed. *Otogizōshi* お伽草紙. Vol. 13 of *Zusetsu Nihon no koten* 図説日本の古典. Tokyo: Shūeisha 集英社, 1980.

Toyoda Takeshi 豊田武. "Tenkai no shakai" 展開の社会. In Ichiko Teiji 市古貞次, ed. *Otogizōshi* お伽草紙. Vol. 13 of *Zusetsu Nihon no koten* 図説日本の古典. Tokyo: Shūeisha 集英社, 1980.

Toyoda Takeshi 豊田武, and Iikura Harutake 飯倉晴武, eds. *Yamashina ke-raiki* 山科家礼記. 5 vols. Tokyo: Zokugunsho ruijū kanseikai 続群書類従完成会, 1967-73.

Toyoda Takeshi 豊田武, and Kodama Kōta 児玉幸多. *Ryūtsūshi* 流通史. Tokyo: Yamakawa shuppansha 山川出版社, 1969.

Tsuji Zennosuke 辻善之助. *Nisshi bunka no kōryū* 日支文化の交流. Osaka: Sōgensha 創元社, 1938.

Tsuji Zennosuke 辻善之助. *Nihon Bukkyōshi* 日本仏教史, vol. 2 and 3. Tokyo: Iwanami shoten 岩波書店, 1960 and 1970.

Tsukushi Yutaka 筑紫豊. *Genkō kigen* 元寇起源. Fukuoka: Fukuoka kyōdo bunkakai 福岡郷土文化会, 1972.

Uejima Tamotsu 上島有. *Tōji jiin keizai ni kansuru ichi kōsatsu* 東寺寺院経済に関する一考察. In Kyōto daigaku bungakubu dokushikai 京都大学文学部読史会, ed. *Kokushi ronshū* 国史論集. Kyoto: Dokushikai 読史会, 1959.

Uejima Tamotsu 上島有. *Keikō shōen sonraku no kenkyū* 京郊荘園村落の研究. Tokyo: Hanawa shobō 塙書房, 1970.

Umehara Takeshi 梅原猛. "Yūgen to shi" 幽玄と詩. In Hayashiya Tatsusaburō 林屋辰三郎, and Okada Yuzuru 岡田譲, ed. *Ami to machishū* 阿弥と町衆. Vol. 8 of *Nihon bunka no rekishi* 日本文化の歴史. Tokyo: Gakushū kenkyūsha 学習研究社, 1969.

Ury, Marian. *Poems of the Five Mountains*. Tokyo: Mushinsha, 1977.

Usuda Jingorō 臼田甚五郎, and Shimma Shin'ichi 新間進一, eds. *Kagura uta, Saibara, Ryōjin hishō, Kanginshū* 神楽歌・催馬楽・梁塵秘抄・閑吟集. Vol. 25 of *Nihon koten bungaku zenshū* 日本古典文学全集. Tokyo: Shōgakkan 小学館, 1985.

Usui Nobuyoshi 臼井信義. *Ashikaga Yoshimitsu* 足利義満. Tokyo: Yoshikawa kōbunkan 吉川弘文館, 1960.

Uwayokote Masataka 上横手雅敬. *Hōjō Yasutoki* 北条泰時. Tokyo: Yoshikawa kōbunkan 吉川弘文館, 1958.

Uwayokote Masataka 上横手雅敬. "Renshosei no seiritsu" 連書制の成立. In *Kokushi ronshū* 国史論集, vol. 2. Kyoto: Dokushikai 読史会, 1959.

Uwayokote Masataka 上横手雅敬. "Kamakura seiken seiritsuki o meguru kingyō" 鎌倉政権成立期をめぐる近業. *Hōseishi kenkyū* 法政史研究 11 (1960): 175-81.

Varley, H. Paul. *Imperial Restoration in Medieval Japan*. New York: Columbia University Press, 1971.

Varley, H. Paul. "Ashikaga Yoshimitsu and the World of Kitayama: Social Change and Shogunal Patronage in Early Muromachi Japan." In John Whitney Hall and Toyoda Takeshi, eds. *Japan in the Medieval Age*. Berkeley and Los Angeles: University of California Press, 1977.

Varley, H. Paul, trans. *Jinnō Shōtōki: A Chronicle of Gods and Sovereigns*. New York: Columbia University Press, 1980.

Varley, H. Paul. "The Hōjō Family and Succession to Power." In Jeffrey P. Mass, ed. *Court and Bakufu in Japan: Essays in Kamakura History*. New Haven, Conn.: Yale University Press, 1982.

Wada hakase kanreki kinenkai 和田博士還暦記念会, ed. *Tōyōshi ronsō* 東洋史論叢. Tokyo: Wada hakase kanreki kinenkai 和田博士還暦記念会, 1951.

Wajima Yoshio 和島芳男. *Eison. Ninshō* 叡尊・忍性. Tokyo: Yoshikawa kōbunkan 吉川弘文館, 1970.

Wakita Haruko 脇田晴子. *Nihon chūsei shōgyō hattatsushi no kenkyū* 日本中世商業発達史の研究. Tokyo: Ochanomizu shobō 御茶ノ水書房, 1969.

Wakita Haruko 脇田晴子. "Muromachi-ki no keizai hatten" 室町期の経済発展. In *Iwanami kōza Nihon rekishi* 岩波講座日本歴史, vol. 7. Tokyo: Iwanami shoten 岩波書店, 1976.

Wakita Haruko 脇田晴子. *Nihon chūsei toshi ron* 日本中世都市論. Tokyo: Tōkyō daigaku shuppankai 東京大学出版会, 1981.

Wakita Haruko 脇田晴子. "Chūsei ni okeru seibetsu yakuwari buntan to joseikan" 中世における性別役割分担と女性観. In *Nihon josei shi - chūsei* 日本

女性史 - 中世, vol. 2. Tokyo: Tōkyō daigaku shuppankai 東京大学出版会, 1983.

Wakita Osamu 脇田修. "Jinaimachi no kōzō to tenkai 寺内町の構造と展開. *Shirin* 史林 41 (January 1958): 1-24.

Watanabe Yosuke 渡辺世祐. *Kantō chūshin Ashikaga jidai no kenkyū* 関東中心足利時代の研究. Tokyo: Yūzankaku 雄山閣, 1926.

Weber, Max. *The Theory of Social and Economic Organization*. New York: Free Press, 1964.

Weinstein, Stanley. "The Concept of Reformation in Japanese Buddhism." In Saburo Ota, ed. *Studies in Japanese Culture*, vol. 2. Tokyo: P. E. N. Club, 1973.

Weinstein, Stanley. "Imperial Patronage in the Formation of T'ang Buddhism." In Arthur F. Wright and Denis Twitchett, eds. *Perspectives on the T'ang*. New Haven, Conn.: Yale University Press, 1973.

Wintersteen, Prescott B. "The Early Muromachi Bakufu in Kyoto." In John Whitney Hall and Jeffrey P. Mass, eds. *Medieval Japan: Essays in Institutional History*. New Haven, Conn.: Yale University Press, 1974.

Wintersteen, Prescott B. "The Muromachi Shugo and Hanzei." In John Whitney Hall and Jeffrey P. Mass, eds. *Medieval Japan: Essays in Institutional History*. New Haven, Conn.: Yale University Press, 1974.

Wright, Arthur F., and Twitchett, Denis, eds. *Perspectives on the T'ang*. New Haven, Conn.: Yale University Press, 1973.

Yamada An'ei 山田安栄. *Fukuteki hen* 伏敵編. 2 vols. Tokyo: Yoshikawa kōbunkan 吉川弘文館, 1891.

Yamada Sōbin 山田宗敏. "Sanmon shūfuku no kiroku" 山門修復の記録. In Haga Kōshirō et al. 芳賀幸四郎他, eds. *Daitokuji to sadō* 大徳寺と茶道. Kyoto: Tankōsha 淡交社, 1972.

Yamada Yoshio 山田孝雄 et al., eds. *Konjaku monogatari* 今昔物語. Vol. 26 of *Nihon koten bungaku taikei* 日本古典文学大系. Tokyo: Iwanami shoten 岩波書店, 1963.

Yamagishi Tokuhei 山岸徳平, ed. *Gozan bungaku-shū, Edo kanshi-shū* 五山文学集 - 江戸漢詩集. Vol. 89 of *Nihon koten bungaku taikei* 日本古典文学大系. Tokyo: Iwanami shoten 岩波書店, 1968.

Yamaguchi Osamu 山口修. *Mōko shūrai* 蒙古襲来. Tokyo: Tōgensha 桃源社, 1964, 1979.

Yamamura, Kozo. "The Development of *Za* in Medieval Japan." *Business History Review* 47 (Winter 1973): 438-65.

Yamamura, Kozo. "Returns on Unification: Economic Growth in Japan, 1550-1650." In John Whitney Hall, Keiji Nagahara, and Kozo Yamamura, eds. *Japan Before Tokugawa: Political Consolidation and Economic Growth, 1500-1650*. Princeton, N. J.: Princeton University Press, 1981.

Yamamura, Kozo. "Tara in Transition: A Study of a Kamakura *Shōen*." *Journal of Japanese Studies* 7 (Summer 1981): 349-91.

Yamamura, Kozo, and Kamiki, Tetsuo. "Silver Mines and Sung Coins: A

Monetary History of Medieval and Modern Japan in International Perspective." In J. F. Richards, ed. *Precious Metals in the Later Medieval and Early Modern Worlds*. Durham, N. C.: Carolina Academic Press, 1983.

Yampolsky, Philip. *The Platform Sutra of the Sixth Patriarch*. New York: Columbia University Press, 1967.

Yanagida Seizan 柳田聖山. *Rinzai no kafū* 臨済の家風. Tokyo: Chikuma shobō 筑摩書房, 1967.

Yanagita Kunio 柳田国男. "Miko kō" 巫女考. In *Teihon Yanagita Kunio shū* 定本柳田国男集, vol. 9. Tokyo: Chikuma shobō 筑摩書房, 1982.

Yashiro Kuniharu 八代国治, ed. *Kokushi sōsetsu* 国史叢説. Tokyo: Yoshikawa kōbunkan 吉川弘文館, 1925.

Yasuda Motohisa 安田元久. *Nihon zenshi* 日本全史 (*chūsei* 1). Tokyo: Tōkyō daigaku shuppankai 東京大学出版会, 1958.

Yasuda Motohisa 安田元久. *Jitō oyobi jitō ryōshusei no kenkyū* 地頭及び地頭領主制の研究. Tokyo: Yamakawa shuppansha 山川出版社, 1961.

Yasuda Motohisa 安田元久. *Shugo to jitō* 守護と地頭. Tokyo: Shibundō 至文堂, 1964.

Yasuda Motohisa 安田元久. "Gokenin-sei seiritsu ni kansuru ichi shiron" 御家人制成立に関する一試論. *Gakushūin daigaku bungakubu kenkyū nempō* 学習院大学文学部研究年報 16 (1969): 81-110.

Yasui Kōdo 安井広度. *Hōnen monka no kyōgaku* 法然門下の教学. Kyoto: Hōzōkan 法蔵館, 1968.

Yokoyama Hideya 横山秀哉. *Zen no Kenchiku* 禅の建築. Tokyo: Shōkokusha 彰国社, 1967.

Yokoyama Shigeru 横山重, and Matsumoto Ryūshin 松本隆信, eds. *Muromachi jidai monogatari taisei* 室町時代物語大成, vol. 3. Tokyo: Kadokawa shoten 角川書店, 1975.

Yokozeki Ryōin 横関了胤. *Edo jidai tōmon seiyō* 江戸時代洞門政要. Tokyo: Bukkyōsha 仏教社, 1950.

Yonehara Masayoshi 米原正義. *Sengoku bushi to bungei no kenkyū* 戦国武士と文芸の研究. Tokyo: Ōfūsha 桜風社, 1976.

Yoshida Tsunenaga 吉田経長. "Kitsuzokki" 吉続記. In Sasagawa Taneo 笹川種郎, comp. *Shiryō taisei*. Tokyo: Naigai shoseki 内外書籍, 1937.

Yoshie Akio 義江彰夫. "Kokuga shihai no tenkai" 国衙支配の展開. In *Iwanami kōza Nihon rekishi* 岩波講座日本歴史, vol. 4. Tokyo: Iwanami shoten 岩波書店, 1976.

Zōho shiryō taisei 増補史料大成, vol. 23. Kyoto: Rinsen shoten 臨川書店, 1975.

Zoku Gunsho ruijū 続群書類従, 33 vols. Tokyo: Zoku gunsho ruijū kanseikai 続群書類従完成会, 1931-33.

Zuikei Shūhō 瑞渓周鳳. *Zenrin kokuhōki* 善隣国宝記. Tokyo: Kokusho kankōkai 図書刊行会, 1975.

Zusetsu Nihon no koten 図説日本の古典. 20 vols. Tokyo: Shūseisha 集成社, 1978-81.

GLOSSARY OF SELECTED TERMS

Akutō 悪党. Literally, "evil bands." Lawless groups of minor warriors and, at times, peasants who banded together to seize tax rice and commit other acts of banditry. They became especially prevalent after the mid-thirteenth century and are known to have acted with or under the direction of other warriors, including military estate stewards (*jitō*), who challenged the political order of the Kamakura and Nambokuchō periods.

Ashikaga bakufu 足利幕府. The second warrior government established by Ashikaga Takauji which ruled between 1338 and 1573 from its headquarters in the Muromachi district of Kyoto after 1378; see also Muromachi period.

Azukari-dokoro 預所. Manager or custodian of a *shōen* who, in some cases, also acted as a deputy of the *shōen* proprietor. This office was often given to the major commender of the land.

Bakufu 幕府. Literally, "tent government." The government of the warrior class headed by a shogun.

Bashaku 馬借. Teamsters who used horses to transport rice and other goods from rural areas to the cities. By the Kamakura period, they had a virtual monopoly over land shipment, and in the Muromachi period, guilds (*za*) were formed to consolidate that monopoly.

Befu (or *beppu*) 別府. Administrative unit of provincial land (*kokugaryō*).

Biwa hōshi 琵琶法師. Literally, "lute priest." Itinerant performers, usually blind, who chanted works of vocal literature to the accompaniment of a lute. First mentioned in contemporary sources in the tenth century, they are believed to have become popular with the spread of Buddhism.

Bu 歩. Unit of land measurement equivalent to 1/360 *chō*; see *chō*.

Bugaku 舞楽. The dance repertoire of the Japanese imperial court. An element of the traditional music (*gagaku*) integral to court life during the Heian period but less popular in the early Kamakura period.

Bugyōnin 奉行人. Administrative stewards originally appointed by the Kamakura bakufu to oversee such administrative functions as the judiciary, shogunal household affairs, matters relating to temples and shrines, and civil engineering projects. They continued to supervise judicial and administrative affairs under the Muromachi bakufu.

Bugyōnin-shū 奉行人衆. Corps of administrators responsible for preparing policy briefs for the shogun.

Buke 武家. Military aristocracy, warrior estate, also referred to as *bushi* or samurai.

Buppō 仏法. Buddhist law.

Bushi 武士. See *buke*.

Buyaku 夫役. Labor service. A tax paid in miscellaneous products and labor. Although initially for agricultural work, labor for such purposes as land reclamation and irrigation projects, repair of roads, transportation of tax rice, and military service was demanded over time by *shōen* proprietors and warrior overlords.

Chanoyu 茶の湯. Tea ceremony. A highly structured method for preparing tea in the

687

company of guests.

Chigyō 知行. Originally meaning "to carry out the functions of office," this term was frequently used to refer to income, especially tax rice, from land. Most commonly used in the medieval to the Tokugawa period to refer to income from fief granted to warriors by their overlord.

Chigyōkoku 知行国. Province (*koku*) held as fief (*chigyō*) by a warrior. Also, in the Heian and early Kamakura periods, an entire province held in proprietorship by a ranking court noble or religious institution appointed by the civil government to serve as provincial proprietor (*kokushu*) of the public land.

Chinjō 陳状. Statement of rebuttal in a judicial inquiry that along with a statement of accusation (*sojō*) and the collection and analysis of evidence, became the basis for judgment.

Chinjufu shogun 鎮守府将軍. General who commanded the headquarters for pacification and defense in northern Honshū established during the Nara period.

Chinsō (or *chinzō*) 頂相. Originally referring to sacred aspects of the Buddha manifested in physical characteristics. In Japan, chiefly a genre of sculpture and painting devoted to the realistic, three-dimensional portrayal of the seated or standing figures of historical Zen priests.

Chinzei *bugyō* 鎮西奉行. A post held in Kyushu by two commissioners appointed by the Kamakura bakufu to oversee local affairs and maintain peace among the Minamoto vassals. Superseded by the Chinzei *tandai* in the late thirteenth century.

Chinzei *dangijo* 鎮西談義所. Office established in 1285 at Hakata as the central judicial and administrative organ for the Kyushu region.

Chinzei *sōbugyōsho* 鎮西総奉行所. Agency established in 1293 to facilitate the authority of two men of the Hōjō family dispatched to Hakata to judge court cases and command military forces. Some scholars regard this agency as the de facto beginnings of the Chinzei *tandai*.

Chinzei *tandai* 鎮西探題. Office of the military governor of Kyushu established in 1293 in the wake of the Mongol invasions and accorded powers similar to those of the Rokuhara *tandai*; also called Kyushu *tandai*.

Chō 町(丁). Unit of land measurement equivalent to 2.45 acres. Because *chō* using the same character can also be a unit of length, when used to refer to land area it is often expressed as *chōbu*.

Chōbu 町歩. See chō.

Daibon Sankajō 大犯三箇条. "Three regulations for great crimes"; also pronounced Taibon Sankajō. Formalized in the Goseibai Shikimoku code of 1232, this phrase referred to the authority of the military governors (*shugo*) under the Kamakura bakufu. Despite the phrase, *shugo* authority under this "regulation" included jurisdiction over the crimes of murder and rebellion and the obligation of mustering the imperial guard. The term continued to be used into the Muromachi period.

Dajō daijin 太政大臣. Post of prime minister. The highest court title accorded authority over both the warrior and court nobility.

Daikan 代官. A deputy or manager entrusted with local administration. Appointed by the bakufu, *shōen* proprietor, or regional military lord (daimyo), *daikan* acted as their local representative in the provinces.

Daimyo 大名. Regional military lords who controlled a region; see *shugo* daimyo and *sengoku* daimyo.

Daimyo *ryōgoku* 大名領国. Domain of a regional military lord (daimyo).

Dazaifu 太宰府. The goverment headquarters in Kyushu established as a regular office in the Taihō code of 701 and charged with diplomatic and defense responsibilities in addition to the administration of the provinces of Kyushu during the Heian period. During the Kamakura period, the office of Dazaifu functioned in name only.

Dengaku 田楽. Literally, "field music." Early medieval theater similar to *sarugaku* and assumed to have included music, dance, and other types of entertainment, which became popular among the newly important military class in the Kamakura period.

Densō 伝奏. Liaison officials who interceded between the civil and religious nobility and the retired emperor (*in*) with the authority to settle lesser political matters.

Dōbōshū 同朋衆. Coterie of artists and aesthetes. Individuals who entered into the direct service of the Ashikaga shogun as arbiters of taste and practitioners of the arts.

Dogō 土豪. Local powers, generally with landed wealth, who acquired local political and military influence.

Do-ikki 土一揆. Leagues of cultivators and low-ranking warriors, especially common in the fifteenth century, organized to demand relief from economic hardships or to redress political grievances; also pronounced *tsuchi-ikki*.

Dōjo 道場. Literally, "training places" for lay devotees of Buddhism.

Dōmeisō 同名惣. An organization of members with the same surname which then allied with other such organizations to establish a much larger league or communal organization (*sō*) within a region.

Dosō 土倉. Originally meant storehouse keepers but referred primarily to pawnbrokers and moneylenders of the Muromachi period.

Emaki 絵巻. Long, horizontal handscroll with illustrations that tell a story, often accompanied by text. This format for painting flourished during the Heian and Kamakura periods.

Enkyoku 宴曲. Literally, "banquet songs." A form of narrative lyric of the Kamakura and Muromachi periods, often a part of the entertainment at banquets held by nobles and warriors.

Erizenirei 撰銭令. Decrees issued in the late Muromachi period by the Ashikaga bakufu, regional overlords (*shugo* daimyo), and even local powers and *shōen* proprietors, specifying acceptable mixes of "good" and "inferior" coins of varying values acceptable for paying dues and, at times, for market transactions.

Fudono 文殿. A management bureau for documents of the emperor, retired emperor (*in*), and courtiers. That of the *in* was transformed in 1286 by the Board of Councilors (*hyōjōshū*) into a subordinate but full-scale judicial organ whose advisory judgments were issued on the basis of documentary evidence rather than open hearings.

Gagaku 雅楽. The traditional musical repertoire of the Japanese imperial court of the Heian period.

Gekokujō 下剋上. Term used to describe the overthrow of a superior by persons of inferior status; often used to refer to the political upheaval of the Sengoku period.

Genin 下人. Those cultivators comprising the lowest level of the peasant class who had no independent control over land. Their status gradually improved during the medieval period, and by the late Muromachi period they had gained some degree of independence and rights to land as tenant farmers.

Gesu (or *geshi*) 下司. *Shōen* manager of the highest local level appointed by the *shōen* proprietor.

Gesu shiki 下司職. See *shiki*.

Gō 合. Unit of cubic measure equivalent to one-tenth *shō*; see *shō*.

Gō 郷. Administrative unit of provincial land (*kokugaryō*) in medieval Japan, having its origins in the *ritsuryō* system.

Gokenin 御家人. Originally, a direct retainer or vassal of the shogun. Later, also used by regional military lords (daimyo) to refer to their major vassals.

Goseibai Shikimoku 御成敗式目. Legal code promulgated by the Kamakura bakufu in 1232 to clarify the extent of its jurisdiction vis-à-vis that of the civil authorities and to strengthen and formalize its relationship with its own vassals.

Gozan 五山. Literally, "five mountains." The temples at the apex of the three-tiered hierarchy of officially sponsored Zen Buddhist monasteries.

Gozen-sata 御前沙汰. Shogunal hearing or council. A procedure under which policy briefs were brought directly before the shogun for his decision.

Gundai 郡代. District deputy or regional intendant.

Gunji 郡司. Local official responsible for the administration of provincial districts (*gun*) under the *ritsuryō* system of government. With the rise of the *shōen* system, the post gradually disappeared.

Gunki monogatari 軍記物語. Literary genre of war tales of the Kamakura and Muromachi periods.

Gun'yaku 軍役. Obligation of military service imposed on vassals by their warrior lords.

Gunyakushū 軍役衆. Cultivators under the command of a retainer of a regional military lord (daimyo) organized into the bottom segment of the daimyo's military force.

Hanzei 半済. Literally, "half-payment." One-half of the tax rice (*nengu*) that vassals of the Ashikaga bakufu were permitted to collect from *shōen* and *kokugaryō* on a temporary basis. Originally yearly grants, they became permanent over time.

Heian period 平安. Historical period that spanned nearly four hundred years, from about 794, when Emperor Kammu established Heiankyō (now Kyoto) as the imperial capital, to 1185, when the Minamoto forces defeated those of the Taira, thus setting the stage for the establishment of the Kamakura bakufu. Emperor Kammu ascended to the throne in 781, and in 784, the capital then located in Heijōkyō (in Nara) was moved to Nagaokakyō. Some classifications prefer either of these two dates as the beginning of the period. In addition, some end it in 1180, when Minamoto Yoritomo established his headquarters in Kamakura. It is noted as a period of great cultural development centered on the imperial court.

Heinō bunri 兵農分離. Historians' term for the strict definition and separation of warriors and peasants that occurred simultaneously with the Taikō *kenchi*; see Taikō *kenchi*.

Hieizan (Mount Hiei) 比叡山. The name Hieizan is often synonymous with the Enryakuji, an important temple founded in 788 by the priest Saichō of the Tendai sect of Buddhism.

Higokenin 非御家人. Nonvassals; see *gokenin*.

Hijiri 聖. Buddhist holy men who led itinerant lives or were ascetic recluses. They were organized into formal groups under the great Buddhist temples in the eleventh and twelfth centuries and played a major role in spreading Buddhism to the Japanese masses.

Hikan 被官. Broadly, warrior retainers, but often meaning retainers of low rank.

Hikitsuke-shū 引付衆. Office of Adjudicants. Investigative office of the Kamakura bakufu formed in 1249 which gradually became the principal organ of inquiry below the Board of Councilors (*hyōjōshū*).

Hinin 非人. Literally, "nonhumans." Those belonging to the lowest social class subject to social discrimination and compulsory "unclean" labor, such as caring for victims of contagious diseases and attending to condemned criminals.

Ho 保. Administrative unit of provincial land (*kokugaryō*).

Hōkōshū 奉行衆. Shogunal military guard of the Ashikaga bakufu.

Hōmei 法名. Buddhist names granted to secular patrons; also pronounced *hōmyō*.

Hompo jitō 本補地頭. Military followers granted the title of military estate steward (*jitō*) and appointed to lands confiscated from the defeated enemy after the Gempei War (1180–5) by Minamoto Yoritomo as reward for their loyalty.

Honjo 本所. A term used to connote the proprietor (*ryōke*) and, from the twelfth century, the guarantor (*honke*) of a *shōen*. Also the administrative headquarters of a *shōen*.

Honjo-ryō 本所領. Land from which a proprietor or guarantor (*honjo*) of a *shōen* received income and to which a military estate steward (*jitō*) had been appointed.

Honke 本家. Titular proprietor or guarantor of a *shōen*. The holder of the highest level of *shiki* rights, often the highest-ranked nobles; see *shiki*.

Hyakushō 百姓. Cultivators or peasants.

Hyōjōshū 評定衆. Board of Councilors established in 1225 by the Kamakura bakufu, the highest decision-making organ of government.

Hyōrō-ryōsho 兵糧領所. Lands from which the military supporters of the Ashikaga bakufu obtained commissariat rice.

Ichizoku 一族. A lineage, including branch family members, that traced its descent from a common ancestor.

Ikki 一揆. Term that originally meant to act in consort but that came to denote both a league of warriors or commoners and an uprising of local warriors and peasants.

Ikkō ikki 一向一揆. Large-scale uprisings by followers of the Jōdo Shin sect of Buddhism in the late fifteenth and sixteenth centuries. These uprisings were often led by local military lords (*kokujin*) who capitalized on the sect's tenets, which encouraged peasant solidarity and millenarian goals to advance their own interests.

Ikkō-shū 一向衆. Regional leagues of local military lords (*kokujin*), peasant warriors (*jizamurai*), and cultivators united by an underlying belief in the teachings of the Jōdo Shin sect that fueled resistance to the authority of the military governor (*shugo*).

Ikoku keigo banyaku 異国警固番役. Obligatory tour of military duty in the Kyushu region imposed on the military governors (*shugo*) and other regional powers by the Kamakura bakufu. The obligation involved mustering a combined unit of vassals from two or three provinces of the region, usually for three months of duty.

Imayō 今様. Medieval Japanese popular song of "modern style."

In 院. Retired emperor (*tennō*); cloistered sovereign.

Inja 隠者. Tonsured male. A person who has taken Buddhist vows and placed himself outside the official class ordering.

Insei 院政. Literally, "cloister government." The system of government of the late Heian period in which a retired emperor (*tennō*) exercised control over the affairs of state. Despite loss of power, the system lasted until 1840.

Isshikiden 一色田. Paddy land of a *shōen* distributed to cultivators but from which only *nengu* is exacted at a relatively high rate; partially exempted fields.

Jinaimachi 寺内町. Towns that grew up within temple grounds rather than in front of its gates; see *monzenmachi*.

Jinin 神人. Dependents of Shinto shrines; persons under the protection of powerful Shinto shrines who were obligated to provide various services in exchange for this protection.

Jinja 神社. Shinto shrine.

Jissatsu 十利. Literally, "ten temples." The temples ranked just below the apex of the offical three-tiered hierarchy of Zen Buddhist monasteries; see *gozan*.

Jitō 地頭. Military estate steward appointed by the Kamakura bakufu. The most important local official of the Kamakura period; see *hompo jitō* and *shimpo jitō*.

Jizamurai 地侍. Literally, "samurai of the soil." Refers to rural warriors not far removed from the peasantry who comprised the lowest level of the warrior class.

Kachōmai 加徴米. Supplementary rice tax or military surcharge.

Kaihatsu ryōshu 開発領主. Local warriors or provincial or district officials who actually developed paddy field lands; also pronounced *kaihotsu ryōshu*.

Kaisen 廻船. Literally, "ships making rounds." Cargo ships used to transport rice tax and other goods or to engage in itinerant trade.

Kaisho 会所. Banquet chamber. A new interior setting for socializing among members of both the warrior and courtier elites that evolved in the late fourteenth and early fifteenth centuries; often discussed in terms of *kaisho* culture.

Kajishi 加地子. Often translated as surtax, additional rent, or cultivation fee; literally, an "added rent" paid by cultivators to those who acquired the right to collect such rents (*kajishi-shiki*). In addition to the rice tax (*nengu*) owed to either the *shōen* proprietor or the warrior overlord, this rent was paid to *myōshu*, religious institutions, moneylenders, and, at times, nobles who bought this right; see Taikō *kenchi, myōshu, shiki.*

Kamakura bakufu 鎌倉幕府. The first warrior government, established by Minamoto Yoritomo at Kamakura, which ruled from 1192 to 1333; see also Kamakura period.

Kamakura period 鎌倉. Historical period corresponding to the life span of the Kamakura bakufu; named after Kamakura, where the government was located. It is generally agreed that the period ended in 1333, the year the bakufu was destroyed. Alternative dates, however, have been proposed to mark its beginning, such as 1180, the year Minamoto Yoritomo established his base at Kamakura, or 1185, when the Minamoto conclusively defeated the rival Taira at the battle of Dannoura, or 1192, the year the imperial court gave official recognition to the de facto military rule of Minamoto Yoritomo by conferring on him the title of shogun.

Kami 神. Indigenous deities.

Kamikaze 神風. Literally, "divine wind" or "wind of the gods," this term refers to the storms that twice destroyed much of the invading Mongol forces in 1274 and 1281 off the coast of Kyushu and forced them to withdraw.

Kan 貫. Unit of weight equivalent to 3.759 grams or 3.759 kilograms. Because the modal weight of one Chinese or illegally minted domestic copper coin (*mon*) was 3.75 grams, one *kan* of coins was roughly equivalent to one thousand coins; see *mon.*

Kandaka 貫高. Putative yield of paddy field expressed in units of cash (*kan*). A means of designating the tax value of paddy field; see also *kokudaka.*

Kangō bōeki 勘合貿易. Tally trade carried on between Japan and the Ming dynasty (1368–1644) of China, from the beginning of the fifteenth century to the middle of the sixteenth century.

Kanjin fuda 勧進符. Strips of wood or paper attesting to receipt of a contribution.

Kanrei 管領. Shogunal deputy. A high official of the Muromachi bakufu who assisted the shogun in all important government affairs. The post was not hereditary but was rotated among members of the Shiba, Hosokawa, and Hatakeyama families, who were thus known as the *sankanrei* or "three deputies"; see Kantō *kanrei.*

Kantō *goryō* 関東御領. Shogunal lands.

Kantō *kanrei* 関東管領. Shogunal deputy for the Kantō region. Official post created in Kamakura by the Muromachi bakufu to assist the members of the ruling Ashikaga family who served as governor generals of the Kantō region (Kantō *kubō*).

Kantō *kubō* 関東公方. Regional bakufu headquarters with administrative control over the Kantō region.

Kantō *mōshitsugi* 関東申次. Court post granted authority over court–bakufu relations.

Karamono 唐物. Art and craft from China including paintings, calligraphic scrolls, ceramic wares, fine porcelains, and lacquerware.

Karita rōzeki 刈田狼籍. Pilfering or otherwise depriving the rightful owners of their harvest.

Kashiage 借上. Moneylenders of the Kamakura and early Muromachi periods who usually accepted pawns; also called *kariage.*

Kawashi 為替. Bills of exchange that began to be used in the mid-thirteenth century that enabled the bearer to receive a specified amount of cash; known variously as *saifu* and *warifu.*

Kemmu restoration 建武. The attempt by Emperor Godaigo in 1333–6 to restore direct imperial rule following the overthrow of the Kamakura bakufu. Kemmu refers to the era name that Godaigo inaugurated in 1334.

Kendan 検断. Provision of law and order which included the power to pursue, arrest, incarcerate, try, and sentence criminals.

Kenmon 権門. A term that refers collectively to the emperor and those of imperial lineage, nobles, leading military houses, and religious establishments who held power and authority in the medieval polity.

Kimon 起文. Pact for unified cultivator action among villages within a province or region.

Kirokushō 記録所. (Kiroku shōen kenkeijo). Office for the Investigation of Shōen Documents, or simply the Records Office. The office, established in 1069 by Emperor Gosanjō, was revived in 1156 by Emperor Goshirakawa and came to function as the body that adjudicated land disputes between local officials and *shōen* proprietors. During the Kemmu restoration this office became the central organ of Godaigo's imperial government.

Kō 講. Religious associations, which originally developed from lecture meetings on Buddhist sutras, organized by religious leaders for spreading their teachings or for some other economic or educational purpose.

Kōan 公案. Literally, "public cases." Conundrums or propositions used as an aid to Buddhist meditation and enlightenment.

Kobyakushō 小百姓. Small cultivators with few rights over land.

Kōden 公田. Public lands the dues from which were paid to the central government.

Kōgi 公儀. The highest public authority of a territory; the principle on which authority to rule was based or justified.

Koku 石. Unit of cubic measure equivalent to ten *to* or one hundred *shō*; see *shō*.

Kokubunji 国分寺. Temples built by the government during the Nara period in each province as state institutions.

Kokudaka 石高. An assessed tax base calculated in terms of *koku*. Official assessment of land value in terms of unpolished rice based on an estimated annual yield.

Kokufu 国府. Provincial capital in which the provincial headquarters (*kokuga*) of the provincial governor (*kokushi*) was located.

Kokuga 国衙. Provincial headquarters.

Kokugaryō 国衙領. Provincial or public land that remained under the administration of the provincial headquarters (*kokuga*), in contrast with lands converted to *shōen*; also called *kōryō*.

Kokujin 国人. Provincial or local warriors. Local figures who acquired political and military power and who from the early Muromachi period frequently took advantage of the weaker military governors (*shugo*) to expand their influence and control. The more powerful succeeded in displacing the *shugo* and becoming autonomous regional lords (*sengoku* daimyo).

Kokushi 国司. Post of civilian provincial governor established under the *ritsuryō* system of government in the Nara period. With the establishment of the Kamakura bakufu, it gradually became an empty title, although it was retained throughout the Muromachi period.

Ko-mokudai 小目代. Resident deputy of the provincial governor.

Kōryō 公領. Public land; see *kokugaryō*.

Kōya hijiri 高野聖. Itinerant *hijiri* of Kōyasan, the Buddhist monastic complex of the Shingon sect on Mount Kōya.

Kubō 公方. An honorific title that originally referred to the emperor and his court. From the Kamakura period, it was used to refer to the shogun. During the Muromachi period, the term referred to the Ashikaga shoguns and their deputies in the Kantō region; see Kantō *kubō*.

Kudashibumi 下文. A type of document that conveyed orders from a superior official or office to a subordinate one. It originated in the Heian period and was used in many offices.

Kuge 公家. A Heian-period term referring to the emperor and court aristocrats. During the Kamakura period, the term was used to differentiate the aristocratic inhabitants of the old capital from the provincial military aristocracy. Often translated as "courtiers," "court aristocracy," or "nobility."

Kugyō 公卿. The families of highest court rank who dominated court society.

Kugonin 公御人. Persons supplying the court with various daily necessities in exchange for exemption from taxes or corvée.

Kuji 公事. A category of tax under the *shōen* system of landholding that can be further divided into corvée labor (*buyaku*) and miscellaneous goods (*zokūji*).

Kumon 公文. A local *shōen* official below the rank of *gesu* charged with handling documents, assigning tax burdens, and the like. Also a certificate of appointment to install an abbot.

Kuni 国. Basic administrative unit of ancient and medieval Japan; province.

Kusemai 曲舞. A lively song and dance form that became a popular part of *sarugaku*.

Kyōgen 狂言. Comic plays that evolved from the earlier tradition of *sarugaku*. Often a part of a noh performance or an independent piece performed between two noh plays; see noh.

Kyūden 給田. Benefice land provided for specific services to be rendered.

Kyushu *tandai* 九州探題. See Chinzei *tandai*.

Machi 町. Administrative unit within a town or city enjoying a degree of self-government.

Mandokoro 政所. Administrative headquarters for political and economic affairs of a powerful family or religious institution. In the Kamakura period, the main executive organ of the bakufu.

Mappō 末法. "Latter days of Buddhist law." A Buddhist concept of historical decline in which society ceases to follow the Buddhist law, and as a result, turmoil replaces order and life becomes submerged in darkness and suffering. This decline was believed to have begun in 1052.

Matsuji 末寺. Branch temples of a monastery.

Menke 免家. Households exempt from dues.

Migyōsho 御教書. Standard documentary form used to transmit orders or directives from a higher authority to subordinates.

Mikkyō 密教. Literally, "secret teachings." A tradition in esoteric Buddhism stemming from the belief that the most profound doctrines of Buddhism should be kept secret, not expounded publicly.

Miko 巫女. A female shaman who played a prominent role in Shinto by acting as medium for the indigenous gods (*kami*).

Miuchibito 御内人. Private vassals of the *tokusō*; see also *tokusō*.

Miyaza 宮座. Shrine guilds that presided over the religious practices of their communities and performed various services for the shrines.

Mokudai 目代. Resident deputy of a capital-based provincial governor (*kokushi*).

Momme 匁. Unit of weight equivalent to 3.75 grams. Because most copper coins weighed approximately this amount, the monetary unit (*mon*) and the weight (*momme*) were often used interchangeably; see *mon*.

Mon 文. Monetary unit of copper coins in pre-Tokugawa Japan; see *momme*.

Monchūjo 問注所. Board of Inquiry. A judicial organ established in the early Kamakura period of both the Kamakura and Muromachi bakufu that adjudicated land disputes and other property cases. It gradually became the chief judicial arm of the bakufu outside Kamakura. Under the Muromachi bakufu, most of the duties of the *monchujō* were taken over by the *mandokoro*, and the former became primarily a records office.

Monzeki 門跡. An imperial residence temple.

Monzenmachi 門前町. Market towns that grew up near the gates of major temples and shrines.

Mōshijō 申状. Petitions.

Mōto 間人. Transient peasants without land who were itinerant agricultural laborers and often similar to beggars.

Mujō 無常. A concept and major theme of medieval literature that emphasizes the transient quality of this world and the impermanence of all things.

Munabechisen 棟別銭. A tax assessed by the number of posts in a residential structure imposed on each household during the Muromachi period. Originally an occasional tax levied to meet the extraordinary expenses of the court or religious institutions, over time it became a permanent levy.

Mura 村. Village. A geographical, social, and economic entity whose members by the mid-1300s had often formed their own organs of self-government.

Muromachi bakufu 室町幕府. See Ashikaga bakufu.

Muromachi period 室町. Historical period named for the location of the shogunal residence in Kyoto; also known as the Ashikaga period, after the warrior house that held the post of shogun from 1338 to 1573. No consensus has been reached regarding when the government gained and lost its legitimacy or effectiveness, and therefore the dates corresponding to this period are a subject of debate. See also Ashikaga bakufu.

Myō 名. See *myōden*.

Myōden 名田. Literally, "named paddy." Land unit by which yearly taxes and services were determined within *shōen* and *kokugaryō*, registered presumably under the name of the head (*myōshu*) of the managing cultivator family, who over time was accorded some degree of private ownership.

Myōshu 名主. Manager and, later, owner of a small amount of land responsible for collecting annual taxes and labor services on *myōden*. Although commoners, *myōshu* often held considerable power in the locale, and in the Muromachi period, some became rural warriors (*jizamurai*).

Myōshu kajishi 名主加地子. A mid-level right to receive income from paddies acquired by *myōshu*; see also *kajishi*.

Myōshu-shiki 名主職. See *shiki*.

Naidaijin 内大臣. Inner minister. An auxiliary government post not prescribed in the Taihō code of 701 as a part of the *ritsuryō* system of administration. In 989, however, the post became permanent.

Namban 南蛮. Literally, "southern barbarian." A term used to describe foreign missionaries, merchants, and sailors who visited or worked in Japan in the sixteenth and seventeenth centuries, as well as the European customs and products they introduced.

Nambokuchō disturbance 南北朝. Literally, disturbance of the "Northern and Southern Courts." The period between 1336 and 1392 when two rival imperial courts existed in Japan, each claiming the legitimate right to rule.

Nara period 奈良. Historical period beginning in 710, the year the capital was moved from Fujiwarakyō to Heijōkyō (in Nara), and ending in 784, when the capital was moved to Nagaokakyō. The ten years between 784 and the beginning of the Heian period in 794 are generally included in the Nara period. It is noted as the period when the *ritsuryō* system of government, which adapted the laws, codes, land policies, and bureaucratic forms of T'ang China, reached its height and other aspects of Chinese civilization were actively introduced.

Nembutsu 念仏. Invocation of the sacred name of Amida Buddha to ensure rebirth in the Pure Land. This fundamental Buddhist practice opened the path of salvation to those without specialized religious training or discipline.

Nengu 年貢. Literally, "annual tribute." The basic dues paid in rice and other commodities. Often translated as land tax, the term can also mean land rent.

Noh 能. A form of musical dance-drama that in the fourteenth century emerged as a distinct form of theater from various performing arts, with its plots drawn from legend, history, literature, and contemporary events. See also *sarugaku, dengaku,* and *kyōgen.*

Ōbanyaku 大番役. Imperial guard service in Kyoto performed by vassals of the Kamakura bakufu.

Ōhō 王法. Imperial law. Unwritten code of behavior for dealing with the emperor and the imperial family.

Okibumi 置文. A testamentary document form in use during the Kamakura and Muromachi periods to regulate matters of inheritance and property.

Ōnin War 応仁. A series of wars fought intermittently in and around Kyoto over a period of eleven years (1467–77) between "western" and "eastern" forces, loose coalitions of *shugo* daimyo led respectively by politically and militarily strong *shugo* daimyo, the Hosokawa and Yamana. Often referred to as the Ōnin–Bummei disturbances by Japanese scholars (from the period names of these eleven years), these wars ushered in a century of civil war known as the Sengoku (literally, "warring states") period. Although the ostensible cause for the Ōnin War was a dispute over the selection of a new shogun, the real cause of the war was the decline in the authority and power of the Ashikaga bakufu and the rise of the *shugo* daimyo as regional military powers who challenged the political stability of the bakufu. The war was prolonged because of the individual ambitions of the leading *shugo* daimyo and fluctuations in their coalitions. Specialists continue to debate the specific political and economic motivations of the *shugo* daimyo and their vassals, as well as of the civil elites who were also involved. See also *shugo* daimyo.

Onryō 怨霊. Malignant spirits of persons of high rank or great influence who died unnaturally or in a state of anger or resentment who, unless placated, would bring harm to the living and haunt their enemies.

Osso 越訴. Appeal to higher authorities, bypassing official channels, for retrial. Such appeals were strictly forbidden before their institutionalization in 1264; see *osso bugyō*.

Osso bugyō 越訴奉行. The post of commissioner of appeals, established in 1264, to which petitions for retrial were permitted. This institution was retained by the Muromachi bakufu but was outlawed by the Tokugawa bakufu, which absolutely forbade, and severely punished, direct appeals.

Ōtabumi 大田文. Provincial land registers. Documents compiled in the Kamakura and Muromachi periods that recorded the size of landholdings and other information on landownership in each province and that were used to apportion taxes.

Renga 連歌. A type of linked verse unique to Japan, with a set number of stanzas that two or more poets generally composed in alternation. The alternated stanzas comprise the traditional two parts of *waka*: a unit of three lines of five, seven, and five syllables; and a couplet of seven syllables each. Usually consists of one hundred stanzas or a multiple thereof.

Rensho 連署. Cosigner. An official subordinate to the regent (*shikken*) of the Kamakura bakufu whose signature was placed beside that of the *shikken* on official documents. After the first assignment to Hōjō Tokifusa (1175–1240) in 1224, the cosignership, like the regency itself, became a prerogative of the Hōjō family.

Ritsuryō 律令. A term referring to the legal codes adopted from China in the seventh and eighth centuries in Japan. The *ritsuryō* government refers to the national, imperial government established by these codes and administered by a bureaucracy; see Nara period.

Rokuhara *tandai* 六波羅探題. Shogunal deputies stationed at Rokuhara in southeastern Kyoto by the Kamakura bakufu to supervise the political, military, and judicial affairs of southwestern Japan. The post was established in 1221 and held concurrently by two men, both chosen from among the ranks of the Hōjō family. The last Rokuhara *tandai* were deposed by Ashikaga forces in 1333.

Rōnin 浪人. Literally, "floating men." Masterless samurai who no longer received income from stipends.

Ryō 両. A unit of weight used in the thirteenth through sixteenth centuries to weigh valuables such as gold and silver. In the late sixteenth century, a unit of currency equivalent to the standard gold coin of the Tokugawa bakufu.

Ryōgoku 領国. Domain.

Ryōgokusei 領国制. See *shugo ryōgokusei*.

Ryōke 領家. The court noble or religious institution to whom a *shōen* was commended who became the central *shōen* proprietor; a level of *shiki* right accorded to the "legal protector."

Ryōshu 領主. General term for warrior overlords and *shōen* proprietors. Historians' term for warriors and others at all levels who exercised political power or possessed various rights to income from land.

Sabi 寂. Aesthetic value of the medieval period that combined elements of old age, loneliness, resignation, and tranquillity.

Sakunin 作人. A broad term referring to cultivators, most often agricultural laborers or small tenant cultivators.

Samurai 侍(士). See *buke*.

Samurai-dokoro 侍所. Board of Retainers. A formal bureau established in 1180 under the Kamakura bakufu to control the activities of its vassals (*gokenin*). Its duties were gradually expanded to include the supervision of the police authority of military estate stewards (*jitō*). Under the Muromachi bakufu, this office assumed responsibility for guarding Kyoto and its environs and overseeing shogunal property.

Sanjo 散所. Literally, "scattered places." A term originating in the late Heian period to distinguish the scattered possessions from the main resident and headquarters (*honjo*) of a *shōen* proprietor. In the Kamakura period, the nonagricultural areas of a *shōen*. The service population congregated in these areas and were themselves often called *sanjo*.

Sansō 山僧. Literally, "mountain monks." The monks of the powerful Enryakuji temple on Mount Hiei in Kyoto.

Sarugaku 猿楽. A genre of early medieval theater which included music, dance, and other types of entertainment. As *sarugaku* developed, it absorbed elements of another performing art known as *dengaku* and became increasingly standardized. The tradition emerging from this process formed the basis on which noh was created in the fourteenth century.

Satanin 沙汰人. Village representatives chosen from the *myōshu* class to serve in the village self-governing organization (*sō*).

Satori 悟り. Enlightenment or awakening. The experience of sudden enlightenment at the heart of the Buddhist faith, particularly the Zen tradition.

Seii tai shogun 征夷大将軍. Generally abbreviated as shogun and customarily translated as "barbarian-subduing generalissimo," this title was derived from ancient titles bestowed on government officials who led campaigns against insurgents or indigenous tribes on the periphery of the realm. The shogunal title, bestowed by the emperor, was resurrected after the Gempei War, and the shoguns became the military rulers whose governments (bakufu) ruled Japan with varying degrees of power, with authority held independently of that of the civil government.

Seisei shogun 征西将軍. General of the Western Pacification Command.

Seitō shogun 征東将軍. General of the Eastern Pacification Command.

Sekisho 関所. Toll barriers.

Sekkan 摂関. Regent; see also *sekkanke*.

Sekkanke 摂関家. The sublineage of the Fujiwara house, whose members served as imperial regents in the Heian period, which split into five branches (*gosekke*) during the Kamakura period, with important offices rotating among them.

Sengoku daimyo 戦国大名. General term for the regional military lords of the Sengoku or Warring States period who gained considerable independent political and economic control over the lands they held and began to fight among themselves for regional hegemony.

Sengoku period 戦国. The period of the warring states which lasted from the beginning of the Ōnin War in 1467 to 1568, when Oda Nobunaga entered Kyoto to assert national hegemony. Some scholars date the beginning of the period in 1490, when the shogunal deputy (*kanrei*) took over actual control of the Ashikaga bakufu. See also *gekokujō*, *sengoku* daimyo, and *shugo* daimyo.

Shariki 車力. Teamsters using carts to transport goods.

Shiki 司記. Originally meaning "office," this term refers primarily, although not exclusively, to the right to receive income from *shōen* accorded to each position within the *shōen* hierarchy. In some instances, such rights developed outside the *shōen* framework, as in the case of *kajishi shiki*. See *honke*, *ryōke*, and *kajishi*.

Shikken 執権. Post of shogunal regent established in 1203 and held in heredity by the Hōjō family under the Kamakura bakufu.

Shimpo jitō 新補地頭. Military estate stewards (*jitō*) newly appointed by the Kamakura bakufu following the Jōkyū war of 1221 to lands confiscated from the defeated army of the imperial court. Most of the new *jitō* were located in central and western Japan, over which the bakufu now enlarged its influence. From this point forward the post of *jitō* became a truly national institution.

Shinden-zukuri 寝殿造. Palace-style architecture typical of the residences of the aristocracy as well as high-ranking Buddhist clerics and warriors in the Heian period, a style that greatly influenced Japanese residential architecture until the mid-fifteenth century. The central feature for which it is named is the master quarters or main hall (*shinden*).

Shitaji chūbun 下地中分. Literally, "halving of land." Division of *shōen* land between a civil proprietor and military estate steward (*jitō*) in order to settle a dispute over rights of tax collection and law enforcement.

Shitaji shinshi-ken 下地進止権. Authority to commend land.

Shō 升. Unit of cubic measure. In measuring rice in the medieval period (as the term is used in this volume), 1 *shō* of rice changed in real quantity from approximately 0.4 *shō* to 1 standard *shō* of the Tokugawa period, from approximately 0.722 liters to 1.805 liters. Because the square wooden container (*masu*) for measuring rice differed over time, by region, and even by *shōen* in the medieval period, the quantities indicated by *koku*, *shō*, and *to* in various chapters cannot be converted to Western measure or even Tokugawa measure with any degree of accuracy.

Shō 荘(庄). Designation for a *shōen* following its name; for example, Ategawa-no-shō is equivalent to Ategawa *shōen*.

Shōen 荘園. Private estates that began to be created in the eighth century through the privatization of public land. At its zenith, the twelfth century, this landholding system became the most important political and economic institution. These estates were created through land reclamation, lands received by religious institutions as gifts from the emperor or the highest officials of the civil government, and, most frequently, commendation of land to the highest-ranked nobles who could exempt them from taxation and prevent entry by civil officials. The means of establishing these estates changed over time, and as a result, those who shared income from these estates also changed and became increasingly complex. These estates were gradually transformed into fiefs controlled by the warrior class in the Kamakura period and had totally disappeared by the late sixteenth century. See *azukari-dokoro*, *daikan*, *gesu*, *honjo*, *honke*, *kuji*, *kumon*, *myōden*, *ryōke*, *ryōshu*, *shiki shitaji chūbun*, *shōkan*, *shugo-uke*, *tsukuda*, *ukeoi daikan*, *ukesho*, *wayo*, *zaike*, and *zasshō*.

Shoin 書院. Interior setting developed in the late fifteenth century, whose principal features were woven rush floor matting (*tatami*), paper sliding screens (*shōji*), a decorative alcove (*tokonoma*), a built-in desk (*shoin*), and asymmetrical shelves (*chigaidana*). Also a style of residential architecture that forms the basis of modern traditional-style Japanese dwellings.

Shōkan 荘官. General term for a variety of *shōen* officials responsible for the management, assignment of duties, tax collection, and protection of *shōen*. Most were dispatched by the *shōen* proprietor or chosen from among local notables. This term usually refers to the principal officer of a *shōen* appointed by the proprietor.

Shokunin 職人. A general term for those engaged in nonagricultural occupations, that is, artisans. Entertainers were also sometimes included in this category.

Shōmon 証文. Documentary proof.

Shōmyō 声明. Liturgical vocal music for the incantation of scriptural texts.

Shōni 少弐. Deputy assistant governor of Dazaifu, the government headquarters in Kyushu.

Shoryō 所領. Individual landholdings.

Shugo 守護. Provincial constable; later, military governor.

Shugo-dai 守護代. Deputy of the military governor (*shugo*) at the local level.

Shugo daimyo 守護大名. Military governors (*shugo*) of the Muromachi period who succeeded in gaining control of a region by adding to their landholdings and attracting local warriors as their direct vassals.

Shugo ryō 守護領. Lands under the personal control of a military governor (*shugo*).

Shugo ryōgokusei 守護領国制. *Shugo* domainal system; not a historical system but, rather, a historiographical concept.

Shugo-uke 守護請. A practice of tax contracting in which a military governor (*shugo*) was entrusted with the collection of taxes and their delivery to the *shōen* proprietor.

Shugo yaku 守護役. In the fifteenth century, ad hoc taxes and labor corvée levied by military governors (*shugo*).

Shukke-tonsei 出家遁世. Literally, "escaping from the world by becoming a monk." Monastic options for males.

Shukuba 宿場. Towns designated as transportation centers along major routes where lodging and other services could be obtained.

Sō 惣. Self-governing organizations that existed in rural Japan from the fourteenth through the sixteenth centuries. Each *sō* took responsibility for its own irrigation, communal lands, law and order, and, in some cases, defense. Decisions were reached and carried out at group meetings (*yoriai*) made up of a headman and a small group of elders selected from among the leading landholders (*myōshu*); also called *sō-mura*.

Sōbyakushō 惣百姓. Resident cultivators of a self-governing organization (*sō*).

Sōhei 僧兵. Warrior-monks employed by the great Buddhist temples.

Sojō 訴状. Complaint; statement of accusation.

Sō-mura 惣村. See *sō*.

Sōroku 僧録. Registrar general of monks with authority over the *gozan* network, especially in Kyoto.

Sōryō 惣領. Internal organization of landholding families of both the warrior and commoner classes which emphasized the absolute leadership of a main heir, usually the eldest son. Most frequently refers to the system as practiced by warrior families of the Kamakura period in which land was divided among multiple heirs.

Sōson 惣村. Post-fourteenth-century medieval village communities in which even small cultivators had full membership rights.

Sōtsuibushi 総追捕使. Provincial-level officers appointed early in the Gempei War; predecessor of the military governor (*shugo*).

Sumi-e 墨絵. Chinese-style monochromatic ink painting adopted by Japanese painters in the fourteenth century and gradually adapted to Japanese aesthetics, although the traditional Chinese themes such as people, flowers, birds, and landscapes were retained.

Taibon Sankajō 大犯三箇所. See Daibon Sankajō.

Taikō kenchi 太閤検地. The cadastral surveys carried out in 1582 by Hideyoshi.

Tan 段(反). Unit of land measurement equivalent to one-tenth *chō*; see *chō*.

Tansen 段銭. During the Kamakura and Muromachi periods, a cash tax per *tan* of land levied on cultivators by the imperial court, the bakufu, military governors (*shugo*), and sometimes temples and shrines, to cover the cost of special events such as imperial enthronements and abdication ceremonies or for the rebuilding of palaces or important temples.

Tatchū 塔頭. Memorial temple for a revered Zen master often supported by warrior patrons, many of which assumed the character of a cultural salon.

Teichū 庭中. A new appeal system adopted in 1293 by which a plaintiff might bring suit directly and in person before a high tribunal, especially if the case had obviously been delayed or mishandled by the assigned investigating officer; also the appeal court under this system.

Tenka 天下. A term that in Chinese political theory refers to the empire or "all under heaven"; Japanese state and polity.

Tennō 天皇. Emperor, sovereign.

To 斗. Unit of cubic measure equivalent to ten *shō*; see *shō*.

Tōcha 闘茶. Tea-judging contests; a precursor of the classical tea ceremony (*chanoyu*) of the later Muromachi period.

Toijō 問状. Formal questionnaires.

Toimaru 問丸. Specialists of the Kamakura and Muromachi periods engaged in sea and land transportation who performed managerial functions and provided other services such as warehousing, delivery of goods, and supervision of porters.

Tokusei 徳政. Literally, "virtuous acts of government." Government decrees issued during the medieval period to give relief to certain groups from taxes and debt.

Tokusei-rei 徳政令. Debt-abrogation decree; see also *tokusei*.

Tokusō 得宗. The patrimonial head of the main branch of the powerful Hōjō family which monopolized the post of shogunal regent (*shikken*) during the Kamakura period. Later, also came to refer to all successors of the main Hōjō line.

Ton'seisha 遁世者. Tonsured males; see *inja* and *shukke-tonsei*.

Tsuchi-ikki 土一揆. See *do-ikki*.

Tsukuda 佃. Paddy fields under the direct administration of the *shōen* proprietor cultivated by peasants and others (*genin*), generally without compensation, as a form of labor service (*buyaku*).

Tsumugi 紬. Cloth made by twisting silk floss into thread by hand, which is then woven on a primitive loom to produce a thick, sturdy fabric.

Udaishō 右大将. A "commander of the inner palace guards." In the Kamakura period, a position without work or duties.

Uji 氏. Lineage group, including lineal and collateral kinsmen and their followers.

Ujidera 氏寺. Temple of a lineage group (*uji*).

Ukeoi 請負. Literally, "contract." A system of tax contracting in which a *shōen* proprietor entrusted the collection of the tax to local warriors or moneylenders.

Ukeoi daikan 請負代官. "Contract stewards" who represented the interests of a weakened proprietor of a *shōen* and negotiated with the military governor (*shugo*) or local warrior (*kokujin*) for the delivery of tax rice; frequently a monk from a Zen temple of Hieizan.

Ukesho 請所. A contractual agreement between a *shōen* proprietor and a military estate steward (*jitō*), authorizing the latter to assume full responsibility for collecting and delivering the annual tax; also called *jitō uke*.

Ukiyo-e 浮世絵. Literally "pictures of the floating world." A genre of art depicting the lives of early modern Japanese that reached its culmination in the mid- to late Tokugawa period.

Utokunin 有徳人. Literally, "men of virtue." Successful merchants of the Muromachi period who had accumulated great wealth and often engaged in moneylending.

Wabicha 侘茶. The classical tea ceremony, which came to symbolize renunciation of the material and celebration of the spiritual values of life.

Wagaku 和学. Japanese scholarship, which consisted of two general areas of study: the corpus of *waka*-centered, classical court literature and the court ceremonial and practice – the accumulated rituals, customs, and minutiae of court life. It reached its peak of development in the late fourteenth and fifteenth centuries.

Waka 和歌. A style of Japanese poetry containing thirty-one syllables; see *renga*.

Wakō 倭寇. Japanese pirates who pillaged the coasts of East Asia from the thirteenth into the seventeenth century.

Wamono 和物. Works of art and craft native to Japan.

Wayo 和与. A compromise agreement, often between a *shōen* proprietor and a military estate steward (*jitō*), regarding distribution of *shōen* revenue; see *ukesho* and *shitaji chūbun*.

Yachida 谷地田. Small landholdings located in the hills.

Yachihata 谷地畑. Dry fields usually planted with millet and buckwheat and sometimes also barley, soybeans, vegetables, hemp, mulberry for sericulture, and other crops.

Yakubuku-mai 役夫工米. Rice paid in lieu of labor service (*buyaku*).

Yamabushi 山伏. The name given to ascetics, usually men, who practiced austerities in the mountains in order to attain holy or magic powers.

Yoriai 寄合. A general term for a meeting, such as of league (*ikki*) leaders and village (*sō*) assemblies, at which important matters were discussed. Also Hōjō family council.

Yūgen 幽玄. An aesthetic value that conveys mystery and depth and that set much of the artistic tone of the medieval age.

Za 座. A trade or craft guild of merchants, artisans, or those offering services that originated in the eleventh century and were most active in the Muromachi period. Each was protected by a patron (usually a religious institution or member of the military or civil elite) who guaranteed its official recognition and protected it from outside competition within its sphere of influence.

Zaichi ryōshu 在地領主. Local warriors who exercised political and military control and possessed the power to collect dues from the cultivators within a locale, by retaining autonomy of power from a higher political authority or military power. Although such warriors existed throughout the medieval period, over time most either became vassals of the military estate steward (*jitō*), military governor (*shugo*), *shugo* daimyo, or *sengoku* daimyo. Others retained their autonomy independently or collectively by forming military leagues (*ikki*). Some, increasingly referred to in the Muromachi period as regional military lords (*kokujin*), themselves became *sengoku* daimyo. See also *jitō*, *kokujin*, *sengoku* daimyo, *shugo*, *shugo* daimyo, and *ikki*.

Zaichō betchimyō 在廳別名. Holdings of local officials of the provincial government (*zaichō kanjin*) within the public domain.

Zaichō kanjin 在廳官人. Local officials attached to the provincial government headquarters (*kokuga*) who handled most provincial affairs and who inherited their offices.

Zaike 在家. Peasants who cultivated the lands of *shōen* proprietors. Originally considered chattel, over time they were able to claim rights over the lands they cultivated and came to resemble small local landholders (*myōshu*).

Zasshō 雑掌. A centrally appointed *shōen* administrator.

Zazen 座禅. Meditation. Meditation and the study of conundrums (*kōan*) are two of the main practices that characterize Zen Buddhism and that prepare the way to enlightenment (*satori*).

Zōkuji 雑公事. Dues paid in various products and labor.

Zōmenbyakushō 雑免百姓. Cultivators of miscellaneous exempt lands; also called "lowly people of exempted households."

Zuryō 受領. Career governors of the mid- to late Heian period appointed by the provincial governor (*kokushi*) to carry out administrative functions in the province while the latter remained in the capital. They were able to enrich themselves through harsh taxation, and thus this term is often translated as "tax manager."

INDEX

An asterisk with an entry indicates that it also appears in the Glossary; ca. denotes circa; fl. denotes flourished; ? denotes that the date of birth or death is not known.

Adachi family, 87, 504
Adachi Tokiaki, 170
Adachi Yasumori: appointed to *osso bugyō*,* 132–3; after Bun'ei invasion, 142, 144; chief of rewards office (*go'on bugyō*), 141–2; killed during Shimotsuki incident, 129, 150; promotes judicial reforms, 150
agriculture: practices, 312–15; productivity, 3, 355, 376–7
Akamatsu family, 196
Akashi no Kakuichi (?–1371), 531–41
akutō*: active in antibakufu movement, 173–4; destabilizing effects of, 129, 131, 171–2, 182–3; rise of, 158–60; suppression of, under Kamakura bakufu,* 136, 149, 158–9
alternate succession, system of, 130, 166–8
Amano Tōkage (fl. 1180–1203), 399
Andō Renshō (?–1329), 153–4
artisans, 345–7, 351–2; *see also* peasants
Ashikaga bakufu,* *see* Muromachi bakufu*
Ashikaga family: background, 177, 179; divided loyalties of, 179; establish branch families, 179–80; holdings of main line, 180; lineage genealogy, 178; rise of, 177–83
Ashikaga Motouji (1340–67), 203
Ashikaga Tadafuyu (1327–1400), 188
Ashikaga Tadayoshi (1306–52), 188, 202
Ashikaga Takauji (1305–58): death of, in 1358, 189; establishes Muromachi bakufu,* 175, 183–9; named *seii tai shogun*,* 191; rift in policy with Tadayoshi, 188; role in

Kemmu restoration,* 174, 180–4, 186–7, 456
Ashikaga Yoshiaki (1537–97), 229–30
Ashikaga Yoshiakira (1330–67), 189, 202
Ashikaga Yoshihide (1538–68), 229
Ashikaga Yoshimasa (1436–90), 470
Ashikaga Yoshimitsu (1358–1408): cultural developments of Kitayama ("Northern Hills") epoch, 461–2; Hana no Gosho (Palace of Flowers), 462; institutionalizes calendar of formal events for warriors, 469; "King of Japan," 433–4, 436–8; Kitayama estate, 470; patronage of Zeami and Kan'ami, 462–3; relations with Ming China, 434–8; reorganizes *gozan** in 1386, 603; succeeds to shogun in 1368, 189; successive court ranks of, 191–2
Ashikaga Yoshimochi (1386–1428), 471
Ashikaga Yoshinori (1394–1441): bakufu reforms under, 209–10; interferes in *shugo** affairs, 210–11; patronage of the arts, 471
Ashikaga Yoshiteru (1536–65), 229
Azuchi–Momoyama epoch (1568–1600), cultural developments of, 491–9
Azuma kagami: account of origins of *shugo** and *jitō** institutions, 59–60, 61–2; account of Jōkyū disturbance, 70–1, 73; discussion of Gempei War, 52; use of term *gokenin*,* 62

Ban'a Shōnin, 102–4
basara daimyo,* 459–61

*bashaku,** 287, 382
bessakuden, 102, 104
Betsugen Enshi (1294–1364), 633–4
*biwa-hōshi,** 535–6
Buddhism, 4, 25–6; adapted to Japanese context, 550–1, 555–6; deities, 518–21; effect on Shinto, 556–7; Eisai and Dōgen, 551–5; esoteric (*mikkyō*), 553; formation and evolution of religious organizations, 571–8; Hōnen and Shinran, 546–51; influence of powerful supporters, 579–80; introduction to Japan, 544–5; new scholastic trends in, 568–71; Nichiren and Ippen, 555–60; origins of Kamakura schools, 580; revival of Nara Buddhism, 562–3, 568–9; role of lay believers, 578–80; significance in Japanese history, 581–2; suppression of Kamakura schools, 564–7; ties to aristocratic society, 545–6; traditional schools, 560–4; and women, 505; *see also* Zen Buddhism
*bugyōnin-shū,** 214–15
*buke**: accumulation of debt, 373; "age of warriors," 447; dependence on central patrons, 48–9; patronage of the arts, 482–3; rise of, 1, 46–8, 55, 355
Bun'ei invasion (1274), *see* Mongol invasions
*bushi, see buke**

*chanoyu**: Azuchi–Momoyama epoch, 497; contrast between forms, 497; development of culture of tea, 488–91; development of politics of tea, 498–9; early settings for, 461; tea-article mania, 497–8
Chao Liang-pi, 135–6
Chiba family, 50–1, 52–3
*chigyōkuku** (proprietary province) system, 49
*chinjō,** 76
*chinsō,** 502–3
Chinzei *bugyō,** 149, 205
Chinzei *dangijo,** 155
Chinzei *sōbugyōsho,** 160
Chinzei *tandai,** 160, 205, 231, 234–5
commerce: absence of uniform measures, 391–3; acceleration of, 360–76; and bills of exchange, 367; capi-
tal trade region, 348–50, 361–4; development of transportation network, 364–6, 381–3; and emergence of *za,** 351–6; and growth in specialized products, 351; growth of, 3, 20–1, 357, 361–2; and growth of cities and towns, 379–80, 356–7; and growth of markets, 356, 364, 380–1; and importation of Sung coins, 366; and *monzenmachi,** 356; and political change, 388–94; and proliferation of moneylenders, 368; as source of artistic expression, 511–14; and use of coins, 360–1, 366–7
commutation (*daisennō*): increase in late Kamakura period,* 368–9; motivations behind, 369–72; prevalence in Muromachi period,* 384–5
corvée, 110–12, 317
courtiers, *see kuge**
cultivators: demands for tax reductions, 284–6; effects of growing commerce on, 372–3; gain greater independence, 284–5; obtain specialized products, 345–8; resistance to proprietor control, 129, 286–9, 321–3; status differences among, 306–10; transformation of lives of, 3–4, 19–20; *see also* peasants
culture, medieval, 4–5, 22–5; Azuchi–Momoyama epoch, 491–9; *biwa-hōshi,** 535–7; *chanoyu,** 488–91, 497–9; decorative screen painting, 492–4; female entertainers, 525–9; genre painting, 495–7; Higashiyama epoch, 470–85; Kamakura period,* 447–55; landscape painting and gardens, 485–8; Muromachi period,* 458–62, 515–16; new interior settings, 468–70; noh* theater, 462–8; *renga,** 473–81; revival of Shinto, 455–7; shamanism, 521–5; *Shinkokinshū,* 452–4; *shirabyōshi** and *kusemai** dance, 529–31

Daibon Sankajō,* 82
Daikakuji line, 167
Dannoura, battle of (1185), 58
Dazaifu,* 76, 205, 399–401
*dengaku,** 462–3
*dōbōshū,** 469–70

Dōgen (1200–53): attitude toward women, 505–6; background, 591; disillusionment with established Buddhism, 553–5, 646–7; promotes Sōtō Zen, 553–5, 573–4, 624–9; retreats to Echizen Province, 566, 628

dogō,★ 253

do-ikki,★ 255, 265, 287–9, 388–9; see also *ikki*★

dōjō,★ 339

Dōshō (629–700), 585

dosō,★ 222–3, 378

dual polity: cooperation in control of *shōen,*★ 124–5; formation of Kyoto *hyōjōshū*★ in 1246, 88; between Heian system of imperial-aristocratic rule and Kamakura bakufu,★ 46–8, 80; and *jitō*★ and *gesu,*★ 62; and Jōkyū disturbance, 70–2; under Muromachi bakufu,★ 191, 216; separate jurisdiction over suits, 77

Eisai (1141–1215), 552–3, 565–6, 573

Eitoku (Kanō, 1543–90), 493–4, 495

Eizon (Eison, 1201–90), 563

Enni Ben'en (1202–80), 591–2

Ennin (793–864), 584

eta, discrimination against, 309–10

Fifth-Month disturbance (1305), 159

foreign relations: in early Muromachi period,★ 423–32; during Hōjō regency, 404–11; under Kamakura bakufu,★ 398–404; with Koryŏ, 406–8; with Ming China, 424–7, 430–2; with Sung China, 396–7, 408–9; see also international relations

Fujiwara family, 49–50, 69, 92–3

Fujiwara no Shunzei (1114–1204), 453

Fujiwara no Teika (1162–1241), 453, 454

Fushimi, Emperor (1265–1317), 164–5

Gazan Shōseki (1275–1368), 629–31

gekokujō,★ 541–2

Gempei War (1180–5), 52–8, 450; aftermath, 59–66; alignment of warrior houses, 52–3; background, 47–52; end of, 58; justification for, 52; and *kuge,*★ 125; spread into provinces, 54–5

genin,★ 309

Genji monogatari (Tale of Genji), 453–4, 465–6

Genkō incident (1331), 173

gesu,★ 62

gō,★ 90–1

Godaigo, Emperor (1288–1339), 167–70; antibakufu movement, 130–1, 172, 174; death of, in 1339, 188; involvement in Genkō incident, 173; and Kemmu restoration,★ 183–7; reign of, 168–70; treatment of Ashikaga Takauji, 184–5

Goen'yu, Emperor (1359–93), 192

Gofukakusa, Emperor (1243–1304), 161–4

gōjichi,★ 283, 331–2

gokenin,★ 67, 68, 74; complaints involving, 77; coordinated under *shugo,*★ 81–2; and Goseibai Shikimoku,★ 78–9; impoverishment of, 130–1; and Jōkyū disturbance, 70; origin and use of term, 62–4; prohibitions against selling land (*tokusei-rei*★), 138, 373–4

Gonijō, Emperor (1285–1308), 166

Gosaga, Emperor (1220–72), 88, 161–3

Goseibai Shikimoku★ (1232), 78–9, 120–1

Goshirakawa, Emperor (1127–92), 97–8, 102; attempts to overthrow Minamoto Yoritomo, 59, 125; reactions to death of, in 1192, 65; relations with Minamoto Yoritomo, 65; studies *imayō*★ under Otomae, 528–9

Gotoba, Emperor (1180–1239), 68–70, 454

Gouda, Emperor (1267–1324), 162–4, 169

gozan★: development of network, 596–610

Gukanshō (Notes on foolish views), 447, 449, 452, 457, 501

gunki monogatari,★ 449–52, 458–60, 533

Gusai (Kyūsai, 1281?–1375?), 474–5, 477

Hakuin Ekaku (1685–1768), 596, 623

Hanazono, Emperor (1297–1348), 166

hanzei,★ 241–2

Hatakeyama Kuniuji, 204

Heike monogatari (Tale of the Heike), 465, 531–3, 534

heinō bunri,★ 300
Heizen-Gate disturbance (1293), 155
Higashiyama ("Eastern Hills") epoch,
  cultural developments of, 470–85
higokenin,★ 64, 68
Hiki family, 67
hikitsuke-shū,★ 213; abolished in 1266,
  133; abolished in 1293, 156; establishment of, 80, 88; reinstituted in
  1269, 137; revived by Hōjō Sadatoki in 1294, 156
hinin,★ 309–10
hiron (false claim), 76
historiography, medieval Japanese: assessment of American scholarship,
  27–31; issues in cultural history,
  500–2; Japanese and English
  works, 6–12
ho,★ 90–1
Hōjō family, 108; aggrandizement of
  shugo★ posts, 83, 142–3; attempt to
  consolidate control under Mongol
  threat, 129, 146, 420; and coalition
  government, 67; factional disputes
  among, 137, 159; foreign relations
  under regency, 404–11; and Jōkyū
  disturbance, 70, 71; patronage of
  the arts, 455; patronage of Zen Buddhism, 455, 598–9; rise of, as
  hegemons, 67–8, 88; strength of, after Shimotsuki incident, 158
Hōjō (Kanezawa) Sanetoki (1224–76),
  132–3
Hōjō Masako (1157–1225), 69, 74, 88
Hōjō Munekata (1278–1305), 159
Hōjō Sadatoki (1271–1311), 148, 155,
  156, 159, 170
Hōjō Takatoki (1303–33), 170
Hōjō Tokimasa (1138–1215), 67, 125
Hōjō Tokimori (1197–1277), 143
Hōjō Tokimune (1251–84), 100, 144,
  148
Hōjō Tokimura (1242–1305), 159
Hōjō Tokisuke (?–1272), 137
Hōjō Tokiyori (1227–63), 593; death of,
  and end of *shikken*★ system, 129;
  succeeds to post of *shikken*, 87
Hōjō Tsunetoki (1224–46), 87
Hōjō Yasutoki (1183–1242): bakufu
  achievements under regency, 74–5;
  death of, in 1242, 87; director of
  mandokoro,★ 74; establishes
  hyōjōshū★ as ranking bakufu organ,

74, 77; establishes *rensho*★ institution, 74; guiding force behind
  Goseibai Shikimoku,★ 78–9
Hōjō Yoshitoki (1163–1224), 68, 70, 74
Hōjōki (An account of my ten-foot
  square hut), 448–9, 450–1, 452
hōkōnin (guardsmen), 217–19
Hōnen (1133–1212): court ban on teachings, 564–5; emphasis on
  nembutsu,★ 547–9, 587; fragmentation of followers after his death,
  575; religious education of, 546–7
honke, 263
Hosokawa family, 229
Hosokawa Kiyouji, 202
Hosokawa Tadaoki (1563–1645), 616
Hosokawa Yoriyuki, 208
hyōjōshū,★ 80; arena for modernization
  of system of justice under bakufu,
  75; in contrast with *mandokoro,*★
  74–5; established as ranking
  bakufu★ organ, 74; rehears cases,
  77; replaced by *yoriai,*★ 144; vehicle
  for Hōjō regent control, 74–5, 87

Ichige Sekiyu (1447–1507), 623–4
Ichijō Kanera (1402–81), 482–3
Ichinotani, battle of (1184), 58
ikki,★ 226–7, 288–9, 394; see also *do-
  ikki*★
ikkō ikki,★ 338–41; see also *ikki*★
Ikkyū Sōjun (1394–1481), 613–14
ikoku keigo banyaku★: changes in, after
  1304, 160; instituted in 1275, 142
Imagawa Ryōshun (1326–?), 206, 427–9
Imagawa Yoshimoto (1519–60), 229
Imai Sōkyū (1520–93), 499
imayō,★ 521
imperial court: administrative changes
  under Gosaga, 161; conflicts at,
  160–4; *in-no-chō* (chancellery) under Gotoba, 68; Northern and
  Southern courts, 164–8; progress in
  courtier law under Kameyama,
  163–4; reorganization of organs of
  justice, 165, 168; sponsorship of
  Zen monasteries, 599–602; see also
  kuge★; Nambokuchō disturbance★
imperial succession: dispute at court under Godaigo, 172–3; terms of
  "*bumpō* mediation" set down by
  Kamakura bakufu,★ 169
in,★ 90

inbutsu, 520
inheritance, patterns of, 86–7
*inja** (or *ton'seisha**), 471–2; *see also* tonsure
international relations, 396–8; changes in East Asian sphere, 440–6; and domestic politics, 21–2; *see also* foreign relations
Ippen (1239–89): contribution to Kamakura Buddhism, 558–60; emphasis on proselytization, 574; spread of early Jishū teachings, 506–7
Ise monogatari (Tales of Ise), 453–4
Ishida Yoshifusa, 204
Isshiki Noriuji: appointed first Kyushu *tandai** by Takauji, 205

Jien (1155–1225), 447, 450
Jimyō-in line, 167
*jinaimachi,** 380
*jinin,** 401
Jinnō shōtōki (Chronicle of the direct descent of gods and sovereigns), 190, 456–7
*jitō,** 64, 70, 74, 80; abuses of post during Gempei War, 60–1; character of post, 83, 93; and commutation, 370–1; competition among, 129; complaints against, 66; disputes with *shōen** proprietors, 83–5, 319–21; extent of authority, 84, 116–19; under Goseibai Shikimoku,* 79; illegal acts, 110–13, 266–7; inauguration of office in 1185, 59; initial appointments, 63, 125–6; under Kamakura bakufu,* 58, 61–2, 84, 127, 260–1; new appointments after Jōkyū disturbance, 72–3, 92; origins of, 60–1; and peasant resistance, 113–15; suits against, 76–7; and tax collection, 85–6, 104, 106–8, 119–20, 318; transition to *kokujin-ryōshu,** 271; usurp control over *shōen*, 261, 265–8
Jōkei (1155–1213), 562, 563
Jōkyū disturbance (1221): aftermath, 70–3; background, 66–70; character, 66, 72–3; contrasted with Gempei War, 71; and installation of *shimpo jitō,** 116; lawlessness engendered by court's defeat, 71; recent research and scholarship on, 73

Josetsu (Buddhist monk-painter, early 15th century), 486

*kaihatsu ryōshu,** 262–3
*kaisen,** 365
*kaisho**: evolution as new interior setting, 469–70; and form of *chanoyu*, 488
Kakitsu affair (1441), 210–11
Kakua (1143–?), 589–90
Kakushin (1168–1243), 563
Kamakura bakufu,* 12–16; antibakufu movements, 173–4; attempt to consolidate rule in Kyushu, 149; balance of power, 60–2; challenges to, 58–9, 71–2; change in organization, 73–4, 128, 132–3; control of *akutō,** 158–9, 171–2; creation of *hikitsuke-shū,** 80; demise of, 160–74; dispute over official birth, 56; effect of Hōjō Yasutoki's death on, 87; foreign relations under, 398–404; and Genkō incident, 173; and Goseibai Shikimoku,* 78–9; instability of, in Nigatsu disturbance, 137; and *jitō** and *shugo,** 60–1, 80–7; Mongol invasions, 131–48, 159, 417–18; patronage of Zen Buddhism, 553; political insecurity after Shimotsuki incident, 151; reforms under Hōjō Sadatoki, 156–7; restrict authority of *shugo*, 82; role and authority of, 56–8; Shōchū incident, 172; shortage of reward lands, 154; system of justice, 3, 72–88, 110–13, 148–50, 155; vassalage, 62–5
Kameyama, Emperor (1249–1305): and problem of imperial succession, 161–4
*kamikaze**: connection with Shinto, 455; and Mongol invasions (1274 and 1281), 139, 140, 147, 418
Kamo no Chōmei (1153–1216), 448–9
Kan'ami (1333–84), 461, 462
Kanenaga, Prince (1329–83), 206
*kanjin fuda,** 520
Kannō disturbance (1350–2), 232
*kanrei**: changes in post after 1441, 211; converted from *shitsuji*, 213; development of *kanrei–yoriai* system, 209; origins and function of, 207–8
Kantō *kubō**: antagonism against bakufu, 233; origins of, 231–2

Kantō *shitsuji*, installed as adviser to Kantō *kubō*,* 232
Kanzan Egen (1277–1360), 618–19
karamono,* 460–1
karita rōzeki,* 159
Keizan Jōkin (1268–1325), 629–30, 647
Kemmu restoration* (1333–6): defeat of Kamakura bakufu,* 173–4; events leading up to, 162; failure of, 456; government established by Godaigo, 185
Kemmu *shikimoku* (Kemmu injunctions), 1336, 474; guidelines for good government, 190; post of *shugo** under, 197; promulgated by Ashikaga Takauji, 187, 211; regulation of *gozan*,* 607–9; supplementary orders (*tsukaihō*), 188
Kira Sadaie, 204
Kitabatake Akiie (1318–38), 187–8
Kitabatake Chikafusa (1293–1354), 204, 456–7
Kitayama ("Northern Hills") epoch, cultural developments of, 461–2
kōan,* 589, 592, 601
Kōan invasion (1281), *see* Mongol invasions
kobyakushō,* 307
Kōgon, Emperor (1313–64), 173
Kokan Shiren (1278–1346): interest in Buddhist history, 570–1; promotion of Chinese secular culture, 644–5
Kokinshū (Anthology of ancient and modern poems), 452–3, 454
kokuga*: and restructuring of *kokugaryō*,* 95–6; and rise of *zaichō kanjin*,* 48
kokugaryō*: of Awaji Province, 91; control over, 93; creation and proprietorship of, 47; in Nara period* (710–94), 89; relationship with private holdings (*shōen**), 90; support of artisans, 345–6; transformation of, 2–3, 94–6, 278
kokujin*: concept of, 253–4; control over *shōen*,* 272; and formation of *ikki** leagues, 226, 254–7; and overlord (*ryōshu**) system, 257–9, 269–72; relationship with *shugo*,* 253–9, 278–9; rise of provincial houses, 217; suppression of, by *shugo*, 231
kokushi,* 90

Kōmyō, Emperor (1322–80), 191
Konoe family, 100
Koryŏ: relations with Japan, 405–8; requests suppression of *wakō** in 1375, 427; role in Mongol invasions, 131–2, 135, 136, 138, 145, 412–14
kōryō,* 90
Koun Ejō (1198–1280), 629
kuge*: and local proprietor (*zaichi ryōshu**) system, 123–5; loss of control over provinces, 47–8; and *mappō*,* 447; superiority over warriors, 48–9; transition to "age of warriors," 452
kugonin,* 349–50
kugutsu, 527
kuji,* 96, 101
Kujō Kanezane (1149–1207), 65–6
Kujō Michiie, 591–2
Kumagai family, 105–7
kusemai*: evolution of, 530; and noh* theater, 464
kyōgen*: development of, 468; peasant entertainment, 337–8; representation of common culture, 516, 519–20
Kyōgoku Tamekane (1254–1332), 165, 168
Kyushu *tandai, see* Chinzei *tandai**

labor service, *see* corvée
land development, forms of, 310–12

mandokoro,* 213; ceases to function, 68; in contrast with *hyōjōshū*,* 74–5; divested of judicial authority, 74; principal organ of government after 1209, 67–8
mappō,* 518; and age of *Shinkokinshū*, 454; dominant tone for outlook of medieval age, 447–8, 449; and revitalization of Buddhism, 587
markets: growth of, 356–8, 364–6, 379–81; and peasants, 327–9; on *shōen*,* 306
meshibumi (official summons), 76
Minamoto family: exile of, after Heiji incident, 51–2; and followers in Gempei War, 52–3; role and influence of, 49–50
Minamoto Sanetomo (1192–1219), 67–8, 69

Minamoto Yoriie (1182–1204), 67
Minamoto Yoritomo (1147–99), 68; actions against kinsmen, 54–5; death of, in 1199, 66; defeat at battle of Ishibashi, 54; deterioration of relationship with Yoshitsune, 59; in early stages of Gempei War, 48; in exile after Heiji incident, 51–2; extends Kamakura's influence in the west, 57–8; and followers, 53, 54; government under, 60–5; marriage to a Taira collateral, 52; negotiates with retired emperor, 56, 59; protection of leading temples and shrines, 53; relationship with Kyoto, 65–6; system of justice under, 75–6
Minamoto Yoritsugu, 87
Minamoto Yoritsune, 74, 87
Minamoto Yoshiie (1039–1106), 50
Minamoto Yoshinaka (1154–84): occupies capital, 54–5; rivalry with Yoritomo, 56
Minamoto Yoshitomo (1123–60), 51; defeat in 1160, 50; and recalcitrant Minamoto branches, 54–5
Minamoto Yoshitsune (1159–89): deterioration of relationship with Yoritomo, 59; establishes Kamakura office in Kyoto, 57; given command of principal Minamoto armies, 58; plots against Yoritomo, 59
Minamoto Yukiie (?–1186), 54–6
miuchibito,* 152–3, 155
Miura family, 50, 87–8
miyaza,* 332, 354
Miyoshi Yasuari, 144
monchūjo,* 76, 213
monetization, 3; and bills of exchange, 367; and commutation (daisennō), 366–9, 383–8; lack of Japanese coins, 385–8; and peasants, 328–9; and prohibitions against Sung coins, 408; and proliferation of moneylenders, 368
Mongol invasions, 66, 88; approaches to study of, 412; background to, 411–19; bakufu* response to Yüan overtures, 137–8; burdens on Japanese, 5, 374; initial Yüan overtures, 131–5, 414–16; invasion of 1274 and aftermath, 138–44; invasion of 1281 and aftermath, 145–50; and kami-

kaze,* 139–40; land rewards following, 141, 149; plans for third invasion, 419–20, 421
monzenmachi,* 356, 379–80
Morinaga, Prince (1308–35), 173–4
mōto,* 308–9
Mugai Nyodai (Mujaku, 1223–98), 502–7
Mugaku Sogen (Bukkō Kokushi, 1226–86), 504–5
Muhon (Shinchi) Kakushin (1207–98), 592
Muin Sōin (1326–1410), 619–20
mujō,* 518
Munetaka, Prince (1242–74), 88
Muromachi bakufu,* 16–18; administrative organs, 211–19; attempt to control shugo,* 200–1, 207–8, 231, 238, 245–7, 280; authority of, 176, 193; changes in structure, 213–14; control of provinces, 201–8, 425; distribution of power, 201–11; economic foundations, 219–25; effectiveness of rule, 175; establish office of kanrei,* 207; founding of, 183–9; and kanrei-yoriai system, 209; landholdings of, 219–22; legitimization of military rule, 189–93; narrowed scope of control, 216–17; patronage of gozan,* 600–2; power of appointment and income, 224, 235; and provincial administration, 193–201, 232–5; relations with Koryŏ, 423–4; relations with Ming China, 424, 432–3; and Sengoku period,* 225–30; suppression of wakō,* 428–9; system of justice, 215–16, 240–1; taxation, 222–5; 377–8;
Musō Soseki (1275–1351), 594–5
Mutō (Shōni) Sukeyori (fl. 1189–1227), 404–5
Mutō (Shōni) Sukeyoshi (1198–1281), 132
myō,* see myōden*
Myōan Eisai (1141–1215), 589–90
myōden,* 101–3, 121–2
Myōe (1173–1232), 562–3
myōshu*: description of, 306–7; growth of, 355; responsibility for tax collection, 101
myōshu kajishi,* 280–3

Nagasaki Enki, 170
Nagasaki Takasuke, 170
Nagoe Mitsutoki, 87
namban,* 496
Nambokuchō disturbance* (1336–92), 232; events leading up to, 456; termination of war between courts, 206–7
Nampo Jōmyō (Daiō Kokushi, 1235–1308), 611–12
nengu, 316
Nichiren (1222–81), 507; contribution to Kamakura Buddhism, 557–8; criticism of other schools of Buddhism, 567; exiled to Izu Province, 566–7; fragmentation of school after his death, 575–6; teachings of, 574
Nigatsu disturbance (1272), 137–8
Nijō Yoshimoto (1320–88), 462, 474–5, 477
Ninshō (1217–1303), 563
Nippō Sōshun (1368–1448), 620–1
Nitta family, 55
Nitta Yoshisada (1301–38), 184, 187–8
noh,* 462–8
Nōnin (priest), and Daruma school, 565
Northern and Southern Courts, rivalry between, 187, 205–6; see also Nambokuchō disturbance*

ōbanyaku,* 81–2
Oda Nobunaga (1534–82), 229–30
Ōgimachi, Emperor (1517–93), 229–30
ōhō,* 451
Ōnin War* (1467–77), 214; basis for conflict, 228; effect on Kyoto commerce, 377; and Sengoku period,* 225
Ōshū Fujiwara family, 63
osso bugyō,* 132, 157
Ōta Mitsuie, 102
ōtabumi*: Awaji Province, 91–2; characteristics and entries of, 90–1; Kamakura bakufu* issues order to submit, 138; Wakasa Province, 93–5, 122
Otomae (1085–1169), 528–9
Ōuchi family, 196
Oyama family, 50

peasants: clothing, 324–5; entertainment, 337–8; expansion in political power of, 120; food, 325–6; form ikki,* 338–41; gain more independence, 122–3; growth in landholding, 329–30; and markets, 327–9; religion, 338–41; and sengoku daimyo,* 341–3; shelter, 326–7; social strata among, 121–3; see also artisans; cultivators

renga*: development of, 473–81; as peasant entertainment, 337
rensho,* 74
roji rōzeki, 159
Rokuhara tandai,* 71, 79–80, 160
Ryōhen (1194–1252), 562
ryōke, 263

sabi*: and common culture, 542; in Shinkokinshū, 453–4; use of, in noh* plays, 466–7
Sagara family, 108
Saichō (766–822), 585
Saigyō (1118–90), 453–4, 466
Saionji Sanekane, 165
samurai, see buke*
samurai-dokoro,* 213–14
sanjo, 309–10, 354
Sanjōnishi Sanetaka (1455–1537), 483–5
sarugaku,* 337, 462–3, 464
Sasaki Dōyo (1306–73), 459–60, 461
Sasaki Tsunetaka, 92
Satake family, 54–5
sekkanke,* 352
Sekkō Sōshin (1408–86), 621–3
Sen no Rikyū (1522–91): and Hideyoshi incident, 617; perfection of wabicha,* 490–1, 497; political and cultural adviser to Nobunaga and Hideyoshi, 499
sengoku daimyo*: and ikki,* 341; origins of, 226–7, 231; patronage of Zen Buddhism, 615–16, 622; and peasants, 341–3; undermine shōen* system, 295–8
Sesshū (1420–1506), 486–7
Sesson Yūbai (1290–1346), 644–5
shamanism, 521–5
shariki,* 365, 382
Shiba Iekane, 204–5
Shiba Ienaga, 202, 204
Shibukawa Mitsuyori, 206
Shida family, 55

shiki,* 89, 100–2; system of, 263–4;
weakening of structure, 270–1
shikken,* 67
Shimotsuki incident (1285), 129, 150–2
Shinkei (1406–75), 477–9
Shinkokinshū (1205), 453–4
Shinran (1173–1262): development of
dōjo,* 577–8; promotion of Jōdo
Shin, 506; separation from Hōnen,
549–50; suppression of, 565
Shinto: deities, 518–21; effects of Buddhism, 556–7; and history of imperial institution, 455–6; revival in
Kamakura period,* 455
shitaji chūbun,* 85–6, 267–8
Shōchū disturbance (1324), 172
shōen,* 2–3, 13–15, 18–19, 110–13,
123–5; characteristics of landholding system, 89, 261–4; and commendation, 261–3, 303–4; creation of,
47, 90–1; dual authority over, 84–
5, 93; governance, 319–21; hierarchy of officials, 100, 102; internal
structure, 101–10; and jitō,* 127,
265–8; jurisdiction over criminal
matters, 320–1; jurisdiction over
land, 319–20; and kokuga,* 91–3;
and kokugaryō,* 93–6; layout of,
304–6; markets on, 306; pattern of
holdings, 103–10, 123; as place to
live, 303–6; regional variations,
101–2; relation to kokugaryō, 90;
self-sufficiency of, 96–7; and
shōkan,* 268–9; social strata within,
120–3; stages in decline, 126–7,
129, 264–5; 298–300; support of artisans, 346–7; and Taikō kenchi,
300; taxation, 348–9; transformation of system, 260–1
shōen* proprietors, 72; absentee proprietors, 47, 93; background, 261–2;
compromise with jitō,* 85–6; conflicts with jitō, 79, 83–4, 319–21;
dependence on myōshu,* 101; domestic economy, 96–101; location
of holdings, 90; neutrality in Jōkyū
disturbance, 69–70; reduction in
shōen income, 289–93; self-
sufficiency of, 96
shogun, post of: court rank, 67, 74; legitimization of, 189–93; significance of, 64–5
shoin,* 469–70, 489

shōkan,* 263; increase control over
shōen,* 268–9
shōmon,* 76
shoryō, 89
Shōtetsu (1380–1458), 477
Shūbun (?–ca. 1460), 486
shugo,* 70, 80; actions against jitō,* 82;
agents of investigation, 76; authority to levy tansen,* 200, 278–9; balance of appointments under
Muromachi bakufu, 206–7, 235–7;
basis of institution, 64; creation of
shugo yoriai,* 213; and Daibon
Sankajō,* 82; development of post,
196–8; division of office, 237–40;
inauguration of office in 1185, 59;
jurisdiction over shōen* proprietors,
81–2; local administration, 208–9,
248–53; patronage of Zen Buddhism, 600–2; relationship with
kokujin,* 253–9, 278–9; relationship with shogun, 209; responsibilities and authority, 64, 80–3, 160,
176, 193, 200, 231, 240–4, 272–4;
and shugo uke,* 279–80; tax collection, 199, 242–4; and usurpation of
kokuga,* 274–7
shugo daimyo*: appearance of, 200; consolidation of territorial control,
242–4; development of domain system, 257–9, 277–80
Shūhō Myōchō (Daitō Kokushi, 1282–
1337), 612–13
shukuba, 358
Shunjō (1166–1227), 563
sō*: and development of ikki,* 334–7;
formation of, 283–6, 331–4; functions of, 332–4
sō-mura, see sō*
Sōgi (1421–1502), 473, 479–81
sojō,* 76
sōtsuibushi,* 61–2
Sōzei (?–1455), 477
sumi-e,* 485–6

Tachibana Kanetaka, 102
Taibon Sankajō, see Daibon Sankajō
Taikō kenchi, 300, 302, 343
Taira family: ascendancy of, 47, 450–2;
destroyed in battle of Dannoura in
1185, 58; flee capital in 1183, 55;
lack of close ties in provinces, 55–
6; role and influence of, 49–50

Taira Kiyomori (1118–1181), 70; becomes chancellor in 1167, 51; coup d'état of 1179, 51; governor of three provinces, 49
Taira Masamori, 49
Taira Tadamori (1096–1153), 49
Taira Yoritsuna (?–1293): autocratic rule of, 152–5; killed in Hiezen-Gate disturbance, 155; and *miuchibito*,* 144, 152, 154; and Shimotsuki incident, 150
Takeno Jōo (1502–55), 490–1
Takezaki Suenaga (1246–?), 141–2; 146–7
tally trade (*kangō bōeki*), 5, 438–40
tansen,* 225
taxation, 315–18
tea ceremony, *see chanoyu**
Tettsū Gikai (1219–1309), 629
Toba, Emperor (1129–59), 90
tōcha,* 460
toijō,* 76
toimaru,* 365, 368, 380, 381–2
tokusei-rei,* 149, 394; abrogation of debts, 372–6; increase in 15th century, 388–9; of 1284 nullified, 154–5; of 1293, 155–6; of 1297, 157, 375–6
tokusō,* 87, 155–8
tonsure: accepted, 507; motivations behind, 509–10; and women, 504, 508–10, *see also inja**
Toyotomi Hideyoshi (1537–98), 617–18
trade, *see* commerce
trade, foreign: with China, 358–9, 422; importance of Kyushu in, 398–9; and importation of Chinese coins, 359–60; with Korea, 440–5; with Ryūkyū Islands, 445–6; with Yüan, 397, 420–1; *see also* international relations
transportation, development of network of, 364–6, 381–3
tribute system, 398, 432–40
tsuchi-ikki, *see do-ikki**; *ikki**
Tsukubashū (1356), 461, 475
Tsurezuregusa (Essays in idleness), 472–3

Uesugi Noriaki (1306–68), 202–3
Uesugi Noriharu, 204–5
ukeoi daikan,* 293–5
ukesho,* 85, 267–8
ukiyo-e,* 496

wagaku,* 454; growth during Higashiyama epoch, 482; influence on aesthetic values, 477
waka,* 452–3; aesthetic values of, 453; classical culture of courtiers, 452–3; ties with *renga*,* 477–8
*wakō**: and China's internal security, 434; and diplomatic friction, 5; first textual reference to, 405; Muromachi bakufu's* response to, 428–9; phases of activity, 397–8, 420; Yüan dynasty demands suppression of, in 1366, 423
wamono,* 461
war tales, literary genre of, *see gunki monogatari**
warrior class, *see buke**
wayo,* 85; *see also shitaji chūbun**; *ukesho**
women: and Buddhism, 505–6; as entertainers, 525–30; in *Heike monogatari*, 534; in medieval Japanese history, 503–4; as shamans, 522–3

yachida,* 310–11
yoriai,* 227
Yoshida Kenkō (1283–1350), 472–3
Yōsō Sōi (1376–1458), 613–14
*yūgen**: and common culture, 542; in noh,* 464, 466–7; in *Shinkokinshū*, 453

*za**: benefits of, 353; decline in power of, 389–91; development of, 354–5; early examples of, 353–4; formation of, 328; growth of, 362–3, 378–9; and growth of commerce, 363–4; origins of, 351; and performers, 462–3; spread of, 380
zaichi ryōshu,* 126–7
*zaichi ryōshu** system: coexistence with *shōen** system of landholding, 126; compared with medieval European feudalism, 124
zaichō betchimyō,* 95
zaichō kanjin,* 48, 57–8, 95
zaike,* 101–2, 123
Zeami (1363–1443), 461–8
Zen Buddhism, 4, 26–7; adapted to Japanese context, 647–52; *ankokuji* (temples for peace in the realm) system, 603–4; Daiō (Rinzai) school,

Zen Buddhism (cont.)
  610–23; economy and administration of monasteries, 637–42; Genjū
  (Rinzai) school, 623–4; growth of
  Zen schools, 597; influence on culture, 489, 605–6; Kamakura period, 586–94; monastic institution,
  596–637; Muromachi period, 594–
  6, 639–40; patronage, 610–11,
  614–17, 631–2, 634–6, 641–2; pre-
  Kamakura period, 584–6; promotion of secular Chinese culture,
  644–5; Rinzai and the gozan,* 596–
  610; role of monks, 651; suppression of, 565–6; Sōtō Zen, 624–37;
  transmission from China, 551–5,
  584–6, 595; see also Buddhism
zōkuji,* 315–17
zōmenbyakushō,* 307–8
zuryō,* 49